SURVEY

OF THE

LAW OF PROPERTY

By

RALPH E. BOYER

Professor of Law, University of Miami

THIRD EDITION

ST. PAUL, MINN.

WEST PUBLISHING CO.

1981

COPYRIGHT © 1956, 1971 WEST PUBLISHING CO.

COPYRIGHT © 1981 By WEST PUBLISHING CO.

Printed in the United States of America

Library of Congress Cataloging in Publication Data

Boyer, Ralph E
    Survey of the law of property.

    Second ed. by C. H. Smith and R. E. Boyer.
    Includes index.
    1. Real property—United States. I. Smith,
Chester Howard, 1893-1964. Survey of the law of
property. II. Title.
KF570.S53   1981   346.7304'3   80-27802

ISBN 0-8299-2128-1

Boyer Law of Prop. 3d Ed. MTB
2nd Reprint—1988

DEDICATION

   To first year law students—whose initial originality, enthusiasm, anticipation, vitality, idealism and candor gradually turn to impatience, bewilderment, despair and ultimate confidence, make each new academic year an exciting challenge and a source of lasting friendships —this edition is gratefully dedicated.

RALPH E. BOYER

*

III

PREFACE

The first edition of this book by the late Professor Chester H. Smith covered most of the material then included in basic Real Property courses in the law schools of the United States. Since that time many changes have occurred in law school curricula, the trend in Property being to compress more material into fewer hours and to decrease the number of required Property courses. The result has been a heavy concentration of Property materials in an allotted number of hours in the Freshman year, and an increase in the use of textual materials in lieu of traditional cases.

The contents of the basic course has also changed with materials on Personal Property being reduced to a minimum, materials on Mortgages and Land Financing being added, and materials on Land Use and Planning being emphasized. The second edition of this book was designed to reflect such curricular changes and to cover most, if not all, of the subjects most likely encountered in the basic Property course.

This third edition is designed primarily to reflect new developments over the past decade, and to make the book even more useful. New contents on Residential Landlord and Tenant Law, Implied Warranties of Fitness in the sale of new housing, Land Use Planning and its relationship to Zoning, and a general updating of all the subjects are the principal features. There are new gems, new illustrative or problem cases, and many new textual notes and case citations. The principal objective of this book, however, has been, and still is, not to present an exhaustive survey of all applicable law, but rather to help the student grasp basic property concepts.

A unique feature of this book is the generous use of problem cases with their accompanying analyses and solutions. These problem cases are used throughout the book including such fundamental topics as the creation of Estates, Future Interests and the Rule Against Perpetuities —areas which are the most difficult to comprehend and which are likely to be covered in a casebook by brief textual and problem materials followed by a few modern complicated cases. The study of these problem cases should be most helpful to the student not only in developing his skill in analyzing and solving legal problems, but also in the acquisition of a better appreciation of the fact that simple principles of law are much less absolute in the context in which the problem is likely to arise. Further explanation of the mechanics of presentation, along with study tips and miscellaneous definitions, are presented in chapter 1.

PREFACE

The author of this third edition, also the coauthor of the second edition, was impressed with the original edition as a most beneficial aid to the beginning student, and this impression has been fortified over the years by enthusiastic endorsements of many users. Hopefully, this third edition may be even more helpful.

RALPH E. BOYER

February, 1981

KEY TO
CITATION OF AUTHORITIES

---

1. Am.Jur., 2d, refers to American Jurisprudence, Second Series, and Am.Jur., 3rd, refers to American Jurisprudence, Third Series.

2. Bigelow, refers to Bigelow, Cases and Materials on Rights in Land (3rd edition 1945) published by West Publishing Company.

3. Brown, refers to Brown on Personal Property, Third Edition (1975) published by Callaghan & Company.

4. Burby, refers to Burby on Real Property, Third Edition (1965) published by West Publishing Company.

5. Casner, refers to American Law of Property, seven volume work by several authors (1952) published by Little, Brown & Company.*

6. C.J., refers to Corpus Juris.

7. C.J.S., refers to Corpus Juris Secundum.

8. Clark, refers to Covenants and Interests Running with Land, Second Edition (1947) by Charles E. Clark, published by Callaghan & Company.

9. Cribbet, refers to Cribbet, Principles of the Law of Property (2d edition 1975) published by The Foundation Press.

10. Gray, refers to Gray, The Rule Against Perpetuities, Fourth Edition (1942) published by Little, Brown & Company.

11. McClintock, refers to McClintock on Equity (2d ed. 1948) published by West Publishing Company.

12. Moynihan, refers to Introduction to the Law of Real Property by Cornelius J. Moynihan (1962) published by West Publishing Company.

13. Osborne, refers to Osborne on Mortgages (2d edition 1970) published by West Publishing Co.

14. Osborne, Nelson and Whitman, refers to Osborne, Nelson & Whitman on Real Estate Finance Law (1979), published by West Publishing Company.

15. Powell, refers to Powell on Real Property, seven volume work published by Matthew Bender & Company.*

---

* This authority is frequently updated, sometimes by pocket parts, and sometimes by textual revision. In case of revision, the page references cited herein, and sometimes even the section or paragraph references, may be changed. In such cases, the researcher is advised to consult the current index of the reference book.

16. Prosser, refers to Prosser on Torts (4th ed. 1971) published by West Publishing Company.

17. Rest., refers to Restatement of the Law, Property, five volumes (1936-1944) published by The American Law Institute.

18. Restatement Second Property (Landlord and Tenant), was published by The American Law Institute in 1977.

19. Restatement Second Torts (1979), published by The American Law Institute.

20. Simes, refers to Simes on Future Interests (2d ed. 1966) published by West Publishing Company.

21. Simes and Smith, refers to Simes and Smith, The Law of Future Interests, (second edition 1956), four volume set published by West Publishing Company.

22. Tiffany, refers to Tiffany Real Property, Abridged Edition by Renard Berman (1970) published by Callaghan and Company; if the volume is cited, then it refers to Tiffany, Real Property, six volume work, Third Edition (1939) published by Callaghan and Company.*

23. Walsh, refers to Commentaries on the Law of Real Property, three volume work (1947) published by Matthew Bender and Company.

24. Williams and Meyers, refers to Williams and Meyers, Oil and Gas Law, abridged edition published by Matthew Bender & Company (1975).*

---

* This authority is frequently updated, sometimes by pocket parts, and sometimes by textual revision. In case of revision, the page references cited herein, and sometimes even the section or paragraph references, may be changed. In such cases, the researcher is advised to consult the current index of the reference book.

SUMMARY OF CONTENTS.

	Page
PREFACE	V
KEY TO CITATION OF AUTHORITIES	VII

PART I. ESTATES AND FUTURE INTERESTS

Chapter

I.	Introduction	1
II.	Classification of Interests in Real Property	6
III.	Freehold Estates Compared With and Distinguished From Non-Freehold Estates	8
IV.	Estates and Future Interests Analyzed and Explained	11
V.	Construction of Deeds and Wills Concerning Present Possessory Estates	41
VI.	Construction of Deeds and Wills Concerning Future Interests	99
VII.	Property Rules Relating to Future Interests: Powers of Appointment	146
VIII.	Landlord and Tenant	197

PART II. RIGHTS INCIDENT TO POSSESSION AND OWNERSHIP OF LAND

IX.	Possession and Adverse Possession	233
X.	Above and Below the Surface	257
XI.	Lateral and Subjacent Support	267
XII.	Water Rights	276
XIII.	Nuisance	310
XIV.	Fixtures and Trade Fixtures	327
XV.	Waste	349
XVI.	Emblements	359

PART III. CONVEYANCING

XVII.	Vendor and Purchaser	366
XVIII.	Conveyances: Types and History	396
XIX.	The Execution and Delivery of Deeds	415
XX.	The Subject Matter Conveyed; Land Description and Boundaries	436
XXI.	Covenants for Title and Warranties of Fitness	455
XXII.	Estoppel by Deed	466
XXIII.	Priorities and Recording	476
XXIV.	Mortgages	499

SUMMARY OF CONTENTS

PART IV.   LAND USE CONTROL

Chapter | Page
XXV. Covenants Running With the Land ------------------- 515
XXVI. Easements and Profits ----------------------------- 560
XXVII. Licenses -- 609
XXVIII. Legislative Control Over Use of Land-Planning and Zoning --- 623
XXIX. Cooperatives and Condominiums -------------------- 659

PART V.   PERSONAL PROPERTY

XXX. Possessor of Personalty ---------------------------- 679
XXXI. Bailment --- 689
XXXII. Gifts, Including Joint Bank Accounts ---------------- 698
XXXIII. Bona Fide Purchaser of Personal Property ------------ 712

Table of Cases --- 717
Index -- 723

TABLE OF CONTENTS

                                                                    Page

PREFACE _____ V

KEY TO CITATION OF AUTHORITIES _____ VII

PART I. ESTATES AND FUTURE INTERESTS

Chapter

I. INTRODUCTION _____ 1

    1. History and Purpose of the Book _____ 1
    2. Study Tips and Review Suggestions _____ 2
    3. Miscellaneous Definitions and Information _____ 3

II. CLASSIFICATION OF INTERESTS IN REAL PROPER-
    TY _____ 6

III. FREEHOLD ESTATES COMPARED WITH AND DISTINGUISHED
    FROM NON-FREEHOLD ESTATES _____ 8

IV. ESTATES AND FUTURE INTERESTS ANALYZED AND EX-
    PLAINED _____ 11

    I. Freehold Estates _____ 12
    II. Non-Freehold Estates _____ 25
    III. Concurrent Estates _____ 28
    IV. Future Interests _____ 33

V. CONSTRUCTION OF DEEDS AND WILLS CONCERNING PRES-
    ENT POSSESSORY ESTATES _____ 41

    1. Rules of Construction Generally _____ 41
    2. Fee Simple _____ 42
    3. Fee Simple Conditional and Fee Tail _____ 54
    4. Life Estates _____ 60
    5. Tenancies Less Than Freehold _____ 69
    6. Concurrent Estates _____ 80
    Summary of Cases in Chapter V _____ 94

VI. CONSTRUCTION OF DEEDS AND WILLS CONCERNING FU-
    TURE INTERESTS _____ 99

    1. Types and Classes Generally _____ 99
    2. Reversions _____ 100
    3. Possibilities of Reverter _____ 105
    4. Rights of Re-Entry for Condition Broken, or Powers
    of Termination _____ 109
    5. Remainders, Vested and Contingent _____ 115
    6. Executory Interests _____ 133
    Summary of Cases in Chapter VI _____ 142

TABLE OF CONTENTS

Chapter		Page

VII. PROPERTY RULES RELATING TO FUTURE INTERESTS: POWERS OF APPOINTMENT 146

    1. Rule in Shelley's Case 146
    2. Doctrine of Worthier Title; Inter Vivos Branch 153
    3. Rule Against Perpetuities 158
    4. Powers of Appointment 179
      Summary of Cases in Chapter VII 191

VIII. LANDLORD AND TENANT 197

    1. Types of Estates 197
    2. General Principles 197
      a. Delivery of possession 197
      b. Warranty of fitness or suitability 199
      c. Tenant's duty to repair and maintain premises .. 203
      d. Illegality and frustration of purpose 205
      e. Eminent domain 208
      f. Quiet enjoyment; miscellaneous provisions 209
    3. Rents 211
    4. Abandonment by Tenant: Remedies of Landlord; Security Deposits 218
    5. Residential Leases 222
      Summary of Cases in Chapter VIII 229

PART II. RIGHTS INCIDENT TO POSSESSION AND OWNERSHIP OF LAND

IX. POSSESSION AND ADVERSE POSSESSION 233

    1. Possession and Prior Possession 233
    2. Adverse Possession 236
      Summary of Cases in Chapter IX 255

X. ABOVE AND BELOW THE SURFACE 257

    Summary of Cases in Chapter X 265

XI. LATERAL AND SUBJACENT SUPPORT 267

    Summary of Cases in Chapter XI 274

XII. WATER RIGHTS 276

    Summary of Cases in Chapter XII 306

XIII. NUISANCE 310

    Summary of Cases in Chapter XIII 325

XIV. FIXTURES AND TRADE FIXTURES 327

    1. Fixtures Generally 327
    2. Trade Fixtures 333

TABLE OF CONTENTS

Chapter | Page

XIV. FIXTURES AND TRADE FIXTURES—Continued

   3. Security Interests in Fixtures (U.C.C.); Stolen Chattels 338

      Summary of Cases in Chapter XIV 347

XV. WASTE 349

      Summary of Cases in Chapter XV 358

XVI. EMBLEMENTS 359

      Summary of Cases in Chapter XVI 365

PART III. CONVEYANCING

XVII. VENDOR AND PURCHASER 366

   1. Brokers' Contracts 366
   2. Statute of Frauds 369
   3. Part Performance 372
   4. Equitable Conversion and Risk of Loss 375
   5. Time of Performance 381
   6. Marketable Title 381
   7. Marketable Record Title Acts 386
      Summary of Cases in Chapter XVII 393

XVIII. CONVEYANCES: TYPES AND HISTORY 396

   Conveyances Outlined 396
   1. Common Law Conveyances 396
   2. Conveyances Under the Statute of Uses 1535 399
   3. Conveyances Under Modern Statutes 409
      Summary of Chapter XVIII and Cases Therein 413

XIX. THE EXECUTION AND DELIVERY OF DEEDS 415

   1. Form 415
   2. Delivery, Escrow and Acceptance 415
      Summary of Cases in Chapter XIX 434

XX. THE SUBJECT MATTER CONVEYED; LAND DESCRIPTION AND BOUNDARIES 436

   1. Description and Boundaries 436
   2. Accretion 449
   3. Exceptions and Reservations 449
      Summary of Cases in Chapter XX 453

XXI. COVENANTS FOR TITLE AND WARRANTIES OF FITNESS 455

   1. Covenants for Title 455
   2. Warranty of Fitness or Habitability 462
      Summary of Cases in Chapter XXI 464

TABLE OF CONTENTS

Chapter   Page

XXII.   ESTOPPEL BY DEED ------------------------------------- 466

        Summary of Cases in Chapter XXII -------------- 474

XXIII. PRIORITIES AND RECORDING -------------------------- 476

        1. At Common Law ------------------------------------- 476
        2. Under Recording Statutes --------------------- 477
            Summary of Cases in Chapter XXIII ------------- 497

XXIV.   MORTGAGES --- 499

        1. Mortgages Generally --------------------------- 499
        2. Mortgage Substitutes or Alternatives and Other Mat-
            ters -- 509
            Summary of Cases in Chapter XXIV ------------- 513

PART IV. LAND USE CONTROL

XXV.   COVENANTS RUNNING WITH THE LAND ---------------- 515

Legal Gems; Introduction ----------------------------------- 515
        1. In Fee -- 518
        2. In Landlord and Tenant Relation ---------------- 530
        3. Equitable Servitudes --------------------------- 539
            Summary of Cases in Chapter XXV -------------- 556

XXVI.   EASEMENTS AND PROFITS ----------------------------- 560

        1. Easements and Profits Defined, Distinguished and
            Classified --- 560
        2. How Created and Extent ------------------------ 569
        3. Extinguishment --------------------------------- 598
            Summary of Cases in Chapter XXVI ------------- 603

XXVII. LICENSES --- 609

        Summary of Cases in Chapter XXVII ------------- 621

XXVIII. LEGISLATIVE CONTROL OVER USE OF LAND-PLANNING
        AND ZONING --------------------------------------- 623

        1. Planning --- 623
        2. Zoning --- 626
            Summary of Cases in Chapter XXVIII ----------- 655

XXIX.   COOPERATIVES AND CONDOMINIUMS -------------------- 659

        1. Introduction ------------------------------------- 659
        2. Cooperatives ------------------------------------ 660
        3. Condominiums ------------------------------------ 667
            Summary of Cases in Chapter XXIX ------------- 676

TABLE OF CONTENTS

PART V. PERSONAL PROPERTY

Chapter   Page

XXX. POSSESSOR OF PERSONALTY: WILD ANIMALS; FINDERS -- 679

     Summary of Cases in Chapter XXX -------------- 687

XXXI. BAILMENT --- 689

     Summary of Cases in Chapter XXXI ------------ 696

XXXII. GIFTS, INCLUDING JOINT BANK ACCOUNTS ------------ 698

     Summary of Cases in Chapter XXXII ------------ 710

XXXIII. BONA FIDE PURCHASER OF PERSONAL PROPERTY ------- 712

     Summary of Cases in Chapter XXXIII ------------ 716

Table of Cases -- 717

Index --- 723

*

SURVEY

OF THE

LAW OF PROPERTY

Part I

ESTATES AND FUTURE INTERESTS

Chapter I

INTRODUCTION

1. History and purpose of the book.
2. Study Tips and review suggestions.
3. Miscellaneous definitions and information.

---

1. HISTORY AND PURPOSE OF THE BOOK

This book is designed as a convenient and fairly comprehensive reference book for students in the first year law school Property Course. Originally published in 1956, the coverage has been expanded and the materials re-arranged, but the unique features are retained. These unique features include the legal gems, the problem cases and answers, and the summary of the cases thereafter. The intelligent use of this book will enable the student to grasp quickly the fundamental legal principles or rules of law, develop an acceptable method of analyzing problems and answering examination questions, and acquire a sufficient knowledge to approach any problem in the area that is likely to be presented.

In most of the chapters the subject matter of each chapter is presented by three distinct methods. First, under the heading "LEGAL GEMS" are presented the fundamental principles which describe the nature of the subject matter of the chapter and which determine the rights of parties concerning such subject matter. Second, the legal gems are followed by hypothetical "CASES". Generally each case is presented in the following form:

(a) a statement of facts and

(b) a question asked, followed by

(c) the specific answer to the question propounded,

(d) a statement of the principle or principles involved, and

(e) the application of such principle or principles to the given set of facts.

The purpose of the "LEGAL GEMS" is to acquaint the student with the subject matter with which the chapter deals. The purpose of the "CASES" is to show the student how to solve legal problems by the application of legal principles to varying sets of facts—in other words, to write legal opinions. The third method of presenting such materials is by a "SUMMARY OF THE CASES" at the end of each chapter. The purpose of the summary is to take advantage of the principle that repetition is a powerful weapon in either teaching or learning.

In recent years pressures on the law school curriculum have resulted in many aspects of property being treated rather summarily or by being presented in abbreviated textural or lecture form. In preparing this revision, traditional real property areas have not been slighted but are retained with adequate illustrations of problems and analyses. The materials on estates and future interests were expanded in the second edition, and are now separated into four chapters in order to facilitate access and increase emphasis. First, in Chapter IV there is a brief analysis and explanation of each estate and future interest, and then each of those estates, future interests, and special property rules relating thereto are explained in detail in Chapters V, VI and VII. All the material, including that which was added in the second edition on mortgages, cooperatives, condominiums and personal property, have been retained and updated.

The material is presented under five principal headings as follows:

I. Estates and Future Interests

II. Rights Incident To Possession And Ownership of Land

III. Conveyancing

IV. Land Use Control, and

V. Personal Property.

The subject matter is further divided into thirty-three chapters and various subheadings thereunder. The book is designed to give the reader a quick comprehension of the principal rules of law and a technique for writing legal opinions or examination questions. It is not intended as an exhaustive treatise, but rather as a helpful tool for the neophyte.

2. STUDY TIPS AND REVIEW SUGGESTIONS

1. For all subjects other than estates and future interests, the student need simply turn to the appropriate subject matter or chapter. The book should be of considerable assistance both in the initial learning and review processes.

2. By carefully studying the legal gems, the abstracted cases, and the case summaries, the essential principles and typical applica-

tions of most subjects should be easily comprehended and remembered.

3. The concepts of estates and future interests, however, covered in the first part of the book, are by far the most difficult subjects of the course, and probably will take additional effort.

4. The student, in using the book as a learning or reinforcement tool, as distinct from a reviewing aid, in studying estates and future interests, will find it helpful to resort to several chapters or pages in order to cover fully a particular estate or interest.

5. For example, to learn fully about the fee simple estates, the student should first look to the chart in Chapter II to obtain a quick list of such estates, then take a glance at the first example of the chart in Chapter III, then pursue slow and thoughtful reading of Part 1 of Chapter IV where the estates are carefully analyzed and described; and finally the student should *study* the first part of Chapter V where typical conveyances are analyzed and the estate created thereby determined.

6. For purposes of reviewing estates and future interests the student or reader can readily decide for himself how much detail is desired—whether a brief review of the chart in Chapter II is sufficient, or whether he should go through the whole process again as in initially learning the subject.

7. Part 3 of this first chapter contains some useful definitions and bits of information, most of which may not be covered in detail in this book but which may be helpful in refreshing your memory and increasing your understanding.

3. MISCELLANEOUS DEFINITIONS AND INFORMATION

1. Alienation by subinfeudation. Subinfeudation under the feudal system involved a vertical transfer whereby the transferee was not a substitute for the transferor, but, instead, held under the transferor-tenant.

2. Alienation by substitution. Under the feudal system, substitution involved a horizontal transfer of the entire interest of the tenant; seisen passed to the transferee and the transferor dropped out of the picture.

3. Allodial ownership. The absolute ownership of land as distinguished from a tenurial system. In a tenurial system the "owner" holds of a lord, the king, sovereign, or state. Burby, 4.

4. Disability. See infra item 9.

5. Duty. See infra item 9.

6. Escheat. If the "tenant" or fee owner died without heirs or was convicted of a felony, the land reverted or escheated to his lord. Moynihan, 21.

7. Free tenure. A life estate or greater. Under the feudal system, only freemen held such estates. See also item 21 infra.

8. Immunity. See item 9 infra.

9. Legal Relations. Legal relations may be reduced to eight fundamental concepts, and all complex relationships and property interests can be analyzed in reference thereto. These relations, listed as correlatives, that is, from the diverse viewpoints of the persons specifically affected, or unaffected, thereby, are as follows:

(a) Right. A right is a legally enforceable claim of one person against another, that the other shall do or not do a given act.

(b) Duty. A duty is a legally enforceable obligation to do or not to do a particular act. Thus, when one person has a right, another person has a duty.

(c) Privilege. A privilege is a legal freedom to do or not to do a given act.

(d) "No Right." The concept of "no right" is the correlative of privilege, and expresses the viewpoint of the person against whom a privilege exists, that such person has no right in respect to whether the person with the privilege does or does not do that particular act.

(e) Power. A power is an ability on the part of a person to produce a change in a given legal relation by doing or not doing a given act.

(f) Liability. Liability refers to a person's particular legal relation being subject to change by the exercise of a power held by another.

(g) Immunity. An immunity is a freedom on the part of one person from having his legal relation altered by a given act or omission to act on the part of another person.

(h) Disability. A disability is an inability to change or alter the legal relation of the person who has the corresponding immunity. See generally Restatement of Property §§ 1–4.

10. Liability. See supra item 9.

11. "No Right". See supra item 9.

12. Power. See supra item 9.

13. Primogeniture. The rule of inheritance under which the oldest male inherits to the exclusion of his brothers, sisters, and other relatives. Stated a bit more broadly, two of the older cannons of descent under British law provided: (1) males exclude females of equal degree; and (2) among males of equal degree, only the eldest inherits. Females inherited equally. Moynihan, 43, n.9.

14. Privilege. See supra item 9.

15. Property Definition. Although property may be defined in many ways, a useful legal definition considers property not as a particular thing but rather as the legal relations relating thereto. Thus, property consists of the legal relations between persons in respect to a thing. Restatement of Property § 3. See also item 9 supra.

16. Right. See supra item 9.

17. Seisin. This somewhat nebulous but previously important concept may be generally explained, if not defined, as possession of land under claim of a freehold estate. However, it should be pointed out that a tenant for years had possession and that the landlord or reversioner had the seisin but not possession. Moynihan, 87–88. See also infra Chapter IV, Case 1.

18. Statute of Tenures (1660). This statute transformed tenure by knight service into tenure of free and common socage. It abolished the incidents of wardship, marriage, aids, primer seisin, fines for alienation, homage and scutage. The only required service became an annual rent. Moynihan, 24.

19. Statute Quia Emptores (1290). The Statute Quia Emptores prohibited further sub-infeudation and permitted alienation by substitution.

20. Tenure or the Tenurial System. The terms tenure or tenurial system are herein used to refer to the technique of "holding" land, or an estate therein, as distinct from owning it. Each tenant held of his lord, who in turn held of a higher lord, with the chief "landlord" at the top of the pyramid being the king.

21. Types of Tenure. Free and Unfree: There were two types of tenure—free and unfree. The type of service required determined the type of tenure. Free tenure, held by barons and other gentry, involved honorable services befitting free men, e. g., knight services, ecclesiastical services and personal or ceremonial services to the king or lord: Unfree tenure, held by peasants, involved menial labors such as those required in the actual tilling of the soil.

22. Unfree Tenure. A term for years or less. Under the feudal system these estates were held by servile or non-free men. See also 21 supra.

23. Words of Limitation. Words of limitation describe the size or quantum of the estate conveyed. The following are typical words of limitation: "and his heirs;" "and the heirs of her body;" and "for life." See Case 1, Chapter IV, infra.

24. Words of Purchase. Words of purchase identify the grantees or indicate who takes the interests being transferred. See Case 1, Chapter IV, infra.

Chapter II

CLASSIFICATION OF INTERESTS IN REAL PROPERTY

Interests in real property may be classified as follows:

I. FREEHOLD ESTATES (these are real property)
  A. Fee Simple (inheritable)
    1. fee simple absolute
    2. fee simple defeasible
        a. fee simple determinable or fee simple subject to special limitation
        b. fee simple subject to condition subsequent
        c. fee simple subject to executory limitation
  B. Fee Tail (successor to fee simple conditional—inheritable) [1]
  C. Life Estates (not inheritable)
    1. created by deed or will
        a. life estate for the life of the grantee
        b. life estate for the life of one other than the grantee—called estate pur autre vie [2]
    2. created by operation of law
        a. fee tail after possibility of issue extinct
        b. dower
        c. curtesy
        d. estate during coverture

II. NON-FREEHOLD ESTATES (chattels real—not inheritable at common law)
  A. Tenancy for years
  B. Tenancy from period to period (meaning year to year, month to month or week to week)
  C. Tenancy at will
  D. Tenancy at sufferance

III. CONCURRENT ESTATES (meaning ownership or possession by two or more persons at the same time)
  A. Joint tenancy
  B. Tenancy by the entirety
  C. Tenancy in common
  D. Tenancy in coparcenary

1. The fee tail after possibility of issue extinct is regarded as a special type of life estate. See infra Chapter IV, Case 11.

2. As to inheritability of a life estate pur autre vie, see infra Chapter IV, Case 10.

IV. SPECIALTY ESTATES
  A. Cooperatives
  B. Condominiums

V. FUTURE INTERESTS
  A. Reversions
  B. Possibilities of reverter
  C. Rights of re-entry for condition broken (more recently called powers of termination)
  D. Remainders
      1. vested remainders
      2. contingent remainders
  E. Executory interests
      1. executory limitations created by deed
          a. springing uses
          b. shifting uses
      2. executory devises created by will
          a. like springing uses
          b. like shifting uses

VI. INCORPOREAL INTERESTS IN REAL PROPERTY (these cannot be possessed physically because they consist of rights of user or rights to enforce agreements as to use)
  A. Easements
  B. Profits
  C. Covenants running with the land
  D. Equitable servitudes
  E. Licenses

Chapter III

FREEHOLD ESTATES COMPARED WITH AND DISTINGUISHED FROM NON–FREEHOLD ESTATES

Freehold estates illustrated

Case 1. Fee simple

A *to B and his heirs*—this gives B a fee simple and leaves nothing in A. B's estate is inheritable by his heirs general, either lineal or collateral.

Case 2. Fee tail

A *to B and the heirs of his body*—at common law this gave B a fee tail and left a reversion in A. B's estate was inheritable only by B's lineal heirs. Today the nature of the estate created by such a conveyance varies from state to state.

Case 3. Life estate

A *to B for life*—this gives B an estate for B's life and leaves a reversion in A. B's estate is not inheritable.

Non-freehold estates illustrated

Case 1. Estate for years

A *to B for 10 years*—this gives B an estate for years and leaves a reversionary interest in A. If B dies during the 10-year period the balance of the term passes to B's personal representative, i. e. his executor or administrator, for purposes of administration. In many jurisdictions the rules as to the intestate transmission of real and personal property are the same.

Case 2. Estate from year to year

A *to B from year to year*—this gives B an estate from year to year and leaves a reversionary interest in A. If B dies during the period of the lease the balance thereof passes to his personal representative.

Case 3. Tenancy at will

A *to B as long as A wishes* (or as long as both A and B agree)—this gives B an estate at will and leaves a reversionary interest in A. B's death (or A's death) during the tenancy terminates the tenancy and A has the right to immediate possession.

NOTE, HOWEVER, that if the limitation is from A *to B for as long as B wishes*, there is a conflict of authority and B has either a life estate determinable (believed to be the better view) or a tenancy at will depending upon the jurisdiction. See infra case 47.

Case. 4. Tenancy at sufferance

A leases to B for 2 years and after the expiration of the 2-year term, B remains in possession without A's permission— B has a tenancy at sufferance which is really no tenancy at all but is called such. A has the right to eject B. B has a mere naked possession without right. See Margosian v. Markarian, 288 Mass. 197, 192 N.E. 612 (1934) and Galjaard v. Day, 325 Mass. 475, 91 N.E.2d 345 (1945).

SIMILARITIES

1. In each case B has possession of the land.

2. In each case B has an estate in the land.

1. In each case B has possession of the land.

2. In cases 1 and 2 above B has an estate in the land but in cases 3 and 4 B does not have an estate but mere possession.

DISSIMILARITIES

1. The interest of B is *real property.*

2. B's interest is *inheritable*— that is, passes to B's heir or heirs in cases 1 and 2 but this is *not true as to case* 3 for a life estate is never inheritable at common law. As to the devolution of a life estate pur autre vie, see infra ch. 4, case 10.

3. B's interest is of *indefinite* or uncertain duration.

4. B is *seised* which means that he is possessed claiming a freehold interest in the land.

1. In cases 1, 2 and 3 B's interest is *personal property*—called a chattel real. In case 4 B has no interest.

2. In cases 1, 2 and 3 B's interest *is not inheritable*—personal property passes to the personal representative and not to the heirs, but the ultimate distributees and the heirs are usually the same under modern statutes.

3. B's interest in case 1 is of *definite* duration, in cases 2 and 3 of indefinite duration.

4. B is *not seised* but only possessed—seisin exists only as to freehold estates.

5. A tenancy at will is a chattel interest in land, of the lowest

nature but it is possession at the mutual wills of the land owner and the tenant, and will support trespass or ejectment; death terminates it.

6. A tenancy at sufferance is no tenancy at all; it is a mere wrongful, naked possession but neither an estate nor property. See Margosian v. Markarian, 288 Mass. 197, 192 N.E. 612 (1934).

Chapter IV

ESTATES AND FUTURE INTERESTS ANALYZED AND EXPLAINED

I. FREEHOLD ESTATES: TYPICAL CASES

1. Typical fee simple absolute.
2. Typical fee simple determinable with possibility of reverter—which is a fee simple estate subject to a special limitation.
3. Typical fee simple subject to condition subsequent—which means fee simple subject to being terminated by exercise of the power of termination or right of re-entry for condition broken.
4. Typical fee simple subject to executory limitation.
5. Typical fee simple subject to executory devise.
6. Typical fee tail.
7. Typical life estate for the life of the tenant.
8. Typical life estate for the life of one other than the tenant.
9. Typical life estate created by fee tail after possibility of issue extinct.
10. Typical life estate by dower.
11. Typical life estate by curtesy.
12. Typical life estate by and during coverture.

II. NON-FREEHOLD ESTATES

1. Typical estate for years.
2. Typical estate from year to year.
3. Typical tenancy at will.
4. Typical tenancy at or by sufferance.

III. CONCURRENT ESTATES: TYPICAL CASES

1. Typical common law joint tenancy.
2. Typical tenancy by the entirety.
3. Typical tenancy in common.
4. Typical tenancy in coparcenary.

IV. FUTURE INTERESTS: TYPICAL CASES

1. Typical reversion.
2. Typical possibility of reverter.
3. Typical right of re-entry for condition broken or "power of termination".
4. Typical vested remainder.
5. Typical contingent remainder.
6. Typical springing use or interest.
7. Typical shifting use or interest.
8. Typical executory devise like springing use.
9. Typical executory devise like shifting use.

I. FREEHOLD ESTATES: TYPICAL CASES

(These are possessed.)

1. TYPICAL FEE SIMPLE ABSOLUTE

CASE 1: A by feoffment or deed conveys Blackacre "to B and his heirs". **(a)** What estate does B get? **(b)** What are the characteristics of such estate?

Answers and Analyses

(a) B has a fee simple absolute.

In the early common law under the feudal system the only way by which a freehold interest in land could be transferred was by the ceremony of feoffment. The owner feoffor went onto the land and made livery of seisin [1] by handing the feoffee a twig or clod of earth symbolical of the land itself, at the same time describing in words the estate intended to be conveyed. The feoffor then walked off the land leaving the feoffee in possession and seised thereof. This method of conveyance is not used in the United States. Conveyances are accomplished today by the delivery and acceptance of deeds.

What then, did A convey to B by the words "B and his heirs"? It was an estate in fee simple absolute which is the largest estate known to the law; it denotes the maximum of legal ownership, the greatest possible aggregate of rights, privileges, powers and immunities which a person may have in land; it is of potentially infinite duration. By the year 1250 the words "and his heirs" had become the *only* ones by which a fee simple could be conveyed. The words "B and his heirs" meant "B in fee simple" without any qualification whatsoever. But the words "B in fee simple" used in a deed would give B only a life estate. The words in the deed had to be "B and his heirs". The words, "and his heirs" used in a deed were construed as *words of limitation* —that is, they described the quantum or size of the estate transferred to B, the grantee, but gave the heirs of B no interest whatsoever. The word B in the example is a word of purchase and indicates the grantee. Words of limitation indicate what is taken; words of purchase indicate the grantees or persons who take. Hence, by the use of the words, "B and his heirs", A conveyed to B a fee simple absolute. See Powell, ¶ 180; Burby, 202.

Note

Will vs. Deed Construction

In construing a *will* it has long been the rule that the technical words, "and his heirs" need not be used to create a fee simple absolute. The intention of the testator determines the interest devised.

---

1. For an explanation of seisin, see Chapter I, part 3, item 17 supra.

Special Note on Creation of Fee Simple Absolute in the United States

Nearly all of the states by statute have changed the common law rule requiring the words of inheritance, "and his heirs", to be used in a conveyance to create a fee simple absolute. The statutes usually provide in substance that if B is named grantee in the conveyance, he takes a fee simple absolute unless the grantor indicates an intention to create a lesser or different estate. Under such statutes a conveyance to "B and his heirs" or "to B" would each create a fee simple absolute. A few states have reached the same result without the aid of a statute. See Restatement of Property § 39: Powell ¶ 180.

(b) The characteristics of the fee simple absolute can best be set forth by answering two simple questions

(1) What can B do with his fee simple absolute? There are five distinct powers which he may exercise over the land, to wit: (I) he may use Blackacre, (II) he may abuse Blackacre, (III) he may have exclusive possession of Blackacre, (IV) he may take the fruits of Blackacre and (V) he may dispose of Blackacre either by deed inter vivos or (since 1540) by will.

(2) How long will B's estate in Blackacre continue? The fee simple absolute is the largest estate in land known to the common law and for all practical purposes it will last forever. Upon B's dying intestate the property will pass to his heirs at law either lineal or collateral. If he dies intestate without any heirs, lineal or collateral, the property escheated to the overlord in feudal days and now either escheats or descends to the state. Hence, it is sometimes said that B's estate will last only as long as he has heirs. But if B disposes of the fee simple either by deed or will to "C and his heirs", the estate will last as long as C has heirs and if C disposes of the fee simple to "D and his heirs" it will last as long as D has heirs, and so on ad infinitum. But the heirs, as such, of any such named grantee, have absolutely no interest in the estate. If the grantee dies intestate, then his heirs take the estate by descent from the grantee, not by purchase from the grantor. An heir is one who takes real property by descent; all others take by purchase and are called purchasers. The word purchaser as here used has nothing to do with the paying of consideration in a commercial transaction—it means merely taking by the act of the parties rather than by descent. See Moynihan 31.

2. TYPICAL FEE SIMPLE DETERMINABLE WITH POSSIBILITY OF REVERTER—WHICH IS A FEE SIMPLE ESTATE SUBJECT TO A SPECIAL LIMITATION

CASE 2: A by deed or will conveys Blackacre "to B and his heirs so long as it is used for school purposes". (a) What estate does B get?   (b) What are the characteristics of such estate?

Answers and Analyses

(a) B has a fee simple determinable. It is sometimes called a base fee or a qualified fee.

(b) A fee simple determinable is a fee simple created to continue until the happening of a stated event. Since the duration of the estate is correlated to the happening of a named event, here the ceasing to use it for school purposes, the estate terminates automatically by operation of law upon the happening of that event. The very important characteristic of this estate is this: the instant it is no longer used for school purposes it reverts to the grantor A, or, if A be dead, then to A's heirs. Such reverting to A or his heirs is automatic and without any act on the part of A or his heirs. The reason for such automatic reverting is in the very language of the conveyance which says the estate in B is to last only so long as it is used for school purposes. The language compels such result and carries out the precisely expressed intent of the grantor in his creation of the estate. It should be noted that the termination of the estate involves no forfeiture. There is no cutting short an estate in B. B's estate was to last as long as he used it for school purposes and when that use ceased, so did the estate.

A the grantor, need not make an entry into the possession of Blackacre when B ceases to use it for school purposes. When B ceases to use it for school purposes, at that instant A becomes the owner in fee simple and has the right to immediate possession. When B ceases such use there is nothing left in him because the conveyance, "to B and his heirs so long as it is used for school purposes", specifically limits B's estate to the time during which he uses the estate for school purposes. See First Universalist Soc'y v. Boland, 155 Mass. 171, 29 N.E. 524, 15 L.R.A. 231 (1892); 3 Walsh, 52; Restatement of Property § 44.

Note

(a) In the above case when A created in B the determinable fee, there remained in A a possibility of reverter. A possibility of reverter, standing alone as it was in A in this case and not attached to a reversionary interest, is inalienable at common law. Most states by statute or decision permit the transfer of a possibility of reverter. Battistone v. Banulski, 110 Conn. 267, 147 A. 820 (1930); Richardson v. Holman, 160 Fla. 65, 33 So.2d 641 (1948); Restatement of Property §§ 159, 163.

(b) The word "until" is often used to create a determinable fee. E. g. A "to B and his heirs until the property is no longer used for church purposes." B has a fee simple determinable.

(c) The words "until" or "so long as" are the words of a special limitation and are usually contained in the granting clause of a deed. However, such words may also appear only in the habendum clause.

In that event the habendum clause is not inconsistent with the granting clause because it merely specifies the type of estate in fee simple that is involved in the conveyance—e. g. A grants to "B and his heirs that certain parcel of land described as . . .. To Have and To Hold unto the said B and his heirs until the property is no longer used for church purposes." B has a fee simple determinable, and A retains a possibility of reverter.

A provision in the conveying instrument that the property is to be used for a specific purpose will not result in the creation of a fee simple determinable, even if there is a provision that the property is to be used for a stated purpose "and for no other." A restriction as to use may be a covenant. See First Presbyterian Church of Salem v. Tarr, 63 Ohio App. 286, 26 N.E.2d 597 (1939); Boone Biblical College v. Forrest, 223 Iowa 1260, 275 N.W. 132, 116 A.L.R. 67 (1937); Beran v. Harris, 91 Cal.App.2d 562, 205 P.2d 107 (1949).

3. TYPICAL FEE SIMPLE SUBJECT TO CONDITION SUBSEQUENT—WHICH MEANS FEE SIMPLE SUBJECT TO BEING TERMINATED BY EXERCISE OF THE POWER OF TERMINATION OR RIGHT OF RE–ENTRY FOR CONDITION BROKEN

CASE 3: A by deed or will conveys Blackacre "to B and his heirs, but if intoxicating liquors are sold on the premises then A has the right to re-enter and repossess the land". (a) What estate does B get? (b) What are the characteristics of such estate?

Answers and Analyses

(a) B gets a fee simple subject to a condition subsequent, which is an estate in fee simple that may be terminated by the conveyor, or those claiming under him, upon the happening of a named event.

(b) Because it is possible that intoxicating liquors will never be sold on Blackacre B's estate may last forever. It is therefore called a fee. But A has retained a right of re-entry or power of termination for condition broken. The important characteristic which distinguishes this type of estate from a fee simple determinable, is that the estate will continue in the grantee, or his successors, unless and until the power of termination is exercised. The estate in fee simple subject to a condition subsequent does not end, *ipso facto*, upon the happening of the named event.

The basic difference, therefore, between a fee simple determinable and a fee simple subject to a condition subsequent, is that the fee simple determinable automatically expires by force of the special limitation when the stated contingency occurs; whereas the fee simple on condition subsequent continues despite the breach of the condition until the estate is divested or cut short by the grantor's exercise of his power to terminate. Upon breach of the condition B's estate does not end automatically but instead continues until A exercises his power of termination. A has the power to terminate or cut off B's fee by making a re-entry onto the premises if and when the condition is broken. It is optional with A whether or not to re-enter. Until A does manifest his election by making an entry on the land or bringing an action to recover it, the grantee's estate continues. A's re-entry causes a forfeiture of the remaining portion of B's estate; it cuts short and brings to an end an existing vested interest in land.

Although no particular words are essential to create an estate on condition subsequent, the use in the conveyance of the traditional words of condition—"upon condition that," "provided that," "but if" —coupled with a provision for re-entry by the transferor on the occurrence of the stated event will normally be construed to manifest an intention to create an estate on condition. According to the older cases, words of condition alone without a re-entry clause are sufficient to create the qualified estate. [See Gray v. Blanchard, 25 Mass. (8 Pick.) 284 (1829)], but the modern trend is to refuse to construe the conveyance as creating an estate on condition in the absence of a provision that the transferor shall have a right to re-enter or words of similar import. Where the language of the instrument is ambiguous the strong reluctance of the courts to enforce a forfeiture will frequently result in a construction that the parties intended to create a covenant or a trust rather than an estate on condition. See Post v. Weil, 115 N.Y. 361, 22 N.E. 145 (1889); Moynihan, 104–105; Burby, 208.

Note

In the above case the right of re-entry or power of termination which remains in A can be exercised by A personally or, if A be dead, then it may be exercised by his heirs. But it was inalienable at common law and could not be exercised by a third person or intended transferee. See Restatement of Property § 160. The power is sometimes alienable by statute.

4. TYPICAL FEE SIMPLE SUBJECT TO EXECUTORY LIMITATION

(a) SUBJECT TO SPRINGING USE OR INTEREST

CASE 4: A, being the owner of Blackacre in fee simple, *by deed* conveys Blackacre "to B and his heirs, B's interest to begin five years from the date of this deed". **(a)** What estate has A? **(b)** What are the characteristics of such estate?

Answers and Analyses

(a) A has a fee simple subject to an executory limitation, the executory limitation being an executed springing use or interest in B. (See also Case 5 and Chapter XVIII–E infra.)

(b) At common law A could not create a freehold estate to begin in futuro because livery of seisin was absolutely essential, and if livery of seisin were made to B, then the estate would take effect at once contrary to A's intention. The conveyance by feoffment at common law had to be effective at once or not at all. Seisin could not remain in the feoffor. Neither could it be in abeyance. The only way there could be an estate to begin in the future was by way of remainder. For example, A could enfeoff B for life, remainder to C and his heirs. But in such case livery of seisin was made to B who held it for life and at B's death the seisin passed to C. This was the only way the common law judges permitted the future estate in C to be created. Hence, in our case the estate attempted to be created in B was void at common law.

However, the Statute of Uses passed in 1535 ultimately permitted the creation by deed of estates which sprang up in the future. By virtue of that Statute, equitable future interests of the springing and shifting type were converted into legal future interests and acquired the name "executory interests." The result is that A in the hypothetical case has a fee simple estate in possession which is subject to the executory limitation in B. When the five years after the making of the deed have passed, A's fee simple will come to an end and B's estate in fee simple will take effect. Technically, B's estate is known as an executed springing use under the Statute of Uses. And it should be carefully noted that a springing use springs up out of the estate of the grantor, in this case out of the estate of A who made the deed to B. Until then A has a presently possessed estate in fee simple. Executory limitations and springing uses will be discussed later. See Cases 28, 30 infra; Restatement of Property § 46; Moynihan, 192.

(b) SUBJECT TO A SHIFTING USE OR INTEREST

CASE 5: A, being the owner of Blackacre in fee simple, *by deed* conveys Blackacre "to B and his heirs, but if B dies without issue living at his death, then to C and his heirs". (a) What estate does B get? (b) What are the characteristics of such estate?

Answers and Analyses

(a) B has a fee simple subject to an executory limitation, the executory limitation being an executed shifting use or interest in C.

(b) At common law there could not be a fee simple in remainder following a fee simple in possession because the remainder was considered repugnant to the estate in possession. Furthermore, at common law a remainder could not take effect in derogation of the preceding freehold estate which supported it. Hence, at common law, under both of these principles, C's estate in this case would be void and he could take nothing. But before the Statute of Uses (1535) the equity courts were not bound by either of these principles and C was permitted to take the estate described in the conveyance if his interest were created by bargain and sale, thus creating a use, instead of a legal interest created by feoffment or livery of seisin. The result was that B's equitable fee simple could be defeated upon the happening of the event, that is, by B's dying without issue surviving him.

After the Statute of Uses, equitable interests were transferred into legal interests, and the shifting interest of C was valid if the conveyance operated under the Statute of Uses. Eventually, deeds creating such interests were liberally construed to effectuate the intent of the parties whether or not a technical use was first created. Hence, in this case when B died without issue surviving, the interest shifted from B to C and C became the owner of Blackacre in fee simple. Technically, C's estate is known as an executed shifting use under the Statute of Uses. And it should be carefully noted that the use or interest shifts from the grantee, B, to a third person, C. B has a fee simple in possession subject to an executory limitation in C. Executory limitations and shifting uses will be discussed later. See Cases 29, 31 infra; Restatement of Property § 46; Moynihan, 193.

5. TYPICAL FEE SIMPLE SUBJECT TO EXECUTORY DEVISE

(a) AN EXECUTORY DEVISE LIKE A SPRINGING USE

CASE 6: A, being the owner in fee simple of Blackacre, *by will*, devises Blackacre "to my brother, C and his heirs, if and when he marries D". A dies leaving B as his sole heir and with no residuary clause in his will. **(a)** What estate does B take? **(b)** What are the characteristics of such estate?

Answers and Analyses

(a) B takes by descent from A the fee simple in Blackacre subject to an executory devise in C. The executory devise in C is like the springing use or interest in a deed under the Statute of Uses.

(b) Upon A's death B took by inheritance a fee simple estate in possession. At early common law it would have been a fee simple absolute because the estate in C would have been void because it was to begin in the future, "if and when C marries D". But the courts took the same liberal view respecting the Statute of Wills passed in 1540 as they had taken concerning estates in futuro created under the Statute of Uses passed five years earlier. Hence, the estate in fee simple in B is one in possession subject to an executory devise. Of course C's estate could not take effect as a remainder because it was not preceded by a particular estate of freehold created by A's will to support it. Executory devises will be discussed later. See Chapter VI–6; Restatement of Property § 46; Moynihan, 195.

(b) AN EXECUTORY DEVISE LIKE A SHIFTING USE

CASE 7: A, being the owner in fee simple of Blackacre, *by will*, devises Blackacre "to B and his heirs but if and when C marries D, then to C and his heirs". **(a)** What estate does B take? **(b)** What are the characteristics of such estate?

Answers and Analyses

(a) B takes a fee simple estate subject to an executory devise in C. The executory devise in C is like the shifting use or interest in a deed under the Statute of Uses.

(b) B's fee simple is a present estate in possession subject to C's right to take possesion if and when he, C, marries D. At common law B would have had a fee simple absolute because C's estate was considered repugnant to that estate which A had already created in B. At common law there could not be created a remainder in fee upon a fee because if the first fee was good, then the second one would necessarily be in derogation thereof and cut it short before its natural termination. But under the Statute of Uses a shifting use was permitted in such cases. The courts used the same liberal rule in construing devises in wills and gave effect to the intention of the testator. Hence, while B had a fee simple estate presently possessed, it was one subject to an executory devise. Executory devises will be discussed later. See Chapter VI–6; Restatement of Property § 46; Moynihan, 195.

6. TYPICAL FEE TAIL

CASE 8: A by deed conveys Blackacre "to B and the heirs of his body". (a) What estate does B get? (b) What are the characteristics of such estate?

Answers and Analyses

(a) B has a fee tail estate.

(b) The characteristics of a fee tail are bound up in its history. This estate came into being as the result of two historical developments: (1) the recognition of the fee simple conditional by the courts; and (2) the passing in 1285 of the Statute De Donis Conditionalibus by Parliament.

Before 1285 the courts had construed the provision, "to B and the heirs of his body" as giving B the power to convey a fee simple in Blackacre if and when a child was born to B. Such an estate was called a fee simple conditional since it was a fee simple conditioned on issue being born to the donee. The effect of such interpretation was to enable B to cut off any rights which the heirs of B's body might have in the land. It also enabled B to cut off the reverter which A had in the land. Of course, this was completely contrary to A's intention but it did make land more freely alienable.

To remedy this evasion of A's intention, the statue "De Donis" was passed in 1285. Its purpose was to keep the family land in the family as long as there was a family or issue. It provided that B could not convey Blackacre so as to cut off the right of the heirs of B's body to inherit the land upon B's death. Nor could he so convey as to cut off A's reversionary interest. So, after the statute, if B conveyed Blackacre to "C and his heirs" and B died leaving child D surviving him, then D could take the land from C; and if B died without heirs of his body surviving him, then A could take the land from C. In other words, after the Statute De Donis, B had the power to convey an estate in Blackacre only for the term of B's life. It should be noted that this tended to create a perpetuity in the family or bodily heirs of B and prevented any tenant on the land, the bodily heir of B, from disposing of an estate for longer than his life. But such was the fee tail estate created by the Statute De Donis in 1285.

The words "of the body" were those commonly used in both deeds and wills to show the intention to create a fee tail rather than a fee simple, but other words having the same meaning, such as "bodily issue," were equally effective. It was permissible for the grantor of a fee tail to restrict the inheritance (by use of proper words in the limitation) to a particular group of the lineal descendants of the grantee. There could be an estate in tail male or in tail female, and either one of these could be a fee tail general or a fee tail special. A grant to a man and the heirs male of his body created a fee tail male. A grant to a man and the heirs female of his body created a fee tail female. If the grant was to a donee and the heirs of his body by a particular spouse the estate was a fee tail special; if no particular spouse was designated it was a fee tail general. Estates in tail female were, in fact, rarely created but estates in tail male were an integral part of the English family settlement and were, therefore, very numerous in the eighteenth and nineteenth centuries. It should be noted carefully, however, that the words, "and the heirs of his body" are words of limitation and not words of purchase; that B has an inheritable estate which passes by descent to his bodily issue upon his death and that B's bodily issue does not take directly as a purchaser from A by A's deed.

This condition of the fee tail did not last long. By 1472 the fee tail tenant, B, could by the fictitious lawsuit known as "common recovery" transfer Blackacre to "C and his heirs" in fee simple, thus cutting off both the heirs of B's body and A's reversionary interest. Thereafter, the fee tail tenant could at any time by this fictitious action, convert his fee tail estate into a fee simple and convey it in fee simple absolute. Another fictitious action, "fine", enabled the fee tail tenant to bar or dock the entail of the bodily heirs. Both fines and common recoveries were abolished in England in 1834 by statute which also provided that the fee tail tenant could convey a fee simple by deed enrolled in Chancery.

In the United States the answer to our question could be given with assurance only after consulting the constitution and statutes of a given state. Only four states would give B a fee tail estate and in each of them B could convey the land in fee simple by deed. These are Mass., R.I. (as to deeds), Me., and Del. In a few states B would take an estate tail for life but the first heir of the body to inherit from B would have a fee simple absolute. Conn., Ohio, and R. I. (as to wills) are in this group. In other states B would take a life estate with contingent remainder in fee simple to his potential heir or heirs of the body, or lineal descendants. Such would be the case in Ark., Colo., Fla., Ga., Ill., Mo., and Vt. Because the estate in fee tail has been considered quite out of harmony with our society and institutions it has been prohibited either by statute or constitution in thirty-three states. Usually under such provisions B would have a fee simple estate either absolute or with limitations. See Rest. Introductory Note Vol. I, p. 201 et seq.; Powell ¶¶ 196–198.

7. TYPICAL LIFE ESTATE FOR THE LIFE OF THE TENANT

CASE 9: A by deed (or will) conveys Blackacre "to B for the term of his natural life". **(a)** What estate does B get? **(b)** What are the characteristics of such estate?

Answers and Analyses

(a) B gets a life estate for B's life.

(b) B has the right to use Blackacre, to take the fruits therefrom, to dispose of his life estate to another. This power of disposition includes the right to mortgage, to create liens, easements, leases or other rights in the property, but none can extend beyond the period of B's life. But B has no right to commit waste or to injure the corpus of the property to the injury of A's reversionary interest. B has the right to the exclusive possession of Blackacre but subject to these qualifications: A is privileged to come onto Blackacre to determine if waste has been or is being committed; to collect rent, if any be due; to make repairs essential to protect his reversionary interest; to remove timber which has been severed and which belongs to A; and to do such acts as may prevent his reversion from being terminated. In general, the life tenant may use Blackacre in the same way as though he were a fee simple owner except that the corpus must be left reasonably intact for the reversioner or remainderman who succeeds to the possession. He must keep the property in repair, except for ordinary wear and tear, he must pay the current taxes, and interest on any mortgage on the premises at the beginning of the life estate. But he has the right to the issues and profits from the land and his personal representative may harvest any crop which he has planted before the life estate terminates, and may remove any fixtures which the life tenant has placed on the ground. If the property is damaged by a wrongdoer, the life tenant may recover for the injury to his life interest and no more. See Restatement of Property §§ 117 to 122; 1 Walsh, 556 et seq.

8. TYPICAL LIFE ESTATE FOR THE LIFE OF ONE OTHER THAN THE TENANT

CASE 10: A by deed (or will) conveys Blackacre "to B for the life of C". **(a)** What estate does B get? **(b)** What are the characteristics of such estate?

Answers and Analyses

(a) B gets an estate for the period of the life of C which is called an estate pur autre vie, that is, for the life of another.

(b) It is obvious that B may predecease or may survive C. But in any event the estate which B has will last only so long and no longer than the life of C. C's life, not B's life, is the measuring life. Of course B's rights and obligations are substantially the same as set forth in Case 7 next above. At common law if B died before C the property was regarded, until C died, as without an owner, hence the first person to take possession, called the common occupant, was entitled to the estate. This conclusion resulted from the fact that the estate pur autre vie was not an estate of inheritance and could not descend to the heirs of the life tenant, and not being personal property it could not pass to the administrator or personal representative. Neither can the reversioner, A, claim the estate because he has granted away his interest during the lifetime of C and C still lives. The general or common occupant can hold the estate until the death of C, not because such person has any right to hold, but because no one has a right to eject him. But if the conveyance were to "B and his heirs for the life of C," then on the death of B during C's lifetime the heir of B took, not by descent but as "special occupant." Some statutes today have made the interest in the property between the death of B and that of C, a chattel real and provided that B's personal representative shall take the property for that period as personal property. Since the life estate possesses the quality of alienability the life tenant can convey his estate, thus giving his grantee an estate pur autre vie. But the life tenant cannot (apart from the common law doctrine of tortious feoffment, or unless he is granted a power in addition to the life estate), convey a greater estate than his own. See Moynihan, 50; 2 Bl.Comm., 259; Restatement of Property § 151.

9. TYPICAL LIFE ESTATE CREATED BY FEE TAIL AFTER POSSIBILITY OF ISSUE EXTINCT

CASE 11: A conveys "to B and the heirs of his body by his wife, W". W dies without issue. **(a)** What estate does B have? **(b)** What are the characteristics of such estate?

Answers and Analyses

(a) B has an estate in fee tail special by the words used in the conveyance. But the death of W without issue leaves B with an estate for life after possibility of issue is extinct because B can have no "heirs of the body by his wife, W" after W has died without issue.

(b) It should be noted that the conveyance itself does not create the life estate named. There must be both the words of the conveyance which creates the fee tail special and the death of W without issue, the death of W being subsequent to the conveyance.

Upon W's death, then, B has a life estate after possibility of issue is extinct. This estate also exists when the conveyance is "to B and W (husband and wife) and the heirs of their bodies" when one of these spouses dies without issue, or, when there is issue, and the issue dies without issue before the surviving spouse. Then the surviving spouse has an estate for life after possibility of issue is extinct. Hence, this estate can arise only in the case of a fee tail special. It can never arise when the fee tail is general such as, "to B and the heirs of his body" because the law presumes B can have issue as long as he lives. The result is that B has a fee tail to the end of his life. In its origin the fee tail special is an inheritable freehold estate and the tenant, B, in the given case above, is not liable for waste. The accidental death of W without issue which transformed the fee tail special into a life estate after possibility of issue is extinct, does not make B liable for waste as life tenants usually are. It is called a life estate because it cannot extend beyond B's life and is no longer inheritable. See Tiffany, § 66; Moynihan, 51.

10. TYPICAL LIFE ESTATE BY DOWER

CASE 12: A conveys Blackacre in a common law jurisdiction to "H and his heirs". H has a wife, W. H dies. **(a)** What estate does W get? **(b)** What are the characteristics of such estate?

Answers and Analyses

(a) At common law a widow was entitled, on the death of her husband, to a life estate in a third of the lands of which her husband was seised in fee simple or in fee tail at any time during the marriage. Hence W is entitled to a life estate in one-third of the land because H was seised thereof during coverture. The conveyance gave H a fee simple, hence seisin. This life estate of W is called the widow's estate of dower.

(b) The right of dower at common law is limited to a particular person and to specific estates. First, it is limited to an actual wife and is not available to one who has been divorced from H. Since the husband must have been seised of an estate of inheritance in order that his widow may be entitled to dower, a widow cannot, at common law, claim dower in land in which he had a life estate, an equitable estate only, or in which her husband had a reversion or remainder expectant upon an estate of freehold. The rule that there cannot be dower in an equitable estate was changed by statute in England in 1833, and similarly extended in most American jurisdictions when and while dower was recognized. The widow's right to dower cannot be defeated by any conveyance by the husband, even to a bona fide purchaser for value, unless the wife joins in the conveyance or releases dower. While the husband is living the wife's dower is said to be inchoate but becomes choate upon the husband's death while the wife still lives. Modern statutes in the United States frequently modify the dower right and change considerably the rights of a married woman in her husband's property. In fact, the trend is to abolish dower, even in name, and to substitute therefore an elective or statutory share of the deceased husband's estate. The law of each state must be examined in detail. See Moynihan, 55; Powell, ¶ 213[1]; Fla.Stat. §§ 732.201–732.215 (1979).

11. TYPICAL LIFE ESTATE BY CURTESY

CASE 13: A conveys Blackacre in a common law jurisdiction "to W and her heirs". W has a husband, H, by whom W has a child, X, now living. W dies. (a) What estate does H get? (b) What are the characteristics of such estate?

Answers and Analyses

(a) In this set of facts H has a life estate in *all* (not in one-third as the wife had in dower) of the wife's lands by curtesy.

(b) Whereas dower exists only for the wife, curtesy prevails solely for the husband. Four requisites are essential to curtesy in H. (1) H and W must be legally married. (2) W must be actually seised of the land in either fee tail or fee simple. Here the conveyance gave W a fee simple estate. H could not have curtesy in W's reversions or remainders because she was not seised of such. Nor could he have curtesy in lands which W held in trust for others. But H did have right to curtesy in equitable estates in fee held by W. (3) W must have issue by H who is born alive and capable of inheriting. In the case given X is the child of H and W and capable of inheriting from W. (4) The wife must predecease the husband, as W did in this case.

A tenancy by curtesy is a life estate to which at common law the husband was entitled to all lands and tenements of which he and his wife were seised in right of the wife in fee simple or in fee tail during the marriage, provided that there was issue born alive capable of inheriting the estate. Curtesy was not allowed unless the issue entitled to inherit the land was actually born alive. At common law the husband acquired an estate by the curtesy initiate immediately on the birth of issue, which became an estate by the curtesy consummate upon the death of the wife. The tenancy by the curtesy initiate has been gradually abolished by statute. The tendency today is to give the husband and wife the same rights in each other's property however such rights might be denominated. See Moynihan, 54; Powell, ¶ 210, 213[2].

12. TYPICAL LIFE ESTATE BY AND DURING COVERTURE

CASE 14: A conveys in a common law jurisdiction "to W and her heirs". W marries H. **(a)** What estates does H get? **(b)** What are the characteristics of such estate?

Answers and Analyses

(a) H has a life estate in W's property during coverture, which at common law means during the joint lives of H and W.

(b) At common law it is said that H and W were one and H was THE one. The wife's personality was merged in that of the husband. She was burdened with the common law disabilities including inability to contract or to use or convey her property. When W, being seised of Blackacre, married H, at that instant she lost and H gained control of Blackacre. He could, during coverture of H and W, enjoy the rents and profits of the property, dispose of same for the period of coverture and it could be levied upon to satisfy his debts. The husband's coverture estate continued until the marriage was dissolved by death or divorce, (an absolute divorce at common law could be obtained only by act of Parliament and so was indeed a rarity), or until issue was born of the marriage at which time it was enlarged into a curtesy estate. Hence, during the joint lives of H and W, H had full control of the land of W. This right extended to land in which W had the fee, fee tail, a life estate for W's life or for the life of another. Of course, upon the death of either H or W before the birth of issue, such control terminated and the land returned either to W or to her heirs. See Moynihan, 52.

Note

Statutes have now changed the common law respecting dower, curtesy and the husband's control of the wife's property by coverture.

II. NON–FREEHOLD ESTATES

(These are possessed.)

1. TYPICAL ESTATE FOR YEARS

CASE 15: L leases Blackacre to T for the period January 1, 1980 to December 31, 1982, a period of three years. **(a)** What estate does T get? **(b)** What are the characteristics of such estate?

Answers and Analyses

(a) T has an estate for years.

(b) Perhaps the most important requisite of an estate for years is that it must have a definite beginning and a definite ending. Note carefully that T's lease begins on a day certain, January 1, 1980, and ends on a day certain, December 31, 1982. It lasts for a specific period of three years. Of course, it is still an estate for years if it does not happen to correspond with the calendar years or does not cover exactly yearly terms, e. g., a lease from April 23, 1977, to August 4, 1982, is an estate for years because it has a definite beginning in time and definite termination date. So also is a lease from August 5, 1981, to August 25, 1981. During the period of the lease the tenant, T, has the right to possess Blackacre, and to use and enjoy the fruits thereof. Of course, he will have to pay rent according to the terms of the lease and must not commit waste on the premises. Upon T's death testate or intestate during the term of the lease, the balance of the term will pass to his personal representative for distribution according to his will or, if none, the statutes on distribution, because such leasehold is personal property, a chattel real. In legal contemplation every estate for years is a smaller estate than a life estate for the reason that a life estate is a freehold and real property, whereas the estate for years (even for 1,000 years) is less than a freehold, a chattel interest. Even though a leasehold is an estate in land and immovable, it is personal property. This is not logical but purely historical. See Restatement of Property § 19; Burby, 123, National Bellas-Hess, Inc., v. Kalis, 191 F.2d 739 (8th Cir. 1951), certiorari denied 342 U.S. 933, 72 S.Ct. 377, 96 L.Ed. 695 (1952).

2. TYPICAL ESTATE FROM YEAR TO YEAR

CASE 16: L leases Blackacre to T for a three year period from March 1, 1975 to March 1, 1978 at a rental of $500 per month payable in advance on or before the 10th day of each month. T holds possession beyond March 1, 1978 and on March 9, 1978 tenders $500 to L which L accepts. (a) What estate does T have? (b) What are the characteristics of such estate?

Answers and Analyses

(a) T now has an estate from year to year.

(b) Of course T by the lease had an estate for years to last for three years. But his holding over and L's acceptance of rent on the same terms as provided in the prior lease, made T a tenant from year to year. The essential characteristic of the year to year (or month to month or week to week) lease is this: it is of indefinite duration whereas the lease for years is for a definite or specific term. It continues indefinitely in the absence of either party's giving notice of termination, and in the case given which was for years but rental payable in monthly installments, the resulting implied periodic tenancy is from year to year and not from month to month. But the terms of the old lease are implied to carry over to the year to year lease with the exception of the term itself.

Notice of termination is an integral element of a periodic tenancy. In our case either party can end the tenancy by giving notice not later than six months preceding the end of the yearly period. The notice must be given on or before September 1st and must state that the lease shall end on the following March 1st. In a month to month tenancy a full month notice must be given and in a week to week tenancy a full week notice must be given. Without such notice the tenancy will continue for another period of a year, month or week. It is important to notice that T was a wrongdoer in his holding over. Such wrongdoing, of course, makes T a tenant at sufferance and gives L an election either to eject T or to accept rent from him and thereby create a tenancy from year to year. If L should give notice of termination of the lease on November 1st of a given year, such notice, in our case would be wholly ineffective and the lease would continue a year after the following March 1st and for the following year indefinitely until either party gives notice on or before September 1st of a given year. Statutes frequently shorten the length of notice required to terminate periodic tenancies.

The above example is the usual method by which year to year tenancies arise. However, they may be created by express agreement and often arise through the making of an oral lease which is void under the Statute of Frauds. For example, L orally leases Blackacre to T for five years when the Statute of Frauds provides that any lease for more than a year must be in writing. T takes possession of Blackacre and pays rent to L. T has an estate from year to year with terms impliedly carried over from the void lease. If, in our typical case given above, T's holding over the term is with L's consent or without wrongdoing and without agreement, then T is not a tenant from year to year, but a tenant at will, and L can recover only the reasonable value for the time T actually holds over the term. See 2 Walsh, 145 et seq.; A. H. Fetting Mfg. Jewelry Co. v. Waltz, 160 Md. 50, 152 A. 434, 71 A.L.R. 1443 (1930); Restatement of Property § 20.

3. TYPICAL TENANCY AT WILL

CASE 17: L leases Blackacre to T for "as long as L wishes".
(a) What estate does T get? (b) What are the characteristics of such estate?

Answers and Analyses

(a) T has a tenancy or estate at will—which means at the will of T as well as at the will of L.

(b) The estate at will is always of indeterminate duration because it can be terminated by either the landlord or the tenant. But the relationship of landlord and tenant must be created with the tenant in possession of the land. L creates no such estate by giving T a mere license and it does not arise if T is a trespasser on Blackacre. Such estate usually arises when no rent is involved but the fact that rent is to be paid either for a month or a year does not prevent its being a tenancy at will if such is the intention of the parties. A tenant for years who holds over with the landlord's consent is a tenant at will as is also one who enters under a void lease unless and until transformed into a periodic tenancy by acceptance by the landlord of rent for a specific period. Such tenancy can be ended by either party without notice, and it is terminated by the death of either party, or by the commission of voluntary waste by the tenant because it terminates the mutual concurrence of the wills of the parties. The estate at will is the lowest form of chattel interest in land and is not assignable. See 2 Walsh, 168 et seq.; Restatement of Property § 21.

Note

If the lease were to T for as long as T wishes, many jurisdictions take the position that T has a life estate determinable. See Thompson v. Baxter, 107 Minn. 122, 119 N.W. 797 (1909); infra Case 47.

4.   TYPICAL TENANCY AT OR BY SUFFERANCE

CASE 18: L leases Blackacre to T for two years, the term ending April 30, 1980. T continues in possession after April 30, 1980 without L's consent. **(a)** What estate does T have? **(b)** What are the characteristics of such estate?

Answers and Analyses

(a) T is a tenant at sufferance but his interest is in no sense an estate. It is a mere naked and wrongful possession.

(b) A tenancy at sufferance arises when any tenant, for years, from year to year, month to month, or life tenant pur autre vie holds possession wrongfully beyond his term. There is no relation of landlord and tenant between such tenant and the reversioner or remainderman. He differs from a trespasser only in that his original entry was rightful. But when the reversioner or remainderman has put him off the land, then by relation back to the beginning of his wrongful holding over, he is liable as though he were a trespasser from the date of the expiration of his lease, and judgment may be rendered against him for mesne profits. Of course, at the election of the reversioner or remainderman, the tenant at sufferance may be transformed into a tenant from year to year or month to month, depending on the facts, by acceptance of rent from him during his wrongful holding over. See 2 Walsh, 177 et seq.; Restatement of Property § 22.

III.   CONCURRENT ESTATES: TYPICAL CASES

(These are owned or possessed by two or more persons at the same time.)

1.   TYPICAL COMMON LAW JOINT TENANCY

CASE 19: G conveys Blackacre "to A, B and C and their heirs forever". **(a)** What estate do A, B and C get? **(b)** What are the characteristics of such estate?

Answers and Analyses

(a) The estate that A, B and C get will depend upon the jurisdiction and the date of the conveyance. At early common law they would get an estate in joint tenancy in fee simple. Of course, the fee simple in A, B and C arises from the use in the conveyance of the words of inheritance "and their heirs". The joint tenancy arises from the fact that the common law preferred joint tenancy over tenancy in common. The reason was clear. The essence of joint tenancy is that the two or more persons named to take the property, take and hold as though they together constituted one person. Each of the joint tenants is a component part of the unity, the fictitious single person. Hence, by calling on one of the joint tenants to do the feudal services, the overlord called on all as a matter of law. Such reason has long since disappeared and our statutes provide that tenancy in common is preferred to joint tenancy. Under such statutes, A, B and C would take as tenants in common since the right of survivorship or joint tenancy is not specified in the conveyance.

(b) Joint tenants are always purchasers, that is, they always take either by deed or will, never by descent. There are always four unities, (1) time—meaning that the tenants take their interests at the same moment, (2) title—meaning the tenants acquire their interests from the same source, the same deed or will, (3) interest—meaning each must have the same identical interest as every other joint tenant, and (4) possession—meaning the possession of each is the possession of all and the possession of all is the possession of each, for, after all, they all constitute a single person. Joint means oneness and in our case A, B and C constitute one person and each owns the whole of Blackacre. A owns ALL of Blackacre, B owns ALL and C owns ALL. Each DOES NOT OWN ONE THIRD. Each OWNS AN UNDIVIDED WHOLE. And this is true irrespective of the number of joint tenants.

The so-called *grand incident of joint tenancy is survivorship.* This means that if A dies without having conveyed during his lifetime, his survivors, B and C, own the whole; if B dies first, then A and C own the whole and if C dies first, then the survivors A and B own the whole. And if A and B die without having conveyed while they lived, then C, the survivor, owns the whole in severalty. If then C dies intestate his heirs only will inherit.

Joint tenancy is destroyed by any act which destroys any unity. For example, A conveys "to X and his heirs an undivided one-third interest in Blackacre". Here is where logic breaks down. A has both right and power to dispose of what he did not own. As a joint tenant he owned all of Blackacre jointly with B and C. Yet here he conveys to X the fractional one-third interest. What are the effects of such conveyance? They are these. First, B and C as to each other remain joint tenants of a two-thirds interest in Blackacre with the four unities still present. X cannot be a joint tenant with B and C because he got his title from a different deed than did B and C, namely from A, and at a different time. Hence, the unities of time and title are both broken. So X, as to his undivided one-third interest, is a tenant in common on one hand, with B and C being a tenant in common of the two-thirds interest on the other, although at the same time B and C remain joint tenants *between themselves* as to their two-thirds interest. (Because the interest of a joint tenant is conveyable, it can be levied upon by his creditors.) Again, suppose, A, B and C agree among themselves to partition Blackacre. A takes the north one-third, B takes the middle one-third and C takes the south one-third. Now we have a breaking up of the unity of possession and each one now owns and possesses his divided part alone and individually. Each is a tenant in severalty of the portion which is given to him in the partition. Suppose, now in the original case A dies testate and in his will he gives his one-third of Blackacre "to X and his heirs". X takes nothing for the reason that upon A's death survivorship becomes effective and B and C as survivors own the whole of Blackacre. In other words, a joint tenant cannot *by will* effectuate a severance of the joint tenancy. Of course, a joint tenancy may exist among two or more persons as to any kind of an estate, fee simple, fee tail, life estate, leaseholders and chattel interests.

The characteristic of survivorship attendant upon a simple conveyance to two or more persons creating a joint tenancy has led to statutory changes in practically all jurisdictions. The statutes vary considerably—some simply reverse the presumption so as to favor a tenancy in common unless the conveyance or transfer clearly indicates otherwise, and others either abolish joint tenancies, especially in land, or abolish the characteristic of survivorship. Insofar as survivorship is concerned, however, it is generally possible to acquire such right if the transfer or conveyance expressly so provides, but the nature of the estate acquired will depend upon the form of the conveyance. It is possible, for example, to create a cotenancy for joint lives with a contingent remainder to the survivor, or a cotenancy in fee with an executory interest in the survivor. In such cases the estate does not have the same characteristics as a joint tenancy. Executory interests (and contingent remainders in many states) are indestructible, and therefore the nature of such estates, particularly as to the survivorship right, cannot be changed (as in a joint tenancy) by a severance of one of the four unities by any one of the coowners. Statutes permitting joint tenancies with the right of survivorship are quite common as to certain types of personal property, such as bank accounts and shares of stock. The law of each jurisdiction must be consulted. See Powell ¶ 616; 2 Walsh 1; 2 Casner, 3; Kane v. Johnson, 397 Ill. 112, 73 N.E.2d 321 (1947); Dennen v. Searle, 149 Conn. 126, 176 A.2d 561 (1961).

2.   TYPICAL TENANCY BY THE ENTIRETY

CASE 20: G conveys Blackacre "to H and W (husband and wife) and their heirs".   (a) What estate do H and W get? (b) What are the characteristics of such estate?

Answers and Analyses

(a) H and W get an estate called tenancy by the entirety in those jurisdictions that recognize such estates.

(b) Tenancy by the entirety is a species of joint tenancy.   To the four unities which obtain in joint tenancy, there is added a fifth one, unity of person, in tenancy by entirety.   This tenancy can exist only between husband and wife who are considered as one person.   It is like joint tenancy in that the doctrine of survivorship obtains. Each owns the whole and upon the death of one spouse the survivor owns the whole and there is nothing in the estate of the decedent.   It is created by deed or will and not by descent.   It differs from joint tenancy in this: neither spouse can voluntarily dispose of his or her interest in the property.   H and W must join in any conveyance. Hence, a creditor of either spouse cannot levy on the spouse's interest in the property owned by the entirety.   Divorce destroys the unity of person and hence, the tenancy by entirety.   The effect of divorce is to make H and W tenants in common if we follow the policy of preferring such tenancy over joint tenancy.   The tenancy by the entirety is not recognized in many states.   See 2 Casner, 23; 52 A.L.R. 886; Moynihan, 229; 41 C.J.S. 458, § 34; Powell ¶ 622; Dorf v. Tuscarora Pipe Line Co., 48 N.J.Super. 26, 136 A.2d 778 (App.Div.1957); Lindenfelser v. Lindenfelser, 396 Pa. 530, 153 A.2d 901 (1959).

3.   TYPICAL TENANCY IN COMMON

CASE 21: G, owner of Blackacre in fee simple, grants "to A, B and C and their heirs each taking a one-third interest therein".   (a) What estate do A, B and C get?   (b) What are the characteristics of such estate?

Answers and Analyses

(a) A, B and C take Blackacre as tenants in common.   While at common law a conveyance to two or more persons usually created a joint tenancy, a tenancy in common could be created when such was the clearly expressed intention as appears in this conveyance by the words, "each taking a one-third interest therein".   While at common law a joint tenancy was preferred over tenancy in common, the reverse is true under state statutory provisions which generally provide that a conveyance to two or more persons shall create a tenancy in common unless it is shown that a joint and not a common tenancy is intended.

(b) Tenancy in common exists when a distinct undivided fractional share is given to each tenant individually.   This is true even when the tenants take similar interests at the same time under a single deed or source of title. Only one unity, that of possession, is required in tenancy in common. It means that the possession of one tenant is the possession of all. But the interests of the tenants need not come from the same source, nor at the same time, and their interests may be quite different one from the other. For example, A, B and C may be tenants in common when A has only a life estate in one-third with remainder to R, B may have a fee in an undivided one-sixth and C a fee in an undivided half of Blackacre. Further, A may have received his interest by deed and B and C by descent. The tenants take equal shares unless the deed or circumstances indicate otherwise. No survivorship exists in tenancy in common and each tenant has the right and power to dispose of his share or any portion thereof by deed or will, and in intestacy the share will descend to the heir of the cotenant. Such tenancy is destroyed either by partition or by purchase when the entire title is owned in severalty by one person. See 2 Casner, 19; 2 Walsh, 16; Dennen v. Searle, 149 Conn. 126, 176 A.2d 561 (1961); In re Horn's Estate, 102 Cal.App.2d 635, 228 P.2d 99 (1951).

4. TYPICAL TENANCY IN COPARCENARY

CASE 22: Ancestor, A, dies intestate in an early common law jurisdiction leaving no son but three daughters, X, Y and Z as his only heirs. (a) What estate do X, Y and Z get? (b) What are the characteristics of such estate?

Answers and Analyses

(a) X, Y and Z take an estate in coparcenary.

(b) A tenancy by coparcenary is created only by descent, never by purchase. It occurred when the ancestor left no son who could take by primogeniture. Three unities existed in such tenancy: title (each took by descent); interest (each had an inheritable estate); and possession (the possession of one was the possession of all). The unity of time need not be present, although it is present in the case given, for X, Y and Z took by descent from ancestor, A, at the instant of A's death. But suppose then, the sister X dies intestate leaving two daughters M and N as her sole heirs. They would take her one-third interest as coparceners with Y and Z although they would take at a different time. M and N would each take a one-sixth undivided interest. Survivorship does not obtain in coparcenary and each coparcener holds an undivided but distinct interest. Hence each of the parceners, X, Y and Z takes from A an undivided one-third interest which will descend to the heirs of each as set forth above with M and N. For all practical purposes today the rules applicable to tenants in common are applicable to coparceners and the latter term is seldom used. See 2 Casner, 33; 2 Walsh, 19.

IV. FUTURE INTERESTS: TYPICAL CASES

1. TYPICAL REVERSION

CASE 23: A, owner in fee simple, conveys Blackacre to B for life. **(a)** What estate does A have? **(b)** What are the characteristics of such estate?

Answers and Analyses

(a) A has a reversion in Blackacre.

(b) A reversion is the residue left in a conveyor or grantor when he conveys an estate which is smaller than that which he had. It arises merely as a matter of simple subtraction. In arithmetic we learned that if A has 5 apples and gives away 3 of them, he has 2 left. The two apples left with A are like a reversion in real property. In the case given A owned a fee. He conveyed away only a life estate to B. Hence, he has an interest left. That interest is a reversion. A fee minus a life estate leaves a reversion in the grantor. The seisin passes to B for his life. When B dies, his life estate comes to an end and the seisin reverts to A, the grantor, if he still lives. If A is already deceased then the seisin returns to his heir or heirs if A dies intestate. If A has left a will disposing of the reversion to a devisee, then the seisin passes from B upon his death to A's devisee. Or, if A during his lifetime and before B's death, has granted or assigned his reversion to a grantee, we shall say to "X and his heirs", then upon B's death the seisin will pass to X in fee simple. A reversion is always retained by the grantor—he has merely conveyed less than he has. He continues to own presently the reversion but he cannot enjoy the occupancy of the land in which the reversion exists until the conveyed estate terminates. In the case given, A owns but cannot enjoy the occupancy of the property Blackacre, until the death of B. The ownership is presently in grantor A but the possession and enjoyment of the property by A are postponed until the death of B. That is the reason for its being called a future interest. But the reversion is always a vested interest in the transferor and he can dispose of such either by deed or will. See 1 Casner, 432; Rest. § 154; Moynihan, 94.

2. TYPICAL POSSIBILITY OF REVERTER

CASE 24: A, owner in fee simple, conveys Blackacre to B and his heirs for *so long as* the property is used for courthouse purposes. **(a)** What interest does A have? **(b)** What are the characteristics of such interest?

Answers and Analyses

(a) A has a possibility of reverter.

(b) A possibility of reverter is an interest which is retained by the grantor after conveying a determinable fee. B is granted a determinable fee in this case. It is true that when a fee simple absolute is granted, there can be nothing left in the grantor. But such estate is bound to last forever or as long as the grantee has heirs general. How long will B's determinable fee in this case last? The answer is in the very words of the grant, "for so long as used for courthouse purposes". Then it is possible that it may not continue in B and his heirs forever or as long as B has heirs general. It may cease to be used for the specific purpose, and if that happens, B's estate comes to an end automatically. That very possibility that it may revert to A is what is left in A and is called a possibility of reverter. The fact that it may remain in the grantee and his heirs forever because it may always be used for courthouse purposes is the reason for B's estate being called a fee. At common law A's possibility of reverter, standing alone and not attached to a reversion, was inalienable. It was descendible only from ancestor to heir. But today many cases and the Restatement of Property § 159a hold a possibility of reverter is alienable. See Restatement of Property § 159a; Collette v. Town of Charlotte, 114 Vt. 357, 45 A.2d 203 (1946) following Restatement of Property; Moynihan, 101.

3. TYPICAL RIGHT OF RE–ENTRY FOR CONDITION BROKEN OR "POWER OF TERMINATION"

CASE 25: A, owner in fee simple, conveys Blackacre to B and his heirs *but if* at any time the premises is not used for courthouse purposes, then A shall have the right to re-enter and terminate B's estate. (a) What interest does A have? (b) What are the characteristics of such interest?

Answers and Analyses

(a) A has a right of re-entry for condition broken or "power of termination".

(b) A right of re-entry for condition broken is an interest in the transferor who has conveyed the property subject to a condition subsequent. In this case B is granted a fee simple but subject to an express subsequent condition that B's estate may be terminated upon the happening of two things: (1) the property is no longer used for courthouse purposes; and (2) A (or his heirs if A has died, for such right of re-entry is descendible) has elected to terminate B's estate and does such acts of re-entry as are necessary to accomplish such termination. Either A's re-entering of the land with intent to terminate B's estate or A's bringing an action for such purpose will terminate B's estate. Failure to do either for a long period of time after the condition is breached may constitute a waiver of the right, or conditions may estop A from asserting the right or exercising the power. This right of re-entry is descendible and can be exercised by A's heirs, but at common law it was not alienable or transferable inter vivos when not attached to a reversion. The reason is plain. The law abhors forfeitures and to cut off B's fee by exercise of the power is strictly a forfeiture. Hence, the exercise of such right or power was and still is not favored by the courts. Some hold an attempt to convey the right extinguishes it. Statutes in some jurisdictions permit the inter vivos transfer of a right of re-entry. When such right is attached to or incident to a reversionary interest, it is transferable. For example, suppose A conveys Blackacre to "B for life but if B sells liquor on the premises then A or his heirs have the right to re-enter and terminate B's estate". A then conveys his reversion including the right of re-entry to C and his heirs. In that case the right of re-entry would pass to C as an incident to the reversion and C or his heirs could exercise the power of termination. And such would be true if the transfer was by will. See Rest. §§ 160, 161; Moynihan, 107–108; Simes & Smith § 1863.

Note

Notice carefully the distinction between the "right of re-entry for condition broken" or "power of termination" on the one hand, and the "possibility of reverter" on the other. It is a question of intention and construing the words of the grant. Compare "A to B and his heirs *so long as* no liquor is sold on the premises" and "A to B and his heirs *but if* liquor is sold on the premises then A shall have the right to re-enter and terminate B's estate". In the former A has a possibility of reverter and in the latter A has a right to re-enter. In both cases B has a fee because it might last forever. But in the former B's estate will come to an end automatically if liquor is sold on the premises because that is as long as the estate is to last. But in the latter B's estate will not come to an end automatically even though he sells liquor thereon. There must be an affirmative act on A's part to terminate B's estate. A may or may not act. But if he does act it will cause a forfeiture of the balance of B's fee. If A does not act, then B's estate continues even though he has breached the condition subsequent. See Moynihan, 99; Simes & Smith § 286.

4. TYPICAL VESTED REMAINDER

CASE 26: A, owner in fee simple, conveys Blackacre to B for life, remainder to C and his heirs. (a) What estate does C have? (b) What are the characteristics of such estate?

Answers and Analyses

(a) C has a vested remainder in fee simple, the words "and his heirs" being words of limitation.

(b) It should be noticed first that A had a fee simple and has granted from himself the fee simple, thus leaving nothing (no reversion) in A. B has an estate in possession for life. B's life estate is a freehold, hence, he is seised. B's life estate is the "particular estate of freehold" which supports C's remainder. *Every remainder must be preceded by a particular estate of freehold*—either a life estate or a fee tail.

At common law, if A granted to B a fee simple there could not be granted also a remainder in fee simple to C because there would have been nothing left to be granted over. Hence, we say a remainder in fee simple could not follow a grant made in fee simple. Also at common law the remainder was the only future estate which could be granted to one other than the grantor or his heirs. And a remainder could become possessory only when the preceding particular estate of freehold came naturally to its end. The remainder could not cut short the preceding particular estate. In our facts C's remainder could give C the right to possession only in case of B's death. If the case were, "A to B for life but if B marry X, then to C and his heirs", C's estate could not be a remainder and would be void at common law because it would, in case B married X, cut short B's life estate. After the Statute of Uses C's future interest in such case would be valid as an executory interest.

In the typical case given, C's remainder is vested because C is in being and the estate granted is a presently created one even though C's enjoyment is postponed till B's death. It is this future enjoyment which classifies it as a future estate. Should C die before B, C's vested remainder will descend to C's heirs in case of intestacy, or C's will may transfer it to a devisee. Similarly, C may convey it during his lifetime. And there could be as many remainders at common law as the grantor saw fit to create subject to the limitation that a fee simple could not follow a fee simple. Thus A, fee simple owner of Blackacre, could convey to "B for life, C for life, D for life, E for life, then to F and his heirs". All except B had vested remainders but if E should predecease B, then E would never enjoy the possession of the property. But it is vested if the person or class to take is certain and the estate is definite. See Moynihan, 110; Rest. § 187; 2 Tiffany, § 319; 3 Walsh, 89.

Note

In each of the following illustrative cases C has a vested remainder:

1. A to B for life, remainder to C for life.
2. A to B for life, remainder to C and the heirs of his body.
3. A to B for life, remainder to C and his heirs.
4. A to B for life, then to X for life if he marries Y, then to C and his heirs.
5. A to B and the heirs of his body, remainder to C and his heirs.

Note

Types of Vested Remainders

There are 3 classes of vested remainders:

(a) Those vested absolutely and not subject to divestment.

e. g. A, fee owner, conveys to B for life, remainder to C for life. C's remainder is absolutely vested and no one can interfere with its becoming an estate in possession at B's death.

Merely enjoyment is postponed until B's death but that has nothing to do with vesting. And the fact that C may predecease B and not enjoy it in possession is immaterial. C's right of ownership of the remainder, not enjoyment in possession, determines the vesting.

(b) Those vested subject to partial defeasance.

e. g. A, fee owner, conveys to B for life, remainder to B's children in fee simple. At the time of the grant B has a child C. Thereafter children D and E are born to B. At the time of the conveyance the remainder in fee simple vested in C. Thereafter, upon the births of D and E, the remainder opens and vests in C, D and E as cotenants. To the extent that D and E participate, C's original interest is divested. In this case it is a two-thirds interest.

(c) Those vested and subject to total defeasance.

e. g. A, fee owner, conveys to B for life, remainder to C and his heirs but if intoxicating liquor is sold on the premises, then A may re-enter and terminate the estates granted. Here C has a vested remainder in fee simple but subject to being completely divested by A's exercising his power of termination upon the sale of liquor on the premises. See Moynihan, 120; Restatement of Property § 157.

5. TYPICAL CONTINGENT REMAINDER

CASE 27: A, owner in fee simple, conveys Blackacre to B for life, remainder to C and his heirs if C pays A $100. (a) What interest does C have? (b) What are the characteristics of such interest?

Answers and Analyses

(a) C has a contingent remainder in fee simple.

(b) A contingent remainder is one which is subject to a condition precedent. In this case the condition precedent was the payment by C of $100 to A. Until that act took place, C's interest remained contingent. If and when he pays A the $100, then the contingent remainder will be transformed into a vested remainder. Because the contingency was a condition precedent, the older common law considered a contingent remainder only a possibility of acquiring an estate in the land. Hence, it was not alienable or transferable inter vivos. However, today the general rule, based more on policy than on logic, is that contingent remainders are alienable like other future interests.

One of the important features of C's contingent remainder at common law was its destructibility. Seisin could not be in abeyance. Hence, upon B's death it had to pass either by reversion to A or by the conveyance to C. But it could not pass by the grant to C unless, before B's death, C had paid the $100 to A. The result was that if B died before C made the payment to A, C's contingent remainder was lost irrevocably and the seisin reverted to A. Here again the inexorible tide of evolution is gradually doing away with the destructibility of contingent remainders in the modern real property law. Statutes are saving them. Under such statutes the seisin would revert to A but if at a later date, even after B's death, C paid $100 to A, then the remainder would become effective as an estate in possession in C, thus permitting it to be effective as a springing or shifting use under the Statute of Uses. Today the doctrine that seisin cannot be in abeyance has little practical value. See Restatement of Property § 162; 2 Tiffany, § 341; Moynihan, 123 to 137.

6.   TYPICAL SPRINGING USE OR INTEREST

CASE 28: A, owner in fee simple, conveys Blackacre to B for life and one year after B's death to C and his heirs. **(a)** What interest does C have? **(b)** What are the characteristics of such interest?

Answers and Analyses

(a) C has a legal springing interest.

(b) Springing and shifting interests are together termed executory interests or executory limitations. They are always created in favor of one other than the conveyor. They are interests which cannot take effect as remainders, either because they are not supported by a preceding particular estate of freehold or because they take effect in derogation of an existing estate.

At common law such executory interests were not possible before the Statute of Uses (1535). Conveyances operating under that Statute (bargain and sale deeds, feoffment to uses, and covenants to stand seised) could raise springing and shifting uses which were transformed into corresponding legal estates. Today, as this typical case illustrates, it is not necessary to first raise a use in order to create executory interests. In the case given, C's interest would fail as a remainder because a remainder had to become effective, in possession not later than the instant of B's death, at which time the seisin would pass to C. But in our case there is a year intervening B's death and when C's interest becomes effective. During that year A's reversion takes effect in possession. Under the Statute of Uses, when the year passed succeeding B's death, a use sprang up in C in fee and the Statute executed it into a legal estate, thus terminating the reversion in A. Thus the springing use or interest in C is an estate created to begin in futuro and vests in derogation of A's estate. In our case then, B is given a life estate, there is then a reversion in fee in A for one year, at which time a use springs up in C. A then holds the legal title to the use of C and his heirs. The Statute of Uses then executes the use (meaning legal title is carried from A to C) so that C has the legal fee simple in derogation of A's vested estate in possession. See Moynihan, 192; Simes & Smith, §§ 30, 221.

7.　TYPICAL SHIFTING USE OR INTEREST

CASE 29: A, owner in fee simple, conveys Blackacre to B for life but if B marries X, then to C and his heirs. **(a)** What interest has C? **(b)** What are the characteristics of such interest?

Answers and Analyses

(a) C has a shifting legal interest.

(b) The following should be carefully noted. (1) C's interest is in one other than the grantor, A. (2) B has a life estate subject to C's executory interest. (3) If and when B marries X, then C's executory interest is executed into a legal estate in fee and vests automatically without any act on C's part. And (4) C's interest is in derogation of B's life estate and cuts it short. These four characteristics distinguish executory interests. They are applicable to springing interests, shifting interests, and executory devises, all of which come under the term executory interests or executory limitations. So, when this conveyance is made, B has a life estate subject to an executory interest and A has a reversion. If the event happens (i. e., B marries X), then C has an estate in possession in fee and B's life estate is cut off and A's reversion passes to C, all of which carries out A's expressed intention. See Simes & Smith, §§ 30, 221; Moynihan, 192 et seq.

8.　TYPICAL EXECUTORY DEVISE LIKE SPRINGING USE

CASE 30: A, owner in fee simple, devises Blackacre to B and his heirs one year after A's death. **(a)** What interest does B have? **(b)** What are the characteristics of such interest?

Answers and Analyses

(a) B has an executory devise.

(b) The characteristics and requirements of such interest are identical with those of springing and shifting uses or interests as set forth in the typical cases next above with this exception: executory devises are created by will whereas springing and shifting interests are created by grant or deed inter vivos. In the case given, there being no residuary clause in A's will, Blackacre would descend to A's heirs for one year in fee simple. The year having passed, the fee simple vests automatically in B, exactly like an executed springing use. This was made possible by the Statute of Wills passed in 1540, and which was construed by analogy to have the same effect on devises as the Statute of Uses, passed in 1535, had on bargain and sale deeds and on covenants to stand seised. If A, owner in fee, bargained and sold Blackacre to B, this deed to take effect one year from its date, the effect would be like the case given. A would remain the owner in fee for one year after which the use springs up in B and the

Statute of Uses makes B the legal owner. Thus an estate is made to commence in the future. See Simes & Smith, § 31; Moynihan, 195.

9. TYPICAL EXECUTORY DEVISE LIKE SHIFTING USE

CASE 31: A, owner in fee, devises Blackacre to B and his heirs but if B sells liquor on the premises, then to C and his heirs. **(a)** What interest does C have? **(b)** What are the characteristics of such interest?

Answers and Analyses

(a) C has an executory devise.

(b) The characteristics of this interest are exactly the same as those that attach to springing and shifting interests but the devise, of course, is created by will and not by deed. It is obvious that C's interest could not be a remainder for two reasons: (1) a remainder cannot follow a fee simple; and (2) a remainder cannot come in and cut short the preceding vested estate. In this case if B sells liquor, C's fee will cut off or vest in derogation of B's fee simple. If an estate can be construed as a remainder it will be so construed rather than an executory interest. But in this case B has a fee simple subject to an executory devise in C. Note carefully that C is intended to have no interest whatsoever unless and until the event of B's selling liquor happens. Then it automatically vests in C and B's fee is cut off. There is no reason why any owner should not be able to create any kind of an estate when no public policy is violated, and none is violated by cutting one fee simple short in favor of another one. It merely carries out the owner's intention. See Simes & Smith, § 31; Moynihan, 192 et seq.

Note

Executory interests and devises are subject to the Rule Against Perpetuities, but the Rule is not violated in this case since C's interest will either vest or fail within the lifetime of B. This is so because B cannot sell liquor after his death. Had C's interest been limited to take effect "if liquor were ever sold on the premises" (instead of "if B sells liquor on the premises"), then the interest would have been void under the Rule Against Perpetuities. See infra, Rule Against Perpetuities.

Chapter V

CONSTRUCTION OF DEEDS AND WILLS CONCERNING PRESENT POSSESSORY ESTATES

1. Rules of Construction Generally.
   Legal Gems.
2. Fee Simple.
   Legal Gems.
   Cases.
3. Fee Simple Conditional and Fee Tail.
   Legal Gems.
   Cases.
4. Life Estates.
   Legal Gems.
   Cases.
5. Tenancies Less than Freehold.
   Legal Gems.
   Cases.
6. Concurrent Estates.
   a. Joint Tenancy.
      Legal Gems.
      Cases.
   b. Tenancy by the Entirety.
      Legal Gems.
      Cases.
   c. Tenancy in Common.
      Legal Gems.
      Cases.
   d. Tenancy in Coparcenary.
      Chart—Common Law Concurrent Tenancies Compared.
Summary of Cases in Chapter V.

---

1. RULES OF CONSTRUCTION GENERALLY

Legal Gems

1. The purpose of construction in conveyances is to find the intention of the parties and all rules of construction are subservient to such purpose.

2. In construing an instrument of conveyance every part thereof should, if possible, be given a meaning in considering the instrument as a whole. This rule might be characterized as the "four corner doctrine," meaning that everything within the four corners of the instrument should be considered in its construction.

3. If possible, the parts of an instrument of conveyance should be construed as consistent with each other.

4. A deed is always construed most strongly against the grantor who has used the language therein.

41

5. Where a deed contains two clauses which are contradictory, the former will govern over the latter. This is part of the old maxim, "the first deed and the last will shall operate". Also, it may take the form, where the granting clause and the habendum clause are repugnant one to the other, that the granting clause will govern. This "rule of repugnant clauses" in modern times will normally not be applied in an arbitrary manner, and it frequently will be rejected in favor of the "four corner doctrine" enunciated in gem 2. See case 34.

6. A deed will be construed to grant a fee simple absolute rather than a fee simple determinable or a fee simple on condition subsequent if the language of the whole instrument makes such interpretation reasonably possible.

7. A provision in a deed or will directing that the transferee of property therein cannot dispose of such is void as a disabling restraint on alienation, spendthrift trusts excepted.

---

2. FEE SIMPLE

LEGAL GEMS

1. Estates in fee simple are
   (a) fee simple absolute
   (b) fee simple defeasible.

2. Estates in fee simple defeasible include
   (a) fee simple determinable
   (b) fee simple subject to condition subsequent
   (c) fee simple subject to executory interests including
      (1) springing uses or interests (by deed)
      (2) shifting uses or interests (by deed)
      (3) springing executory devises (by will)
      (4) shifting executory devises (by will).

3. The *only way* a fee simple estate could be created at common law was by the use of the words of inheritance, "and his heirs" or "and their heirs". These magic words were indispensable.

4. Under modern statutes the words of inheritance are not necessary to create a fee simple estate. It is presumed that the named grantee will take a fee simple estate unless a lesser estate is described.

5. Under many modern statutes the fee tail estate is deemed a fee simple estate. In jurisdictions where such is the case there is but one inheritable freehold estate, the fee simple.

6. A fee simple determinable comes to an end automatically upon the occurence of some specified event or act, whereas a fee simple subject to a condition subsequent requires both a breach of the

specified condition and an affirmative act by the grantor or his heirs to terminate the estate.

7. Any disabling restraint on the power to alienate a fee simple estate is void.

Note

At this point Cases 1 through 7, supra, setting forth the characteristics of the fee simple absolute and the fee simple subject to limitations should be carefully re-read. In the following cases, unless otherwise indicated, it is assumed that the grantor had a fee simple absolute at the time of the initial transaction.

CASE 32: A, owner in fee simple of Blackacre, executes a deed thereto in these words, "I hereby grant Blackacre to B". In the jurisdiction where the land is located a statute provides in substance this—every grant or conveyance of an estate in lands made to a person shall be deemed a fee simple unless a lesser estate is described in the instrument. (a) What estate would B take at common law? (b) What estate would B take under the statute?

Answers

(a) At common law B would take a life estate in Blackacre, and under the statute B would take a fee simple estate in Blackacre. At common law no conveyance could pass a fee simple without the use of the magic words of inheritance, "and his heirs". Hence, without those words following the grantee's name, B would take a life estate at common law.

(b) Under the statute it is intended that the named grantee shall take a fee simple estate in every conveyance unless by express words in the deed it is stated that such grantee shall take an estate less than a fee simple. It is obvious then that by the statute B would take a fee simple estate in Blackacre. This is a simple but a very important case to the practitioner for the reason that many states have adopted statutes similar in substance to the one given. Furthermore, in some jurisdictions it is held that B takes a fee simple in such case even without the aid of a statute. See 1 Restatement, § 39.

Note

Special Constructions at Common Law

(a) A conveys to B corporation (whether sole, aggregate or municipal). B takes a fee simple without the use of words of inheritance. (b) A conveys to B as trustee. B takes such estate as is necessary to carry out the trust, including a fee simple, without use of the words of inheritance. (c) A conveys to B for life remainder to the heirs of C while C is still living. The heirs of C take as purchasers and as a class of heirs a contingent remainder in fee simple. If and when C dies before B, they then take a vested remainder in fee simple without words of inheritance being used in the deed. (d) A and B are *joint tenants* in fee simple of Blackacre. A releases his interest to B. B now is owner in fee simple in severalty without use of the words of inheritance in the deed. The reason is that B, as well as A, had previously owned the fee in the whole. (e) A and B are *tenants in common*, each owning an undivided one half of Blackacre in fee simple, and A grants to B A's interest in Blackacre. B will take at common law only a life estate in A's undivided half unless words of inheritance are used. This is because A's estate is wholly separate and distinct from B's fee simple, each having a different interest. (f) A devises Blackacre to B. B takes a fee simple without the use of words of inheritance if such is the intention of the testator. See Restatement of Property §§ 29–37; Moynihan, 31, 32; Simes, 181–185.

CASE 33: A, being owner in fee simple of Blackacre, executes a deed thereto in the following language, to wit: "I hereby convey Blackacre to B and his heirs forever, to have and to hold to B and his heirs forever. Provided, that should B die without issue before C, then Blackacre is to go to C". What estate does B take under the deed?

Answer and Analysis

The answer is this—a fee simple. Here we have a granting clause creating a fee simple in the grantee. The habendum clause confirms the fee simple in the grantee. The proviso then attempts to limit the estate of the grantee to a "life" estate [1] on the contingencies that he die before C and without issue. In this set of facts it is not clear, by reading the entire deed, just what the grantor's intention is. Hence, there is justification to resort to rules of construction. One of those rules is this: when there are two contradictory clauses in a deed, the former will govern. Another is this: the grantor having once granted an estate in an instrument of conveyance, no subsequent clause therein can operate to nullify the grant. Either of these rules of construction may apply to and solve this case. Here we have two clauses, the granting clause and the habendum clause, granting a fee simple to B. Then we have a proviso wholly separated from the granting and habendum clauses, which cuts short the estate in B. This proviso, being wholly repugnant to the granting and habendum clauses, is void, and the grantee takes a fee simple estate. Such rules

---

1. Although on the happening of the contingencies B's estate would terminate on his death, it is not correct to classify it as a life estate. Rather, it should be termed a fee simple subject to an executory interest. It appears certain that a definite failure of issue construction is intended since the estate is to "shift" over to C only if B dies without issue in the lifetime of C. If B should die after C, either with or without issue, the estate would not go over to C but would be distributed through B's estate. The fee simple at that point would become absolute. See Note following this case.

of construction should be resorted to with caution and always on the premise that the reading of the entire instrument does not disclose a contrary intention of the grantor. See Carllee v. Ellsberry, 82 Ark. 209, 101 S.W. 407, 12 L.R.A.,N.S., 956, 118 Am.St.Rep. 60 (1907); Burby, 105; Simes, 196–203.

Note on Death Without Issue

Problems of construction frequently arise in a conveyance or devise to "A and his heirs but if A dies without issue, then to B and his heirs." Depending upon additional words in the instrument and surrounding circumstances, several interpretations may be possible. Two interpretations are common—namely, the definite versus the indefinite failure of issue construction.

By "definite failure of issue" is meant that it will be determined whether A dies without issue at a definite period of time, and such definite period, unless another is specified, will be the death of the named grantee, namely A in the above hypothet. Under such a construction, if A dies leaving any lineal descendant, he dies leaving issue and the contingency of his dying without issue can never happen. Thus, his estate is now a fee simple absolute which will either descend to his heirs or go to a devisee.

On the other hand, if A dies without leaving any issue surviving him, the estate will go over to B. Thus, under this definite failure of issue construction, A received a fee simple subject to an executory interest in B. It may also be noted in the instant case that since B's interest will either vest both in interest and possession or fail at the death of A, a life in being, B's interest is valid under the Rule Against Perpetuities. See infra Chapter VII.

By "indefinite failure of issue" is meant that if A's line of lineal descendants ever become extinct, then at that time, although it may be long after his actual death, A will die without issue. This describes a fee tail estate. Thus, in the above hypothet, if an indefinite failure of issue construction is employed, then A will receive a fee tail and B will have a vested remainder in fee simple absolute. See Simes, 196–203.

CASE 34: A, being fee simple owner of Blackacre, executed his deed thereto as follows: "I hereby grant Blackacre to my son-in-law, B, and his heirs, to have and to hold for his lifetime, and at his death to be equally divided among his heirs, they being my grandchildren then living". What estate does B take under this deed?

Answer and Analysis

The answer is this—a life estate. Here is an inconsistency between the granting clause which gives B a fee simple and the habendum clause which limits B's estate to a life estate. If we follow the rule of construction that if the granting clause is repugnant to or inconsistent with the habendum clause, the former will govern, then, of course, B takes a fee simple estate. But such rule will be resorted to only when the intention of the parties cannot be ascertained from the entire instrument. And it is believed such intention in this case can be gleaned by reading the entire instrument.

In analyzing the entire instrument not too much stress should be placed on the order in which the words, phrases or clauses appear. In the first place, the grantee, B, is a son-in-law of the grantor, A. In the second place, the deed provides for a division of the estate after the death of B. And among whom is the division to take place? "Among B's heirs, they being my grandchildren then living". A is here providing for a remainder among B's children, A's grandchildren. True, there can be no heirs of a living person and it cannot be foretold who B's heirs will be. But there is reason for believing A is using "B's heirs" as synonymous with "B's children," and if such be the case, then it is clear that B takes a life estate and there is a contingent remainder to B's children living at B's death.

Furthermore, by taking such view, the words, "and his heirs" used in the granting clause might well be read as "and his children". This construction would give effect to every part of the deed and reconcile the granting and the habendum clauses. Under such interpretation, B takes a life estate in Blackacre and his children living at his death take a contingent remainder, and there is a reversion in A. From a reading of the entire deed such seems to be A's intention. See Combs v. Fields, 211 Ky. 842, 278 S.W. 137 (1926); Simes, 181–185.

———

CASE 35: In State X a statute provided that a conveyance which prior to the enactment of the statute would create a fee tail estate should thereafter create a fee simple estate in the conveyee. In such a state, A, being fee simple owner of Blackacre, by deed or by will executes an instrument of conveyance using these words, "I hereby transfer my Blackacre to B and the heirs of his body". What estate does B take under the instrument?

Answer and Analysis

The answer is this—a fee simple. Prior to the statute and at common law the expression "to B and the heirs of his body" created in B a fee tail estate. Such estate was limited to lineal heirs. Many states have statutes which provide substantially that an estate which was at common law a fee tail, shall be deemed a fee simple. Under such statutes and the one given in the question above B would take a fee simple estate which would not be limited to lineal heirs but upon intestacy would or could pass to collateral heirs as well. Statutory modification of the fee tail is common, but the treatment is diverse.

See Restatement of Property § 42, Simes, 196–202; Moynihan, 41–48, and the law of particular states.

CASE 36: A, being fee simple owner of Blackacre, executes a conveyance thereto in the following language: "I hereby grant my Blackacre to B for life and thereafter to B's heirs". What estate is granted to B?

Answer and Analysis

The answer is this—a fee simple, if the Rule in Shelley's Case is in effect. The Rule in Shelley's Case is a rule of law. It is this: when the ancestor is given a life estate and in the same conveyance the ancestor's heirs are given the fee, then the ancestor takes a fee simple estate and his heirs take nothing by the conveyance. Applying the rule to the set of facts, B is the ancestor and is given a life estate. In the same deed B's heirs are given the fee. Result: B has the fee simple. This being a rule of law rather than one of construction, means that B takes the fee simple irrespective of the intention of A, the grantor. A rule of construction interprets the intention of the parties. There is no rule of construction applicable here. The Rule in Shelley's Case will be considered under future interests later. See Restatement of Property § 31; Simes, 43–55; Moynihan, 138–139; 1 Coke Rep. 93b (1581).

CASE 37: A, being fee simple owner of Blackacre, conveys it to B in the following language, "I hereby grant Blackacre to B and his heirs so long as Blackacre is used for school purposes". What interest has B in Blackacre?

Answer and Analysis

The answer is this—B has a fee simple determinable in Blackacre. B has a fee because words of inheritance, "and his heirs" were used following the grantee's name, which indicate the estate in B may last forever or as long as B has heirs. But they are words of limitation describing the fee in B. Also, the property may always be used for school purposes in which case the special limitation, "so long as used for school purposes" will neither add nor detract from B's estate. However, should Blackacre cease to be used for school purposes, then B's estate would *automatically* terminate and revert to A because the very words of the conveyance state that B's estate shall last just that long. Hence, there is no forfeiture involved. In that event B's estate would come to an end naturally. But the point here is this—B had a fee simple determinable. A has a possibility of reverter a subject which will be dealt with later under future interests. See Collette v. Town of Charlotte, 114 Vt. 357, 45 A.2d 203 (1946); Restatement of Property § 44.

CASE 38: Within X County A owned Blackacre which comprised an area of several blocks of land. The land was unimproved and undeveloped. A offered to convey one block of such land, Whiteacre, in the center of the tract to X County to be used for courthouse purposes. The proper county officers agreed to receive the property on behalf of the county and to locate the courthouse thereon. A made a deed to the county as grantee in these words, "I hereby grant, convey and forever set over to X County, State of Missota, all of my right, title, claim, interest and estate in and to Whiteacre, but upon this condition that Whiteacre shall be used forever as the site on which the courthouse of X County shall be erected". The courthouse was built on Whiteacre and so remained and was used as such for more than 100 years, when it was abandoned as a courthouse. When the structure ceased to be used for courthouse purposes, H was the sole heir of A. H sues X County for possession of Whiteacre contending that the above deed created in X County either a determinable fee simple or a fee simple on condition subsequent. May H succeed?

Answer and Analysis

The answer is no. A determinable fee is a fee which is created by an instrument of conveyance which provides that such estate shall come to an end automatically upon the happening of some described event. A fee simple subject to a condition subsequent is a fee which is created in an instrument of conveyance which provides that upon the happening of some certain event, then the grantor or his successors or heirs shall have the power to enter and terminate the estate of the grantee. The principal difference between the two is this: in the determinable fee the estate *automatically* comes to an end when the stated event happens, whereas in the fee subject to a condition subsequent the termination of the estate is *not automatic* but must be terminated by an entry or exercise of the reserved power by the grantor or his successor in interest. The former involves no forfeiture, the latter does. It is plain that whether a given deed conveys a fee simple absolute on the one hand or a determinable fee or one on condition subsequent on the other, is a matter of construction of the words used in the instrument.

In the construction of limitations the courts favor unconditional estates rather than conditional ones for the reason that estates once vested should not be uprooted after long periods of time unless it was the intention of the grantor expressed in the deed that such should happen. Following this principle the deed should be construed in favor of the defendant County unless it is fairly clear that the grantor, A, intended either a determinable fee or a fee upon condition subsequent. In the deed A grants to the County, a quasi-municipal corporation, "all of his right, title, claim, interest and estate in and to Whiteacre". Words of inheritance are not only not required but are quite inappropriate in such a case with a public corporation as grantee, so it is quite clear that A intended to grant a fee simple estate to X County.

The words following, "but *upon this condition* that Whiteacre shall be used *forever* as the site" of the courthouse, are the only words on which it can be contended there was either a determinable fee or fee upon condition subsequent. These words show no intention whatsoever that the fee simple in X County should automatically revert to A or his heirs. True, they limit the use to which Whiteacre shall be put, but they put no limit on the time during which the estate shall last. The typical words for creating a determinable fee are "so long as", "during", "until" or "while". None of these or similar expression was used but the use was to be "forever". Hence, it seems there is no expression of intention by A in the deed that there should be a determinable fee simple in X County. Was there a fee simple on condition subsequent? A fee simple on condition subsequent is generally introduced by such phrases as "provided that," "on condition that," "subject to the condition that," or "but if." An express reverter clause giving the grantor the right to re-enter is generally appended. Such reverter clauses, however, are not absolutely necessary. The fee simple subject to a condition subsequent always involves a forfeiture of a vested interest. The law abhors forfeitures and the courts will not construe the words of a deed to create such an estate unless the language is so clear as to admit of no other interpretation. In this case the deed did say, "upon the condition" that the tract be used "forever" as a courthouse site. But there is not one word used by A in the deed as to what should happen in case the site were not so used. There is no right of entry or power to terminate the estate reserved in A or his successors in interest. Without such express reservation of such power, the court ought not to imply such, when the result of which would cause a forfeiture of an estate which has lasted for more than a century. Hence, we conclude that there was no fee simple estate upon condition subsequent created in X County.

There is a further economic argument in such a case which should not be overlooked. It may be that A's grant of Whiteacre to X County was not wholly altruistic. If the county courthouse could be located in the middle of land owned by the grantor, such institution would no doubt enhance and stabilize the value of the lots surrounding the courthouse. Reading the language of the deed as a whole and considering the conditions under which it was executed, it seems quite correct to conclude that X County took a fee simple absolute estate in Whiteacre and that no defeasible fee simple was intended. Hence, H should not succeed in his action. See Chouteau v. City of St. Louis, 331 Mo. 781, 55 S.W.2d 299 (1932); Restatement of Property §§ 44, 45; Burby, pp. 205–209.

Note

It seems appropriate at this point when dealing with an interest claimed after the passing of a century to say that the common law rule against perpetuities has no application either to (a) a possibility of reverter or (b) right of re-entry for condition broken or power of termination. This subject will be considered in Chapter VII.

CASE 39:   A, being fee simple owner of Blackacre, executed a deed in B's favor as grantee as follows: "I hereby grant Blackacre to B and his heirs, provided that if intoxicating liquors are ever sold on the premises, then I reserve the right to enter and terminate the estate hereby created". What estate does B take under this deed?

Answer and Analysis

The answer is this—a fee simple subject to a condition subsequent. The older cases used the expression "right of re-entry for condition broken" to describe A's right. The more recent cases describe A's right as a "power of termination". But our question seeks to determine B's estate. He has a fee simple because words of inheritance "and his heirs" are used to describe the quantum of his estate. B's estate may last forever provided intoxicating liquors are not sold on the premises. It may also last forever although intoxicating liquors are sold on the premises provided A or his successors in interest do not terminate such estate of B by making entry and causing the forfeiture thereof.

The usual words for creating a condition subsequent are, "on condition that", "but if", "on the express condition that", "provided that" or similar expression. The usual expressions for reserving the power to terminate are that the grantor may: "reenter and take the property", "enter and terminate the estate", "in such case cause the title to revert back to the grantor", or other words evincing an intention to take back the property. The power to terminate may even be implied from such expressions as "every thing herein shall be null and void" or "this deed shall be null and void and the title shall revert to the grantor".

In our case both the condition subsequent and the power to terminate are provided for expressly in the deed. "Provided that if intoxicating liquors are ever sold on the premises" describe the condition subsequent. "Then I reserve the right to enter and terminate the estate hereby created" describe the power to terminate or right to make reentry for breach of the condition. It is clear then that A intended to create a fee simple in B and that if a certain event or condition happened, namely, the selling of intoxicating liquor on the premises, then A would have the right or power to enter and put an end to that fee simple. But it should be noted carefully that B's estate would not end automatically. It would end only if and when the condition happened AND thereafter the grantor or his successors in interest performed the requisite affirmative act of reentry for terminating such estate. See Restatement of Property § 45; Simes, 30.

CASE 40: A, being the fee simple owner of Blackacre, executed his deed to B as grantee in the following words, "I hereby grant Blackacre to B and his heirs, but upon the express condition that it shall not be competent for B to dispose of or alienate said Blackacre for a period of five years after he receives the title to such property". Ten days after the deed was delivered to B and B had duly recorded same, B executed his deed to Blackacre to "C and his heirs". What estate does C have in Blackacre?

Answer and Analysis

The answer is this—C has a fee simple absolute in Blackacre. This question does not involve either a determinable fee simple or a fee simple on condition subsequent for no such intention appears on the face of the deed. Here is a fee simple estate vested in B. The grantor then attempts to impose on the grantee, B, a restraint on his power to alienate or dispose of such fee simple estate. Is such restraint valid? The answer is an unequivocal no.

The power to dispose of the fee simple estate is an integral part and parcel of such estate in the hands of its owner, B. Such estate cannot exist apart from power in its owner to dispose of it any and every minute of the day. This type of restraint on power to alienate is classified as a disabling restraint and is void in all cases except when connected with spendthrift trusts. Where such restraint appears in a deed the grantee takes the property free of such restraint and with full power to dispose of the property. This is true whether such restraint refers to real or personal property, whether it refers to legal or equitable interests (spendthrift trusts excepted), and whether the estate involved is a fee simple, fee tail, life estate or an estate for years. In other words there is no power on the part of a grantor or testator to convey a fee simple estate to a person sui juris and deny such person the power to dispose of such estate for five years, for one year, for one day or one minute. Such is the doctrine of the common law. In this case then, A's attempted restraint on B's power to alienate the estate created in him was void and B took the fee simple absolute in Blackacre. Having such estate with no restraint thereon, B had both the right and power to convey the fee simple estate to anyone. Having granted the estate to "C and his heirs", C took from B the estate which B had which was a fee simple absolute. See Mandlebaum v. McDonell, 29 Mich. 78 (1874); In re Anderson's Estate, 267 Minn. 264, 126 N.W.2d 250 (1964); Simes, 237, 238.

Caveat

The disabling restraint illustrated in this case is a type of direct restraint on alienation. Other types of direct restraints are the promissory and forfeiture restraints. Unlike the disabling restraint, which is generally held invalid except in the case of spendthrift trusts, promissory and forfeiture restraints are generally held valid when imposed on interests less than fees simple. Simes, 237–241. See also Index, Restraint on Alienation, for additional text materials.

CASE 41: T, being fee simple owner of Blackacre, dies testate and devises Blackacre in the following language, "I hereby devise my Blackacre to B and his heirs, said estate in B hereby created to commence five years after my death". There is no residuary clause in T's will and no other reference to Blackacre therein. Upon T's death H is his sole heir. What interest, if any, has H in Blackacre?

Answer and Analysis

The answer is this—H has a fee simple estate in Blackacre subject to a springing executory devise in B. B's interest in Blackacre cannot be a remainder for two reasons: (a) it is not preceded by a freehold estate created in the same instrument as creates B's interest; and (b) a remainder could not follow a fee simple estate. Indeed, an estate such as T has created in B could not exist at common law for the reason that, apart from remainders, an estate could not be made to commence in futuro. Hence, B's interest must be of the executory type either under the Statute of Uses (1535) or Statute of Wills (1540).

Under the Statute of Uses, always created by deed, are two types of such interests: (a) springing uses which are carved out of the estate left in the conveyor; and (b) shifting uses which, upon the happening of a stated event, will shift from one person to another, other than the conveyor. Under the Statute of Wills, by analogy to uses, and always created by will, are two types of executory interests: (a) executory devises of the springing type which are carved out of the estate not disposed of by the testator; and (b) executory devises of the shifting type which upon the happening of a stated event, will shift to another person other than the heir. Of these four it is obvious that the interest created in B is an executory devise of the springing type because it is created by will and is carved out of the estate left undisposed of by the testator, T, which descended to his heir, H, and it does not shift to any other person. Today it is generally not necessary to distinguish between executory interests created by deed under the Statute of Uses and those created by devise under the Statute of Wills.

Thus, in our problem H has a fee simple estate which descended to him from the ancestor, T, and he holds such fee simple estate subject to an executory limitation which creates in B an executory springing devise. This means that T did not devise Blackacre to anyone to take effect immediately upon T's death. It then descended to H in fee simple. H can enjoy the possession of Blackacre as a fee simple owner for a period of five years immediately following T's death. When the five year period has expired the executory devise in B will spring up and he, B, will be possessed of a fee simple absolute in Blackacre. See Restatement of Property §§ 25, 46, 47; Simes, 25–28; Moynihan, 196–199. See also supra Cases 4–7, infra Chapter XVIII, part 2, Conveyances Under The Statute of Uses.

CASE 42: T, being owner of Blackacre in fee simple, dies testate and devises Blackacre in the following words, "I devise Blackacre to my three sons, A, B, C and their heirs forever and upon the death of any one of said three sons, the survivors shall take the share of the decedent share and share alike, to them and their heirs; and in case all three should die without issue, then Blackacre shall go to D and E and their heirs". The will is admitted to probate. A and B died intestate and without issue. C is in possession of Blackacre and opens new mines thereon. D and E sue C for damages for the commission of waste. May they recover?

Answer and Analysis

The answer is no. C is a fee simple owner and has the right to open new mines on his property. This conclusion depends upon the intention of T, the testator, and the construction of the words used in the will. First, it is obvious that the sons, A, B and C were given the fee simple estate in Blackacre for words of inheritance "and their heirs" limited such estate in them. Whether we consider A, B and C as joint tenants with the doctrine of survivorship, or whether we consider them tenants in common with an executory devise over to the survivor or survivors, is immaterial as under either theory C became the owner in fee simple upon the deaths of A and B. Secondly, it is necessary to determine the interests of D and E. D and E cannot have remainders because remainders cannot follow a fee simple estate. Specifically there cannot be a remainder following C's presently existing fee simple estate. D and E have shifting executory devises which are like shifting uses or interests created by deed. If it should happen that C should die without issue, which probably means children as used in T's will, then the estate will shift to D and E who will take Blackacre in fee simple.[2] But until that event happens, they have no vested estate in Blackacre but only an expectancy. The common law indulges in the conclusive presumption that a person is capable of procreation as long as he lives. That being the case there is a presumption in favor of C's having children. Until C dies without children he has an estate in fee simple defeasible, subject to a shifting executory devise in D and E in fee simple. As long as C has a fee simple estate in Blackacre he has the right to open new mines on the property and by so doing he does not commit waste. Hence, D and E

---

2. There would seem to be an implied gift to the issue or lineal descendants of the first two dying (A and B under the facts) in case the last survivor (C) died without issue, but such an implied gift cannot take effect in this case since A and B had already died without issue.

cannot recover in their action against C. See Gannon v. Peterson, 193 Ill. 372, 62 N.E. 210, 55 L.R.A. 701 (1901); Simes, 25, 26; Moynihan, 196–199.

See also supra Cases 4–7; infra Chapter XVIII, part 2, Conveyances Under The Statute of Uses; Note following Case 33 on Death Without Issue.

3. FEE SIMPLE CONDITIONAL AND FEE TAIL

LEGAL GEMS

1. The fee simple conditional estate was the forerunner of the fee tail estate and existed prior to the Statute De Donis Conditionalibus which was passed in 1285. This statute destroyed the fee simple conditional estate.

2. The fee simple conditional was an estate conditioned on the donee having a child with the donor retaining a reverter interest. After such child was born the donee had the power to convey a fee simple estate, and having exercised the power, both the rights of the donee's bodily heirs and the possibility of reverter of the donor were barred.

3. The Statute De Donis (1285) created the fee tail estate and made it a substitute for the fee simple conditional estate.

4. The typical words which created the fee simple conditional estate before 1285 and the fee tail estate after 1285 were, "to A and the heirs of his body".

5. The fee tail tenant owned a freehold inheritable estate but with limited powers thereover. He could use it during his lifetime, but he could make no disposition thereof so as to prevent its descending to his bodily heirs, if any, or if no bodily heirs, he could not prevent its reverting to the donor. Each succeeding fee tail tenant had the same rights.

6. Because the fee tail estate restricted the free alienability of land, the courts did not favor it. Fictitious legal proceedings were evolved to enlarge the powers of the fee tail tenant. The fine empowered him to cut off the rights of his bodily heirs and the common recovery empowered him to cut off both the rights of his bodily heirs and the reversion of the donor.

7. A fee simple estate is a larger estate than a fee tail estate. Hence, when a fee simple owner conveys a fee tail estate, there is a reversion left in the donor. In most jurisdictions recognizing the fee tail estate, the fee tail tenant now has the power, by giving a deed in fee simple, to cut off both his bodily heirs (called barring the entail) and the reversion in the donor.

8. Many states by statutes have abolished the fee tail estate by transforming it into a fee simple, or into a life estate in the first taker with a remainder in fee simple to his issue or lineal descendants.

Note

At this point Case 8, supra, setting forth the characteristics of the fee tail estate should be carefully re-read.

CASE 43:   In the year A.D. 1275, A, being the owner in fee simple of Blackacre in England, enfeoffed Blackacre to "B and the heirs of his body".   Thereafter there was born to B a son, S, who is an infant aged 5 years.   B enfeoffs Blackacre to "C and his heirs".   B dies leaving S his sole heir.   S sues C for the possession of Blackacre.   May he succeed?

Answer and Analysis

The answer is no.   For some years prior to A.D. 1285 when the Statute De Donis Conditionalibus (called De Donis) was passed, feoffments had been made of the type here set forth.   It was a device of the landed gentry to limit the descent of land to lineal heirs of the body and to keep the land in the family.   It is probable that the feoffor, A, intended that the feoffee, B, should take a life estate in Blackacre and that the words, "heirs of his body", should be words of purchase designating the persons to take after B's death.   In any event the feoffor did not intend that the feoffee, B, should have a fee simple estate, and he did intend that his deed should direct the course of descent of Blackacre down the lineal line of heirs only.   Had such intention been effective the land could have been kept indefinitely within the family line.   Titles thus fettered are not readily saleable.

The courts, apparently motivated by the theory that land should be freely alienable, construed the words, "to B and the heirs of his body" as a fee simple conditional, the condition being the birth of a child alive to B.   Once such birth took place, the donee, B, had power to convey a fee simple estate.   Hence, in our case when B's son, S, was born, such event empowered B to transfer the fee simple to C.   Having done so, C has a fee simple estate, and both the heirs of the body of B, on one hand, and the feoffor's right to have the estate if B's lineal heirs became extinct on the other hand, were cut off completely.   The conveyance by B to C having cut off S's right to Blackacre, S cannot maintain his suit to dispossess C.

Until birth of issue to B, in our hypothetical case, in essence B had only a life estate with a possibility of reverter in A, the feoffor.   When a child was born to the donee, then the reverter could be barred.   Thus, B could inter vivos convey the land in fee simple but if he did not so convey, then the land would descend, not to B's heirs generally, but only to his lineal descendants.   Fee simple conditional estates continued in England until the passage of the Statute "De Donis" in 1285 by which such estates were transformed into fee tail estates.   These two types of estates did not exist in England at the same time; the fee simple conditional preceded the fee tail and was the forerunner thereof.   Fee simple conditional estates have been recognized in South Carolina, Iowa and Oregon. See Antley v. Antley, 132 S.C. 306, 128 S.E. 31 (1925); Restatement of Property §§ 59–67, 68–77.

CASE 44:   In the year A.D. 1295, A, being the owner in fee simple of Blackacre in England, enfeoffed Blackacre to "B and the heirs of his body".   Thereafter there was born to B a son, S, who is an infant aged 5 years. B enfeoffs Blackacre to "C and his heirs". B dies leaving S his sole heir. S sues C for the possession of Blackacre. May he succeed?

Answer and Analysis

The answer is yes. It should be noticed that this set of facts is identical with the facts given in Case 43 next above, with this exception, the date in this case is 20 years later. It should be noticed too that the answer is just the opposite of that in the former case. Why? Because in the year 1285 Parliament passed the statute De Donis Conditionalibus. That statute destroyed the fee simple conditional estate in England and created the fee tail estate for the first time. This set of facts created a fee simple conditional estate in 1275 but under the statute De Donis, passed in 1285, created a fee tail estate in 1295.

The landed gentry was not at all pleased with the interpretation put by the courts on the expression, "to B and the heirs of his body" whereby a fee simple conditional was recognized, and the landed gentry was in control of Parliament. So the statute De Donis was passed for the very purpose of taking from the donee, B, in the above expression in a deed, the power to convey a fee simple estate upon the birth of issue alive to him, thereby cutting off the rights of B's bodily heirs and the reversionary interest in the feoffor, A. The statute bluntly provided in substance that the feoffor's intention should be carried out.

This statute De Donis is considered the most stringent restraint on the alienation of land in English law. Of course, the courts were bound by the statute. They were compelled to hold in the case given, that the feofee, B, took a fee tail estate under the feoffment. Such holding meant, (a) that B had an inheritable estate because the words, "and the heirs of his body" were construed to be words of limitation, (b) that such estate would last as long as B had heirs of his body, (c) that while B could use Blackacre as a fee owner, still that use could not extend beyond the period of B's lifetime, (d) that B could not convey any interest which would last beyond B's lifetime, (e) that B could do nothing by conveyance inter vivos or otherwise which could deflect the course of descent from the bodily issue of B, and (f) that B could do nothing which would prevent Blackacre reverting to A, or to his heirs, if B did not have descendants.

Applying these principles to the set of facts given as of the year 1295, the court would have to hold that B had a fee tail estate but with no power by conveying to "C and his heirs" to cut off the right of his son, S, to inherit Blackacre from B at B's death. Hence, C took no more than an estate pur autre vie, for the life of B. Upon B's death, Blackacre descended from B to his bodily heir, S, who then had the right to possess Blackacre from anyone to whom B had conveyed it. Hence, S could eject C from the land. And of course, S, now being a fee tail tenant, had the same rights with the same restrictions as had his father, B, before him, and could not cut off his own issue from inheriting Blackacre. And so it went ad infinitum. And had B died without descendants, then the feoffor, A, could have ejected C. (A's reversion arose, of course, out of the fact that A had a fee simple estate and out of it he carved in B's favor a lesser estate, a fee tail.) Such was the effect of the statute De Donis. But the struggle between the landed gentry who favored the statute on the one hand, and the commercial classes who were in favor of free alienation of land on the other, was not over.

The courts were hostile to the statute. By the year 1472 the court procedure called "common recovery" was devised. By this fictitious lawsuit the fee tail tenant, B in our case, was empowered to cut off the interest of his bodily heirs (called barring the entail) and also the reversion of the donor, A in our case. By this bold stroke the courts severed the restraint on alienation which had fettered the fee tail tenant and permitted him to dispose of the estate in fee simple, thus barring both the entail and the reversion in the donor. Logically, both the statute De Donis and the power by common recovery to defeat it, should have become part of the American common law. These concepts were not so received. Today in the United States nearly all of the states have either constitutional or statutory provisions covering the subject.

See Restatement of Property pp. 201–327 where the subject is exhaustively covered as to each state; typical case of fee tail herein, Case 8, supra.

Note

Once the principle of the fee tail was established, that one could limit descent to a class of heirs narrower than the heirs general in a fee simple estate, the donor was permitted to restrict the course of descent still further as appears in the classification of fee tail estates below.

1. Fees tail general
   - A to B and the heirs of his body
   - A to B and the heirs male of his body
   - A to B and the heirs female of his body

2. Fees tail special
   - A to B and the heirs of his body by wife, W
   - A to B and the heirs male of his body by his wife, W
   - A to B and the heirs female of his body by his wife, W.

CASE 45: A owned Blackacre in fee simple in State X where, by statute, a fee tail tenant could bar the entail by giving a deed to the premises in fee simple. A conveyed Blackacre "to B and the heirs of his body". B became indebted to C who took judgment against B and levied upon and sold Blackacre to D. The sheriff's deed issued to "D and his heirs". B married W and had a son of such marriage, S, who survived B's death and who was B's sole heir. B made no conveyance of Blackacre during his lifetime. Upon B's death, his bodily heir, S, sues D to eject D from Blackacre. May he recover?

Answer and Analysis

The answer logically can go either way. First the question will be answered yes with complete analysis and reasons, and then it will be answered no with similar coverage in the Note following the first discussion.

As to the yes answer, two important principles are involved in this set of facts, (a) the rule of the common law obtains unless changed by statute, and (b) the rights of a creditor are wholly derivative; the creditor can take no more right upon execution than the debtor had in the property involved. What interest or right, then, did the debtor, B, have in Blackacre?

At common law B was a fee tail tenant with no power to bar the entail or the reversion, except by the use of the fictitious lawsuits of fine or recovery. [The common recovery barred both the reversion and the entail. See Case 44 supra. The fine barred only the entail.] In State X the statute has substituted a deed of conveyance for these fictitious lawsuits as a means by which the tenant in tail could bar the entail and the reversionary interest of the grantor, A. But the statute goes no further. It does not say that someone other than the tenant in tail, B in our case, can exercise that power. And the facts tell us that B made no conveyance of Blackacre during his lifetime. Until B and B alone exercised that power, B remained a fee tail tenant having the right to use Blackacre only during his lifetime. So the sheriff's levy and sale under C's judgment affected only B's life interest in Blackacre. Hence, the sheriff's deed could and did convey to D only B's life interest in the property and the entail in S's favor was not barred. Upon B's death then, the fee tail estate descended to S unaffected by the judgment levy and sale. Hence, S can eject D, the purchaser at the judgment sale, from Blackacre.

Of course, under the statute, had B conveyed to a "straw man", "Z and his heirs" and taken a conveyance back from Z to "B and his heirs", then B would have exercised the power given him by the statute and would have owned Blackacre in fee simple. Then the sheriff's deed on sale of the fee simple estate of B would have lodged the fee simple in D, and S's rights would have been barred and he could not have ejected D. But unless the statute gives a creditor of a fee tail tenant the power to bar the entail, such creditor can levy only on the fee tail tenant's life interest in the property. See Hazzard v. Hazzard, 29 Del. 91, 97 A. 233 (1916).

Note

The Alternative Answer

This is the type of case in which the student can be bold and independent and solve the case not only on what he "guesses" a court would do but also upon his own philosophy as to whether a statute should be given a restrictive or an expansive interpretation. In the Hazzard case the Delaware court, and the answer previously discussed, gave a restrictive construction to the statute. By using the same set of facts and giving an expansive interpretation to the statute, the opposite, and perhaps a more satisfactory, result can be obtained.

Two principles are involved: (a) any interest which an owner of property can convey voluntarily, a creditor can take from him involuntarily, and (b) a general power over property is considered the equivalent of property. Applying these principles to the set of facts we conclude that the fee tail tenant not only had a fee tail estate but also had a power to convey a fee simple estate in the property; that when the levy was made on Blackacre it was made both on the fee tail estate and also on the power to convey a fee simple, both of which were vested in the debtor, B. This power was part and parcel of the subject of the levy of execution and was sold by the execution sale to the purchaser, D. C's rights being derivative, he sold to D what rights and powers B, the debtor, had over Blackacre. By the sale on execution the judgment creditor, C, had exercised the power which B had over Blackacre and conveyed to D a fee simple estate. Thus the entail in S, the bodily heir of the fee tail tenant, B, is barred and he cannot recover from D. Both this result and that previously reached in this Case, are legally sound, depending on the premise and philosophy used and the result desired to be attained. See Restatement of Property § 90.

CASE 46: T died testate and in her will devised Blackacre which she owned in fee simple, "to my daughter, W, and the heirs of her body". A residuary clause in T's will devised all the residue of my real property "to my children, A, B and W and their heirs, share and share alike." In the jurisdiction a statute provided that if a spouse died intestate without issue, the decedent's property would descend to the surviving spouse. Another statute preferred tenancy in common over joint tenancy, and another empowered a fee tail tenant to convey a fee simple. After T's death W married H and died intestate and without issue her surviving. W and H had been in the possession of Blackacre and after

W died H continued in the possession of the property.   A and B sue to eject H from Blackacre.   May they succeed?

Answer and Analysis

The answer is no.   When one owns a fee simple estate in land and conveys a fee tail estate in the same land, there is a reversion left in the conveyor for the reason that the fee simple estate is larger than the fee tail.   The fee simple will last as long as the owner has heirs general, lineal and collateral, whereas the fee tail will last only as long as the owner has heirs of the body which are lineal.   When T in her will devised a fee tail estate to W, there was left in T a reversion which fell within the residuary clause of T's will in favor of A, B and W.

Under T's will, then, W was donee of a fee tail estate in Blackacre which would descend to her bodily heirs, if any, and was beneficiary under the residuary cause of an undivided one third interest in the reversion left in T.   Upon W's death intestate without bodily issue, the estate tail came to an end and the reversionary interest which W owned descended to her surviving spouse, H.   Hence, H is a tenant in common with A and B of Blackacre in which tenancy the unity of possession exists so that H's possession is the possession of A and B as a matter of law.   Each tenant in common has the same right of possession as every other such tenant and one cannot eject another.   So A and B must fail in their suit against H.

Of course, had W conveyed her fee tail estate to another in fee simple during her lifetime, then the defeasible reversion which T devised to A, B and W in the same will by which she devised the fee tail to W, would have been cut off and the grantee from W in fee simple would have owned Blackacre in fee simple absolute.

See Ewing v. Nesbitt, 88 Kan. 708, 129 P. 1131 (1913), a most interesting case on fee tail estates.

Note

The student should note carefully this peculiar anomaly about a fee tail—the words, "and the heirs of his body", are words of limitation which describe an estate in the donee which will last as long as there are bodily heirs or lineal descendants of such donee; that such bodily heirs take their successive fee tail estates by descent, and still no fee tail tenant had the power to convey an estate which would continue beyond his lifetime.   Such situation continued from the statute De Donis in 1285 till 1472 when the common recovery permitted the fee tail tenant to convey in fee simple cutting off the entail and the reversion.

4.   LIFE ESTATES

LEGAL GEMS

1.   Life estates include (a) life estate for the life of the tenant, (b) life estate for the life of one other than the tenant (pur autre

vie), (c) life estate resulting from a fee tail special tenancy after possibility of issue extinct, (d) life estate by dower, (e) life estate by curtesy, and (f) life estate by and during coverture.

2.   A life estate is one in which the duration is measured by the life or lives of one or more human beings and is not otherwise terminable at a fixed or computable period of time.

3.   If an estate MAY last for a lifetime, it is a life estate, even though it may be cut short before it runs its natural course.   However, if a limitation is made expressly subject to the will of the grantee or lessee, there is a conflict, and the interest created is either a life estate determinable or a tenancy at will, depending upon the jurisdiction.

4.   If a conveyance identifies the grantee but fails to describe effectively the estate which he is to take, then the conveyee takes a life estate at common law, but today the estate conveyed will usually be construed to be a fee simple or whatever estate the conveyor had.

5.   A life tenant, in addition to his estate for life, may be given a power to convey, sell, appoint, or mortgage the fee.   Upon the exercise of such power, the rights of the remaindermen or reversioners are affected accordingly.

6.   The Rule in Shelley's Case as a rule of property rather than as a rule of construction, defeats the intention of the grantor to create a life estate, and gives the named life tenant either a fee simple or a fee tail estate.

7.   A life estate may be limited to B for the lives of B, C, D and E and the survivor of them, and will not terminate until the death of the survivor of the four.

8.   A life estate to B for and during his life and the lives of all the persons of a given state would give B a life estate for his life only, the provision for the lives of the others being void because of impracticability of learning of the death of the survivor.

9.   Forfeiture restraints on the power to alienate a life estate, usually phrased so as to make the life estate defeasible on an attempted alienation, are valid.   The reasons for upholding such restraints are: (1) life estates are not readily alienable in a commercial sense anyway; and (2) the restraint may have been imposed for the benefit of the reversioner or remainderman.

10.   Like other estates, a life estate may be subject to termination by a special limitation or by a power of termination.

Note

At this point Cases 9 through 14, supra, setting forth the characteristics of the various types of life estates should be carefully reread.

———

CASE 47:   A, being fee simple owner of Blackacre, made a lease to B "during the full term of while B shall wish to live

in this city of X". A then granted his reversionary interest
in Blackacre to P while B remained in possession under the
lease and was not in default in paying rent or otherwise. P
gave B notice to quit which B refused to do. P brings suit
to eject B and contends that B has only a tenancy at will.
May P succeed in his action?

Answer and Analysis

The preferred answer is no. We say that if an estate in land
MAY last forever, it is a fee, a fee tail or fee simple, even though it
may be a determinable fee or one subject to condition subsequent or
to an executory limitation. The same is true of a life estate. If the
estate described in the grantee MAY last for a life time, then it is a
life estate. In the case before us it is quite obvious that B MAY "wish
to live in this city of X" during the term of his natural life. Therefore B has a life estate which is determinable at his option.

Another principle which may be applied to bring about the same
conclusion is that the terms of a conveyance are construed most
strongly against a grantor or lessor. The language of the instrument
leaves the power in the conveyee to terminate the estate by leaving
the city of X and construing such words against the conveyor, that
power to end the estate should be in B and in no one else. Thus B
takes a life estate determinable. However, see Notes *infra*.

Note 1

There are many contra cases which hold that B gets a tenancy at
will. These cases are based on the ancient dictum of Coke, "when
the lease is made to have and to hold at the will of the lessee, this
must be also at the will of the lessor." This appears to be based on
the doctrine of mutuality, but since a conveyance is not an executory
contract, there need be no mutuality. The intention of the conveyor
governs, and since the lessor left the estate at the "wish" of the lessee, which might be for B's life, B should obtain a life estate. Conversely, however, if the lease or conveyance were at the wish of the
lessor or conveyor, then it is generally, if not universally, held that
the limitation creates a tenancy at will. Cf.: Thompson v. Baxter,
107 Minn. 122, 119 N.W. 797, 21 L.R.A.,N.S., 575 (1909), and Foley v.
Gamester, 271 Mass. 55, 170 N.E. 799 (1930). See Restatement of
Property §§ 109, 112; Moynihan, 83–85.

Note 2

In some limitations the possibility of there arising a fee simple
determinable might also be considered. Since words of limitation are
no longer necessary to create a fee simple, a fee simple determinable
rather than a life estate determinable may be created if there is no
indication that the estate cannot last longer than a life. For example, a limitation to "W for life or until she marries" creates no more
than a life estate because the words "for life" are expressed. However, if the instrument reads simply to "W until she marries" without

a gift over on the death of W, it is necessary to determine whether the conveyor intends W's estate to become absolute on her death without marrying, or whether in any event the estate is to terminate at her death. Thus, in determinable estates it is necessary to determine the maximum duration of the estate, and in addition, to be aware of the rule in some jurisdictions that if the estate is terminable at the will of the grantee or lessee, then it is also terminable at the will of the grantor or lessor. See Moynihan, 50–51.

CASE 48: H and W were husband and wife who had five minor children. H was fee simple owner of Blackacre at the time of his death testate. H devised Blackacre "to my wife, W, for the term of her natural life, remainder to our children share and share alike, but if my wife, W, determines it to be for the welfare of the family to sell Blackacre, then she is hereby empowered to sell the land and pass a fee simple title thereto". W did decide that it was for the family welfare to dispose of the property so she made a conveyance thereto to "B and his heirs". W died and the five children sue B for possession of Blackacre. Should they succeed in their action?

Answer and Analysis

The answer is no. Sometimes an estate is given with a power in someone to cut short or destroy it. Sometimes an estate is given with a power to enlarge it. This case involves both types—a life estate in W with a power to dispose of the fee simple and a remainder in fee simple defeasible in the children with power in W to destroy it. By W's conveyance to B in fee simple she exercised that power, which single act both enlarged her life estate to a fee in her grantee and destroyed the remainder in fee simple which had vested in her children. But until the exercise of the power by W, she had only a life estate, and her creditors could not exercise such power for her because the devisor, H, intended such power to be based upon W's judgment and discretion as to whether it was for the family welfare. See Smith v. Teel, 35 Ariz. 274, 276 P. 850 (1929); Restatement of Property § 108, comment e.

CASE 49: Testator, T, being fee simple owner of Blackacre, devised it "to my son, B, for life, remainder, in fee simple to the heirs of B's body". In the state where Blackacre is located a fee tail estate is permissible and the tenant in tail has the power to convey a fee simple title inter vivos. B during his lifetime conveyed to "C and his heirs". B died. Immediately X and Y, the two children of B, both of whom survived him, brought suit to eject C from Blackacre. May

X and Y succeed? (NOTE: Read Case 36, supra, before going further.)

Answer and Analysis

The answer is yes. Of course, the answer depends upon what estate was created in B by the devise of T. And that depends upon the interpretation of the words in the will. It is clear that B took a freehold estate, (a) a life estate, (b) a fee tail, or (c) a fee simple. It is just as plain that if he took either a fee tail or a fee simple, such could have been true only by the application of the Rule in Shelley's Case. [Case 36 supra, 87 infra] Could such apply under the words used in T's will? The Rule applies both to fee tail and fee simple estates. It will create a fee tail in the following language in a conveyance, "to B for life, remainder to the heirs of B's body." Result: B takes a fee tail—his bodily heirs take nothing. Why? Because as a rule of property, the words "the heirs of B's body" are words of limitation describing, not persons to take, but the size of the estate given to B. But the words used in T's will are not those just used for illustration. The will says, "remainder *in fee simple* to the heirs of B's body". If the Rule applied, then the remainder would be in fee tail only, but T says such remaindermen are to take in fee simple, and his intention governs unless the Rule applies.

The Rule will create a fee simple in the following expression in a conveyance, "to B for life, remainder to B's heirs". Result: B takes a fee simple and his heirs take nothing. Why? Because the Rule makes "to B's heirs" words of limitation describing the estate which B is given. But T did not use the words used in the illustration. He limited the heirs to "bodily heirs" but said they were to take in "fee simple". So the Rule in Shelley's Case cannot apply to make a fee simple when the heirs are limited to those lineal; and it cannot apply to make a fee tail when the heirs are lineal but they are to take a fee simple. If we are at liberty to follow T's intention, that is not difficult to find. He intended B should have a life estate and says so in ipsis verbis, "for life". Then the remainder shall go to his bodily heirs in fee simple. Who are B's bodily heirs? That is not determinable until B dies. Hence, they take a contingent remainder. And it must be noticed that the words, "heirs of B's body" are construed as "words of purchase" meaning words designating persons to take rather than "words of limitation" describing the size of the estate to be taken.

The solution of our problem is this: B had a life estate, the heirs of his body had a contingent remainder in fee simple. B, having only a life estate, could convey only such to C, who took an estate in Blackacre for the life of B. When B died, C's estate came to an end. At the instant of B's death, his bodily heirs were determinable and determined to be X and Y. At the instant of B's death, the contingent remainder of X and Y was transformed into an estate of possession and X and Y had as of that instant the right to immediate possession of Blackacre. See Meyer v. Meyer, 146 Kan. 907, 73 P.2d 1007 (1937).

CASE 50: A, being fee simple owner of Blackacre, executed a deed thereto in these words, "to B for the lives of B, C, D and E and the survivor of them". B conveyed to X all of B's right, title and interest in Blackacre. B then died with C, D and E surviving. A sues to eject X from Blackacre and argues that B's death terminated X's interest in the premises. May A succeed?

Answer and Analysis

The answer is no. It should be noted that the tenant's name, B, is listed among the measuring lives so that this is not wholly an estate pur autre vie. Further, of course, if B should be the survivor of the four, then it would have terminated as a life estate for the tenant B. But that would not be true in its creation or origin. But B has a valid estate for the lives of B, C, D and E *and the survivor of them.* The *underscored* phrase makes the life of the survivor of the four the maximum term of the estate which B had and which he assigned to X. Hence, A, as reversioner has no right to eject X until all of the four are dead. Had the conveyance read, "for the joint lives, of B, C, D and E", then the "joint lives" could only last until the first of the four died and when B died, then A could have ejected X. But the deed did not so provide. Had the measuring lives been "for the life of B and the lives of all the persons now living in the State of South Dakota and the survivor of them", the provision for the lives beyond that of tenant, B, would be void for the reason that it would be impracticable if not impossible to determine the time of death of the survivor, and B would take a life estate for his own life only. See Restatement of Property § 107, illustrations 1, 4, 5.

CASE 51. T devised Blackacre to his daughter, D, for life, and at her death to his two grandchildren, X and Y, and their heirs, and provided further that Blackacre should not be sold until X and Y reached 45 years of age. Is the provision against sale valid?

Answer and Analysis

The answer is no in almost all states, but yes in Mississippi during the life of D. The provision against sale is a restraint on alienation of the disabling type. A disabling restraint is a direction in the creating instrument that the estate shall not be alienated; thus, if valid, it would create a non-transferable estate. The general rule, with the exception of a disabling restraint on the beneficial interest under a spendthrift trust, is that all disabling restraints on alienation are void. This rule of invalidity applies whether the disabling restraint is attached to a fee simple, life estate, or lesser interest. It also applies whether the restraint is total or partial, limited or unlimited as to duration. When applicable, the rule of invalidity invalidates the illegal restraint on alienation and makes the estate freely alienable. Thus, in most jurisdictions, in the instant case, D acquires a life estate which she can alienate, and X and Y can freely alienate their remainder interests during the lifetime of D, and they can freely alienate the fee simple after the death of D regardless of whether or not they reach the age of 45.

Forfeiture and promissory restraints on fees simple have generally been held invalid, but forfeiture and promissory restraints on life estates and lesser interests are generally held valid. A forfeiture restraint exists when the creating instrument provides that on an attempted alienation the estate created or transferred shall be forfeited or terminated with a provision for the estate to go over to another person or revert to the grantor. A promissory restraint is in the form of a covenant that the grantee will not alienate the estate. Thus, in the instant case, if the will provided that should D transfer or alienate her life estate, then her estate should end and the entire estate vest in X and Y, the provision would be perfectly valid and enforceable. See also Note 2 following this case.

In Mississippi, however, as a result of the statute prohibiting the fee tail, [Miss.Code Ann. § 89–1–15 (1972 as of 1979)], the courts have upheld disabling restraints on alienation during the lifetime of a life tenant. The restraint on alienation in Mississippi may not exceed the life of the life tenant or a succession of life tenants living at the time the estate is created. Thus, in the above case, a restraint on alienation during D's life is valid, but the restraint until X and Y become 45 might well exceed D's life and hence is excessive. In such a case, the courts have two alternatives: (1) they can invalidate the entire restraint and make the respective interests freely alienable at once; or (2) they can uphold the restraint in part and invalidate only the part that is excessive. Mississippi follows the second alternative; therefore the restraint on alienation is valid in that state during the lifetime of D but no longer.

Forfeiture restraints on life estates may be justified on two grounds: (1) they may be imposed for the benefit of the reversioner or remainderman; and (2) life estates are somewhat inalienable (at least in a commercial sense) anyway. Because the life tenant may die the next day, no one is willing to pay very much for a life estate. Forfeiture restraints on leaseholds are common and are valid. These restraints customarily take the form of affording the landlord the right to re-enter and terminate the estate if the leasehold is transferred without the landlord's consent. The interest of the landlord in protecting his rental income and reversionary estate are sufficient justification for upholding such restraints. See: In re Estate of Kelly, 193 So.2d 575 (Miss.1967); Simes, 237–248.

Note 1

Life estates are also subject to termination by special limitation such as "to B for life so long as he does not sell liquor on the premises," or "to W for life for so long as she remains a widow (or until she remarries)", and to a power of termination such as, "to B but if he does not keep the fences in repair, then I reserve the right to re-enter and take back the premises." See: McCray v. Caves, 211 Ga. 770, 88 S.E.2d 373 (1955); Restatement of Property § 18.

Note 2

Effect of Condominium and Close-in Living

The modern trend to condominium and cluster housing has given rise to increased restrictions on the use and transfer of such housing units. The close interrelationships of the community members, whether controlled by a home owners', a condominium or a cooperative association, have resulted in the use of restrictions in order to achieve a community of compatible and financially responsible persons. The restrictions frequently involve not only restrictions on use, i. e., single family residence, no children under a certain age, or no pets, but also restrictions on sale or transfer.

A wholly disabling restraint on sale most likely would not be used, and even if it were, most likely would be held invalid although limited as to duration. However, provisions are common that grant the association a right of first refusal. In other words, when an owner wishes to sell, the association may either approve the prospective buyer and sale, or instead, may buy the unit on the terms and conditions offered by the prospective buyer.

As long as the association does not have an unreasonably long period of time in which to exercise its purchase option, such provisions have been, and should be upheld as long as the particular terms do not violate the rule against perpetuities.[3]

3. See infra Case 101 and the Note following holding that options in gross are subject to the common law rule against perpetuities, but that options to renew or purchase in connection with leases are not subject to the Rule because such options promote rather than hinder alienability.

Thus, prima facie in a cooperative housing situation, where usually the occupant owns stock in a corporation and leases his apartment from the corporation, a right of first refusal or option to buy vested in the association-lessor, as distinct from an option in the lessee, because of its desirability should withstand the perpetuities test. On the other hand, in a typical homeowners' association where the individual owns his separate home and lot while the association takes care of and may own certain property used in common, prima facie, an option or right of first refusal granted to the association would have to be so limited as to comply with the rule against perpetuities. The same situation logically should apply to a condominium community where the occupants own their individual units in fee simple.

Some states have avoided the problem in condominiums by express provisions in the statute that the rule against perpetuities shall not be applied to defeat a right given any person or entity by the declaration for the purpose of allowing unit owners to retain reasonable control over the use, occupancy, and transfer of units.

One court expressed the opinion that a right of first refusal was not a restraint on alienation since the seller in effect had two purchasers instead of one. Watergate Corp. v. Reagan, 321 So.2d 133 (Fla. 4th D.C.A.1975). Such reasoning is questionable. Where there exists a right of first refusal, any prospective purchaser that the seller gets must be prepared and willing to wait until the association decides whether or not to exercise the option. If the association is given too long a period of time to decide, many prospective purchasers will refrain from making an offer because they will not want to be bound for a long time without an assurance that they will get the land. Thus, there will definitely be a restraint on alienation. Reasonable controls, however, are common and even desirable.

In view of these recent developments, statements about direct restraints on alienation should be phrased as follows: reasonable restraints on alienation are upheld, but unreasonable restraints on alienation are invalid. See Coquina Club, Inc. v. Mantz, 342 So.2d 112 (Fla. 2d D.C.A.1977), holding that unit owner must tender a qualified purchaser (here with no children under 12), before association has duty to purchase or provide another purchaser; Hoover & Morris Dev. Co., Inc. v. Mayfield, 233 Ga. 593, 212 S.E.2d 778 (1975), holding that owner didn't comply with declaration requirements concerning notice to the association so as to require exercise of the option or consent, but that there was evidence of a waiver; and Ritchey v. Villa Nueva Condominium Ass'n, 81 Cal.App.3d 688, 146 Cal.Rptr.

See, e. g., West's Fla.Stat.Ann. § 718.-104(5); Utah Stat.Ann. § 57–8–28 (1979); and Mo.Stat.Ann. § 448.210 (1979), the latter two also excluding the rule prohibiting unreasonable restraints on alienation from invalidating such provisions. In the absence of an express statute, the option can be phrased in reference to both an arbitrary standard which will not exceed the period of the Rule and also in reference to the life of the condominium regime. Under this technique options can be exercised for a considerable period of time.

Even when there is no statute specifically exempting repurchase options from the rule against perpetuities in cluster housing developments, a good policy argument can be made in support thereof, particularly in the case of condominiums. The following is a brief excerpt from Boyer, Florida Real Estate Transactions, § 39.17[2] (1977).

". . . Policy arguments have been advanced that the rule should not be applied to essentially commercial transactions seeking to accomplish reasonable objectives. [Leach, Perpetuities: 'New Absurdity, Judicial and Statutory Correctives,' 73 Harv.L.Rev. 1318, 1321–1322 (1960)]. Further, the interest of the individual owners is different from that of an ordinary fee simple owner in severalty. This is essentially a new type of ownership. Each owner has in addition to his separate ownership an undivided interest in the common elements and underlying fee. The association of owners, if we can disregard a possible corporate entity and elevate reality over legal fiction, are in fact the collective owners of various fee and easement interests in the building, and it is to such a group that the pre-emptive option is given. The analogy to the leasehold interest and the exception of options connected therewith from the rule against perpetuities is strong. Clearly, an option annexed to one owner's interest in favor of all the owners is substantially different from a simple option in gross. It should be held that such an option, although it may fetter alienation, is socially desirable and should be upheld." [See Powell, ¶ 771 for a discussion of the traditional approach to option cases and the policy involved].

695 (1978), holding that age restrictions on occupancy and sale were reasonable and valid, and that coupled with a right of first refusal as provided in the documents would impose on the association the duty within fifteen days to either provide a qualified purchaser, purchase itself, or waive the restriction.

5. TENANCIES LESS THAN FREEHOLD

LEGAL GEMS

1. Tenancies less than freehold include

(a) estate for years, which is by far the most important class,

(b) periodic tenancy, being year to year, month to month, week to week, etc.; these are generally called "year to year" tenancies, or "estates from year to year",

(c) tenancy at will, being at the will of either tenant or lessor, and

(d) tenancy at sufferance, which is no tenancy at all but a mere naked possession of land without right.

2. To be a tenancy or estate for years, the term must have a definite and specific time for beginning and a definite and specific time or date for its termination. If a specific date cannot be found when the estate shall end, it is not an estate for years.

3. The word "years" as used in the phrase, "estate for years", is only a name and does not mean the term must be for years. Any definite leasehold period indicates an "estate for years", such as, one year, one month, six weeks, 90 days, half a year, January 31st, 1970 to August 4, 1970, or June 30, 1970 to June 30, 1975.

4. An ineffective creation of an estate for years usually results in an estate at will or, under some additional facts such as payment of rent for specific periods, may create an estate from year to year.

5. An estate for years at common law is a chattel real and always PERSONAL PROPERTY; upon the death of the owner of such estate intestate, it passes as any other personalty to his personal representative. While it is an estate in real property it is NOT REAL PROPERTY.

6. The creation of an estate for years is a conveyance and no contractual provision need be included. Thus, in each of the following instances B receives an estate for years: (1), A, being a fee simple owner of Blackacre, conveys to B for ten years with no reservation of rent and with no contract provision therein; or (2), A, being fee simple owner of Blackacre, conveys "to B for 10 years, then to C and his heirs forever".

7. However, because almost all leases for years include contractual provisions, an analysis of any lease will disclose both: (a) privity of estate, the tenant being owner of an estate for years with a reversion in the landlord; and (b) privity of contract by which each party to the lease undertakes personal obligations.

8.   Every leasehold includes the following elements:

(a) an estate in the tenant;

(b) a reversion in the landlord;

(c) exclusive possession and control of the land in the tenant; and

(d) generally, a contract between the parties.

Note: a, b and c constitute privity of estate, and d is privity of contract.

9.   Whereas in a lease exclusive possession must lodge in the tenant, in a license the possession remains in the licensor and the licensee has a mere privilege of being on the land without being treated as a trespasser.

10.   When a tenancy for years fails because of the Statute of Frauds, the tenancy becomes one at the will of the parties, but subsequent events, such as the payment and acceptance of rent for a year or a part thereof, may transform the tenancy at will into one from year to year, month to month or week to week.

11.   An estate for years may in its creation be subject to a special limitation, right of re-entry for condition broken or an executory limitation.

12.   When a tenant holds over after the termination of lease, the landlord has a choice of several remedies: (1) he may treat the tenant as a trespasser, evict him, and recover damages for use and occupation; (2) at common law and in most states he may treat the tenant as a tenant from period to period on the same terms as the prior lease insofar as they are applicable; (3) he may demand double rent in accordance with statutory provisions in some states; or (4) he may notify the tenant that continued occupancy will be on such terms as L then specifies, including an increased rental, and if the tenant remains, he then impliedly agrees to such changed terms.

Note

At this point Cases 15 through 18, supra, setting forth the characteristics of the various types of estates less than freehold (non-freehold estates) should be carefully re-read.

CASE 52:   L., owner of Blackacre in fee simple, leased it to T for a period of 10 years. When 3 of the 10 year period had passed T died intestate. D promptly took possession of Blackacre. H was T's sole heir and A was appointed and duly qualified as his administrator. H sued D for possession of Blackacre and D moved to dismiss for failure to state a claim upon which relief could be granted. How should the court rule on the motion?

Answer and Analysis

The answer is that the motion should be granted in those jurisdictions following the common law. By the common law upon the death of a person intestate the title to his real property passes to his heir and the title to his personal property passes to his personal representative, executor or administrator. Estates for years were classified as chattels real and regarded as personal property at common law. Therefore, in a common law jurisdiction the right of action belongs to A and not to H; hence the motion should be granted. In many jurisdictions, however, statutes modify the common law and the term for years is regarded as real property for many purposes. Thus, if the action arises in a jurisdiction treating the leasehold as realty for devolution purposes, the motion should be denied.

Historically a leasehold involved no interest at all in land. It was a mere contractual relationship between the parties. If the tenant were prevented by some third person from using the leased land, his remedy was exclusively against the landlord on his contract to protect the tenant in his use of the land. Early in the 13th century the tenant was allowed a trespass action for damages against the landlord but it was not until 1499 that the tenant was allowed specific recovery of the land through ejectment. But ejectment was a personal and not a real action. Because such was the case and because during the centuries from 1200 to 1500 the leasehold had taken so many of the characteristics of personal property, it retained its status as personal property and still remains such in the American law except where changed by statute. See McKee v. Howe, 17 Colo. 538, 31 P. 115 (1892); Burby, 113; Thompson, § 1016.

———

CASE 53: L being fee simple owner of Blackacre, a residence in which L and his family lived, made a written instrument, bearing the title "lease" at the top thereof, by which it was agreed that T might occupy a room in the house on Blackacre which had an outside as well as inside entrance. T's term of occupancy was to be from September 15, 1980 to March 15, 1981. It was agreed that T should eat no meals on the premises and that L would be responsible for T's bed being made every day and his room being cleaned not less than once per week. There was a bathroom in connection with T's room of which he should have the exclusive use. The amount which T agreed to pay for the use of the room called "rent" in the written instrument, was $80.00 per month. T was not in default in any way when L evicted him and his baggage from the premises on January 15, 1981. T sues L in ejectment to recover possession of the room. May T succeed?

Answer and Analysis

The answer is this: this question raises a question of fact concerning the intention of the parties which ultimately must be determined by the trier of fact under proper instructions from the court. It would be error to withdraw it from the trier of fact and decide the matter as a pure question of law. This agreement would seem to be an ordinary lodging contract by which one person is permitted to occupy a room in the dwelling house of another. Such agreements usually do not create a landlord-tenant relationship but only that of licensor and licensee with a contractual obligation on the part of the occupant to pay for the use of the occupied area. But there are at least three items in this instrument which might well be considered evidence of an intention to create a landlord-tenant relationship. The instrument is labelled a "lease". The payment to be made from T to L is called "rent". The term for occupancy has a definite beginning, Sept. 15, 1980, and a definite date for termination, Mar. 15, 1981. But these items alone are not controlling. They must be considered with all the other items which evidence the intention of the parties.

There is no landlord-tenant relationship unless the owner delivers to the occupant the exclusive possession of the premises to be occupied. The room was part of L's dwelling house, it could be entered from inside as well as outside the house, L retained the right to enter the room to make the bed and clean the occupied area. This is hardly consistent with exclusive possession on T's part. It is usually held under such circumstances, that such an arrangement constitutes a lodging contract and consists primarily of a contract for use of the room and facilities, but that no interest in the land, the actual exclusive possession thereof, passes to the occupant, and that the possession remains in the landowner. There is privity of contract but no privity of estate, and the occupant, as to the land itself, is only a licensee, and that such license is revocable at the will of the owner of the premises even though he may be liable to the occupant for breach of contract. It should be added that such an arrangement does not as a matter of law preclude there being a lease. It is possible for the owner to supply services to an occupant of a room in the former's house without retaining possession thereof and to relinquish such possession to the occupant. Whether or not such is done is ultimately a fact question for the trier of fact under proper instructions from the court. If the trier of fact should find that there was an intention on the part of L and T that T should have the exclusive possession of the room and bathroom in L's house, then T should succeed in his attempt to repossess such area. If, on the other hand, the trier of fact should decide that there was no intention that T should have the exclusive possession of the occupied area but that such remained in L, then T's action would fail. See White v. Maynard, 111 Mass. 250, 15 Am.Rep. 28 (1872); Powell, ¶222[4].

CASE 54: L, being owner in fee simple of Blackacre, orally agreed that T might take possession of Blackacre on March 1, 1979 and hold the same exclusively as a tenant for a period of 10 years thereafter at a rental calculated at $2400.00 per year but which was to be paid at the rate of $200.00 per month. In the jurisdiction where the land was situated the Statute of Frauds provided that no lease for a period of more than one year could be enforced unless some memorandum thereof be in writing and signed by the party to be charged. At the end of six months following T's taking possession of Blackacre, and when T was in no way in default, L gave T notice to quit the premises. T refused to quit and L sues to eject him. May L succeed?

Answer and Analysis

The answer is no. This oral lease for 10 years is not valid and is not enforceable. But T took possession of Blackacre with L's consent and is not a trespasser. All the cases seem to agree that if a lease is not valid under the Statute of Frauds and the tenant goes into possession, he is in any event at least a tenant at will. Such tenancy at will is, of course, based on an implied intention of the parties, the express oral lease having failed. But it is not unreasonable to find an implied intention under the circumstances of this case to have a valid lease from year to year. The rental was calculated on an annual basis even though the rent was to be paid monthly. T has already occupied and had possession of Blackacre for a period of half a year. T was not in default which must mean that he has paid at least six months rent and L has accepted such. Under these circumstances it would seem that the tenancy at will which existed upon T's taking possession has been transformed by the subsequent events into a year to year lease binding on both the parties. If this be true, then T may remain in possession as against L's notice to quit for at least the balance of the year, and L's action must fail. See Davis v. Lovick, 226 N.C. 252, 37 S.E.2d 680 (1946); Burby, 125–127; 128–134.

Note

The description and characteristics of the tenancy resulting from similar circumstances may vary from the above common law solution as a result of local statutes. See, for example, West's Fla.Stat.Ann. § 83.01, creating a tenancy at will from period to period.

––––––––

CASE 55: L, being fee simple owner of Blackacre, made a lease in writing to T which included the following language, "to T for a period of 10 years beginning next March 1, 1978, or until intoxicating liquors are sold on the premises, and provided if T does not pay the taxes on the premises on or before their due date, then L reserves the right to re-enter and terminate this lease". T took possession of Blackacre, and when during the second year of the 10 year period the taxes became due, T did not pay them and they became delinquent. L paid the taxes but did nothing more. Sixty days after the taxes became delinquent, T sold intoxicating liquors on the premises. Within 30 days thereafter L sues to eject T from Blackacre. May he succeed?

Answer and Analysis

The answer is yes. Here was the establishment of a landlord-tenant relationship and the creation of a valid estate for a 10 year period. But such leases are sometimes determinable leases or may be subject to a condition subsequent or a power of termination. This lease is both determinable because, while it may last 10 years and is therefore an estate for years, it is also to last only "until intoxicating liquors are sold on the premises", and it is also subject to L's re-entry and exercising his power to terminate such upon T's failure to pay the taxes before they became delinquent. Applying these principles to the facts, we find that the condition subsequent happened, to wit: T did not pay the taxes in time and that L paid same. But L did not exercise his power of termination by making re-entry. Indeed, while we are not given sufficient facts to determine the matter, L may have waived such right of re-entry. In any event, when T sold intoxicating liquors on the premises, then the estate for years automatically came to an end because it was to last only until such sale of liquors on the premises. At the instant after such sale T was a tenant at sufferance. He was holding over his term as a mere possessor with no right. Hence, he was subject to ejectment by the owner, L, whose reversionary interest had been transformed into an estate in possession. See Burby, 135–139; Restatement of Property § 19.

CASE 56: L, being owner in fee simple of Blackacre, a farm on which crops of corn, barley, oats, etc., are raised, made a written contract with T by which it was agreed that T would "work" the farm, preparing and seeding the fields, cultivating and harvesting the crops, and would deliver one third of all the crops harvested to L as payment of "rent", or for the use of the farm. It was specifically agreed that T should have possession of the farm during the term of Mar. 1, 1979 to Mar. 1, 1980, and that L and T should, until division thereof, be tenants in common of all the crops grown on Blackacre. T raised 1,200 bushels of shelled corn on Blackacre, among other crops. He hauled all of such corn to D's elevator and was about to receive cash from D for the corn when L served process on both T and D in a suit in equity to enjoin T's selling and D's buying said corn unless and until there had been a partition thereof and an agreement as to what settlement should be made. Should the injunction issue?

Answer and Analysis

The answer is yes. This is one type of what is commonly called a "croppers" contract in which the parties share in the crops which are grown on the premises. The term is ambiguous and has no specific and definite meaning. Its use should be avoided. It is applied to various sets of facts as will be illustrated in the note below. The rights of the parties under such contracts, in the absence of a specific agreement as to the issue in dispute, generally depend upon whether a landlord-tenant, licensor-licensee, or master-servant relationship is created.

In the above case it should be noted that T is given possession of Blackacre for a specific period of time and agrees to pay rent therefor in "kind", that is, in a share of the crops as distinct from cash rent. It should be carefully noticed also that the crops when harvested do not belong either to T or to L. They belong to both parties as tenants in common, T owning an undivided two thirds and L owning an undivided one third of the crops. It appears that T was about to convert L's one third of the 1,200 bushels of corn by attempting to sell it to D. L's security in the payment of his rent was bound up in his co-ownership of the crops with T. T did not own 800 of the 1,200 bushels of corn and L 400 bushels. T and L each owned an undivided fractional interest in every kernel of corn in the entire 1,200 bushels taken to D's elevator. And neither had the right nor the power to sell any single kernel of such corn to D or to anyone else. And technically neither could replevy his share from the other for the reason that replevin presupposes a right on the part of the plaintiff to the exclusive possession of the property claimed, and in the case of cotenancy, the plaintiff already has possession legally by virtue of the unity of possession in which the possession of one cotenant is the possession of the other cotenant. Hence, L's remedy at law is not adequate and he should have an injunction against the defendants until the 1,200 bushels of corn have been divided between the coowners and each is paid for his proportionate share.

In this case it is clear that all the elements of a term of years are present and that the relationship of landlord-tenant obtains between L and T. In this case the duty of the tenant, T, was plain. When he had harvested the 1,200 bushels of corn it was T's duty to divide the corn into two parts, two thirds for himself and one third for L, and to deliver the one third part to L. In attempting to sell the entire lot of corn to D without making any division thereof, T was violating his obligation under the lease. See Harrison v. Ricks, 71 N.C. 7 (1874); Smith v. McNew, 381 S.W.2d 369 (Mo.App.1964); Burby, 117; Powell, ¶222[4].

Note

It is often important to distinguish the landlord-tenant relationship from that of landowner and hireling (master and servant) in cases involving the sharing of crops. It is usually a matter of construction but the six cases following will give the proper perspective.

1. L, owner in fee simple of Blackacre, a farm, makes a written agreement with T for one year whereby T does all the physical work in the operation of the farm for which he is to be paid $250.00 per month cash. T with his family is also permitted to occupy a house on Blackacre during the year he is working for L. L retains possession of the land, that is, he is in control of the farm. The relationship is that of landowner and hireling or master and servant.

2. Same set of facts except that instead of being paid in cash for his services, T is paid in the form of one half of the crops harvested on the premises. This is sometimes called a croppers contract but the relationship between the parties remains that of landowner and hireling. T has no interest in either the land or the crops until division of the latter is made.

3. Same set of facts except that instead of being paid in cash for his services, T is paid by being co-owner with L of an undivided one half of the crops harvested on Blackacre. Here again T is sometimes called a share cropper with a croppers contract but there is no landlord-tenant relationship because L still retains complete possession of and control over Blackacre. The relationship is still essentially that of master and servant, except that the parties are cotenants of the crops, through which T is paid for his services.

4. Same set of facts except that T is given exclusive possession and control of Blackacre and the parties are to be cotenants of the crops, each owning an undivided one half thereof. This too is called a croppers contract. But in this case instead of T's being paid in kind for his services, L is being paid rent in kind for the use of his land. Here is a landlord-tenant relationship. The important distinguishing item is that L has relinquished possession and control of Blackacre to T.

5. Same set of facts except that T is given possession of Blackacre, the crops all belong to T and T agrees to pay L one half of the crops as rent for use of the premises. This again is a simple landlord-tenant relationship, with T owning an estate for years in land and paying rent in kind.

6. Same set of facts except that T is given possession of Blackacre, all crops belong to T and T pays cash rent to L for the use of the land. This again is a landlord-tenant relationship.

Comment: The important item is not how payment is made, in cash, in crop sharing or in common ownership of crops, but in whether L retains possession of the land and pays for services or whether L relinquishes possession to T and T pays rent for the land. If the former, the relationship is that of master and servant as in the first three cases above; if the latter, then the relationship is that of landlord and tenant as in the last three cases given. See cases cited supra preceding this note; McCutchen v. Crenshaw, 40 S.C. 511, 19 S.E. 140 (1893); Burby, 117; Powell, ¶¶222[4], 261.

CASE 57:   L, being fee simple owner of Blackacre, leased it to T for a period of 5 years, the term being from March 1, 1975 to February 28, 1980, the rent being $6,000.00 per year payable at the rate of $500.00 per month in advance. Several months prior to the termination of the lease period T notified L that he did not intend to renew the lease and would vacate the premises when the term expired. Complications in T's business prevented T's vacating Blackacre on February 28th, 1980 but he did succeed in moving completely from the premises on March 3, 1980. He had held over the term of the lease three days. T tendered a month rent of $500.00 to pay for the three days occupancy. L refused to accept such unless it were to be considered payment of rent for the first month of another entire year. T then refused to make any payment at all. In May 1980 L sues T for $1,000.00 rent for the months of March and April. May he recover?

Answer and Analysis

The answer is yes. In a lease for years no notice to quit is necessary on the part of either landlord or tenant. The term comes to an end at the expiration date with or without notice. So it was immaterial that T notified L of his intention to vacate Blackacre on February 28, 1980. The important question is the effect of T's holding over the term and becoming a tenant at sufferance, which means that T is a bare possessor with no right. However, the landlord, L, does have rights in such a situation. He may at common law do one of two things, (a) he may treat T as a wrongdoer and proceed to eject him, and hold him for use and occupation, or (b) he may treat T as a tenant from period to period on the same terms as the prior lease for years as far as those terms are applicable. The new tenancy is usually from year to year where the term of the original lease was one year or more.

In this case L exercised his election and decided to hold T as a tenant from year to year and promptly notified T of such determination. The theory upon which T's liability is based depends upon the circumstances. If L merely accepts rent from T and T continues to occupy the premises, then T's liability is based on a contract implied in fact. If, on the other hand, as in this case, there is no intention on the part of T to agree to a year to year lease, then such obligation is one imposed by law in quasi-contract. In either event, the option is with L to decide whether to treat T as a wrongdoer or a tenant from year to year. L having made the election to hold T for another year, T is liable for the rent for such entire year. Such is the rule of the common law. See A. H. Fetting Mfg. Jewelry Co. v. Waltz, 160 Md. 50, 152 A. 434, 71 A.L.R. 1443 (1930); Moynihan, 82; Burby, 131; Powell, ¶254. Cf. Commonwealth Bldg. Corp. v. Hirschfield, 307 Ill.App. 533, 30 N.E.2d 790 (1940), denying the landlord's right to hold the tenant for another year when the tenant's vacation of the premises was not complete until the day after the lease expired, the court concluding that the landlord was entitled only to double rent for the period of actual occupancy in accordance with a provision of the lease.

The common law rule might be modified by statute, as, for example, West's Fla.Stat.Ann. § 83.04, which provides that a holding over without a renewal of the lease in writing shall constitute only a tenancy at sufferance, and that a holding over with the written consent of the lessor is necessary to convert such tenancy into a statutory tenancy at will which is similar to a common law periodic tenancy. See also infra Case 59.

————

CASE 58:   L, being fee simple owner of Blackacre, leased it to T on a year to year lease, the first year term being from March 1, 1978 to February 28, 1979. On August 30, 1978, T notified L that T would vacate the premises on February 28, 1979 and that the present lease would terminate on that date. On February 26, 1979 when T was preparing to move from the premises he became seriously ill and the doctor advised him that he must remain in bed until his health improved. The sole cause of T's holding over the term until March 10, 1979, when he vacated the premises, was his serious illness. L elected to hold T for another year and sued him for rent on such theory. T set up in defense that he had given notice to terminate the tenancy and that the interposition of an Act of God made it impossible for him to vacate Blackacre on the last day of the term. Is T's defense good?

Answer and Analysis

The answer is no but there are contra cases. The most important characteristic of a year to year, or period to period, lease is that it continues indefinitely unless and until notice is given by either landlord or tenant that it shall be terminated. Such notice must be given not less than six months before the end of the lease year if it is a year to year tenancy. If it is from month to month, then an entire month notice is necessary to terminate the tenancy. If it is a tenancy from week to week, then notice for a week is essential to terminate such at the end of the week following. If notice to terminate the lease is properly given at the proper time and the tenant holds beyond the date of termination, then such notice may be considered as waived and the other party may hold the one who gave the notice for an additional period during which another notice must be served to terminate the tenancy.

In our case T gave proper notice six months before the end of the year. He had no intention of remaining on the premises for another year so it cannot be said that he impliedly contracted to do so. But, of course, when T held beyond February 28, 1979, the last day of the term, the effect of his notice was rendered nugatory and it was within the power of L either to eject T or to treat him as a tenant for another year just as though no notice had ever been given. But does the fact that an Act of God which caused T's illness affect the application of the rule? In the field of contract, express or implied in fact, the answer would be clearly in the negative, for an Act of God is no defense to an obligation voluntarily assumed unless the contract specifically so provides. The fact that the individual finds it impossible to perform is immaterial if, indeed, the contract could be performed by anyone. But in our case it would seem clear that T's obligation, if any, to pay rent for another entire year, is imposed by law and is quasi-contractual, not contractual. In some such cases the courts have taken the view that an Act of God constitutes impossibility and excuses T from liability for the entire year but holds him liable only for the hold-over time of occupancy plus any damage which may have been caused the landlord. Such exception to the application of the common law rule is of doubtful validity. Does it mitigate the harshness of the rule merely to shift it from the tenant to the landlord? Is it a greater hardship to compel the tenant to find another lessee rather than the landlord? We apply the common law rule to the set of facts and hold that T's defense is not good and L should be able to recover the rent for the entire year. See Mason v. Wierengo's Estate, 113 Mich. 151, 71 N.W. 489, 67 Am.St.Rep. 461 (1897); Herter v. Mullen, 159 N.Y. 28, 53 N.E. 700, 44 L.R.A. 703, 70 Am.St.Rep. 517 (1899); Burby, p. 131.

Caveat

In the case of a residential lease, recent developments may relieve tenants of some of the rigors of the common law in situations analogous to the above. Statutes imposing a duty of good faith, for example, might be interpreted as requiring the landlord to exert efforts to obtain a new tenant for purposes of mitigating damages, and if an unconscionable provision is also in the statute, it is conceivable that a sympathetic court would find unconscionable the result in Case 58 of holding the tenant for another whole year. See also infra Chapter VIII, part 5.

———

CASE 59: Ancillary to the sale of land from T to L, the parties entered into a lease, in which L leased to T the commercial premises theretofore occupied by T as owner for a term to end on a specified date two months later. The consideration was one dollar, and it was expressly agreed that T would vacate the premises at or before midnight on the date specified. T failed to vacate, and a few days later, L wrote T a letter notifying him to vacate immediately and that any continued occupancy would be at T's risk and that L would charge him rent at the rate of $500 per month. A year later, T was still in possession, and L sent him a bill for rent at the rate of $500 per month, and again instructed T to leave or continue to be charged at that rate. T vacated the premises 22 months after the date of the letter specifying the rental increase. Thereupon L sued T for $11,000 representing a claim for 22 months rent at $500 per month. May L recover?

Answer and Analysis

The answer is yes. When T holds over after the expiration of the term of the lease, L has a choice of several remedies: (1) when applicable as in this jurisdiction, he may demand double the monthly rent as provided for by statute [West's Fla.Stat.Ann. § 83.06]; (2) he may treat the tenant as a trespasser and claim damages for the deprivation of any reasonable rental value plus any special damages; or (3), he can waive the wrongful holding over and demand an increased rent if the tenant chooses to remain. [In this particular jurisdiction (Florida), L cannot elect to make the holdover a statutory tenant at will from period to period (periodic tenancy), as in Case 57 supra, unless L consents thereto in writing. West's Fla.Stat.Ann. § 83.04.] The election is L's and not T's, and in this case L clearly elected the third alternative. Further, as to the statutory penalty of double rent, it is only applicable in this particular jurisdiction when such a demand is made, and in the instant case there was no such demand. T is liable for the increased rent on the basis that when L demands such an increased rent and T remains after receiving notice, then T impliedly agrees to pay the rent demanded. See David Properties, Inc. v. Selk, 151 So.2d 334 (Fla. 1st D.C.A. 1963), Powell, ¶ 254, n. 31.

6. CONCURRENT ESTATES

a. JOINT TENANCY

LEGAL GEMS

1. Joint tenancy is always created by deed or by will, never by descent.

2. In joint tenancy there must always be two or more grantees or devisees.

3. A "to B and C and their heirs" are typical words for creating a joint tenancy at common law, but today in the absence of a clearly expressed intent to create a joint tenancy with the right of survivorship, such a limitation creates a tenancy in common.

4. At common law joint tenancy was preferred over tenancy in common; under modern codes tenancy in common is preferred over joint tenancy.

5. Every joint tenancy requires the four unities of

(a) time—meaning all tenants take their interest in the premises at the same instant of time

(b) title—meaning all tenants take their interest from the same source, the same deed or the same will

(c) interest—meaning every tenant has the same identical interest in the property as every other tenant, such as fee simple, fee tail, life estate, etc.

(d) possession—meaning the possession of one joint tenant is the possession of all the joint tenants and the possession of all the joint tenants is the possession of each joint tenant.

6. Every joint tenant owns the undivided whole of the property, he does not own a fractional interest; he is part and parcel of the unit group which owns the whole—such is the meaning of joint or oneness.

7. The grand incident or characteristic of joint tenancy is that of SURVIVORSHIP which means that upon the death of one joint tenant, the survivor or survivors own the whole of the property and nothing passes to the heirs of the decedent.

8. Upon the death of a joint tenant the survivors take nothing from the decedent but take the whole from the original conveyance which created the joint tenancy and which whole they have owned all the time.

9. A severance of the joint tenancy can be made by conveyance inter vivos only, never by will because survivorship is prior to and defeats the effect of the will.

10. If all joint tenants except one die without having severed their interests, the lone survivor owns the whole property in severalty.

11. Joint tenancy is destroyed by severance inter vivos, by partition or by any act destroying any one of the four unities.

12. Except in those jurisdictions where the joint tenancy has been abolished, husband and wife may, by a clearly expressed intention in the conveyance, take and hold as joint tenants.

Note

At this point Case 19, supra, setting forth the characteristics of the estate in joint tenancy should be carefully re-read.

———

CASE 60: A, being fee simple owner of Blackacre, made a conveyance thereof in these words, "I hereby convey Blackacre to B, C and D and their heirs as joint tenants with right of survivorship in the survivors, and not as tenants in common". In the jurisdiction where the land was located a typical statute provided that all concurrent tenancies shall be deemed tenancies in common and not joint tenancies unless it is expressly declared that the grantees or devisees shall take as joint tenants. B died testate devising all of his interest in Blackacre to X and his heirs. X immediately took possession of Blackacre. C and D. sue X in ejectment. May they succeed?

Boyer Law of Prop.3d Ed.MTB—4

Answer and Analysis

The answer is yes. Under modern statutes the doctrine of survivorship is not popular. Many such statutes in express terms prefer tenancy in common over joint tenancy which is the reverse of the common law. To create a joint tenancy under the type of statute given in the question there must be a clear expression of intention that the conveyor intends the conveyees to take as joint tenants. Any doubt is and should be resolved in favor of their taking as tenants in common. It would seem that A has succeeded in his deed in creating in the grantees a joint tenancy. He uses these words, "as joint tenants with right of survivorship . . . and not as tenants in common". Three distinct ideas are expressed: (a) the grantees are called joint tenants; (b) they are to have the right of survivorship; and (c) they are not to be tenants in common. Any one of these expressions by itself may not overcome the preference for tenancy in common. But when all three are put in the conveyance, and it is expressly declared to be joint tenancy as the statute requires, then B, C and D would take as joint tenants. Such being the case when B died testate or intestate, the survivors, C and D, continue as survivors to hold Blackacre in fee simple in joint tenancy. To destroy the joint tenancy by severance the joint tenant must make a conveyance inter vivos. Such destruction will take place even by the conveyance of a lesser interest than the joint tenant has. The joint tenant's interest being in fee simple, a severance occurs by his conveyance of a fee tail, life estate or, according to some cases, by his transfer of a nonfreehold estate for years. But the will of a joint tenant is wholly ineffective to pass any interest in the jointly owned property; at the instant of death the doctrine of survivorship takes effect and the attempted severance comes too late. Hence, B's devisee, X, takes nothing under the will, has no interest in Blackacre and can be ejected from the premises by the owners and possessors, C and D. See Burby, 215–218; Mustain v. Gardner, 203 Ill. 284, 67 N.E. 779 (1903).

––––––––

CASE 61: T owned a regular section of land, Blackacre, in a given township and effectively devised it to A and B as joint tenants. A executed a deed to X as follows, "I hereby convey all of my right, title and interest in the North East Quarter of Blackacre to X and his heirs". Thereafter, Y, a judgment creditor of A, levied upon and sold to M on execution sale, all of "A's right, title and interest in the South Half of Blackacre". A died intestate leaving W his widow and Z his sole heir at law. Who owns Blackacre?

Answer and Analysis

The answer is this: (1) B and X are tenants in common of the North East Quarter of Blackacre, (2) B and M are tenants in common of the South Half of Blackacre, and (3) B is the owner in severalty of the North West Quarter of Blackacre. Each part of this answer will be discussed in the order above.

(1) That every joint tenant owns the whole of the jointly owned property and that he does not own a share or a fractional part thereof are clearly inherent in the oneness or jointness of such ownership. It is also clear that each joint tenant has the right and power to dispose of that which he does not own. This means that A and B as a unit owned Blackacre and that A owned Blackacre and B owned Blackacre. And it means that by a conveyance inter vivos A had the right and power to dispose of an undivided one half interest in Blackacre which he did not own. If A could dispose of his entire interest in Blackacre, then he could dispose of part of such interest by limiting his conveyance to the North East Quarter of Blackacre. Thus, A's deed to X carved out and vested in X an undivided one half interest in the North East Quarter of Blackacre. But as to that Quarter, X and B are tenants in common because the unities of time and title have been severed by A's deed. X takes his title from a different source than did B and takes his title at a different time than did B. Hence, B and X cannot be joint tenants where the four unities must exist. Result: B and X each owns an undivided one half interest as tenants in common in the North East Quarter of Blackacre in fee simple.

(2) Because a joint tenant has the right and power voluntarily to dispose of his interest in the jointly owned property, his creditors have the right and power to take that interest involuntarily. Then A's judgment creditor, Y, had the right to levy upon and sell A's interest in the South Half of Blackacre. Having done so, when M purchased at the execution sale, the unities of time and title were destroyed because M took his interest in Blackacre from a different source and at a different time than did B. The result is that M and B are tenants in common of the South Half of Blackacre, each owning an undivided one half interest therein.

(3) The North West Quarter of Blackacre remained unaffected by the conveyances to X and M. A and B remained joint tenants of that Quarter until A's death. Survivorship defeats any dower right which a widow may have in the estate of a joint tenant. It also defeats the rights of the heirs of such joint tenant. Therefore, A's widow, W, and his heir, Z, can claim no interest in the North West Quarter of Blackacre. That Quarter belongs to B in severalty in fee simple by the doctrine of survivorship. See Lessee of White v. Sayre, 2 Ohio 110 (1825); Burby, 220–221; Klajbor v. Klajbor, 406 Ill. 513, 94 N.E.2d 502 (1950).

Note

For an explanation of a section of land and the government survey, see infra Chapter XX.

CASE 62:   T, being fee simple owner of Blackacre, devised it effectively to A and B as joint tenants. The property consisted of a 50 foot lot fronting on a very busy street in a city. One half of the 50 foot frontage was covered by a store building. The other half was vacant. The land was worth $16,000.00. The building was worth $5,000.00 but needed $1,000.00 worth of repairs on the roof as an absolute necessity to make it habitable for business purposes. The other half of the lot could be used for store purposes if a building costing $4,000.00 were built thereon. A asked B to contribute $500.00 towards repairing the roof of the existing building and $2,000.00 towards the construction of another store building on the lot for rental purposes. B refused to do anything. A then repaired the roof for $1,000.00 and built another store building on the lot for $4,000.00 and with B's approval, rented both buildings. A then asked B to repay to A one half of the sums he had expended in repairs and in building the new store. A then sued B to partition Blackacre, it being conceded that it was not partitionable in kind but only by making a sale and dividing the proceeds. Under order of the court Blackacre was sold to X for $26,000.00. The court then ordered the $26,000.00 divided as follows: $10,500.00 to B and $15,500.00 to A, to which division B objects. Was the court correct?

Answer and Analysis

The answer is yes. A partition suit is in equity and an equity court should do equity. It seems that joint tenant, A, at common law might have had a cause of action to compel B, the other joint tenant, to contribute for the making of repairs which are absolutely necessary, provided he brought the action BEFORE the repairs were made but that no such action lay AFTER the repairs were made. Furthermore, one joint tenant has no cause of action against his other joint tenants for contribution for improvements. Hence, under these principles, it is plain that A had no right against B for contribution either for repairs or the improvement. But this suit is for partition and each joint tenant has the right to have the jointly owned property partitioned. Under the circumstances, by A's making and paying for repairs and improvements he has enhanced the value of Blackacre by $5,000.00. By returning to A the $5,000.00 which he has expended in repairing and improving the property, he is made whole as to such and B is not injured. Had there been no such repairs or improvements the property was worth $21,000.00. There is still that sum left after reimbursing A for his expenditures for repairs and improvements. So it would seem the equity court made an equitable partition of the proceeds and that B has no valid objection to such division. Of course in such cases partition is the only practicable remedy. See Calvert v. Aldrich, 99 Mass. 74 (1868); Moynihan, 227–229; Burby, 228–230.

CASE 63: H, being fee simple owner in severalty of Blackacre, makes a deed thereto to himself and his wife, W, in the
following language, "I, H, hereby grant Blackacre to H and
W, husband and wife and their heirs forever, in joint tenancy with right of survivorship, and not to them as tenants by
the entirety or as tenants in common, it being my intention
that all the rights and powers of joint tenants shall accrue
to said H and W". H died intestate leaving S his sole heir
at law. In whom is the title to Blackacre?

Answer and Analysis

The preferred answer is this: W is the fee simple owner in severalty of Blackacre. There is no question concerning H's intention.
In unmistakable language he has expressed an intention that H and
W shall hold Blackacre in joint tenancy. There is no question either,
(except in those jurisdictions that do not recognize all types of concurrent estates), that a husband and wife may hold real property either as tenants by the entirety, as joint tenants or as tenants in common, depending on the intention expressed in the conveyance. The
only real question is this: can a grantor grant to himself and another
and thereby create a joint tenancy, (or tenancy by the entirety),
when such is the grantor's clearly expressed intention. It seems that
a proper analysis can bring only an affirmative answer. The cases
present at least three distinct views as to the effect of such a conveyance.

One view is this. At common law the husband and wife were
one and he was THE ONE. Hence, when the husband granted to
himself and wife, he was granting to himself. When one grants to
himself, nothing happens. So the conveyance is void. But this concept is wholly an anachronism in the law. Today the wife is a legal
person and her personality is no longer merged in that of the husband. He is no longer THE ONE.

The second view holds that the effect of such a conveyance is to
create a tenancy in common between the husband and wife, each
owning an undivided one half interest in Blackacre. There are two
objections to this result. The first is that it does violence to the
grantor's clearly expressed intention that H and W shall NOT TAKE
AS TENANTS IN COMMON. The second is that it treats H, the
grantor, as the same person, as H, the grantee. Thus it comes to the
conclusion that one part of the conveyance wherein H conveys to H is
void and of no effect, and H therefore remains the owner of one half,
whereas the other part of the conveyance from H to W affects only
an undivided half of Blackacre which H originally owned and therefore W becomes an owner of such other undivided half. Ergo, we
have tenants in common.

The third view and the one which is believed to be the correct
one is this. Joint means oneness. In joint tenancy when two, three
or a dozen persons are named as grantees, those joint tenants take as
a unit, as one juristic person. When husband and wife are named as

joint tenants they take as one person, not because HE IS THE ONE, but because the two in legal contemplation, like any other joint tenants, constitute one single juristic person. No other concept fits into the idea of jointness, oneness or unity of ownership. Applying such concept to our set of facts we have this, "H to H and W" as joint tenants. In such conveyance H is one person and "H and W" constitute in the singular number quite another person. For the purpose of joint tenancy (or tenancy by the entirety) such grantees or devisees take as a unit personage. For such purpose they are united or merged in a single juristic person. Why do all the cases say that when one joint tenant dies, the survivors take nothing from the decedent but take wholly from the original conveyance? Because each owned the whole and they all owned the whole as a unit. When one died the survivors still continued as a unit owning the whole until there was but one survivor. Hence, when H conveyed Blackacre to "H and W" intending them to take as joint tenants, the grantor, H, was one person, and "H and W" was (singular number) another person, and they *as a unit* took Blackacre as JOINT TENANTS. Such grantee, "H and W", takes title from the same source, at the same time with the same interest and with unity of possession. When H died W held in fee simple by survivorship.

In this modern day there is much to be said in favor of carrying out the clearly expressed intention of the grantor in the creation of estates, even though technically all of the so-called unities may not be present. Too often the unities are the tail which wags the dog and the form governs the substance. In the instant case, even if the state still recognized dower rights, the fact that W does not join in H's deed to H and W should not result in the joint estate being encumbered with W's dower. Her acceptance of the deed as a joint tenant (or tenant by the entireties) should take the place of her actual joinder in the deed to release dower. Further, the problem will be moot in most cases anyway. If W should die first, any inchoate dower will never become consummate; if she should survive H, her larger estate in fee simple will extinguish by merger any dower interest. The procedure of direct conveyances is sometimes expressly authorized by statute. See Boehringer v. Schmid, 133 Misc. 236, 232 N.Y. S. 360 (1928), affirmed in 254 N.Y. 355, 173 N.E. 220 (1930); Matter of Klatzl, 216 N.Y. 83, 110 N.E. 181 (1915); Therrien v. Therrien, 94 N.H. 66, 46 A.2d 538, 166 A.L.R. 1023 (1946); Pegg v. Pegg, 165 Mich. 228, 130 N.W. 617, 33 L.R.A.,N.S., 166, Ann.Cas.1912C, 925 (1911); Schuler v. Claughton, 248 F.2d 528 (5th Cir. 1957); West's Fla.Stat.Ann. § 689.11; Burby, 224; Moynihan, 219.

Note

If one spouse owns Blackacre in fee simple in severalty and desires to transform it into either a tenancy by the entirety or a joint tenancy so that the survivor of the spouses will hold by survivorship, and the court of last resort in the jurisdiction has not expressly held as set forth in Case 63, supra, there is only one sensible and practicable way to accomplish such result without risking litigation. The owning spouse should convey to a third person and have the third person convey to the spouses as joint tenants or tenants by the entirety.

———

CASE 64: T, being owner in fee simple of Blackacre, effectively devises it to A, B and C as joint tenants. A then conveys all of his right, title and interest in the premises "to X for the period of his natural life". (a) What is the effect of this conveyance? (b) Who now owns Blackacre?

Answers and Analyses

The answers are these: (a) this conveyance destroys the joint tenancy as to A's interest and (b) X owns a life estate as a tenant in common in an undivided one third interest in Blackacre; A owns the reversionary interest in that same undivided one third interest; B and C own the remaining two thirds interest as joint tenants between themselves but with X as a tenant in common for his life. Any conveyance inter vivos by a joint tenant of his entire interest or a freehold interest therein, or probably of an estate for years therein, constitutes a complete severance of his interest in the jointly owned property and destroys the joint tenancy as to his interest. Thus, by conveying a life estate to X, A has severed his entire interest in Blackacre from the joint tenancy. Having carved out of the whole estate an undivided one third portion, and having created in that undivided portion a life estate in X, there is left in A the reversionary interest in such undivided one third in fee simple. Such conveyance by A destroyed the unities of time, title and interest without which, of course, joint tenancy could not continue.

However, the four unities still obtain as to the two thirds interest remaining in B and C which was unaffected by A's conveyance to X. As to that undivided two thirds interest B and C remain joint tenants and if one of them should die without having made an inter vivos conveyance, the survivor of those two would own that undivided two thirds by survivorship. But we also have two tenants in common with the one unity of possession, to wit: X is possessed of an undivided one third and B and C as a unit are possessed of the other two thirds. Thus, B and C occupy two roles. Between themselves they are joint tenants of two thirds interest. As to X they as a single unit person constitute a tenant in common of the two thirds interest. It will be noticed that A, the owner of the reversion in an undivided one third interest, is not called a tenant in common. The reason is this. He owns a future interest, of course, in an undivided one third. But the term concurrent estates, including joint tenancy, tenancy by the entirety, tenancy in common and coparcenary, is limited to possessory estates. It involves presently possessory estates owned by two or more persons. Thus, in our case, B, C and X, but not A, have immediate possessory estates in Blackacre and the possession of B or C or X of Blackacre is in law the possession of all three together. See Burby, 219–221; Moynihan, 221–222.

---

b. TENANCY BY THE ENTIRETY

LEGAL GEMS

1. A tenancy by the entirety is a form of concurrent ownership based upon the common law concept of unity of husband and wife.

2. Tenancy by the entirety is a species of joint tenancy and as in joint tenancy each spouse owns the whole estate and not a fractional part thereof.

3. Tenancy by the entirety can exist only between husband and wife.

4. The doctrine of survivorship obtains in tenancy by the entirety, the survivor taking all, the heirs nothing.

5. Five unities are essential in tenancy by the entirety: (a) time, (b) title, (c) interest, (d) possession and (e) person. The first four are the same as in joint tenancy. The fifth involves the common law concept of unity of person in husband and wife.

6. Tenancy by entirety is created only by deed or will, never by descent.

7. In most jurisdictions that recognize the estate by the entirety, neither spouse can dispose of any interest in the estate by entireties, both must join in the conveyance.[4]

8. In most jurisdictions that recognize the estate by the entirety, a creditor of one spouse cannot levy upon the estate owned by the entirety, nor is a judgment against one spouse a lien against the estate held in entirety.[5]

9. Divorce eliminates the unity of person, destroys the tenancy by entirety and the divorced persons become tenants in common of the property.

10. Because the tenancy by entirety is to protect the family, neither spouse has a right to have partition thereof, and neither has power, without the consent of the other, to destroy such tenancy.

---

4. In some states in a tenancy by the entirety, the husband has the sole right to possession during the joint lives, and a fee simple absolute in all of the estate if he survives the wife. The wife, on the other hand, has no present estate but she does have a fee simple absolute in all of the estate if she survives her husband. The husband can convey his interests subject only to the right of the wife to absolute ownership if she survives; but the wife, during their joint lives, cannot convey her possibility of ac-quiring the estate. See Powell, ¶ 623. See D'Ercole v. D'Ercole, 407 F.Supp. 1377 (D.Mass.1976).

5. In those states that preserve the estate by the entirety in all its common law flavor, see supra n. 4, creditors of the husband can attach and sell under execution all of his interest in an estate by the entirety, but separate creditors of the wife cannot reach her interest. See Licker v. Gluskin, 265 Mass. 403, 164 N.E. 613 (1929); Powell, ¶ 623.

Note

At this point Case 20, supra, setting forth the characteristics of the tenancy by entirety should be carefully re-read.

CASE 65: T, being the fee simple owner of Blackacre, devised it "to H and W, husband and wife, and their heirs forever, jointly". Thereafter H executed to M a mortgage on Blackacre. H then procured a divorce from W and on a later date married Y. H then died intestate, leaving Y his widow, and X as his sole heir. W sues Y and X seeking to quiet in her the title to the whole of Blackacre. May W succeed?

Answer and Analysis

The answer is no. By appropriate language in the conveyance a husband and wife can hold real property as tenants in common, as joint tenants or as tenants by the entirety. But there was always a presumption that a conveyance to a husband and wife jointly created a tenancy by the entirety. Under such presumption the conveyance in this case would be construed to make H and W tenants by the entirety rather than joint tenants.

Assuming then that H and W are tenants by the entirety, in most jurisdictions recognizing such estates, neither had the right or power to dispose of or incumber such estate without the consent of the other spouse. Therefore, the mortgage which was executed alone by the husband, H, to M was wholly ineffective at that time to create a lien or incumbrance on the land. M's remedy must be limited to his personal action on the debt owed by H to M.

When H procured a divorce from W, the unity of person which is essential to the creation and continued existence of an estate by the entirety, was destroyed, and with it the tenancy by entirety was destroyed. But, of course, H and W continued in some form of concurrent tenancy to be the owners of Blackacre. In joint tenancy or tenancy in common? If pure logic is used to answer this question, it would be in joint tenancy because of the five unities in tenancy by the entirety, only one, unity of person, was destroyed by the divorce. The other four unities of time, title, interest and possession, remain. Ergo, joint tenancy! But that generally is not and should not be the law. Policy rather than logic dictates with better reason that H and W after the divorce should be strangers in their property ownership as far as possible, as well as strangers in person. Tenancy in common is the concurrent tenancy most nearly approximating such concept. It is also more probable in accord with their intent. The cases so hold.

H and W were then each owner of an undivided one half interest in Blackacre when H married Y. Upon H's death intestate the title to H's undivided one half interest in Blackacre descended to his heir,

X, but subject to Y's right of dower in such half interest. Hence, Blackacre is now owned by W and X as tenants in common, each owning an undivided one half thereof, with X's undivided half interest being subject to the choate right of dower in the widow, Y.

There is also a good possibility that X's undivided one half interest may be also incumbered by the mortgage to M as a result of the doctrine of estoppel by deed. Although the mortgage was initially invalid, on divorce H acquired an undivided one half interest which was freely alienable and mortgageable. Thus, as to this after-acquired severable interest, H can be estopped to deny the effectiveness of M's mortgage in the same way he would be estopped as to previously conveyed or incumbered other after-acquired property. Thus, if estoppel is invoked against H, his new wife, Y, and his heir, X, take their interests subject to such mortgage. See infra, Chapter XXII, Estoppel By Deed; Hillman v. McCutchen, 166 So.2d 611 (Fla. 3d D.C.A.1964).

See also: Steltz v. Shreck, 128 N.Y. 263, 28 N.E. 510, 13 L.R.A. 325, 26 Am.St.Rep. 475 (1891); Hoag v. Hoag, 213 Mass. 50, 99 N.E. 521, Ann.Cas.1913E, 886 (1912); 166 A.L.R. 969 et seq.; Burby, 221 et seq. That a joint tenancy between husband and wife is not affected by divorce see Westerlund v. Myrell, 188 Wis. 160, 205 N.W. 817 (1925); 27 C.J.S. 838.

Finn v. Finn, 348 Mass. 443, 204 N.E.2d 293 (1965), held that on divorce formerly held entireties property became a joint tenancy, pursuant to a property settlement incorporated into the divorce decree.

----

c. TENANCY IN COMMON

LEGAL GEMS

1. Tenancy in common may be created by deed, by will or by operation of law.

2. Under modern statutes tenancy in common is preferred over joint tenancy.

3. Only one unity, that of possession, need be present in tenancy in common.

4. Each tenant owns an undivided fractional part of the property, none owns the whole as in joint tenancy.

5. Each tenant can dispose of his undivided fractional part or any portion thereof, either by deed or by will.

6. Upon the death intestate of a tenant in common his interest descends to his heirs. There is no right of survivorship.

7. Tenancy in common may be destroyed by partition or by merger when the entire title vests in one person, either by purchase or otherwise.

8. When one cotenant ousts from possession his cotenant, the ousted tenant has a cause of action against the possessor, not to put him out, but to regain possession for himself with the possessor.

9. There is no real fiduciary relationship between cotenants merely because of the cotenancy, but good faith between cotenants prevents one cotenant from buying up an adverse title and asserting it against his cotenants if such cotenants offer to share their part of the expense of gaining such title. The buyer of such adverse title is made to hold in constructive trust for his cotenants.

Note

At this point Case 21, supra, setting forth the characteristics of tenancy in common should be carefully reread.

CASE 66: T, owner in fee simple of Blackacre, devised it "to A and B and their heirs forever, share and share alike". A died intestate leaving H as his sole heir. B conveyed one half of his undivided interest in Blackacre "to C for life, remainder to D and his heirs". H then took exclusive possession of Blackacre and ousted B and C from the possession thereof and threatened them with physical violence if they returned to possess the premises. H permitted the taxes on Blackacre to become delinquent and purchased the tax title thereto in the hope of cutting off the interests of B and C. For such tax title H paid $400.00. B and C each tendered to H the sum of $100.00 as his share of the taxes paid by H which H refused to accept. B and C join in an action against H to compel H to hold the tax title for the benefit of B and C as well as H and to compel H to permit B and C to share with H in the possession of the premises. The court held for B and C on both counts. Was there error?

Answer and Analysis

The answer is no. First, let us determine the state of the title to Blackacre. When T devised Blackacre to "A and B and their heirs, share and share alike", it is clear that T intended them to take as tenants in common for each was to take a share equal to that of the other. Each then took an undivided one half interest in the premises. The one unity of possession is present, meaning that A's possession is B's possession and vice versa. When A died intestate his undivided one half interest descended to his heir, H. Now H and B are tenants in common of Blackacre, each owning an undivided one half interest. When B conveyed one half of his interest to C for life with remainder in such portion to D in fee, then H, B and C were tenants in common of the premises, H owning an undivided one half interest in fee simple, B owning an undivided one fourth interest in fee simple, and C having a life estate in an undivided one fourth interest. Tenants in common need not have the same fractional interests nor the same estates in the property.

As a matter of law when H took possession of Blackacre, his possession was the possession also of B and C. However, such theory does not prevent B and C from having a right physically to be on the premises as well as H. Such right is enforceable by an action at law in court and the court will order the sheriff to put B and C in possession with H. It will not of course order the sheriff to put H out of possession for his right to such is coextensive with the rights of B and C. Irrespective of the fractional interest or the size of the estate which a tenant in common has, he has the right with his other cotenants to possess every part of the coowned premises. Thus, B and C have the right to be in possession of Blackacre with H and the court did not err on that count.

As to the tax title some other questions arise. Having paid the $400.00 taxes on Blackacre, would H have had a cause of action against B and C for $100.00 each? If in the jurisdiction a real property owner is bound personally to pay such taxes, then the answer would be yes. But if in the jurisdiction such owner is not personally liable to pay the taxes but taxes merely become a lien on the property in favor of the State, which is the usual case, then the answer is no. In that case H should be subrogated to the rights of the State and be able to enforce such lien against the interests which B and C have in Blackacre. But these questions were not involved when B and C each tendered to H his proportionate share of the taxes which H had paid. One cotenant is not permitted to buy up an outstanding adverse lien or title to the premises which is coowned and assert it against his coowners to their detriment if and when they agree to bear their proportionate share of the burden. Such purchased title by one cotenant inures to the benefit of all the cotenants. Hence, when B and C tendered to H their proportionate share of the taxes paid by H, he was duty bound to accept such and to use such title for their benefit. When H refused to accept the money, H became a wrongdoer and a constructive trustee of a one fourth interest in the tax title for B, and likewise for C. Hence, the court did not err in holding that H must hold a half interest in the tax title for the benefit of his cotenants, B and C. See Dolan v. Cummings, 116 App.Div. 787, 102 N.Y.S. 91 (1907); Burby, 228–232; Powell, ¶ 605.

----

d.   TENANCY IN COPARCENARY

Note

At this point Case 22, supra, setting forth the characteristics of tenancy in coparcenary should be carefully reread. For all practical purposes in the United States, coparceners are treated as tenants in common and the laws applicable to tenancy in common are alike applicable to tenancy in coparcenary. See Moynihan, 235.

COMMON LAW CONCURRENT TENANCIES COMPARED*

Kind of tenancy	How created	Typical words in deed or will	Unities present	Interest owned by tenant	Power of disposition	How can disposition be made	Rights on intestacy	How destroyed
Tenancy by the entirety	By act of the parties, *deed or will*	A "to H & W and their heirs."	Time, Title, Interest, Possession, Person	Husband and wife as a unit own the whole, *joint* ownership	Both husband and wife must join in conveyance	By deed only and not by will. Survivorship defeats effect of will.	Survivor continues to own all but in severalty	Divorce terminates the tenancy and makes them tenants in common
Joint tenancy	By act of the parties, deed or will	A to "B & C and their heirs as joint tenants with the right of survivorship and not as tenants in common."	Time, Title, Interest, Possession	All tenants as a unit own the whole, *joint* ownership	All may join and dispose of whole or each tenant can dispose of share he did not own as such	By deed only and not by will. Survivorship defeats effect of will.	If only one survivor he continues to own but in severalty. If more than one survivor they continue to own in joint tenancy.	1-One tenant conveys his interest. 2-By partition in kind among tenants. 3-By any act which breaks any unity.
Tenancy in coparcenary	By law of inheritance	A dies intestate leaving 3 daughters, B, C & D, his only heirs	Title, Interest, Possession	Each tenant owns an *undivided* portion which portions are not necessarily equal	Each tenant can dispose of his undivided share or part thereof	By deed or by will	Heir or heirs inherits undivided interest of deceased parcener.	1-By partition. 2-By conveyance by one parcener. 3-By whole descending or vesting in one parcener
Tenancy in common	By act of the parties, deed, will, or by law	A "to B and C and their heirs share & share alike as cotenants."	Possession	Each tenant owns an undivided portion which portions are not necessarily equal	Each tenant can dispose of his undivided share or part thereof	By deed or by will	Heir or heirs inherits undivided interest of deceased co-owner	1-By partition among tenants. 2-By uniting all titles in one tenant in severalty by purchase or otherwise

[C2454]

* Of course such an outline at best is not complete but is intended merely to set forth and compare the outstanding characteristics of the tenan-

SUMMARY OF CASES IN CHAPTER V

2. FEE SIMPLE

Case 32. Words of inheritance, "and his heirs", were indispensable to the creation of a fee simple estate at common law. Under modern statutes the use of such words is usually not necessary and a fee simple estate may be created without the presence of such words in a deed.

Case 33. When two clauses of a deed are contradictory and the intention of the grantor cannot be found from a reading of the entire instrument, then the former clause will govern over the latter.

Case 34. Even if two clauses in a deed are in conflict, still if the grantor's intention can be found by a reading of the entire instrument, such intention shall govern.

Case 35. Under many modern statutes a conveyance which would have created a fee tail estate at common law now creates a fee simple estate.

Case 36. Under the Rule in Shelley's Case a grant to B for life and thereafter to B's heirs, creates in B a fee simple estate.

Case 37. A grant to B and his heirs so long as the land is used for school purposes creates in B a fee simple determinable and leaves in the grantor a possibility of reverter.

Case 38. This case distinguishes a determinable fee simple from a fee simple subject to a condition subsequent. The provisions of a deed will be construed to create a fee simple absolute rather than a fee simple determinable or a fee simple subject to a condition subsequent, if such interpretation is reasonable.

Case 39. A grant to B and his heirs provided that if intoxicating liquors are ever sold on the premises the grantor or his heirs has the right to re-enter and terminate the estate, creates in B a fee simple subject to a condition subsequent and leaves in the grantor a right of re-entry for condition broken which today is called a power of termination.

Case 40. A restraint which disables a fee simple owner of land from alienating the property is void and the owner may dispose of the property in fee simple.

Case 41. A devise to B in fee simple to begin five years after the testator's death creates in the testator's heir a fee simple estate subject to a springing executory devise in B.

Case 42. A devise to B and C and their heirs and upon the death of either the other shall take in fee simple creates in each devisee a fee simple subject to a shifting executory devise.

3. FEE SIMPLE CONDITIONAL AND FEE TAIL

Case 43. This case presents the characteristics of the fee simple conditional estate which existed in England prior to 1285 when the Statute De Donis was passed making such estates fee tail estates. The donee of a fee simple conditional estate had a fee simple conditioned on issue

cies mentioned. Many variations exist among the jurisdictions; the chart reflects the characteristics prevailing in the majority of jurisdictions that recognize the particular estate.

born to him alive and the donor retained a possibility of reverter. When a child was born the donee had the power to convey to another person a fee simple estate thereby cutting off the rights of the donee's bodily heirs as well as the reverter rights of donor.

Case 44. This case presents the characteristics of the fee tail estate created by the Statute De Donis Conditionalibus in 1285. The fee tail tenant had an inheritable estate which lasted as long as he had bodily heirs, and which estate the donee himself could use only during his lifetime. He was without power to cut off his bodily heirs or the reversionary interest of the donor. Each such succeeding fee tail tenant had such limited power until the recognition of common recoveries whereby the interests of the bodily heirs and the reversioner could be defeated.

Case 45. This case involves the rights of a creditor of a tenant in tail in a modern jurisdiction. The conflicting answers involve the following principles: (a) The rule of the common law will govern unless changed by statute. (b) The rights of a creditor are derivative and he can take no greater interest in property than the debtor has. (c) What a debtor can convey voluntarily, his creditor can take involuntarily. (d) A general power over property is the equivalent of property. By placing on a statute a restrictive interpretation the first answer does not permit a creditor of the fee tail tenant to exercise the power to bar the entail even though the tenant himself could do so. The second answer in the note by using an expansive interpretation of the statute, reaches an opposite result.

Case 46. (a) When a fee simple owner conveys a fee tail estate, there is a reversion in the donor. (b) Such reversion may be cut off by an inter vivos conveyance of the fee simple by the fee tail tenant. (c) If the fee tail tenant dies without issue the fee tail is at an end and the donor has an estate in possession which the donor can dispose of by deed or by will.

4. LIFE ESTATES

Case 47. (a) If an estate MAY last for a lifetime, it is a life estate, even if it may be cut short before its natural end. (b) A lease at the will of the lessee creates a life estate determinable, although there is some authority that it creates a tenancy at will.

Case 48. A tenant may have a life estate in possession with a power to enlarge his life estate by conveying the fee simple, which conveyance also defeats the vested remainder.

Case 49. The Rule in Shelley's Case, being a rule of property law, and not a rule of construction by which the intention of the grantor is found, when applied to the proper fact situation, will create either a fee simple or a fee tail estate; it is not applicable to the words of a grant, "to B for life, remainder in fee simple to the heirs of B's body" where the intention governs and gives B a life estate and the "heirs of B's body", as purchasers, take a contingent remainder in fee simple.

Case 50. A "to B for the lives of B, C, D and E and the survivor of them", is valid as a life estate in B until the death of the survivor of the four; A "to B for the joint lives of B, C, D and E" is valid and lasts as long as all four live, and ends upon the death of the first of the four; A "to B for B's life and the lives of all the people who live in State X and the survivor" is a valid life estate for the life of B only, the provision for the other lives and survivor being void for impracticability of determining the death of the survivor.

Case 51. (a) Disabling restraints on alienation (spendthrift trusts excepted) are generally void regardless of the estate to which they are attached, but such restraints are valid in Mississippi if they do not exceed the lives of a succession of life tenants living at the time the estate is created. (b) Forfeiture and promissory restraints on life estates and lesser interests are generally valid. (c) All unreasonable restraints on the alienation of fees simple are invalid. (d) Life estates are subject to termination by special limitations and powers of termination.

5.   TENANCIES LESS THAN FREEHOLD

Case 52. At common law an estate for years is a chattel real, personal property, and upon the death of the owner passes to his personal representative and not to his heir.

Case 53. No estate for years is created and no relationship of landlord and tenant exists unless (a) the term created has a definite time of beginning and definite date for ending, (b) exclusive possession and control for the term are given to the occupier tenant, and (c) the reversion is retained by the landowner landlord.

Case 54. If a lease for a term of years fails to be effective because of the Statute of Frauds, the tenant becomes a tenant at will. Subsequent events such as payment of rent for a year or a fraction thereof may indicate an implied intention to transform such tenancy at will into a periodic tenancy from year to year or month to month or week to week.

Case 55. An estate for years may be a determinable lease and it may be subject to a power of termination for breach of condition subsequent.

Case 56. The term "cropper's contract" is ambiguous and may mean any of several situations involving the sharing of crops. When the landlord and tenant share crops and are co-owners thereof, and it is made the duty of the tenant to divide and deliver to the landlord a specific fractional part of same, the landlord may enjoin a sale of such crops pending division of them and payment to each his proportionate share. (See six cases in note following this case.)

Case 57. When a tenant for years holds over the term and becomes a tenant at sufferance, at common law and unless changed by statute, the landlord has an election either (a) to treat such tenant as a wrongdoer and proceed to eject him and hold him for the use and occupation of the land, or (b) to treat him as a tenant from year to year on the same terms as the prior lease, as far as applicable, in which case the tenant is liable for rent for an entire additional year.

Case 58. A tenancy from year to year will continue indefinitely unless and until either party gives notice to the other that the tenancy shall end. If proper notice is given and the tenant holds over the term, the landlord may claim that the notice is waived and hold the tenant for another year, and the fact that sickness caused the holding over is no defense to the tenant.

Case 59. When a tenant for years holds over after the expiration of his term, the parties can agree to a continuation on different terms than that provided in the original lease. If the landlord notifies the tenant that the rent will be increased if the tenant holds over, and the tenant remains after receiving such notice, then the tenant impliedly agrees to such increased rent. In some jurisdictions the landlord by statute also has the option of demanding double rent from the holdover tenant, and, of course, he has the option of treating the holdover tenant as a trespasser and recovering for use and occupation. See also Case 57 supra.

6. CONCURRENT ESTATES

a. JOINT TENANCY

Case 60. (a) Joint tenancy must under many modern statutes be expressly declared to overcome the preference for tenancy in common. (b) A joint tenant cannot convey his interest by will; only by an inter vivos conveyance can he defeat the doctrine of survivorship.

Case 61. A joint tenant owns the whole of the jointly owned property, not a fractional part thereof, but he can dispose of his entire interest and his conveyee will take a fractional part as a tenant in common. A joint tenant may dispose of his interest in a specific part of the jointly owned property. The interest of a joint tenant can be levied upon and sold by his creditors. Upon the death of a joint tenant his widow cannot claim dower and his heirs have no interest in the property.

Case 62. A joint tenant has no right of contribution against the other joint tenants for repairs or improvements he has made, but if partition is had the court in making an equitable division of the proceeds will take into consideration the expenditures made by one tenant for repairs and improvements.

Case 63. A husband and wife can hold real property in joint tenancy if such be the expressed intention. Such joint tenancy (or tenancy by the entirety) in most jurisdictions can be created by husband, H, making a grant "to H and W, husband and wife" with clearly expressed intention to that effect.

Case 64. A, B and C, being joint tenants in fee simple, A conveys to X for life. This constitutes a severance and a destruction of the joint tenancy as to A's entire interest. Thereafter X owns a life estate in one third as tenant in common and A owns the reversion in that same one third; B and C remain fee simple owners in joint tenancy between themselves as to the other two thirds, but as to X they own the two thirds as a tenant in common.

b. TENANCY BY THE ENTIRETY

Case 65. There is a presumption that a conveyance to husband and wife jointly creates a tenancy by the entirety. A divorce eliminates the unity of person in tenancy by the entirety, destroys such tenancy and the husband and wife become tenants in common of the property. During the existence of the tenancy by entirety, in most jurisdictions neither spouse without the joining of the other, has the right or power to dispose of or incumber the property.

c. TENANCY IN COMMON

Case 66. In tenancy in common each cotenant owns an undivided fractional part of the property, and upon his death intestate such interest passes to his heirs. A cotenant who has paid the entire taxes on the property may either compel contribution by his cotenants or enforce a lien against the property for such. When one cotenant purchases an outstanding adverse lien or title on the co-owned property, the other cotenants upon offering to bear their share of the burden, may compel the purchaser to hold such title in constructive trust for them.

Chapter VI

CONSTRUCTION OF DEEDS AND WILLS CONCERNING FUTURE INTERESTS

1. Types and Classes Generally.
     Legal Gems.
2. Reversions.
     Legal Gems.
     Cases.
     Chart—Reversions Compared with and Distinguished from Vested Remainders at Common Law.
3. Possibilities of Reverter.
     Legal Gems.
     Cases.
4. Rights of Re-entry for Condition Broken, or Powers of Termination.
     Legal Gems.
     Cases.
     Chart—Possibilities of Reverter Compared with and Distinguished from Powers of Termination.
5. Remainders, Vested and Contingent.
     Legal Gems.
     Cases.
     Chart—Vested Remainders Compared with and Distinguished from Contingent Remainders at Common Law.
6. Executory Interests.
     Legal Gems.
     Cases.
     Chart—Future Interests Compared with and Distinguished from Each Other.
Summary of Cases in Chapter VI.

---

1. TYPES AND CLASSES GENERALLY

LEGAL GEMS

1. There are five classes of future interests

    a. reversions (the only one created by operation of law)

    b. possibilities of reverter

    c. powers of termination—also called rights of re-entry for condition broken

(these three are always in favor of the conveyor)

    d. remainders

    e. executory interests

(these two are always in favor of one other than the conveyor—that is—a conveyee).

2. The first four classes were recognized by the common law. Executory interests are products of the Statute of Uses (1535) and

99

the Statute of Wills (1540). See supra Cases 28–31, infra Chapter XVIII, part 2.

3. Remainders were the only future interests which the common law recognized which were in favor of a transferee, that is, in favor of one other than the conveyor. Remainders are created by will or by deed.

4. There are two types of estates with respect to right of possession,

　　　a. possessory estates, those which are presently possessed by the owner, and

　　　b. future estates, those which are presently owned but the enjoyment or possession of which is postponed until a future time; the element of futurity having reference, not to the ownership, but to the time when the estate may be possessed.

5. Each class of future estates is subject to further classification and is in itself a complex and important subject in the field of real property.

2. REVERSIONS

LEGAL GEMS

1. When a person owns an estate in land and conveys to another an estate the duration of which is less than that which the conveyor owns, there is an undisposed of residue remaining in the conveyor. That undisposed of residue is called a reversion.

2. Because the conveyor in his conveyance simply does not deal with that undisposed of part of his estate which remains with him, a reversion is said to be created by operation of law.

3. Because the conveyor has disposed of his entire estate in the land, there is no reversion in any of the following examples: (a) A, being fee simple owner of Blackacre, conveys Blackacre to B and his heirs, (b) A, being owner of a life estate in Blackacre, conveys to B "my life estate in Blackacre", (c) A, being owner of a 50 year lease in Blackacre, assigns or conveys to B "all of my right, title, and interest in Blackacre".

4. All reversions are vested and are of two classes, (a) those which cannot be divested, and (b) those which are subject to being completely divested.

5. Examples of reversions which cannot be divested:

A, being fee simple owner of Blackacre, conveys

　　　a. "to B and the heirs of his body". A has a reversion in those jurisdictions which recognize a fee tail.

　　　b. "to B for life". A has a reversion.

　　　c. "to B for 99 (or 10) years". A has a reversion.

A, being a life tenant of Blackacre, conveys

    a. "to B for 99 years". Historically an estate for years was always less than a life estate, so A has a reversion.

    b. "to B for the life of B." Historically a life estate in another is always less than the life estate in the tenant, so A has a reversion.

    c. "to B for such portion of my life as B continues to support me". A has a reversion.

6. Examples of reversions which are subject to being completely divested:

A, being fee simple owner of Blackacre, conveys it

    a. "to B for life, and if C pays B $100 before B's death, then to C and his heirs". A has a reversion which is subject to complete divestment if and when C pays B $100.

    b. "to B for life, and two years after B's death, to C and his heirs". A has a reversion for two years after B's death but which will then be divested by the executory interest in C.

7. An attempt to create a remainder in an intervivos conveyance in favor of the heirs of the grantor is ineffective under the doctrine of worthier title (except in those jurisdictions where the doctrine has been abolished), and the grantor retains a reversion. Worthier title is discussed in Chapter VII.

CASE 67:   A, being fee simple owner of Blackacre, conveys it "to B and the heirs of his body, remainder to C for life." C dies. Then B dies leaving a son, X. X dies without issue and without having made any conveyance of Blackacre. A still lives. Who has the right to possess Blackacre?

Answer and Analysis

The answer is A in jurisdictions recognizing the fee tail. A owned a fee simple estate, the largest estate one can have in land. He conveyed a fee tail estate to B, followed by a remainder to C for the life of C. At common law there could be as many remainders following the prior particular estate as the feoffor or grantor wished. But if the prior particular estate, B's fee tail in our case, and the remainders were all estates of lesser duration than that which the grantor had in the premises, there was still a reversion in such grantor. In our case B's fee tail was of lesser duration than A's fee simple. So also was C's life estate in remainder. Therefore, there was left in A a reversion which he did not dispose of. Such reversion is indefeasibly vested in A. This means that nothing can prevent its reverting to A (or if A be dead to his heirs or devisees) and becoming an estate in possession upon the natural termination of B's fee tail and C's life estate. In our set of facts, C had a vested life estate in remainder but because he died before B and his issue, C never was able to possess or enjoy Blackacre. When B died, not having barred his entail, or A's reversion, either by fine, common recovery or deed, X became possessed of a fee tail estate. When X died without bodily issue and without barring either the entail or reversion, then the possession of Blackacre reverted (turned back) to A. See Simes, 17–19; Burby, 335–337; Restatement of Property § 154.

CASE 68: T, being fee simple owner of Blackacre, provided in his will, "I hereby give and devise to A a 15 year estate in my Blackacre". There was no residuary clause in the will, nor any disposition of Blackacre other than A's 15 year term. T died leaving H as his sole heir. When the 15 years following T's death had expired, A refused to give up possession of Blackacre and H sues him in ejectment. May H succeed in ejecting A?

Answer and Analysis

The answer is yes. By T's will A was given a term of years in Blackacre. This is a non-freehold estate and a chattel real. At an earlier date when a fee simple owner conveyed an estate for years in his land, he was said to have a fee simple subject to a term of years rather than a reversion. Today it is considered that the landowner has a reversion even though the term carved out of his fee simple is a non-freehold interest. Such being the case when T died and his will became effective, there was vested in A the possessory interest in Blackacre for the 15 year term. There was a reversion left in someone. It could not be in T because he is deceased. Such reversion not being disposed of in T's will, it passed to his heirs by intestate succession. H, being the sole heir of T, received the reversion by descent. It was at that time a future interest. It was owned by H but could not be possessed or enjoyed by him until the expiration of the 15 year term. But when that time had passed, the possession of Blackacre reverted to H, who as T's heir is as to Blackacre, an extension of the personality of the deceased T. H therefore had the right to eject A. See Simes, 17–19; Burby, 335–337; Restatement of Property § 154.

CASE 69: A, owner in fee simple of Blackacre, conveyed it "to B for life, remainder to the children of B who survive him in fee simple". A then made a deed conveying "all of my right, title and interest in Blackacre, to X and his heirs forever". What interest, if any, has X in Blackacre?

Answer and Analysis

The answer is this, X has in Blackacre a reversion subject to complete defeasance. When A executed his first deed there was created in B a life estate in possession. Such life estate is the prior particular estate which supports the contingent remainder which was created in the children of B who survived their parent. As long as there is a condition precedent to the vesting of the fee simple remainder in the children of B, there is a reversion in the grantor, A. If no children survive B, then, of course, the reversion remains in A and he is entitled to possession of Blackacre on the death of B childless. If on the other hand, a child or children of B do survive B, then and at the instant of B's death, the contingent remainder in fee simple is transformed into an estate in fee simple in possession and the reversion is completely defeated. But two events must happen to defeat such reversion. B must die and he must have a child who survives him. Until these happened there was a reversion in A. A reversion is a future estate and not one in possession. Hence, it lies in grant and not in livery. A's deed to X conveyed the interest which A had in Blackacre. That was a reversion subject to complete defeasance in case B died leaving a child or children surviving him. A's conveyance to X did not make X a remainderman. He became the assignee of the reversion with rights which are substantially the same as though he were a remainderman. See Restatement of Property §§ 154, 159; Simes, 70; Powell, ¶ 281.

CASE 70: A, being fee simple owner of Blackacre, conveyed it "to B for life, remainder to my heirs in fee simple". Thereafter A granted "to C and his heirs all of my right, title and interest in Blackacre". A died leaving H his sole heir. B then died and H took possession of Blackacre. C sues H in ejectment. May C succeed?

Answer and Analysis

The answer is yes. A's conveyance created in B a valid life estate. By the very words of that conveyance it is obvious that A intended his own heirs to take a remainder following B's life estate. But the rule of the common law which, contrary to the situation today, was a rule of property rather than a rule of construction, provided without equivocation that one could not make his own heirs his purchasers. This is called the doctrine of worthier title which is discussed later. By applying such rule it was beyond A's power to convey to his heirs as remaindermen which would make them take by purchase rather than by descent. If A's heirs were to take at all it would be because there was a reversion left in A and he might die without having disposed of it by deed or by will. In such case A's heirs would take by descent by operation of law rather than by purchase, title by descent being a worthier title than a title by purchase. So under the rule A's conveyance would read simply this without more, "A to B for life". The provision, "remainder to my heirs in fee simple" was treated as being void. There was then a reversion in A which he could and did convey to C in fee simple. A's heir, H, took nothing and was subject to ejectment by C who had the right to immediate possession on B's death. This is the simplest case illustrating the creation of a reversion by applying the doctrine of worthier title which doctrine will be discussed in more detail later. See Robinson v. Blankenship, 116 Tenn. 394, 92 S.W. 854 (1906); Simes, 56–57; infra Doctrine of Worthier Title in Chapter VII.

REVERSIONS COMPARED WITH AND DISTINGUISHED FROM VESTED REMAINDERS AT COMMON LAW

SIMILARITIES

REVERSION	VESTED REMAINDER
1. is future interest	1. is future interest
2. is preceded by an estate in possession	2. is preceded by an estate in possession
3. is not destructible	3. is not destructible
4. is transferable	4. is transferable
5. is subject to claims of creditors	5. is subject to claims of creditors
6. is vested	6. is vested
7. sometimes subject to defeasance	7. sometimes subject to defeasance
8. is an estate	8. is an estate
9. has right to possess when prior estate ends	9. has right to possess when prior estate ends
10. not subject to Rule against Perpetuities	10. not subject to Rule against Perpetuities
11. has right against prior estate owner for waste	11. has right against prior estate owner for waste
12. may force prior estate owner to pay taxes and interest on encumbrances	12. may force prior estate owner to pay taxes and interest on encumbrances
13. does not take effect in derogation of prior estate	13. does not take effect in derogation of prior estate

DISSIMILARITIES

1. is created by operation of law	1. is created by act of the parties—by deed or will
2. is always in favor of transferor	2. is always in favor of transferee, one other than transferor
3. there was tenure between reversioner and holder of prior estate	3. there was no tenure between the remainderman and the holder of the prior estate

3. POSSIBILITIES OF REVERTER

LEGAL GEMS

1. A possibility of reverter is the interest left in conveyor who transfers a determinable fee. It is a future contingent interest.

2. A determinable fee is usually limited or described by the words "so long as", "until", "while" or "during".

3. An example illustrating both a determinable fee and possibility of reverter is this: A, fee simple owner, conveys "to B and his heirs so long as used for court house purposes". B has a determinable fee simple and A has a possibility of reverter.

4. A possibility of reverter is always in favor of the transferor or his successors in interest.

5. Today a possibility of reverter is considered alienable, descendible and devisable. At common law it was considered inalienable when standing alone.

6. A possibility of reverter is not subject to the common law Rule against Perpetuities, but an executory interest following a fee simple defeasible is subject to the Rule.

7. A possibility of reverter arises by implication of law from failure on the part of the conveyor to convey the interest left in him, although the intention may be expressed.

8. A possibility of reverter cannot be a reversion because a reversion cannot remain after the conveyance of a fee simple, even though it be a fee simple determinable.

9. A possibility of reverter may be attached to or be an incident to a reversion. E. g., A, fee owner, leases Blackacre to B for 10 years or so long as intoxicating liquors are not sold on the premises. A has a reversion with a possibility of reverter as an incident thereto. If intoxicating liquors are sold on the premises the leasehold automatically terminates and the possession reverts to A even before the end of the 10 year term.

10. The fact that the instrument says the property is to be used for one purpose only does not create a possibility of reverter; neither are express words of reverter essential to create a possibility of reverter.

11. The outstanding characteristic of a possibility of reverter is this: *the estate given to the grantee automatically comes to an end and that estate automatically reverts to the grantor upon the happening of the event named in the conveyance.*

12. Examples of possibilities of reverter standing alone:

a. A, fee owner, conveys to B and his heirs *while* the buildings thereon are kept in repair. A has a possibility of reverter but no reversion.

b.   A, fee owner, conveys to X Corporation *so long as* used for school purposes. A has a possibility of reverter but no reversion.

13.   Examples of possibilities of reverter attached to or as an incident to a reversion:

a.   A, fee owner, conveys to B for life *during* the time B personally lives on the premises. A has a reversion with possibility of reverter attached as an incident thereto.

b.   A, life tenant, leases to B for 20 years or *as long as* B continues to support me with food and shelter. A has a reversion with a possibility of reverter as an incident thereto.

c.   A, having a 10 year estate, transfers to B for 5 years or *until* intoxicating liquors are sold on the premises. A has a reversion with a possibility of reverter as an incident thereto.

———

CASE 71:   A, being fee simple owner of Blackacre, conveys it "to B and his heirs so long as a brick yard is operated on the premises, then to X and his heirs". A died intestate leaving H his sole heir. The premises ceased to be used for brick yard operations. X took possession of Blackacre. H sues to eject X from the premises. May he recover?

Answer and Analysis

The answer is yes. If there were no gift over to X, A's conveyance created in B a fee simple determinable as evidenced by the words "so long as" a brick yard is operated thereon. Of course, such brick yard may be operated thereon forever and words of inheritance "and his heirs" were used to indicate a fee simple in B. So there was no reversion left in A. But there was a possibility that the premises would cease to be used for brick yard operations. Hence, if X were not in the picture, A retained a possibility of reverter. Such interest is always in favor of the conveyor, never in favor of a third person or transferee.

What interest then did X take under the conveyance? It is quite obvious that the interest of X might vest far beyond any life or lives in being and 21 years and is therefore void under the common law Rule against Perpetuities, if such Rule applies. The Rule does not apply to possibilities of reverter. But it does apply to executory interests. Because a possibility of reverter cannot be in favor of one other than the conveyor or his successors in interest, X's interest was an attempted executory interest. As such it is void under the Rule against Perpetuities. So the conveyance should be read as though the phrase, "then to X and his heirs" were not included therein.

With X's interest invalidated, it is easy to see that there is a possibility of reverter in the conveyor A at the time of the conveyance. A possibility of reverter is always descendible and upon A's death it descended to his heir, H. H, then, was owner of the possibility of reverter at the time Blackacre ceased to be used for brick operations. At that time the fee simple automatically terminated in B and reverted to H, who now has immediate right to possession and may eject X therefrom. See Restatement of Property § 154; Leonard v. Burr, 18 N.Y. 96 (1858), Simes, 12, 28–30, 234; Moynihan, 95–103; Burby, 344–345.

Note

It is important to understand the nature of a possibility of reverter. It is bound up with the nature of a determinable estate. Notice in each of the following examples that each of the determinable estates comes to an end of its own limitation; this means by the very words which describe its duration. (a) A, fee simple owner, "to B and his heirs *until* liquor is sold on the premises". When liquor is sold on the premises B's estate automatically comes to an end because it is described to last just that long. There is no forfeiture. And of course, when B's estate ends, A's possibility of reverter becomes an estate in possession. (b) A, being life tenant, "to B for my life or *until* liquor is sold on the premises". When liquor is sold on the premises B's life estate pur autre vie comes to an end and A's possibility of reverter becomes an estate in possession because A's life estate reverts to A. There is no forfeiture. (c) A, being tenant for 10 years, "to B for ten years or *so long as* liquor is not sold on the premises". When liquor is sold on the premises B's estate automatically terminates and the possibility of reverter left in A automatically takes effect and the 10 year term, or what is left thereof, reverts to A. There is no forfeiture.

———

CASE 72: A, owner in fee simple of Blackacre, conveys it "to B and his heirs for school purposes, but when said property shall no longer be used for school purposes, it shall revert to A, his heirs and assigns". A then granted to X and his heirs, "all my right, title and interest in Blackacre". After Blackacre had been used for school purposes for 50 years such use was abandoned and X took possession thereof. B sues X in ejectment. May he succeed?

Answer and Analysis

The answer is no.

(1) It was once argued that under the statute Quia Emptores a possibility of reverter could not exist. Today that question is academic for it is universally held that there can not only be determinable fees, but also determinable fees tail, determinable life estates and determinable estates for years, with consequent possibility of reverters in each case. Had A conveyed merely "to B and his heirs" it is obvious A would have had nothing left. But when A conveyed for school purposes and the deed provided in substance that such estate should be in B only so long as it was so used, and then it should "re-

vert to A, his heirs and assigns", there was some interest retained in A. That interest is a possibility of reverter. Even though it may never be enjoyed, even though it is not presently enforceable as a right, even though it does not rise to the dignity of an estate, nevertheless, it is a presently existing thing, an interest in real property which will descend from ancestor to heir.

(2) At common law a possibility of reverter could be released to the owner of the determinable fee, and the effect would be to transform such determinable fee into a fee simple absolute. To that extent it was universally held to be alienable. If, in our case, A had made a release to B, then B would have had a fee simple absolute.

(3) Had A in our case granted "to B for life so long as used for school purposes", so that a reversion as well as a possibility of reverter had remained in A, then the common law permitted A to alienate his reversion and the possibility of reverter was also transferred as an incident to the reversion.

(4) But for no very satisfactory reason the common law did not permit a possibility of reverter, unconnected with a reversion, to be alienated by a deed inter vivos. Today, in line with the modern philosophy that a possibility of reverter is an existing thing presently owned, and that any thing which can exist and be owned, although its enjoyment be postponed or may never be enjoyed as a possessory interest, the better considered cases, with or without a statute, hold contrary to the common law view, and give effect to a conveyance of a possibility of reverter and recognize the grantee as having the same rights as had the grantor before the transfer. Applying such doctrine to the facts of our case, when A executed his deed to X, there was transferred to X the possibility of reverter. When, thereafter, Blackacre ceased to be used for school purposes, the determinable fee simple in B immediately and automatically came to an end, the possibility of reverter immediately and automatically took effect and the fee simple estate immediately and automatically reverted to X. X is now the owner of Blackacre in fee simple absolute and has a good defense in ejectment against the whole world including B. Such is the general and the better rule. See Restatement of Property § 159; Simes, 28–30, 73–75; Collette v. Town of Charlotte, 114 Vt. 357, 45 A.2d 203 (1946), which follows the Restatement; Burby, 345.

Note

The difference in result between Cases 71 and 72 simply because of the difference in conveyancing attempts is significant. In Case 71 the grantor did not attempt to retain a possibility of reverter in himself, but instead, attempted to create its equivalent, actually, an executory interest, in a third party. Since executory interests are subject to the Rule Against Perpetuities, the particular executory interest was void, and the grantor retained a possibility of reverter. In Case 72 the grantor made no effort to create an executory interest but, instead, left the possibility of reverter in himself, and then in a separate instrument transferred it to a third party. The possibility of reverter is transferable and is not subject to the Rule Against Perpetuities. Therefore, the transferee of the possibility of reverter acquired such interest in Case 72, but since the creation and transfer were in effect attempted in one transaction in Case 71, the third party interest was invalid in that situation.

4. RIGHTS OF RE–ENTRY FOR CONDITION BROKEN, OR POWERS OF TERMINATION

(These two expressions mean the same thing. From now on, because it is modern, shorter and more accurate, we shall use the expression, powers of termination).

LEGAL GEMS

1. A power of termination is a future interest retained by the transferor who conveys an estate subject to a condition subsequent.

2. A power of termination is always in favor of the transferor and his heirs, never in favor of a transferee.

3. A power of termination is just what those words say, a power retained by the transferor to put an end to the estate created if and when the transferee has broken the condition subsequent.

4. This power *never takes effect automatically* even when the condition subsequent has been broken by the transferee.

5. *Two things must happen* for a power of termination to become effective,

(a) *the transferor must elect* to exercise the power and

(b) *the transferor must do some affirmative act* to terminate the estate in the transferee.

6. The exercise of a power of termination *always causes a forfeiture* of the estate of the transferee.

7. Until the exercise of the power by the transferor, the estate of the transferee continues.

8. A power of termination is always created by appropriate language in a deed or a will. Typical words creating the condition subsequent are, "provided that", "but if it should happen that", "but if"; "subject to the condition that", or "in the event that".

9. A power of termination may stand alone or may be an incident to a reversion. Examples follow.

(a) A, fee owner, conveys "to B and his heirs, *but if* liquor is sold on the premises the right to enter and terminate the estate is reserved". A has a power of termination which stands alone unconnected with a reversion.

(b) A, fee owner, conveys "to B for life, *provided that if* liquor is sold on the premises, then I or my heirs have the right to reenter". A has a reversion attached to which is a power of termination.

(c) A, fee owner, conveys "to B for 10 years, *but on the express conditions* that if liquor is sold on the premises or B does not pay the rent, I may take back the premises". A has a reversion with a power of termination as an incident thereto which may be exercised in case of breach of either of two conditions.

10. A power of termination standing alone, unconnected with a reversion, was not alienable or transferable by deed inter vivos at common law. This inalienability rule is still in effect in some jurisdictions, but others permit alienability.

11. A power of termination standing alone will descend from the ancestor to the heir, is devisable in most jurisdictions, and can be released to the owner of the granted estate.

12. A power of termination attached to a reversion is alienable, descendible and devisable as an incident to the reversion.

13. To effectuate a power of termination at common law the grantor had to make an actual entry onto the granted premises. Today he may make such power effective by bringing an action in ejectment.

14. The grantor, by failing to act for an unreasonably long time after breach of the condition, may waive the power to terminate. Other acts such as acceptance of rent after breach of condition may also constitute a waiver of the power to terminate.

15. In construing an instrument the courts will not construe it to create a power of termination unless the language to create such is unmistakably clear. The courts are hostile to powers of termination because the effect is harsh and causes forfeiture. The courts prefer to construe language as creating a covenant for the breach of which only an action for damages lies, rather than a power of termination.

16. Equity will often give relief against forfeiture caused by the exercise of a power of termination in instances of hardship, accident or mistake.

17. A power of termination is not subject to the common law Rule against Perpetuities.

CASE 73: A, being fee simple owner of Blackacre, conveys it "to B and his heirs, but upon the express condition that if B does not live on the premises personally, then I or my heirs have the right to eject him therefrom". Two years later and while B still lived on Blackacre, A conveyed all of his right, title and interest in Blackacre to X and his heirs. A then died testate devising all of his interest in Blackacre to C. A's sole heir is H. Three years thereafter B moved off Blackacre and leased it to M for a term of 10 years. H then entered on Blackacre and evicted M therefrom and notified B that his estate had been terminated. C now sues H in ejectment and gives notice to B and M that he has terminated

B's estate and consequently, M's interest in Blackacre.   May
C succeed?

Answer and Analysis

The answer is yes in jurisdictions following the traditional common law.   In A's conveyance to B, he has used appropriate language, "but upon the express condition", to create a condition subsequent. In addition he has in express words reserved the right to terminate B's estate by ejecting him from the premises.   It should be noted too that such power of termination was reserved, not to any third person, but to the grantor and his heirs.   It seems clear then that B was granted a fee simple estate subject to a condition subsequent that if he did not live on the premises the grantor could exercise the power of termination.

While the condition had not yet been breached, A conveyed, or attempted to convey, his power of termination to X.   This was a power of termination standing alone.   There was no reversion left in A who had conveyed a fee simple estate to B, to which the right of re-entry or power of termination could be attached as an incident.   At common law, and also today in some jurisdictions, a power of termination unconnected with a reversion was not alienable inter vivos. The reason given was that to allow the transfer of what was considered a mere possibility would encourage maintenance and champerty.[1]   This reason has ceased to have any practical importance in the law but the rule persists.   Curiously enough it has been held in some cases that even though the power of termination is not alienable inter vivos, nevertheless, an attempt by its owner to transfer it will result in its annihilation and that thereafter the owner of the possessory estate owns it without being subject further to the condition subsequent.   There seems no proper foundation for the imposition of such a penalty or result and the general rule is to the effect that the attempted transfer is void and just simply has no effect at all, and the power of termination still exists and remains with the transferor.

Applying such rule, to the instant case, A's conveyance to X had no effect and A still owned the power of termination.   A then died testate, his will devising his interest in Blackacre to C.   It is held generally that a power of termination is an interest in real property which will descend from the ancestor to the heir and that in this case

---

1.   The policy behind the rule of non-assignability was to prevent the stirring up of law suits.   Black's Law Dictionary (1979), gives the following definitions:

   Champerty.   A bargain by a stranger with a party to a suit, by which such third person undertakes to carry on the litigation at his own cost and risk, in consideration of receiving, if successful, a part of the proceeds or subject sought to be recovered.   Schnabel v. Taft Broadcasting Co., Inc., Mo.App., 525 S.W.2d 819, 823.   **Maintenance** consists in maintaining, supporting, or promoting the litigation of another.

   Another explanation of the non-alienable rule was simply the lack of a remedy for the assignee under medieval law.   Moynihan, 107, n. 2.

had A died intestate his power of termination in Blackacre would have passed by intestate succession to his heir, H. It is also generally true that an interest which will descend is likewise subject to testamentary disposition and can be devised. This is true as to a power of termination. Hence, when A's will devised to C his interest in Blackacre, his power of termination passed to his devisee, C.

However the fact that C owns the power of termination and that the owner of the possessory estate, B, has breached the condition subsequent, does not automatically revest the estate in the owner of the power of termination. At common law the owner of the power would have to (a) elect to terminate the estate and (b) make an entry onto the premises. Today he has to (a) elect to terminate the estate and (b) do some affirmative act towards its termination. Bringing an action in ejectment and sometimes mere giving of notice have constituted such affirmative act. In this case C's bringing ejectment against H and giving notice to B and M, should be sufficient affirmative acts to terminate the possessory estate and revest it in C, the owner of the power of termination. C may therefore eject H from Blackacre.

One more point requires consideration. What rights did M acquire under his lease from B? The answer is this. When the owner of an estate subject to a condition subsequent creates estates or encumbrances on the land, all persons who take such estates or encumbrances are bound by the condition and if the power of termination is exercised, such estates and encumbrances are rendered wholly nugatory as to the owner of the power of termination, who now owns the estate as though he had never parted therewith ab initio. Under such doctrine when C exercised the power of termination, he not only cut off B's estate but also effectively terminated any interest which M had in the premises. See Restatement of Property §§ 154, 155, 159–161, 165 comment a, Illustration 5; Burby, 346–348; Moynihan, 103–109; Simes, 30–32, 73, 76; Richardson v. Holman, 160 Fla. 65, 33 So.2d 641 (1948), dicta to the effect that a power of termination was alienable inter vivos.

CASE 74: A, being life tenant of Blackacre, leases it "to B for 10 years upon the express understanding and conditions that if B sells liquor on the premises or makes an assignment of this lease without the written consent of the lessor, in either such event, then said lessor, A, or his successors in interest have the right to enter the premises and terminate this lease". The rent was $100 per month, payable in advance. A then assigned all of his right, title and interest in Blackacre to X. B then began selling liquor on the premises. On the month following the first sales of liquor on Blackacre, B made his monthly rent check to X for the sum of $125.00 instead of $100.00 and told X the additional $25.00 was because he was selling liquor on the premises. This procedure continued for a year at which time, without any consent from X, either written or oral, B assigned the lease to M. Thereupon, X promptly entered the premises, evicted M and notified both M and B that the lease had been terminated. B and M join in action against X to regain possession of Blackacre. May they succeed?

Answer and Analysis

The answer is no. The provisions in A's lease to B are typical of those in many leases. When A provided that the lease was "upon the express understanding and conditions" and that the lessor and his successors in interest "have the right to enter the premises and terminate this lease", it seems quite clear there was created a condition subsequent with power of termination and not mere covenants that the lessee would not do the things forbidden. A power of termination was therefore reserved in favor of the transferor lessor, A. But such power did not stand alone. It was attached to or an incident to the reversion which was also in A, because the 10 year lease was a lesser estate than A's life estate.

At the early common law a power of termination, even when attached to a reversion, was not alienable. However, by the statute of 32 Henry VIII, c. 34 (1540), which statute is considered part of the American common law, such power of termination when incident to a reversion, was made alienable. Hence, when A assigned to X, both the reversion and power of termination incident thereto, passed to the assignee, X. When, thereafter, B breached the condition concerning the sale of liquor on the leased premises, X could have terminated the lease. Not having done so, it continued. But X was not merely passive concerning such. He accepted additional rent from the lessee who had breached the condition. That acceptance of such additional rent for the breach of the very condition in the lease constituted a waiver of such breach as a matter of law. A waiver is the intentional giving up of a known right. It is usually a question of fact but no reasonable men could differ on there being a waiver in this case in which case it is a question of law. Hence, X could not exercise the power of termination for the breach of the condition not to sell liquor on the premises.

However, the condition against assignment of the lease is wholly separate and independent from the one concerning liquor and the waiver of the latter did not affect the continued efficacy of the former. When, then B made an assignment of the lease without the written consent of X, there was a breach of such condition subsequent which gave X the right to exercise his power of termination. Having elected to exercise such power and having exercised such power by entry on Blackacre, B's leasehold and all rights of the assignee thereunder, were effectively terminated. Neither B nor his assignee, M, has a right against X. See Moynihan, 103–109 and citations under Case 73 supra.

POSSIBILITIES OF REVERTER COMPARED WITH AND DISTINGUISHED FROM POWERS OF TERMINATION

SIMILARITIES

POSSIBILITY OF REVERTER	POWER OF TERMINATION
1. it is a future contingent interest in real property	1. it is a future contingent interest in real property
2. it is always in favor of the transferor only	2. it is always in favor of the transferor only
3. it is not an estate in land	3. it is not an estate in land
4. it is descendible, will pass from the transferor as ancestor to his heir, and is devisable	4. it is descendible, will pass from the transferor as ancestor to his heir, and in most states is devisable
5. it can be released by the transferor to the owner of the determinable estate	5. it can be released by the transferor to the owner of the determinable estate
6. when attached to a reversion, it is alienable, descendible and devisable	6. when attached to a reversion, it is alienable, descendible and devisable
7. *at common law* a possibility of reverter, standing alone and unconnected with a reversion, was not alienable (NOTE—today this is changed—see under dissimilarities and see Case 72)	7. at common law a power of termination, standing alone and unconnected with a reversion, was not alienable (Note—this is true today in some but not all jurisdictions—see under dissimilarities)
8. it is not subject to the common law Rule against Perpetuities	8. it is not subject to the common law Rule against Perpetuities
9. the owner has no right against the owner of the granted estate for waste unless it is reasonably probable that the interest will become possessory and the threatened injury is wanton and unconscionable	9. the owner has no right against the owner of the granted estate for waste unless it is reasonably probable that the interest will become possessory and the threatened injury is wanton and unconscionable

DISSIMILARITIES

POSSIBILITY OF REVERTER	POWER OF TERMINATION
1. IT **ALWAYS TAKES EFFECT AUTOMATICALLY** UPON THE HAPPENING OF THE EVENT UPON WHICH IT IS LIMITED	1. IT **NEVER TAKES EFFECT AUTOMATICALLY** UPON BREACH OF THE CONDITION SUBSEQUENT UPON WHICH IT IS LIMITED
THIS IS ITS CHIEF CHARACTERISTIC	**THIS IS ITS CHIEF CHARACTERISTIC**
2. no affirmative act on the part of its owner is necessary to make it effective	2. to make it effective its owner must (a) elect to exercise the power and (b) must do some affirmative act to terminate the estate
3. it is created by implication of law when a deed or will creates a determinable estate	3. it is created only by clear and express language in a deed or will providing for a condition subsequent to the estate conveyed
4. typical words limiting the determinable estate are "until", "while", "so long as", "during"	4. typical words limiting the condition subsequent are, "but if", "provided that", "upon the express condition that", "but if it should happen that"
5. it is alienable when standing alone unconnected with a reversion	5. it is *not* alienable in many states when standing alone unconnected with a reversion
6. its operation does not cause a forfeiture of any estate	6. its operation causes forfeiture of an estate
7. it cannot be waived after the event	7. it can be waived after breach of the condition

See Simes, 28–32, 73–76, 280; Moynihan, 95–109, Restatement of Property §§ 154, 155, 159–161; Burby, 344–348, 420.

5. REMAINDERS, VESTED AND CONTINGENT

Legal Gems

1. In the creation of a remainder the following elements must be present:

    a. the remainder must be in favor of a transferee who is one other than the conveyor,

    b. the remainder must be created at the same time and in the same instrument as the prior particular estate which supports it,

c. the remainder must be so limited (described) that it can take effect as a present interest in possession immediately upon the termination of the prior particular estate, and

d. the prior particular estate must be an estate of lesser duration than the interest of the conveyor at the time of the conveyance so that there can be an interest to pass in remainder.

2. At common law the particular estate which preceded and supported a remainder had to be a freehold estate, that is, either a fee tail or a life estate, but modern usage permits such prior estate to be either (a) a fee tail, (b) a life estate, or (c) an estate for years; it cannot be a fee simple estate because if a fee simple estate has vested in the prior tenant, then there is nothing left in the conveyor to pass to the remainderman, and in addition, such remainder would have to take effect in derogation of (that is by cutting short) such preceding particular etate.

3. The remainder itself may be either (a) a fee simple, (b) a fee tail, (c) a life estate, or (d) an estate for years.

4. Remainders are classified as

a. vested remainders, and

b. contingent remainders.

Vested remainders include those that are:

(1) indefeasibly vested;

(2) vested subject to partial defeasance or subject to open; and

(3) vested subject to total defeasance.

5. A remainder is always created by deed or by will and the remainderman takes as a purchaser.

6. Vested remainders have always been alienable, devisable and descendible. At an earlier date in the common law contingent remainders were considered inalienable. Today, all remainders are considered alienable, and unless terminated by the death of the owner, are devisable and descendible.

7. Every remainder is subject to the claims of the creditors of the owner thereof.

8. A remainder cannot take effect in derogation of, that is by cutting short, the prior particular estate; it can take effect only when such prior particular estate comes to an end naturally according to its limitation.

9. A remainder is called a remainder because when the prior particular estate comes to an end, it "remains" away from rather than reverts to the conveyor.

10. At common law there can be created in any conveyance as many remainders as the conveyor desires, subject, of course, to the limitation that he cannot dispose of a greater estate than that which he has.

11.   If an instrument can be so construed as to create either a vested or a contingent remainder, that construction is preferred which will result in the creation of a vested remainder.

12.   If an instrument can be so construed as to create either a contingent remainder or an executory interest, that construction is preferred which will result in the creation of a contingent remainder.

13.   A vested remainder, being vested, is not subject to the Rule against Perpetuities; a contingent remainder is subject to the Rule.

14.   If a vested remainder is in fee simple, there is no reversion left in the conveyor; there is always a reversion left in the conveyor in case of a contingent remainder, as long as the remainder remains contingent.

15.   A vested remainder, if not defeated, has an absolute right to become a possessory interest at the end of the prior particular estate; a contingent remainder has only a conditional right to become possessory when the particular estate ends.

16.   A vested remainderman has a right against the prior estate owner for waste; a contingent remainderman, suing for himself alone, has no such right.

17.   A vested remainderman has a right to compel the prior estate owner to pay taxes and interest on incumbrances to the extent of the value of rents and profits; the contingent remainderman has no such right.

18.   Examples of vested remainders

    a.   indefeasibly vested (subject to *no condition*)

        (1) A to B for life, remainder to C and his heirs. C has such a remainder.

        (2) A to B and the heirs of his body remainder to C and his heirs. C has such a remainder.

    b.   vested subject to partial defeasance (subject to *condition subsequent*)

        (1) A to B for life remainder to B's children, B having one child, C. C has a vested remainder subject to open and let in later born children. C's remainder will be partially defeated as each additional child is born to B.

    c.   vested subject to total defeasance (subject to *condition subsequent*)

        (1) A to B for life, remainder to C and his heirs, but if C predeceases B, then to D and his heirs. C has a vested remainder subject to being completely defeated.

19.   Examples of contingent remainders (subject to *condition precedent*)

    a.   A to B for life, remainder to C and his heirs if C marries before B's death. C has a remainder contingent upon his marriage before B dies.

b.   A to B for life, remainder to C for life if C survives X.   C has a remainder contingent upon X's predeceasing both B and C because the contingency of C's surviving X must happen on or before the termination of B's life estate.

20.   To avoid the doctrine of destructibility when applicable, every contingent remainder must vest at or before the termination of the preceding particular estate.   E. g., A to B for life, remainder to C and his heirs if C marries X.   If C does not marry X before B dies, then the seisin will revert to A and C's contingent remainder is destroyed forever at common law.   If he marries X but after B dies, that will not save or revive the irretrievably lost contingent remainder.   The destructibility rule is abolished in most but not all states.

21.   Example of a conveyance creating several remainders

a.   A to B for life, then in order to C for life, D for life, E for life, F for life, and finally to G and the heirs of his body.   B has a life estate in possession.   C has a vested remainder for life. Same as to D, E and F.   G has a vested remainder in fee tail.   A has a reversion.   It is quite immaterial that any one of the vested remainders for life may never be enjoyed because of the remainderman's, e. g., E, dying before B, or that G may die without bodily heirs before B's life estate in possession terminates.   The seisin will pass regularly to those named who are living and then revert to the grantor, A, or if he be dead the reversion will have descended to his heirs.

22.   Remainders may be created by implication as well as express provisions in conveyances.   See Restatement of Property §§ 156, 157, 162; Simes, 19, 33, 90, 98, 279; Burby, 33, 338, 418.

———

CASE 75:   A, being fee simple owner of Blackacre, conveys it "to B for life, remainder to C and his heirs".   What interest, if any, does each party have in Blackacre?

Answer and Analysis

The answer is this, A has no interest, B has a life estate in possession, and C has an indefeasibly vested remainder in fee simple.

(a) It is clear that A, who owned a fee simple estate in Blackacre, has conveyed away that fee simple estate by the life estate in B and the fee simple in remainder in C, so there is no reversion left in A.   Hence, he has no interest whatsoever in the premises.

(b) If A's conveyance to B were at common law, it would involve the ceremony of feoffment whereby A went onto Blackacre and made livery of seisin to B for B's life.   A would walk off the premises and leave B in possession seised of a life estate.   If A's conveyance were a bargain and sale deed under the Statute of Uses (1535) and recited a consideration, then mere delivery of the deed to B would vest in B a life estate.   The consideration in the deed would raise a use in B and the Statute would transfer the legal title. In either event the conveyance would give B a valid legal life estate. At common law every remainder had to be supported by a preceding particular estate of freehold. Such particular estate could be either (1) a life estate or (2) a fee tail estate, but it could not be a fee simple estate because if the prior tenant had a fee simple estate there was nothing left to pass in remainder to the remainderman. Hence, B has an estate which will qualify as the particular freehold estate which supports a remainder, namely, a life estate.

(c) Every remainder must qualify as such by complying with the common law requirements: (1) it must be in favor of a transferee who is one other than the conveyor; (2) it must be created at the same time and in the same instrument as the particular estate of freehold which precedes and supports it; (3) it must be so limited (described) that it will take effect, if at all, as a present interest in possession *at* (neither before nor after) the natural and regular termination of the particular estate of freehold which precedes and supports it; and (4) the prior particular estate of freehold must be an estate of lesser duration than the interest of the conveyor at the time of the conveyance so that there can be an interest to pass in remainder. We now apply these tests to C's so-called remainder. (1) The remainder is in favor of C who is a transferee, he being one other than the conveyor, A. (2) C's interest is created at the same time and in the same instrument as is the prior particular estate of freehold, B's life estate. (3) C's interest is so limited or described that it is to take effect at once or immediately upon the termination of B's life estate, that is upon B's death. (4) The prior particular estate of freehold, B's life estate, is a lesser estate than the estate held by the conveyor at the time of the conveyance, A's fee simple. Clearly C's interest possesses all the elements required of a common law remainder. Hence, C has a remainder in fee simple in Blackacre.

Of what class is C's remainder? It is a vested remainder because it is presently owned by C and is subject to no other condition to becoming an estate in possession than that B's life estate terminate by B's death. And it is indefeasibly vested because nothing can defeat it. If C survives B, C will enjoy the possession of Blackacre. If C conveys the remainder, then his grantee will enjoy the possession. If C devises it, then his devisee will enjoy the possession. If C dies intestate before B dies, then C's heir will take the possession. Hence, we say C has an indefeasibly vested remainder in Blackacre. See Simes 19–25; Restatement of Property § 157.

CASE 76: A, being fee simple owner of Blackacre, conveyed it "to B for life, remainder to C for life, remainder as C shall by will appoint and in the absence of the exercise of such power by C, then to D and his heirs". What interests do C and D have in Blackacre?

Answers and Analyses

The answers are: (a) C has a vested remainder for life subject to complete defeasance, and (b) D has a vested remainder in fee simple subject to complete defeasance.

There are three classes of vested remainders, (1) those indefeasibly vested (see Case 75 supra), (2) those vested subject to complete defeasance and (3) those vested subject to partial defeasance or subject to open (see Case 77 et seq.). A remainder which is vested and subject to complete defeasance is one which is presently owned but which may or may not ever be enjoyed by the remainderman as an estate in possession. In this case C's life estate is presently owned by C and cannot be enjoyed as a possessory estate until the death of B. If at that time C still lives, then C will have an estate in possession and will occupy Blackacre. But suppose C dies before B. In that event C's remainder will never be transformed into an estate in possession. Whether such an estate comes to an end by its own limitation or by some extrinsic executory limitation, would seem to make no difference analytically. In either event the remainder is completely defeated. The modern view classifies it as a remainder subject to complete defeasance.

The same is true of D's interest. D has a remainder in fee simple. He owns it presently but the enjoyment as an estate in possession is not only postponed, it is subject to the *condition subsequent,* the exercise of the power vested in C, which may defeat it completely. If C by his will exercises the power vested in him and appoints X in fee as remainderman following C's life estate in remainder, then, of course, D's remainder in fee will be destroyed. Such is the nature of a vested remainder subject to complete defeasance. It is always subject to a condition subsequent. See Simes, 19 et seq.; Restatement of Property § 157. For powers of appointment, see infra Chapter VII, part 4.

CASE 77: A, being fee simple owner of Blackacre, conveys it "to B for life, remainder to the children of B in fee simple". At the time of this conveyance B had no child but within a year following he had child C, and thereafter had in succession children D, E and F. After C attained adulthood, his creditor, X, levied upon and sold C's interest in Blackacre, to Y. What interest, if any, did Y take by the execution sale?

Answer and Analysis

The answer is this, Y took the interest which C had in Blackacre which is a variable, but which is at present an undivided one fourth interest in the remainder but which is subject to open if more children are born to B.

Following the facts in this case the interests of the conveyees are as follows. B was given a life estate which is the preceding particular estate which supports the remainder in B's children. That B's children have a remainder interest is not open to doubt. It is in favor of one other than the conveyor, A. It is created in the same instrument and at the same time as B's life estate. It is to take effect, if at all, when B's life estate naturally ends. And B's life estate is a lesser estate than A's fee simple when he made the conveyance. These are all the elements of a remainder. But there is at the time of the conveyance a condition precedent to the vesting of such remainder because B had no child. There was therefore a reversion in A subject to defeasance and a contingent remainder in B's children.

When C was born to B, the contingent remainder was transformed into a vested remainder in C in fee simple and the reversion in A was totally divested. And just what interest does C have? He has a vested remainder which he owns in severalty but which is subject to open in favor of further children born to B. C's remainder is also described as one subject to partial defeasance. When C's brother, D, came along, then C and D were owners of the remainder in fee simple, each owning an undivided one half interest therein. When E was born to B, then the estate opened up still further and C, D and E each owned an undivided one third in the remainder in fee simple. When F was born to B, there was still further division and C, D, E and F each owned an undivided one fourth interest in the remainder in Blackacre. It just did not pay C to have brothers and sisters. But that is not all. B is by the common law conclusively presumed able to have children as long as he lives. Hence, during B's lifetime the estate in remainder is subject to open in favor of any other children which may be born to B. As each child is born, as is seen above, the interest of each child remainderman, is partially defeated by having to "divide up" with his later born brothers and sisters.

Each remainderman who is sui juris has the right and power to dispose of his interest in the remainder. There being such power in the owner, then the owner's creditor, has the right to levy upon the interest which is owned. Hence, C's creditor, X, had the right to levy upon C's remainder interest in Blackacre. And upon the execution sale by X, just what did the purchaser, Y, take? He took what the debtor, C, had for the rights of the creditor are derivative. Y bought C's one fourth interest in his vested remainder but this purchased fourth interest in the hands of Y would be subject to open in favor of any child or children thereafter born to B. At common law contingent remainders were not considered alienable but today, with recording statutes under which anyone can look at the records and find out what interest anyone has in land, all remainders are alienable. See Restatement of Property § 157, comment 1, illustration 2, §§ 162, 167; Simes, 19–25.

CASE 78: A, fee simple owner of Blackacre, conveys it "to B for life, but if B becomes bankrupt, then remainder to B's children share and share alike". B has children living. What interest do B's children have?

Answer and Analysis

The answer is this—B's children have an executory interest in fee simple; they do not have a remainder. This interest fails to meet one of the tests required of a remainder.

(1) The children's interest is in favor of a transferee who is one other than the conveyor, A. (2) It is created at the same time and in the same instrument as the particular estate of freehold which supports it, B's life estate. (3) The prior particular estate of freehold, B's life estate, is a lesser estate than the conveyor's fee simple. Thus far the remainder meets all the requirements. But (4) a remainder must be so limited that it will take effect in possession *at the natural or regular termination of the prior particular estate of freehold*. The natural or regular termination of the prior estate of freehold in our case is when B's life estate comes to an end by B's death. A future interest cannot be a remainder if it takes effect in derogation of or cuts short such prior particular estate. By the terms of A's conveyance if B becomes bankrupt, then the so-called remainder is to become effective. If that occurred, then the children's future interest would come in in derogation of and would cut short B's life estate. Such is a violation of one of the requirements of a remainder that it must take effect *at* the termination of the prior particular estate and *not before* or *after* such termination. Hence, the future interest to B's children is void as a remainder. If, in its inception, a future interest can be construed as a remainder it will be so construed. If it cannot be so construed when it is created, then it may take effect as an executory interest. In this case the children of B have an executory interest which will, if B becomes bankrupt, cut off B's life estate. Executory interests regularly cut short the vested interests which precede them. See Blackman v. Fysh, 3 Ch.Div. 209 (1892); Moynihan, 198; Burby, 349; Powell ¶ 273.

Note

(a) The thin line between remainders and executory interests can be readily discerned by comparing the case given which creates an executory interest, with the following case which creates a remainder: A, being fee simple owner of Blackacre, conveys it "to B for life or until he becomes bankrupt, then remainder to B's children share and share alike". Here the remainder would be effective, not in derogation of the preceding particular estate, but *at* the termination of the determinable life estate.

(b) There is little difficulty in distinguishing a remainder from either a reversion, a possibility of reverter or power of termination, because a remainder is always in favor of a transferee whereas the other three are always in favor of the conveyor or transferor.

(c) The real difficulty is in distinguishing a remainder from an executory interest. The following may help. A remainder *must always* be able to take effect, if at all, at the termination of the particular estate of freehold which precedes it, *never* in derogation thereof. An executory interest, with *one exception* given below, *always* takes effect in derogation of or by cutting short the vested estate which precedes it. In one instance an executory interest takes effect *at* the termination of the preceding estate. E. g., A, being fee simple owner of Blackacre, conveys it "to B and his heirs so long as the property is used for courthouse purposes, and if it ceases to be so used, and while my friend X is living, then to X and his heirs". X's interest cannot be a remainder because no remainder can follow a fee simple, whether absolute or determinable. It is an executory interest but it will vest as an estate in possession *at* the termination of the preceding freehold estate in B. See Moynihan, 196–199; Simes, 25–28; Burby, 348–350.

CASE 79: A, being fee simple owner of Blackacre, conveys it "to B for life and one year after B's death, remainder to C and his heirs". B died and A took possession of Blackacre. One year after B's death and while A was in possession, C demanded possession of Blackacre from A. A refused. C sues A in ejectment. **(a)** May C recover? **(b)** What type of interest, if any, does C have?

Answers and Analyses

The answers are: (a) Yes; (b) An executory interest.

Every remainder must conform to the legal requirements for its existence. They are, (1) it must be in favor of a transferee, that is one other than the conveyor, (2) it must be created at the same time and in the same instrument as the prior particular estate which supports it, (3) it must be so limited (described) that it will take effect as a present interest immediately upon the termination of the prior particular estate, and (4) the prior particular estate must be an estate of lesser duration than the interest of the conveyor at the time of the conveyance.

We apply these tests to the facts given. (1) The so-called remainder in C is in favor of a transferee, that is, C is a different person than the conveyor, A. (2) C's so-called remainder is created in the same instrument and at the same time as B's life estate which is the prior particular estate which supports it. (3) The interest in C is limited, *not to take effect immediately upon the termination of the prior particular estate,* that is, B's life estate, but one year after the termination of such prior particular estate. (4) The prior particular estate, B's life estate, is of lesser duration than the interest of the conveyor at the time of the conveyance, that is, A's fee simple. C's interest conforms to all the requirements of a remainder except (3) above. Without conforming to all four, it cannot be a remainder. If a future interest is to take effect one second *after* the termination of the particular estate of freehold which precedes it, such future interest cannot be a remainder. The reason is that at common law the seisin could not be in abeyance for an instant. When B died the seisin had to go somewhere. It could not go to C for such was not intended until the passing of one year after B's death. So the seisin reverts to the conveyor, A. At common law, once the seisin has reverted to A it will take another conveyance to divest him thereof. Hence, C's interest described in A's conveyance will fail *as a remainder*.

However, after the Statute of Uses, two new types of future interests quite unknown to the common law were permitted in favor of transferees. And these new future interests took effect in derogation of preceding estates. One, the springing use or interest, cut short the prior estate which was vested in the conveyor. The other, the shifting use or interest, cut short the prior estate which was vested in one other than the conveyor. In our case when B died there was a reversion to the conveyor, A, who is now possessed of a fee simple estate for the period of one year after B's death. When that year has expired a use springs up in C in fee simple which use draws the legal title to itself by means of the Statute of Uses. C now owning the legal title in fee simple has the right to immediate possession and can eject the conveyor A whose prior estate has been cut off by C's executory interest which A himself created. See Simes, 19–25; Burby, 348–350; Moynihan, 110, 196; Note to Case 78, supra, for one exception to rule that executory interests always cut short preceding estates. See also infra Chapter XVIII, part 2 for the Statute of Uses.

CASE 80: A, being fee simple owner of Blackacre, conveyed it "to B for a period of 10 years, remainder to C and his heirs". (a) Is the remainder to C valid? (b) Would it make any difference if the remainder were to "the heirs of C," a living person?

Answers and Analyses

The answers are: (a) no, not as a remainder at common law; C acquired a present fee simple subject to a term for years in B. Today it is permissible to refer to C's interest as a remainder. (b) yes, it would make a difference if the remainder following a term for years were contingent. Such a contingent interest was void at common law; today it could take effect, subject to the rule against perpetuities, as an executory interest.

(1) The answer given to (a) is a technical answer based on a technical reason. At common law every remainder had to be preceded by a particular estate of freehold, either a fee tail or a life estate. Every freehold estate (fee simple, fee tail or life estate) had to be created by livery of seisin. No freehold estate could be made to com-

mence in futuro because there had to be the ceremony of feoffment and that had to take place in the present. However, the creation of a remainder was not considered a violation of the rule. For example, suppose X, being fee simple owner, wished to enfeoff Y for life, with remainder to Z and his heirs. X would go onto the land, make livery of seisin to Y with the declaration that such seisin was for Y for Y's life and thereafter for Z and his heirs. Both estates were considered as being created at the same time and the feoffor was considered as having put the seisin out of himself for the entire time during which the declared estates would exist. X would then walk off the land leaving Y in possession claiming a life estate therein, he being therefore seised, and holding such seisin for himself and the remaindermen who followed. Indeed, the remainder was the only future estate which was recognized by the common law which was in favor of a transferee, one other than the transferor. But Y's life estate is a freehold estate and a life tenant is seised. When, then, Y dies the seisin will pass immediately to Z in fee simple. There will be no break in the continuity of the seisin, the seisin will not be in abeyance.

However, in the problem given for solution B was to have a non-freehold estate, an estate for years. A tenant for years, having only a chattel real, could not be seised. He could be possessed only. The conveyor could not deliver seisin to a tenant for years to pass naturally to the remainderman at the end of the term for years. A could not deliver seisin to B for 10 years which would then pass to C in fee simple. Strictly speaking, then, there could be no remainder following an estate for years, and in the case given C's so-called remainder would be void and there would be a reversion in the conveyor, A.

(2) Nevertheless even at common law, there was a procedure by which the entire conveyance of A in our case could be made valid and effective, but not as a technical remainder. It was done as follows. A made livery of seisin to B, the tenant for years, but at the same time declared that such livery was made for the benefit of C. Thereupon, the seisin passed immediately through B to C, who then held the fee simple estate in possession but subject to a term of 10 years in B. It should be noted in this procedure that the seisin never lodged in B, nor was it in abeyance for an instant because it passed immediately through B to C who was intended to be seised. In this case C's interest today is often referred to as a remainder, even though it did not technically qualify as such.

(3) If C's interest following the 10 year term was intended to be a contingent remainder as in question (b), rather than an estate in possession subject to a term, not even this procedure described in (2) above could save it. For example, A, being fee simple owner, conveys, "to B for 10 years, remainder to the heirs of C", C being a living person. Here there could be no livery of seisin to B for C's heirs, because C's heirs are not, until C's death, determinable. Thus the seisin would be in abeyance and the intended contingent remainder in C's heirs would be absolutely void.

(4) Of course, in the set of facts given as to question (a), under the Statute of Uses (1535), C would take an executory interest following B's 10 year term. It would work as follows. Assume A's conveyance is a bargain and sale deed which recites a consideration. Now, the grantor, A, is seised of Blackacre. By the consideration in the deed a use is raised in accordance with A's declaration in the deed for B for the 10 year period. The Statute of Uses executes the use and carries the legal title to B for the 10 year period. That makes the 10 year term in B effective. When the 10 year term has expired a use springs up in C in fee simple and the Statute of Uses again carries the seisin and legal title from the grantor, A, to C and makes C the legal owner of Blackacre in fee simple. But C takes an executory interest by way of a springing use, not a remainder. Thus, operating in this manner, the fact that the end limitation may be contingent is immaterial today. Such interest will take effect, if at all, by divesting the reversion in the grantor. Executory interests, however, must satisfy the rule against perpetuities or else they will be held void. See Tiffany, Abridged Edition, 101–102, 110–111, 126; Moynihan, 167–170, 176–179; Burby, 348–350.

Note

The answer in Case 80, supra, is intended to explain the historical development and logic in the common law requirements of a remainder in land. Today livery of seisin is obsolete. The reason for requiring continuity of seisin has long since disappeared. The modern view permits remainders not only in land but also in chattels real and in chattels personal. The conveyor's estate need not be a freehold and a remainder may follow an estate for years. See Simes, 19; Restatement of Property § 156, comment e, illustration 9 (saying C in Case 80, supra, has a remainder).

CASE 81:   A, being fee simple owner of Blackacre, conveys it "to B for life, and upon B's death, to C and his heirs". Does C take a vested or contingent remainder under this conveyance?

Answer and Analysis

The answer is, C takes a vested remainder. This problem raises a question of construction which requires the finding of the intention of the transferor from the language he has used in the instrument. There is no question that C takes a remainder. But is it a vested remainder or a contingent remainder?

A vested remainder is one which is limited to an ascertained person who has the right to immediate possession if and when the prior estate is terminated. It may be subject to no condition, in which case it is said to be indefeasibly or absolutely vested. In that case it is certain to become an estate in possession. But it may be subject to a condition subsequent which will divest the remainderman of his estate. But it is nevertheless vested until divested. E. g., A to B for life, remainder to C and his heirs but if C does not pay $100 to X before B dies, then to X and his heirs. C's remainder is vested subject to condition subsequent which may defeat it completely.

On the other hand a contingent remainder is one which is subject to a condition precedent. It is one which will not vest until the happening of an event or the ascertainment of a person. So, subject to the doctrine that all remainders must take effect at the time the preceding estate terminates, we have three propositions, (1) a remainder which is indefeasibly vested is subject to *no condition*, (2) a remainder which is vested but may be partially or totally divested is subject to a *condition subsequent*, and (c) a contingent remainder is subject to a *condition precedent*. So our question requires a determination whether on the one hand there is no condition or a condition subsequent and therefore a vested remainder, or on the other hand, whether there is a condition precedent and therefore a contingent remainder.

It is of course arguable that the language in the instant case "upon B's death" evinces an intention that C shall have no interest in Blackacre until the death of B, that B's death is a condition precedent to the vesting of any interest in C, and therefore C has a contingent remainder. On the other hand, the language in the conveyance says nothing more than this, "to B for life, then to C and his heirs". The words, "upon B's death", add nothing to the meaning of the other words used in the conveyance. But if there is any doubt concerning whether the words of a conveyance create a vested or a contingent interest, that interpretation is always preferred which will result in the interest being vested. So, in our case, the courts hold that there is a vested remainder in C and that the words, "upon B's death" are mere surplusage.

If the meaning of the words is clear, the courts will not do violence to such meaning. Compare these two cases: A, fee owner, devises Blackacre, (1) "to B for life, then to B's children in fee simple, but if any one of B's children predeceases B, then the share of the decedent shall go to the surviving children", and (2) "to B for life, then to the children of B, who survive B, in fee simple". In (1) it is clear that B's children (assuming he has children at the time), take a vested remainder subject to defeasance, that is, they take subject to a condition subsequent, and in (2) it is just as clear that none of B's children is to take any interest until such children are ascertained by their surviving the death of B, that is, it is a condition precedent that such children survive B, and therefore they have a contingent remainder. See Simes, 19–25, 186; Moynihan, 116–125.

———

CASE 82: A, being fee simple owner of Blackacre, conveys it "to B for life, remainder in fee simple to the heirs of C",

C then being a living person. B then died. A then took possession of Blackacre. Then C died leaving H his sole heir. H sues A to eject him from Blackacre. May he succeed?

Answer and Analysis

The answer is at common law, no, but yes today in most states. (See Note C below).

What is the effect of A's conveyance? It gave B a life estate in possession. It gave C no interest, he being merely the ancestor through and at whose death the remaindermen would be determined. The heirs of C were given a contingent remainder, the contingency being their ascertainment at or before the death of B. That was the condition precedent which made the remainder contingent. As long as there is a contingent remainder, there is a reversion in the conveyor, A. What was the effect of B's death? B left no inheritable estate to pass either to his heirs or devisees. But B was seised and at his death the seisin had to pass to someone. That someone had to be either A, the reversioner, or the remaindermen. But there can be no heir of a living person and C was still alive. Hence, his heirs were not, at the death of B, ascertainable. Therefore, the seisin could not go forward to the unascertained and unascertainable remaindermen. So the seisin reverted to A, the reversioner. Once that happened there was no way at common law by which such seisin could be gotten out of A except by another conveyance. And what then happened to the contingent remainder? It was destroyed forever. This set of facts illustrates the doctrine known as the destructibility of contingent remainders. It was based on the principle that every remainder must vest at or before the termination of the prior particular estate or it was forever destroyed. That was a settled doctrine of the common law. In our case then, when B died before C, at that instant the remaindermen being unascertainable, the seisin reverted to A who had the right to immediate and continued possession of Blackacre, and the contingent remainder was completely and forever destroyed. Thus, H had no right and could not eject A.

What would have happened had C predeceased B? Such event would have had three distinct legal effects. (1) Upon C's death his heirs would have been immediately ascertainable and ascertained as H. That which had been the condition precedent would have occurred. Such event would have transformed the contingent remainder into a vested remainder, indefeasibly vested in H in fee simple. (2) The instant such remainder became vested in H, the reversion in the conveyor, A, would have been defeated and A would no longer have any interest in Blackacre. (3) Then, upon the death of B, H's vested remainder (the future interest, presently owned but the enjoyment of which is postponed) would have become an estate in possession and presently enjoyed by H. Had that occurred, then H could have ejected A or anyone else from Blackacre. See Moynihan, 128 et seq.; Simes, 37 et seq.

Note

(A) Generally, the condition precedent which makes a remainder contingent is either (1) the happening of an event or (2) the ascertainment of the remainderman because he is yet unborn or because some event must happen as is illustrated by Case 82. An example of (1) follows. A to B for life, remainder to C if C pays A $100. C has a contingent remainder. If C pays A before B dies, then C's contingent remainder becomes a vested remainder. If C does not so pay before B's death, then C's contingent remainder is destroyed. An example of (2) follows. A to B for life, remainder to the children of C, a bachelor. C's children have a contingent remainder. If C has a child before B dies, such child has a vested remainder subject to open. If he has no child before B dies, then the contingent remainder is destroyed.

(B) At common law there were three ways by which a contingent remainder could be destroyed, (1) by the condition precedent failing to happen which permitted the contingent remainder to vest at or before the termination of the particular estate as is illustrated in Case 82, supra, (2) by merger and (3) by forfeiture. An example of (2) is this. A to B for life, remainder to B's eldest male heir. B has a son born, X. Now, in order there are (i) life estate in B, (ii) contingent remainder in B's male heir (no one can be an heir male of B till B's death) and (iii) reversion in A. Note that the contingent remainder intervenes the life estate and the reversion. Now, either A grants his reversion to B or B transfers his life estate to A. In either event there is a merger of the life estate in the fee and the intervening contingent remainder is destroyed. Thereafter, upon B's death, his heir male has no rights. An example of (3) is this. Take the same set of facts just given above. B, the life tenant, makes a tortious feoffment to M and his heirs in fee simple. B dies leaving X his male heir. B's tortious feoffment destroyed the contingent remainder and X has no rights. (Archer's Case, 1 Co.Rep. 66B, 1597, is leading case.)

(C) Only a few of the states now permit a contingent remainder to be destroyed as at common law. The destructibility rule has been abolished in the other jurisdictions. In most of the states of the Union the answer to Case 82 would be yes instead of no, because by statute or decision, if the condition precedent to a contingent remainder does actually happen, regardless of when it happens, the contingent remainder takes effect as of the date of the happening of the required event. See Simes, 41; Restatement of Property § 240.

CASE 83: A, fee simple owner of Blackacre, devises it "to B for life, and if B predeceases C, then to C and his heirs, but if B does not predecease C, then to D and his heirs". D conveyed "all my right, title and interest in Blackacre to X and his heirs". C died. Then B died. In the jurisdiction a

typical statute provided that all future interests are alienable, devisable and descendable as are estates in possession.
Who is entitled to possess Blackacre?

Answer and Analysis

The answer is, X. This conveyance gave B a life estate in possession which would support any succeeding remainders. With respect to the interests created in C and D it should be noticed that
there is no contingency as to the persons. They are ascertained and
the only contingencies are concerning events. In determining the interests of C and D, two rules of construction should be considered,
(a) a construction which results in a vested remainder or interest is
preferred over one which results in a contingent remainder or interest, and (b) a construction which results in a contingent remainder is
preferred over one which results in an executory interest. If we apply the first rule to the facts given, then C has a vested remainder
subject to being defeated or cut off completely by the executory interest in D. An executory interest can but a remainder cannot cut
short a prior vested estate. If we apply the second rule, then we
have alternative contingent remainders in C and D or which are
sometimes called contingent remainders with a double aspect. By the
first rule D has an executory interest and by the second rule D has a
contingent remainder. Insofar as the particular conveyance is concerned, the usual construction is that C and D. have alternative contingent remainders. However, if the conveyance were altered just
slightly to read "to B for life and then to C and his heirs, but if B
does not predecease C, then to D and his heirs," a different construction will usually prevail. In this case, C would have a vested remainder subject to defeasance, and D would have an executory interest.
Where the classification is in doubt, probably the vested remainder
and executory interest classification will be adopted.

Under the common law both contingent remainders and executory interests were considered mere possibilities of having an interest
in land and were wholly inalienable. By the better rule today, either
because of a statute such as is given in the facts or by judicial decision without statute, such future contingent interests are considered
as presently existing things and are therefore freely alienable. The
fact that perhaps only a "speculator" might buy such an interest is
wholly immaterial. In this day and age when the public records are
available for everyone to examine, and such records disclose the exact
interest owned, there is no reason why such future contingent interests should not be freely alienable if persons sui juris wish to deal
with them. If the contingency prevents the ascertainment of the person who may dispose of the interest, either because not yet born or
otherwise, that also is quite immaterial, for it merely means that
when that person is ascertained and sui juris, then he can alienate
the interest.

Applying such principles to our facts, when D conveyed to X and
his heirs, he conveyed either a contingent remainder or an executory

interest [a contingent remainder in the original form; an executory interest in the altered form.] Either being alienable, X got exactly the interest which the conveyor, D, had, and it is subject to the same condition either subsequent or precedent. The interest may turn out to be an interest in possession or it may be completely defeated. In this case C's interest was completely defeated by his death before the death of B. When B died D's interest became an estate in possession and had he not conveyed to X, D would have had the fee simple in Blackacre and the right of possession. And that is exactly the interest which X received under D's conveyance. So X is now entitled to possess Blackacre. Even were we to take the view that D's interest was not alienable, his deed might well estop him from denying title in X, or had there been consideration paid, equity might well have treated the conveyance as a contract to convey. But these topics will be dealt with later under estoppel by deed. See Simes, 24, 186 et seq.; Moynihan, 198; Restatement of Property § 162.

CASE 84: A, being fee simple owner of Blackacre, devises it "to B and C as tenants in common for their lives and after the deaths of B and C, to D and his heirs". A residuary clause in A's will gave the residue of his property to M. B died. C leased Blackacre to E for $1,200 per annum net to C. M sues C for one half of such net rent. May M recover?

Answer and Analysis

The answer is no. By express language A has given B a life estate in an undivided one half of Blackacre. The same as to C. D has been given an indefeasibly vested remainder in fee simple. The specific question raised is this. If B dies before C, in whom vests the remainder as to B's undivided one half interest during the continued life of C. If C dies before B, in whom vests the remainder as to C's undivided one half interest during the continued life of B. Surely D has no right to either because his remainder is specifically limited to take effect upon the deaths of both B *and* C. If this is an undisposed of residue of A's estate, then M should be able to claim under the residuary clause and recover against C one half of the rent provided for by the lease. But such is not the law. In the case of a will there is a presumption that the testator intends to dispose of all of his property and that he does not intend intestacy. This would seem doubly clear where the residue intervenes the life estate and the ultimate remainder and as to only an undivided fractional part of the property. This is a case of the creation of cross-remainders by implication. In detail, then, the effect of A's will is to give B a life estate in an undivided one half of Blackacre and a vested remainder subject to divestment in the undivided one half owned by C; likewise, C is given a life estate in an undivided one half of Blackacre and a vested remainder subject to divestment in the undivided one half owned by B; and D has an indefeasibly vested remainder in fee simple. Hence, A having disposed of his entire estate M has no right. In the case of a will this result is based on the presumption that the testator intends to dispose of the whole of Blackacre. Such cross remainders are implied also in case of a conveyance inter vivos based on the rule of construction that an ambiguity in a deed is construed most strongly against the grantor. See, Restatement of Property § 115, Appendix, 16; Burby, 359.

VESTED REMAINDERS COMPARED WITH AND DISTINGUISHED FROM CONTINGENT REMAINDERS AT COMMON LAW

SIMILARITIES

VESTED REMAINDER	CONTINGENT REMAINDER
1. is a future interest	1. is a future interest
2. called a remainder because it *remains* away from the conveyor instead of reverting to him	2. called a remainder because it *remains* away from the conveyor instead of reverting to him
3. must be in favor of a transferee, one other than the conveyor	3. must be in favor of a transferee, one other than the conveyor
4. must be created at same time and in same instrument as the prior particular estate	4. must be created at same time and in same instrument as the prior particular estate
5. must become an estate in possession at the termination of the prior particular estate of freehold	5. must become an estate in possession at the termination of the prior particular estate of freehold
6. must be preceded by particular estate of freehold—a fee tail or a life estate (see 10 below)	6. must be preceded by particular estate of freehold—a fee tail or a life estate (see 10 below)
7. is created either by will or deed, never by descent	7. is created either by will or by deed, never by descent
8. remainderman always takes as a purchaser	8. remainderman always takes as a purchaser
9. there may be as many as the conveyor wishes	9. there may be as many as the conveyor wishes
10. TODAY—may be preceded by an estate for years	10. TODAY—may be preceded by an estate for years but then it is an executory interest
11. it is descendible and devisable	11. it is descendible and devisable

DISSIMILARITIES

VESTED REMAINDER	CONTINGENT REMAINDER
1. is not destructible	1. is destructible
2. is transferable	2. is not transferable
3. is subject to the claims of creditors	3. is not subject to the claims of creditors

Today contingent remainders are no longer destructible in most states; they are transferable and are subject to the claims of creditors. The above three dissimilarities should *now* be moved up into the similarities column.

4. is vested	4. is not vested
5. is an estate	5. is not an estate
6. no reversion left in conveyor if remainder in fee	6. reversion is always left in conveyor as long as remainder is contingent
7. has absolute right to possess when prior estate ends	7. has only conditional right to possess when prior estate ends
8. not subject to Rule against Perpetuities	8. is subject to Rule against Perpetuities
9. vested remainderman has right against prior estate owner for waste	9. contingent remainderman has no right against prior estate owner for waste
10. vested remainderman may force prior estate owner to pay taxes and interest on encumbrances	10. contingent remainderman cannot force prior estate owner to pay taxes or interest on encumbrances

6. EXECUTORY INTERESTS

LEGAL GEMS

1. An executory interest is a future contingent interest created in favor of a transferee under the Statute of Uses (1535), or Statute of Wills (1540), in the form of a springing or shifting use which, on the happening of the contingency described, will be executed into a legal estate, and which cannot be construed as a remainder.

2. An executory interest could not exist at common law; it could be created only after and by the authority of the Statute of Uses and Statute of Wills. See infra Chapter XVIII, part 2 for the Statute of Uses.

3. The following elements are essential to the creation of an executory interest:

a. it is always in favor of a transferee, one other than the transferor;

b. it is always contingent and can never become vested, because when it vests either as a future or present interest, it ceases to be an executory interest;

c. it must take effect either (1) *before the natural termination of the preceding estate,* therefore in derogation thereof or by divesting it, or (2) *after the termination of the preceding estate.* (If it took effect *at* the natural termination of the preceding estate, it was a remainder. There is one exception—an executory interest can take effect *at* the termination of a determinable fee. See Note to Case 78, supra, explaining this exception.)

4. An executory interest always divests a preceding vested estate either

a. of the grantor, in which case it is a springing interest,
or

b. of another grantee, in which case it is a shifting interest.

5. By the better view all executory interests are alienable inter vivos, descendible and devisable.

6. An executory interest is indestructible. Out of the indestructibility of executory interests has evolved the Rule against Perpetuities. See infra Chapter VII, part 3.

7. If a limitation could take effect as a contingent remainder, it was construed to be a remainder and it could not take effect as an executory interest even to save the interest from destruction. Of course, where, as in most states today a contingent remainder is not destructible, the question of contingent remainder or executory interest is usually academic.

8. Executory interests include (a) springing and shifting uses which are *created by deed* and (b) executory devises which are *created by will.* Executory devises are interests which are identical with executed springing and shifting uses except that they are created by will instead of by deed. So all executory interests are either of the springing or shifting type.

9. Equitable future interests of the springing and shifting types were enforceable in equity before the Statute of Uses. Examples:

a. A, fee owner, enfeoffed B and his heirs to the use of C and his heirs three years after this feoffment. B had a legal fee simple subject to C's equitable *springing use* which equity would enforce three years after the feoffment.

b. A, fee owner, enfeoffed B and his heirs to the use of C for life but if C became bankrupt then to D for life. B had a legal fee simple subject to C's equitable life estate. C's equitable life estate was subject to a *shifting use* which equity would enforce in D's favor if C became bankrupt, thus cutting off C's equitable life estate. After the Statute of Uses these equitable future interests were converted into legal future interests, examples of which appear below.

10.   Examples of legal statutory interests after the Statute of Uses

a.   Illustrating a freehold estate made to commence in futuro and divesting the vested estate of the grantor:

(1) by springing use created by deed of bargain and sale—A, fee owner, conveys "to B and his heirs, this deed to take effect three years after its date."

This deed leaves the fee simple in A for three years at which time a use springs up in B and the Statute of Uses executes the use in B into a legal estate in fee simple, thus divesting the fee simple which was in A, the grantor. By this deed A held a fee simple estate subject to an executory interest in B. B's interest could not be a remainder because it is not preceded by a particular freehold estate in another grantee.

(2) by executory devise by will—A, fee owner, devises "to B and his heirs three years after my death" (no residuary clause in will).

This will leaves the fee simple in A's heir for three years by intestate succession at which time a use springs up in B and under the Statute of Wills by analogy to uses under the Statute of Uses the use is executed into a legal estate in fee simple, thus divesting the fee simple which was in A's heir who represents the testator. The heir held a fee simple estate subject to an executory devise in B. B's interest could not be a remainder because it is not preceded by a particular freehold estate in another devisee.

b.   Illustrating freehold estates made to commence in the future and following gaps in successive estates to grantees, each time divesting the vested estate in the grantor:

(1) by springing uses by deed of bargain and sale—A, fee owner, conveys "to B for life and one year after B's death, to C for life and one year after C's death to D and his heirs."

This deed leaves a fee simple in A for one year after B's death and again for one year after C's death. These are reversions. After B dies the estate reverts to A for a year and after C's death the estate reverts again to A for a year. When the year after B's death has ended a use springs up in C for life and the Statute of Uses executes such use into a legal life estate in C. C's life estate divests A's reversion after the one year period. Then when C dies and another year has ended, a use springs up in D in fee simple and the Statute of Uses executes such use into a legal estate and gives D a fee simple in possession, thus again divesting the grantor, A, of the reversion after one year.

In short, the legal effect of A's deed is this: a life estate in B, a reversion in fee simple for a year in A subject to an executory interest in C, then a life estate in C, a reversion in fee simple for a year in A subject to an executory interest in D, then a fee simple estate in D. Neither C's interest nor D's interest in its creation could be a remainder because neither was preceded by a particular freehold estate created in the same instrument in favor of another grantee at the natural termination of which either interest could take effect.

(2) by executory devise, by will—

A, fee owner, devises "to B for life and one year after B's death to C for life and one year after C's death to D and his heirs".

This is the identical case given in (1) next above except that it is created *by will* instead of by bargain and sale deed and is solved in exactly the same way. Being created by will it is called an executory *devise*.

c.   Illustrating a contingent freehold interest as an executory interest following a term of years:

(1) by a springing use by bargain and sale deed—

A, fee owner, conveys "to B for 10 years then to the heirs of C in fee simple", C then being a living person.

This deed gives B a legal estate for a term of 10 years followed by an executory interest in C's heirs and a reversion in A. If C dies and his heirs are determined before the end of the 10 years, then at the end of the 10 year term a use is raised in C's heirs and by the Statute of Uses such use is executed into a legal fee simple, which divests the reversion in A. If C dies after the 10 year term the same holds true. If and when C dies, the contingency determining the identity of those to take under the executory limitation will have happened. The use is then raised in said heirs in fee simple and the Statute of Uses executes the use into a legal estate in favor of such heirs of C and the reversion in A is thereby divested.

In short, A's deed creates a 10 year term in B, a reversion in A subject to an executory interest in C's heirs in fee simple, which executory interest is indestructible. C's heirs' interest could not be a remainder because it is not preceded by a particular estate of freehold. (See Case 80, supra.)

(2) by executory devise by will—

A, fee owner, devises "to B for 10 years then to the heirs of C in fee simple", C then being a living person. This is the identical case given in (1) next above except that it is created *by will* and is called an executory devise.

d. Illustrating a future freehold interest taking effect by cutting short or divesting the vested estate of another grantee:

(1) by shifting use by bargain and sale deed—

A, fee owner, conveys "to B and his heirs but if B dies without leaving children surviving him, then to C and his heirs".

This deed leaves nothing in the grantor, A. It gives the fee simple to B, but subject to an executory interest of the shifting type in C. Upon B's death without children surviving him, the use shifts from B to C, and the Statute of Uses executes the use in fee simple in C into a legal fee simple which cuts off and completely divests B's fee simple estate. C's interest in this case could not be a remainder because (a), a remainder cannot be created to follow a fee simple estate, and (b), a remainder cannot cut short or take effect in derogation of a preceding vested estate.

(2) by an executory devise by will—

A, fee owner, devises "to B and his heirs but if B dies without leaving children surviving him, then to C and his heirs".

This is the same identical case given in (1) next above except that it is created *by will* and is solved in the same way and is called an executory devise.

———

CASE 85: A, fee simple owner of Blackacre, bargains and sells it "to B for life, then to his children who attain the age of 21 years in fee simple, but if B becomes bankrupt then to his children in fee simple". B became bankrupt and then died leaving children, C, D and E, all of whom were under 21 years of age. A then took possession of Blackacre. After C, D and E had all attained the age of 21 and before any statute of limitations had passed, they joined in an action to eject A from Blackacre. May they succeed as against A's contention that the plaintiffs had a contingent remainder which had been destroyed?

Answer and Analysis

The answer is yes.

B, of course, acquired a life estate. In determining the interest of the children, two rules of construction are important: (1) if the limitation can be construed as creating either a vested or contingent interest, then that construction is preferred which will result in a vested interest; (2) if the limitation can be construed so as to create either a contingent remainder or executory interest, then the construction creating a contingent remainder is to be followed. If the interest of the children is construed as a contingent remainder, then under the common law the interest failed or was destroyed by their failing to reach 21 before the life estate of B ended. If their interest is construed as an executory interest, then, because executory interests are not destructible, their interest was not destroyed and they can eject A.

The initial limitation to the children of B who attain 21 is prima facie a contingent interest, reaching 21 being a condition precedent to vesting and not simply a postponement of the time of enjoyment. Thus, although B will undoubtedly have children (if at all) within his lifetime (or within the period of gestation thereafter which is sufficient to satisfy the condition of birth), the interest will not vest in the children on birth, but only on their reaching 21. Further, they might reach 21 (at least some of them might), before the death of B or before the life estate otherwise ends. Thus, under such circumstances they could take as remaindermen. Hence, applying the rule that the interest must take effect as a remainder if it can, the interest of the children is construed as a contingent remainder and not as an executory interest. Therefore, if the limitation had stopped at this point, "to the children of B who attain the age of 21 years," the children would have only a contingent remainder, and it would have been destroyed by their not attaining such age before the termination of the life estate.

However, the conveyance also provided that if B were to become bankrupt, then the estate was to go to the children of B without any age contingency. In this instance the interest of the children takes effect by cutting short the preceding life estate. Remainders never take effect by cutting short the preceding estate, but executory interests can take effect in this manner. Hence, under this contingency the children have to take by way of executory interest. Executory interests, unlike contingent remainders, are indestructible. Since in our facts B did become a bankrupt, the title vested in the children by way of executory interest. Hence, they can now eject A.

If in the instant problem B had died leaving only minor children and without ever having become bankrupt, the result presumably would have been different. The conveyance created two separate interests in the children of B—(1) a contingent remainder on reaching 21; and (2) an executory interest on B's becoming bankrupt. Since under our second assumption B died without becoming a bankrupt, the children would have to take by way of the contingent remainder and not by way of the executory interest. Since the remainder did not vest at or before the termination of the life estate (the children were minors at B's death), under common law the remainder failed or was destroyed. Thus, the children would not be able to eject A, whose reversion had become a possessory estate. Of course, in those jurisdictions where the destructibility rule has been abolished, it would make no difference whether the children take by way of contingent remainder or executory interest. See Blackman v. Fysh [1892], 3 Ch.Div. 209; Simes, 25–28, 33–42; Moynihan, 198–200; Burby, 349–350.

CASE 86: A, owner in fee simple of Blackacre, conveys it "to B and his heirs, and upon C's death to C's children who survive C in fee simple, but upon C's death without children surviving him, then to D and his heirs." A's judgment creditor, X, levied upon A's interest in Blackacre. D's judgment creditor, Y, levied upon D's interest in Blackacre. **(a)** Did X take any interest by virtue of his levy? **(b)** Did Y take any interest by virtue of his levy?

Answers and Analyses

The answer to (a) is probably no. The answer to (b) is yes.

These answers are based on two premises, (1) that a vested interest, a contingent remainder and an executory interest, in land are each alienable and are therefore subject to the claims of the owner's creditors, and (2) that when a creditor levies on the interest which his debtor has in land, the creditor takes the same interest as the debtor had, including the rights, the contingencies and the defeasances attached thereto. With these assumptions we proceed to discuss question (a). The proper construction of the conveyance is important. Either A had a reversion upon which X could levy or A had no interest left in Blackacre. If we take the view that A conveyed to B a fee simple "to B and his heirs" then there was no interest left in A on which X's levy could be made. If we take the view that because B's interest was in any event to terminate at the death of C, with or without children him surviving, and that B therefore, had only an estate pur autre vie, that is, for the life of C, then there was a reversion in A on which X could and did levy. Either view can in reason be justified.

Executory interests of the springing type may be created to take effect on an event certain to happen. Thus A, fee owner, conveys "to B and his heirs, this deed to take effect five years from its date". It is agreed in this case of a springing interest that during the five years after the date of the deed, A has a fee simple estate and not a mere five year term. If such be true in case of a springing interest which cuts short the fee simple estate of the grantor, it seems quite as reasonable to say that grantee B in the principal case has a fee simple estate which will be cut short by a shifting interest which is certain to happen at the death of a designated person, C. Logically there should not be one rule for springing uses and another for shifting uses. However the Restatement of Property appears to draw the line at this point, and concludes that executory interests limited on an event certain to occur may not be created if they are of the shifting type. [See citation at end of case.]

The real difficulty in classifying the future interests in these cases arises from the nature of the fee simple estate. We define it as an estate which may last forever. Then in these cases we say that there is a fee simple estate in a grantor or grantee when we know that such estate will be cut short by an event certain to happen either in

years or at the end of a life. Of course there is no logic in saying a
fee simple is an estate which must have the possibility of lasting forever and at the same time say this is a fee simple estate when we
know it must end in a specific number of years or at the death of a
particular person. A possible reconciliation is to say that the rule
that a fee simple is an estate which may last forever is qualified by
the law applicable to executory interests. We adopt such view and
base our answer in this case on the proposition that A conveyed to B
a fee simple estate subject to executory interests in the children of C
on the one hand or D on the other. Hence, there was no reversion
left in A and X took no interest by his levy.

(b) Having determined that B takes a fee simple estate by A's
deed, there are two good reasons why the interest created thereafter
cannot be a remainder. First, a remainder cannot follow a fee simple
estate. Second, a remainder cannot cut short or take effect in derogation of the preceding particular estate of freehold. Hence, the interests created in the children of C and in D, must be executory interests. They are contingent rather than vested interests because it
seems quite clear that it is a condition precedent to the vesting of
any estate in C's children that he have children and they survive him,
and that it is a condition precedent to any vesting in D that C dies
without children surviving him. D then has an executory interest
subject to a condition precedent. This is a contingent future interest
which may or may not ever become an estate in possession. But by
the better view such an interest is an existing thing and is freely alienable inter vivos for what it is worth even though a market for
such would be extremely limited. It seems the principle that an interest which can be voluntarily alienated should also be subject to involuntary alienation by the creditors of the owner, should be applied
in this case. Of course it may be a hardship on the owner to have
his contingent future interest sold at forced sale for a nominal sum.
But in times of depression that has also been true in forced sales of
vested estates. If the hardship is too great, the court usually has
power to postpone a sale. But it seems wise to keep all interests in
land freely alienable and subject to the claims of creditors except
where such are exempt for the protection of the family such as homestead interests. Hence, D's judgment creditor, Y, took D's executory
interest by virtue of his levy. If thereafter the interest is sold the
purchaser will take what D had. If C should then die without surviving children the purchaser would have the fee simple estate in Blackacre, but if C died leaving children surviving him, then the purchaser
would have nothing. See Simes, 26, 67–80; Restatement of Property
§§ 14, 46, comment i, illustrations, 8–12; Restatement of Property §
166, comment d.

Note

If the position is taken that there cannot be an executory interest of the shifting type limited on an event certain to occur, then the
conveyance is construed as follows: B has a life estate for the life of

C; A has a reversion; D and the surviving children of C have alternative contingent remainders in fee simple. Reversions were always alienable, and contingent remainders are generally held alienable today. Thus, both interests are reachable by creditors, and therefore, the answers to both questions, (a) and (b), in the principal problem would be yes.

FUTURE INTERESTS COMPARED WITH AND DISTINGUISHED FROM EACH OTHER

THE FUTURE INTEREST	HOW CREATED	IN WHOSE FAVOR	VESTED OR CONTINGENT	ALIENABLE INTER VIVOS	DESCENDIBLE AND DEVISABLE	SUBJECT TO DEFEASANCE	DIVESTS PRIOR ESTATE
REVERSION	BY OPERATION OF LAW	ALWAYS IN FAVOR OF GRANTOR	ALWAYS VESTED	ALWAYS ALIENABLE	ALWAYS DESCENDIBLE AND DEVISABLE	SUBJECT TO DEFEASANCE FOLLOWING CONTINGENT REMAINDER AND BY SPRINGING USE	NEVER DIVESTS PRIOR ESTATE
POSSIBILITY OF REVERTER	BY IMPLICATION OF LAW	ALWAYS IN FAVOR OF GRANTOR	ALWAYS CONTINGENT *	NOT ALIENABLE AT COMMON LAW WHEN UNCONNECTED WITH A REVERSION; *TODAY* IT IS ALIENABLE WITH OR WITHOUT A REVERSION	DESCENDIBLE AND DEVISABLE WITH OR WITHOUT A REVERSION	NOT SUBJECT TO DEFEASANCE	NEVER DIVESTS PRIOR ESTATE
POWER OF TERMINATION	BY CLEAR, EXPRESS WORDS IN DEED OR WILL	ALWAYS IN FAVOR OF GRANTOR	ALWAYS CONTINGENT *	NOT ALIENABLE AT COMMON LAW WHEN UNCONNECTED WITH REVERSION—LIKEWISE TODAY IN SOME STATES —*TODAY* IT IS ALIENABLE WHEN CONNECTED WITH REVERSION**	DESCENDIBLE AND DEVISABLE WITH OR WITHOUT A REVERSION	NOT SUBJECT TO DEFEASANCE	ALWAYS DIVESTS PRIOR ESTATE
VESTED REMAINDER	BY WORDS OF DEED OR WILL	ALWAYS IN FAVOR OF GRANTEE	ALWAYS VESTED	ALWAYS ALIENABLE	ALWAYS DESCENDIBLE AND DEVISABLE	MAY BE SUBJECT TO DEFEASANCE PARTIAL OR TOTAL BY SHIFTING USE	NEVER DIVESTS PRIOR ESTATE
CONTINGENT REMAINDER	BY WORDS OF DEED OR WILL	ALWAYS IN FAVOR OF GRANTEE	ALWAYS CONTINGENT	NOT ALIENABLE AT COMMON LAW; *TODAY* IT IS ALIENABLE	DESCENDIBLE AND DEVISABLE	NOT SUBJECT TO DEFEASANCE	NEVER DIVESTS PRIOR ESTATE
EXECUTORY INTEREST	BY WORDS OF DEED OR WILL	ALWAYS IN FAVOR OF GRANTEE	ALWAYS CONTINGENT	TODAY ALIENABLE	DESCENDIBLE AND DEVISABLE	NOT SUBJECT TO DEFEASANCE	ALWAYS DIVESTS PRIOR ESTATE

[C2453]

Note to Foregoing Chart

(1) Of course no interest is descendible or devisable which is terminated by death, and no interest is alienable except by one identifiable and qualified to convey.

(2) Of all the future interests, only the contingent remainder was destructible at common law; today all future interests, including contingent remainders in most states, are indestructible.

Summary of Foregoing Chart

(a) Reversions and possibilities of reverter are created by law —powers of termination, vested and contingent remainders and executory interests are created by deed or by will (first column).

(b) Reversions, possibilities of reverter and powers of termination are always in favor of the grantor or his successors in interest —remainders and executory interests are always in favor of the grantee (second column).

* Possibilities of reverter and powers of termination were not subject to the common law rule against perpetuities, however.

** Some states do permit the alienation of powers of termination unconnected with a reversion.

(c) Reversions and vested remainders are always vested—possibilities of reverter, powers of termination, contingent remainders and executory interests are always contingent (third column). Reversions, vested remainders, possibilities of reverter and powers of termination are not subject to the common law rule against perpetuities. Indestructible contingent remainders and executory interests are subject to the rule.

(d) At common law possibilities of reverter, powers of termination and contingent remainders were not alienable inter vivos—today a power of termination unconnected with a reversion is still not alienable inter vivos in most states—all other future interests, including a power of termination connected with a reversion, are alienable inter vivos (fourth column).

(e) All future interests are descendible and devisable (fifth column).

(f) Only reversions and vested remainders (the vested future interests) are subject to defeasance (sixth column).

(g) Only powers of termination and executory interests divest prior estates (seventh column).

SUMMARY OF CASES IN CHAPTER VI.

2. REVERSIONS

Case 67. All reversions are vested and one is vested indefeasibly when it is absolutely certain to revert to the conveyor and become an estate in possession upon the natural termination of all prior estates.

Case 68. A reversion vests in the conveyor, if alive, but if the conveyor be dead, then the reversion vests in his successor in interest which is the heir or devisee as to a reversion in fee simple. A reversion may follow a term of years.

Case 69. A reversion is alienable but being a future interest and not an estate in possession, lies in grant and not in livery. A fee simple owner who conveys a life estate followed by a contingent remainder in fee simple, has a reversion until the contingency is resolved and the reversion defeated.

Case 70. When fee simple owner, A, grants to B for life with remainder to the heirs of A, the doctrine of worthier title makes the remainder void and leaves the reversion in the grantor, A.

3. POSSIBILITIES OF REVERTER

Case 71. A possibility of reverter follows a determinable fee, is descendible and is not subject to the common law Rule against Perpetuities. An executory interest is subject to the Rule against Perpetuities and if it offends the Rule, is void ab initio. A possibility of reverter is in favor of the conveyor, or his heirs if he be dead intestate, and arises by implication of law without any express words describing it as such.

Case 72. At common law a possibility of reverter unconnected with a reversion was not alienable by a deed inter vivos. Today according to the better view a possibility of reverter can be transferred by a deed inter vivos and the grantee takes the same interest as the grantor had in the property. At common law a possibility of reverter could always be released to the owner of the determinable fee, thus making the fee simple absolute, and it could be alienated as an incident to the reversion of which it was a part.

4. RIGHTS OF RE–ENTRY FOR CONDITION BROKEN, OR POWERS OF TERMINATION

Case 73. A power of termination can be created only in the transferor, who in traditional common law jurisdictions can devise it but cannot alienate it inter vivos when unconnected with a reversion. It will descend from ancestor to heir. A power of termination never takes effect automatically upon breach of the condition subsequent by the owner of the possessory estate. To make it effective the owner of the power must (a) elect to terminate the estate and (b) do some affirmative act towards its termination. All estates and encumbrances created by the owner of the possessory estate exist subject to the exercise of the power, and if the power is exercised such estates and encumbrances are rendered nugatory.

Case 74. A power of termination connected with a reversion is alienable inter vivos as an incident to the reversion. When an instrument creates an estate subject to more than one condition subsequent, one may be waived after its breach, without affecting the other. The question of waiver is usually a fact question but if it is so clear that reasonable men cannot differ thereon, it is a question of law. Re-entry on the premises is an effective exercise of the power of termination.

5. REMAINDERS, VESTED AND CONTINGENT

Case 75. Every remainder (a) must be in favor of a transferee, (b) must be created at the same time and in the same instrument as the prior particular estate of freehold which supports it, (c) must be so limited that it will take effect as an estate in possession at the termination of the prior particular estate of freehold, and (d) the prior particular estate of freehold must be a lesser estate than that of the conveyor at the time of the conveyance. Such prior particular estate must be either a life estate or a fee tail. It cannot be a fee simple. A remainder is indefeasibly vested when it is bound to take effect in possession when the preceding particular estate of freehold terminates. It is subject to no condition.

Case 76. A vested remainder subject to complete defeasance is one which is presently owned but which may or may not ever be enjoyed as an estate in possession. Such a remainder is always subject to a condition subsequent.

Case 77. A vested remainder may be subject to partial defeasance as by a limitation to the children of a living person. As the number of children increases, the interest of each remainderman decreases proportionately and to that extent is defeated. Every remainder is alienable by its owner and is subject to the claims of his creditors.

Case 78. If a future interest will take effect, if at all, *at* the termination of the particular estate of freehold which precedes it, then it is a remainder. If a future interest will take effect in derogation of the preceding particular estate of freehold, or after its termination, then it is an executory interest, with one exception, where the executory interest follows a determinable fee it takes effect *at* the termination of the prior estate. All reversions, possibilities of reverter and powers of termination are in favor of the transferor; all remainders and executory interests are in favor of a transferee, one other than the transferor.

Case 79. If a future interest is to take effect but one second after the termination of the preceding particular freehold estate, it cannot be a remainder; it will take effect as an executory interest.

Case 80. At common law every remainder had to be preceded by a particular estate of freehold to prevent abeyance of the seisin. Hence, there could be no remainder following an estate for years, a nonfreehold estate. In such case the so-called remainderman took an executory interest by way of a springing use under the Statute of Uses. Modern usage permits a remainder to follow an estate for years.

Case 81. Indefeasibly vested remainders are subject to no condition; defeasibly vested remainders are subject to conditions subsequent; contingent remainders are subject to conditions precedent. A vested remainder is one limited to an ascertained person who has the right to immediate possession when the prior estate terminates, even though it may be divested. If the language of an instrument can be construed as creating either a vested or a contingent remainder, the preference is for a vested remainder.

Case 82. At common law if the condition precedent to a contingent remainder did not happen before the termination of the prior particular estate, then the contingent remainder could not vest at or before the termination of such particular estate and the contingent remainder was destroyed forever. The condition precedent to a contingent remainder was either the happening of an event or the ascertainment of the remainderman either because he was yet unborn or for some other reason such as the ancestor still being alive. The destructibility of contingent remainders took place in three ways, (1) by its failure to vest at or before the termination of the preceding particular estate, (2) by merger or (3) by forfeiture. In only a few states today is a contingent remainder permitted to be destroyed. In most states by statute or decision the contingent remainder takes effect when the condition precedent happens, even if it happens after the termination of the preceding particular estate.

Case 83. Provisions of an ambiguous conveyance may be construed to create either alternative contingent remainders or a vested remainder followed by an executory interest, depending on whether the rule (a) that a vested remainder or interest is preferred over a contingent remainder or interest or (b) a contingent remainder is preferred over an executory interest, is followed. At common law neither contingent remainders nor executory interests were alienable. Today, with or without statute, both such future contingent interests are considered presently existing things and are freely alienable.

Case 84. Remainders may be created by implication as well as by express provisions in conveyances. Cross-remainders are implied in case of tenants in common for life when the entire estate is dealt with in remainder thereafter. In case of a will such implication is based on the presumption that the testator intended to dispose of his entire estate. In case of a deed it is based on the rule that a deed is construed most strongly against the grantor.

6. EXECUTORY INTERESTS

Case 85. A construction resulting in a vested remainder is preferred over one which results in a contingent remainder; a construction resulting in a contingent remainder is preferred over one resulting in an executory interest. A contingent remainder is destructible, an executory interest is not destructible. A remainder cannot cut short the particular freehold estate which supports it. An executory interest always cuts short the vested estate which precedes it. A contingent remainder and an executory interest can be created in favor of the same person or persons in the same instrument, in which case the interest takes effect (or fails possibly) either as one or the other in accordance with the occurrence of the events.

Case 86. Usually an interest in land which is alienable by its owner voluntarily can be taken by his creditors and alienated involuntarily. An executory interest in land is alienable inter vivos and is subject to the claims of the creditors of the owner. The creditor takes only what the debtor has. A grantor may hold a fee simple estate subject to an executory interest which will cut it short at a definite future date, or on an event certain to happen, and it seems reasonable that such principle should permit a fee simple estate to vest in a grantee even though it will be cut short by an event certain to happen either at the end of a period of time or at the end of a life.

Chapter VII

PROPERTY RULES RELATING TO FUTURE INTERESTS: POWERS OF APPOINTMENT

1. Rule in Shelley's Case.
   Legal Gems.
   Cases.
2. Doctrine of Worthier Title; Inter Vivos Branch.
   Legal Gems.
   Cases.
   Chart—The Rule in Shelley's Case Compared with and Distinguished from the Doctrine of Worthier Title.
3. Rule Against Perpetuities.
   Legal Gems.
   Cases.
4. Powers of Appointment.
   Legal Gems.
   Cases.
Summary of Cases in Chapter VII.

---

1. RULE IN SHELLEY'S CASE

LEGAL GEMS

1. In its simplest form the rule may be stated as follows: When in the same conveyance an estate for life is given to the ancestor with remainder to the ancestor's heirs (or heirs of his body) then the ancestor takes the fee simple (or fee tail) remainder estate and his heirs take nothing. E. g., A, fee owner, conveys "to B for life, then to B's heirs". B takes both the life estate and the remainder in fee simple. By merger then, the life estate is merged in the fee and B has the fee simple absolute. By the rule this conveyance is then made to read as though it merely provided, "A to B and his heirs". This statement of the rule will solve most simple cases.

2. A more complete statement of the rule is this: "If a life estate in land is conveyed or devised to A, and by the same conveyance or devise, a remainder in the land is limited, mediately or immediately, to the heirs of A, or to the heirs of A's body, and the life estate and remainder are of the same quality, then A has, in addition to his life estate, a remainder in fee simple or in fee tail". Simes, 45.

3. The origin of the rule is lost in antiquity but it seems sufficient to say that it arose in the feudal system and protected the feudal lord in his benefits of relief, wardship and marriage, which were his when an heir took land by descent but were lost to him if the same person took as a purchaser. It persisted in England from 1324 to 1925 when it was abolished by statute.

146

4. The rule had almost universal acceptance in the United States but has now been abolished by statute in not less than three fourths of the states.

5. The rule is a rule of law and not one of construction. This means if the requisites are present the rule applies even though the result is wholly contrary to the clearly expressed intention of the grantor.

6. It applies to fees simple and fees tail alike.

7. It applies when both the life estate and the remainder are legal estates and when they are both equitable estates, but it does not apply when one is legal and the other is equitable in quality.

8. The Rule requires:

a. the deed or will must create a life estate in the ancestor; and

b. the same instrument must create a remainder in the ancestor's heirs or heirs of his body; and

c. the life estate and remainder must be either both legal or both equitable.

9. Examples illustrating the operation of the Rule—

a. A, fee owner, conveys "to B for life, remainder to B's heirs". *By the deed* the life estate is given to B. *By the rule* the remainder in fee simple is given to B. *By merger* the life estate is swallowed in the remainder making B the owner of the fee simple estate.

b. A, fee owner, conveys "to B for life, remainder to the heirs of B's body". *By the instrument* B has a life estate and *by the Rule* B takes the remainder. *By merger* the life estate is swallowed in the fee tail in remainder; B has the fee tail estate, and the heirs of his body take nothing.

c. A, fee owner, conveys "to T in an active trust for B for B's life and thereafter T to hold in active trust for B's heirs". *By the instrument* B is given an equitable life estate, and *by the Rule* the equitable remainder stated to be in favor of B's heirs, is given to B. *By merger* the life interest is merged in the equitable fee and B owns the equitable fee simple, both being of the same quality, that is, equitable estates.

d. A, fee owner, conveys "to T in active trust for B for life and upon B's death, title is to vest in the heirs of B in fee simple". The Rule does not apply because B's life estate is equitable and the remainder to B's heirs is legal. The trust is not to continue beyond B's life. Therefore, B takes only a life estate (equitable), and the heirs of B take a legal contingent remainder, the contingency being that they are not determinable until B's death. But they take as purchasers and not by descent as heirs.

e. A, fee owner, conveys "to B for life, then to C for life, remainder to B's heirs". The fact that another life estate intervenes the ancestor's life estate and the remainder in fee simple does not prevent the operation of the Rule. The remainder belongs to B. The intervening life estate does, however, prevent a merger at the time of the operation of the instrument. But if C dies before B, a merger takes place at the instance of C's death. If B predeceases C, then the remainder passes to B's heirs by descent and not by purchase.

    f. A, fee owner, conveys "to B for life, and if B pays A $100, then to B's heirs". Here again the Rule operates at once and gives the contingent remainder to B. But *it affects the remainder only*. It does not affect the life estate. And a merger cannot take place as long as the contingent remainder remains contingent. But if and when B pays $100 to A, at that instant the contingent remainder becomes a vested remainder and merges B's life estate therein so that B then would have the fee simple estate. It must be kept in mind that the Rule gives the remainder to the ancestor. Thereafter the doctrine of merger when applicable makes the estates one.

10. Historically the rule applied only to conveyances and devises of real property; it had no application to transfers of personal property and chattels real. Some jurisdictions, however, applied an analogous rule to personal property as a rule of construction. See Moynihan, 138–149; Simes, 43–55; Burby, 338–340; Restatement of Property §§ 312, 313.

———

CASE 87: A, owner in fee simple of Blackacre, devises it "to B for life, then to C for life and only for life and no longer, remainder to the heirs of C". B dies. C dies testate devising all of his interest in Blackacre to M. C's sole heir is X. X's judgment creditor, Y, levies upon Blackacre and threatens to sell it at execution sale. M sues Y to enjoin such sale. May M succeed?

Answer and Analysis

The answer is yes. This problem is designed to illustrate the basic requirements of the Rule, and also to raise the issue as to whether the Rule applies when the testator clearly indicates an intent that it should not.

(1) It is obvious that A's will creates in B a life estate in possession, a vested remainder in C for life and (but for the Rule in Shelley's Case) a contingent remainder in C's heirs in fee simple. The Rule in Shelley's Case is not limited in its application to a remainder following a life estate in possession. The life estate may be a remainder as is C's estate in our case. Thus the first requirement of the Rule, that there be a conveyance creating a life estate in the ancestor, is met in A's will. The Rule applies only to freehold estates in land such as we have here, never to chattel interests, personal or real.

(2) The second requirement of the Rule is that the same instrument which created the life estate must also create a remainder in the heirs of the ancestor or in the heirs of the ancestor's body. In our case we have but one instrument, A's will. It creates both the life estate in the ancestor, C, and the remainder in the ancestor's heirs. Had A by will created C's life estate and by a codicil to such will created the remainder in C's heirs, this would have met the requirement of the Rule because a will and a codicil thereto constitute the last will of the testator and are "the same instrument". So the second requirement is complied with.

(3) The third requirement is that the life estate and the remainder be of the same quality, either both legal or both equitable interests. In our case C's life estate and the remainder to C's heirs are both legal remainders. Hence, they are of the same quality and meet the third requirement of the Rule. So our conclusion must be that the Rule in Shelley's Case applies and the remainder "to the heirs of C" belongs to C by virtue of its application. Hence, if we read A's will as it is in legal effect by application of the Rule, it would provide, "to B for life, then to C for life remainder to C and his heirs", with the words "and his heirs" being words of limitation. By the doctrine of merger C's life estate in remainder would merge in his remainder in fee simple. Hence, by reading into A's will the legal effects of both the Rule and merger, it will read simply, "to B for life, remainder to C and his heirs". Of course such a result leaves nothing in C's heirs. When B died the fee simple in possession vested in C. When he died testate devising Blackacre to M the devise carried to M the fee simple. There was no interest at any time in X, the heir of C. Hence, X's judgment creditor, Y, took no right by virtue of his levy on Blackacre and had no right to sell the property. Therefore, M's suit for an injunction should succeed.

One more point requires attention. Notice A's will provides that after B's life estate the property shall then go "to C for life and only for life and no longer". A could not have made his intention clearer. He did not intend C should have more than a life estate. He intended C's heirs to have a contingent remainder. And, but for the Rule in Shelley's Case, that is just what would have happened. But the Rule in Shelley's Case is a *rule of law*. It is not a rule of construction whereby the intention of the grantor is sought to be given effect. The requirements of the Rule being present, the remainder passes to the ancestor, regardless of the grantor's intention. Such a rule has no justification in modern jurisprudence. It has only one merit, it does make the land more freely alienable. But that alone cannot justify its existence when it nullifies the intention of the grantor. See Moynihan, 138–149; Simes, 43–55; Burby, 338–340; Restatement of Property §§ 312, 313.

CASE 88: A, owner of Blackacre in fee simple, devises it "to my son B for life, then to his heirs who survive him in fee simple, but if none of his such children or heirs survive him, then to B's brothers and sisters share and share alike". At A's death B is a widower having two adult children, C and D. Thereafter B marries W and dies testate devising all of his interest in Blackacre to W. C and D survive B. C and D take possession of Blackacre and W sues them in ejectment. May she succeed?

Answer and Analysis

The answer is no. Whether this is the correct answer depends, of course, upon whether or not the Rule in Shelley's Case applies in this fact situation. While this Rule is one of law rather than one of construction, its application often involves the interpretation of the provisions of an instrument to see if the requirements of the Rule are satisfied. This particular problem presents one of the most difficult and most litigated questions concerning the application of such Rule. The difficulty is determining the meaning of the word "heirs" as used in the particular deed or will. For the Rule to apply the word "heirs" must be used in its technical sense and not as a substitute for "children," "lineal descendants," or other group of people.

Depending upon the setting in which it is used by the particular grantor or devisor, the word "heirs" has no less than four distinct meanings. (1) In England the word "heirs" usually refers to the group of persons who are to take land by descent from generation to generation indefinitely. For instance, A to B for life, then to B's heirs, means not only that B's heirs will take from B by descent but that the heirs of those heirs, and heirs of those heirs on ad infinitum will continue to take without limitation in time. Unless the word "heirs" is used in this broad technical sense in a conveyance in England, the Rule in Shelley's Case was not applied.

(2) But suppose the case is, A to B for life, then to B's heirs who will take from B by descent at B's death. Here the word "heirs" is used to indicate persons who will take by descent but it is used in a much narrower sense. It means here merely the first generation of heirs, those who take from B only, not those who will take in indefinite succession. This use of the word would fall short of meeting the requirements for applying Shelley's Rule in England. But by the modern American view such narrower use of the word calls for the application of the Rule, and in our supposed fact situation the remainder "to B's heirs who will take from B by descent at B's death" would be a remainder to the ancestor, B, and his heirs would take nothing.

(3) Sometimes the word "heirs" is used to mean "issue" which is a term broad enough to include lineal descendants of all generations, children, grandchildren, great grandchildren, etc. For example, A to B for life, then to B's heirs or issue. In this case the Rule in Shelley's Case has no application and should B die leaving two sons, X and Y, and two grandsons, M and N, the children of B's deceased son, Z, then

X, Y, M and N would take the property share and share alike as purchasers from A. The remainder "to B's heirs or issue" is construed as a contingent remainder belonging to B's issue who are determined upon B's death, and not to B under the Rule.

(4) "Heirs" may also be used to mean the first generation of lineal descendants of the life tenant in which case it is synonymous with the usual meaning of the word "children". This is a still narrower meaning than that given to the word "issue". The word "children" is usually a word of purchase, meaning persons to take, and not a word of limitation describing the quantum of the estate taken. When the word "heirs" is used to mean "children" the Rule in Shelley's Case does not apply and the remainder goes to the children and not to the life tenant as ancestor.

Now our question is this: in what sense did A use the word "heirs" in his will. The answer given above is based on the conclusion that A used the word "heirs" as a synonym of the word "children", and that the Rule in Shelley's Case has no application. There seem to be three good reasons for such conclusion. First, in the clause introducing the executory interests in the brothers and sisters, "but if none of his such *children or heirs* survive him", the word "heirs" is used interchangeably with "children". Second, in the quoted clause the word "such" modifies the word "children" and must refer back to the word "heirs" in the clause creating the remainder, "then to his heirs who survive him". So A has used synonymously "heirs" and "such children". Third, the gift over to B's brothers and sisters would seem to be surplusage if A had used "heirs" as "heirs" technically because if B had died without lineal descendants, then his brothers and sisters might well have been his collateral heirs.

This indicates that A must have used the word "heirs" to mean B's children as persons to take. If we apply this meaning to the words of A's will, it will read in effect as follows, "to my son B for life, then to his children who survive him in fee simple, but if none of his children survive him, then to B's brothers and sisters share and share alike". From this we conclude that B took only a life estate under A's will and that B's will devising his interest in Blackacre to W was wholly nugatory because B had no interest in the property which would survive his death and which he could devise. On the other hand, the contingent remainder in favor of B's surviving children became a vested estate in fee simple in possession in C and D upon B's death. Therefore, W may not eject C and D from Blackacre. See McRorie v. Creswell, 273 N.C. 615, 160 S.E.2d 681 (1968); Simes, 50; Restatement of Property §§ 312, 313.

Note

Of course the reverse of what appears in the above case may be true. If the word "issue" or the word "children" is used in a given instrument to mean "heirs" in its technical sense, the Rule in Shelley's Case will apply. The question is one of construction.

CASE: 89: A, being fee simple owner of Blackacre, conveys it "to B for life, then to the heirs of B". B dies testate devising all of his interest in Blackacre to X and leaving Y as his sole heir. Y takes possession of Blackacre. In the jurisdiction a statute abolishes the Rule in Shelley's Case, and provides that in such a case the ancestor or first taker acquires a life estate only and his heirs take the remainder. X sues to eject Y from Blackacre. May he succeed?

Answer and Analysis

The answer is no. Statutes abolishing the Rule in Shelley's Case exist in at least three fourths of the states. Such statutes frequently provide that limitations which previously would have operated under the Rule have the effect of giving the ancestor a life estate only with a contingent remainder going to his heirs. However, the statutes are not uniform, and the exact wording of the applicable statute must be consulted.

When the Rule is abolished, it is necessary first of all to determine if the words of the limitation are such as would have otherwise given rise to the application of the Rule, and also to determine if the limitation is within the terms of the statute. The answer to both questions will usually be the same, that is, both will be either yes or no, but it is conceivable that contrary answers might arise in situations where the statute, for example, is less than all inclusive in its operation or as to its specific applications. The usual rule of construction of ascertaining the intent of the grantor or devisor is still of paramount importance in determining the effect of the limitation. This intent must be determined before the statute can be applied.

In the instant case, the conveyance expressly provides for a life estate in B with a remainder to B's heirs. All of the requirements for the application of the Rule exist: (1) a life estate in an individual with a remainder to his heirs; (2) both interests are created in the same instrument; and (3) both interests are of the same quality— both legal in this case. Also, there is nothing to show that the word "heirs" is used in other than its technical sense. Thus, the Rule would have applied, and the statute governs. Therefore B acquires a life estate, and a contingent remainder is given to B's heirs, such heirs to be ascertained at B's death. Under the facts of the case, Y is B's sole heir.

Upon B's death Y became the fee simple owner of Blackacre but he took the title not from B by descent but from A under A's deed as a purchaser. In this case the word "heirs" is used to mean persons to take by purchase as contingent remaindermen. Hence, X, the devisee of B who had only a life estate, took nothing under B's will. Result: Y owns Blackacre and X cannot eject him therefrom.

2. DOCTRINE OF WORTHIER TITLE; INTER VIVOS BRANCH

LEGAL GEMS

1. The Doctrine is this: Any limitation in an inter vivos conveyance of real property *to the heirs of the conveyor* is void and there is a reversion in the conveyor.

2. The typical illustrative case is this: A, fee owner, conveys to B for life, then to *the heirs of A*. Effect of the Doctrine: B has a life estate and there is a reversion in the grantor, A. The Doctrine affects only the remainder and has no effect on the life estate.

3. The doctrine arose in the feudal system apparently to preserve the feudal benefits of relief, wardship and marriage to the overlord, which were available to him from one who took land by descent but not from one who took by purchase.

4. The doctrine, or rule, requires only that there be (a) a conveyance inter vivos of real property and (b) that there be a limitation to the grantor's heirs, or its equivalent, e. g., sometimes the word children or issue is used to mean heirs.

5. The rule has no application to a conveyance to a named person even if that person turns out eventually to be the heir of the grantor. E. g., A to B for life remainder to my son, John. The remainder is valid in John's favor even though upon A's death John is A's heir.

6. The rule has no application to the case where the word "heirs" is used to mean "children"; for the rule to apply the word "heirs" must mean heirs in its technical sense, meaning the persons to take by intestate succession at the time of the grantor's death, not persons who would be the grantor's heirs at some other time.

7. The estate which precedes the limitation to the grantor's heirs is immaterial. It may be a life estate or an estate for years or a determinable fee. E. g., A, fee owner, conveys to "B and his heirs so long as B keeps the fences in repair, then to my heirs." The expression "then to my heirs" is void and the possibility of reverter is in A.

8. The type of interest or estate given the grantor's heirs is immaterial. It may be a remainder or an executory interest. E. g., A, fee owner, conveys to "B for life but if B becomes insolvent, then to my heirs." The executory interest over "to my heirs" is void under the rule. Perhaps B then has a determinable life estate which would be construed as "to B for life or until he becomes insolvent". The interest may be either equitable or legal. E. g., A, fee owner, conveys "to T in fee in active trust for B for life and then in active trust for my heirs." The limitation in favor of A's heirs is void, and A has a reversion. The reversion is equitable. Upon the death of B, A can compel the termination of the trust since A has the entire beneficial interest. As to active uses or trusts, see infra Chapter XVIII, B.

9. The doctrine applies only to inter vivos conveyances of real property; it has no application to devises of real property by will.

At common law there was a testamentary branch of the doctrine to the effect that if a will devised to a person a freehold estate of the same quality and quantity which that person would have taken had the devisor died intestate, then the devise was void and the person took by descent. This particular rule is obsolete and no longer in effect.

10. In the earlier law it was a rule of law and not a rule of construction; in modern law it has become a rule of construction under which the intention of the grantor is given effect. However, the presumption favors the doctrine and the grantor must use words in the deed to overcome the presumption and show he intends his heirs to take as purchasers.

11. A minority of states have abolished the doctrine of worthier title and some have modified it.

———

CASE 90: A, being fee simple owner of Blackacre, conveys it "to B for life, remainder to the heirs of A". A then makes a will devising all of his interest in Blackacre to X. A dies leaving H his sole heir. B dies. H takes possession of Blackacre and X sues to eject him. May X succeed?

Answer and Analysis

The answer is yes. This case is the simplest illustration in which the doctrine of worthier title is applicable. The doctrine requires (a) a conveyance of real property inter vivos and (b) a limitation to the heirs of the grantor. When A conveys to B for life with remainder, it is a conveyance of real property which meets the first requirement. When the remainder is "to the heirs of A", A being the grantor, it meets the second requirement. Result: B has a life estate and the remainder is void, thus leaving the reversion in the grantor A.

The legal effect of A's conveyance is simply this: A to B for life. Here it should be noted that the grantor in his deed has limited the remainder to the persons who would take by descent, that is, his heirs. Under the Doctrine the title by descent being considered worthier than the title by purchase, then let the heirs take by that title which is worthier. Such is the theory of the Doctrine of Worthier Title. Applying it to the facts of our case, H, the heir of A, will take, if at all, by descent as heir of A and not through A's deed as a purchaser. But in this case H just does not take at all, for the reason that the reversion left in the grantor, A, is subject to testamentary disposition. So when A devises his interest in Blackacre to X, there is nothing left in A to descend to his heir, H, by intestate succession. That which appears to be a contingent remainder in favor of the heirs of the grantor, is by the Doctrine of Worthier Title, made only an illusion. Hence, X being the owner in fee simple of Blackacre, can eject H who has no interest therein. See Moynihan, 149–162; Simes, 56–65; Restatement of Property § 314.

————

CASE 91: A, being fee simple owner of Blackacre, conveys it "to B for life, remainder to my heirs, it being my intention that those persons who would take my Blackacre were I to die intestate, shall take such property through and by virtue of this deed". Thereafter A executed a will devising all of his interest in Blackacre to W. A died without changing such will. H is A's sole heir. W took possession of Blackacre and H sues to eject W therefrom. May he succeed?

Answer and Analysis

The answer is yes. In the earlier stages of the Doctrine of Worthier Title, it was a rule of law and not a rule of construction. At that time the remainder in a conveyance being in favor of the grantor's heirs was void and there was a reversion in the grantor. The grantor's intention was quite immaterial. If we were to follow such doctrine as a rule of law today, then the devisee, W, in our case would be the owner of Blackacre and H could not eject him. But the law on this subject has evolved and with such evolution has come a great consideration for the intention of the grantor in making a conveyance of land.

The modern view is that the Doctrine of Worthier Title is no longer a rule of law but a rule of construction under which the intention of the grantor determines the effect of the limitations in the deed. The Doctrine remains in force in the typical case, A to B for life remainder to the heirs of A. But if the grantor in his deed evinces an intention that his "heirs" shall take as purchasers under the provisions in the deed, they will so take.

In our case it seems clear that the inference of the Doctrine of Worthier Title that the grantor does not intend to create an interest in his heirs which he cannot thereafter destroy by his own act, has been overcome by the express limitations in the deed. The deed provides that A's heirs "shall take such property through and by virtue of this deed". This clearly shows that such "heirs" are to take as "purchasers" and that they are not to take Blackacre by descent at a later time on A's death. Such plain words in the deed overcome any inference to the contrary and make A's heirs contingent remaindermen. Of course, this leaves a reversion in A but one which is subject to defeasance upon the ascertainment of the remaindermen. At the instant of A's death his heirs, who turn out to be H, were determined and the contingent remainder was transformed into an estate in possession owned in fee simple by H. Therefore, W, the devisee of A, took no interest in Blackacre by virtue of A's will because A had already disposed of such in favor of his "heirs" as purchasers. Result:

H can eject W from the property. Such is an application of the modern view of the Doctrine of Worthier Title. See Restatement of Property § 314, comment e; Simes, 56–65; Doctor v. Hughes, 225 N. Y. 305, 122 N.E. 221 (1919).

CASE 92: A, fee simple owner of Blackacre, dies testate devising it "to B for life, remainder to my heirs in fee simple". Upon A's death his sole heir is H. B died and H took possession of Blackacre. H died testate devising "all the property which I received by purchase to my son, John, and all the property which I received by descent to my son, Paul". Both John and Paul claim Blackacre. Which should prevail?

Answer and Analysis

The answer is John. At one time in our legal history there was a rule analogous to the Doctrine of Worthier Title in inter vivos conveyances, which was applicable to devises. The reasons for such rule have long since disappeared; the rule has become obsolete and modern statutes on wills have completely superseded any such rule. Today there is no reason for differentiating a title received by descent from one received by purchase. In construing a will the testator's intention should be followed. In our case it is clear that the testator intended to dispose fully of Blackacre. Otherwise he would not have added the remainder following B's life estate. Furthermore, by the use of the words "in fee simple" following the word heirs, the testator has evinced an intention that such estate shall pass to the persons who are identified on his death as his heirs. He did not use the word "heirs" as indicating indefinite succession. In other words, A has used the word "heirs" as a word of purchase and not as a word of limitation and the remainder should be given effect. The Doctrine of Worthier Title today is limited to inter vivos conveyances and has no application to wills or devises thereunder. H, then, took a vested remainder under A's will. It is vested because H was determined at the very instant of A's death when the will took effect. The remainder being valid, H took Blackacre by purchase and not by descent. Hence, under H's will Blackacre goes to his son, John. See Restatement of Property § 314, comment j; Simes, 57.

THE RULE IN SHELLEY'S CASE COMPARED WITH AND DISTINGUISHED FROM THE DOCTRINE OF WORTHIER TITLE

THE RULE IN SHELLEY'S CASE	THE DOCTRINE OF WORTHIER TITLE
SIMILARITIES	
1. it arose in the feudal system to preserve the feudal benefits to the overlord	1. it arose in the feudal system to preserve the feudal benefits to the overlord
2. in a typical case it affects only the remainder—e. g., A to B for life, remainder to the heirs of *B* (under the rule the remainder is given to the ancestor B)	2. in a typical case it affects only the remainder—e. g., A to B for life, remainder to the heirs of *A* (under the doctrine the remainder is void and there is a reversion in A)
3. in the early common law it was a rule of law and not a rule of construction (it is still a rule of law)	3. in the early common law it was a rule of law and not a rule of construction (it has become a rule of construction)
4. it defeats the expressed intention of the grantor	4. it defeats the expressed intention of the grantor except in modern times when by construction it is concluded that the grantor intended it to apply
5. it was abolished by statute in England in 1925	5. it was abolished by statute in England in 1833
DISSIMILARITIES	
1. the rule always operates in favor of the *transferee*—e. g., A to B for life remainder to the heirs of *B*—the rule gives the remainder *to B* and his heirs take nothing	1. the rule always operates in favor of the *transferor*—e. g., A to B for life remainder to the heirs of *A*—the rule makes the remainder void, gives the reversion *to A* and his heirs take nothing
2. after the rule has operated, then by *merger* B's remainder in fee swallows B's life estate and makes B the fee simple owner	2. after the rule has operated, A owns the reversion subject to B's life estate and there is *no merger*
3. it is still *a rule of law* and not a rule of construction	3. it was a rule of law, but in modern law *has become a rule of construction*

4. it applies *only to freehold interests* in land	4. it applies *to real property and to chattel interests*, personal and real
5. it applies *both to conveyances inter vivos and to devises* by will	5. it applies *only to conveyances* of real property *inter vivos—it has no application to devises* by will
6. it has been abolished in most states.	6. it has not been abolished in most states.

3. RULE AGAINST PERPETUITIES

LEGAL GEMS

1. The common law rule in its simplest form is, "No interest is good unless it must vest, if at all, not later than twenty-one years after some life in being at the creation of the interest". Gray, Rule Against Perpetuities (4th ed. 1942) 191.

2. The stated rule analyzed:

a. "no interest is good" means that any contingent interest which does not conform to the rule is void ab initio.

b. "must vest" means that the contingent interest must become a vested interest (or fail) within the period of the rule. Thus, if A conveys to B for life remainder to the heirs of C, and C predeceases B, the contingent remainder becomes a vested remainder. The rule is satisfied by a vesting in interest even though possession is postponed.

c. "if at all" means that if the contingent interest is absolutely certain either to "vest" or "fail" entirely within the period of the rule, it is valid.

d. "not later than 21 years after some life in being" includes within the period, (1) all relevant lives in being, provided they are not so numerous as to prevent practical determination of the time when the last one dies, plus (2) 21 years, plus (3) such actual periods of gestation as come within the proper purpose of the rule.

e. "at the creation of the interest" means that in the ordinary case the period of the rule begins when the creating instrument takes effect.

3. The rule is directed entirely against remoteness of vesting—the sole test being, *must* the interest vest (or fail) within the period of the rule. If it *may* vest beyond the maximum period permitted by the rule it is void.

4. While the rule is directed toward remoteness of vesting, its ultimate purpose is to prevent the clogging of titles beyond reasonable limits in time by contingent interests, and to keep land freely alienable in the market places.

5. The following interests *are not* subject to the common law rule:

    a. present interests in possession

    b. reversions

    c. vested remainders

    d. possibilities of reverter

    e. powers of termination

    f. charitable trusts [1]

    g. resulting trusts

6. The following interests *are* subject to the rule:

    a. contingent remainders

    b. executory interests

    c. options to purchase land not incident to a lease for years

    d. powers of appointment [2]

7. The rule does not per se apply to the duration of indestructible private trusts, and a trust is not void merely because it may last longer than the period of the rule. However, if a private trust is created to be indestructible for a period beyond lives in being and twenty one years, the provision for indestructibility is probably void and the trust made terminable.

8. The rule is applicable to contingent interests whether they be legal or equitable and whether they be in land or chattel property.

9. In solving any case under the rule against perpetuities the first thing to be observed is this: is the creating instrument *a deed* inter vivos *or a will* making a devise.

10. Under the rule: (a) the lives in being must be human lives, not the lives of any of the lower animals or lives of corporations; (b) the lives in being must precede, they cannot follow, the 21 years; (c) every human being is conclusively presumed capable of having children during his lifetime; (d) the lives in the measuring group or class must not be so numerous or so situated that the survivor cannot be practically determined by the ordinary evidentiary processes. E. g., if the lives in being were all the persons now living in the State of Arizona, or in Great Britain, the interest would be void.

11. The common law rule against perpetuities as above stated is in force, without material alteration, in a substantial number of states, but the rule is in a state of transition, and basic modifications exist. Simes, 260–262.

1. A perpetual trust for charity is valid, but this is not necessarily an exception in the strict sense to the common law rule against perpetuities, since the rule is concerned primarily with remoteness of vesting and not the duration of interests. A clear exception exists, however, in the case of a gift over from one charity to another charity on a condition precedent that may not necessarily occur within the period of lives in being and twenty one years. Simes, 296.

2. As to the validity of powers, see infra Cases 104 and 105.

12. In recent years criticism of the Rule has led to various reforms, the most common of which are as follows:

a. The wait and see doctrine.

The essence of this reform is that the validity of the contingent interest is determined not at the inception of the period but at the time the contingency occurs. Some jurisdictions have adopted by statute a limited wait and see doctrine whereby the validity is determined at the end of one or more relevant life estates.

b. The cy pres doctrine.

Under this doctrine the limitations which would violate the rule are redrafted or reformed to conform to the intent of the settlor as nearly as possible without violating the rule. A simple example is the case of an age contingency, as when there is a gift to an unborn person who reaches 25. If by reducing the age contingency to 21 an otherwise invalid gift would be saved, the limitation is reformed accordingly.

c. Statutory enactments modifying the application of the rule to specific typical situations, such as:

(1) time limitations on the duration of possibilities of reverter and powers of termination;

(2) reduction of age contingencies of unborn persons to 21 years;

(3) declaring the legal effect of interests limited on certain administrative contingencies such as the probate of an estate. See Simes, 269 et seq.; Note following case 102 for more references relating to modern reforms. These modifications are not further discussed in this volume.

13. Statutes prohibiting the suspension of the power of alienation and the absolute ownership of personal property for designated periods of time exist in some states. The New York statutes were the subject of significant amendments in 1958 and 1960. See Simes, 298–313. The New York Rule is not discussed in this volume. As to the common law rule generally, see Restatement of Property §§ 370–377; Simes, 253–297; Burby, 412–426.

––––––––

Offending interest void ab initio; contingent remainders and destructibility; possibilities not probabilities

CASE 93: A, fee owner, *by deed* conveys Blackacre to B for life then to the first child of B who reaches age 25. At the time of the conveyance B is alive and has two children, age 6 and 2 respectively. **(a)** Is the interest to the child who reaches 25 valid under the common law rule? **(b)** What is the state of title?

Answers and Analyses

The answers are:

(a) The interest of the first child to reach 25 is valid if the jurisdiction follows the rule of destructibility of contingent remainders. It is not valid if the destructibility rule is abolished.

(b) If the interest of the child is valid, the state of title is: B has a life estate, the first child to reach 25 has a contingent remainder in fee, and A has a reversion. If the destructibility rule is not in effect, the state of title is: life estate in B, reversion in fee simple in A, and the interest of the first child to reach 25 is void.

Under the conveyance, B takes a life estate. It is a presently vested estate in possession, and the rule against perpetuities has no application to it. Likewise, the common law rule has no application to A's reversion as it is vested in interest. The rule does apply, however, to the contingent interest of the child. Since the conveyance is to the first child of B to reach 25, and since no child has yet reached 25, the interest is contingent. Because a child could reach 25 before the death of B, the interest could take effect as a remainder at the end of the life estate; hence it must be construed as a contingent remainder rather than an executory interest. If the destructibility rule is in effect, then the interest will either vest no later than, and take effect in possession at the end of the life estate, or else it will fail completely. Thus, it is valid under the rule because it *will vest, if at all,* within the period of the rule, in this case no later than the end of B's life estate.

If the destructibility rule is not in effect in the jurisdiction, then the fact that no child of B has reached 25 at the end of his life estate, does not prevent a child from taking if he reaches 25 after the death of B. In the instant case the fact that B has two children, 6 and 2, does not necessarily mean that one of these two children will take. It is possible that both of these children will die before reaching 25, that B will have another child and will die before that child reaches four years of age, and that that subsequent born child will reach 25 more than 21 years after the deaths of B and his presently living children. Thus, the gift to the first child of B who reaches 25 is void, leaving the state of title—life estate in B and a reversion in fee simple in A. The fact that it is highly probable that one of B's present children, or even an after born child, will reach 25 within 21 years after the death of B does not save the gift. There must be an absolute certainty that the gift will either fail or vest within the period of the rule. See Simes, 264–265, 280.

The interest must vest either in interest or possession during the period permitted by the rule.

CASE 94: A, fee owner, *devises* to B for life, then to B's children for their joint lives and to the survivors of them for the life of the survivor, then to all of my lineal descendants who survive B, share and share alike. What interests are valid under the common law rule?

Answer and Analysis

The answer is this—all interests are valid. First, it should be noticed this is a devise. Hence, A's life is removed. Second, B's life estate is vested in possession so the rule has no application to it. Third, if at A's death B has children then they would have a vested remainder subject to open as other children are born to B. Further, all children of B will be born within his lifetime, or the period of gestation thereafter. Thus, the interest of every member of the class of B's children will necessarily vest (if at all) within the period of the rule, namely within the period of B's life.

If at A's death B has no children then the remainder would remain contingent until B has a child at which time it would become a vested remainder subject to open. But it would *vest in interest* in such child or children of B at least during B's lifetime and would, therefore, comply with the rule. Further, the interest of such children would vest in possession not later than B's death, that is, not later than a "life in being" at the creation of the interest which was when A's will took effect at A's death. So the interest of B's children is valid.

Fourth, of course B may have several children after A's will became effective and each may live to be 80 years of age and such child or children will possess far beyond B's life and 21 years. And A's lineal descendants cannot possess till then. But how does that affect, if at all, the validity of the interest of A's lineal descendants? It affects the possession only and not the vesting. Those lineal descendants will be determined at B's death and at that time their interest will *vest in interest* even though their right to possess may be postponed far beyond the period of the rule against perpetuities. So the interest of the lineal descendants must vest (if at all, if there be such descendants, or fail if none) not later than B's death, the life in being as the measuring life for vesting, and is quite a valid future interest under the rule.

Of course, had A's will provided "then to my lineal descendants then living," instead of providing for "lineal descendants who survive B", the interest of such lineal descendants would have been void because it might not have vested within the period of the rule. See Simes, 264.

––––––––

If the interest MUST EITHER vest or fail within the period of the rule it is valid

CASE 95: A, fee owner, conveys to B for life, remainder to such children only of B who are living at B's death. Is the remainder valid under the common law rule?

Answer and Analysis

The answer is yes. It seems clear that A intended survivorship of B as a condition precedent to any vesting in B's children. Hence, such children have a contingent remainder. Now, to apply the rule! (1) The rule has no application to B's life estate which is vested in possession. (2) The rule has no application to A's reversion even though it is subject to defeasance by B's leaving surviving children. (3) At B's death the contingent remainder in favor of B's children either vests in possession at that instant or it fails completely. The interest fails if B has no children living at his death because thereafter it will be impossible for him to procreate any children, and a child *en ventre sa mere* at his death will both avoid the destructibility rule and qualify under the rule against perpetuities. Hence, the contingent remainder is perfectly valid under the rule because it MUST EITHER vest or fail at the end of one life in being, that is the life of B. The rule does not stop by saying the interest "must vest". It says "must vest, *if at all*", meaning it must vest or fail within the allowable period. See Simes, 265.

The vesting must take place not later than 21 years after some life in being

> CASE 96: A, fee owner, by deed conveys to B for life, then to the first child of C who attains the age of 21 years whether that be before or after the death of B. At the time of the conveyance C is a living single person having no child. Are all the interests valid under the common law rule?

Answer and Analysis

The answer is yes. (1) Because the interest of C's child is contingent there is a reversion in A subject to being divested. But every reversion is vested and the rule has no application thereto. (2) B's interest is presently vested in possession and the rule does not apply to it. (3) The interest of C's first child to attain the age of 21 is a contingent interest, contingent both on being born and surviving to the age of 21. Whether technically the child might be considered as having both a contingent remainder and an executory interest, or whether he is considered as having a single future interest, is immaterial insofar as perpetuities is concerned since the rule applies to both. Is there any possibility that this interest will vest later than a life in being and 21 years? The answer is no.

The measuring life is that of C. No child can be born to C later than the period of gestation (the period of gestation is normally 9 months but 10 months is allowed) after C's death. Any such child must attain the age of 21 years, if at all, within 21 years after its birth. So the longest possible time when such interest must either vest or fail is, C's life plus a period of gestation plus 21 years. Under the rule a child in the womb is in being. Therefore, the rule does not invalidate any interest because the period stated is extended by an actual period of gestation. Hence, the interest of C's first child who may attain the age of 21 must either vest or fail within the allowable period with no possibility that it can vest at any later time. Therefore, it is valid.

Measuring lives may be determined by implication

CASE 97: A, fee owner, devises Blackacre "to my grandchildren who arrive at the age of 21 years", A leaving three children, X, Y, and Z, but no grandchildren, living at A's death. Is the devise to the grandchildren valid under the common law rule?

Answer and Analysis

The answer is yes. Without a residuary clause in A's will, Blackacre would pass to A's heirs for the period intervening A's death and when some grandchild became 21 years old. The interest in A's grandchildren would be an executory devise of the springing type which would cut short the interest left in A's heirs. The rule against perpetuities applies to such executory devises.

In this case there is no life expressly mentioned which can be the "life in being" or "lives in being", but the mention of grandchildren implies there must be an intervening generation of A's children in order that A may have grandchildren. So by implication the children of A become the "lives in being" during which, plus 21 years, the devise must vest. But such vesting cannot by any possibility take place after the period of the rule because every grandchild of A, if any, who attains the age of 21 years must do so not later than the death of the survivor of X, Y and Z, and a period of gestation, and 21 years.

Let us spell this out very specifically. The devise did not take effect until the testator, A, died. Hence, A's life is terminated when the interest is created. Then we begin with the lives of A's children. Suppose X dies first followed by the death of Y. Then Z dies and a child is born to him posthumously, whom we shall call M. M is the last possible grandchild of A. M arrives at the age of 21. At that instant M's interest in Blackacre vests. How long has it taken after A's death for such interest to vest? The answer is this—the lifetime of Z, he being the surviving child of X, Y and Z, plus that part of the period of gestation between Z's death and M's birth, plus 21 years. Hence, the executory devise to A's grandchildren who attained the age of 21 years, did not offend the rule and was effective. And, had there been no grandchild of A who attained such age, then the executory devise would have failed within the period of the rule and the reversion would have remained in A's heirs.

Note

If instead of a devise A made an inter vivos conveyance to those of his grandchildren who reach 21 (there being no grandchildren in existence who are 21), then the children of A could not be the measuring lives because of the possibility that A could have an afterborn child, and such afterborn child could produce a grandchild who could reach 21 more than 21 years after the deaths of A, his existing children, and grandchildren, if any. Therefore, such an inter vivos conveyance would be void. See Simes, 265–266.

———

The time for vesting is generally calculated from the time the creating instrument takes effect—if a will from the testator's death —if a deed from delivery

> CASE 98: A, being fee owner, devises Blackacre "to the children of my son, B, who reach the age of 25". At A's death B has four sons ranging in age from 14 to 22. B dies 10 days after the death of A, leaving no other children. Is the devise to the children valid under the common law rule against perpetuities?

Answer and Analysis

The answer is no. It appears that one or more of the sons will surely arrive at the age of 25 and they probably will in fact. But to say that the provision in favor of B's children is valid, is only an illusion. It is void under the rule against perpetuities.

The validity of an interest created by a will must be determined as of the date when the will takes effect, that is in our case at A's death. Looking forward from that date these possibilities, and we are dealing with possibilities not probabilities, must be observed. First, as long as B lives he is conclusively presumed capable of having more children. Second, it is possible that he will have other children after A's death. Third, it is possible that all of B's four sons living at A's death will die before any one of them arrives at the age of 25. Fourth, then it is possible that the only one, if any, of B's children who will arrive at the age of 25 will be a child who is born after A's will took effect. Fifth, it is possible that such child may be born posthumously, that is, after the death of B and that it will take 25 more years for him to arrive at the required age for an interest in Blackacre to vest in him.

Conclusion: it is possible that any interest in B's children will vest at a time later than any life in being and 21 years after the will of A took effect. Therefore, the devise in favor of B's children who reach the age of 25 years, as provided for in A's will is void ab initio under the rule against perpetuities. See Simes, 267–268.

Note

Unlikely Possibilities; Case of the Unborn Widow.

The common law rule's emphasis on possibilities rather than probabilities may lead to unexpected results and constitute a trap for the unwary. This may be illustrated by the famous case of the "unborn widow."[3] To illustrate, testator, T, leaves property in trust "to pay the income to his son, A, for life, then to pay the income to A's widow for her life, and then to pay the principal to the children of A then living." At the time of T's death, A was 50 years of age, married, and the father of grown children. The gift of principal is invalid.

The reason for invalidity is that there is a possibility that A's present wife will die before him, that A will remarry, and that his new wife will be a woman who was born after the initial transfer. If this happens, the second wife would not be a life in being at the creation of the interest. Hence, for the principal to vest in the surviving children, it would be necessary to wait until the end of a life not in being at the creation of the interest.

To summarize: The devise gave A a vested equitable life estate. A contingent equitable remainder for life was given to his widow. This remainder was contingent because it was limited to his widow, not necessarily his present wife, and the identity of the widow would only be known at the time of A's death. The ultimate remainder of principal to the children of A is also contingent since they must survive both A and his widow. Further, since it is a class gift, every member of the class must be able to take for the gift to be valid. Thus, since the class includes possible after born children who must survive a possible "unborn" widow, all these contingencies might not necessarily be resolved within lives in being and twenty-one years. Thus, the remainder to the surviving children is invalid. It should be noted, however, that the life estate to the possibly unborn widow is perfectly valid. She necessarily will take, if at all, at the time of A's death at which time her interest will either vest both in interest and possession, or it will fail altogether.

———

Power of termination is exempt from the rule

CASE 99: A, owner in fee simple of Blackacre, by deed conveys it "to B and his heirs, but if liquor is ever sold on Blackacre, then to C and his heirs, and if for any reason the interest hereby conveyed to C is not valid, then I reserve to me and my heirs the right to re-enter Blackacre and take back the property". B sells liquor on the premises and C sues B to eject him therefrom. In a separate action A sues

3. Leach, Perpetuities in a Nutshell, 51
Harvard L.Rev. 638, 644 (1938).

B in ejectment. The court decides to hear the two actions together. Who should prevail?

Answer and Analysis

The answer is, A should prevail. First, C's interest cannot be a remainder for two reasons, (a) C's interest is to cut short the preceding particular estate and that a remainder cannot do, and (b) a remainder cannot follow an estate in fee simple which B has in this case. So C's interest must be an executory interest of the shifting type, if it is anything. However, executory interests are subject to the common law rule against perpetuities and it is obvious that liquor may not be sold on Blackacre for an indefinite time in the future, if ever. Hence, the contingent executory interest of C *might not* vest until some remote time far beyond the maximum time provided by the rule and is therefore void ab initio.

Thus, with C's interest void, A's conveyance would read in legal effect as follows, "to B and his heirs but if liquor is sold on the premises then I reserve the power to enter and terminate B's estate". This means that B has a fee simple estate subject to a condition subsequent, and that there is reserved in the grantor, A, a right of re-entry for condition broken or power of termination. Of course, it is possible that liquor will not be sold on the premises until a very remote time and far beyond the period of time provided by the rule against perpetuities. But in the United States, contrary to the English view, the rule against perpetuities has no application to powers of termination or rights of re-entry for condition broken. Hence, the reserved power of termination in the grantor, A, is valid and A having sued in ejectment has done the two things essential to make such power effective. He has (a) elected to exercise the power and (b) he has done such affirmative act as the law requires, namely, brought a suit in ejectment. Result: C's action in ejectment must fail; A's action to eject B must prevail. Simes, 280; Burby, 420.

Note

Statutes which limit the duration of possibilities of reverter and powers of termination are rather common.

An absolute interest conditioned on an administrative contingency, such as after probate of a will, is void under the common law rule

CASE 100: A, being owner in fee simple of Blackacre, devises it to "B and his heirs after the probate of this will." There is no residuary clause in the will and X is A's sole heir. Upon A's death B takes possession of Blackacre, X brings ejectment. May X recover?

Answer and Analysis

The classical answer is yes. As worded the estate given to B is contingent on the probate of A's will. Thus, the question is whether B's estate must vest or fail within the period of the rule. Viewed from the moment of A's death, and considering all possibilities, the answer is clearly no. Of course, A's will may be probated promptly after his death, and in all probability it will occur within 21 years, but there is no absolute certainty of that. Some wills are never probated. Further, B need not be alive to take. Thus, because the will might not be probated until after 21 years, and because no measuring life is involved, B's interest is void. Therefore Blackacre descends to A's heir X, who may eject B.

In cases of this type, the limitation is sometimes saved by one or another construction techniques. Thus, a devise on probate of an estate may be construed as not contingent at all but simply as a recognition of the fact that no ultimate distribution can be made of the estate until probate. Similarly, a devise to take effect after settlement of the estate may be held valid under the doctrine that the holder of the will is duty bound to deliver the will promptly, that the executor has a fiduciary duty to settle the estate promptly, and that the testator expected both of these things to be timely done and certainly within 21 years. Of course, if the limitation following the "after probate" contingency is to a named individual for life, the gift is necessarily valid because the devisee himself is a life in being. Thus, a devise "after probate of my estate to B for life," is necessarily valid since B, having only a life estate, will have to take, if at all, within his own lifetime. See Restatement of Property § 374; Simes, 286; Leach, Perpetuities In A Nutshell, 51 Harv.L.Rev. 638, 645 (1938); Leach, Perpetuities, The Nutshell Revisited, 78 Harv.L.Rev. 973, 979 (1965).

Options unconnected with leases are subject to the common law rule against perpetuities

> CASE 101: A, being fee simple owner of Blackacre, agrees for a valuable consideration that B, his heirs or assigns, may have an option to purchase such property for a stated amount of $5,000.00 at any time, upon 30 days notice, within 22 years from the date of such option agreement. One year thereafter B gives proper notice and tenders the $5,000.00 to A and demands performance by A, which is refused. May B compel A to perform?

Answer and Analysis

The answer is no. It is well settled in this country that the common law rule against perpetuities applies to option agreements which are not connected with leases or incident thereto. It is obvious in this case that it is possible that no interest will vest in B or his successor within a gross period of 21 years from the time the agreement is made. Such being the case the option is void under the rule. It is considered that such an agreement fetters the alienability of Blackacre for longer than the allowable period under the rule and is a deterrent to A, the owner, from selling to any one else during the period provided for in the option. Here again it should be kept in mind that the validity of the interest is determined at the time of the creation of the interest and not by events as they happen thereafter. It is quite immaterial that the option was attempted to be exercised by B within one year after the agreement was made. The option being void under the rule against perpetuities, B cannot enforce it either by specific performance or by an action for damages. Of course, the rule against perpetuities does not apply to contracts as such, but is limited to interests in lands and chattels. See Simes, 281; Burby, 419–421.

Note

An option to renew a lease is valid although it may be exercised beyond the period of the rule. Similarly, an option in a lease to purchase the reversion is valid although remotely exercisable. A justification for these exceptions is that the option, being an accepted commercial device, may aid rather than hinder alienation. Simes, 282. See also supra Chapter V, fn. 3 following Case 51.

In applying the common law rule there is a conclusive presumption of fertility

CASE 102: A, being fee simple owner of Blackacre, devises it "to the children of B for their lives and the life of the survivor of them, then to B's grandchildren in fee simple". There is a residuary clause in M's favor. At the time A dies, B is a woman of the age of 85 and she has three children, X, Y and Z. When the survivor of X, Y and Z dies M takes possession of Blackacre and sues to quiet title in himself. May he succeed?

Answer and Analysis

The answer is yes. At the outset the following items should be carefully noted. The creating instrument is a will; B, a woman of 85 is not a donee under the will but she does constitute a generation; B's children, X, Y and Z, are given life estates which are to last until the death of the survivor, and such children constitute a second generation; the children of X, Y and Z, are the grandchildren of B and constitute the third generation.

For the purpose of the rule against perpetuities every living person is conclusively presumed capable of having children as long as he lives. And the rule says *"life in being at the creation of the interest"*. So it must be kept in mind that even though B is 85 years of age she can legally have children until her death, regardless of the fact that biologically she may be quite incapable of reproduction. Hence, it is legally possible that B may have another child, H, who will have children who will qualify as B's grandchildren and who were not in being at A's death and may not come into being until more than 21 years after the deaths of X, Y and Z. It is possible then that all of B's children and grandchildren except H's children, who were not "lives in being at the creation of the interest", will have dropped out before the interest created by A's devise, will vest, and that H's children will be the only ones who can take such interest. This provision fetters the alienation of Blackacre for a longer time than is permissible under the rule, thus making the gift "to B's grandchildren in fee simple" absolutely void ab initio.

In such cases there is often a thin line between what is valid and what is void. Notice in this case, had A's will limited B's grandchildren to the children of X, Y and Z, then the devise to such grandchildren would have been valid because the lives in being as measuring lives would have been X, Y and Z, and their children were bound to take vested interests not later than the death of the survivor of X, Y and Z, and a period of gestation, from "the creation of the interest". Of course the life estates to the children of B were valid even though they were to open and let in afterborn children of B. The limitation in A's will to B's grandchildren, being void under the rule against perpetuities, the will would read in legal effect merely, "to the children of B for their lives and for the life of the survivor of them". Result: the fee simple thereafter passes under the residuary clause to M who now has the right to have the title quieted in him, the life estates in X, Y and Z having been terminated by death. See Simes, 287; Burby, 415.

Note

For a brief synopsis of statutes designed to overcome such improbable assumptions as the "fertile octogenarian" and unlikely possibilities involved in administrative contingency cases, see Leach, Perpetuities: The Nutshell Revisited, 78 Harv.L.Rev. 973, 987–991; Simes, 269–279.

For suggested more comprehensive reforms, see: Restatement, Second, Property, Tentative Draft, §§ 1.1–1.6 for recommended modifications of the common law rule with lots of references; Maudsley, Perpetuities: Reforming the Common Law Rule—How to Wait and See, 60 Cornell L.Rev. 355 (1975); Comment, Rule Against Perpetuities: The Second Restatement Adopts Wait and See, 19 Santa Clara L.Rev. 1063 (1979).

A class gift, subject to two exceptions, stands or falls as a unit under the common law rule

CASE 103: A, being fee simple owner of Blackacre, devises it "to B for life, then to the brothers and sisters of B who reach the age of 25 years". At the death of A, the parents of B, H and W, are both living, as are three brothers, M, N, and O. While B still lives two other brothers are born, R and S. B dies. X, the heir of A takes possession of Blackacre. M, N, O, R and S join in an action to eject X. May they succeed if contingent remainders are not destructible?

Answer and Analysis

The answer is no. B's life estate is valid. The limitation to B's brothers and sisters is a class gift. Such a gift is considered a unit and is not divisible into parts, and unless all members of the class can qualify under the rule against perpetuities the gift fails in its entirety. In other words, if one member of the class cannot qualify under the rule, then the entire gift fails even though as to the other members of the class the interest has vested. Such principle can be justified upon the theory that the grantor or devisor must have intended all members of the class to take and did not intend that only part of the class, described in the deed or will as a class, should take and some would not take in case some did not qualify under the rule.

Applying such principles then, if one of B's brothers and sisters cannot qualify to take a vested interest within a life in being and 21 years after A's death, then the entire gift to B's brothers and sisters must fail. Of course such conclusion must be determined by construing A's will at A's death, not by the facts as they actually did happen after A's death. When A's will took effect B's parents, H and W, were still alive and conclusively presumed capable of having children. If thereafter a child is born to them, being a brother or sister of B, the life tenant, such child would not be "a life in being at the creation of the interest". Such child would have to attain the age of 25 years before his interest could vest. That time could be longer than "a life in being and 21 years" after "the creation of the interest" by A's will. In fact, both R and S are such afterborn children. If either or both attain the age of 25 years, it may be at a time more remote from the creation of the interest than is allowable under the rule. For example, if R and S were under 4 years of age at the death of B, and if H, W, M, N and O had predeceased B, then the interest of R and S would vest (if at all) beyond lives in being and 21 years measured from the effective date of the will. Since we consider possibilities from the inception of the interest, such brothers cannot qualify to take the contingent interest in Blackacre as a member of the class, "brothers and sisters of B who reach the age of 25 years". Hence, the entire gift to such class must fail even though some members of the class, M, N and O, did in fact qualify and their interests became vested. This is an exception to the rule that the rule against perpetuities does not apply to vested interests.

In our case then in legal effect A's will would read merely, "to B for life", leaving the reversion to descend by intestate succession to A's heir, X, who now owns and has the right to possess Blackacre as against B's brothers, M, N, O, R and S, who must fail in their ejectment action.

Here again there may be a thin line between the valid and the void. Had A provided in his will for separability of the interest of each brother and sister of B so that the interest of each as an individual (rather than as a member of a class as a unit), would have been tested under the rule of perpetuities, then only part but not all of the gift would have failed. For example, suppose A had provided, "then to each brother or sister of B such fractional interest in Blackacre as he or she can qualify to take if and when he arrives at age 25". Under such provision M, N and O, being "lives in being" at A's death would each, upon attaining age 25, have qualified to take Blackacre in fee simple. The interest of each would depend on which, if any, of the three reached age 25. But such might not have been A's intention. The problem is one of construction. See leading case Leake v. Robinson, 35 Eng.Rep. 979 (1817); In re Wanamaker's Estate, 335 Pa. 241, 6 A.2d 852 (1939); Leach, The Rule Against Perpetuities and Gifts to Classes", 51 Harv.L.R. 1329 (1938); Simes, 289; Burby, 422.

Note

Two important limitations on the unitary class gift rule are in effect. The first is the case of a per capita gift to each member of the class, illustrated in the last paragraph of the above discussion, but more commonly illustrated by a gift of a specific sum of money to each member of a class who attains an age in excess of 21. In such instance, the gift is valid as to those members who are in existence when the limitation takes effect, but is invalid as to those who are born afterwards.

The second exception is the sub-class rule. Under this exception, when there is a gift to a class of sub-classes, the gift to a particular sub-class may be valid although the gift to other sub-classes may be too remote. This rule applies when there is a gift to a class, the membership in which is certain to be determined within the period of the rule, and this is followed by a gift over of the share of each member of the class, or of the share from which each member of the class has been given income, to his children, issue, heirs or the like. See Leach, Perpetuities in a Nutshell, 51 Harv.L.Rev. 638, 648–651 (1938); Simes, 289–292; Burby, 422–424.

A general power presently exercisable is valid if the donee must acquire the power within the period of the rule against perpetuities

CASE 104: A, being fee simple owner of Blackacre, devises it "to B for life, then to the first child born to B for life, said child to have the general power by deed or will to appoint to whomsoever he will, including himself, to take the fee simple in said property". At the time of A's death B is a single person having no child. A's will gives the residue of his property to M. B dies leaving surviving him his first born child, X, who is 25 years of age and competent, and who has not yet exercised the power given him by A's will. M disputes the validity of the power given to X in A's will whereupon X executes a deed appointing himself as the owner of the fee simple estate in Blackacre. X then sues M seeking to quiet title in X. May X succeed?

Answer and Analysis

The answer is yes. (1) There is no question in this case as to the validity of B's life estate or of the life estate in his first born child, X. (2) The dispute between X and M concerns merely the validity of the power of appointment limited to X. In determining the validity of such power the ultimate purpose of the rule against perpetuities should be kept in mind. While it is directed towards remoteness of vesting, it is intended to prevent the fettering of property over long periods of time. A general power of appointment by deed or will means that the donee of such power can exercise it during his lifetime whenever he so desires. Such general power of appointment is considered the practical equivalent of the ownership of the property itself.

The test for the validity of such a general power is not when it is exercised in fact but whether it can be exercised within the period of the rule against perpetuities. In our case such general power could be exercised by B's first born child at any time from the date of its birth. Indeed, the time when the donee of the power could exercise it from the time of its creation could not be longer than a life in being (B's life) and the period of gestation if his first born child were born posthumously.[4] This is clearly within the rule. Furthermore, it

---

4. This is only theoretically true; pragmatically it is not since a one day old baby could hardly in fact exercise a power of appointment. It is possible, theoretically at least, for the donor to provide for the exercise of a power by an infant, but in this case the directions are for the exercise by a deed or will (not by an instrument in the nature of a deed or will). In such a case it is generally held that the donee must have the capacity to execute the particular instrument in question, which, in the case of a deed or will, means that the donee must be of sound mind and of the age of majority or otherwise have the disability of infancy removed. Thus, pragmatically, in the instant case, the longest period of time that the power could remain unexercisable would be for B's life, the period of gestation, and 21 years thereafter. This, however, is within the period of the rule. See Simes, 142, as to the capacity of a donee of a power.

would have been within the rule had such power been limited to B's first born child who arrived at the age of 21 years.[5] It is true that X could in fact exercise the general power given him at a time more remote from its creation than is permissible under the rule. But that is because the purpose of the rule is not offended. As long as there is some person who has the power to acquire the absolute property for his own benefit within the period of the rule, he can do so and alienate the property. Thus the property is freely alienable within the period of the rule.

The power to acquire the absolute interest in the real property must exist within the period allowed by the rule against perpetuities, but its exercise may be at a more remote time. Had A's will limited the existence of the general power in B's first born child to the time when such first born child had attained the age of 25 years, then such general power would have been void under the rule and not exercisable by X at any time. But in our case, X having exercised the general power in his own favor, he became the fee simple owner of Blackacre and title should be quieted in him as against A's residuary devisee, M. See Restatement of Property § 391; Simes, 292–293; Bray v. Bree, 6 Eng.Rep. 1225 (1834).

––––––––

A special power, and a general power exercisable by will only, is void if it is capable of being exercised beyond the period of the rule

CASE 105: A, being fee simple owner of Blackacre, devises it "to B for life, then to B's first born child for life, such first born child to have power by will to appoint among his brothers and sisters who shall take the fee simple in Blackacre". There is no residuary clause in A's will. H is A's sole heir. B is a single person having no child at A's death. B dies leaving his first born child, M, who at B's death is 30 years of age. M executes his will appointing his brother, N, among his several brothers and sisters, to take Blackacre in fee simple. M dies and N takes possession of Blackacre. H sues N to eject him from the premises. May H succeed?

Answer and Analysis

The answer is yes. The correctness of this answer depends upon the validity of the power given to B's first born child who turned out to be M. But here is a special testamentary power because it could be exercised only by will and only among a limited class of persons, namely, the donee's brothers and sisters. In case of a special power (whether testamentary or inter vivos, and also in case of a general testamentary power), its validity under the rule against perpetuities is de-

––––––––

5. That this is the practical effect of the limitation as written if the age of majority is 21, see n. 4 supra.

termined by whether or not it must be exercised within a life in being and 21 years from its creation. In other words, in our case, the power granted to B's first born child to be valid would have to be exercised not later than "a life in being and 21 years" from the death of A whose will created the special power. The measuring life would be the life tenant, B. Such special power to be valid, must be required to be exercised, within 21 years after B's death. If its exercise is possible under the limitations of A's will, at a later time, then it is void in its inception. In this case the power can be exercised only by will. The will of M cannot take effect until his death. If, then, the first born child of B should live longer than 21 years after B's death, then such special power would be exercised at a date more remote than is allowed by the rule. Therefore, the special power given to B's first born child is void ab initio and its attempted exercise by M in favor of his brother, N, is wholly ineffective and N has no interest in Blackacre. The result is that A's will in effect reads as follows, "to B for life, then to B's first born child for life". This left the reversion in Blackacre to descend to A's heir, H, who is now the owner in fee simple of the property and can eject N therefrom.

The reason for requiring the exercise of a special power of appointment within the rule against perpetuities is this. Such special power is not in any sense the equivalent of ownership as is a general power. Hence, it is the exercise of the special power which vests ownership in the appointee. If the exercise of such special power were not required within the period allowed by the rule, then a vesting in interest in property could take place at a time more remote than is allowed by the rule. In the meantime there would be no person who could alienate the property. This would offend the rule. See Restatement of Property §§ 390, 391; Simes, 292; Burby, 424; Leach, Perpetuities in a Nutshell, 51 Harv.L.Rev. 638, 651 (1938).

Note

The result in the above case would be the same if the power given to B's first son were (1) to appoint by deed or will to his brothers and sisters, or (2) if the power were to appoint to anybody by will only. In (1), although M could appoint as soon as he reached 21, which obviously could not be more than 21 years after B's death, he is under no obligation to do so, and thus the power might be exercised beyond the period of the rule. In (2), although M has a general power, since it is exercisable by will only, the property in fact is not alienable during the lifetime of M. See citations noted above.

Period of gestation may precede as well as follow lives in being; accumulations within the period of the rule are valid

CASE 106: A, being fee simple owner of Blackacre, devises it "to T and his heirs in trust for the purpose of accumulating the net income from such real property during the lives of my several children and when my first grandchild has arrived at the age of 21 years, then T is directed to deliver to such grandchild both the accumulated net income from Blackacre, and the legal title to Blackacre". In the residuary clause of A's will all of the undisposed-of property of A is given to B. B brings suit to have the provision concerning Blackacre determined to be void, contending that he, B, takes Blackacre by virtue of the residuary clause. May B succeed?

Answer and Analysis

The answer is no. As in private indestructible trusts the rule against perpetuities applies to accumulations and makes them void if the interest created is not to vest within the period of the rule. But the rule against perpetuities cannot apply to vested interests. In the case above the legal title both to Blackacre and to the net income therefrom is vested presently in the trustee, T. But the interest of B's first grandchild to arrive at the age of 21 is not vested for the reason that such beneficiary cannot be ascertained and identified until such child, if any, arrives at the required age.

This, then, is a case to which the rule against perpetuities does apply, and the equitable interest to be valid must vest in interest or in possession within the period permitted by the rule. So it is essential to determine whether such interest must vest within or without the period of the rule. The rule says the interest must vest within some life in being at the creation of the interest and 21 years thereafter. Applying this principle to our set of facts, the latest time at which the equitable interest in this case could possibly vest would be as follows, (a) a period of gestation, plus (b) a life in being, plus (c) a period of gestation, plus (d) 21 years from the creation of the interest.

The foregoing conclusion is reached by the following reasoning. First, the only child which the testator might leave surviving him and whose child might reach the required age of 21 as a grandchild of the testator, A, may be born to A posthumously. But if there be such child he is considered in being if conceived and in the womb of his mother at A's death. Second, such child of A is then a life in being at the time of the creation of the interest by A's will. Third, the only grandchild of A who may reach the age of 21 years may be born posthumously to the posthumously born child of A. But he will be considered in being at the death of his parent, the posthumously born child of A. Thus we might have a second period of gestation. Fourth, when such child, if any, reaches the age of 21 years as the first grandchild of A to attain such age, the equitable interest in this trust involving accumulations will vest. In such case the rule allows as a maximum period of time (a) a life in being at the creation of the interest, plus (b) 21 years, plus (c) any number of periods of gestation actually involved in the limitation being construed. Thus, the equitable interest *must vest* (if at all), within the period of the rule and *there is no possibility of its vesting an instant later* than such period. The equitable interest created by A's will is therefore valid and defeats any conflicting claim which may exist as to it in the residuary devisee, B, who must fail in his suit involving the validity of the limitation in A's will concerning accumulations.

An accumulation as here used means the withholding of income by the trustee for a longer period than is required in the ordinary administration of the trust. If the beneficiary is identified in such a trust and the interest is vested and the period of accumulation is longer than the rule against perpetuities, the trust is valid but the limitation for accumulations is void and the trust is terminable by the beneficiary. It should be carefully noted that the equitable interest in such case of accumulations is either vested or it is contingent. If it is contingent, then the rule against perpetuities applies. If it is vested the rule against perpetuities does not apply, but a common law rule analogous thereto prevents accumulations from taking property out of commerce for a longer period than the rule against perpetuities. Provisions for accumulations to continue beyond the rule are void. The trustee may actually continue to make such accumulations long past the period of the rule but if he does so it is simply because the beneficiary thereof does not require the corpus and the income to be paid over to him. And as long as the beneficiary has power to require the accumulations to be turned over to him, he is for all intents and purposes the owner with power to alienate it, and there is no public policy violated. See Simes, 258, 265–267, 279, 321, 322, 324; Burby, 432; Restatement of Trusts, § 62, comment *l*; and the leading case of Thellusson v. Woodford, 11 Ves. 112 (1805).

Provisions in private trusts for indestructibility beyond the period of perpetuities are void

CASE 107: A, being fee owner of Blackacre, devises it "to T and his heirs to hold in trust for C and his heirs for 40 years". At the time of A's death C is a boy of the age of 15 years. When he arrives at the age of 25 years he demands that the trust be terminated and that T turn over to him the trust res. T refuses. C sues T seeking a court decree terminating the trust. May he succeed?

Answer and Analysis

The answer is yes. There is no question that the rule against perpetuities applies to the vesting of the equitable interest in the beneficiaries of a private trust. If C or his successors in our case was not to have the benefit of the equitable interest in Blackacre until a period in gross of 40 years after the creation of the interest, the equitable interest would fail under the rule. But that is not our case. In the given facts both the legal and the equitable interests are vested in fee simple in the trustee and in the cestui respectively. The rule against perpetuities is directed at remoteness of vesting. If the rule is taken literally it can have no application to our case where both the legal and equitable interests are vested.

Thus, the question resolves itself into whether or not there is a common law rule that a private indestructible trust cannot endure longer than the period of the rule against perpetuities. Both the cases and the authorities on the subject of trusts are divided on the answer to this question. A private trust is indestructible when the court will not decree its termination because contrary to the intention of the settlor and when none of the parties has power to terminate it. It is quite obvious, for instance, if the settlor has reserved the power to revoke a trust at any time and retake the trust property as owner, or the beneficiaries can require the trustee to turn over the property to them at any time, there is no need of having a rule concerning the duration of a private trust for the very reason that in such cases the settlor or beneficiaries can, as an owner, alienate the property whenever they see fit to exercise the powers which they have. Such trusts are destructible. In such case a rule would accomplish nothing of importance.

Nevertheless it must be admitted that the splitting of the equitable from the legal title which takes place in the ordinary private trust, does fetter and place a clog upon the alienability of the trust property. The trustee is bound by the terms of the trust instrument and even though he has power to sell the trust property and reinvest the proceeds, he cannot do the things an owner can do such as give it away or use it for his own purposes. And while the equitable interest can be sold by a cestui que trust (beneficiary) who is sui juris, the fact remains that there are not buyers in the market who are willing to buy such interests with the same liberty or abandon as they would buy property not subject to a trust. The very fact that he might have to bring an action against the trustee to get possession of the trust res would be some deterrent to any reasonable purchaser. Hence, no reasonable person can escape the conclusion that the private indestructible trust is one device for tying up wealth for long periods of time if there is not some legal rule or machinery for limiting the duration of such device. It would seem wise then as a matter of public policy to place some restriction on the limit in time during which a private indestructible trust can continue.

The rule against perpetuities is well known and available and it seems wiser to use it than to try to develop a new and untried principle. We therefore adopt it in this case as the time limit for the duration of an indestructible private trust. Its adoption can impose no unreasonable hardship on anyone. But how shall we apply it to our facts? One method which has been used is to treat only the surplus time provided for in the trust instrument as invalid. When a life in being at the creation of the interest and 21 years is used, then we have the two elements of the lifetime and the term for years. But if no life in being is involved then a gross period of 21 years is the maximum time permitted under the rule. Under such view the trust created by A for C's benefit could last 21 years and the balance of 19 years would be cut off as void. But such application of the period of the rule is not at all consistent with the generally applied doctrine that when a limitation in an instrument offends the rule against perpetuities, the entire limitation, not just part of it, is void. By adopting such view, the trust in our case is a valid private trust, but the attempt to make it endure for 40 years is in its entirety void in its inception and the result is that the beneficiary, C, can at any time upon reaching his majority, or if a cestui be sui juris when such a trust is created, then such beneficiary can immediately require a termination of such trust by applying to the court for such.

In the problem given the beneficiary, C, being of the age of 25 years has the right to a decree terminating the trust and should succeed in his action against the trustee, T. Such a trust may actually last for 40 years but that is immaterial so long as the beneficiary has the right to terminate it. See Scott on Trusts, § 62.10; Simes and Smith, §§ 1391–1395; Claflin v. Claflin, 149 Mass. 19, 20 N.E. 454, 3 L.R.A. 370, 14 Am.St.Rep. 393 (1889); Restatement of Property §§ 378, 381; Restatement of Trusts § 62.

Note

The rule applied in the above case is applicable to honorary trusts and to trusts for the benefit of unincorporated associations. It is considered consistent with good public policy to permit charitable or public trusts to be created to last in perpetuity and the cases hold the rule against perpetuities does not prevent such even though the trust is indestructible. Statutes permitting the perpetual maintenance of cemetery lots are common.

4. POWERS OF APPOINTMENT

Legal Gems

1. A power of appointment is an authority created by a donor (one having property subject to his disposition as owner or otherwise) and conferred upon a donee enabling such donee either to appoint persons to take the property or to appoint the proportionate shares which designated persons shall take in the property.

2. Persons who take by the donee's appointment are appointees.

3. Persons who take either because the power of appointment is not exercised at all or is ineffectively exercised are called takers in default of appointment.

4. Powers of appointment are generally classified as

  a. general powers;

  b. special powers;

  c. powers purely collateral;

  d. powers in gross;

  e. powers appendant;

    f.   powers in trust;

    g. powers not in trust;

    h. exclusive powers; and

    i. non-exclusive powers.

5. A general power of appointment is one which enables the donee to appoint any person including himself or his estate as appointee.

6. A special power of appointment is one which limits the exercise of the power in favor of a person or persons other than the donee or his estate.

7. A power purely collateral exists when the donee has no interest in the property other than the power itself.

8. A power in gross exists when the donee has an interest in the property in addition to the power, but the exercise of the power does not affect the interest of the donee, as, for example, when the donee has a life estate and a power to appoint the remainder.

9. A power appendant exists when the donee has an interest in the property and the exercise of the power disposes of all or part of such interest. The modern view is that there is no power appendant as the power merges in the property.

10. A power in trust exists when the donee, under some circumstances and within some period of time, is under a duty to exercise it. A power in trust is also called an imperative or mandatory power. It can exist only where there is a special power whose permissible objects are not too broad or numerous, and there are no takers in default.

11. A power in which the donee is under no duty to exercise it is a power not in trust. A general power can never be a power in trust; nor can a power be a power in trust when there are takers in default.

12. An exclusive power is one in which the donee of a special power may exclude one or more of the permissible objects and appoint all of the property to the others.

13. A non-exclusive power is one in which the donee of a special power must appoint something to each of the permissible objects of the power. According to some authorities, if all the permissible objects do not receive a substantial share as a result of an appointment (but receipt of a share as a result of a partial default of appointment is sufficient), the appointment is void as illusory. This doctrine of illusory appointments is difficult in application and is not universally followed.

14. The instrument creating a power of appointment may be either a deed or a will.

15. The creating instrument may require the power of appointment to be exercised only by deed, or only by will, or by either as the donee shall determine. The creating instrument might also provide

that the power can be exercised by an instrument in the nature of a will or deed, as well as by a valid will or deed.

16. If the creating instrument requires the power of appointment to be exercised only by deed, it cannot be effectively exercised by will; and if it is required to be exercised by will it cannot be effectively exercised by deed.

17. A donee of a special power of appointment may exclude one or more members of the objects of the power unless the creating instrument evinces an intent that all shall benefit. In other words, the presumption is in favor of an exclusive power. See gems 12 and 13 supra.

18. Creditors of a donee of a special power of appointment cannot subject to their claims the property subject to the special power.

19. Creditors of a donee of a general power of appointment cannot subject to their claims the property subject to the general power when the power remains unexercised; but such creditors can, if the power is exercised in favor of a volunteer or a creditor of the donee, subject the property to their claims, because in such case the exercise of such power is considered substantially the equivalent of ownership.

To the rule that the affected property of an unexercised general power cannot be reached by creditors of the donee, there are two exceptions:

a. If the donee is also the donor of the power, and the conveyance creating the power is deemed fraudulent, then the donee's creditors can reach the property to the same extent as in the case of other conveyances in fraud of creditors;

b. If the donee who is also the donor creates the power by transferring property in trust and reserves for himself the life income and a general power to appoint the corpus, then, on the donee's death, his creditors can reach the trust property to the extent that their claims cannot be satisfied from his owned estate. The creditors can reach the corpus in this case because the donee/donor has retained substantially all the benefits of ownership.

20. When an appointment is made it is usually considered that the title to the property passes to the appointee from the donor of the power and not from the donee.

21. If an attempted exercise of a power is void or ineffective, the property ordinarily passes to the takers in default, or if there are none, it reverts to the donor or his heirs. This rule, however, does not apply if the doctrine of capture is employed.

The doctrine of capture in essence is an implied alternative appointment to the donee's estate in the case of an ineffective exercise by will of a testamentary general power. The property is "captured" for the donee's estate and taken from the control of the original dispositive provisions of the donor. [See Case 110.]

22. Failure to exercise a power of appointment other than a power in trust results in the property passing to the takers in default, or if there are none, to the donor or his estate.

23. Failure to exercise a power in trust results in the property passing to the objects of the power in equal shares. [See Gem 10; Case 111.]

24. a. A contract to exercise a general power presently exercisable is valid.

b. A contract to exercise a testamentary power, and a contract to exercise a special power in order to benefit a non-object, is void.

25. An exercise of a special power of appointment to objects of the power for the purpose of benefitting non-objects is fraudulent and void. [See Case 112.]

26. a. All powers other than powers in trust are releasable.

b. Although a contract to exercise a testamentary power is invalid, a contract not to appoint may be valid as a release, and this is true although the release may benefit a non-object of the power. [See Case 113.]

27. In reference to the rule against perpetuities:

a. The validity of an appointment under both a special power and a general testamentary power is determined by measuring the period from the time the power is created; but

b. The validity of an appointment under a general power presently exercisable is determined by measuring the period from the time the power is exercised. [See Case 110.]

See Restatement of Property §§ 318–330, 360, 361; Burby, 398 et seq.; Simes, 121, 292 et seq.

———

CASE 108: A, fee simple owner of Blackacre, devises it "to T and his heirs in active trust for my son, B, for life, remainder as B shall by will appoint among B's children in fee simple, and in default of such appointment such remainder shall be equally divided among B's children living at B's death". At B's death four of his children, M, N, X and Y, are living. B's will exercises the power of appointment by excluding Y entirely and appointing M, N and X, each to take an undivided one third interest in fee simple in Blackacre. B dies wholly insolvent. C, a judgment creditor of B, presents his claim for $500.00 to B's executor, E, and asks that it be satisfied out of Blackacre. Y seeks a decree of final distribution giving him an undivided one fourth interest in Blackacre. (a) Should E allow C's claim as against Blackacre? (b) Should the final decree provide for Y as to any interest in Blackacre?

Answers and Analyses

The answer to (a) is no. The answer to (b) is no.

This set of facts represents perhaps the most typical case of the creation of a special power. A testator leaves property in active trust for his son for life and then leaves the disposition of the trust res subject to a special power in the son to appoint among the grandchildren of the testator. This is a special power because it cannot be exercised in favor of the donee, B, or in favor of his estate. It is limited in favor of a group, namely, B's children. Further, the power is testamentary since it can be exercised only by will, and it is in gross since B has a life estate in the property and the exercise of the power will not affect his interest.

A special power is either exclusive or non-exclusive. It is exclusive when it permits the donee of the power to exclude one or more of the permissible objects entirely from the benefits to be derived from the exercise of the power. It is non-exclusive when the donee in the exercise of the power must include all the members of the permissible class and none may receive less than a substantial share of the property subject to the power. However, the exercise of such power may make the shares quite unequal. But a special power shall be construed to be an exclusive power unless the donor of the power has expressed an intention that it shall be non-exclusive.

Applying this doctrine to our set of facts, it would seem clear that A has included in his will no expression which would evince an intention to make the power given to B a non-exclusive power. That being the case it was within B's power to exclude from its benefits one or more of B's children. It was therefore wholly within the power granted to B, to exclude the child, Y, from any interest in the remainder in Blackacre. Hence, the answer to question (b) is that the final decree of distribution in B's estate should make no provision for the excluded child, Y. Indeed, the probate court would have no power to make such a provision for the reason that no interest in Blackacre is a part of B's estate. B had a life estate in that property and upon his death his interest therein ceased completely.

Blackacre was part of A's estate and by A's will the remainder was given to the children of B living at B's death in default of the exercise of the power. Thus, the children of B had a contingent remainder, the remainder of each being contingent on surviving B and also subject to being divested in favor of his brothers and sisters by an exercise of the power so providing. Now, by the exercise of the special power of appointment by his will, B has limited such remainder to three of his four children, M, N, and X. Y is effectively excluded from any participation in such remainder. Furthermore, by the exercise of this special power the remainder passed to M, N, and X, not from the donee of the power, B, but from the donor of the power, A. So the source of the title of M, N and X is A, their grandfather, not B, their father.

Such remainder never became any part of B's estate. Hence, B's creditor, C, has no right against Blackacre and indeed, E, B's executor would have no power to subject any interest in Blackacre to the claim of such judgment creditor. This follows the general rule that property subject to a special power of appointment cannot be taken by the creditors of the donee of the power, whether such power be or be not exercised. See Restatement of Property §§ 326, 360, 361; Simes, 136 et seq.; 159 et seq.

CASE 109: A, being fee simple owner of Blackacre, devises it "to T and his heirs in active trust for B for life, remainder to such person or persons whom B shall by will appoint, and in default of any appointment, then to X and his heirs in fee simple." B by will appointed his friend, Y, to take Blackacre in fee simple. Y gave no consideration for such appointment. Blackacre is of the value of $5,000.00. B's property is valued at $10,000.00 above administration expenses. But B owes creditor, C, $20,000.00. E is appointed and qualifies as B's executor. E pays all expenses of administration, applies the $10,000.00 assets in his hands to C's debt, leaving $10,000.00 still due C, and demands that T turn over Blackacre to E for administration as part of B's estate to satisfy C's debt pro tanto. Y also demands Blackacre from T. In a proper proceeding T seeks instructions from the Court which orders him to deliver Blackacre to E for administration as part of B's estate. Is the order of the Court correct?

Answer and Analysis

The answer is yes. A's will gave B an equitable life estate with a general power of appointment as to the remainder in fee simple in Blackacre. If a general power of appointment is not exercised then the creditors of the donee of the power can not subject to their claims the property subject to the power. The reason for such principle is this—the donee of the power has in no way exercised over the property the dominion of an owner and it is still a part of the property or estate of the donor of the power. But when the donee of a general power of appointment has exercised the power in favor of either a volunteer or a creditor of the donee, then to the extent that the donee's other property is insufficient to pay his debts the property subject to the power may be subjected to the claims of the donee's creditors.

The reason for the above principle is this—for some purposes a general power of appointment is the equivalent of ownership itself. When the donee of such a general power of appointment has exercised the power, he has for all practical purposes exerted a dominion over the property which is equivalent to the power an owner exercises over property of which he is the absolute owner. This is true whether he exercises such general power by deed or by will. He could do no more by executing a deed or devising by will than he is doing by exercising the general power of appointment. One cannot by devising property by will, cut off his creditors from subjecting such property to their claims if there is not enough other property of the testator. The devisees take subject to the claims of the devisor's creditors.

By analogy an appointee under a general power of appointment also takes subject to the claims of the donee's creditors. Of course this process of reasoning is in conflict with the general view that the appointee under a power takes title from the donor and not from the donee of the power, and that the donee is not the owner of the property. But it seems to be settled as part of our common law procedure in satisfying the creditors of the donee of a general power of appointment to take the property subject to the power to the extent only that other property of the donee is insufficient to pay his creditors. Applying such principle to our case when the donee's executor, E, had exhausted all other property in B's estate and there still remained $10,000.00 as an unpaid debt to creditor, C, then Blackacre may be subjected to such debt. In this case it will exhaust all of Blackacre and C will still have $5,000.00 unpaid on his debt due from the decedent donee of the power, B. The result is that the appointee under the general power, Y, will take no interest in Blackacre. Whether the trustee, T, or the executor, E, should make the distribution of Blackacre or the proceeds therefrom to the creditors of the donee of the power or the appointee, or to both, is a matter of convenience and local procedure. See Restatement of Property §§ 327, 329; Simes, 136 et seq.

Note

For more detailed treatment of Powers of Appointment, see Restatement of Property §§ 318–369; Simes, 121–179.

Appointment and Perpetuities; Class Closing; Capture

CASE 110: T bequeaths a fund to F in active trust for A for life and then for whomever A by will appoints, and in default of appointment to the M charity. At the time of T's death, A is single and has no children. Years later A dies testate, his will providing that he "bequeaths, devises and appoints all my property, real and personal, including all property with respect to which I have a power of appointment, to all the children of my son B, it is my express wish that no children of B shall be excluded regardless of when they are born." At A's death, B is 32 years old, married, and the father of two minor children, C1 and C2. B and W, the surviving widow of A, are A's sole heirs, each being entitled to one half of A's intestate property. F asks the court for instructions as to the proper distribution of the trust fund and his obligations thereto, and he joins as defendants X, the executor of A's estate, B, M, C1, C2, W, and requests a guardian to represent unborn children of B. Who is entitled to the trust fund?

Answer and Analysis

The answer is this—X is entitled to the fund to be distributed as intestate property of A to B and W equally.

This case involves a number of important principles concerning the rule against perpetuities, powers of appointment and class gifts. Starting with perpetuities, the general testamentary power given to A is itself valid since it will necessarily be exercised if at all at A's death. See supra case 105. In determining the validity of an appointment under the rule, the courts distinguish between an appointment under a general power presently exercisable on the one hand, and an appointment under a special power or a general testamentary power on the other. In the case of a general power presently exercisable, the period of the rule is measured from the time of the exercise of the power. In the case of an appointment under a special power, and under a general power to appoint by will only, the period of the rule is measured from the time of the creation of the power.

Applying these principles to the above case, since we are dealing with a general testamentary power, the period of the rule is measured from the death of T, the time the power was created. A later appointed to all the children of his son B. The facts tell us at the time of T's death (creation of the power), B was not yet born since A was single and had no children. Thus, as viewed from the creation of the power, we have a limitation to the children of an unborn person. It is obvious that the interests of such persons might vest beyond the period of the rule, and therefore the gift to such children is invalid.

In testing the validity of an appointment and measuring the period from the creation of the power, the courts take cognizance of the appointment as actually made rather than invalidate an appointment simply because an invalid appointment could have been made. This so-called "second look" doctrine, however, is of no help in the instant case. A did in fact appoint to the children of an unborn person, and the interests of these children might well vest too remotely.

Class closing rules may sometimes save a gift under the rule by excluding potential afterborn persons. In the instant case A appointed the children of B, and there were two children of B living at A's death. Measured from the creation of the power, A was a life in being, and if the class would close to exclude other children of B so that C1 and C2 would take immediately, the gift would be valid since it vested at the end of a life in being, namely A's. Since this is an immediate gift to the children of B, the class would normally close at A's death, and C1 and C2 would be the only ones entitled to share in the trust funds. However, A specifically provided that no child of B should be excluded regardless of when he should be born. Thus, the normal class closing rule, being only a matter of construction and convenience, will not apply. The class is treated as a unit in applying the rule, and since as to afterborn children the interest might vest too remotely, the gift to the children of B fails.

In the case of the non-exercise of a power of appointment, (powers in trust excluded), the property normally passes to the takers in default, or if there are none, it reverts to the donor's estate. An invalid or ineffective appointment can, of course, be regarded as no appointment, but in the case of a general power of appointment by will, the doctrine of "capture" is frequently used to "capture" the property for the donee's estate. This is based on the theory of an implied alternative appointment to the donee's estate. In the instant case, the donee exercised the power by a blending provision in which he expressly disposed of both owned and appointed property in the same manner. In such a case, the courts generally conclude that the testator treated the appointive property as his own, and if the appointment fails, there is an implied alternative appointment to his own estate. The presence or absence of a taker in default should have no bearing on the application of capture since it is the donee's intent that controls, and not the donor's. Thus, in the instant case M charity, the taker in default, is not entitled to the fund since it is captured for the donee's estate.

Thus far, we have concluded that the appointment is invalid, and that M charity does not take. If there is an appointment to the donee's estate, can the blending provision in the will then dispose of the funds to the children of B as owned property of A? If so, since the period of the rule concerning owned property of A is measured from A's death, and since B is now a life in being, the gift in favor of all of B's children would be valid since the interest of each must vest no later than the death of B and the period of gestation. To so hold, however, would in effect abolish the rule that the effectiveness of an appointment under a general testamentary power is measured from the creation of the power. Thus, the appointment cannot be validated by that circuitous reasoning. Since there is no other clause mentioned which disposes of this appointive property, it shall pass as intestate property of A. Since B and W are A's sole heirs, the fund shall be divided between them. See Simes, 149, 207, 292 et seq.; Burby, 385, 405, 410, 424 et seq.; Fiduciary Trust Co. v. Mishou, 321 Mass. 615, 75 N.E.2d 3 (1947).

CASE 111: A devises his estate in trust to pay the income to B for life and then to transfer the estate to such of B's children as B shall by will appoint. B dies intestate survived by three children, B1, B2 and B3, and no children predeceased him. What happens to the property that was in A's estate?

Answer and Analysis

The answer is this —B1, B2 and B3 share equally. Here there is a special power of appointment with no gift in default, and a failure to exercise the appointment. It would be possible, of course, to have the property revert to A's estate and have it pass by intestacy, but the courts do not do this. Instead, they give it to the permissible appointees equally on the rationale that this was a power in trust, a mandatory or imperative power, or that there was an implied gift in default of appointment to the class of permissible appointees.

The theory of a power in trust or mandatory power is that the donee is under a duty to exercise the power at some time and under some circumstances. When the donee fails to exercise such a power, the property is distributed to the objects of the power in equal shares. One theory by which this is accomplished is that equity imposes a constructive trust on those who take in default in order to prevent unjust enrichment. In some jurisdictions statutes expressly provide for distribution to the permissible objects on failure to appoint. Another theory employed is an implied gift in default of appointment to the objects of the class equally.

If in the above case, a child of B had predeceased him, that child's estate would not have shared in the appointive property. This is because B could not have appointed him, and there was no direct gift to the children of B. If, however, the devise had been ".   .   . to pay to B for life and then to give the corpus to B's children but B can appoint by will and divide the property amongst his children .   .   .," then, on default of appointment, there is authority that the estate of the deceased child would take a share. This is because there is a direct and immediate gift to all the children of B, subject, of course, to be divested on his exercise of the power, but not contingent on surviving and not subject to being divested on not surviving B. See Lambert v. Thwaites, Court of Chancery, 1866, L.R. 2 Eq. 151; Simes, 169 et seq.

———

CASE 112: S devised a fund in trust to pay the income to his daughter, D, for life, and then to transfer the fund as D shall by last will appoint among her children and other blood relatives, and in default of appointment to the X charity. On her death without children, D's will appointed $250,000 to her cousin, C, and the balance, about $500,000, to her brother B. Among D's papers was a letter written by C in which he stated: "I am informed that by your last will you have bequeathed to me $250,000. In the event that you predecease me and I receive that bequest, I promise and agree to pay to your husband, H, $100,000." Additional evidence shows that in a former will C had been appointed $50,000, and that D had reached an understanding with C to increase his appointment to $250,000 in return for C's promise to give $100,000 to H. To how much is C entitled?

Answer and Analysis

The better answer, it is believed, is $150,000; but it is conceivable that a court might permit him to receive only $50,000; while the case on which the hypothet is based voided the entire appointment to C and let him keep nothing.

This case deals with fraudulent or excessive execution of powers of appointment. The invalidity of D's appointment stems from the fact that D appointed an object of the power, C, for the purpose of benefiting a non-object, H. In the case of special powers, the donee, of course, is limited in his choice of appointees to those designated in the creating instrument. Since the donee cannot appoint directly to a non-object, he cannot accomplish such a purpose indirectly by appointing to an object for the purpose of benefiting a non-object. In the instant case, H, not being a blood relative of D, is not a permissible appointee.

In case of an excessive appointment, the courts frequently categorize it as fraudulent and void. The term fraudulent may be somewhat of a misnomer since actual fraud need not be involved, and a more accurate categorization might be voidable rather than void, since it is generally held that a bona fide purchaser of the appointed property is protected. Where there is such an excessive or fraudulent appointment, sometimes the entire appointment is regarded as inseparable and invalid. This should follow, of course, when there is no intent to confer any benefit on the appointee but, instead, the intent is to benefit solely the non-object. However, there is authority that the appointment should stand to the extent that there is an intent to benefit objects of the power independent of the purpose to benefit non-objects. Thus, in the instant case, since C was to have $150,000 even if he carried out his agreement, the appointment can be sustained to the extent of $150,000. On the other hand, if the court concludes that the intent was to benefit C only to the extent of $50,000 as provided for in the revoked will, and that the additional $100,000 appointment was only an inducement to get him to enter into an unauthorized transaction, the appointment seemingly could be sustained to the extent of $50,000. Finally, it is possible to view the entire appointment as part of an illegal scheme to benefit a non-object and void the entire appointment to C. This was the result in Matter of Carroll, 274 N.Y. 288, 8 N.E.2d 864 (1937); but see the report of the Appellate Division, 247 App.Div. 11, 286 N.Y.S. 307 (1936), which would have sustained the appointment to the extent of $150,000.

In the instant case, the appointment of $500,000 to D's brother, B, is valid and will be sustained. To whatever extent the $250,000 appointment to C is held invalid (and at least $100,000 will be so held), such sums should go in default of appointment to the X charity. See Simes, 157–159; Matter of Carroll, supra.

CASE 113: A devises $600,000 to T in trust to pay the income to B for his life and then to transfer the fund to such of B's children as he shall appoint by will, and in default of appointment to transfer the fund to the children of B equally.

Problem (1). B enters into an agreement with his son, B1, whereby B in consideration of B1's agreement to enter into the family business agrees to appoint the entire $600,000 to B1. At B's death, his will appoints the fund to be divided equally among his three children, B1, B2 and B3. May B1 get specific performance of the contract to appoint to him alone, or in the alternative, may he recover damages from B's estate for breach of contract?

Problem (2). B executes a deed of release and delivers it to B1 on B1's entering into the family business which deed recites that B releases, gives up and quitclaims his power of appointment. At B's death, his will purports to exercise the power of appointment in favor of his other children, B2 and B3. Is B1 entitled to anything?

Problem (3). On B1's entering into the family business, and in consideration therefor, B enters into an agreement with B1 whereby B agrees that he will not exercise his power of appointment in such a manner that B1 will receive less than $100,000. On B's death, his will purports to exercise the power of appointment in favor of his other children, B2 and B3 equally. Is B1 entitled to anything, and if so, how much and by what means?

Answers and Analyses

Answer to Problem (1). B1 may not get specific performance of the contract to appoint, nor can he get damages from B's estate for breach of contract. He is entitled to $200,000 pursuant to the appointment, and no more.

The power in the instant case is a special testamentary power. A contract to appoint under a special power in a manner to benefit a non-object is void. Thus, in this case, the purpose of the contract may be viewed as intended to benefit B, a non-object, by persuading B1 to enter into the family business. Further, since B is a non-object of the power and he is a party to the contract, upholding the contract could be viewed as benefiting B, a non-object, to the extent that he or his estate would be liable for damages in the event that he breached the contract. Thus, on this basis the contract is void and unenforceable.

Further, the contract is void for another reason. B had a power to appoint by will only. The donor intended the donee to have discretion as to the exercise of the power all during the donee's lifetime. To the extent that a contract to appoint such a power would be upheld, the donee in effect has exercised a testamentary power inter vivos. The American courts hold that a contract to appoint a testamentary power is wholly void, and that such a contract can neither be enforced by specific performance nor by damages. A contract to appoint a general power presently exercisable, however, is valid as such a contract can be considered equivalent to an appointment. See Simes, 166 et seq.

Answer to Problem (2). Under the facts of problem (2), B1 is entitled to $200,000.

Although testamentary powers cannot be exercised inter vivos, and although contracts to enforce such powers are void and unenforceable, it is now generally held that all powers of appointment, except powers in trust, are releasable. In the instant case B's release was effective to terminate his power of appointment. Therefore, his later purported exercise was invalid, and the property passed on his death to the takers in default equally, namely B1, B2 and B3. Many jurisdictions have statutes providing for the release of powers of appointment, but even in the absence of statute, such powers are generally releasable except for powers in trust. See Simes, 173 et seq.

Answer to Problem (3). Under the facts of Problem (3), B1 is entitled to $100,000.

The agreement that B1 should receive no less than $100,000 cannot, of course, take effect as a contract to appoint, as such a contract is invalid in the case of a testamentary power. Testamentary powers, however, are releasable, and a contract not to appoint can be given effect as a release. There is no requirement that a release be total, but, instead, a power which is releasable may be released as to part of the property. It is also believed that a releasable power can be released as to all but a designated class or classes of persons who are its objects, but this, of course, is not involved in the instant case.

With the foregoing principles in mind, what was the effect of the contract not to exercise the power in such a manner that B1 would receive less than $100,000? It was a pro tanto release of the power. In order for B1 to get $100,000 by way of release, B had to give up his power of appointment to the extent that there would be sufficient sums to go to the takers in default so that each would get $100,000 in default of appointment. In this case, since there were three remaindermen or takers in default, of which B1 was one, there was a release of the power to the extent of $300,000. Thus, B1 gets $100,000 as a taker in default along with B2 and B3, and B2 and B3 share the other $300,000 equally as appointees. See In re Evered, [1910] 2 Ch. 147; Simes, 178.

SUMMARY OF CASES IN CHAPTER VII

1.   RULE IN SHELLEY'S CASE

Case 87. The Rule in Shelley's Case is not limited in its application to a remainder following a life estate in possession—the life estate may be one in remainder. The Rule applies only to freehold interests, never to chattel interests. If the requirements of the rule are met, it operates as a rule of law, regardless of the clearly expressed intention of the grantor to the contrary. The requirements are: (1) a conveyance creating a life estate in the ancestor; (2) the same conveyance must create both the life estate, and a remainder in favor of the ancestor's heirs; and (3) both estates must be of the same quality, either legal or equitable. Two steps are essential to the ultimate result giving the fee simple (or fee tail) to the ancestor: (a) the rule must operate giving the remainder to the ancestor; and (b) there must be a merger by which the remainder swallows the life estate. Result: fee simple in the transferee.

Case 88. The Rule in Shelley's Case does not apply in a case where the word "heirs" is used to mean "children" or "issue". In the United States the rule will apply when the word heirs is used merely to indicate the first generation of persons to take by intestate succession. Whether the word "heirs" is used in one sense or another is a problem of construction.

Case 89. In a jurisdiction where the Rule in Shelley's Case has been abolished, the intent of the grantor and the applicable statute control. Thus, A to B for life remainder to B's heirs, gives B a life estate and his heirs, determinable at his death, a contingent remainder under a commonly employed statute. In such case the contingent remainder becomes immediately an estate in possession at B's death.

2. DOCTRINE OF WORTHIER TITLE; INTER VIVOS BRANCH

Case 90. The simplest case representing the doctrine and its application is, A to B for life, remainder to the heirs of A. Result: B has a life estate, the remainder is void and there is a reversion in A. In effect it reads merely, A to B for life. The doctrine or rule requires only (1) a conveyance of real property inter vivos, and (2) a limitation to the heirs of the grantor. Taking title by descent was considered worthier than taking title by purchase, so if A makes a limitation to his heirs he must have intended such heirs to take by the worthier title.

Case 91. Originally the Doctrine of Worthier Title was a rule of law and not a rule of construction. Today it has become a rule of construction by which the intention of the grantor is found and followed. But the inference that the grantor's heirs are to take by descent rather than by purchase still continues, and the grantor by express language in the deed must show that he intends his "heirs" to take as purchasers for the Doctrine not to apply.

Case 92. At one time there was a rule analogous to the Doctrine of Worthier Title applicable to devises by will. Today there is no such rule and the Doctrine of Worthier Title is not applicable to devises by will—it is limited to inter vivos conveyances of land.

3. RULE AGAINST PERPETUITIES

Case 93. If an interest offends the rule it is void ab initio. The destructibility rule, if applicable, will save a contingent remainder in real property from invalidity under the rule against perpetuities when the remainder is limited to take effect at the end of one or more life estates of persons in being. This is because of the fact that the remainder will either vest in possession or fail completely at the end of the preceding life estate. In considering the certainty of vesting or failing, possibilities and not probabilities control.

Case 94. An interest is valid under the common law rule if it vests in interest within the period of the rule; it is not necessary that it vest in possession within the period of the rule.

Case 95. A gift is valid if it is certain either to vest or fail within the period of the rule. Thus, a remainder to the children of an individual living at his death is valid under the common law rule.

Case 96. An interest is valid under the common law rule against perpetuities if there is no possibility that it may vest beyond relevant lives in being plus the period of gestation plus 21 years. Thus, a limitation to the first child of a living person who attains the age of 21 is valid.

Case 97. The measuring lives need not be specifically mentioned in the instrument if they can be determined by implication. Thus, a devise to the testator's grandchildren who reach 21 is valid as the testator's children are the measuring lives. However, an inter vivos conveyance to the grantor's grandchildren who reach 21 is invalid if no grandchildren are 21 at the time because of the possibility that the grantor may have more children, and such subsequent born children are not in being when the instrument takes effect.

Case 98. The period of the rule is measured from the time the instrument takes effect, and the time for vesting is calculated accordingly. In the case of a will, the period is measured from the death of the testator; in the case of a deed, from the date of delivery. Circumstances at the effective date of the instrument control; and possibilities rather than probabilities determine the validity of the limitations.

Case 99. A remainder cannot follow a fee simple estate nor take effect in derogation of the preceding freehold estate. An executory interest in fee simple following a fee simple subject to a remote condition subsequent is void as being in violation of the rule against perpetuities. The rule against perpetuities in the United States, contrary to the rule in England, has no application to a right of re-entry for condition broken or power of termination.

Case 100. When, under the rule against perpetuities, no life in being appears as a measuring life, then the contingent interest must vest within the gross period of 21 years from the time of its creation, which, in the case of a will is counted from the time of the death of the testator. Absolute interests limited to vest after administrative contingencies are frequently held void.

Case 101. The rule against perpetuities applies to an option agreement to purchase land not connected with or incident to a lease, and if the interest of the optionee may not vest within the period of the rule, the option is void. The validity of the option is determined as of the time when the option is created and not by events which happen subsequent thereto.

Case 102. For the purpose of the rule against perpetuities every living person is conclusively presumed capable of having children as long as he lives. Under such rule a limitation in the conveying instrument must be construed as of the time when such instrument takes effect which, in the case of a will, is the time of the death of the testator.

Case 103. A gift limited to a class is considered a unit and is not divisible, and if any member of the class cannot qualify to take under the rule against perpetuities, the entire gift must fail. If, on the other hand, the members of the class are to take not as a class but as individuals, then the gift will not fail and those individuals who can qualify will take according to the limitations in the instrument. Similarly, where there are sub-classes, the validity of each sub-class is determined separately.

Case 104. A general power of appointment presently exercisable is considered the equivalent of ownership of property. Hence, if one has such a general power of appointment over property he can exercise such power and alienate the property. Thus, if one can alienate the property the rule against perpetuities is not offended. So in order for a general power to be valid under the rule it must be exercisable, but not necessarily exercised, during the period allowed by the rule.

Case 105. A special power of appointment is not the equivalent of property because it must be either exercised in a limited way or in favor of a limited class of persons. To be valid under the rule against perpetuities, a special power of appointment is required to be exercised so that the interest in property thereby created will vest within the period of the rule. If it is possible to exercise a special power of appointment later than a life in being and 21 years after its creation, then the power is void from its inception.

Case 106. An accumulation is the withholding of income by the trustee for a longer period than is required for ordinary trust administration. If a limitation requires accumulations to be made by the trustee for a period longer than the rule against perpetuities, and the beneficial interest is contingent, then the rule applies and the equitable interest is void for failure to vest within the period of the rule. If the interest must vest within the period of the rule, the interest is valid. If the interest is vested and the accumulations are to continue for a period longer than the rule against perpetuities, then a rule at common law analogous to the rule against perpetuities, makes void the limitation for accumulations, and the beneficiary may require the trustee to turn over the assets to such beneficiary.

Case 107. An indestructible private trust is one which the court will not terminate by decree when contrary to the settlor's intention and which cannot be terminated by any of the parties. Even though in such trust both legal and equitable titles are vested, it does clog the alienability of the property and should not be permitted to last longer from its creation than the period permissible under the rule against perpetuities. Any limitation requiring an indestructible trust to last longer than the rule against perpetuities is void and the beneficiary has the right immediately to a decree terminating the trust. Such principles apply to honorary trusts and to trusts for the benefit of unincorporated associations, but charitable or public trusts are valid even though indestructible and in perpetuity.

4. POWERS OF APPOINTMENT

Case 108. A special power of appointment is one in which the donee is limited in his appointment to a person or persons other than himself or his estate. A general power of appointment permits the donee to exercise the power in favor of himself or his estate or to any other person or persons. A special power of appointment is exclusive when the donee in its exercise may exclude one or more persons from the group to be benefited; it is non-exclusive when the donee in the exercise of the power must include all members of the designated class or group, and each must get a substantial benefit under the power, but the donee in the exercise of the power may make the shares of the appointees quite unequal. The creditors of the donee of a special power of appointment cannot subject to their claims the property subject to the special power. The appointees under a special power of appointment take their title from the donor of the power and not from the donee of the power of appointment.

Case 109. If a general power of appointment is not exercised the creditors of the general power cannot subject to their claims the property subject to the power of appointment. But if such general power of appointment is exercised in favor of a volunteer or a creditor of the donee, then the appointee takes the property subject to the claims of the creditors of the donee, to the extent that the donee's other property is insufficient to satisfy his creditors. In such case the exercise of the general power of appointment is considered equivalent to the dominion of an owner over the property.

Case 110. The validity of an appointment under a general testamentary power is measured for purposes of the rule against perpetuities from the creation of the power. The circumstances existing at the time the power is exercised and the appointment actually made are taken into consideration. Rules of construction as to closing of classes yield to contrary expressions of intent in the creating instrument. An ineffective or invalid exercise of a general power of appointment in the will of a donee results in the appointive property being captured for the donee's estate when the ineffective or invalid appointment is exercised by a general blending provision. The doctrine of capture is also employed according to substantial authority when there is an invalid testamentary appointment of a general power in trust, although logically whether the appointment is in trust or not should make no difference. The real basis for the application of "capture" in the case of an ineffective testamentary appointment of a general power is that of an implied alternative appointment to the donee's estate.

Case 111. A power in trust or mandatory power exists when there is a special power in favor of a reasonably defined class of persons and no takers in default. On failure to exercise such a power, the appointive property is distributed to the class of permissible appointees equally. This result is sometimes sustained on the theory of an implied gift in default of appointment.

Case 112. The appointment to objects of a special power for the purpose of benefiting non-objects is fraudulent and void. To the extent that there is a purpose to benefit objects of the power, the appointment may be sustained according to some authorities, but others maintain that the appointment is inseparable and void in its entirety. In those cases where there is no intent to benefit permissible objects, the entire appointment should be held void, but when there is an intent to benefit objects, the appointment should be held valid to that extent. When the appointment is partially invalid, the valid should stand unless it can be fairly inferred that the donee would rather have the entire sum pass in default.

Case 113. (1) A contract to exercise a special power to benefit a non-object is void. Similarly, a contract to exercise a testamentary power is void.

(2) All powers of appointment, except powers in trust, are releasable even in the absence of statute.

(3) Releasable powers may be partially as well as totally released. A contract not to appoint may be given effect as a release, and a contract not to appoint in such a manner that a permissible object, who is also a taker in default, will receive no less than a designated amount may be given effect as a partial release.

Chapter VIII

LANDLORD AND TENANT

1. Types of Estates.
2. General Principles.
    a. Delivery of Possession.
        Legal Gems.
        Cases.
    b. Warranty of Fitness or Suitability.
        Legal Gems.
        Cases.
    c. Tenant's Duty to Repair and Maintain Premises.
        Legal Gems.
        Cases.
    d. Illegality and Frustration of Purpose.
        Legal Gems.
        Cases.
    e. Eminent Domain.
        Legal Gems.
        Cases.
    f. Quiet Enjoyment: Miscellaneous Provisions.
        Legal Gems.
        Cases.
3. Rents.
    Legal Gems.
    Cases.
4. Abandonment by Tenant: Remedies of Landlord; Security Deposits.
    Legal Gems.
    Cases.
5. Residential Leases.
    Legal Gems.
    Cases.
Summary of Cases in Chapter VIII.

---

1. TYPES OF ESTATES

For the different types of estates held by tenants and their characteristics, see Chapter V—5, Tenancies Less than Freehold.

2. GENERAL PRINCIPLES

LEGAL GEMS

a. DELIVERY OF POSSESSION

1. A landlord impliedly warrants that the tenant will have a legal right to possession of the premises at the beginning of the term.

2. There is a conflict of authority as to whether the landlord has an obligation to deliver actual possession of the premises to the tenant at the beginning of the term.

(a) Under the "American" view, the landlord does not have an obligation to deliver actual possession, but under the "English" view he does.

(b) There is substantial authority for both positions in the United States, but modern policy favors the "English" position. Restatement, Second, Property (Landlord and Tenant) § 6.2, Comment (a).

3. Either the new tenant or the landlord may evict a former tenant who wrongfully holds over into the term of the new tenant.

———

CASE 114: L, owner in fee simple of Blackacre, by a writing leased the premises to T for a 10 year period, March 1, 1980 to March 1, 1990. When this lease was made Blackacre was occupied by tenant D whose term expired at midnight on February 28, 1980. D held over his term and remained in continuous possession of Blackacre. There was no express agreement in the lease that L agreed to deliver possession of Blackacre to T on March 1, 1980, nor for quiet enjoyment thereof by T. On Mar. 3, 1980, T commenced two actions in court: (a) one against L for breach of contract for not delivering possession of Blackacre to T on March 1st; and (b) the other against D to eject D from Blackacre. May T succeed in either action?

Answer and Analysis

As to T's action against L for breach of contract, the result depends upon the jurisdiction. The suit against L must be based on an alleged implied contract by the landlord to put the lessee in possession at the beginning of the term. The "English" rule applied in many American cases holds there is such an implied obligation or duty on the part of the landlord. The "American" rule is to the contrary. All the cases agree that the landlord impliedly agrees that the lease gives the tenant a legal right to the possession of the demised premises with quiet enjoyment, and assures the tenant that there is no legal obstacle to the enforcement of such right. But the question is not that. It is whether the landlord has impliedly agreed to enforce such right against a trespasser or a holdover tenant.

In support of the "American" rule, it is argued that although T would not knowingly have purchased a lawsuit by having to run the risk of suing D, it is also true that T could have protected himself against such by an express provision in the lease. Not having done so, should the law impose on the landlord the burden of holding the tenant harmless as to the torts of a third person? The traditional "American" view would answer in the negative and leave T to his action against the wrongdoer, D. All the cases agree that except as to the first day of the term, T's exclusive remedy is against the wrongdoer, and that T has no action against the landlord for any trespass by a third person after the term has begun.

Arguments in favor of imposing on the landlord the duty of delivering actual possession reason that this is what the tenant has bargained for, that the landlord is in a better position to know the status of the property and whether any possessor is there rightfully, that only the landlord can dispossess any person in possession prior to the effective date of the lease, and that the tenant will obtain less than his bargain if he has to pay the costs of ousting the wrongful possessor. Modern policy favors this "English" rule.

As to the eviction of the holdover tenant, either L or T may bring the action. As between T on the one side and the holdover tenant, D, on the other, it is clear that T has a right to eject D. D is a typical tenant at sufferance having a bare possession with no right at all. When L leased to T there was a conveyance of an estate in the land demised and with it went the right of immediate possession. T had the right to enforce such right against D and against anyone else without title paramount to that of L. See Hannan v. Dusch, 154 Va. 356, 153 S.E. 824, 70 A.L.R. 141 (1930), for the traditional "American" view; Cheshire v. Thurston, 70 Ariz. 299, 219 P.2d 1043 (1950); Restatement, Second, Property (Landlord and Tenant) § 6.2, Comment and Reporter's Note for the "English" view.

b. WARRANTY OF FITNESS OR SUITABILITY
LEGAL GEMS

1. Traditionally, the landlord did not impliedly warrant that the leased premises were suitable for any particular purpose, and he was not liable for a dangerous condition existing on the leased premises. Normally, the doctrine of caveat emptor prevailed, but there were exceptions as noted in Gems 5, 7 and 8 infra.

2. As to the implied covenant of habitability, see RESIDENTIAL LEASES, Part 5 infra, Gem 7.

3. The trend toward greater protection of the residential tenant by applying contract principles is not as widespread in the commercial setting where traditional property concepts are still likely to prevail.

4. A landlord may be liable in tort to the tenant, his guests, licensees and invitees, if at the commencement of the lease there is a dangerous condition which the landlord knows or should know about, and the discovery of which would not likely occur by the tenant exercising due care.

5. Even before the modern trend of extensive protection for residential tenants, in many jurisdictions a landlord in the lease of a completely furnished dwelling for a short period of time impliedly warranted the fitness of the premises and the furnishings. Thus, if injury resulted from defects therein, the landlord was liable.

6. Today, many jurisdictions have abrogated the landlord's tort immunity in favor of a caveat vendor (lessor) approach. The land-

lord in these states may now be held liable in tort to the tenant, his guests, licensees, and invitees on either a theory of negligence or breach of an implied warranty of habitability. See Case 117.

7.   Under the common law and in the absence of a statute or a covenant in the lease, and except as changed in modern times as to residential leases, the landlord is under no duty to maintain the leased premises in a state of repair.

8.   Although he may be under no duty to repair, if the landlord does undertake to repair and does so negligently, he is liable in tort for resulting injuries.

———

CASE 115: L owned a two-story building in which the first floor was rented and used as a grocery store and the second floor was divided into two apartments. Both apartments were served by an inside stairway and the back apartment was served by an outside stairway of wooden construction which was built sometime prior to 1923. In July 1955, L rented the back apartment to T. There was no covenant to repair by L. The outside stairway was leased as part of the back apartment and was not used in common by the other tenant. On October 3, 1955, T's invitee P, fell to the ground and suffered injuries when one of the treads gave way while he was using the back stairway. P sues L for damages for his injury. May he recover?

Answer and Analysis

The answer is yes. Under the common law, in the absence of a written agreement, the lessor is under no obligation to make repairs on things damaged or deteriorating after the start of the lease. The lessor has no responsibility to persons on the land for conditions developing after the lease begins. The lessor is, however, under an obligation to disclose to the lessee concealed, dangerous conditions existing when the possession is transferred and which are known to the lessor. Today some courts require that the lessor have actual knowledge of the existence of the condition before he is under any duty to disclose it. The majority of courts hold, however, that it is sufficient if the lessor has information which could lead a reasonable man to suspect that the danger exists, and that he must at least disclose such information to the lessee. Since the lessor in this case was negligent in not correcting the dangerous situation or making the lessee aware of the dangerous condition, liability is imposed.

The common law required that the lessor have actual knowledge of the existence of the dangerous condition before he was under any duty to take precautions against such a hazard. In the instant case, since L knew or should have known that the stairs were in a state of disrepair, he had a duty to correct the situation or to warn the tenant. Thus, he is liable for injuries sustained by P. Even if L did not have actual knowledge of the danger he would still be liable if he had information which would lead a reasonable man to suspect that the danger existed. Today in many states statutes impose a duty upon lessors to maintain leased premises in a state of repair. This is especially true with respect to multiple dwellings. See Johnson v. O'Brien, 258 Minn. 502, 105 N.W.2d 244, 88 A.L.R.2d 577 (1960); Burby, 119–122.

CASE 116: L owned Blackacre in fee simple and leased it to T for 30 days. It was a fully furnished utility apartment. Among the furnishings was a double decker bed. Access to the upper bunk was by means of a ladder which hooked over the side board of the upper deck. The hooks on the end of the ladder were secured by ¾ inch screws which were screwed in "with the grain of the wood". T ascended the ladder for the purpose of making the bed. The screws securing the hooks on the end of the ladder came loose, the ladder fell, and with it the tenant, T, who was injured. T sues L. May he recover?

Answer and Analysis

The answer is yes. The general common law rule is that the landlord does not impliedly warrant that the leased premises are fit for the purpose for which they are leased. However, even before the modern developments in residential leasings (see infra Part 5), many cases made an exception to such rule when the lease was for a very short time and the dwelling unit was fully furnished, and when it was considered that the furnishings and equipment constituted the principal subject of the lease. Under such circumstances it is held that the lessor impliedly covenants that the premises and the equipment are fit for the purpose for which they are apparently intended. While the cases indicate such liability is based on breach of contract and should be confined within narrow limits, it is reminiscent of the liability imposed on the manufacturer and retailer of chattels such as ladders and automobile wheels where the furnishers of such articles are held liable in tort on implied warranty of fitness. See Hacker v. Nitschke, 310 Mass. 754, 39 N.E.2d 644, 139 A.L.R. 257 (1942), Burby, 148–149.

CASE 117: L occupies the ground floor of a two-story apartment building which he owns. The second floor of the premises, which is serviceable by an outside stairway, is occupied by T, who is the regular babysitter for P's four-year-old daughter. While in the control of T, the child falls to her death from the outside stairway. There is no apparent cause for the fall except that the stairway is dangerously steep, and that the railing is insufficient to prevent the child from falling over the side. P sues L in tort for the death of the child. May P recover?

Answer and Analysis

The answer is yes according to recent authorities. Under the old common law the landlord was generally held immune from tort liability. This immunity was subject to a few strictly construed exceptions. The landlord would be held liable if: (1) there was a hidden and undisclosed defect or danger known only to the landlord; (2) the particular dangerous area was a common area over which the landlord had exclusive control; or (3) the landlord had negligently repaired the premises. Thus, in the instant case, L would not be held liable under the old common law because there was no hidden defect, common area under the exclusive control of the landlord, or negligent repairs by the landlord.

However, the trend of authority has been to abolish the landlord's tort immunity and to hold the landlord liable on either a theory of negligence or breach of implied warranty of habitability. Thus, in those jurisdictions, the landlord now has the affirmative duty of repairing and maintaining the premises in a nondangerous manner. In the instant case, L's failure to provide a more protective railing and a safer angle of descent will subject him to liability for the death of the child. See Sargent v. Ross, 113 N.H. 388, 308 A.2d 528 (1973); Restatement, Second, Property (Landlord and Tenant) § 17.1, and Reporter's Note to Introductory Note to Ch. 17.

––––––––

CASE 118: Landlord, the owner of a multi-level building, executed a written lease of designated space to T for five (5) years at a stipulated rent. T was going to use the premises as a jewelry store and the specific business purpose was made clear to L both in the contract negotiations and in the lease. Six months after the store opened a burglary occurred in which entry was made through the ceiling of the vault area, which ceiling was also the floor of the second story of the building. A mechanical equipment access room was located over the jewelry store, and the floor of this room formed the ceiling of the jewelry store. This design allowed easy entry into the vault from above. May T recover against L?

Answer and Analysis

The answer is yes in a growing number of jurisdictions. Under traditional property concepts there would not exist any cause of action since the doctrine of caveat emptor, or in this case caveat lessee, would be strictly applied. L has no duty to inform about or repair any undesirable conditions at common law. However, some modern courts hold that L is under a basic duty to inform the prospective tenant of the conditions of the premises which might affect their suitability for the intended use. L breached this basic duty when he failed to inform T of the special ceiling condition. The particular needs of commercial tenants often require the leased premises to have specific attributes. Therefore, the duty of disclaiming any condition which might reasonably be undesirable from the tenant's point of view is basic. Further, because the duty to disclose under these circumstances *is* basic and the ultimate consequences foreseeable, liability may be imposed in spite of a broad exculpatory clause. Vermes v. American Dist. Tel. Co., 312 Minn. 33, 251 N.W.2d 101 (1977).

CASE 119: T was in possession of L's premises pursuant to an oral lease which was converted into a periodic tenancy from month to month by operation of law. T remained in possession for seven years, near the end of which time the plaster of the ceiling in the bedroom cracked and bulged. L repaired and replastered the ceiling thereby causing it to appear safe, but in fact it was not. Shortly after the repairs, and while T was asleep in bed, the plaster suddenly became loose and fell on T, causing injuries. In a suit by T against L for the injuries sustained, may T recover?

Answer and Analysis

The answer is yes. Under the common law there is no duty on L to make repairs during the continuance of the lease, unless, of course, the parties contract otherwise. Nevertheless, if the landlord undertakes to make repairs, he must make them in a nonnegligent manner. In the instant case the landlord did make the repairs and the evidence would warrant a finding that they were negligently made. Thus, he is liable whether he adds to the danger or simply fails to improve the defect.

Another point to note is that the periodic tenancy is a continuing one and that a new lease does not begin every month. Thus, L cannot rely on the principle that he is not liable unless there is a latent defect known to him and unknown to the tenant at the beginning of the lease. In this case the lease began many years before; the defect developed during the tenancy, and L made negligent repairs. See Janofsky v. Garland, 42 Cal.App.2d 655, 109 P.2d 750 (1941); Burby, 119.

---

c. Tenant's Duty to Repair and Maintain Premises

Legal Gems

1. Unless the tenant covenants to make repairs, his obligation in respect to maintenance is governed by the law of waste. A tenant is liable for permissive as well as voluntary waste, and thus is under an obligation to make tenantable repairs.

2. Where the subject matter of the lease is land with improvements, as distinguished from a lease of a part of a building, the tenant remains liable under his lease and is obligated to pay rent although the building or buildings are destroyed by fire, flood or other casualty, in the absence of a statute or covenant in the lease to the contrary.

———

CASE 120: L, being owner of Blackacre in fee simple, leased it furnished as a dwelling house to T for a period of five years. Towards the end of the second year of the term, a violent whirlwind dislodged and blew off two asbestos shingles from the roof of the house. T noticed a little rain leak through the roof where the shingles had been blown off but no damage was done at that time. Two weeks later and when T had had ample time to repair the roof, a violent rain came and the water which leaked through the hole in the roof did serious and extensive damage to the valuable oak floors in the rooms below. Later T looked at the public records and discovered that L had not paid his taxes on Blackacre. T proceeded to purchase tax title on Blackacre and thereafter refused to pay rent to L, making the claim that Blackacre was his own property. L sues T for rent and for damage to his floors. May L recover either?

Answer and Analysis

The answer is, he may recover the rent and also for the damage. This set of facts raises two principles concerning the position of a lessee: (a) the tenant is estopped to deny his landlord's title; and (b) the tenant for years is liable for permissive waste, which is another way of saying the lessee for a term is duty bound to make ordinary repairs. Every tenant gets his estate and the possession of the demised premises through his landlord. Having accepted such at the hands of the lessor the law does not thereafter permit him to deny the source of his benefits. Hence, while T had the right like any other person to buy in the tax title to Blackacre, he had no right to assert it against L during the term of the lease, at least, not without first surrendering the term to L. This estoppel finds its base on the permissive possession rather than on the lease, and upon giving up such possession to the landlord, then the lessee may assert a title hostile to that of the landlord or deny the latter's title. But such procedure does not necessarily relieve the tenant of his contractual liabilities to his landlord. In our case T is bound by the principle set forth. As to damage to L's floors caused by T's failure to replace the shingles on the roof, the liability rests squarely on T. A tenant for years is not bound to prevent the mere depreciation of structures on the leased premises on the one hand, nor is he required to rebuild a structure on the other. He is bound to make such ordinary repairs on the leased property as will avoid serious injury to the property from the elements. It would seem the replacing of the two shingles (of which T had knowledge), to prevent the serious injury to the floors would properly be classified as ordinary repairs, and that T should be liable for such permissive waste. See Townshend v. Moore, 33 N.J.L. 284 (Sup.Ct.1869); Suydam v. Jackson, 54 N.Y. 450 (1873), as to T's duty to make tenantable repairs; Burby, 35, 151; Cribbet, 209, 213.

---

d. ILLEGALITY AND FRUSTRATION OF PURPOSE

LEGAL GEMS

1. If land and improvements are leased for a particular purpose and such purpose cannot be accomplished because of structural defect or other violation of law which prevents use of the building for any purpose authorized under the lease, the tenant may rescind or avoid the lease. Under such circumstances the lease is considered illegal, and neither party can enforce it.

2. In those situations when the only use intended is legal and plausible at the inception of the lease but later becomes illegal or impossible because of a change of law, a typical "frustration of purpose" situation, the following principles apply:

> (a) If the lease permits the tenant to use the premises for only a single purpose, a later prohibition of law against such use will, according to the prevailing view, terminate the contract and relieve the tenant of any obligations thereunder. Kahn v. Wilhelm, 118 Ark. 239, 177 S.W. 403 (1915).

> (b) If the business of the lease is simply made less profitable by a law, rule, regulation or order, the tenant is not relieved of his obligations under the lease. Wood v. Bartolino, 48 N.M. 175, 146 P.2d 883 (1944).

> (c) Further, in some jurisdictions, even when there is complete or almost complete frustration of purpose, the obligation to pay rent is not relieved. Imbeschied v. Lerner, 241 Mass. 199, 135 N.E. 219 (1922). See generally Restatement, Second, Property (Landlord and Tenant) § 9.2, Reporter's Note.

CASE 121: L leased Blackacre to T for a period of five years at a designated rental to be paid monthly. At the end of two years of the term a fire burned and completely destroyed the dwelling house which was the principal subject of the lease. T moved to another dwelling house and refused to pay rent under his lease of Blackacre. There was no provision in the lease excusing the payment of rent by T. L sues T for rent under the lease. May he recover?

Answer and Analysis

The traditional answer has been yes in a majority of jurisdictions, but recent developments, particularly in residential housing, would change the result in most states, and relieve T of liability for any additional rent. In this case T has made an agreement under which he has covenanted to pay monthly for the use of land. This is rent. In another sense it is payment on the installment plan for an estate in land, a five year leasehold. It is always possible for the parties to provide in the lease for certain excuses for nonpayment of rent. But in this case there is no such provision in the lease. At common law the rule was this, if a tenant agreed to pay rent for land and the premises became totally uninhabitable during the term either by destruction thereof by fire, flood, unforeseen action of the elements or otherwise, nevertheless the tenant continued to be liable for the rent unless exempted therefrom by express provision of the lease. Hence, following the common law rule, T remains liable to L for the payment of rent under the lease. This is a harsh rule and an increasing number of states by statute, particularly in the residential area, have given relief against it. See Suydam v. Jackson, 54 N.Y. 450 (1887); also Standard Indus. Inc. v. Smith, 214 Md. 214, 133 A.2d 460, 61 A.L.R.2d 1433 (1957); Burby, 178–179; Restatement, Second, Property (Landlord and Tenant) § 5.4 and Reporter's Note; West's Fla.Stat.Ann. § 83.63 (1979).

———

CASE 122: L leased a building to T for a period of 9 years on the condition that it was only to be used as a restaurant and night club. After the payment of the first month's rent of $300., T applied for a restaurant and night club license. The department of licenses refused T a license on the grounds that the building was not fireproof. The Building Code provisions stated that the premises could not lawfully be used as a night club because it was not a fireproof building. T sues L for recovery of the rent paid and L counterclaims for past due rent. Who recovers?

Answer and Analysis

T does. Usually, when there is a lease which restricts the use of the property, and such use depends upon obtaining a license, the lessee assumes the risk of obtaining the license and if he doesn't, he still is held to the lease. This is because the granting or withholding of the license rests on the discretion of the licensing official and the lessee assumes the risk. If the lessee takes a lease without conditions under such circumstances, and binds himself absolutely for the payment of the rent, the courts will not relieve him from the contract. But where the granting of the license does not rest on discretion, but rather on an ordinance which made such a contemplated use illegal, and there are no other uses which the property can be used for under the lease, then the lessee is not liable under the lease and is entitled to his paid in rents because of the complete failure of consideration. See Economy v. S. B. & L. Bldg. Corp., 138 Misc. 296, 245 N.Y.S. 352 (1930); Burby, 148–150, 180 n. 45.

———

CASE 123: L, being owner in fee simple of Blackacre, leased it to T for 10 years with an express stipulation in the lease that no use of the land be made by T or his assigns other than carrying on the liquor business thereon. During the term, the 18th amendment to the U.S. Constitution and laws thereunder made it illegal to continue to carry on the liquor business. T refused to pay the rent provided for and L sues T for such rent. May L recover?

Answer and Analysis

The answer depends on the jurisdiction. In the majority of cases today the landlord will not be able to recover where there is a total or almost total frustration of purpose. The courts look for a way to avoid the harsh result under the old rule. Here the lease had an express stipulation to use the property only for carrying on a liquor business. When this became impossible because of a change in the law, complete frustration of purpose occurred, and many courts will allow the tenant to terminate the lease.

Under the traditional view, still followed in many states, the tenant would remain liable under the lease although he can no longer carry on the liquor business on the leased premises. This view admits that T is in substance deprived of the beneficial use of the land, but reasons that T still owns the estate in Blackacre and that the risk of loss generally follows the ownership. Also under the facts, the ownership of the estate for years and the contract to pay rent are not rendered illegal by the 18th amendment. T did not make a contract to carry on the liquor business which contract is now made illegal, but if he had made such an agreement, then impossibility of performance would be a defense in the field of contracts. In the lease T was merely permitted to use the land for the liquor business; he was not obligated to do so. See Kahn v. Wilhelm, 118 Ark. 239, 177 S.W. 403 (1915); Imbeschied v. Lerner, 241 Mass. 199, 135 N.E. 219, 22 A.L.R. 819, with note (1922); Note, " 'Commercial Frustration' as Applied to Leases of Real Property," 43 Mich.L.Rev. 598 (1944); Casner § 3.-104; The Federal Soldiers and Sailors Relief Act of 1940, 50 U.S.C.A. § 534, as to tenants who enter the military service; Burby, 178; Restatement, Second, Property (Landlord and Tenant) § 9.2, Reporter's Note.

e. EMINENT DOMAIN

LEGAL GEMS

1. Condemnation of the leased premises in their entirety terminates the relation of landlord and tenant and relieves the tenant of any further obligation to pay rent under the lease.

2. In the case of a partial taking under eminent domain, whether of a part of the physical premises, or whether of all of the premises for a part of the term, in the absence of a lease provision to the contrary, the relationship of landlord and tenant continues and the tenant remains liable to pay the rent reserved without an abatement.

CASE 124: L, being owner in fee simple of Blackacre, leased it for a 10 year period to T. After 3 years of the term had expired, Uncle Sam condemned Blackacre for temporary use by the military services. L and T were, of course, each paid just compensation in the proceeding for his particular injury. T, finding he could no longer occupy the premises, refused to pay rent. L sues T for the rent according to the terms of the lease. May L recover?

Answer and Analysis

The traditional answer is yes. Every such lease as here set forth involves two distinct elements, (a) privity of contract under which T has agreed to pay rent, inter alia, and (b) privity of estate under which T has an estate for years and L has a reversionary interest to which is attached the right to the rent. When Uncle Sam condemned the property for temporary use, just what did he "take"? Probably little more than T's right of use, control and exclusive possession as long as needed for military purposes, which time might be far less than the balance of the term of the lease. Of course it might be longer. At any rate, if Uncle Sam should give up the premises during the term of the lease, the right of exclusive possession would revert to T for the rest of the term. The relationship of landlord and tenant would remain unaffected. And as to the interest of either which had been taken, Uncle Sam would have paid each. T, having been paid for what was carved out of his estate for years through the condemnation proceedings, should pay L in full for his leasehold.

Suppose Uncle Sam had taken only part of the physical property leased. Here it is clear that T would continue to occupy the rest of the premises not taken and the relation of landlord and tenant would still exist, and T should pay rent on the whole. The only case in which condemnation proceedings would seem to relieve T of his obligation to pay rent is the one in which the condemner takes the entire fee to the leased property, thus causing a complete merger of the leasehold in the fee in the taker. In such case the payment of just compensation would necessarily include full payment for the fee simple, including the values of both the leasehold and the reversion. Both interests would be completely extinguished as such in the hands of the condemner and there could no longer be a relationship of landlord and tenant. The privity of estate would have disappeared by merger and any contractual obligations would seem to have been fully performed by the fact that landlord and tenant has each been fully paid for his interest. And such seems to be the law. Summarizing, in condemnation proceedings where a landlord-tenant relationship exists and the condemner takes only part of the property, either in time or space, the tenant remains liable for the rent; but if the entire fee simple is taken and the estates of both tenant and landlord are extinguished by merger and each is paid in full for his entire interest, the tenant is no longer liable for the rent. See Leonard v. Autocar Sales & Serv. Co., 392 Ill. 182, 64 N.E.2d 477, 163 A.L.R. 670 (1945); Kentucky Dept. of Highways v. Sherrod, 367 S.W.2d 844, (Ky.Ct. of Appeals, 1963), involving a partial taking; Powell, ¶ 247[2], criticizing the rule of no abatement in partial takings; Burby, 176–178; Restatement, Second, Property (Landlord and Tenant) § 8.1 favoring rent abatement in partial takings.

---

f. Quiet Enjoyment: Miscellaneous Provisions

Legal Gems

1. In the absence of a lease provision to the contrary, a covenant of quiet enjoyment is implied in every lease.

2. An eviction by the landlord breaches the covenant of quiet enjoyment and relieves the tenant of his obligation to pay rent. There is also a failure of consideration.

3. An eviction by the landlord may be constructive as well as actual. A constructive eviction results from conduct or neglect by the landlord which makes the premises uninhabitable. To take advantage of the defense of constructive eviction, the tenant must actually vacate the premises; if he remains in spite of the landlord's conduct, he waives the defense of constructive eviction.

4. A violation by the landlord of a vital and material covenant in the lease may justify the tenant's rescission and termination of his obligations under the lease.

5. An increasing number of jurisdictions impose on the landlord a duty to inform a prospective tenant about conditions which might render the premises unsuitable for the tenant's particular commercial purpose, thus reversing the traditional doctrine of "caveat lessee."

6. A tenant in possession under a lease is generally estopped to deny his landlord's title.

7. A tenancy from period to period is a continuing tenancy and not the inception of a new tenancy at the beginning of each rental period.

Note

Fixtures and trade fixtures are discussed infra, Chapter XIV; emblements are discussed infra, Chapter XVI.

CASE 125: L, being fee simple owner of Blackacre, leased it to T for a period of two years for the purpose of conducting the business of selling pearls as a specialty therein. The lease specifically provided that L covenanted not to lease any other room in the same building to any other person who made a specialty of selling pearls. T took possession and began operating his business. L leased another room in the same building to X covering the same term as T's lease, and in the lease to X was a provision in which X covenanted that he would not sell pearls in the leased premises. X violated this covenant and made a specialty of selling pearls in the room leased from L. Shortly after T started business, L changed his heating system in the building from one operated by soft coal to one operated by oil. For two months following the changeover, soot, smoke and oil fumes came through the floor and baseboards in T's leased area to such an extent that T's physician advised him to vacate the premises to preserve his health. T notified L who promised to correct the situation but he was unable so to do. T then rescinded the lease, vacated the premises and refused to pay the rent. L sues T for rent. May he recover?

Answer and Analysis

The answer is no. In this set of facts L has violated his implied covenant to T of quiet enjoyment and there has been a failure of consideration for the reason that L has constructively evicted T from the premises. Further, L has violated his express covenant not to lease any room in the same building to another who would specialize in the sale of pearls, a vital element in the leasehold from T's standpoint. On both these counts—constructive eviction, and breach of an express covenant—T has a good defense to the payment of rent. In the lease L sold T an estate for years. He impliedly covenanted that L should have exclusive possession and quiet enjoyment of the leased premises. By sending smoke, soot and oil fumes into the leased premises to the extent described, L made it impossible for T to occupy the very premises leased. L could not have been more effective had he manually evicted T from the premises. That L did not have an actual intent to oust T is quite immaterial for in such circumstances one is held to intend the natural and probable consequences of his acts. He constructively evicted T, thereby violating L's covenant that T might quietly enjoy the premises and thereby causing a failure of the consideration for which the rent was to be paid.

Furthermore, it was a vital and important part of the lease that T was not to have a competitor in the sale of pearls in the same building. The fact that L put a provision in X's lease that X would not sell pearls in the building did not in itself comply with L's express covenant in the lease. The burden was on L to enforce such provision for T's benefit. Otherwise form would take the place of substance. The violation of the express provision of the lease that L would not lease any other room in the building to one specializing in the sale of pearls, entitled T to rescind the lease which he did. Hence, T is not liable to L for the rent provided for in the lease. See Westland Housing Corp. v. Scott, 312 Mass. 375, 44 N.E.2d 959 (1942); University Club of Chicago v. Deakin, 265 Ill. 257, 106 N.E. 790, L.R.A. 1915C, 854 (1914); Burby, 147–148.

3. RENTS

LEGAL GEMS

1. Today rent is the consideration paid by a tenant to his landlord for the use and enjoyment of the land.

2. The amount of rent is determined by agreement between the landlord and tenant and is contractual in nature. A change in the amount of rent during the continuance of the lease requires new consideration, but in particular cases a theory of executed agreement or promissory estoppel may be employed to enforce the new agreement.

3. At common law there are three classes of rent—

    a. *rent service* which is an incident of a reversionary interest in the land. E. g., L, fee simple owner of Blackacre, leases the land to T for 10 years at a rent of $500.00 per month. In theory rent issues out of and is "rendered" by the land itself. Distress is an incident to rent service.

    b. *rent seck* (or dry rent) is a right to rent when there is no reversionary interest in the land. E. g., L, fee simple owner of Blackacre, leases the land to T for 10 years at a rent of $500 per month. Now L owns two real property rights: (1) the reversion; and (2) the rent. L conveys the rent to A. Now A owns rent but no other interest in Blackacre. A owns the *rent seck*. Distress is no part of rent seck.

    c. rent charge exists when one becomes the owner of rent seck and there is an express provision in the grant of the rent that distress may be used.

4. Distress is the right of the rent owner to enforce the payment of rent either, as at common law, by personally going onto the land and seizing chattels thereon, or by having the seizure accomplished by a public official in accordance with a statute. Distress, when recognized, is usually regulated by statute. To the extent that

the statute permits seizure without some prior notice and hearing, it is likely to be held unconstitutional.[1]

5. Rent service, which we simply call rent, is the only rent in general use today. Rent seck and rent charge are used only in limited areas.

6. Rent which is not yet due is real property. When rent becomes due it is a chose in action and personal property. E. g., L, fee simple owner of Blackacre, leases it to T for 10 years at $500.00 per month. The rent yet to be collected when the lease is made is an incorporeal real property right and to transfer such requires compliance with statutes for conveying real property. When the first month's rent of $500.00 is due and not paid by T to L, the right of L against T is a chose in action and a transfer thereof is governed by the requirements for the assignment of such choses.

7. When the lessor dies intestate his reversionary interest in the land and the undue rent incident thereto descend to his heir, and the rent which is due at the time of his death, but unpaid, passes to his personal representative.

8. A conveyance of the reversion by a lessor carries with it the rent as an incident unless there is an agreement to the contrary. The lessor may transfer the reversion and reserve the rent or he may transfer the rent and reserve to himself the reversion.

9. Both the benefit and the burden of a covenant in a lease to pay rent run with the land, the benefit with the reversion and the burden with the leasehold.

10. At common law rent is not apportionable as to time. It does not accrue like interest from day to day but, instead, fully accrues only at the time of payment. E. g., L, fee simple owner of Blackacre, leases it to T for 10 years at an annual rent of $3000.00, the rent to be paid on December 31st of each year. During the term L conveys his reversion to A on November 1st of a given year. When the rent becomes due on the following December 31st the entire rent of $3000.00 is due to A and none to L. Of course, this may be changed by agreement or statute.

11. Rent is apportionable as to amount. E. g., L, owner in fee simple of Blackacre, leases it to T for 10 years at an annual rent of

---

1. See Sniadach v. Family Fin. Corp., 395 U.S. 337, 89 S.Ct. 1820, 23 L.Ed. 2d 349 (1969), invalidating prejudgment wage garnishment; and Fuentes v. Shevin, 407 U.S. 67, 92 S.Ct. 1983, 32 L.Ed.2d 556 (1972), rehearing denied 409 U.S. 902, 93 S.Ct. 177, 34 L. Ed.2d 165, invalidating provisions of a replevin statute allowing chattels to be taken without a prior hearing. Relative to the breadth of the *Fuentes* doctrine, Mitchell v. W. T. Grant Co., 416 U.S. 600, 94 S.Ct. 1895, 40 L.Ed.2d 406 (1974), and North Georgia Finishing, Inc. v. Di-Chem, Inc., 419 U.S. 601, 95 S.Ct. 719, 42 L.Ed.2d 751 (1975), should be consulted.

The following cases have held the particular distress statute unconstitutional: MacQueen v. Lambert, 348 F. Supp. 1334 (M.D.Fla.1972); Barber v. Rader, 350 F.Supp. 183 (S.D.Fla.1972); Hall v. Garson, 468 F.2d 845 (5th Cir. 1972); Musselman v. Spies, 343 F. Supp. 528 (M.D.Pa.1972).

$3000.00. Blackacre is a section of land, the north half and south half thereof being equally valuable and productive. During the period of the lease L conveys his reversion in the north half of Blackacre to A, and his reversion in the south half to B. A and B each has a right to half the rent from T.

12. A rent is extinguished or suspended by—

a. a release by the rent owner,

b. a merger, e. g., L, fee simple owner of Blackacre, leases it to T for 10 years at a rent of $500.00 per month. L dies intestate during the term and T is his sole heir. The reversion and the rent incident thereto and the leasehold of T are all merged in the fee simple.

c. expiration of the lease,

d. eminent domain which takes both the leasehold and the reversion (supra case 124),

e. eviction of the tenant by the landlord or by one under paramount title (supra case 125),

f. the complete, or almost complete, frustration of purpose in some jurisdictions, as, for example, when the sole use provided for in the lease becomes illegal (supra case 123),

g. a surrender, either by express agreement or by operation of law. See infra case 131 this Chapter, case 208, chapter 18.

13. When there is an express covenant in the lease to pay rent, the original tenant, in the absence of a release, remains liable after an assignment. This liability is based on privity of contract. As between the tenant and his assignee, the assignee is primarily liable and the tenant-assignor is secondarily liable, somewhat similar to that of a surety.

14. An assignee of the leasehold is liable for rent as long as privity of estate continues, but in the absence of an express assumption agreement or covenant to pay the whole rent for the balance of the term, his liability ceases when he in turn assigns the lease to a third person.

15. A landlord has no action against a subtenant for rent or for breach of other covenants in the lease in the absence of a statute to the contrary since there is neither privity of contract nor privity of estate between them.

16. There is a conflict of authority as to whether the reservation only of a contingent right of re-entry in the transfer of the leasehold estate constitutes the transfer an assignment or sublease.

––––––––

CASE 126: L, fee simple owner of Blackacre, a store building, executes a written lease to T for three years at a rent of $500.00 per month. At the end of the first year when the lease still has 24 months to run, L and T orally agree that the rent during the remaining 24 months will be $400.00 instead of $500.00 per month. During such remaining 24 months of the lease T pays L promptly $400.00 per month. When the lease expires L demands that T pay the remaining amount of rent as provided for in the lease, namely, $100.00 per month for the last 24 months of the term, or a sum of $2400.00. T refuses and L sues T for that amount. May L recover?

Answer and Analysis

The traditional answer is yes but there is considerable contrary authority. Of course the answer to this question is determined on the basis of contract law. The lease between L and T involves both privity of estate and privity of contract. L conveys to T a leasehold estate for three years. For this estate T makes a contract in the lease whereby he agrees to pay L the sum of $500.00 per month for 36 months. Once such agreement is made both parties are bound thereby and any agreement to modify the terms of the agreement must be based on a new consideration. Whether the modifying agreement is in writing or oral seems immaterial except that in the first instance the writing might import a consideration but that is rebuttable. There being no consideration[2] for the modifying agreement reducing the rent from $500.00 to $400.00 per month, such modifying agreement is nudum pactum and unenforceable. Thus T remains liable to L for the $100.00 per month rent for the last 24 months of the lease which he has not paid. L is entitled to judgment against T for $2400.00. Such represents the prevailing rule. Some cases deny L's right to judgment on the ground that the oral agreement is executed and the result is the equivalent of a gift. Others reach a similar result on the basis of promissory estoppel. Some refuse recovery to L for more than that actually paid under the modification agreement, but would allow recovery in accordance with the lease terms for any time remaining under the lease. See Levine v. Blumenthal, 117 N.J.L. 23, 186 A. 457 (Sup.Ct.1936); Perry v. Farmer, 47 Ariz. 185, 54 P.2d 999 (1936); Burby, 168–169; Restatement, Second, Property (Landlord and Tenant) § 12.1, Comment (d).

CASE 127: L, fee simple owner of Blackacre, leases it to T for a 10 year period at a rent of $600.00 per year beginning January 1, 1945, the rent to be paid annually on the 31st

---

2. If the facts were such that T threatened to vacate the premises and go out of business unless L reduced the rent, and the parties then agreed to the lesser rental, and T remained in possession, the requirement of consideration would seem to be satisfied. T obtained the advantage of not having to vacate the premises because of poor business, and L obtained the advantage of continued occupancy. See Burby, 168–169, citing Ma-Beha Co., Inc. v. Acme Realty Co., Inc., 286 Ky. 382, 150 S. W.2d 1 (1941), and others.

day of December of each year. On December 1, 1954, at T's suggestion L accepts a surrender of the leasehold and takes possession of Blackacre. L demands that T pay the rent from January 1, 1954 to November 30, 1954, the period during which he occupied Blackacre and for which T has paid no rent. T refuses. L sues T for 11 months rent at the rate of $50.00 per month. May L recover?

Answer and Analysis

The answer is no. At common law rent is not apportionable as to time. That means that rent does not accrue from day to day as does interest on money loaned. It means that there is no rent due until the day on which it is to be paid. Applying such doctrine to our facts there is no rent due to L from T during the year 1954 until the last day of the year, December 31, 1954. Therefore, when L accepted the surrender of the leasehold from T and took possession of Blackacre the lease was terminated by merger of the leasehold in the fee ownership and no rent for the first eleven months of 1954 has ever become due. There must be judgment for the defendant, T. Of course such common law rule can be altered by express provision in the lease or by statute. See Willis v. Kronendonk, 58 Utah 592, 200 P. 1025, 18 A.L.R. 947 (1921); Hammond v. Thompson, 168 Mass. 531, 47 N.E. 137 (1897); Burby, 170–171.

———

CASE 128: L, fee simple owner of Blackacre, a store building containing many trade fixtures including shelves, counters, show cases and other similar items, leases it with the fixtures to T for a 10 year period at a rent of $500.00 per month. X, an enemy of T's breaks into the store at night, destroys the fixtures and takes and keeps possession of the store as against T's protests for a period of two months. During such two month period T pays no rent and refuses to pay L for such period. L sues T for the $1000.00 rent for the two months during which X has possession of Blackacre. May he recover?

Answer and Analysis

The answer is yes. Had L withheld possession of Blackacre or had one having paramount title taken possession from the tenant, T, then rent would be extinguished or suspended during the period while T is evicted. But a lessor does not assume responsibility for the wrongful acts of third persons in evicting a lessee from the leased premises. The lessee has his proper remedies for such wrongful interference with his right of exclusive possession of the premises and such remedies do not include the suspension or the extinguishing of his obligation to pay rent. Neither does the destruction of the trade fixtures by a third person or other fortuitous event relieve the lessee of his duty to pay rent according to the terms of his lease. The reason is plain. The lease conveys to the lessee an estate in the land. The responsibility for payment of rent is based upon the ownership of that estate and the right of exclusive possession thereunder. The destruction of the fixtures has nothing to do with the ownership of the leasehold estate and the tenant's duty to pay for the use and enjoyment of such estate in the form of rent. Such are the rules of the common law. See Burby, 178–179.

CASE 129: L and T enter into a written lease giving T an estate for five years at a stipulated rental payable in monthly installments at the beginning of each month. Thereafter, and during the term, T assigns the lease to A who subsequently defaults in the payment of rent. **(a)** May L recover against T in a suit for past due rent? **(b)** May L recover against A in a suit for past due rent? **(c)** If L should recover a judgment against A, and the judgment is not satisfied, may L then recover against T? **(d)** If A in turn assigns the leasehold to B and B defaults in the payment of rent, may L recover against A for rents accruing after the assignment?

Answers and Analyses

(a) The answer to (a) is yes. This is based on the assumption that the lease between L and T contained a covenant that T would pay the rent reserved. Such a covenant is customarily inserted in leases, and the requirement can be satisfied not only by an express promise in exact words to pay the rent, but also by any language necessarily importing an undertaking to that effect. The lease between L and T created both privity of estate and privity of contract between the parties. The assignment by T transferred his entire leasehold estate to A as such is the definition of an assignment. The assignment, therefore, terminated the privity of estate between L and T. However, the assignment had no effect on the privity of contract existing between L and T, and T remains liable to L on the basis of privity of contract. Of course, L could release T, or a novation between L, T and A could be effectuated but there was no indication of either in the instant case. Therefore, L can recover from T. Samuels v. Ottinger, 169 Cal. 209, 146 P. 638 (1915); Cauble v. Hanson, 249 S.W. 175 (Comm. of Appeals, Texas, 1923).

(b) The answer to (b) is yes. The assignment to A transferred the entire leasehold to A and, therefore, A and L were in privity of estate. Liability for rent and for observing the other covenants that run with the leasehold can be based on privity of estate as well as privity of contract. Therefore, L can recover from A rent obligations accruing while privity of estate continues or until A in turn assigns the leasehold. See cases cited (a) supra and (d) infra.

(c) The answer to (c) is yes. After an assignment without a novation both the tenant and the assignee are liable to the landlord for rent thereafter becoming due. The suit by L against A is not an election of remedies and is not inconsistent with L's right to collect from T if in fact he does not collect from A. As between A and T, A has the primary responsibility for payment of rent since he has the use of the premises. The landlord, however, does not have to sue A first before going against T, but, instead, may rely on T's obligations based on privity of contract. If the landlord does proceed against A first, he should not be prejudiced if the judgment against A is not satisfied. A satisfaction of A's judgment, however, satisfies the claim and thereafter T is not liable so far as that claim is concerned. Should T have to pay the rent which A should have paid, then T should be subrogated to L's rights against A and would be able to proceed accordingly. In certain instances, other theories of recovery may sustain an action by T against A for sums which T had to pay L on behalf of A. See generally, Burby, 140 et seq.; Casner §§ 3.61, 3.-64.

(d) The answer to (d) is no. As indicated above in the absence of an express agreement, A's liability is based on privity of estate. This privity of estate is terminated when A assigns the leasehold to B. Thus, A is no longer liable for rent or other obligations under the lease. Since past due rent becomes a chose in action, A should be liable to L for any sums accruing while he was in privity of estate, but there is a little authority contra. Reid v. Wiessner Brewing Co., 88 Md. 234, 40 A. 877 (1898); A. D. Juilliard & Co. v. American Woolen Co., 69 R.I. 215, 32 A.2d 800, 148 A.L.R. 187 (1943).

―――――

CASE 130: L and T enter into a valid ten year lease. Thereafter T subleases to ST, and then ST defaults in the payment of rent. (a) May L recover from ST the past due rent? (b) If the transfer between T and ST is for the entire balance of the term but T reserves a contingent right of re-entry in case of default by ST, is the transfer properly denominated an assignment or sublease?

Answers and Analyses

(a) The answer to (a) is no. In the case of a sublease, privity of estate and privity of contract exist between the original landlord and tenant. Similarly, privity of estate and privity of contract exist between the tenant and subtenant. However, neither privity of contract nor privity of estate exist between the original landlord and subtenant. Therefore, the landlord cannot sue the subtenant. Of course, it is possible to change this result by contract. In the original lease the landlord might reserve the right to go against subtenants in case the tenant defaults, and in the sublease, the agreement might provide for direct payments by the subtenant to the landlord.

(b) The answer to (b) depends upon the jurisdiction. There is a conflict of authority. By definition an assignment occurs if the tenant transfers the entire estate, or the balance thereof, to the third party. If a lesser estate is conveyed so that the tenant retains an interest in the leasehold, the transfer is properly denominated a sublease. Historically, a contingent right of re-entry or power of termination was not regarded as an estate. Thus, if the only interest retained by the tenant was a contingent right of re-entry, the transfer otherwise covering the entire balance of the term, the transfer was an assignment and not a sublease. There is substantial authority in modern cases, however, that a contingent right of re-entry is a sufficient estate or interest in land to constitute the transfer a sublease and not an assignment. See Davis v. Vidal, 105 Tex. 444, 151 S.W. 290 (1912); Burby, 140–141; Restatement, Second, Property (Landlord and Tenant) § 15.1, Comment i.

4. ABANDONMENT BY TENANT: REMEDIES OF LANDLORD; SECURITY DEPOSITS

LEGAL GEMS

1. When a tenant abandons the premises and renounces the lease, in the absence of statutes or lease provisions to the contrary, the landlord may

    a. accept a surrender of the leasehold and relieve the tenant of all further liability;

    b. retake possession on behalf of the tenant for the purpose of mitigating damages;

    c. treat the tenant's conduct as anticipatory breach of contract, accept a surrender of the premises and sue for damages, present and prospective; or,

    d. in a majority of jurisdictions, since the landlord does not have a duty to mitigate damages, he may let the premises lie idle and sue the tenant for rent as it becomes due; but

    e. in a growing number of jurisdictions, recent cases require the landlord to make reasonable efforts to re-rent in order to mitigate damages.

2. Advance rental payments may not be recovered by a defaulting tenant.

3. A security deposit in the absence of a lease provision or statute to the contrary creates simply a debtor-creditor relationship.

4. The landlord is obligated to return a security deposit, less actual damages, to the tenant at the end of the lease.

5. Penalty provisions in leases are void and unenforceable.

6. Lease provisions for liquidated damages, in the absence of a statute to the contrary, are valid.

7. Whether a particular lease provision constitutes a valid provision for liquidated damages or an invalid penalty is for the court to decide.

CASE 131: During the term of a lease, T abandons the premises, returns the key to L, and states that he no longer wants to use the premises and that he is giving up his interest in the lease. What are L's rights and liabilities?

Answer and Analysis

The answer is that the landlord has the choice of at least four alternatives in the absence of lease provisions to the contrary or statutes limiting his courses of action.

(1) The landlord, treating the tenant's abandonment as an offer of surrender, may resume possession on his own behalf, thus accepting a surrender of the leasehold from the tenant, thereby terminating the leasehold estate and relieving the tenant from further liability.

(2) The landlord may notify the tenant that he does not accept a surrender of the leasehold but that he will retake possession on behalf of the tenant for the purpose of mitigating damages. When the landlord pursues this course of action, the tenant is held liable in general damages for the difference between the amount of rent stipulated in the lease agreement and the amount recoverable from a reletting. The tenant is also liable for any special damages. The majority of jurisdictions permit the landlord to mitigate damages but do not require him to do so. Under this procedure, a final accounting and settlement of claims between the landlord and tenant must await the end of the lease term. There appears, however, a growing minority in favor of requiring the landlord to mitigate damages by making a reasonable effort to relet the premises to a new tenant. See Wright v. Baumann, 239 Or. 410, 398 P.2d 119 (1965); (dicta since instrument was in reality a contract to make a lease); Mar-Son, Inc. v. Terwaho Enterprises, Inc., 259 N.W.2d 289 (N.D.1977).

(3) The landlord may stand by and do nothing, and sue the tenant as each installment of rent matures, or sue for the whole when it becomes due. Under this course of action the leasehold estate and the concomitant obligations continue unaffected by the tenant's abandonment. As stated above, in a growing number of jurisdictions this is no longer possible because the courts and legislatures have imposed a duty on the landlord to make a reasonable effort to relet the premises in order to mitigate damages caused by the defaulting tenant. See Wilson v. Ruhl, 277 Md. 607, 356 A.2d 544 (1976), involving a statutory duty to mitigate in residential leases.

(4) The landlord may regard the tenant's breach as an anticipatory breach of contract, resume possession of the premises, and sue immediately for full damages, present and prospective. This remedy recognizes that the lease is a contract as well as a conveyance, and the right to recover damages is unaffected by the existence or nonexistence of the leasehold estate. The measure of damages is the difference, reduced to present worth, between the rent fixed in the lease and the present fair rental value of the premises for the remainder of the term, together with such special damages as may have resulted

from the breach. Under this course of action, the leasehold estate is surrendered, and the landlord recovers damages, not rent. See Kanter v. Safran, 68 So.2d 553 (Fla.1953), subsequent proceedings, 82 So.2d 508 (Fla.1955), 99 So.2d 706 (Fla.1958). See also infra, Chapter XVIII case 208 for a discussion of surrender by operation of law.

CASE 132: L leased to T a hotel for a five year term for a total rental of $169,000.00. The lease required a deposit of $33,000 by the tenant as "security for the performance of all the terms of the lease as well as security for the rent." The lease also provided that if the lease were cancelled through the fault of the lessee, the deposit would be retained by the lessor as agreed and liquidated damages, that in such event no part of the fund should be returned to the tenant, but that if actual damages should exceed the deposit, then the landlord should recover such actual damages including past due rent at the time of vacating the premises by the tenant. In the second year of the lease, tenant notified L that he was going to abandon the premises, return the keys to the landlord, and no longer operate the hotel. L notified T that he would not accept a surrender of the estate but that he would resume possession and control of the premises as agent of T for the purpose of mitigating damages. Thereafter the parties met, took inventory of the personal property, and L accepted the keys from T. Thereafter L operated the hotel for about a year when he entered into a new lease with A. After the new lease was signed, and before the original lease would have expired, T sued L to recover his $33,000 deposit. May T recover?

Answer and Analysis

The answer is this. T may not at this time recover his "security deposit," but after the period when his original lease would have expired, he may recover the balance of the deposit after the landlord deducts the damages or losses suffered as a result of T's breach of the lease.

As indicated in case 131 supra, on default of T, and in the absence of lease provisions to the contrary, L has the choice of several remedies insofar as the continuation or surrender of the leasehold estate is concerned. In this case L initially pursued the remedy of reletting on behalf of T for the purpose of mitigating damages. In order to arrive at the problem presented in this case we will assume that nothing thereafter transpired which would amount to an abandonment of that course of action, and that L's conduct did not operate as a surrender by operation of law. Parenthetically, however, it might be added that in some jurisdictions, at least, the fact that L makes some repairs or even alterations before reletting, the fact that he relets for a period of time extending beyond the original lease period, or that in releting he includes premises not in the original lease, does not require a finding that a surrender by operation of law occurred.

The proper characterization of a deposit made by T on entering into a lease is important in determining the rights of the parties in respect to that deposit. Further, the determination of the nature of the deposit is justified substantively and analytically and is not, or should not be, an idle exercise in semantics to justify a foregone conclusion concerning L's right to retain the deposit. The various possibilities are explained in the following paragraphs.

The deposit might be an advance rental. Rent becomes due in accordance with the terms of the lease, and provisions for payment of rent in advance are valid and enforceable. If the deposit is an advance rental payment, the landlord is entitled to the payment beneficially when made, and further, a defaulting tenant is not entitled to recover advance payments of rent. In the instant case, although the problem did not so state, the deposit was to be returned to the tenant in the last year of the lease but not as rent. Further, the lease referred to it as security and liquidated damages, not as rent. Clearly, therefore, the deposit was not an advance rental payment.

The deposit might be simply security to protect the landlord against the tenant's defaults. A simple security deposit would entitle the landlord to retain the deposit until the lease expires, at which. time he is obligated to return the deposit but may deduct damages or other sums owing by the tenant. In particular cases the deposit might secure physical damages to the premises, rental payments or other obligations of the tenant. In the absence of statute to the contrary (such statutes are becoming rather common in the case of multiple residential units), or prevailing lease provisions, a security deposit creates only a debtor-creditor relationship, and does not require the landlord to place it in escrow or trust account. The above lease provision did refer to the deposit as security, but if the lease were not surrendered, it would seem that the tenant would not be able to recover until the temporal termination of his lease.

The deposit might be a penalty. Provisions in leases designed simply to induce performance are generally considered against public policy and will not be enforced. The deposit will likely be construed as a penalty if it provides for a forfeiture without regard to the probable losses or damages of the nonbreaching party. The fact that the parties do not label the provision for a deposit a penalty is, of course, not controlling. The proper characterization of the provision is within the province of the court.

Finally, the deposit might be a bona fide provision for liquidated damages. In the absence of a statute to the contrary, the courts generally assert that provisions for liquidated damages are valid and will be enforced. Again, of course, the label that the lease attaches to the provision is not controlling. It is a question as to whether the court concludes the parties in good faith attempted to determine their damages in advance. In the instant case the provision stated that the landlord would retain the deposit as liquidated damages, but that if he could prove more damages, then he could collect them also. Under such circumstances it is obvious that the parties did not intend to liquidate their damages. Thus the provision is in the nature of a penalty. Therefore, since L acted to mitigate damages and the extent of the damages will not be ascertained until the lease is terminated, T is not at this time entitled to recover the deposit. At the end of the lease T will be able to recover the deposit less such damages as proved by L. See Kanter v. Safran, 68 So.2d 553 (Fla.1953), subsequent proceedings, 82 So.2d 508 (Fla.1955), 99 So.2d 706 (Fla. 1958); cf. Ricker v. Rombough, 120 Cal.App.2d Supp. 912, 261 P.2d 328 (1953); Powell, ¶ 231.

5. RESIDENTIAL LEASES

LEGAL GEMS

1. Recent years have witnessed an increasing disenchantment with traditional landlord-tenant concepts in the area of residential leasings, particularly in the case of indigent tenants and sub-standard dwellings.

2. Among the most commonly agreed shortcomings of traditional concepts are:

    a. The theory of independent covenants in leases;

    b. The lack of implied covenants such as that of habitability and fitness;

    c. The doctrine of caveat emptor; and

    d. The theory of freedom of contract and the assumption that landlords and tenants have equal bargaining power.

3. Recent litigation has been chiefly concerned with such issues as:

    a. Must the landlord deliver and/or maintain the premises in an "habitable" condition;

    b. If the premises are uninhabitable, must the tenant nevertheless pay rent;

    c. Can a tenant be subjected to rent increase or eviction in retaliation for his complaining to authorities about the condition of the premises; and

    d. Must a tenant accept and comply with various unconscionable or onerous terms of a lease?

4. Retaliatory eviction refers to the dispossession of a tenant in revenge for his attempting to better housing conditions by employing statutory remedies, court action, or reporting to housing authorities.

5. Recent cases recognize that a tenant has a right to inform proper government authorities of violations of the Law and that he may not be injured or punished by anyone for having availed himself

of such right. While a landlord may evict a tenant at will, or one from period to period by giving appropriate notice, for any legal reason, or for no reason at all, he is not free to evict in retaliation for his tenant's report of housing code violations.

6. Traditionally, if a tenant attempted to recover damages by withholding all or some rent, the landlord could use a summary dispossession action to evict the tenant. Some jurisdictions now hold that if a landlord fails to make repairs and replacements of vital facilities necessary to maintain the premises in a livable condition, the tenant may resort to self-help. If the tenant gives timely and adequate notice to the landlord, giving the latter an unexercised opportunity to repair, the tenant may repair and deduct the cost thereof from future rents.

7. Many modern jurisdictions, by statute or common law, impose a warranty of habitability. In that event, the covenant by a tenant to pay rent and the express or implied covenant of a landlord to maintain the leased premises in a habitable condition are mutually dependent. In order to constitute a breach of the warranty, the defect must be of such a nature and kind as to render the premises unsafe or unsanitary and unfit for living therein. The extent of the landlord's obligation is usually measured by applicable housing and health codes. In an action by a landlord for unpaid rent, a tenant may use as a defense the breach by the landlord of his continuing obligation to maintain an adequate standard of habitability. In such cases the tenant may be liable for the reasonable rental value.

8. A lease entered into when serious housing violations exist may be held illegal and, therefore, null and void. Hence, in an action by the landlord to recover possession for nonpayment of rent, the landlord cannot sue on the lease or rental agreement, and the tenant cannot be dispossessed for nonpayment of the agreed rent. In some jurisdictions the tenant might be held liable for the reasonable rental value of the premises in its then condition under the doctrine of quasi-contract.

9. Exculpatory clauses, or provisions by which a landlord seeks to relieve himself of liability for the consequences of his own negligence, in the absence of statute, have met with varying degrees of approval and disapproval depending upon numerous factors such as the breadth of the exculpatory provision, the declared public policy of the state, and special circumstances such as the adequacy of the supply of rental property. The trend, however, is toward strict construction so as to impose liability, and even explicit disapproval of exculpatory clauses in residential leasings. The new residential acts, see infra Gem 10, contain provisions which will facilitate invalidating such clauses.

10. Recently enacted Residential Landlord and Tenant Acts codify many aspects of the residential landlord-tenant relationship, substitute modern contractual principles for archaic conveyancing con-

cepts, and strike a balance between the rights and obligations of the respective parties.

11.   These acts, which standardize to a large degree all residential leases, either expressly or by implication, incorporate many of the innovations heretofore mentioned. The implication or imposition of a covenant of habitability, the recognition of retaliation as a defense to eviction, the utilization of the doctrine of apportionment and abatement of rent, the application of the concept of unconscionability, and the requirement of good faith on the part of both parties are common features.

12.   Good faith is imposed in the performance or enforcement of rental agreements which come within the jurisdiction of a Residential Landlord and Tenant Act. Defined as "honesty in fact," good faith can be used by a court to prevent a landlord from unduly harassing a tenant, or conversely, against a tenant who refuses to allow a landlord reasonable access to examine or repair the premises.

13.   A concept of unconscionability is commonly encompassed within the Residential Landlord and Tenant Acts. Upon a finding of unconscionability, a court may:

   a.   Refuse to enforce the entire rental agreement; or

   b.   Enforce the remainder of the agreement without the unconscionable provision; or

   c.   Limit the application of any objectionable provision so as to avoid any unconscionable result.

14.   Residential acts commonly provide that a tenant may terminate the rental agreement if the landlord fails to comply with applicable housing codes, statutory duties, or otherwise breach material provisions of the agreement. In case such failure is due to causes beyond the control of the landlord and he seriously attempts to comply, the statute may permit modification of the agreement as follows:

   a.   If the landlord's failure to comply renders the dwelling untenantable and the tenant vacates, the tenant shall not be liable for rent during that period of uninhabitability.

   b.   If the tenant remains in occupancy and only part of the dwelling unit is untenantable, the rent for the period of non-compliance shall be reduced in proportion to the loss of rental value.

15.   Under modern residential acts, the landlord is generally required to account for his claim to any part of the security deposit within a stated period of time after the lease is terminated. If the landlord fails to comply with such requirements, he becomes subject to penalties ranging from forfeiture of his claim to punitive damages for wrongful withholding of the funds.

16.   The landlord is generally required to pay interest under modern acts on any deposit he retains for a stated period, and in addition, he may be required to hold the funds in trust for the tenant and thus be prohibited from commingling them.

17. A landlord generally is under no duty to protect his tenants against the intentional torts or crimes of third persons in the common areas of an apartment complex without the landlord's consent. However, some modern cases impose such a duty to take reasonable means to protect tenants in particular cases because of the inability of the tenants to protect themselves, the landlord's control, the tenant's reliance on security measures which were allowed to degenerate, or the foreseeability of the landlord of such activity.

CASE 133: T rented a two bedroom apartment from L on a month-to-month basis. The apartment was kept in poor repair, exhibiting numerous housing, health and building code violations: the walls were cracked and structurally defective, the ceilings leaked from visible holes, the elevator shaft in the hallway remained open, and the basement incinerator was in faulty repair. T, after having made several demands on L to make the necessary repairs, reported the conditions to the appropriate local governmental authorities pursuant to the housing code regulations. When L learned of these actions, he demanded T's eviction within thirty days. In L's suit for unlawful detainer and eviction against T, may T successfully plead the defense of retaliatory eviction?

Answer and Analysis

The answer is yes. Although the general rule is that upon proper notice a landlord may evict a month-to-month tenant for any legal reason, or for no reason at all, the modern trend holds that he is not free to evict a tenant in retaliation for having reported housing code violations to the authorities. In establishing housing code regulations, the legislature intended to secure safe and sanitary living accommodations. Such a system of regulations and governmental investigation is predicated upon the initiative of private citizens. To permit retaliatory eviction of the tenant for reporting housing code violations would be to frustrate the effectiveness of the legislation. If a tenant in sub-standard housing is prevented from reporting code violations because of the practical threat of eviction, better housing and living conditions would remain merely an illusory legislative promise. Thus, legislative intent and landlord-tenant realities dictate the existence of the retaliatory eviction defense.

To establish the defense of retaliatory eviction, the tenant must show that:

(1) a condition existed which in fact did violate the housing code,

(2) the landlord knew that the tenant had reported the condition to the enforcement authorities, and

(3) the landlord, for the sole purpose of retaliation, sought to terminate the tenancy.

However, although the landlord may not evict the tenant for retaliatory purposes, once the illegal purpose is dissipated, the landlord, in the absence of contract, may evict the tenant for any other reason or may raise the rental. See Edwards v. Habib, 397 F.2d 687 (D.C.Cir. 1968), certiorari denied 393 U.S. 1016, 89 S.Ct. 618, 21 L.Ed.2d 560; Dickhut v. Norton, 45 Wis.2d 389, 173 N.W.2d 297 (1970), requiring the tenant to prove the defense by clear and convincing evidence; and Robinson v. Diamond Housing Corp., 463 F.2d 853 (D.C.Cir. 1972), indicating the difficulty that such a "blemished" landlord may encounter in ultimately evicting the tenant.

CASE 134: T rented a three room apartment in a multi-family dwelling. At the time of signing the rental agreement, the apartment was habitable and acceptable to T. Over a period of time, however, the apartment complex, without the fault of T, deteriorated: the structure was materially damaged, rodent and insect infestation was evident, heat and hot water were not provided, and garbage was not collected on a regular basis. Upon being notified of these conditions, L refused to take the necessary corrective measures in repairing the premises. Due to the unavailability of other suitable housing, T remained on the premises. L now brings suit for the past due rent which T had withheld in protest. T counterclaims that L has violated applicable building and housing codes. May L recover?

Answer and Analysis

The answer is no in many modern jurisdictions. At least, he may not recover the contract rent. Traditionally, in the absence of an express covenant or statute, the landlord had no duty to make any repairs once the tenant had commenced occupancy. This no-repair rule, however, has been substantially modified or completely rejected by many modern courts.

The complexities of the modern landlord-tenant relationship have caused many modern courts to reject totally the doctrine of caveat emptor, thus creating an implied warranty of habitability. Under the common law, a lease was equivalent to a sale of the premises for a term. Since it was primarily the land and its use which was the subject of the lease, both the landlord and the tenant possessed equal knowledge as to the qualities of the land. Such an equality of knowledge, however, cannot exist as to modern multi-family dwellings. Further, the tenant is no longer primarily interested in the land, but rather is interested in the right to enjoy the premises for living purposes. Thus, the tenant in effect seeks a contractual package of goods and services.

The court's modern treatment of the lease as a contract rather than solely as an interest in land stems from many practical aspects of the modern landlord-tenant relationship. First, the prospective tenant lacks the requisite knowledge and skills for determining an apartment's condition, compliance with building codes, or the existence of latent defects. Furthermore, even if the tenant had the knowledge, skill, and financial capability to make the necessary repairs, the increasing complexity of modern dwellings would require access to equipment and areas in the control of the landlord. And thirdly, as in other areas of consumer protection, the courts recognize the inherent inequality of bargaining power between the parties as created by standardized leases, shortages of available adequate housing, and racial and class discrimination.

Thus, many courts have found an implied warranty of habitability and fitness in the residential landlord-tenant relationship analogous to the warranty of merchantability in products liability cases. When housing codes establish a duty on the landlord to provide habitable tenements, it has been held that these guidelines shall form the standards for the implied warranty of habitability. As such, contractual remedies are available to the tenant for breaches of the warranty as defined by case law or by housing code guidelines.

In order to constitute a breach of the warranty of habitability, the defect must be of such a nature as to render the premises unsafe or unfit for habitation. In order for the tenant to rely upon the warranty, it is *not* necessary for him to vacate the premises as required in the case of constructive eviction. Since the covenant of the tenant to pay rent and the implied covenant of the landlord to maintain the leased premises in a habitable condition are mutually dependent, the tenant may raise a breach of the warranty of habitability as a defense to the landlord's action for unpaid rent. However, although the tenant may not have to pay all past rent due, he may still remain liable for the reasonable rental value of the premises in its deteriorated condition. See Javins v. First Nat'l Realty Corp., 428 F.2d 1071 (D. C.Cir. 1970); Lemle v. Breeden, 51 Haw. 426, 462 P.2d 470 (1969).

CASE 135: T rented an apartment from L which at the time of contract exhibited various housing code violations including broken railings, cracked ceilings, shattered windows, obstructed commodes and insufficient ceiling height in the basement. L knew that the condition of the apartment was in violation of the local housing code, which in part provided that:

"No person shall rent any habitation unless such habitation is in a clean, safe and sanitary condition, in repair, and free from rodents or vermin."

After T took possession, L refused to make the necessary repairs, and T withheld his rent. L now sues for possession of the apartment and for past rent due. May L recover?

Answer and Analysis

The answer is no. The modern trend is that when an apartment is rented with serious housing code violations which are known to the landlord at the time of contract, the rental lease will be declared illegal and void ab initio. In general, an illegal contract is void and confers no right upon the wrongdoer. As such the landlord may neither bring an action for past due rent nor for possession, thus making the tenant a tenant at sufferance.

Although the landlord may not bring suit based upon the illegal contract, some modern courts do grant the landlord a form of quasi-contractual relief based upon the reasonable rental value of the premises on the day of contract and the period of tenant occupancy.

The question, however, is raised as to whether a landlord may evict a tenant solely because the tenant has successfully pled the defense of illegality. Some modern courts have held that the defense of retaliatory eviction protects tenants who protest housing code violations through the defense of illegality.

Thus, when a lease is declared to be illegal due to the landlord's knowledge of housing code violations existing at the time of contract, the landlord may not sue on the lease, may only recover in quasi-contract, and may not evict the tenant for retaliatory purposes. Brown v. Southall Realty Co., 237 A.2d 834 (D.C.App.1968); William J. Davis, Inc. v. Slade, 271 A.2d 412 (D.C.App.1970); Robinson v. Diamond Housing Corp., 463 F.2d 853 (D.C.Cir. 1972).

———

CASE 136: T rented a plush apartment in Gilded Towers from L, relying upon representations of adequate security. Gilded Towers, which consists of four apartment buildings in a wealthy suburban community, provides 24-hour security guard service for the protection of its tenants. One evening at approximately 8:00 p. m., T was approached in the foyer of his apartment building by two gunmen who demanded T's jewelry. When T resisted, he was brutally beaten and robbed. It was later revealed that on the night of T's attack, the security guard was absent from his post. T now sues L for the injuries he sustained. May T recover?

Answer and Analysis

Traditionally the answer is no, but some recent decisions have made inroads on such immunity. Generally there is no duty to protect another against the intentional torts and criminal acts of third persons. This common law rule has been applied by a majority of the courts to the landlord-tenant relationship, even when security precautions were voluntarily provided by the landlord. See Gulf Reston, Inc. v. Rogers, 215 Va. 155, 207 S.E.2d 841 (1974); Goldberg v. Housing Auth. of Newark, 38 N.J. 578, 186 A.2d 291 (1962). But cf,

Braitman v. Overlook Terrace Corp., 68 N.J. 368, 346 A.2d 76 (1975); and Kline v. 1500 Massachusetts Ave. Apartment Corp., 439 F.2d 477 (D.C.Cir. 1970).

Some modern courts, however, have imposed upon the landlord a duty of protecting residential tenants. One theory for imposing such a duty analogizes landlord-and-tenants to innkeepers-and-guests. Under the common law, the innkeeper owed a duty to protect his guests from the criminal acts of third persons due to the existence of a "special relationship." This special relationship doctrine has been extended by some courts to include the modern day tenant. On the theory that the modern tenant has rented a package of goods and services, a few courts have recognized an implied contractual obligation on the part of the landlord to provide those protective measures which are within his reasonable capacity.

Other courts have found liability in tort based upon (1) the inability of tenants to adequately protect themselves against intruders, (2) the landlord's exclusive control of the common areas and the areas of access to the apartment complex, (3) the tenant's reliance and the subsequent degeneration of security features existing at the time of rental, and (4) the foreseeability of or the landlord's actual knowledge of criminal activities within the apartment complex. See Kline v. 1500 Massachusetts Ave. Apartment Corp., 439 F.2d 477 (D. C.Cir. 1970).

Thus, although many courts still follow the strict rule that the landlord is not responsible for the criminal acts of third persons, there is a modern trend toward imposing liability on the part of the apartment landlord under certain circumstances.

SUMMARY OF CASES IN CHAPTER VIII

2. GENERAL PRINCIPLES

a. DELIVERY OF POSSESSION

Case 114. The lessor impliedly covenants that the lease gives the lessee the legal right to possess the premises demised and that as between the parties the lessee shall have quiet enjoyment of the premises. There is a conflict among the jurisdictions as to whether the lessor impliedly covenants to put the lessee into actual possession on the first day of the term. Either the lessor or the new tenant may evict a hold-over tenant.

b. WARRANTY OF FITNESS OR SUITABILITY

Case 115. This case applies the following general common law principles concerning the liability of the lessor for dangerous condition of the leased premises. (1) The lessor is not liable for injury from the dangerous condition of the leased premises because the lessee buys the leasehold under the doctrine of caveat emptor. (2) But if there is a hidden defect in the premises which is known or should be known to the lessor and would not be disclosed by the tenant exercising due care, and injury flows therefrom, then the lessor is liable for he has enticed the lessee into a trap and has violated his duty to warn of the hidden danger. (3) If the lessee can recover from the lessor, then so also can the invitee or business guest of the lessee.

Case 116. A lessor generally does not impliedly warrant that the leased premises are fit for the purpose for which they are leased, but an exception has been made where the lease is of a fully furnished dwelling unit for only a short time, and the furnishings are considered the principal subject of the lease.

Case 117. The modern trend is to impose liability on the landlord for injuries occurring on the leased premises under general principles of tort law or, in the case of residential leasing, for breach of an implied covenant of habitability. Thus, the landlord was held liable for the death of a child when the stairway was too steep and without an adequate protective railing.

Case 118. Landlords have a duty to inform prospective commercial tenants of conditions which might render the premises unsuitable for the tenant's particular commercial use. Thus, failure to disclose a weak ceiling as a possible means of access for purposes of burglary rendered the landlord liable. Further, the duty to disclose such conditions is so basic that liability may be imposed despite an exculpatory clause.

Case 119. Under the common law there is no duty on the part of the lessor to make repairs on the leased premises. However, if the lessor undertakes to repair and does so negligently, and injury results, he is liable in tort. A periodic tenancy is a continuing one and not a series of successive tenancies.

c. Tenant's Duty to Repair and Maintain Premises

Case 120. A tenant is estopped to deny his landlord's title and is liable for permissive waste, which means the tenant must make ordinary repairs to prevent serious injury to the leased premises.

d. Illegality and Frustration of Purpose

Case 121. Under the traditional common law rule, in the lease of land, even if improved, a tenant remains liable to pay rent although the property is rendered totally uninhabitable because of fire, flood or other casualty, unless the lease provides otherwise.

Today, because the building, or parts thereof, rather than the land is considered the principal subject of the lease, the common law rule has been reversed and the tenant relieved of liability after casualty loss of the building. This is particularly true in residential leasing.

Case 122. When the granting of the license does not rest on discretion, but rather on an ordinance which made such a contemplated use illegal, and there are no other uses for which the property can be used under the conditions of the lease, then the lessee is not liable under the lease and is entitled to his paid in rents because of the complete failure of consideration.

Case 123. In most modern jurisdictions, when complete frustration or nearly complete frustration of business purpose occurs, the tenant can terminate his contract and relieve himself of any further obligations thereunder. This view is contrary to the traditional common law rule which holds in the absence of a specific stipulation in the lease to the contrary, that the tenant remains liable under the lease.

e. EMINENT DOMAIN

Case 124. When a relationship of landlord and tenant obtains and in a condemnation proceedings only part of the leased property, either in time or space is taken, under the traditional view the relationship continues and the tenant is liable to pay the rent, but if the entire fee is condemned and taken, then the interests of both parties are extinguished by merger in the taker, the contractual obligations have been performed and the tenant is no longer liable for rent.

f. QUIET ENJOYMENT: MISCELLANEOUS PROVISIONS

Case 125. If, after creating an estate for years in and delivering possession to a tenant, the landlord actually or constructively evicts the tenant from the leased premises, the landlord thereby violates his implied covenant of quiet enjoyment and causes failure of consideration which relieves the tenant of the obligation to pay rent. If the landlord violates any vital and material covenant in the lease the tenant may rescind the lease and his obligations thereunder are terminated.

3. RENTS

Case 126. When a valid lease is made providing for a stipulated rent to be paid, a later agreement reducing the rent provided for in the lease is not binding on the parties unless such later modifying agreement is based on a new consideration.

Case 127. At common law rent is not apportionable as to time. It does not accrue from day to day as does interest on money loaned. If a lease provides for the payment of annual rent on the last day of the calendar year and the lessor accepts a surrender of the leasehold any time during the year, he can collect no rent for any portion of such year.

Case 128. The withholding of possession of leased premises from the tenant by the lessor, or eviction therefrom by one having paramount title, will suspend or extinguish rent, but eviction from the premises by the wrongful acts of a third person, or the destruction of the trade fixtures on the leased premises, does not release the tenant from his obligation to pay rent, according to the common law.

Case 129. (a) A tenant who expressly covenants to pay rent remains liable therefore after an assignment although as between the tenant and assignee, the assignee is primarily liable. (b) An assignee remains liable for rent during the period he has the leasehold estate on the basis of privity of estate. (c) A tenant who has assigned the estate may recover from his assignee sums which the tenant is obligated to pay the landlord. An unsatisfied judgment of the landlord against an assignee does not preclude the landlord from proceeding against the tenant. (d) An assignee terminates his privity of estate when he in turn assigns the leasehold; therefore an assignee is not liable for rent accruing after he in turn assigns the leasehold.

Case 130. (a) In the absence of express contract provisions, the landlord has no action against a subtenant for rent. (b) There is a conflict of authority as to whether a transfer of the entire balance of the leasehold estate, but with a reservation of a contingent right of re-entry or power of termination by the tenant, constitutes an assignment or sub-lease.

4. ABANDONMENT BY TENANT: REMEDIES OF LANDLORD; SECURITY DEPOSITS

Case 131. On abandonment and renunciation by T, L may: (1) accept a surrender of the leasehold and relieve T of all further liability; (2) retake possession of the premises for the purpose of mitigating damages; (3) do nothing and sue for rent as it comes due in a majority of jurisdictions, but a growing minority require the landlord to mitigate damages; or (4) sue immediately for damages on the basis of anticipatory breach of contract.

Case 132. The proper characterization of a deposit made by T at the inception of a lease to insure his performance is a question for the court. Advance rentals cannot be recovered by a defaulting tenant. Valid provisions for liquidated damages are generally upheld, but if the court construes the provision as a penalty, it will not be enforced. In case the deposit is security as such, or invalid as a penalty, the landlord in either case is entitled to recover his provable damages.

5. RESIDENTIAL LEASES

Case 133. Generally, a landlord may evict a month-to-month tenant for any legal reason or for no reason at all. However, the landlord may not evict a tenant in retaliation for the tenant's having reported housing code violations to governmental authorities.

Case 134. Under the common law, a landlord was under no duty to make any repairs once the tenant had commenced occupancy. The modern trend, however, is to reject caveat emptor, and impose an implied warranty of habitability. By recognizing the modern lease to be a contract instead of solely creating an interest in land, the courts have made available contractual remedies for the landlord's failure to supply a habitable residence.

Case 135. When an apartment is rented with serious housing code violations known by the landlord to exist at the time of contract, the courts may declare the lease to be void. As such, the landlord may not bring any suit based upon the lease, but he may collect in quasi-contract for the reasonable rental value of the apartment while occupied by the tenant.

Case 136. Under the common law, a landlord was under no duty to protect his tenants against the intentional torts and criminal acts of third persons. A modern trend, however, is to imply such a duty in certain circumstances. The implied duty may stem from a special relationship existing between the landlord and tenant, an implied warranty of protection, the foreseeability of criminal acts and the reasonable ability to take protective measures, or the deterioration of relied on security programs.

Part II

RIGHTS INCIDENT TO POSSESSION AND OWNERSHIP OF LAND

Chapter IX

POSSESSION AND ADVERSE POSSESSION

1. Possession and Prior Possession.
     Legal Gems.
     Cases.
2. Adverse Possession.
     Legal Gems.
     Cases.
Summary of Cases in Chapter IX.

------

1. POSSESSION AND PRIOR POSSESSION

LEGAL GEMS

1. The possession of real property consists of dominion and control over the property with the intent to exercise such dominion and control to the exclusion of others.

2. To constitute possession, the acts of dominion and ownership must reasonably correspond to the size of the tract, its condition and appropriate use, and must be of a character that usually accompany the ownership of land similarly situated.

3. In controversies concerning possession, it is normally the function of the jury to determine what the physical acts of dominion and control were, and then to determine whether those acts constituted possession in accordance with the standard (see Gem 2 supra) set by the court.

4. The prior possessor of real property has title against the whole world except the rightful owner.

5. A possessory interest in real property (omitting leaseholds) is real property. Such interest can be conveyed by deed, or devised by will and upon intestacy will descend from ancestor to heir. It will support ejectment and if taken in condemnation proceedings, will require compensation for its value and some cases hold for the value of the fee.

CASE 137: Blackacre is a large peninsula containing about 1,000 acres, surrounded on three sides respectively by a creek, a bay, and a marsh. S repaired an ancient stone wall

which crossed the mouth of the peninsula at his own expense. He also erected a gate and a gatekeeper's hut. By
these actions he controlled land access to Blackacre. He
used the peninsula to graze horses. S later deeded the land
to R. R continued to use the land for grazing live stock. D
entered the land and R brought an action for ejectment. R
died during the pendency of the action and P, as administrator of his estate, was duly substituted as plaintiff. During
the trial the court charged the jury as follows:

> "If the jury are satisfied from the evidence given in this
> cause, that S entered upon Blackacre in the year 1850,
> and are further satisfied that he then made a complete
> enclosure of the same, and that such enclosure was suf-
> ficient to turn and protect stock, and that he actually
> used such enclosure for such purpose up to the time of
> the alleged conveyance to R, and that he deeded the
> same to R, and that the land was used by R subsequent
> thereto, for the purpose of pasturage, and that the land
> was suitable for pasturage; and that the defendant en-
> tered adversely and subsequent to the completion of
> said enclosure, and while the said land was being so
> used by said S prior, and, by said R, after said convey-
> ance, you will find for the plaintiff against such defend-
> ant, provided such defendant was occupying the prem-
> ises at the time of the commencement of this suit."

After a judgment for the plaintiff, defendant appealed, assigning the above instruction as error. Should the judgment
be reversed for improper instruction?

Answer and Analysis

The answer is yes. The general principle is that the acts of dominion and ownership which establish a possession must correspond,
in a reasonable degree, with the size of the tract, its condition and
appropriate use, and must be such as usually accompany the ownership of land similarly situated. However, it is the function of the
jury, under proper instructions from the court, to decide whether or
not the acts of dominion relied upon, considering the size of the tract,
its particular condition and appropriate use, were of such a character
as usually accompany the ownership of land similarly situated. Under the instruction given, the court invaded the province of the jury
by instructing it that certain acts were sufficient to constitute possession. It should have let the jury decide whether such acts of dominion which it found to have taken place were sufficient to comply with
the standard of possession as set forth by the court.

It will be noted that this case, like the next one, involves a conflict between two possessors, and that the plaintiff is not claiming title as a result of adverse possession or otherwise. The problem in
these two cases involves the rights of a possessor, and what is neces-

sary to constitute possession. The task is to distinguish between a series of trespasses and possession. This is normally the function of the jury under proper guidance from the court. Unless none of the facts are in dispute, and the results are so clear that reasonable minds can not differ, the jury should determine what the physical facts are, and then applying the standard set forth by the court, whether the facts are sufficient to constitute possession. Because the court, instead of the jury, in effect decided that certain acts constituted possession, the judgment is reversed and a new trial ordered. See Brumagim v. Bradshaw, 39 Cal. 24 (1870).

CASE 138:   O was the owner of Blackacre in fee simple. He went on a hunting expedition to Africa. While he was gone A took possession of the land and claimed it as owner. A died intestate leaving P his only heir. D took possession of Blackacre. P sues to eject D, and D sets up in defense the paramount right of O. May P recover?

Answer and Analysis

The answer is yes. Note carefully two facts; O is not in the case; the case is strictly between two possessors. The principles involved are these: prior possession is good against the whole world except the rightful owner; a possessory interest in land will descend from ancestor to heir, and a defendant in ejectment cannot set up the right of a third person as a defense. Applying these principles it is obvious that as to D, the decedent A was a prior possessor. Upon A's death intestate, his possessory interest descended to his heir P. P then had possessory title which drew to itself constructive possession of Blackacre. Hence, upon A's death, his heir, P, had possession constructively which possession was prior to the possession of D. P, having prior possession which gives right against the whole world except the rightful owner, O, can eject D. Further, D cannot set up the jus tertii, right of a third person, in defense unless: (a), D can show that he is holding under the real owner, O, (in which case he is really asserting his own superior right); or (b), D can show that P never did have prior possession by showing that O possessed Blackacre continuously right down to the instant when D took possession (in which case he is disputing P's claim of prior possession). Neither of these propositions appearing, the rule applies and D has no defense. Neither would D have had a defense had P brought trespass q. c. f. for damages. Of course, O, the real owner, can eject P or D.

Another principle commonly asserted is that the plaintiff in ejectment must recover on the strength of his own title and not on the weakness of the defendant's. As a corollary to this principle it is sometimes stated that the defendant can effectively defend by showing that the title is not in the plaintiff but in a third person. However, an exception to that rule is stated to exist when the plaintiff is relying not on title as showing a right to possession but simply on his rights as a prior peaceful possessor. Under this rationale, a prior peaceful possession is an exception to the rule that the jus tertii is a defense. The cases generally are in accord in result regardless of how the jus tertii rule is stated. It is believed, however, that the rationale stated in the first paragraph above is the better approach and that it is not at all inconsistent with the rule that the plaintiff in ejectment must recover on the strength of his own title. As against a wrongdoer or trespasser, the prior peaceful possession of a plaintiff in ejectment is a sufficient and superior title. In ejectment, the question at issue is the right to possession, and peaceful possession is a protected interest. See Asher v. Whitlock, L.R.1865 1 Q.B. 1; Tapscott v. Cobbs, 52 Va. (11 Grat.) 172 (1854).

---

2. ADVERSE POSSESSION

LEGAL GEMS

1. The doctrine of adverse possession is based on statutes of limitation for recovery of real property. Statutes of limitation operate not only to bar one's right to recover real property held adversely by another for a specified period of time, but also they operate to vest the disseisor with a perfect title as if there had been a conveyance by deed.

2. For one to acquire title to real property by adverse possession, his possession must be:

> a. actual and exclusive (meaning sole physical occupancy);

> b. open, visible and notorious (meaning not secret or clandestine but occupying as an owner would occupy, for all the world to see);

> c. continuous and peaceable (meaning without abatement, abandonment or hiatus in occupancy by the claimant, and also without interruption by either being physically evicted or by action in court, in other words an unbroken continuity of possession for the statutory period which may be 5, 7, 10, 15 or 20 years); and

> d. hostile and adverse (meaning that the possession is held against the whole world including the dispossessed owner; that the possessor claims to be the owner whether or not there is any justification for his claim, or whether or not there is color of title which is a paper or instrument which cannot operate as a conveyance but which the claimant may believe is effective).

3. All of these elements must co-exist to enable the adverse possessor to acquire title by adverse possession.

4. Whether each of these elements exists is primarily a question of fact.

5. For one person to take real property from its owner by adverse possession is a very drastic procedure and requires the adverse

possessor to bear the burden of proof to show the elements exist by a preponderance of the evidence and some courts say by "clear and positive evidence". Most courts say that the possession of realty is presumed to be in subordination and not adverse to the legal owner. See Lewis v. Farrah, 65 Ariz. 320, 180 P.2d 578 (1947); Van Meter v. Kelsey, 91 So.2d 327 (Fla.1956); West's Fla.Stat.Ann. § 95.13.

6. Unless required by statute, good faith on the part of the adverse possessor is immaterial. He may mature his title with no rightful claim at all if the above elements exist.

7. The purpose and policy of the statute of limitations is to suppress long dormant claims, to quiet men's estates, and to require diligence on the part of the owner.

8. Unless the statute so requires, the adverse possessor need not pay taxes to mature his title by adverse possession.

9. Adverse possession for the statutory period matures in the possessor an original substantive law title which is as real and effective as a valid title by deed or will. It is good as a sword, as a basis for suit, or as a shield, as a defense. Nor can such title be abandoned.

10. No adverse possessor can acquire by his adverse possession a larger estate in the land than that which he has claimed throughout the entire period of his adverse possession. E. g., if he has claimed only a life estate he can mature title only to a life estate.

11. The statutory period on adverse possession begins to run when a cause of action accrues against the adverse possessor.

The time when a cause of action accrues depends, of course, upon the facts in a particular case. In a simple situation, the cause accrues and the statute starts to run when a claimant without right enters into clearly visible possession of another's land claiming title.

12. No one claiming less than a freehold estate in land can get title by adverse possession; he must claim either a life estate, a fee tail or a fee simple because only one claiming a freehold can be seised. (But see 22 Harv.L.Rev. 138; 4 Tiffany, § 1173.)

13. Constructive adverse possession applies only when the adverse possessor holds possession under color of title, never when he holds under mere claim of title. Color of title means a writing which the adverse possessor may believe is effective but which is not operative as a conveyance.

Constructive possession is a fiction by which an actual possession of a portion is extended to include the remaining area of the tract encompassed within the instrument or decree constituting color of title. For constructive adverse possession there must be an actual possession by the claimant of at least a part of the tract in question.

14. The recording statutes have no application to title by adverse possession, but some states require the recording of the instrument upon which the claim is based in order to satisfy the require-

ments of adverse possession under color of title. Perhaps the only way to record an adverse possession title is through obtaining a judgment to quiet title.

15. The period of adverse possession of one possessor can be tacked to the period of adverse possession of another possessor when there is privity between the two. Such privity exists when the possession is passed from one to the other by deed, will, descent, written contract, oral contract, mere oral consent or permission. A parol transfer, however, is not sufficient for tacking periods of constructive adverse possession under color of title.

16. One who is under a disability *at the time of the accrual of the cause of action against the adverse possessor*, is given by statute in most states, time beyond the removal of his disability in which to bring his action.

17. Under some but not all statutes, the protection which is afforded by a disability is wholly personal to the disabled person and is not available to anyone who may be his successor, either as heir or purchaser.

18. The running of the statute on adverse possession is not affected by either an intervening or a supervening disability. Thus there is no tacking of disabilities, either of successive disabilities in the same owner or of disabilities in successive owners.

19. If two or more disabilities exist in the original owner at the time the cause of action accrues, the owner may take advantage of the disability which lasts the longest.

20. The statute of limitations does not run against the holder of a future interest when the future interest exists at the time the adverse possession begins.

21. The title acquired by adverse possession is an original title and not derived from the dispossessed owner. Thus, the adverse possessor takes the title and estate freed from all claims which could have been asserted against the former owner during the statutory period.

22. Certain relationships, as, for example, that of cotenants, give rise to a presumption or inference that the possession of one of the parties is with the permission of, and in subordination to, the rights of the other party or parties. However, if the possessor makes an open disclaimer or repudiation of the title or rights of the other parties, and knowledge of such disclaimer is brought home to them, and such possession and disclaimer is continued for the statutory period, then title will vest in the possessor in derogation of the rights of the others.

23. The adverse possessor's title does not affect the interest of any person unless that person had a cause of action because of the adverse possession. E. g., when there is a severance of the surface and sub-surface when adverse possession starts, adverse possession of the surface does not give a cause of action to the owner of coal under the surface. Similarly, if at the time adverse possession begins the

estate is divided into present and future interests, adverse possession of the parcel does not give rise to a cause of action in favor of the reversioner or remainderman.

Thus, in these two instances the adverse possessor would gain title only to the surface in the first case, and only to a possessory interest in the second.

24. An adverse possession begun when the title is held as a unified whole is not affected solely by a subsequent division of the title. Thus, if after adverse possession starts, the rightful owner separates the mineral estate, or creates possessory and future interests, the adverse possession will continue to run against all parties, with the adverse possessor ultimately getting a fee simple absolute unless the owner of the sub-surface starts mining operations or otherwise ousts the adverse possessor, or unless the owners of the future interests effectively assert their titles, which may require filing a law suit.

25. Possession under a mistaken belief that one is the owner is adverse under the majority view.

26. Statutes vary considerably as to specific requirements on such matters as adverse possession under color of title and not under color of title, types of disability and the effect of a disability in specific instances, and whether or not the statute of limitations may run against governmental entities.

———————

CASE 139: O was the owner of Blackacre in fee simple. A took possession of the land as an adverse possessor. While A was in adverse possession as indicated, O gave a deed to such land to B purporting to convey to B the fee simple estate in the land. Before A had possessed the land for the statutory period for adverse possession, B sued A in ejectment. May B recover?

Answer and Analysis

The answer is yes. This answer is arbitrary but represents the answer in a majority of the states. There are many cases contra. This answer is based on analysis and reason whereas the cases holding otherwise are based on historical concept. There were two good reasons at the early common law why B should not recover. First, A was in possession and claiming a freehold interest in the land. Hence, he was seised, and no one but he could transfer the fee in the land because there had to be livery of seisin. Feoffment was the only way by which a freehold could be transferred. With O out of possession and not being seised and having only a right of re-entry, how could he convey a present interest in the land? He couldn't. Therefore, the early common law judges had to hold that O's deed conveyed no interest to B. Second, O had only a right of re-entry which was a chose in action. Choses in action were not transferable. Transactions involving such were considered tainted with champerty and maintenance contrary to public policy. Hence, the early common law judges had to hold that O's deed did not transfer to B the chose in action which O held to eject A. The most that it could do was to permit or empower B to sue in O's name to eject A. Such are the reasons for saying B could not eject O. But both of these reasons are now quite obsolete.

Where recognized, the rule that a conveyance by the owner of adversely possessed land is void should be limited in effect so that the conveyance is void only as to the adverse possessor. Such a conveyance is generally valid between the parties, and presumably also to parties other than the adverse possessor. The invalidity pertains (or should pertain) only to the fact that the grantee cannot in his own name maintain an action against the adverse possessor. The action is brought by, or at least in the name of, the grantor, but the recovery inures to the benefit of the grantee.

Today, no feoffment or livery of seisin is essential to the transfer of a freehold estate in land. Since the Statute of Uses this can be done by a mere deed such as involved in this case. Also, choses in action are freely transferable with no public policy opposed to such. When the reasons for the rule disappear, so also should the rule. Following this line of reasoning most states seem to hold that B can maintain an ejectment action against A based on a deed to B while the land was actually in the adverse possession of the defendant, A. Such holdings are sometimes based on state statutes and sometimes on the idea that the original rule is quite obsolescent. Today we take the view that one can dispose of what he owns and under such view O owned Blackacre until A's adverse possession matured title in A. When O gave his deed to B, then B owned Blackacre until A's title by adverse possession had matured. Hence, when B brought ejectment he was the owner and had the right to possess Blackacre, and should recover. See Tiffany, Vol. 5, § 1331, and note 35 L.R.A.,N.S., 758 for the then position of each state on the question; also Powell, ¶ 882.

––––––––

CASE 140: O owned Blackacre which was the northeast quarter of a given section of land. A was the owner of the northwest quarter of the same section. These quarter sections had a common boundary line one half mile long determined by the points X and Y, O's land being to the east and A's land being to the west of such line. By an honest mistake A placed his boundary line fence on a line exactly four rods or 66 feet to the east of the line XY and occupied such strip on O's land for the period of the statute on adverse possession. O then had a survey made and discovered that A had occupied such strip of O's land for such time. A refused to give up the strip and O sued to eject him. At the trial A testified, "I occupied that strip of land because I thought it was my own but I never intended to take the land of anyone else." Thereupon the court directed a verdict for O. Was the court correct?

Answer and Analysis

The answer is no in most jurisdictions but there is a minority viewpoint. This is a question of honest mistake in the possession of land. There is no question that A occupied and used the land as an owner. His possession was (a) actual, (b) exclusive, (c) peaceable, (d) open and notorious, and (e) continuous for the statutory period. But was it adverse? All the cases agree that the intention of A, the adverse possessor, is controlling. Some of the cases state that the possessor does not hold adversely unless he intends to hold against the whole world, including the rightful owner, but the really significant fact is that he hold against, that is, not in subordination to the rights of the legal owner. Maas v. Burdetzke, 93 Minn. 295, 101 N. W. 182 (1904). Thus, under this view the holding is adverse.

The minority, following the more subjective test of adverse possession, would conclude that when A testified he did not intend to hold any but his own land and that he did not intend to hold land which belonged to another, he testified himself right out of court. In many cases of this type the principal issue may be more a question of evidence than of property law. Testimony of the purely subjective intent of the adverse possessor may be circumspect since there is ample motive for coloring the actual intent. The whole case can succeed or fail on a single yes or no to a question as to whether the claimant intended to claim the land irrespective of whether or not it was his. Thus, the view expressed by the Connecticut court is believed the sounder position:

> "The possession alone, and the qualities immediately attached to it, are regarded. No intimation is there as to the motive of the possessor. If he intends a wrongful disseisin, his actual possession for fifteen years, gives him a title; or if he occupies what he believes to be his own, a similar possession gives him a title. Into the recesses of his mind, his motives or purposes, his guilt or innocence, no inquiry is made. It is for this obvious reason: that it is the visible and adverse possession, with an intention to possess, that constitutes its adverse character, and not the remote views or belief of the possessor." French v. Pearce, 8 Conn. 439 (1831). Cf. Preble v. Maine Cent. R. R. Co., 85 Me. 260, 27 A. 149, 21 L.R.A. 829, 35 Am.St.Rep. 366 (1893), contra.

See also: Norgard v. Busher, 220 Or. 297, 349 P.2d 490 (1960); Schertz v. Rundles, 48 Ill.App.3d 672, 6 Ill.Dec. 674, 363 N.E.2d 203 (1977), agreeing that possession under mistake may be adverse.

CASE 141: O owned Blackacre in fee simple. A took possession of Blackacre and held it adversely for more than the

statutory period and matured title to such land. Then O re-
gained possession of the property and after being in possession for about a month, conveyed it to B who traced the record of title and found it to be a perfect chain of title down
to O. B had no actual notice or knowledge of A's claim and,
of course, nothing on the record disclosed such. Immediately following B's purchase of Blackacre and taking possession
of same from O, A brought suit against B to eject him.
May A succeed?

Answer and Analysis

The answer is yes. This set of facts involves two questions: (a)
what is the effect of A's adverse possession for the statutory period;
and (b) assuming B to be a bona fide purchaser, may he rely on the
record of title as against an adverse possessor? The answer to question (a) is this: A's title, matured by adverse possession is not merely a defensive weapon but is a substantive law title as valid as though
he had received the title by deed from O. It is an original title which
will support an action to recover the land. Hence, A can eject any
possessor from Blackacre who does not derive title through A or who
does not take title from A by adverse possession.

The answer to the second question is this: the recording acts
have no application to title by adverse possession. Even though B is
a bona fide purchaser, even though he had no actual knowledge or
notice of A's claim because A was not in possession, and even though
the records showed O to be the record title holder, and even though O
was actually in possession, nevertheless, the legislature never intended the recording acts to be applied to titles by adverse possession and
B could not rely on such under the circumstances of this case. There
is only one way by which such a bona fide purchaser can protect
himself in such case and that is by inquiring around the neighborhood and learn of the facts concerning the adverse possession of the
land. Not having done such, B is not protected by the recording statutes and in his reliance thereon. See Hughes v. Graves, 39 Vt. 359,
94 Am.Dec. 331 (1867); Schall v. Williams Val. R. R. Co., 35 Pa. 191
(1860).

CASE 142: O was the owner in fee simple of Blackacre on
which was a weatherbeaten old house. A asked O if he, A,
might move into the house on Blackacre. O granted the request and A moved in. Shortly thereafter O sold Blackacre
to B. The statute of limitations was 10 years in the jurisdiction. A knew nothing about O's sale to B and occupied
the premises for 12 years after such sale but thinking during
such time that he was still occupying with O's permission.
B demands that A leave the premises which A refuses to do.
B sues to eject A and A sets up in defense that he is an ad-

verse possessor and is the owner of Blackacre. Is the defense good?

Answer and Analysis

The answer is no. No one who possesses real property by permission or with the consent of the owner can claim title by adverse possession, irrespective of how long he so occupies. Of course, as a matter of law when O sold Blackacre to B, the license which O extended to A, was revoked. But A did not know of the sale and was still possessing under the mistaken belief that such permission or license was still effective. Hence, in A's subjective mind, he was a licensee. His subjective attitude of mind and not the revocation of the license determines the character of his possession and as long as he believed he was possessing under the permission of the owner, he could not hold adversely. On such state of facts A's defense is not good and B can eject him. See Bond v. O'Gara, 177 Mass. 139, 58 N. E. 275, 83 Am.St.Rep. 265 (1900).

Note

A grantor left in possession, a mortgagor, purchaser in possession, joint owner, co-tenant, trustee, guardian, agent and others having permission to possess land, do not hold adversely to the other party to the relationship unless and until the relationship is repudiated and intention so to hold is made unmistakably clear to such other party. See Casner, Vol. 3, p. 798.

———

CASE 143: A owned Blackacre in fee simple and B owned Whiteacre in fee simple. They made a trade of the two tracts on even terms under which agreement A took possession of Whiteacre and B took possession of Blackacre. This condition of affairs continued for a period of 12 years in a jurisdiction in which the statute on adverse possession was 10 years. B became dissatisfied with his deal with A and demanded that A return possession of Whiteacre to B which A refused to do. B then sued A in ejectment claiming that the trade concerned real property and was oral and contrary to the statute of frauds. In defense A set up title by adverse possession but made no issue of partial performance. During the trial A offered evidence of the oral agreement and the possession which followed. B objected to the introduction of such testimony on the ground of the statute of frauds. Should the court admit such evidence?

Answer and Analysis

The answer is yes. The principle involved in this case is this: if evidence is admissible for any purpose, it should be admitted, even though it would not be admissible for another purpose. It is obvious that A is not claiming title to Whiteacre by virtue of the oral trade. For such purpose the statute of frauds would be a valid objection. But A's defense is that of adverse possession and he is entitled to show every fact which establishes his title by adverse possession. And how better can he establish the adverseness of his possession than by showing he went into possession as an owner because of the trade of properties with B? Hence, the evidence is admissible, not for the purpose of showing a transfer of title under the oral trade which would be contrary to the statute of frauds, but for the purpose of showing the character of A's possession as adverse. A's possession is adverse because it is not in subordination to the rights of B. Although an entry under a parol gift is permissive and friendly in the popular sense, the possession in the instant case is adverse and hostile in the legal sense because there is an assertion of ownership in the occupant. See Cook v. Stevens, 51 Ariz. 467, 77 P.2d 1100 (1938).

Note

In the type of case given it is sometimes contended that A could not claim by adverse possession because he took possession by B's consent. This contention is not good when the consent is intended either by deed or trade or oral gift, because thereafter the possession is held not in subordination to the former owner's title but against it, even though it is derived through such. In these cases the possession is asserted because of claimed ownership. See Burby, 275.

––––––

CASE 144: T owned Blackacre which consisted of a block of land in City X with paved streets on all four sides. T built a church thereon and gave Y Church congregation permission to occupy such for church purposes which was done for many years. T died leaving an invalid will in which Blackacre was devised to Y Church Corporation. Y Church Corporation continued to occupy and use the church building in all respects as it had before T's death, conducting services therein and parking cars around the church building, thus covering the entire block on Sunday. All this was done, however, under the devise in the invalid will. T's heir, H, wrote several letters to Y Church Corporation advising it that T's will was invalid and that H insisted that Y Church Corporation cease and desist from using such premises for church purposes, and in the absence of such cessation that the Church occupy the premises under H's permission. Y Church Corporation did not answer H's letters and continued so to use the premises for church purposes, for a period longer than the statute on adverse possession after T's death. H sues Y Church Corporation in ejectment. May H recover against Y's defense of title by adverse possession?

Answer and Analysis

The answer is no—IF Y's possession was (a) actual and exclusive, (b) open and notorious, (c) continuous and peaceable, (d) hostile and adverse, for the entire statutory period. These will be discussed in order.

(a) Actual and exclusive possession requires only that the premises be occupied and used as the average owner of similar property would occupy and use it and not necessarily that it be occupied every minute of the day and night. Y Church seems to have occupied Blackacre during its Sunday services and presumably during perhaps one or two evenings of the week as churches usually do. Presumably no one was around the premises during several days and nights of each week. Such is the occupancy of a church. If, then, Y Church occupied and used the premises *as a church* and no one else shared such possession, then the church's possession was actual and exclusive.

(b) Apparently Y Church continued to use the church premises as when T lived. That being so it would seem that its possession was neither secret nor clandestine but open and notorious for all the world to see and visible to everyone in the neighborhood including T's heir, H. If such be the case this element obtains.

(c) The facts seem to say specifically that the Y Church "continued" to use the church as a church for the statutory period unless H's acts of writing letters to Y Church constituted an interruption. An occupancy of property is continuous and peaceable if it is not interrupted either by physical eviction by another or by the bringing of an action in court for possession of the premises. The interruption must be such that, had the occupant been the owner and title holder, the act of interruption would have given him a cause of action. The writing of letters by H to Y would not, had Y been the title holder, given it a cause of action against H. Hence, there was no interruption on that score as a matter of law. If these be the facts, then Y Church's possession was continuous and peaceable.

(d) If Y Church's corporate mind was to the effect that it was possessing and using Blackacre as the devisee in T's will, whether justified or otherwise, then Y Church was possessing and using Blackacre in its role as owner and not in subordination to any other title or owner. It was occupying and holding Blackacre against the whole world, including T's heir, H. Such being the facts, then Y's possession would be hostile and adverse to everyone, and this required element would be present. Hence, the answer is, if all of these elements be true, then H cannot recover. If they are not true, then H would be the victor. So it will be noted that many of the items in adverse possession are factual and to be determined by the trier of fact. See Casner, Vol. 3, p. 765 et seq.

CASE 145: O was the owner of Blackacre, a tract 300 feet wide and 1,500 feet long containing approximately 10 acres. O died intestate and X thought he was O's sole heir. In this belief he was mistaken for H was in fact and in law O's sole heir. X executed a deed to Blackacre to A in fee simple. Under X's deed A took actual possession of the east end of Blackacre, comprising an area of 300 by 500 feet, and built a small house thereon and fenced it. Y claimed to own all of Blackacre under a will left by O under which alleged will Y took possession of the west end of Blackacre comprising an area 300 by 500 feet, built a small house thereon and fenced it. This alleged will was invalid and gave Y no title to the premises. Between the two areas occupied and claimed by A and Y respectively, was an area 300 by 500 feet, which was the center part of Blackacre. From this center tract a third person, Tim Todd, cut a tree. Does either A or Y have a cause of action against Tim Todd?

Answer and Analysis

The answer is this: A has a cause of action against Tim Todd. Y does not have such. It is obvious that upon O's death the title to Blackacre descended to H. Such title drew to it constructive possession in H. When A entered Blackacre he trespassed upon this possession of H. He entered under a deed which was inoperative for lack of any interest in the premises held by the grantor, X. Every adverse possessor enters property either under a claim of title, which involves no paper or instrument, or under color of title which always involves a paper or instrument. Under a mere claim of title an adverse possessor can claim no greater area than that which he actually occupies. Under color of title an adverse possessor can claim not merely that which he occupies, but in addition thereto he may claim the area described in his "color of title" (X's deed in this case) provided such additional area is a "reasonable appendage" to the area he actually occupies. Under such doctrine, assuming the obvious, that A's possession is adverse, he took actual possession of the east $3\frac{1}{3}$ acres of Blackacre and took constructive adverse possession of the rest of the tract which was only $6\frac{2}{3}$ acres. Such small tract is clearly a "reasonable appendage" to that part which was actually occupied. No definite limitation can be laid down as to the extent of one's constructive adverse possession. Such depends on the facts of each case. It may seem reasonable that one who occupies one acre only under a deed describing 800 acres, may not claim the additional 799 acres by constructive adverse possession. But it depends upon the kind of land involved, for what it is used or may be used and where it is located, together with other pertinent facts. But in our case it seems clear that A had constructive adverse possession of the west two-thirds of Blackacre.

When Y took actual possession of the west end of Blackacre covering 300 by 500 feet and fencing the same, at that time Y ousted A's constructive adverse possession of that area. But who possesses the center area from which Tim Todd cut the tree? The answer takes the form of a rule, to wit: a subsequent constructive adverse possession cannot oust a former constructive adverse possession. Hence, A's prior constructive adverse possession takes priority over Y's later constructive adverse possession and A possesses the center area of 3⅓ acres from which Tim Todd took the tree. Then it was the possession of A on which Todd trespassed and to whom Todd is liable in an action for trespass. See Casner, Vol. 3, p. 819 et seq.; Ralph v. Bayley, 11 Vt. 521 (1839).

CASE 146: O was the owner of Blackacre. In a jurisdiction where the statute on adverse possession was 20 years, A went into adverse possession of Blackacre and held for 5 years and died intestate leaving H his sole heir. H took possession and held 3 years and by deed conveyed all of his interest in Blackacre to M, who took and held possession of the premises for 2 years, at which time he died testate devising Blackacre to P. P held possession of Blackacre for 5 years and orally gave the premises to his son, X. X possessed the premises for 3 years and leased it to L for one year. When the lease was terminated X retook possession of Blackacre and on the same day received notice that Uncle Sam desired his person and presence in the army. Before leaving for military service the following day he called his friend, D, to the place and advised him to take over Blackacre and make the most of it and that X would make no further claim to it. D took possession at X's suggestion and remained in possession for 2 months, when he was called to another state on account of his father's serious illness. He went and stayed with his father for 3 months and then returned to Blackacre and remained in possession for more than 3 years thereafter. D then called O by telephone and said to him this: "O, I have decided to abandon Blackacre. It is yours if you want it." D then moved off Blackacre with no intent to return. Who owns Blackacre?

Answer and Analysis

The answer is D. One can abandon an adverse possession which has not yet matured title. But one cannot abandon a fee simple title acquired either by a conveyance or by adverse possession. In this case, assuming that the possession of each occupant was adverse, then D had acquired the fee simple to Blackacre and could not abandon it, even to the original owner, O. In the main this is a case involving "tacking" of adverse possessions one to another. This can be done provided there is privity between the adverse possessors. Privity exists when the possessory interest of an adverse possessor is passed from one to another by descent, deed, will, agreement oral or written, by oral gift or by mere permission. Hence the descent from A to H, the deed from H to M, the devise from M to P, the oral transfer from P to X, the mere permission from X to D to take possession from X, each of these constituted privity and permitted the tacking of the adverse possession of each to that of his successor to make up the total period of adverse possession. The periods consisting of 5 years, 3 years, 2 years, 5 years, 3 years and 3 years and 2 months, make up more than the 20 year period.

Two questions remain; what was the effect of X's one year lease to L, and of D's three months visit to his father. X's lease to L meant nothing more than that L's possession was the possession of his landlord X for the purpose of adverse possession. So that during that year X was still legally in possession as to the owner, O. D's three months visit to his father's bedside had no effect in the absence of his intention to abandon his possession of Blackacre and no such intention appears. He appears still to be occupying the property as an owner since owners often are required to be temporarily absent from their property. Hence, these adverse possessions when tacked to each other making more than the 20 year period required by the statute, make D the owner of Blackacre and he cannot abandon such. The rule seems well nigh universal that the effect of the running of the statute of limitations on adverse possession is to lodge title to the premises in the adverse possessor, and to divest the former owner of all of his right, title and interest in the property in addition to taking from him any remedy for recovering the possession thereof. This is true even though the statute does not expressly so provide. See Casner, Vol. 3, p. 828 et seq.

Note

For an interesting case on tacking see Howard v. Kunto, 3 Wash.App. 393, 477 P.2d 210 (1970), where several successive purchasers received record title to tract A under the mistaken belief that they were acquiring tract B, immediately contiguous thereto. The various grantees took possession and occupied tract B. The court held that there was sufficient privity of estate to permit tacking and to establish adverse possession. The court also held that summer occupancy only of a summer beach home was sufficiently continuous.

CASE 147: O owned Blackacre in fee simple and conveyed all the coal underneath the surface thereof to B. He gave a mortgage thereon to C, and conveyed to D a right to install and maintain a pipeline through Blackacre 3 feet beneath the surface. D installed the pipes. A took adverse possession of Blackacre and held it during the entire time required by the statute on adverse possession. Under a statute permitting A to quiet title he sues for such a decree and makes O, B, C and D parties defendant. Should he succeed as to any of these defendants?

Answer and Analysis

The answer is this: He should succeed as to O. He should not succeed as to B, C or D. Prior to the running of the statute of limitations and while A was an adverse possessor, he had title to the surface of Blackacre against the whole world except O. When the statutory period had run A acquired title against O too and O's rights were terminated. Hence, as to O, A has a right to have quieted his title to Blackacre. But did A's adverse possession of the surface of Blackacre give B, C or D a cause of action against him? The answer is no for the reason that there is no inconsistency between the existence of B's ownership of the coal under the surface and A's occupancy of the surface, nor between the lien of C's mortgage and A's occupancy of the surface, nor between the existence of D's easement involving pipes under the surface and A's occupancy of the surface. If no cause of action accrued in favor of each of these parties, then no statute of limitation could run against any one of them. Had B's ownership of coal involved surface rights with which rights A had interfered, had C reduced his mortgage by decree to a right to possess Blackacre before A took possession, or had D's easement involved the use of the surface of the ground and A had interfered with such use, then A's adverse possession would have given each of them a cause of action and their respective rights would have been cut off by A's matured title by adverse possession. The test would seem to be whether or not the adverse possession gives the person claiming an interest a cause of action at the time the adverse possession commences. Of course, if the State or the United States has in its patent reserved an interest in Blackacre, such interest is not affected by adverse possession because in the absence of a specific statute to that effect, no statute of limitations begins to run against the sovereign. See Casner, Vol. 3, p. 828 et seq.; Failoni v. Chicago & N. W. Ry. Co., 30 Ill. 2d 258, 105 N.E.2d 619 (1964).

CASE 148: O owned Blackacre in fee simple and conveyed it to B for life remainder in fee to C and his heirs. A took adverse possession of Blackacre and held it for the statutory period claiming a fee simple interest therein. B then died and C sues A in ejectment. May he recover?

Answer and Analysis

The answer is yes. At the time of the commencement of A's adverse possession B had a life estate and was in possession and C had a vested remainder in fee simple. When A took possession of the premises he trespassed on the possession of B only, not on the possession of C. Indeed, C had no right to possess Blackacre until the death of the life tenant, B. Hence, C had no cause of action against A and no statutory period began to run against C. When A had held for the statutory period he had matured title to a life estate in Blackacre, an estate pur autre vie, that is, for the life of another, namely, B. Not until the death of B did C have the right to possess Black-acre. At that time a cause of action for the first time accrued in C's favor. So when C sues to eject, A he may recover. See Casner, Vol. 3, p. 802.

———

CASE 149: O, a boy of the age of 5 years, was the fee sim-ple owner of Blackacre, when A took possession thereof ad-versely. The statute of limitations on adverse possession in the jurisdiction was 20 years with an added provision that if one was under a disability at the time the cause of action accrued then such person would have 10 years after the re-moval of his disability in which to bring his action. How long must A continue his adverse possession against O to gain title?

Answer and Analysis

The answer is 26 years if the age of majority is twenty one. The first thing to be noticed very carefully is this: the owner O was under a disability AT THE TIME OF THE ACCRUAL OF THE CAUSE OF ACTION. Without such fact the provision of the statute for extended time has no application. Were it not for the disability, of course, A would mature title in 20 years. But A is under such dis-ability and it will take 16 years for him to arrive at adulthood when the disability of infancy terminates. Thereafter, O has 10 years to bring his action. When we add the 16 years to the 10 years, we have a total period of 26 years during which A must hold to gain title against O. See Casner, Vol. 3, p. 822 et seq.

Note 1

Not always does one with disability under such statutes have a longer period than one not under a disability. E. g., suppose in Case 149 the boy O had been of the age of 16 years when A took adverse possession. Then A could mature title in 20 years, the same as against an adult. Why? Because we add 5 years it will take for O to arrive at age 21, then 10 years after such disability is removed, which makes 15 years. But A cannot gain title in any event until he has held adversely for 20 years. So A would have 5 more years, making 20 years in all. Thus, under such a statute, the disability ex-tension may be wholly within the 20 year period.

———

Note 2

Caveat as to Disability Provisions

The condition or status of an individual that will constitute a dis-ability depends, of course, upon the explicit terms of the appropriate statute. Common disabilities are minority, insanity and imprison-ment.

The age of majority for a long time had been twenty-one, but in recent years that age has been reduced to eighteen, at least for some purposes. Thus, the statute and law of a particular jurisdiction will have to be consulted. At least one state, Florida, has eliminated entirely the disability provisions from the limitations period relating to real estate. See West's Fla.Stat.Ann. §§ 95.12–95.18 (1979).

The disability cases in this chapter, except as may be otherwise indicated, are based on a statute which is similar to the following:

". . . but if a person entitled to bring such action, at the time the cause thereof accrues, is within the age of ___ years, or of unsound mind, or imprisoned, such person, after the expiration of ___ years from the time the cause of action accrues, may bring such action within ___ years after such disability is removed."

Thus, applying the statute literally as discussed infra in Case 152, an heir or successor to the owner during the extended or grace period after the disability is removed would not be able to take advantage of the extended period.

The reader is again cautioned that the statutes vary and the wording of a particular statute must be consulted. It is possible that the statute may provide that adverse possession or the statute of limitations will not run against a person under a disability, in which case the result or rationale would be different from that herein discussed.

———

CASE 150: O, a boy of the age of 9 years on March 1, 1960, was the owner in fee of Blackacre. On that date A took adverse possession of Blackacre and continued to hold such. O died at the age of 15 and Blackacre passed by descent to O's sole heir, his younger brother, P. On March 1, 1981, P brought suit in ejectment to oust A from his possession of Blackacre. The statute of limitations in the jurisdiction on adverse possession was 20 years, with an added 10 years after the removal of any disability which existed at the time of the accrual of the cause of action. May P eject A?

Answer and Analysis

The answer is no. There are two principles of law involved in this set of facts: (a) the defense of disability, under our model or typical statute,[1] is purely personal to the person under disability at the time of the accrual of the cause of action; and (b) no intervening disability will stop the running of the statute of limitations. Applying the first principle to the facts discloses that O and O alone can take advantage of the 10 year extended period. Applying the second principle, it is noted that P's disability is an intervening one, and will have no effect at all on the running of the statute. Had O continued

1. See supra Note 2 following Case 149.

to live he would have been 21 in 1972. Assuming the age of majority is 21, he personally would have had until 1982, when he was 31 years of age, to bring his action against A. But he was the only person who could claim the benefit of the extension of time because he was the only person described in the statute as being under a disability at the time the cause of action accrued in his favor against A in 1960. A's adverse possession had run 20 years on March 1, 1980. Because P's intervening disability was not intended to be protected by the statute, P must bring his action within the 20 year period from the original adverse possession. Not having brought his action before March 1, 1980, P's suit is too late and A is the owner of the land. Were this not so, it is readily seen that a series of intervening disabilities would prolong for an indefinite period the time during which an adverse possessor would have to hold. Of course, if a statute provided for such protection of intervening disabilities, the statute would be applied according to its terms. See Casner, Vol. 3, p. 822 et seq.

CASE 151: O, a child of the age of 2 years, owned Blackacre in fee simple at which time A took adverse possession thereof. When O was 5 years of age he was injured in an automobile accident which rendered him non compos mentis. The statute of limitations on adverse possession in the jurisdiction provided for a period of 20 years but with an added provision of 10 years after the disability was removed for one who was under a disability at the time of the accrual of the cause of action. How old will O be when the statute will have run against him and in A's favor?

Answer and Analysis

The answer is this—O must bring his action before he is 28 years of age if the age of majority is 18. O was under one disability, that of infancy, when A's action gave O a cause of action against him. A disability added later to the one existing at the time of the accrual of the cause of action and affecting the same person is a supervening disability. Such supervening disability does not stop or affect the running of the statute of limitations. The only disability which gives an additional time, is the one existing when the cause of action accrues against the wrongdoer. Hence, the disability of insanity or non compos mentis, has no effect at all and O must bring his action within 10 years after the infancy disability is removed, that is, before he becomes 28 years of age. See Casner, Vol. 3, p. 822 et seq.

Note

Suppose in Case 151, O had been both insane and an infant when A took adverse possession. In that case O would have 10 years after the removal of the longer of the two disabilities to bring his action against A.

CASE 152: O, a boy of the age of 2 years, was the fee simple owner of Blackacre when A took possession thereof adversely. A continued his adverse possession for a period of 24 years at which time O was 26 years of age and was killed in an automobile wreck. O's sole heir was an uncle, P, aged 35 years. The statute on adverse possession provided for a period of 20 years with an additional 10 years after the removal of the disability for one who was under a disability at the time of the accrual of the cause of action. The age of majority was 18. Immediately following O's death, P sued A in ejectment. May he recover?

Answer and Analysis

The strict answer is no under our typical statute [2] in the absence of an additional provision extending the time in favor of a decedent's successors. The statute of limitation is a statute of repose. Its policy is to let things remain as they are after long periods of time. A had possessed adversely for 24 years, four years longer than the statutory period except for the extension of time given to O. This period was for the protection of O and no one else. It was wholly personal to him. Hence, upon O's death without having brought his action, title vested in the adverse possessor A. P, being O's heir, cannot take advantage of an extension of time which the statute provides for O's protection. It must be carefully noted that O's death occurred during the 10 year extended period. A liberal jurisdiction might allow P the balance of the extended period applicable to O.

Note

Many states have statutes which extend the time for bringing actions when persons die near the end of the period of the statute of limitations. The period of the extension is frequently rather short, from six months to one year. Of course if the statute specifically provides that the statutory period would not run during the disability, then the adverse possessor would have to hold for the statutory period after the disability is removed. See Casner, Vol. 3, p. 822 et seq. and Taylor, 20 Iowa Law Review 738 et seq.

Likewise, the result would be different if the statute read as follows:

"If the person entitled to an entry or action dies under any of the disabilities specified in this chapter, any other person claiming from, by, or under him, shall have the same benefit which the person first entitled would have had, by living until the removal of the disability." 10 Del.Code § 7904 (in effect as of 1978).

Special Note on Color of Title

The specific wording of an applicable statute is most important. State A has different statutory requirements for adverse possession

---

2. See supra Note 2 following Case 149.

under color of title and adverse possession without color of title. Although the length of time for title to accrue is the same, the requirements are somewhat different. For adverse possession without color of title it is necessary for the claimant to make a return of the property to the county appraiser and thereafter pay all taxes. For adverse possession under color of title, nothing is said about paying taxes, but it is necessary to record the color of title. After recording, the tax bill no doubt will naturally follow.

The question has arisen as to whether a person who has a perfectly valid title to a parcel of land but goes into possession of that parcel plus an adjacent strip, believing his title carries to the enclosed additional strip, occupies that land under color of title. In the usual situation the claimant will not satisfy the particular requirement for adverse possession without color of title because he will not make a return of the additional land to the tax appraiser, and will not specifically pay taxes on the encroached parcel. Can he qualify as an adverse possessor under color of title?

Prior to a recent statutory amendment, a state Supreme Court had held that such a person would not satisfy the requirements of adverse possession under color of title. Logically it seems that this position is correct. It is difficult to see how a person who has a valid title, or even color of title, to parcel "A", can by enclosing parcels "B" and "A" as a unit get color of title to parcel "B". Meyer v. Law, 287 So.2d 37 (Fla.1973).

When the statute was amended, it eliminated some of the language relied on in the Meyer case, supra, and provided:

"(2) For the purpose of this section, property is deemed possessed in any of the following cases: . . .

(b) When it has been protected by a substantial enclosure. All contiguous land protected by the enclosure shall be property included within the written instrument, judgment, or decree, within the purview of this section. . . ." West's Fla.Stat.Ann. § 95.16 (1979).

An appellate court concluded that under the statutory amendment, it was not necessary to have paper title accurately describing the disputed land in order to establish adverse possession under color of title. Therefore, the claimant who had a valid title to parcel "A" and enclosed therein the adjoining parcel "B", did satisfy the requirements of adverse possession under color of title. The court decided that the statute should not be applied retroactively, however, so that the claimant would have to remain in possession with his fenced in enclosure for the full statutory period after the effective date of the statutory change. In addition, since this decision was by an intermediate court, it referred the case to the Supreme Court as being a matter of great public interest. As of the time of this writing, the state Supreme Court has not passed on this question. Seddon v. Harpster, 369 So.2d 662 (Fla. 2d D.C.A. 1979).

SUMMARY OF CASES IN CHAPTER IX

1. POSSESSION AND PRIOR POSSESSION

Case 137. Possession of real property requires acts of dominion and control with an intent to possess and exclude others. It is normally the function of the jury to determine what physical acts of dominion and control were exercised, and then to apply the standard set by the court to those physical acts in order to determine whether or not the claimant was in possession.

Case 138. (a) Prior possession is good against the whole world except the rightful owner. (b) A possessory interest in land will descend from the ancestor to the heir. (c) One having mere prior possession can maintain an action in ejectment. (d) A defendant in an ejectment action cannot set up the right of a third person as a defense. (e) A plaintiff in ejectment must rely on the strength of his own title, but as against a wrongdoer, prior possession is sufficient.

2. ADVERSE POSSESSION

Case 139. The owner of land in the possession of an adverse possessor can pass title thereto in most states, and the grantee will have the right to eject the adverse possessor who has not matured original title. At the early common law such a disseisor had only a right of re-entry and could not transfer such chose in action.

Case 140. Adverse possession must be (a) actual and exclusive, (b) hostile, (c) peaceable, (d) open, (e) notorious, (f) continuous, (g) adverse, and (h) for the statutory period. The intention of the adverse possessor is all important. Such intention may be proved either by objective acts or by testimony of the adverse possessor as to his subjective intention. Under the better view a possession is adverse although the occupant believes that the land is his.

Case 141. When the adverse possessor has complied with all the requirements for adverse possession for the statutory period, his title is good as a sword as well as a shield—it is a substantive law title. The recording statutes have no application to a title matured by adverse possession.

Case 142. A license given to a licensee to be on the land is revoked by a sale of the land by the licensor. The licensee cannot be an adverse possessor as long as he thinks the license is still effective and that he is occupying the premises thereunder.

Case 143. If evidence is admissible for any purpose, it is admissible, even though it may be inadmissible for another purpose. In adverse possession oral evidence that the adverse possession was taken under an oral trade or sale of the property to the adverse possessor is admissible to show the adverseness of the possession, even though it would not be admissible under the Statute of Frauds to show a valid and enforceable trade or sale of real property.

Case 144. This case explains each item of adverse possession. Most of the questions involved in adverse possession are factual and must be determined by the trier of fact.

Case 145. Constructive adverse possession must be based on paper title, called color of title. One who goes into possession under such color of title, such as a deed, may extend the boundaries of the area claimed by constructive adverse possession beyond the area actually occupied. A later constructive adverse possession cannot oust a former constructive adverse possession.

Case 146. (a) An adverse possessor can abandon his interest in the land possessed at any time *before* the statute has fully run. (b) An adverse possessor cannot abandon his interest in the land possessed *after* the statute has run and he has matured a substantive law title thereto. (c) The interest of one adverse possessor may be tacked to that of another if there is privity between the two. (d) Privity exists between adverse possessors if the interest of one is passed to the other by descent, deed, will, written contract, oral contract, oral gift or by mere oral permission.

Case 147. An adverse possessor matures title only against those having an interest in the land who, because of the adverse possession, have a cause of action against the adverse possessor.

Case 148. An adverse possessor cannot mature title against a remainderman because the remainderman has no cause of action against the adverse possessor until the death of the life tenant.

Case 149. An adverse possessor cannot claim the benefit of the running of the statute of limitations until he has done such act of occupancy that a cause of action accrues to the owner. A disability, to be protected by an extension of time by statute, must exist at the time of the accrual of the cause of action.

Case 150. The defense of disability under many statutes is wholly personal to the one who is under a disability at the time of the accrual of the cause of action—no other person can claim the benefit of such. An intervening disability in most jurisdictions will not stop the running of the statute, which means there is no tacking of disabilities.

Case 151. A supervening disability will not stop the running of the statute. Supervening disabilities refer to more than one disability in the same person whereas intervening disabilities refer to disabilities in different persons. There is no tacking of either intervening or supervening disabilities.

Case 152. An adverse possessor cannot mature title by adverse possession in any event during a period less than the statutory period. No one except the person under a disability at the time of the accrual of the cause of action can take advantage of a statutory extension of time meant to be wholly to protect the disabled person. Frequently statutes grant brief extensions to successors of decedents dying near the end of the period of limitations.

Chapter X

ABOVE AND BELOW THE SURFACE

Legal Gems.
Cases.
Summary of Cases in Chapter X.

LEGAL GEMS

1. The possessor of real property has the right to the exclusive possession of the surface of the ground, the airspace above and the soil underneath, the extent of which is determined by his exterior boundaries extended vertically upward and downward.

2. An owner of land does not own all the space above his land projected outward to infinity, but he is entitled to have free from intrusions of noise, transit and other incursions so much of the space as is necessary for the reasonable use and enjoyment of the surface.

3. A landowner owns at least as much of the space above the ground as he can occupy or use in connection with the land.

4. The superadjacent airspace at low altitude is so close to the land that continuous invasions of it affect the use of the surface of the land itself, and invasions of such space are in the same category as invasions of the surface.

5. Flights over private land are not a taking unless they are so low and so frequent as to be a direct and immediate interference with the enjoyment and use of the land.

6. Repeated and continuous invasions of excessive noise and vibrations concomitant to airport operations are held to constitute a taking of property without direct overflights in some jurisdictions.

7. Inverse condemnation is the term applied to a cause of action against a governmental defendant to recover the value of property which has in effect been appropriated by the governmental defendant's activities when no eminent domain proceedings were utilized.

8. A landowner is entitled to the natural processes of cloud formation and rainfall above his own land.

CASE 153: P was the owner of Blackacre and was engaged in raising chickens and maintaining a small dairy thereon. D operated an air field in such position that when his planes took off and landed they traveled immediately over P's house at a height of less than 100 feet. This was a constant procedure day and night. P's chicken and dairy business was ruined because P's chickens and cows were frightened so that they produced almost no eggs or milk. P's nights were sleepless and his nervous system injured. P sues D on the theory that D has taken P's property and must make compensation therefor. May P recover?

Answer and Analysis

The answer is yes. Prior to the day of aviation the courts had no difficulty in declaring that the owner of the soil owned up to the high heavens and down to the center of the earth. This was called the "ad coelum" doctrine as to the upper space and was expressed in the Latin maxim, "cujus est solum ejus est usque ad coelum". Translated literally it is this, "whose is the soil, his is to the sky or high heavens". With the coming of the airplane the courts were compelled to revisit such doctrine, with the result that now statutes and cases usually say either that the landowner owns to the sky subject to the right of flight, or that the landowner owns upwards only so far as he can effectively possess. Under either theory it would seem correct to say that the aviator has no right to fly his airplane so low that it materially interferes with the landowner's use of the land, whether the landowner maintains a skyscraper thereon or his land is occupied only by packrats or prairie dogs. If and when the plane is operated at so low an altitude that there is substantial interference with the landowner's normal and legitimate use of his land on the surface, then the aviator should be liable.

In the case given, the defendant, D, used the airspace above P's land at so low an altitude that not only his cows and chickens were frightened but he himself was in constant and continuous fear. His chicken industry and dairy were destroyed by the use of the lower air strata by D. If P owned the airspace to the sky subject to the right of flight, that right of flight was violated by D's flying at too low a level. If P owned only so far upwards as he could effectively possess, then P must be held to have owned sufficiently high that he, his cows and chickens would not be substantially injured by D's flying above his land. In either event D materially interfered with P's rights in the airspace above his land and is liable for the injury done.

In Hinman v. Pacific Air Transport, 84 F.2d 755 (C.C.A.Cal. 1936) the court used the following language concerning the "ad coelum" doctrine, "We reject that doctrine. We think it is not the law, and that it never was the law. . . .   When it is said that man owns, or may own, to the heavens, that merely means that no one can acquire a right to the space above him that will limit him in whatever use he can make of it as a part of his enjoyment of the land. To this extent his title to the air is paramount. No other person can acquire any title or exclusive right to any space above him."

In U. S. v. Causby, 328 U.S. 256, 66 S.Ct. 1062, 90 L.Ed. 1206 (1946) the court said such doctrine has no place in the modern world and "The air is a public highway, as Congress has declared. Were that not true, every transcontinental flight would subject the operator to countless trespass suits. Common sense revolts at the idea. To recognize such private claims to the airspace would clog these highways, seriously interfere with their control in the public interest and transfer into private hands that to which only the public has a just claim". In the Hinman case where the planes took off and landed regularly within a few inches of the surface of the landowner's land which was unoccupied, the court said, "We therefore hold that it is not legally possible for appellees (operators of the airplanes) to obtain an easement by prescription through the airspace above appellants' land". This is because such space not used by the landowner belongs to the public, and the question of how much airspace above the land is possessed by the landowner depends wholly on the use to which he is putting the land at the given time, and that is a question of fact.

Note

Had P sued D for an injunction the equity court would balance the convenience and determine whether it would do more good than harm by granting such. Such suit is brought either on the theory of continuing trespass or continuing nuisance. In cases where the court has found that an injunction would do more harm than good, the plaintiff is left to his remedy at law for damages. See the cases cited in the answer above and Smith v. England Aircraft Co., 270 Mass. 511, 170 N.E. 385, 69 A.L.R. 300 (1930); Burnham v. Beverly Airways, Inc., 311 Mass. 628, 42 N.E.2d 575 (1942); Restatement, Second, Torts § 159; Swetland v. Curtiss Airports Corp., 55 F.2d 201, 83 A.L.R. 319 (1932).

CASE 154: The Port Authority of City A owns and operates and airport. Private third parties use the airport facilities and the entire operation is regulated by a federal agency. P owns and resides in a dwelling house adjacent to the airport. P sues the Port Authority for inverse condemnation and alleges that noise produced by the jet planes causes windows in the house to break, makes conversation and sleep impossible, and generally makes life unbearable and the land unusable. Assuming that plaintiff's allegations can be proved: **(a)** May P recover if the excessive noise is caused by flights at low altitudes directly over his house? **(b)** May P recover if the excessive noise is caused by flights not passing over P's house but in close lateral proximity thereto, or is caused by planes warming up on the ground in close lateral proximity to P's house? **(c)** Does it make any difference whether or not governmental agencies in the particular jurisdiction are immune to tort liability? **(d)** Does it make any difference if governmental agencies in the particular jurisdiction are required to compensate property owners only when there is a taking of property or if they are also required to pay compensation when there is a damaging of property?

Answers and Analyses

(a) The answer to (a) is yes. This is essentially the case of United States v. Causby, supra case 153. It may be noted that at the time of the Causby case, the federal government was immune to tort suits but that the Fifth Amendment prohibited it from taking private property without compensation. Since that time, the doctrine of the case has been generally accepted and many cases have held governmental authorities liable for a taking when overflights have substantially interfered with the use and enjoyment of neighboring land. The amount of compensation required depends, of course, upon the quantum of interest taken which, in many instances of this nature, will be an easement and not a complete appropriation of the realty. The term applied to "takings" of this nature where there has not been formal condemnation proceedings is inverse condemnation.

(b) There is a conflict of authority on this point, but it is believed that the preferred view is yes. In United States v. Causby, supra case 153, the court stressed the unreasonable interference with the use and enjoyment of the land and did not clearly distinguish between trespass and nuisance. Use and enjoyment would seem to be the principal property right of the possessor of land, and if this right is taken, it would seem logical that the taker would have to pay. In this regard, the following quotation seems appropos:

> "IF we accept, as we must upon established principles of the law of servitudes, the validity of the propositions that a noise can be a nuisance; that a nuisance can give rise to an easement; and that a noise coming straight down from above one's land can ripen into a taking if it is persistent enough and aggravated enough, then logically the same kind and degree of interference with the use and enjoyment of one's land can also be a taking even though the noise vector may come from some direction other than the perpendicular."

Thornburg v. Port of Portland, 233 Or. 178, 192, 376 P.2d 100, 106 (1962); subsequent proceedings, 244 Or. 69, 415 P.2d 750 (1966).

Among the cases taking a contrary position on this proposition is Ferguson v. City of Keene, 108 N.H. 409, 238 A.2d 1 (1968). This case justified in part the distinction between the overflight case and the noise case from non-overflights as follows:

> "A genuine distinction may reasonably be thought to exist between the nature of the injury suffered by the owner whose land is subjected to direct overflight, and that suffered by his neighbor whose land is not beneath the flightpath. Only the former has lost the use of the airspace above his land, and he is subjected to risks of physical damage and injury not shared by the latter." 108 N.H. at 412, 238 A.2d at 3.

(c) The answer to (c) is that logically it should make no difference whether or not governmental agencies are immune to tort liability, but that pragmatically it might. In U. S. v. Causby, supra case 153, and in Thornburg v. Port of Portland, supra (b) of this case, the defendant was either immune or assumed to be immune from tort liability and compensation for a taking was authorized. In Ferguson v. City of Keene, supra (b) of this case, on the other hand, the city was liable in tort and the court held that it was not liable for a taking but that it could be liable for a nuisance. In the case of governmental immunity for torts, the courts might well be more favorably inclined to recovery on a theory of a taking because this is the only avenue by which the property owner can recover compensation. If the government is liable in tort, however, the finding that there was no taking does not preclude a recovery in trespass or nuisance according to the facts of the case. It is believed that recovery in inverse condemnation is to be preferred to a recovery on a nuisance theory since full damages for the scope of the interest taken can be recovered in one law suit, and only in the event that circumstances would so change as to justify a conclusion that a greater interest were later taken, would a subsequent suit be permitted. See infra chapter 13 as to nuisance and the difference between a temporary and continuing nuisance.

(d) The answer to (d) is that logically it should make no difference whether the governmental unit must pay only when there is a taking or whether the government must pay also when there is a damaging to property. Pragmatically, however, there might be a difference. The court in Ferguson v. Keene, supra (b) of this problem, pointed out that Martin v. Port of Seattle, 64 Wash.2d 309, 391 P.2d 540 (1964), permitted recovery where there were no overflights but noted that the Constitution of Washington required compensation when there was a damaging as well as a taking of property. However, in Thornburg v. Port of Portland, supra (b) of this problem, the state Constitution did not require compensation for a damaging of property but the court nevertheless held that a taking could occur without an overflight. Although it might be easier to justify recovery when the constitution requires compensation for damaging, in inverse condemnation the question is really whether there was a taking. A taking need not be of the entire ownership but can consist of an easement or other interest less than the fee. Thus, if the interference with the use and enjoyment is so substantial as to prevent the reasonable use of the property for which it is then being used, there would appear to be a taking and compensation should be awarded.

Note

The fact that the glide path is now defined as within the navigable air space should have no bearing as to whether or not a particular landowner should be entitled to compensation. The question is how the activity affects the particular landowner and not whether the planes fly within or below the prescribed glide path. The airport authority should be required to pay for sufficient land so that aviation activities will not unreasonably interfere with adjacent land.

CASE 155: Corporation D is engaged in experimentation with artificial means to seed clouds in an attempt to suppress damaging hail storms. D was hired by farmers to the east of P's land. The hail storms apparently originated in and over the area within which P's land is located. P brought suit to enjoin such cloud seeding activity. At the trial it was found that D had been conducting its activities over clouds above P's land. P testified that D's seeding dissipated the potential rainclouds over his land. There was considerable conflicting expert testimony as to whether this was possible. There was also considerable lay testimony that D's seeding operations caused the clouds to dissipate completely. The trial judge issued a temporary injunction with reference to any activity of D over land in the vicinity of P's land. D appeals both the propriety of granting the injunction and also the breadth of the injunction granted. What result?

Answer and Analysis

The answer is this—the judgment should be affirmed as to P's right to an injunction but the decree should be modified to prohibit D's activity only over the land of P. It should be pointed out first that no governmental agencies are involved in this weather modification program, and that the dispute is entirely between private parties. The right to use and enjoy property should include the benefits of natural rainfall, and a duty should be imposed on adjoining landowners not to interfere with such natural rainfall. The landowner, of course, does not own the clouds, nor can he prevent flights over his land at such altitudes that do not interfere substantially with the use and enjoyment of the surface. However, any use of the space above his land which is unreasonable, improper, or interferes with the use and enjoyment of the surface can constitute a trespass.

In the instant case there was sufficient evidence to support the trial court's findings that clouds were destroyed over the land of P by the activity of D. The trial court chose to believe the evidence to that effect and disbelieve the contrary evidence. This was within its powers so long as there was sufficient evidence to support the finding, as there was. Thus, the issuance of the injunction was proper. However, the injunction prohibited D's activity in the area of P's land. The court at this time is not prepared to say that a landowner has any right to prevent or control weather modification over land not his own. The proper limits of the doctrine herein recognized will have to be determined in the future. For the present, let it suffice to say that a landowner as against another private party has a right to prevent such a party from interfering with cloud formations above the landowner's property. Thus, the injunction should be modified to prevent D from engaging in cloud seeding activity only above the land of P. See Southwest Weather Research, Inc. v. Duncan, 319 S.

W.2d 940 (Texas Ct. of Civil Appeals, 1958); affirmed 160 Tex. 104, 327 S.W.2d 417.

———

CASE 156: A was in possession of Blackacre, a rectangular lot 50 feet wide and 150 feet along. B owned lots on both sides of Blackacre and without A's permission strung a wire above the surface thereof at a height of 30 feet extending from one of B's lots to the other. What, if any, remedy has A?

Answer and Analysis

The answer is this: A has five possible remedies. (1) A may use self-help, remove the wire himself and place it on B's property. (2) A may sue B for damages in trespass quare clausum fregit. (3) A may sue B in ejectment. (4) A may in equity sue for an injunction for continuing trespass. (5) A may in equity sue for an injunction for continuing nuisance. Each of these will be discussed briefly. In all these the basic principle involved is that A has the right to possess Blackacre exclusively as to B and B has violated such right by breaking the close of A.

Self-help by A is sometimes a practical and certainly cheap remedy. But if the wire happens to be one carrying high voltage electricity, then it becomes a highly dangerous operation and would usually be quite unwise. A's recovery in trespass is in damages and he may sue time and time again and collect for such trespass, but such remedy is inadequate because the wire is still there.

A judgment in ejectment is to the effect that the defendant's act has put the plaintiff out of possession and that plaintiff has the right to be returned to his exclusive possession. An execution of such judgment would require the sheriff to put the plaintiff in possession by removing the objectionable thing—in this case by removing the wire from over A's land. Rarely will a sheriff undertake such a hazardous undertaking because he is not prepared for such. To the extent that B's wire occupies the cylindrical space over A's property, A is ousted from possession, but if the sheriff will not remove the wire, then such remedy is quite inadequate.

Because the wire is a physical intrusion, it is a trespass by B, and because it is a continuing thing, it is a continuing trespass. The suit in equity seeks removal of the wire by B himself through mandatory injunction. This remedy is adequate to accomplish the desired result. Because the wire interferes substantially with A's enjoyment of his Blackacre, it is a nuisance. Because it is a continuing thing over A's land, it is a continuing nuisance. Here again, A seeks removal of the wire by B himself through mandatory injunction, and he should have such. This remedy is adequate and orders B to remove the wire from over A's land. Such decree being given, B would be in contempt of court were he not to comply. See Butler v. Frontier Tel.

Co., 186 N.Y. 486, 79 N.E. 716, 11 L.R.A.,N.S., 920, 116 Am.St.Rep. 563, 9 Ann.Cas. 858 (1906), Restatement, Second, Torts §§ 158, 159.

Note

The remedies in the case above are likewise available for all artificial physical intrusions over land, such as cornices on buildings, leaning walls and buildings projecting eaves, and roofs. When trees or growing things by natural growth extend from B's land over A's land, and cause damage by shade, clogging sewers, etc., A is usually limited to his remedy of self-help by cutting off the offending branches and placing them back on B's land, and has no cause of action against B.

CASE 157: A and B owned adjoining mining claims. Within about three feet of the common boundary line B dug a shaft straight down into the earth and located at a depth of 20 feet a valuable vein of ore. The shaft was four feet in diameter. The soil nearest A's land was sandy and kept slipping into B's shaft. On that side of his shaft B dug away more sand and put in a concrete wall and by mistake the solidified concrete projected two inches onto A's claim for the entire depth of the shaft. B then began mining operations and followed the vein of ore along its top edge or strike, both under his own claim surface and by mistake also under the surface of A's claim. B had no actual intention of taking ore which belonged to A. A now sues B for damages for removal of A's ore and to compel B's removal of the two-inch projection of his concrete wall onto A's land under the surface. May he recover on either?

Answer and Analysis

The answer is this—A may recover on both causes. B made two mistakes. He put his concrete where it extended two inches onto A's mining claim. He dug ore from under A's claim. In both instances he punctured the imaginary plane which separated his property from A's. Subjective intent is no part of trespass. Hence, it was immaterial that B did have no intention of being on A's property. A had the right to possess exclusively his entire mining claim as against B, and that right included the soil below the surface of the ground. B violated this right. And when B took A's soil, including the ore, he was liable in trespass quare clausum fregit. And when B projected his concrete wall two inches into A's possessory domain, he was guilty of continuing trespass and maintaining a continuing nuisance, and he became subject to a mandatory injunction in equity to remove such projection. It should be noticed that B was following the vein on its strike and not on its dip so there was no question of extra-lateral rights. Only real property rights are involved in this case. See Tom Reed Gold Mines Co. v. United Eastern Mining Co., 39 Ariz. 533, 8 P.2d 449

(1932); Pile v. Pedrick, 167 Pa. 296, 31 A. 646, 46 Am.St.Rep. 677 (1895); Restatement, Second, Torts 2d §§ 158, 159.

Note

Subsurface Rights—Caves and Minerals

The old maxim that he who owns the surface also owns "ad coelum ad infernos" can no more be applied literally in a downward direction than it can be applied literally in an upward direction. If every surface owner owned to the center of the earth, that little parcel would have a lot of co-owners. The general concept of subsurface ownership, however, may be practically employed as long as the depths aren't too great.

An interesting problem may arise in connection with a cave—does the surface owner also own the empty space below? To illustrate: A and B are adjoining landowners. On A's parcel there is an opening to a large cave. A installs lighting and adds other facilities to make the cave a tourist attraction for which he charges a fee. B believes that part of the cave extends under his land, but the only access is from A's land. After considerable litigation it was held that a court could compel A to permit inspection so as to secure evidence as to whether the cave extended under the adjoining land. Then, when it was discovered that the cave did in fact extend under B's land, it was also held that B was entitled to a percentage of the net profits realized over a period of five years plus interest, and also an injunction against further trespasses. See Edwards v. Sims, 232 Ky. 791, 24 S. W.2d 619 (1929); Edwards v. Lee's Adm'r, 265 Ky. 418, 96 S.W.2d 1028 (1936).

Solid minerals sufficiently close to the surface for purposes of extraction belong to the surface owner (unless, of course, he conveys them to someone else), and little or no conceptual difficulties arise therefrom. In the case of oil and gas, however, the migratory or mobile characteristics thereof cause some conceptual problems. The analogy to solid minerals on the one hand, and subterranean or percolating water on the other, is apparent. As might be expected, different jurisdictions have adopted different theories as to ownership, but the differences in practical results are not very great. Those jurisdictions that have adopted an "ownership in place" theory have qualified or modified it by the "law of capture." See generally: Williams & Myers, Oil and Gas Law, §§ 203—204.

SUMMARY OF CASES IN CHAPTER X

Case 153. The owner of the surface of land either (a) owns to the sky (coelum) above his land subject to the right of flight, or (b) owns the space above his land which he can effectively possess, and he has the right to peaceful and quiet enjoyment of such surface. Frequently repeated flights at such a low altitude as to interfere substantially with the use and enjoyment of the surface constitute a taking of property for which compensation must be paid.

Case 154. The operation of an airport in such a manner that noise and vibrations interfere substantially with the use and enjoyment of neighboring land may constitute a taking of property for which compensation must be paid. Logically in these cases of inverse condemnation it should make no difference whether or not the noise and vibrations emanate from low flying airplanes passing directly over plaintiff's land, whether or not the government is immune to tort liability, or whether or not the government is required to compensate property owners when there is a damaging as well as a taking of property. There is, however, a conflict of authority and the aforementioned factors have been cited in various opinions.

Case 155. A landowner has the right to receive natural rainfall, and private third parties have the duty not to interfere with the natural development of clouds and precipitation over one's land. Accordingly, a landowner may enjoin others from engaging in cloud seeding activities above his land.

Case 156. A landowner has the right of exclusive possession of the airspace above his land which is necessary to the enjoyment of the surface thereof, and he has at least five remedies to enforce such right.

Case 157. At common law a landowner owns the land and space below his surface, and he has remedies both to prevent interference with such space, and for damages in case there is such interference.

Chapter XI

LATERAL AND SUBJACENT SUPPORT

Legal Gems.
Cases.
Summary of Cases in Chapter XI.

LEGAL GEMS

1. The right of a landowner to have his land supported laterally by the neighboring land is an absolute right inherent in the land itself and a part thereof.

2. The right of lateral support means the *land in its natural condition* is entitled to be held in place from the sides by the neighboring land.

3. The right of lateral support does not include the right to have the additional weight of buildings or artificial structures on the land supported from the sides by the neighboring land.

4. Neighboring land includes all the land laterally from the supported land which is necessary to support such land in its natural condition. Neighboring land may include land owned by several different owners. How far distant from the supported land neighboring land extends depends entirely on the structure of the soil. If it is of solid granite the neighboring land may extend only a few feet from the supported land. If it is of sand or ash the neighboring land necessary to support the land may extend several hundred feet distant from the supported land.

5. One who by excavation or otherwise withdraws lateral support from his neighbor's land is liable for the injury done to such land in its natural condition, regardless of negligence. Taking away lateral support is interfering with a property right.

However, when the excavation on one's land is caused by an Act of God, e. g., by high winds and tidewaters generated by a hurricane, then the owner of that land is under no duty to refurnish the lateral support that was removed by the forces of nature. Carrig v. Andrews, 127 Conn. 403, 17 A.2d 520 (1941).

6. If one excavates on his land and such excavation releases water or oil from under his neighbor's land causing the neighbor's land to sink, there is no liability.

7. If one excavates on his land and such excavation releases semi-fluid or semi-solid material from under his neighbor's land causing the neighbor's land to sink, there is liability.

8. The right to subjacent support means support from underneath the surface of the land as distinguished from the sides, and the

267

rights involved are substantially the same as those involved in lateral support.

9. The basis for liability for removal of lateral support is the same in England as in this country—it is the injury to the land in its natural condition.

10. If the land be in its natural condition with no artificial structures thereon it is obvious the recovery in damages would be the same in England and in this country to wit: the injury to the land. But there must be more than nominal damage, there must be substantial damage to the land.

11. If there are artificial structures on the land, and the land in its natural condition would be injured by the taking away of lateral support, then there are two distinct views as to the damages recoverable;

a. in some states the recovery will include both the damage to the land and as parasitic thereto the damage to the artificial structures thereon (called the English rule),

b. in other states the recovery is limited to damage to the land in its natural condition and may not include any damage to the artificial structures on the land (called the American rule).

12. In both England and the United States if there is negligence on the part of the wrongdoer who removes lateral or subjacent support, then the wrongdoer is liable for all damages which naturally and proximately flow from his negligence, including damages to both land and artificial structures.

13. An excavator has a common law right to go on his neighbor's land to shore up his neighbor's land and buildings to prevent injury to such land and buildings, but as to such neighbor he is a volunteer and must stand the expense of such activities on his neighbor's land. This is true even though he gives notice to the neighbor and demands that the neighbor perform the necessary acts to protect his land and buildings.

14. An excavation may be done at one time and the subsidence caused thereby may occur at a later date. The cause of action accrues to the land owner in almost all jurisdictions when the subsidence occurs and causes damage, rather than when the excavation was made. Thus, the statute of limitations does not begin to run until the date of the subsidence.

15. State statutes or local ordinances may vary the common law rules. See, for example, Ohio Revised Code §§ 723.49 and 723.50, (1976), which provide that if an owner or possessor in a municipality excavates to a depth in excess of nine feet he shall be liable for any damage done to an adjoining wall, house, or other building, but that he may excavate to the full depth of any foundation wall of any building on an adjoining lot or to the full depth of nine feet without incurring such liability.

16. In the United States it is not possible to obtain a prescriptive easement for the support of a building since the construction of a building entirely on one's own land does not constitute a use adverse to the adjoining landowner.

17. An easement by implication for the support of a building may arise by implication incidental to a conveyance of a portion of land improved with a building. See Tiffany, 333; Burby, 40–44.

CASE 158: A and B are adjoining lot owners, each lot being 50 feet wide and 150 feet long, and the common boundary line being a side line 150 feet in length. The lots face north and abut Market Street on the south side thereof. A's lot is west of B's lot. On B's lot is a one story commercial building used for store purposes. The exterior boundaries of this building coincide exactly with the exterior boundaries of B's lot, being 50 feet wide and 150 feet long. It is a brick structure with all exterior walls being supported by reinforced concrete footings which extend 3 feet into the ground. The entire floor of the building is constructed of reinforced concrete six inches in thickness. A's lot is vacant and he decides to build a 20 story skyscraper thereon. The plans for such new building call for a basement and a subbasement which will require an excavation below the surface of not less than 40 feet in depth. These basements and the building are to cover A's entire lot. The excavation for A's building is begun and proceeds without incident to a depth of about 36 feet when a stratum of quicksand is encountered. The more quicksand that is removed from the floor of the excavation, the more flows in; particularly from under B's building there is almost a continuing flow of bubbling, gurgling semi-fluid and semi-solid black material. This movement of earthy material exists along the entire length of B's building abutting A's lot. The solid material which supports B's building on the west side of his lot begins to crumble and slide into A's excavation, until all the land which supports the west 10 feet of B's building has moved away, and leaves said west 10 feet of B's building jutting out in space with no support except that from the cement floor and footings.

There is no negligence on the part of A in his excavation or otherwise. He notifies B to shore up his building lest it sink on the west side and slide into A's excavation. B does nothing. B's building begins to sink on the west side taking on the semblance of the Leaning Tower of Pisa. A then at great expense shores up B's building but considerable damage has been done thereto. At this point B sues A for damages to his land and building for A's wrongful removal of lateral support. A counterclaims for damages caused to A for B's failure to shore up his own building when A notified him to do so. It is stipulated (a) that B's land is damaged to the extent of $8,000, (b) B's building is damaged to the extent of $1,000 and (c) A has expended $4,000 in shoring up B's building which is his damage and the amount of his recovery on his counterclaim if he has any right thereon. B files a motion to dismiss A's counterclaim on the basis that it fails to state a claim which entitles him to any relief. (1) How should the court rule on B's motion to dismiss A's counterclaim? (2) How much, if any, may B recover from A?

Answers and Analyses

The answers are, (1) the court should grant B's motion to dismiss A's counterclaim and (2) B should recover from A the sum of $9,000.

(1) The counterclaim does not state a cause of action against B. Sometimes it is said that an excavator must give the adjoining owner notice of the excavation to be made if he would be free from negligence. In this case A gave B notice to shore up his building and furthermore, the facts state that A is free from negligence. When A's lot remained in its natural condition with no excavation thereon, B's building was safe and secure and created no hazard to anyone. If B's building and the weight thereof became a hazard, if it endangered A in his excavation or building process, such hazard and danger were caused solely by the affirmative acts of A and in no way by any act of B. There was no duty on B to act before A's excavation, and A's affirmative acts can cast no duty upon B. There is no concept in the common law which, under such circumstances, would cast upon B any duty to support his own building. He has a right to do nothing and if the building slides into A's excavation who would have caused it? Only A. So when A went onto B's land, as he has a right to do for the purpose, not alone of saving B's building but for the purpose of freeing himself both from possible danger and possible liability, he was acting wholly for himself and in the role of a volunteer. Therefore the expense he suffered in shoring up B's building is of his own making and he alone must bear same. There being no basis for A's casting such liability onto B, B's motion to A's counterclaim must be granted.

(2) On the subject of A's liability to B, it should be carefully noticed again that A is wholly free from any negligence. Hence, his liability, if any, must be predicated on the removal without negligence of the lateral support from B's land which is entirely within the realm of real property rights. B's right to have his land in its natural condition remain free from interference by the removal of its lateral support by any neighbor is absolute. If A's land is essential to the lateral support of B's land in its natural condition and A removes such support, then A is liable irrespective of negligence. If A's land is so far distant from B's land that it is not essential to the

lateral support of B's land then A's land would not be "neighboring land". But even if A's land is neighboring land owing lateral support to B's land *in its natural condition,* A's land does not owe lateral support to the artificial structures on B's land. Applying such principles to the given set of facts we find that A removed solid earth and quicksand which is semi-fluid and semi-solid material from the area adjacent to B's land. Both such solid earth and semi-fluid material which are natural in origin and give lateral support to neighboring land may be the basis for liability if removed. Then it will be noticed that the earth under B's building subsided into A's excavation leaving the building for some time thereafter in the exact position in which it was built. Hence, the weight of the building could have had no effect on the subsidence of the land below it, which subsidence must have been caused solely by the weight of the land in its natural condition. In other words, the weight of B's building was no part of the cause of the subsidence of B's land into A's excavation. Causation is usually a question of fact but when reasonable men cannot differ thereon, as in this case, it is a question of law. Therefore, it may be said that A's excavation which removed both lateral and subjacent soil and support from B's land caused B's land *in its natural condition* to subside and to be damaged substantially. This conclusion without more establishes A's liability to B.

Now the question of damages—the amount of recovery! On this subject there are two distinct views each having some merit in its favor. The English view, which is also followed in some states, permits the wronged land owner to recover both for injury to the land in its natural condition and for damage to the buildings thereon as parasitic to damage to the land. The theory is this—liability having been established, then all damage which naturally results therefrom should be permitted the wronged person. There being no question that the damage to both land and buildings flows from the removal of the lateral support, the plaintiff should recover for both. The liability being predicated solely on the damage to the land in its natural condition, without the weight of the buildings thereon, such rule does not make the adjoining land furnish support both for land and buildings; it merely allows damages for both after the liability is established, based on injury to the land alone. On the other hand the so-called American rule, being similar to the English rule with respect to the basis for liability, namely: damage to the land in its natural condition, permits recovery in damages for injury to the land only and no recovery for injury to the artificial structures thereon. The theory of this rule is that to permit the wronged landowner to recover for damage to his buildings is in substance a requirement that the adjoining landowner's land furnish lateral support for both the land and the buildings of the plaintiff. And it is thought that the result of such rule is to compel or put pressure on every landowner to put an adequate foundation under the artificial structures which he builds on his own land. This being true, each landowner improves his own land and makes sure that the foundations under his buildings are supported by his own subjacent soil and does not depend on lateral support from the neighbor's land. Adopting the English rule we conclude that B can recover for injury to his land and also for injury to the building thereon. B may therefore recover the sum of $9,000 from A for the removal of the lateral and subjacent support from B's land. See a leading case, Prete v. Cray, 49 R.I. 209, 141 A. 609, 59 A.L.R. 1241 (1928) following the English rule; Braun v. Hamack, 206 Minn. 572, 289 N.W. 553, 129 A.L.R. 618 (1940); Tiffany, 315 et seq.; Burby, 40–44; 36 A.L.R.2d 1253 (re damages); 87 A.L.R.2d 710.

CASE 159: Three adjoining lots, each 50 feet wide and 150 feet long, abut Arizona Avenue on the south, the lots facing north. A owns the west lot, B the center lot and C the east lot. The lots are all vacant and the soil in all is of a sandy loam type with some clay therein. As a fact, if C were to remove all of the soil on his lot to a depth of 100 feet, lot B would laterally support lot A in its natural condition. Many years before there had been some mining under the surfaces of lots B and C so that a considerable subsoil around the 25 foot level below the surface had been removed and timbers had been substituted for the removed subsoil. These timbers in time became so rotten that they gave no support to the surface. On July 1, 1948 C began excavating on his lot preparatory to building a dwelling house thereon and dug down to a depth of 12 feet below the surface. Temporarily for lack of money C was compelled to halt his building project. On July 1, 1950 a substantial part of the surface and subsurface soil on A's lot subsided into the old mine shafts on B's lot and a substantial part of B's lot was thereby caused to subside into C's excavation. There is no negligence on the part of C, yet had C not dug his basement the subsidences mentioned would not have occurred. In the jurisdiction the statute of limitations for damages caused by removal of lateral support is six years. On August 1, 1954 A commences an action against C for damages to his lot based on C's wrongful removal of lateral support. May A recover?

Answer and Analysis

The answer is no. It is well settled that the cause of action for the removal of lateral support accrues when the subsidence or damage actually takes place and not when the excavation is made.[1] The cause of action, if any, then accrued to A, not on July 1, 1948 but on

---

1. See, e. g., Pollock v. Pittsburgh B. & L. E. R. Co., 275 Pa. 467, 119 A. 547 (1923), involving excavation near a highway but leaving enough buffer to support the highway for many years. When eventually a car driving near the edge of the highway was precipi- tated into the excavation because the land gave way, it was held that the action was not barred by the statute of limitations because the cause of action did not accrue until the damage occurred.

July 1, 1950. The statute of limitations being six years has not then run on August 1, 1954, the date on which A commenced his action against C. Hence, procedurally A may maintain his action. But the question in the substantive law remains, is C liable to A for the removal of lateral support. It is given as a fact that had all three lots described been in their original natural condition, the removal of all the soil on C's lot to a depth of 100 feet would not have affected A's lot in the least. That means that the center lot owned by B and in its natural condition would have given full and complete lateral support to the lot owned by the plaintiff A. That being true, the only land to the east of A's lot and which owes lateral support to A's lot is B's lot. Only B's lot is then "neighboring land" to A's lot on the east. No part of C's lot is "neighboring land" to A's lot and it owes no duty of lateral support to the lot of A. The fact that miners many years before had dug out the subsoil of the lots owned by B and C cannot alter the common law doctrine that lateral support applies only to land in its natural condition, unaffected by artificial structures on the surface or by artificially created cavities under the surface. If C's lot when the lots of A, B and C were all in their natural condition was not neighboring land owing lateral support to A's lot, then any later act by any human being could not make it such neighboring land. If C's lot is not neighboring land to A's lot, then C may make any excavation he wishes on his lot without any liability to A therefor. The question of C's possible liability to B is not before us. The case is A against C. C, not being the owner of neighboring land, is not liable to A for the removal of lateral support. Of course, had C been negligent and his negligence had caused injury to A's land, then C would be liable to A. But the facts eliminate such question also. See the leading case, Corporation of Birmingham v. Allen, L.R. 6 Ch.Div. 284 (1877); Bonomi v. Blackhouse, 120 Eng.Rep. 652.

CASE 160: O constructs a building on part of his land, and then conveys that part to P, the division line being very close to the building. O makes no improvements on that part of his land adjacent to the parcel conveyed to P, and this situation continues for more than twenty years. Thereafter O excavates in preparation to construction, and P's land caves in causing substantial damage to P's building. P sues O for damages, and at the trial it is established that P's land would not have subsided had it not been for the pressure of the building on the land. Nevertheless, P contends that he is entitled to recover because (a) he has acquired an easement by prescription for the support of his building, and (b) at the time of the original conveyance he acquired an easement by implication for the support of his building. May P recover on either theory?

Answers and Analyses

The answer to **(a)** is no; the answer to **(b)** is yes. An easement by prescription can be acquired if the claimant exercises such right for the full period of prescription (20 years at common law), and such user satisfies the following characteristics: open and notorious, adverse and hostile, continuous and uninterrupted, with the knowledge and acquiescence of the servient owner. Under English common law it was possible to acquire a prescriptive right to the support of a building, but this is generally not possible in the United States, at least it is not possible under the circumstances of the problem case. At the outset the requirement of adverseness is not satisfied. The construction and maintenance of a building on one's own land cannot be considered a use adverse to the neighbor when the landowner has a perfect right to build or otherwise use the land as he wishes so long as he does not unreasonably interfere with the use and enjoyment of his neighbor. Similarly, the adjoining owner has a perfect right to let his land remain unimproved; he cannot be compelled to improve now or forever be required to support his neighbor's building. The construction of a building does not give the neighbor a cause of action until that building interferes in some way with the neighbor's use and enjoyment of his own land. Thus, since P's building did not constitute a use adverse to O during the past twenty years because O had no cause of action against P during that period, P did not acquire an easement by prescription.

(b) An easement by implication arises incidentally to the conveyance of land and is predicated on the inferred intent of the parties. In the instant case the alleged easement would be created by implied grant since it would arise in favor of the grantee. Historically the courts were more willing to imply a grant than a reservation because of the doctrine that a grantor could not derogate from his conveyance. Today the tendency is to minimize the distinction between implied grants and implied reservations, and to base the conclusion simply on the inferred intention of the parties. When O erected his building it was logical to assume that he would use the surrounding land to support it. When he conveyed to P the land with the building and made the dividing line such that there was insufficient land conveyed to support the building, it can be assumed that he impliedly granted an easement to P in respect to the land retained for the support of P's building. Thus, P can recover for damage to his building. See Tunstall v. Christian, 80 Va. 1 (1885); infra Chapter XXVI for easements; Burby, 72–75, 76–83.

SUMMARY OF CASES IN CHAPTER XI.

Case 158. The right to lateral support is an inherent part of the ownership of real property. Such duty of lateral support is owed only by one piece of land to another piece of land when it is in its natural condition. It does not owe the duty to support any artificial structure thereon. Any liability for the removal of lateral support is based on damage caused thereby to land in its natural condition. Under the American rule in a suit for damages for the removal of lateral support the recovery is limited to the damage to the land alone. Under the English rule recovery is allowed for injury to the land and as parasitic thereto recovery is also allowed for damage to the buildings thereon.

Case 159. A cause of action for removal of lateral support arises only when the subsidence occurs and not when the excavation is made. The statute of limitations, therefore, begins to run from the time of the damage. Neighboring land is that land which is close enough to another piece of land so that an excavation thereon will cause substantial damage to that other piece of land in its natural condition. If land is not neighboring land to other land there can be no liability for removal of lateral support thereon because no duty is owed to the other land. The common law doctrine of lateral support applies only when the lands are in their natural condition unaffected by artificial structures thereon or artificially created cavities underneath.

Case 160. (a) It is not possible to obtain a prescriptive easement for the support of a building since the erection and maintenance of a building on one's own land is not adverse to the rights of a neighboring landowner. (b) An easement by implication for the support of a building arises when a portion of land improved with a building is conveyed without sufficient neighboring land for the building's support.

Chapter XII

WATER RIGHTS

Legal Gems.
Chart—The Common Law Rules of Riparian Water Rights Compared with
and Distinguished from the Doctrine of Prior Appropriation.
Cases.
Summary of Cases in Chapter XII.

LEGAL GEMS

1. Title to lands under water

   a. Title to lands under non-navigable streams is generally in the abutting owner and extends to the center of the stream. The same holds true in the case of lakes.

   b. A stream or lake is considered navigable if it can be used for commerce. The title to lands under navigable streams or lakes is usually in the state through which the stream flows or in which the lake is located.

   c. The owners of lands bordering on the ocean usually own to the high water mark, the line to which the high tide comes. The title to the land between the high water mark and the low water mark, called the shore, is usually owned by the state.

2. Under the commerce clause of the United States Constitution all waters which are navigable as interstate highways are subject to control of the federal government. Both states and individuals which use such waters do so merely because the federal government has taken no action respecting such. If the federal government does act as to such waters, such as dredging or building dams, and the state or individual interests are injured, it is damnum absque injuria and there is no right to compensation, unless there is a "taking" of the property of the state or of the individual. E. g., P builds a dam in a navigable interstate stream for the purpose of developing power. The United States then builds another dam just below P's dam which backs up water in the stream so as materially to interfere with P's fall of water and its capacity to develop power. P has no right against the United States for he has no more property interest in the continued level of the water of the navigable stream than an abutting owner of land has in the grade of the highway beside his land. The damage to P's water power project is not a "taking" and is damnum absque injuria.

3. Waters (like Caesar's Gaul), may be divided into three parts or classifications:

   a. Lakes and streams on the surface. A lake is a body of water of reasonable size resting on a bed, having well defined banks and the surface of which is perpendicular to the radius of the earth. A stream of water flows on a bed, has well defined banks and its surface upstream forms an obtuse angle and downstream an acute angle with the radius of the earth.

b. Underground or percolating water. This water is below surface and merely seeps, oozes or filters into the earth from the surface and moves, drips or flows among the interstices of the earth.

c. Surface water. This is water on the earth's surface which has come from rains, springs and melting snow and ice, and which follows the contours of the land and has not yet reached a well defined water course or basin. It should be distinguished from flood waters. Surface waters have not yet reached a stream or lake. Flood waters have already been in a stream or lake and have overflowed its banks.

4. Each of the three separate categories of water in turn has three different rules of law relating to the use of the water that may be applicable. Which rule is applicable, of course, depends upon the jurisdiction.

5. Lakes and Streams—"Riparian" Rights: One or a combination of the following rules govern the rights of the parties abutting a lake or stream:

a. the natural flow theory;

b. the reasonable use theory; or

c. the prior appropriation doctrine.

6. "Natural flow" and "reasonable use" are common law concepts whereas "prior appropriation" is based on statutory or constitutional provisions. [See Gem 12 infra.]

7. The common law doctrine of riparian rights consisting of either the natural flow or reasonable use rule, or a blending of the two, is predominant in the Eastern United States and is in effect to some extent in a number of other states west of the Mississippi River. Legislation implementing and modifying common law riparian doctrines is becoming increasingly common as the water problems become more complex.

The prior appropriation doctrine is the sole basis of water rights in some western states, and is enforced in combination with common law rules in others.

8. Characteristics of the natural flow theory of riparian rights:

a. Each proprietor of land on a stream or lake has a fundamental right to have the stream or lake remain substantially in its natural state, free from any unreasonable diminution in quantity and free from any unreasonable pollution in quality.

b. Each riparian may use the water for either natural or artificial wants so long as he uses it only on riparian land and does not sensibly affect the quantity or quality of the water.

c.   The rights of all riparians are equal.

d.   A lower riparian has a right of action against an upper riparian whenever the latter's use of the water materially affects either the quantity or quality of the lake or stream waters, even though such use results in no injury or damage to the lower riparian.

e.   This rule or theory has the merit of being relatively certain and definite so that the riparian owner knows fairly well just how far he can go in his use of the water.   It is non-utilitarian in its restricted use and wastage of water.

9.   Characteristics of the reasonable use theory of riparian rights:

a.   Each riparian proprietor has the fundamental right to make the maximum use of the water in the stream or lake provided such use does not unreasonably interfere with the like use by other riparians.   Under this theory the stress is laid, not on the effect the use has on the stream or lake in its natural condition, but upon the effect the use has on other riparians.

b.   Each riparian may use the water for any beneficial use either on riparian or non-riparian lands so long as the use does not interfere with the reasonable use by other riparians.   Reasonable use alone constitutes the measure and the limit of the water right.   Reasonableness is a question of fact under the circumstances of each case measured by the importance of the use on one hand and the gravity of the effects on other riparians on the other.

c.   The rights of all riparians are equal.

d.   A lower riparian has no right of action against an upper riparian until he can show that the use is unreasonable and that such use has caused damage to the lower riparian.

e.   This theory has the merit of giving to each riparian the right to make the maximum beneficial use of the water available in the lake or stream, but its weakness is its indefiniteness for no riparian can determine the extent of his rights as against his fellow riparians.

10.   The following case illustrates the fundamental differences between the two common law theories of riparian rights.   A, an upper riparian along a stream of water, diverts the water from the stream for the purpose of irrigating both his riparian and non-riparian lands.   The diversion of the water causes the level of the water in the stream to go down six inches below its normal level.   However, there is plenty of water in the stream to supply all of the possible and reasonable uses to which the lower riparian, B, can put the water.   B sues A to enjoin A's unreasonable use of the water in the stream. Under the natural flow theory the injunction would issue because B has the right to have the natural level of the water in the stream maintained.   Under the reasonable use theory the injunction would

not issue because B can show no injury to himself as a lower riparian. Furthermore, under the natural flow theory it is an unreasonable use per se that A is using the water on non-riparian lands. To be riparian, land must border the stream and be within the watershed. The theory is that water used on riparian lands as thus restricted will eventually return to the same stream and therefore the water in the stream will remain undiminished in quantity.

11.   England and a few states follow the natural flow theory and a growing number of states follow the reasonable use theory. In most jurisdictions the doctrine of riparian rights is applied without making any distinction between the two theories.

COMMENT: Today there is a shortage of fresh water everywhere in the country. Those principles of the doctrine of riparian rights should be adopted which will permit the maximum beneficial use of the available supply of fresh water for human needs.

12.   The arid western states have found the common law doctrine of riparian rights quite inapplicable to their local conditions and have abolished it by constitution and statute, and in its place have adopted the prior appropriation doctrine as more suitable for governing water rights within their borders.

13.   The sole aim and purpose of the prior appropriation doctrine is to make possible the maximum beneficial use of the limited supply of water available.

14.   The underlying theory of this doctrine is this—he who first appropriates a supply of water to a beneficial use is first in right.

15.   The wisdom of this policy in a land where there is not enough water to supply all who would and could apply it to a beneficial use is illustrated by the following example. Suppose A and B each owns 40 acres of arable and irrigable land; that it takes 3 acre feet of water to raise a crop on each acre of such land. This means there must be during the season for raising the crop a total amount of water three feet deep on each acre or that amount spread over each acre of the entire irrigated area. The available supply of water is just enough to cover 40 acres three feet deep during the season. If the entire available water supply is spread over the entire 80 acres owned by both A and B, thus making 18 inches of water over the whole surface area, it is obvious that neither A nor B will raise a crop and all the water will have been lost or wasted. On the other hand if the entire available supply is used exclusively either on A's 40 acres or on B's 40 acres, there will be at least one 40 acre crop raised. Hence, if A first appropriates the 3 acre feet of water and puts it to a beneficial use on his 40 acres of land, his right to the water is recognized prior to any right of B to use any of such limited supply under the prior appropriation doctrine. If B makes such appropriation first, then A will have no right to such water supply.

16.   Under both the doctrine of riparian rights and the doctrine of prior appropriation the waters of lakes and streams belong to the

public. Water is not the subject of private ownership, it can only be used. One may own water when he has it in a cup or vessel but when it is released it returns to public ownership.

17. There are three different rules relating to the use of percolating waters:

    a. The common law rule regards the water beneath the surface as belonging to the landowner whose ownership and power of disposition is absolute. This absolute dominion is modified in some jurisdictions which require the water to be used for a beneficial purpose, do not protect a disposition motivated solely by malice, or by statute prohibit waste of such water.

    b. The reasonable use rule authorizes only such use by the landowner as is regarded reasonable in the light of all relevant circumstances, including the effect on neighboring landowners.

    c. The prior appropriation doctrine recognizes state ownership of percolating waters and protects the appropriators who comply with the law in order of seniority of appropriation, that is, a prior appropriator is protected against a subsequent appropriator who interferes with his available supply.

18. There are three different rules applicable to the conduct of a landowner in regard to surface waters:

    a. The common law rule, also known as the common enemy rule, permits the landowner unlimited discretion in dealing with surface waters regardless of the effect on others.

    b. The civil law rule states that each landowner has to accept the natural flow of surface waters and a duty not to interfere with such natural flow, thus in effect imposing on each parcel of real estate a servitude to receive the natural flow of surface water from above.

    c. The rule of reasonableness requires that the landowner's conduct in regard to surface water be reasonable in the light of all relevant circumstances, including the benefit to himself and the harm which results to others.

19. The rights of riparian proprietors to the use of waters in a non-navigable lake for boating and other recreational purposes are equal, and each riparian owner, under the civil law rule, which is the more utilitarian, has the right to use all the water in the lake for such purposes so long as his use is not an unreasonable interference with the rights of the other riparian owners. The common law rule, on the other hand, restricts each landowner to the use of the water overlying the land he owns.

THE COMMON LAW RULES OF RIPARIAN WATER RIGHTS COMPARED WITH AND DISTINGUISHED FROM THE DOCTRINE OF PRIOR APPROPRIATION

Common Law Riparian Rules

1. THE DISTINGUISHING FEATURES OF THE COMMON LAW RIPARIAN RULES ARE EQUALITY OF RIGHTS AND REASONABLE USE—there is no priority of rights, the reasonable or permitted use by each is limited by a similar use in every other riparian.[1]

2. To be a riparian one needs only to be an owner of riparian land. Riparian land is land which abuts or touches the water of a lake or stream.

3. No one can be a riparian who does not own riparian land.

4. Riparian lands are lands bordering the stream and within the watershed. Under the natural flow theory a riparian cannot use water on non-riparian lands. Un-

Prior Appropriation Doctrine

1. THE DISTINGUISHING FEATURE OF THE PRIOR APPROPRIATION DOCTRINE IS FIRST IN TIME IS FIRST IN RIGHT—there is no equality of rights and no reasonable use limited by the rights of others.

2. To be a prior appropriator one must do four things, (a) have an intent to appropriate water, (b) divert the water from the source of supply, (c) put such water to a beneficial use, and (d) when applicable follow the necessary administrative procedures.

3. One need not own any land to be a prior appropriator. There is one exception—in some jurisdictions like Arizona if the appropriation is for irrigation purposes then the appropriator must own arable and irrigable land to which that water right is attached.

4. The prior appropriator may use the appropriated water on riparian and on non-riparian lands alike. The character of the land is quite immaterial.

1. The above statements are applicable whether the jurisdiction technically follows the natural flow or reasonable use theory. Since the "reasonable" concept is very flexible, a use to be reasonable in a natural flow jurisdiction may be more limited than in a reasonable use jurisdiction. See supra Gems 8 and 9.

Common Law Riparian Rules	Prior Appropriation Doctrine
der the reasonable use theory a riparian may use water on non-riparian lands if such use is reasonable.	
5. Under the common law riparian rules the use of water for *natural* purposes is paramount and takes precedence over the use of water for *artificial* purposes. Natural uses include domestic purposes for the household and drinking, stock watering and irrigating the garden. Artificial purposes include use for irrigation, power, mining, manufacturing and industry.	5. The prior appropriation doctrine makes no distinction between uses of water for natural wants and for artificial and industrial purposes.
6. The riparian owner, simply because he owns riparian land, has the right to have the stream of water flow to, by, through or over his land, under the riparian rights doctrine.	6. An owner of land, simply as such owner, has no right to have a stream of water flow to, by, through or over his land, under the prior appropriation doctrine.
7. The riparian has the right to have the water in its natural state free from unreasonable diminution in quantity and free from unreasonable pollution in quality.	7. The prior appropriator has the right to the exclusive use of the water free from interference by anyone, reasonable or unreasonable.
8. The rights of the riparians are equal.	8. The rights of the appropriators are never equal.
9. The basis, measure and limit of the riparian's water right is that of reasonable use. [But see fn. 1 supra.]	9. The basis, measure and limit of the water right of the prior appropriator is the beneficial use to which he has put the water. He has no right to waste water. If his needs are smaller than his means of diversion, usually a ditch, then his needs determine his right. If his ditch is smaller than his needs, then the capacity of his ditch determines his right.

Common Law Riparian Rules	Prior Appropriation Doctrine
10. The doctrine of riparian rights came to this country from the common law of England although it seems to have had its origin in the French law.	10. The doctrine of prior appropriation is statutory in our western states although its origin seems lost in antiquity.

See, Tiffany, 307–315; Burby, 45–61; Powell, ¶¶ 710–723, 733–744.

CASE 161: A is the owner in fee simple of Blackacre through which naturally flows Clear Creek. B is a mining company engaged in working mines in the vicinity of Blackacre. For many years from a point below Blackacre, and before A ever used any of the water from Clear Creek, B has been using all of the water from Clear Creek in its mining operations. A is a widow living alone on Blackacre and uses the water from Clear Creek for domestic purposes, for watering her cow, a few pigs and chickens, and for irrigating her small garden. B now finds it convenient in opening and operating a new mine above Blackacre to divert all of the water of Clear Creek from a point above Blackacre. It diverts all of the water of Clear Creek and carries it over the watershed and uses it in its mine on non-riparian land. This leaves no water at all flowing in Clear Creek which reaches A's Blackacre. She is left wholly without any water from that or any other source. A brings suit against B to enjoin B from interfering with A's supply of water flowing to Blackacre through Clear Creek. A alleges all of the facts given above and B demurs to the complaint. How should the court rule on the demurrer?

Answer and Analysis

The answer is this—(a) if the court in that jurisdiction is governed by the doctrine of riparian rights it should overrule the demurrer, but (b) if the court is governed by the doctrine of prior appropriation it should sustain the demurrer.

(a) Under the riparian rights doctrine, whether the jurisdiction follows the natural flow or reasonable use rule, there are three reasons why the court should overrule B's demurrer and hold that A has stated a claim or cause of action against B. First, as a riparian under the natural flow theory, A has the right to have Clear Creek flow in its natural condition to, by, through and over Blackacre, free from unreasonable diminution in quantity or quality. Further, under a reasonable use theory of riparian rights, B could not successfully claim the right to divert all of the water from this natural stream to be a reasonable use as to a lower riparian who has an equal right to the use of the waters of Clear Creek. Second, as between two riparian users, the use of water to supply *natural* wants is preferred over and takes precedence of the use of water to supply *artificial* wants. In our case A's use of the water of Clear Creek is wholly to satisfy natural wants. She is using it for household and domestic purposes, for watering her cow, pigs and chickens and for watering her garden. On the other hand B is using the water solely for mining purposes which is entirely to satisfy artificial wants. Hence, A's use of the water should take priority over B's use of the water. Third, under the natural flow theory of riparian rights no riparian has the right to use stream water on non-riparian lands. B is violating such principle of riparian rights by using the water of Clear Creek on non-riparian lands and A has a right to enjoin such use. Under the reasonable use theory of riparian rights, use on non-riparian lands could not be reasonable as to the lower riparian when the upper riparian is using all of the stream water on non-riparian lands and is leaving none for the lower user. So it seems very clear that if the court is bound by the principles of riparian rights the demurrer of B should be overruled.

(b) However, if the court is governed by the doctrine of prior appropriation it must apply the distinguishing feature of that doctrine, *first in time is first in right*. According to the facts *B put to a beneficial use all of the water of Clear Creek before A ever used any of such water*. Our conclusion must then be this—B is first in time, he is therefore first in right, and A has no right to the use of any of the water of Clear Creek as against the prior appropriator B. Furthermore, B having the prior right to use all of the water of Clear Creek, has the right to divert the water from any point in the stream as long as vested rights of other appropriators are not thereby injured. And under this doctrine it is wholly immaterial whether the prior appropriator uses the water on riparian or non-riparian lands and whether he uses it for the satisfaction of natural or artificial wants. As to such land and as to such wants the doctrine of prior appropriation makes no distinction whatsoever. Under this doctrine B is first in time and is first in right and the injury to A is damnum absque injuria. B's demurrer must be sustained for A's complaint has stated no claim or cause of action against B. See a most instructive case, Mettler v. Ames Realty Co., 61 Mont. 152, 201 P. 702 (1921).

CASE 162: In state X, the prior appropriation doctrine of water rights governs. In 1902, A, owner of Blackacre, diverted all of the water of Clear Creek into his large diversion ditch which then carried the water two and one-half miles to his property. The base of the ditch was soil, and five-sixths of this water was lost en route to his property by absorption into the soil base, and only, negligibly, by evaporation. The water which actually arrived at his property originally was sufficient to irrigate fifteen acres of alfalfa, a family orchard, vegetable garden, and to satisfy household and cattle uses. Over the years the water reaching A's ranch was diminished considerably, so that from 1956 through 1965 there was only enough water for agricultural and livestock use of a domestic and non-commercial nature. Farther upsteam, in 1966, B diverted, under authority of an appropriation permit, approximately half of the water from Clear Creek for use on his ranch. B's use of the water was clearly a beneficial use. B's diversion caused a further decline in the amount of water coming into A's ditch downsteam. A brought an action against B to quiet title as to all the waters of Clear Creek; will A be successful?

Answer and Analysis

The answer is no but there are some qualifications. The policy behind the prior appropriation doctrine adopted by the relatively arid western states is to prevent waste, unreasonable use, and unreasonable method of use of water. Here, the method of A's use of the water from Clear Creek was unreasonable since five-sixths of the water was never put to use. Under the prior appropriation doctrine, the accent is placed upon the beneficial use of water. Here, most of the water from Clear Creek was not put to beneficial use by A, but was lost in his diversion ditch.

An appropriative right is not measured by the flow originally appropriated, and not by the capacity of the diversion ditch, but by the amount of water put to beneficial use at the delivery point and such additional flow as is reasonably necessary to deliver it. No matter how great in extent the original quantity had been, an appropriator can hold as against one subsequent in right only the maximum quantity of water which is devoted to beneficial use at some time within the period by which his right would otherwise be barred for non-user. Thus, A was entitled to one-sixth of the water from Clear Creek plus such additional water as may be necessary to propel it to his property if reasonable means of transportation is used. However, an appropriator who has transported the water for many years by an open ditch may not be compelled at his own expense to install impervious conduit. But if a junior appropriator is willing to bear such an expense in order to capture some of the lost water, he should be entitled to do so.

The water that actually did irrigate A's property was put to a beneficial use. Domestic uses of water, such as the irrigation of pastures, gardens, and fruit trees, and the watering of livestock are all beneficial uses of water. A's use of the water was reasonable, but only to the extent of the quantity that was reasonable to use to achieve his purposes. The excess water of Clear Creek that was not reasonably used by A can be used by a subsequent appropriator. Erickson v. Queen Val. Ranch Co., 22 Cal.App.3d 578, 99 Cal.Rptr. 446 (1971).

The last paragraph of the court's opinion in the preceding case reveals the following interesting facts: (1) for two and one half miles the irrigation ditch traverses land under the jurisdiction of the United States Forest Service; (2) over the years leakage from the ditch has generated vegetation; (3) the water and vegetation support a population of deer and quail; and (4) plaintiffs had sought permission to replace the ditch with a pipeline but the Forest Service declined for the sake of the animal and bird life. The court conjectured that Defendants might be able to work out a solution with the Forest Service, but that if a three-way extrajudicial solution were impossible, a three-way lawsuit in an appropriate forum would be necessary to resolve the problem.

Note

The 4 cases following deal with riparian rights.

CASE 163: A is a lower riparian owning Blackacre which is a 160 acre tract abutting the waters of Red River. A maintains a mill on his land which is operated by power from the water flow of Red River. B is an upper riparian owning Whiteacre which abuts Red River. B also owns Greenacre which does not touch the waters of Red River and is not contiguous to Whiteacre but is located farther from the River than the most remote corner of Whiteacre. On Greenacre B maintains a manufacturing plant which uses 50,000 gallons of water per day. B obtains all of this water from Red River by leading it over a ditch on Whiteacre to Greenacre. B has been running his manufacturing plant since Jan. 1, 1935 and has always used water from Red River on Greenacre for such purposes. But only since 1948 has B's plant grown to the point where he has used 50,000 gallons per day, and not until 1948 did B's use of the water from Red River actually lower the level of the water at A's mill six inches below its normal level, and make it impossible for A's water power to be sufficient to operate his mill. Also, during 1948 B's use of 50,000 gallons of water per day diverted across Whiteacre to Greenacre caused such a shortage of water power at A's mill that he had to shut it down much of the time. A sues B on Sept. 1, 1955, to enjoin his interfering with the operation of A's mill. B sets up a prescriptive right to the use of the water under a 10 year statute of limitation. Should the injunction issue?

Answer and Analysis

The answer is yes. One may gain a prescriptive right to use more water than he as a riparian owner normally has a right to use. But no such right can be had without there being a cause of action against the claimant thereof. A cause of action must accrue to the lower riparian to start the statute of limitations running. When, if at all, did B so act respecting the water of Red River as to give A a cause of action against him? Under the reasonable use theory of riparian rights an upper riparian has the right to make a reasonable use of the water of the stream on which he owns riparian land. Such reasonable use includes the right to use the water on either riparian or non-riparian lands. Riparian lands are lands which (a) touch the water of a stream or lake and (b) which are within the watershed, that is land which drains into the stream or lake. The theory of this requirement that land be within the watershed to be riparian is this: if water is taken out of the stream and is used on land within the watershed, then that water will either flow back into the stream or by percolation will join the stream farther down on its course. Furthermore, when the rains come it is this land within the watershed which feeds the stream and makes it possible for the stream to exist. Hence, there is good reason for permitting such land within the watershed to use the water of the stream which it supplies with water, and equally good reason for not permitting land outside the watershed to use the stream water without limitation.

B's Whiteacre is riparian land which makes B a riparian with rights as such. But B's Greenacre is non-riparian land. That it is noncontiguous to Whiteacre is immaterial. Every riparian may make reasonable use of the water but when he uses the water on non-riparian land there is this important limitation. The use on non-riparian land ceases to be reasonable when such use materially interferes with or injures the lower riparian in his use of the water of the stream. Prior to 1948 B's use of Red River water on Greenacre did not affect the level of the water at A's mill and it did not affect the water power generated to operate the mill. During the period of 1935 to 1948 B's use of the water from Red River was, as to A, entirely reasonable and therefore legal. After 1948 B's use of 50,000 gallons per day on Greenacre was, as to A, entirely unreasonable and therefore illegal. Why? Because the facts disclose that such use materially interfered with and injured A's use of the water by destroying part of his water power essential to the operation of A's mill. Usually what is a reasonable use of water by a riparian is a question of fact. To determine whether a use is or is not reasonable many factors must be considered such as, the supply of water, the character of the soil to be irrigated, the area to be irrigated, the climatic conditions, the means of diversion and loss of water by evaporation and seepage, the purposes to be served by the use to which the water is put, the effect such use has on lower riparians, and all the surrounding circumstances attending its use. However, when the fact is established that the use is on non-riparian land and that such use injures the lower riparian, then the use is unreasonable as a matter of law. But such injury or damage to A did not occur till 1948.

The cause of action did not accrue when the water was first used back in 1935 for there was then no damage to A. The cause of action first accrued to A when he was first injured which was in 1948.

Then the statute of limitations in B's favor began to run. But the 10 year period had not run when the action was brought in 1955. Therefore, B can claim no prescriptive right to use more water than that to which his position as a riparian entitles him. Thus, A has a right to an injunction. But how far should the decree enjoin B's use of water? Should it decree that B use no more water from Red River on his Greenacre? Certainly not. An equity court should and will save as many claims of each of the parties as possible. The decree should provide that B is enjoined from using such water from Red River on Greenacre as causes injury to A in the operation of his mill. That means that B may continue to use as much water from Red River as does not interfere with A's operating his mill. The number of gallons may be 20,000 or 40,000 gallons per day more or less, but the burden of letting enough water flow down to A to enable him to operate his mill is on B. Otherwise B would be in contempt of court. See Stratton v. Mount Herman Boys' Sch., 216 Mass. 83, 103 N.E. 87, 49 L.R.A.,N.S., 57, Ann.Cas.1915A, 768 (1913); Harris v. Harrison, 93 Cal. 676, 29 P. 325 (1892).

Note

The threefold classification of waters into diffused surface waters, streams, and percolating waters, as well as the concomitant differentiation between riparian and non-riparian land, no doubt functioned fairly well in a largely agrarian society with limited technological knowledge. Today, with a greater understanding of the complete hydrological cycle this approach seems somewhat arbitrary and elementary. There is constant evolution of the water cycle through various stages of rainfall, surface waters, streams, ground seepage, percolations, evaporation, cloud formation and back again to rainfall, and all of these natural processes know no legal or political boundaries. Water is the same substance whether it be aloft in clouds, descending in torrents, babbling in brooks, raging in floods, or percolating beneath the surface. To treat water at each stage of the cycle as if it were a distinct commodity is somewhat unrealistic, but until now, at least, it seemingly has served fairly well in solving immediate controversies between individuals with that resource at a particular stage of the cycle. As population pressures and industrial demands for this scarce resource increase, more comprehensive approaches to the problem may be necessary.

See Pendergrast v. Aiken, 293 N.C. 201, 236 S.E.2d 787 (1977), while adopting the rule of reasonable use as to surface drainage, made some interesting comments concerning the artificiality of the traditional three-fold classification of waters.

CASE 164: A owns 160 acres of land, Blackacre, which abuts Red River on the east side thereof where the stream runs almost due north. All of Blackacre is within the watershed. He has been irrigating all of Blackacre from the water of Red River. He conveys the east 80 acres of Blackacre to B. None of such 80 acres is closer than 80 rods to Red River. B diverts water from Red River to irrigate the 80 acres of land which he purchased from A. X, a lower riparian, then sought and obtained an injunction against B from using any water from Red River on such 80 acres. B then reconveyed the 80 acres to A who now has his original 160 acres again. X now sues A to enjoin A's use of water from Red River on the 80 acres which were reconveyed from B to A. May X succeed?

Answer and Analysis

The answer is no under the "unity of title" test. Only riparian owners have the right to use the water of a stream or lake. One is a riparian owner if he owns land which is riparian. Land is riparian if (a) it touches the water of a lake or stream *and* (b) it is within the watershed. It will be noticed that all of Blackacre is within the watershed so there can be no question as to meeting that requirement. As long as A was the sole owner of all of Blackacre, such land was riparian. It is immaterial how small or how large a tract of land is and the length of frontage on the water is immaterial. If it has the two essentials mentioned above it is riparian and the right to use the water from the stream or lake to which it is riparian attaches to every part of the land. But these requirements must continue to exist for the land to remain riparian. When A sold his east 80 acres to B that 80 acres continued to be within the watershed but it did not touch the water of Red River. Therefore it ceased to be riparian and its owner had no rights of a riparian. It was therefore correct for the court to grant the injunction in favor of X and against B. But when B reconveyed that 80 acre tract to A and all of Blackacre was again under one single ownership, that reinstated all of Blackacre to the position of riparian land. A can therefore irrigate all of Blackacre, including the 80 acres reacquired from B, from the waters of Red River. Thus, the court should deny the injunction sought by X. The test used in this case is that called "unity of title". Under it when the title to land comes within a single ownership and is all within a contiguous whole and all within the watershed, it is all riparian land regardless of the time when ownership is acquired. Under another view, called "source of title" test, the east half of Blackacre once having lost its position as riparian land, it cannot thereafter ever regain the status of riparian land. Under such test the right of irrigation is limited to the smallest tract touching the water and owned by any one ownership in the whole history of the title. This view permits the riparian land area to get smaller but not larger. See 36 Mich. Law R 346; Jones v. Conn, 39 Or. 30, 65 P. 1068, 87 Am.St.Rep. 634, 54 L.R.A. 630 (1901); Restatement, Second, Torts § 843, comment c; Burby, 50; 27 Cal.Law R. 92.

CASE 165: City B owns a 40 acre tract of land, Blackacre, abutting Clear Creek, on which tract it has built a waterworks plant for supplying its inhabitants and industrial units with water from Clear Creek. For this service and water B makes a regular charge monthly which is paid regularly by the water users. B City has so grown that it requires nearly all of the creek water to supply its needs. A is the owner of a lower riparian tract of land on which he operates a mill by the use of water power from Clear Creek. He has been so using the water for more than 50 years. Within the past 4 years and unaffected by any statute of limitations B's use of the water from Clear Creek has been so enormous in quantity that it has caused too little water to flow to A's mill to enable A to continue its operation. A seeks an injunction against B. May he succeed?

Answer and Analysis

The answer is yes. There is no reason why a municipality may not be a riparian the same as an individual person with similar riparian rights. In this case City B should be able to divert water from Clear Creek for the purpose of irrigating its Blackacre of 40 acres or for other purposes in its position of owner of the riparian tract. But City B is appropriating the water from Clear Creek and selling it to the inhabitants of the City. As to any inhabitant whose land abuts Clear Creek there can be no objection to B's acting for such a riparian inhabitant and furnishing water which the inhabitant himself could use. But for the great number of inhabitants and industrial units within City B who have no riparian lands, the City has no power or right to furnish them water as such. To hold otherwise would be to permit a municipal corporation to take from the lower riparians their water rights, and to transfer such to non-riparians who have no connection with the stream or with lands riparian to the stream. In substance it would be permitting the municipality to transform all of the non-riparian inhabitants of the city into riparians at the expense of the lower riparians and for which the municipality is being paid. Such is a clear taking of property for which the lower riparians have a right to compensation when it is used for public purposes. A is therefore entitled to have B enjoined from using the water of Clear Creek in such amount as to injure A's mill operations. If such injunction will result in B's having a supply of water insufficient in quantity to care for its inhabitants, then the injunction decree may be delayed in the discretion of the equity court until City B has the proper time to bring condemnation proceedings against the lower riparians for the purpose of determining the just compensation due them for the taking by City B of the water rights of such lower riparians, including A. See City of Emporia v. Soden, 25 Kan. 588, 37 Am.Rep. 265 (1881); notes, 22 L.R.A.,N.S., 386, 9 Ann.Cas. 1236; City of Canton v. Shock, 66 Ohio St. 19, 63 N.E. 600, 58 L.R.A. 637, 90 Am.St.Rep.

557 (1902); 12 Ky.L.J. 10 (1923). See Burby, 56, as to *Pueblo Rights.*

CASE 166: B is a mining company which owns Blackacre on which it has erected valuable buildings and mining equipment. The mines on Blackacre are some of the largest and most valuable in the state. B has over $25,000,000.00 invested and hires more than 1,500 men in the operation of its mines on Blackacre. This land is upper riparian land on Red River. A owns Whiteacre, a lower riparian tract used for farming and worth $8,000.00. A by a deed grants to C and agrees that C may use A's riparian water right attached to his Whiteacre, for the irrigation of C's Greenacre which abuts Whiteacre but does not abut Red River but is in the watershed of Red River. In the operation of its mines on Blackacre B casts into Red River poisonous material which makes the water therein totally unusable for irrigation purposes on either Whiteacre or Greenacre. C sues B for damages for injury to C's crops on Greenacre caused by the pollution of the water of Red River. May C recover?

Answer and Analysis

The answer is yes. The first question to be determined is the effect of A's deed to C of A's riparian water right. Some cases say that such a riparian water right cannot be conveyed away from the land of which it is a part and that the most such an attempted conveyance can be is an agreement between the parties thereto. But an owner of real property can convey the trees thereon, or the coal thereunder or the sand or gravel thereunder. Hence, other cases and the majority reason that the riparian water right is also an interest in land which can be conveyed. Of course, the grantee of such a right can have no more than his riparian grantor had and the grantee can exercise no greater or different use of the water than the grantor could as to other riparian owners. Thus we may conclude that C owns the riparian right which A had as part of his Whiteacre.

Every riparian has the right to have the water of the stream to which his land is riparian, come down to, by, or over his land free from unreasonable diminution in quantity and free from unreasonable pollution or deterioration in quality. A had that right and transferred it to C so that now C has that right. It should be carefully noticed that C's suit is not for an injunction. It is at law for damages. In an equity suit for an injunction the equity court would balance the equities of the parties and might well conclude that it would do more harm than good by granting the injunction when the result of granting such injunction might put 1,500 men out of work and shut down a major industry of the state, if such in fact would be the result. But in a case for damages at law no such balancing of interests can take place. If there is an injury caused by B's acts then there must be a remedy therefor and an action for damages is a proper remedy. And the fact that the defendant is large and powerful and the plaintiff may be poor and impotent is not a factor for consideration in a law case in a land which boasts of equality under the law. The facts disclose that the poisonous material cast into Red River by B makes the water of that stream totally unusable for irrigation purposes. While reasonable use is usually a question of fact under the circumstances, it is a question of law when no reasonable men can differ thereon. When the water of a stream is rendered totally unusable for one of the basic uses such as irrigation for the raising of crops, then no reasonable men can differ that the use being made of the water in Red River by B is unreasonable in its pollution of the water and therefore illegal. It deprives the lower riparians and their grantees of their equal use as riparians. Hence, C has a right to damages from B for its unreasonable pollution of the waters of Red River. This same result would obtain in a state where the prior appropriation doctrine governs. Suppose B is a subsequent appropriator upstream from A, the prior appropriator. B pollutes the waters of the stream which injures the use thereof by A. A has a cause of action against B for damages or an injunction or both. See 56 Am.Jur. p. 710 et seq.; Stockport Waterworks Co. v. Potter, 159 Eng.Rep. 545; Arizona Copper Co. v. Gillespie, 230 U.S. 46, 33 S.Ct. 1004, 57 L.Ed. 1384 (1913).

CASE 167: Red River is a small stream of water which flows due south to a point where it splits into the East Fork and the West Fork. This split in the river is caused by a sharp rock promontory appearing in the middle of the stream behind which rises Razor Back Knoll which continues to keep the waters of Red River separated as it continues its flow in a southerly direction. From the air Red River appears like a huge letter Y upside down with the prongs of the letter pointed to the southward. Lying across Red River at the point where it forks and extending north and south thereof is a 40 acre tract, Blackacre, which is owned by A. Abutting Blackacre on the north is B's Whiteacre. South of Blackacre and lying across the West Fork of Red River is C's Greenacre. South of Blackacre and lying across the East Fork of Red River is D's Brownacre.

At the fork of Red River A builds a dam which backs up the water of the river onto B's Whiteacre causing a large artificial lake thereon. When the level of the water of the lake has reached the top of his dam A turns the entire flow of the river down the West Fork of Red River and leaves the East Fork totally dry. Thereafter B builds a hotel, cottages and boat houses on the edge of the artificial lake on his land

and makes a resort on his land.　D levels off what was once the natural channel of the East Fork of Red River and makes it into an area of fields and gardens producing grains and vegetables.　Other land owners along East Fork do likewise. With the increased water supply along the West Fork C establishes a fish hatchery and builds ice houses for the storage of ice.　Other land owners along the West Fork build permanent structures depending on the continuation of the increased water supply.　In the jurisdiction the statute of limitations for gaining a prescriptive right is 10 years.　The conditions described continue for 40 years.　There grow up around the artificial lake on B's Whiteacre and along the edge of the water of West Fork large trees which make the lake and West Fork appear natural in origin.　Over the dam built by A grow moss, shrubbery and vines which make it appear as though it were a natural dam not built by human hands.　In what was once East Fork channel are now fields, gardens, houses and parts of villages.

A now threatens to tear down his dam and let Red River pursue its natural course.　This would leave B's hotel, cottages and boat houses "high and dry".　It would flood the fields, gardens, structures and parts of the villages in the original channel of East Fork.　It would leave C's fish hatchery and ice houses without access to the water of West Fork. B, C, and D join in an action seeking to enjoin A from demolishing his dam.　May they succeed?

Answer and Analysis

The answer is yes.　If this case were to be solved purely on logic and legalistic grounds a negative answer would result.　This side of the problem will be presented first.　A few important principles will help to reveal the analysis necessary to understand the problems presented by this set of facts.

1.　Damming, Diversion and Prescription

First, any riparian has a right to build a dam in the stream to which his land is riparian and the right temporarily to stop the stream flow while creating the artificial lake behind the dam provided it does not unreasonably interfere with the lower riparians. Such a use is reasonable and when the water level of the artificial lake reaches the level of the top of the dam, the theory is that the natural flow of the stream will continue without unreasonable diminution in quantity or quality.　But no riparian has the right to back up stream water on the land of the upper riparian.　If he does so the upper riparian has a cause of action against the actor.　So when A backed up the water of Red River onto B's Whiteacre there accrued in B's favor a cause of action against A for the wrongful act.　Such accrual of a cause of action in B's favor set the statute of limitations running in A's favor, and if the wrong continues for the statutory period, 10 years in our set of facts, then A will gain a prescriptive right to maintain the backed up water on B's land. And that is exactly what happened. A gained a prescriptive right to maintain the water of Red River on B's Whiteacre.

Second, no riparian has a right to divert a natural stream from its natural channel. When he does so a cause of action accrues against him in favor of each lower riparian. Thus in our case when A diverted East Fork from its natural channel a cause of action accrued in D's favor against A. And when A continued such diversion for more than the statutory period, 10 years in our case, A acquired a prescriptive right against D and other lower riparians to continue to divert the water of East Fork.

Third, no riparian has a right to divert a natural stream into another natural stream. When he does so each lower riparian on the stream into which the additional water is diverted has a cause of action against him. Thus, when A diverted the water from East Fork into West Fork there accrued in C's favor a cause of action against A. And when that diversion was continued for longer than the statutory period, A acquired against C and each other lower riparian a prescriptive right to maintain such diversion.

Summarizing, it should be carefully noticed that A has acquired three distinct easements by prescription: (a) one against B to maintain backed up stream water on B's Whiteacre; (b) one against D to divert all of the water of East Fork from its original natural channel; and (c) one against C to divert the water of East Fork into the channel of West Fork. And in each of these easements A is the dominant tenant. This means that A, by the inaction of B, C and D for the statutory period when each had a cause of action against A, is now in the controlling position having complete command of the situation. And in each of these easements B, C and D are respectively the servient tenants.

2. Rights of Dominant Tenant

Thus, in our case, B, C and D, by their inaction, have become as to their properties affected by A's wrongful acts and subject to A's domination. As to the lands, the legal effect of these facts is that it makes A's Blackacre the dominant tenement and Whiteacre, Greenacre and Brownacre servient tenements. Hence, in logic and on purely legalistic grounds, the conclusion would be that A, being a dominant tenant and the owner of the dominant tenement, has the right to maintain or demolish his dam at will, and no one may interfere with the exercise of such will even though A has no reason but only a whim to raze the dam.

On the other hand it must be noticed that this is not a law case, it is a case in equity which is a court of conscience. A litigant does not have a right as a right to equitable relief. It is a matter of grace and in the sound discretion of the equity court. The court will balance the equities of the parties and determine whether the granting of the injunction will do more good than harm or whether the denying of the injunction will result in more harm than good. On the one hand it seems A is injured little by leaving things as they are. On the other hand irreparable damage will be done if the injunction is denied and A removes his dam. B's resort with all its facilities will be rendered almost worthless, D's fields and gardens and parts of villages along East Fork will be destroyed and the established structures and businesses built along the higher water level of West Fork will be rendered worthless or almost so. By refusing the injunction on such determination the court would arbitrarily take from A his position and rights as a dominant tenant without satisfactory reason.

And to say that B, C and D have reciprocal easements is a conclusion wholly without merit and without any justifiable legal reason to support it. Why? Because an easement by prescription (and it can be none else in this case) must have for its foundation the accrual of a cause of action in favor of the servient tenant and against the dominant tenant. As to the reciprocal easements A would be the servient tenant and B, C and D the dominant tenants. Has either B, C or D committed any act which might constitute a cause of action in A's favor against any of them? Of course not. They have merely been passive as to A's wrongful acts of backing up water on B's land and diverting the East Fork water into the West Fork. So such conclusion, even though reaching a proper result, is wholly without legal reason to support it.

The court might use the doctrine of estoppel against A but the trouble with estoppel is this—A has done no act on which B, C or D had the right to rely and without right of reliance the doctrine is not properly applicable.

3. New Natural Conditions

Most of the cases which have had to solve the problem presented here have concluded that A has no right to change the conditions which he has created. They reason that when conditions have been created artificially but have been maintained for as long as the forty year period in our case, then the element of time has transformed such conditions from artificial conditions into natural conditions and the law should treat them as such. Furthermore, such transformation is justified when to permit a change would cause irreparable damage to many quite innocent persons. With that premise as the first step, the next logical conclusion must be that the lake on B's land is a natural lake, that West Fork with all the water from Red River flowing therein, is a natural stream and that East Fork as a stream no longer exists. Conclusion—A has no right to turn loose the water of a natural lake, no right to divert any of the water naturally flowing in West Fork and no right to cast water from a natural stream into the fields and gardens and villages in the valley of what was once in the dim and distant past the channel of a natural stream, East Fork. Perhaps this is an arbitrary determination also but it is probably the best reason yet devised on which to base what is considered a fair and just result. However, in the absence of a long period of time and irreparable injury, the law should protect A in his dominant estate. See Goodrich v. McMillan, 217 Mich. 630, 187 N.W. 368, 26 A.L.R. 801 (1922); Kray v. Muggli, 84 Minn. 90, 86 N.W. 882, 54 L.R.A. 473, 87 Am.St.Rep. 332 (1901); Hammond v. Antwerp Light & Power Co., 132 Misc. 786, 230 N.Y.S. 621 (1928); Burby, 49; 36 Mich.L.R. 1432.

CASE 168: In state X the prior appropriation doctrine of water rights governs, and the water of running streams, either on the surface or underground, is made subject to prior appropriation. In that state percolating water is governed by the common law and is not subject to prior appropriation. A is a prior appropriator of all the water of Clear Creek which water is being used to irrigate A's Blackacre. Farther upstream from where Blackacre is located, B is digging a series of wells on his own land, Whiteacre, across which Clear Creek flows. Some of B's wells are within 25 feet of the banks of Clear Creek. B is pumping water from his wells and storing it in large reservoirs for stock watering. As B continues to dig more wells and pump more water, the supply of water which comes to A's Blackacre decreases in amount, and A concludes that B's pumping water from his wells is the cause of the diminishing supply of water to which A has a prior right as an appropriator. A sues to enjoin B's pumping water in such a way as to diminish his water supply. It is stipulated that B's pumping is causing the diminution of A's water supply, but B contends he has a right to continue pumping because the water which he is extracting from under the surface is percolating and therefore belongs to him as surface owner, and is no part of the stream water which A has appropriated. Should the injunction issue?

Answer and Analysis

The answer is yes. At common law percolating water may be taken and used by the owner of the surface under which the water is found. And it is presumed that underground water is percolating water, and the burden is on him who says it is otherwise to show it. So it is necessary to find out just what A appropriated when he became prior appropriator of all of the water of Clear Creek.

A stream of water consists of (a) a bed (b) banks and (c) a flow of water. Usually the flow of water is evidenced by water which is seen on the surface of the ground held in place by well defined banks. If the bed and banks of a stream are composed of impervious granite that would be all there is to it. But the soil through which streams of water flow are not ordinarily composed of granite but of other soils such as clay, loam or sand or a mixture of these. When such is the case it usually takes a great deal of water under the bed and beyond the banks of a stream to support the surface flow. In other words, the ground which constitutes the bed and banks of a stream must be saturated with water before the surface flow can appear as a visible stream of water. And of course the more porous the soil the more water it will take to saturate the bed and banks to support the flow on the surface. This water which saturates the bed and banks of a stream and moves slowly through the soil in the direction of the surface stream constitutes the subflow and the lateral flow of the stream. But such subflow and lateral flow are part and parcel of the stream of water.

When A became the prior appropriator of all of the water of Clear Creek his prior right not only included the right to the surface flow of the stream at the point of diversion, it also included a right that the subflow and the lateral flow remain without interference so that they might continue the support of the surface flow and carry it undiminished to A's point of diversion on Blackacre. When it was stipulated that B's pumping of water was diminishing the amount of water which was reaching A's Blackacre for irrigation purposes, this was an admission on B's part that his pumping was in an area wherein Clear Creek's subflow and lateral flow are located. Such stipulation carried A's burden of proof as to causation which is usually a fact question. Hence, B's pumping is drawing out of the earth the subflow and the lateral flow of Clear Creek at least to the extent that it is diminishing A's surface supply of water for the irrigation of Blackacre. To that extent it is taking stream water which is subject to A's prior appropriation right.

The test for determining what underground water is percolating and what is the subflow or lateral flow of a stream is one which is easy to state but very difficult to apply to a given set of facts. It is this—if the drawing off of the underground water affects the flow of the stream, then the water being drawn off is a part of the subflow or lateral flow of the stream. If the drawing off of the underground water does not affect the flow of the stream, then such water is percolating water. In our case the usual fact question of causation is settled by the stipulation. It applies the test and shows that A is entitled to a decree enjoining B from pumping any water which interferes with the subflow or lateral flow of Clear Creek which detracts from A's prior appropriation. See a very instructive case, Maricopa County Municipal Conservation Dist. No. 1 v. Southwest Cotton Co., 39 Ariz. 65, 4 P.2d 369 (1931).

———

CASE 169: A is the owner of Blackacre, an 80 acre tract on which he operates a small dairy. Through the tract flows a small stream called Squaw Creek. A spring flows out of the side of a small hill near A's dairy and a well nearby furnishes a plentiful supply of water. All three of these sources of water are used for operating A's dairy, for household purposes, and for irrigation of a garden and a small field. City X buys a section of land above A's dairy farm and expends $1,000,000.00 in erecting a waterworks plant, including 20 large artesian wells in order to supply water to the inhabitants of the city. The withdrawal of such amounts of underground water by City X causes the drying up of Squaw Creek, the spring and the well on A's dairy farm. A sues City X for damages. All of the above facts are stipulated by the parties to be true but City X contends that the injury to A is damnum absque injuria which prevents his recovery. May A recover?

Answer and Analysis

The better answer is yes. Under the English rule as to percolating waters the owner of the surface is the owner of all underneath the soil whether the substance thereunder be solid or semi-solid or fluid like water. If such rule were applied in this case then X's withdrawal of percolating water from under its own land would constitute mere extracting of its own property and indeed A would have no recovery. His loss of his water supply would be damnum absque injuria for which the law can give no redress. But there are at least two flaws in the reasoning in such rule. One is that such rule assumes no difference between substances which underlie the surface soil. But solid rock under the soil which remains fixed in place should not be treated like a fluid such as water which is mobile in nature. Then again, if each surface owner owns all the substance underneath his surface, how can the conclusion be reached that if A pumps out all the water under A's soil, and also through the same well pumps out all of the water under B's soil, that A owns all the water he has pumped including that which was under B's soil? Such reasoning is not satisfactory for it first says the water under B's soil belongs to B, and then says that if A pumps out such water it belongs to A.

The so-called American rule of "reasonable use" as to percolating water is based on better reasoning and brings about a more just and equitable result between landowners competing for the use of such underground water. The substance of such rule is this—every surface owner has the right to withdraw and make a reasonable use of the percolating water under the surface of his land, and such use is reasonable if the water is used beneficially on the land from under which it is withdrawn or used in the development of such land. Such use may be reasonable even when the water is used on other land provided it does not interfere with or injure neighboring landowners. But the use of such water on land other than that from under the surface of which it is withdrawn is unreasonable and illegal when it interferes with or injures the use thereof by neighboring proprietors.

Applying this doctrine to our set of facts, it is clear that A should recover from City X. The City was pumping percolating water from under the surface which it owned. That it had a right to do. And it had a right to use such water on the section of land which it owned to the extent that it benefited such land or developed it. The City would have no right to waste such water simply because it pumped it from under the ground. The law has no interest in protecting any landowner in wasting water. But the facts do not disclose any use by City X on its owned section of land from under which the water is withdrawn. The water is used for the benefit of the inhabitants of the City. Therefore, when City X carries the percolating water from the land from under which it is withdrawn, and such use on other land injures the neighboring proprietor, A in our case, then such neighboring landowner can say such use is unreasonable and illegal.

The doctrine of "reasonable use" does not prevent a landowner from withdrawing and using the percolating water from under his soil to develop his own land even though it may damage his neighbor, but it does prevent the use of such water as an article of merchandise or the use on other land at the expense of the neighbor. Thus, City X, which is using the percolating water on land other than its own from which it has been extracted, and for the purpose of furnishing it to the inhabitants of the City is liable to A, the neighboring proprietor, for the damage it has caused him. See the leading case, Meeker v. City of East Orange, 77 N.J.L. 623, 74 A. 379, 25 L.R.A.,N.S., 465, 134 Am.St.Rep. 798 (E. & A.1909); Acton v. Blundell, 12 M. & W. 324 (1843); 14 Mich.L.R. 119.

CASE 170: A is the owner of Blackacre, a section of land. It is used for the purpose of raising cattle. A's house with its outbuildings stands in the northeast corner of the tract. B owns the section abutting Blackacre on the north and C owns the section abutting Blackacre on the south. The general slope of the area is from north to south and southwest. When the heavy rains come a short low valley which is in no sense a natural water course carries the surface water from B's land directly against A's house, flows into his basement and into his outbuildings. A builds a concrete wall three feet high along his north border and across the low valley which carries the surface water to his buildings. This causes the surface water to stand and become stagnant on B's property. In the southwest corner of Blackacre A builds a dike which impounds most of the surface water which falls from the rains on Blackacre and drains to the southwest. Behind this dike a large reservoir of water is formed from the natural drainage of the surface water on Blackacre and is used the year around by A for stock watering. B sues A to compel him to remove the concrete wall along his north border which prevents the natural flow of the surface water to the south. C sues A to compel him to remove the dike which impounds the surface water in the southwest corner of Blackacre contending that C has used this surface water for years on his land for the benefit of his crops. **(a)** May B succeed in his action? **(b)** May C succeed in his action?

Answers and Analyses

The traditional answer to (a) is no, but the trend of cases would answer yes if A's conduct were considered unreasonable and resulted in substantial damages to B. The answer to (b) is no. Surface waters are those which come from rain, springs and melting snow and ice, simply follow the contours of the land and have not yet reached a natural water course or basin with well defined bed and banks. Waters in marshes and swampland are usually considered surface waters. In our set of facts all of the waters involved are obviously surface waters. None of such water has reached a natural water course and all has come from the rains. There are three doctrines governing rights over surface waters: (a) the *civil law rule*; (b) the *common law rule*; and (c) the *reasonable use* or *reasonable conduct* rule. The first two of these rules permit the surface owner of land to impound and make use of any and all of the surface waters which he is able to capture on his land. The result would be the same under the third rule if the landowner's conduct were considered reasonable. The principal difference in the application of the rules comes in the obstruction of the flow of surface water.

Under the civil law rule every lower piece of land is burdened with a servitude in favor of the higher land to receive and carry the natural flow of surface water and the owner of the lower tract has no right to obstruct the natural flow of the surface water. Under the common law rule, sometimes called the common enemy rule, the lower tract is not burdened with any servitude in favor of the higher land and the owner of the lower tract has the right to protect his lower tract from "the common enemy" or the flow of surface water by making any improvements which are suitable for the purpose.

The common law rule had been applied in most of the states, but an increasing number is adopting the rule of reasonable use. Under this rule each possessor is privileged to make a reasonable use of his land, even though an altered flow of surface water may cause some harm to others, but liability is incurred if his conduct is unreasonable and causes substantial damages.[2] What then are the rights of B and C against A in their respective actions?

(a) Under the civil law rule it is clear that B would have the right to compel A to remove his wall which obstructs the flow of the surface water onto Blackacre for the reason that Blackacre, being the lower tract as to B's land, is burdened with a servitude in favor of B's higher tract and is bound to receive and carry off such surface water which naturally flows from B's land onto Blackacre. Hence, under

---

2. See Pendergrast v. Aiken, 293 N.C. 201, 236 S.E.2d 787 (1977); also, Armstrong v. Francis Corp., 20 N.J. 320, 120 A.2d 4 (Sup.Ct.1956).

this doctrine A has no right to obstruct the flow of such surface water. On the other hand under the common law rule every landowner has the right to obstruct and shut out a common enemy. He has the right to treat surface water as such common enemy and the right to protect his land against it. Under this doctrine A's concrete wall or any improvements he makes on his land such as building, grading or planting which obstructs the flow of surface water onto his lower tract are considered reasonable use of the land and if such improvements affect injuriously the owner of the higher land, then such damage is damnum absque injuria for which the law affords no redress. This rule permits every landowner the freedom to improve his land as he sees fit so long as he does no affirmative act in the direction of his neighbor such as actually casting water on his neighbor's land, or does not commit a nuisance on his own land. Under the reasonable use rule, A would be privileged unless the court concluded that his conduct was unreasonable and resulted in substantial damages. Under the common law rule B has no right against A and should fail in his suit. Under the reasonable use rule the result would probably be the same.

(b) C's action is simple and easy of solution. Under either the civil law rule or the common law rule the landowner has the right to capture and use any and all surface waters which fall on or flow onto his land. When it is said that the has the right to "appropriate" such surface waters it should be carefully noted that this word is used in its generic sense and has nothing to do with the doctrine of prior appropriation. As here used it means merely the right to capture and use the surface water. Hence, when A impounded the surface waters on his Blackacre he was doing an act which he had a right to do and the fact that such act deprives C of the surface water he had been accustomed to use on his land is quite immaterial. C's damage, if any, is damnum absque injuria and he has no cause of action against A. The result would appear to be the same under the reasonable use rule.

Of course if the surface water on A's Blackacre had entered a natural water course with well defined bed and banks, then such water would cease to be surface water and would have become stream water and subject to the rights of riparians. Then A would have no right to impound and use such waters to the exclusion of C who would then be a lower riparian with the right to have such stream flow down to, through or over his land free from unreasonable diminution either in quantity or quality. Much litigation in this field turns on the question as to whether the water has ceased to be surface water and has become stream water. This is usually a question of fact. See Burby, 59–61; 59 A.L.R.2d 424; Haferkamp v. City of Rock Hill, 316 S.W.2d 620 (Mo.1958), re common law rule; Ambrosio v. Perl-Mack Constr. Co., 143 Colo. 49, 351 P.2d 803 (1960), re civil law rule; Pendergrast v. Aiken, 293 N.C. 201, 236 S.E.2d 787 (1977), re reasonable use rule.

CASE 171: A owns Blackacre, a quarter section of land. B owns Whiteacre, the quarter section which abuts Blackacre on the north. C owns Greenacre, the quarter section which abuts Blackacre on the south. Through the center of the three quarter sections and extending from north to south is a low marshy, swampy area created and fed wholly by rains and having no well defined banks. The natural drainage is from north to south but the slope is so gradual as to be almost imperceptible. Within this wet spongy ground and lying across the boundary line between A's Blackacre and B's Whiteacre is an area containing about six acres, half on each quarter section, whereon water usually stands in depth from one to two feet. On his side of the boundary line B has developed a small business in which he raises and sells water lilies which grow naturally in this marshy pool of water. C has partially drained the bog on his Greenacre and uses most of the area which was once spongy earth as fields for growing crops.

A now conceives the idea of draining the swampland on his Blackacre so that he may grow crops thereon. By means of small ditches carefully constructed which follow the natural contour of the land he drains the pool of water from his side of the boundary line between Blackacre and Whiteacre. But of course the draining of the part of the pool on Blackacre also causes the water from the pool on Whiteacre to flow south and leaves B's lily pool without water. At the other end of A's drainage project the water slowly flows, oozes or seeps onto C's Greenacre thus interfering with C's crops. A is not negligent. B sues A for damages for draining the water from Whiteacre and C sues A for damages for draining the water from Blackacre and causing it to drain onto Greenacre. **(a)** May B recover? **(b)** May C recover?

Answers and Analyses

The answer to (a) is no. The answer to (b) is no. No landowner has the right to gather together surface water and cast it on his neighbor's land. He is liable in damages for doing so. He is not liable if by natural flow or drainage, surface water passes from his land onto the land of his neighbor. Between these two situations is the case in which the landowner by artificial means assists nature in draining his land. Some cases lay down the rule that if the landowner by artificial means discharges surface water onto his neighbor's land and thereby injures him there is liability. This treats the case as though any artificial means is a casting of water onto the land of the neighbor. Such a holding can be justified. On the other hand, a landowner should be able to improve his land and not be compelled in perpetuity to let his land lie unimproved and unproductive. In our case it should be noticed that A is free of negligence and that his efforts are directed solely to the improvement of his land. Further, it should be noticed that the artificial means used by A do not gather together the surface water and cast it onto C's land. They merely assist the surface water to drain along the natural slope of the land. Of course it is a matter of degree. If a heavy rain should come and wash small ditches through the spongy material of the swamp or marsh and the same drainage would take place as is now occurring through A's artificially made ditches, then there would obviously be no liability on A. Taking all the facts into consideration it appears that the principal ingredients of the cause of injury to C's land is not the act of A but the combined natural elements involved, towit: the surface water lodged in the swamp, the natural slope of the drainage area and the weight of the spongy earth which squeezes out the water therein. Thus, in substance the forces of nature are causing a drainage of surface water from A's land and the damage to B and C is damnum absque injuria, and neither can recover from A. In such case it seems better to leave B and C to their remedies of self help.

Under the civil law rule A's land would have to receive and carry the surface water from B's land. But that B does not want. He wants the surface water of the swamp to remain and support his water lily business. All he has to do then is to improve his own land by erecting a wall or other improvement by which he captures such water and retains it on his Whiteacre. He can do the same under the common law and reasonable use rules. As to C, he could not object to the drainage of the surface water from Blackacre under the civil law rule for his Greenacre is bound to receive and carry away such surface water. And under the common law rule C has the right to erect an obstruction along his north border to protect his Greenacre from the drainage surface water from Blackacre. Under the reasonable use rule both A and C are entitled to act reasonably. A's conduct clearly seems reasonable here, and C could take reasonable means to drain his lands. Thus, each landowner is free to improve his own land and is burdened with the problem of disposing of the surface water on his particular land, keeping in mind that any landowner is liable for negligent acts which cause injury to his neighbor and is liable for unreasonably casting water on his neighbor's land. See Terry v. Heppner, 59 S.D. 317, 239 N.W. 759 (1931); Stouder v. Dashner, 242 Iowa 1340, 49 N.W.2d 859 (1951); Burby, 60.

CASE 172: A's railroad track runs due north and south. Indian Creek has a channel about 30 feet in width and 4 feet deep. Most of the year it is a dry wash. But when the heavy rains come the channel is full and much water overflows its banks and covers the country on either side thereof. The channel of Indian Creek runs in a southwesterly direction as it approaches A's railroad track. When it gets within about 300 feet of the railroad track its course turns almost a right angle and following a southeasterly direction. On several occasions during the rainy season the channel of

Indian Creek has not been of sufficient capacity to contain
the great supply of water which flows down from the surrounding hills. The water overflows the banks of the Creek
and drives onto A's railroad tracks and so saturates the soil
which supports the track that A's trains are impeded in their
progress and large additional sums of money are spent in
track maintenance. To remedy this condition A builds large
dikes between its tracks and Indian Creek and parallel with
the tracks. B is the owner of agricultural land on the east
side of Indian Creek, the opposite side of the Creek from
where A's dike is located. The floods theretofore have not
materially affected B's land or the crops grown thereon. In
the rainy season following the construction of A's dike B's
land and the crop growing thereon are flooded and the crop
is destroyed. The effect of A's dike has been to cast the
flood waters back into Indian Creek from where they continue across the channel of the Creek and overflow B's land. B
sues A for damage to his crop. May he recover?

Answer and Analysis

The answer is no. There is nothing in this set of facts to indicate any negligence on the part of A, and in the absence of such, the
injury to B's crops is damnum absque injuria. Surface water is that
which comes from rains, springs and melting snow and ice and follows the contours of the land and has not yet reached the waters of a
stream or lake. On the other hand flood water is that which has
been in the water of a stream or lake and has overflowed the banks
of the stream or the lake. In the facts of our case the waters of Indian Creek have overflowed its banks and are flood waters. Any landowner is entitled to treat flood waters like surface waters as a common enemy and has a right to protect his land against its depredations. Therefore, when A built a dike to protect its railroad track
from the encroachments of the flood waters of Indian Creek, it was
doing only what good sense and reason would dictate, and the law
will protect it even when such act on A's part will result in injury
to the neighboring proprietor. If B would protect his land and his
crops from the flood waters of Indian Creek he will have to do as A
has done and build a wall or a dike which will obstruct the destructive
force of those flood waters. Hence, B's action against A must fail.
See Southern Pacific Co. v. Proebstel, 61 Ariz. 412, 150 P.2d 81 (1944).

CASE 173: Lake A is a lake of approximately 75 acres. It
is non-navigable and landlocked, and is wholly owned by the
parties litigant and other adjoining landowners. D owns a
29 acre tract on the lake and operates thereon a public
beach. D leases portions of his tract to B. B operates a
water skiing school on the lake. The school operates every-
day in the week, from early morning until dark, and the

skiers use the entire surface of the lake, frequently going close to shore and sending large waves and assorted debris onto the beaches. The boats make considerable noise, emit large quantities of exhaust fumes, and are frequently operated in congested areas thereby endangering the lives and safety of plaintiff and other landowners using the lake for bathing and other recreational purposes. The operation is alleged to be such as to interfere unreasonably with the use and enjoyment of P's property and that of other landowners. P owns two parcels, one westerly near the northern end and the other at the southwestern portion of the lake. P's northern tract has a common boundary with the southern property line of D's tract. If the property lines are extended into the lake, they intersect at a point which gives D only a small wedge-shaped area on the lake surface. P brings an action against B and D seeking: **(a)** an injunction against the water skiing activities on the basis that they constitute a nuisance; and **(b)** a decree that D and B shall be restricted in the use of the lake to the waters overlying the wedge-shaped area which is owned by D. Is P entitled to the injunction and the decree?

Answer and Analyses

The answers are as follows: (a) D and B should be enjoined from carrying on water skiing activities in such a manner as to constitute a nuisance; and (b) D and B, under the more practical civil law rule, should not be restricted to the area of the lake which overlies the bottom owned by D, but instead, their right to use the surface of the entire lake for recreational purposes should be recognized.

(a) The facts stated in the problem are sufficient to support the allegation that the operation of the water skiing activities constitute an unreasonable interference with the use and enjoyment of the property of the other landowners. Such activities therefore amount to a nuisance. The facts indicate a continued annoyance, discomfort, and even danger to the lakefront community. Accordingly, relief is authorized. Water skiing, however, is itself not a nuisance per se. The injunction should be phrased so as not to enjoin the defendants from engaging in water skiing activities entirely, but only from engaging in them in such a manner as to substantially interfere with the rights of the other landowners. The injunction should be framed in terms of restrictions on the hours of operation, the area of operation, and the number participating at any one time so as to protect the rights of all the landowners.

(b) In regard to the use of waters of privately owned landlocked lakes, there are two different theories—the common law rule and the civil law rule. The common law rule restricts each landowner to the use of the waters overlying the land he owns, whereas the civil law rule permits all the owners of a portion of the lake bottom to use all of the waters for boating, bathing, and recreational purposes. The civil law rule commends itself as being more practical and utilitarian. Each landowner may find himself severely restricted if he is limited to waters overlying his owned land, whereas each will get a far greater benefit if all are entitled to use all of the waters. Each, however, must use the water in a reasonable manner so as not to interfere with the use of the other adjoining landowners. The right of each landowner is equal, and the rights must be so exercised as to recognize the similar rights of the other landowners. Adopting, then, the civil law rule, the defendants in the instant case are entitled to use all of the waters, and the plaintiff is not entitled to a contrary decree. See Florio v. State ex rel. Epperson, 119 So.2d 305 (Fla.2d D. C.A.1960) (water skiing); Duval v. Thomas, 114 So.2d 791 (Fla. 1959) (use of lake water). See also infra Chapter XIII as to nuisance.

SUMMARY OF CASES IN CHAPTER XII

Case 161. Under the doctrine of riparian rights every riparian has the right to have the stream of water flow down to, by, through and over his land free from unreasonable diminution in quantity and from unreasonable pollution in quality. This statement should apply equally in either a natural flow or reasonable use jurisdiction. Under such rules the use of water for the satisfaction of natural wants takes precedence over the use of water for the satisfaction of artificial wants. Under either theory of riparian rights it would be unreasonable for an upper riparian to use all of the water in a stream and on non-riparian lands and leave no water at all for the lower riparian. The rights of riparians are equal. Under the doctrine of prior appropriation the distinguishing feature is first in time is first in right, and such doctrine makes no distinction whatsoever between the use of water on riparian and non-riparian lands, and none between the use of water for natural and for artificial wants.

Case 162. The extent of an appropriation right is measured not by the flow originally appropriated and not by the capacity of the diversion ditch, but rather by the amount of water put to beneficial use at the delivery point plus such additional flow as is reasonably necessary to deliver it. Domestic non-commercial uses for agricultural, irrigation and animal raising are beneficial uses for which an appropriation may be obtained. If a prior appropriator wastes water by use of inefficient diversion ditches, a later appropriator may be entitled to an appropriation of the wasted water if he invests in a more efficient transfer method on behalf of the prior appropriator.

Case 163. To be riparian land it must (a) touch the water of a lake or stream and (b) be within the watershed. By prescription a riparian owner may gain a right to use more water than he is entitled to as a riparian, but to do that he must do an act which gives the lower riparian a cause of action against him and the statute of limitations must run its full course. Under the reasonable use theory of riparian rights a riparian owner may use water on either riparian or non-riparian land, but if the water is used on non-riparian land and such use causes injury to the lower riparian, that use is unreasonable as a matter of law, and a cause of action accrues to the injured lower riparian.

Case 164. Land is riparian if it touches the water of a lake or stream and is within the watershed. It is not material how small or large the tract is, and the length of frontage on the water is unimportant. When title to riparian land is severed and the part conveyed has no frontage on the water of the lake or stream, it ceases to be riparian and the owner has no riparian rights. If land within the watershed which is not riparian is purchased by a riparian and the two properties are contiguous, then that land which was non-riparian becomes, under the "unity of title test", riparian land. Under the "source of title" test once a piece of land ceases to be riparian it can never thereafter regain a riparian status. Under this test riparian status is limited to the smallest tract touching the water during the entire history of the title.

Case 165. While a municipality which owns riparian land may exercise the same rights as any other riparian concerning the use of water, the better rule is that it cannot claim to be a riparian as to all and each of the inhabitants thereof and furnish water to such inhabitants at the expense of the lower riparian owners. For doing such the city should be liable to the lower riparians, and if it would continue to furnish water from the stream to its inhabitants, it may do so through condemnation proceedings and paying just compensation to the lower riparians for taking their water rights.

Case 166. The general rule is that a riparian water right can be conveyed by its owner from the land of which it is a part and that the grantee has the same rights with the same limitations as had the riparian grantor, including the right to sue an upper riparian who unreasonably pollutes the water of the stream. Every riparian or his assignee or grantee has the right to have the water of the stream to which his land is riparian come down to, by or over such land free from unreasonable diminution in quantity and free from unreasonable pollution or deterioration in quality. If the lower riparian or his grantee sues the upper riparian for an injunction in equity the court will balance the equities in deciding whether or not to grant the injunction, but in an action at law for damages there is no such balancing of interests, and the plaintiff has a right to damages for unreasonable pollution of the waters of the stream by the upper riparian.

Case 167. A riparian owner has the right to build a dam on the stream to which his land is riparian and a right to impound the water of the stream behind the dam. He has the right to stop the flow of the stream temporarily for such purpose provided he does not unreasonably interfere with the lower riparians. A riparian owner does not have the right to back stream water onto the land of an upper riparian. If he does do so and continues to maintain the water thereon for the statutory period he gains a prescriptive right to maintain such water on the land of the upper riparian. A riparian owner has no right to divert the flow of a natural stream of water. If he does so and continues the diversion for the statutory period he gains a prescriptive right to continue the diversion as against the lower riparians. If a riparian creates an artificial lake above his dam or creates an artificial stream by diversion of the waters of a natural stream, and continues to maintain such artificial lake or stream for a long period of time, the law may treat such lake or stream as a natural lake or stream and subject to the common law governing natural lakes and streams.

Case 168. A stream of water consists of (a), a bed (b), banks and (c), a flow of water. This flow of water consists of a subflow, a lateral flow and a visible flow on the surface, if the water is sufficient in amount that a surface flow appears. Under the prior appropriation doctrine one who appropriates all of the water of a stream has prior right to the subflow, the lateral flow and the surface flow, which means that he has the right that the supporting subflow and lateral flow which support the surface flow be not interfered with. At common law one who owns the surface of the land has the right to take and use the percolating water under the surface.

Case 169. Under the English law percolating water under the surface is subject to the absolute control of the surface owner, and if the withdrawal thereof affects the neighboring proprietor injuriously, it is damnum absque injuria. Under the American doctrine of "reasonable use" the owner of the surface may withdraw the percolating water from under the surface of his land and make reasonable use thereof. Using such water beneficially on his land or to develop such land is reasonable even though it injures his neighbor landowner. But using such percolating water on land other than that from which it is withdrawn, or using it as an article of merchandise elsewhere, is unreasonable when such use injures the neighboring proprietor and creates in such neighboring landowner a cause of action for damages.

Case 170. Surface waters are governed either by the civil law rule, the common law rule, or the rule of reasonable use. Under each or all of these rules the landowner may impound and use any or all surface water which falls on or flows onto his land, and if such causes injury to his neighbor it is damnum absque injuria. The difference in the rules appears when the flow of surface water is obstructed by the lower owner to prevent its reaching his land. Under the civil law rule the lower tract of land is burdened with a servitude in favor of the higher tract to receive and carry off surface water which naturally flows from the higher to the lower tract. Under the common law rule, the lower tract of land is not burdened with a servitude in favor of the higher tract. Any landowner may treat surface water as a common enemy and protect his land against it by obstructing the natural flow thereof, and if such obstruction injures the owner of the higher tract it is damnum absque injuria. Under the reasonable use rule each owner's conduct will be measured by the test of reasonableness. Surface water includes water which comes from rains, springs, melting snow and ice, the water in marshes and swamplands, none of which has yet reached a natural water course or basin.

Case 171. When the owner of lower land drains swamps and marshes on his own land and such act also drains similar areas on the higher land, it is damnum absque injuria as to the owner of the higher land. If the owner of the higher land drains his land along the natural course of drainage and in the improvement of his land injures a lower owner, it is damnum absque injuria as to the lower owner even if the drainage is onto the land of the lower owner. But a landowner is liable for gathering together surface water and forcefully casting it on his neighbor's land, and for negligent acts which cause injury to his neighbor.

Case 172. Surface waters are those which come from rains, springs and melting snow and ice, which follow the contour of the land and have not yet reached the water of a stream or lake. Flood waters are those which have already been a part of stream or lake waters and have overflowed the banks of the stream or lake. Any landowner may treat flood waters or surface waters as a common enemy and may protect his land against the depredations thereof. If in the protection of one's land against the encroachments of flood or surface waters the land of a neighbor is injured it is damnum absque injuria for which the law furnishes no redress.

Case 173. Water skiing activities are not a nuisance per se but they become a nuisance when carried on in such a manner as to interfere unreasonably with the use and enjoyment of the property of adjoining landowners. Under the civil law rule each proprietor of a portion of a nonnavigable lake is entitled to use the waters of the entire lake for boating and other recreational purposes.

Chapter XIII

NUISANCE

Legal Gems.
Cases.
Summary of Cases in Chapter XIII.

LEGAL GEMS

1. A private nuisance consists of conduct which interferes with or disturbs the use and enjoyment of land. To be actionable three essential elements must occur—

    a. the interference with the plaintiff's use and enjoyment of his land must be both substantial and unreasonable,

    b. the defendant's conduct must be either (1) intentional and unreasonable (which is the usual case), or (2) negligent, reckless, wanton or unusually hazardous, and

    c. the defendant's conduct must cause the interference.

2. A public nuisance is conduct which injures the public health, morals, safety or general welfare. It is criminal in nature although the same act which gives rise to criminal liability often entails civil liability also. The subject of public nuisance will not be dealt with in this treatise.

3. The essential basis for liability in a private nuisance is the interference with the use and enjoyment of land. A fee owner, a life tenant, a tenant for years or from week to week, or an adverse possessor may maintain the action. But a mere licensee or laborer on the land, having no interest in the land as such, cannot maintain an action for private nuisance.

4. Notice carefully the following four cases and distinctions—

    a. In trespass land is invaded by a tangible physical object which interferes with the right of exclusive possession. E. g., A walks on or throws a rock on B's land. B's action against A is one of trespass.

    b. In the case of a private nuisance, land is invaded, not by any tangible matter, but by intangibles such as noises or odors which unreasonably interfere with the use and enjoyment of the land. E. g., A operates on his land a soap factory within a few feet of B's house. The noise from A's engines and the odors from the materials he uses invade B's bedroom windows 24 hours each day in the week. A's unreasonable conduct or unreasonable use of his land interferes both substantially and unreasonably with B's use and enjoyment of his land. B's action is for A's maintenance of a private nuisance.

c.   A trespass which is continued through a series of acts or recurring events may become a private nuisance. E. g., A, over a period of time, swings his crane in an arc over B's land or strings and maintains a wire over B's land. B may sue A either in trespass or in trespass on the case for maintaining a continuing nuisance.

d.   The same act may constitute both a trespass and a nuisance. E. g., A builds a dam on his land causing the water in a stream to back up and flood B's land. B may sue A either in trespass or for maintaining a nuisance. A has invaded B's land with tangible matter, water, and is at the same time interfering substantially and unreasonably with B's use and enjoyment of his land.

5.   A private nuisance may interfere with—

a.   the land itself, such as polluting the water of a stream or causing the ground to vibrate and shake down the house, or

b.   the occupant's comfort or health, such as causing smoke and noxious vapors to fill the house, or

c.   the occupant's peace of mind, such as maintaining nearby a funeral parlor, a small-pox hospital, or a dynamite factory.

6.   Private nuisances are of infinite variety, but for the disturbance caused by the defendant to be a nuisance, it must be such as would be offensive to the average normal person with ordinary sensibilities. An interference with the use and enjoyment of land which is offensive only to the hypersensitive person is not a nuisance. E. g., during the weekend when A's children are not in school they play, laugh, scream and holler in A's back yard. B who lives nevt door on the adjoining lot and because of several operations is an extremely nervous person, is actually made sick by the noise made by A's playing children. His use and enjoyment of his land are substantially interfered with. But A is making a reasonable use of his own property by permitting his children to play as normal children play. This is a circumstance which accompanies normal living in a civilized community. This noise would be quite inoffensive, and indeed often very enjoyable, to a normal person with ordinary sensibilities. Thus, B has no cause of action against A for the law of private nuisances does not undertake to protect the supersensitive. Also A might defend by showing B could neutralize the noise by moving to the other side of the house temporarily and closing his windows.

7.   Unsightliness alone, without other elements of harm, traditionally is not actionable as a nuisance. However, unsightliness connected with other elements may be an important item in determining whether or not the defendant's use of his land is reasonable. E. g., A maintains an ugly junkyard surrounded by a barbed wire fence in a residential neighborhood. There is no noise, no odor, no vibrations or other objectionable features. B owns a house just across the street which faces A's junkyard. This interference with B's use and occupation of his land is considered a trifle and unsubstantial. B tra-

ditionally has had no cause of action against A but some of the recent cases indicate by holding or dictum that nuisance law should
give relief. Further, in the case of a junkyard there can usually be
found some additional factors affecting the comfort, health, morals or
welfare which can bring the offensive use into the concept of a nuisance. See Powell, ¶ 705 at n. 21.

Today "nuisances" such as the above junkyard most likely would
be prohibited or regulated by applicable zoning ordinances. See
Beuscher & Morrison, Judicial Zoning Through Recent Nuisance Cases. 1955 Wis.L.Rev. 440; Chapter XXVIII infra on Zoning.

8.   A nuisance may be temporary or it may be permanent.

a.   A nuisance is temporary when active operation is essential to its continuance as a nuisance. E. g., A operates a fertilizer factory in an area used entirely for residences and apartment
houses. Because A may cease to operate the business tomorrow
it is considered temporary. In the case of a temporary nuisance
the plaintiff can recover only for (1) *past and* (2) *present damages*. Injunctive relief is also available in a proper case.

b.   A nuisance is permanent when it is passive and created
by a durable artificial thing. E. g., a dam as permanent as anything built by human hands causes water of a stream to back up
on plaintiff's land. If such a structure and its effects are reasonably certain to continue in the indefinite future, it is a permanent nuisance. In such case the plaintiff may recover for (1)
past, (2) *present and* (3) *future damages*. Such a nuisance by
its very existence is considered as having caused all the damage
it can ever create. Permanent nuisances are rare.

9.   The question whether the use of property is reasonable or
unreasonable is one of degree and is usually a question of fact depending upon all the surrounding circumstances including: (a) the use
being made of the defendant's property; (b) the use being made of
the plaintiff's property; (c) the character of the neighborhood; (d)
the time of day or night when the interference occurs; (e) the fre-
quency and extent of the injury; (f) the sensitivity of the persons affected or the sensitivity of the business affected; (g) the effect upon
the health, life and property, and other relevant facts. It is really determined by weighing the utility of the defendant's conduct against
its effect on the plaintiff. See generally 40 A.L.R.3d 601 (1971).

10.   If the facts are settled or are such that reasonable men can
not differ thereon, then the question of the reasonableness of the user
of the property is a question of law.

11.   Because a plaintiff proves that the defendant is operating
his business as a nuisance does not necessarily mean that the defendant will be enjoined from continuing his business entirely. E. g., the
operation of A's factory on power generated by the use of soft coal
emitting great clouds of smoke and soot may constitute a nuisance as
to B, but the same operation on power generated by anthracite coal

which emits little or no smoke may constitute no nuisance at all. In such a case A should be enjoined merely from operating his factory in such a manner as to constitute a nuisance. This leaves it open to A to work out the manner of operation which will not be a nuisance.

12. Although a defendant may be enjoined from continuing activity which constitutes a nuisance, under particular circumstances he may be entitled to damages or compensation for being required to terminate or move his business. Thus, when a developer built a new city near cattle feedlots, which feedlots became a nuisance to the new residents, the feedlots were enjoined but the court held that the developer, who brought the people to the nuisance, should indemnify the defendant for the reasonable cost of moving or shutting down. Spur Indus. Inc. v. Del E. Webb Dev. Co., 108 Ariz. 178, 494 P.2d 700 (1972).

13. Because each case depends upon its own peculiar circumstances, a business in one area may be a nuisance while the same business conducted in the same manner in another area may be no nuisance at all. The following uses of land have been charged with being nuisances: (a) maintaining in a residential area a slaughterhouse, a funeral home, an asylum for the insane, a tuberculosis sanitarium, a light and gas manufacturing plant, a fertilizer factory, a pig sty, a livery stable, large electric lights and signs, sand and gravel plant, cement plant; (b) a sewage disposal plant casting unsterilized sewage into a stream of water; (c) operating a smelter emitting sulphur fumes which destroy crops on neighboring land; (d) operating a baseball field near residences, causing dust, excess traffic, noise, parking on lawns, and breaches of the peace; (e) maintaining powerful flood lights on a race track which interfere with outdoor movie theater; and (f) operating powerful machines which vibrate earth and buildings.

14. One may gain a prescriptive right to maintain a private nuisance, but the statute of limitations begins to run from the time the injury is suffered by the plaintiff, not from the time the defendant commits the act, unless these concur in point of time.

See Restatement, Second, of Torts § 822; Prosser, 571–612; Powell, ¶¶ 704–707.

CASE 174: A, owner and possessor of Blackacre, had a personal grudge against his neighbor and abutting owner, B. B's house was built about two feet from the common boundary line separating Blackacre from B's lot. A's house on Blackacre was twenty feet from the common boundary. A built a high brick wall within one inch of the common boundary but wholly on Blackacre which wall was ugly and unsightly on B's side and which substantially darkened B's windows. The wall was built wholly for spite and for no useful purpose on A's land. B seeks to compel A's removal of the wall by mandatory injunction. May he succeed?

Answer and Analysis

The answer is no according to the traditional view but yes according to most modern authority. The basis of the traditional view is that every possessor of land at common law had the right of exclusive possession of the surface thereof and the right to use such surface in any way he saw fit so long as he did not commit a nuisance thereon. Within his exterior boundaries he had the right to build as he pleased and the motive with which he built and the effect the building had on his neighbor were quite immaterial. The foregoing principles are involved in this case. A's ugly wall was wholly on his own land and within his exterior boundaries. True, he built the wall for spite—to irritate his neighbor, B. Apparently he succeeded or B would not have brought this suit. The reason of the common law seems to be embraced in the idea, that A could not be committing a wrong while he was building wholly within his rights. How could A be doing a wrong while he was doing right, merely because his motive was wrong?

Most modern states, however, and the Restatement of Torts, take the view that the law does not protect a landowner in his building on his land for the sole purpose of gratifying his ill will against his neighbor. In determining the existence of a nuisance the utility of the defendant's conduct is weighed against the gravity of the plaintiff's harm. Where the defendant's conduct is motivated solely by malice, his use cannot be found to be reasonable. When the defendant's conduct has mixed motives, however, some useful, some malicious, there is less likelihood that there will be a finding of nuisance. Traditionally, offense to the esthetic senses was insufficient for a finding of a nuisance, but there is an increasing awareness of the importance of esthetic values. Thus, in the instant case, because the fence serves no useful purpose, is motivated solely by spite, and is definitely offensive in an esthetic sense, the better view is that the court should compel its removal. See and compare Hornsby v. Smith, 191 Ga. 491, 13 S.E.2d 20 (1941), with Cohen v. Perrino, 355 Pa. 455, 50 A.2d 348 (1948). See also Prosser, § 89 at 598; Restatement, Second, Torts § 829; Powell, ¶¶696 at n. 6, 705 at ns. 21, 23 and 35.

CASE 175: A is the owner of Blackacre on which he maintains his dwelling house. B owns abutting Whiteacre on which he maintains and operates a cement factory and a sand and gravel pit. A sues to enjoin B's operating such business alleging that B has dug an ugly hole within 20 feet of A's dwelling house which hole is 25 feet deep in some places and is half a block wide and a block long, that in the operation of such sand and gravel pit B uses big machinery with open exhaust pipes which make loud and objectionable noises from 7 o'clock in the morning until 6 o'clock in the evening, that such machines in digging and hauling large loads of sand and gravel cause great clouds of dust to rise and envelope A's dwelling house, passing in the windows and settling on the beds, furniture and floors, making life and the use and enjoyment of Blackacre extremely burdensome. A does not ask for any damages.

B sets up in his answer that since this action was commenced B has placed mufflers on all exhaust pipes on the machines described in A's complaint, has used sprinklers on all areas from which sand or gravel is being moved so that almost no dust arises therefrom, that even without such alterations by B, there should be no relief given A because in front of A's house and within 30 feet thereof is an unpaved and much-traveled street from which great clouds of dust arise and envelope A's house, passing in the windows thereof and settling on A's beds, furniture and floors, and that such is the real cause of A's dust troubles, that behind A's house and within 100 feet thereof is a railroad switchyard from which much more noise comes to A's house during the hours mentioned in A's complaint and that just across the railroad switchyard and within 300 feet of A's house is a stockyards which adds to the noise and dust of which A complains, that because of the character of the neighborhood and the businesses being carried on within the immediate vicinity of A's dwelling house, the granting of an injunction against B would accomplish little or nothing to relieve A of the burdens of which he complains and would in no way change the essential character of the neighborhood in which A lives.

To this answer A demurs. The court overrules A's demurrer and the case comes on for trial before the trial judge. After all the evidence has been presented both parties request the trial judge to view the premises. He does so. Both the evidence and the judge's view of the premises confirm, almost without conflict, all of the allegations of both the complaint and the answer. The court then denies the injunction. Is the denial of the injunction correct?

Answer and Analysis

The answer is yes. If a plaintiff states a cause of action in his complaint he has a right to relief as of the time when he brings his action. The fact that the defendant changes the conditions thereafter does not take from the plaintiff the right to relief. But in the given set of facts B's changing the conditions to make the operation of his business no longer a nuisance would prevent A's having a right to an injunction. It might well give A a right to damages up to the time when B placed mufflers on his machines and wet down his sand and gravel pit to prevent the dust menace. However, A has not asked for damages and perhaps cares nothing for such. The second item worthy of mention is that which involves the hours during which B operates his business. They are normal hours of carrying on business

and B's use of his property can hardly be said to be unreasonable
from the standpoint of the time element. It seems that A has in his
complaint stated facts which constitute a cause of action for nuisance
against B, were those facts standing alone. But B's answer discloses
that such facts as alleged by A, even though true, do not stand alone.
They exist in a setting and that setting constitutes the circumstances
surrounding A's fact situation. The equity court will not indulge in
granting a decree which will be futile in its effect. Now that B has
cut down the noise and dust of which A complains, there remains
merely a large ugly hole which B has dug on his premises. It does
not appear that such hole constitutes a dangerous condition. It appears only as being unsightly for which the law does not afford A a
remedy when that condition stands by itself. Hence, the granting of
an injunction against B would do little to alter A's condition since
the surrounding neighborhood includes a much-traveled unpaved highway, a railroad switchyard, and stockyards, all with accompanying
noise and dust. Practically the only effect which an injunction
against B would have under these circumstances is to burden B greatly without any reasonable benefit to A. Thus, to grant such injunction would be a futile act on the part of the equity court. Fair and
just equitable relief does not include such. The court was right in
holding that B's answer stated a good defense and in denying the injunction against B. Ordinarily whether or not B's use of his property was reasonable or unreasonable would be a fact question. If it
were such in this case then the equity court sitting as a trier of fact
has, by denying the injunction, found the fact against A. But in this
case the facts seem to exist without conflict, and being thus settled,
the reasonableness of B's use of his property is a question of law
which the court properly determined in B's favor. See Prosser,
599–600; Restatement, Second, Torts §§ 827(d) and 828(b); Bove v.
Donner-Hanna Coke Corp., 236 App.Div. 37, 258 N.Y.S. 229
(1932); Boomer v. Atlantic Cement Co., 26 N.Y.2d 219, 309 N.Y.S.2d
312, 257 N.E.2d 870 (1970), affirmed 42 A.D.2d 496, 349 N.Y.S.2d
199, granting injunction but authorizing its vacation on payment of
permanent damages.

––––––––

CASE 176: A and B own adjoining city lots on which they
maintain their respective dwelling houses. B's lot is the
higher of the two so that when the rains come a large
amount of surface water flows from the rear end of B's lot
to and over the front part of A's lot including the lawn and
sidewalk in front of A's house. B builds a board fence
around the rear part of his lot in which he keeps two horses.
B depends on the flow of the surface water to keep his horse
yard clean. The rains come and large quantities of manure
and refuse are washed over A's front yard and sidewalk. A
builds a cement wall on his lot in such position as to prevent
such refuse from being washed down onto his lot. B sues A

to enjoin A's maintenance of such cement wall. May B recover?

Answer and Analysis

The answer is no. On these facts it seems B's use of the rear of his lot together with the pollution of the surface water which regularly flows onto A's lot constitutes a nuisance. A, the victim of such private nuisance, has three remedies, to wit: (a) an action for damages at law, (b) a suit in equity for an injunction or (c) self help. In this case A has seen fit to use self help to protect himself against the nuisance. Under the common law rule (see Chapter XII, Gem 18 supra), one may treat surface water as a common enemy and use whatever means is necessary to protect his property from such. This A has done in this case. The result of his act is merely to compel B to take care of his own refuse and manure pile produced in his own back yard. A having acted within his common law rights, the damage to B is damnum absque injuria for which the law affords him no relief against A. The fact that A could have sued B either for damages at law or for an injunction for the pollution of the surface water constituting a nuisance, does not prevent A's using what may be the cheaper and more effective remedy of self help. See Gibson v. Duncan, 17 Ariz. 329, 152 P. 856 (1915); Prosser, 601–02; Restatement, Second, Torts §§ 832 and 833.

NOTE

A's conduct might well be considered reasonable in a jurisdiction applying the reasonable use theory, thus leading to the same result. Not even in a jurisdiction following the civil law rule would B be allowed to drain polluted waters onto A's land. In such a jurisdiction the validity of A's defensive action would probably depend upon its reasonableness in reference to all relevant circumstances.

CASE 177: A is the owner of Blackacre on which he maintains a gasoline filling station in the rear of which station and in part of the same physical structure, A, his wife and three small children make their home. Directly across Car Avenue, a street only 30 feet in width, B owns Whiteacre on which he operates a business of keeping and boarding dogs. B has some 90 dog kennels in which he keeps about 40 dogs during the winter and about 80 dogs during the summer. Automobiles travel Car Avenue day and night almost the year around. As a car goes by one or more of the dogs howls and barks. This sets up among the other dogs similar barking and howling which continues long after the car has gone by and often until the next car comes along. This almost continuous barking and howling so disturbs the sleep and rest of A and his family as to make life in such atmosphere extremely burdensome and interferes materially with the use and enjoyment of his Blackacre. A sues for an injunction. B sets up in defense that A is a supersensitive person and that the barking and howling of the dogs as set forth in A's complaint would not substantially bother an average person with ordinary sensibilities.

The evidence disclosed without contradiction that all of the above facts are true but that the barking and howling of the dogs resulting in A's lack of rest and sleep over a period of three years, has transformed A from a normal and average person with ordinary sensibilities into a nervous, supersensitive person. The court found B was committing a nuisance and made an order granting B six months in which to see if he could operate his business without its being a nuisance and if by the end of that time, he had not succeeded, then a permanent injunction should issue against him. Was the court correct?

Answer and Analysis

The answer is yes. It should be noticed that there is no trespass in this case. B has made no invasion of A's right of exclusive possession. The invasion is by an intangible which affects only the sense of hearing, namely, noise. The facts tell us that the noise of the barking and howling dogs "interferes materially with the use and enjoyment of his (A's) Blackacre". This must mean that there is a substantial interference with A's enjoyment of his property. The fact that the court has seen fit to grant an injunction unless B can within six months find a way of operating his business without its being a nuisance means that the court has found two additional facts (a) that B's use of his land under the circumstances is unreasonable and (b) that such unreasonable use has caused the substantial injury to A in his enjoyment and use of his property. Hence, there is a nuisance being committed by B in the manner in which he is using his property. Such determination also means that the court has agreed with the uncontradicted evidence that A was, when B began using his property unreasonably or when it first affected A, an average person with ordinary sensibilities, and that the unreasonable use by B of his own property has materially affected A's health by making him nervous and unreasonably sensitive. The test used in the field of private nuisances for determining the effect of a use of land on a person is the effect on an average person of ordinary sensibilities. The law does not provide protection for the ultrasensitive, but when one is ultrasensitive as a result of a nuisance, it ill behooves the maintainer of the nuisance to use such condition as a defense for his own wrongful use of his property.

Thus it is clear A has a right to relief. But what relief? Both A and B are operating legitimate businesses. B's business is not necessarily per se a nuisance. It is only the manner of his operating the business under the circumstances which makes it a nuisance. If B can by enclosing his kennels within walls and a roof, or by moving them to the back of his lot at a sufficient distance from A's living quarters as not materially to affect the enjoyment of Blackacre, or by some other manner make the use of his property reasonable and therefore free from the present substantiated charge that it is a nuisance, then he can go right on operating his business. The court, by its decree is trying to save as many of the legitimate claims of both parties as possible and it would seem that giving B six months is a reasonable time for him to make such changes as he may to bring the use of his property within the sphere of reasonable use. In this connection it should be noticed that the equity court has retained jurisdiction over the subject matter of the suit and of the parties thereto. There is an increasing tendency to retain such jurisdiction until the court is relatively sure of a final determination of the issues of the case. See Krebs v. Hermann, 90 Colo. 61, 6 P.2d 907, 79 A.L.R. 1054 (1931); Herbert v. Smyth, 155 Conn. 78, 230 A.2d 235 (1967); Larsen v. McDonald, 212 N.W.2d 505 (Iowa 1973). Prosser, 596–99.

CASE 178: A is the owner of an apartment house building which he maintains on Blackacre, a lot in the residential district of City X. B is an electrical street railway company engaged in operating street cars throughout City X and authorized by city ordinances to operate the street cars on the streets of the city. B's car barns are located in the residential area of the city and are surrounded by apartment houses and single dwelling units. Within a couple of blocks of Blackacre are a few shops and a lumberyard. The center of City X is about 10 blocks from the properties of A and B above described. B's street cars are operated from about 4 o'clock in the morning until 1 o'clock in the morning of the next day. During those hours the cars are continuously running in and out of the car barns. From 4 o'clock in the morning until 6 o'clock each morning the cars are pulled out of the barns and lined up for their respective drivers to take them to their various routes in the city. During such process the cars are pulled around curves making a sharp grinding noise and in making up trains the cars make bumping noises as they are coupled to each other. Also during that period there is loud talk by employees of B and sometimes considerable noise from hammering the cars while they are cleaned and small repairs made. In addition the car gongs are sounded from time to time as signals are required. B has car barns in four other similar locations in City X. It is admitted there is no negligence on the part of B in its operation of its cars and car barns. A sues B to enjoin its operation of its cars and car barns in or near his apartment house or in the residential area, and in case an injunction should be denied, then he asks for damages, alleging the above facts and that the noises described at such unreasonable hours keep A and his tenants awake at night and have reduced the rental value of Blackacre. May A recover?

Answer and Analysis

The answer is no. There can be no doubt that the facts in this case disclose substantial and unreasonable interference with A's use and enjoyment of Blackacre. There can be no doubt that such interference is caused by B's conduct in the operation of its cars and car barns. But the ultimate decision in the case will have to come from the determination whether or not B is making a reasonable use of its property, the car barns, and of the streets. The answer to such question involves settling two other questions, (1) are B's car barns properly located and (2) is the use by B of the switches and curves in its tracks a proper street use. In some fact situations it is not difficult for a court to decide that the business of the defendant can be as effectively carried on in some other place as in the place where it is a nuisance. Such is not the case in our facts. The very business of the street car company is transporting residents of the city from their homes to the places of their business or labor. Its business is in the residential area where it can perform the function for which it exists. Its lines traverse the residential areas to pick up and discharge passengers whom it serves. B's cars and car barns must be located within the city for it is authorized by ordinance only to operate within the city. If its barns are located beyond the residential area, residences soon build up around the car barns and B would be in the same position it now is. If a nuisance in fact exists it is immaterial whether the victim or the offender were there first. Moving to a nuisance does not prevent the one who moves in from having a cause of action of reasonable use and enjoyment of his property. So it is immaterial whether the car barns and tracks were there first or whether A's apartment was there first. To carry out B's public obligations imposed on it by law, it must have its barns located where it can make its street cars promptly available to the traveling public. Thus, it must be said that B's car barns in the residential area which it serves are properly located under all the circumstances and that the use to which B is putting its property is a reasonable use.

Is B's use of the streets a proper use thereof? The use of streets is acquired for the purpose of making public travel expeditious and convenient. B's building of its street car tracks with their switches and curves together with the use of the street cars themselves, have for their primary purpose the very same object, namely—to make convenient and expeditious public travel. Such use by B cannot then be an additional burden on street use. Hence, the use of the streets of City X by B in its operation of its street car business is a reasonable use thereof under all the circumstances. The question of what is and what is not a reasonable use of one's property is a question of degree. It involves the weighing of the utility and the necessity of the defendant's conduct and business operation against the seriousness of the effect of such conduct or business operation on the plaintiff's use and enjoyment of his land. People who choose to be city dwellers must tolerate and acquiesce in some, indeed in many, annoyances and inconveniences with which the rural resident need not be burdened. On the other hand the urban dweller also enjoys many conveniences, including travel by street car, which are not available to the country denizen. If in our case the court had to consider only the plaintiff, the defendant and the noise, the plaintiff might well succeed in his action. But in the process of determining reasonable use the court sometimes has to consider also the interests of others than the immediate parties. Here the public interest is an important, if not the decisive, factor. Were an injunction to issue in this case it might well be the end of street car travel in City X. If A could recover damages, it might well be that the number of damage suits and recoveries therein, would spell the end of such travel because such an economic burden would put the street car company out of business. Hence, A's injunction must be denied and his injury must be considered damnum absque injuria. See Romer v. St. Paul City R. R. Co., 75 Minn. 211, 77 N.W. 825, 74 Am.St.Rep. 455 (1899); 90 A.L.R. 1203; 82 U.Pa.L.R. 567; Brown v. Allied Steel Products Corp., 273 Ala. 184, 136 So.2d 923 (1962). Cf. Altman v. Ryan, 435 Pa. 401, 257 A.2d 583 (1969). See also Restatement, Second, Torts §§ 822, 826, 827 and 828; 40 A.L.R.3d 601 (1971).

CASE 179: A owns Blackacre on which he resides. Across a 20 foot alley therefrom B resides in his dwelling house on Whiteacre. These tracts are in a strictly residential neighborhood. B converts his dwelling house into a tuberculosis sanitarium with a capacity for accommodating 10 patients. The effect of B's maintaining such institution is to depreciate the value of the surrounding property from one third to one half in value and the property is not salable even at such lower values. A sues to enjoin B's operation of the sanitarium in this residential neighborhood, alleging the above facts and that it constitutes a private nuisance for its very existence in such locality detracts substantially and unreasonably from the comfortable use and enjoyment of A's Blackacre. B's defense is that the fear and dread of the disease is, in the light of scientific investigation, wholly unfounded, imaginary and fanciful. Should the injunction issue?

Answer and Analysis

The answer is yes. To be actionable as a nuisance (a) the plaintiff's use and enjoyment of his property must be interfered with both substantially and unreasonably, (b) it must have been caused by the defendant's conduct and (c) the defendant's conduct must be intentional and unreasonable on the one hand or negligent, reckless or ultrahazardous on the other.

(a) Is the disturbance to A's enjoyment of his property substantial and unreasonable? Nothing appears in the facts to make us believe that A is a supersensitive person and in the absence of such it must be assumed that A is a normal person with ordinary sensibilities. A says that the dread and horror of the disease substantially disturbs him in the enjoyment of his property. Is that disturbance peculiar to A alone? It seems it is quite generally shared by the entire public in the jurisdiction where this property is located when the presence of B's sanitarium has depressed values of the surrounding real property from a third to a half in value. Is the question of comfortable enjoyment of property a question to be determined by the result of scientific investigation or by the effect of the defendant's conduct on the average normal person who lives on and uses property? Does it depend on what goes on in the scientist's mind or by the impact made on the mind of the normal person? The answer is this—it is immaterial whether or not a fear is scientifically well founded if the fear in fact exists; it is immaterial whether or not it is an imaginary fear if it in fact exists. If the fear is such that it determines the thoughts, the acts and conduct of men, it is such that a court cannot ignore it. So in this case if A's fear of tuberculosis, he being a normal person with ordinary sensibilities, interferes substantially with his enjoyment of Blackacre situated within a few feet of B's sanitarium, it must be concluded that his use and enjoyment is substantially and unreasonably disturbed and that the first element of a nuisance is present.

(b) There can be no doubt that B's conduct is the sole cause of A's discomfort and that the second element of nuisance is present.

(c) A private nuisance may be based on the defendant's negligent, reckless or extrahazardous conduct. Nothing in our facts suggests any of these. B's operation of his sanitarium is intentional. This means only that B is voluntarily conducting the institution. It does not mean that he has any intention of injuring A or that he has any ill will towards A. So the question remains, is B making a reasonable use of his land under all the circumstances? This requires a weighing of the utility and necessity of B's use of his land against the gravity or seriousness of the effect which such use has on A in the enjoyment of his land. First, it should be noticed that here is a sanitarium squarely in the midst of a neighborhood which is exclusively residential. It is true that such institutions are necessary to care for the people who are afflicted with the disease. But there is no necessity or requirement that such an institution be in a residential area. It can be just as effectively operated in some area dedicated to or principally used by sanitariums and hospitals or in a rural community. It is just a right thing in a wrong place like the pig in the parlor instead of in the barnyard. Comfortable enjoyment of property is not limited to physical comfort. It includes also peace of mind. When we compare the effect which B's conduct has upon A's use and enjoyment of his land with the utility or necessity of B's operating his sanitarium in this strictly residential community, it would seem that this sanitarium is not properly located and that B is making an unreasonable use of his Whiteacre. Then it appears that all the essential elements of a private nuisance exist in this case and that A is entitled to an injunction against B. If, at any given time and place, the attitude of the people generally in the community would reflect the attitude of the scientist to the effect that tuberculosis is not contagious, not communicable, readily cured, and that such a sanitarium would have no effect on property values and people would as soon live beside such an institution as beside a home housing healthy people, then, of course, B's use of his property would have to be considered reasonable under all of the circumstances, and if A were then substantially disturbed it would be because he is ultrasensitive, and the injunction would be denied. Thus the determination of reasonable use depends on time and place and the enlightenment of the people in the community. See Everett v. Paschall, 61 Wash. 47, 111 P. 879, 31 L.R.A.,N.S., 827, Ann.Cas.1912B, 1128 (1910); Park v. Stolzheise, 24 Wash.2d 781, 167 P.2d 412 (1946); Prosser, 591–602; Restatement, Second, Torts § 822. Cf. Florida East Coast Properties, Inc. v. Metropolitan Dade County, 572 F.2d 1108 (5th Cir. 1978), certiorari denied 439 U.S. 894, 99 S.Ct. 253, 58 L.Ed.2d 240, holding a jail/work-release facility not a nuisance.

CASE 180: A is the owner of Blackacre on which he maintains his dwelling house. B owns Whiteacre which is a lot adjacent to Blackacre to the east thereof. The lots are separated by a brick wall 6 feet high. For nearly 20 years B has been regularly refinishing furniture in his back yard and in the open. To take the old finish such as glue, varnish, shellac, paint, etc. off the old furniture B has used a sandblasting machine. In the process a fine dust has been produced much of which has found its way over the wall separating Blackacre and Whiteacre and has settled down on the rear of Blackacre which has been used by A for the family garden. A has often noticed the dust as it settled down in his garden but it did not materially disturb either his peace of mind or his use and enjoyment of Blackacre. Within the past year A has changed his garden to another part of Blackacre and along the wall mentioned has strung four clothes lines on which to hang the family laundry. The effect of the dust from B's sand blasting is to cover A's clean damp laundry with particles of glue, paint, varnish, sand, soil and other foreign substances, much of which clings to and makes permanent stains on A's clothes hanging on the lines. The statute of limitations for maintaining a private nuisance in the jurisdiction is 10 years. A sues B to enjoin B from operating his business in a way which constitutes a nuisance. B sets up the statute of limitations. Is the defense good?

Answer and Analysis

The answer is no. In this case A has one complaint only—the dust from B's Whiteacre is spoiling his laundry as it hangs on the line. It must be admitted that A's using his property for clothesline purposes is an ordinary occupancy. There is nothing supersensitive or extraordinary about such use of anyone's land. It would seem rather clear that this is a substantial and unreasonable interference with A's use and enjoyment of his land. The sole cause, of course, is B's sand blasting. Is B's use of his land reasonable under the circumstances? One of the important circumstances to be considered in such question is the ease with which either the plaintiff or the defendant can avoid the effects of the objectionable use. In this case it would be difficult for A to avoid the effects of B's conduct without building an enclosure, but doing that would be thwarting the very purpose of having his laundry on the line to dry in the open air. On the other hand it would seem quite reasonable and not too burdensome on B to require him to carry on his sand blasting in some manner which would prevent the dust from going over the wall and onto A's clothes. With little labor and inexpensive materials B could readily and without changing his location enclose his sand blasting operations and keep his dust in his own back yard. Under the circumstances it seems A should have an injunction against B unless B's defense of the statute of limitations is good.

If one trespasses on the land of another a cause of action immediately accrues whether or not there has been any actual damage because there has been an interference with the exclusive possession. The statute of limitations begins to run at once.[1] In the case of a private nuisance it sometimes happens that substantial damage is done at once and a cause of action accrues. For example, suppose B obstructs A's highway, or backs up stream water onto A's land, or builds a spite fence between A's and B's properties where such fence is considered a nuisance—in these cases the cause of action accrues at once and the statute of limitations begins to run. But this is not always true in case of a private nuisance. Sometimes the same act is carried on for years by the defendant without in any way interfering with the plaintiff's use and enjoyment of his land. Then when conditions change or another use is made of the plaintiff's land, the conduct of the defendant becomes an annoyance of magnitude. In the field of private nuisances as elsewhere the statute of limitations begins to run when a cause of action accrues. But the cause of action does not accrue until the nuisance actually exists and that is not always when the act is committed but when the act does damage by interfering substantially and unreasonably with the plaintiff's enjoyment of his land. Applying such doctrine to our case we find that B

---

1. See, e. g., Fletcher's Gin, Inc. v. Crihfield, 423 F.2d 1066 (6th Cir. 1970), holding that the erection of a dam which caused backwater to damage neighboring land was a permanent nuisance and that the statute of limitations started to run when the harm was first inflicted.

has been sand blasting in his back yard for nearly 20 years. But during nearly all of that time the dust which came from his operations fell harmlessly and without substantial injury, if any, to A in the use or enjoyment of his land. Hence, there was no nuisance. But when A put up his clothesline where his garden had theretofore existed, then for the first time was there any material interference with A's enjoyment of his Blackacre. Only then, within the past year, did a nuisance exist and a cause of action therefor accrue in A's favor and the statute of limitations begin to run in favor of B. The statute of limitations being 10 years and less than a year having run since the cause of action accrued, such defense is not available to B. See the leading case of Sturges v. Bridgman, L.R. 11 Ch.Div. 852 (1879); Prosser, 595. See also footnote 1.

Note

See also supra, case 173, Chapter XII, as to water skiing activities constituting a nuisance.

SUMMARY OF CASES IN CHAPTER XIII

Case 174. At common law every landowner had the right to the exclusive possession of the surface of his land and the right to use such surface in any way he chose, provided he did not commit a nuisance thereon, including the right to build a "spite fence". Today, however, many jurisdictions would hold unreasonable conduct motivated solely by malice although the offense were only to the esthetic senses.

Case 175. A may have a cause of action for an injunction against B for operating his business in such a way as to be a nuisance as to A if A's property and B's business are standing alone. But if the character of the neighborhood in which A's property and B's business are located is such that the granting of relief to A would be futile because it would give A little benefit and substantially result in merely a burden on B, the relief will be refused. Equity will not grant relief the effect of which would be futile. The question whether the use of property is or is not reasonable under the circumstances is usually a fact question but if the facts are settled then it is a question of law.

Case 176. The victim of a private nuisance has three remedies: (a) an action for damages at law, (b) a suit in equity for an injunction, and (c) self help. If he uses self help in abatement of a private nuisance any damage caused to the one who maintains the nuisance is damnum absque injuria. The pollution of surface water by the owner of the higher tract of land may constitute a private nuisance as to the owner of a lower tract.

Case 177. Whether a particular interference or annoyance may be a nuisance depends on its effect on an average person with ordinary sensibilities and not its effect on a person who is supersensitive. But if such interference has caused an average reasonable person with ordinary sensibilities to become nervous and supersensitive, it is no defense in a nuisance case that the victim is now supersensitive. If a business is a nuisance only because of the manner or the circumstances involved in its operation, the equity court in its decree may properly permit the defendant time in which to change the method or circumstances so that the business can be operated without being a nuisance.

Case 178. The question of reasonable use by the defendant of his property is primarily determined by weighing the utility and necessity of his conduct or the operation of his business against the seriousness of the effect on the plaintiff's use and enjoyment of his property. But in a given case the public interest in the continuation of the defendant's conduct, business or service, may be an important or decisive factor in such determination. Street car barns maintained in a residential area may be a reasonable use by the street car company because of the public interest in having street car service, even though the noise may affect substantially and unreasonably the plaintiff's use and enjoyment of his land. City dwellers may enjoy many conveniences which the country denizen may not have, but he must also tolerate annoyances and inconveniences which do not exist in the rural areas.

Case 179. To be an actionable nuisance: (a) the plaintiff's use and enjoyment of his property must be interfered with substantially and unreasonably, (b) it must have been caused by the defendant's conduct, and (c) the defendant's conduct must be intentional and unreasonable on the one hand or negligent, reckless or ultrahazardous on the other. In the absence of evidence that a person is ultrasensitive it must be assumed that he is normal and with ordinary sensibilities. The reasonableness of use of property is determined by weighing the utility and necessity of the defendant's conduct against the gravity or seriousness of the effect upon the plaintiff in the use and enjoyment of his property. Comfortable enjoyment of property includes peace of mind as well as physical comfort. A sanitarium for tuberculars in a strictly residential area may or may not be a private nuisance depending on the enlightenment and attitude of the people in the community as to the disease.

Case 180. If one person trespasses on the property of another a cause of action accrues at once and the statute of limitations begins to run. That is true also in the case of a private nuisance when the act which constitutes the nuisance causes immediate damage. But in the case of a private nuisance when the act occurs at one time and the damage does not take place until a later date, then the cause of action accrues and the statute of limitations begins to run as of the date when the damage is done.

Chapter XIV

FIXTURES AND TRADE FIXTURES

1. Fixtures Generally.
   Legal Gems.
   Cases.

2. Trade Fixtures.
   Legal Gems.
   Cases.

3. Security Interests in Fixtures (UCC); Stolen Chattels.
   Legal Gems.
   Cases.
   Exhibit A—UCC § 9–313.

Summary of Cases in Chapter XIV.

---

1. FIXTURES GENERALLY

LEGAL GEMS

1. *A fixture is a chattel which has become real property.*

2. *To be differentiated from the law of fixtures is the doctrine of accession.* However, in *accession* the chattel loses its identity (example: beam built into house—no more beam—all house), but in *fixtures* it does not (example: metal bathtub built into house—still bathtub).

In other situations chattels used in connection with realty retain their classification as chattels (example: ordinary movable and removable furniture such as chairs, tables and beds—still chattels).

3. *An article* of personal property *may become a fixture*

    a. *without any physical attachment to the land* other than the fact that it rests thereon of its own weight, e. g., a prefabricated house is moved onto Blackacre and is set on a pre-constructed cement foundation thereon with no other annexation, or

    b. *by being set in and annexed to the soil itself,* e. g., a fence post placed in a hole in the ground and dirt solidly tamped around it, or

    c. *by being annexed to a thing which is itself an accession to or a fixture on the land,* e. g., a house is already an accession to or a fixture on Blackacre and a pre-constructed window frame is fitted and attached to the house, or a table too large to be taken out any door or window is built in a room of the house.

4. *Whether or not a particular article is a fixture is primarily a question of the intention of the annexer.* This intention, however, *means the objective intention* as determined by external indicia and

by the circumstances surrounding the annexation. *The actual subjective intention* or what actually goes on in the mind of the annexer *is usually immaterial.*

5. Notice the effect of intention in the following five cases.

a. A is the owner of a furnace. He also owns Blackacre on which there is a dwelling house. He entertains no intention of putting the furnace in the house on Blackacre. The furnace is a chattel for all purposes.

b. A prepares a basement room in the house on Blackacre for the purpose of installing the furnace therein and moves the furnace into the house on Blackacre for that purpose. By the intention of A and the location of the furnace in the house on Blackacre it is constructively annexed to the land and is a fixture. A sale of Blackacre to B will carry with it the title to the furnace as a fixture in the absence of an agreement to the contrary.

c. A affixes the furnace by bolts to the basement floor of the house on Blackacre. It is a fixture actually annexed.

d. A removes the furnace from Blackacre temporarily for the sole purpose of repairing it but with the intention of returning it to the basement from which it is taken. The furnace is still a fixture and part of Blackacre.

e. A removes the furnace from Blackacre with no intention of returning it to the house on Blackacre. From the time the furnace is severed from the basement on Blackacre with the intention of having it permanently severed therefrom the furnace is reconverted into a chattel for all purposes.

6. For a chattel to become a fixture three essential elements must concur.

a. *The chattel must be annexed to the realty either actually or constructively.* E. g., an engine which is bolted to the cement floor of a building is actually annexed to the land; a key which is the only one which will unlock and lock the door to a building on the land is constructively annexed to the land even though it is carried in the landowner's pocket; a wheelbarrow used on a farm is neither actually nor constructively annexed to the land.

b. *The chattel must be appropriated to the purpose for which the land is used.* E. g., an air compressor used to hoist automobiles for greasing purposes in a gasoline station is appropriated to the purpose for which the land is used; an air compressor solidly bolted to the cement floor of a factory building and used exclusively for the purpose of hoisting automobiles for greasing purposes in a gasoline station across the street is not appropriated to the purpose for which the land is used.

c. *It must be the intention of the annexer that the chattel become a fixture. This is an objective intention* which is inferred from: (1) the nature of the article; (2) the manner of annexation to the land; (3) the injury to the land, if any, by its removal; (4) the completeness with which the chattel is integrated with the use to which the land is being put; (5) the relation which the annexer has with the land such as licensee, tenant at will or for years or for life or fee owner; (6) the relation which the annexer has with the chattel such as owner, bailee or converter; (7) the local custom respecting treating such chattel as personal property or a fixture; (8) the time, place and degree of social, economic and cultural development, (e. g., a luxury in one generation is a necessity in another—a bathtub on legs was a chattel in the State of Washington in 1900 but a "built in" fixture in 1946—Strain v. Green, 25 Wash.2d 692, 172 P.2d 216); and (9) all other relevant facts surrounding the annexation.

E. g., if a fee owner builds on his land a dwelling house made of brick and mortar and based on a cement foundation two feet thick and extending into the ground five feet, the house is a fixture on the land as a matter of law because the objective intention is so clear that reasonable men cannot differ thereon. (In such a case the law of fixtures and the law of accession shade into each other. By the law of fixtures the house is still house, but it is a fixture on the land. By the law of accession the house loses its identity and is merged in the land. There is no more house—it is all land.)

7. Whether or not a chattel has become a fixture is usually a question of fact to be determined by the trier of fact under proper instructions of the trial court, but of course if the facts are stipulated or are so clear that reasonable men cannot differ thereon it is a question of law for the court to decide.

8. The determination of whether a chattel is a fixture depends in many instances upon the relationship of the parties contesting the status of the item. Therefore in solving a fixtures problem it will assist in the analysis if it is first determined which of the following cases is involved,

a. the case in which both the chattel and the land to which it is annexed are owned by the annexer; e. g., A, fee owner of land, buys and installs a steam radiator in his house on the land, or

b. the case in which the chattel belongs to the annexer and the land belongs to another; e. g., a tenant buys and installs a steam radiator in the house owned by his landlord, or

c. the case in which the land belongs to the annexer and the chattel belongs to another; e. g., A, fee owner of land, being bailee or converter of X's steam radiator, installs the radiator in his house on his land, or

d. the case in which the annexer owns neither the chattel nor the land; e. g., A, licensee or tenant at will on B's Blackacre, converts X's steam radiator and installs it in B's house on Black-acre.

9.   An oral agreement that a chattel shall not become a fixture even though later affixed to the land is valid between the parties and as to all others except a subsequent bona fide purchaser without no-tice.   E. g., A, owner of Blackacre, purchases a furnace from B and it is orally agreed that even though the furnace is to be installed in and annexed to the house on the land it shall, until paid for, retain its chattel character.   If not paid for B may remove it if that be the agreement.   However, if Blackacre is sold by A to a bona fide purchas-er, C, who takes without notice of the oral agreement and for value, the furnace will be considered a fixture and real property as to C, and as to him B cannot remove it.

10.   The Statute of Frauds applies to an unremovable fixture and an oral contract for its sale is unenforceable for it involves an in-terest in land.   E. g., L owns Blackacre a two-story store building. He leases it to T who installs a two-story cold storage system extend-ing from the floor to the roof of the building including cutting away the floor of the second story.   Either T or L orally agrees to sell the cold storage system to X.   Because this cold storage room or system cannot be removed without substantial injury to the land it is an un-removable fixture.   Because it is an unremovable fixture it is part of the land and X cannot enforce his oral contract to buy the cold stor-age system.   Here again fixtures and accession shade into each other. This "room" could be an accession.

11.   The Statute of Frauds does not apply to a sale of a remova-ble fixture.   E. g., L leases Blackacre to T for the purpose of operat-ing a store in the building thereon.   T installs shelves along the walls in the building, and by nails securely affixes them to the floor but in such a way that they can be removed without substantial inju-ry to the building.   T orally sells the shelves to X.   This agreement is valid and enforceable because, although the shelves are trade fix-tures, T has a right to remove them.   Hence, X is considered as buying the right to remove the fixtures rather than the fixtures themselves.   Until actual severance the fixtures remain realty.   After severance they belong to the purchaser X as personal property.   Of course some cases hold otherwise and say the agreement must be in writing.

CASE 181: A is the owner of Blackacre, a 6-story apartment house containing 24 efficiency apartments, 4 such apartments being on each of the 6 floors. In each apartment the floors are covered with linoleum which extends from wall to wall and is glued to the floors. In each there is also an exterior window blind outside each window which is fastened to the outside wall of the building by two metal hinges. Above each window inside each apartment there are two metal brackets screwed to the wall. Across the brackets extends a metal curtain rod which rests on the brackets by its own weight. Each curtain rod is cut in length to fit the space across the top of the window and is of the same wrought iron design as the brackets. On each rod hang the curtains which cover the windows from public view and excessive light. In the single bedroom in each apartment there is an in-a-door bed which is intended to be folded up during the daytime and hidden from view by being rolled into a closet specially constructed for size to contain such in-a-door bed. All of this equipment was purchased by A and placed in each apartment for use by his tenants while occupying and using same. A trades Blackacre to B for a farm, each conveying title to the other by deed. After the transaction is complete A insists on removing from each apartment the curtain rods, window blinds, linoleum and in-a-door bed. This is resisted by B who insists all of these items are fixtures and hence were conveyed to him by A's deed of Blackacre. A sues B to recover possession of these articles in each of the 24 apartments on Blackacre. May he recover?

Answer and Analysis

The answer is no. Three essential elements must co-exist in order that a chattel be held to be a fixture. (1) The chattel must be annexed to the realty either actually or constructively. (2) The chattel must be adapted to the use to which the realty is put. (3) There must be an intention on the part of the annexer that such chattel become a fixture. This means the objective intention inferred from all the surrounding circumstances and not the secret, subjective intention, if any, which may actually be in the mind of the annexer. The circumstances to be considered in inferring the intention of the annexer include: (a) the nature of the article; (b) the manner of annexation to the land; (c) the injury, if any, caused by its removal; (d) the completeness with which the chattel is integrated with the use to which the land is put; (e) the relation which the annexer has with the land such as licensee, tenant at will, for years, for life or fee owner; (f) the relation which the annexer has with the chattel such as owner, bailee or converter; (g) the local custom, if any, respecting treating such chattel as personal property or a fixture and other pertinent facts.

(1) **The annexation.** (a) The linoleum, blinds and curtain rod brackets are physically affixed to the realty by glue, hinges and screws respectively. There are three substantial reasons why the curtain rods should be considered as constructively annexed to the brackets on which they rest. First, each curtain rod is cut specifically in length to reach across the window below it. It is not a rod which can be used anywhere, but is made to fit this particular space in A's apartment house. Second, the rods are of the same design as the brackets on which they rest. It is the obvious intention of the

owner who put them up that the brackets and the matching rods are to go and remain together in the scheme of decoration used in the apartment house. Third, these rods and brackets are furnished by the fee owner of Blackacre to his tenants who live in the apartment house and are obviously intended to be permanent decorations in the various efficiency units of the building. Therefore, it seems clear that these rods are to be considered as constructively annexed to the brackets which support them, and the brackets themselves are securely affixed to the walls of the apartments on Blackacre.

The in-a-door bed is not actually annexed to the floor or wall of the apartment in which it is located. Nor is it intended to remain stationary like the curtain rod resting on its brackets. Indeed, were it to be affixed to the building it could not accomplish the purpose for which it is intended, namely, to be folded up and rolled into the closet during the daytime. There are two reasons why the in-a-door bed should be considered as constructively annexed to the efficiency apartment in which it is located. First, the closet of the bedroom in the apartment is specially built and located to receive and store this particular type of in-a-door bed. The closet and the bed are selected to fit each other in their combined use in the apartment. Second, this closet is built and this in-a-door bed is furnished by the fee owner of Blackacre for the purpose of use by his tenants in the various apartments. It is obvious that his intention must have been to make this bed an integral and permanent part of the efficiency apartment in which it has been placed and in which it is being used. Therefore it must be concluded that each in-a-door bed is constructively annexed to that particular efficiency apartment in which it is located and that all of the 24 in-a-door beds are constructively annexed to the apartment house on Blackacre.

(2) **The adaptation of the chattel to the use made of the efficiency apartment.** There can be no doubt that each of the chattel items is peculiarly adapted to be used in connection with the use being made of the efficiency apartment in which it is located. The apartment is being used for living purposes. The linoleum on the floor, the blinds on the windows, the curtain rods on which hang the curtains, and the in-a-door bed, each serves its particular purpose directly connected with the comfort and enjoyment of the apartment in which it or they are located. Thus, this required element for a fixture is present as to each of the items in controversy.

(3) **The intention.** For a chattel to become a fixture there must be an actual or constructive annexation to the freehold, there must be an adaptation of the chattel to the use to which that part of the land to which it is annexed is put, and there must be an inferred objective intention on the part of the annexer that such article become a fixture. All three of these items must concur, but if there is any one of them more important than the others it is this third item of intention. What is actually in the mind of the annexer subjectively, what he is actually thinking, if anything, when he makes the annexation, is

quite immaterial. It is the objective surrounding circumstances which constitute the basis for inferring the intention that the chattel shall become a fixture. In our case the facts from which such intention must be inferred are these. (a) The linoleum is glued to the floor and may be ruined if there is an attempt to remove it. The blinds and curtain rods with brackets are screwed to the wall, but they might be removed without substantial injury to the building. The in-a-door bed can be removed without any injury to the physical structure of the building. (b) All these items are completely integrated with the use of the apartment as a living unit and each is essential to the comfortable enjoyment of the apartment. (c) Each of these items has been placed in the apartment, not by one having a temporary relation to the realty, but by the fee owner thereof. (d) Each of these items belonged as a chattel to the same fee owner of the land prior to his placing such in the apartment. (e) The fee owner has made a large investment in building the apartment house and is in the business of renting furnished apartments. Given these facts, one can only conclude that when A, as owner of Blackacre in fee simple, annexed each of these items to its particular apartment, that he had an intention permanently to dedicate the use of each to that use to which the apartment was dedicated, namely for permanent dwelling quarters and that each of such items is intended by A to be a fixture in such apartment.

(4) **Conclusion.** Each of the chattels—the linoleum, the blinds, the curtain rods and the in-a-door bed—being either physically or constructively annexed to the apartment building, and each being specially adapted to the use which is made of that part of the realty to which it is annexed, and there being a clear intention on the part of A, the fee owner annexer, that each such chattel become a fixture to the realty, it is concluded that each of such items is a fixture on Blackacre. Thus, the title to each of such items passed to B, the grantee, and A, the grantor, cannot recover any of such fixtures. See the leading cases, Teaff v. Hewitt, 1 Ohio St. 511, 59 Am.Dec. 634 (1853) and Doll v. Guthrie, 233 Ky. 77, 24 S.W.2d 947 (1930).

---

2. TRADE FIXTURES

LEGAL GEMS

1. "Trade fixtures" are chattels annexed to the land by a tenant for pecuniary gain during his tenancy. They are removable by the tenant, be he a tenant for life, tenant for years or tenant at will.

2. If the tenancy is for a definite time and ends on a day certain, the trade fixtures must be removed *before* the end of the term. E. g., L leases Blackacre to T as a store for three years. The term expires December 31, 1980. T during the term firmly affixes shelves to the floor of the store building. He does not remove them before midnight of December 31, 1980. The shelves remain fixtures on the

property and belong to the landlord L. They are forfeited by T as an implied condition of the lease.

3. If the tenancy is for an indefinite time and the termination date remains uncertain, the trade fixtures must be removed within a reasonable time after the expiration of the lease. This applies to a life tenancy or to a tenancy at will.

E. g., L owns Blackacre, a vacant lot and permits T, as a tenant at will, to move a building thereon for the purpose of carrying on a business for profit. L notifies T on February 1, 1980 that his tenancy is terminated as of May 1, 1980. T does nothing. On June 15, 1980 L gives T formal notice to remove the building forthwith. T does nothing. On September 30, 1980 L sells the building to P. P severs the building from Blackacre preparatory to moving it onto P's Whiteacre. T takes the building to T's Brownacre. P sues T in trover for conversion. P may recover. When T failed to remove the building from Blackacre within a reasonable time after the termination of his tenancy on May 1, 1980 he forfeited his right to remove the building and it remained a fixture on Blackacre and became the property of the landlord, L. When L sold the building to P and P severed it from Blackacre it became P's chattel property. When T wrongfully took the house and appropriated it to his own use he became a converter thereof and is liable to P in trover. See 6 A.L.R.2d 342.

4. The better considered cases refuse to follow the common law rule that a tenant forfeits his trade fixtures by renewal of his lease unless he provides for no forfeiture in the renewal lease or actually removes and then replaces his fixtures.

E. g., L leases a store building to T for three years the lease expiring November 1, 1980. T annexes to the building valuable trade fixtures including, shelves, counters and a refrigeration unit. On October 1, 1980 L and T renew the lease till November 1, 1981. On October 15, 1981 T starts removing his trade fixtures. L seeks to enjoin such removal. By the common law rule the injunction would issue because nothing is said about such removal in the renewal leases and T did not remove his fixtures prior to November 1, 1980. The harshness of this rule is quite without justification. The injunction should be denied. It is absurd to require of T the futile and expensive act of removing and replacing his fixtures at the risk of forfeiting them. To read into a lease such an implied condition borders on the ridiculous. The renewal lease should be considered an extension of the same rights of removal of trade fixtures as are implied in the former lease. See Greenspan-Greenberger Co. v. Goerke Co., 111 N. J.Eq. 249, 162 A. 87 (Ch. 1932).

————

CASE 182: L, fee simple owner of Blackacre, a 320-acre farm, leases it to T for a period of 5 years, the term coming to an end December 1, 1980. There is nothing in the lease about fixtures. Blackacre is a farm used for the raising of corn and hogs. T so uses it. To increase and preserve his productivity while farming Blackacre T builds thereon a corncrib made of lumber which is 20 feet wide and 30 feet long and set on loose bricks which hold it about 6 inches off the ground. At each corner of the corncrib T sets a wood post in the ground 18 inches deep and nails the corncrib to the four corner posts. He also builds a hog house of brick and mortar on the premises. It is set on a cement foundation which extends into the ground 18 inches. This hog house is 15 feet wide by 40 feet long and used to keep the brood sows warm during the cold seasons. Between November 15, 1980 and November 30, 1980 T disengages the corncrib from the four corner posts which anchor it to the ground and moves both corncrib and posts to another farm which he has rented for future use. He tears down the hog house brick by brick and removes the mortar from each of them. He loads the bricks on his truck and hauls them to his new location. He fills the post holes with dirt, removes the cement foundation on which the hog house has been resting and fills with dirt the space which the cement foundation had occupied. Then he hauls all the mortar and cement to a proper dumping ground, thus leaving Blackacre in the same condition that it was before he rented it. After the lease has expired L sues T for waste (a) for removing the corncrib and (b) for removing the hog house. May he recover?

Answers and Analyses

The answers are these. (a) L may not recover for the removal of the corncrib. (b) L may recover for the removal of the hog house.

For an article of personal property to become a fixture on land it is necessary that: (a) there be an annexation of the article to the land either actually or constructively; (b) the article be adapted to the use for which the land is used; and (c) there be an intention on the part of the annexer that the article become a fixture. This intention is not the secret, subjective intention of the annexer. It is the objective intention which is inferred from the facts surrounding the annexation such as the nature of the article, the manner of annexation, the effect its removal would have on the article or on the land, the relation the annexer has to the chattel and to the land, together with any other pertinent facts.

(1) **The annexation.** The hog house being built of brick and mortar and affixed to a cement foundation which extends into the ground 18 inches is actually annexed to the soil of Blackacre. The corncrib is nailed to posts which are firmly set in terra firma. Both these structures for the purpose of becoming fixtures are annexed to the land as a matter of law.

(2) The adaptation of the chattel to the use to which the land is put. On this question there is no difficulty. The facts show why these two structures were built and how they are used. The farm is a corn and hog farm. The hog house and the corncrib are used in the feeding and raising of hogs. Therefore, the buildings are not only suited to the use to which Blackacre is put—they are actually used for the purpose of feeding and raising hogs. So the second element required for a fixture is present as to both buildings.

(3) The intention that the chattel become a fixture. The fact that the hog house is attached to the land by means of a cement foundation and that the corncrib is nailed to posts firmly set in the ground seem to indicate an intention to make the buildings part of the land as fixtures. The fact that the annexer owns the buildings and the chattels which go into their constructions but that the annexation is to land which belongs to another, raise some doubt concerning such inferred intention. That the annexer is a tenant for only a five year period raises still more doubt about the intention. That the corncrib can be removed from Blackacre with practically no injury to the freehold would indicate that it might be a part of the realty, while the fact that the hog house is actually built into the soil and that it cannot be removed without actually lifting the cement foundation out of its resting place and causing complete destruction of the hog house as a building clearly indicates an intention to make it a fixture. Taking into consideration all of these physical indicia it seems reasonable to infer that T, the annexer of the two buildings to Blackacre, intended them to be fixtures thereon. If that be true the third requirement for a fixture is present. It is therefore concluded that both the corncrib and the hog house are fixtures on Blackacre. But, because these buildings are fixtures it does not necessarily follow that T is liable for their removal from Blackacre.

(4) Trade fixtures. Trade fixtures are chattels which are annexed to the land by a tenant for the purpose and convenience of his trade or business on the land. They are affixed to the land for the purpose of increasing the pecuniary profit from the business or trade conducted on the land. In the early law it was said that anything attached to the land partook of the nature of land and was not to be removed therefrom. To encourage trade and industry that rule has been relaxed in favor of trade fixtures. And under the doctrine of trade fixtures such fixtures can be removed by the tenant. But in England such doctrine did not extend to fixtures added to the land for agricultural purposes. In the United States the business of raising and selling grain, cattle or hogs is as much a business as the buying and selling of shoes over a store counter and is entitled to the same protection. Hence, in this country the doctrine of trade fixtures includes fixtures which are annexed to the farm for the purpose of pecuniary benefit therefrom as well as shelves or counters attached to the floor of a store building. Usually such doctrine is applied to factory machinery, store and shop equipment or temporary partitions in industrial establishments and the like. There is more difficulty in applying the doctrine to buildings or to additions or extensions to buildings already present on the land. But the principle remains the same and difficulty in applying it should not prevent the use thereof in a proper case.

The truth is that the difficulty usually stems from the injury done to the freehold by the removal of the structure. Such injury does not mean simply decreasing the freehold in value, but it includes such physical injury that an unreasonable burden is cast on the landlord in restoring his property to its former condition. When such is the case the doctrine of trade fixtures ought not to be applied and the tenant ought not to be permitted to remove the building from the land even though the landlord did not contribute anything to the building thereof. However, that is not our case. The removal of the hog house by T is not an injury to L's Blackacre in the sense that the corpus of the land is materially injured. It is not. Indeed T has restored the land to its former condition. Then why should L have a claim against T? The reason is founded in public policy and economics. True, T or any other owner of a building may destroy his own brick building if he so desires and no one can complain. But the brick hog house which T built on L's land is a fixture. It is joined to and integrated with the freehold as such. It became such by T's affirmative act. There is a vast difference between moving a large stationary engine piece by piece on the one hand, and moving a brick building brick by brick on the other. The engine is taken to pieces and the pieces are reassembled in another location as the same identical engine as before. Its identity as an engine is preserved and the cost of moving it is not out of proportion to the value of the engine. Indeed, it is a small fraction thereof.

However, the taking down of a brick house constitutes a complete destruction of the building as a building and reduces it to mere materials. The saving of such materials to the tenant is so slight compared with the injury to the land by the removal of the building that it ought not to be permitted. Add to the value of the saved materials the cost in labor of wrecking the brick building, removing the mortar from the bricks, the removal and disposal of the cement foundation, the labor involved in building another structure of those saved bricks, and the total is all out of proportion to the value of the materials saved by the destruction of the hog house on Blackacre. This economic waste is quite unjustified and T should not be permitted to remove the hog house from Blackacre and is liable in damages to L for having done so.

On the other hand the corncrib falls within the doctrine of trade fixtures for the removal of which before the end of the tenancy T is not liable in waste to L. Its connection with the land is relatively slight. Its removal from the land does no injury to the realty. It can be used intact on other land as well as on Blackacre and the expense of removing it is not at all out of proportion to its value. In other words, there is little economic waste in its removal. Therefore, it seems proper to permit T to remove the corncrib from the farm, Blackacre, as a trade fixture. See Elwes v. Maw, 102 Eng.Rep. 510 (1802 King's Bench); Cameron v. Oakland County Gas & Oil Co., 277 Mich. 442, 269 N.W. 227, 107 A.L.R. 1142 (1936); 6 A.L.R.2d 322–355.

---

3. SECURITY INTERESTS IN FIXTURES (UCC); STOLEN CHATTELS

LEGAL GEMS

1. The most significant impact of the UCC on the law of real property is in the area of fixtures. Article Nine of the UCC governs security interests in goods with § 9–313 specifically applying to fixtures.

2. Much confusion has arisen in this mixed area of commercial and real property law. Many states adopted the 1962 version of the UCC, § 9–313 of which has been criticized by both commercial and property lawyers for its ambiguity as well as for certain priority rules. Thus, the 1972 revision of § 9–313 is substantially different from its predecessor. [See Exhibit A infra following the cases]. Of course, the statutes of a particular state must be consulted to determine local law.[1]

3. In determining the priority of a security interest in fixtures in relation to competing interests in the same good, the concepts of *attachment* and *perfection* are most important. A security interest *attaches* when it becomes enforceable against the debtor in respect to the collateral (fixture). (UCC § 9–203(2), 1972 version). This is usually accomplished by the execution of a *security agreement*.

4. Under both the 1962 and 1972 versions of the UCC, the filing of a *financing statement* will *perfect* a security interest in a fixture. The 1972 revision—the better approach—creates a special type of financing statement: the *fixture filing*. (UCC § 9–313(1)(b). The fixture filing is recorded in the same place as interests in the realty so that a search of the real estate records for a piece of realty will reveal any security interests in the fixtures annexed thereto. The required contents of a fixture filing are set out in UCC § 9–402.

5. PRIORITIES; 1962 CODE: Although it is not explicitly stated in the Code, the 1962 version of UCC § 9–313 is intended to cover primarily purchase-money security interests. A purchase-money security interest is one held by a creditor whose money has been used to buy goods. But for his financing the goods would not be in

---

1. As of 1979 most of the states adhered to the 1962 version of U.C.C. § 9–313, but some had adopted the 1972 version. Of course, it is always possible in the adoption of any uniform or model act that the legislature may make substantial changes. See, e. g., West's Fla.Stat.Ann. § 679.313 (1979), which is a substantially amended form of the 1962 version.

the hands of the debtor at all; therefore a purchase-money financer receives special priority.

6. The purchase-money financer in a state which retains the 1962 Code need only have his interest attached before installation to achieve priority over even *prior* recorded interests in the realty. However, if the interest is not perfected by filing, a *subsequent BFP* of the realty *without notice* of the fixture encumbrance will take free of it. An interest which attaches *after* installation will be *subordinate* to existing realty interests as well as to subsequent ones (if the subsequent holder qualifies as a BFP) which arise before the fixture interest is perfected.

7. 1972 CODE PRIORITIES: The 1972 Code places a heavier burden on the fixture financer who seeks to achieve priority. Under the revised UCC § 9–313, a security interest in fixtures will have prioity over prior realty interests if it:

    a. is a purchase-money interest,

    b. arose *before* installation,

    c. is perfected before or within ten days after installation (the 1962 Code required only attachment), and

    d. is in goods annexed to realty in which the debtor has a recorded interest or is in possession. (UCC § 9–313(4)(a)).

8. A perfected non-purchase-money interest (which is rare) will have priority over conflicting realty interests if the security interest is perfected by a fixture filing before the competing interest is recorded. (§ 9–313(4)(b)) (1972 Code).

9. SPECIAL RULES:

    a. *Construction Mortgage:* The 1972 Code gives "super priority" to construction mortgages. Such a mortgage will prevail over any fixture interest if (1) the construction mortgage is recorded before fixture installation; and (2) fixture installation occurs before completion of construction. (UCC § 9–313(6)).

    b. *Factory & Office Machines, Domestic Appliance Replacements:* A security interest in these goods (when they are readily removable) may be perfected by filing *any* type of financing statement, and when so perfected has priority. (UCC § 9–313(4)(c)). This exception from the fixture filing was made because: (1) local laws differ as to whether certain machinery and appliances become fixtures; and (2) continual filing of interests on domestic appliances would be an undue burden on real estate record agencies and creditors.

    c. *Judicial Liens:* Liberal provisions for fixture filing and priority are also applicable when the conflicting interest is a lien obtained through court action. (UCC § 9–313(4)(d)). In this case a security interest perfected by any method permitted under the Article has priority over a subsequent real estate lien.

d. *Fixture Interests Arising through Real Property Law:* UCC § 9–313 is not the exclusive rule for creation of interests in fixtures. An interest in a fixture may arise through real property law independent of the Code. (UCC § 9–313(3)).

e. *Non-debtor Owners of Realty:* UCC § 9–313(7) states that in cases not governed by other subsections of the Code Section (i. e. the rules previously mentioned), . . . a security interest in fixtures is subordinate to the conflicting interest of an encumbrancer or owner of the related real estate *who is not the debtor*. (emphasis added)

f. *Subordination Agreements:* A party with priority status (usually an owner or encumbrancer of the realty) may surrender his preferred status by *written* agreement. See UCC § 9–313(5)(a). This is often done to make it easier to obtain financing from sources which demand priority status. In the case of a subordination agreement the fixture interest need not be perfected in order to obtain priority.

10. DEFAULT: If a fixture financer has priority over any conflicting interests in the goods and the debtor defaults on his payments (or some terms of the security agreement), the financer may remove the installed goods. However, he will be liable to the owner or encumbrancer of the realty for *damage* caused by removal and no removal may be made if it constitutes a breach of the peace. Further, the financer may be required to provide security for repair before removal is allowed. (UCC § 9–313(8)) (1972 version).

11. Although the removing financer will be liable for physical damage to the realty caused by the fixture removal, any diminution in the value of the realty is *not* a proper measure of damages. E. g., the fixture lender on a room air conditioner installed in a wall properly removes it after default. He will have to pay for repair to the wall, but will not be liable for the difference in value between the air conditioned and non-air conditioned room or building.

12. As between the parties, an agreement that the chattel shall remain a chattel is effective unless accession occurs. Thus, when a landowner buys a chattel with the intention of annexing it to the realty and there is an agreement that it shall remain a chattel until it is paid for, the article retains its chattel character.

E. g., A, landowner, buys a furnace from B under a conditional sales contract or by giving a chattel mortgage thereon. A defaults in his payment. B may remove the furnace.

E. g., (b) A, landowner, buys from B a steel "I" beam to be used in the construction of his house for the support of the second story thereof, under a conditional sales contract or by giving a chattel mortgage thereon. The "I" beam is built into the house and A defaults on his payments. The beam has become an accession to the house and has lost its identity therein. B cannot remove the "I" beam. In such a case the removal of the beam would substantially destroy the house. Under such circumstances no agreement can preserve the chattel character of the annexed article. B is limited to his action against A personally on the debt.

Note 1

The result in these two examples should be the same under the Uniform Commercial Code. § 9–313 of the UCC, set forth in Exhibit A, infra, governs security interests in fixtures. Subsection (1) of the 1962 version and subsection (2) of the 1972 version provide that the section shall not apply to cases of accession. Thus, the second example above is not affected by the Code. The first example above is governed by subsection (2) of the 1962 version since the security interest in the fixture would attach at the time of the purchase of the furnace. Subsection (2) provides that if the security interest attaches before the good becomes a fixture, then it has priority over interests in the real estate except as noted in subsection (4). Since the landowner is not one of those mentioned in subsection (4), here for purposes of convenience generically described as subsequent purchasers for value without notice, the security interest in the furnace has priority. Subsection (5) of the 1972 version would give B the same right as long as there was a written, or probably even an oral agreement, to that effect.

Note 2

The statutes of particular states should be consulted because legislatures in enacting uniform acts frequently change specific provisions thereof.

13. If a chattel is wrongfully taken from its owner and annexed to another's land the innocent owner of the chattel has a right to recover it either from the owner of the land to which it has been annexed or from a grantee or mortgagee of such landowner, unless such article has lost its identity by accession and its removal would result in substantial injury to the real property.

E. g., (a) A wrongfully takes B's steam radiator and annexes it to A's heating system in his house on Blackacre after which he sells Blackacre to C who knows nothing of the above facts. B can recover the radiator which still retains its chattel character for the reason that there is no intention of the rightful owner that the radiator become a fixture.

E. g., (b) A wrongfully takes B's bricks and builds them into a wall of A's house on his Blackacre after which he sells Blackacre to C who may or may not know of the above facts. B cannot recover the bricks which have become an accession to the house in which they have lost their identity. In other words there are no more bricks legally, they are all house. The reason for B's inability to recover the bricks is the practical fact that such recovery would necessarily cause substantial destruction of the house. B may find his remedy in a personal tort action against A for the conversion of the bricks.

Note

The UCC does not apply to either of these cases since no security interest in chattels is involved, and, additionally as to example 2, it is a case of accession.

References

UCC Authorities: Uniform Commercial Code (1962, 1972), Secs. 9–313, 9–314, 9–203, 9–402 and comments thereto; White and Summers, Handbook of the Law Under the Uniform Commercial Code, West Publishing Co. (1972), Sec. 25–17 et seq.; Henson, Handbook on Secured Transactions Under the Uniform Commercial Code, West Publishing Co., Ch. 8 (1979).

———

CASE 183: A purchased Blackacre in 1968 using a loan secured by a mortgage to M recorded March 4, 1968 with a life of thirty years. On June 18, 1980, A buys a furnace from C using a "retail financing security agreement" executed by A to C. The agreement, dated June 19, 1980, recites that payments are to be made monthly over a ten year period and that the furnace is to be collateral. On June 20, C files a regular UCC–1 financing statement in the personal property records of Blackacre County. The furnace is installed on July 1, 1980 and two weeks later, on July 15, C files a fixture filing with the Recorder of Deeds of Blackacre County. One year later A defaults on both the mortgage and the furnace security agreement because he has insufficient funds to pay both. In conflicting suits on the debts, who will prevail (a) under the 1962 UCC? and (b) under the 1972 UCC? (c) Would it make any difference if the mortgage to M was for the purchase of land and construction of the house on Blackacre?

Answers and Analyses

(a) The answer to (a) is that C will have priority over the mortgage to M. Under the 1962 version of the UCC a security interest in a fixture will have priority over *prior* recorded real estate interests as long as the security interest *attaches* prior to the installation of the fixture. Here, the security interest in the furnace attached on June 19, 1980 when the security agreement was executed. Installation was not completed until after that, so C's interest will have priority over the mortgage. This may seem unfair to M, but remember that but for C's financing, the furnace would never have been installed on Blackacre.

(b) The answer to (b) is that C will lose and M will prevail. Under the 1972 revised UCC, C may not rely on the mere attachment of his security interest; he must perfect it by filing in accordance with the UCC. Here he has failed to do so in two ways: (1) the filing on June 20 is ineffectual under the 1972 Code because it was not a fixture filing and was not filed in the office where *real estate* records are kept; (2) further, while the July 15 fixture filing might cure this problem, a fixture filing must be made *before* installation of the fixture or within the ten-day grace period thereafter. C has failed to do so, therefore he cannot claim priority over the mortgage.

(c) If the mortgage to M was a construction mortgage, under the 1972 Code it would have priority over C's interest even if C had properly filed within the allowable time. This is because of the "super priority" given construction mortgages on the theory that but for such financing, no real property would exist on which the fixture could be installed. Note that no such provision exists under the 1962 Code, thus leaving priority to the purchase money fixture security interest. [Answer based on analysis of the two Code provisions; see Exhibit A infra].

CASE 184: Assume the same facts in the preceding case as to the mortgage and security interest in the furnace. In addition, on October 12, 1980, A obtained additional financing on his house from S, secured by a second mortgage duly recorded on that date. A used part of these funds to have a roof repaired by R company, but failed to pay for the repairs. Consequently R obtained a lien on Blackacre through judicial proceedings. Will C—the fixture financer—have priority over S and/or R: **(a)** under the 1962 Code; **(b)** under the 1972 Code?

Answers and Analyses

The answer to (a) is that as to S, C will have priority. Under the 1962 Code the attachment of the security interest on either one of the two filings would be sufficient to give priority over the *later-recorded* second mortgage interest. As to R, the judicial lienor, C's interest would prevail only if R had knowledge of the security interest, and the prior fixture filing in the land records should constitute such notice.

The answer to (b) is that C would have priority over both S and R under the 1972 version of the UCC. As to S, the usual "first to file or record" rule would give C priority. R, however, falls under the special rule pertaining to judgment lienors (UCC § 9–313(4)(d)). Although the Code may not require a fixture filing as a prerequisite to priority over a judgment lienor, there was in fact a perfected security interest prior to the perfection of the creditor's lien, and therefore the fixture security interest would have priority. [See Exhibit A.]

CASE 185: D, owner of Whiteacre, buys an airconditioner from X which is installed in a wall. D finances this purchase with an installment sales contract which is covered by a duly filed fixture filing made in the proper place before installation by D. Whiteacre is encumbered by a mortgage held by M. D subsequently defaults on payments to both X and M and prior to a foreclosure sale of Whiteacre X seeks to remove the unit. M objects, arguing that such removal will impair his security by (1) physically damaging the realty, and (2) diminishing its value. Will M prevail under the 1972 version of the UCC?

Answer and Analysis

The answer is no, but M is not completely without rights. First of all X's interest has priority over M's because X's interest was perfected before the unit became a fixture. It is essential that X establish his priority before he may remove the fixture. Once it is established, M may exercise his right to have X post a bond to cover any damage to Whiteacre caused by the removal. On posting a bond, X may proceed with removal. If M does not require a bond, X will nonetheless be liable for *physical* damage, but *not* for diminution in value of the realty. Of course, if X's removal would constitute a breach of the peace (e. g., by breaking into the building), he could not remove. Further, if the cost of removal and repair exceeded the recoverable value of the air conditioner, X would be foolish to remove it.

Note that UCC § 9–313(5)(b) (1972 version), gives X an alternative route to take. If D had a right to remove the air conditioner himself (as against M), X may do so and *not* be liable for damages, unless D was.

M would also prevail under the 1962 version of the UCC since M's interest *attached* before it became a fixture and M's mortgage was an existing encumbrance on the real estate.

EXHIBIT A

UCC § 9–313

1962 Text

(1) The rules of this section do not apply to goods incorporated into a structure in the manner of lumber, bricks, tile, cement, glass, metal work and the like and no security interest in them exists under this Article unless the structure remains personal property under applicable law. The law of this state other than this Act determines whether and when other goods become fixtures. This Act does not prevent creation of an encumbrance upon fixtures or real estate pursuant to the law applicable to real estate.

(2) A security interest which attaches to goods before they become fixtures takes priority as to

1962 Text

the goods over the claims of all persons who have an interest in the real estate except as stated in subsection (4).

(3) A security interest which attaches to goods after they become fixtures is valid against all persons subsequently acquiring interests in the real estate except as stated in subsection (4) but is invalid against any person with an interest in the real estate at the time the security interest attaches to the goods who has not in writing consented to the security interest or disclaimed an interest in the goods as fixtures.

(4) The security interests described in subsections (2) and (3) do not take priority over

    (a) a subsequent purchaser for value of any interest in the real estate; or

    (b) a creditor with a lien on the real estate subsequently obtained by judicial proceedings; or

    (c) a creditor with a prior encumbrance of record on the real estate to the extent that he makes subsequent advances

if the subsequent purchase is made, the lien by judicial proceedings is obtained, or the subsequent advance under the prior encumbrance is made or contracted for without knowledge of the security interest and before it is perfected. A purchaser of the real estate at a foreclosure sale other than an encumbrancer purchasing at his own foreclosure sale is a subsequent purchaser within this section.

(5) When under subsections (2) or (3) and (4) a secured party has priority over the claims of all persons who have interests in the real estate, he may, on default, subject to the provisions of Part 5, remove his collateral from the real estate but he must reimburse any encumbrancer or owner of the real estate who is not the debtor and who has not otherwise agreed for the cost of repair of any physical injury, but not for any diminution in value of the real estate caused by the absence of the goods removed or by any necessity for replacing them. A person entitled to reimbursement may refuse permission to remove until the secured party gives adequate security for the performance of this obligation.

1972 Text

(1) In this section and in the provisions of Part 4 of this Article referring to fixture filing, unless the context otherwise requires

    (a) goods are "fixtures" when they become so related to particular real estate that an interest in them arises under real estate law.

    (b) a "fixture filing" is the filing in the office where a mortgage on the real estate would be filed or recorded of a financing statement covering goods which are or are to become fixtures and conforming to the requirements of subsection (5) of Section 9–402.

    (c) a mortgage is a "construction mortgage" to the extent that it secures an obligation incurred for the construction of an improvement on land including the acquisition cost of the land, if the recorded writing so indicates.

1972 Text

(2) A security interest under this Article may be created in goods which are fixtures or may continue in goods which become fixtures, but no security interest exists under this Article in ordinary building materials incorporated into an improvement on land.

(3) This Article does not prevent creation of an encumbrance upon fixtures pursuant to real estate law.

(4) A perfected security interest in fixtures has priority over the conflicting interest of an encumbrancer or owner of the real estate where

(a) the security interest is a purchase money security interest, the interest of the encumbrancer or owner arises before the goods become fixtures, the security interest is perfected by a fixture filing before the goods become fixtures or within ten days thereafter, and the debtor has an interest of record in the real estate or is in possession of the real estate; or

(b) the security interest is perfected by a fixture filing before the interest of the encumbrancer or owner is of record, the security interest has priority over any conflicting interest of a predecessor in title of the encumbrancer or owner, and the debtor has an interest of record in the real estate or is in possession of the real estate; or

(c) the fixtures are readily removable factory or office machines or readily removable replacements of domestic appliances which are consumer goods, and before the goods become fixtures the security interest is perfected by any method permitted by this Article; or

(d) the conflicting interest is a lien on the real estate obtained by legal or equitable proceedings after the security interest was perfected by any method permitted by this Article.

(5) A security interest in fixtures, whether or not perfected, has priority over the conflicting interest of an encumbrancer or owner of the real estate where

(a) the encumbrancer or owner has consented in writing to the security interest or has disclaimed an interest in the goods as fixtures; or

(b) the debtor has a right to remove the goods as against the encumbrancer or owner. If the debtor's right terminates, the priority of the security interest continues for a reasonable time.

(6) Notwithstanding paragraph (a) of subsection (4) but otherwise subject to subsections (4) and (5), a security interest in fixtures is subordinate to a construction mortgage recorded before the goods become fixtures if the goods become fixtures before the completion of the construction. To the extent that it is given to refinance a construction mortgage, a mortgage has this priority to the same extent as the construction mortgage.

(7) In cases not within the preceding subsections, a security interest in fixtures is subordinate to the conflicting interest of an encumbrancer or owner of the re-

1972 Text

lated real estate who is not the debtor.

(8) When the secured party has priority over all owners and encumbrancers of the real estate, he may, on default, subject to the provisions of Part 5, remove his collateral from the real estate but he must reimburse any encumbrancer or owner of the real estate who is not the debtor and who has not otherwise agreed for the cost of repair of any physical injury, but not for any diminution in value of the real estate caused by the absence of the goods removed or by any necessity of replacing them. A person entitled to reimbursement may refuse permission to remove until the secured party gives adequate security for the performance of this obligation.

SUMMARY OF CASES IN CHAPTER XIV

1. FIXTURES GENERALLY

Case 181. For a chattel to become a fixture three elements must co-exist. (1) There must be either an actual or a constructive annexation of the chattel to the realty. (2) The chattel must be adapted to the use which is made of the real property to which it is annexed. (3) There must be an intention on the part of the annexer that the chattel become a fixture. This is the objective intention inferred from the circumstances surrounding the annexation and not the secret, subjective intention which is in the mind of the annexer. Objective facts which determine the intention include: (a) the nature of the article; (b) the manner of its annexation to the realty; (c) the injury, if any, caused by its removal; (d) the integration of the chattel with the use to which the land is put; (e) the relation to the annexer to the land; (f) the relation of the annexer to the chattel; (g) the effect of local custom, if any; and all other pertinent facts. Applying these tests the linoleum glued to the floors of an apartment house, the window blinds and curtain rods, and in-a-door beds placed therein by the fee simple owner as permanent furnishings are fixtures, and title thereto passes with a deed to the land.

2. TRADE FIXTURES

Case 182. For a chattel to become a fixture there must be: (a) an annexation to the land actually or constructively; (b) an adaptation of the chattel to the use to which the land is put; and (c) an objective intention inferred from the circumstances on the part of the annexer that the chattel become a fixture. A trade fixture is one which is annexed to land by a tenant for the purpose of pecuniary gain in the business he conducts on the land. To encourage trade and industry a tenant is permitted to remove trade fixtures from the land. Such doctrine extends to agricultural trade fixtures in the United States. Trade fixtures usually include factory machinery, store counters and shelves, temporary partitions in buildings and the like. In proper cases the doctrine is applied to buildings, but it should not extend to the destruction of a brick building (put on the land by a tenant) for the purpose of saving the materials from which the building is made because that would involve unreasonable economic waste.

3. SECURITY INTERESTS IN FIXTURES (UCC); STOLEN CHATTELS

Case 183. Under the 1962 version of the UCC, a security interest in a fixture will have priority over a prior recorded interest in the realty as long as it *attaches* before installation—perfection is not required. The 1972 version puts a heavier burden on the fixture financer. Mere attachment prior to installation is insufficient to give the interest priority. Likewise, neither a non-fixture filing nor a fixture filing after the permissible period will suffice for priority purposes. However, if the conflicting realty interest is a construction mortgage and the 1972 Code is in effect, the fixture interest will be subordinate. The 1962 version would give priority to the fixture interest.

Case 184. The UCC adopts the "first to file or record" rule of priority in regard to otherwise equal security interests. Thus a recorded fixture interest will prevail over a later-recorded mortgage interest. Special rules under the 1972 Code give the fixture financer more leeway in filing as against a subsequent judicial lienor. All that is required is *any* type of security filing, because the lienor will not be relying on real estate records. Under the 1962 Code, the fixture interest need only attach before installation to prevail over a lienor with knowledge of the interest.

Case 185. The holder of a priority security interest in a fixture may remove the fixture as against a mortgagee of the real estate, but the holder of the fixture security interest will be liable to the mortgagee for any physical damage to the realty caused by such removal, but will not be liable for any diminution in value of the realty. Also, under the 1972 version of the UCC, if the realty owner has a right to remove a fixture as against a real estate mortgagee, then the holder of the fixture security interest may likewise remove it.

Chapter XV

WASTE

Legal Gems.
Cases.

Summary of Cases in Chapter XV

Legal Gems

1. Waste is not a subject which can be defined with precision. Generally it consists in an act by a life tenant or a tenant for years which results in damage to the corpus of the property or the estate in remainder or reversion. If the act done is consistent with good husbandry and is substantially what a fee simple owner of the land would do were he occupying and using the land, the act does not constitute waste. E. g.,

  a. A, life tenant of Blackacre, clears the land of timber standing thereon for the purpose of using it for raising annual crops, thus enhancing the value of the land from $50.00 per acre to $100.00 per acre. This is not waste.

  b. A, life tenant of Blackacre, a lot in an exclusively residential area tears down the dwelling house and builds a store building in its place. This is waste as to the reversioner. But if that which was once a residential area has become completely a business area and A does the same thing it is not waste as to the reversioner. See Melms v. Pabst Brewing Co., 104 Wis. 7, 79 N. W. 738 (1899).

  c. A, a life tenant of Blackacre, opens a new mine or quarry thereon and proceeds to dig out and dispose of the minerals or rock therefrom. This is waste. If A continues to operate a mine or quarry already open and being mined when A's life estate takes effect, it is not waste.

  d. A, a life tenant of Blackacre, gathers up and sells manure which has been produced by feeding cattle the crops grown on Blackacre. This is waste. A does the same thing as to manure which has been produced by feeding cattle grain which has been grown on other land and bought by A. This is not waste.

  e. A, life tenant of Blackacre, which has not been used for producing timber, cuts timber thereon to be used for repair of the buildings thereon, or as posts for repairing the fences thereon or for firewood (called estovers). This is not waste. A cuts the same timber for the purpose of sale. This is waste.

  f. A, life tenant of Blackacre, cuts down a beautiful big shade tree in the prime of its life in front of the house on Blackacre. This is waste. But if the same tree is old and rotting and about to fall on the roof of the dwelling house and A cuts it down to preserve the dwelling house such act is not waste. In each of the above cases the same results would follow if A were a tenant for years instead of a life tenant. The question in each case is whether or not the act gives the reversioner or remainderman a reasonable ground for objection on the theory that the act is not consistent with good husbandry.

2.   There are four types of waste—

    a.   voluntary waste is injury to the inheritance caused by an affirmative act of the tenant: e. g., A, life tenant or tenant for years, opens a new sand pit on the occupied land and digs out and sells the sand therefrom.

    b.   permissive waste is injury to the inheritance caused by the tenant's failure to act when it is his duty to act: e. g., A, life tenant or tenant for years, fails to cover a hole in the roof of the dwelling house on the leased premises when the mere putting on of a few shingles would do it. The rain leaks through the hole in the roof and ruins the hardwood floors of the house. The tenant is bound to make ordinary repairs.

    c.   ameliorating waste is a change in the physical charactertistics of the occupied premises by an unauthorized act of the tenant which increases the value of the land: e. g., A, life tenant or tenant for years, razes an old and outmoded building on the leased premises and builds a modern building conforming to new conditions and thereby increases the value of the land from $10,000.00 to $15,000.00. Ordinarily the tenant is not liable for ameliorating waste.

    d.   equitable waste is an injury to the reversionary interest in land which is inconsistent with good husbandry and is recognized only by the equity courts and does not constitute legal waste as recognized by the courts of law. It usually arises where the expression "without impeachment of waste" appears in the lease to a life tenant or tenant for years. E. g., A, fee simple owner of Blackacre, grants to B a life estate in the premises "without impeachment of waste". Blackacre is a lot in a business district on which stands a six story hotel building and is being used as such. B threatens to raze the hotel building and build a single dwelling house thereon. "Without impeachment of waste" means that the life tenant or tenant for years may use the leased premises as a fee simple owner might use the land. At law a fee simple owner may raze his hotel building and build a mansion house on the land. But because no reasonable fee owner of Blackacre would raze the hotel building and because it is inconsistent with good husbandry and under the circumstances would be an unconscionable and unreasonable destruction of the inheritance an equity court will enjoin B's tearing down of the hotel building. Such is equitable waste.

3. If a tenant for life or for years commits waste on land by cutting down trees thereon or opening new mines and taking minerals therefrom, the trees cut and the minerals severed belong to the reversioner or remainderman and not to the tenant. And if such trees or minerals have been sold the proceeds of the sale belong to the reversioner or remainderman.

4. A tenant for life or for years is liable to the reversioner or the remainderman for voluntary waste and for permissive waste but he is not liable for injury to the leased premises caused by accident for which he is in no way at fault.

5. For legal waste, voluntary or permissive, the reversioner or remainderman may sue the tenant for life, or for years, either in tort for damages or in contract for breach of the implied covenant in the lease to preserve the leased premises in a reasonable state of repair. If either of such remedies is inadequate the suit may be brought in equity. For equitable waste the owner of the reversionary interest may sue in equity, usually for an injunction.

6. The general purpose of the law of waste is to give the life tenant or tenant for years the maximum use of the leased premises and at the same time to preserve the substance of the corpus of the property for the person who takes the land at the end of the tenancy. It deals with a balancing of the interests of the two and the line of demarcation is often in a twilight zone.

7. Liability for waste applies generally to holders of limited possessory interests, such as life tenants and tenants for years. It does not apply to owners of fees simple absolute as such parties, subject to the law of nuisance, zoning and police power regulations, are free to use the land as they wish and may diminish the inheritance.

8. Tenants in common or joint tenants, however, may be liable to their cotenants if they extract more than their share of minerals or timbers. See White v. Smyth, 147 Tex. 272, 214 S.W.2d 967, 5 A. L.R.2d 1348 (1948); Kirby Lumber Co. v. Temple Lumber Co., 125 Tex. 284, 83 S.W.2d 638 (1935).

9. A legal action for waste is available to holders of a vested future interest, e. g., reversioners and vested remaindermen.

10. Usually the holders of possibilities of reverter and rights of re-entry do not have actions for waste. However, if the concomitant fee interest is almost certain to end in the near future, then such interest holders should be entitled to equitable protection as in Gem 11 infra.

11. A contingent remainderman, and the same principle would seem to apply to holders of other contingent future interests, may obtain relief only if the contingency is *fairly certain to occur*. Appropriate relief could be an injunction against waste, or, if waste has already occurred, an assessment of damages and impoundment of the proceeds pending resolution of the contingency. If chances are *re-*

mote that the contingency will occur, courts will not give relief of any kind to a contingent remainderman. See Case 189 infra.

See Restatement of Property §§ 139–146, 188–191; Tiffany, p. 258 et seq.; Burby, 33 et seq.; Powell, ¶¶ 636–650.

———

CASE 186: A is the fee simple owner of Blackacre, a section of land. Half of Blackacre is swampland totally unfit for cultivation but heavily covered with valuable hardwood timber. The other half of Blackacre is also covered with valuable timber but is land which is fit for the raising of crops when cleared of the timber thereon. And such land is more valuable for cultivation than for the growing of timber. A grants to B a life estate in Blackacre. B takes possession and clears 40 acres of the timber thereon so that such 40 acres can be used for cultivation and the growing of annual crops. He also cuts timber from the swampland. He sells the timber cut on the swampland for $1,000.00 and the timber from the field to be used for cultivation for $1,200.-00. B has cut some timber on the land and used it as estovers. A sues B seeking an injunction against any further cutting of timber on Blackacre and for an accounting of the proceeds received from the timber sold. What decree, if any, should issue in A's favor?

Answer and Analysis

The answer is this: A should have a decree providing as follows: (a) B is permanently enjoined from cutting any more timber on the swampland other than for estovers and must account for the proceeds received from the sale of the timber taken from the swampland; (b) the injunction is denied as to cutting further timber on the land which can be used for cultivation and B need make no accounting for the proceeds received from the sale of the timber from the land cleared for cultivation; and (c) the injunction is denied as to the cutting of timber on any of the land and using such for estovers.

(1) **Estovers.** A tenant for life or for years has a right to cut and appropriate timber on the leased premises as "estovers" for the purpose of use in repairing on the land, fences, buildings, equipment, machinery and the like, and for use as fuel in his own and his servants' dwellings. A tenant at will has no such right. But it is waste for the tenant to cut growing, healthy trees for such purposes if dead or inferior timber will serve the purpose just as well, or to use more than is reasonably necessary to accomplish the required result. In our case B is a tenant for life of Blackacre and has a right to make proper use of the timber on the land for estover purposes. Therefore, as to such item no injunction should issue in the absence of a showing that such right has been exceeded.

(2) The timber cut to clear land for cultivation. Any change in the characteristics of land which makes it more productive and adds to the store of consumable goods should be given all the protection which sound legal principles permit. It takes much time, labor and power to convert timberland into tillable fields for the production of annual crops. It is a simple task to cut down the trees. But it is a stubborn task to remove the stump and roots of a single tree. And to remove the stumps and roots of trees covering a 40 acre tract is an undertaking of Herculean proportions. When, then a tenant for life or for years does clear land of timber and make it available for the growing of crops he is due some consideration by way of compensation for the time, labor and power expended. The law takes account of such by awarding to him the timber which is removed for such purpose. Furthermore, the tenant for life or for years has a right to use land as good husbandry dictates. This usually includes the right to transform timberland into arable land for the plow, provided of course the soil can be made suitable for such purpose. Therefore, in our case B should not be enjoined from clearing more timberland for crop purposes and is not required to account for the proceeds which he has received from the sale of timber taken from the land cleared for cultivation.

(3) The timber cut from the swampland. The swampland is not now and cannot be made usable for the growing of crops. It seems to be capable of growing trees only. This swampland, as far as the facts disclose, has never been used and at the time of the taking effect of B's life estate was not being used for the production of lumber. B is the first to cut timber thereon. At this point an analogy may assist in the analysis and understanding of the problem. It is well settled that a tenant for life or for years has a right to continue the operation of old mines on the leased premises for the reason that such is the use to which the land has been put or is being put at the time of the beginning of the tenant's estate. The lease implies that such use may be continued. On the other hand such tenants have no right to open new mines and appropriate the minerals therefrom. The reason is clear. It has taken eons of time to produce the minerals which underlay the land. It is the very substance of which the land is made and that corpus should not be available for consumption or destruction by a tenant of a limited interest in the premises, unless of course the lease is made for the very purpose of mining. Likewise it has taken generations of time to produce the hardwood forests of the swampland and the value of that forest is the very heart and substance of that portion of Blackacre. It should not be available for consumption and destruction by a tenant of a limited estate as against the reversioner or remainderman who owns the inheritance. To hold otherwise would be giving to the owner of the temporary interest the kernel of the nut and the holder of the permanent interest the mere shell thereof. Therefore, B should be permanently enjoined from cutting any more trees on the swampland except for estover purposes, and should account for the proceeds from the sale of the timber which was cut on the swampland. This accords with the law and good sense. See Tiffany, pp. 258–268; Davis v. Gilliam, 40 N.C. 308 (1848); 8 Va.L.R. 289 (1922); Restatement of Property § 140.

CASE 187: L, owner in fee simple of Blackacre, leases it to T for a period of 5 years to be used as a soap factory. On one side of the large building on Blackacre is another factory building between the two being a party wall one foot in thickness. Between the rear wall of the factory on Blackacre and the alley is a vacant area about 15 feet in width in which there is a patch of dry weeds. In the front of the soap factory building is a rendering tank. Without L's consent T cuts a hole in the party wall between the soap factory and the adjoining factory, and puts a door therein which is 6 feet high and 3 feet wide so that he can have access to the adjacent building. The weeds in the rear of the soap factory catch fire from an unknown cause. T discovers the fire when it can easily be stamped out without difficulty or danger to anyone. He negligently fails to extinguish the blaze and because of such negligence it damages the rear doors and wall of the soap factory before the fire department puts it out. The rendering tank in the front of the building accidentally explodes and damages the building. The lease expires and the soap factory building still remains in its damaged condition. T refuses to restore the party wall where the door now is or to repair any of the damage done by either the fire or the explosion. L sues T for damages (a) for injury to the party wall, (b) for injury done to the rear doors and wall by the fire and (c) for injury done by the explosion. May L recover for any?

Answers and Analyses

The answer is yes as to (a), yes as to (b) and no as to (c).

(a) **The injury to the party wall.** At common law neither a tenant for life nor a tenant for years has a right to destroy or alter materially the physical structure which is the principal subject matter of the lease in the absence of consent from the lessor. The tearing down of a house or a wall in the house is waste unless such is authorized by the lease. In our case the tearing out of the party wall without the consent of the lessor, either in the lease or otherwise, is a destruction of the party wall to the extent that the bricks and mortar thereof are removed. It is immaterial whether or not the other party wall owner consents to such. The half of the wall owned by the lessor, L, is part and parcel of his building and for the tenant to destroy it without L's consent is voluntary waste for which the tenant is liable in damages. Therefore as to the removal of the part of the party wall the plaintiff has a right to damages. Had the lease not expired and the defendant were still in possession the plaintiff would be entitled to a mandatory injunction to compel immediate restoration of the party wall. However, with the plaintiff in possession of the property it is better that damages be awarded and that the plaintiff restore the party wall to its original position.

(b) The injury caused by the fire. At common law a tenant for life or for years is not only liable for voluntary waste caused by his affirmative acts in altering or injuring the leased premises; he is also liable for permissive waste caused by his failure to keep the leased premises in a reasonable state of repair, so that when they are returned to the reversioner or remainderman at the end of the lease the property is unimpaired except for usual wear and tear. There is an implied obligation inherent in every lease in the absence of provision to the contrary that the tenant will make ordinary repairs to the property and will guard and preserve such property. These are affirmative duties cast upon a lessee of property and his failure to perform such with resultant injury makes him liable for permissive waste. In our case when T discovers fire in the dry weeds behind the soap factory building it is his duty to protect the building therefrom. His negligent failure to perform such duty caused damage to the leased building and premises. For such damage T is liable to L in damages.

(c) The injury caused by the explosion. For voluntary waste the tenant is liable in damages to the lessor. For permissive waste caused by the tenant's negligent failure to preserve the leased property the tenant is liable in damages to the lessor. Voluntary waste is a sin of commission. Permissive waste is a sin of omission, there being a duty to act. But a tenant for life or for years is not liable for injury to the leased premises which is caused by forces wholly beyond his power to control such as Act of God, public enemies, tempest or flood. Neither is he liable for such injury which is caused by accident for the happening of which he is in no way at fault. The common law has not carried the implied duty in the lease or liability for permissive waste so far as to make the tenant liable without fault. Thus in our case when the rendering tank exploded causing damage to the leased premises without any fault on the part of T, there is no liability for such injury. The loss must lie where it falls because there is no reason either in intentional or negligent act to shift it. Hence, L cannot recover damages from T for such injury. See Earle v. Arbogast, 180 Pa. 409, 36 A. 923 (Sup.Ct.1897); Klie v. Von Broock, 56 N.J.Eq. 18, 37 A. 469 (Ch.1897); Restatement of Property § 139; Restatement, Second, Property, § 12.2; Townshend v. Moore, 33 N.J.L. 284 (Sup.Ct.1869).

CASE 188: L, owner in fee simple of Blackacre on which is a large barn for the storage of hay, leases it for that purpose to T for a period of three years. T fills the barn with some hay and with several other materials which are much heavier than hay including, grain, meal, fertilizer and rock salt. The excess weight of these other materials causes the floors of the barn to sink, the joists and rafters to break and come loose from their fastenings and the roof to cave in so that the barn is in a state of collapse at the end of the lease. T pays the entire rent due. The fact is that T's use of the leased premises is quite unreasonable under the circumstances. L sues T for damages for breach of contract for failure to use Blackacre in a tenant-like and proper manner. May L recover?

Answer and Analysis

The answer is yes. In this case T uses the hay barn for the storage of more weighty materials and the excessive weight causes the barn to collapse. Such use is unreasonable under the circumstances. The damage caused by such excessive weight and unreasonable use is waste. It is not mere permissive waste for failure to perform a duty enjoined upon the tenant. It is waste caused by a positive and unreasonable act. Such is voluntary waste for which a tenant for life or a tenant for years or a tenant at will is liable to the lessor. However, a tenant at will is liable only in an action in trespass, the theory being that the act of voluntary waste terminates his tenancy at will and makes him a trespasser. But the tenant for life or for years is liable for an action for waste and may be sued either in tort or in breach of contract for such voluntary waste. And this is true whether or not the lease expressly provides for such. There are implied covenants in every lease that the tenant will preserve the leased property in a reasonable state of repair and that he will occupy and use such property in a tenant-like and proper manner. For the unreasonable use of the leased premises which causes damage the lessor may sue the tenant in tort for damages. For the breach of the implied covenants in the lease the lessor may sue the tenant in breach of contract. In a jurisdiction where such causes of action may be joined the lessor may sue on both theories under different counts of the same complaint without being made to elect on which one to proceed. In this case the commission of voluntary waste by the tenant gives the lessor a cause of action in contract for which he has a right of recovery. Therefore L may recover in contract against T for the collapse of the barn caused by T's using the leased premises in an untenant-like and improper manner. See Chalmers v. Smith, 152 Mass. 561, 26 N.E. 95, 11 L.R.A. 769 (1891); Tiffany, p. 264.

––––––––

CASE 189: H and W are fee simple owners of Blackacre, a sheep farm with extensive unharvested timber. H and W made identical wills devising to each of three daughters a life estate in an undivided one-third of Blackacre, with the remainder to such of the children as should survive each daughter. They also provided for "the descendants of any deceased daughter to take by right of representation." D is one of H and W's daughters, and has a life estate in one-third of Blackacre. D and her three adult children, X, Y and Z, all agreed to sell timber cut from "their" land (Blackacre had been partitioned subject to contingent future interests), to Q Corporation. The corporation had logged timber from the land of the reasonable value of $180,000 when D's son, X, died. X's son, S, brings suit to enjoin further logging and to have his rights in and to the timber proceeds adjudicated. What are S's rights?

Answer and Analysis

The answer is this. As long as the court finds that S's contingent interest is fairly certain to vest, the court will grant S relief. In this instance, S is the grandchild of D, who has only a life estate in the land in question. D's children have contingent remainders, which would vest upon D's death. The term: "descendants of any deceased daughter to take by right of representation" is construed to mean that the lineal heirs of any descendant is intended to be substituted in the place of a parent who fails to survive the preceding generation. Consequently, S is deemed to have the same right in the land as his father, X, had—a contingent remainder subject to his surviving D. Since S is D's grandson, the court could reasonably conclude that he is fairly certain to survive D, and the court would grant relief.

What is S's relief? First, he may be entitled to an injunction against further logging.[1] What about the $180,000 worth of timber already cut? The loss of timber need not diminish the sheep ranch-value of Blackacre to constitute waste. The depreciation in the value of the property caused by the removal of the timber could be more than the net value of the timber, but it could not be less. S's grandmother, D, owned a one-third life interest in the land. Each of her children therefore have a contingent remainer in an undivided one-ninth interest. S replaces his father, X, as contingent remainderman in a one-ninth interest. S therefore is entitled to one-ninth of the proceeds of the sale, or $20,000. But since S's interst, though likely to vest, is still contingent, the court will impound the proceeds to await distribution according to the interests of the parties after the contingencies upon which their interests vest have been resolved. See Pedro v. January, 261 Or. 582, 494 P.2d 868, 51 A.L.R.3d 1235 (1972), citing Watson v. Wolff-Goldman Realty Co., 95 Ark. 18, 128 S.W. 581 (1910), and Restatement of Property §§ 189, 192.

1. In the instant case based on Pedro v. January, cited at end of hypothet, the Plaintiff, S, had only a ⅑ contingent future interest, the other future interest holders did not join in the suit, and S did not file a class action. The only remedy granted was the impoundment of S's share of the proceeds of the timber sale. In the Watson case, also cited at the end of the hypothet, all, or nearly all, contingent remaindermen sought the injunction also, and the relief granted was both an injunction and impoundment of the damages. Double or triple damages are frequently allowed by statute. See Pedro v. January.

SUMMARY OF CASES IN CHAPTER XV

Case 186. A tenant for life or for years has a right to use the timber on the leased premises as "estovers" for the purpose of fuel and to repair fences, buildings, equipment and machinery on the land. A tenant at will has no such right. A tenant for life or for years has a right to clear land of timber and convert such land into fields for growing crops provided the soil is suitable for such. If such is done the timber removed from the land belongs to the tenant. A tenant for life or for years has no right to cut virgin timber from swampland on the leased premises when such swampland is suitable for no other purpose than growing timber, and it has not been used for the production of lumber before the beginning of the tenancy, estovers excepted. Such cutting of timber constitutes waste and the tenant must account to the reversioner or remainderman for the proceeds of the sale of such timber and should be enjoined from cutting more timber from the swampland.

Case 187. A tenant for life or for years is liable in damages to the lessor for injury done to the leased premises by acts constituting either voluntary waste or permissive waste. But such tenant is not liable to the landlord for injury to the leased premises which is caused by forces beyond his control such as Act of God, public enemy, tempest, flood or accident.

Case 188. A tenant for life or for years or at will is liable to the lessor for voluntary waste. But the tenant at will can be sued only in an action on trespass on the theory that such wrongful act terminates his tenancy and makes him a trespasser on the land. In every lease there are implied covenants that the tenant will preserve the leased premises in a reasonable state of repair and will occupy and use the premises in a tenant-like and proper manner. For voluntary waste the lessor may sue the tenant either in tort for the unreasonable use which causes damage, or in contract for breach of the implied covenant to occupy and use the premises in a tenant-like and proper manner.

Case 189. A contingent remainderman, and logically any other holder of a contingent future interest, has an action for waste if the contingency is fairly certain to occur and the interest likely to vest. The relief granted will generally include an injunction against future waste. As to waste already committed, a monetary judgment may be awarded, but the award will be impounded until the contingency is resolved and the person or persons who succeed to the fee simple title are ascertained.

Chapter XVI

EMBLEMENTS

Legal Gems.
Cases.
Summary of Cases in Chapter XVI.

LEGAL GEMS

1. Mother earth produces *two types of crops,*

   (a) *fructus naturales,* those which come from nature's bounty without the aid of man, such as trees, bushes, grasses and the fruits of these, and

   (b) *fructus industriales,* those which come primarily from man's industry, that is, man's annual planting, cultivating, and fertilizing, such as grains, beans, corn, pineapple, citrus fruits in orchards.

2. *Fructus industriales are* called *emblements. Emblements are usually annual crops* but if a crop such as apples, pears, grapes, raspberries, oranges, grapefruit or lemons is a *perennial,* it *is* nevertheless *an emblement if it is produced primarily by the application of man's labor and industry.*

3. *Fructus naturales are* and remain *real property* for all purposes *until they are actually severed from the land.*

4. *Fructus industriales are for most purposes personal property but for some purposes are real property.* The following cases illustrate emblements as real property.

   (a) A, fee simple owner of Blackacre, has growing crops of corn, beans and barley growing thereon. He dies testate and provides in his will that all of his real property shall go to his friend, D. Both Blackacre and the growing crops as emblements pass to the devisee as real property on the theory that such is A's intention.

   (b) A, fee simple owner of Blackacre, has growing crops of oats, wheat and oranges growing thereon. A conveys Blackacre to B, orally reserving to himself the emblements thereon. In such a transaction the better rule is that these growing crops constitute an interest in land and the reservation thereof must be in writing under the Statute of Frauds and that the evidence of the oral agreement is not admissible. Hence, in this case under A's deed to B the emblements or growing crops would pass to the grantee B as part of the real property. This is true whether the crops are matured or unmatured if they are still unsevered from the land. On all these points are conflicting cases.

(c) A, fee simple owner of Blackacre, mortgages the land to B, the mortgage becoming due April 1, 1970. On June 1, 1970 B sells Blackacre on foreclosure sale to purchaser P. At the time of the foreclosure sale A has annual crops of flax, potatoes, cotton, carrots and melons growing on the land. These emblements pass as real property to P, the purchaser at the foreclosure sale as of June 1, 1970.

The following cases illustrate emblements as personal property.

(d) A, fee simple owner of Blackacre, has growing crops of rye, hemp, turnips and barley growing thereon. A dies intestate. Blackacre descends as real property to A's heir. The emblements or growing crops are treated as personal property and as such pass to A's administrator.

(e) A, fee simple owner of Blackacre, has growing crops of grapes, grapefruit, wheat and corn growing thereon. A mortgages Blackacre to B, the mortgage to run over a five year period. During the period of the running of the mortgage the mortgagor, A, is usually entitled to possession of Blackacre, and also is entitled to the profits of the land in order that he may pay the mortgage. Therefore, during the period of the running of the mortgage and up till the time of foreclosure sale the emblements or growing crops are considered as being owned by the mortgagor, A, as personal property.

(f) A, fee simple owner of Blackacre, has growing crops of hops, beans, rice and parsnips growing thereon. A makes an oral sale of these emblements to B. He then conveys Blackacre to C and at the time of the sale tells C that the growing crops have been sold to B and belong to B. Thereafter C claims the emblements. The better rule is that the emblements belong to B under the oral sale. In other words the owner of land may sell the emblements thereon as personal property without complying with the provisions of the Statute of Frauds concerning the conveyance of an interest in land. It follows therefore that such owner may give a valid and enforceable chattel mortgage on such emblements. These propositions are true whether the crops are matured or not matured.

Note

This example should be compared with 4(b) supra. The two are not contradictory. 4(b) illustrates that growing crops are generally treated as realty and pass ancillary to a conveyance thereto, and to prevent such, a reservation in writing is necessary. 4(f), on the other hand, indicates that an oral sale of crops is valid as a sale of personalty, and that a subsequent sale of the realty to one with notice will not defeat the rights of the prior purchaser of the crops.

5. Crops which have been severed from the land are from the time of severance personal property for all purposes whether they be fructus naturales or emblements.

6. An oral agreement by the landowner to sell the wild grass or other wild crops growing on the land or standing timber, fructus naturales, is a sale of personal property to which the Statute of Frauds does not apply, the theory being that such crops are constructively severed from the land. This, of course, is practical although not logical.

7. Two rules govern the right of a tenant to remove and claim emblements.

(a) If the term of the tenancy is definite and certain and comes to an end on a day certain, then the tenant must remove the growing crops or emblements before the end of the term or they will belong to the landlord.

(b) If the term of the tenancy is of uncertain duration such as a tenancy at will, a life estate for the life of the tenant or for the life of a third person, the tenant has a right to remove the growing crops or emblements during a reasonable time after the termination of the tenancy. This common law rule is modified in some modern jurisdictions and other means of protecting the rights of all the parties are employed. See infra case 192.

See Brown, pp. 588–610; Burby, 14–21, Restatement of Property § 121; Tiffany, pp. 243–247; Powell, ¶ 663.

CASE 190: L, owner in fee simple of Blackacre, leases it to T for a period of 5 years, the tenancy coming to an end at midnight of May 31, 1981. In March 1981 T plants oats, wheat and corn on Blackacre all of which are in the growing stage and not ripe for harvesting at the termination of the lease on May 31, 1981. T moves off Blackacre when the term ends but returns and removes the emblements therefrom when they become ripe. L sues T in damages for the trespass on Blackacre and for the removal of the crops therefrom. May L recover?

Answer and Analysis

The answer is yes. The lease of Blackacre constituted a tenancy for years. It had a definite beginning and a definite day of termination. When the term came to an end T's right to remain on Blackacre and his right to remove any crops therefrom were terminated. That means that after midnight of May 31, 1981 T had no right to be on Blackacre and had no right to remove any crops, ripe or unmatured, which were still standing and attached to the soil on the land. There is good reason for this view. When both parties to the lease can foresee and understand in advance that their respective rights will come to an end on a day certain, then they should provide in their agreement for the conditions which will obtain on that day. If they make no provisions for the crops as they can be foreseen to exist as of the date of the termination of the lease, then their intention can only be construed as leaving things as they are as of that date. Whether it be folly, inadvertence, stupidity or an actual intention on the part of the tenant to cast a material benefit on the landlord by planting when he cannot reap is not a matter for the law to determine. Their rights are settled as of May 31, 1981 in this case. At that time the growing crops are still attached to the soil and on the second after midnight of that date they are no longer removable by the tenant, T, and remain part and parcel of the reversionary interest of the landlord, L. Therefore, L has a cause of action against T for his trespass on Blackacre and removal of the standing grain thereon. It seems clear also that L could have chosen to treat the severed grain as personal property and sued either in replevin or trover for T's wrongful taking of such. But the doctrine set forth above has no application to emblements severed before the end of the tenancy and left on Blackacre. For example, had T cut and shocked wheat or corn and left it in the shock or in bundles on the ground, such severed grain would still be the personal property of the tenant, T, with the privilege to go onto Blackacre and retrieve such the same as his machinery thereon. See the leading case, Whitmarsh v. Cutting, 10 Johns. (N.Y.) 360 (1813); Brown, p. 590 et seq.; Powell, ¶ 663.

————

CASE 191: L, owner in fee simple of Blackacre, a farm on which annual crops are regularly grown, leases it to T on a month to month lease. In the jurisdiction a month notice is required to terminate such a tenancy. In the month of April 1980 T plants wheat, rye and oats on Blackacre. On April 30, 1980 L gives T notice that his tenancy will be and by such notice is terminated as of June 1, 1980. After receiving such notice T plants corn in one field on the premises. On June 1, 1980 none of the crops is ripe and ready to be harvested. Thereafter T returns to Blackacre and harvests the wheat, rye, oats and corn within a reasonable time after each matures. L sues T for trespassing on Blackacre and removing the crops therefrom. May L recover?

Answer and Analysis

The answer is this. (a) L may not recover for T's removal of the wheat, rye or oats. (b) L may recover for the removal of the corn. The rule is well settled that when a tenant has a tenancy of uncertain duration and such term comes to an end between the time of his planting crops and the time for harvesting such crops on the leased premises, the tenant has a reasonable time after the termination of the tenancy to remove the growing crops as emblements from the leased land. Of course this rule is limited to a single annual crop. This principle is applied regularly to a tenancy at will and to a tenancy for life. There has been some difficulty in classifying a tenancy from year to year. Is it a tenancy like an estate for years to which the above announced principle of the tenant's removal right has no application, or is it one of uncertain duration to which the doctrine applies? The cases which have reached what appears to be the most reasonable and fair result have not troubled themselves about giving such periodic tenancy an arbitrary classification. They have laid down the proposition that in a year to year lease the time of notice by the landlord of the termination of the lease determines the rights of the parties respecting the right to remove the growing crops. If at the time of such notice of termination by the landlord to the tenant, the tenant has planted the crops, then as to those crops already planted when notice is given by the landlord and received by the tenant, the tenant has a right to remove such crops within a reasonable time after the termination of the tenancy. But the crops must be planted at the date of the notice of termination. On the other hand, as to any crops planted by the tenant after the notice of termination of the lease is given, there is no right on the part of the tenant to remove such after-planted crops.

Applying such principles to our set of facts the conclusion is clear that T had the privilege to remove the wheat, the rye and the oats. The lease itself is a month to month lease. By name or classification such a lease is termed a "year to year" lease even though the term itself is only for a month. It is a periodic tenancy. This lease is terminable by either party, L or T, upon his giving the other party one month's notice. L gives the required notice to T on April 30, 1980. Such notice terminates the lease as of June 1, 1980. When such notice was given T had already planted the wheat, rye and oats on Blackacre but he had not yet planted the corn. But the wheat, rye and oats were not ready for harvesting by the time the lease came to an end on June 1st. Therefore it is but reasonable and fair, because T could not foresee and plan for the termination of the lease until he received notice of the termination thereof, that he be given a reasonable time after such termination to remove the crops which he had already planted when the notice was received. Such reasonable time must surely continue to the time when such planted crops are ready for harvesting, and must include a reasonable time thereafter for the harvesting of the crop to be completed. Our facts raise no question concerning such reasonable time for we are told that T did remove the crops within such time. Therefore, T is not liable to L for trespass on Blackacre and removing the rye, wheat and oats therefrom. On the other hand when L notified T that the lease was terminated as of June 1, 1980 and such notice was given on April 30, 1980, such notice transformed the lease into one of certain duration. Thereafter T has neither the right nor the power to burden his lessor, L, with a privilege on T's part to enter upon Blackacre and remove any crop which he plants on the premises after such notice is given. It is immaterial how far T has proceeded in the preparation of the land for the planting of additional crops. The fact that he has plowed, harrowed and rolled the land for the purpose of planting the corn on Blackacre is just one of the risks which accompany such a tenancy. The doctrine applies only to the crops which are in the ground when the notice of termination is given. Consequently, T is liable to L in damages for the trespass upon Blackacre and the removal of the corn therefrom. See Fuglede v. Wenatchee Dist. Co-op. Ass'n, 134 Wash. 350, 235 P. 790, 39 A.L.R. 953 (1925); Brown, p. 590; Fox v. Flick, 166 Kan. 533, 203 P.2d 186 (1949); Powell, ¶ 663. ¶ 663.

CASE 192: L was a life tenant in possession of an orange grove pursuant to the will of her late husband who devised the land to her for life with a remainder to his children by a former marriage. L maintained the grove after her husband's death and each year she received the proceeds from the sale of the fruit. At the time of L's death there was growing on the land an immature orange crop, in the cultivation of which crop L had expended the sum of $3200. As between L's personal representative and the remaindermen, who is entitled to the orange crop?

Answer and Analysis

The answer is that L's personal representative should be entitled to the crop under the common law rule of emblements, but there is conflict of authority and the Florida case, hereinafter cited, awarded the crop, (actually the proceeds from the sale thereof), to the remaindermen but required them to reimburse the personal representative the $3200 expended by the life tenant in order to prevent unjust enrichment. Oranges, of course, are grown on trees which are perennials, but, nevertheless, the annual crops are produced primarily by man's labor and skill and so should be treated as fructus industriales or emblements. The tenancy of a life tenant is, of course, of uncertain duration. Thus, if the common law rule of emblements is applied, then the personal representative of the life tenant should be entitled to the immature crop that was in existence at the time of L's death.

In Florida, however, crops of fruit growing trees, whether regarded as fructus industriales or fructus naturales, are regarded as parts of the realty unless severed, actually or constructively as by an agreement for sale. Thus, the orange crop as part of the realty vested in the remaindermen on the death of L. L, however, had expended $3200 to produce this crop. To permit the remaindermen to obtain the crop without reimbursing the estate of the life tenant would result in unjust enrichment. Therefore, the personal representative is entitled to recover $3200 from the proceeds of the crop's sale.

Either result can be justified. That he who sows should also reap has an appeal of fundamental fairness and it seems no undue hardship to let the remaindermen wait another year for the next crop which they will have to cultivate before reaping these particular benefits from their land. On the other hand the purpose of the original testator was to provide for L only during her life. Her life has now ended, and the growing crop can do her no good whatsoever. To the extent that she has expended money or labor in producing the crop, her estate should be reimbursed, but there is no need to otherwise deprive the remaindermen of the benefits of Blackacre until the next crop is harvested. L has enjoyed the benefits of the land all during her life; apparently the desires of the former testator have been fulfilled as to her; and arguably he would want his remaindermen children to get the benefits of Blackacre as soon as the life estate expires. There is really no need to give her estate the whole crop. Substantial justice is done if the estate recoups the amount she spent in cultivating the crop. See Peer v. Wilson, 210 So.2d 495 (Fla. 2d D.C.A.1968); Lloyd v. First Nat'l Trust and Sav. Bank of Fullerton, 101 Cal.App.2d 579, 225 P.2d 962 (1951); reaching the same result based on testator's intent; 1 Casner 142 et seq.

SUMMARY OF CASES IN CHAPTER XVI

Case 190. If a tenancy is an estate for years having a definite time of beginning and a definite day of termination the tenant's right to remove growing crops or emblements is terminated when the tenancy comes to an end. Any crops not removed by the end of the tenancy belong to the landlord. If the tenant has severed the crops by the end of the tenancy but the severed grain still remains on the land such severed grain is personal property belonging to the tenant and he has a right to remove such the same as any other personal property such as machinery.

Case 191. If a tenancy is of uncertain duration having no day certain for its termination, then the tenant has a reasonable time after the termination of the tenancy in which to remove the crops which are planted and growing at the time of the termination of the term. This doctrine is regularly applied in the case of a tenancy at will or tenancy for the life of the tenant or for the life of a third person. There has been difficulty in solving cases which involve tenancies from year to year. The solution which seems most reasonable and fair permits the tenant to remove all growing crops within a reasonable time after the termination of the tenancy if such crops are actually planted in the ground at the time of the notice of termination of the tenancy and denies to the tenant the privilege to remove any crop which is planted after the notice to terminate the tenancy is given. Of course, the doctrine for the removal of emblements after the end of the term is limited to one annual crop.

Case 192. Contrary to the common law rule of emblements, in some jurisdictions on the death of the life tenant the title to an immature orange crop vests in the remainderman. However, in order to prevent unjust enrichment, the personal representative of the deceased life tenant is entitled to recover the sums expended by the life tenant in the cultivation of the crop.

Part III

CONVEYANCING

Chapter XVII

VENDOR AND PURCHASER

1. Brokers' Contracts.
   Legal Gems.
   Cases.
2. Statute of Frauds.
   Legal Gems.
   Cases.
3. Part Performance.
   Legal Gems.
   Cases.
4. Equitable Conversion and Risk of Loss.
   Legal Gems.
   Cases.
5. Time of Performance.
   Legal Gems.
6. Marketable Title.
   Legal Gems.
   Cases.
7. Marketable Record Title Acts.
   Legal Gems.
   Cases.
Summary of Cases in Chapter XVII.

---

1. BROKERS' CONTRACTS

LEGAL GEMS

1. Traditionally, a real estate broker's contract has been regarded as a contract for the performance of services rather than a contract for the sale of an interest in land. Such a contract, therefore, is not within the usual statute of frauds and is enforceable although oral. 12 Am.Jur.2d § 38; Seay v. Bennett & Kahnweiler Associates, 73 Ill.App.3d 945, 29 Ill.Dec. 912, 392 N.E.2d 609 (1979).

2. Many states, however, have a statutory requirement that precludes recovery of a real estate commission unless there is a written contract or authorization signed by the seller or party to be charged for the commission. See, e. g., Seaman v. King Arthur Court, Inc., 35 Conn.Sup. 220, 404 A.2d 908 (1979).

3. Under a nonexclusive or ordinary listing contract, a real estate broker earns his commission when he has produced a purchaser who is ready, willing and able to buy the property on the terms and conditions set by the vendor. A sale need not actually be consum-

mated under this traditional view. E. g., Judd Realty, Inc. v. Tedesco, — R.I. —, 400 A.2d 952 (1979).

4. Under a minority view, which may be illustrative of a more recent trend, the broker, under an ordinary listing contract, is not entitled to a commission unless he fulfills the following requirements:

(a) he produces a purchaser ready, willing and able to buy on the terms fixed by the owner;

(b) the purchaser enters into a binding contract with the owner to do so, and

(c) the purchaser completes the transaction by closing the title in accordance with the provisions of the contract.

In other words, under this view, there is no right to a commission if the contract is not consummated because of the buyer's financial inability or because of any default of the buyer. However, if the failure to consummate the contract results from the wrongful act or interference of the seller, the broker's claim is valid and must be paid. Tristram's Landing, Inc. v. Wait, 367 Mass. 622, 327 N.E.2d 727 (1975), citing and adopting the rule of Ellsworth Dobbs, Inc. v. Johnson, 50 N.J. 528, 236 A.2d 843 (1967), and adopting the philosophy thereof, although the court previously had reached the same decision on a technical analysis of the case.[1] The court referred to this new approach as a growing trend in a minority of recent decisions.

5. A broker may properly fill in blanks on forms of commonly used earnest money contracts or offers to purchase, when such activity involves merely the supplying of simple factual data, such as the names of the parties, the time for closing, the amount of the sales price, and how it shall be paid. A broker, as distinct from an attorney, however, is not allowed to fill in blanks on deeds, mortgages, and other legal instruments subsequently executed in relation to the sales transaction. See infra Case 193.

6. The broker and seller may enter into any one of several types of agreement relating to the sale of realty:

(a) nonexclusive, open or ordinary listing wherein the broker is entitled to a commission only if he is the first to procure a purchaser; if the property is sold by the seller himself, or by someone else, the broker has no claim;

(b) exclusive listing or agency agreement wherein the broker is entitled to a commission if he or any other broker sells the property, but he is not entitled to a commission if the owner himself sells the property; exclusive listing frequently becomes multiple listing with the members of a local real estate board who agree to divide the commission if one other than the listing broker effects the sale; and

(c) exclusive right to sell agreement whereby the broker is entitled to a commission if the property is sold by anybody, even

---

1. The contract in Tristram's Landing did in fact contain the provision that the commission was to be paid "on the said sale."

the owner himself, during the term of the agreement. See generally 12 Am.Jur.2d §§ 224–231.

7.   A common type of listing agreement provides that the broker's commission will be a designated percentage of the sales price. Another possibility is a net agreement whereby the owner/seller agrees to accept a specified price for the realty with the broker being entitled to anything for which the property is sold above that price.

CASE 193:   Benny Broker is a licensed real estate broker who, in connection with his business and as a service to his clients, prepares offers to purchase real estate, draws contracts of purchase and sale, prepares deeds and other instruments necessary to clear or transfer title, and supervises the closing of the transaction.   No separate fee is charged for these services, his compensation consisting solely of brokerage commissions.   The local bar association files a complaint against Benny Broker, alleging that he is engaged in the unauthorized practice of law, and seeks to enjoin him from carrying on such activity as above mentioned.   Will the injunction be granted?

Answer and Analysis

The answer is no as to sales contracts and yes as to deeds, mortgages and other legal instruments.

Broker will not be enjoined from properly filling in the blanks on a form of an earnest money contract or offer to purchase where such activity involves merely the supplying of simple factual data.   Such factual data includes the names of the parties, the time for closing, the sales price, and the method of payment.   However, after he has completed the form by the insertion of the data and has secured the necessary signatures, he has fully performed his obligation as broker. The preparation of or filling in blanks on deeds, mortgages, and other legal instruments subsequently executed requires the skill of an attorney and constitutes the practice of law.   "Such instruments are often muniments of title and become matters of permanent record.   They are not ordinarily executed and delivered until after title has been examined and approved by the attorney for the purchaser.   Their preparation is not incidental to the performance of brokerage services but falls outside the scope of the broker's function."   Chicago Bar Ass'n v. Quinlan and Tyson, Inc., 34 Ill.2d 116, 214 N.E.2d 771 (1966).[2]

2. A similar result was reached in State Bar v. Arizona Land Title & Trust Co., 90 Ariz. 76, 366 P.2d 1 (1961), rehearing denied 91 Ariz. 293, 371 P.2d 1020.   Thereafter, the realtors succeeded in obtaining a constitutional amendment.

1. "Any person holding a valid license as a real estate broker or a real estate salesman . . . shall have the right to draft or fill out and complete, without charge, any and all instruments incident hereto including, but not limited to, preliminary purchase agreements and earnest money receipts, deeds, mortgages, leases, assignments, releases, contracts for sale of realty, and bills of sale."

Ariz. Const. Art. 26, § 1, added by election Nov. 6, 1962.

Note—Minimum Fees

In Goldfarb v. Virginia State Bar, 421 U.S. 773, 95 S.Ct. 2004, 44 L.Ed.2d 572 (1975), rehearing denied 423 U.S. 886, 96 S.Ct. 162, 46 L.Ed.2d 118, the Supreme Court held that Section 1 of the Sherman Anti-Trust Act had been violated by conformance with a bar association's minimum fee schedule that established fees for title examination services performed by attorneys in connection with the financing of real estate purchases.

In McLain v. Real Estate Bd. of New Orleans, Inc., 444 U.S. 232, 100 S.Ct. 502, 62 L.Ed. 441 (1980), the court held that a complaint based on violation of the Sherman Act because of an agreement among real estate brokers in a market area to conform to a fixed rate of brokerage commission on sales of residential property should not have been dismissed. It was held that the evidence submitted to the District Court was sufficient for satisfying the jurisdictional requirements under the effect on commerce theory, and the case was remanded for further proceedings.

2. STATUTE OF FRAUDS

Legal Gems

1. All states have a Statute of Frauds relating to the enforceability of contracts for the sale of land or for the sale of an interest therein.

2. These statutes are based on an English predecessor and have similarity in substance while exhibiting diversity in phraseology and style.

3. The English Statute provides that no action shall be brought upon real estate contracts or upon any agreement not to be performed within one year unless the agreement or some memorandum thereof shall be in writing and signed by the person sought to be charged or by his lawfully authorized agent.

4. The contract provisions of the Statute are applicable only to executory obligations. If the contract is executory on both sides, then the promises of both the buyer and seller are equally within the statute. If the buyer pays the full purchase price, the executory contract of the seller to convey is still within the statute; but if the seller conveys and the buyer does not pay, the buyer's promise is simply to pay a sum certain and is not within the statute.

5. The statute is satisfied if a sufficient memorandum is in writing and signed by the person sought to be charged.

6. There is room for considerable flexibility in the construction of what constitutes a sufficient memorandum. Basically, however, it would appear that the writing or memorandum would have to contain the following: (a) an identification of the parties; (b) a sufficient description or identification of the land to be conveyed; (c) the pur-

chase price and the manner of payment; and (d) the promises on both sides.

7. The writing must be signed. Under the English type statute the required signature is of the person sought to be charged or of his authorized agent. The person sought to be charged is the person against whom the contract is attempted to be enforced, either the seller or the buyer as the case may be. However, in some states, either by construction or by express statutory provisions, the writing or memorandum must be signed by the vendor or grantor.

8. The memorandum may consist of several writings if they are sufficiently connected and are signed by the party to be charged.

9. The authority of the agent may rest in parol unless there is a statute to the contrary. See 3 Casner 18 et seq.; Powell, ¶ 927.

CASE 194: V and P entered into an oral contract for the sale of V's real estate. P gave V $500 at the time they entered into the agreement, and V gave P a receipt as follows:

"March 21, 1980

"For the sum of twenty thousand dollars ($20,000.00), I, the undersigned, agree to sell my property, located at the corner of Black and White Streets and known as 120 Black Street. Received as earnest money five hundred dollars ($500.00).

V"

One month later P tendered nineteen thousand five hundred dollars ($19,500.00), to V and demanded a deed. V refused saying that he changed his mind and offered to return the five hundred dollars ($500.00) deposit. P refused to accept the return of the money and thereafter filed a suit for specific performance. May P recover?

Answer and Analysis

The answer is no. The Statute of Frauds requires a writing for a contract for the sale of real estate to be enforceable. The Statute does not require that the entire contract be reduced to writing, but it does require a sufficient memorandum signed by the party sought to be charged. The only memorandum in the instant case is the receipt set out above. The memorandum is deficient in that it does not identify the parties to the contract. The purchaser is in no place referred to or identified in the instrument. Since the purchaser is the one bringing the action, it is not necessary that the purchaser sign the memorandum. The person sought to be charged in this case is V, and V did sign the writing. Although V promised to convey his land, he nowhere promised to convey it to any particular party. Thus, the memo is insufficient.

Is the instrument otherwise sufficient? The property is identified by street number and located at the intersection of two streets. There is no mention of any city, state or county, however. If the city were sufficiently identified, the description by street number is probably adequate as parol evidence can be used to supply the exact dimensions or boundaries. Perhaps if there were an averment that O owned only one such parcel of real estate which satisfied the street description and that such parcel was located in a particular city and state, the description might be considered satisfactory. There is no such allegation in the instant case, however.

Another matter to consider is the purchase price and manner of payment, or the terms and condition of sale. The receipt states the down payment and the total purchase price. It does not state how the balance is to be paid or when the sale shall be completed. Although financing is an important factor in many, if not most, sales today, an all cash transaction, at least as far as the vendor is concerned,[3] is not uncommon. Thus, if there is nothing specified as to the manner of payment, it might be inferred that an all cash transaction is intended. Further, in this case the purchaser is tendering cash. Therefore, if the other requirements of the memorandum were sufficient, the absence of provisions as to the manner of payment could be immaterial as an all cash transaction might be inferred.[4] Similarly, the lack of a date specified for consummating the transaction is not fatal since in the absence of an agreement to the contrary, a reasonable time can be inferred.

The receipt, however, in addition to not identifying the purchaser, contains no promise on his part. The seller promises to convey, but no buyer is identified and no one promises to buy. Thus, the memorandum seems insufficient in this regard, also. Other matters such as the quality of the vendor's title need not be specified since, in the absence of a provision to the contrary, the requirement of a marketable title will be inferred. Likewise, the custom in the community can supply such missing items as to who pays what taxes, documentary stamps if any, the costs of preparing instruments, the type of deed to be given, and other incidental matters.

To recapitulate—in the instant case, P will not be entitled to specific performance because the memorandum is insufficient in that it does not indicate a buyer nor any promises on his part. See Kohlbrecher v. Guettermann, 329 Ill. 246, 160 N.E. 142 (1928); 3 Casner 16 et seq.

3. The text statement has reference to the fact that in a typical home or condominium purchase transaction, the purchaser commonly borrows money and executes a mortgage to finance the purchase. The seller, however, receives all cash some of which, of course, may be needed and used to satisfy existing mortgages or encumbrances.

4. On the other hand, particularly in the case of larger transactions, because of the impact of income taxes, it may be equally or even more reasonable to infer an intent to sell on an installment basis. See Cohodas v. Russell, 289 So.2d 55 (Fla. 2d D.C.A. 1974), where the court, for the above reason, refused to infer that an all cash transaction was intended, and denied specific performance.

CASE 195: Vendors, a hospitalized mother and two daughters, one of which was out of state and contacted by telephone, generally agreed with purchaser on terms for the sale of 160 acres. Immediately following the discussion the daughter who was present wrote out an agreement in longhand in the presence of purchaser. It was decided at the time the agreement was signed that the parties would meet that same afternoon in the office of purchaser's attorney where a formal contract would be executed. The lawyer was unable to draft the contract immediately, and when it was later drawn, the sellers objected to certain provisions therein, and the formal written contract was never signed by the vendors. The vendors, instead, entered into a formal sales contract with another party. The deposit had been left with the purchaser's attorney and never delivered to the sellers. The purchaser sues for specific performance. Will he prevail?

Answer and Analysis

The answer is no. Whether parties to an informal agreement become bound prior to the drafting and executing of a contemplated formal writing is largely a question of *intent* of the parties as determined by the surrounding facts and circumstances. The fact that the parties contemplate execution of a final document is some evidence, not in itself conclusive, that they intend not to be bound until it is executed. Under the facts and circumstances here, no binding contract was made by the parties. The informal agreement was executed by only one of the three owners of the property. The earnest money provided for in the informal agreement was never paid to the vendors. The intent of the parties was clear that they were negotiating with the understanding that the terms of the contract were not fully agreed upon and a written formal agreement was to be executed. Since the vendors rejected the terms set out in the formal contract, no enforceable contract was made by the parties. King v. Wenger, 219 Kan. 668, 549 P.2d 986 (1976).

---

3. PART PERFORMANCE

LEGAL GEMS

1. The doctrine of part performance permits an oral contract for the sale of land to be enforced specifically in equity.[5]

2. There is considerable diversity among the states as to the kind and amount of part performance which is necessary in order to

---

5. All but a very few states permit an oral contract to be specifically enforced when there is sufficient part performance. North Carolina, Kentucky, Mississippi and Tennessee have been listed as the only states that do not recognize the doctrine. 3 Casner 41, 1952—76 Supp., n. 13 to p. 27, § 11.7.

permit the contract to be enforced in equity. The acts of performance commonly relied on are:

> (a) payment of all or part of the consideration or purchase price;

> (b) delivery of possession to the vendee;

> (c) construction of permanent and valuable improvements by the vendee, or in the absence thereof, proof of such facts as would make the transaction a fraud on the purchaser if the contract were not enforced.

3. A very small minority of states may hold that payment of all or a very substantial portion of the purchase price is sufficient part performance.

4. A minority of states hold that delivery of possession to the purchaser may be sufficient part performance, but the continuance of a prior possession by the purchaser is generally held insufficient.

5. Most jurisdictions require either a combination of payment plus possession, or possession plus improvements in order to permit the oral contract to be enforced specifically. The more strict jurisdictions require a combination of all three types of part performance specified in Gem 2 supra in order to permit the contract to be enforced in equity. See McClintock 139 et seq.; 3 Casner 25 et seq.; Powell, ¶ 925[2][a].

CASE 196: P, by oral agreement, on April 5, 1978, leased from V a dwelling house for a term of one year beginning May 1, 1978, at a rental of $200 per month. V also gave P an option (definite as to terms), to purchase the property at the expiration of the lease with the provision that P be allowed credit for the total rent paid. P then entered into possession, and before the expiration of the lease, notified V that he wished to exercise his option. V stated at that time that he did not have time then to draw the contract, but that he would do so later. P stayed in possession beyond the stipulated lease date, but V refused to honor P's option. P now brings an action against V for specific performance of the contract. Should the court grant P's request for specific performance?

Answer and Analysis

The answer is yes. The option, prior to its acceptance, is, of course, simply a continuing offer to sell and conveys no interest in the land. It merely vests in the optionee a right to buy at his election. An oral lease of real estate for a term of one year to commence in the future is, however, within the Statute of Frauds. The oral lease in the instant case was not capable of performance within one year from the date of its inception on April 5, 1978, and would be subject to the Statute of Frauds unless removed or performed.

The acts of taking possession and of making part payment in reliance upon, and with unequivocal reference to, the vendor-vendee relationship, is sufficient to avoid the Statute of Frauds. The majority of jurisdictions holds that there need not be simultaneously any proof of such irreparable injury as would result if there were fraud.

P was in possession of the land and V's conduct and statements were consistent with that of a vendee-vendor relationship because of his unequivocal reference to the oral contract. This is illustrated by V's statement that he did not then have time to draw the contract, but would do so later. The evidence is clear that the parties intended a vendor-vendee relationship from the beginning, and that the landlord-tenant relationship was only incidental. Thus P's possession and part payment under the rental agreement is in furtherance of the contract to convey. Accordingly, P is entitled to specific performance of the oral contract because of part performance. See Shaughnessy v. Eidsmo, 222 Minn. 141, 23 N.W.2d 362 (1946).

———

CASE 197: In June, 1918, one James Halsey, an aged widower, told A that if he gave up his business and cared for him that the house, lot, and furniture belonging to Halsey would belong to A upon Halsey's death. No writing of the agreement was made. A accepted the offer, moved in and attended to Halsey until Halsey's death five months later. No deed, will, or memorandum of the agreement signed by Halsey was ever found. A now brings an action for specific performance to enforce the agreement. The defense is the Statute of Frauds. Should A's request for sepcific performance be granted?

Answer and Analysis

The answer is that it depends somewhat on the jurisdiction and whether the services rendered can ordinarily be obtained by hiring someone else. In jurisdictions holding that the acts of part performance must have unequivocal reference to a contract for the sale of land, the answer is no. Under this theory the acts done must supply the key to what is promised. Rendition of services alone may justify recovery of the value of the services, but such services of themselves are not significant of ownership, either present or prospective. What is needed is occupancy as owner and acts, such as improvements, which clearly indicate that a conveyance will be made.

In the instant case the plaintiff did not even have possession during the life of Halsey. The possession was that of Halsey and the occupancy of A was that of a servant or guest. Presumably Halsey could have dismissed him at any time. There might be an inference of a reward, but not necessarily that of a conveyance of the land.

Accordingly, under this view, the acts of part performance are not solely and unequivocally referable to a contract for the sale of land, and A therefore is not entitled to specific performance. See Burns v. McCormick, 233 N.Y. 230, 135 N.E. 273 (1922).

Note 1

Some jurisdictions base the part performance doctrine on the theory that the conduct of the vendee shows such reliance on the contract as will result in irreparable injury if the contract is not enforced. Under this theory of injurious reliance, the rendition of services is not sufficient part performance if the services can ordinarily be obtained by hiring. If such services cannot be valued in money, however, then the rendition of services is sufficient part performance. Accordingly, the result in particular cases of the instant type will depend upon the circumstances of the particular case and the jurisdiction. It would seem that in any event the contract should be enforced if the circumstances were such that the court should conclude that not to enforce it would amount to a fraud on the one performing the services. See Bick v. Mueller, 346 Mo. 746, 142 S.W.2d 1021 (1940); McClintock, 144–145.

Note 2

According to some jurisdictions an act which is purely collateral to an oral contract, although done in reliance thereon, is not sufficient part performance to authorize the enforcement of the contract by a court of equity. Thus, a purchaser was denied specific performance when there was no relationship of trust or confidence with the vendor, when there was no misrepresentation of existing facts, when the vendor repeated a promise that he would perform the oral contract and would enter into a written contract, and the purchaser sold another farm in reliance on the prospective purchase of the one in issue. Walker v. Ireton, 221 Kan. 314, 559 P.2d 340 (1977). The sale of the other land in reliance on the oral contract was not contemplated by the vendor, and the sale was not shown to have resulted in a loss.

An exception to the collateral rule, supra, however, is said to be recognized where the agreement was made to induce the collateral act or where the collateral act was contemplated by the parties as a part of the entire transaction. The direct case authority, however, seems minimal. See 81 C.J.S., Specific Performance § 63, p. 860.

4. EQUITABLE CONVERSION AND RISK OF LOSS

LEGAL GEMS

1. The doctrine of equitable conversion treats interests in land as if the land had already been converted into personal property.

2. Equitable conversion is based on the maxim that equity regards as done that which ought to be done.

3. Equitable conversion applies when there is an enforceable obligation to sell land. The obligation may be created by will, court order, or contract. Discussion herein is limited to equitable conversion as a result of a contract to convey land.

4. For equitable conversion to apply, the contract must be specifically enforceable.

5. Under equitable conversion the purchaser is regarded as the owner of the land for many purposes, and the vendor, although he still owns the legal title, is regarded as the beneficial owner of personal property, primarily the right to the purchase price and to impress a security interest on the legal title to enforce the payment of the purchase money.

6. When the vendor dies during the existence of a specifically enforceable contract, the beneficial interest descends as personal property and the heir gets only a bare legal title which he must convey to the purchaser when the purchaser performs.

7. When the purchaser dies during the existence of an enforceable contract, the right to receive the land goes to his heir but the duty to pay the purchase price is imposed upon the personal representative.

8. In the absence of a contract provision to the contrary, the traditional view and probable weight of authority applies the equitable conversion doctrine and puts the risk of loss on the vendee for casualty losses which occur without the fault of either party during the existence of the vendor-vendee relationship. A minority view imposes the risk on the vendor, and two Uniform Acts in effect place the risk of loss on the one in possession.[6]

---

6. Uniform Vendor and Purchaser Risk Act

"1. Any contract . . . for the purchase and sale of realty shall be interpreted as including an agreement that the parties shall have the following rights and duties, unless the contract expressly provides otherwise:

(a) If, when neither the legal title nor the possession of the subject matter of the contract has been transferred, all or a material part thereof is destroyed without fault of the purchaser or is taken by eminent domain, the vendor cannot enforce the contract, and the purchaser is entitled to recover any portion of the price that he has paid;

(b) If, when either the legal title or the possession of the subject matter of the contract has been transferred, all or any part thereof is destroyed without fault of the vendor or is taken by eminent domain, the purchaser is not thereby relieved from a duty to pay the price, nor is he entitled to recover any portion thereof that he has paid.

. . ."

Uniform Land Transactions Act

Section 2–406.

"(a) This section does not apply to transfers of leaseholds. . . .

(b) Risk of loss or of taking by eminent domain and owner's liabilities remain on the seller until the occurrence of the events specified in subsection (c). In case of a casualty loss or taking by eminent domain while the risk is on the seller:

(1) if the loss or taking results in a substantial failure of the real estate to conform to the contract, the buyer may cancel the contract and recover any portion of the price he has paid, or accept the real estate with his choice of (i) a reduction of the contract price equal to the decrease in fair mar-

9.   In the absence of a contract provision to the contrary, equitable conversion does not give the purchaser the right to possession before the contract is consummated and a deed executed. Accordingly, the vendor is normally entitled to possession, and rents or profits during the existence of the relationship.

10.   In the absence of a contract provision to the contrary, the obligation to pay taxes is usually imposed on the party in possession.

11.   The granting of specific performance rests in the sound judicial discretion of the court. Thus, specific performance will not be granted if the contract is deemed grossly unfair or unconscionable, or, if its enforcement would entail undue hardship on the defendant or a third party. See McClintock, 188, 284 et seq.; 3 Casner 22 et seq.

12.   Both the vendor and vendee have an insurable interest while the contract is executory.

———

CASE 198: A contracted to sell to B a certain piece of land which was to be used for the purpose of erecting a storage plant for ice cream and frozen fruits. However, between the time the contract of sale was made and the time for delivery of the deed, the city council rezoned the lot so that it could only be used for residential purposes. The rezoning caused a substantial depreciation in the land, and B refused to honor the contract. A now brings an action for specific performance arguing that the doctrine of equitable conversion places the loss on the buyer. B argues that to enforce the contract would be harsh and oppressive to him. Should A recover?

ket value caused by the loss or taking, or (ii) the benefit of the seller's insurance coverage or the eminent domain payment for the loss or taking, but without further right against the seller; or

(2) if the real estate substantially conforms to the contract after the loss or taking, the buyer must accept the real estate, but is entitled to his choice of (i) a reduction of the contract price equal to the decrease in fair market value caused by the loss or taking or (ii) the benefit of the seller's insurance coverage or the eminent domain payment with respect to the loss or taking but without further right against the seller.

(c) Risk of loss or taking and owner's liabilities pass to the buyer:

(1) if sale is not to be consummated by means of an escrow, at

the earlier of delivery of the instrument of conveyance or transfer of possession of the real estate to him; or

(2) if sale is to be consummated by means of an escrow, at the earlier of transfer of possession or fulfillment of the conditions of the escrow.

(d) Any loss or taking of the real estate after risk of loss or taking has passed to the buyer does not discharge him from his obligations under the contract of purchase.

(e) For the purposes of any provision of law imposing obligations or liabilities upon the holder of legal title, title does not pass to the buyer until he accepts the instrument of conveyance."

Answer and Analysis

The answer is no. The doctrine of equitable conversion states that when the sales contract is made, equity then considers the vendee as the owner of the land and the vendor as the owner of the purchase money. This rule, however, is limited in its application to cases where the intention of the parties will not produce an inequitable result, and where nothing has intervened which ought to prevent a performance. The intent of A was to sell to B a lot usable for the erection of a storage plant. The intent was defeated by the supervening act of the city council. Under these circumstances the granting of specific performance would be unduly harsh and oppressive to B. Of course, the parties could have contracted in reference to this particular event, and equity will not relieve B of a bad bargain. The refusal to grant specific performance is not the same as rescission. The contract remains in effect; it is not terminated as it would be if rescission were granted. The denial of specific performance does not end the matter in this case, but, instead, the vendor may proceed against purchaser B in a suit at law. See Clay v. Landreth, 187 Va. 169, 45 S.E.2d 875, 175 A.L.R. 1047 (1948).

Note

That a loss resulting from zoning changes should be treated the same as a casualty loss, see DiDonato v. Reliance Standard Life Ins. Co., 433 Pa. 221, 249 A.2d 327 (1969).

————

CASE 199: In October, 1967, P contracted to purchase from V for $150,000 certain property on which was erected a hotel. The contract required P to pay V in installments, and to pay a sum in escrow out of which all taxes and fire insurance premiums were to be paid. P then entered into possession. In December, 1970, a fire occurred on the property causing substantial damage. At this time a substantial balance was still owing on the purchase price. Payment by the insurance company was insufficient to restore the building, and P vacated the premises. P now claims that all money paid by him pursuant to the installment contract should be repaid since V cannot now deliver a sufficient building as contracted. V claims that under the doctrine of equitable conversion, the loss should fall upon the vendee. May P rescind the transaction and recover the payments made?

Answer and Analysis

The answer is no. An executory contract for the sale of land requiring the seller to execute a deed conveying legal title upon payment of the full purchase price works an equitable conversion so as to make the purchaser the equitable owner of the land and the seller the equitable owner of the purchase money. The result is that the purchaser, the equitable owner of the land, takes the benefit of all subsequent increases in value and, at the same time, becomes subject to all losses not occasioned by the fault of the seller. This is the rule in most jurisdictions. Some jurisdictions, however, place loss from fortuitous destruction upon the purchaser in an installment situation only if at the time of entry into the contract the purchaser is put into possession of the land and thereafter exercises full rights of control. Under either view, P must bear the loss in the instant case and is not able to recover payments made to date. In fact the vendor is entitled to specific performance.

Under the common law rule, the purchaser, to protect himself, either must procure his own insurance, or by appropriate provision in the contract, cast the risk upon the seller. Consequently, some jurisdictions have attempted to ameliorate the possible inequities in the doctrine of equitable conversion by the adoption of the Uniform Vendor and Purchaser Risk Act. This act provides that, unless provided otherwise in the contract of sale, the vendor may not enforce the contract if property is destroyed by no fault of the purchaser or is taken by eminent domain if neither legal title nor possession has been transferred to the purchaser.[7] A minority of jurisdictions reverse the common law rule and place the risk of loss on the vendor. See Briz-Ler Corp. v. Weiner, 39 Del.Ch. 578, 171 A.2d 65 (1961).

Note 1

A state statute provides that if the matter being sold is partially destroyed, the purchaser has the choice of abandoning the sale or retaining the preserved part and having the price proportionately reduced. Thus, a purchaser of property which was severely damaged by a hurricane prior to the completion of the sale was entitled to abandon the sale, was relieved of his obligation under the agreement to purchase, and was entitled to have his deposit returned. Williams v. Bel, 339 So.2d 748 (La.App.1976).

Note 2

As a result of equitable conversion, the purchaser under a contract may be considered the owner of the land for the purpose of remonstrating against a special or local assessment or for protesting the formation of a local improvement district. Committee of Protesting Citizens, Etc. v. Val Vue Sewer Dist., 14 Wash.App. 838, 545 P.2d 42 (1976).

CASE 200: Vendor and Purchaser entered into a contract for the sale of improved realty. Purchaser went into posses-

---

7. See also Uniform Land Transactions Act, § 2–406, n. 6 supra.

sion and acquired a fire insurance policy in the face amount of $10,000. At a time when purchaser's total expenditures pursuant to the contract and building repairs was approximately $2,000, the building was damaged by fire to the extent of $9,000. Outstanding title defects were also discovered. The insurance company offers to pay Purchaser only $2,000, but he insists that he should recover $9,000. Should the Purchaser be entitled to recover $9,000 when the risk of casualty loss rests on the vendor because of a contract provision between the parties?

Answers and Analyses

The court held yes. Both the vendor and purchaser have insurable interests in the property irrespective of the party on whom the risk of loss is placed. It is always possible that the other party may be uninsured and without sufficient assets to cover the loss. In the instant case the Purchaser is both in possession and is regarded as the equitable owner. The court held that the Purchaser could recover the amount of the fire loss and was not limited to his actual expenditures. There was no evidence in regard to the title defects that the Purchaser would be unable to ever acquire title, and since the vendor was not a party to the litigation, it could not be decided whether recovery by the vendee might otherwise inure to the benefit of the vendor via a constructive trust theory. [On this latter point, see Note following]. Cooke v. Firemen's Ins. Co., 119 N.J.Super. 248, 291 A.2d 24 (1972).

Note

The above case illustrates an erosion of the basic principle that casualty insurance is strictly a personal contract of indemnity to reimburse the insured for actual losses sustained. A similar result may be illustrated by a Florida case which allowed the *vendor*, who had a lien to secure the balance of the purchase price, to recover an amount equal to the unpaid purchase price, not exceeding the face amount of the policy, of course, without proving an actual loss. Rutherford v. Pearl Assur. Co., 164 So.2d 213 (Fla. 1st D.C.A.1964).

Some jurisdictions hold that when the parties agree that the vendor will carry insurance on the property until the exchange of possession and/or title is transferred, under the doctrine of equitable conversion the purchaser is entitled to the benefit of insurance proceeds paid to the vendor for damage loss occasioned by fire or other casualty. The proceeds are held by the vendor as trustee for the purchaser. Fellmer v. Gruber, 261 N.W.2d 173 (Iowa 1978).

A practical approach to the insurance problem in an ordinary executory contract situation, and one that should result in substantial justice, would be for the vendor pursuant to an agreement with the purchaser to have his policy endorsed "payable to the vendor or vendee as their interests shall appear."

5. TIME OF PERFORMANCE

LEGAL GEMS

1. In equity time is not of the essence in a contract for the sale of land unless

(a) the contract specifically so provides; or

(b) special circumstances surrounding the execution of the contract so require.

2. Where time is not of essence, equity will allow a reasonable time for performance. See Hochard v. Deiter, 219 Kan. 738, 549 P.2d 970 (1976).

3. The parties to a contract for the sale of land may make time of the essence by specific provision to that effect.

4. Although time is made of the essence, the parties may waive that provision of the contract.

5. Although time is not originally made an essential part of the contract, it may later be made of the essence by the party not in default serving on the other a proper notice and specifying a reasonable date for performance. See McClintock, 208.

6. MARKETABLE TITLE

LEGAL GEMS

1. The concept of marketability generally denotes a title that is reasonably free from doubtful questions of law or fact, or a title not likely to result in litigation.

2. The terms "good" and "marketable" and the terms "bad" and "unmarketable" generally designate titles a court of equity will or will not compel a purchaser to accept in a suit for specific performance.

3. In the absence of an agreement to the contrary, there is an implied undertaking in the contract that the vendor has a marketable title. The contract usually provides that on failure of the vendor to deliver a marketable title, the vendee may rescind and be entitled to his money.

4. Unless otherwise specified a fee simple is the type of title or estate required.

5. If a deed is delivered and it contains no warranty of title, the vendee has no redress, since the deed supersedes the contract which is no longer in effect. To the rule that the contract merges into the deed, there is an exception as to those provisions which the parties obviously did not intend to merge. For example, if the contract provides that possession will be delivered one month after closing, then the provision as to possession will continue to regulate the rights of the parties for one month after the deed is delivered.

6. The vendor is only obligated to tender a "good" and "marketable" title on the date when the conveyance is to be executed and a purchaser may not rescind a land sale contract before the time for performance.

(a) Knowledge by the purchaser of the vendor's lack of title at the time he entered into the contract is immaterial, since he has a right to rely upon the vendor either having a title, or procuring it so as to carry out his agreement.

(b) A vendor may lack title at the time of entering the contract, e. g., in a situation where the vendor is himself a vendee under a contract with the owner, without being in default prior to the time for performance.

7. The real estate sales contract may expressly stipulate that the vendor furnish an "abstract" showing his title to be good and marketable. This is equivalent to a marketable title of record. Marketability in this instance must be deduced from the public records or abstract entries and resort to parol evidence is not permissible.

8. Title to land acquired by accretion does not constitute merchantable title of record because there must be resort to matters outside the record and abstracts in order to establish such title. Gaines v. Dillard, 545 S.W.2d 845, (Tex.Civ.App.1977).

9. If, either by express provision or by construction, the vendor is required to have only a marketable title as distinguished from a marketable title of record, it is generally held that the vendor may rely on matters outside the record to establish his title, and that a title by adverse possession may be marketable.

10. Common defects which may render land titles unmarketable include variations in names of grantors and grantees in the chain of title, breaks in the chain of title, outstanding dower interests, outstanding mortgages, defectively executed instruments in the chain of title, defective judicial or tax sales in the chain of title, and incompetency of grantors in the chain of title.

(a) The existence of restrictive covenants, although not coupled with a reverter so as to subject the estate to possible forfeiture for their breach, renders the title unmarketable. There is an exception in favor of reasonable restrictions imposed by governmental authority.

(b) Outstanding reverter rights render the title unmarketable.

(c) An incumbrance which the vendor cannot or will not remove and which the vendee cannot remove by application of the purchase money is such a defect that renders the title unmarketable.

(d) As a general rule an easement upon any appreciable part of a city lot constitutes an incumbrance and renders the title unmarketable.

(e) If a vendor places a mortgage on the land without prepayment privilege and such mortgage makes it impossible for him to convey a marketable title free of the mortgage on the due date, then the vendee is entitled to rescission without waiting until the date of performance. This rule applies where the term of the mortgage is to expire beyond the date fixed for conveyance to the vendee.

(f) If vendor's title is only slightly imperfect, equity may not rescind the contract but may require a reduction in the purchase price.

11. There are in existence a large number of curative acts which operate on defective instruments or bar claims which otherwise might be asserted because of defects. Typical examples of curative legislation include statutes which: validate tax or other deeds which have been on record for twenty or other specified number of years; cure deeds defective for want of witnesses or a seal after a lapse of seven, ten or other specified number of years from recording; and impose a statute of limitations on the enforcement of mechanics liens and mortgages.

12. There is diversity of opinion as to whether a provision for conveyance by quitclaim deed is sufficient to dispense with the requirement of a marketable title. That a marketable title is still necessary appears to be the sounder view.

13. The fact that a title is insurable merely means that it is capable of being insured, and not that it is also good or marketable. See Powell ¶ 925[2][b]; 3 Casner 123 et seq.

———

CASE 201: During a period of great excitement in the real estate market A entered into negotiations with B to purchase a tract of land, receiving from the vendor an instrument which said: "Title to prove good or no sale, and this deposit to be returned." No time was specified within which such examination should be made nor was any mention made that the condition of the title should be ascertained from any particular abstract. A received a letter saying the title was imperfect. Thereafter A commenced an action against B to rescind the sale. Will A prevail?

Answer and Analysis

The answer is no. Since no time was specified within which such examination should be made, a reasonable time is therefore implied. Also, since no mention was made that B would furnish an abstract, it was incumbent upon A to search the records or to procure an abstract and to satisfy himself as to the condition of the title. A could not pronounce the title defective without examination. If, upon examination, it appeared that the title was defective, it then became his duty to report to B the defects and allow him a reasonable time to correct them. The burden is on A, the vendee, to point out defects in the title. If the vendor fails to remedy the defects, the purchaser, in an action to recover the deposit upon the ground that the title is defective, is limited to asserting such defects as were then pointed out.

In every executory contract for the sale of land, there is an implied condition that the title of the vendor is good and marketable, and that he will transfer to the vendee, by his deed of conveyance, a title apparently unencumbered and without defect.[8] In addition, a vendee may maintain an action to rescind an agreement on the ground that the vendor at the time of entering into the agreement knew that he could not make the conveyance, or that he fraudulently represented himself as the owner of the premises. Also, if the vendor subsequently voluntarily puts it out of his power to complete the contract,—as if he should sell the land to another during the existence of the agreement—the vendee may treat the contract as rescinded, and bring his action for the deposit. In these cases the ground for the rescission is fraud of the vendor, either at the time of entering into the contract or by his subsequent acts. In the present case there is no indication of fraud or misrepresentation. Thus, the principles delineated in the first paragraph apply. The acts of payment and conveyance being mutual and dependent, neither party is in default until after tender and demand by the other. See Easton v. Montgomery, 90 Cal. 307, 27 P. 280 (1891).

CASE 202: A entered into a contract with B to purchase a parcel of real property. A deposit was made and the balance was to be paid in monthly installments for eight years. Two years after entering into the contract A learns that an adverse claim has been asserted against B and that the outcome is uncertain. A brings an action to be relieved from paying further installments pending the outcome of B's litigation. Will A succeed?

---

8. The buyer, of course, wants a perfect title, and he correctly will refuse to take a title subject to known defects or encumbrances to which he objects. It should be noted, however, that a marketable title is one that is reasonably free from doubtful questions of law or fact. See Gem 1 supra. It is a title that a reasonably prudent person, e. g., a title attorney, will accept. It is not necessarily a perfect title in fact. As a practical matter, a marketable title may in fact be invalid, as, for example, if a recent instrument in the perfect record title had been forged, and such forgery is not known, and the statute of limitations has not yet run against the real owner. On the other hand, an unmarketable title may in fact be a perfectly valid title. This could occur, for instance, if there were a gap in the chain of title because of an unrecorded instrument, which instrument had been properly executed and delivered but not recorded, or it could occur if certain doubtful factual situations not shown in the record had in fact occurred so as to have resulted in a perfect title in the vendor.

See generally Gem 21, Chapter XXIII on Recording, for interests not protected by the recording acts.

Answer and Analysis

The answer is no. There can be no rescission by A of an executory contract of sale merely because of lack of title in the vendor prior to the date when performance is due. Neither can A place B in default by tendering payment and demanding a deed in advance of the time and under circumstances not contemplated by the contract. See Luette v. Bank of Italy Nat'l Trust and Sav. Ass'n, 42 F.2d 9 (9th Cir. 1930).

CASE 203: A, interested in buying land from B, is told by B that the property has extensive shore lines and included within its boundaries is a trout creek. A and B enter into an agreement under which B agreed to sell the property and supply an abstract showing the title to be good and marketable. A discovered from a survey that the description included considerably less area than that which had been pointed out. B claims that he occupied this area for more than the statutory period for adverse possession and refuses to set aside the transaction. May A rescind?

Answer and Analysis

The answer is yes. By the terms of the agreement B was required to convey to A a good and marketable title as shown by the abstract. Title established through adverse possession is free from encumbrance and of a character to assure quiet and peaceful enjoyment of the property by A, but it is not a marketable title of record until there has been a judicial determination of such title. To show a record title by adverse possession requires a suit and the recording of a decree. B has not quieted title to the property through statutory proceedings; hence, there is nothing on public record which could be placed in an abstract to indicate defendant's ownership of the property outside of the boundaries established by survey. Although a court may determine that B had title by adverse possession, A did not bargain for that kind of title. Accordingly, A may rescind. See Escher v. Bender, 338 Mich. 1, 61 N.W.2d 143, 147, 46 A.L.R.2d 539 (1953).

Note

In the above cited case A discovered the discrepancy in the size of the tract after the sale had been consummated and a deed delivered. Normally the function of marketable title is to enable the purchaser to check the vendor's title prior to consummation of the sale and to decide whether the title is satisfactory or not before accepting the deed. The problem case, however, is a little different in that the abstract showed a marketable title to the land legally described, but it took the acts of a surveyor to locate the land encompassed within the confines of the legal title. B, the vendor, had assured the purchaser that he owned all the land intended to be conveyed, and in fact he may have been able to establish his asserted boundaries by acquiescence and adverse possession. A, however, does not want to run the risk of being able to defend successfully his title in subsequent litigations because of matters in pais. A relied on the assertions of B to his detriment. Both parties were mistaken as to the legal boundaries. Thus, the transaction, although consummated, should be rescinded because of mutual mistake. See McClintock, 238–239, 253 et seq.

———

CASE 204: A entered into a contract of sale for certain designated premises and provided that upon receipt of the price, B would execute a "quitclaim deed of said premises," and said nothing as to the quality of the title to be conveyed. On the closing date A refused to take the deed because of the existence of an inchoate dower interest or other encumbrance. A sued to recover the deposit and the reasonable expense of examining the title. Will A be successful?

Answer and Analysis

The answer is probably yes. There is a split of authority as to whether a purchaser may recover when the contract calls for a quitclaim deed and the title is not good or marketable. There is authority to the effect that if it clearly appears from the contract itself that the parties contemplated and bargained for nothing more than a conveyance which would pass such rights as the vendor may have, whether defective or not, that is all the vendee can claim or insist upon.

However, the weight of authority would hold that a contract provision for conveyance by quitclaim is not of itself a waiver of the implication of the required marketable title. Even knowledge by the vendee of the vendor's lack of title at the time he entered into the contract is immaterial since he has a right to rely upon the vendor either having a title, or procuring it, so as to carry out his agreement. The agreement of the vendee to accept a quitclaim deed as the means of transfer is not a waiver of any defects. A quitclaim deed is as effective as any other to convey all the title the grantor has, and a deed with all the covenants cannot strengthen a defective title, but can only provide a remedy by legal action against the vendor for breach of covenant because of the defective title. See McManus v. Blackmarr, 47 Minn. 331, 50 N.W. 230 (1891); Wallach v. Riverside Bank, 206 N.Y. 434, 100 N.E. 50 (1912).

7. MARKETABLE RECORD TITLE ACTS

Legal Gems

1. Marketable Record Title Acts are designed to reduce the period of title search, to limit the period of title examination, and to clear titles from ancient and outmoded encumbrances.

2. Marketable Record Title Acts combine the essential features of statutes of limitations, curative acts, and recording acts.

3. A Marketable Record Title Act is a statute of limitation in that the filing of a notice is a prerequisite to preserve a right of action against the real estate founded upon any transaction which occurred prior to the period specified in the act. The filing of such a claim is necessary whether the claim or interest is mature or immature and whether it is vested or contingent.

4. Such an act is a curative act in that it may operate to correct certain defects which have arisen in the execution of instruments in the chain of title.

5. A Marketable Record Title Act is also a recording act in that it requires notice to be given to the public of the existence of conditions and restrictions, whether such interests be vested or contingent, growing out of ancient records which fetter the marketability of titles.

6. The period commonly specified for a marketable record title under such acts is either thirty or forty years.

7. The purpose of such an act is to extinguish all claims in existence for the statutory period or more which conflict with a record chain of title which is at least that old. This is accomplished by declaring as marketable record title any estate or interest reflected by the recorded chain of title for the statutory period. All interests which are older than the root of title, subject to certain designated exceptions, are extinguished.

8. Under such an act a root of title is a conveyance or other title transaction in the claimant's chain of title purporting to create the interest claimed by such person, such transaction being the most recent to be recorded as of a date prior to the statutory number of years before the time marketability is being determined.

9. A statutory marketable record title is made subject to certain enumerated exceptions, common examples of which are as folows:

    (a) all interests and estates, easements and use restrictions disclosed by, and defects inherent in the muniments of title;

    (b) all interests preserved by the filing of a proper notice;

    (c) rights of any persons in possession;

    (d) interests arising out of a title transaction recorded subsequent to the effective date of the root of title;

    (e) rights of variously described easement holders;

    (f) interests of the federal or state governments; and

    (g) rights of persons to whom the land has been assessed for taxation within a designated recent period of time.

10. Subject to the exemptions designated, a marketable record title under such an act is freed from all claims and charges which

predate the effective date of the root of title. All such pre-root claims are declared null and void.

11. A marketable record title under such an act does not necessarily mean a marketable title in a commercial sense. However, the extinction of ancient claims is expected to increase marketability in a commercial sense. Nevertheless, under many marketable record title acts, it would be possible to have, for example, a marketable record fee simple determinable title which would not be marketable in a commercial sense.

12. Marketable record title acts operate against persons under a disability as well as against persons sui juris, and they invalidate future interests as well as present interests.

13. A pure quitclaim deed can probably not be a root of title under most marketable record title acts. See Simes & Taylor, Improvement of Conveyancing by Legislation (1960); Boyer and Shapo, Florida's Marketable Title Act: Prospects and Problems, 18 U. Miami L.Rev. 103 (1963); Barnett, Marketable Title Acts—Panacea or Pandemonium, 53 Cornell L.Q. 45 (1967); Wichelman v. Messner, 250 Minn. 88, 83 N.W.2d 800, 71 A.L.R.2d 816 (1957).

———

CASE 205: The patentee of Blackacre conveyed the land to X and Y by a metes and bounds description in 1892. A small portion of Blackacre was not included in the conveyance and it is this parcel which is now in dispute. X died intestate leaving Y and Z as his sole heirs. In 1912 Z conveyed to Y, via a quitclaim deed, all interest which Z had to the whole of Blackacre, the deed describing the entire parcel including that portion of Blackacre not conveyed to X and Y by the patentee. The 1912 quitclaim deed provided:

> The grantor does remise, release and quitclaim all the right, title, interest, claim and demand which the grantor has in and to Blackacre.

Y died intestate leaving A and B as his sole heirs. A then died devising all of her property to B. By warranty deed in 1943, B purported to convey Blackacre to C.

D brings an action against C for that portion of Blackacre not included in the conveyance by the patentee to X and Y. The sole basis of D's claim is his ancestor's patent and his proof of heirship. C relies on the 1912 quitclaim deed as a valid root of title under the recording act although it is a wild deed with respect to the parcel of Blackacre here in question.

May C prevail, and is the wild quitclaim deed of 1912 a valid root of title under the Marketable Record Title Act?

Answer and Analysis

Both answers are no. The Act, as a marketable title act, is not concerned with the quality of the title conveyed by the root of title *so long as the root purports to convey the estate claimed.*

Here, it cannot be determined from the face of the instrument exactly what interest the deed purports to convey. If the deed evidenced an intent to convey an identifiable interest in Blackacre, it would suffice as a valid root of title under the recording act. For example, if the deed in question stated:

> The grantor does remise, release, and quitclaim all the right, title, interest, claim and demand, *which consists of a fee simple interest,* that the grantor has in and to Blackacre,

the deed would be a valid root of title under the recording act. In the instant case it is impossible to determine from the face of the instrument what interest the deed purports to convey. Therefore C cannot prevail on the basis of the Marketable Record Title Act, and D, being heir of the patentee of land which was never conveyed, is entitled to recover. See Wilson v. Kelley, 226 So.2d 123 (Fla. 2nd D. C.A.1969).[9]

CASE 206: In 1899 Blackacre was conveyed to A by deed, and the deed was recorded that year. A conveyed to B by deed dated November 4, 1965, which deed was recorded November 19, 1965. By mesne conveyances title passed to C, through and under whom D claims Blackacre. This chain of title originates with a grant from the United States. E, through his grantors, held a record chain of title for over forty (40) years (the period required under the applicable Marketable Record Title Act), prior to 1965 (the year A conveyed to B), but E's chain originated subsequent to D's

9. Cf. Wilson, supra, holding that a quitclaim deed cannot be such a title transaction as to constitute a root of title because it doesn't purport to convey any particular interest, with Kittrel v. Clark, 363 So.2d 373 (Fla. 1st D.C.A.1978), certiorari denied, 303 So.2d 909 Fla.1980). This case, construing an exception to the marketable record title such as indicated in Gem 9(d) supra, held that the probate of an estate of a former party in interest within thirty years after the recording of a root of title preserved the prior interest (an oil and mineral estate) from extinguishment although there was no description, inventory or mention of the property in the probate proceedings of the deceased prior owner. The appellate court had observed that it would be appealing to construe a title transaction as requiring a description of the land it purports to affect, but concluded that it should not supply that which the legislature did not choose to include. 363 So.2d at 374.

The Supreme Court denied certiorari without opinion, but Justice Boyd, joined by two associates, wrote a convincing dissent, expressed an opinion that the result may be a large increase in the number of quiet title suits, and suggested that such interpretation may result in the marketable record title act causing more harm than good. The reader is again cautioned that the phraseology of a particular statute and the interpretation thereof is most important.

chain (i. e. after 1899). E's defense to D's claim to Blackacre is the above mentioned Marketable Record Title Act.
No one in D's chain of title filed any claim to Blackacre
within forty (40) years after his interest arose as is provided in the act.

Is E's title, based on a deed which is foreign to D's title,
entitled to the protection of the Marketable Record Title Act
and therefore superior to D's?

Answer and Analysis

The answer is no according to the Supreme Court of Illinois in
applying their marketable record title act to the above problem.
However, such marketable title acts are relatively new and there is
considerable diversity in phraseology and in the exceptions delineated
in the various acts; hence, it is difficult to proclaim a general proposition which would be applicable to such facts in most states having
similar legislation.

In analyzing the problem, it is seen that A acquired the title in
1899 and simply held on to it until 1965, when he conveyed, and that
such title eventually lodged in D. This chain of title was based on a
grant from the United States, and therefore would appear to be the
better paper title. E is claiming a recorded chain of title more than
40 years old at the time A conveyed to B in 1965, and during such 40
year period A did not record his title so as to preserve it under the
provisions of the act. E's source of title, however, is entirely different from that of D's, and as to D, E's root of title is a wild one. As
the problem is presented, there is no evidence of possession by either
party, payment of taxes, or other circumstances which would specifically preserve D's rights under the marketable record title act. Thus,
there is presented a pure question as to whether a chain of title based
on a wild deed can divest a senior chain of title simply because the
senior chain had no title activity for the period specified in the act.

The policy of permitting such a wild chain to divest a senior
chain was significant in the Illinois decision. The court pointed out
that to so hold could result in the grantee of a complete and even
fraudulent stranger to the title divesting the title of a record owner.
This could happen although the record owner may have satisfied the
usual responsibilities of ownership such as paying taxes simply because he did not re-record his title or claim in order to preserve his
interest. The court concluded that the act contemplated the existence of only one chain of title since its purpose was stated as that of
"simplifying and facilitating land title transactions by allowing persons to rely on a record chain of title." Thus, since the act did not
contemplate the problem of two chains and purport to solve the enig-
ma, the court concluded that the act was not controlling and that the
title dispute would have to be solved by traditional doctrines. See
Exchange Nat'l Bank of Chicago v. Lawndale Nat'l Bank of Chicago,
41 Ill.2d 316, 243 N.E.2d 193 (1968).

Note 1

Cf. Whaley v. Wotring, 225 So.2d 177 (Fla. 1st D.C.A.1969), also involving two chains of title, one of which was inactive for the statutory period. In this case the senior chain of title dated back to 1863 before a patent from the U.S. government. The patent was issued in 1897, but was not recorded until 1966, and there was no connection between the senior chain and the patent. The court applied the marketable record title act of Florida, quieted title in the senior chain, and invalidated the junior chain. The court concluded that the government had no interest after the patent was issued so that the junior title was not preserved under an exception to the act in favor of the United States, and that the senior chain did satisfy the requirements of the act. Under the exception to the act by which interests can be preserved by recording, the junior chain had until July 1, 1965, to record the claim because of its existence when the act went into effect. Having failed to record until 1966, the junior claim was held invalidated by the Florida intermediate appellate court. Note that in this case the invalidated chain had not been recorded until after the act had operated on the senior chain. This could make a difference. See Simes & Taylor, Improvement of Conveyancing by Legislation (1960); Boyer and Shapo, 18 U. of Miami L.Rev. 103, 117 (1963); Barnett, 53 Cornell L.Q. 45 (1967).

Note 2

In Wichelman v. Messner, 250 Minn. 88, 83 N.E.2d 800, 71 A.L. R.2d 816 (1957), the Supreme Court of Minnesota applied the state's marketable title act to convert a defeasible fee simple title into a fee simple absolute. Most marketable title acts would not be construed in such a manner since interests disclosed by and defects inherent in the muniments of title, including the root, are usually excepted from the provisions of the act. See, for example, West's Fla.Stat.Ann. § 712.03(1) (1979).

CASE 207: Title to the real property was originally acquired in 1913 by the Atlantic Beach Company. In 1923 a majority stockholder of the company, Mathew Marshall, died. His widow had no knowledge of her deceased husband's interest in the company.

In 1924 one Terry, pretending to be president of the Company, falsely signed the minutes of a purported stockholder meeting authorizing the conveyance of the assets of the company to Terry. The forged deed was recorded on February 15, 1924. On February 14, 1924, Terry executed a deed to Hollywood Realty Company, which deed was recorded on April 11, 1924. On August 6, 1924, a deed was then executed by Hollywood Realty Company to Homeseekers Realty Company and recorded on August 22, 1924.

On April 25, 1929, the Highway Construction Company obtained a judgment against Homeseekers Realty Company. Following a levy and a sheriff's sale, a sheriff's deed to the Highway Construction Company was recorded on December 30, 1930. This deed purported to convey substantially all of the real property involved in this litigation. On February 21, 1931, the Highway Construction Company conveyed the subject property to the defendant, Hollywood, Inc., and the deed was duly recorded.

The administrator of Mathew Marshall's estate brought suit in 1966 to have a trustee appointed to convey the legal title to the property to the heirs of the deceased on the ground that the deed executed in the name of the Atlantic Beach Company by Terry to himself in 1924 was void as a forgery. Should the Marshall estate recover title to the subject property?

Answer and Analysis

The answer is no. The purpose of the Marketable Title Act as enacted in 1963 is to simplify and facilitate land transactions by allowing persons interested thereon to rely on a record title. West's Fla.Stat.Ann. § 712.02 reads as follows:

"Any person having the legal capacity to own land in this state, who, alone or together with his predecessors in title, has been vested with any estate in land of record for thirty years or more, shall have a marketable record title to such estate in said land . . . .."

The question then is whether the Act confers marketability to a chain of title arising out of a forged deed, so long as the strict requirements of the Act are met. The Florida Court held that the marketable Title Act may be applied to validate a record title based on a forged or void deed, although the forged deed itself perhaps could not constitute a root of title. Marshall v. Hollywood, Inc., 236 So.2d 114 (Fla.1970), certiorari denied 400 U.S. 964, 91 S.Ct. 366, 27 L.Ed.2d 384 (1970), affirming 224 So.2d 743 (Fla. 4th D.C.A.1969).

See also City of Miami v. St. Joe Paper Co., 364 So.2d 439 (Fla. 1978), holding specifically that a wild deed may constitute a root of title.

Note

Marketable title legislation in many states is based upon the Model Marketable Title Act, which traces its history to legislation earlier adopted in Michigan, Wisconsin and Ontario. This Act codified the New England tradition of conducting title searches back not to the original creation of title, but for a reasonable period only. The Model Act is designed to assure a title searcher who has found a chain of title starting with a document at least thirty or forty years old that he need not search any further back into the records.

SUMMARY OF CASES IN CHAPTER XVII

1. BROKER'S CONTRACTS

Case 193. Real estate brokers and salesmen may fill in the blanks on printed sales contracts when such activity involves simply the supplying of factual data. They may insert the names of the parties, the time for closing, the sales price, and the method of payment. Brokers and salesmen may not draft or complete deeds, mortgages and similar legal instruments as those documents should be prepared by attorneys.

2. STATUTE OF FRAUDS

Case 194. To be sufficient under the Statute of Frauds a memorandum must: (a) identify the parties to the contract; (b) describe the land to be conveyed; (c) contain the sales price and the essential terms of the agreement; and (d) state the promises to be performed on each side. The writing need not contain all the details of the agreement since some items such as the quality of the vendor's title, the type of deed to be delivered, and the allocation of incidental costs can be inferred from the general customs of the community, and parol evidence can be used to make certain some of the essential terms which otherwise might be indefinite.

Case 195. A memorandum or informal writing, even if possibly otherwise sufficient to satisfy the Statute of Frauds, will be effective to obligate the parties to carry out a land sales agreement only if the parties so intend at the time the writing is signed. If the facts and circumstances indicate that the parties understand that all the terms are not agreed upon, and that a formal document or contract encompassing all the details will be drafted and signed, then either party may withdraw from the transaction prior to the approval and signing of such a formal contract.

3. PART PERFORMANCE

Case 196. An oral lease for one year to commence in the future cannot be performed within one year and is thus within the Statute of Frauds. When an option to purchase is appended to such an oral lease under circumstances showing that the parties intended a vendor-vendee relationship from the beginning and that the lease was only incidental, then when the option is accepted part performance consisting of the delivery of possession and acceptance of part of the purchase price is sufficient in many jurisdictions to permit the contract to be enforced specifically.

Case 197. Whether the rendition of services is sufficient to remove from the Statute of Frauds a promise to convey or devise land depends upon the jurisdiction and the theory therein employed as to part performance. Under the so called unequivocal reference theory, services rendered are not sufficient, whereas under the injurious reliance theory, the rendition of such services as ordinarily cannot be equated to a monetary value are sufficient.

4. EQUITABLE CONVERSION AND RISK OF LOSS

Case 198. The granting of specific performance is within the sound judicial discretion of the court, and it will not be granted when to do so would result in undue hardship or oppressiveness. The denial of specific performance in such cases, however, is without prejudice to the non-defaulting party bringing an action at law. Accordingly, specific performance has been denied when there was a contract for the sale of land to be used for commercial purposes and a change of zoning prevented such use.

Case 199. Under the doctrine of equitable conversion the risk of loss from casualty and other fortuitous events is normally placed on the purchaser in the absence of controlling provisions in the contract. A minority of jurisdictions, however, place such risk on the vendor, and those jurisdictions which have adopted the Uniform Vendor And Purchaser Risk Act place the loss on the one in possession. Thus, when the premises are destroyed by fire and the risk is placed on the vendee, the vendee is not entitled to rescission and, conversely, the vendor may still obtain specific performance.

Case 200. The vendee under a sales contract has an insurable interest and may recover up to the policy limits the full extent of casualty damages without regard to actual out of pocket expenses. Such recovery is permitted although the risk of casualty loss is placed on the vendor. The case did not decide whether such proceeds should ultimately inure to the benefit of the vendor on whom the risk of loss was placed, nor did it decide whether the result would be different if the title were so defective that the vendor could never convey a good title.

6. MARKETABLE TITLE

Case 201. In every executory contract for the sale of land, there is an implied condition that the title of the vendor is good and marketable, and that he will transfer to the vendee, by his deed of conveyance, a title unencumbered and without defect so far as can be ascertained. If no time is specified within which such examination should be made, a reasonable time is implied. Also, if no mention is made for the vendor to furnish an abstract, it is incumbent upon vendee to provide the abstract and to satisfy himself as to the condition of the title. The burden is on the vendee to point out defects in the title.

Case 202. There can be no rescission of an executory contract of sale merely because of lack of title in the vendor prior to the date when performance is due. Neither can a vendee place the vendor in default by tendering payment and demanding a deed in advance of the time and under circumstances not contemplated by the contract.

Case 203. Title established through adverse possession is free from encumbrance and of a character to assure quiet and peaceful enjoyment of the property by the vendee, but it is not a marketable title of record until there has been a judicial determination of such title. To show a record title by adverse possession requires a suit and the recording of a decree. Even though a court may determine vendor had title by adverse possession, the vendee did not bargain for that kind of title when the contract required a marketable title of record. A transaction, although consummated, may be rescinded because of mutual mistake as to the location of the boundaries.

Case 204. There is a split of authority as to whether a purchaser may recover his deposit and rescind when the contract provides for a quitclaim deed and the title is not good or marketable. The weight of authority would hold that knowledge by the vendee of the vendor's lack of title at the time he entered into the contract is immaterial since he has a right to rely upon the vendor either having a title, or procuring it so as to carry out his agreement. The agreement of the vendee to accept a quitclaim deed as the means of transfer is not a waiver of the requirement of a marketable title according to the better view.

7. MARKETABLE RECORD TITLE ACTS

Case 205. A pure quitclaim deed which does not purport to convey any particular estate cannot be a root of title under the marketable record title act. To be a root of title the deed or other title transaction must purport to convey some particular estate or interest.

Case 206. The Supreme Court of Illinois has held that state's marketable title act inapplicable to a situation involving two independent chains of title each more than 40 years old, and left the resolution of the controversy as to the ownership of the land to more traditional property concepts. Because these acts are relatively new and without extensive interpretation, and because the contents of the acts and the possible fact situations vary considerably, no general statement as to the applicability of such acts to competing chains of title is justified at this time.

Case 207. A marketable Record Title Act may validate a chain of title originating in a forged or void deed. Possibly the forged deed itself could not constitute a root of title because of the inherent defects therein, but a subsequent deed in the chain, and even a "wild" deed can constitute a root of title. Title will be perfected in the remote grantee under the "invalid" chain of title if there is no recorded activity for the statutory period under the otherwise superior chain of title.

Chapter XVIII

CONVEYANCES: TYPES AND HISTORY

1. Common Law Conveyances.
    a. Feoffment.
    b. Grant.
    c. Lease and Release.
    d. Surrender.
    e. Dedication.
    Cases.

2. Conveyances under the Statute of Uses 1535.
    a. What's a Use?—Brief Historical Sketch.
    b. Additional Background.
    c. Periods of Development.
    d. Uses Illustrated—Cases.
    e. Effect of Statute of Uses on Modern Law.

3. Conveyances under Modern Statutes.
    Legal Gems.
    Cases.

Summary of Chapter XVIII and Cases Therein.

1. COMMON LAW CONVEYANCES

a. FEOFFMENT

Example, A enfeoffs B and his heirs of Blackacre. The ceremony of feoffment consisted of: (a) livery of seisin in which the feoffor, A, picked up a twig or piece of turf symbolical of the land itself, and handed it to the feoffee, B, with appropriate words such as, "I hereby enfeoff you and your heirs of Blackacre"; and (b) A's walking off the land leaving B in possession claiming the freehold estate in such land, that is, B claimed either a life estate, a fee tail or a fee simple. B was then seised of the land. A feoffment always transferred the physical possession of corporeal property. It is said to "lie in livery" because the possession of the land could be physically handed over to the feoffee.

b. GRANT

Example, A makes a deed to B and his heirs conveying incorporeal property such as a reversion, a remainder or an easement. These were not subject to physical possession and were therefore said to "lie in grant", which meant they could be transferred only by a deed.

c. LEASE AND RELEASE

Example, A leases to B Blackacre for a week and after B takes possession of the premises A makes to B a deed releasing to B and his heirs A's reversionary interest in Blackacre. The purpose of this type of conveyance was to save the owner, A, the burden of having to go to and onto the land to make a feoffment. By first making to B a lease, B was in possession and A now had a reversion. The reversion "lying in grant" could be transferred by deed. When the landlord conveys his reversion to his tenant it is called a release. B is then the owner in fee simple.

d. SURRENDER

Example, A leases Blackacre to B for five years and at the end of three of those five years, B, the tenant, agrees to give up the last two years of the lease and A agrees to receive such. B then gives up the possession of the land to A. This is the reverse of release and is called surrender. When the landlord conveys his reversion to the tenant it is a release. When the tenant transfers his leasehold estate to the landlord it is a surrender. The two types of surrender, by agreement and by operation of law, are explained in Case 208 below.

e. DEDICATION

Example, A, fee owner of Blackacre, which consists of 9 blocks or squares of land in the form of a square area, three blocks long and three blocks wide, decides that he can sell the property most advantageously if he makes the block in the center of the tract a park. He orally declares his intention by telling his neighbors that he hereby dedicates such block for use of the public as a park. This is followed by people in the community using such block for picnics, playground and recreation. That constitutes a dedication of the said block. Dedication at common law requires no particular form and could be made by any method by which the dedicator expressed his intention, by words, conduct or writing. When it is accepted by the public by using it as a park, there is a conveyance of an easement for such public use as a park, the fee remaining in A, the dedicator.

———

CASE 208: L, owner in fee simple of Blackacre, a store building, leases it to T for a term of 5 years. At the end of 2 years and when the lease still has 3 years to run, T offers to surrender the premises to L and requests L to accept such surrender of the leasehold. L refuses to accept such surrender whereupon T tosses the keys to the building to L which L catches in his hands. L tells T that he, L, will be glad to mitigate T's damages by re-letting Blackacre for T's benefit but that he, L, will not accept a surrender of the possession of Blackacre for his own benefit until the term has expired. T says nothing and leaves. L takes possession of Blackacre for the sole purpose of mitigating T's damages and re-lets the premises to X on the best terms possible for the balance of the three years of the tenancy. Whereas T's lease provides for rent at the rate of $300.00 per month, X's lease provides for rent at the rate of $250.00 per month. At the end of X's lease L sues T for the difference between the rent received from X and that which is provided for in T's lease, that is, $50.00 per month for a three year period or $1,800.-00. May L recover?

Answer and Analysis

The answer is yes. The relation of landlord and tenant involves two privities, (a) privity of estate and (b) privity of contract. When L leased Blackacre to T he carved out of his fee simple estate a five year term and sold it to T for the sum of $18,000.00 which T agreed to purchase and pay for at the rate of $300.00 per month for the five year period of 60 months. One thing is certain in such a relationship. The tenant owns an estate for years and cannot by unilateral action abandon it. Therefore, even though T intends to abandon his five year term in Blackacre, such estate still remains with him. There are two ways by which he can voluntarily dispose of his leasehold, (a) he may assign it to a third person or (b) he may surrender it to his landlord. But these presuppose the willingness of an assignee to accept the assignment or the landlord to accept the surrender.

There are two ways to effectuate a surrender, (a) by act of the parties and (b) by operation of law. In our case had L accepted the possession of Blackacre voluntarily from T and on his own account there would be a surrender of the balance of the term to L, and T would no longer be liable for rent. Such is a surrender by the act of the parties. Had L made a new and valid lease to T for a longer or shorter term than the balance of the term in the first lease and nothing had been said about the former lease, such former lease would have been surrendered by operation of law for the reason that there cannot be two valid leases for the same period of time as to the same premises. But neither of these types of surrender took place in our case for the reason that L did not accept the surrender from T for and on his own account, that is, for L's benefit.

However, the law does permit, although in most jurisdictions it does not require, L to mitigate T's damages. Therefore, if L mitigates T's damages and does so by re-letting the premises, the law will not release T from liability to perform his contractual obligations. In such case the landlord is permitted to take possession of the premises for and on behalf of the faithless tenant, and to re-let the premises on behalf of such tenant and, of course, must account to such tenant for the rent received from the re-letting.[1] Furthermore, the re-letting of the premises to a third person by the landlord, being an act quite inconsistent with the continuation of the original lease, would normally constitute a surrender of the premises and termination of the original leasehold and a termination of the privity of estate created thereby. But it does not necessarily terminate the privity of contract between the landlord and the tenant respecting the latter's liability to pay for

---

1. In the event that L re-rents for a greater sum than the original rent, many jurisdictions would not permit T to recover the excess from L on the basis that T should not be able to benefit from his wrongful misconduct. See Whitcomb v. Brant, 90 N. J.L. 245, 100 A. 175 (E. & A. 1917).

the leasehold estate which he purchased from L in the first instance. Thus, L can elect to proceed on a contractual basis, take possession of the balance of the term, sell it on behalf of the tenant, T, give him credit for the money received on the re-letting, and hold T liable in contract for the difference between the value of the balance of the term and the purchase price therefor agreed to in the lease.

As another rationale accomplishing the same result, suppose with the landlord's consent the tenant assigns the balance of his term to a third person. This transaction will terminate the privity of estate between L and T but it does not release T from his personal liability in contract to pay the agreed rent to L in case the assignee does not pay the rent for T to L. In this situation the leasehold estate is not terminated or surrendered. Nor is it surrendered in the case of a sublease. Thus it seems clear that when L takes possession of the premises, not for his own benefit but for and on behalf of T, and relets the premises on T's behalf and gives T credit for the rent received, T is not thereby released from his contractual obligation to pay the rent provided for in the lease. In other words, the fact that there is a termination of the privity of estate between the landlord and the tenant does not necessarily terminate the privity of contract between the two. Under this approach, whether or not there is a technical surrender of the leasehold estate is really immaterial. Most jurisdictions, however, seem to indicate that there is no technical surrender of the leasehold estate, at least there is no surrender for the purposes of determining L's damages resulting from T's abandonment, and for the purposes of determining such damages L is fictionally regarded as acting as agent of T in re-renting the premises. It is a question of the intention of the landlord when retaking possession, and in our case we are told that L took possession and re-let the premises on behalf of T and solely for T's benefit. Thus, L may recover the remaining rent of $1,800.00 from T.

Note

Whether or not there is a surrender may affect the *theory* of L's recovery. If L accepts a surrender of the leasehold he may still be able to recover damages for breach of contract since a lease is a contract as well as a conveyance. If L does not accept a surrender of the leasehold, then L can recover rents not received on the reletting.

See Novak v. Fontaine Furniture Co., 84 N.H. 93, 146 A. 525 (1929); Gray v. Kaufman Dairy & Ice Cream Co., 162 N.Y. 388, 56 N.E. 903, 49 L.R.A. 580, 76 Am.St.Rep. 327 (1900), 110 A.L.R. 368; also supra Chapter VIII case 131.

2. CONVEYANCES UNDER THE STATUTE OF USES 1535

a. WHAT'S A USE?—BRIEF HISTORICAL SKETCH

(1) Example: A enfeoffs "B and his heirs for the use of C and his heirs."

The purpose was to give B the legal title only and to give C the possession and enjoyment. These conveyances were common in feudal England before the Statute of Uses.

(2) Why a Use?

There were many advantages or reasons for creating uses but among the most important were the avoidance of such feudal incidents of tenure as primer seisin, wardship and marriage. See infra b for illustration

(3) Enforcement of Uses

By Whom? After uses became common they were enforced by the chancellor, the keeper of the King's conscience. The reasons were primarily ethical or spiritual: (a) a man, e. g., the feofee to uses, ought to keep his promise, and (b) to prevent unjust enrichment, i. e., the feofee to uses would be unjustly enriched if he did not recognize the beneficial interest of the cestui que use.

How? The method of enforcement was and is characteristic of equity jurisprudence—in personam, e. g., by injunction, fine and imprisonment against the defendant.

Against Whom? The use was enforced against four different categories of persons: the feofee to uses (analogous to the modern trustee); the feofee's heir; a donee of the feofee; and also a purchaser from the feofee if the purchaser had knowledge of the use. All of these persons would be unjustly benefitted if the use were not enforced against them.

Not Against Whom? There were also four categories of persons against whom the use was not enforced: a bona fide purchaser from the feofee if the purchaser had no notice of the use; the overlord if he obtained the land by escheat, the dower right of the feofee's wife, and a disseisor. The good faith purchaser would acquire both the legal title and an equity from his purchase, and this prevailed over the prior equity of the cestui que use. The overlord had a superior interest and logically the land would escheat free of the use; the dower of the feofee's wife was conferred by law but it is difficult to see how she could get a beneficial estate when her husband had none; and the disseisor, of course, acquired a new and independent title as a result of his own actions and operation of law. See Moynihan, 173–184. Bigelow, 77–96.

(4) The Statute of Uses—Effect

The Statute of Uses, 1535, converted the use estate into a legal estate. Thus in our example under (1) supra, after the Statute of Uses C acquired a legal fee simple absolute and B had nothing.

Additional examples and more information follows.

---

b. ADDITIONAL BACKGROUND

Why was the Statute of Uses passed? It was forced upon an unwilling Parliament by a strong willed monarch, Henry VIII, for the purpose of enhancing the depleted royal revenues. This depletion was largely due to the fact that perhaps four-fifths of all land in England was held to uses to avoid the heavy burdens of a dying feudal system of land tenures. Much of the royal revenues were gained from the burdens of wardship and marriage in the feudal system.

To illustrate the incidents of wardship and marriage, suppose A is an elderly person who owns Blackacre in fee simple and has a son, B, who is ten years of age. If A should die shortly while B is still a minor, then A's overlord would have the right to the profits of the land till B became of age and would have the right to determine whom B should marry. These were rights which brought the overlord a substantial income. To avoid such results, A could enfeoff a young man, M, of Blackacre for the use of A's son B. Then A's death would not affect M's rights at all for M is of age. Nor would M's overlord have any rights of wardship or marriage concerning B. Further, M would then hold Blackacre for the benefit and profit of B, and would accumulate the net profits for B till B became of age.

The King, being the one lord who was not also a tenant in the system, was most directly affected by the fact that land was held to uses. He introduced and forced the passage of the Statute of Uses for the purpose of eliminating uses. He succeeded as to passive uses. See Casner, Vol. 1, p. 31 et seq. and Moynihan, 181 et seq.

c. PERIODS OF DEVELOPMENT

At this point the student should recognize three distinct periods of time in the development of the law of uses: (1) the "law period" between 1066 and about 1433, during which period the law courts did not recognize a use as giving any rights at all; (2) the "equity period" from 1433 to 1535 when the Statute of Uses was passed, during which period equity emerged and began to recognize a use as being an enforceable right; and (3) after 1535 when the Statute of Uses was in force, during which period the passive use was automatically executed into a legal estate. Immediately following will be given five cases and each will be solved respecting the rights of the parties in each of the three periods set forth above.

----

d. USES ILLUSTRATED—CASES

(1) Uses executed on a feoffment on transmutation of possession, that is, delivery of possession from feoffor to feoffee

(a) Use expressly declared by the feoffor at the ceremony of feoffment: example—A enfeoffed B and his heirs of Blackacre *to the use of C and his heirs.*

(i) In the law period A had no rights, B had the fee simple and C had no rights at all because the law did not recognize a use. C could merely entreat B to hold the land for C.

(ii) In the equity period A had no rights, B had the fee simple and C could bring a suit in equity and petition the court for a decree ordering B to hold the land for C. The court would issue the decree and B would have to do as ordered or be in contempt of court. This carried out A's expressed intention that the feoffment was for the use of C.

(iii) After the Statute of Uses in 1535, A would have no rights, B would have no rights and the legal title in fee simple would be in C. The Statute executed the use by carrying the legal title from B to C in fee simple. This was automatic because the Statute so provided, whereas under (ii) above before the statute, the use was enforced by proceedings in court.

Note

The words of the Statute of Uses are: "where any person or persons stand or be seised . . . of lands . . . to the use of any other person . . . such person . . . that have any such use . . . in fee simple, fee tail, for term of life or for years . . . shall from henceforth stand and be seized, deemed and adjudged in lawful seisin, estate and possession of and in . . . such like estates as they had or shall have in use . . . in the same; and that the estate . . . that was in such person that were . . . seised of any lands . . . be from henceforth . . . in him or them that have . . . such use. . . ."

In plain English this says that if B is seised to the use of C, the title is carried from B to C. It should be noticed that B, the feoffee to uses, must be seised for the use of C, the cestui que use, but that C need not claim a freehold estate but may have a use for only a term of years. Example: A to B and his heirs for the use of C for 10 years. The Statute of Uses carries the legal title to C giving C a 10-year lease.

Note, Resulting Use

In the above example last given the reversion in fee simple is in A. Because equity would not raise a use unless there was consideration for the conveyance or a use expressed, it became customary to imply a resulting use in favor of the grantor when the entire beneficial estate was not otherwise disposed of. After the Statute of Uses this resulting use was also executed so that the grantor, A, in the above example, would have a legal reversion in fee simple. This principle of resulting uses has a modern counterpart in the law of trusts, the usual rule being that the trustee acquires a legal estate just large enough to accomplish the purposes of the trust, and the trustee takes no beneficial interest unless such an intent is clearly expressed. See infra example (d).

(b) Use raised on consideration actually paid at the ceremony of feoffment: example—A enfeoffed B and his heirs of Blackacre, nothing being said by A that it was for the use of C, but C actually pays money to A at the time.

Here the rights of the parties are identical with those given under (a) next above, to wit:

(i) In the law period A had no rights, B had the fee simple by the feoffment and C had no rights because, while the payment of consideration by C raised a use in him, the law courts did not recognize the use or any rights in the cestui que use, that is, C.

(ii) In the equity period A had no rights, B had the fee simple because of the feoffment, but C, whose use was raised by the consideration paid by C, could petition the equity court for a decree ordering B to hold Blackacre for the use and benefit of C. The decree would issue and B would obey or be jailed for contempt of court.

(iii) After the Statute of Uses, A had no rights, B would have no rights and the legal title in fee simple would be in C. The Statute of Uses executed the use by carrying the legal title from B to C in fee simple. This was automatic because the Statute expressly so provided that if one, B in this case, were seised to the use of another, C in this case, then the seisin would be deemed and adjudged in the one who had the use, which was C in this case.

(c) Use raised by consideration recited in a deed of feoffment: example—A enfeoffed B and his heirs of Blackacre, followed by a deed of feoffment on which both A and B, feoffor and feoffee, placed their seals which was customary in England, the deed reciting that C had paid consideration for the feoffment. This recital of payment of consideration by C in the deed was not rebuttable and raised a use in C whether or not he had in fact paid any consideration. The rights of the parties were then identical with those set forth in (a) and (b) next above and for the same reasons.

(d) Resulting use: when the feoffor did not declare at the ceremony of feoffment that the feoffee was to hold for the use of another, nor was there a consideration paid in fact by anyone, nor recited in a deed: example—A enfeoffed B and his heirs of Blackacre—nothing more.

(i) In the law period A had no rights and B was the fee simple owner because of the feoffment.

(ii) In the equity period the equity courts presumed that one did not intend to give away his property unless he so declared or expressed himself to that effect at the feoffment ceremony, or he received consideration for same, or recited receipt of such in a deed. Hence, in this case the equity courts found a resulting use in A, that is, that B was holding seisin to the use of the feoffor, A. Then we have the feoffee holding to the use of the feoffor. A could then petition the court of equity for a decree ordering B to hold the land for the benefit of A and such order would issue. And if B did not comply with the order he would be in contempt of court and punished accordingly.

(iii) After the Statute of Uses passed in 1535, B was seised to the use of A *by virtue of the feoffment* and the seisin or title was carried right back to A *by the Statute*. So we have the anomalous situation of A's conveying the seisin to B by feoffment and the Statute carrying it back to A. It was like A's snapping a rubber to B and it coming right back to him, unless there was either declaration that it was for B's use or consideration paid by B to prevent it, as appears in the use to a legal grantee in the next illustration.

(e) Use to a legal grantee with declaration of use in favor of the feoffee: example—A enfeoffed B and his heirs of Blackacre *to the use of B and his heirs.*

(i) In the law period A had no rights and B was the fee simple owner because of the feoffment.

(ii) In the equity period A had no rights and B was the fee simple owner because of the feoffment. And the declaration of the feoffor, A, that the use was for the feoffee, B, prevented a resulting use in the feoffor, A, as in the case (d) next above.

(iii) After the Statute of Uses A had no rights and B was the fee simple owner because of the feoffment, and the Statute of Uses had no application because B was not seised to the use of another but to the use of himself. So B continued to hold in fee simple exactly as though it were in the law period. Hence, it is said to be a use to a *legal* grantee.

———

(2) Uses executed without transmutation of possession, that is, without a feoffment in which possession is delivered by feoffor to feoffee

Note

At this point the student should note carefully that in the five cases given next above [examples (a) through (e)], there was a feoffment in each case. It was the common law conveyance in which physical possession was delivered to the feoffee by the feoffor on the land. At common law that was the *only* way a present free-hold estate could be transferred in a single transaction. Now comes the revolutionary method of conveying freehold estates in land *without* making such delivery of possession. It is the method used today and the method which is codified in the modern statutes. It eliminates the inconvenience of going onto the land to be conveyed. The conveyance is made by merely executing a deed in the lawyer's office. Such is made possible by virtue of the Statute of Uses as will appear below.

(a) Bargain and sale deed: example—A, being fee simple owner of Blackacre, executes and delivers his bargain and sale deed to such land to B. The deed recites, "for and in consideration of $1.00 and other valuable considerations, the receipt of which is hereby acknowledged, I, grantor, A, hereby bargain, sell and convey Blackacre to B and his heirs   .   .   .," and the deed is signed and sealed by A. What was the legal effect of this transaction in each of the three periods mentioned above? The answers follow.

(i) In the law period this deed had no effect at all. The reason was plain. This was not a feoffment and the ceremony of feoffment wherein there was livery of seisin or delivery of possession of the land from feoffor to feoffee was the *only* method by which A could convey Blackacre in fee simple to B at common law. Hence, A remained the fee simple owner of Blackacre and B had nothing and no right in Blackacre because the deed could give him none.

(ii) In the equity period the equity courts recognized that the recital of the $1.00 consideration in the deed raised a use in B. It was immaterial whether or not the $1.00 was paid, because the recital of such payment being in an instrument under seal, could not be rebutted. Now, A who was seised before the execution of the deed, is still seised because he has not made livery of seisin to any other person. The result was that B, having the use, could petition the equity court for a decree ordering A to let B occupy the land or otherwise use the land for B's benefit. The court would make the order and if A did not obey, he would be punished for contempt of court. But the point is this: the equity court before the Statute of Uses in 1535, did enforce the use in B's favor, such use being raised by the recital of the consideration in the bargain and sale deed.

(iii) After the Statute of Uses A had no further interest in Blackacre and B was the owner in fee simple. By the recital of the consideration in the deed, the use was raised in the grantee, B. Then A was seised to the use of B. That is the exact situation to which the Statute of Uses applies. In substance it says, when one is seised to the use of another (A seised to the use of B) then he who is seised (A in our case) shall lose such seisin to that other (B in our case). Why did it work that way? Because A had the fee simple before the deed was executed. The deed did not transfer the seisin or possession. Neither did A make livery of seisin or deliver possession of Blackacre to anyone. But the deed by its recital of consideration did raise the use in B. Then A being still seised, is seised to B's use. Then the Statute of Uses carries the seisin and legal title to B.

The result is this: the bargain and sale deed by its recital of consideration raised the use in B, the grantee. Then the grantor, A, is seised to the use of the grantee, B. Then the Statute of Uses carries the legal title from A who is seised, to the grantee, B, who has the use. This is the modern method of conveyancing and exists because of the Statute of Uses. The deed raises the

*use in the grantee and the Statute of Uses completes the convey-
ance by automatically carrying the legal title from the grantor
to the grantee.*

Note

To be effective as a bargain and sale deed *three elements are essential.* To be a deed it must be under seal. To be a bargain and
sale deed the deed must recite a valuable consideration, and it must
be delivered, which means it must be intended by the grantor to take
effect as a conveyance. A *valuable* consideration means a money
consideration or its equivalent; it means the type of consideration
which exists in the commercial world and will support a contract.
This must be distinguished from *good* consideration which means the
establishment of a house or family. Good consideration means relationship by blood or marriage. Such consideration will support a
covenant to stand seised as explained below, but will never support a
contract.

(b) Covenant to stand seised: example—A, owner in fee simple
of Blackacre, executes and delivers to B an instrument under seal
which provides, "For the love and affection which I have for my son
(or son-in-law) B, I hereby covenant to stand seised of Blackacre for
the use of B and his heirs" or "For the love and affection which I
have for my son (or son-in-law) B, I hereby convey my Blackacre to
B and his heirs". What are the rights of A and B in each of the
three periods set forth above?

(i) In the law period, 1066 to 1433, A.D., A remained fee
simple owner and B had no rights at all for the reason that at
common law only a feoffment could convey a freehold estate of
which the fee simple is one. The law courts did not recognize a
use.

(ii) In the period of equity between 1433 and 1535 when the
Statute of Uses was passed, A still held the seisin because he had
made no transfer of possession by the ceremony of feoffment.
However, this sealed instrument raised a use in B which B could,
by petition in equity, have enforced by decree against A. In equity the relationship by blood or marriage of the covenantor, A
in this case, and covenantee, B in this case, was sufficient to
raise a use in the covenantee. On the face of the instrument it
appears that B is the son (related by blood, or son-in-law, related by marriage to A) of A. Hence, a use was raised in B so that
thereafter A was seised to the use of B. This permitted B to
procure a decree in equity ordering A to let B occupy or otherwise use Blackacre for the benefit of B. It should be noticed
that this instrument could not operate as a bargain and sale deed
because it did not recite a *valuable* as distinguished from a *good*
consideration. But, the instrument being under seal was a covenant, and reciting relationship of blood or marriage showed a
good consideration, which raised a use in B. And such use was
enforceable in equity.

(iii) After the Statute of Uses in 1535, which provided that one who was seised to the use of another, should lose that seisin to the other, A had no rights in Blackacre and B was the owner thereof in fee simple.

The analysis is simple. A being seised in fee simple executed the covenant to stand seised to B and his heirs. This did not transfer the seisin but did raise a use in B. Hence, A was seised to the use of another and that other was B. The Statute of Uses then carried the seisin or legal title from A to B and his heirs. If an instrument under seal cannot operate as a bargain and sale deed for lack of recital of a valuable consideration but there is relationship by blood or marriage between the parties, it is construed as a covenant to stand seised. This is another example of a modern conveyance without the inconvenience of physical transfer of possession by feoffment out on the land. To be effective as such there must be a sealed instrument, a *good* consideration and delivery.

Modern statutes on conveyancing are codifications of bargain and sale deeds or covenants to stand seised, both of which grew out of the effects of the Statute of Uses. The Statute of Uses executed the use raised by the instrument of conveyance into a legal title in the grantee or covenantee.

———

(3) Unexecuted uses, that is, uses which were not affected by the Statute of Uses

(a) Uses on chattel interests: example—A, being owner of a thousand head of sheep and of a 99 year lease on Blackacre, transfers them to B for the use of C. What effect had the Statute of Uses on this transaction?

It had no effect at all in this case. The reason is simple. The Statute of Uses applied only to cases where "any person   .   .   . stand or be seised   .   .   . to the use   .   .   . of any other person".   .   .   . One could only be seised of a freehold estate in land, that is, of a fee simple, fee tail or life estate. One could not be seised either of personal chattels such as sheep in this case or of chattels real such as the 99 year lease in this case. Hence, by the very words of the Statute itself, it has no application to the facts in this case.

The result is this: A has no longer any interest in the sheep or the lease. B has the legal title to the sheep and the lease but he holds such for the use and benefit of C according to A's declared intention. C can enforce such use in equity and compel B to hold for C. This use being unaffected by the Statute of Uses is said to be unexecuted. Unexecuted uses became trusts, and out of such concept has grown our modern law of trusts.

(b) Active uses: example—A, being fee simple owner of Blackacre, makes a feoffment thereof to B and his heirs for the use of C and his heirs, it being the duty of B to keep the buildings on Black-acre in repair, keep the property rented, collect the rents, pay the expenses of the property and account to C for the balance of the rent. What effect had the Statute of Uses on this conveyance? The courts held that it had no effect at all in this case.

The courts were hostile to the Statute of Uses and hence, gave a restrictive rather than an extensive interpretation thereto. They then reasoned that B could not perform his active duties of renting the property, collecting the rents, keep it in repair and other active duties if the use was executed in favor of C, that is, if the Statute of Uses were permitted to carry the legal title or estate from B to C. So it was held that if and when active duties were imposed on the feoffee to uses, B in our case, the Statute of Uses had no application and did not execute the use in favor of the cestui que use, C in our case.

The corollary to this proposition is this: the Statute of Uses executed only passive uses, that is, those in which there were no active duties imposed on the legal title holder. Active uses became trusts.

(c) Use upon a use: example—A, being fee simple owner of Blackacre, made a feoffment thereof to B and his heirs to the use of C and his heirs to the use of D and his heirs. How did the Statute of Uses affect this transaction? The answer is this—it executed the first use in favor of C but it did not execute the second use in favor of D.

There was no reason in logic, after the Statute of Uses had carried the legal title from B to C and C was then seised to the use of D, why it should not have carried the legal title from C right over to D. But the hostility of the courts to any expansive interpretation would seem to be the reason. They simply held the Statute had spent its force in the execution of the first use and could go no further. Here, then, was simply an unexecuted use in D with the legal title in C. The effect of the statute was simply to eliminate B from the scene. And the case remained as though it were the following case before the Statute of Uses was passed, to wit: A to C and his heirs to the use of D and his heirs. So C then held to the use of D.

Historically for about 100 years after the Statute of Uses was passed the courts held the second use void as being repugnant to the first use. But thereafter that position was abandoned and the second use was held to be valid but simply unaffected by the Statute.

e. EFFECT OF STATUTE OF USES ON MODERN LAW

(1) *Conveyancing.* Land became transferable by a single written deed, livery of seisin no longer necessary.

(2) *Estates.*

(a) Executory interests, i. e., springing and shifting legal interests become possible. See supra Chapter VI; infra case 211.

(b) Rule against perpetuities was formulated to prevent indestructible future interests from unduly cluttering titles. See supra Chapter VII.

(3) *Trusts*. The modern law of trusts developed out of the unexecuted uses, namely, the active use, use estates in personalty, and uses on uses.

On the subject of uses see; Tiffany, Vol. 1, p. 388 et seq.; Casner, Vol. 1, p. 24 et seq.; Moynihan, 173–215.

3. CONVEYANCES UNDER MODERN STATUTES

LEGAL GEMS

1. Every sovereign state of the Union has exclusive jurisdiction over the land within its borders.

2. Each state has the power to prescribe the form which a conveyance of real property shall take and the power to determine the legal effect of such conveyance.

3. Whether the prescribed form set forth in a statute is to operate as a common law "grant", or is to operate under the Statute of Uses, or is to operate independently of both, is to be determined by construing the words of the particular statute and finding the legislative intention.

4. In most of the states of the Union the Statute of Uses 1535, being in force in England at the time of the Revolution 1776, and being a statute of general application, is considered part of the common law.

––––––

CASE 209: In State X a simple form of conveyance of real property is set forth as follows, "For the consideration of _____, I hereby convey to A. B. the following real property (describing it)." In such State, Alley Oop is the owner of Blackacre in fee simple. He signs, acknowledges and delivers a deed in the above form to A. B. He properly describes the property and fills in $1.00 as the consideration. On what theory would this deed operate as a conveyance in State X?

Answer and Analysis

The answer is this: assuming the acknowledged instrument to be the equivalent of a common law deed with seal, this deed could operate as a conveyance on any one of three theories.

(a) The deed could be a common law "grant". At common law only incorporeal rights or hereditaments lay in grant, that is, could be transferred by deed. The reason was simple—such rights having no physical existence, could not be delivered over to the grantee. Only physical property was subject to livery of seisin and required delivery of possession by feoffment. If the legislature of State X intended, by prescribing the above form of conveyance, to say that corporeal real property lay in grant as well as in livery, then such deed can operate as a conveyance equivalent to a common law "grant".

(b) The deed could be operative under the Statute of Uses. The recital of the $1.00 consideration in the deed raises a use in the grantee, A. B. Then the grantor, Alley Oop, is seised to the use of A. B. The Statute of Uses then automatically carries the legal title from Alley Oop, grantor, to A. B., grantee. This statute seems to be a codification of the doctrine of conveyances under the Statute of Uses by bargain and sale deed. The fact that there is recital of consideration set forth in the prescribed instrument seems to indicate such intention of the legislature.

(c) This statutory prescribed form can operate as a conveyance wholly independently of the past methods of transfer of real property, either at common law, in equity or under the Statute of Uses, simply because the legislature of State X has so declared. The local statute gives such form the efficacy of a conveyance and no reasons are needed beyond the fact that the legislature has power to prescribe forms of conveyance and this is the form so prescribed. See Tiffany, Vol. 4, p. 14, Sec. 958; Casner, Vol. 3, p. 223.

———

CASE 210: In State Y the legislature declared that a grant of an estate in real property may be made in substance as follows: "I, AB, grant to CD all that real property situated in JJ county, State of Y, bounded or described as follows: (here insert boundaries or description by name as 'The N Ranch'). (date) (signed) AB." The statute then defined "transfer" as an act of the parties by which title to real property is conveyed from one person to another. It continued, by saying that a written transfer is a grant and can be explained by circumstances under which it is made and that a fee simple is presumed to pass in a conveyance unless a lesser estate is intended.

M owned Blackacre in State Y. She wrote several letters to her son, Sam, in a distant state requesting him to leave his job there and go to State Y and live in and take care of Blackacre and to send other property to M. In her letters which were dated and signed by her she wrote, "Blackacre is your property" and "I have written you several times that the little place with the garden, Blackacre, is your property". M was a citizen of Germany and lived there. Sam was a United States citizen and lived in the United States. Sam then left his job, traveled to State Y, moved his family onto Blackacre and claims the property as his own. Is his claim valid?

Answer and Analysis

The answer is yes. There are two questions involved in this problem, the intention of the legislature and the intention of M. It is obvious that the statutes in State Y did not intend to require any definite formula of words to constitute a conveyance. No consideration is required by them. It appears that a mere writing signed and dated by the property owner would constitute a conveyance if that be the intention of the owner. And such writing is a grant according to the statute. Such seems to be the intent of the legislature. And the statute providing that a fee simple is presumed unless a lesser estate is intended, is a typical one. It makes unnecessary the common law requirement that words of inheritance "and his heirs" be used with the name of feoffee or grantee.

The intention of M seems clear. She wrote "The property is yours". The present tense leaves little doubt but that there was an intention that the property was to be the property of her son, Sam, from the instant her words were written in the letter. If such be the case, these informal letters constituted a compliance with the statutory requirements and conveyed Blackacre to Sam. The State has power to prescribe methods of conveying real property. If it prescribes merely a signed and dated writing, then compliance with such statutes will convey land and wholly without reference to technical requirements of the common law or former statutes. See Metzger v. Miller, 291 F. 780 (D.C.Cal.1923).

———

CASE 211: H and W were husband and wife. H owned Blackacre and executed, acknowledged, delivered and recorded a deed thereto in favor of W. The deed provided, "This deed is not to take effect and operate as a conveyance until my decease, and in case I shall survive my said wife, this deed is not to operate as a conveyance, it being the sole purpose and object of this deed to make a provision for the support of my said wife if she shall survive me, and if she shall survive me then and in that event only, shall it be operative to convey to my said wife said premises in fee simple." It named the wife specifically as grantee and recited a consideration of $1.00 as paid. The statute provided, "a person owning real estate and having a right of entry into it, whether seised of it or not, may convey it, or all his interest in it, by a deed to be acknowledged and recorded as hereinafter provided." Other statutes provided how the acknowledgment and recordation should be made and that such deed should be effective as a conveyance. No specific provision dealt with the time when a conveyance should take effect. H then cut down trees on the premises and W sues him for

damages for waste.   Assume no problem because a wife is
suing a husband.   May she recover?

Answer and Analysis

The answer is no.   Two reasons are given why a common law
conveyance could not take effect in the future.   One is that there had
to be livery of seisin which had to be made on the land as evidence of
change of possession then or not at all.   The other was that seisin
could not be in abeyance, for the feudal overlord had to know who
was seised at all times so that he would know on whom to call for the
feudal services.   Under such rule it is obvious this deed could not operate as a common law conveyance, even though the reasons for the
rule have long since disappeared.   Under the doctrine of springing
uses a valid conveyance could be made to commence in futuro.   There
being in this instrument of conveyance a recital of consideration, in
addition to the love and affection for a spouse, a use would spring up
in the grantee, and the Statute of Uses would execute the use into a
legal estate.   The executed use will be a legal executory interest of
the springing type.   It will become possessory at the moment of H's
death if W survives him.   Should W not survive H, W's interest will
cease and terminate.   And what interest, if any, does W have in Blackacre during the lives of H and W?   The answer is that W has an irrevocable assurance that the land will be hers if she survives H, but
in the interim she has no interest in the land which will support an
action for waste.

Another view may be taken, namely, that the local statute makes
the deed effective as a conveyance wholly independently of the Statute of Uses.   By analogy the Maine Supreme Court took the view
that the publicity and notoriety which livery of seisin gave a common
law conveyance, the acknowledgment and recording of a deed gives to
this statutory conveyance.   Such Court says, "Our law now says to a
party having such an interest in real estate as is mentioned in (the
statute quoted above), you may convey that interest or any part
thereof in any manner herein prescribed with such limitations as you
see fit, provided you violate no rule of public policy, and place what
you do on record so that all may see how the ownership stands".
Further, that Court concludes that deeds "executed in accordance
with the provisions of our statutes and deriving their validity therefrom may be upheld thereby, as well as under the statute of uses, notwithstanding they purport to convey freeholds to commence at a future day".   The attitude of the Court concerning modern statutory
conveyances appears in the following quotations, "The mere technicalities of ancient law are dispensed with upon compliance with statute requirements.   The acknowledgment and recording are accepted
in place of livery of seisin, and it is competent to fix such time in the
future as the parties may agree upon as the time when the estate of
the grantee shall commence.   No more necessity for limiting one estate upon another, or for having an estate (of some sort) pass imme-

diately to the grantee in opposition to the expressed intention of the parties.

The feoffment is to be regarded as taking place, and the livery of seisin as occurring at the time fixed in the instrument, and the acknowledgment and recording are to be considered as giving the necessary publicity which was sought in the ancient ceremony. The questions, did anything pass by the conveyance, if so, what, and when, are to be determined by a fair construction of the language used, without reference to obsolete technicalities." With such construction put upon the statute and with the intention of H, the grantor, being clear to the effect that the deed was not to take effect until and unless W survived H, and that it was not to take effect at all if H survived W, it is evident that W had no present interest in Blackacre until the event happened, that is, until the death of H with W surviving. Hence, W could not maintain an action of waste against H who still continued to be the fee simple owner of the land. See Abbott v. Holway, 72 Me. 298 (1881).

SUMMARY OF CHAPTER XVIII AND CASES THEREIN

1. COMMON LAW CONVEYANCES

This chapter presents in text and short case form an explanation of the important features of the common law methods of conveyancing by feoffment, grant, lease and release, surrender and dedication.

Case 208. The landlord-tenant relation involves two privities: (a) privity of estate; and (b) privity of contract. There are two types of surrender: (a) surrender by the act of the parties; and (b) surrender by operation of law. There may be a surrender of the leasehold from the tenant to the landlord, thereby terminating the privity of estate without thereby releasing the tenant from his contractual liability to pay the rent provided for in the lease if such is the intention of the lessor, and he takes possession of the premises solely for the benefit of the tenant and for the purpose of mitigating damages. The tenant cannot abandon his leasehold estate by unilateral action. He may assign it to a third person or he may surrender it to the landlord provided such assignee or the landlord is willing to accept it.

2. CONVEYANCES UNDER THE STATUTE OF USES 1535

Under this heading this chapter presents in text and short case form the motive which brought about the passage of the Statute of Uses, the development of uses recognized in equity before the Statute of Uses, and the effect of such Statute on uses, including executed uses upon a feoffment or transmutation of possession, and executed uses without transmutation of possession by bargain and sale deeds and covenants to stand seised (from which has developed the modern law of conveyances), and unexecuted uses which were not affected by the Statute of Uses (from which has developed the modern law of trusts).

3. CONVEYANCES UNDER MODERN STATUTES

Case 209. A conveyance under a modern statutory form may be effective on any one of three theories: (a) as a common law grant; (b) under the Statute of Uses; or (c) merely as a prescribed form set by the Legislature.

Case 210. Mere informal letters from the conveyor to the conveyee may constitute an effective conveyance of real property under a modern statute which defines a "transfer" as an act of the parties by which title to real property is conveyed from one person to another.

Case 211. Estates to commence in futuro may be created under modern statutes. This could not be done at common law.

Chapter XIX

THE EXECUTION AND DELIVERY OF DEEDS

1. Form.

2. Delivery, Escrow and Acceptance.
   Legal Gems.
   Cases.
   Chart—Summary of Delivery of Deeds to Real Property.

Summary of Cases in Chapter XIX.

---

1. FORM

The common law ceremony of feoffment by which a freehold estate was conveyed was oral and no writing was required. The common law "grant" conveying such incorporeal interests as remainders, reversions, easements and profits was a deed and had to be under seal. The Statute of Frauds required a writing and a signature by the conveyor of an interest in real property, excluding short term leases. Covenants to stand seised and bargain and sale deeds under the Statute of Uses were required to be under seal. No general statement concerning the requirements of conveying instruments in the United States can have wide spread, much less, universal application. The statute of frauds and the statute on conveyancing in each state should be consulted.

In most states a seal is no longer required for the validity of a deed, but North Carolina (at least as of 1978), is an exception to that rule. See Garrison v. Blakeney, 37 N.C.App. 73, 246 S.E.2d 144, at 147–148 (1978), where the court states that a seal is necessary in North Carolina and then gives a brief but interesting history of the role of seals and why they were used.

2. DELIVERY, ESCROW AND ACCEPTANCE

LEGAL GEMS

1. *Delivery of a deed means an intention on the part of the grantor that it shall operate or take effect as a conveyance.*

2. There must be in existence a physical deed duly executed by the grantor before delivery is possible.

3. If the grantor intends the deed to be effective, delivery takes place irrespective of whether the physical paper be in the possession of the grantee, the grantor or a third person.

4. Delivery is primarily a question of fact and what the grantor does with the physical deed may be some evidence of his intention concerning its taking effect.

5. If the grantor hands the deed to the grantee with no intention that it operate as a conveyance, it is ineffective and there is no delivery; if he keeps possession of the deed but intends that it operate as a conveyance in favor of the grantee, there is a delivery.

6. Delivery, being the state of mind of the grantor, is wholly dehors the deed, and the parol evidence rule should have no application thereto.

7. Delivery to a third person to be delivered to the grantee upon the happening of an event or the performance of a condition is commonly referred to as a delivery in escrow. Nevertheless, a distinction between the commercial transaction and a donative transaction is believed helpful in analyzing the cases and arriving at the correct solution.

8. In a commercial escrow transaction the delivery is truly a conditional one. The condition may be the payment of the balance of the purchase price, the obtaining of certain quitclaim deeds, the satisfaction of mortgages or other incumbrances, or the performance of other acts or conditions which may or may not take place. In all of these cases, however, the performance of the condition is beyond the control of the grantor. Control is vested either in the grantee or in third parties.

9. A delivery in escrow in the typical commercial transaction is a valid delivery.

10. There cannot be an escrow or conditional delivery to the grantee under the traditional view. Conditional delivery to the grantee, the grantor retaining no other control over the instrument, takes effect presently. But see Chillemi v. Chillemi, 197 Md. 257, 78 A.2d 750 (1951) under important note following Case 217 infra, holding contra.

11. A true escrow requires the grantor to give up all control over the operation of the deed, subject only to the performance of the condition or the happening of the event which is involved. It vests in the grantee the power to become the owner upon the performance of the condition or the happening of the event.

12. The delivery in escrow or conditional delivery must be to a third person and requires the manual handing over of the deed to the escrow depositary.

13. The escrow depositary is neither an agent nor a trustee of either the grantor or grantee; it is his duty merely to carry out his instructions, with or without contractual obligations therein.

14. In a commercial escrow the title to the property passes to the grantee upon the performance of the condition or upon the happening of the event, that is, from the so-called "second delivery". In case of death of the grantor, however, or his becoming non compos mentis, or a grantor feme sole becoming feme covert, or for other reasons simply to do justice, title relates back or passes from the date

of the "first delivery", that is, from the time when the grantor hands the deed to the escrow depositary.

15.   When the grantor makes a commercial escrow delivery of a deed, it is irrevocable and he loses all control over the operation of the instrument as a conveyance subject only to the failure of the grantee to perform or failure of the other conditions. There is authority that a commercial escrow delivery is revocable unless there is an ancillary underlying enforceable contract to convey, but it is believed that this position is unsound. The question at this stage of the transaction is not whether there is an enforceable contract to convey but whether the grantor has sufficiently divested himself of control over the deed and title.

16.   In a donative escrow transaction the grantor delivers the deed to a depositary to be delivered to the grantee upon the happening of an event or the occurrence of a condition. Depending upon the amount of control relinquished by the grantor, the delivery may be either valid or invalid.

17.   In a donative escrow transaction where the delivery to the grantee is to occur on the death of the grantor whenever and however that occurs, there is a valid delivery.

    a.   The death of the grantor is a certainty; the only contingency is when.

    b.   The grantor in this case gives up all control.

    c.   When necessary to determine the rights of the parties before the death of the grantor, the analogy to a fee simple and executory interest or life estate and remainder is employed.

    d.   The deed in this type of case takes effect on the initial deposit with the depositary. However, it does not then vest the entire estate in the grantee; rather it vests presently a valid future interest.

18.   In a donative escrow transaction where the depositary is subject to further instructions and control by the grantor, there is no delivery at all. Such a transaction is illustrated by a direction to the depositary to "deliver this deed to the grantee on my death if I don't recall it before then." In this case it is clear that the grantor reserves the right to control the deed in the hands of the depositary; thus the depositary is his agent, and there is no delivery.

19.   In the case of a donative transaction where the deed is to become effective upon the happening of an event within the control of neither the grantor nor the grantee, there are conflicting decisions. This situation may be illustrated by the direction to "deliver this deed if I die before the grantee, but if he dies before me, then return it." It is clear that the grantor does intend to retain (or get back) the entire title if one contingency happens, but to divest himself completely of the title if another contingency happens. It is believed that the more logical view is that such delivery is valid and that the

418 CONVEYANCING Part 3

grantee will acquire title if the specified event occurs. The analogy to the commercial escrow situation seems appropriate.

20. An instrument of conveyance may, and usually does, arise out of a pre-existing contract, and it may include within its terms a contract such as a warranty of title, but it is not a contract.

21. In logic, a conveyance being merely a transfer of title from grantor to grantee, like a gift from donor to donee in personal property, no express acceptance thereof is required because the law presumes one will accept that which is to his financial benefit or advantage.

22. An heir cannot prevent title coming to him by descent by operation of law, but a conveyance cannot be forced upon a purchaser against his will; every grantee in a conveyance has the right to make disclaimer and cast the title back upon the grantor.

23. Assuming delivery by the grantor, he who says title does not vest in the grantee has the burden of showing affirmative disclaimer by such grantee.

24. Many American cases assert but far less such cases actually hold that acceptance of a deed by the grantee is essential to an inter vivos conveyance.

25. All cases agree that infants and persons non compos mentis may hold title by purchase even though they have no capacity to accept contractual responsibility.

26. In the absence of evidence to the contrary, a valid delivery to one of several co-grantees serves as a delivery to all of them. Arwe v. White, 117 N.H. 1025, 381 A.2d 737 (1977); LeMehaute v. LeMehaute, 585 S.W.2d 276 (Mo.App.1979).

See Tiffany, Vol. 4, § 1033 et seq.; 25 Mich.L.R. 171; 19 Harv.L. R. 612; Casner, Vol. 3, p. 311 et seq.; Burby, 293 et seq.

CASE 212: A, owner of Blackacre in fee simple, was negotiating with B for a sale of the premises for cash. A made out a complete deed to the land, named B as grantee therein and acknowledged it before a notary public. When B came to A's house to talk further about the possible deal, A handed B the deed with these words, "If we make this deal and you pay me the $5,000.00 cash, this is the deed which I will give to you." B replied, "I'll take the deed home and show it to my wife. If she likes it we may buy the property tomorrow." B left with the deed, placed it on record in the proper county office and now sues to eject A from Blackacre. Should he succeed?

Answer and Analysis

The answer is no. A was the owner of Blackacre. He can convey title thereto by deed by doing two things: (a) making a deed; and

(b) making delivery thereof to the intended grantee. In this case he made out the deed. He did not make delivery. It is true, A handed over the deed physically to the named grantee, B. B had physical possession of the deed with no wrongdoing on his part. But *delivery is a question of the intention of the grantor. It is the intention of the grantor that the instrument shall operate as a conveyance,* that it shall pass title to the grantee, that the grantee be empowered to use it as a muniment of title. It means that the grantor must relinquish all control over the instrument as an effective transfer of title. It does not mean giving up control over the mere physical piece of paper on which the writing or printing appears. It is much more than that. It means that the writing or printing on the paper shall have the legal effect of conveying title to the named grantee. Such intention is in the mind of the grantor and is usually a question of fact. In this case it is probably so clear that no reasonable men could differ as to the intention of A. The grantor's words were, "If we make this deal . . . I will give it to you. . . ." This indicates no present but a future time when A intends to give efficacy to the deed, and on a condition. The words of the named grantee likewise show no misunderstanding. He said, "If she likes it we may buy tomorrow." He too understood there was no present intention on A's part to part with the operation of the instrument as a conveyance even if A did part with the physical possession thereof. Hence, A, while he did intend to hand over physical control of the deed, had no intention to relinquish control of the deed as a deed transferring title to Blackacre. Hence, there was no delivery and as between A and B, A is still the owner of Blackacre. What effect had the recordation? It had none as between these parties. Had A recorded the deed there would have been a presumption of delivery by him but such is not the case when the named grantee records the deed. See Tiffany, Vol. 4, Sec. 1034; Burby 295.

Note

This case should be distinguished from the one involving a conditional delivery to the grantee. See infra case 217 and Important Note following that case. The difference is between no delivery at all and a conditional delivery. In this case there was no intent to make any kind of delivery. There was only a handing over of a written instrument for purposes of inspection, a bailment of the document, in effect.

CASE 213: A, owner in fee simple of Blackacre, makes out a completed deed to the premises in favor of B as grantee therein. A puts the deed in the drawer of his office desk. B who has been negotiating with A for the purchase of Blackacre hands A the agreed price of $5,000.00 which A accepts and says to B: "Blackacre is yours". Thereafter, A having refused to turn over the physical deed to B, B sues A in ejectment and alleges all of these facts to which A demurs. How should the court rule on the demurrer?

Answer and Analysis

The court should overrule the demurrer. On the demurrer all the above facts being well pleaded are admitted for the purpose of testing the sufficiency of the complaint. These facts being admitted, can they constitute delivery as a matter of law? The deed being made and delivery being a question of the grantor's intention, it is clear that the words of the grantor, A, "Blackacre is yours", could well mean that he intended the deed to operate as a transfer of title to B. It is important that B have possession of the physical deed so that he can record it as evidence of his title. But he need not have the physical piece of paper or deed in order to have the title as against A when it is established there is such physical deed, and that A intended it to be operative as a legal conveyance of title from A to B. See Kanawell v. Miller, 262 Pa. 9, 104 A. 861 (1918); Tiffany, Vol. 4, § 1034; Burby, 294.

CASE 214: A, being owner in fee simple of Blackacre, makes and delivers his deed thereto to B as grantee. B takes the deed and puts it in his pocket, remarking, "Well, now I'm a landowner for the first time in my life. I belong to the landed gentry." An hour later B returned to A and said this, "A, I've decided that this transaction which made me the owner of Blackacre also made me morally indebted to you and I prefer to be indebted to no man. Here is your deed back again. Thanks, anyway!" B handed the deed to A and A tore it up and threw it in the stove where it was totally destroyed by the fire. Who is the owner of Blackacre?

Answer and Analysis

The answer is this—B is the owner of Blackacre. The facts state that A "delivers" his deed to B. That means that he intended such deed to pass title to B. It did transfer title to B, subject only to B's disclaimer which would cast title back on A ab initio. But B did not disclaim. He declared himself a landowner and a member of the landed gentry. So title was in B. When B later changed his mind, such change of mind did not change the title which was in B. There are only two ways by which B can be divested of the title to Blackacre: (1) by a deed voluntarily executed by B as grantor to another and; (2) by some other person taking it from B involuntarily by adverse possession. When B returned the deed to A, he was returning A's voluntary conveyance or deed. It was not B's deed to A. B had not executed a deed of his own and delivered it to A. Title had vested in B and a voluntary conveyance executed by B was essential to reconvey the property to A. All that A destroyed was evidence. The deed to A had already taken effect, and that effect remained with title in the grantee, B. This may be a "trick" question, but it is fundamental to one's understanding of the nature of a conveyance. The fact that such facts may be difficult or impossible of proof is totally immaterial here because the facts are given as such. See Burby, 294; Tiffany, 459.

CASE 215: A, being owner in fee simple of Blackacre, made a complete deed to B as grantee and placed it in his safe deposit box in the bank where it was found upon A's death. A's will did not mention Blackacre but disposed of all the rest of his property. A dispute arose between B and A's heirs as to who was the owner of Blackacre. Who owns Blackacre?

Answer and Analysis

This question cannot be given a yes or no answer in its present form because it merely raises a question of fact. The answer depends upon whether or not A made a delivery of the deed during his lifetime. If, during A's lifetime, he intended that deed to be effective to convey title to B, then B is the owner of Blackacre. If, during A's lifetime, he had no intention that such deed convey title to B, then the heirs of A are the owners of Blackacre. No deed can be effective unless delivered during the lifetime of the grantor for the simple reason that there can be no intention in one who is deceased. Only a will can take effect the instant following death. The fact that A made a deed to Blackacre is no evidence of and raises no presumption of delivery thereof. The fact of delivery is wholly outside of and extrinsic to the instrument itself. Delivery must be proved as an independent fact, and the burden is on him who claims there was a delivery to prove such. In this case the burden would be on B to show by a preponderance of evidence that A during his lifetime intended the deed to be effective. And whether he did or did not so intend would be a question of fact for the trier of fact. See Erbach v. Brauer, 188 Wis. 312, 206 N.W. 62 (1925); Tiffany, Vol. 4, § 1039.

CASE 216: A, being fee simple owner of Blackacre, made a complete deed to Blackacre in favor of B who was named grantee therein. A authorized C to place the deed on record which was done. When the deed was recorded it was mailed to C who returned it to A. A remained in possession of Blackacre. B died and D was his sole heir. A now brings suit against D to remove the cloud which the recorded deed casts upon his title. The only evidence adduced at the trial on the question of delivery were C's statement that A told him, C, to record the deed and A's bald assertions that the physical deed was never in B's possession and that he, A, had never "delivered" the deed to B. The trial court, sitting without a jury, found for and gave judgment to the defendant and A appeals. How should the appellate court rule?

Answer and Analysis

The answer is, the appellate court should affirm the decision of the lower court. Here again the question of delivery is a question of fact. But when a grantor records his deed in favor of a grantee, there is a presumption that he intends to deliver the deed and that it shall pass title to the grantee. The burden of overcoming such presumption is then on the grantor. A mere assertion by the grantor that he did not intend to deliver the deed is ordinarily not sufficient to overcome the presumption of delivery. He must prove no delivery by clear and positive proof. In this case he might have done so by showing clearly that C was not authorized by him, that is by A, to record the deed. This he did not do by merely saying he did not deliver the deed. In any event the question of delivery was a question of fact for the trier of fact, and the trial court found such question in favor of the defendant with plenty of evidence to sustain such finding. Hence, the upper court should affirm the judgment. See Stiegelmann v. Ackman, 351 Pa. 592, 41 A.2d 679 (1945); Tiffany, Vol. 4, § 1044; Burby, 296.

CASE 217: A, owner in fee simple of Blackacre, made a complete deed thereto in favor of grantee, B. A handed the deed to B with this admonition, "I'm going on a dangerous journey. If during such trip I am killed, then put this deed on record". A returned safely from the journey. B had put the deed on record and claimed the property. May A set aside the deed?

Answer and Analysis

The answer is no. This holding is anomalous. There is no reason in logic why, if delivery is a matter of the grantor's intention, a deed cannot be handed to the grantee to take effect on a condition. But the great majority of the cases hold that if the grantor hands the deed to the grantee with the intention that it be a conditional delivery, then it is an absolute delivery. The grantee cannot be an escrow depositary. If effective delivery means what the cases hold, that the grantor intends to give up all control and dominion over the operation of the deed as a conveyance, it should be wholly immaterial whether the physical deed be in the hands of the grantor, the grantee or a third person. But in this instance where the grantor hands the paper to the grantee to be effective on a condition which may or may not happen, the shades of the past which treat the deed like a feoffment which must take effect presently or not at all, seem to continue to govern the more enlightened view on the subject.

For statements consistent with the above result, see Wipfler v. Wipfler, 153 Mich. 18, 116 N.W. 544, 16 L.R.A.,N.S., 941 (1908), in which appear the following: "a delivery of a deed by a grantor to a grantee in escrow or upon condition is effectual to pass title presently" and "Nor do we know of any authority which goes to the extent of holding that a deed delivered to a grantee with an intention on the part of the grantor that it shall be subject to a future condition, but with no express provision for recall by the grantor and requiring for its validity no additional act on the part of the grantor or any third person, can be defeated by parol proof of such condition." See also Tiffany, Vol. 4, p. 227, where appears this: "The manual transfer of the instrument, which is ordinarily assumed to be essential to a conditional delivery, must, according to a great majority of the authorities in this country, be to a person other than the grantee, it being held that if the grantor, intending to make a conditional delivery, hands the instrument to the grantee, there is necessarily an absolute delivery." See also Sweeney, Adm'x v. Sweeney, 126 Conn. 391, 11 A.2d 806 (1940), accord; Burby, 304.

Important Note Contra

In a fairly recent case the Maryland Supreme Court turned the light of reason and logic on the shades of the historical past which determined the common law rule set forth in Case 217 above and refused to follow it. In such case H and W, husband and wife, owned Blackacre in fee simple as tenants in entireties. H was ordered by the government to perform a dangerous mission in Korea and Japan. He made a deed to W of his interest in Blackacre and handed it to her on condition (a) that she would not record the deed until such time as he "should be reported missing, killed or had failed to return", and (b) that if he should return, the deed would be returned and destroyed. W recorded the deed contrary to the condition and refused to return it to H upon his return. H sued to have the deed annulled.

The court found that the deed had been conditionally delivered by H to the grantee, W, and that it should be annulled, saying, "there is actually no logical reason why a deed should not be held in escrow by the grantee as well as by any other person. The ancient rule is not adapted to present-day conditions and is entirely unnecessary for the protection of the rights of litigants. After all, conditional delivery is purely a question of intention, and it is immaterial whether the instrument, pending the satisfaction of the condition, is in the hands of the grantor, the grantee or a third person. After the condition is satisfied, there is an operative conveyance which is considered as having been delivered, although the ownership does not pass until satisfaction of the conditions. We therefore *hold* that it is the intention of the grantor of a deed that determines whether the delivery of the deed is absolute or conditional, although the delivery is made directly to the grantee."

The court explained the origin of the common law rule in the following words, "It has long been held at common law that there cannot be a valid delivery of a deed to the grantee named therein upon a condition not expressed in the deed. The ancient rule that the mere transfer of a deed from the grantor to the grantee overrides the grantor's explicit declaration of intention that the deed shall not become operative immediately is a relic of the primitive formalism which attached some peculiar efficacy to the physical transfer of the deed as a symbolical transfer of the land. . . . In England in ancient times there could be no change of possession of land until a livery of seisin had taken place. A knife was produced and a piece of turf was cut, and the turf was handed over to the new owner. Later, under the Roman influence, the written document came into use. These documents, which few people had the art to manufacture, were regarded with mystical awe. Just as the sod had been taken up from the ground to be delivered, so the document was laid on the ground and then solemnly lifted and delivered as a symbol of ownership. In this way the principle developed that the delivery of the deed was the mark of finality." The court then explained that the first sign of breaking away from this strict formalism was the recognition that there could be a conditional delivery to a third person in escrow. But such conditional delivery was not allowed when the deed was handed to the grantee.

Comment

This case presents the law as it should be and it is hoped that others will follow its lead. See Chillemi v. Chillemi, 197 Md. 257, 78 A.2d 750 (1951); Lerner Shops of North Carolina, Inc. v. Rosenthal, 225 N.C. 316, 34 S.E.2d 206 (1945) accord; Burby, 304.

CASE 218: A, owner in fee simple of Blackacre, executed a specifically enforceable contract to sell Blackacre to B. He also executed a deed in B's favor as grantee and placed it in the hands of X bank, an escrow depositary, with written instructions to X that X should hand the deed to B when B paid the full purchase price to X. Thereafter B paid the full purchase price to X. A then instructed X not to hand the deed to B. X refused to give the deed to B. B sues for possession of the deed. May he recover?

Answer and Analysis

The answer is yes. This type of escrow transaction gives little difficulty. The rights of the parties are clear. When the specifically enforcable contract was executed, equitable conversion took place whereby B became the equitable owner of Blackacre and A retained the legal title as security for the payment of the purchase price. Had there been no escrow, B, having performed in full, could have sued in specific performance and compelled A to execute to him a deed to Blackacre. These are the rights of the parties under the contract.

Under the escrow transaction it was clearly intended that title should remain in A until B had fully performed his contractual obligations. Conversely, it was just as clear that the deed should take effect as an operative conveyance when B had fully performed. Hence, when B paid the full purchase price to X, the deed became effective and title passed to B irrespective of whether the physical paper were handed over to the grantee, B, because such was A's intention and delivery is merely a question of intention of the grantor that the deed operate as a conveyance. Consequently B had the right to the possession of the physical deed for the purpose of evidence and to place same of record.

The following principles should be carefully noted in connection with this and every escrow transaction. (a) There must be a deed. (b) It must be delivered to a third person. (c) Title remains in the grantor until the happening of an event or performance of the condition. (d) Title passes to the grantee upon the happening of the event or performance of the condition irrespective of who holds the physical deed. (e) The escrow depositary has merely the duty to carry out his instructions or perform his contract if there be such. (f) The escrow depositary is not an agent for either party nor trustee for either for if he be such, then he is not an escrow depositary. In this case when A delivered the deed to X, the escrow depositary, (called the *first* delivery) A invested B with a power to become the owner of Blackacre by performing his obligation. Thereafter A had no control over the deed or its operation unless B failed to perform. Neither did A have any control over the escrow depositary X and X's refusal to make the *second* delivery to B was without authority. Such is the nature of a true escrow. See Burby, 300; 3 Casner 322 et seq.

CASE 219: A, owner in fee simple of Blackacre, orally agreed to sell Blackacre to B. A executed a deed thereto in B's favor as grantee and placed the deed in the hands of X bank as escrow depositary with oral instructions to deliver the deed to B when B paid the full purchase price, which was to be paid in five installments of $1,000 each. B paid four installments. A then instructed X to return the deed to A which X refused to do. B then paid the last installment to X, making full payment of $5,000 according to the original oral agreement, and demanded the deed from X which X refused. A offered to repay to B the entire $5,000 which B refused. Who owns Blackacre?

Answer and Analysis

The answer is this—B owns Blackacre, and has the right to the deed thereto according to the better reasoned cases, but there is substantial authority contra. It should be carefully noticed that here is a contract based on a consideration but unenforceable under the Statute of Frauds. In this respect it differs from Case 218 ante. The answer to this question requires a presupposition as to the very nature of an escrow transaction. If a conveyance is not a contract, and it is not, and if delivery is merely a question of the grantor's intention, and it is, then it would appear that a grantor has the power and right to invest a grantee named in a deed with a power to become the owner of property by performance of a condition, or, or by an act of payment of money. Further, it would appear that he could make such power in the grantee irrevocable as to the grantor, subject only to the performance by the grantee. If such be the case, then the Statute of Frauds has no application to the case and the grantor is bound by his irrevocable delivery to the escrow depositary, subject, of course, to performance by the grantee. Such seems to be the true nature of an escrow transaction and gives to it great practical utilitarian value in the field of conveyancing. To require in such case a specifically enforceable contract is to thwart the intention of the grantor at the time of establishing of the escrow and permit him to change his mind to the detriment of the grantee, and at the same time to detract materially from the value of escrows as a practical method of carrying on conveyancing business. Neither does it negate the Statute of Frauds which applies, and was intended to apply, to an oral contract for the sale of land when no escrow is involved. Surely the grantor intended more than an oral contract for the sale of Blackacre when he executed a deed and placed it in escrow. Tiffany's Abridged Edition at page 457 says that the view which requires a specifically enforceable contract in an escrow transaction "has no considerations of policy or convenience in its favor and considerably detracts from the practical utility of the doctrine of conditional delivery." See also 14 Col.L.Rev. 399; 16 Mich.L.Rev. 569; 29 Yale L.Jour. 826.

Further, delivery is a requirement in addition to the requisite formalities pertaining to the execution of sales contracts and deeds of conveyances. If it is possible to have a fully completed delivery when there was no ancillary contract at all, and it is, then it should also be possible to show that there was a conditional delivery when there was either no contract at all or only an unenforceable one. The question is not whether there was an enforceable ancillary contract, but whether the grantor had either completely effectuated the conveyance by delivery or had gone so far in that direction as to put it beyond his power to revoke. It is submitted that a conditional delivery in escrow should be irrevocable except for the non-performance of the condition although there is no enforceable ancillary contract. There are, however, considerable cases to the contrary. See generally 3 Casner 323; Burby, 300; Campbell v. Thomas, 42 Wis. 437 (1877), holding contra to the views expressed above.

CASE 220: A, owner in fee simple of Blackacre, executes his deed thereto in favor of B and hands it to X bank with instructions to deliver said deed to B upon A's death. A dies and his heirs or devisees claim Blackacre. Who is the owner of Blackacre?

Answer and Analysis

The answer is this—B is the owner. Here it should be noted there is no contract at all—merely an event to happen. This is a donative transaction in which the grantor gave up all control over the operation of the deed as a conveyance, subject only to the happening of an event.

The event in this case is certain to happen since death is inevitable. Thus, construing A's instructions as meaning to deliver the deed whenever and however A dies, the only contingency is that of time. A has thus given up all control over the title's eventually vesting completely in B; thus there is a valid delivery.

In the instant case no controversy arose before A's death so that the only question to be decided was whether there was a delivery and whether B now has title to Blackacre. Suppose, however, a dispute should arise as to the rights of the parties after the initial deposit and before the death of A, as, for example, if B should learn of the deed and bring ejectment against A, or creditors of B should attempt to levy on Blackacre, or B should sue A for waste. What is the status of the parties during the interim? In donative cases of this type, it is frequently held that the deed takes effect on the initial deposit or it doesn't take effect at all. It is not necessary, however, that the deed take effect initially to convey an entire fee simple; it can take effect presently to convey a future interest. The analogy in this case to the creation of a springing executory interest with A retaining the fee simple subject thereto, or A vesting in B a remainder with the reservation of a life estate, is rather striking and often construed accordingly. As to the specific questions raised, it should be decided that B should not be able to eject A during his lifetime; that B's creditors could reach by whatever means are available only his future interest in Blackacre; and that B should not be able to recover for waste. See Smith v. Fay, 228 Iowa 868, 293 N.W. 497 (1940); Smiley v. Smiley, 114 Ind. 258, 16 N.E. 585 (1888); Rathmell v. Shirey, 60 Ohio St. 187, 53 N.E. 1098 (1899).

Note

If on depositing the deed with the third party the grantor evidences an intent to control the deed and title, as, for example, he states that unless he should give contrary instructions or ask for the deed back, then the depositary should deliver the deed on the death of the grantor, the depositary is simply an agent of the grantor and there is no delivery. The transaction is testamentary and fails for lack of compliance with the statute of wills.

The most troublesome cases are donative transactions in which the deed is to become fully effective on the happening of an event within the control of neither party and not certain to occur. An example might be the death of the grantor before the grantee. By analogy to the commercial escrow situation the delivery should be sustained because the grantor has put beyond his control whether or not the title will fully vest in the grantee. On the other hand, he has not irrevocably parted with title and he will recover full ownership on the condition or event not occurring. The cases are divided with probably the majority finding no delivery. See Dunlap v. Marnell, 95 Neb. 535, 145 N.W. 1017 (1914), upholding delivery; Kenney v. Parks, 125 Cal. 146, 57 P. 772 (1899); Atchison v. Atchison, 198 Okl. 98, 175 P.2d 309 (1946), holding no delivery; Burby, 299.

CASE 221: A, owner in fee simple of Blackacre, executed his deed in B's favor as grantee and delivered it to X bank as escrow depositary with instructions to deliver said deed to B when B paid the full purchase price to X in installments. Before all payments were made and without the knowledge or consent of A, X let B have the deed. B put the deed on record and sold Blackacre to C, a bona fide purchaser, who knew nothing of the escrow transaction. Blackacre is undeveloped land with nobody in possession. A sues B and C to cancel the deeds and to quiet title. May A succeed?

Answers and Analyses

The answer is yes according to the majority and what is believed the better rule. This result is based on logic and the reasoning is as follows: A owned Blackacre. He placed his deed to B in escrow. Until B had performed the condition of making full payment no title could pass from A to B. X is not A's agent so as to bind A by his act contrary to his instructions. A is just as innocent as the bona fide purchaser, C. In such case the law should be followed. Title being in A, he has the right to quiet title against C, and the recording acts do not change this result. The recording acts invalidate unrecorded instruments as against subsequent bona fide purchasers for value without notice. They have absolutely nothing to do with recorded but void deeds, and the fact that the deed may be void because of forgery, non-delivery, or for other reasons is entirely immaterial. Thus, the non-delivered deed is invalid and the innocent purchaser relying on the recording act gets no protection.

In the instant case it should be noted that the grantee did not have possession of the land, and the grantor did not know that the deed had been delivered. If either of these situations had occurred, then as against the grantor the bona fide purchaser from the grantee of the wrongfully procured escrow deed should be protected either on the basis of estoppel or ratification.

In the event that the grantor lets the escrow grantee into possession, then the grantor, in the case of a wrongfully procured deed, has in effect permitted the grantee to be clothed with a double indicia of title—both possession and deed. If the grantor remains in possession, then his possession constitutes notice of his interest and there can be no bona fide purchaser without notice. In case nobody is in possession, then the equities should be regarded as equal and the law, holding no title passed, should prevail since the recording acts do not deal with recorded but undelivered deeds. In case the grantor learns of an improperly delivered deed and takes no action to invalidate such deed, then the grantor should likewise be subordinated to the rights of the bona fide purchaser on the basis of either estoppel or ratification. See Mays v. Shields, 117 Ga. 814, 45 S.E. 68 (1903), accord with the principles herein expressed. Everts v. Agnes, 4 Wis. 343, 65 Am.Dec. 314 (1855), indicated that a bona fide purchaser from a grantee of a wrongfully procured deed from an escrow agent would get no title; whereas Schurtz v. Colvin, 55 Ohio St. 274, 45 N.E. 527 (1896), spoke very sympathetically of the policy behind the recording acts and the desire of protecting bona fide purchasers relying thereon. However, in *Schurtz* the grantee was also let into possession so the exception applicable in Mays v. Shields, supra, would apply. See also Burby, 302–303.

———

CASE 222:   A, being owner in fee simple of Blackacre, executed a deed thereto in B's favor and placed it in the hands of X bank as escrow depositary with instructions to X that the deed should be handed to B upon B's payment of the last installment of the purchase price. Before the last installment was paid by B, the grantor, A, died. Thereafter B paid to X the last installment and demanded possession of A's deed. In whom is the title to Blackacre?

Answer and Analysis

The answer is this—the title is in B and he has the right to the deed. The courts speak of "first" and "second" deliveries in the escrow cases. The first one has reference to the handing over by the grantor of his deed to the escrow depositary and the second has reference to the handing over of the deed to the grantee by the escrow depositary. Of course, the first is not a technical delivery for the grantor does not intend title to pass to the grantee at that time. If it is a true escrow the first delivery merely makes the grantor's deed irrevocable and empowers the grantee, by fulfilling the condition or by the happening of the event, to become the owner of the property. Further, upon the fulfilling of the condition or happening of the event the deed operates to pass title even without any handing over of the deed to the grantee because such is the intention of the grantor. However, there can be no intention of a deceased grantor. The rule that a deed in escrow takes effect at the "second" delivery cannot apply when the grantor has predeceased the time when the condition is fulfilled. This situation, then, illustrates an exception to such rule, and by relation back for the purpose of doing justice, the deed is made effective as of the date of the first delivery by the grantor to the escrow depositary. At common law there were two other exceptions to the rule that the deed became effective on the "second" delivery: one when the grantor became non compos mentis between the first and second deliveries; and the other when the grantor, being a single woman, became a married woman between first and second deliveries, such marriage burdening her with the common law disabilities. Generally, it may be said that the theory of relation back to the first delivery will operate whenever the court finds it necessary to do justice in the case. See Burby, 303; Tiffany, 456.

CASE 223: A, being fee simple owner of Blackacre, agreed to sell same to B for $5,000.00, payable in installments of $1,000 each year for five years. A placed his deed to Blackacre naming B as grantee, in the hands of X bank as escrow depositary. When B had made three payments totalling $3,000.00 to X, C, a creditor of A, took judgment against A for $6,000.00 and levied upon Blackacre, which was put up for sale by the Sheriff and was sold to C to whom was issued Sheriff's Certificate of Sale. Immediately when levy was made on Blackacre C notified B and demanded that all future payments on his contract with A be made to C. When the Sheriff later executed his deed to C, C tendered title to Blackacre to B and demanded that B pay C the entire purchase price of Blackacre, namely, $5,000.00. How much may C recover from B?

Answer and Analysis

The answer is $2,000.00. Two principles are important in this case. One is that the rights of a creditor are derivative. The other is that title in an escrow transaction passes at the second delivery unless justice requires that it be related back to pass as of the time of the first delivery. The first principle applied to this set of facts prevents C from having any greater or higher right than his debtor A. A had been paid $3,000.00 of the purchase price and had only $2,000.00 still coming to him. Hence, C, his creditor, can claim from B no more than A could claim which is $2,000.00. But if we apply the rule that title in escrow passes only as of the time of the second delivery, we must conclude that A was the total owner of Blackacre when the levy was made, and hence the entire title vested in the creditor, C. But this would be unjust to B, the purchaser grantee. Hence, for the purpose of doing justice, we relate the passing of title back to the first delivery and permit the levy to affect only the balance of the unpaid purchase price which, after notice to B, should be paid to C, the judgment creditor of A. See May v. Emerson, 52 Or. 262, 96 P. 454, 16 Ann.Cas. 1129, rehearing denied 52 Or. 262, 96 P. 1065, 16 Ann.Cas. 1129; Burby, 303.

Note

Suppose that in Case 223 there were no contract involved and that the escrow was one of the donative transactions discussed in Case 220. The results may well be different and may depend upon a number of factors. If the contingency is simply the death of the grantor and the jurisdiction employs the rationale of the deed taking effect on deposit to convey a future interest, then the possessory estate of the grantor should be able to be reached by the creditors. In the donative transaction neither the donee nor the creditors have any special equities requiring the employment of relation back or other fiction to do substantial justice. Thus, the situation should be simply analyzed in terms of title passing as between the parties, and then the creditors should be permitted to attach whatever interests, if any, their debtors have. In some jurisdictions judgment creditors are within the protection of the recording acts; hence in those states such creditors of the grantor may acquire rights superior to those of the "escrow grantee" when the deed is not recorded.

CASE 224: A, owner in fee simple of Blackacre, executed a deed to the premises in favor of B as grantee and placed it on record. B died intestate thereafter without any knowledge of the deed and leaving X as his sole heir. A, having remained in possession of Blackacre, then executed a deed to D who was given possession of Blackacre. D paid A full purchase price for the land. X now sues D in ejectment. A testifies to the above facts but is asked nothing and states nothing concerning his intention as to the recorded deed in B's favor. D's sole defense is that the recorded deed which remained in A's possession was never accepted by B. May X recover possession of Blackacre?

Answer and Analysis

The answer is yes. D's defense is without merit. The law presumes that a grantee will accept that which is to his financial benefit and in the absence of affirmative disclaimer by the grantee title vests in such grantee. There are two ways by which derivative title to real property may be obtained: (a) by descent; and (b) by purchase. An heir cannot prevent title being thrust on him by descent by operation of law. But title cannot be forced by purchase on anyone. Hence, in our case B could have disclaimed title under the deed from A, and thereby cast title back upon A. But the burden is on him who says there was disclaimer to prove such as against the presumption that the grantee will and does accept that which is to his benefit. In this case when A executed and recorded his deed in B's favor as grantee there is a rebuttable presumption that A intended to deliver such deed to B. That presumption could have been but was not overcome by A's testimony in the case for he said nothing about his intention at the time of his making and recording such deed. Therefore the presumption of delivery stands and the title vested in the grantee in the absence of a showing that B disclaimed. B, the grantee, having no knowledge of the deed, could neither accept such nor disclaim such. So the presumption of acceptance stands and B became the owner of Blackacre, and upon his death intestate the title descended to X who has the right to possession thereof. Hence, X should recover from D in ejectment.

There are many cases which say, but far less which actually hold, that affirmative acceptance of a conveyance inter vivos is essential to a completion of the transfer. Such cases seem to be based upon the erroneous assumption that a conveyance is a contract and that delivery is an offer, and, therefore, acceptance is as essential to a completed conveyance as it is to the consummation of a contract. Perhaps most conveyances arise out of pre-made contracts and some conveyances contain contracts such as covenants of warranty within their terms, but a conveyance is not a contract. It is merely a transfer of title. The analogy to contracts is specious and wholly without merit. The following words from Welch v. Sackett, 12 Wis. 243, illustrate this erroneous point of view: "All agree that it is necessary to the validity of every deed or conveyance, that there be a grantee who is not only willing, but who does in fact accept it. It is a contract, a parting with property on the part of the grantor, and an acceptance of it by the grantee. Like every other contract, there must be a meeting of the minds of the contracting parties, the one to sell and convey, and the other to purchase and receive, before the agreement is consummated." If this be true, then how is it possible for an infant one year of age or one who is non compos mentis to become the owner of Blackacre? Yet there is no dissent from the proposition that such persons own property as purchasers but without capacity to accept contractual obligations. We conclude that affirmative acceptance by the grantee is no necessary part of a conveyance. See Thompson v. Leach, House of Lords 1691, 2 Vent. 198; Tiffany, p. 727; Mitchell's Lessee v. Ryan, 3 Ohio St. 377; Meade v. Robinson, 234 Mich. 322, 208 N.W. 41 (1926); Burby, 304.

Note—Losses During Escrow

In the event that the depositary misappropriates property held in escrow, it becomes necessary to determine who as between the grantor and grantee shall bear the loss. In spite of occasional representations to that effect, the commercial escrow before the conditions are performed is really not an agent of either or both parties; hence an agency rationale should not be used for locating the risk of such losses occurring at that stage of the transaction. The general rule for losses occurring before the condition is performed is that such losses fall on the one who deposited the property involved. If the escrow absconds with property after the condition is performed, the grantee is generally protected in his ownership of the land. After performance of the condition, the status of the depositary is similar to that of an agent of the grantor for delivering to him the purchase money, and that of an agent for the grantee for delivering to him the deed. Thus, if the money is diverted at this time, the loss should fall on the grantor and the title of the grantee should be protected. As a general proposition applicable to all unauthorized misappropriations of an escrow, the loss may be said to fall on whoever is entitled to the misappropriated property at the time of its diversion. See Shreeves v. Pearson, 194 Cal. 699, 230 P. 448 (1924); Cradock v. Cooper, 123 So.2d 256 (Fla.2nd D.C.A.1960); Comment, "Escrow Agreements," 8 Miami L.Q. 75 (1953); Burby, 302.

SUMMARY OF DELIVERY OF DEEDS TO REAL PROPERTY (excluding escrows)

ASSUME: (1) a deed complete to conform to statutory or other requirements, and (2) that delivery of a deed means the intention of the grantor that the deed shall operate as a conveyance; (3) delivery is usually a fact question so that no summary could possibly cover more than a few important principles on the subject. See 26 C.J.S. p. 231 et seq.; 16 Am.Jur. p. 654 et seq.

Disposition of the physical deed	Grantor's intention	Is there effective delivery?
1. Remains in grantor's possession	No intention deed shall operate	No effective delivery
2. Remains in grantor's possession	No evidence concerning such	Directed verdict for grantor for two reasons (a) presumption of no delivery when still in grantor's possession and (b) burden is on one claiming delivery to show such by preponderance of evidence. 16 Am.Jur. 657. No effective delivery.
3. Remains in grantor's possession	Grantor intends deed to operate	Delivery is effective. See 26 C.J.S. p. 237, Sec. 42.
4. Grantor records deed or has it recorded after which it is returned to grantor	No other evidence of grantor's intention	Recording by grantor raises rebuttable presumption he intended deed to operate. The burden is then on him to overcome such presumption by showing no such intention by clear and positive evidence. Mistake or lack of authority to one who recorded might do such. Delivery is effective.
5. Grantor puts deed in safe deposit box or in drawer of desk or bureau where it is found at his death.	No other evidence of intention	This is question of fact for trier of fact with burden on him who claims there was delivery to show such by preponderance of evidence. If no other evidence, then directed verdict for grantor—no effective delivery.
6. Grantor hands deed to grantee	Intention the deed shall not operate	No effective delivery. See 26 C.J.S. p. 240, Sec. 42, c.
7. Grantor hands deed to grantee	Grantor intends deed shall operate	Delivery is effective
8. Grantor hands deed to grantee	No other evidence of grantor's intention	Possession of the deed by grantee raises rebuttable presumption of delivery and burden is on grantor to show no intention to deliver. With no other evidence verdict should be directed for grantee. There is effective delivery.
9. Grantor hands deed to grantee	Deed on its face says it is to take effect only at a specific future day and grantor intends deed to be effective as written	Delivery is effective under Statute of Uses as springing use. Deed is irrevocable but the estate passes at the day certain in futuro. See Am.Law of Property, Vol. 3, p. 315.
10. Grantor hands deed to grantee	Grantor intends it to operate only at a certain future day such as at grantor's death or if he dies during operation, but such is not written on face of deed	There is effective delivery at once and not in the future. Three reasons appear (a) deed is equivalent to livery of seisin in feoffment and takes effect presently or not at all, (b) deed reads in present tense and parol evidence not admissible to alter such, (c) grantee cannot be an escrow depositary. This is an anomaly and reasons not satisfactory. Of course if grantor retains some control over the operation of the deed, then there is no delivery at all. See Am.Law of Property, Vol. 3, p. 316. But see Important Note following Case 217 supra.

SUMMARY OF CASES IN CHAPTER XIX

2. DELIVERY, ESCROW AND ACCEPTANCE

Case 212. Delivery of a deed to real property means that the grantor intends that the deed shall operate as a conveyance. To effectuate such a conveyance there must be a physical deed and an intention on the part of the grantor that it take effect as a conveyance. It is not material where the physical deed is.

Case 213. Title will pass to the grantee if there be a physical deed and the grantor intends it to operate as a conveyance, even though the grantor retains possession of the physical paper on which the deed is written.

Case 214. Once title has lodged in the grantee, he cannot abandon such title. Title can leave him only by his act by deed or will, or by another taking from him by adverse possession. Once title has lodged in the grantee without his disclaimer he cannot reconvey to the grantor by returning to the grantor the same deed which the grantor delivered to the grantee.

Case 215. (a) Delivery is a question of intention and intention is a fact question to be determined by the trier of fact. (b) Delivery is in the mind of the grantor and wholly dehors the deed. (c) The burden is on him who says there was a delivery to prove such.

Case 216. When the grantor makes out a deed and has it recorded in favor of the grantee, there is a presumption of delivery and the burden is on the grantor to overcome such presumption.

Case 217. A grantee cannot be an escrow depositary—conditional delivery cannot be made to the grantee—the deed either takes effect at once or not at all. This is an anomaly but seems to be the law in most states—but see note contra following case.

Case 218. A delivery in escrow is a conditional delivery. When the condition is fulfilled or the event happens on which the delivery depends, then title passes to the grantee even when the physical deed is retained wrongfully by the escrow depositary, and the grantee has the right to the possession of the physical deed as evidence of his title. There must be a physical deed and it must be handed over to the escrow depositary who is not an agent of either party but has merely the duty to carry out his instructions.

Case 219. A conveyance is not a contract. In an escrow transaction the grantor invests the grantee with a power to become the owner of the land represented by the deed and such power is irrevocable as to the grantor who loses all control over the operation of the instrument as a conveyance subject only to the failure of the grantee to perform. Under the better reasoned cases, the Statute of Frauds has no application to such and an oral placing of the deed in escrow is enforceable by the grantee who performs. A specifically enforceable contract is not essential to a valid escrow under this view.

Case 220. A delivery in escrow in a donative transaction in which the deed is to be delivered on the death of the donor whenever and however that occurs is a valid delivery. When necessary, the relationship of the parties prior to the happening of the certain event is analogized to that of a fee simple and executory interest, or life estate and remainder. If the grantor makes the depositary his agent subject to further control, there is no delivery. In donative escrow transactions where the event or condition is not certain to occur, the cases are divided as to whether there is a valid delivery.

Case 221. When the escrow depositary wrongfully hands the deed over to the grantee before the grantee has performed or has a right to the deed and the grantee records such deed and sells to a bona fide purchaser, the grantor is not estopped to deny the efficacy of his deed and the bona fide purchaser is not protected unless the grantee is let into possession, the grantor knows of the delivery of the deed and takes no action to revoke, or for other reasons the grantor is estopped. If the grantor retains any control over the operation of the deed it is not a true escrow.

Case 222. The deed in escrow takes effect to pass title on the so-called "second delivery" with the following exceptions: (a) when the grantor dies between the "first" and "second" delivery; (b) when during that time the grantor becomes non compos mentis; (c) the grantor being a feme sole and during that period becomes a feme covert burdened with the common law disabilities; or (d) justice requires it—by relation back in these cases the title passes as of the first delivery, that is, when the deed was handed to the escrow depositary.

Case 223. The rights of a creditor are derivative and an escrow passes title as of the second delivery unless justice requires relation back to the first delivery; justice requires such relation back to prevent the grantor's creditor from claiming more from the grantee than the grantee still owes on the escrow transaction.

Case 224. An heir cannot prevent title being cast on him by descent but a purchaser can disclaim any title by purchase. A conveyance is not a contract. No affirmative acceptance of a deed is necessary because the law will presume the grantee will accept that which is to his financial benefit. The burden is on him who says that a deed is ineffective for lack of acceptance to prove a disclaimer.

Chapter XX

THE SUBJECT MATTER CONVEYED; LAND
DESCRIPTION AND BOUNDARIES

1. Description and Boundaries.

    Chart   I—Showing "Principal Base Line" and "Principal Meridi-
               an" by Which Townships and Ranges in Land De-
               scriptions are Measured.
    Chart II—Township Map Showing Section Numbers.
    Chart III—Section Map Showing Subdivisions Thereof.
    Legal Gems.
    Cases.
2. Accretion.
3. Exceptions and Reservations.
    Cases.

Summary of Cases in Chapter XX.

---

1. DESCRIPTION AND BOUNDARIES

Note

In 1796 Congress adopted the rectangular system of surveys as the official method of land measurement in the United States. The principal units of such system used in land descriptions are townships, ranges and sections and subdivisons thereof. Each regular township is six miles square and contains 36 sections. Each section is one mile square and contains 640 acres. Chart I below with explanation following shows how the system is used in locating townships in any given state. Chart II below shows the method of numbering the sections within any given township. Chart III below shows how each section may be subdivided and the number of acres in each subdivision and is followed by a description of each of such subdivisions.

CHART I

SHOWING "PRINCIPAL BASE LINE" AND "PRINCIPAL MERIDIAN" BY WHICH TOWNSHIPS AND RANGES IN LAND DESCRIPTIONS ARE MEASURED

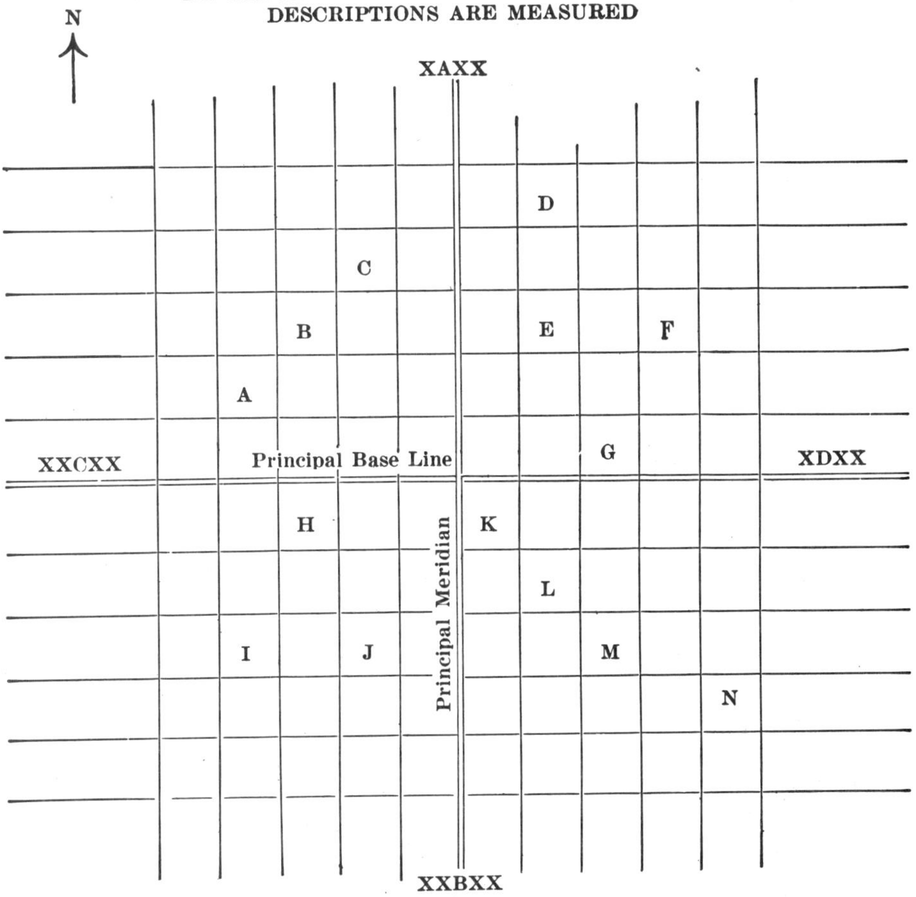

In each state using the rectangular system of surveys there are drawn arbitrary lines perpendicular to each other, one called the "principal base line" running east and west and the other called the "principal meridian" running north and south. Townships are measured north and south of the principal base line and ranges are measured east and west of the principal meridian. Each of the squares indicated in the above chart lettered from A to N indicates a township six miles square.

[A2175]

Some of these squares will be described as they would appear in a land description, to wit: the square indicated by letter A would be described as "Twp. 2 N, Rn. 4 W". By counting north from the Principal Base Line we find A in the second tier and by counting west from the Principal Meridian we find A in the fourth tier, thus the description given above. Continuing, square B would be "Twp. 3 N, Rn. 3 W"; square F would be "Twp. 3 N, Rn. 4 E"; square J would be "Twp. 3 S, Rn. 2 W" and square N would be "Twp. 4 S, Rn. 5 E", etc. Of course the abbreviation Twp. means township and the abbreviation Rn. means range. In land descriptions the township always precedes the range.

CHART II

TOWNSHIP MAP SHOWING SECTION NUMBERS

6	5	4	3	2	1
7	8	9	10	11	12
18	17	16	15	14	13
19	20	21	22	23	24
30	29	28	27	26	25
31	32	33	34	35	36

The method of numbering the sections within a township should be carefully studied even though it is a simple process. Beginning with section number 1 in the northeast corner of the township, the sections are numbered to the left from 1 to 6 in the top tier of sections, then down one tier and the counting is to the right to section 12, then down one tier and to the left, then down one tier and to the right, then down another tier and to the left and down one tier and to the right, ending with section 36 in the lower right hand corner of the township.

[A2174]

CHART III
SECTION MAP SHOWING SUBDIVISIONS THEREOF

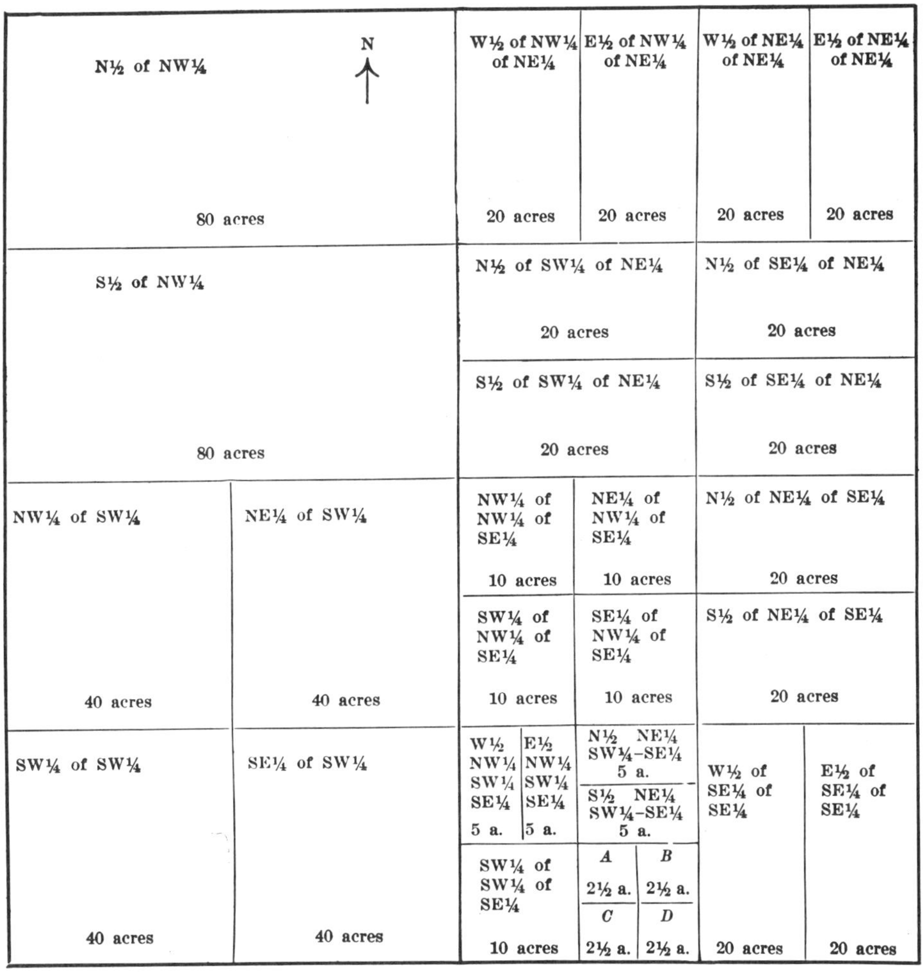

N½ of NW¼ N↑ 80 acres	W½ of NW¼ of NE¼ 20 acres	E½ of NW¼ of NE¼ 20 acres	W½ of NE¼ of NE¼ 20 acres	E½ of NE¼ of NE¼ 20 acres
S½ of NW¼ 80 acres	N½ of SW¼ of NE¼ 20 acres		N½ of SE¼ of NE¼ 20 acres	
	S½ of SW¼ of NE¼ 20 acres		S½ of SE¼ of NE¼ 20 acres	
NW¼ of SW¼ 40 acres	NE¼ of SW¼ 40 acres	NW¼ of NW¼ of SE¼ — 10 acres	NE¼ of NW¼ of SE¼ — 10 acres	N½ of NE¼ of SE¼ 20 acres
		SW¼ of NW¼ of SE¼ — 10 acres	SE¼ of NW¼ of SE¼ — 10 acres	S½ of NE¼ of SE¼ 20 acres
SW¼ of SW¼ 40 acres	SE¼ of SW¼ 40 acres	W½ NW¼ SW¼ SE¼ — 5 a. E½ NW¼ SW¼ SE¼ — 5 a. / SW¼ of SW¼ SE¼ — 10 acres	N½ NE¼ SW¼–SE¼ 5 a. / S½ NE¼ SW¼–SE¼ 5 a. / A 2½ a. B 2½ a. / C 2½ a. D 2½ a.	W½ of SE¼ of SE¼ — 20 acres E½ of SE¼ of SE¼ — 20 acres

Tract *A* is the NW¼ of SE¼ of SW¼ of SE¼
Tract *B* is the NE¼ of SE¼ of SW¼ of SE¼
Tract *C* is the SW¼ of SE¼ of SW¼ of SE¼
Tract *D* is the SE¼ of SE¼ of SW¼ of SE¼

See note A, B & P, Vol. 1, p. 601

[A2176]

LEGAL GEMS

1. To be effective as a conveyance of land the deed must so describe the land as to identify it.

2. A deed which fails to describe a specific divided part of a larger tract but describes a distinct fractional part thereof may be upheld as a conveyance of an undivided part.

3. If a deed in describing the land to be conveyed, refers to a particular map or plat, such map or plat is part of the deed for the purpose of identifying the land conveyed.

4. A metes and bounds description is the oldest known method of describing land. Literally, the term means measurements and boundaries. This method describes the tract by using compass directions and distances from an ascertainable starting point. Monuments, when applicable, are frequently included, as, for example, " . . . then proceed N. 30 degrees E. for 200 ft. to the South side of Utopia Avenue."

5. In a metes and bounds description, two things are vital: (1) the description must begin at some readily identifiable known point of a substantial character so that it can be relocated if the marker is removed; and (2) the description must close, that is, if the courses and distances are followed step by step, one will return to the place of beginning.

6. When a deed describes the boundaries of the land to be conveyed by reference to monuments, natural or artificial, *the intention of the parties is the controlling factor* and all rules of construction are mere aids in determining such intention.

7. In a description of land a monument is any object on the ground which helps to identify the land conveyed. It may be either natural or artificial and may be a tree, a stone, a stake, a river, a lake, a highway, a wall, a house, a ditch, a graveyard, an ocean, a farm or a mining claim.

8. The "course" of a line in a description means the direction it takes across the country and is usually determined by its angle with some other known line.

9. The "distance" means the length of a line from one point to another point, and the "contents" means the area of a tract of land.

10. When the terms of a deed conflict, then generally: (a) monuments, either natural or artificial, govern over courses and distances; (b) courses govern over distances; (c) a specific description will govern over a general description; and (d) any of these will govern over an estimated "contents" or area. These rules, however, are rules of construction only, not rules of law, and different priorities will prevail if there is evidence of such an intent.

11. Parol evidence is not admissible to determine the identity of land described in a deed unless it is first found that the description is ambiguous. Even then it is not admissible to alter, but only to explain the ambiguity, unless the suit is in equity for reformation.

12. When the description of land in a deed carries it "to", "by", "from" or "along" a street, road, alley, way, highway, creek, stream or similar monument, the common-law rule is that the grantee takes title to the land to the center of such street, road, alley, way, highway, creek, stream or similar monument, assuming, of course, that the grantor owned to the center of such monument.

13. If the description of land in a deed carries it to or from *a point on the side of a street,* stream, road or similar monument, *and along such street,* stream, road or similar monument, still the grantee

should take title to the center of such monument under the common law rule, but there are contra cases.

14.   If the description of land in a deed carries it to or from *a point on the side of a street,* stream, road or similar monument and *along the line on the side* of such street, stream, road or other similar monument, still the grantee should take title to the land to the center of such monument under the common law rule unless it is expressly excluded from the grant.   Such seems the better rule.

15.   An oral agreement made between adjoining owners of land settling an uncertain boundary line or one in dispute is valid and binding and does not come within the Statute of Frauds.

A related but not necessarily identical doctrine is that of acquiescence.   See Day, Validation of Erroneously Located Boundaries by Adverse Possession and Related Doctrines, 10 U.Fla.L.Rev. 245, 263–264 (1957); 2 Tiffany, §§ 652–653.

16.   When the boundary of a tract of land is the thread or center line of a stream of water, such boundary is a variable and changes with the thread of the stream.

17.   Title to the land under the waters of a non-navigable stream belongs to the abutting riparian owners and title to the land under the waters of a navigable stream belongs to the state.

18.   When a landowner owns to the water of a stream, lake, pond or ocean, but owns no land under the water, his boundary line and land area may be extended by the imperceptibly slow addition of soil by the action of the water, called accretion, or by the land rising and water receding, called reliction.   The newly made land is called alluvion.

19.   Alluvion belongs to the owner of the land abutting the water for three reasons: (a) he is the only person who is in a position to use it advantageously and make it produce; (b) such owner runs the risk of losing his land by erosion and should have a corresponding right to the gain by water deposits; and (c) his access to the water as a littoral or riparian owner should be preserved.

20.   When a river by sudden and violent change (called avulsion) alters its course and overflows privately owned land the title to such lands is not changed.

21.   In the United States private ownership as to tidal lands stops at the high water mark.
See Burby, 51; Tiffany, pp. 272, 391, 432; and leading case Gifford v. Yarborough, 5 Bing. 163 (1828).

22.   An exception is an exclusion from the operation of a deed of some part of the corporeal property described therein.   Such excepted portion is wholly unaffected by the deed and remains in the grantor.   E. g., A conveys Section 14 to B and his heirs except the northeast quarter thereof.

23. A reservation in the United States today is the creation of a new right in the land conveyed for the benefit of land retained by the grantor. E. g., A conveys Blackacre to B and his heirs but reserves an easement across such tract in favor of A's Whiteacre. (See also Case 233 infra, reservation to third person.)

24. In the United States the word "reservation" is sometimes construed as an exception and the word exception is sometimes construed as a reservation. The intention of the grantor is the all important consideration.

————

CASE 225: A, owner of Blackacre in fee simple, borrowed $500 from B to secure which indebtedness A executed his mortgage to B describing the land to be mortgaged as follows: "That certain tract of land, gristmill and storehouse, said tract to contain three acres and within my 40-acre farm". Thereafter A gave a mortgage to C covering A's 40-acre farm and properly describing it, said tract being the same farm referred to in B's mortgage. B was about to sell the land under foreclosure proceedings when C brought suit to enjoin such sale on the ground that B's mortgage was void for want of description identifying any specific land. Should the injunction issue?

Answer and Analysis

The answer is yes. No deed or mortgage is valid unless the description of the land sought to be conveyed or mortgaged is sufficient to identify such land. What land is identified in A's mortgage to B? The tract is three acres in area. But where is it? It is some place within a 40 acre tract. But no words locate it at any particular place within the 40 acres, and no words describe the shape of the three acres. Even if the buildings are intended to be within the three acres, a specific shape and location is lacking. Neither do the words used refer to any map or plat from which the 3 acre tract can be located. No monuments, no lines and no points give any indication of how to identify the land intended to be mortgaged to B. Hence, B's mortgage is void and the injunction should issue at the instance of the mortgagee, C, whose mortgage appears to be valid. See Harris v. Woodard, 130 N.C. 580, 41 S.E. 790 (1902); Burby, 307.[1]

1. Suppose, however, that the larger tract, Luvacre, is square in shape and the deed reads: "A one acre parcel located in the N.E. corner of Luvacre." In this situation the description would no doubt be held adequate since the court would assume a square parcel was intended to be conveyed. Thus, by measuring equal lengths along the northern and eastern boundaries the requisite number of feet to enclose a square acre by drawing parallel lines, the parcel would be identified. Of course, a triangular or other different shaped parcel of one acre could be carved out of the northeast portion of Luvacre, but unless there was clear evidence to show that such an odd shaped parcel was intended, the court would probably decide on the square lot. See Cribbet, 171–172, citing Bybee v. Hageman, 66 Ill. 519 (1873).

CASE 226: A, being owner in fee simple of Blackacre, executed a deed in favor of B as grantee in which he used the following language, "I hereby grant to B and his heirs that certain piece of land, it being one half of my Blackacre". What are the rights of the parties?

Answer and Analysis

The answer is this—A and B are tenants in common of Blackacre. The parties to this transaction intended that something should be conveyed by the deed. If possible the courts give effect to the language used. It is obvious that the words in the deed describe no specific "certain piece" or a divided part of Blackacre. Hence, the deed would fail if it were to be applied to any specific piece of land. On the other hand the language, "it being one half of Blackacre", does describe that which can be the subject matter of a conveyance, an undivided half. Hence, the deed should be construed as transferring an undivided half interest in Blackacre to B, thus making A and B tenants in common of Blackacre. If, on the other hand such a deed had attempted but had failed to describe a distinct piece of Blackacre, and if the intention of the grantor were clear that he intended to convey a divided portion of the tract, and the words, "it being one half of my Blackacre" were meant to describe merely the area of the piece intended to be conveyed, then the deed would fail for lack of description. See Morehead v. Hall, 126 N.C. 213, 35 S.E. 428 (1900); Tiffany, p. 427.

CASE 227: A, being owner in fee simple of Blackacre, executes his deed thereto in the following language in favor of B as grantee, "I hereby grant to B and his heirs that certain Lot 1, Block 1 of Veterans Addition to the City of Tucson, State of Arizona, according to that certain map on page 66 of Book 5 of Maps and Plats filed in the Office of the County Recorder of Pima County, State of Arizona." This described Blackacre. B paid full value for the lot and recorded the deed. Thereafter A borrowed money from X bank and executed a mortgage on several pieces of land to secure the payment of such mortgage debt. Blackacre was included in the mortgage to X. X foreclosed the mortgage and was about to sell Blackacre thereunder. B seeks to enjoin such sale and X contends that the description in B's deed is insufficient to pass title. In the trial B seeks to introduce in evidence the map and plat of Lot 1 Block 1 as it appears on page 66 of Book 5 of Maps and Plats in the Recorder's Office. Is such evidence admissible?

Answer and Analysis

The answer is yes. On this point there seems to be striking unanimity among the cases. The cases hold that if a deed in its description of the land to be conveyed refers to a map or plat, such reference makes such map or plat a part and parcel of the deed for purpose of identifying the land. It is obvious in the facts given that the description of the land as Lot 1, Block 1, etc., does not describe any land or locate any property which could be the subject of the conveyance apart from the map or plat. But by construing the deed and the map or plat together there is a piece of land with specific and accurate dimensions which is located on the terrain in reference to other pieces of land which bound it. In fact, with the map or plat the deed is complete; without it the deed is incomplete and void. Thus the courts carry out the expressed intention of the grantor by treating the deed and map or plat as one for purpose of making the conveyance complete. Hence, the evidence is admissible and B appears to be the title holder of Blackacre. See Deery v. Cray, 77 U.S. 263, 19 L. Ed. 887 (1842); Tiffany, Vol. 4, 3d ed., § 992.

Note

Deeds describing land by street number or "all my land" are considered valid descriptions provided they are identified as within a particular city, town, county or state. Of course it is the reference in the deed to extraneous material which makes such material available in evidence to identify the land. Were the reference in the deed not made the extraneous matter would not be admissible. Burby, 305 et seq.

CASE 228: A owned Blackacre in fee simple. Blackacre was a lot 80 feet wide and 200 feet long. The front 40 feet of Blackacre was subject to an easement for street purposes and was not usable by the owner as long as Market Street was used over such area. Market Street was 80 feet wide and the south line of Blackacre formed the center line of such Street for a distance of 80 feet. The long sides of Blackacre extended due north and south and were perpendicular to Market Street which extended due east and west. A executed a deed to B of such property using the following language therein, "I hereby grant to B the following described property to wit: Beginning at a steel stake in the north side line of Market Street exactly 100 feet west of the intersection of said north side line of Market Street with the west side line of Spruce Street, in the City of Dover, State of Arisota; thence due north at right angles to the north side line of Market Street 160 feet to another steel stake; thence due west and at right angles to the line just drawn 80 feet to another steel stake; thence due *north* and at right angles to the line just drawn 160 feet to Market Street; thence along Market Street to the place of beginning." (a) Is this deed valid to transfer to B any part of Blackacre?

(b) If so, does B take title to the 40 feet of the lot which is covered by Market Street?

Answers and Analyses

The answers are these, (a) the deed is valid and passes title to B, and (b) title to the 40 feet covered by Market Street passes to B. Question (a) will be discussed first. It raises a very important rule of construction which is this: in the description in a deed when there is a conflict between the calls of a deed as to courses and distances on one hand and monuments natural or artificial on the other, the MONUMENTS WILL GOVERN OVER COURSES AND DISTANCES. The reason for the rule is this: in the experience of mankind it has been learned that one is much more apt to be correct when referring to a monument than when turning off an angle for the direction of a line (a course) or in measuring a distance. Reverting to our set of facts it will be noticed that the description started at a monument, a stake specifically located in the north line of Market Street. The first course went north to another monument, a stake; the second course went west to another monument, a stake. Thus far the courses and distances and monuments coincide. Next comes the parting of the ways. The course turns due north but the monument, Market Street, is south. If the course is followed, there will be no land inclosed and the deed will fail for the courses describe only a broken line. If the monument governs, then the course will be carried not due north as the words indicate, but due south where the monument is located on the ground. Furthermore, by carrying the third course to the monument, Market Street, it will be possible by following the fourth course, "along Market Street to the place of beginning" to enclose a piece of land which could be the subject matter of the conveyance. Thus, by using the rule of construction that MONUMENTS GOVERN OVER COURSES AND DISTANCES, the deed with its calls will enclose an area of ground and will be valid. Our conclusion is that the third course runs "due south" to Market Street, the monument, and not "due north" as the deed states in words, and the deed is valid to pass title to B.

Question (b) involves another very important common law principle of construction. It is this: when the description of land in a deed carries it "to", "by", "from" or "along" a street, road, alley, way, highway, creek, stream or similar monument, the common law rule is that the grantee takes title to the land to the center of such street, road, alley, way, highway, creek, stream or similar monument, provided the grantor owns to the center of such monument. In our case the calls of the deed start from a point on the side line of Market Street and take a northerly direction "from" such point or Street. When the calls return to the monument, Market Street, they run "along" Market Street to the place of beginning. If the view is taken that the stake in the north side line of Market Street indicates an intention on the part of the grantor that the land conveyed shall be no further south than that point, then it can be argued that the grantee takes only to the north side line of Market Street and the tract which B gets is only 80 ft. by 160 ft. and no part of the lot under Market Street passes to B. But it is believed the general rule stated above should apply and that the stake on the north side line of Market Street is but a measuring point from which the area to be conveyed is to be identified, and that the location of that stake does not, in the absence of other factors, constitute a basis for determining the grantor's intention as to the area to be conveyed. The reason for the rule is this: that the only purpose which the retention in the grantor of a narrow strip of land in a street can possibly serve is to be the subject in the future of vexatious litigation. Such possibility is eliminated by construing the deed in B's favor. This application of the rule may be more policy than logic but it is valid. The truth is that the parties actually rarely think of the strip in the road when the transaction is made. See the leading case Hoban v. Cable, 102 Mich. 206, 60 N.W. 466 (1894); Low v. Tibbets, 72 Me. 92 (1881); Burby, 308.

Note

Another rule of construction is that COURSES GOVERN OVER DISTANCES in the calls of a deed when the two are in conflict. To illustrate, suppose the third call in a deed is from a point to a given line on the side of a road south of said point. The deed reads, "then south to the road a distance of 66 feet, such line forming a right angle with the line on the north side of said road". The fact is that a line between the point and the line and forming a right angle therewith will be exactly 60 feet long. If the line is to be 66 feet, then it will do one of three things as it swings in an arc: it will go 6 feet past the line; or it will form either an acute or an obtuse angle with such line. In such case the COURSE, the direction of the line from the point to the road and making a right angle therewith, will govern over the length of the line, the DISTANCE, and the deed will be so construed that the line will be 60 instead of 66 feet in length. See Hall v. Eaton, 139 Mass. 217, 29 N.E. 660 (1885); Burby, 308. Suppose the lengths of two lines in a deed both cannot be correct. One or the other must be in error. In such case there is an ambiguity and parol evidence is admissible to explain what was actually done on the ground. In Temple v. Benson, 213 Mass. 128, 100 N.E. 63 (1912), the court permitted a remote grantor to testify to the boundaries as they were marked out on the ground.

————

CASE 229: A owns Blackacre, a quarter section of land which abuts Lincoln Highway, a road 80 feet wide, on the north. The south 40 feet of Blackacre is covered by the pavement of Lincoln Highway. In his deed to B as grantee, A uses this language, "thence south to a point on the north side line of Lincoln Highway, thence along the north side line of said Highway to the place of beginning, being a steel stake in the north side line of said Highway." The rest of the description was accurate as to Blackacre lying north of Lincoln Highway. Lincoln Highway was then abandoned and B took possession of and struck oil on the 40 feet of Blackacre which had been used as part of said Highway. A sues to eject B from said 40 foot strip. May A recover?

Answer and Analysis

The answer is no according to the better view. The cases are not uniform on the question. The specific question is this: when the description in the deed describes two points or a line which constitutes one side of a monument, such as a road, street, highway, stream, alley or the like, and the grantor owns to the center of the monument, does the description carry title to the grantee to the center of the monument, or does the grantor retain the strip between the side line and the center of the monument? In logic it can be said that two points determine a line and a line determines a boundary. The grantor has described the boundary line of the land conveyed as the "side line" of the Highway. Hence, no part of the Highway passes to the grantee. The result is that the strip in the highway still belongs to A and A can eject B. Some cases so hold and their logic is unassailable.

The contrary view is this. The general rule, that when a description carries the boundary of land conveyed to a monument such as a street, stream, road and the like, title to the center of the monument passes to the grantee, should apply unless the strip between the center and the side line thereof is expressly excluded from the grant. This view is based on policy and seeks to avoid vexatious litigation which may and does arise by the grantor's retention of long narrow strips of land. Such litigation is just about the only purpose which such retention of title can serve, for until the street is abandoned the grantor is in no position to make a beneficial use thereof. But what of the intention of the grantor? Under this view the following may be said. The parties usually do not think of the strip under the monument when the deed is delivered. Their minds do not advert thereto. Of course, the grantor has the right to retain such strip, and also the grantee would have the right to reject the deal if the strip were retained. However, it is not inconsistent with the general rule allowing title to the center of the monument to pass to the grantee, to treat the two points, or the line on the side of the highway where it is more convenient to place stakes than in the road, not as a boundary line as such, but merely as the measuring points from which to identify the land conveyed, and indicating the side of the road on which the land lies. Thus the grantor's intention may be found as granting to the middle of the highway or road. It is believed such is the better rule and that the grantee, B, owns to the center of what was Lincoln Highway and that A cannot eject him.

See Salter v. Jones, 39 N.J.L. 469 (E. & A.1877), where the court quotes: "The rule, therefore, which the Pennsylvania courts regard as the true one, and which, perhaps, on the whole is the wisest one, would seem to be that nothing short of an intention expressed in ipsis verbis, to 'exclude' the soil of the highway, can exclude it;" and 58 A.L.R. 231 where the West Virginia court in 1928 rejected the rule. See also 42 A.L.R. 228; Tiffany, p. 434; Burby, 308–309.

Note

The student should notice three fact situations:

(a) The description is to and along a road, but no point on the side of the monument is given.

(b) The description is to or from a point on the side of the road and along the road. Here one point is fixed.

(c) The description is to or from a point on the side of the road and along the side line of the road. Here two points are fixed.

Solutions of the cases are as follows: All the cases solve (a) by giving the grantee to the middle of the road. In situation (b) some cases hold for the grantee and some for the grantor. The same is true in situation (c). The "catch all" rule applied in Case 229 solves all three cases the same way. It gives the grantee title to the land to the middle of the road or stream or alley, unless the grantor in the deed expressly excludes the portion in the road or stream or monument.

––––––––

CASE 230: A owned Blackacre in fee simple which consisted of a tract 180 feet square and bounded on the north by the line AB, on the east by the line DA, on the south by the line CD and on the west by the line BC. A was at the northeast corner, B at the northwest corner, C at the southwest corner and D at the southeast corner. A executed his deed to a portion of Blackacre to B and therein used the following language to describe the tract conveyed, to wit: "I grant to B that certain portion of Blackacre bounded as follows, on the east by the line AD, on the north by the line AM which is the easterly 100 feet of the line AB, on the south by the line DN which is the easterly 100 feet of the line DC and on the west by the line joining the two points M and N, which enclosed tract is the easterly one half of my Blackacre". B fenced in the easterly 100 feet of Blackacre which left the westerly 80 feet thereof in the possession of A. A sues B to eject him from the westerly 10 feet within B's fence. May A succeed?

Answer and Analysis

The answer is no. It is obvious that the first part of the description in the deed defines with particularity the boundary lines of the east 100 feet of Blackacre. It is just as obvious that the east 100 feet of such tract is more than half thereof by an excess of 10 feet in width. Consequently, if B owns such 100 feet to the east, then A has only 80 feet to the west and has retained less than half of Blackacre. Here, then is a conflict between a specific description or description by metes and bounds on the one hand, and a general description by fractional part or area on the other. In such case the rule is well settled that the clear specific description governs over the general description which is inconsistent therewith. Applying such rule to our set of facts, title to the east 100 feet of Blackacre passes to B, and A's general description that such property conveyed was one-half of Blackacre has no force and effect. See Morse v. Kelley, 305 Mass. 504, 26 N.E.2d 326, 127 A.L.R. 1037 (1940); Burby, 308.

---

2.   ACCRETION

(See Legal Gems 18–21, *supra*.)

---

3.   EXCEPTIONS AND RESERVATIONS

(See Legal Gems 22–24 above.)

CASE 231:   A, being the fee simple owner of Blackacre, used the following language in his deed in favor of B as grantee, to-wit: "I hereby grant to B and his heirs my Blackacre except the east half thereof and except the standing timber on Blackacre and except the coal under Blackacre". What interest did B take under the deed?

Answer and Analysis

The answer is this—B took the west half of Blackacre minus the standing timber thereon and minus the coal thereunder. An exception merely subtracts from the entire tract described in a deed, some corporeal portion thereof which is not to pass to the grantee and is to remain in the grantor unaffected by the deed or conveyance. Of course the portion excepted must be clearly described so that it can be identified, and it must not except the entire subject matter of the deed in which case there would be total repugnancy, and the deed would operate without the exception. Such exception would be void. The deed given describes Blackacre. It then, by exception, subtracts therefrom or from its operation, the east half thereof, all the standing timber on the whole tract, and all the coal under the entire tract. That leaves for the conveyance to operate upon the west half of Blackacre, less the standing timber thereon, and less the coal thereunder. Such is the property granted to B. It should be noted that all three subjects of exception, the east half, the standing timber and the coal, are all corporeal property, and they are retained by the grantor, unaffected by the deed. The grantor can dispose of such excepted property by deed or by will, and such will descend in intestacy to his heirs. See Burby, 69; Tiffany, pp. 240, 421.

CASE 232: A, being fee simple owner of Whiteacre and Blackacre which abutted each other, and there being a visible roadway from a highway to the house on Whiteacre running across Blackacre (a quasi-easement), executed his deed in favor of B as grantee to Blackacre, and used these words in the conveyance, to wit: "I hereby grant Blackacre to B and his heirs, reserving to me and my heirs an easement from my house on Whiteacre to the highway along our usual roadway". (a) What interest was conveyed to B? (b) What interest, if any, was retained by A in Blackacre?

Answers and Analyses

The answers are as follows: (a) B received Blackacre in fee simple burdened with an easement appurtenant in favor of Whiteacre, and (b) A retained in Blackacre an easement appurtenant to Whiteacre in the way running from the house on Whiteacre across Blackacre to the highway over the road which had been the usual way of passage thereto.

In the field of exceptions and reservations in the common law, history has played an important role which cannot be ignored when solving cases on those subjects. In England, a reservation created a right or incorporeal interest which was theretofore non-existent, and which issued out of the land as a feudal service. Perhaps rent would be the only present concept to which it could apply. In England it was created as a "regrant". It was considered that the grantor conveyed the entire property to the grantee free from any burden, then the grantee in the same deed "regranted" the interest reserved to the grantor. But this was possible in England where both grantor and grantee signed or sealed the deed. But such theory could hardly work in this country where only the grantor usually signs the deed. How, then, did our courts reach the result given as the answer above? They solved the case given as though it were an exception rather than a reservation. Because exceptions applied only to presently existing interests, such concept could not be applied to an easement or profit which was to be newly created by the deed and which did not exist before. So the courts simply took the view that a "quasi-easement" (case in which the grantor had two properties and used one to serve the other, which, of course, in law, was no easement at all for one could not have an easement in his own land), constituted a sufficiently existing "present interest" to be the subject of an exception. By so treating the matter in our case, the grantor, A, simply excepted his "quasi-easement" over Blackacre, and it became an actual easement over the now servient tenement, Blackacre, in favor of the dominant tenement, Whiteacre, which was retained by A. It will be noticed that the given set of facts presents a case with a "quasi-easement".

Suppose, however, that Blackacre had never been used by A to serve Whiteacre when he owned both Blackacre and Whiteacre. The same fiction obtains and the same result was achieved and A was considered the owner of an easement over Blackacre without any previously existing quasi-easement. After all, if a "quasi-easement" which is no easement at all, can be made into an easement just by calling it such, the courts had no difficulty in saying a non-existing "quasi-easement" is an easement, if the grantor so intended. The result is that the word reservation may now actually create a new, incorporeal interest in the grantor in the land conveyed, whether it be easement or profit, which was not a feudal service and which did not issue out of the land.

Another item needs attention. Notice that the set of facts given uses words of inheritance, "reserving to me *and my heirs*" an easement, etc. Words of inheritance were never necessary in an exception because exceptions were simply unaffected by the conveyance. But on the theory of a regrant in a reservation, only an easement or profit for life of the grantor could be created unless words of inheritance were used. And some cases held such reservation lasted only for the lifetime of the grantor and could not be claimed by his heirs. Of course, in a jurisdiction which has a statute dispensing with words of inheritance to create an estate of inheritance (fee simple or fee tail), the easement or profit reserved to the grantor without using the words "and his heirs" could last beyond his lifetime. Reverting to our questions and answers then, it may be seen that the answers are correct on one theory or fiction or another, and that the results carry out the intention of the grantor. Thus, after the conveyance given, B owns Blackacre as a servient tenement and A owns Whiteacre as a dominant tenement. See Restatement of Property §§ 472, 473; Tiffany, pp. 240, 421; Burby, 69, 70.

CASE 233: A owned Blackacre in fee simple. B owned Whiteacre in fee simple. These properties abutted each other and were so situated that a road over Blackacre would be a great convenience to Whiteacre as a much shorter way to go to and from a small town, Z, nearby. A executed a deed to his Blackacre in which he used the following language, "I hereby grant Blackacre to X and his heirs, reserving to B and his heirs a way across Blackacre in favor of Whiteacre to town, Z, such way to be over a 10 foot strip along the east edge of Blackacre". The deed was delivered to X. B starts to use the road described in the deed. X seeks to enjoin such use by B. Should the injunction issue?

Answer and Analysis

The answer is no. X's suit must be based on the proposition laid down in the cases that a reservation must be wholly and solely for the benefit of the grantor or conveyor and in favor of no one else. In this case the reservation, if it be such, is in favor of B, a third party to the deed. Here is another case in which history on the one side conflicts with logic, common sense and the intention of the grantor on the other. History dictates that an exception or a reservation can be in favor of the grantor only. Obviously the way attempted to be created in favor of B cannot be an exception for it was not in existence before the deed. Also, it must be admitted that there is no grant to B of an easement in ipsis verbis. It seems fair to assume, however, from the very words of the instrument taken as a whole, that the grantor A intended to create in B an easement appurtenant to Whiteacre. In logic there is no reason why a grantor cannot in the same deed create a possessory estate in one person and an easement in another. Perhaps no one would question the effectiveness of A's deed had it read, "I hereby grant to B and his heirs an easement appurtenant to Whiteacre over my Blackacre over a 10 foot strip along the east edge of Blackacre, and thereafter I hereby grant Blackacre, subject to such easement in favor of B and his heirs, to X and his heirs." No one could question A's power to create such interests had A used two instruments, first, one to B granting the easement, and second, one to X creating the fee. It should make no difference that two interests, one possessory and the other nonpossessory, are created in the same instrument if such be the intention. If these propositions be true, then the fact that A used the word "reserving" instead of "granting", or "I hereby grant", should be immaterial, provided A intended to create in B an easement over Blackacre. It seems clear that A so intended. Thus, X takes Blackacre subject to B's easement, and the injunction should be refused. This seems the better rule. See Restatement of Property §§ 572, 573; Burby, 71.

See also Willard v. First Church of Christ Scientist, Pacifica, 7 Cal.3d 473, 102 Cal.Rptr. 739, 498 P.2d 987 (1972), upholding a reservation in favor of a third party. The deed to X contained a provision "subject to an easement . . . parking . . . for the benefit of [Y] Church . . ." The court repudiated the old rule of no reservation in favor of a third party, and gave effect to the intent of the parties.

Note

It seems safe to say that the intention of the grantor in a deed should be carried out irrespective of whether he has used the word "exception" or "reservation"; that cases have used the words interchangeably; that the reasons for the historical limitations on the use of the word "reservation" have long since disappeared and so should such limitations. Tiffany, Abridged Edition, on page 423 says this: "In construing conveyances creating, or attempting to create, rights in the land granted in favor of the grantor, the courts will construe the language used as an exception or a reservation, according to the nature of the rights sought to be created, and hold that a 'reservation' is an exception and that an 'exception' is a reservation".

SUMMARY OF CASES IN CHAPTER XX

1. DESCRIPTION AND BOUNDARIES

See Text for explanation of rectangular system of surveys.

Case 225. No conveyance is valid unless the description of the land sought to be conveyed is sufficient to identify the land.

Case 226. The courts will give effect to the language of the instrument of conveyance if possible, even making the parties tenants in common when an undescribed "piece" of land is mentioned but which was to be a distinct fractional part of the whole tract.

Case 227. If a deed in its description of the land to be conveyed refers to a map or plat, such reference makes such map or plat a part and parcel of the deed for the purpose of identifying the land.

Case 228. (a) If in the description in a deed there is a conflict between the calls of a deed as to courses and distances on the one hand, and monuments, natural or artificial, on the other, the monuments will govern over the courses and distances. (b) When the description in a deed carries it "to", "by", "from" or "along" a street, road, alley, way, highway, creek, stream or similar monument, the common law rule is that the grantee takes title to the center of such street, road, alley, way, highway, creek, stream or similar monument, provided the grantor owns to the center of such monument. (c) Courses govern over distances.

Case 229. If the description in a deed is carried to two points constituting a line or the "side line" of a street, road, alley, way, highway, creek, stream or similar monument, still the grantee takes title to the center of such monument unless in express words the grantor excludes any part of such monument from the operation of the deed. This is considered the better rule but many cases are contra.

Case 230. When there is a conflict in the description in a deed between a specific description or description by metes and bounds on the one hand, and a general description by fractional part or area on the other, the clear specific description will govern over the general description.

3. EXCEPTIONS AND RESERVATIONS

(See Legal Gems 22–24 above)

Case 231. An exception in a deed merely subtracts from the entire tract described in the deed some corporeal portion thereof which is not to pass to the grantee, but is to remain in the grantor wholly unaffected by the deed or conveyance, and such portion must be sufficiently described so that it can be identified.

Case 232. This case distinguishes exceptions and reservations as they existed at common law, the former applying only to corporeal property which remained in the grantor wholly unaffected by the conveyance, and a reservation being limited to incorporeal rights newly created by the deed and issuing out of the land as a feudal service, such as rent. In the United States today both easements and profits may be created by "reserving" such to the grantor if such be his intention. Indeed, the intention of the grantor will govern whether the word "exception" or "reservation" is used. Words of inheritance never had to be used in case of an exception. Such words must be used in creating a reservation to last longer than the grantor's lifetime unless a statute dispenses with such in the creation of a fee simple estate.

Case 233. A reservation of an easement made in favor of a third party to the deed should be valid if such be the intention of the parties. Most cases, however, hold that a reservation can be in favor of no one other than the grantor. Of course, an exception, being unaffected by the conveyance, remains solely in the grantor.

Chapter XXI

COVENANTS FOR TITLE AND WARRANTIES OF FITNESS

1. Covenants for Title.
   Legal Gems.
   Cases.

2. Warranty of Fitness or Habitability.
   Legal Gems.
   Cases.

Summary of Cases in Chapter XXI.

---

1. COVENANTS FOR TITLE

LEGAL GEMS

1. There are six covenants for title to real property:

   a. Three of these are in the present tense and are breached, if at all, when the deed is delivered:

   (1) Covenant for seisin

   (2) Covenant of the right to convey

   (3) Covenant against incumbrances.

   b. Three of these cover breaches which occur after the deed is delivered, that is, in the future:

   (4) Covenant for quiet enjoyment

   (5) Covenant of general warranty

   (6) Covenant for further assurances.

2. A deed providing for "usual covenants" is construed to include the first five covenants given above, and a deed providing for "full covenants" is construed to give protection afforded under all six of the covenants listed.

3. Covenants for seisin and of the right to convey are usually construed as synonymous and guarantee to the grantee that the grantor owns the estate which the deed purports to convey. Of course, a grantor conveying under a power could have a right to convey without being seized of an estate; and if in a particular jurisdiction seizin is construed as meaning only being in possession and claiming title, then an owner when the land is in the adverse possession of another may have a right to convey without being seized, and similarly, an adverse possessor would be seized without a right to convey a fee.

4. The covenant against incumbrances is a guarantee to the grantee that the property conveyed is not subject to outstanding

455

rights or interests which would diminish the value of the land, examples of which are mortgages, liens, restrictions on use of land, easements, or profits.

The existence of zoning restrictions does not constitute a breach of the covenant against incumbrances, but the existence of a violation of zoning or building restrictions may constitute such a breach. Cribbet, 276.

5. Covenants of quiet enjoyment and covenant of general warranty are construed to have the same legal effect. They undertake to defend the grantee-covenantee against all lawful claims of the grantor himself or of third persons who would evict the grantee-covenantee, actually or constructively.

6. The covenant for further assurance (not much used in the United States) is an undertaking on the grantor's part to do such further necessary acts within his power to perfect the grantee's title.

7. None of these covenants protects the grantee against the trespass or aggression of a mere wrongdoer.

8. The construction of these covenants, which are varied by the language used in each case, is governed by the principles of contract law.

9. Under the traditional view, the first three covenants cannot run with the land because they become personal choses in action when they are breached at the very time the deed is delivered. (But see Note following Case 237.)

10. The last three covenants are covenants which run with the land and can be enforced by remote grantees who take through the covenantee.

11. More than one remote grantee may enforce a given covenant which runs with the land. E. g., A conveys to B in fee with covenant of general warranty. B conveys the east half of the property to C and the west half to D. Each is evicted by O who has paramount title. Both C and D may hold A on his covenant.

12. Covenants for title are in their nature contracts of indemnity and damage must be shown as a condition precedent to recovery for breach thereof; it is not enough merely that there has been a breach.

13. The maximum recovery for breach of title covenants in a large majority of jurisdictions is the purchase price paid plus interest.

Interest is usually allowed only when the grantee has not had possession or the benefits of rents or profits from the land, or has had to surrender them to the holder of the paramount title. Additionally, the grantee can usually recover the costs of his unsuccessful defense of the title.

14. In case of a total breach of the covenant of seisin or right to convey, the measure of damages is the purchase price paid plus interest. These covenants are breached, if at all, on delivery of the

deed. In the case of a partial breach, recovery is for a proportionate part of the purchase price plus interest.

15. For breach of the covenant against incumbrances, the measure of damages is the cost of removing the incumbrance when that is possible, and the amount by which such incumbrance reduces the value of the land when removal is not possible.

16. For a breach of the covenants of quiet enjoyment and warranty, the measure of damages is the value of the land at the time of breach (eviction) but not to exceed the purchase price paid by the plaintiff-grantee. For a partial breach, recovery is based on the amount expended by the plaintiff to perfect his title, or on the value of the land lost to the superior title.

17. When a covenant for title runs with the land an intermediate grantee often occupies a dual role. He is a covenantor as to subsequent grantees if he included the covenant in the deed when he conveyed, and he is a covenantee as to prior grantees. For such intermediate grantee to maintain an action against the original covenantor, or a prior covenantor, he must show both (a) a breach of the covenant and (b) damage to himself.

E. g., A conveys to B with covenant of general warranty or quiet enjoyment. B conveys to C with like covenant. C conveys to D with like covenant. X evicts D because of paramount title. B sues A for the breach. B cannot maintain the action by merely showing the breach by D's eviction. He must show in addition that D or C has sued him, B, and that B has been made to pay damages. Then only does B have a right to indemnity because that is the actual contract made by A.

18. Each remote grantee has a right to judgment on a covenant running with the land against each and all of the preceding covenantors when the covenant is breached, but such remote grantee has a right to but one full recovery. E. g., A conveys to B with covenant of general warranty or quiet enjoyment. B conveys to C with like covenant. C conveys to D with like covenant. D is evicted by X who has paramount title. D sues and takes judgment for $10,000.00 damage against C, B and A. C pays D in full. C then has a cause over against B and A. B pays C in full. B then has a cause over against A.

19. Payment in full made by the original covenantor to the evicted last covenantee-grantee for his damage, constitutes a good defense to such original covenantor to any action by an intermediate covenantee-grantee.

E. g., A conveys to B with covenant of general warranty or quiet enjoyment. B conveys to C. C conveys to D. D is evicted by X who has paramount title. A pays D in full for his damage. B then sues A for breach. A's payment to D is a complete defense to B's action because B can show no damage. But suppose B has also paid D in full for his damage. If such payment was after A's payment to D, then A's payment is still a good defense and B's remedy is against D for overpayment for money had and received. If B's payment was made to D before A's payment, then it would seem B's action may be maintained against A and A must look to D for reimbursement.

20. As a general rule, no warranties are implied in a conveyance of real property, and covenants must be specifically inserted to be effective, although so-called "short-forms" are allowed by legislatures in many states. These statutory deeds incorporate by reference the covenants designated in the statute.

21. The rule of Gem 20 of not implying covenants in deeds is accurate in relation to covenants for title and should be so limited. In present times there is a growing trend to imply a covenant of fitness in the sale of new homes. See part 2 infra.

22. Title covenants, of course can be modified so as to exclude certain mortgages, restrictive covenants, or other outstanding interests.

When the land is conveyed specifically subject to certain interests, as for example, an outstanding mortgage in accordance with the understanding of the parties, the title covenants should be construed as warranting only the estate granted, that is, subject to the mortgage. This construction should apply whether or not the covenants are expressly so modified, but there are some cases to the contrary, especially older ones. See, for example, case 242 infra, relating to estoppel by deed, and whether the title covenants should be construed independently of the granting clause.

23. The type of deed to be conveyed, if not stipulated in the sales contract, will be the type determined by the custom of the community.

See Tiffany, Vol. 4, § 999 et seq.; 21 C.J.S. 907 et seq.; 20 Am. Jur.2d 615; Chicago, Mobile Development Co. v. G. C. Coggin Co., 259 Ala. 152, 66 So.2d 151 (1953).

————

CASE 234: D executed a deed conveying Blackacre in fee simple to P and in the deed covenanted that "D is lawfully seised in fee simple of such premises; that he has good right and lawful authority to sell the same". This deed was delivered in April 1950. In October 1962 P sued D alleging that "D's covenants are not true; that D was not seised of Blackacre and had no good right or authority to convey the same". The statute of limitations of ten years is set up as a bar. Has the statute run?

Answer and Analysis

The answer is yes. The plaintiff alleges that defendant has broken the covenants of seisin and of right to convey. These two covenants are synonymous and constitute a guarantee by the grantor, D, that he owns the land when the deed is executed and delivered. If then D did not own the land when he made the conveyance, these covenants were immediately broken in April 1950. There being more than 10 years elapsed between the breach which gave rise to the cause of action in April 1950 and the time when the action was brought in October 1962, the statute of limitations has run and constitutes a bar. See Mitchell v. Kepler, 75 Iowa 207, 39 N.W. 241 (1888); Bernklau v. Stevens, 150 Colo. 187, 371 P.2d 765, 95 A. L.R.2d 905 (1962); Powell, ¶¶ 896, 897.

CASE 235: T owned Blackacre in fee simple and in his will devised such land to his friend, D. T died and it was discovered that one of the two required witnesses on the will was not qualified. Hence, the will was invalid and Blackacre descended to T's heir, H. In the meantime and after T's death, D had conveyed Blackacre to P for $4,000.00 with covenant for quiet enjoyment and of general warranty. P is in possession of Blackacre and is threatened with eviction by H. P pays H $5,000.00 for a deed in fee simple to Blackacre and sues D for damages for breach of his covenants. May he recover, and if so how much?

Answers and Analyses

The answer is yes, P may recover. These two covenants are construed to mean substantially the same thing, and bind the covenantor to defend the grantee against eviction, actual or constructive, by anyone under paramount title, including the covenantor. They are breached when the covenantee is disturbed in his enjoyment of the premises conveyed. In this case it is obvious that H, being the heir of T, and the will under which D claimed being invalid, held paramount title. It is also clear that had H ejected P either by action or physically, P would have had a cause of action against D for breach of the covenants made. But actual eviction is not necessary to a claim. Constructive eviction is sufficient. In this case the assertion of paramount title by H and P's paying him for such, is constructive eviction which will support a claim for breach of the covenants made in D's deed. Of course, in his suit against the covenantor for damages the plaintiff-covenantee must prove that he was evicted by one having paramount title.

The damage which P can recover is usually the consideration paid which in this case is $4,000.00 and not the value of the land at the time of the eviction. When there are legal proceedings to evict the grantee, if such grantee would bind or estopp the covenantor by the judgment itself, he must give the covenantor notice of the proceedings and request that he defend the action. Even without such notice to the covenantor, if the grantee-covenantee is evicted, he may still recover from the covenantor but he has a heavier burden in having to prove that the party who evicted him had a paramount title. As to the measure of damages for breach of such covenants there should not, in principle, be any difference between the breach of this kind of a contract and any other kind. But there is a difference. In this case P can recover the value of the land, measured by the consideration paid at the time of the conveyance, which is $4,000.00, with interest, not from the time of its payment but from the time of the eviction. The covenantee should not have both interest on his money and use of the land and he has had the latter until eviction. See Tiffany, Vol. 4, ¶¶ 899–900; Burby, 313–319; Haley v. Morgan, 13 Ann. Cas. 206 and note following Powell ¶ 908.

CASE 236: A owned Blackacre in fee simple worth $10,000.00 on which land A executed to X a mortgage of $5,000.00. A then conveyed Blackacre to B in fee simple with a covenant against incumbrances. X threatened foreclosure and B paid off the mortgage with interest. B now sues A for breach of the covenant. May he recover?

Answer and Analysis

The answer is yes. First, it is clear that A's covenant against incumbrances was breached the very instant he conveyed to B because the incumbrance of the mortgage burdened Blackacre at that time. Second, the recovery by B on the covenant should be the loss which the breach has caused B. In this case it would be the amount which B has been compelled to pay X in principal and interest, with interest thereon from the time of such payment. This is compensation for an actual damage done, the covenant being one of indemnity. But suppose the mortgagee never forecloses or threatens to foreclose and B is never called upon to pay off the incumbrance. In such case there is a breach of covenant but no actual damage and B can recover merely nominal damages. If the statute of limitations is 6 years on the covenant and 10 years on the right of foreclosure, it would be possible for the mortgagee to wait so long to foreclose that the covenantee would actually be limited to his cause for nominal damages. If the incumbrance is not one measured in money like the note and mortgage given, but one such as an easement, restrictive covenant, or a lease, then the measure of damages is the difference between the value of the land with and without such incumbrance. See In re Meehan's Estate, 30 Wis.2d 428, 141 N.W.2d 218 (1966), indicating that substantial encroachment would be an encumbrance but finding no damages; Burby, 318, 319; Tiffany, Vol. 4, ¶ 898; note 61 A.L.R. 10.

CASE 237: O owned Blackacre in fee simple. A, who was in possession of Blackacre, conveyed the land to B with "the usual covenants" of title. B paid A $4,000 for the property and took possession. B conveyed the property to C for $4,000 and C took possession. O ejects C from the land and

C brings suit against A for breach of covenants in the deed. May he recover?

Answer and Analysis

The answer is yes, but not on all of the covenants. First, A's "usual covenants" include: (a) covenant of seisin; (b) covenant of right to convey; (c) covenant against incumbrances; (d) covenant of quiet enjoyment; and (e) covenant of general warranty. Of course, A is liable on his covenants, but to whom? He made them to B. B is not suing A. B's assignee is suing A. The assignee, C, was no party to the covenants and cannot be unless the covenants "run" with the land conveyed to him by the covenantee, B. So the question resolves itself into this: which, if any, of the five covenants runs with the land? The answer to such question is this: the first two covenants were breached at the very instant the deed was delivered from A to B and at that instant became choses in action which B held against A personally. Such a chose cannot run with the land because it is no longer a covenant and because it was not expressly assigned by B to C. (Some contrary cases hold either that the covenant runs, or that the deed itself constitutes an assignment of the chose in action, so as to permit the grantee, C, to hold A liable.) Hence, in most jurisdictions C cannot maintain the action against A on the first two covenants. One can hardly say the third covenant, the one against incumbrances, is involved when A had no title at all to Blackacre. But, if it were such, it would be breached at once and would not run with the land to C.

The fourth and fifth covenants which can be breached only after the delivery of the deed, that is, in the future, were breached when O evicted C. At that time C had a cause of action if, and only if, such covenants "ran" with the estate which B conveyed to C. If the benefit of these covenants was attached to the land as it passed from B to C, then C can enforce it against A. For such covenants to run there must be an intention not only that the covenant shall protect the immediate covenantee but also any of his successors, heirs, grantees and assignees, who take the land from the covenantee and who may be evicted by paramount title such as O held in this case. And there must be privity of estate which seems in this connection, to mean no more than that the person attempting to enforce the covenant has succeeded to the interest of the covenantee. In our given case it would seem clear that A's fourth and fifth covenants were intended to protect anyone who took through A's deed containing the covenants if such covenants are to be given their ordinary meaning and the owners of the land, including remote grantees, were to be given full protection. And, of course, there was privity of estate between the covenantee, B, and C, the plaintiff. Consequently, C can recover against A on the covenants of quiet enjoyment and general warranty but not on those of seisin, of right to convey and against incumbrances. See Solberg v. Robinson, 34 S.D. 55, 147 N.W. 87 (1914); Burby, 316–318; Tiffany, pp. 446–448; Chicago, Mobile Develop-

ment Co. v. G. C. Coggin Co., 259 Ala. 152, 66 So.2d 151 (1953); Peters v. Bowman, 98 U.S. 56, 25 L.Ed. 91 (1878); Bernklau v. Stevens,
150 Colo. 187, 371 P.2d 765, 95 A.L.R.2d 905 (1962), holding that
purpose of statute providing that covenant shall run is not to change
the time of the accrual of the cause of action, but rather to extend
the benefit of such covenants to subsequent purchasers and encumbrancers.

Note

The solution in the case above represents the American view by
the great majority of the cases. But it is worth while looking at the
opposite side of that holding. A conveys to B with covenant of seisin
which means that A covenants that he is, at the time he gives the
deed, seised of the property. The fact is that he is not seised at all
and has no interest in the property. Then B conveys to C and the
real owner, X, evicts C. C has paid B full value for the land. C now
sues A for breach of the covenant. The purpose of the covenant is to
give security to the grantee, immediate or remote. Today many
technicalities have been erased from our real property law and choses
in action are readily assignable. This covenant is no good to B after
he has conveyed for full value to C. The only one needing the security of the covenant is the last owner who has been evicted by paramount title. This is C in our case. Chancellor Kent called the doctrine that the covenant could not run with the land because it was
breached at the instant the deed was given, a mere "technical scru-
ple". It prevents justice and takes the indemnity from C, the very
person who should have it. The deed should be considered as an assignment of the chose in action from B to C and C should have an action against the covenantor, A, because C alone has suffered from the
breach. See Schofield v. Iowa Homestead Co., 32 Iowa 317, 7 Am.
Rep. 197 (1871) which follows the English rule in principle.

2. WARRANTY OF FITNESS OR HABITABILITY

LEGAL GEMS

1. At common law covenants for title or other warranties had
to be expressed in the deed—they were not implied. Warranties or
representations in the sales contract did not survive the consummation of the transaction. After closing, the rights of the buyer, except
for possible actions based on fraud, duress or mistake, depended upon
covenants contained in the deed.

2. In recent years many states have rejected the doctrine of caveat emptor in the sale of housing, particularly in the sale of new
housing, and have held that there is an implied warranty of fitness or
habitability in the sale of such units.

3. The possibility of disclaimer or waiver of the implied covenant of fitness has not been extensively litigated. If the obligation is
contractual, then it would seem that a clear and unambiguous waiver

intelligently agreed to should be enforced, but if strict liability is imposed on the basis of products liability, then such waiver would probably be ineffective and not upheld.

Cf. Tibbitts v. Openshaw, 18 Utah 2d 442, 425 P.2d 160 (1967), giving effect to an "as is" provision in the contract, with Casavant v. Campopiano, 114 R.I. 24, 327 A.2d 831 (1974), holding that a provision that the purchasers were taking the premises "in the same condition in which they now are" was not sufficiently specific to exclude implied warranties. At the very least, attempted disclaimers will be strictly construed.

CASE 238: A purchased a new home from B, a builder-vendor. Within a year of A's occupancy, the septic tank system had backed up to a depth of three inches in A's basement. A called B and informed him of the situation. B dug down to the discharge pipe, perforated the line, and let the sewage flow into an open trench. B refused to do anything further. The stench became increasingly unbearable. A had to have the septic tank replaced at a cost of $2,000 because of the inadequacy of B's original installation. A brings an action against B for the recovery of the expenses incurred in installing the new system. Will A prevail? Why or why not?

Answers and Analyses

The answer is that A will prevail according to a growing number of recent cases. According to these cases, recovery of the $2,000 is predicated on an implied warranty of fitness in the sale of a new house by a builder-vendor. The judicial trend is away from the harsh results of caveat emptor and toward the more equitable doctrine of implied warranty of fitness in cases involving sales of new houses by builder-vendors. The doctrine of caveat emptor was based on arms-length transactions and contemplated comparable skill and experience. In view of modern technology and marketing practices, these circumstances no longer exist. The purchaser of a house generally has neither the bargaining power to insist on a warranty, nor the expertise to detect what could be wrong with the workmanship. Today's purchaser of a new house *must* rely on the builder-vendor's expertise and knowledge. Therefore, the courts adopting this modern rule infer an understanding between the buyer and the builder-vendor that the house will be reasonably fit for habitation, in other words, an implied warranty of fitness or habitability. Tavares v. Horstman, 542 P.2d 1275 (Wyo.1975); David v. B & J Holding Corp., 349 So.2d 676 (Fla. 3d D.C.A.1977).

Note: Parameters of the Doctrine—Privity Consideration

Casavant v. Campopiano, 114 R.I. 24, 327 A.2d 831 (1974), also involved the doctrine of implied warranty of fitness. In this case the purchasers of a home discovered a defective roof and sought to recover damages from the builder-vendor. Prior to the sale the builder-vendor had rented the home to a married couple for a year. The Rhode Island Supreme Court applied the doctrine of implied warranty of fitness despite the intervening occupancy. The court felt that the intervening occupancy should not per se deprive the buyers of the implied warranty of fitness. The court stated that the very purpose of the doctrine was to protect buyers from overreaching by knowledgeable builder-vendors. The court also rejected the argument that the intervening occupancy rendered the home "used" instead of "new." The court felt that the intervening occupancy was neither causally connected with the defective condition of the roof, nor of such an extended duration as to make the application of warranties unreasonable.

Other cases involving an implied warranty of fitness are: Bethlahmy v. Bechtel, 91 Idaho 55, 415 P.2d 698 (1966); Humber v. Morton, 426 S.W.2d 554 (Tex.1968); Gable v. Silver, 258 So.2d 11 (Fla. 4th D.C.A.1972), involving a condominium.

A very liberal extension of the implied warranty of fitness doctrine is expressed in Berman v. Watergate West, Inc., 391 A.2d 1351 (D.C.App.1978), which authorized recovery by a tenant shareholder in a cooperative (see Chapter XXIX infra, as to cooperatives), against a defendant company, a subsidiary of the sponsor of the project, which marketed the apartments, and also authorized recovery against the sponsor of the project, and also against the builder, another subsidiary of the sponsor, although there was no privity of contract between the plaintiff and any of the defendants.

In *Berman*, the court, reversing a directed verdict for the defendants, held that each of the defendant entities was an integral part of an overall producing and marketing enterprise that placed a defective product into the stream of commerce, and each of them *could* be held accountable to the ultimate consumer for damage caused by the defective product. The court decided that the law of products liability should apply even if the sale of a cooperative unit did not appear as a sale of "goods," since such liability does apply to the sale of new homes. The difference between tort and warranty or contract law was minimized, and the case was remanded.

SUMMARY OF CASES IN CHAPTER XXI

1. COVENANTS FOR TITLE

Case 234. Covenants of seisin and right to convey are synonymous in most instances. They covenant that the grantor owns the land when the deed is executed and delivered. If he does not own the land these covenants are breached immediately and a cause of action accrues at the time of the delivery of the deed.

Case 235. The covenants for quiet enjoyment and of general warranty are generally construed to mean the same thing. They bind the covenantor to defend the grantee-covenantee against eviction, actual or constructive, by anyone under paramount title, including the covenantor. These covenants are breached when the covenantee is disturbed in his enjoyment of the premises conveyed.   Actual eviction need not take place. If a valid paramount title is asserted and the grantee is compelled, to avoid actual eviction, to buy title from the holder of the paramount title, then there is a constructive eviction which will support a claim for breach of the covenants.   Damages recoverable are usually the value at the time of the purchase measured by the price paid plus interest from the time of the eviction.

Case 236.   If an owner of land conveys it with a covenant against incumbrances and there is at the time a mortgage on the premises, the covenant is breached at the time the deed is given.   On foreclosure of such mortgage the covenantee who pays such incumbrance is entitled to recover from the covenantor the amount of money paid in principal and interest, plus interest from the date of such payment.   If the incumbrance is an easement or a profit or a lease, the damage is the difference between the value of the land with and without such incumbrance thereon.

Case 237.   A remote grantee can recover against a covenantor only in case the covenant sued upon runs with the land.   The expression "with usual covenants" includes: (a) covenant of seisin; (b) covenant of right to convey; (c) covenant against incumbrances; (d) covenant of quiet enjoyment; and (e) covenant of general warranty.   Under the majority view, the first three of these cannot run with the land because they are breached, if at all, at the time of the delivery of the deed and at that instant are turned into a chose in action, and such chose does not run with the land.   The covenants of quiet enjoyment and of general warranty are breached, if at all, after the deed is delivered and are the type of covenants which run with the land.   Hence, a remote grantee can sue on such covenants against the original covenantor.

2.   WARRANTY OF FITNESS OR HABITABILITY

Case 238.   A purchaser of a new dwelling from a builder-vendor can recover damages for construction or materials defects which amount to a breach of an implied covenant of fitness or habitability.   The growing trend of cases reject the old rule of caveat emptor and replace it with a rule of implied warranty of fitness.

Chapter XXII

ESTOPPEL BY DEED

Legal Gems.

Cases.

Summary of Cases in Chapter XXII.

Legal Gems

1. Estoppel by deed has reference to the doctrine by which if a person executes a deed purporting to convey an estate in land which he does not have or which is larger than he has, and such person at a later date acquires such estate in such land, then the subsequently acquired estate will, by estoppel, pass to the grantee.

2. This doctrine is based on the intention of the parties as expressed in the deed—the grantor intends to transfer the estate described in the deed, and the grantee intends to receive the estate described in the deed.

3. The doctrine is an outgrowth of the common law rules relating to warranty of title, but covenants for title are not necessary today for the doctrine to apply.

4. Whether or not the doctrine operates in a given case is wholly dependent on the language which is used in the deed and which appears on the face of the instrument.

5. By the better rule the doctrine may be invoked in favor of a stranger to the deed and is not limited to the parties to the deed and their privies. See infra case 240.

6. The doctrine will operate in favor of the grantee even though the deed contains neither a misrepresentation nor a covenant of title.

7. There are two distinct theories on which the doctrine is claimed to operate—

    (a) the deed having been given and the estate having been subsequently acquired by the grantor, then as a matter of law, the estoppel operates on the estate itself and passes it to the grantee—it is objective and wholly impersonal and the grantee takes even as against a bona fide purchaser of the after acquired title from the grantor.

    (b) the deed having been given and the estate having been subsequently acquired by the grantor, then the grantor is only personally estopped to deny that he owned the estate at the time the deed was given, or he is personally estopped to deny the estate has passed to the grantee, but the estate itself is not affected, and the grantor is bound to convey to the grantee the after acquired title or estate. Under this theory, the estoppel is personal, and a bona fide purchaser from the grantor of the after acquired title would have priority over the original grantee.

8. Under either theory, if there be a covenant of title in the deed, the grantee cannot be compelled to accept the after acquired title either in partial or total satisfaction of the covenant. Instead, the grantee has an election either to sue for damages for the breach or to accept the after acquired title.

9. The doctrine has no application to the case in which the grantor in his deed undertakes merely to convey whatever right, title or interest, if any, he may have at the time of the deed.

10. For purpose of clear understanding note carefully these three cases—

(a) A, having no interest in Blackacre, but not knowing whether or not he has an interest, makes a deed to B as follows: "I hereby convey to B all of my right, title and interest in Blackacre and hereby warrant to the said B any interest which I presently own in such property". Thereafter A inherits the fee simple estate in Blackacre. Here no estoppel applies for the reason that the deed purports to convey and warrants no particular estate in Blackacre but undertakes merely to convey whatever interest A has at the time of the making of the deed.

(b) A, having no interest in Blackacre, and not knowing whether or not he has an interest, makes a deed to B as follows: "I hereby convey to B and his heirs the fee simple estate in Blackacre and hereby warrant such title in him and covenant to defend such against the whole world". Later A inherits the fee simple estate in Blackacre. A's deed contains a granting clause purporting to convey the fee simple. It also contains a clause warranting such title in the grantee. The doctrine of estoppel by deed clearly applies because A intended to convey and B intended to receive the fee simple title in Blackacre. This would be true under either theory of estoppel.

(c) A, having no interest in Blackacre, and not knowing whether or not he has an interest, makes a deed to B as follows: "I hereby convey to B and his heirs the fee simple estate in Blackacre". Later A inherits the fee simple estate in Blackacre. A's deed contains a granting clause purporting clearly to convey the fee simple estate in Blackacre. The doctrine of estoppel applies. The deed contains no misrepresentation of fact and contains no covenant of warranty but it does contain a clearly expressed intent to convey a fee simple estate which the grantor, A, did not have. And later A acquired the very estate which his deed purported to convey to B, and which B intended to receive from A. These two items, then: (1) an expressed intent in the deed to convey an estate larger than the grantor has; and (2) later acquisition by the grantor of such estate, are sufficient to support the doctrine of estoppel by deed.

See 144 A.L.R. 554; 23 Am.Jur.2d 326 et seq.

CASE 239: A owns Blackacre in fee simple. B, having no interest in Blackacre, executes to C a 5 year lease on Blackacre such term to begin March 1, 1970. Shortly thereafter A executes to B a 20 year lease on Blackacre to begin March 1, 1970. B makes a sublease to D for 5 years to begin March 1, 1970 and stating orally to D at the time of the sublease, "I made a 5 year lease to C for the same period but of course I had no interest in the land at the time so C's lease is no good". D takes possession of Blackacre on March 1, 1970. C demands possession thereof which D refuses. C sues to eject D. May he succeed?

Answer and Analysis

The answer is yes. The doctrine of estoppel by deed is as applicable to leases as to other estates in land. When B made the lease to C for 5 years, of course C received no interest in Blackacre when B, his lessor, had none. However, when the owner of the land, A, leased to B for 20 years, B immediately had a 20 year term in such land and by estoppel such after-acquired estate inured to the benefit of B's lessee, C. But it is D who is in possession of the land. D is a privy of B, the lessor of C. Both the grantors and their privies are bound by the doctrine of estoppel by deed. And, of course, D cannot claim to be a bona fide purchaser because he was told by B of B's prior lease to C. So whether we take the theory that the doctrine of estoppel operates as a matter of law on the estate which does not protect bona fide purchasers, or that the doctrine operates only to charge the conscience of the grantor or lessor personally and does not affect the estate, D is bound by the doctrine because he is not a bona fide purchaser from B. The result is that C has a right to eject D from Blackacre and to hold possession thereof for the period of 5 years under his lease. Of course, this answer presupposes that the lease to C will satisfy the formal requisites of a deed under the doctrine. Today when seals have been widely abolished, this question should cause little difficulty. See Doe ex dem. Christmas v. Oliver, 10 B. & C. 181, Kings Bench 1829; Burby, 320–322.

––––––––––

CASE 240: A, being fee simple owner of an undivided one half interest in Blackacre, conveys "to B and his heirs the fee simple estate in the whole of Blackacre and agrees to warrant and defend such title in B against the whole world". Thereafter D took possession from B as an adverse possessor and is presently possessed but the statute of limitations has not yet run fully in his favor. A inherits the fee simple in the undivided half of Blackacre which he did not own when he conveyed to B. A dies intestate and P is his heir. P sues D in ejectment. May he succeed in ejecting D?

Answer and Analysis

The answer is no. When A owned only an undivided one half interest in Blackacre and executed to B a deed which on its face purported to convey a fee simple estate in the whole property, his deed covered a larger estate than he, the grantor, owned in the property. When thereafter, such grantor, A, by inheritance acquires the very estate which his deed purported to convey to B, the benefit of such subsequent acquisition inures to the benefit of the grantee, B. Such is the plain doctrine of estoppel by deed. Hence, it is perfectly obvious had B been the defendant in this case, he could have claimed the benefit of such doctrine for he was a party to the original deed in which A both granted to B and warranted in him the fee simple in all of Blackacre. Such doctrine operates in favor of both the parties to the original transaction and in favor of their privies who claim by consent through them. In other words, had D been a grantee of B, there would be no doubt of his having the benefit of the doctrine.

Here D is not claiming through B by privity of estate but is claiming against him as an adverse possessor. Hence, D is not in privity with B in any sense. However, taking the position that the doctrine of estoppel by deed does not merely bind the consciences of the parties and their privies, but that it operates objectively in rem on the estate itself and as a matter of law, then when the grantor, A, inherited the fee simple estate in the undivided one half interest in Blackacre, which he did not own when he gave his deed to B, the title to that undivided half passed eo instante to B and is presently vested in B. In an action of ejectment the plaintiff must recover on the strength of his own title and not on the weakness of his adversary's title. (See supra Case 138 as to this principle and the role of the jus tertii as a defense in an action of ejectment.) But the adversary can show that the plaintiff has no title at all. In this case then, the defendant adverse possessor, D, can show that estoppel by deed passed A's inherited title to B, and that A had no title or interest in Blackacre at the time of his death. Thus P received no interest therein by being the heir of A. Therefore, D, a stranger to the original deed from A to B, and not in privity with either party, is permitted to set up estoppel by deed as a defense in this action in ejectment.

On the other hand, if the view were taken that estoppel by deed does not pass the estate by operating in rem, but only operates on the persons and binds their consciences, then D, a stranger to the original deed between A and B, and not being in privity with either, could not claim the protection of the doctrine. Under that approach the title would still be in A or his heir P, although A or his heir, as against B would be estopped from denying B's title. Under this theory, the after acquired title would still be in A if he were alive and in P, his heir, if he be deceased. However, A or his privies would be prevented from denying that the title is in B or from denying A had title when he gave the deed to B. Under such theory the estoppel is only a rule of evidence and does not effectuate an actual passing of the title. Thus A, or his heir, P, would not be estopped as to wrongdoer D, and P should win the ejectment suit. See Perkins v. Coleman, 90 Ky. 611, 14 S.W. 640 (1890), applying the first theory; Tiffany, p. 501.

CASE 241: A, having at least an estate pur autre vie for the life of X in Blackacre but being quite uncertain of any further interest therein, conveyed to B "all of my right, title and interest in Blackacre and hereby warrant and agree to defend such title to B in the premises". Thereafter by inheritance the fee simple in Blackacre came to A. X died and A demanded from B the possession of Blackacre. B refused. A sues to eject B from the premises. May A succeed?

Answer and Analysis

The answer is yes. B's only defense must be estoppel by deed against A. Whether that doctrine applies in any given case depends upon the language actually used in the deed and the construction to be given thereto. It may be said generally that the granting clause in a deed determines the estate which is intended to be conveyed to the grantee and that any covenant of warranty thereafter does not enlarge upon the estate granted but merely warrants that the estate described in the granting clause is to be defended. In the facts given there is no doubt at all but that the granting clause describing the estate conveyed as "all of my right, title and interest in Blackacre" purports only to convey whatever interest the grantor, B, at the time of the deed actually owned in the premises, and no greater or different interest or estate. Does the covenant of warranty which follows the granting clause enlarge the estate described in the granting clause? Such covenant says, "warrant and agree to defend *such title* to B *in the premises*". Surely the expression, "such title" must refer to the "right, title and interest" described in the granting clause. It does no more. What does the phrase "in the premises" mean? It can mean no more than the estate which the granting clause has described "in Blackacre". It seems clear then that the covenant of warranty does not in any way enlarge the estate described in and purported to be conveyed by the granting clause. That being the case the effect of A's deed was merely to convey to B any and every interest which A owned in Blackacre at the time the deed was made. Such deed did not purport to convey an estate which A did not have in Blackacre. Neither did it purport to convey a larger estate than A had in Blackacre. One of these last two stated propositions is essential to the operation of the doctrine of estoppel by deed. Therefore, it was the intention of the parties, A, the grantor, and B, the grantee, as appears on the face of the deed, that A was conveying and B was receiving only the interest in Blackacre which A owned presently when the deed was delivered to B. To such a situation the doctrine of estoppel by deed has no application and any after-acquired estate which comes to the grantor belongs to the grantor free from such doctrine. The result is that B's estate in Blackacre came to an end with the death of X. Thereafter by virtue of A's inherited fee simple, A has the right to immediate possession of the property and the right to eject B therefrom. See Baker v. Austin, 174 N.C. 433, 93 S.E. 949 (1917); Brown v. Harvey Coal Corp., 49 F.2d 434 (D.Ky. 1931); Burby, 321.

CASE 242: A, being fee simple owner of Blackacre, gave to B a first mortgage on the property. He then executed a second mortgage to C which second mortgage contained the following language, "this mortgage is given subject to the first mortgage hereinafter described, and I do hereby covenant with the mortgagee herein that I am seised in fee simple of Blackacre and that said Blackacre is free of all incumbrances and I will warrant and defend said fee simple title to said mortgagee against all claims whatsoever". Thereafter B foreclosed the first mortgage making A and C parties defendant in the action. A then purchased Blackacre from the purchaser at the foreclosure sale. Both mortgages and the deed to A following the foreclosure were on record from the time they were executed. A then conveyed to D by a deed purporting to convey the fee simple estate in Blackacre. D paid full price for the property and knew nothing about the above transactions except what appeared on the records. C now seeks to foreclose his mortgage, making both A and D parties defendant. May, C succeed?

The facts may be illustrated as follows:

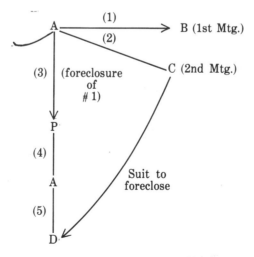

Answer and Analysis

The answer should be no.   When B foreclosed his first mortgage there is no doubt that such proceedings effectively cut off all rights which the original mortgagor, A, and the second mortgagee, C, had in Blackacre.   Indeed, that is the very purpose and effect of such foreclosure proceedings.   On the records neither A nor C appears to have any interest in Blackacre.   But A's general covenant of warranty still appears in the second mortgage to C.   The question whether C might hold A liable for damages for the breach of such covenant of warranty is not our question.   C is seeking to gain title to Blackacre through the doctrine of estoppel by deed and foreclosure.   Does the doctrine apply?   In the language of the mortgage to C it is stated, "this mortgage is given subject to the first mortgage" etc.   There was as to such first mortgage then no misrepresentation of fact.   But the mortgage continues, "said Blackacre is free of all incumbrances and I will warrant and defend said fee simple title to said mortgagee against all claims whatsoever".   When all of this quoted language is read as a whole it may be construed as saying, "Blackacre is subject to a first mortgage but I hereby warrant it to be free from all incumbrances and will defend in the second mortgagee a clear fee simple title".

The doctrine of estoppel by deed does not require for its operation that there be a misrepresentation of fact.   It is a technical doctrine requiring merely that the covenant or representation which is made in the deed concerning title be made good.   In this case under the foregoing interpretation the language shows that the mortgagor, A, intended the mortgagee to have a fee simple title for the subject of his mortgage and that the mortgagee intended to receive such.   The recital of the existence of the first mortgage does not prevent the assumption by the mortgagor by his covenant that he hereby estops himself from denying the fact of such prior mortgage.   The reason such estoppel should operate is simply this—it is the obvious intention of both parties that it should operate.

On the other hand a different interpretation is not only possible but more reasonable.   Applying the principle that a document should be considered in its entirety in order to arrive at its proper construction, then when the instrument itself shows that the land is conveyed or mortgaged subject to an outstanding interest, and this granting clause is followed by a covenant for title, the title covenant should be construed as warranting only the estate granted or mortgaged in the preceding clause.   In effect, the title covenant is construed as if it stated ".   .   . warrant and defend the title against the claims of all persons *except as above noted.*"   Under this interpretation the grantor, A in the instant case, is not estopped to assert his after acquired title.

Assuming, however, a jurisdiction that would follow the earlier interpretation and would construe the title covenant most strictly against the grantor and without modification, then we would find that C's mortgage with its covenant of warranty is a conveyance by A of a larger interest than he had in the property at the time it was given. After B's foreclosure A had no interest in the property because it had been completely cut off by B's foreclosure action. Thereafter A acquires by purchase the fee simple in the property. At the instant of such reacquisition the benefit thereof inures to C under the doctrine of estoppel by deed. Such doctrine is binding both on A, a party to the original second mortgage, and on those who take through him, D in our case. This is true whether or not D is a bona fide purchaser. Such was the common law rule and were we to stop at this point the answer to our question would be yes instead of no, and C could foreclose his mortgage. In other words, if this case were to be determined wholly on the doctrine of estoppel by deed, and if it were applicable, then C should have the benefit of A's after acquired property.

In the event that estoppel by deed would apply to this situation, the further effect of the recording act should be considered. Although there is a conflict of authority, it is believed that the better view is that estoppel by deed is modified by the recording act, and that a BFP thereunder takes free of the rights of the grantee under the estoppel deed. To illustrate, let us assume that A in this case had executed two warranty deeds, one first to B and then one to C. C's deed, of course, was ineffective to convey any title since A had already conveyed it to B. When A later reacquired title by another conveyance (there would, of course, be no foreclosure if no mortgage were involved), and then A conveyed to D, the question of D's status as a BFP becomes important. D, in checking the chain of title, would normally disregard A after finding the recorded deed from A to B, and would pick up A again after finding the recorded deed back to him from the subsequent purchaser. Thus, D would not normally find the deed from A to C which was executed at a time when A did not have title. Therefore, D would be a BFP relying on record title, and to give full effect to the policy behind the recording act, D should prevail over the estoppel grantee, C. Of course, the recording act in so many words pertains only to unrecorded instruments, but to give full effect to the policy of the act, instruments recorded *out of the chain of title* should be regarded as not recorded.

This theory of protecting the bona fide purchaser as against the grantee of the estoppel deed was not applied to the mortgage situation in the principal case. Ayer v. Philadelphia & Boston Face Brick Co., 159 Mass. 84, 34 N.E. 177 (1893). If applied to the mortgages in such a situation, the application would be subject to criticism for the following reason: it is difficult to see how D can become a BFP under the recording act. A purchaser in D's position in checking title is not justified in disregarding A after A executes a first mortgage because A still retains a substantial interest which is subject to further mortgage and conveyance. Further, the second mortgage was recorded and C was made a party to the foreclosure suit. D should necessarily check the foreclosure proceedings and is charged with notice of everything that would be revealed by a search of the records. Thus, he should be charged with constructive notice of C's mortgage and of the covenant of title therein. Under such circumstances it would not be unjust to let the estoppel grantee, C, prevail over D who is charged with notice of his rights.

In conclusion, the result should be that D prevails over C because A's title covenant should be considered modified by the recital in the deed that it was a second mortgage. Thus, estoppel by deed should not apply, but there are cases to the contrary. If estoppel by deed does apply, there are conflicting decisions as to whether the doctrine is modified by the recording act. In those jurisdictions in which the BFP normally prevails over the estoppel grantee, still, in this case, D should not be regarded as such a BFP although there may be decisions to the contrary. See Wack v. Collingswood Extension Realty Co., 114 N.J.Eq. 253, 168 A. 639 (E. & A.1933); Ayer v. Philadelphia & Boston Face Brick Co., 159 Mass. 84, 34 N.E. 177 (1893); Wheeler v. Young, 76 Conn. 44, 55 A. 670 (1903); Midland Realty Co. of Minnesota v. Halverson, 52 P.2d 159 (Mont.1959), this latter case for the proposition that title covenants do not operate to enlarge the particular estate granted and that no estoppel would apply in such a case to an after acquired title; Tiffany, pp. 502, 507; 58 A.L.R. 348; 144 A.L.R. 556.

SUMMARY OF CASES IN CHAPTER XXII

Case 239. The doctrine of estoppel by deed that when a person executes an instrument conveying a larger estate than he has in land and subsequently acquires such larger estate, it inures by estoppel to the benefit of the grantee, is as applicable to leases as to other estates in land. If the conveyor transfers his after-acquired interest to one who is not a bona fide purchaser, then such conveyee is also bound by the doctrine of estoppel by deed and takes title subject to the prior right of the original grantee, whether on the theory that the estoppel operates on the estate as a matter of law or merely personally and on the conscience of the grantor or his privies.

Case 240. Under the theory that the doctrine of estoppel by deed operates in rem and actually conveys the after-acquired estate of the grantor to the grantee, such doctrine will protect a stranger to the original deed as well as the parties to it and their privies; but if such doctrine operates only on the consciences of the persons, and does not affect the estate, it is available only to the parties to the original deed and those in privity with them.

Case 241. If when a deed is made it purports to convey only the interest which the grantor presently owns in the property and the covenants of warranty therein do not enlarge the estate described in the granting clause, the doctrine of estoppel by deed has no application and any after-acquired estate which comes to the grantor may be kept by him free from the operation of the doctrine. The doctrine must be based solely on the language used which appears on the face of the instrument and the construction placed thereon.

Case 242. The doctrine of estoppel by deed does not require for its operation that there be any misrepresentation of fact on the face of the deed; it requires merely that the representations on the face of the deed concerning the title be made good whether such representations be in the form of a grant or a covenant or both. In some jurisdictions, however, the scope of title covenants may be construed as modified in terms of the estate granted. Under the recording statutes the general rule is that a subsequent purchaser is not charged with notice of a recorded instrument of conveyance by a person in the chain of title unless such record was made at a time later than the records disclose such person to have acquired such title. This means the record must show a conveyor to be a grantee before he can be a grantor. While some cases treat title through estoppel by deed as an exception to such general rule, the better rule is that it is governed by the general rule and that the subsequent purchaser has priority over the one who claims the benefit of the doctrine but through an instrument which is outside the chain of title. This is the only holding in harmony with the purpose of the recording acts.

Chapter XXIII

PRIORITIES AND RECORDING

1. At Common Law.
   Legal Gems.
2. Under Recording Statutes.
   Legal Gems.
   a. Types of Acts.
   b. Constructive Notice.
   c. Purchaser and Subsequent Purchaser.
   d. Recorder's Errors.
   e. Duly Recorded.
   f. Void Instruments.
   g. Adverse Possession.
   h. Chain of Title.
   i. Persons Protected, BFPs.
   j. Hazards Not Covered.
   k. Indices.
   Cases.
   Chart Comparing Recording Acts.
Summary of Cases in Chapter XXIII.

---

1. AT COMMON LAW

LEGAL GEMS

1. At common law the question of priority of title was usually simply a question of time. The doctrine was first in time is first in right. E. g., A, owner of Blackacre in fee simple, conveys to B in fee simple. A then conveys the same Blackacre to C in fee simple. B is the owner merely because there was no interest left in A to convey to C.

This rule of priority applied both to competition between equitable interests and also to competition between legal interests. Further, a prior legal interest prevailed over a subsequent equitable interest.

2. There is one exception to the rule of priority based on time. A bona fide purchaser for value without notice takes priority over a former equity or equitable interest. E. g., A, being fee simple owner of Blackacre, declares himself trustee of the property for B. A then conveys the legal title in Blackacre to C in fee simple. C pays full value for the property and has no knowledge of the declaration of trust in B's favor. C owns Blackacre in fee simple and B's equity, even though earlier in point of time, is cut off.

The above example is an illustration of the common law rule that a subsequent equity when combined with the legal title prevails over a prior equity. Thus, in the above illustration, C acquires the legal title as a result of the conveyance and he also acquires an equity from his status as a bona fide purchaser without notice. He accordingly prevails over B.

3. Two early English statutes provided that conveyances made for the purpose of defrauding creditors or subsequent purchasers should be null and void. E. g., (a) A, fee simple owner, owes creditor, C. To prevent C's being able to collect the debt A fraudulently conveys to B as a donee, B giving no consideration for the deed and knowing the purpose of the conveyance. C may have such deed set aside as null and void. (b) A, fee simple owner, conveys to C as donee, C paying nothing for the deed. A, intending to defraud B, conveys to B who pays full price for the property and is given no notice of the prior conveyance to C and buys bona fide. B may have the conveyance to C set aside as null and void.

4. The above common law rules as to priority still prevail when the controversy is not governed by an applicable recording act.

2. UNDER RECORDING STATUTES

Legal Gems

a. Types of Acts

1. Although the specific provisions of the recording acts of the several states vary considerably as to their phraseology, and even as to substantive matters in relation to the parties protected thereby, there are four basic types of recording acts in the United States. These four types are as follows:

(a) Notice: An unrecorded conveyance or other instrument is invalid as against a subsequent bona fide purchaser (creditor or mortgagee if the statute so provides) for value and without notice.

Under this type of statute the subsequent bona fide purchaser prevails over the prior unrecorded interest whether the subsequent purchaser records or not. Insofar as the subsequent purchaser is concerned, there is no premium on his race to the recorder's office; his priority is determined upon his status at the time he acquires his deed or mortgage. Of course he should record to protect himself from the possibility of a still later subsequent bona fide purchaser.

(b) Race: No conveyance or other instrument is valid as against (lien creditors or other specified parties and) purchasers for a valuable consideration but from the time of recordation.

Under this type of statute, the first to record wins, and a subsequent purchaser need not be bona fide and without notice since he will prevail if he records first. Priority is determined simply by who wins the race to the recording office.

(c) Race-Notice: An unrecorded conveyance or other instrument is invalid as against a subsequent bona fide purchaser for value without notice (and possibly other designated parties such as mortgagees and creditors), who first records.

This statute combines the essential features of both the notice and race type recording statutes. In order for a subsequent party to prevail in a race-notice jurisdiction, he must be both a bona fide purchaser for value without notice of the prior interest and record first.

(d) Period of Grace: A period of grace statute is usually coupled with the features of a notice type statute.

Under such a statute, the prior grantee (or holder of other interest) is allowed a period of grace (e. g. 15 days) in which to record his instrument in order to preserve his priority. If a prior grantee does not record within the period of grace, then a subsequent bona fide purchaser will prevail.

Notice and race-notice are the most common types of recording statutes, with only a few jurisdictions having a pure race or period of grace type statute.

b. CONSTRUCTIVE NOTICE

2. Under the recording acts in England a recorded instrument of conveyance *does not* give constructive notice of its contents to subsequent purchasers and incumbrancers.

3. Under the recording acts in the United States, a recorded instrument of conveyance, usually a deed or mortgage, *does give* constructive notice of its contents to subsequent purchasers and incumbrancers. Constructive notice is notice implied by law and is not dependent on actual notice or notice of facts from which knowledge of an unrecorded instrument would be implied. Constructive notice is a rule of law.

4. Such constructive notice prevents a subsequent purchaser or incumbrancer from being a bona fide purchaser. E. g., A conveys Blackacre to B who records his deed. A then executes a deed to Blackacre in fee simple to C as grantee. C pays full value in good faith for the property and has no actual notice of the former deed to B. C is not a bona fide purchaser as a matter of law because he is bound to examine the records and is *construed* to have notice of B's recorded deed whether or not he knows about it.

5. Constructive notice applies whether the interest conveyed by the recorded instrument is a legal or an equitable interest. E. g., A, owner of Blackacre, declares himself trustee of Blackacre for B and records the declaration of trust. Thereafter A makes a deed to C covering the fee simple in Blackacre. C is charged with notice of what appears on the record in the declaration of trust and takes his deed subject to B's prior equitable interest in the property. C cannot be a bona fide purchaser.

c. Purchaser and Subsequent Purchaser

6. The term purchaser as used in the recording acts generally refers to a purchaser of the legal interest, i. e., a grantee for value, mortgagee, or other person who acquires a legal estate or interest in the property. In some jurisdictions, however, either by decision or statute, a subsequent purchaser of an equitable interest, e. g. a vendee under a contract for sale, is protected by the recording act.

d. Recorder's Errors

7. A subsequent purchaser or incumbrancer acting in good faith and with no actual knowledge of a former conveyance is normally entitled to rely on what appears on the records.

E. g., A conveys to B and B does not record. Then A conveys to C who is a bona fide purchaser. C prevails in a notice jurisdiction whether or not C records before B. C prevails in a pure race and a race-notice jurisdiction only if he records ahead of B. In a period of grace jurisdiction, C prevails if B fails to record within the period of grace allowed by the statute.

In the event that B delivers the deed to the proper office for recordation before A's conveyance to C, and the recorder fails to record the deed at all, or the recorder makes a mistake in recording B's deed, then there is a split of authority as to whether C gains priority over B. Under one view, C should be protected on the theory that it was B's responsibility not only

    (a) to see that the deed was recorded but also

    (b) to see that the recordation was accurately made.

Under the other view protecting B, B's instrument is constructive notice of its actual contents as soon as it is deposited in the proper office, any mistake as to actual recording or copying it into the record having no effect on constructive notice.

e. Duly Recorded

8. To be duly recorded and thus constitute constructive notice, the instrument must be properly executed, proved, acknowledged in some jurisdictions, and within the chain of title as a condition precedent to being properly recorded. Under such a statute the actual physical recording of an improperly executed instrument does not impart constructive notice to such subsequent purchaser or incumbrancer, the legal effect being the same as though no record had in fact been made. However, if one sees such an improperly executed deed or mortgage, or actually knows about it, then he is charged with at least inquiry notice and is held to have knowledge of such facts as a reasonable inquiry would have disclosed.

f. Void Instruments

9. An instrument of conveyance which is void for reasons such as forgery or lack of delivery is ineffective for any purpose and re-

cording such has no legal effect. E. g., A is fee owner of Blackacre. B forges A's name to a deed to Blackacre in which deed B is the grantee. B then mortgages the property to C who lends the money in good faith and without notice of the forgery except as it appears on the record. The mortgage is wholly ineffective as to A and gives C no interest in Blackacre.

g. ADVERSE POSSESSION

10. The recording statutes have no application to a title procured by adverse possession or prescription; they apply only to title procured by instruments of conveyance which can be recorded. See CASE 141 supra.

h. CHAIN OF TITLE

11. The chain of title to a piece of land means the regular series of recorded instruments from the patent from the United States Government, or former sovereign, down to and including the instrument through which the party claims ownership, each instrument representing a regular link in the chain. E. g., United States makes patent to A; A deeds to B; B deeds to C; C deeds to D; D mortgages to X; D deeds to E subject to X's mortgage; X executes a satisfaction of the mortgage; E deeds to F; etc., each grantee becoming the subsequent grantor.

12. Every subsequent purchaser or incumbrancer takes his interest in the property conveyed subject to prior interests properly recorded, which proper recording means either

(a) an instrument in the direct chain of title or

(b) a recital in an instrument in such direct chain of title. E. g., A, who is grantee in a deed in the direct chain of title, gives to B a mortgage on the property, which mortgage is not recorded. A then gives a deed to C which deed recites, "subject to a mortgage given to B on said property". This recital, being properly recorded gives C constructive, or at least inquiry notice of the mortgage to B and prevents C being a bona fide purchaser.

13. An instrument which does not constitute a regular link in the chain of title or which is not identified by a recital in an instrument in such chain, is not considered properly recorded and does not give constructive notice to subsequent purchasers or incumbrancers.

E. g., A is a grantee in a deed which is a regular link in the chain of title. A makes a deed to B but B does not record his deed. This failure on B's part to record his deed breaks the chain of title subsequent to the deed in which A is the grantee. B then makes a deed to C. B, not having appeared as a grantee in any former instrument of record, now appears as an interloper and a deed by him is no part of the regular chain of title. Then A makes a deed to the same property to D. D puts his deed on record. As to D the deed of B to C, being no part of the regular chain of title, imparts no constructive notice. Hence, D is the owner of the property as against B and C, provided in other respects he is a bona fide purchaser.

i. PERSONS PROTECTED, BFPs

14. The recording statutes are construed to give protection to two persons only, (a) a bona fide purchaser or incumbrancer, or (b) one who claims through such a bona fide purchaser or incumbrancer.[1]

15. In order to be a bona fide purchaser protected under the recording act, one must

(a) be subsequent,

(b) pay value,

(c) be without notice, (the value must have actually been paid before notice), and

(d) be of good faith.

16. Recording statutes do not protect a subsequent claimant who has not paid more than a nominal consideration because he is not a purchaser; nor one who takes with either actual or constructive notice of a prior interest because he does not take in good faith; to be protected he must acquire his interest both (a) for value and (b) in good faith.

17. One who takes a mortgage to secure a pre-existing debt without at the same time relinquishing any right or claim as a consideration for the mortgage is not a purchaser for value. But if the mortgagee surrenders other security for the debt or extends the time of payment by a binding contract, he is regarded as a purchaser for value.

With respect to one who takes an absolute conveyance of land in satisfaction of an antecedent debt, the cases are divided on the question as to whether he is a purchaser for value, but since the debt is cancelled instead of being secured, the position that he does qualify as a purchaser seems sound.

18. If a person is in possession of land, then any person taking an interest in that land is charged with notice of the interest which the possessor claims in the land. This rule is most properly confined to possession inconsistent with record title.

19. A subsequent purchaser who takes under a quitclaim deed, under what is believed the better view, is protected by the recording statutes because a quitclaim deed is considered a conveyance and not merely a release.

20. A mortgagee, although not specifically mentioned in a recording act, is considered a purchaser to the extent of his interest

---

1. A notable exception is Colorado. See Eastwood v. Shedd, 166 Colo. 136, 442 P.2d 423 (1968), concluding that a subsequent donee was entitled to the protection of the recording act when the act extended to ". . . any class of persons with any kind of rights, except between the parties thereto, . . ." See Colo.Rev. Stat. § 38–35–109.

and is protected by the recording act if he otherwise qualifies as a subsequent bona fide purchaser for value without notice.

j. HAZARDS NOT COVERED

21. The recording acts generally afford purchasers and other subsequent parties either no or inadequate protection against the following interests:

    a.   forged and other void deeds or instruments;

    b.   deeds by incompetents;

    c.   fraudulent statements in the instruments as to marital status;

    d.   claims of undisclosed and pretermitted heirs;

    e.   falsification of records;

    f.   undelivered but recorded deeds;

    g.   false personation of record owner; and

    h.   adverse possession.

In addition, some statutes afford no protection against

    i.   recording mistakes;

    j.   indexing mistakes; and

    k.   possibly other undisclosed interests.

k. INDICES

22. Gems 11–13 supra relating to the chain of title, as well as the cases following when applicable, are based on an official grantor-grantee index. Many of the recording problems would be eliminated if official tract indices were used since then all recorded instruments pertaining to a particular tract or parcel would be discovered despite "gaps," out of turn recording, and "wild" instruments. Many professional title companies do in fact use their own tract indices regardless of the official index.

See Tiffany, pp. 514–530; Burby, 323–331; Powell, ¶¶ 912–918.

Note

Because the provisions of recording statutes vary greatly, the cases construing them often reach opposite results. The statutes and cases of each state should be consulted. In the main the Legal Gems above present the general principles.

———

CASE 243: A, owner of Blackacre in fee simple, conveys it to B. B does not record his deed. A then executes a deed to C purporting to convey Blackacre to C. C, having no notice of the deed to B, pays full value of the property to A. B then records his deed after which C records his deed. At the time C receives his deed B is not in possession of Blackacre, but later when C goes to possess Blackacre he finds B is already in possession thereof. The recording statute in the jurisdiction provides, "Every conveyance of real property shall be void as to subsequent purchasers and incumbrancers who give value and take without notice, unless such conveyance is duly recorded before such subsequent purchase or incumbrance". C sues to eject B. May C succeed in the action?

Answer and Analysis

The answer is yes. The legislature of a state has power to determine the form, effect and priorities of conveyances of land within the borders of the state. In this case the legislature by its recording statute has undertaken to make void a conveyance as to "subsequent purchasers and incumbrancers . . . unless . . . duly recorded before such subsequent purchase or incumbrance". This is a notice type statute which protects the subsequent BFP from claims arising under a prior unrecorded instrument. In our case A's deed to B is a conveyance of real property which was not recorded. C is a subsequent purchaser who gave full value and had no notice of B's deed. C's purchase preceded in time the recording of B's deed. Every item of the statute specifically applies to C's claim and by the very words of the statute, B's deed is made "void" as to C's purchase. The fact that B's deed was recorded before C's deed is immaterial for the statute does not consider or make any provision for priority of recording, as some statutes do. Hence, but one conclusion can be reached in this case and that is this, C having purchased for value and in good faith subsequent to B's deed and B having failed to record his deed before C's purchase, B's deed is void as to C and C has priority and is the owner of Blackacre in fee simple under the terms of the recording statute quoted. In such case it may usually be said that B's failure to record his deed has made it possible for C to be injured which is the very reason for the statute. It is therefore just and fair as between the parties that C should have priority.

However, the provisions of such a statute can work a similar injustice on B. Suppose for instance B receives his deed late in the evening when the office where recording is made is closed. Immediately following his transaction with B, A goes to C and sells the same property to C. When the recording office opens the following morning B is there and presents his deed for recordation. Shortly thereafter C records his deed. Under such statute as is quoted in our case C has priority. And yet B has been as diligent as it is possible for a person to be. It is quite unjust and unfair to B in such case to give C priority. Such a case has led some legislatures to give priority to the grantee who first records his deed. However, it is for the legislature and not for the court to promulgate the statute and under the statute given in our case C must be given priority over B and may eject B from Blackacre. See Randall v. Hamilton, 156 Ga. 661, 119 S.E. 595,

32 A.L.R. 342 (1918); Craig v. Osborn, 131 Miss. 323, 98 So. 598 (1924), noted in 37 Harv.L.R. 1141; Tiffany, p. 518.

CASE 244: A, being fee simple owner of Blackacre, conveys it by deed to B for which B pays A $2000.00. B records his deed and takes possession of Blackacre. C goes to A and expresses a desire to purchase Blackacre. A advises C that he has already sold the property to B. C hands A $1.00 and asks A to execute to him a deed to Blackacre in fee simple which A does. C records his deed and brings an action against B to eject him from Blackacre. In the jurisdiction a typical recording statute provides that any conveyance or incumbrance of real property shall be void as to subsequent purchasers or incumbrancers for value and without notice unless the instrument is duly recorded. May C eject B?

Answer and Analysis

The answer is no. There are four specific reasons why C cannot eject B from Blackacre, any one of which would give B a good defense. (1) The recording statute is of the notice type intended to protect bona fide purchasers and incumbrancers. To be a bona fide purchaser or incumbrancer one must both (a) give value and (b) take without notice of a prior claim. In this case the subsequent purchaser, C, gave the sum of $1.00 for what appears to be a piece of property worth $2,000.00. Such a nominal consideration does not make one a purchaser for value. Therefore, C is not a bona fide purchaser who is protected by the recording statute. (2) B's recording of his deed from A did two things, it made inapplicable the recording statute making his deed void as to subsequent purchasers and incumbrancers for the deed was "duly recorded", and prevented C's being a bona fide purchaser because such deed on record gave C constructive notice of B's prior claim regardless of whether C had actual knowledge of such. (3) When C sought to buy Blackacre from A, he was told by A that the property had been sold to B. Such actual knowledge prevents C from being a bona fide purchaser. Even had B's deed not been recorded such actual notice from A would have prevented C's having any protection under the recording statute given. B's deed would have been perfectly valid as to C simply because C took his deed with notice of B's prior deed or title. (4) If we assume that B did not record his deed, that C gave full value for Blackacre and that A had not told C of his deed to B, still C would not be a bona fide purchaser and could not eject B. The reason is this, B is in actual physical possession of Blackacre at the time A delivered the deed to C. When C makes such a purchase the law puts the purchaser right out on the land and charges him with notice of what appears thereon, and it is immaterial whether or not the purchaser actually goes to and inspects the land. So, in our case C saw what was on the land whether he did or not. He is charged with seeing B in possession of Blackacre and that makes C responsible to make inquiry of B to learn just what B's interest in or claim to Blackacre actually is. Hence, with the prior claimant actually being on the land, the subsequent purchaser is charged with notice of such possessor's claim to the land and has no protection under the recording statute.

However, there are some instances in which possession of the land may give the subsequent purchaser no notice of any adverse or inconsistent claim in which case the doctrine of inquiry notice does not apply. For example, suppose A and B are on the record equal cotenants of Blackacre. A conveys his undivided one half interest in the property to B. B does not record his deed. A then gives a deed to C of an undivided one half interest in Blackacre. C records his deed. B's possession would not give C notice that B claimed more than an undivided one half interest because his possession as a coowner would be entirely consistent with the record because of the unity of possession involved in cotenancy. There is authority, however, that possession of a tenant, although consistent with record title, may constitute notice of an inconsistent claim because of the fairly common practice of landlords and tenants entering into supplemental agreements and arrangements. See 25 Mich.L.R. 812; 105 A.L.R. 845; Tiffany, p. 523; Burby, 328; Galley v. Ward, 60 N.H. 331 (1880).

———

CASE 245: A, owner in fee simple of Blackacre, conveys it by deed to B. This deed is recorded. B executes to A a purchase money mortgage dated June 1, 1965. This mortgage is not recorded until June 1, 1970. B conveys by deed to C and on the face of the deed it is recited, "subject to the mortgage given to A". This deed is dated June 1, 1966 and is not recorded. C gives a mortgage on the premises to D on January 1, 1970 which is recorded January 2, 1970. A brings an action to foreclose his mortgage in which D contends that his mortgage is prior to that of A's. May A have a decree of foreclosure?

Answer and Analysis

The answer is yes. For a party to prevail under most of the recording acts, he must at least satisfy the requirements of being a subsequent bona fide purchaser or mortgagee for value without notice, and the prior interest must not be recorded at the time the subsequent party obtains his interest. The chronology of events in the above set of facts is as follows: (1) A conveys to B. (2) B's deed is recorded. (3) B mortgages to A. (4) B conveys to C "subject to the mortgage". (5) C's deed is not recorded. (6) C mortgages to D. (7) D's mortgage is recorded Jan. 2, 1970. (8) A's mortgage is recorded June 1, 1970. From this set of facts the record alone shows (a) B owns Blackacre, (b) C mortgages to D and (c) B mortgages to A.

Any priority which D claims must be based on his taking as a subsequent incumbrancer without notice, there being no question on the subject of value given. So the question is this—does D take with or without constructive notice of A's mortgage? It is quite obvious that had B's deed to C been recorded prior to D's mortgage, D would have been given constructive notice by such recordation because C's deed is an essential link in D's chain of title, and a subsequent purchaser takes with notice either (a) of a deed on record which is a part of his chain of title or (b) of a recital in an instrument which is a part of his chain of title. So if C's deed had been on record D would have taken with notice of A's mortgage, whether or not such mortgage was on record, because C's deed recited that it was "subject to the mortgage given A". But on the face of the record C seems an interloper. The record discloses no interest in C prior to his giving the mortgage to D. This should have put D on inquiry to learn the source of C's title, if any. Either there is such a source or there is not. If there is none, then D has no interest under C's mortgage. If there is such a source, D should have discovered it and in the absence of such discovery he should be and is charged with notice of the contents of such source whether or not it is recorded. Such being the law, D is charged with constructive notice of the recital in C's deed that it is given "subject to the mortgage given to A". Hence, A's mortgage from B is prior to that of D who takes with constructive notice and is not a bona fide purchaser from C as to A's mortgage.

In the cases involving priorities of instruments of conveyance the underlying principle should be constantly kept in mind. It is this— one is protected by the recording statutes if he is diligent but he is not protected if he is negligent. The purchaser of real property is duty bound to make diligent search of the records for prior claims and he is duty bound to make diligent inspection of the property respecting claims of possessors thereof. If (a) the record gives the purchaser constructive notice, or (b) the record is such as to leave him in doubt and puts him on inquiry so that to be diligent he must search further, or (c) one in possession of the land is inconsistent with the record, or (d) the possession of the land leaves the purchaser in doubt and to be diligent he must make inquiry concerning the interest which might be claimed by one on the land; then, in all of these cases the purchaser is charged with notice and cannot be a bona fide purchaser entitled to protection under the recording statutes. See Baker v. Mather, 25 Mich. 51 (1872); Tiffany, pp. 523–526; Burby, 329 et seq.

———

CASE 246: A, being fee simple owner of Blackacre, conveys it to X. X does not record the deed. X conveys to Y. Y records his deed. Then A executes a deed to B. B records his deed. B executes a deed to C. C records his deed. Neither B nor C knew of the deeds to X and to Y. Blackacre is vacant land with no one actually in physical possession thereof. Y then moves onto the premises and C sues to eject him. May C succeed?

Answer and Analysis

The answer is yes.[1] Of course if this were a case at common law where priority in time is priority in right, Y would be the title holder of Blackacre and have the right to possession because after A's deed to X there would be no interest in A to convey to B. But under the recording statutes the common law rule does not always prevail and the question of priority often depends, as in this case, upon the recordation of instruments and the constructive notice which such recordation imparts. When we are told that A is a fee simple owner, such conclusion presupposes a perfect recorded chain of title from the patent of the United States Government, or other former sovereign, down to and including A. It presupposes no break in the recorded chain and that every link properly binds the links preceding and succeeding it. Then what happens? A conveys to X but X does not record his deed. Thus the title in X is good between the parties, A and X. But on the record the chain is not complete without the last link. Then X conveys to Y. Y records his deed. But the record discloses a good chain with all links there down to A. But there is no link on the record between A and Y. Y now appears to be an interloper, a stranger to the chain of title because there is no link connecting him with A, the last link in the chain connected with the original source of title. Now A conveys to B and B to C. Both deeds are recorded. Now the chain of title *on the record* is perfect from the patent down to and including C. So the question is this—are the subsequent purchasers B and C bound by any constructive notice imparted to them by Y's recorded deed from X when X, and therefore Y, are *strangers to the chain of title*?

The general rule answers this question in the negative. Such "general rule" may be stated as follows. A subsequent purchaser or incumbrancer is not bound by constructive notice of any recorded instrument of conveyance unless such instrument constitutes an essential link in the chain of title. Stated in another way it may be said that no recorded instrument of conveyance gives constructive notice to a subsequent purchaser or incumbrancer unless that recorded in-

---

1. The answer should be the same under any of the four types of recording statutes, but the reasons would be somewhat different. (1) Under a notice statute both B and C are subsequent BFP's because the X–Y deed is outside the chain of title and doesn't constitute constructive notice. (2) Under a race statute, recording should be construed as meaning the recording of a complete chain of title; therefore the non-recording of the A–X deed precludes Y from claiming a prior recording, and the entire competing chain—A to B to C—is recorded first. (3) In a race-notice jurisdiction, both B and C can each qualify as a subsequent BFP whose conveyance was first recorded insofar as Y is concerned because of the reasoning under (1) and (2) supra. (4) In a period of grace statute if the period of grace for X's recording has expired, the result is the same as in a notice jurisdiction, and C will prevail. See also the first NOTE in text following this case for further discussion.

strument is made after the time when some other recorded instrument shows the grantor to have obtained the title. In short, *on the record the grantor must first appear as a grantee before he can be a grantor.* Applying this rule to our facts, X is a *complete stranger* to the chain of title. He does not appear on the record as a grantee at all, much less before he appears as a grantor. On the other hand C's chain of title is perfect and complete. As a subsequent purchaser C is bound by constructive notice only of the instruments in his chain of title. This does not include the instrument from X to Y. Hence, C holds priority as a bona fide purchaser under the recording statutes and can eject Y from Blackacre. It should be noticed that B took his interest without notice of any interest in Y and that C took whatever interest B had and notice to C would be immaterial. In other words if B, a subsequent purchaser, takes without notice, then he is empowered to transfer his interest to another who does or does not have notice of the prior claim. Of course, this does not mean that one who holds with notice can improve his position by selling to a bona fide purchaser and buying back again. See Board of Educ. of City of Minneapolis v. Hughes, 118 Minn. 404, 136 N.W. 1095, 41 L.R.A.,N.S., 637 (1912); Tiffany, p. 517; Burby, 326.

Note 1

If we were to approach the above case (no. 246), from a literal application of the recording act, it might seem that a different result would ensue. Take a typical notice type statute which provides in effect that no deed shall be valid until recorded as against a subsequent bona fide purchaser for value and without notice. In the instant case Y did place his deed on record before A conveyed to B and B in turn conveyed to C. Thus, it could be argued that Y did record his instrument before B entered the picture; therefore the recording act has no application, and the common law rule of first in time governs. However, the break in the chain of title from A to X affords such persons as B and C no opportunity to find the conveyances to X and Y. Thus, in order to give effect to the policy behind the recording act, the concept of recording should be construed to mean the recordation of a complete chain of title. Under such an interpretation, Y's deed is not recorded within the intent of the act when it is a wild deed unconnected with a prior deed of record in the chain of title. Thus, the result is the same as previously indicated.

Note 2

If the jurisdiction had an official tract index in which all instruments were recorded in reference to the legal description of the land instead of in reference to grantors and grantees, then the chain of title concept would be inapplicable, and B and C in case 246 supra would have no difficulty in finding the recorded deed to Y and they would be charged with notice thereof.

CASE 247: A, having no interest in Blackacre, mortgages the property to X. X assigns the mortgage to Y. Both the mortgage and the assignment thereof are recorded. Thereafter A acquires title to Blackacre and executes a deed thereto for full value to B who conveys to C who conveys to D. All these deeds are duly recorded. Y seeks to foreclose his mortgage against all of the above parties and all resist his effort to foreclose. May Y succeed?

Answer and Analysis

The answer is no according to the better view. Both at common law and under modern conveyances the doctrine of estoppel by deed will operate in favor of a grantee and against a grantor as to after acquired property, and such doctrine extends to the successors in interest of these parties. However, it does not follow that because there is such a doctrine as between the parties and their successors, that it is not affected by the modern recording statutes. It will be noticed that when A made his mortgage to X and when X assigned the mortgage to Y, A had no interest in Blackacre. His mortgage, therefore, was completely outside the chain of title. He had by such mortgage become on the record a conveyor before any record showed him to be a grantee or a conveyee.

By the general rule subsequent purchasers or incumbrancers are not bound by such recorded instruments because such recordation gives no constructive notice to bona fide subsequent purchasers and incumbrancers. Indeed, it may be said that when X and Y took A's mortgage they did not carry out their duty of due care with respect to searching the record of the chain of title because the exercise of such diligence would have disclosed that A was not a grantee in the chain of title of Blackacre. Applying the general rule, then, the purchasers from A after A acquired the title to Blackacre were subsequent purchasers without notice of the mortgage to X and assigned to Y, because such mortgage was outside the chain of title. B and his successors, C and D, are therefore entitled to protection under the recording statutes as subsequent purchasers and take their title free from the encumbrance of Y's mortgage. This is the only holding which complies with the purpose and the spirit of the recording statutes, and should hold true whether we take the theory that the estoppel operates only on the person or on the estate itself.

There are many cases holding contra, thus making the passing of title by estoppel by deed an exception to the general rule that an instrument of conveyance not in the chain of title does not give constructive notice to subsequent purchasers and incumbrancers. The exception seems unjustified in view of the fact that the one claiming the benefit of the exception is either himself guilty of negligence in searching the record or he holds through one who is negligent and the record discloses such. Of course, as between parties who are unaffected by the recording statutes the doctrine of estoppel by deed still continues to operate. See Wack v. Collingswood Extension Realty Co., 114 N.J.Eq. 253, 168 A. 639 (E. & A.1933); McCusker v. Mc-Evey, 9 R.I. 528, 11 Am.Rep. 295 (1870); Burby, 326–327; Tiffany, pp. 517–518.

Note

For further discussion of this problem, see supra Case 242.

————

CASE 248: A, being owner in fee simple of Blackacre, conveys it to B. B takes his deed to the proper public officer whose duty it is to make a proper record of the deed, and B pays the statutory fee for such recordation. The public officer sets aside the deed for the purpose of making a record thereof but loses it among other papers on his desk with the result that it is not recorded at all. A then executes a deed to Blackacre to C who takes his deed to the same public officer who properly records it. Blackacre is vacant land and C has no knowledge of A's former deed to B. C takes possession of the land and B sues to eject him therefrom. May B succeed?

Answer and Analysis

The answer is no in many jurisdictions, but there is contrary authority. The rationale for putting the loss on B is as follows: Under the recording acts it seems the better rule to require the holder of an instrument of conveyance not only to present his deed to the proper official for recordation but also to require such holder to see that such instrument is properly recorded, if he would give notice to subsequent purchasers and incumbrancers. It is true that the public should be able to rely on a public servant or official to do his duty. But a public servant or officer is human and he makes errors. Now the question is, as between two quite innocent persons, B and C in our case, which one should bear the loss or injury caused by the failure on the part of a public officer to do his duty? Only one of those two persons could have prevented the injury because he alone had complete control of the situation at the time of the attempted recordation. That person is B, the holder of the deed. There is no way imaginable by which C, who could only act as a result of what B did or did not do, could protect himself. To require C to do more than examine the record with care and diligence would be a determination that the public or subsequent purchasers cannot rely on the public records as to titles. Hence, it seems proper in carrying out the purpose and intent of the recording statutes to require B to use due diligence not only in presenting his instrument for recordation but also to require him to see that such recordation is made. Therefore, the bona fide subsequent purchaser, C, takes priority over B and may remain in possession of Blackacre as the owner thereof. This principle applies not only where no record at all is made but also when a record is made but it is erroneously made. For example, suppose in our case the owner A had made a first mortgage on Blackacre for $5,000 to B.

B takes the mortgage for recordation. By an error the record shows the mortgage for only $500. Then A gives a second mortgage for $2,500 to C. B sues to foreclose his $5,000 mortgage. C is made a party defendant and agrees that B has the right to foreclose for $500 but not for $5,000. Here again B is bound to see that his mortgage is correctly recorded and, as to C, he can foreclose only as to $500. Such doctrine is the only one which gives full effect to the principle that subsequent purchasers and incumbrancers are entitled to rely on what they find on the title records.

The rationale for protecting B and putting the loss on C in the above case is as follows: B has done all that is required of him under the recording act when he files his instrument for record with the proper official. Further, necessarily some delay will occur between the deposit of the instrument in the registry and spreading it on the records, and even further delay in compiling the index. Unless the deed is deemed recorded from the time it is deposited in the registry and not from the time it is spread on the record and then indexed, there is a possibility that a person in B's position above will be defeated by a subsequent bona fide purchaser from the original grantor in spite of the fact that B has done all that pragmatically is within his power to do. An ordinary layman cannot literally perform the recorder's job for him, and it is essential that the deed or other instrument be deemed recorded from the moment of its deposit in the registry. Thus, although it is hard for an innocent purchaser to suffer a loss as a result of the recorder's mistake, it is equally hard for an innocent owner to suffer such a loss. Under such circumstances there is no more reason to protect the subsequent purchaser than the owner. Such errors in recording, like forged and other void instruments, are simply matters against which the recording act offers no protection. The remedy of the innocent purchaser in such cases should be against the recorder. See 70 A.L.R. 603–608; Terrell v. Andrew County, 44 Mo. 309 (1869); Burby, 325–326.

CASE 249: A, being fee simple owner of Blackacre, was negotiating with B for the sale of the property to B. B requested A to make out a deed in B's favor as grantee, saying he would be back the day following to examine the proposed deed. The day following B returned to A's house and A handed to B for examination the deed which A had signed and acknowledged as B had requested. B examined the deed and pronounced it satisfactory but stated that he would have to think over the matter a little longer. B returned the deed to A who put it in his pocket. Without A's knowledge or consent and without negligence on the part of A, B clandestinely picked the deed from A's pocket and put it on record and sold Blackacre to C, executing a deed to C as grantee therein. Blackacre was vacant property and C had no knowledge other than what the records imparted to him.

C took possession of Blackacre and A sues to eject him therefrom. May A succeed?

Answer and Analysis

The answer is yes. These facts show conclusively that A did not deliver his deed to B. Furthermore, they overcome any presumption of delivery which may be indulged in because the grantee, B, had possession of the instrument. And the facts state that A was not negligent in respect to B's gaining possession of the instrument which he recorded. Hence, estoppel cannot be used against A. There being no delivery of the deed by the owner and he having been guilty of no conduct which could estop him from denying delivery, A is still the owner with the right to possess Blackacre unless the recording acts preclude him from recovery.

The recording acts are intended to protect bona fide subsequent purchasers. There is no doubt that C should be so classified. We may assume that he examined the records and found a deed properly signed and acknowledged by A and that he paid full value for Blackacre. But the recording statutes are not intended to be a means by which wrongdoers, tortfeasors, criminals and forgers can deprive innocent owners of their real property. Such statutes are intended to protect the innocent and when two persons are equally innocent and one is no more to be blamed than the other for the predicament in which they find themselves, then the statutes will have no application and the title will remain where the law would recognize it to be. In our case the title was in A. He made no delivery of a deed to anyone. Any undelivered deed is a nullity and leaves the title in the owner as though there had been no deed at all.

Placing an undelivered deed on record can not give life to the dead paper and pass title, even though it may place a cloud thereon. But the result of B's wrongfully taking the deed from A's pocket and placing it on record can have no legal effect upon the title to Blackacre. A still remains the owner of Blackacre with the right of immediate possession and can eject anyone, including C, therefrom. C will have to be content with his personal action against B. And why does not the record assist C? Because the recording statutes presuppose a valid delivery of the instrument in order that they have any application. There is no such delivery in our case. The same would be true in case B forged A's name to a deed and placed it on record. It would have no legal effect at all and anyone who claimed through such forged deed would have no interest in the premises. Nor is an owner bound to examine the records himself from time to time to see if anyone has placed a forged or an undelivered instrument of conveyance on record for the purpose of depriving him of his land or clouding his title. In short, the recording acts protect subsequent parties against prior otherwise valid and delivered but unrecorded instruments; they have no application whatsoever to recorded but void deeds. See Stone v. French, 37 Kan. 145, 14 P. 530, 1 Am.St.Rep. 237 (1887); Burby, 323, 324.

CASE 250: O conveyed Blackacre, vacant land to A. A did not then record the deed. Later, O conveyed the land to B who had notice of the earlier deed. B recorded. Sometime later, A recorded his deed, and still later, B conveyed the same land to C. C had no notice of the deed to A. A brings suit to quiet title against C. Will he succeed?

Answer and Analysis

The answer is no according to the better view. For C to prevail in either a notice or race-notice jurisdiction he must, of course, qualify as a BFP without notice of A's deed. If the contest were between A and B, A would clearly win since B had notice of A's deed. But B recorded before A, and then conveyed to C. At the time C entered the picture, A's deed was filed for record. Looking at the recording statute literally, it might appear that A would be preferred since at the time C entered the picture the prior deed to A had been placed on record, and A had not been divested by the conveyance to B who took with notice.

However, the realities of tracing title through grantor-grantee indices suggest that C should win. The recording of A's deed out of turn puts it out of the chain of title, since a subsequent purchaser such as C would not be likely to find it in tracing title from O. In checking such title, C would find first the conveyance to B. If thereafter C ignored O on the reasonable assumption that O having conveyed once would have no further title to convey, C would never find the prior deed to A. Thus, C does qualify as a subsequent BFP without notice of the prior deed to A which is outside the chain of title.

This rule is logical and gives due consideration to the practicalities of tracing title when it is applied to deeds as stated in the case. It has also been applied to successive mortgages in the above situation, but the rationale to mortgages is less sustainable. For example, after O mortgages to A, O still has a substantial interest in Blackacre which is subject to further mortgage or conveyance. Hence, a subsequent person such as C would not be as justified in ignoring O after he finds first the recorded mortgage to B. Of course, C, in taking an assignment of the mortgage from B is primarily interested in getting a first mortgage and not a junior one. Hence, it is logical to say that he can disregard O after finding the recorded mortgage to B since C is only interested in getting a first mortgage and having found that B was the first mortgagee, all that concerns C from then on is to be sure that B did not assign the mortgage to someone else. At any rate, the leading case of Morse v. Curtis, citation below, did apply the doctrine of chain of title to mortgages in this situation.

There is a little authority contra which regards such out of turn recordings as within the chain of title. This position is believed unsound because of the difficulty it imposes on the title examiner. See

Morse v. Curtis, 140 Mass. 112, 2 N.E. 929 (1885); Woods v. Garnett, 72 Miss. 78, 16 So. 390 (1894), contra.

CASE 251: L owned 2 parcels of adjoining land. He conveyed one parcel to M, covenanting that he would not convey the other parcel unless the grantee entered into a covenant similar to that contained in the deed from L to M with respect to certain building restrictions. L's heirs conveyed the other parcel to G without inserting the covenant. The deed to M was duly recorded. G had no actual knowledge of any restrictions upon the land conveyed to him. G brings an action for breach of covenant for title against L's heirs. Will he succeed?

Answer and Analysis

The answer depends upon the jurisdiction. Of course, for G to be obligated to observe the building restrictions, (see infra chapter 25 as to equitable servitudes), he must take with notice of the restriction in the deed from L to M. Since G had no actual notice, the question is whether he is charged with constructive notice under the recording act of the covenant in the deed from L to M. Under one line of authority he is charged with such notice. Under this view, G must not only check to see that his grantor had not conveyed the very parcel of land which he is acquiring, but in addition must check deeds out from the common grantor to see that in conveying such neighboring land the grantor did not impose a covenant or servitude which affects the remaining land and which is ultimately conveyed to him. Thus, under this view, G takes with notice of the prior servitude. Therefore, his land is so incumbered, and he does have an action against his grantors for breach of the covenant against incumbrances.

Under the other view, G is charged with notice only of those things appearing in his direct chain of title. Under this view G need only check prior recorded deeds of his grantor to see that the land he is purchasing has not been previously conveyed. He need not check the contents of the other deeds out by a common grantor. Under this view, since G did not have actual notice of the servitude, he takes free therefrom. Thus, the grantors did not breach the covenant against incumbrances, and G has no action therefor.

The question presented in this problem is sometimes stated in terms of the meaning of "subsequent purchaser" under the recording act. Does the term refer to a subsequent purchaser from the same grantor or simply to a subsequent purchaser of the same land. As indicated previously, the courts take different positions, some thinking that the burden is too great to require a purchaser to examine prior deeds out by a common grantor; others take the contrary view-point. See Glorieux v. Lighthipe, 88 N.J.L. 199, 96 A. 94 (E. & A.1915); Finley v. Glen, 303 Pa.St. 131, 154 A. 299 (1931); Burby, 326.

CHART COMPARING RECORDING ACTS

Hypothet I:

1. O, owner of Blackacre, executes and delivers to A a deed conveying Blackacre to A, A does not record.

2. O, then executes and delivers to B a deed of the same land and at that time B knows of A's prior unrecorded deed.

3. B records his deed.

4. B executes and delivers to C a deed of the land and C does not know of A's prior unrecorded deed.

5. A then records.

6. C then records.

At the end of each numbered transaction the location of title would be as follows under the various recording acts:

Steps	1	2	3	4	5	6
Notice	A	A	A	C	C	C
Reason	Rec'd not necessary between the parties	B not a BFP	B not a BFP	C is a subseq. BFP	C is a subseq. BPF	C is a subseq. BFP
Race	A	A	B	C	C	C
Reason	Same as above	B did not record	B recorded first	Because B had title-chain of title concept	Because B had title-chain of title concept	Because B had title
Race-Notice	A	A	A	C	C	C
Reason	Same as above	Both of the above	B not a BFP	Subseq. BFP who can rely on B's record	Subseq. BFP who can rely on B's record	Subseq. BFP who can rely on B's record

Hypothetical II.

1. O, owner of Blackacre, executes and delivers to A a deed conveying Blackacre to A, A does not record.

2. O then executes and delivers to B a deed of the same land. B does not know of A's prior unrecorded deed. B does not record.

3. A then records his deed.

4. B then executes and delivers to C a deed to Blackacre. C does not record.

5. A then deeds Blackacre to D who does not know of either B or C. D does not record.

6. B then records.

7. C then records.

8. D then records.

At the end of each numbered transaction the location of title would be as follows under the various recording acts:

Steps	1	2	3	4	5	6	7	8
Notice	A	B	B	C	D	D	D	D
Reason	Rec'd not necessary between the parties	He is a subseq. BFP	B was a subseq. BFP	C gets B's title	Most subseq. BFP	Need not record as to prior parties	He had already divested C's title	was subseq. BFP and has now recorded
Race	A	A	A	A	D	D	D	D
Reason	Same as above	Neither recorded so A wins as before	A recorded 1st	A recorded 1st	He gets A's record title	B & C had been divested by A's record	same as ← and chain of title concept	same as ← and D has now recorded
Race-Notice	A	A	A	A	D	D	D	D
Reason	Same as above	Although B is a subseq. BFP, he did not record	B did not record 1st	C had constr. notice of A's title; A recorded 1st	D is subseq. BFP & can use A's recording	Same as ←	Same as ←	D is subseq. BFP and his chain recorded b/4 B's & C's

SUMMARY OF CASES IN CHAPTER XXIII

2. UNDER RECORDING STATUTES

Case 243. The recording statutes are intended to protect subsequent purchasers and incumbrancers who give value and take title in good faith without notice of a prior claim. Under notice type statutes bona fide purchasers or incumbrancers have priority over prior purchasers who do not record their deeds until after such subsequent purchasers have expended their money and taken their deeds in good faith.

Case 244. To be a bona fide purchaser entitled to protection under the recording statutes one must give a value which is more than nominal and he must take without notice of a prior claim or interest in the land. One cannot be in good faith if: (a) he takes with constructive notice given by a properly recorded instrument of conveyance; or if (b) he takes with actual notice of a prior claim or interest; or if (c) there is an actual physical possession of the land by one who has a prior interest even though such possessor's deed is not recorded. When one buys land the law charges him with notice of any interest claimed by one in possession of the land, but possession consistent with the record title does not constitute notice of the possessor's inconsistent claims in many jurisdictions, except in the case of tenants.

Case 245. A purchaser of land is duty bound to use due diligence both in searching the records and in inspecting the land respecting prior interests which may be claimed by others. If either the record or an inspection of the land discloses a circumstance which puts him upon inquiry he must pursue such inquiry to the point where he has used due diligence and is bound by such notice which due diligence would disclose. A subsequent purchaser is charged with constructive notice of every recorded instrument of conveyance which is a link in his chain of title. He is also charged with constructive notice of recitals in a recorded instrument which is a link in his chain of title, which recitals may refer to unrecorded instruments. He is also charged with constructive notice of recitals in an unrecorded instrument of conveyance which is an essential link in his chain of title and through which unrecorded instrument his own claim must be made.

Case 246. Under the recording statutes priority in right often depends upon the constructive notice imparted by recordation of instruments rather than on the common law rule, priority in time is priority in right. The chain of title means the unbroken continuity of title with every link in the chain being present from the patent to the claimant. A recorded instrument of conveyance outside the chain of title does not impart constructive notice to a subsequent purchaser or incumbrancer. If a grantor appears as a grantor in an instrument on the record without appearing on the record as a grantee, the instrument is a wild deed and not in the chain of title. A subsequent bona fide purchaser takes priority over a grantee in a recorded instrument which is outside the chain of title.

Case 247. An instrument of conveyance which operates by way of estoppel by deed is outside the chain of title and does not give constructive notice to subsequent purchasers and conveyancers according to the better view. Hence, the general rule, that a subsequent purchaser or incumbrancer of the after acquired property takes priority over the grantee or mortgagee in an earlier recorded instrument of conveyance which is outside the chain of title, applies to the ordinary case of estoppel by deed when the recording statutes are involved.

Case 248. Subsequent purchasers and incumbrancers are entitled to rely on the title records. If a holder of a deed presents it for recordation to the proper public official and the officer fails to record it, the loss or injury under one view must fall on the one who presents such instrument for record and not on a bona fide subsequent purchaser. Likewise, if the officer records the instrument but makes an error in its recordation, the loss or injury under this view must fall on him who had the instrument recorded and not on a subsequent purchaser or incumbrancer. Under this position the duty lies on the holder of an instrument of conveyance not only to see that the instrument is recorded when he presents it for record, but also to see that it is correctly recorded. Under the contrary position, the loss falls on the subsequent purchaser when the recorder makes a mistake. The reason is that the holder of the instrument does all that is required of him when he deposits such instrument for recordation.

Case 249. A forged or an undelivered deed is a nullity and no one can claim any interest through such. Placing such a deed on record does not add any legal efficacy to such a forged or undelivered instrument. The recording statutes are not intended to be a means of conveyance nor are they intended for the purpose of assisting wrongdoers, tort-feasors, criminals and forgers in depriving innocent owners of their real property. The original owner continues his ownership over one who claims even as an innocent purchaser through a forged or an undelivered deed.

Case 250. A subsequent purchaser is not charged with notice of a prior deed or other instrument which is out of the chain of title although it may be placed on record. A prior deed recorded after a second deed to the same property from the same grantor is out of the chain of title. If a purchaser finds a conveyance from the owner to his grantor which gives him a perfect record title, he is entitled to rely thereon and is not obliged to search the records further to see if there were any prior deeds recorded out of sequence.

Case 251. There is a conflict of authority as to whether the term subsequent purchaser as used in the recording acts means only subsequent purchaser of the same land or whether it means subsequent purchaser from the same grantor. Under the latter view, the subsequent purchaser is charged with notice of servitudes or incumbrances contained in deeds out by a common grantor when such incumbrances affect the land he is purchasing. Under the former view, the subsequent purchaser is charged with notice of incumbrances which appear only in recorded documents pertaining to his direct chain of title, i. e., the very land he is purchasing.

Chapter XXIV

MORTGAGES

1. Mortgages Generally.
   Legal Gems.
   Cases.

2. Mortgage Substitutes or Alternatives and Other Matters.
   Legal Gems.
   Cases.

Summary of Cases in Chapter XXIV.

---

1. MORTGAGES GENERALLY

LEGAL GEMS

1. A mortgage is an interest in land created by a written instrument providing security for the performance of a duty or the payment of a debt.

2. The debt may be antecedent, existing, or one which is to arise in the future.

3. The debt is usually evidenced by a promissory note or bond, and frequently a copy of such note is appended to or incorporated into the mortgage instrument.

4. The original note or bond is not incorporated into the mortgage or recorded but is retained in the mortgagee's possession. The mortgage should be and is generally recorded.

5. The mortgagor creates the mortgage. He is the "landowner" and debtor. The mortgagee is the creditor and the holder of the mortgage.

6. At common law, and still in some states, the mortgage operates as a conveyance of the legal title to the mortgagee, but such title is subject to defeasance on payment of the debt or performance of the duty by the mortgagor.

7. In other states the mortgage creates only a lien on the land regardless of the operative words of the mortgage instrument.

8. The difference between lien theory and title theory states is not great insofar as the substantive rights of the parties are concerned since, even in title theory states, it is universally recognized that the mortgagee's title is only for purposes of security.

9. The term equity of redemption most accurately refers to the interest of the mortgagor in a title jurisdiction after default. It was in this situation that the mortgagor needed the aid of equity to provide relief from the conveyance which at law had become absolute in the mortgagee. Had the mortgagor performed on law day, his title

499

would have reverted and the law would have afforded a remedy. Nevertheless, common usage refers to the mortgagor's interest as an "equity," presumably a shorthand expression for equity of redemption, at all times. The term "equity" also is commonly used to refer to the value of the mortgagor's interest over and above the amount of the debt owing to the mortgagee.

10. A mortgagor may convey his land encumbered by the mortgage or subject it to further mortgages.

11. In a conveyance of the land "subject to" a mortgage, the grantee is not personally liable for the debt which the mortgage secures, but if he doesn't pay the debt, the mortgage may be foreclosed and he will lose the land. The practical effect of an individual not being personally liable for the debt is that the mortgagee cannot get a deficiency judgment against him in case of a foreclosure in which the property does not bring enough at the foreclosure sale to satisfy the debt.

12. In a sale of the land in which the purchaser assumes the mortgage, the purchaser or grantee is personally liable for the mortgage debt and is subject to a deficiency judgment in case of a foreclosure with the sale not realizing enough to satisfy the debt.

13. There is a conflict of authority as to the personal liability of an assuming grantee who derives title from a prior grantee who had not assumed the mortgage obligation. Under one view, when there is an hiatus in the chain of assumption agreements, the promise of the assuming grantee is a nullity and he is not personally liable. Under the other view, such an assuming grantee is personally liable on the basis of a third party beneficiary contract theory.

14. Mortgages are assignable. Both the mortgage (the security), and the note (the debt), should be transferred to the same person.

15. When there is a purported transfer of the note or debt to one party, and an assignment of the mortgage to another, the general rule is that the mortgage follows the note or debt. It should be borne in mind that the debt (or note) is the principal relationship, and that the mortgage is only ancillary thereto for purposes of security. If there is no debt or obligation, there is no mortgage. Therefore, in case of conflict, the holder of the debt will usually prevail.

16. The mortgage and assignments thereof should be recorded. Failure to record the mortgage may make it possible for the mortgagor to convey to a bona fide purchaser who would take free of the mortgage under the recording act. Similarly, failure of an assignee to record his assignment may make it possible for the assignor to execute a fraudulent satisfaction of the mortgage which would enable the mortgagor to convey to a bona fide purchaser who could take free of the mortgage under the recording act.

17. Foreclosure in modern practice is the method by which the security (i. e. the mortgaged property), or proceeds from the sale

thereof, is applied to the satisfaction of the debt or obligation. Depending upon the jurisdiction, there may be more than one method of foreclosure available, but foreclosure by sale pursuant to judicial or equitable proceedings of one type or another is available in all jurisdictions. Such method of foreclosure is the most common one.

18. In early times foreclosure meant literally foreclosing or barring the equity of redemption. It was a remedy afforded the mortgagee to prevent the mortgagor from redeeming his land from the mortgage after default. In essence, the mortgagee sought and obtained a decree to the effect that if the mortgagor did not satisfy the mortgage debt by a specified date, then he would be foreclosed (barred) from ever redeeming. This is strict foreclosure and is still applicable in some states.

19. Strict foreclosure is contrary to the theory of mortgages in lien theory states. In lien theory states, the mortgagor retains title until it is divested at foreclosure sale; foreclosure is a method of enforcing the lien by selling the property and applying the proceeds to the satisfaction of debt.

20. Other methods of foreclosure, such as foreclosure under power of sale, and foreclosure by entry, are available in some states.

21. Foreclosure by sale under judicial supervision facilitates the determination of the value of the mortgaged property and thus aids in the determination of the amount of any deficiency decree that might be awarded where the proceeds realized from the sale are insufficient to satisfy the mortgage debt.

22. The granting of a deficiency decree is within the sound judicial discretion of the court. In many jurisdictions, at least, the mortgagee need not seek a deficiency in the foreclosure proceedings but may bring a separate action at law on the note.

23. In order to protect fully the redemption right of the mortgagor, equity developed several doctrines to prevent the mortgagee from exacting agreements or concessions which would interfere with or clog the equity of redemption. The most common of these rules, and the only one which has attained substantial significance in the United States, is the maxim "once a mortgage, always a mortgage." This simply means that if in fact a mortgage is created, then the usual incidents of a mortgage attach regardless of the apparent form of the transaction, and that any ancillary device entered into at the inception of the transaction to impinge on the mortgagor's rights as a mortgagor is ineffective.

24. Subrogation is the substitution of one person to the position of another, an obligee, whose claim he has satisfied. Thus, when a mortgagor conveys land to a grantee and deducts the amount of the mortgage from the purchase price, as between the mortgagor and grantee, either the grantee (in the case of an assumption agreement), or the land itself (in the case of a "subject to" sale), is regarded as being primarily liable for the debt, and the mortgagor's liability is

secondary or similar to that of a surety. Therefore, if the mortgagor is required to pay the mortgage debt, he is subrogated to the mortgagee's rights to proceed against the grantee, or the land, or both, as the case may be.

CASE 252: C executed a mortgage on real property to P to secure P for any indorsements or guarantees he had made or should thereafter make on promissory notes for the mortgagor, C, up to the amount of $6,000.00. It was dated May 2, 1967, and was recorded May 3, 1967. The first indorsement was made on May 7, 1967, and the last on October 16, 1970. P has been compelled to pay the indorsed paper and has advanced $5,000.00, over and above all payments made by the mortgagor. This action was brought to foreclose the mortgage. The issue presented is that of priority between P and X, a judgment creditor of C. X's judgments were obtained subsequent to the mortgage but prior to the indorsements by the plaintiff of some of the notes which enter into and form a part of the mortgage debt. Who has priority?

Answer and Analysis

The answer is that P's lien has priority to the full extent of $5,000.00. A mortgage to secure future advances or liabilities is valid as long as the amount of the incumbrance can be rendered certain. The critical question is the effective date of the mortgage. A mortgage is simply security for a debt or other obligation. If there is no obligation, there is no necessity for security. In the case of a mortgage for future advances, there is no actual debt until the advances are made. Thus, if the transaction is regarded as a series of mortgages coming into effect at the time each advance is made, then the judgment creditor should have priority over the mortgage as to all advances made after the judgments were perfected. Such an approach, however, would seriously limit the utility of mortgages for future advances, inhibit commerce, and would be unrealistic as to the true nature of such mortgages.

Mortgages for future advances are of great utility. A simple example of a construction loan mortgage will illustrate. With such a mortgage the funds are advanced as the building progresses; the mortgagor saves interest by not having all of the loan from the beginning, and the mortgagee obtains adequate security by advancing money only as the building is constructed. If intervening parties were able to obtain priority as to later payments under the single mortgage, such arrangements would be impractical as many such lenders can by law and prudent business practice only lend on first mortgage security. Of course, a distinction can, and frequently is, made between mortgages for future advances when such advances are obligatory, and when such advances are optional. In the case when such advances are obligatory, there would seem to be more compelling reasons for giving priority to the mortgagee from the date of the execution of the mortgage. Under such a mortgage the mortgagee is compelled to make the advances and therefore his priority should be secured as of the date he obligated himself.

Even in the case of optional advances, however, there is persuasive if not compelling reason for affording the mortgagee priority from the time of the original agreement. In a mortgage for future advances, the obligation secured is not the series of individual advances, but rather the single promise of the mortgagor to repay all specified future advances. The making of the advances is but a condition precedent to the *performance* of the promise; it is not necessary to its existence. Thus, the mortgage is to secure the single obligation—the promise to pay advances when made.

In spite of the foregoing logic, however, most courts do place a limitation on the priority of mortgages for future advances when the advances are optional instead of obligatory. In the case of both optional and obligatory advances, the mortgagee has priority over all subsequent parties to the extent of advances already made. In the case of obligatory advances, he has priority over all later liens to the extent of his original obligation and in spite of notice by later lienors. Some states have enacted statutes which afford optional advances the same priority as obligatory ones. (E. g., West's Fla.Stat.Ann. § 697.-04. Nevertheless, in the absence of legislation most courts hold that the mortgagee in the case of optional advances has priority over subsequent parties only to the extent of advances made before receiving notice that the liens of such subsequent parties attached. For such a subsequent party to obtain priority over a prior mortgagee for optional future advances thereafter made, the weight of authority requires actual notice to the mortgagee, constructive notice being insufficient. Since in the instant case there is no evidence that X served notice on P prior to any advancements of P, P should have priority as to the full extent of his advancements, $5,000.00. See McDaniels v. Colvin, 16 Vt. 300, 42 Am.Dec. 512 (1844); Ackerman v. Hunsicker, 85 N.Y. 43, 39 Am.Rep. 621 (1881); Osborne, Nelson & Whitman, 756, 759 et seq.

CASE 253: A was the owner of Blackacre and, having become indebted to X, executed to him a deed absolute to the property. This deed, although absolute in form was intended only as security for the payment of the debt. Later A also conveyed the personal property on the farm and delivered possession of the farm and everything on it to X. This was done upon the express agreement that such was to be additional security for his indebtedness to X and also security for his indebtedness to his laborers. P was one of those laborers. X died soon afterward and D was appointed as administrator of his estate. X's claim was satisfied out of the proceeds from the sale of the crops and Blackacre was reconveyed to A. There was a sufficient residue from the sale of the crops to pay P, but the general creditors of the deceased contested his right to such proceeds. The trial court decided that P had no right to the proceeds and appealed. What result?

Answer and Analysis

The answer is that the judgment should be reversed and remanded with directions to enter a decree for P. It has long been recognized in equity that a deed absolute in form intended for security will in fact be given effect as intended and construed as a mortgage. This is not really surprising when it is remembered that the traditional form of the mortgage was a conveyance subject to defeasance, and that the equity of redemption was created by the equity court to protect the mortgagor after default. In order to preserve this equity of redemption various rules were formulated to prevent mortgagees from limiting or clogging the equity of redemption. The most common example of such rules is the principle "once a mortgage, always a mortgage." This, in effect, means that a mortgagee cannot circumscribe the mortgagor's right to redeem by disguising the transaction as an outright conveyance or by entering into ancillary contracts limiting his right of redemption. Thus, a deed absolute when intended as security is in fact a mortgage with all the ancillary rights and obligations pertaining thereto.

In the instant case all the parties apparently conceded that the original deed absolute was a mortgage and no complaint was made when the land was reconveyed to A after the satisfaction of the debt owing to X. There seems to be no reason for distinguishing between the absolute conveyance of the land itself and the absolute conveyance of the personalty and delivery of possession of the land for security purposes. Since both transfers were intended as security, they were both mortgages. Further, the delivery of possession of the farm and personalty to X would constitute X a mortgagee in possession. As such, X has a duty to account; he is not authorized to acquire from the transaction any advantage over and beyond the repayment of his claim. Further, such transfer was expressly conditioned also upon securing the obligation to P. Therefore, X, and consequently his administrator, had the duty to pay P's claim if there were sufficient proceeds to do so. The facts state that there were such proceeds after the satisfaction of X's claim; hence, P can recover.

Although the above analysis may correctly describe the rights of the parties inter sesse, additional problems or issues remain. One such problem is whether or not parol evidence is admissible to prove that a deed absolute on its face was intended as a mortgage. The answer to this question is yes; equity has long since permitted it. The introduction of such testimony must overcome two strong objections —the Statute of Frauds and the parol evidence rule. The great majority of jurisdictions permit such parol evidence, but the rationales and theories differ. As to the Statute of Frauds, the best rule is that it is inapplicable because the evidence to be introduced deals with the retention, and not the creation or transfer, of an interest. In other words, the evidence is being introduced to show the equity of redemption, an interest retained in the grantor and not created by the deed absolute. As to the parol evidence rule, one explanation is that such evidence is not used to contradict or vary the terms of the instrument but to establish an equity superior to its terms. Another explanation is that the parties did not intend to embody their whole agreement in the deed, and still another is that the omission of the defeasance clause was the result of mistake, fraud, ignorance or undue advantage.

An additional problem in the deed absolute mortgage cases is whether the true nature of the transaction is valid as to third parties. This entails a problem as to priorities and the recording act. Since the mortgagee appears to have the fee simple title, there is a good possibility, unless the mortgagor is in possession, that the mortgagee may convey to a bona fide purchaser for value without notice of the mortgagor's equity. Under such circumstances, such bona fide purchaser generally prevails over the mortgagor even apart from statute. In the instant case, however, there are no such parties. Although lien or judgment creditors are protected under some recording acts, there are none in the instant case. General creditors were complaining, and general creditors are entitled to reach only the assets of their debtor. Thus, in the instant case, the true nature of the transfers can be shown and P is entitled to be satisfied from the proceeds of the crop sale. See Pierce v. Robinson, Adm'r, 13 Cal. 116 (1859); Osborne, §§ 69, 72, 73, 77, 79, 83, 84, 85; Osborne, Nelson & Whitman, pp. 37–58.

Note

When the "mortgagee" under a deed absolute mortgage transfers to a BFP, the mortgagor has no rights against the BFP, but he does have an action for redemption against the "mortgagee" for the value of the land, or, at his election, the proceeds of the sale. The theory is that the mortgagee now has the value of the land in his hands as a separate fund, and such fund as a substitute for the land may be redeemed by the mortgagor. See Mooney v. Byrne, 163 N.Y. 86, 57 N. E. 163 (1900); Havana Nat'l Bank v. Wiemer, 32 Ill.App.3d 578, 335 N.E.2d 506 (1975); Osborne, § 79; Osborne, Nelson & Whitman, pp. 46–48.

————

CASE 254: MR executed a mortgage on his real property in favor of ME to secure an indebtedness represented by a note. ME assigned the mortgage to P. Thereafter P brought an action against MR to foreclose the mortgage. P proved the assignment of the mortgage but failed to prove a transfer of the note or otherwise satsifactorily accounting for it. May P obtain a decree of foreclosure?

Answer and Analysis

The answer is no, but there is supporting contrary authority. Those jurisdictions that deny recovery under the circumstances of this case do so on the basis that the mortgage is simply security for the debt (note), and that the plaintiff in foreclosure must show that both the note (debt) and the mortgage were assigned to him. Although it is well established that the mortgage follows the note, the converse is not necessarily true. Hence, the plaintiff, having not shown that he is entitled to the debt, may not foreclose.

Cases supporting a contrary result do so on the basis of the probable intent of the parties and on the popular meaning ascribed to the term "assignment of mortgage." By popular usage "assignment of mortgage" connotes the transfer of the mortgagee's total interest, that is both the debt and the security, and not just the bare security. As a matter of fact, transfer of the security alone would be a nullity since its only purpose is to secure the debt or obligation. Transactions should be construed so as to effectuate the intent of the parties, and it should not be presumed that they intended a futile act. Thus, where the debt is not represented by a separate written instrument (note), it is not uncommon to assume that the parties intended a transfer of the debt also. Even when the debt is represented by another instrument, it should be remembered that the mortgage secures the debt itself and not simply the evidence of it. Hence, if it is possible for the mortgagee to assign the debt without the instrument, or to transfer at least an equitable interest therein, an assignment of the mortgage alone may indicate such intent and should be given effect. Any inference that the mortgagee intended to keep the debt and assign only the security may be offset by the improbability that he intended such a futile act.

The second approach, however, should be used with caution. When there is a separate instrument representing the debt, the assignee of the mortgage should be required to explain his position, and, if possible, to account fully for the outstanding note or other instrument. It is possible for such an instrument to get into the hands of a third party, even a holder in due course if the instrument is negotiable. Where there are separate transfers of the note and mortgage, it would seem that the person entitled to the note or debt would be entitled also to the security, and hence have the right to foreclose. See Cleveland v. Cohrs, 10 S.C. 224 (1878); Sobel v. Mutual Dev., Inc., 313 So.2d 77 (Fla. 1st D.C.A.1975); Osborne § 226; Osborne, Nelson & Whitman, p. 320.

———

CASE 255: MR mortgaged Blackacre to ME to secure an indebtedness of $20,000.00. Thereafter MR conveyed Blackacre to A who "assumed the mortgage;" after that A conveyed Blackacre to B "subject to the mortgage;" and still later B conveyed to C who "assumed the mortgage." The mortgage is in default and ME is about to bring foreclosure proceedings. State the rights and obligations of the parties.

Answers and Analyses

The answer and the reasons therefore will be indicated in the following paragraphs. ME has a security interest in Blackacre which he can enforce and a personal claim against MR for the amount of the debt outstanding. ME can proceed against Blackacre, sue MR on the note, or do both at the same time. When MR conveyed the land to A, MR did not terminate his obligation on the debt, nor did he free Blackacre from the "lien" of the mortgage. The amount of the indebtedness would normally be taken into consideration in establishing the purchase price between MR and A, (in other words, A would pay MR the value of the land less the mortgage debt outstanding), so that as between them, A should pay off MR's indebtedness to ME. This is clearly the case where, as in this instance, A expressly assumed the mortgage. Such assumption does not relieve MR of his contractual obligation to ME, but it does establish that as between MR and A, A should be primarily liable, and MR secondarily liable. Similarly, MR is entitled to have Blackacre regarded as the principal source of payment of the indebtedness. Thus, if ME should sue MR and collect on the debt without foreclosing, MR would be subrogated to ME's rights against Blackacre and could bring foreclosure proceedings. If from the foreclosure there remained a deficiency, MR could recover a judgment for such amount against A because A promised to pay such indebtedness when he assumed the mortgage.

The result is similar to an extent as to the other transferees in all cases. The mortgage remains a valid incumbrance against Blackacre as to all grantees, including B and C. MR remains personally liable on his indebtedness, but as to all the grantees, whether the conveyance was subject to or assuming, MR is entitled to have Blackacre applied first to the satisfaction of the debt. Thus, should MR have to pay the debt, he would be subrogated to ME's right of foreclosure.

The difference between a transfer of the mortgage property "subject to" and "assuming" the mortgage is the difference between personal liability and the lack thereof on behalf of the grantee. Thus, in the initial conveyance, A assumed the mortgage and became personally liable therefore as between him and MR, and, as previously pointed out, should MR have to pay either the outstanding indebtedness or any deficiency resulting from foreclosure, MR then has a suit against A on the contractual obligation.

When A conveyed the land to B "subject to the mortgage," this meant that B did not personally become liable for the outstanding indebtedness. Of course, the land was incumbered and could be foreclosed to satisfy the debt, but B is personally liable to no one for such debt. Thus, although B stands to lose the land while it is in his possession if the debt is not paid, he cannot be liable for any deficiency realized from foreclosure. Now that B has sold the land, he is in effect out of the picture and is liable to no one on the outstanding indebtedness. No deficiency decree can be had against him.

The only question remaining is that of the personal liability of C. On this there is a conflict of authority. Under one line of authority C's promise to B to pay the indebtedness to ME is a nullity because B was not personally liable and owed no obligation to ME. Other jurisdictions permit ME to hold C personally liable and to recover a deficiency judgment against C on the basis of a third party beneficiary contract—the assumption agreement between B and C being for the benefit of ME. If MR is required to pay any deficiency to ME, then he should be entitled to recover from C on the basis of subrogation in those jurisdictions that would permit ME to recover from C. Until MR has to pay, it is doubtful that he has any rights against C personally. See Osborne §§ 248, 252, 253, 258, 259, 260 and 261; Osborne, Nelson & Whitman, pp. 249–278.[1]

———

CASE 256: A, owner of Blackacre, borrowed money to finance some improvements and executed a mortgage thereon in favor of B to secure the loan. Later, A borrowed money from C and executed a second mortgage on Blackacre to secure that loan. Both mortgages were promptly recorded, and C had notice of the mortgage to B. C's mortgage is in default and he brings foreclosure proceedings against A. C joins B as a party defendant, and B moves that he should be dismissed from the action. Should B's motion be granted?

Answer and Analysis

The answer is yes. The holder of a prior incumbrance cannot be made a party to a foreclosure action without his consent. In the instant case B has the first mortgage or prior incumbrance. After the execution of the mortgage to B, A still had an interest in Blackacre

---

1. Provisions applicable to a UCC section or other specific statute may vary the results in a particular case, and may even lead to unfair results. Thus: MR conveyed a parcel of land subject to a mortgage; the grantee executed another mortgage; and the first mortgage went into default. ME–1 then obtained payment from MR and assigned the mortgage and endorsed the note to MR. MR then assigned the note and mortgage to P1 who sought foreclosure. ME–2 counterclaimed for foreclosure and claimed priority. It was held that P1 had no cause of action.

The decision was based on an application of UCC 3–601(3) providing:
"The liability of all parties is discharged when any party who has himself no right of action or recourse on the instrument . . . reacquires the instrument in his own right . . . ."

Thus, when MR paid the amount due on the note the debt was extinguished and all rights thereunder were discharged, including any rights of subrogation. Thus, MR had nothing to transfer to P1. The court reasoned that there cannot be subrogation rights in a "subject to" situation when the debt paid was the obligation of the person who paid it. Best Fertilizers of Arizona, Inc. v. Burns, 116 Ariz. 492, 570 P.2d 179 (1977).

The case is criticized in Osborne, Nelson & Whitman, pp. 262–264.

which he could further incumber or convey. He could do nothing, however, (assuming B recorded his mortgage which he did), to defeat such prior right or interest of B. All subsequent mortgagees or grantees must take their interest subject to the prior mortgage of B. If B's mortgage is not in default, or if B simply does not yet wish to foreclose, C cannot compel him to do so. If there is doubt as to the relative priority of the claims, however, then joinder may be permitted for the limited purpose of determining priority.

If C cannot join B in a foreclosure, does this mean that C must forego the possibility of realizing on his security, or wait until B decides to foreclose? Not at all. C can foreclose against A and have the land sold at foreclosure subject to the first mortgage. The relationship of the parties is most readily explained in terms of lien theory states. Thus, after A mortgaged to B, A could have sold the land subject to B's mortgage lien, or he could have executed a second mortgage lien thereon, which he did. The security for this second mortgage to C was the land subject to the first mortgage lien of B. Thus, when C realizes on his security, he is foreclosing on the land subject to the prior mortgage lien in favor of B, and the purchaser at the foreclosure sale gets just that. Any proceeds from the foreclosure of the second mortgage will go first to the payment of the costs of foreclosure, then to satisfaction of the debt owing C, and any surplus will go to A. B will not share in the proceeds of such a foreclosure, but B still has his mortgage security and a personal action against A. The result is the same in title theory jurisdictions although the terminology is somewhat different.

If the situation were reversed, however, and B, the first mortgagee, were bringing the foreclosure action, then he could join C as a party defendant. In fact, he must join C in such a foreclosure action in order to divest C's mortgage and sell the land free and clear of all mortgages. C must be joined as a party defendant in order to be given an opportunity to redeem the security from the claim of the first mortgage. If C is not joined, his rights as to the security remain unaffected. In a foreclosure of a first mortgage with all juniors properly joined, the proceeds of sale are applied first to the payment of costs, then to the first mortgage obligation, then to junior incumbrances in order of priority, and finally to the mortgagor if any sums remain. On such a foreclosure of the senior claim with all incumbrancers properly joined, the land is sold free and clear of all incumbrances. See Osborne, §§ 321, 323, 324; Osborne, Nelson & Whitman, pp. 447 et seq.

2. MORTGAGE SUBSTITUTES OR ALTERNATIVES AND OTHER MATTERS

LEGAL GEMS

1. The installment land contract is frequently used as an alternative or substitute for a mortgage, particularly as a substitute for a purchase money mortgage.

2.   In an installment land contract the purchaser generally goes into possession, agrees to make installment payments over a long period of time, agrees to pay taxes, insurance, and to maintain the property, while the vendor agrees to execute a deed when the purchaser has fully performed.

3.   The installment contract usually states that time is of the essence and then provides for summary contract remedies if the purchaser defaults, i. e., that the vendor has the option to declare the contract terminated, to retake possession without legal process, and to retain all payments as liquidated damages. In fact, it is the desire to take advantage of such remedies and to avoid the more cumbersome process of mortgage foreclosure that influences many vendors to use this device.

4.   Although installment land contract forfeiture provisions had been routinely enforced in the past, there is considerable variation in treatment not only from state to state, but also frequent variations within a state depending upon the precise contract remedy sought, the exact terms of the contract, and the facts of the case. Many jurisdictions, however, do in fact confer on the vendee under an installment contract an equity of redemption.

As to installment land contracts, see generally, Osborne, Nelson & Whitman, pp. 79–110; Hoffman v. Semet, 316 So.2d 649 (Fla. 4th D.C.A.1975).

5.   In addition to the installment land contract, parties frequently use other substitutes or alternatives to the traditional mortgage. Such devices include:

(a) the deed absolute with an oral agreement to reconvey (see *supra* case 253) ;

(b) the conditional sale which may take one of several forms:

(1) a deed (sale) and option to repurchase;

(2) a deed (sale) and leaseback with option to repurchase; or

(3) a sale (deed) and contract to repurchase; and

(c) the deed of trust. See Osborne, Nelson & Whitman, pp. 13–14, 62–68.

6.   Whether the conditional sale will be construed as the device indicated by the terms of the instruments, or whether it will be construed as a mortgage, depends on a number of factors, but the primary test is the intention of the parties at the time of the transaction. Osborne, Nelson & Whitman, pp. 67 et seq.

7.   The deed of trust, unlike the other mortgage substitutes mentioned in Gem 5, was not developed to circumvent the rule prohibiting the clogging of the equity of redemption. Rather, it was probably developed to provide a more rapid foreclosure technique than judicial sale, and at the same time permit such lenders at fore-

closure under a power of sale to be bidders at such sale. Frequently, mortgagees exercising a power of sale are prohibited from bidding at such sale. See Osborne, Nelson & Whitman, p. 13.

8. A deed of trust is a security device used as an alternative to a mortgage; it is a three party transaction instead of a two party, mortgagor-mortgagee, arrangement. In a deed of trust, the borrower or debtor, analogous to the mortgagor, transfers the legal title to a trustee, the third party, to hold the property as security for payment of the debt to the lender, creditor or financier, analogous to the mortgagee in the traditional mortgage.

9. Deeds of trust usually contain a power of sale vested in the trustee authorizing him to sell the property if the grantor-mortgagor defaults on his obligation.

10. "Due on sale" clauses gained increasing popularity in recent years when interest rates were rising rapidly. This clause permits the mortgagee to accelerate the debt when the mortgagor sells the property unless the mortgagee and the new buyer agree on the interest rate to be charged. Some states enforce the clause as written, but many states refuse to let the mortgagee accelerate unless he can show an impairment of the security or some other default by the mortgagor. Osborne, Nelson & Whitman, p. 303.

11. A wrap-around mortgage is a subsequent, and therefore junior, mortgage which is written to secure a debt or obligation which includes the amount of outstanding mortgages as well as any new funds advanced. It may be illustrated thus:

> MR is the owner of Debtorsacre, worth $200,000, but subject to an existing mortgage in favor of ME–1 with a balance due of $80,000, at an interest rate of 7%. MR borrows $70,000 from ME–2, and executes a mortgage and note to ME–2 for $150,000 at an interest rate of 10%, and ME–2 agrees to make the payments on the first mortgage out of the payments made by MR to him. Thus, the second mortgage is "wrapped around" the first. See Osborne, Nelson & Whitman, pp. 278–280.

12. Marshalling is an equitable principle employed to adjust the rights of various parties by ranking their priorities and determining the order in which the mortgaged property will be sold to satisfy the mortgage debt or debts. Two common techniques are the "two funds" doctrine, and the "inverse order of alienation" rule. See generally Osborne, Nelson & Whitman, pp. 614 et seq.; Gems 13–14 infra.

13. The "two funds" doctrine applies when a senior mortgagee has a first mortgage on two or more parcels and a junior mortgagee has a security interest on only one. The doctrine applies to require the senior creditor to proceed first against the parcel which is subject only to his lien. In this way, the junior lienor will receive the maximum possible protection and will not be arbitrarily deprived of his security by the prior mortgagee proceeding first against the property

subject also to the junior's claim. The doctrine is not applied automatically; it is incumbent on the one asserting the right to request the equity court to apply it.

14. The "inverse order of alienation" rule applies when a mortgaged tract of land is "sold off" or conveyed in parcels and the various grantees pay full value to the mortgagor without getting a release from the mortgagee. Thereafter, if the mortgagor defaults and the mortgagee forcloses, the "inverse order" rule will require the mortgagee to proceed first against the lands still owned by the mortgagor, and then proceed against the other parcels in the inverse order in which they were sold until the mortgage is fully satisfied. The rationale is that the buyer of the first parcel sold acquired the most equity, and likewise down the line until the land still held by the mortgagor has the least. As between the mortgagor and the grantees, the mortgagor should pay the debt, and his land should be sold first for that purpose.

15. The opposite of the "inverse order" rule should apply when one or more grantees of a portion of the mortgaged property assumes the mortgage debt. In this situation, as between the grantee and the mortgagor, the equity resides with the grantor-mortgagor, and the grantee should pay and his land be sold to satisfy the debt. Thus, the "direct order of alienation" rule would apply in this situation, and the mortgagor's remaining land would be last sold to satisfy the debt.

––––––

CASE 257: Vendor and vendee execute an installment contract for a period of twenty years. Vendee complies for five years and thereafter is in default for four years. Vendor remains silent throughout this period and the vendee remains in possession. Vendee tenders full payment and brings an action for specific performance, and vendor counterclaims for removal of the contract as a cloud on his title. What result?

Answer and Analysis

Vendee is awarded specific performance. Vendor's silence throughout the four year period constituted a waiver of the default, and thus the contract for sale was specifically enforceable. Upon tender of the balance due the court found that vendee was entitled to a right of redemption.

The judicial creation of a right of redemption is in effect providing that same equitable remedy to a vendee that he would have had if the parties used a deed and purchase money mortgage in consummating the transaction. Forfeiture provisions of installment land contracts, although once regularly enforced as written, have met with sharp attacks in most jurisdictions. The courts will consider the type of action brought, the terms of the contract and the respective postures of the parties, including but not limited to the percentage of purchase price paid. In addition, several states have enacted statutes limiting the right of forfeiture.

Thus, the trend is to virtually eliminate the forfeiture provisions of the installment contract and treat it like a mortgage. There are, of course, tax advantages of an installment sale, and there is always the possibility that the vendee may not assert his legal rights. It should be noted that only the installment land contract is likely to be treated as a mortgage; the ordinary executory contract for the sale of the land is not. See H & L Land Co. v. Warner, 258 So.2d 293 (Fla. 2d D.C.A.1972); Osborne, Nelson & Whitman, 79–110.

SUMMARY OF CASES IN CHAPTER XXIV

1. MORTGAGES GENERALLY

Case 252. A mortgage is security for a debt or other obligation of the mortgagor. A mortgage for future advances is valid from its inception, the obligation being the single promise to pay all the subsequent advances and not the individual advances as they are made. Such a mortgage, when the advances are obligatory, has priority over all persons obtaining an interest in the security after the mortgage is executed, regardless of when the advances are made. As to such mortgages when the subsequent advances are optional, most courts hold that the mortgagee has priority over subsequent parties only to the extent of advances made before receiving actual notice that the liens or interest of such subsequent parties have attached.

Case 253. A deed absolute in form and intended as security is in fact a mortgage. Parol evidence can be introduced to show that a deed absolute in form was intended as a mortgage, and the Statute of Frauds and the parol evidence rule do not preclude such evidence. Under some circumstances the grantee ("mortgagee") under a deed absolute given for security may transfer the land to a BFP, and if he does so the BFP takes free of the grantor-mortgagor's equity of redemption. The relationship between the original parties, however, is not affected by the superior claim of the BFP.

Case 254. In a mortgage transaction, the underlying debt or obligation is the principal and the mortgage is the accessory. The mortgage follows the obligation (debt, note), but the converse is not necessarily true. An assignment of the mortgage without a transfer of the obligation is a nullity, and some jurisdictions will not permit an assignee of the mortgage to foreclose without expressly showing that he is also a transferee of the obligation. Some jurisdictions in some circumstances will infer that an assignment of the mortgage carries with it an assignment of the obligation also. Whoever under applicable law is entitled to the obligation is entitled to the security also.

Case 255. A mortgagee has both an in personam claim against the mortgagor on the debt or obligation and an in rem action against the security. An assuming grantee becomes personally liable on the mortgage debt whereas a grantee from the mortgagor who takes simply subject to the mortgage does not become personally liable. Where there is a break in the chain of assumption agreements, there is a split of authority as to whether an assuming grantee who takes from a nonassuming grantee is personally liable on the debt to the mortgagee. If a mortgagor who has transferred the mortgaged property is required to pay the mortgage debt, he can be subrogated to the rights of the mortgagee to proceed against the security.

Case 256. A prior mortgagee cannot be made a party against his will to a foreclosure action by a junior mortgagee or incumbrancer. A junior incumbrancer, however, can be made an involuntary party to a foreclosure action by a senior incumbrancer. In fact junior incumbrancers must be made parties in order to have their claims eliminated. In a foreclosure sale by a junior incumbrancer or mortgagee, the senior incumbrance or mortgage is unaffected by the proceedings.

2. MORTGAGE SUBSTITUTES OR ALTERNATIVES AND OTHER MATTERS

Case 257. An installment land contract wherein the vendee goes into possession and makes periodic payments over a long period of time is often treated as a mortgage or security device. When treated as a security transaction, the provisions for forfeiture on default are rarely enforced. The proper remedy of the vendor on default of the vendee is an action to foreclose the vendee's interest, and until he does so, the vendee is entitled to redeem and get a deed by paying the balance owed plus interest and any enforceable additional charges.

Part IV

LAND USE CONTROL

Chapter XXV

COVENANTS RUNNING WITH THE LAND

Legal Gems; Introduction.
1. In Fee.
   Cases.
2. In Landlord and Tenant Relation.
   Legal Gems.
   Cases.
3. Equitable Servitudes.
   Legal Gems.
   Cases.
Summary of Cases in Chapter XXV.

LEGAL GEMS; INTRODUCTION

1. Generally speaking the legal effect of a contract is to *bind person to person.* Thus only the promisor is bound to perform the promise and only the promisee has a right to compel performance of the promise. Among the exceptions to this general principle are: (a) the case in which a third person for whose benefit a contract is made may, without being a party to the contract, enforce it against the promisor; (b) the case in which the promisee assigns the benefit of the contract to an assignee who may, without being a party to the contract, enforce it against the promisor; and (c) covenants running with the land under which one may, without being a party to the contract, and simply by virtue of becoming owner of the estate in the land, enforce the contract or be compelled to perform the contract.

2. Generally speaking the legal effect of an easement (or profit) appurtenant is to *bind land to land.* The dominant tenant owns "an interest in the land of another". If he transfers his dominant tenement the easement (or profit) appurtenant thereto passes as an incident to the conveyee and a transfer of the servient estate carries with it the burden of the easement (or profit) appurtenant. The successor in interest to either estate must recognize the easement (or profit) as an interest in the land and not as a personal obligation or right of either tenant.

3. A covenant running with the land is more than a mere personal contract and it is less than an easement (or profit) in the sense that it is not "an interest in land". It is a concept somewhere between a personal contract on one side and "an interest in land" on the other. A homely analogy may be of assistance. Whereas a dom-

515

inant tenement and an easement appurtenant thereto are of the same species, all land, so also are a cottonwood tree and one of its branches of the same species, all tree. On the other hand a covenant running with the land is of a different species than the estate in the land to which it is attached or connected, but connected it is. The covenant is to the estate in the land as the mistletoe is to the cottonwood tree out of whose trunk it grows. The mistletoe and the cottonwood tree are of a different species but the former is attached to and connected with the tree and gets its sustenance and vitality therefrom.

This attachment or connection between the estate in the land and the covenant which "runs" therewith is the essential factor differentiating a covenant running with the land from an easement. Such attachment or connection with the estate in the land is called "privity of estate" and no covenant or contract has the quality to "run with the land" unless such privity of estate exists.

4. The running of the covenant with the land means that the burdens or benefits, or both, of the covenant, pass to the persons who succeed to the estate of the original contracting parties, the idea being that the covenant runs because it is attached to the estate in the land as it is conveyed from one to another in the chain of title.

5. CAVEAT: It is customary, as in these gems, to speak of *covenants* running with the land. It must be pointed out, however, that the *benefit* and *burden* of a covenant are tested separately, that either the *benefit* or *burden* can run independently of each other, or they can both run if all the requirements are satisfied. See also gem 6(c) *infra*.

6. For a covenant to run with the land at law the following essential characteristics must concur—

(a) There *must be a covenant* which originally meant a sealed instrument. Today when seals have been largely abolished by statute a writing which is signed and complies with the Statute of Frauds is usually sufficient. Indeed, in the case of a grantee's accepting a deed containing a covenant by the grantee, such grantee is bound by the covenant without even signing the deed.

(b) There *must be an intention* that the covenant shall run with the land. If the word assigns or the word successors is used in the instrument the intention is usually clear that the covenant is intended to run. But it is sufficient if the intention can be gleaned from the terms, the purpose and the circumstances surrounding the making of the writing.

(c) The covenant *must be the type which touches and concerns the land*. This means that the effect of the covenant is to increase the use or utility of the land or to make it more valuable in the hands of the covenantee or to curtail the use or utility of the land or make it less valuable in the hands of the covenantor. Usually if the benefit of the covenant touches and concerns the land of the covenantee, the burden also touches and concerns the land of the covenantor. The reverse is also true. It must be noted, however, that it is possible for the benefit to touch and concern the land without the burden doing so, and for the burden to touch and concern the land without the benefit doing so. It is essential in solving a problem to treat separately the running of the benefit on the one hand and the running of the burden on the other. The covenant must affect the legal relations of the parties as landowners and not as members of the community at large.

(d) There *must be privity of estate*. This element gives little difficulty when the landlord-tenant relationship is present in a case because privity of estate always exists between the original covenanting parties, the landlord and the tenant. But in cases involving the running of a covenant in connection with the fee simple estate there is the greatest uncertainty as to its meaning and application. In Clark's Covenants and Interests Running with Land (2d ed.) at p. 111, three distinct meanings are set forth: (1) "succession to the estate of one of the parties to the covenant"; (2) "succession of estate also between covenantor and covenantee"; and (3) "mutual and simultaneous interests of the parties in the same land", with the comment that (1) is the only proper meaning, but admitting on p. 116 that the rule as generally stated requires privity of estate between the covenantor and covenantee.

7. Because a covenant running with the land encumbers the land and fetters its free alienability there is a tendency to restrict rather than expand the legal effect of the covenant. The "running" is disfavored rather than favored.

See Clark, p. 92 et seq.; Restatement of Property § 530 et seq.; Powell, ¶¶ 670–686.

———

Note

In solving a case involving covenants running with the land the analysis will be materially aided if each of the following items is carefully considered—

(a) First, *draw a figure* showing the position of the parties, a triangle if only one of the original covenanting parties has assigned, a rectangle if both have assigned.

(b) If more than one covenant is involved, then each should be analyzed and treated separately.

(c) There is always *privity of contract* between the original covenantee and covenantor—*is there also* a conveyance of an interest in land between them constituting *privity of estate* to which the contractual relationship is or can be connected? In some jurisdictions the privity of estate between the original covenantee and covenantor is a prerequisite to the running of the covenant. It is always present between landlord and tenant.

(d) The covenantor is always the promisor and he or his assignee always has the burden of the covenant.

(e) The covenantee is always the promisee and he or his assignee always has the benefit of the covenant.

(f) Is the original conveyor of an interest in land the covenantor or the covenantee?

(g) Is the original conveyee of an interest in land the covenantor or the covenantee?

(h) Does the assignment of the interest in land run from the covenantee or covenantor or both?

(i) In determining whether or not a covenant touches and concerns the land, the running of the benefit and the running of the burden should be treated separately. Usually if one end of the covenant runs the other end will run also but that is not necessarily true.

(j) Is the defendant in the action the covenantor or his assignee?

(k) Is the plaintiff in the action the convenantee or his assignee?

The cases below will illustrate the application of these suggestions.

———

1. IN FEE

(covenants running at law with the land in fee)

CASE 258: A is the fee simple owner of Blackacre, the NW¼ in Section 18. B is the fee simple owner of Whiteacre, the NE¼ of Section 18. By a deed poll A grants to B and his heirs a right of way along the northernmost six feet of Blackacre for the purpose of an irrigation ditch which will carry water across Blackacre for use on Whiteacre. B accepts the deed from A. In the deed B, the grantee, covenants to build and maintain in perpetuity a barbed wire fence of definite specifications along each side of the six-foot strip in which the irrigation ditch is located. B constructs the ditch and the fences. Then A dies intestate leaving H his sole heir. Thereafter both fences are permitted to be in a state of disrepair. H demands that B fix the fences which B refuses to do. H sues B in damages for breach of contract. May he recover?

Answer and Analysis

The answer is yes. This conclusion presupposes a determination that the covenant set forth in the instrument runs with the land. Figure 1 below discloses an analysis of the facts and the position of the parties.

FIGURE 1

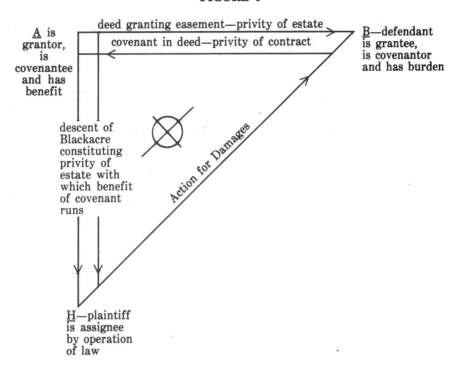

For a covenant to run with the land at law four elements must co-exist. (1) There must be a covenant. (2) There must be an intention that the covenant run with the land. (3) The covenant must touch and concern the land. (4) There must be privity of estate.

(1) The covenant. At common law a covenant meant an instrument in writing under seal. Under modern statutes seals have either been abolished completely or their legal effect has been greatly curtailed in most of the states. In general today an instrument which is in writing and which is signed by the party to be charged as required by the Statute of Frauds may for practical purposes be considered a covenant for the purpose of running with the land. Covenants which run with land are often called *real* covenants to distinguish them from purely *personal* covenants which bind the person only. In our set of facts we are given a deed poll from A to B in which the covenant is contained. But a deed poll is one which is signed by the grantor only and not by the grantee. It is now settled that a grantee in a deed poll, by accepting the deed, becomes bound by the covenants therein contained even though he does not actually sign the instrument. The facts state that B accepted the deed poll from A. Therefore, B is bound by the covenant or promise contained in the deed by which B agreed to construct and maintain the fences on either side of the irrigation ditch. Hence, the first required element is present.

(2) **The intention.** In the early cases on this subject it was said that no covenant could run with land unless the word "assigns" was used to express the intention that the covenant run. When the word assigns or the word successors is used it is clear that there is an intention that the covenant shall run. But the use of such words is only one of the items to be considered in determining the intention of the parties to a covenant. If the terms, purpose and circumstances surrounding the making of a covenant disclose the intention of the parties it is immaterial whether or not any particular words have been used in the body of the instrument. In our set of facts neither the word assigns nor the word successors has been used in the deed. But it seems quite plain that A and B did not covenant for the fencing of the irrigation ditch solely for the benefit of A personally. Such covenant was entered into to benefit A not merely as a member of the community but as the owner and possessor of Blackacre. And it is provided that those fences on both sides of the irrigation ditch should be maintained, not merely during A's lifetime, but in perpetuity because it was intended that such maintenance should continue beyond the lifetime of A and for the benefit of those who succeed A as the owners and occupiers of Blackacre. Thus it seems clear that the original covenanting parties, A and B, intended that the covenant run with the land and that the second required element is present.

(3) **The covenant must touch and concern the land.** Neither the cases nor the commentators present an exact test for determining whether or not a particular covenant touches or concerns land. It is a question for the court in using his best judgment when a given set of facts is presented. If the effect of a given covenant is to enhance or increase the use or the utility of the land or make it more valuable in the hands of the covenantee, then it is said that the *benefit* of the covenant touches and concerns the land. On the other hand if the effect of a given covenant is to curtail the use or the utility of the land or make it less valuable in the hands of the covenantor, then it is said that the *burden* of the covenant touches and concerns the land. In applying these principles to our set of facts, the easement granted by A to B for the irrigation ditch should be carefully distinguished from the covenant made by B to A concerning the building and maintenance of the fences on both sides of that ditch. As to the easement A is the grantor and B is the grantee. As to the covenant B is the covenantor and A is the covenantee. The benefit of the covenant is in favor of A. The burden of the covenant is to be performed by B. These appear in graphic form in FIGURE 1 above. Without the covenant, B, the dominant tenant as to Blackacre, has the right to come onto the land for the purpose of constructing the irrigation ditch and keeping it in proper repair for carrying water to Whiteacre. But he has no obligation to build and maintain a fence on either side of the ditch without the covenant providing for such. The covenant being performed by B, A's relationship to his Blackacre is somewhat altered thereby. The fences on either side of the irrigation ditch give privacy and protection to A in his use of Blackacre. It protects the

northern border of his Blackacre from trespassing animals and prevents his own live stock from leaving the premises. The property is more valuable in A's hands merely because the fence is there and is maintained by B without expenditures on the part of A as the owner of Blackacre. It seems clear then that the benefit end of the covenant touches and concerns Blackacre.

The other end of the covenant seems clearly to touch and concern Whiteacre and the easement appurtenant thereto because it alters in some respect B's relationship to the land. For our purposes here the easement as well as Whiteacre is considered as land. Without the covenant B could use and enjoy the appurtenant easement without building or maintaining the fences. With the covenant his use of the easement in connection with Whiteacre is curtailed to the extent that it is necessary for him to build the fences and from time to time go onto the six foot strip and repair the fences. And surely the use and utility of Whiteacre and its appurtenant easement are less valuable to B because that covenant is contained in the deed poll which B accepts from A. It is not material that the fences may also be beneficial to B in keeping live stock from obstructing the ditch by pushing mud and soil into it while drinking therefrom, and in saving for irrigation the water which might be thereby consumed. The point is that the effect of the covenant is to burden Whiteacre and the easement and make them less valuable in the hands of their owner, B. Such covenant therefore touches and concerns Whiteacre and the easement appurtenant thereto. However, as to this end of the covenant involving the burden thereof our problem raises no question because B has made no assignment or transfer of Whiteacre and the appurtenant easement.

(4) There must be privity of estate. Referring to the deed poll from A to B and the covenant therein and to FIGURE 1 above it should be noticed, (1) that *the covenant* itself *creates a contractual privity* between the original parties, A and B, (2) that *the conveyance of the easement* for the irrigation ditch *creates privity of estate* between the covenantor and covenantee, and (3) that *the covenant is of and concerning the easement*.

Privity of estate as here used means that one of the contracting parties succeeds to an interest in the land of the other party. It means that B succeeds to an interest (the easement) in Blackacre and by the deed is made the dominant tenant. Thus there is privity of estate between A and B to which privity of estate the covenant is attached or connected. It means that the benefit end of the covenant is connected with or "touches and concerns" Blackacre and that the burden end of the covenant is connected with or "touches and concerns" Whiteacre and its easement appurtenant. When A dies intestate Blackacre is assigned by operation of law (descent) to his heir, H. In such cases there is no distinction between a voluntary assignment and one by operation of law. Because H succeeds to A's interest or estate in Blackacre there is privity of estate between A and H. To this privity of estate the benefit end of the covenant is annexed and passes to H with the estate. There being privity of estate between the covenanting parties, A and B, by virtue of A's deed to B, and there being privity of estate between A and H by virtue of descent, there is present privity of estate in this case as the fourth required element in the running of the covenant.

Conclusion as to the running of the covenant. There being present in our given set of facts: (1) a covenant; (2) an intention that the covenant run with the land; (3) a touching and concerning the land by the covenant; and (4) privity of estate, the benefit of the covenant by B to build and maintain fences on Blackacre runs with the land, Blackacre, to H.

Legal effect of the running of the covenant. The legal effect of a covenant which runs with land is either to benefit or to burden a person who is not a party to the making of the contract. And such effect comes about through no other reason than that the person has become the owner of an interest in the land involved. In this case A and B were the only parties to the original covenant in A's deed to B. Ordinarily in the field of contracts no one other than A or B would have any rights or liabilities under that contract. But in this case because the covenant is one which runs with the land, either its benefit or its burden, or both, in case of assignment of the interest in the land, will affect the assignee. When, therefore, the law assigns Blackacre to A's heir, H, upon A's dying intestate, the benefit of the covenant runs with Blackacre to H, and he is thereby empowered to sue for its breach in the same way and to the same extent as A, had he lived, had a right to do. And B has made no assignment but is sued as an original promisor on the covenant in the deed poll which he accepted from A. Hence, H may recover in his action against B for damages for breach of the covenant. See Morse v. Aldrich, 19 Pick. (36 Mass.) 449 (1837); Burbank v. Pillsbury, 48 N.H. 475, 97 Am.Dec. 633 (1869); Clark, p. 92 et seq.

———

CASE 259: A is the fee simple owner of Blackacre, the NW¼ in Section 18. B is the fee simple owner of Whiteacre, the NE¼ of Section 18. By a deed poll A grants to B and his heirs a right of way along the northernmost six feet of Blackacre for the purpose of an irrigation ditch which will carry water across Blackacre for use on Whiteacre. B accepts the deed from A. In the deed B, the grantee, covenants to build and maintain in perpetuity a barbed wire fence of definite specifications along each side of the six-foot strip in which the irrigation ditch is located. B constructs the ditch and the fences. B dies intestate leaving H his sole heir. Thereafter H permits the fences to come into a state of disrepair. A demands that H repair the fences which H refuses to do. A sues H in damages for breach of contract. May he recover?

Note

This set of facts is identical with those in the preceding case with these exceptions. Here the covenantor, B, dies. The heir is defendant. The question involves the running of the burden rather than the benefit end of the covenant. Compare FIGURES 1 and 2.)

Answer and Analysis

The answer is yes. This conclusion presupposes a determination that the covenant set forth in the instrument runs with the land. Figure 2 below discloses an analysis of the facts and the position of the parties.

FIGURE 2

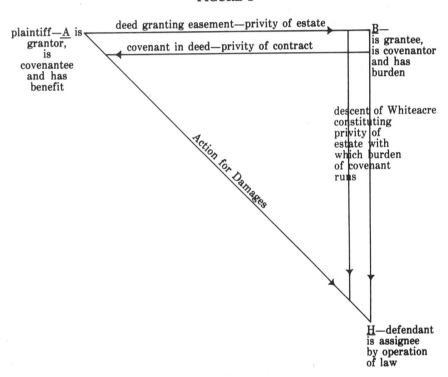

For a covenant to run with the land four elements must co-exist. (1) There must be a covenant. (2) There must be an intention that the covenant run with the land. (3) The covenant must touch and concern the land. (4) There must be privity of estate. What has been said concerning each of these topics in the preceding case is equally applicable here. And the conclusions are the same as drawn and explained in that case. One item deserves attention. In the preceding case the benefit of the covenant ran with the descent of Blackacre. In this case the burden runs with the descent of Whiteacre and the easement appurtenant thereto. In the case of a voluntary assignment the assignee has the power to refuse to receive the property. He can reject it. In the case of descent the heir cannot prevent the vesting of the title in him. Such is not objectionable when there is a benefit conferred. But in this case by the descent of Whiteacre with the burden end of the covenant running therewith, H finds himself in the position of being personally liable on a covenant he never made and which has come to him without right or power to prevent it. But the law makes no distinction between a voluntary assignment and one by operation of law and there is nothing H can do to escape the personal liability imposed on him by this set of facts. And perhaps Whiteacre and the appurtenant easement are sufficiently valuable so that he does not deserve too much sympathy in the matter. In any event, all of the elements for the running of the burden of the covenant being present, H is liable to A for breach of the contract to keep the fences on either side of the irrigation ditch in repair.

Note

Recording and Bona Fide Purchaser

If a covenant is not properly recorded and a later grantee qualifies as a subsequent bona fide purchaser without notice, he generally will take free of the burden of the covenant. In the instant case, the defendant H is not a purchaser and, therefore, he cannot escape liability on that basis. See supra Case 251.

CASE 260: A is the fee simple owner of Blackacre, the NW¼ in Section 18. B is the fee simple owner of Whiteacre, the NE¼ in Section 18. By a deed poll A grants to B and his heirs a right of way along the northernmost six feet of Blackacre for the purpose of an irrigation ditch which will carry water across Blackacre for use on Whiteacre. B accepts the deed from A. In the deed B, the grantee, covenants to build and maintain in perpetuity a barbed wire fence of definite specifications along each side of the six-foot strip in which the irrigation ditch is located. B constructs the ditch and the fences. A dies intestate leaving H his sole heir. B dies intestate leaving X his sole heir. The fences are permitted to come into a state of disrepair by X. H demands that X repair the fences and X refuses to do so. H sues X in damages for breach of the contract. May he recover?

(Note: This set of facts is identical with those in the two preceding cases with these exceptions. Here both covenantor and covenantee die. One heir is suing another heir. The question involves the running of both the benefit and the burden of the covenant. Compare FIGURES 1, 2 and 3.)

Answer and Analysis

The answer is yes. This conclusion presupposes a determination that the covenant set forth in the instrument runs with the land. Figure 3 below discloses an analysis of the facts and the position of the parties.

FIGURE 3

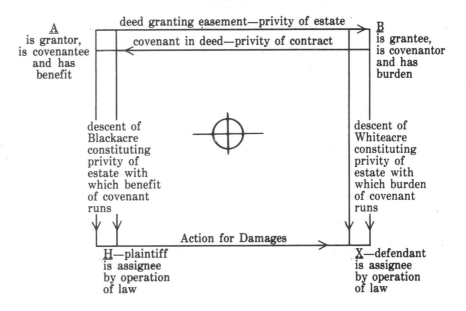

What has been said in the two preceding cases is equally applicable in the solution of this case. Whereas in each of those cases there was but one assignment of the land, in this case there are two assignments, one by the covenantor and one by the covenantee. The result is that both ends of the covenant run and the assignee of the covenantee is suing the assignee of the covenantor. Both the benefit and burden having run with the land the assignee of the covenantee, H, may recover damages for breach of the covenant from the assignee of the covenantor, X. Figure 3 above discloses five factors on privity of estate which should be carefully noted. (1) A conveys an easement to B which constitutes successive privity of estate between the original covenanting parties. (2) A and B own interests simultaneously in Blackacre, A owning Blackacre is a servient tenement and B owning an easement therein. (3) The descent of Blackacre to H constitutes successive privity of estate between A and H, the assignee. (4) The descent of Whiteacre and the appurtenant easement to X constitutes successive privity of estate between B and X, the assignee. (5) H and X own interests simultaneously in Blackacre, H owning Blackacre as a servient tenement and X owning an easement therein.

CASE 261: A is the owner of Blackacre in fee simple on which tract he operates a mill which is powered by the water of River Y which flows through Blackacre and is fed by a continuous flow from Lake M. The principal value of Blackacre is the mill thereon. City K has riparian water rights in Lake M and is taking water out of the lake for the purpose of supplying the inhabitants of City K. The quantity of water which City K takes from Lake M increases with the growth of the City and finally reaches a point where the level of the lake is so low that there is insufficient flow from Lake M through River Y to run A's mill. A threatens to sue City K for wrongful interference with A's water supply. To prevent such suit and settle A's claim amicably City K and A execute a written acknowledged agreement by which A covenants not to sue City K and City K covenants to desist from taking any water from Lake M which will interfere with A's mill on Blackacre and covenants not to take water out of Lake M which will lower the surface of the water in Lake M below a specific level. Thereafter A conveys Blackacre to B and assigns with it the covenant made with City K. City K violates the covenant by taking so much water from Lake M that it causes B's mill to shut down for lack of a sufficient head of water. B sues City K for damages for breach of the covenant. May B recover?

Answer and Analysis

The answer is yes. This answer presupposes a determination that the covenant runs with Blackacre into the hands of B, the assignee of A, the original covenantee. See Figure 4 below which discloses an analysis of the facts and the position of the parties.

FIGURE 4

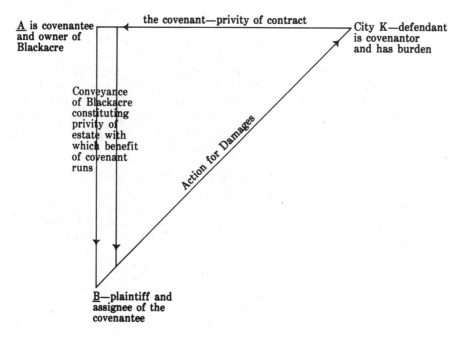

A is covenantee and owner of Blackacre

the covenant—privity of contract

City K—defendant is covenantor and has burden

Conveyance of Blackacre constituting privity of estate with which benefit of covenant runs

Action for Damages

B—plaintiff and assignee of the covenantee

For a covenant to run with the land four elements must co-exist. (1) There must be a covenant. (2) There must be an intention that the covenant run with the land. (3) The covenant must touch and concern the land. (4) There must be privity of estate.

(1) The covenant. This item presents no difficulty on the facts. A written, acknowledged agreement executed by both parties constitutes a covenant which can run with land.

(2) The intention. While it does not appear that the word assigns or the word successors is used in the covenant, and it would have made B's case easier had they been used, especially on the benefit side, still it seems quite clear that under the circumstances of this case, A did not require the execution of the agreement by City K merely to benefit A as a member of the community. The entire purpose of the agreement is to benefit A in his ownership of Blackacre. And we can hardly ascribe to A an intention that the covenant is to benefit the ownership of Blackacre only during A's lifetime for we are told that the principal value of Blackacre is in the value of the mill thereon. And the value of the mill is saved only by saving the water level in Lake M as provided for in the covenant. So it must have been intended that permanent value be assured Blackacre by keeping the water level in Lake M at a point where it will continue in perpetuity to run the mill on A's property whether A continues to own the property or there is another subsequent owner. Hence, the required intention for the running of the covenant is present in this case.

(3) The covenant must touch and concern the land. The sole purpose of the covenant is to make Blackacre usable, productive and valuable. Without the covenant Blackacre cannot be used for mill purposes. The facts say the mill constitutes its principal value. That must mean that without the operation of the mill thereon Blackacre is rendered practically unproductive and valueless. With the covenant the mill runs and Blackacre is made productive and its value is assured. This covenant not only changes A's relationship to the property, it actually saves it from destruction as a productive and valuable property enterprise. Thus it clearly touches and concerns the land if that expression has any significance at all.

(4) There must be privity of estate. This item raises the only real important issue in the problem. Privity of estate may be mutual or successive. If X and Y are co-owners of land there is said to be mutual privity of estate between them. If X owns land and conveys it to Y there is said to be successive privity of estate between them because Y succeeds to X's interest in the land. The cases seem to agree that if there is: (1) privity of estate between the original covenanting parties; and (2) simultaneous ownership by the covenanting parties in the same land; and (3) privity of estate between either of the covenanting parties and his assignee, then the covenant will run with the land.

In the preceding cases on this subject all of the above mentioned elements were present. But in this case it should be noticed that there is no privity of estate, either mutual or successive, between the original covenanting parties, A and City K. A simply owns Blackacre and City K has no interest therein either as a co-owner or as a conveyee of an interest therein. Between A and City K there is simply the covenant which constitues privity of contract. Dicta in the great majority of cases would require privity of estate between the original covenanting parties as a condition prerequisite to the running of the covenant with the land. But there seems neither logical nor historical basis for such requirement. Privity of contract between the original parties seems quite sufficient provided there is privity of estate in the assignment of the interest in the land with which either the burden or the benefit of the covenant can run. In our case there is privity of estate between A, the covenantee, and B, the assignee. When A conveys Blackacre to B there is successive privity of estate because B succeeds to the interest or estate which A has in the land. To this privity of estate the benefit of the covenant can adhere and therefore run with it. When then such conveyance of Blackacre is made to B and the covenant is assigned to B therewith, the necessary privity of estate for the running of such benefit of the covenant is present and B, the assignee, can recover damages from the covenantor, City K, for its breach of the covenant. Furthermore, the result is just because it is clearly doing no more than carrying out the intention of the parties. See Shaber v. St. Paul Water Co., 30 Minn. 179, 14 N.W. 874 (1883); Clark, p. 111 et seq.; Lingle Water Users' Ass'n v. Occidental Bldg. & Loan Ass'n, 43 Wyo. 41, 297 P. 385 (1931).

Note

There is considerable controversy as to the requirement of privity of estate in cases such as 261. It should be noted that in that case it is only a question of the benefit running. Under such circumstances, the Restatement of Property adopts the liberal view of privity of estate indicated above, and would permit the benefit to run. Under similar circumstances, however, the Restatement would not permit the burden to run, but would require in such cases either "simultaneous interests" in the same land, or a succession of interests (even in fee) between the promising parties. For more discussion see Powell, ¶674; see also Restatement of Property §§ 547, 548.

———

CASE 262: A is the owner of Blackacre in fee simple adjoining which is B's Whiteacre. They are city lots having a common boundary line. A and B enter into a covenant in writing which is signed and adknowledged by both and put on record under the terms of which A agrees to build a party wall twelve inches in thickness half of which wall is to be on Blackacre and half on Whiteacre located over the common boundary line separating the two lots. B agrees to the building of such wall for which A is to pay in full. B covenants for himself and his assigns that if and when either he or his assigns shall use such party wall on Whiteacre that he or his assigns will pay A personally the original cost of one half of such party wall. A builds the party wall and a four-story building on Blackacre. A then conveys Blackacre to X but reserves to himself the right to receive from B or his assigns the payment for half of the party wall. B conveys Whiteacre to Y who has actual notice of the party wall agreement. Y starts to build on Whiteacre and attaches the joists of his building to the party wall. A demands from Y payment for half the original cost of the party wall which Y refuses. A sues Y for the amount he paid for half of the party wall. May A recover?

Answer and Analysis

The answer is yes. This conclusion presupposes a determination that the party wall agreement constitutes a covenant whose burden runs with the land.

(1) There is no question about there being a covenant executed by A and B. The facts so state.

(2) Neither is there any question about the intention of the parties. The covenantor, B, covenanted for himself and his assigns that he or his assigns would pay for half of the cost of the party wall. Thus it is clear that it was intended that the burden of the covenant should run with the land. It is also clear that the parties intended that the benefit of the covenant should not run with the land because it specifically provides that the payment for the half of the party wall shall be paid to the covenantee, A, personally. Furthermore, when A conveys Blackacre to X the conveyance provides that the payment to be made for half of the party wall is reserved to A.

(3) The legal effect of the party wall agreement is the creation of cross-easements on Blackacre and Whiteacre making each a dominant tenement as to the easement on the other and each a servient tenement as to the right of the other to use the party wall. The covenant, apart from the easement, is an agreement on the part of B, the covenantor, to pay for half the cost of the wall. If such covenant is valid between the parties it constitutes a credit device by which the use of Whiteacre is enhanced and made more valuable in the hands of B because it produces a party wall immediately available to B for building purposes whenever he chooses to build on Whiteacre. It is easy to argue that an agreement merely to pay money is quite personal and has no connection with the use or value of land as land. That argument is not realistic and is clearly extrinsic to the intention of the parties. In our case the agreement to pay for half the cost of the party wall is inextricably bound up with the creation of the incorporeal easement and with the building of the physical wall. It therefore touches and concerns Whiteacre and the easement appurtenant thereto to use that part of the party wall on Blackacre.

(4) There is privity of estate. The party wall agreement creates in A an easement appurtenant to his Blackacre. Thus A succeeds to an interest in B's Whiteacre so there is successive privity of estate. The party wall agreement also creates in B an easement appurtenant to his Whiteacre because by it B succeeds to an interest in A's Blackacre. So again there is successive privity of estate. When B conveys his Whiteacre to Y there is successive privity of estate between the two to which the burden end of the covenant may be attached and with which it can run. Thus, all of the required elements for the running of the burden end of the covenant are present.

The only question left concerns the benefit. The benefit end of the covenant does not run to the covenantee's assignee, X, for the reason that it is intended to be personal to A and is not intended to run. In this case there is both reason and justice for permitting the burden to run with the land even though the benefit does not so run. The benefit has already been conferred by A, the plaintiff covenantee, on the covenantor and his assigns by A's building an entire party wall and making full payment therefor. Furthermore, there is no reason in principle why either a benefit should not run without the running of the burden, or why the burden should not run without the running of the benefit, if such is the intention of the parties and the other required elements for the running of either are present. Thus, A can recover from the assignee, Y, the original cost of one half of the party wall between Blackacre and Whiteacre. See Conduit v. Ross, 102 Ind. 166, 26 N.E. 198 (1885); Clark, p. 101 et seq.

---

2. IN LANDLORD AND TENANT RELATION

(covenants running with the land in landlord and tenant relation)

LEGAL GEMS

1. In a landlord-tenant relation *there is always privity of estate.*

2. For a covenant to run with the land in a landlord-tenant relation three elements must co-exist—

(a) *there must be a covenant,*

(b) *there must be an intention that the covenant run with the land, and*

(c) *the covenant must touch and concern the land.*

3. The covenant touches and concerns the land if the legal effect of the enforcement of the covenant is either

(a) to enhance the use or utility of or make more valuable the leasehold or the reversion, or

(b) to curtail the use or utility of or make less valuable the leasehold or the reversion.

4. The covenant may run either with

(a) the leasehold which is land for this purpose, although technically it is personal property, or (b) the reversion.

5. (a) An assignee of a covenant running with the land *is not liable* for a breach of the covenant which occurs *before he becomes assignee* of the land.

(b) An assignee of a covenant running with the land *is liable only* for a breach of the covenant which occurs *while he owns the estate* in the land.

(c) An assignee of a covenant running with the land *is not liable* for a breach of the covenant which occurs *after he has assigned* the estate in the land.

———

CASE 263: L is the fee simple owner of Blackacre, a section of land. By an instrument signed by both L and T he leases it to T for the ten year period March 1, 1965 to March 1, 1975. The NE¼ of Blackacre is presently a field of alfalfa. In the lease T covenants to leave this NE¼ in alfalfa for the years 1965 and 1966; that he will plow such alfalfa field in 1967 and plant corn therein; that during the year 1968 he will raise oats on that NE¼ and in the year 1969 such field will be sowed to buckwheat. T plows up the alfalfa field in 1966 and assigns the lease to A who in 1967 plants the field to barley. In the autumn of 1967 A assigns the lease to B who in 1968 sows the NE¼ to flax, and in 1969 sows it to corn. L sues A for damages for breach of the covenant for the years 1966, 1967, 1968 and 1969. May he recover for breach of the covenant?

Answer and Analysis

The answer is yes. But A is liable only for the breach of the covenant during the year 1967. The answer to this question presupposes that the covenant in the lease runs with the land. For such a covenant to run with the land in a tenant-landlord relationship three elements must co-exist. (1) There must be a covenant. (2) There must be an intention that the covenant run with the land. (3) The covenant must touch and concern the land.

(1) The covenant. The lease between L and T is in writing and signed by both parties. The promise made by T to L is contained in such lease. For the purpose of running with the land this instrument constitutes a covenant between T and L.

(2) The intention. While the word assigns or the word successors is not used in the lease it is nevertheless clear that the purpose of the covenant is to benefit the land itself by rotating the crops thereon. Such covenant is intended not merely to benefit the landlord personally or as a member of the community but it is intended to

benefit him as the owner of the reversion in Blackacre. It is intended to improve the very soil which makes up the subject matter of the
lease. So it is plain that the parties intended this covenant to run
with the land, including both the leasehold and the reversion.

(3) **The covenant must touch and concern the land.** There is no
type of covenant which more plainly touches and concerns the land
than the type set forth in this set of facts. It provides that the very
soil on Blackacre is to be plowed or left unplowed. A field is to be
sowed to certain crops and not to be sowed to other crops. The covenant provides how Blackacre, the subject matter of the lease, is to be
used and how it is not to be used. The legal effect of the covenant is
to limit the use of the leasehold estate to the rotation of crops and to
make it, because of such restrictions, less valuable to the tenant, T.
The burden of the covenant therefore touches and concerns the leasehold estate. On the other hand the restrictions placed on the use of
Blackacre during the leasehold period improves the soil and enhances
the value of the reversion. When the possession is returned to L the
land will be in better condition by virtue of the enforcement of the
covenant. Therefore the benefit of the covenant touches and concerns the estate in reversion. Conclusion: the covenant runs with
the land.

(4) **The liability of T.** When a person makes a contract he is personally liable thereon and he cannot assign to another that liability
and thereby divest himself of the responsibility of performance, unless it is expressly provided for in the contract. The covenants contained in a lease constitute a contract and the covenantor cannot by
assigning the leasehold estate rid himself of the duty to perform.
Hence, T is personally liable to L for all of the breaches of the covenants he has in the lease promised to perform. Why? Because he
signed the lease and the covenants therein.

(5) **The liability of the assignees.** The liability of an assignee of
a covenant running with land is imposed upon him solely because he
becomes the owner of the land. The converse of that proposition is
also true. If the assignee is not the owner of the land he is not liable
on the covenant which runs with the land. From these two propositions evolve three legal conclusions concerning the liability of assignees of covenants running with land: (a) an *assignee* of an estate in
land *is not liable* for a breach of a covenant which runs therewith if
that breach has occurred *before he becomes such assignee*; (2) an
assignee of an estate in land *is liable* for a breach of a covenant which
runs therewith if such breach occurs *while he is the assignee of such
estate*; and (3) an *assignee* of an estate in land *is not liable* for a
breach of a covenant which runs therewith if such breach occurs *after
he ceases to be such assignee.*

(6) **Application of these principles to the facts.** (a) When the
covenantor, T, plowed up the alfalfa field in 1966, thereby breaching
the covenant in the lease, T and he alone is liable for such breach.

This part of the covenant is a non-continuing provision and can be breached only in 1966 because it applies only to that year. When such a covenant is breached it is transformed into a cause of action in favor of the covenantee and does not thereafter run with the land. Therefore the liability incurred by T cannot be passed on to his assignee of the land. (b) When T assigned the leasehold to A in 1966 the burden of performing the covenant came to A with the acquisition of the estate. When A planted barley instead of corn in the NE¼ in 1967 there was a breach of the covenant for that year for which A is liable in damages to the covenantee, L. Here again this is a breach of a non-continuous covenant because it can be breached only in 1967. The breach thereof transforms such provision of the covenant into a chose in action in L's favor and cannot longer run with the land. Therefore A cannot pass such incurred liability on to his assignee by assigning his estate in the land. (c) When A assigned the leasehold to B in the autumn of 1967 A ceased to be the assignee or the owner of the leasehold and cannot be liable for any breach of the covenant which occurs thereafter because by the assignment both the estate and the covenant which runs therewith pass to B. When therefore B, while he owns the estate to which is annexed the burden of the covenant, breaches such covenant by sowing flax instead of oats in 1968 and by sowing corn instead of buckwheat in 1969, B becomes personally liable for such breaches to the covenantee, L. Conclusion: L can recover damages from A only for A's breach of the covenant during the year 1967. See Cockson v. Cock, 79 Eng.Rep. 109 (1606); Clark, p. 96 et seq.; 34 A.L.R. 779.

––––––––

CASE 264: A is the fee simple owner of Blackacre and Whiteacre, two abutting city lots. On Blackacre is a three story building which is being used as a hotel. The rooms in the third story of the hotel have large windows facing Whiteacre which is a vacant lot. A leases Whiteacre to B for a period of 99 years. Both A and B sign and acknowledge the lease. In the lease B covenants not to build any building on Whiteacre which will be higher than the floor of the third story rooms on Blackacre, it being the expressed intention of the parties that the free flow of light and air into the third story windows of the hotel on Blackacre shall not be interfered with by any building on Whiteacre. Thereafter A conveys his reversion in Whiteacre to X. B starts to build on Whiteacre a building six stories high which will tower far above the hotel on Blackacre and shut out completely the air and light from the third story windows of the hotel. A sues B to enjoin the extension of B's proposed building beyond the height provided for in the lease. B's defense is that the covenant in the lease not to build beyond the specified height is a covenant running with the land and therefore only A's assignee, X, can sue on such covenant. Is the defense valid?

Answer and Analysis

The answer is no. This case can be solved by the simple statement that it is immaterial whether or not this covenant runs with the land. A and B made a contract and both are personally liable thereon. Therefore A may enjoin B's breach thereof, especially in a case such as this when A still owns Blackacre and has a genuine interest in the continued enforcement of the covenant. Consequently the rest of this opinion may well be classified as dicta.

A covenant not to build can be construed either as a negative easement, an equitable servitude or as a covenant running with land. But did the covenant run with *the* land in this case? In a landlord-tenant relationship there are only two interests which can be called "land" for the purpose of the running of a covenant. They are the leasehold estate in the tenant and the reversion in the landlord. It is clear in this case that the burden of the covenant is such that it can run with the leasehold. There is a covenant in the lease. The parties intended that Whiteacre should not be built upon higher than the height specified in the covenant irrespective of who owned the leasehold estate. And the covenant touches and concerns the leasehold estate because it curtails the use of such estate by limiting the right to build thereon and makes such leasehold less valuable to the tenant. So the burden of this covenant could clearly run with the land. But can the benefit end of the covenant run with the land? The answer is no insofar as the reversionary interest in Whiteacre is concerned. "The land" as to the benefit of a covenant in a landlord and tenant relationship means either the leasehold or reversion; thus in this case it would mean the reversionary interest in Whiteacre.

This covenant not to build is not intended to benefit the leasehold reversion, the landlord's interest in the leased property. In the covenant it is expressly stated that the intention of the parties and the purpose of the covenant are to benefit Blackacre in the use and enjoyment of the third story of the hotel thereon. This is *other land*. It is not Whiteacre and it is not the reversionary interest in Whiteacre. The benefit of a covenant cannot be enforced by one who owns *the land* when the benefit of the covenant is intended to enhance and make more valuable *not the land but other land*. There was clearly no intent for the covenant to run with the reversionary interest in Whiteacre. Whether or not the benefit of this covenant can run with Blackacre is another matter, but it would seem that it could under the circumstances of this case. At least it should be enforceable in equity by the owner of Blackacre. However, since there was no intent that it should run with the reversion in Whiteacre, A's assignee of the reversion of Whiteacre which is *the land* cannot enforce the covenant against his tenant B. But A, the original covenantee in the lease still has his contract right against B, the covenantor and the other original party to the contract. Further, A still owns Blackacre and is vitally interested in the continued observance of the covenant. For a covenant to run with the land in a tenant-landlord relationship the burden must affect either the leasehold or the reversion and the benefit must affect either the leasehold or the reversion. Either the benefit or the burden may run independently of the other. Each should be tested separately as to the intent and touch and concern requirements. See Thruston v. Minke, 32 Md. 487 (1870); Clark, p. 101 et seq.

CASE 265: L, fee simple owner of Blackacre, by an instrument signed by both L and T, leases Blackacre to T for a period of 10 years for dwelling house purposes. In the lease L covenants to keep the house in repair during the lease and particularly to keep the roof so covered that it does not leak when the rains come. After two years T assigns to A the remaining eight year period of the leasehold estate. L does not keep the roof in proper repair. A sues and recovers damages from L for such breach of the covenant. A assigns the remaining five year period of the leasehold to B. During B's occupancy of Blackacre the roof leaks and B notifies L to repair the roof. L does nothing and B sues L for damages for breach of the covenant. L's defense is that he has already paid damages to A and that his responsibility for the repair of the roof is thereby terminated. May B recover?

Answer and Analysis

The answer is yes. This answer presupposes a determination that the covenant contained in the lease runs with the land and that it is a continuing covenant. The lease from L to T is in writing and signed by both parties. It is thus a covenant. The lease does not in express language say that L will keep the house in repair for T's assignees but it does say that L will keep the house in repair "during the lease". And in the absence of a provision in the lease that the tenant has no right to assign without the consent of the landlord or otherwise, the tenant has a common law right to convey his leasehold estate. So there is an intention that the covenant to repair shall run with the land. In the absence of a statute or an express agreement in the lease there is no common law duty on the part of the landlord to keep the leased premises in repair. The fact that in this case the landlord reversioner has covenanted to keep the house in repair makes the leasehold of greater utilitarian value in the hands of the tenant and the reversion is so burdened by it that it is of less value in the hands of the landlord. Such effect of the covenant shows that it touches and concerns the land in both its burden and benefit. It is generally agreed that a covenant to repair the property which is the subject matter of a lease runs both with the leasehold and with the reversion. Whether such a covenant is a continuing or a non-continuing covenant is a question of construction.

In this case it seems clear that keeping the house repaired "during the lease" is an agreement that the house will be kept in repair not only during the occupancy of the original tenant but throughout the period of the tenancy irrespective of who happens at a given time to be the tenant. That being true the original tenant or any assignee of the term has the benefit of the covenant and the right to enforce it against the covenantor landlord. And the fact that the assignee, A, compels the landlord, L, to pay damages during A's occupancy of Blackacre does not at all affect the running of the continuing obligation which L assumed when he executed the lease to T. Thus L may be liable as many times as he breaches the covenant during the period of the lease and is liable to any assignee thereof when the breach occurs during the assignee's occupancy. It is therefore no defense to B's action against L that L has for a previous and different breach of the continuing covenant satisfied a judgment which A procured against him. B may recover for L's breach of the covenant during B's period of occupancy. In this case it will be noticed that it is the original landlord reversioner who is the defendant. Because the burden end of this type of covenant runs with the land the tenant could maintain such action either against L, the original reversioner, or against his assignee. See Stoddard v. Emery, 128 Pa. 436, 18 A. 339 (1889); Clark, p. 96 et seq.; p. 116 et seq.; Burby, 153.

CASE 266: L is the owner in fee simple of Blackacre, a business lot used personally by L for the purpose of operating a barber shop therein. L leases Blackacre to T for 10 years and in the lease signed by both parties L covenants that he (L), will not compete with T's barber business on Blackacre, within a radius of two miles during the term of the lease. Two years later T assigns the leasehold to A who continues operating the business of barbering on the premises. Shortly thereafter L conveys the reversion in Blackacre to B. B opens up a barber shop only two doors from Blackacre and within 60 feet thereof. A sues B seeking damages for breach of the covenant in the lease and an injunction against B's operating a barbershop within two miles of Blackacre. May A recover?

Answer and Analysis

The answer is no. For a covenant to run with the land in the landlord-tenant relation three elements must co-exist. (1) There must be a covenant. (2) There must be an intention that the covenant run with the land. (3) The covenant must touch and concern the land.

(1) The covenant. That there is a covenant in this case can admit of no doubt because both parties, L and T, signed the lease containing the agreement.

(2) The intention. The intention of the parties concerning the running of the covenant seems clear also. They intended that the leasehold in the hands of T, the tenant, should be benefited by not having to compete with L in the business of barbering. That intention was not solely for the benefit of T personally. It was for his benefit as owner of the 10 year term in Blackacre. Therefore it is clear that as to the benefit of the covenant it was intended that it run with the land, the leasehold estate. On the other hand when L covenanted not to compete as a barber, did this mean L personally, did it mean L as the owner of the reversion of Blackacre, or did it mean L as merely a citizen in the community? Such covenant clearly had reference to L as a barber. It referred to him personally including his personality and his capacity to attract business away from T in his operating of the shop on Blackacre. Therefore, it must be concluded that there was no intention on the part of L and T that the burden of the covenant was to run with the reversion in Blackacre.

(3) The covenant must touch and concern the land. Some cases say that a covenant which casts a physical benefit on land such as plowing it, repairing structures thereon or rebuilding a destroyed house, runs with the land, and that a covenant which casts only a business, financial or economic benefit on the land cannot run therewith. No fault can be found with the conclusion that the covenant casting the physical benefit runs but there is just as much reason and often more for permitting the running of a covenant which casts a business, financial or economic benefit on the land. Taking that view the covenant in our case benefits T's leasehold in its capacity to produce income by removing L as a business competitor. Indeed the use and utility of T's barbershop in Blackacre may be very materially affected by the enforcement of the covenant. T may be able to operate three chairs in his barbershop without L as a competitor whereas he might not be able to operate more than a one-chair barbershop if L is competing in the business. So it seems the better rule that such a covenant on the benefit end touches and concerns the land, T's leasehold. On the other hand the burden end of this covenant cannot possibly touch and concern L's reversionary interest in Blackacre because by the very nature of the covenant it affects only persons and does not bind any other land.

(4) The running of the benefit of the covenant. There being a covenant, there being an intention that the benefit of the covenant run with the land, the leasehold, and the benefit of the covenant being such as touches and concerns the leasehold it must be concluded that the benefit of the covenant runs with the leasehold and may be enforced either by the original tenant, T, or his assignee. Therefore T's assignee, A, may enforce the covenant. But against whom?

(5) The running of the burden of the covenant. No covenant can run with land unless it is intended that it shall run and it is of the type which touches and concerns the land. If there is an intention that the covenant shall run but it is personal and not the type which touches and concerns the land, it cannot run. If the covenant is the type which can touch and concern the land but there is no intention that it shall run, it cannot run. The intention and the type to touch and concern the land must both be present for the covenant to run. The same is true respecting either the benefit or the burden separately. In our case there being no intention that the burden of the covenant not to compete should run with the land, it cannot run. Further, the nature of the covenant being purely personal and not of the type which touches and concerns the land, it cannot run. Therefore, the burden of the covenant does not run with the conveyance of the reversion in Blackacre from L to B and B is not bound by the covenant not to compete with the original tenant, T, or his assignee. A is therefore limited in his action on the covenant to a suit against L only. But L has not breached the covenant. Therefore, A's action against B must fail. See Hebert v. Dupaty, 42 La.Ann. 343, 7 So. 580 (1890); 33 Yale L.J. 447; Clark, p. 105 et seq. If of course such a covenant is objectionable because it unreasonably restrains trade that is another matter.

Note

The following types of covenants have been held to touch and concern land and therefore run; covenant to pay rent, to insure the buildings on leased premises, to pay taxes on the leased premises, to renew or extend a lease, an option to purchase the leased premises, not to permit a particular person to participate in the management of the business on the leased premises, not to sell intoxicating liquor on the leased premises, to build a structure on the leased premises, not to assign or sublease the leased premises without the lessor's consent, to supply water, light or heat on the leased premises, not to purchase supplies for resale on the leased premises from one other than the lessor. The following types of covenants have been held collateral and not to touch and concern the land and therefore do not run; covenant to pay taxes on land other than the leased premises, to pay a promissory note of the covenantee, covenant not to compete in business (but see next paragraph), to perform acts on land other than the leased premises, covenants purely personal.

Modern business leases commonly employ non-competitive and exclusive use clauses, the covenants frequently extending not only to the leased premises themselves but also to other land within a designated radius from the premises leased or the boundaries of the shopping center within which the premises are located. Although such covenants are strictly construed, if the intent is clear they are generally enforceable in equity if not at law. As to the requirements for covenants to run in equity, see subsection 3 infra. See generally Clark, 96 et seq.; Burby, 156–157; Rest. § 537, Comment f which would permit the benefit but not the burden to run; Dick v. Sears-Roebuck & Co., 115 Conn. 122, 160 A. 432 (1932), covenant between fee owners and permitting the burden to run; Carter v. Adler, 138 Cal.App.2d 63, 291 P.2d 111 (1956), permitting the burden to run as to adjoining land with a transfer of the landlord's interest; See Shell Oil Co. v. Henry Ouellette and Sons, Inc., 352 Mass. 725, 227 N.E.2d 509 (1967), covenant between fee owners and not permitting enforcement by a successor of the covenantee against a successor of the covenantor; 90 A.L.R. 1462; 97 A.L.R.2d 72, 76.

3.   EQUITABLE SERVITUDES

LEGAL GEMS

1.   The industrial revolution of the last half of the 20th century transformed the population of a rural America into an urban population dwelling in crowded conditions in great metropolitan cities. Accompanying this change in living conditions came an insistent demand for the setting aside of areas of land restricted solely for residential purposes.   The common law of easements and covenants running with the land being both confused and restricted was quite incapable of satisfying this demand.   Out of this inadequacy of the common law of property and the activities of the equity courts has developed the doctrine of equitable servitudes.

2.   In England covenants will not run with land unless there is a landlord-tenant relation.   In the United States such covenants will run at law with the fee provided there is privity of estate.   The meaning and application of this expression, privity of estate, are in a state of hopeless confusion.   Such concept is wholly unusable as an effective and dependable device for guiding and governing the development of restricted areas, residential and otherwise, as demanded by modern society and conditions.   In brief this is a disclosure of the inadequacies of common law concepts to cope with and properly serve modern life.

3.   The *real basis for the enforcement of equitable servitudes is the doctrine of notice* as recognized in the equity courts to the effect that *a person who takes land with notice* of a restriction thereon *cannot in equity and good conscience be permitted to violate that restriction.*

4.   *An equitable servitude is a restriction on the use of land enforceable in a court of equity.   An equitable servitude* is more than "a covenant running with the land in equity" because it *is an interest in land.*   The term, *equitable servitude,* is broader than "equitable easement" because it *applies not only to land but also to chattel property* such as a business.

5.   Despite the statement in Gem 4 that the equitable servitude is more than a covenant running in equity, the approach of a covenant running in equity will greatly aid the neophyte scholar in comprehending the subject.

a.   For a covenant to run in equity the following requirements must be satisfied:

(1)   Intent (See Gems 7 and 9)

(2)   Touch and Concern (See Gem 10)

(3)   Notice (See Gems 3 and 8)

b. For a covenant to run at law, as demonstrated in part 1 of this chapter, the following requirements must be satisfied:

(1) Intent

(2) Touch and Concern

(3) Privity of Estate

c. Thus, privity of estate is not required for a covenant to run in equity, and notice is generally not listed as a requirement for a covenant to run at law. However, if a covenant is not properly recorded and a transferee qualifies as a subsequent BFP without notice, then, under the recording acts, the burden will not be enforced against him even at law. Thus, the most significant difference is that privity of estate is not required for equitable enforcement of a covenant or servitude.

6. For our purposes, dealing only with real property, an equitable servitude will be considered as the equivalent of an "equitable easement".

(1) For example, compare the cross-easements created by a party wall agreement with equitable servitudes created in a subdivision building scheme.

(a) A party wall is built on the common boundary line between A's Blackacre and B's Whiteacre. A owns the part of the wall on his side of the boundary line. B owns the part of the wall on his side of the boundary line. A as owner of Blackacre has an easement appurtenant to his land which entitles him to use Whiteacre and B's half of the party wall for the support of A's side of the wall and for the purpose of supporting any building joists inserted into the party wall. B has equal rights in Blackacre in his position as owner of Whiteacre. A may enforce such easement by enjoining B from interfering with A's use of the party wall. B may do the same as to A.

(b) X owns Brownacre on the edge of City M. He subdivides it into 100 lots which he numbers from 1 to 100. He places on record a "declaration of restrictions" which restricts each of the 100 lots in Brownacre to use for family dwelling only and provides that only a single dwelling house shall be built on each lot. X sells all of the lots to 100 persons and in the deed to each there is a reference to the "declaration of restrictions" by record book and page number and a provision that the grantee of the lot and his successors are bound to use the lot conveyed only as the declaration of restrictions provides, that is, for a single dwelling house only. A, B, C and D are among the buyers of lots in the subdivision. A's lot is a dominant tenement as to the lots owned by B, C and D. A may enforce the restriction as to B, C and D or as to a grantee of any one of them. On the other hand A's lot is also a servient tenement as to B's or C's or D's lot and each of these lot owners can enforce the restriction as to A's lot. The rights of the lot owners are mutual and reciprocal, and on each lot there is a running burden and a running benefit. But it should be noticed that each of the lot owners takes his lot with actual notice of the restrictions by provisions in his deed and with constructive notice of the restrictions as given by the recorded declaration of restrictions. Also it should be noticed that whereas there is privity of estate in the party wall agreement case, there is no privity of estate between the lot owners of the subdivision except that all the lot owners derive their titles from a common source. See supra Part 1, Gem 6(d).

(2) Now compare the equitable servitudes created in (b) next above with the dividing into lots of a dominant tenement and its effect on the servient tenement when there is a common law easement. A owns Blackacre, a quarter section of land, abutting B's Whiteacre, another quarter section of land. B grants to A an easement appurtenant to Blackacre for a right of way across Whiteacre which right of way is to serve Blackacre in its present single ownership and also to serve Blackacre and all its parts if and when it is ever divided into smaller pieces including blocks and lots. Thereafter Blackacre is divided into 100 lots all of equal size. The easement over Whiteacre still continues and adheres to every part of Blackacre including each of the 100 lots but the number of users of the easement has been increased from one to 100. By this division of the dominant tenement the benefit of the easement runs to each of the 100 lots whereas the burden remains alone on the servient tenement, Whiteacre. (See infra Cases 280–281 relating to increased usage of easements.)

In the equitable servitudes case under (b) above the benefit of the servitude runs in favor of each of the 100 lots as a dominant tenement and the burden of the servitude runs to each of the 100 lots as a servient tenement, there being mutual and reciprocal cross-servitudes as to each lot in the development or building scheme. From these comparisons it can readily be seen that there is a striking similarity between easements at common law and equitable servitudes as applied to land.

7. *An equitable servitude may be created by any writing complying with the Statute of Frauds evincing an intention that such servitude exist.* A deed poll accepted by the grantee providing for an equitable servitude will create such a servitude without the signature of the grantee on the deed. The restriction creating a servitude may take the form of a promise, a covenant, a reservation or a condition. But there must be found an intention to bind the land to a restricted use, and not merely bind the person. Of course, the case may be tak-

en out of the Statute of Frauds by either estoppel or part performance.

8. Under modern recording statutes either a common law easement or *an equitable servitude can be enforced against one who purchases the servient land with notice* of the existence of the easement or the equitable servitude. Conversely, under such statutes a common law easement or *an equitable servitude cannot be enforced against a bona fide purchaser* who takes the servient land for value and without notice of the easement or the equitable servitude.

9. *The intention of the parties determines who may and who may not enforce an equitable servitude.* Such intention is to be gathered from the terms of the instrument and the circumstances surrounding its execution.

10. The transferees of the original parties to an equitable servitude are bound by the servitude if it is intended to bind the land, and not merely the persons, and the benefits and burdens of the servitude are intended to run to such transferees.

11. If the owner of a dominant tract for the benefit of which an equitable servitude exists conveys such dominant tract, the benefit of the servitude passes to the conveyee as an incident to the principal thing.

12. An equitable servitude may be enforced against one of the parties or his transferee with notice, as to land acquired after the creation of the original relationship between the parties.

13. A court of equity may refuse to enforce an equitable servitude: (a) if its purpose is contrary to public policy; or (b) the granting of relief would do more harm than good; or (c) when the granting of the relief prayed for would be futile; or (d) the plaintiff is guilty of laches or violating the servitude.

14. Adverse possession of the land subject to an equitable servitude will not extinguish the servitude if the possession is not inconsistent therewith. E. g., A owns Blackacre and Whiteacre and conveys Whiteacre to B, the deed providing that Whiteacre shall not be used for commercial purposes by B or his successors in interest. X gains title to Whiteacre by adverse possession. X's possession alone and without violating the servitude is quite consistent with the existence of the servitude and does not extinguish it.

15. An equitable servitude may be extinguished by (a) the doing of an act which violates the servitude and continuing such for the period of the statute of limitation, (b) a release by the dominant tenant or tenants or (c) by the existence of conditions which make the purpose and object of the servitude impossible of achievement, such as change in the character of the neighborhood from a residential to a business area.

16. An equitable servitude is created if two elements co-exist—

(a) an instrument which complies with the Statute of Frauds and

(b) an intention that there be a restriction on the use of the land involved.

Note that (b) satisfies the intent and touch and concern requirements of Gem 5 supra. Notice becomes important in enforcing the servitude against particular defendants.

17. For the burden of an equitable servitude to run with the land and be enforceable against a transferee of one of the original parties three elements must co-exist—

(a) there must be an instrument which complies with the requirements of the Statute of Frauds, and

(b) there must be an intention that there be a restriction on the use of the land involved, and

(c) the transferee must take the land with either actual or constructive notice of the existence of the servitude.

See Clark, pp. 170–186; Burby, 100–109; McClintock, 341–353.

———

CASE 267: A is the owner of two adjoining city lots, Blackacre and Whiteacre. He conveys Whiteacre to B by a deed poll accepted by B containing the following provision, "with this express reservation, that no building is to be erected by the said B, his heirs or assigns, upon the land herein conveyed". Any building on Whiteacre will destroy a view of the ocean from Blackacre. B conveys Whiteacre to C by a deed which refers to the restriction in the deed from A to B. C then conveys to D who has no actual knowledge of the restriction, the deed to D making no reference to the restriction, and D makes no examination of the records concerning Whiteacre. A then conveys Blackacre to P. All deeds in the chain of title are properly recorded immediately following execution. D buys Whiteacre for the purpose of building thereon. Before D begins building on Whiteacre P notifies him of the restriction and warns him not to build on Whiteacre. D starts to build on Whiteacre and P brings suit against him seeking to enjoin such building. Should the injunction issue?

Answer and Analysis

The answer is yes. This answer presupposes the determination of the existence of an equitable servitude and the running of the benefit and burden thereof. Figure 5 below discloses an analysis of the facts and the position of the parties.

FIGURE 5

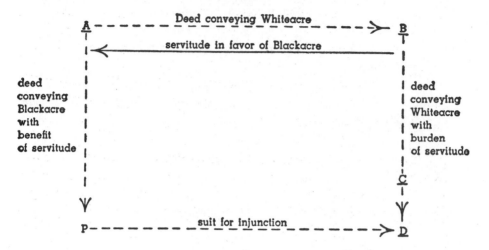

[A2177]

For an equitable servitude to exist there must be (a) an instrument which complies with the requirements of the Statute of Frauds, and (b) an intention that there be a restriction on the use of the land involved.

(a) The instrument. The deed conveying Whiteacre to B is in writing and signed by the grantor, A, but being a deed poll it is not signed by the grantee, B, and B is the party to be charged or the party against whom the burden of the servitude is to run. But this is an exception to the requirement that the instrument has to be signed. When B accepts the deed poll he is bound by the provisions of the deed even though it is not signed by him. Thus the instrument satisfies the requirement for the creation of an equitable servitude.

(b) The intention. No particular words are essential to the creation of an equitable servitude provided that an intention to bind the land and not merely the persons to the transaction can be found from the instrument and the circumstances surrounding its execution. In this case the words of the deed are in the form of a reservation, namely, "with this express reservation, that no building is to be erected by the said B, his heirs or assigns, upon the land herein conveyed". And the circumstances add clarity to the expressed meaning for it appears that any building built on Whiteacre will destroy the view to the ocean from Blackacre, the land retained by the grantor. The reservation in the deed and the circumstances make it clear that the land conveyed, Whiteacre, is to be bound, and not merely B personally, and that the purpose of such restriction on the use of Whiteacre is for the protection of Blackacre. Furthermore it is not difficult to find the intention concerning the duration of such restriction. Not only B but "his heirs or assigns" are not to build on Whiteacre. Hence, the restriction is not only to last for a few years or for the life of A or the life of B, or while A continues to be the owner of Blackacre, but such restriction is to continue indefinitely and in fee. At this point then it can be concluded that A's deed to B of Whiteacre created an equitable servitude on the use of Whiteacre for the benefit of Blackacre and that such servitude is to continue indefinitely. But for an equitable servitude to run with the land there must be not only (a) an instrument and (b) an intention as set forth above, the intention relating to both the running and touching and concerning the land, but there must also be actual or constructive notice to the person or persons against whom it is sought to be enforced.

(c) **The notice and the running of the burden.** An equitable servitude is enforceable against any person who takes land with either actual or constructive notice that such land is burdened with a restriction on its use. On the other hand such a servitude cannot be enforced against a person who gives value and has no notice of the existence of the servitude, a bona fide purchaser. These propositions are true under modern recording statutes. What is the position of D, the person against whom the servitude is sought to be enforced? The facts state that he has no actual notice of the servitude at the time he purchased Blackacre. Further, there is no reference in his deed from C that such restriction exists. In addition he purchases Whiteacre for the very purpose of doing an act which will be a violation of the servitude, namely, erecting a building on Whiteacre. But these do not determine either the question of notice or D's rights. When D purchased Whiteacre he did not examine the records in his chain of title to Whiteacre. Every purchaser of land is bound by notice of the contents of the deeds and other instruments which are on record and are a part of his chain of title. The deed from A to B is an essential link in D's chain of title to Whiteacre and imparts constructive notice to D of its contents. Part of those contents is the reservation that neither B nor his "assigns" shall erect a building on Whiteacre. Therefore, when D purchased Whiteacre from C he took Whiteacre with constructive notice from the records that he has no right to build on such land. Hence, the burden of this equitable servitude is binding upon and enforceable against the defendant, D, in his position as owner of Whiteacre.

(d) **The running of the benefit of the servitude.** The intention of the parties determines who may and who may not enforce an equitable servitude. In our case the fact that Blackacre is retained by A and that any building on Whiteacre would cut off the view to the ocean from Blackacre makes it plain that the servitude created in the reservation of the deed to B is intended not merely to benefit A personally but is intended to benefit Blackacre and preserve to it an unrestricted view to the sea. It is intended then that such servitude shall redound to the benefit of any successive owner of Blackacre, which includes A's grantee, P. Nothing appears to indicate that the deed from A to P expressly granted or assigned to P the benefit of the servitude. But such servitude is merely an incident to Blackacre, the land for the benefit of which it is created. Therefore, when Blackacre is conveyed to P, the incidental servitude passes with the principal thing, Blackacre, without express mention. The result is that P can enforce the equitable servitude against D, and the injunction should issue in his favor.

(e) Dicta. The servitude created in this case might well satisfy also the requirements for a negative easement appurtenant to Blackacre as the dominant tenement with Whiteacre as the servient tenement, or the requirements of a covenant running with the land at law in the United States. There is: an instrument containing a covenant; an intention that the covenant run with the land; the covenant touches and concerns the land because it restricts the use of Whiteacre; and there is successive privity of estate between the original parties, and between B and D as to Whiteacre as to the burden, and between A and P as to the benefit which runs with Blackacre. Of course, in England where a covenant cannot run with the fee it could not be a covenant running with the land. The reason why such servitude may have such multiple classification is due to the fact that the concepts for easements, covenants running with the land at law and equitable servitudes became crystallized at different times in our legal history. Therefore, a solution of this problem under any one of these three concepts would be valid. See the leading case on equitable servitudes, Tulk v. Moxhay, 2 Phillips, 774 (English Chancery 1848); Peck v. Conway, 119 Mass. 546 (1871); Clark, p. 174 et seq.

CASE 268: A is the fee simple owner of Blackacre, a 40 acre tract which he subdivides, exclusive of streets, a park and alleys, into 240 lots numbered 1 to 240. He puts on record a plat of the area and a declaration of restrictions both of which are signed and acknowledged covering all the lots in the tract which disclose a complete scheme of development for the subdivision. The restrictions are declared to be "covenants running with the land constituting equitable servitudes upon the lots lying within Blackacre" and include the following:

1. All lots shall be used for residence purposes only except Lots 5, 7 and 9 in Block 3 and Lots 6, 8 and 10 in Block 15 and Lots 3, 5 and 7 in Block 9.

2. No part of said Blackacre or any building thereon, except Lot 7 in Block 9 shall be used directly or indirectly for the sale or manufacture of intoxicating liquor of any kind.

3. All adobe and tile buildings shall be plastered on the exterior surface and all frame buildings shall be painted.

4. No temporary residence shall be built upon the front half of any lot.

5. No residence shall be built of scrap metal but garages may be built of corrugated iron on the rear half of the lot.

6. No residence shall cost less than $20,000.00.

7. No residence shall be built within 25 feet of the front property line or within 5 feet of the side line.

8. No business building shall be built within 10 feet of the front property line.

9. Any lot may have a separate garage.

10. Not more than a single dwelling house shall be built on any one lot.

11. No part of said property shall be sold, conveyed, rented or leased to or be used by any person of negro descent.

A sells 150 of the 240 lots and in each deed there is a reference to the recorded declaration of restrictions with a statement to the effect that the grantor, the grantee and their heirs and assigns and successors are bound by each of the restrictions. P is the purchaser and owner of Lot 7 in Block 9 in Blackacre and is engaged in operating a tavern and selling intoxicating liquor thereon. D is the purchaser and owner of Lot 3 in Block 9 in the subdivision and is engaged in operating a drug store on his lot. He has purchased trade fixtures, has procured a license to sell liquor on Lot 3 from the State and is making arrangements to purchase large quantities of intoxicating liquors and threatens to sell such liquors in his drug store on Lot 3 in Block 9 of Blackacre. It appears that there have been violations of the above restrictions as follows: (a) 3 residences have been used for religious meetings; (b) 9 residences made of adobe are not plastered on the exterior; (c) one house owner has sold a few chairs and a few stoves, and in a limited way has used his residence as a "second hand" store; and (d) 4 frame houses have not been painted. There are 125 small dwelling houses on the tract. P sues D to enjoin his selling liquor on Lot 3 in Block 9 of Blackacre. The owners of 10 residential lots in the subdivision join with P as party plaintiffs. Should the injunction issue?

Answer and Analysis

The answer is yes. It is obvious that the restrictions on the use of Blackacre constitute equitable servitudes. The declaration of restrictions and reference thereto in each of the deeds to the lot owners constitute instruments complying with the Statute of Frauds. The declaration of restrictions and the deed to each lot owner in express terms disclose an intention that such restrictions shall bind not only the persons of the grantor and grantee but shall also bind their heirs, assigns and successors. In addition they provide that these restrictions shall run with the land and constitute "equitable servitudes upon the lots" in the subdivision. If that is not enough it may be pointed out that the surrounding circumstances disclose a general scheme or plan for developing the subdivision. And the fact that the plat of the subdivision and the declaration of restrictions are signed, acknowledged and recorded, and that the deed to each lot owner refers to the declaration of restrictions, gives each lot owner notice of the existence of the servitudes. There is therefore present the three requisites for the existence and enforceability of the equitable servitudes, namely, an instrument, an intention and notice. Alternatively, the requirements for a covenant to run in equity are satisfied: there is a covenant or instrument, intent, touch and concern, and notice. Then each of the restrictions contained in the declaration of restrictions is enforceable unless it is invalid or it has been waived or abandoned.

(1) **The validity of the restrictions.** Every one of the restrictions set forth in this declaration of restrictions is typical of the kind found in general schemes for the development and protection of a residential area as such. And every one of them individually and specifically, with one exception, is valid and enforceable as an equitable servitude. Restriction number 11 is unenforceable in the courts. It provides, "No part of said property shall be sold, conveyed, rented or leased to or be used by any person of negro descent". The 14th Amendment to the United States Constitution provides, "No State shall deny to any person within its jurisdiction the equal protection of the laws". The above restriction cannot be enforced without judicial action. Judicial action is "state action" and to enforce such restriction by state action is denying a "person of negro descent" equal protection of the laws. Prior to 1948 many such racial restrictions concerning minority groups such as Chinese, Japanese, Mexicans, Hawaiians, Puerto Ricans, Filipinos and others, were sustained as valid in state courts and such persons were excluded from being the owners or users of real property. Since the now famous Shelley v. Kraemer case such racial restrictions cannot be enforced. See Note following this case.

(2) **Waiver or abandonment of the restrictions.** Several principles may be considered at this point.

(a) A plaintiff who is guilty of laches is not entitled to relief in equity. There is nothing in this case which indicates delay, reasonable or otherwise. The action is commenced even before any liquor is actually sold on Lot 3 of Blackacre so it appears there is prompt action on the part of the plaintiffs.

(b) If an area is restricted to use for residential purposes only and the character of the entire neighborhood has in the process of evolutionary change and development become so affected or used or surrounded by business or industry that the purpose and object of the restrictions can no longer be realized or achieved, then the burden of the servitude is extinguished and cannot be enforced. This principle is not applicable to our state of facts. Here we have 240 lots with 125 dwelling houses in the area protected by equitable servitudes. It is inevitable that there be some violation, great or small, of rigidly worded restrictions, human beings being what they are with all degrees of intelligence and understanding of what restrictions mean and having utmost freedom under a benign and free government. The violations listed, if indeed they are real violations, are relatively minor when considered in the light of the possible values, physical and spiritual, which are protected by the servitudes as they are applied to all of the lots and all of the lot owners in Blackacre. Consider the fact that a single dwelling house in the area is to cost only $20,000.00. This indicates that the lots in the subdivision are expected to be sold to persons of small means who, for the most part, may build their own houses and may in the process be required to build part of a house and then wait to save more money with which to finish it. During such waiting period a frame house may be without paint and an adobe house without stucco. But the yearning of the man of small means to live in an area exclusively residential, thus giving his family the benefit and protection of comfortable, quiet and attractive surroundings, is as great as that of the man of wealth. And in this land of equality and opportunity the right of the poor man to be protected in his limited possessions is equally as important as the protection of the more expansive possessions of the rich. These restrictions in their ultimate effect are not limited to the defense of physical lands and structures. They control businesses and the conduct of lot owners in the community, and by so doing often give meaning and inspiration to the spiritual life of the neighborhood. Is there no difference between owning a house, establishing a home therein and rearing one's children in a neighborhood where the business district and tavern are restricted to an area three blocks away than doing the same things with the tavern next door? Hence, simply because there are in the subdivision a few unpainted and unplastered houses, some chairs and stoves are sold from a residence, and a few houses are used for religious meetings, that does not mean that the character of the neighborhood has been changed from its exclusively residential character.

(c) Each valid and enforceable restriction constitutes a separate and independent servitude casting its benefit and a reciprocal burden on each lot within the purview of the development scheme. And because one restriction has been violated and nothing done about it does not mean that there is universal waiver or abandonment of or acquiescence in the violation of another restriction. Nor does it mean that acquiescence in the violation of several restrictions constitutes a waiver of the right to enforce another restriction. The restriction concerning the sale of liquor in our case is different in kind from each of the other restrictions. Its desirability, its value and its purpose to each lot owner in the subdivision are quite distinct from the desirability, the value and purpose of any other restriction covering the tract. It can be enforced for its own purpose without regard to such other restrictions. Further, it cannot be maintained that there has been any waiver or abandonment of such liquor servitude on Lot 3 in Block 9 of Blackacre. The fact that the defendant has procured a liquor license from the State is totally immaterial. The servitude governs. The fact that the defendant may have invested heavily in trade fixtures and liquor is totally immaterial. The servitude governs. He bought his lot with notice of the restriction which governs the use thereof and he is bound thereby.

(3) Who may enforce the restrictions. The intention of the parties determines who may enforce an equitable servitude. This case admits of no doubt. Both the benefits and the burdens of the restrictions are made expressly to run with the land and in favor of the grantor, the grantees, their heirs, assigns and successors. In addition the subdivision development scheme evinces a clear intention that every lot and the owner thereof has the right and a reciprocal duty concerning the preservation of that plan. Thus, it may be said that the servitudes created by the restrictions on the use of Blackacre may be enforced by every person who owns a lot in the subdivision whether he be the grantor or his successor or a grantee or his successor. And this includes the plaintiffs in this action. Therefore, the injunction should issue prohibiting the defendant, D, from selling intoxicating liquor on his Lot 3 in Block 9 of Blackacre. See Shelley v. Kraemer, 334 U.S. 1, 68 S.Ct. 836, 92 L.Ed. 1161, 3 A.L.R.2d 441 (1948); Condos v. Home Development Co., 77 Ariz. 129, 267 P.2d 1069 (1954).

Note on Racial Discrimination: Prior to the case of Shelley v. Kraemer, noted supra, it was generally considered that racial discriminatory covenants on use and occupancy were simply private agreements and valid. The Fourteenth Amendment was thought to be inapplicable since it prohibited only states from discrimination and not private parties. Shelley v. Kraemer, however, held that if the state enforced such covenants, there was state action within the prohibition of the Fourteenth Amendment. Shelley v. Kraemer specifically involved enforcement in equity, but any doubt as to the enforceability of such covenants by legal action were dispelled by Barrows v. Jackson, 346 U.S. 249, 73 S.Ct. 1031, 97 L.Ed. 1586 (1953). Barrows held that a covenantor who breached such a covenant could not be forced to pay damages in a legal action by the covenantee since such a coerced payment would be state judicial enforcement of the covenant. The fact that the two parties to the action were parties to the covenant, neither of whose constitutional rights had been violated, was held immaterial, and the defendant covenantor could plead the constitutional rights of the discriminated persons.

Some of the discriminatory covenants in the past had taken the form of not only prohibiting use and occupancy by designated groups but also prohibited selling or leasing to such persons. Since it has been the policy of the common law to prohibit or greatly restrict restraints on alienation, prior to Shelley v. Kraemer, some courts had invalidated the restraints on alienation but upheld the restraints on use and occupancy. Under such a holding, the covenant could not preclude a person from purchasing or leasing the land, but it could preclude him from occupying it.

The policy of achieving racial discrimination by use of the fee simple determinable or other limitation wherein the estate would automatically determine and revert to the grantor if the land should be occupied by the designated type of person has been considered. In Charlotte Park and Recreation Comm'n v. Barringer, 242 N.C. 311, 88 S.E.2d 114 (1955), the Supreme Court of North Carolina upheld such a reverter provision as to land conveyed by private grantors to be used as a golf course for white persons only. The Supreme Court of the United States denied certiorari in 350 U.S. 983, 76 S.Ct. 469, 100 L.Ed. 851 (1956). Similarly, in Evans v. Abney, 396 U.S. 435, 90 S.Ct. 628, 24 L.Ed.2d 634 (1970), the Supreme Court upheld a reversion to the heirs of a devisor who had devised the land in trust for a municipal park for white persons only. When the purpose of the trust failed, the Georgia Supreme Court decided that the property reverted, and this decision was upheld by a majority of the Supreme Court, noting that the decision eliminated all discrimination since the whites as well as the blacks were now prevented from using the land as a park. The state court had decided that the cy pres doctrine (changing the terms of the trust to carry out as nearly as possible the intent of the settlor), could not be utilized to alter the will of the testator.

The above "public use" cases should be compared with Capitol Fed. Sav. & Loan Ass'n v. Smith, 136 Colo. 265, 316 P.2d 252 (1957), involving private restrictions on subdivision lots with a provision that if the lots were sold or leased to black persons, then the estate would terminate and vest in other lot owners in the block. The court decided that the provision was void under the 14th Amendment, and that no rights, duties or obligations could be based on such a restriction. Technically, in this case the persons to whom the title would shift on violation of the restrictions would have had an executory interest which was to last for a period of 48 years from its creation. Such an interest is, of course, subject to the rule against perpetuities, and it would seem that such common law rule would have been violated in any event. That rule, however, was not discussed.

Philosophically it may be difficult to distinguish the above cases on strictly a "state action" and automatic termination of the estate basis. Perhaps it is significant that in one situation a donor is simply attempting a gift for an illegal purpose to last "for so long as," whereas in the other situation unenforceable private housing patterns are attempted.

Club membership devices are a commonly employed method of controlling who purchases or occupies land in a sub-division or vertical development such as a high rise apartment complex. No doubt such devices may be used as a subterfuge to discriminate against designated minority groups, but such practices are not legally permissible. In Harris v. Sunset Islands Property Owners, Inc., 116 So.2d 622 (Fla.1959), the Supreme Court of Florida held invalid such a scheme where the bylaws of the Association restricted membership to Caucasian Gentiles, and membership in the association was necessary to become an owner or occupant of the subdivision. Where the bylaws are not so explicit but where discrimination is nevertheless practiced, the court no doubt will be able to disregard form for substance.

Federal Civil Rights legislation is now of prime importance in invalidating racial discrimination in real estate transactions. The Civil Rights Act of 1866 provides that all citizens shall have the same right as is enjoyed by white citizens to inherit, purchase, lease, sell, hold and convey real and personal property. 42 U.S.C.A. § 1982. In Jones v. Alfred H. Mayer Co., 392 U.S. 409, 88 S.Ct. 2186, 20 L.Ed.2d 1189 (1968), the Supreme Court stated that the Act meant exactly what it said, and that it prohibited *all* racial discrimination, private as well as public, in the sale or rental of property. The power of Congress to enact such statutes was predicated on the Thirteenth Amendment. In 1968 Congress enacted a comprehensive open housing law, (Civil Rights Act of 1968, Title VII, Fair Housing, Pub.L. 90–284, 82 Stat. 73), which the Supreme Court in the *Jones* case was held to be supplementary and complimentary to the 1866 legislation and not a replacement thereof. The 1968 legislation in most respects is much more comprehensive than the 1866 legislation, but in one respect it is not. Whereas there are exceptions written into the 1968 legislation, there are none in the brief 1866 legislation.

In brief, it is believed that *all* discrimination based on race in the sale and leasing of housing, except for the minor exceptions provided for in the 1968 legislation, is now invalid and illegal. Further, the 1968 act prohibits discrimination based not only on race, but also discrimination based on color, religion and national origin.

CASE 269: A, B and C each own 48 lots in a tract three blocks square and containing 9 blocks. The lots of each are scattered throughout the entire area. The three own all of the 144 lots within the subdivision. No other person owns a single lot therein. A, B and C join in signing and acknowledging and putting on record a map of this subdivision and designate it Fairview. There is no general declaration of restrictions and no agreement among the owners concerning restrictions to govern the area involved. Each owner is interested in selling all of his lots and in getting the maximum price for each. A sells his 48 lots to 48 persons over a period of time including one to D and in each deed he provides as follows: "Fairview is an attractive residential subdivision. Only one single dwelling house may be built on any lot and must cost not less than $30,000.00 and the house must be set back at least 30 feet from the front property line. These restrictions shall run with the land and shall continue as long as the grantor or his heirs own any lot in Fairview. Any violation of one of the restrictions shall cause the lot to revert to the grantor or his heirs". B sells his 48 lots to various persons including two lots to D and provides in each deed: "Only one single dwelling house may be built on any lot and must cost not less than $30,000.-00. These restrictions shall run with the land as long as the grantor or his heirs own any lot in Fairview. The violation of any restriction may be enjoined by the grantor or his heirs". C sells his 48 lots to 48 different persons and there is no restriction placed in any of his deeds. P is the owner of three lots in Fairview one lot being purchased from each of the three original owners. The three lots which D purchased from A and B are adjoining lots and D makes plans for building a large store building on the three lots. P seeks to enjoin such construction on the ground that each of the three lots is subject to a restriction for one dwelling house on each. Should the injunction issue?

Answer and Analysis

The answer is no. There are several sound reasons for this answer.

(1) **Methods of imposing equitable servitudes in subdivision schemes; ascertainment of benefit and duration.** There are three general types of subdivision schemes by which equitable servitudes are imposed. (a) In one plan there is a common owner or grantor who executes and records a declaration of restrictions setting forth a general scheme of building and development in the subdivision. Each deed issued to a lot in the tract binds the grantee to adhere to the restrictions contained in the recorded declaration. In such cases the servitudes created are made to run with the land and are made enforceable by and against the assignees and remote grantees of the original parties. The case next above illustrates this type of scheme. (b) In another plan all of the owners of lots in an unrestricted subdivision get together and draw up and execute a formal agreement in writing whereby they subject their respective lots to restrictions for residential purposes only and provide that each lot owner may enforce such restrictions against the owner of every other lot in the subdivision including remote assignees and grantees. Such agreement is recorded to constitute constructive notice to all subsequent purchasers. The legal effects are the same as in type (a) above. (c) Then there are the cases in which the owners of lots in a particular subdivision exact restrictive covenants from all of their grantees for the benefit only of the remaining lots which the owners hold in the tract. In such cases only the grantors or their heirs can enforce the restrictions and then only so long as they continue to own a lot in the tract. In such cases the servitudes are intended to benefit only the

grantors as owners of the remaining lots. And the servitudes are intended to endure only during the time while the grantor or his heirs still own part of the tract. But it should be noticed that the servitude is intended to protect the sale value of the grantor's remaining lots. Therefore it is made to run with the land until the grantors' last lot is sold and is not merely a personal contract. In such case none other than the grantors or their heirs can enforce the covenant. As far as endurance and enforcement are concerned this is the type of case we have in our problem. C placed no restrictions on the use of the lots he sold. A subjects his sold lots to servitudes but expressly provides that such servitudes shall endure only until his last lot is sold. The same is true as to B. But at the time P brings his suit against D all of the original owners of lots in the subdivision have disposed of all of their lots. Therefore, because it was so intended in the original grants, all of the servitudes have been extinguished by the expiration of the time during which they were to endure. This is enough to solve this case and to support the conclusion that the injunction should be denied. But there are other reasons.

(2) **Who may enforce an equitable servitude.** Whether or not a particular person may enforce an equitable servitude is determined by the intention of the parties. In our case it was intended that the grantor or his heirs and no one else is to enforce the restrictions. The plaintiff, P, is not one of these and therefore cannot maintain his action against D.

(3) **Extinguishment of equitable servitudes.** As a general principle it may be stated that equitable servitudes may be extinguished in the same way as easements or profits. This includes release, merger, abandonment and so on. But in equity the granting of relief is said to be a matter of grace and not of right. Hence, if a plaintiff is guilty of laches or of violating the very restriction he seeks to enforce it may be quite inequitable to give him the relief prayed for. Also if the granting of an injunction would work great hardship on the defendant with small benefit to the plaintiff the relief may be denied. Furthermore, when conditions work such a change in a neighborhood that the purpose of the restrictions are impossible of achievement then the servitude is extinguished. This principle, although there is no change in the conditions in the neighborhood, is involved in this set of facts. Here we have an apparent attempt by three owners to develop a residential subdivision. One places restrictions of one type on the lots he sells. Another places different restrictions on the lots he sells. The third owner places no restrictions at all on the lots he sells. There can be no effective general scheme of restrictions covering a subdivision unless the restrictions are universal and cover the entire tract and apply to all lots of like character brought within the total scheme. If it does not cover all lots it cannot be reciprocal. If it does not involve and require reciprocity the scheme as such must fail and is not binding on the lot owners. The reason is this; such a scheme presupposes a benefit to all and if only

some lots are benefited without burden and some lots carry all the onus of the restrictions without reciprocal benefit, then the intended purpose of the scheme is impossible of attainment. Such a result is not intended by the parties. For this reason alone P should be denied the injunction. Then the question comes up, suppose A or B still owned lots in the subdivision and one or the other or both brought the suit against D. For the reasons given above they should be denied the injunction. Some cases seem to permit recovery of damages at law in such cases but if the burden of the servitude has ceased to be, then damages ought not to be allowed for the reason that the benefit of the servitude is not intended to be merely personal. This is quite apart from the weighing of the hardship on the defendant with the benefit to be derived by the plaintiff. See O'Malley v. Central Methodist Church, 67 Ariz. 245, 194 P.2d 444 (1948); Clark, pp. 181–186; Restatement of Property §§ 560–564.

PUDS, HOA'S, CONDO'S AND CO–OP'S

Modern housing development often encompasses large areas and many units, and frequently the project encompasses different uses, or restrictions on uses, in different portions of the development. The developer may resort to various techniques and different types of housing to accomplish his goals, but whenever restrictions on use are imposed it should be noted that the heart of the concept is the equitable servitude or covenant running with the land. This note briefly explains some of the commonly used techniques for creating a controlled and compatible community.

The PUD, or Planned Unit Development, generally refers to a subdivision which provides for a mixture of land uses—residential, commercial, service, industrial—all in a single district but, of course, segregated by the planner so as to provide close-in recreational, service, and work facilities, and at the same time maintain quiet and peaceful residential sections.

An important characteristic of the PUD is flexibility. Portions of the subdivision may be developed as condominiums, cooperatives, or single family ownership. There also may be a combination of apartment, town houses, closely located single homes, and areas of widely separated single homes.

The HOA, or Home Owners' Association, is commonly used in connection with individual ownership of separate parcels. As a result of a Declaration of Restrictions each parcel owner may be compelled to be a member of the association and to pay assessments levied by the association. Commonly owned areas, parks, possibly streets, club house, swimming pools, and the like, are usually owned by the association, and the various members pay for the operating expenses via assessments, and the association is frequently accorded a lien on the member's property for unpaid assessments. The association may also be given wide powers over such things as approving building and renovation plans so as to preserve not only the residential character of the neighborhood but also its architectural compatibility. See Anthony v. Brea Glenbrook Club, 58 Cal.App.3d 506, 130 Cal.Rptr. 32 (1976), upholding mandatory membership; Heritage Heights Home Owners' Ass'n v. Esser, 115 Ariz. 330, 565 P.2d 207 (1977), upholding restrictions against fences; and Kell v. Belle Vista Village Property Owners' Ass'n, 258 Ark. 757, 528 S.W.2d 651 (1975), upholding generally the association's lien for assessments.

The condominium form of ownership is statutorily regulated, and usually the title to the common areas is vested in the various unit owners as tenants in common. Major restrictions on use and other regulations are made a part of the Declaration of Condominium, others may be incorporated into the by-laws of the association, and reasonable rules and regulations may be promulgated by the Board of Directors. Failure to pay the assessments results in the condominium association having a lien on the unit, which lien can be foreclosed.

The cooperative is frequently organized in a manner so that the association owns the building and leases it to the tenant-shareholders of the cooperative organization. Shares of stock or membership interest and the "proprietary lease" are bound together and cannot be partitioned or transferred separately. Control over the members may be even more strict and more readily sustainable than in the other two types of organizations because of the landlord-tenant analogy. However, the cooperative owner is in reality more than a tenant in the usual sense—he is a part owner of the project, and such ordinary landlord-tenant remedies as summary eviction might not be applicable. See Earl W. Jimerson Housing Co., Inc. v. Butler, 425 N.Y.S.2d 924, 97 Misc.2d 563 (1979), holding summary eviction not applicable; In re Pitts' Estate, 218 Cal. 184, 22 P.2d 694 (1933), upholding the association's lien on the unit. For cooperatives and condominiums generally, see infra Chapter XXIX.

SUMMARY OF CASES IN CHAPTER XXV

Case 258. The legal effect of a covenant which runs with land is to make an assignee of the land either benefit by or be burdened by the covenant without being a party to the making of the contract. For a covenant to run with the land at law there must be: (a) a covenant; (b) an intention that the covenant run with the land; (c) a covenant which touches and concerns the land; and (d) privity of estate. Today with seals largely abolished or curtailed by statute, a signed writing constitutes a covenant. A deed poll accepted by the grantee and containing a promise by the grantee constitutes a covenant by the grantee. A covenant touches and concerns the land if it makes the land in the hands of its owner either more usable and more valuable or less usable and less valuable. Privity of estate usually has reference to the succession to the interest in the land of one of the covenanting parties. An assignee of the benefit end of a covenant which runs with the land may recover damages from the covenantor for breach of the covenant.

Case 259. An assignee of the burden end of a covenant which runs with the land is personally liable to the covenantee in damages for breach of the covenant. This is true even when the covenant comes to the assignee by descent by operation of law and he has neither the right nor the power to reject it.

Case 260. If both the benefit end and the burden end of a covenant run with the land and both covenantee and covenantor assign their interests in the land, then the assignee of the covenantor is personally liable to the assignee of the covenantee for breach of the covenant.

Case 261. There are two types of privity of estate, mutual and successive. Co-owners of land, or of separate interests therein, represent mutual privity of estate, and when X conveys his land to Y there is successive privity of estate because Y succeeds to X's estate in the land. The majority of the cases say that there must be privity of estate between the original contracting parties in order that the covenant may run with the land. There seems little basis for this requirement. If there is privity of contract without privity of estate between the original covenanting parties and an assignee succeeds to the estate of one of the covenanting parties, and the other requirements are met, then the benefit or burden of the covenant should run to the assignee.

Case 262. A covenant for the building of a party wall is a conveyance creating cross-easements and constitutes privity of estate between the contracting parties. The benefit end of a covenant may run with the land without the running of the burden, and the burden may run with the land without the running of the benefit, if such is the intention of the parties and the other required elements for the running of the covenant are present.

2. IN LANDLORD AND TENANT RELATION

Case 263. For a covenant to run with the land in a landlord-tenant relation three elements must co-exist. (1) There must be a covenant. (2) There must be an intention that the covenant run with the land. (3) The covenant must touch and concern the land. Privity of estate always exists between landlord and tenant. An assignee of an estate in land with which a covenant runs is liable only for the breach of the covenant while he owns the estate in the land. Such assignee is not liable for a breach which occurs before he becomes assignee of the land, and he is not liable for a breach of the covenant which occurs after he has transferred the land. When there is a breach of a noncontinuing covenant running with the land, the covenant is transformed into a chose in action and no longer runs with the land.

Case 264. In a covenant running with the land in a landlord-tenant relation the expression "the land" means either the leasehold of the tenant or the reversion of the landlord. In such relation the benefit of a covenant cannot run with *the land* if it is intended to benefit and does benefit only *other land*. The benefit and burden should be tested separately in determining whether either or both runs with the land.

Case 265. In a landlord-tenant relation, a covenant to repair the property which is the subject matter of the lease runs with the land, the benefit with the land of the covenantee and the burden with the land of the covenantor, whether it be the leasehold or the reversion. In a continuing covenant the covenantor or his assignee is liable for any breach thereof and the fact that the covenantor has been compelled to pay damages for breach of the covenant at one time is no defense to a later action for a subsequent and different breach of the covenant.

Case 266. For a covenant to run with either the leasehold or the reversion in a landlord-tenant relation it must be intended to run and must be of the type which touches and concerns the land. An intention that the covenant shall run cannot cause it to run if it is personal and not the type which touches and concerns the land. Conversely if the covenant is the type which touches and concerns the land but there is no intention that it shall run, it will not run with the land. If a lessor covenants not to compete with the lessee in the operation of his business on the leased premises, the burden of the covenant is personal and will not run with the reversion. But the benefit of such covenant will run with the leasehold and the lessee's assignee can enforce it against the lessor personally. Either benefit or burden of a covenant may run separately without the running of the other.

3. EQUITABLE SERVITUDES

Case 267. An equitable servitude may be created by (a) an instrument which complies with the Statute of Frauds, and (b) an intention that there be a restriction on the use of the land involved. A deed poll providing for a restriction on the use of the land conveyed and accepted by the grantee may create an equitable servitude without the grantee's signature. The intention to create an equitable servitude may be determined by the words of the instrument and the circumstances under which it is executed. There must be an intention that the land be bound. An equitable servitude may be enforced against any person who takes land with either actual or constructive notice that such land is burdened with a restriction on its use. Such servitude cannot be enforced against a bona fide purchaser who takes land for value and with no notice of the restriction on its use. Whether or not a particular person can enforce an equitable servitude is determined by the intention of the parties. If land, and not merely the owner thereof personally, is to be benefited by the servitude, then a transferee of the land for the benefit of which the servitude exists may enforce the restriction.

Case 268. A declaration of restrictions which is signed, acknowledged and recorded, evincing an intention to restrict the use of the lots in a subdivision to residential purposes only, and disclosing an intention to set forth a comprehensive development scheme for the subdivision, is competent to create an equitable servitude on each lot within the tract and each owner of a lot therein is bound by such restrictions. There being an intention that such servitudes shall run with the land, any lot owner or his assignee may enforce such restrictions and such restrictions are enforceable against any assignee. Restrictions which prohibit either the ownership or the use of real property on the ground that a person belongs to a particular race such as Negro, Chinese, Japanese, Mexicans, Filipinos and the like, are no longer enforceable in the courts. Every valid restriction on the use of land constitutes a separate and independent servitude and can be enforced for its own purpose. This is true even though other restrictions have been violated and the dominant lot owners have acquiesced in such violations. However, if a subdivision is restricted to residential purposes only and the neighborhood has so changed that the purpose of the restrictions can no longer be accomplished, then the servitude is extinguished.

Case 269. There are three types of schemes for subdivision development: (a) one in which a common owner records a declaration of restrictions setting forth the general scheme and binds all his grantees to adhere to such restrictions; (b) one in which all the owners of an unrestricted area join in a formal agreement creating equitable servitudes on their respective lots; and (c) one in which an owner of a subdivision places restrictions on all lots in the tract but such restrictions being for the sole benefit of the remaining lots owned by the owner in the tract. In schemes (a) and (b) the servitudes are to continue indefinitely and are enforceable by and against remote grantees and assignees of the original parties. In scheme (c) such servitudes are intended to endure only while the grantor continues to own a lot in the tract and they are enforceable only during that period and only by the grantor or his heirs. Equitable servitudes may be extinguished in the same way as easements or profits. But a plaintiff seeking to enforce an equitable servitude may be denied relief on equitable grounds such as laches, hardship or there being no equity in his favor. If and when the purpose of a servitude in a development scheme is impossible of attainment the servitude should be extinguished and damages should not be permitted for a breach thereof. A development scheme which is not universal and applicable to all lots in the subdivision is not reciprocal and if reciprocity is not required the plan must fail because its effectiveness must be based on the intention to benefit all lots in the tract. If some lots are restricted in one way and others in another way and some lots not restricted at all the scheme must fail.

EASEMENTS AND PROFITS

1. Easements and Profits Defined, Distinguished and Classified.
    Legal Gems.
    Cases.
2. How Created and Extent.
    Legal Gems.
    a. By Prescription.
        Cases.
    b. By Express Provision in Deed or Will.
        Cases.
    c. By Implication.
        Cases.
3. Extinguishment.
    Legal Gems.
    Cases.
Summary of Cases in Chapter XXVI.

---

1. EASEMENTS AND PROFITS DEFINED, DISTINGUISHED AND CLASSIFIED

LEGAL GEMS

1. An easement is the *right* of one person to go onto the land in possession of another and make a limited use thereof. E. g., A has a *right* to walk across, lay pipes or string wires over Blackacre which is in the possession of B.

2. A profit (short for profit a prendre) is the *right* of one person to go onto the land in possession of another and take therefrom either some part of the land itself or some product of the land. E. g., A has a *right* to go onto Blackacre which is in the possession of B, and take off sand, oil, gravel, marble, stone, grass, trees, shrubbery, or fish.

3. The distinguishing element between an easement on one hand and a profit on the other is this: an easement gives its owner only the right to use the land of another with no right to take anything from such land, whereas a profit gives its owner the right to take either the soil itself such as sand, dirt or gravel, or the right to take a product of the land such as grass or trees which grow thereon, and in addition, the owner of the profit may use the land to the extent necessary to enable him to enjoy the profit. E. g., A, having the right to take coal and grass from B's Blackacre, has (a) the right to go onto Blackacre to where the coal and grass are, (b) the right to cut the grass and sever the coal, and (c) the right to carry off the grass and coal after they are severed.

560

4. In the United States the rules and principles governing the classification, creation, extinguishment, the right of succession to and determining the scope thereof, are alike applicable to easements on the one hand and profits a prendre on the other. Some authorities use the term easement to include both easements and profits, differentiating when necessary between easements with a profit and easements without a profit.

5. Easements (or profits) are classified as

(a) easements appurtenant and

(b) easements in gross.

6. An easement (or profit) is appurtenant when in its creation it is attached to a piece of land and benefits the owner of such land in his use and enjoyment thereof. E. g., A owns Blackacre which is separated from Town X by B's Whiteacre which lies between A's land and the Town. B conveys to A a right of way to go across Whiteacre to Town X from Blackacre, such right of way being intended to benefit A in his use of Blackacre. This right of way over Whiteacre is an easement appurtenant to A's Blackacre and can be used only in connection with Blackacre.

7. Easement (or profit) appurtenant analyzed—

Every easement appurtenant requires for its existence *two pieces of land* which are *owned by two different persons*. The two pieces of land involved are—

(a) the *dominant tenement,* which is the land whose owner is benefited by the easement and is Blackacre in the example given under paragraph 6 above, and

(b) the *servient tenement,* which is the land whose owner is burdened by the easement and is Whiteacre in the example given under paragraph 6 above.

(c) The owner of the dominant tenement is called the *dominant tenant,* and is A in the example given under paragraph 6 above, and

(d) the owner of the servient tenement is called the *servient tenant*, and is B in the example given under paragraph 6 above.

(e) It is said that the servient tract, Whiteacre, serves the dominant tract, Blackacre, but this really means that A's use of Blackacre is enhanced by his being able to use the right of way over Whiteacre in his use of Blackacre, and that Whiteacre in the possession of B is subject to the right of way in A's favor and to that extent B's use of Whiteacre is curtailed.

8. An easement (or profit) is in gross when in its creation it is not intended to benefit the owner or possessor of land as such but is intended to exist without a dominant tenement. E. g., A owns Blackacre on which is a gravel pit. B is a road contractor who owns no land but who uses gravel. A conveys to B the right to come onto

Blackacre and take off gravel. B owns a profit in gross which exists wholly independently of B's ownership of land.

9. Easement (or profit) in gross analyzed—

Every easement in gross requires for its existence *one piece* of land which is owned by a person other than the owner of the easement in gross. Only *one piece* of land is involved—

(a) the *servient tenement*, which is the land subject to and burdened by the easement, and which is Blackacre in the example given under paragraph 8 above.

(b) The owner of the servient tenement is called the *servient tenant*, and is A in the example given under paragraph 8 above, and

(c) the owner of the easement in gross is called the *dominant tenant*, and

(d) there is *no dominant tenement*.

10. By analogy to estates in land an easement (or profit) is real property if its period of duration is either: (a) for an indefinite time like a fee simple estate; or (b) for the life of a human being; and is personal property, a chattel real, if its period of duration is either: (c) for a specific time like an estate for years; or (d) from period to period like an estate from year to year.

11. For purposes of use easements are classified as

(a) *affirmative easements* which entitle the easement owner to do affirmative acts on the land in the possession of another— e. g., A owns a right of way across B's Whiteacre. A is entitled to go onto Whiteacre, move across Whiteacre and may repair and improve the way on Whiteacre. A has an affirmative easement as to the servient tenement, Whiteacre.

(b) *negative easements* which take from the owner of the servient tenement the right to do some things which, were it not for the easement, he would have a right to do on his own land. E. g., B, being owner of Whiteacre which is located between A's Blackacre and the ocean, by an effective instrument agrees with A that no building will be built on Whiteacre which will in any way interfere with A's view from Blackacre to the ocean. A has a negative easement on Whiteacre. A negative easement is negative in another sense; it does not permit the dominant tenant to do any affirmative act on the servient tenement. In the case given A has no right to do any act on Whiteacre. The effect of such negative easement is merely to curtail B's rights on Whiteacre and to permit A to enforce such curtailment.

12. An easement appurtenant construction is preferred over that of an easement in gross. Hence, if there is doubt as to whether an easement is appurtenant or in gross, it is construed as an easement appurtenant.

13. By the better rule easements (or profits) are alienable either by deed or by will and are descendible.

14. Whether or not an easement (or profit) is apportionable is determined by the intention of the parties as expressed in the instrument if created by deed or by will, and by the manner of its creation if it arises by prescription. E. g., B grants to A and his heirs the right to pasture on B's Blackacre four head of cows. A conveys to C and his heirs the right to pasture two head of cows on Blackacre, A reserving his right to pasture two head of cows thereon. Because this apportionment of his profit in gross by A is admeasurable and will not surcharge or place any additional burden on the servient tract, Blackacre, and because it seems to have been intended by the parties to the original conveyance, the profit in gross created by B in A is apportionable.

15. An easement (or profit) is an interest in land requiring compliance with the Statute of Frauds in the creation or transfer thereof. Such principle is not applicable to an easement by implication which arises by inference of the intention of the parties in connection with a conveyance of part of a tract of land. See Gem 16 infra. The intention of the parties can be shown by the surrounding circumstances which are provable by parol evidence. It seems also that if in a given jurisdiction an oral lease for one year is valid that an orally created easement for one year should likewise be valid.

16. To establish an easement by implication the following must be shown:

(a) that at the time of the conveyance one part of the land is being used for the benefit of the other part (a quasi-easement);

(b) that the use is apparent;

(c) that the use is continuous; and

(d) that the use is reasonably necessary to the enjoyment of the quasi-dominant tract.

17. If the implied easement is in favor of the conveyee and is appurtenant to the tract conveyed, it is called an implied grant; if the implied easement is in favor of the conveyor and is appurtenant to the tract retained, it is called an implied reservation.

18. Because an implied easement is based on the inferred intention of the parties, all the circumstances surrounding the conveyance, including the following, are important and provable by parol evidence if necessary:

(a) the language used in the conveyance;

(b) the fact as to whether the easement is claimed by the grantee or grantor;

(c) the degree of necessity that the easement exist or the hardship, if any, if it does not exist;

(d) the determination as to whether the easement will, if implied, confer benefits on both parties to the conveyance;

(e) the manner in which the property was used before the conveyance; and

(f) the knowledge the parties had concerning the use of the property before the conveyance.

See Restatement of Property §§ 450–486; Burby, 72–75.

———

CASE 270: A, the fee simple owner of Blackacre under the surface of which is a thick seam of coal, makes a conveyance to B "granting to B and his heirs the right to come onto Blackacre and sever and take away any or all the coal he may find therein or thereunder, he to have hereby all the right which the grantor A has over such coal". Ten days thereafter while B is exploring for coal on Blackacre he discovers that A is digging and transporting coal therefrom. B brings an action to enjoin any further digging or removal of coal from Blackacre. Should the injunction issue?

Answer and Analysis

The answer is yes. There is a fine but highly important distinction between the ownership of coal on the one hand and a right to take coal on the other. In our case where words of inheritance, "B and his heirs", are used, each would constitute real property which would descend from the ancestor to the heir. But the difference is this—if A's conveyance to B transfers to B the property in the coal as coal, then the corpus of all of the coal under Blackacre belongs to B and A no longer has any interest therein and has no right to take or remove any of it. If, however, A's conveyance to B transfers to B no coal as coal, but only a right to come onto Blackacre and take and carry away coal, then the corpus of the coal still belongs to A until B has exercised the right, severs such coal from its natural position, and makes an appropriation thereof. In this latter case B would have a profit in gross and A could still continue to dig and transport any coal he wishes from Blackacre.

To determine whether B now owns coal or a right to take coal, resort must be had to the words of the conveyance. The first part of A's conveyance, "granting to B and his heirs the right to come onto Blackacre and sever and carry away any or all coal he may find therein or thereunder" is a typical description of a *right* which would constitute a profit. If these words alone described the grant to B, it should be construed as a profit in B's favor, A would still own the coal, and the injunction should not issue against him for digging and transporting his own coal. But when we add to the above quoted words the remaining words in the grant, "he (B) to have hereby all the right which the grantor A has over such coal", then it seems clear that the fee simple in the coal has been granted to B. Why? Because in specific words the conveyance says the grantee, B, is to have all the rights which the grantor, A, has over such coal, and A, the grantor has a fee simple over the coal as coal. And if there is doubt on the point the instrument is construed more strongly against the grantor, who is A in our case, and in favor of the grantee, who is B in our case. There are two ways of describing the subject of a transfer in real property. One is by metes and bounds and the other is by describing the power and control over the subject matter. The second method is used in this conveyance and gives to the grantee B the same right over the coal as A had which was in fee simple. Hence, B having been granted the coal as coal under Blackacre, is now the owner of the corpus of the coal, and A has no right therein. Thus, the injunction should issue. But B's ownership of coal would be of little value if he could not use the surface of Blackacre as a means by which to discover and remove the discovered coal. Hence, under such circumstances B not only owns the corpus of the coal in and under Blackacre, he has also an easement by implication to a right of way to find and remove such coal. Such must have been intended by the parties to the conveyance even though nothing is said about it expressly. Thus we infer from the circumstances an implied easement in favor of B. This easement is appurtenant to B's fee simple estate in the coal as coal which is the dominant tenement. Blackacre is the servient tenement as to such easement. A is the servient tenant and B is the dominant tenant. See Caldwell v. Fulton, 31 Pa. 475, 72 Am.Dec. 760 (1858); Restatement of Property § 474 et seq.

Note

Fee Versus Easement Construction

In Midland Val. R. R. Co. v. Arrow Indus. Mfg. Co., 297 P.2d 410 (Okl.1956), it was held that an instrument labelled "Right of Way Deed" conveyed not an easement for railroad purposes but rather a strip of land in fee simple. The operative words were: ". . . hereby conveys and warrants to . . . a strip of land for right of way over and across the following described tract . . . "

Although the rationale was bolstered by a statute preferring a fee simple construction unless clearly limited otherwise, the court noted that the deed stated that it "conveys . . . a strip of land." In effect, the words "for right of way purposes" were an expression of purpose, motive or use, but the land itself was conveyed.

The issue is important when the land is no longer used for railroad or other designated purposes: if a fee was conveyed, the narrow strip of land remains with the grantee or his successor; if an easement was conveyed, the land reverts to his grantor or his successor. Careful draftsmanship can avoid the problem. If an easement is intended, the deed should read that it "grants or conveys a right of way for . . . purposes across the following parcel . . . " If a fee is intended, the deed should simply state that it "conveys the following described parcel: . . ."

———

CASE 271: A is the owner of Blackacre, a section of land on which there is a small lake almost in the center of the tract and which is fed entirely by springs from the adjoining hills. Abutting Blackacre on the south is B's quarter section, Whiteacre. B's land is lower than Blackacre and the natural drainage is from north to south, from Blackacre to Whiteacre. B is in the business of supplying water and ice to some of his neighbors and maintains on Whiteacre a large artificial reservoir and an ice house for such purposes. A conveys to B and his heirs forever the right to come onto Blackacre, pipe water from Blackacre into B's reservoir on Whiteacre and the right to take the ice from the lake on Blackacre for storage on Whiteacre. It is further provided that the right to take such water and ice may be exercised by piping the water to or storing the ice on any other property in case B should dispose of Whiteacre.

B then purchases Greenacre, another quarter section which also abuts A's Blackacre on the south. B then conveys Whiteacre to X and his heirs, it being understood that the conveyance includes none of B's rights to water or ice from the lake on A's Blackacre. B then runs a pipe from the lake on Blackacre to his Greenacre and builds an ice house on Greenacre and continues his business of supplying ice and water to his neighbors by contract. B then sells Greenacre and his rights to ice and water from the lake on Blackacre to Y and executes a conveyance thereof to Y and his heirs. A refuses to permit Y to take any water or ice from the lake on Blackacre. Y sues seeking to enjoin A from interfering with Y's piping water and taking the ice from the lake. Should the injunction issue?

Answer and Analysis

The answer is yes. (1) What interests did A convey to B? From an historical perspective, A conveyed to B an easement to take water and a profit to take ice from the lake on Blackacre. Because water in nature is owned by no one but belongs to everyone, it is not considered as connected with any particular piece of land and is not considered a product of the soil. Thus, a right to take water from the land of another is treated merely as a right to use the land and therefore only an easement. On the other hand when that same water is frozen and becomes a solid on a particular piece of land, it had been considered a product of that soil while it was so frozen and therefore the right to take it was considered a profit. The distinction between profit and easement, however, is no longer important in this country since the rules relating to both are essentially the same.

(2) Are the interests which A conveyed to B appurtenant or in gross? The answer to this question is found in the deed which provides that these rights may be exercised by B on any land which he may see fit to use in connection therewith. It is evidently not the intention of A and B then to attach them or make them appurtenant to Whiteacre or any other land even though at the time of the conveyance B did own Whiteacre and piped the water thereto and stored the ice thereon. That being the case these rights are not appurtenant to Whiteacre but belong to B wholly independently of his ownership of any land in particular. Hence, it must be concluded that these rights are rights in gross which involve only one piece of land in its creation. That piece of land in our case is Blackacre, the servient tenement. As to such easement to take water and profit to take ice, B is the dominant tenant and A is the servient tenant.

(3) May B transfer his easement in gross to take water from the lake on Blackacre? Historically this is an important question. In England an easement in gross can not exist, much less be assigned. The English courts recognized only easements appurtenant to land, and if one not an owner of land to which an easement could be appurtenant was given a right of way across land or right to take water from land, such right was considered wholly personal and in no sense a right in the land, and such right was not transferable. However, in the United States this English doctrine has not been followed. In this country an easement in gross which is of a commercial nature, such as the one involved in our case in B's favor, is an interest in land and can be conveyed like any other property interest. In this respect it is treated exactly like a profit in gross which could exist and was alienable in the English common law. Thus, it was competent in this country for B to transfer to Y the easement in gross to take water from the lake on Blackacre.

(4) May B transfer his profit in gross to take ice from the lake on Blackacre? Both in England and in the United States a profit in gross has always been considered an interest in land and alienable as such. Hence, B's conveyance to Y of the right to take ice from Blackacre was effective and Y becomes the owner of such profit. It might be added that had this easement and this profit been appurtenant to Whiteacre in their creation then they would have been alienable with the dominant tenement, Whiteacre, because an incident passes with the conveyance of the principal thing. Both in England and in the United States a conveyance of the dominant tenement carries with it all easements and profits appurtenant thereto unless it is otherwise expressly provided. From the above it must be concluded that Y is now the owner of the easement in gross to take water from the lake on Blackacre, and also owner of the profit to take ice from the lake on Blackacre, and A has no right to interfere with Y's exercise of those rights. Thus the injunction should issue. See Restatement of Property §§ 450, 489, 490; Huntington v. Asher, 96 N.Y. 604, 48 Am.Rep. 652 (1884); Akroyd v. Smith, 138 Eng.Reprint 68 (1850); Standard Oil Co. v. Buchi, 72 N.J.Eq. 492, 66 A. 427 (Ch.1907).

CASE 272: A is the fee simple owner of Blackacre on which is an apartment house six stores high, the exterior boundaries of which building are coextensive with the exterior boundaries of Blackacre. B owns Whiteacre which bounds Blackacre on the east. B makes an effective written agreement for and on behalf of himself, his heirs and assigns, that neither he nor they will build any building on the west 25 feet of Whiteacre abutting Blackacre so long as the apartment building stands on Blackacre and has windows in the east side thereof, such agreement being in favor of A and his heirs as owners of Blackacre. B threatens to build a 10 story building on Whiteacre and contiguous to A's apartment house. A seeks to enjoin such building within 25 feet of A's apartment house building. Should the injunction issue?

Answer and Analysis

The answer is yes. There are two kinds of easements with respect to the use to be made of the servient tenement by the dominant tenant. One is affirmative and the other is negative. When the dominant tenant has the right to do affirmative acts on the servient tenement, then it is called an affirmative easement. For example, X has a right to lead water by means of a ditch across Y's Brownacre. X, the dominant tenant, has a right to go onto Brownacre, the servient tenement, for the purpose of keeping the ditch open and free from obstructions so that the water will flow through the ditch. X's easement is an affirmative easement. When the dominant tenant has no right to do any affirmative act on the servient tenement, then the easement is called a negative easement.

The case given is an example of a negative easement [1] because A, the dominant tenant, has no right to go onto B's Whiteacre, the servient tenement, and do any affirmative act thereon. The easement consists simply of an assurance by B and his successors that A, the dominant tenant, shall have a limited use of the west 25 feet of Whiteacre by having light and air diffused thereover without any obstruction thereon by a building. B has effectively conveyed to A part of the rights which B had over the west 25 feet of Whiteacre. But having made such conveyance, B is curtailed in his right to use his property to the extent of the limitations contained in the negative easement. B may still continue to use such 25 feet for parking space, for a garden or other uses which will not obstruct A's light and air by means of a building thereon.

Easements, as already stated, are classified as (a) appurtenant and (b) in gross. The easement created by B in our case is an easement appurtenant to Blackacre, and is of benefit to A solely as the

---

1. Although there was no grant or deed creating the easement, the valid covenant is enforceable and the result is the same as if the agreement had been incorporated into a deed granting A an easement for light and air with appropriate descriptions as to the building restrictions.

owner of Blackacre. It can benefit no other property and no person other than the owner of Blackacre. Here are both dominant tenement, Blackacre, and servient tenement, Whiteacre. Here are also the dominant tenant, A, and the servient tenant, B. Thus, all the elements of an easement appurtenant exist. Should A convey Blackacre to C, then C would take Blackacre as the principal thing and would also take the easement as an incident to the principal thing. See Restatement of Property §§ 450–456.

---

2. HOW CREATED AND EXTENT

Legal Gems

1. Easements (or profits) are created as follows:

    (a) by prescription

    (b) by express provision in a deed or will

    (c) by implication

    (d) by estoppel

    (e) by eminent domain.

In addition irrevocable relationships amounting to easements may be created by

    (a) licenses which have become irrevocable, and

    (b) refusal to enjoin a trespass or nuisance.

2. An easement by prescription arises by adverse user of the servient tenement by the dominant tenant for the period of the statute of limitations. To mature such an easement against a landowner the user must be:

    (a) adverse as distinct from permissive; in derogation of right rather than in subordination to the rights of the landowner;

    (b) open and notorious;

    (c) continuous and without interruption; and

    (d) for the period of prescription.

3. The extent of the rights matured by prescription is determined by the use of the servient tenement continued during the period of prescription.

4. An easement created by deed arises when the deed is delivered, and an easement created by will arises at the death of the testator. If the easement is in favor of the transferee or grantee, it is created by express grant; if it is in favor of the grantor, it is created by exception or reservation. See supra Chapter XX, Cases 232 and 233 for creation by exception or reservation.

5. The extent of the rights under an easement created by deed or by will is determined by the words of the instrument which describe the easement.

6. An easement by implication arises from the circumstances surrounding the dividing by the owner of a piece of land into two pieces and conveying one of such pieces to another. From such surrounding circumstances an inference is drawn that the parties intend the creation of an easement.

Easements by implication include (a) easements of necessity, and (b) easements created by conveyances in reference to a plat depicting streets, parks and other places thereon.

7. The extent of the rights under an easement created by implication is determined by the circumstances surrounding the conveyance which divides the single ownership.

In easements created by conveyance in reference to a plat, the extent of the easement is determined by reference to one of three divergent rules according to the jurisdiction and the nature of the easement. These rules are referred to as: (1) the "broad" view or "unity" rule; (2) the intermediate or "beneficial enjoyment" rule; and (3) the "narrow" view or "necessary" rule. These rules are discussed at length in 7 A.L.R.2d 607, 612.

8. Disabilities may extend the period of time for the acquisition of prescriptive easements. By way of analogy the disabilities applicable to adverse possession are applied to prescription cases and they are applied in the same manner.

9. Tacking of successive periods of adverse use to satisfy the time period is permissible in prescription cases in the same manner as applied to adverse possession cases.

10. Ordinarily adverse user does not run against a future interest holder, but when the adverse user involves taking the corpus of the property and the remainderman has notice, then the prescription is effective against the remainderman as well as against the possessory interest.

See Restatement of Property §§ 457–486; Powell, ¶¶ 407–416.

a. BY PRESCRIPTION

CASE 273: B is the owner of Blackacre on which is a marble quarry. A goes onto Blackacre in plain view of B's house and without right for a period of 8 consecutive years severs and removes 15 cubic yards of marble therefrom. Then for each of the 4 years following he continues the process but removes 25 cubic yards of marble from Blackacre. The statute of limitations for prescription is 10 years and for recovery of damages for trespass on real property is 3 years within the jurisdiction. B sues A to enjoin any further removal of marble from Blackacre and for damages for all the marble he has removed therefrom. **(a)** Should any injunction issue? **(b)** Should B recover any damages?

Answers and Analyses

The answer to (a) is yes, but the injunction should be limited to the removal of any marble in excess of 15 cubic yards per annum. The answer to (b) is yes, but the damages should be limited to the value of 10 cubic yards for each of the last 3 years. The first question is whether or not A has gained any prescriptive right and second what is the extent of such right. The facts given state that A severed and carried away marble without right and that such was done within sight of B's house. This must mean that the taking was (a) wrongful, (b) not in subordination to B's rights, and (c) open and notorious. Such acts were carried on for 12 consecutive years so the taking was (d) continuous. Because B did not interfere with A's taking either by physical obstruction or by legal proceedings, it must be concluded that A's taking was (e) uninterrupted. Furthermore A's taking continued (f) during the 10 year period of prescription. All of these elements having concurred during the entire period of the statute of limitation, it must be concluded that the actor, A, acquired a profit to take marble from B's Blackacre. No dominant tenement appearing it must be a profit in gross.

The next question involves the extent of A's prescriptive right. A has the right to continue to take as much marble as he has continued to take each year during the period of prescription which is 15 cubic yards. During no single year did he take less than that amount. During each of 2 years of the 10 year period he took 10 cubic yards in excess of that amount. So A's profit is limited to a right to take from Blackacre 15 cubic yards of marble per year. As to that amount he has a right and no decree of the court should interfere with it. However, he has no right to take any more than 15 cubic yards per year and to the extent that he does take more he is a wrongdoer and should be enjoined. Hence, the decree should enjoin A from taking any marble from Blackacre in excess of 15 cubic yards per year. When once the prescriptive period has passed, then the landowner has no right to recover for any marble taken during any of the prescriptive period which is within the minimum taken. However, the landowner can recover damages for any excess marble taken within the statute of limitations for recovery for trespass to real property. Thus in our case where the statute on this action is three years, B has a right to recover in damages for the value of 10 cubic yards of marble for each of the last three years or for a total of 30 cubic yards of marble. Had A continued for 8 more years to take 25 cubic yards of marble, then he would have acquired a prescriptive right up to 25 cubic yards of marble per annum. See Restatement of Property §§ 457–460, 465, 477, 478.

CASE 274: A is fee simple owner of Blackacre and Greenacre. Between these two tracts lies B's Whiteacre. Each tract contains 80 acres. Town X is located just north of

Greenacre which is north of Whiteacre. For a period of 15 years both the public generally and A have used a road across Blackacre, Whiteacre and Greenacre which is the shortest way from south of Blackacre to Town X. The period of prescription in the jurisdiction is 10 years. B puts a fence across the road and A seeks a mandatory injunction compelling B to remove the fence. During the trial A testifies that he used the way openly and graded it every year for 15 years, that he has never received permission from anyone to use the road across B's Whiteacre, and denies that he ever talked to B about obtaining permission to use or purchasing a right of way over Whiteacre as B testifies. The trial court grants the injunction and B appeals. How should the appellate court rule on B's appeal?

Answer and Analysis

The judgment should be affirmed. There is a difference between gaining title to land by adverse possession and gaining title to an easement by adverse user, even though both must be gained without the consent of the landowner. Adverse possession requires that the adverse possessor have exclusive possession of the land for the statutory period. The title gained by adverse possession is said to be title to corporeal property. But title gained by prescription is always to incorporeal property, merely a right to use. To gain such title the adverse claimant does not have possession of the land and very often the use which he makes of the servient tenement is not exclusive. An adverse claimant may gain title by prescription to a right of way while the same way is being used both by the public and by the owner of the servient tract. Hence, in our case the fact that the public is also using the road over Whiteacre does not prevent A's gaining a right of way over such road by prescription. The facts state that A has used the road for 15 years which exceeds the statutory period by 5 years.

There are three possible rules as to the legal effect of the use of a way over the land of another for the prescriptive period. (1) Some cases say that such use raises a presumption that the use is adverse. (2) Other cases say that unless there is direct and specific proof that the use has been adverse, then there is a presumption that the use is permissive. (3) The third view is that there is no presumption either in favor of adverseness or in favor of permissiveness and that the burden of proof is on him who claims by adverse user to prove all of the elements required to gain a prescriptive right. In addition to differences in jurisdictions, the circumstances of the case may be significant as to which rule is applied. (see Powell ¶ 413).

Under the third view which is believed to be the correct one, there is usually just one question for the appellate court and that is whether or not there is evidence to support the findings of the trier of fact. Under this view the claimant of the prescriptive right must prove that the use is adverse, that is, that it is wrongful, not in subordination to the owner of the land claimed to be burdened with the easement, and open and notorious. He must also prove that such use is continuous and uninterrupted for the entire statutory period. It is quite obvious that these are questions of fact to be determined by the trial court. In the facts it appears that A used the way for more than the statutory period of 10 years. There is evidence that he received no permission to use such way and that he used it openly and notoriously. The question of continuity is for the trier of fact and there appears no evidence that there was any interruption. The most that can be said concerning B's testimony that A came to him to buy a right of way across Whiteacre and sought permission to use it, and that A thereby recognized B's paramount title and attempted to make his acts subordinate thereto, is that it raised a conflict in the evidence. Even if that be granted, it remained a question of fact, and when the trial court on the conflicting evidence found for the plaintiff, A, the facts are settled that the use was wrongful, without subordination to B or B's interests, open and notorious, continuous and uninterrupted for the statutory period. There being evidence to support such finding, there is nothing for the appellate court to do but to affirm the judgment of the lower court. See O'Banion v. Borba, 32 Cal. 2d 145, 195 P.2d 10 (1948); LaRue v. Kosich, 66 Ariz. 299, 187 P.2d 642 (1947); Restatement of Property §§ 457–460.

Cf. Lunt v. Kitchens, 123 Utah 488, 260 P.2d 535 (1953), involving use of a neighbor's driveway between the houses. The two families were on friendly terms for many years, and the court assumed an implied consent to accommodate the neighbor—hence permissive and no prescriptive easement.

CASE 275: A owns Blackacre, a city lot, on which there is no water supply. B owns Whiteacre abutting Blackacre on which there is a spring from which flows plenty of pure water. A has his dwelling house on Blackacre and during the year 1940 starts trespassing on Whiteacre by going to the spring thereon and bringing home buckets of water for use on Blackacre. In the year 1942 B notices a path from Blackacre to the spring on Whiteacre and places a sawhorse across the path. A pushes the sawhorse to one side and continues to use the path and to take water from the spring on Whiteacre. Such condition continues until the year 1950 when B writes a letter to A telling him in no uncertain terms to stay off Whiteacre and to take no more water from the spring thereon. A pays no attention to the letter and continues to use the path and take water from the spring. During all of the time from 1940 to 1955 A has continued to take substantially the same amount of water from the spring which is 30 gallons per day. The local statute on prescription is 10 years. In 1955 B sues A both for damages for trespassing and to enjoin further trespass on Whiteacre. Should B recover?

Answer and Analysis

The answer is no. For purposes of analysis it may be assumed that A's use of Whiteacre for the years 1940 to 1942 is adverse. To acquire an easement by prescription the use must also be continuous and without interruption. The terms are not synonymous. Continuous refers to the behavior of the claimant; without interruption refers to the conduct of the potential "servient owners." By the year 1942 it is clear that B had notice of A's trespasses on Whiteacre and that he placed a physical obstruction in the form of a sawhorse across the path which A was using. There is no doubt that such an obstruction may interrupt the running of the statute of limitation in A's favor. Either a legal proceeding against the wrongdoer or any interference with the use which, if the right of way or easement actually existed, would give rise to a cause of action, will stop the running of the statute of limitation. Using this test it is clear that had A actually had an easement over Whiteacre to take water from the spring thereon, B's placing a sawhorse or other physical obstruction across the way would have given A a cause of action against B. Hence, we could conclude that when B put the sawhorse across A's path in 1942, it stopped the running of the 10 year statute in A's favor. The facts, however, indicate that A simply moved the sawhorse aside and continued to exercise his "easement." B did assert his right by placing the obstruction in A's path, but A's use was hardly interrupted in fact.

B's conduct, however, would tend to show a non-acquiescence (also frequently stated to be a requirement), and hence may be a sufficient interruption. If B's conduct was a sufficient interruption, then A's adverse user would have to start anew in 1942. In any event, however, A continued to use the path and to take water from the spring. So the instant A pushed the sawhorse to one side and continued to trespass, at that instant a cause of action accrued in B's favor against A and the statute of limitations began to run in A's favor. Such statute does not begin to run to protect the wrongdoer but to compel the landowner to be diligent, and if he does not thereafter act within the prescriptive period the wrongdoer will gain an easement. What is the effect of B's letter to A in 1950 telling A to keep off Whiteacre? Using the test given above the question is this—if A actually had an easement over Whiteacre would the writing of such letter by B to A give A a cause of action. Of course it would not. It would in no way interfere with A's use of his right of way. Then the answer to the question is this—the letter of B to A had no legal effect at all on the running of the statute of limitations. In some states where acquiescence, consent by silence, is considered an essential element of prescription, such a letter is held to stop the running of the statute because it breaks the silence. This is not the better rule and is not applied in this case. So the statute of limitations kept right on running in A's favor from 1942, if not from 1940, to the time of the bringing of this action in 1955, a period of 13 years which is in excess of the 10 year statutory period. So the facts show that for more than the prescriptive period A used the way on Whiteacre wrongfully, openly and notoriously, without subordination to B, continuously and without interruption after 1942. Thus, he has matured title by adverse user to a right of way on Whiteacre, to go to and from the spring, and take water therefrom, and use the same on Blackacre. Hence, the injunction should not issue in B's favor.

But should B have damages for the trespassing? The answer to that question is no. The facts state that A has taken substantially the same amount of water each day from Whiteacre. The extent of the use in an easement by prescription is determined by the minimum use to which the dominant tenant, A in our case, has put the servient tenement, Whiteacre in our case, during the entire period of prescription. Because such minimum use during the 10 year period from 1942 to 1952 was 30 gallons per day, and during that time A did not take more than that number of gallons, B has no right to damages. Once the prescriptive easement has matured, then the law considers all damages caused during the entire period as barred from the beginning of the running of the statute. So all damages done by A on Whiteacre from 1942 forward are barred. Thus, B cannot recover. See Lehigh Val. R. R. Co. v. McFarlan, 43 N.J.L. 605 (E. & A.1881); Conness v. Pacific Coast Joint Stock Land Bank, 46 Ariz. 338, 50 P. 2d 888 (1935); Dartnell v. Bidwell, 115 Me. 227, 98 A. 743, 5 A.L.R. 1320 (1916); Restatement of Property §§ 459, 460, 465, 477.

CASE 276: X is the owner of Whiteacre in fee simple and is a boy 10 years of age. A has a life estate in Blackacre, and the remainder in fee in Blackacre is in B. These properties are adjacent to each other. A, without justification or excuse, builds a road across Whiteacre which he uses in connection with Blackacre. At the age of 25 years X is rendered non compos mentis by an automobile accident and remains in that condition until the age of 45 when he regains his sanity. A does not limit his claim to the right of way across Whiteacre to the interest which he has in Blackacre, a life estate only, but denies that X has a right at any time to prevent either A or his remainderman from using the road on Whiteacre. A continues without interruption to use the road across Whiteacre until X reaches the age of 35 at which time X, through his guardian G, sues A for damages for trespassing on Whiteacre. In the jurisdiction the period of prescription is 20 years with an additional 10 years beyond the removal of any disability existing at the time of the accrual of the cause of action. A wins this suit and dies. B continues to use the road over Whiteacre and X, through his guardian G, when X is 36 years old sues to enjoin B from using the road. Should the injunction issue?

Answers and Analyses

The answer is no. This problem presents two important subjects, (a) disability and (b) the duration of an easement by prescription. No disability has any legal effect as far as the running of the statute of limitations is concerned unless it exists at the time of the accrual of the cause of action. This means that any intervening or supervening disability which occurs after the accrual of the cause of action has no effect upon the running of the statute of limitations. It means that disabilities are wholly personal and cannot be tacked one to the other. Of course, if there are two or more disabilities existing at the time of the accrual of the cause of action, the longer of the two or the longest of more than two disabilities will govern. But no disability can have any effect on the statute of limitations unless it exists when the cause of action accrues. In no event, however, will a prescriptive right mature unless the wrong has continued for the minimum period of the statute of limitations. Applying these principles it should be first noted that X's cause of action against wrongdoer, A, accrued when X was 10 years of age and at that time he was laboring under one disability only, that of infancy. Therefore, the fact that he was rendered incompetent at age 25 is wholly immaterial and has no legal effect. It is an intervening disability occurring after the disability of infancy has ceased. X's disability of infancy is removed when he becomes of age, probably 18 today but formerly 21. Thereafter he has 10 more years in which to bring his action against A which would be no later than until he is 31 years of age. On the other hand, under no circumstances could A mature a prescriptive right in less than the 20 year statutory period. But X did not bring his action until he was 35 years old. The result is that A has gained a prescriptive easement over Whiteacre appurtenant to Blackacre. Therefore, A was properly awarded judgment against X in X's suit for damages.

The next question is this—what is the durational extent in point of time of the easement which A matured in his favor. It is usually said and is usually the case that one who gains an easement by prescription gains no larger interest in point of time than that which he claims during the period of prescription. If A in our case had claimed an easement only for the period of his interest in Blackacre, that is, during his lifetime, he would have had an easement to last only that time and it would have ceased upon his death. But the claim of the wrongdoer is not the test. The test is the extent of the denial of rights made by the wrongdoer as to those against whom he claims the easement. In this case it will be noticed that A denied that X had any right to prevent either A or the remainderman, B, from using the road over Whiteacre. Thus the denial of rights was for an indefinite period of time and matured in A, appurtenant to Blackacre, an easement in fee simple which can be enjoyed not only by A during his lifetime but by his remainderman in fee simple, B.

The result is that the injunction should not issue against B. See Restatement of Property §§ 460–463.

CASE 277: A is fee simple owner of Blackacre which abuts Whiteacre in which B has a life estate and C has the fee simple in remainder. On Whiteacre is a marble quarry which has been used many years. On Blackacre A conducts a business of processing marble for building purposes. A adversely uses Whiteacre by taking marble from the quarry thereon and uses it in his business on Blackacre. B immediately advises C of A's taking of the marble. After such use by A for two years A dies and Blackacre descends to A's son, H, who continues such adverse use of Whiteacre for three years when H's creditor, X, levies upon and under execution sale sells Blackacre and appurtenances to Y who continues the same adverse use of Whiteacre for seven years at which time, B having died during Y's seventh year of use, C sues to enjoin Y from further use of the quarry on Whiteacre. During all of the time mentioned both B while he lived and C thereafter quarried marble on Whiteacre. The local statute of limitation on prescription is 10 years. Should the injunction issue?

Answer and Analysis

The answer is no. This set of facts raises three questions for discussion. (1) May periods of adverse use be tacked one to another to make up the period of prescription? (2) Does adverse use of a piece of land in the possession of a life tenant affect the remainderman? (3) To what extent may a servient tenant use the servient tenement? In this case the facts tell us that the use is adverse so we may assume there is no problem on that score. On the question of tacking the rule is that periods of adverse use may be added one to another provided there is privity between such adverse users. And the rule applies whether a conveyance is voluntary or involuntary. Thus in our case there is privity by descent between A and his heir, H. There is likewise privity between H and the purchaser of Blackacre on execution sale, Y, even though such sale is involuntary. Hence, the 2 years of adverse use by A, the 3 years of such use by H and the 7 years of such use continued by Y, may be tacked to make up a continuous period of adverse user of 12 years. There is no question then that Y matured against B, the life tenant of Whiteacre, a profit appurtenant to Blackacre to use Whiteacre for the quarrying of marble thereon. And the reason is clear. When A first quarried marble on Whiteacre a cause of action accrued in B's favor against A and continued in his favor for the statutory period. Having done nothing to interrupt the running of the statutory period the effect of B's lack of diligence is to give Y a profit by prescription.

But how did these adverse acts on Blackacre affect C, the remainderman. Had the user been such as to affect the possession. only, such as using a way over Whiteacre, then C would not have been affected in the least for no cause of action would have accrued in his favor. Under such circumstances the death of B would have terminated the easement. However, the acts of A, H and Y did not affect the possession of the life tenant, B, only. They were adverse to C, the remainderman, also because the corpus of the soil itself was actually being taken and disposed of. In such cases the only real question is whether the adverse acts are committed openly and notoriously so that the remainderman has notice thereof. In our case we are told that B advised C of the depredations being committed on Whiteacre. Hence, the use was adverse to the remainderman as well as to the life tenant and the injunction should not issue. The prescriptive profit is in fee simple, is binding on C and constitutes a burden on C's servient tenement, Whiteacre, and is a profit appurtenant to Y's dominant tenement, Blackacre.

The third question involves the right of the servient tenant to use the servient tenement. The answer to that question is this—the servient tenant has a right to use his servient estate in any and every way and to every extent as an owner so long as his use thereof does not in any way interfere with the easement or profit which burdens the servient property. Thus in our case the profit in Y's favor is not exclusive and the servient tenant, C, may continue to take marble from the quarry to any extent he wishes so long as his operations do not interfere with those of Y. See Restatement of Property §§ 462–464, 481.

CASE 278: A is the owner in fee simple of Blackacre which adjoins Whiteacre which is owned in fee simple by B. A maintains a large two story dwelling house on Blackacre in which dwell A and his wife and four minor children. By adverse user A acquires a right of way to walk across Whiteacre which way is used by A and the members of his family. During the time of the acquisition of the way by prescription domestic servants are available at reasonable wages and A has a maid to assist his wife in the keeping of the house in order and in caring for the children. But with the evolution of society and economic conditions domestic help becomes unavailable. A's children grow to adulthood and leave home. A and his wife occupy the mansionhouse alone. The neighborhood changes from one occupied by single dwelling houses to one of apartment houses. A then remodels his house and makes it into a modern apartment house which furnishes dwelling space for four families. The members of these families all use the way across Whiteacre which A has acquired by prescription. B sues to enjoin what he alleges to be excess use. Should the injunction issue?

Answer and Analysis

The answer is no. The only thing in this world which does not change is change. Families and the members thereof change. The character of neighborhoods changes. Social and economic orders change. The use to which a property is put in a neighborhood is never static over a long period of time. It changes with the evolution of the community. Such changes are always foreseeable in the aggregate even though not in detail. During the prescriptive period a right of way is used to serve the needs of a dominant tenant in his use of the dominant tenement. But while the nature of the use and its extent during the prescriptive period set the general pattern which determines the extent of the use to be made of the servient tract after the easement is matured, it cannot be maintained that such use is limited to the use for the benefit of the dominant tenement in the condition in which the dominant tract existed during the prescriptive period. Both the adverse user and the servient tenant must be charged with foreseeing normal, natural and reasonable evolution and development in the use of property in the neighborhood, including such changes in the use of the dominant tenement. In this case it seems quite reasonable to charge B, during the period of adverse user, with foreseeing the changes which have taken place in the use of A's Blackacre, and to hold as to him that Whiteacre is burdened with an easement appurtenant to Blackacre, which easement may be used for serving Blackacre in its normal, natural and reasonable alteration as time changes the neighborhood from one of single dwelling houses to one of apartment houses.

In determining the extent of the use permitted under a prescriptive easement there should be a comparison of the use during the prescriptive period and the claimed use after the easement has been established. Such process should compare: (a) the physical use during the prescriptive period with the physical use claimed under the easement; (b) the purpose of the use during the prescriptive period with the purpose of the claimed use under the easement; (c) the burden on the servient estate during the prescriptive period with the burden thereon under the claimed use under the easement; and in case of an easement appurtenant, (d) the needs of the dominant tenant in his use of the dominant tenement which are due to normal changes in the use of the dominant tenement balanced with the additional burden, if any, which results to the servient estate from the claimed use. By applying these comparisons in our case we see that the physical use of the way over Whiteacre is by a single family during the running of the statute of limitations. Thereafter it is used by four families. Thus it will be seen the use remains the same in kind but differs only in degree. Being used only by a few more people it would seem that the physical use as to the servient tract remains substantially the same use as during the prescriptive period.

The general purpose of the use during the running of the statutory period is to serve the dominant tract and the dominant tenant in his use of such tract for family dwelling purposes. After the easement is matured the purpose is to serve four families instead of one family. Hence, the purpose seems to be the same as during the period of prescription. As for the burden cast on the servient tenement by the four-family use instead of the one-family use, the use seems different only in degree and not different in kind, and the degree of burden does not seem sufficiently different as to say it is at all unreasonable especially when balanced with the needs of Blackacre. Thus, it seems a fair conclusion to say that the use of the servient tenement under the changed conditions under which the dominant tenement is being utilized, is a reasonable and normal use which could have been reasonably foreseen by B, who became the servient tenant, during the prescriptive period and a use which should be permitted under the prescriptive easement matured by A. Thus, the injunction should be denied.

Suppose (a) the dominant tract has been transformed into a bicycle shop and the way is used by A and his family and his customers to support bicycle traffic. This new physical use of the way cannot be justified for it is quite different in kind from the physical use of the way for walking purposes during the maturing of the prescriptive right. Furthermore, the purpose which this new use would serve would be quite different in kind than that during the prescriptive period. And it may be added that the operation of bicycles on the foot path would constitute an additional burden on the servient tract which cannot be justified. Indeed, it might well be assumed that the servient tenant, B, would have interrupted the use of the way for bicycles during the prescriptive period whereas he did not do so for foot traffic. Suppose (b) A has transformed the dominant tract into a cement factory with great truck loads of cement and cement products coming to and leaving the servient tract over the prescriptive foot way. It is clear in such case that this use could not have been foreseen by B in the normal and reasonable evolution and development of the dominant tract and that it would be wholly unreasonable to allow such use under the conditions under which the prescriptive easement was gained. Such use would be a different physical use of the way, would serve an entirely different purpose and would be an additional and unjustifiable burden on Whiteacre, quite beyond the scope of use during the period of prescription. Restatement of Property §§ 477–479; Burby, 84.

---

b. By Express Provision in Deed or Will

CASE 279: A is the fee simple owner of Blackacre which lies between B's two tracts, Whiteacre and Greenacre. B has a flowing well on Whiteacre and wishes to pipe some of the water therefrom across Blackacre to Greenacre. A by deed conveys to B and his heirs a right of way across a strip of land 6 feet wide along the north edge of Blackacre, in which B may bury and maintain a pipe not to exceed 8 inches in diameter and not closer to the surface of the ground than 2 feet, for the purpose of carrying water from Whiteacre to Greenacre. The easement is to be appurtenant both to Whiteacre and Greenacre. The pipe was installed and the surface of the ground was made level. Thereafter B objects to A's continued use of the six foot strip for raising crops as A has done before and which use in no wise interferes with B's pipe under ground. A objects to B's coming on to Blackacre and trampling the crop above the pipe which is essential to repair the pipe which springs a leak. Then B discovers oil on Whiteacre and uses the pipe for transporting oil from Whiteacre to Greenacre. A sues to enjoin (a) B's use of the pipe for transporting oil and (b) B's coming onto the 6 foot strip of Blackacre to repair the pipe. B counterclaims to enjoin A from plowing the soil and raising crops on the 6 foot strip. Should any injunction issue? If so, to whom and for what?

Answers and Analyses

The answers are these: (1) B should be enjoined from using the pipe for transporting oil. (2) B should not be enjoined from coming onto the 6 foot strip to repair his pipe. (3) A should not be enjoined from using the 6 foot strip for raising crops thereon.

In this case we have an easement created by deed which in express terms gives the dominant tenant, B, the privilege of using exclusively a cylindrical space through the land of Blackacre for the purpose of maintaining a pipe therein under the ground and which pipe is to be used for carrying water from Whiteacre to Greenacre. That pipe is to be used for no other purpose. Had the deed contained a provision that the pipe might be used for the transporting of water "or for any other lawful purpose", or other such expression which would permit other uses, then such pipe might well be used for transporting oil, gas or other liquid. But the extent of the use permitted by an easement created by deed must be determined by the words of the instrument of conveyance. When that instrument in unambiguous language limits the use to the carrying of water by an 8 inch pipe, then that is the extent of the use, and any other and different use is excessive and beyond the scope of the created easement. It is quite immaterial that transportation of oil takes no more room in the pipe or in the ground than the transportation of water. The servient tract, Blackacre, belongs to A and he may parcel out such uses therein as he wishes, and when he limits a use to a pipe and the carriage of water therein that is the limit of the use. Therefore, B should be enjoined from transporting oil in the pipe across Blackacre. Of course, the easement for transporting water from the flowing well on Whiteacre to Greenacre still exists in B's favor.

When one has such an affirmative appurtenant easement as has B in this case, such easement carries with it the right to do such affirmative acts on the servient tract as are necessary to the enjoyment thereof. Such right includes the right to repair, maintain and improve the means by which the easement is made effective. Therefore B should not be enjoined from going onto Blackacre and repairing his pipe so long as he does no unnecessary damage to A's crops or his land.

On the other hand the owner of a servient tract has the right to make the maximum use of his land as long as such use is not inconsistent with the rights which he has granted to the dominant tenant in creating the easement. In our case A has the right to raise crops on the strip of land encasing B's water pipe so long as it does not interfere with B's easement. But of course A runs the risk of having those crops trampled by acts which are necessary to repair the pipe in the ground and under the growing crop. And of course, in the absence of agreement, the servient tenant has no duty to do any affirmative act to keep the easement effective. Thus there should be no injunction against A as sought in B's counterclaim. See Restatement of Property §§ 482, 485, 486; Missionary Soc'y of Salesian Congregation v. Evrotas, 256 N.Y. 86, 175 N.E. 523 (1931); Pinkerton v. Pritchard, 71 Ariz. 117, 223 P.2d 933 (1950); Gray v. City of Cambridge, 189 Mass. 405, 76 N.E. 195, 2 L.R.A.,N.S., 976 (1905).

CASE 280: A is the owner in fee simple of Blackacre, a 5 acre tract, on which he maintains a dwelling house for himself and family. On Blackacre A has a very deep well from which A can draw an abundance of pure clear water. B owns Whiteacre, an abutting 5 acre tract, on which B maintains his dwelling house for himself and family but upon which there is no water supply. These tracts are within a residential neighborhood. A conveys to B and his heirs the right to come onto Blackacre and draw water from the well thereon for use on Whiteacre. B converts his dwelling house into a hotel, adds a few rooms thereon, so that his physical plant will accommodate 50 guests. B continues to take water from A's well to supply his hotel needs. A sues to enjoin such use as excessive. Should the injunction issue?

Answer and Analysis

The answer is yes. When an easement is created by a conveyance, and the words describing the extent of the use granted are clear and unambiguous, and the scope of the use is easily measured, then the words of the instrument determine the extent of the use under the easement. But when the words of a conveying instrument are not complete as to the extent of the use when applied to the future development of the dominant tenement, then the real meaning of the instrument must be found in the circumstances surrounding the execution of the conveying instrument. The parties to such instrument must be charged with foreseeing normal change and development in the condition of the dominant tenement. And with such change must come some alteration in the use to which the servient tenement will be subjected under the easement granted. Such must be assumed to be contemplated by the parties when the privileges granted are to be exercised through an indefinite future. Had the deed in this case provided that water might be drawn from A's well for use on White-acre so long as used for private family dwelling purposes, or to the extent of 400 gallons per day, then the duration of the use on one hand, or the maximum use on the other, would have been readily determined. Had the deed provided that water might be drawn from A's well for use on Whiteacre for any and every purpose irrespective of the condition and use of Whiteacre, then it would be clear that the easement is to serve such dominant tenement without limit. It would be a general easement for all purposes.

However, the deed provided neither of the above. It provided merely that water might be taken from A's Blackacre for use on Whiteacre, and one of the important circumstances surrounding the execution of A's deed is that Whiteacre at that time was used exclusively for a private family dwelling as were the other tracts surrounding it. It would be unfair and unreasonable to say, in the absence of specific provisions, either that the deed and circumstances surrounding its execution conveyed to B an unlimited use of White-acre, on the one hand, or, on the other, a use limited to Whiteacre while it remained strictly in the condition it was in at the time of the deed.

The fair and reasonable scope of the easement created is somewhere between these two extremes, and is found by applying the test of what at the time of the making of the conveyance can or should be contemplated by the parties as the normal and evolutionary development of the dominant tenement. Normal and evolutionary development means the common, not the uncommon, the ordinary, not the extraordinary, experience of mankind concerning such matters. In the common experience of mankind it might well be assumed that A and B could and should contemplate that B's family might grow in numbers and that additional rooms might be added to his house and that more water would be required from the servient tenement. If the neighborhood is near the edge of a district in which multiple dwelling units such as duplexes are being built, it would not be unreasonable to assume that B's Whiteacre might be transformed into a duplex. But that is not this case. Here is a single dwelling house in a residential area transformed overnight into a hotel with capacity to accommodate 50 persons. Surely that is such a change in the condition of the dominant estate which the experience of mankind would not contemplate as a common experience. Such things may and do happen but they are not the common but the uncommon, not the ordinary but the extraordinary experience of mankind. And the par-

ties to the conveyance, A and B, should not be charged with foreseeing the happening of such drastic changes in the development of the
dominant tenement. Indeed, the use of A's Blackacre to serve Whiteacre when used as a hotel accommodating 50 persons, seems a use
of the servient tenement which is different in kind, not merely different in degree, from that which must have been contemplated by the
parties at the time of the making of the deed. It seems clear then
that such use of Blackacre by B is excessive and should be enjoined.
See Restatement of Property § 484; Man v. Vockroth, 94 N.J.Eq.
511, 121 A. 599 (E. & A.1923).

CASE 281: A is the owner of Blackacre in fee simple, a section of land used for agricultural purposes. B owns an abutting section, Whiteacre, also used for farming. A conveys
to B and his heirs a right of way appurtenant to Whiteacre
over a road through the center of Blackacre which road has
been used by A for the purpose of passing from one part of
Blackacre to another in his farming operations. Thereafter
B conveys the NE¼ of Whiteacre to C, the NW¼ to D, the
SE¼ to E and the SW¼ to F. These four grantees continue to use the way over Blackacre. A sues to enjoin such
use. Should the injunction issue?

Answer and Analysis

The answer is no. When B conveys the quarter sections of Whiteacre to the named grantees, each grantee takes under the conveyance not only the land itself but also all appurtenances thereto. This is
true whether or not "appurtenances" are expressly mentioned in the
conveyance. Hence, each grantee takes an easement appurtenant to
his particular quarter section of Whiteacre, which easement consists
of a right of way across the center of Blackacre if the easement as
originally created in A's deed to B is apportionable.

Easements appurtenant are considered apportionable upon the
subdivision of the dominant tenement unless the conveyance creating
the easement otherwise provides. There are two reasons for this
principle. First, the subdivision and sale of parts of tracts of lands
nowadays are so common as to be assumed to be within the contemplation of the parties when they create easements appurtenant. Second, usually the subdivision of the dominant tenement and the apportionment of the easement cast a relatively slight additional burden on
the servient tenement when compared with the benefit and enjoyment
which the easement adds to the dominant tenements. Thus it may be
assumed in our case that A and B contemplated at the time of the
creation of the easement that the dominant tract, Whiteacre, would
not always remain in a single ownership, and that the easement
would attach to every part of Whiteacre if and when it was subdivided. Hence, it is reasonable to assume that it was within the intention
of A, the grantor, when he created the easement appurtenant to White-

acre, that if such tract were subdivided that the benefit of the easement as an appurtenance would accrue to each subdivision thereof, and that the grantee of each such subdivision would be permitted to enjoy such easement. That being the case it must be concluded that: (a) C has an easement over Blackacre which is appurtenant to his NE¼ of Whiteacre; (b) D has an easement over Blackacre which is appurtenant to his NW¼ of Whiteacre; (c) E has an easement over Blackacre which is appurtenant to his SE¼ of Whiteacre; and (d) F has an easement over Blackacre which is appurtenant to his SW¼ of Whiteacre. Thus, the injunction should not issue. See Restatement of Property § 488; Hall v. Lawrence, 2 R.I. 218, 57 Am.Dec. 715 (1852); Southern New England Ice Co. v. Town of West Hartford, 114 Conn. 496, 159 A. 470 (1932).

CASE 282: A, a private detective who makes his living by sleuthing and finding facts for private persons, owns an airplane by which he makes rapid trips from one part of the country to another for the purpose of carrying on his business. A lives in the state of Texas and concludes that if he has a private airport, or the right to use land for such in the state of Illinois, he can carry on his business in the eastern part of the country most effectively from such base. A has a brother, B, living in central Illinois who owns Blackacre, a level section of land, in one corner of which is a meadow used wholly for raising wild grass. This land is worth $200 per acre for such purposes. Along the edge of Blackacre on the meadow A stakes out a strip of land 80 feet wide, containing about 5 acres, and pays B $1000 for a deed granting A for life the privilege of using such strip of land for the purpose of an airport, for landing and taking off in airplanes for the purpose of carrying on his detective business. A establishes a gasoline pump on the strip and improves it sufficiently for his purpose and uses it for a period of five years at which time A becomes ill and is quite unable to carry on his business further. He sells his detective business to C, his most effective and trusted employee, including his airplane and an assignment of his interest in Blackacre. B seeks to enjoin C's use of the strip along the edge of Blackacre for use as an airport. Should the injunction issue?

Answer and Analysis

The answer is no. When B executed to his brother, A, a right to come onto Blackacre and land and take off with his airplane and otherwise use the strip along Blackacre in connection with his detective business, he created an easement in gross in Blackacre for the period of A's life. Easements in gross which are of a commercial nature are interests in real property which are alienable as a matter of law unless the manner in which they are created, by prescription or the terms of the conveying instrument by deed or will, determine otherwise. On the other hand an easement in gross of a noncommercial nature may or may not be alienable depending on the terms of the conveyance or the manner of its creation. A commercial easement is one the principal purpose of which is to benefit its owner economically or financially. An easement is of a noncommercial nature when its principal purpose is to benefit its owner primarily in a personal way. If in our set of facts B had granted to his brother A the use of the strip of land on his farm for the mere purpose of assisting him personally, had charged him a nominal sum for the privilege and with no intention that anyone else would enjoy the privilege, then it is obvious such an easement would be noncommercial in nature and would have been inalienable by A. But that is not what happened. True, A and B are brothers. But A paid B not a nominal sum for the privilege of using a strip on Blackacre, but $1,000 which was not far from the actual value of the land used had it been granted in fee simple. And it was not granted in fee simple. Only an easement for the period of A's life was granted to A. The fact that the grant is for A's life is, of course, some evidence that only A was to use the easement. However, such grant was made for the primary purpose of enhancing A's capacity to carry on his detective business more effectively. Its function was to benefit A economically and financially. Just as a life estate in fee simple in land may be conveyed to another who then has an estate pur autre vie, so a commercial easement in gross for life may be so conveyed. Properly construed, the grant from B to A, under the terms of the instrument and the circumstances surrounding its execution, seems to convey to A a commercial easement in gross which is alienable by the grantee. That being true, C is the owner of such easement by the assignment from A and has a right to continue the use of the strip on Blackacre during A's lifetime. Therefore, the injunction should not issue. See Restatement of Property §§ 489–492; Burby, 67–68; Standard Oil Co. v. Buchi, 72 N.J.Eq. 492, 66 A. 427 (Ch. 1907).

CASE 283: A is the owner of Blackacre, a quarter section of land on which is a sand pit containing a large quantity of sand having commercial value. B is a road contractor who uses a substantial amount of sand in performing his road contracts. A grants to B for 10 years the right to come onto Blackacre and take any or all sand which he can find thereon together with right of ingress thereto and egress therefrom. B is to pay for the sand at a specific rate per cubic yard as it is removed from Blackacre. B digs and uses the sand for about a year at which time he assigns his right to take sand from Blackacre to C, D and E, individual contractors, each to have a right to dig and take sand from the premises wholly independently of the acts of any other. Each of the three assignees comes onto Blackacre with trucks and other machinery and starts digging and removing sand therefrom. A sues to enjoin their taking any sand. Should the injunction issue?

Answer and Analysis

The answer is yes. In determining what interest A conveyed to B there are three concepts which should be distinctly differentiated. (1) A landowner may convey the *corpus of sand* in which case the sand belongs to the grantee and the grantor has no interest left therein. (2) A landowner may convey *an exclusive right* to come onto land and take sand in which case the sand continues to belong to the landowner until it is severed from the land and appropriated by the grantee. In this case the grantee only has the right to take the sand, but neither the grantor nor any third person may take any sand from Blackacre. (3) A landowner may convey *a nonexclusive right* to come onto land and take sand in which case the grantor or any third person to whom the grantor may convey such a right, may dig and take sand from the property as well as the grantee.

It is obvious in our case that the corpus of the sand on Blackacre is not granted to B. A right merely to come onto land and take sand does not describe sand as sand. It merely describes an incorporeal right to take sand. Granting that A has conveyed to B only a right to take sand from Blackacre, is such right exclusive or nonexclusive? According to the cases, an easement or profit is construed as a nonexclusive right unless the contrary clearly appears either by the words of the instrument or because of the nature of the right conveyed. For example, a right of way granted to a railroad to be used as a road bed or as a depot site would necessarily have to be exclusive. But such is not the case when it involves the taking of sand or the mining of minerals. In these cases there is nothing inconsistent in the grantor's having the right to make use of his soil or the products thereof at the same time the grantee is using the soil or taking some of it. In our case there are no words in the conveying instrument indicating an intention to transfer to B an exclusive right to take sand. Thus, the grantor, A, still has the right to take sand from Blackacre. The fact that B's profit is to continue only 10 years and is therefore personal property does not alter the parties' rights. There is little question as to the nature of B's right. It is a nonexclusive profit in gross of a commercial nature. It is a profit because it involves a right to take some of the corpus of the soil. It is in gross because B's right to take and use the sand is not appurtenant to any other property as a dominant tenement. Indeed, so far as the facts appear, B does not own any other property which could be a dominant estate. It is of a commercial nature because it benefits B economically and financially in his business as a contractor. Such a commercial profit in gross is therefore alienable.

But because an easement or a profit is alienable does not mean it is divisible or apportionable. The rule on that subject is this. If an easement or a profit is exclusive there is an inference that it is intended that it should be apportionable. This is particularly true when the dividing of the right is advantageous to the grantor as well as to the grantee. For example, when sand is to be paid for by the cubic yard as it is removed from the servient tract it is obvious that if divisibility results in more sand being removed it will benefit the grantor financially as well as the grantee who is permitted to apportion the right. Suppose M conveys to N and his assigns the exclusive right to mine copper on M's Blackacre. N assigns to X the right to mine copper on the north half and to Y the right to mine copper on the south half of Blackacre. In this case M has created an apportionable profit in N whose assignments to X and Y are valid. X and Y may mine the copper. This accords with M's intention and does not overburden M's Blackacre. But if apportionability of the exclusive right will result in overburdening or surcharging the servient tenement to an extent which could not have been intended by the terms of the conveying instrument, or in the manner of use during a prescriptive period, then such excessive use may be enjoined.

However, with respect to a nonexclusive right such as we have in our case as set forth under (3) above, the easement or profit is not apportionable unless the terms of the instrument or manner of its creation clearly indicate an intention that it shall be apportionable. The reason is this. When the grantee has an easement or a profit which is nonexclusive, it means that the grantor himself has a right to make a similar use of the servient tenement, or the grantor may convey to others the same or similar right. If the grantee is permitted to divide or apportion his nonexclusive right, he is being permitted to create rights in his assignees which are inconsistent with the rights reserved by the grantor in the servient estate. And if the assignees of the owner of the nonexclusive easement or profit are permitted individually to use the servient property, then they are empowered to make use of more than one right when the original grantor created only one.

In our case B has the right and power to alienate his profit in gross. He can transfer it to a single person or he can transfer it to two or more persons *jointly*. By transferring a single right to "X, Y and Z jointly", the right remains intact because "jointly" means that X, Y and Z take as a unit, as a single aggregate person. As a unit these persons may exercise the right of taking sand from the servient tenement. But they must operate the right as a "common stock". They cannot exercise the right individually and independently of each other. And that is exactly what is provided for in B's assignment to C, D and E, "each to have a right to dig and take sand independently from Blackacre". This constituted a dividing of an indivisible right. Whereas A conveyed to B a single living legal organism, B has conveyed to C, D and E this living legal organism severed into three distinct parts. It is no different in legal contemplation than A's selling a cow to B and B dividing the cow into three distinct parts and selling one part to each of C, D and E. The cow no longer exists. That is not like B's selling the cow to C, D and E jointly, in which case the cow remains intact as a living organism. This is an attempt to overburden the servient tenement, Blackacre. But the overburdening is not merely because there will be more trucks and other physical machinery on Blackacre removing greater quantities of sand than the original parties ever contemplated. Indeed, C, D and E acting jointly as a unit might well remove as much sand as they would when acting independently. It is of course argued that the removal of such quantities of sand by C, D, and E acting or operating independently might well ruin or destroy the servient tenement. That is true but the legal overburdening comes from the fact that when acting independently as assignees of B, these contractors are attempting to exercise *three distinct and separate rights* or *profits* when the original conveyance from A to B created but one indivisible and unapportionable right in B, and B could not assign more than that which he owned. Hence, when B apportioned among his assignees, C, D and E the single profit which he owned, the right was thereby destroyed and the assignees have no right to take any sand from Blackacre. Therefore, the injunction should issue. See Restatement of Property § 493; Stanton v. T. L. Herbert & Sons, 141 Tenn. 440, 211 S.W. 353 (1919); Miller v. Lutheran Conference & Camp Ass'n, 331 Pa. 241, 200 A. 646, 130 A.L.R. 1245 (1938).

Note

A owns Blackacre in fee simple to which is appurtenant a right of way over B's Whiteacre. A conveys Blackacre to C and in the conveyance reserves to himself the right of way across Whiteacre. May A use the right of way? No. This is an attempt on the part of A to convert an easement appurtenant into an easement in gross. Usually the easement appurtenant bears the same relation to the dominant tenement as a tail does to the cow. When the tail is severed from the cow it dies. When the easement appurtenant is severed from the dominant tenement it is extinguished. However, if in this case A's deed provides that the easement may be severed from the dominant tenement and used by A as an easement in gross, then it may be so severed and used in gross. The general principle is this —the severance of an easement appurtenant from the dominant tenement extinguishes the easement unless the manner or terms of its creation evinces an intention to the contrary. See Cadwalader v. Bailey, 17 R.I. 495, 23 A. 20, 14 L.R.A. 300 (1891).

———

CASE 284: A is the owner of Blackacre which abuts B's Whiteacre. A matures by prescription a right of way over Whiteacre by which he carries water along a ditch from Whiteacre to Blackacre. B finds the location of the ditch on Whiteacre very inconvenient for some uses he wishes to make of his property. B changes the location of the open ditch by moving it 6 feet south and enclosing the running water in a cement tile pipe which carries the same amount of water as the open ditch and delivers it at the same place on Blackacre. A seeks a mandatory injunction compelling B to open the ditch exactly where it was when the prescriptive right matured and to permit the water to run through it as before without further obstruction by B. Should the injunction issue?

Answer and Analysis

The answer is yes. When A matures by prescription a right to maintain the ditch over Whiteacre appurtenant to Blackacre he has an incorporeal right in Whiteacre. It is real property and the right is fixed in its location as definitely as are the boundaries of the physical tract, Whiteacre. Neither A, the dominant tenant, nor B, the servient tenant, has any right whatsoever to change the boundaries or location of the ditch on Whiteacre regardless of how inconvenient it may be to either. In the newly located ditch A has no right either by prescription or by deed. Indeed, he has no right in such, and it might well be determined, if he makes no objection to the new location of the ditch, that he has abandoned his easement by prescription. Suppose then B closes the new ditch on Whiteacre. To say the least A's position concerning an easement over Whiteacre would be precarious and uncertain. Reasonable user of an easement does not empower either the servient or the dominant tenant to change the location of such on the servient estate even if the same benefit, or even greater benefits, would accrue therefrom to the dominant tenant. This is true whether the easement be created either by prescription or by conveyance. See Sakansky v. Wein, 86 N.H. 337, 169 A. 1 (1933); Stamatis v. Johnson, 71 Ariz. 134, 224 P.2d 201 (1950), on rehearing judgment modified 72 Ariz. 158, 231 P.2d 956 (1951).

––––––––

CASE 285: A owns Blackacre, a city lot 50 feet by 150 feet. B owns Whiteacre which is a city lot 50 feet by 150 feet abutting Blackacre and having a common boundary line therewith of 150 feet in length. A and B in writing agree to build a party wall on their common boundary line which wall is to be 16 inches in width, two stories high and extend along the common boundary line from the front of the lots toward the rear for a distance of 100 feet. Half of the wall is to be on Blackacre and half on Whiteacre. Nothing is said in the agreement concerning their respective rights in the use of the party wall.

A builds a two story building on Blackacre and extends his joists which support his floors and roof into the party wall only to the center thereof which is exactly above the common boundary line. Thus A is using only the party wall on his side of the common boundary to support his joists. B then begins building a two story building on his Whiteacre and extends his joists through the party wall so that his joists rest on the entire thickness of the party wall. A objects to B's using that part of the party wall which is on A's side of the common boundary line extended upwards. B completes his building using the entire party wall to support his joists. Thereafter B raises the party wall at his own expense to a height of three stories and adds a third story to his building on Whiteacre. A then decides to add a third story to his building on Blackacre but refuses to pay B for his proportionate cost of the added height of the party wall. B seeks to enjoin A's use of the third story portion of the party wall until A has paid for his share of such part of the wall. **(a)** Should the injunction issue? **(b)** Is A's objection to B's use of the entire party wall to support his joists well taken?

Answers and Analyses

The answer to (a) is yes. The answer to (b) is no. Discussing first the answer to question (b), there are three distinct views concerning the rights of abutting owners in a party wall when the wall is bisected by the common boundary extended vertically upward through the center of the party wall. (1) One view is that the abutting owners are tenants in common of the party wall with each having the right to use the entire wall. This is the common English view. (2) Another view is that each abutting owner owns the party wall only to its center which represents the common boundary line and can use only that part of the wall which is on the owner's side of the common boundary line for support of his building joists. This is the claim of A in our case. (3) A third view is that each abutting owner owns the wall only to the common boundary line, that is, he owns only the half of the wall on his side of the common boundary line, but has an easement to use the entire thickness of the wall for the support of his building joists. This is the common American view and will be applied in this case. In all three views there are cross-easements under which each abutting owner has the right to have his building and his half of the party wall supported by the half of the party wall on the land of the abutting owner. In this case taking view number (3) above, B has the right to use the entire thickness of the party wall for the support of his joists and A cannot object when B extends such joists completely through but not one particle beyond the thickness of the party wall. Hence, under this view A's objection to B's using the entire wall for the support of his joists is not well taken.

Answering question (a), it may be said that every party wall owner has a right at his own expense to increase either the height or the length of the party wall provided the foundation will support such additional height. And the party wall owner who does extend the party wall either in height or length has no right to contribution for such extension from the other party wall owner until such time that the other party wall owner undertakes to use such extended wall. But when such party wall owner does use or undertake to use such extended wall which has been fully paid for by the one who built it, then a right to have contribution accrues to the one who built and paid for the extension. And there is no right on the part of the non-builder to use such extension until he has paid for the reasonable value of his share of the wall as it then exists. Thus A has no right to attach his proposed third story joists to the party wall until he has made proper payment to B and the injunction should issue against A until such payment has been made. In a party wall each owner, in the absence of express agreement to the contrary, has equal and reciprocal rights with the owner of the other part of the wall. Neither has a right which is denied to the other. For example, one owner may not monopolize the top of the party wall exclusively for the maintenance of an advertising sign thereon for the reason that such wall must at all times be immediately available to both parties for extension thereof and building thereon. See Tiffany, Vol. 3, p. 371 (3d ed.); Varriale v. Brooklyn Edison Co., 252 N.Y. 222, 169 N.E. 284 (1929); Wait v. Newman, 284 Mich. 1, 278 N.W. 742 (1938).

---

c. By Implication

CASE 286: L is the owner of an apartment house, Blackacre. He shows a 4th story apartment to T for the purpose of renting it to him. They ride in the elevator from the street floor to the 4th floor and L points out to T the stairway leading to the 4th floor for use when the elevator may not be in working order. In the jurisdiction an oral lease is valid if for one year or a lesser period of time. L orally leases the 4th story apartment to T for 3 months at a rent of $300.00 per month. T pays L the rent for the first month and moves into the apartment. During the negotiations for renting the apartment, nothing is said between L and T concerning the use of the elevator leading to the 4th story apartment, or concerning use of the entrance to Blackacre or the lobby of the building on the ground floor. L objects to T's using the elevator in connection with his apartment for the reason that they made no agreement concerning it when the lease was made. May T use the elevator as a means of ingress to and egress from his 4th story apartment on Blackacre?

Answer and Analysis

The answer is yes. T has an implied easement for the period of his lease which is 3 months. Usually an easement is created by grant in a deed. An implied easement is created and proved not by the words of the deed or conveyance but by the circumstances surrounding the execution of the deed or conveyance. It is based on the intention of the parties as inferred from the circumstances. Of course that assumes that the circumstances are within the knowledge of the parties and that they intended or would have intended such easement had they foreseen what they might have anticipated from the information before them at the time of the making of the conveyance. And in some cases without doubt it is ascribing to the parties an intention they never entertained. But under the circumstances set forth in the problem presented, there is little doubt that there should be inferred from the circumstances surrounding the making of the lease from L to T an intention creating an implied easement in T's favor, and against L, that T was to have the use of the elevator in the enjoyment of his 4th story apartment.

There are five distinct requirements for the existence of an implied easement all of which are present in the facts above.

(1) *There must be two properties owned by one person who uses one of the pieces of property to serve the other piece of property.* One cannot have an easement in his own property so when he uses one piece of his property for the purpose of serving another piece of his property there is said to exist *a quasi-easement*. In the case given this means that before any lease is made by L to T, there is the 4th story apartment owned by L and he uses as a means of getting to and going from such apartment some of the other parts of Blackacre, namely, the elevator, stairway and lobby of the building. This space occupied by the elevator, stairway and lobby, serves the 4th story apartment as they are used by L. The 4th story apartment is then a quasi-dominant tenement and the lobby, elevator and stairway are the quasi-servient tenement because as the entire property is used by its owner, L, the lobby, elevator and stairway are used by L to serve the 4th story apartment. There is therefore said to be a quasi-easement as to the two pieces of Blackacre. The word "quasi-easement" has no legal significance in itself. The word "quasi" means "as if" or "seeming" or "as it were". An easement as such requires that one person has the right to make a limited use of the property of another. But when the same person owns the two properties and uses one in connection with the use of another it is merely "as if" there were an easement. Hence, the requisite that there exist a "quasi-easement" as a condition precedent to an implied easement is present in our set of facts.

(2) *There must be a conveyance of one part of the property to another person, the other part being retained by the conveyor.* The creation of a lease constitutes a conveyance. Therefore, when L conveyed to T the 4th story apartment for 3 months and retained the rest of Blackacre, there is the requisite conveyance of one part of L's property and the retention of the other part, that is, the lobby, the stairway and the elevator.

(3) *The quasi-easement must be apparent at the time of the conveyance.* This does not mean that the use made by the grantor prior to the conveyance is necessarily visible. The word apparent as here used is a broader term than visible and includes such knowledge as would have been gained at the time of the conveyance by a reasonably prudent investigation or inspection of the premises. This meaning becomes important when the quasi-easement involves the use of

underground pipes, sewers and drainage facilities. In our set of facts this item is simple because the elevator and lobby were actually used by both L and T at the time of the making of the lease and the stairway was pointed out by L to T. Hence, they were all actually visible and known to the purchaser and lessee, T, at the time of the lease or conveyance.

(4) *The quasi-easement must be continuous, which means that the use of the quasi-servient tenement must be permanently adapted to serve the needs of the quasi-dominant tenement.* There has been some difficulty in the meaning of the word continuous as it has evolved in the cases. Unfortunately it has been limited in some cases to situations in which the quasi-easement can be enjoyed only when no affirmative act by man is involved. Such narrow meaning includes easements in drains, flowing water in ditches and negative easements not to build on particular land, but it excludes such common and usual rights of way for foot or vehicular traffic, easements to obtain water by bucket or other artificial means as by pump. The broader meaning is far more realistic and utilitarian and is used in the majority of the more recent cases. If the use of the quasi-servient tenement is permanently adapted to serve the quasi-dominant tenement, then it is continuous as required for an implied easement. It is obvious in our set of facts that the lobby, stairway and elevator are permanently adapted to the serving of the 4th story apartment and that the quasi-easement is therefore continuous as required for an implied easement in T's favor.

(5) *The quasi-easement must be (a) "reasonably necessary" to the convenient enjoyment of the quasi-dominant tenement if that tract is the property conveyed to the grantee, and (b) "strictly necessary" to the enjoyment of the quasi-dominant tenement if that tract is retained by the grantor.* A greater degree of necessity is required for an implied easement in favor of the grantor than for one in favor of the grantee because the grantor usually draws the deed, and when he grants the quasi-servient tenement to the grantee and then claims an easement on such property, he is considered as derogating from his grant. An implied easement in favor of the grantor is created by an *implied reservation* whereas one in favor of the grantee is created by an *implied grant*. Hence, it is always very important to consider whether the grantor conveys to the grantee the quasi-servient or the quasi-dominant tenement. If he conveys to the grantee the quasi-servient tenement and retains the quasi-dominant tenement, then the grantor will be claiming an implied easement by implied reservation. If he conveys to the grantee the quasi-dominant tenement then the grantee will be claiming an implied easement by implied grant. In the case to be solved L conveys to T the quasi-dominant tenement, the 4th story apartment and retains the quasi-servient tenement, the elevator, stairway and lobby. Thus, T is claiming an implied easement by implied grant. In such case he needs to show only that the quasi-easement is *reasonably necessary* to the enjoyment of the quasi-dominant tenement. It seems clear in this case that the use of the

elevator, stairway and lobby are reasonably necessary to the comfortable enjoyment of the 4th story apartment. Surely T's use of the elevator rather than climbing and descending four flights of stairs each time he enters or leaves his apartment is reasonably necessary to the enjoyment of the apartment. That being the case, T has by implied grant an implied easement to use the elevator in his enjoyment and use of the 4th story apartment in Blackacre. It is often said that the grantee has an implied easement to use the quasi-servient tenement retained by the grantor if the use thereof merely adds to the convenience in the enjoyment of the quasi-dominant tenement. See Restatement of Property § 476; 38 A.L.R. 1310; 58 A.L.R. 837; Burby, 72–74.

CASE 287: A is the owner of Blackacre and Whiteacre, two city lots each 50 feet wide and 150 feet long having a common boundary line of 150 feet. A builds a house on each lot each having all modern conveniences and runs a common sewer pipe six feet undergound from Whiteacre to and across Blackacre to the main sewer in the street along the side of Blackacre. This common sewer pipe runs behind each house and is about 100 feet from the front of the lots and about 50 feet from the rear of the lots. There is no main sewer in the street in front of the two lots and there is no alley in the rear of the lots. Both the street in front of the lots and along the side of Blackacre are paved with reinforced concrete about 8 inches thick. Unless the common sewer pipe carrying sewage from Whiteacre over Blackacre is used, the only other way of disposing of the sewage on Whiteacre is by installing a pipe to the front of Whiteacre from the rear of the house thereon and then under the cement paving along the street in front of both lots to the main sewer in the street along the side of Blackacre. A sells Blackacre to B without reserving in the deed a right of way for the sewer pipe across Blackacre. During the negotiations for the sale and purchase of Blackacre B learns that the houses on Blackacre and Whiteacre are both modern and equipped with all modern facilities and conveniences including sewage disposal. But B does not know of the existence of the sewer pipe from Whiteacre across Blackacre and A forgets about it completely at the time of the conveyance. B plugs up the sewer pipe at the boundary line between Blackacre and Whiteacre and A sues to enjoin such obstruction. Should the injunction issue?

Answer and Analysis

The answer is yes. By an implied reservation A has an implied easement for his sewer pipe from Whiteacre across Blackacre. (1) Before the conveyance from A to B there is a quasi-easement as to

A's two properties, Blackacre and Whiteacre, under which Blackacre is the quasi-servient tenement and Whiteacre the quasi-dominant tenement. (2) One of the properties, Blackacre, is sold to B and the other, Whiteacre, is retained by the grantor. (3) The quasi-easement is continuous for the sewer pipe running through Blackacre is permanently adapted to use in the service of Whiteacre. The two problems presented by this case are whether (4) the quasi-easement is apparent and (5) strictly necessary to the grantor's enjoyment of Whiteacre.

It is quite certain that the sewer pipe six feet under the soil of Blackacre is not visible. But is it apparent if the word apparent includes such information which a reasonably prudent investigation and inspection of Blackacre, the quasi-servient tenement, by the purchaser and grantee, B, would have disclosed? B knew at the time of the conveyance that the houses on both Blackacre and Whiteacre were equipped with a sewage disposal system. It seems rather clear that a reasonably prudent investigation and inspection of the premises would have disclosed the existence of the quasi-easement. Indeed, it is possible that the investigation would have required no more than asking A about the sewage disposal system from the two tracts. If such be the fact then it seems reasonable to conclude that the quasi-easement is apparent as required for the creation of an implied easement in favor of the quasi-dominant tenement, Whiteacre.

But is such quasi-easement strictly necessary to the enjoyment of the retained quasi-dominant tenement by the grantor, A? It is probably correct to say that the majority of cases say and adhere to the principle that in case of an implied grant in favor of the grantee there must be reasonable necessity and in case of an implied reservation in favor of the grantor there must be strict necessity for the existence of the implied easement. And it is agreed in all the cases that a greater necessity is required for an implied reservation than for an implied grant. But the expressions, "reasonably necessary" and "strictly necessary" are variables, not absolutes, and their application to a given set of facts leaves wide range for differences of opinion as to the final result. It is clear that an implied easement is the result of an inference of the intention of the parties drawn from all the circumstances surrounding the conveyance. While there is and should be a difference in the degree of necessity required for an implied reservation and an implied grant, yet the fact that the implied easement is claimed by the grantor rather than the grantee, is only one of the many circumstances to be considered in inferring the intention of the parties.

In addition to such circumstance the Restatement of Property lists the following as important, namely: the terms of the conveyance; the consideration given; whether there are reciprocal benefits to both parties; the manner of use of the property under the quasi-easement; and the extent of the parties' knowledge as to the prior use. This list is not intended to be complete. But surely the expression, "strictly necessary" to the enjoyment of the quasi-dominant tenement retained by the grantor, does not mean without which the quasi-dominant tenement could not be used at all by its owner. And surely it does mean that the continued use of the quasi-easement is more than a mere convenience in the use of the quasi-dominant tenement. And it means more than "reasonably necessary". It is a meaning somewhere between "reasonably necessary" and "absolutely necessary" to the use of the retained quasi-dominant estate. In our facts the burden of the underground sewer pipe on Blackacre is probably relatively slight. It is a circumstance to be considered in inferring the intention of the parties. On the other hand the extent of the burden on A if the quasi-easement is not to continue is evidence of the necessity for its continuance. It will compel A to run a sewer line around the rear of his house on Whiteacre, then extend it 100 feet to the front of such lot, then dig through the 8 inch thick reinforced concrete in front of both Whiteacre and Blackacre and continue such under the street which runs along the side of Blackacre to the main sewer thereunder. A continuance of the quasi-easement will avoid this burden of labor, capital investment, use of additional materials and tearing up of the concrete pavement in the public streets. In the field of degree of necessity it seems not unreasonable to say that the continuance of the quasi-easement over Blackacre is strictly necessary to the use and enjoyment of Whiteacre and that this requirement to create an implied easement is present in our given facts. All of the elements prerequisite to the creation of an easement by implication being present, it is concluded that the grantor, A, has by implied reservation an implied easement appurtenant to Whiteacre over and through the servient tract, Blackacre, and that B should be enjoined from obstructing such easement. See Restatement of Property § 476; Van Sandt v. Royster, 148 Kan. 495, 83 P.2d 698 (1938); Brown v. Fuller, 165 Mich. 162, 130 N.W. 621, 33 L.R.A.,N.S., 459, Ann.Cas.1912C, 853 (1911); 34 A.L.R. 238.

Note

If A owns Blackacre and Whiteacre and there exists a quasi-easement in favor of Blackacre over Whiteacre and A *simultaneously* conveys Blackacre to C and Whiteacre to D, C is entitled to an easement by implication across Whiteacre on the same principles set forth above.

An easement by implication whether an implied grant in favor of the grantee or an implied reservation in favor of the grantor, is a true easement having permanence of duration, and should be distinguished from a "way of necessity" which lasts only as long as the necessity continues. E. g., A owns Blackacre which is completely "bottled up" or surrounded by lands owned by other persons and there is no way for A to enter or leave Blackacre without trespassing on the land of another. The shortest way and the way which will do least damage to a highway from Blackacre is across a narrow strip of land 200 feet wide owned by B, the grantor of Blackacre. A may have a way of necessity over B's 200 foot strip. Later A buys another piece of land which gives him access to another highway but is far less convenient than the use of B's strip. The way of necessity ceases when A has access to the highway regardless of how inconvenient it may be. A real way of necessity is a "rare bird".

---

3. EXTINGUISHMENT

LEGAL GEMS

1. An easement (or profit) may terminate in either of two ways, (a) by expiration of time determined at the time of its creation, or (b) by extinguishment which is determined by events subsequent to its creation.

2. The termination of an easement by expiration of time usually presents little difficulty. Examples of such follow.

(a) A grants to B the right to come onto A's Blackacre and dig and carry away gravel for a period of 10 years. The profit terminates with the expiration of the 10 year period.

(b) A grants to B the right to pasture any number of B's cattle on A's Blackacre during B's lifetime. Upon B's death the profit terminates.

(c) A owns Blackacre and Whiteacre. He leases Whiteacre to B for five years with the right to use a way over Blackacre appurtenant to Whiteacre during the lease. When the lease expires the right of way terminates.

(d) A owns Blackacre on which is a gravel pit. B is a road contractor. A grants to B the right to come onto Blackacre and dig and carry away gravel for B's use in constructing the X Highway only and when B has completed his contract to build the X Highway such right is to cease. When X Highway is completed the profit terminates.

(e) A and B agree to construct a party wall on the boundary line separating their respective lots. The wall is built. A fire destroys both buildings attached to the wall and the wall itself. The cross easements created by a party wall are based on necessity. When the necessity ceases by destruction of the party wall the cross easements are terminated. Any easement dependent on an artificial structure for its continuance terminates when the artificial structure is destroyed.

3. The termination of an easement (or profit) takes place by extinguishment by operation of law when any of the following events happen:

(a) When an easement appurtenant exists and both the dominant and servient tenements come under the ownership of the same person. Example (1). A owns Blackacre in fee simple and B owns Whiteacre in fee simple. A grants to B a right of way over Blackacre appurtenant to Whiteacre. B then conveys

Whiteacre in fee simple to A. One cannot have an easement in his own property. The easement is merged in the fee simple ownership in A.

Example (2). A owns Blackacre in fee simple and B owns Whiteacre in fee simple. A grants to B an easement appurtenant to Whiteacre providing B with a right of way to pass over Blackacre. A then leases Blackacre to B for a period of 10 years. The easement is extinguished during the 10 year lease. This is a partial extinguishment. When the lease expires and A repossesses Blackacre, B has the right to use the right of way over Blackacre.

(b) When an easement is appurtenant to another easement and the owner of the dominant easement becomes the owner of the servient tenement. Example—A owns Blackacre in fee simple. B owns Whiteacre in fee simple. There is on Whiteacre valuable timber. C is a lumber merchant. B grants to C the right to come onto Whiteacre and cut timber. A grants to C the right to haul across Blackacre the timber which he cuts on Whiteacre. Now the easement over Blackacre is appurtenant to the profit on Whiteacre. A conveys Blackacre in fee simple to C. This extinguishes the easement on Blackacre because C's easement on Blackacre is merged in his fee simple ownership thereof.

(c) When the owner of an easement in gross becomes the owner of the servient tenement on which the easement is a burden. Example—A owns Blackacre in fee simple and grants to B the right to come onto the premises and take water from a spring thereon for use in B's steam engine. A then sells and conveys to B Blackacre. The easement is merged in the fee simple ownership in B and is thereby extinguished.

(d) When the dominant tenant executes either a deed or a will releasing the easement in favor of the owner of the servient tenement. Example—B has a right of way over A's Blackacre. B executes either a deed or a will which provides that B releases to A the right of way over Blackacre. The easement is extinguished by release. A release of an easement must comply with the Statute of Frauds.

(e) When the dominant tenant has abandoned the easement and such abandonment is evidenced by conduct showing an intention to relinquish the right. Non-user of an easement without more will not establish abandonment. Example—B has a right of way over A's Blackacre appurtenant to B's adjoining Whiteacre. Where the way enters Blackacre from Whiteacre B builds on Whiteacre a permanent cement wall as part of a patio surrounding his house on Whiteacre. B tells A he has given up his right of way over Blackacre. The oral statement of B alone is not sufficient to constitute abandonment of the easement, but it is admissible and together with the conduct of B in building the wall constitutes an extinguishment of the easement by abandonment.

(f) When the servient tenant has used his land continuously and uninterruptedly for the statutory period of prescription in a way inconsistent with and adverse to the easement and without consent of the dominant tenant. Example—B has a right of way across A's Blackacre. Without B's consent A plows up the road used as the way and continues to cultivate it for the raising of crops during the prescriptive period. The easement is extinguished by prescription.

(g) When the servient tenant, in reasonable reliance on conduct of the dominant tenant, uses his servient tenement in a manner inconsistent with the existence of the easement and it would be inequitable to permit further use of the easement, such easement is extinguished by estoppel. Example—B has a right of way over A's Blackacre and tells A he has no intention of ever using the way again and has not used it for several years. A builds a house on his Blackacre over the space B used as the easement. Each day as the house is being built B watches the progress and might stop it by asserting his right but he does nothing until the house is completed. B then asserts his right to use the way. B is estopped to deny that the easement is extinguished.

(h) Under the recording statutes, if an easement (or profit) is created by grant and the deed is not recorded, and the servient tenement is conveyed to a bona fide purchaser for value without notice, the easement is extinguished. Example—A owns Blackacre in fee simple, and grants to B the right to come onto the premises and take any and all coal and sand which he can find thereon. B does not record the deed. A conveys Blackacre to C, a bona fide purchaser who pays A full value for the property and has no notice actually or constructively of B's profit in the land. C takes title to Blackacre without the burden of the profit on the land. The profit is extinguished. The recording statutes have no application to easements (or profits) created by prescription.

See Restatement of Property §§ 497–506; Burby, 90–93.

CASE 288: A owns Blackacre in fee simple and B owns adjoining Whiteacre in fee simple, Whiteacre being the lower tract. B grants to A the right to construct and maintain a drain across Whiteacre for the purpose of draining excess water from Blackacre. A small stream flows from Blackacre to and over Whiteacre. After procuring the easement from B, it occurs to A that he might accomplish the drainage of Blackacre by deepening the bed of the natural stream, and he does it. Forty years after the easement is granted, C offers to buy Whiteacre from B, but C does not want the property burdened with the easement. For the purpose of making the sale to C free from the easement, B brings an action against A to quiet title to Whiteacre and thereby clear it from the burden of the easement. It is B's contention that since A has not acted on the granted right for a period of 40 years, he has thereby abandoned it. The case is tried to the court without a jury; the court finds no evidence of A's intention to abandon the easement, and denies the decree quieting title. B appeals. What rule on appeal?

Answer and Analysis

The judgment below should be affirmed and the appeal dismissed. An easement is an incorporeal right in real property which comes within the purview of the Statute of Frauds. It cannot be created, transferred or released without a writing. Neither can it be abandoned by mere oral declarations. It can be abandoned if the dominant tenant intends to abandon it and such intention is evidenced by conduct, usually physical acts, on either the dominant or servient tenement. Whether or not there is an abandonment of an easement or profit is a question of fact and not a question of law unless the facts are so clear that reasonable men cannot differ thereon. However, non-user of an easement or profit, no matter how long continued, cannot by itself constitute abandonment. When other facts indicate an intention to abandon an easement, then evidence of non-user is admissible on the question of intention. But in this case there is no evidence on the part of the dominant tenant, A, that he intended to abandon the easement or the use of it. The deepening of the stream which temporarily drained Blackacre might not be in the future an adequate means of drainage, in which case A might wish to use his easement on Whiteacre. Such a substantial right as an easement is not and should not be easily destroyed. In any event, in our case the lower court found as a fact that A had not intended to abandon his use of the easement, and that settled the matter as effectively as the verdict of a jury. No facts appearing to the contrary, Whiteacre remains burdened with the easement of drainage appurtenant to Blackacre and the lower court was right in refusing to quiet title thereto in B. See Richardson v. Tumbridge, 111 Conn. 90, 149 A. 241 (1930).

CASE 289: Greenacre, Blackacre and Whiteacre are three business lots abutting each other with Blackacre between the other two lots. A owns Blackacre in fee simple and maintains his dwelling house thereon. He has a right of way across Whiteacre, appurtenant to Blackacre, for the use of himself and his family for crossing Whiteacre on foot or by bicycle or automobile. B is the owner of Whiteacre. C owns Greenacre and conveys it to A in fee simple. A builds a 20 story office building covering Greenacre and Blackacre which houses 8,000 persons during working hours each day. All of these persons use the way over Whiteacre and A uses the way for trucking as many as 20 loads of coal per day to

the building situated on Blackacre and Greenacre. B brings
suit seeking to enjoin any use of Whiteacre by A or any of
the 8,000 persons who work in A's office building and argues
that the easement is extinguished. **(a)** Is the easement extinguished? **(b)** Should the injunction issue?

Answers and Analyses

The answer to (a) is no. The answer to (b) is yes.

(a) Mere excessive user of an easement (or profit) does not forfeit or extinguish the easement. In the case of excessive user the
owner of the easement is simply making use of the servient tenement
beyond the scope or extent of the user permitted by the easement in
its creation. The easement as it was originally created still exists
and within its scope can be used. But the user in excess of the scope
of the easement can be enjoined and damages may be had for injury
caused by the excess user.

(b) Then why should the injunction sought by B issue forbidding any use of Whiteacre by A or the 8,000 persons who work in the
office building? In this case there are two quite distinct factors
which contribute to the excess user of the easement over Whiteacre.
First, the condition of the dominant tenement Blackacre has been
materially altered. Second, by building the office building on both
Greenacre and Blackacre these two lots have been integrated into a
common unit, one of which is a dominant tenement as to Whiteacre
and the other of which has no legal relation whatsoever to the servient tenement, Whiteacre. As to the change in the condition of the
dominant tract, Blackacre, if such could be separated from Greenacre,
B might well have a decree enjoining the excess use of the easement
over Whiteacre, but which decree would still permit A and his family
to use the way over Whiteacre for walking, bicycles and automobiles.
However, the facts of the instant case do not permit such a solution.

The use of the office building as a unit makes it impossible to
separate the use A is making of Whiteacre in his role as owner of
Blackacre, the dominant tenement, from the use A is making of Whiteacre in his role as owner of Greenacre, the non-dominant tract.
Some of the use which A is making of Whiteacre in connection with
the use of Blackacre may be proper, but some of it is merely excessive.
But any use at all which A is making of Whiteacre in connection
with Greenacre is not merely excessive, it is wholly unauthorized.
But when the lawful use of the servient tenement is inextricably integrated with the illegal use of such tract, then the dominant tenant
has no right to make any use at all of the servient tract until the
lawful use can be separated from the improper use thereof. Therefore,
although the easement is not extinguished, it is wholly suspended and
no use thereof can be made by the dominant tenement while the
present condition obtains. None of the 8,000 persons who work in
the office building have any relationship to Whiteacre under the
terms of the creation of the easement, and, therefore, they have no

right to use such servient tenement. Hence, the injunction should prohibit any use of Whiteacre by A or any of the persons who work in the office building as long as the present condition of affairs continues. If there comes a time when the office building is removed and A's dwelling house or relatively similar condition is restored to Blackacre, then A and his family may again use the easement over Whiteacre. See McCullough v. Broad Exchange Co., 101 App.Div. 566, 92 N.Y.S. 533, 16 N.Y.Ann.Cas. 51 (1905); 18 Harv.L.R. 608.

SUMMARY OF CASES IN CHAPTER XXVI

1. EASEMENTS AND PROFITS DEFINED, DISTINGUISHED AND CLASSIFIED

Case 270. If a conveyance transfers the corpus of the coal under the surface of real property, then the grantor has no interest therein and has no right to appropriate it to his own use. But if a conveyance conveys only the right to take coal, a profit, then the grantor still owns the coal until it is severed and appropriated by the grantee, and may continue to sever and use it. Whether a conveyance transfers the corpus of the coal or only the right to take the coal depends upon the construction of the words of the conveyance. There are two ways of describing in a conveyance the subject of the conveyance, one being by describing the thing itself such as by metes and bounds and the other by describing the power and control which the grantee shall have over the property. If a conveyance transfers coal in a particular property an easement by implication to go onto the land and take the coal is inferred.

Case 271. A right to come onto property and take water is an easement whereas a right to come onto property and take ice is historically a profit because ice was considered a product of the soil. If in its creation an easement or a profit is not intended to be attached to or appurtenant to a particular piece of land, the dominant tenement, it is an easement or a profit in gross. In England an easement in gross cannot exist but a profit in gross can exist and is transferable. In the United States an easement in gross of a commercial nature is recognized and is alienable like any other property interest. So also is a profit in gross. A conveyance of a dominant tenement carries with it all easements and profits appurtenant thereto as incidents unless it is otherwise expressly provided.

Case 272. There are two classes of easements with respect to the use of the servient tenement by the dominant tenant. One is affirmative and the other negative. An easement is affirmative if the dominant tenant has a right to go onto the servient tenement and do any affirmative act thereon. An easement is negative if it curtails the servient tenant in the use of his own servient tenement and the dominant tenant has no right to do any affirmative act on the servient tenement. Easements are also classified as easements appurtenant and easements in gross. An easement appurtenant is attached to a dominant tenement and permits the owner thereof, the dominant tenant, to make a limited use of another property, the servient tenement, in connection with his use of the dominant estate. It cannot be used in connection with the use of property other than the dominant tenement. In an easement appurtenant there are always a dominant tenement and a servient tenement.

2. HOW CREATED AND EXTENT

A. By Prescription

Case 273. To acquire an easement (or profit) by prescription the use, as to the land owner, must be: (a) wrongful; (b) not in subordination to the land owner; (c) open and notorious; (d) continuous; (e) uninterrupted by physical obstruction or legal proceedings; and (f) continued for the prescriptive period. The extent of the right acquired by prescription is determined by the use to which the landowner's land has been put by the user during the prescriptive period. When one has acquired an easement by prescription over a piece of land, the owner of the easement is not liable to the servient tenant for any damage done on the servient tenement during the acquisition of the prescriptive right if the damage is within the scope of the easement. But the dominant tenant is liable for damages done on the servient tenement for those damages which are not within the scope of the easement.

Case 274. Title by adverse possession is a title to corporeal property. Title by prescription is a title to incorporeal property, a right only. Neither such title can be gained if the possession or use is with the consent of the landowner. In prescription the adverse user does not have possession of the land—he only uses it, and that use need not be exclusive but may be used in common with the public and the landowner.

There are three distinct views as to the legal effect of a showing that land has been used for the prescriptive period. (1) One view is that it raises a presumption of adverseness. (2) Another is that unless there is specific evidence of adverseness there is a presumption of permissiveness. (3) The third, and believed the correct view, is that there is no presumption either way and the burden of proof is on the claimant to show all the elements of prescription, including adverseness. When the trier of fact has found in favor of the claimant of an easement by prescription or against him, if there is evidence to support the finding, then the appellate court must affirm the judgment of the trial court.

Case 275. The running of the statute of limitations in prescription may be stopped either by, (a) legal proceedings brought against the wrongdoer or, (b) by such obstruction or interference on the land that, if the easement actually existed, would give the easement owner a cause of action. A physical obstruction placed across a right of way will normally toll the running of the statute of limitations, but oral or written protestations, such as a letter, in most states will not affect the running of the statute of limitations. The statute of limitations begins to run in favor of the wrongdoer when a cause of action accrues to the landowner. The statute is not for the protection of the wrongdoer but requires diligence on the part of the innocent party.

Case 276. No disability has any effect on the running of the statute of limitations unless it exists when the cause of action accrues. Intervening and supervening disabilities which occur after the cause of action accrues do not affect the running of the statute of limitations. A disability is wholly personal and the only person who is protected by an extension of the statute of limitations is one who is under a disability at the time of the accrual of the cause of action. Disabilities cannot be tacked one to another. In no event can an adverse user mature a prescriptive right in less time than the period provided for in the statute of limitations.

In the usual case a prescriptive right will last no longer than that which is claimed by the adverse user during the period of the statute of limitations. But the claim is not the test. The test for the durational extent of the easement by prescription is the extent of the denial by the adverse user of the landowner's rights during the period of the statute of limitations. Thus, a life tenant may by prescription create an easement in fee appurtenant to his property which will inure to the benefit of his remainderman.

Case 277. Periods of adverse user may be tacked one to another if there is privity between the adverse users and such privity may exist where a conveyance from one adverse user to another is voluntary or involuntary. Adverse user of land in the possession of a life tenant does not ordinarily affect the remainderman, and a prescriptive easement is acquired generally only against the life tenant because the user does not give the remainderman a cause of action when possession alone is affected. But when the adverse user involves taking the corpus of the property and the remainderman has notice of such user, he has a cause of action against the adverse user and the statute of limitations runs against the remainderman. In such case the profit acquired by prescription is binding on the remainderman. In all cases of profits and easements the servient tenant may use the servient tenement in any way he wishes so long as his use does not interfere with the profit or easement of the dominant tenant.

Case 278. The extent or scope of an easement acquired by prescription is determined by the extent of the use during the period of prescription. In determining whether a claimed use is permitted by the easement there must be a comparison of the use made of the servient estate during the prescriptive period with the claimed use after the easement has been established. Such process must compare: (a) the physical use during the prescriptive period with the physical use claimed under the easement; (b) the purpose of the use during the prescriptive period with the purpose of the claimed use under the easement; (c) the burden on the servient estate during the prescriptive period with the burden thereon under the claimed use under the easement; and in case of an easement appurtenant; (d) the needs of the dominant tenant in his use of the dominant tenement which are due to normal changes in the use of the dominant tenement must be balanced with the additional burden, if any, which results to the servient estate. If the claimed uses is due to the change in the condition of the dominant tenement, and such changed condition is the result of the normal and reasonable evolution and development in the use of the dominant tenement, then the servient tenant may be charged with having foreseen such development, and it is reasonable to say that the matured easement includes the claimed use. On the other hand, if the claimed use in connection with the altered condition of the dominant tenement is beyond the normal evolution and development of the dominant estate, then such claimed use should not be allowed under the easement.

b. By Express Provision in Deed or Will

Case 279. The extent of an easement created by deed or will is determined by the words of the instrument. When the language describing the purpose for which the easement is to be used is clear and unambiguous, and limits such use to a single purpose, then the servient tract cannot be used for any other purpose. The dominant tenant has the right to enter on the servient tenement for the purpose of repairing, maintaining and improving the means by which the easement is enjoyed and to make such means effective. The servient tenant has the right to make the maximum use of his servient tenement consistent with the rights which he has conveyed to the dominant tenant in creating the easement. In the absence of agreement there is no duty on the part of the servient tenant to do any affirmative act to keep the easement effective.

Case 280. When an easement is created by conveyance and the words of the instrument are not complete in describing the future use to be made of the easement, then resort must be had for the meaning of the easement to the circumstances surrounding the execution of the instrument. Parties to such a conveyance must be held to contemplate a normal evolution and development in the use of the dominant tenement, and an altered use of the servient tract to accommodate such normal development will be within the scope of the created easement. But when there is such a drastic change in the use of the dominant tract that the change can hardly be contemplated in the normal development of the use of such property, then the use of the servient tract to serve the dominant owner in his altered use of the dominant tenement is not within the scope of the created easement. Normal development of the dominant tenement means that which accords with the common, not the uncommon, experience of mankind.

Case 281. When an easement appurtenant is created by deed it attaches to every part of the dominant tenement. Such an easement appurtenant is apportionable upon the subdivision of the dominant tenement unless the instrument creating the easement otherwise provides. Such easement becomes an appurtenance to each part of the subdivision and the owner of each part is entitled to use and enjoy such easement as a dominant tenant.

Case 282. An easement in gross is of a commercial nature when its principal purpose is to benefit the easement owner economically or financially. Such an easement is alienable as a matter of law. An easement in gross which primarily benefits its owner only personally is in nature noncommercial. Whether or not such an easement is alienable depends upon the manner and nature of use by which it is created when acquired by prescription, and on the terms of the conveying instrument and the surrounding circumstances if created by deed or will. An easement in gross of a commercial nature may be transferred like a life estate in property and the transferee will then have an easement pur autre vie.

Case 283. Three concepts should be differentiated. (1) A landowner may convey the corpus of sand on his land leaving him no interest in the sand. (2) A landowner may convey the exclusive right to come onto his land and take the sand therefrom. Only the grantee can exercise the right to take the sand but until the appropriation of the sand the servient tenant owns the corpus of the sand. (3) A landowner may convey a nonexclusive right to come onto the land and take sand. In such case the grantor still has the right to use the sand from the land and he has a right to convey a similar right to others.

In the case of an exclusive easement or profit in gross there is an inference that it is apportionable. In the case of a nonexclusive easement or profit in gross it is considered unapportionable unless by the terms of the conveyance or the manner of its creation it clearly appears that it is apportionable. When one has a nonexclusive profit in gross which is not apportionable and conveys it to two or more persons not jointly but independently as individuals, the profit in gross is destroyed.

Case 284. When an easement appurtenant is created either by prescription or by conveyance over a servient tenement the boundaries and extent of such easement become fixed and are binding on both the servient and dominant tenants. Neither such tenant has any more right to change the location of such easement than he has to change the boundaries of the physical servient or dominant tenement. The easement is an incorporeal right which is real property.

Case 285. In the absence of express agreement to the contrary, the owners of a party wall, bisected by the common boundary line extended vertically upward, have equal and reciprocal rights to the use of the party wall, and each has an easement on the other's half of the wall for the support of his building and his half of the party wall. The general American view is that each party wall owner has the right to use the entire thickness of the party wall to support his building joists. Each party wall owner has a right to extend the party wall upward or lengthwise at his own expense with no right of contribution from the other party wall owner until such other uses or undertakes to use the extension of the wall. When the non-builder of the extension does use or undertake to use the extended wall, then he is bound to make payment for the reasonable value of his share of the wall.

c. By Implication

Case 286. An implied easement is created and proved not by the words of the conveyance but by all the circumstances surrounding the execution of the conveyance. It is based on the intention of the parties as inferred from those surrounding circumstances. There are 5 prerequisites to the creation of an implied easement. (1) There must be a quasi-easement. (2) There must be a conveyance of one part of the property and a retention of another part of the property by the grantor. (3) The quasi-easement must be apparent at the time of the conveyance. (4) The quasi-easement must be continuous, meaning that the quasi-servient tenement is permanently adapted to serve the quasi-dominent tenement. (5) The quasi-easement must be (a) *reasonably necessary* to the enjoyment of the quasi-dominant tenement if that tract is conveyed, and (b) *strictly necessary* if the quasi-dominant tenement is retained by the grantor.

Case 287. For purposes of creating an implied easement by implied reservation in favor the grantor, the quasi-easement (which becomes a true easement by implication) is apparent if it would have been disclosed by a reasonably prudent investigation and inspection of the quasi-servient tenement. For the grantor to have an implied easement by implied reservation the use of the quasi-servient tenement must be strictly necessary to the enjoyment of the quasi-dominant tenement retained by the grantor. The expression "strictly necessary" is a variable and its meaning lies somewhere between "reasonably necessary" on one hand and "absolutely necessary" on the other. In this field of degree of necessity there is wide latitude for difference of opinion in the application of what is "strictly necessary" and such difference of opinion may result either in there being or not being an easement by implication.

3. EXTINGUISHMENT

Case 288. An easement (or profit) is an incorporeal right in real property and comes within the purview of the Statute of Frauds. It cannot be created, transferred or released without a writing. Neither can it be abandoned by mere oral declarations. But an easement (or profit) can be extinguished by abandonment by the dominant tenant provided his intention to abandon the use of the easement is evidenced by conduct evincing such intention. Non-user of an easement, however long continued, standing alone, cannot constitute abandonment of an easement. When there are other facts indicating an intention to abandon an easement, then evidence of non-user is admissible on the question of intention. But abandonment is a question of intention of the dominant tenant, and intention is always a question of fact and not one of law unless the facts are so clear that reasonable men cannot differ thereon.

Case 289. Excessive use of an easement does not forfeit or extinguish the easement. In such a case the servient tenant may enjoin the dominant tenant's excessive use of the easement but the dominant tenant may still use the easement within the scope or extent thereof as created. The dominant tenant of an easement appurtenant has no right to use the servient tenement in connection with a tract of land which is not part of the dominant tenement. If the use of the dominant tenement is so integrated with the use of another piece of land which is no part of the dominant tenement that the use of one is the use of the other, then the dominant tenant has no right to make any use of the easement over the servient tenement in connection with these integrated properties. This result is based on the principle that when a legal use is inextricably integrated with an illegal use, then any use is illegal or unauthorized.

Chapter XXVII

LICENSES

Legal Gems.
Cases.
Summary of Cases in Chapter XXVII.

LEGAL GEMS

1. The term license is enmeshed in ambiguity, frequently being used in the same context to refer both to the act of giving permission and to the legal effect of the permission given.

2. It would be preferable to define the term license in reference to the legal relationship resulting from the consent given, although such usage is far from universal. To distinguish the legal relationship "license" from the more substantial relationship "easement," license should be limited to a revocable relationship. Under such a classification, an irrevocable relationship would constitute an easement (except for the *license coupled with an interest*), no matter how created, because an irrevocable license in legal effect is no different than an easement.

The term "license coupled with an interest," however, is deeply embedded in legal literature; the relationship is unique with irrevocability quite limited; there is no equivalent terminology; and thus the concept of *license coupled with an interest* is useful and cannot readily be discarded.

3. With the foregoing caveats in mind, and with apologies for the subsequent semantic gymnastics, e. g., differentiating between a license and a mere license, the following additional gems are offered.

4. A license may be one of *three classes*:

   (a) A *license* or mere license which *is always revocable;*

   (b) A *license coupled with an interest* which is *irrevocable;* or

   (c) An *executed license* (oral license acted upon), which *is irrevocable.*

5. A *license* simply *permits one person to come onto land in the possession of another without being a trespasser.*

6. A license can be created by either an express or implied agreement.

7. *A license arises from consent* given by the one in possession of land. Hence, consent being given, *no prescriptive right* can arise through a license.

609

8. A *license* must be *distinguished from a lease*. A licensee never has possession of land whereas a lessee always has possession of land. For example, A being fee simple owner of Blackacre permits B to come onto Blackacre as a tenant at will. B has possession of the land. Possession means occupancy with an intent to control for one's own purposes. B is a lessee, even though his tenancy can be terminated at any minute by either A or B. On the other hand suppose A permits B to come onto Blackacre to use the land but A retains the possession of the land and simply consents to B's presence on the property without being a trespasser. B is a mere licensee whose license is terminable at the will of A. The difference in the two cases is this—in the first case B is given possession of the land whereas in the second case A retains possession of the land. In the first case B is a lessee. In the second case B is a licensee.

See Note following Case 294.

9. A *license* must be *distinguished from an easement*. An easement is a substantial incorporeal interest in the land of another and is created by a deed of conveyance. It is said to lie in grant. It is an interest in land which requires for its creation a compliance with the Statute of Frauds.

On the other hand a *mere* license is no such interest in land and requires no formalities for its creation. However, there are fact situations in which a license and an easement approach similarity and care must be used in determining which is present. For example, suppose A, fee simple owner of Blackacre, in a jurisdiction wherein either a lease for not more than one year or an easement or profit in gross to last for a period not more than one year may be created orally, permits B to come onto Blackacre for the purpose of fishing in a stream on the land from the hour of 2 o'clock in the afternoon to 6 o'clock in the afternoon of a specific day. Is this a profit in gross or a license? The answer is this—if the privilege is at the will of the landowner, A, it is a license, but if the right is irrevocable creating an interest in Blackacre for the 4 hour period, then it is a profit in gross.

An easement or a profit cannot exist at the will of the servient tenant whereas *a mere license is alway revocable* by either licensor or licensee at any time. The question is usually one of fact as to the intention of the landowner, but if the facts are not in dispute or are agreed upon, it is then a question of law. Usually B's right to fish for 4 hours would be considered a license.

10. A *license* must be *distinguished from a contract*. A contract is always based on a consideration. There may or may not be a consideration for a license. Compare:

(1) A permits B to come onto A's Blackacre to fish for 2 hours with no consideration involved and the permission being revocable at any time by A. B has a mere license.

(2) A permits B to come onto A's Blackacre to fish for 2 hours for which B pays A $1.00 for the sole purpose of not being considered

a trespasser and for no other purpose. B has a mere revocable license.

(3) A permits B to come onto A's Blackacre to fish for 2 hours and B pays A $1.00 for A's agreement that B may fish for the 2 hours without interruption. B has a license to fish on Blackacre which is revocable but he also has a contract under which A has promised for a consideration not to revoke the license. A has the right and the power to revoke the license as such, but he has only a power but no right to breach the contract and is liable if he does so.

Nothing is consideration which is not intended to be such. In such a case it is a question of intention as to what the consideration is for and that is usually a fact question.

11. An attempt to create an easement or profit which fails because the deed of conveyance is defective will result in a license. E. g., A executes a deed granting to B a right to mine coal on property which is not described in the deed. The deed is ineffective for failure to describe the property on which the coal is to be mined. No other facts appearing B has a license to go onto the intended land to mine coal. Such license is, of course, revocable.

12. A *mere license is generally personal* and not assignable but such *a license is assignable if the licensor so intends*. E. g., A, a theater operator, issues tickets to his theater on the face of which appears "this ticket is transferrable". B buys such ticket and assigns it to C. The assignment is valid and C has a license to attend the theater.

13. *If one owns personal property on the land of another with a privilege incidental to such personal property, such privilege is a license coupled with an interest* and *is assignable with the transfer of the personal property*. E. g., A sells to B a wheelbarrow which is located on A's Blackacre and tells B to go onto Blackacre and get the wheelbarrow. B has a license coupled with an interest. B without getting the wheelbarrow from A's Blackacre sells it to C with the privilege of taking the article from the land. B has assigned the license coupled with an interest by transferring the wheelbarrow to C with the privilege of getting it from A's Blackacre. A has no right to revoke C's license coupled with an interest if it prevents his getting the wheelbarrow. The license is irrevocable at least for a reasonable time. If A revokes such license without giving C a reasonable opportunity to obtain the wheelbarrow, A becomes a converter of the wheelbarrow and is liable as such.

14. If *a licensee in exercising his license and in reasonable reliance upon representations made by the licensor as to the duration of the license, has made expenditures of capital or labor so that it is inequitable for the license to be discontinued, it is termed an executed license, or an oral license acted upon, and is irrevocable. An executed license is based on estoppel and is equivalent to an easement.*

E. g., A owns Blackacre a riparian tract of land on the east fork of X Creek. B owns Whiteacre a riparian tract of land on the west fork of X Creek. A wishes to build a mill on Blackacre but the water supply in the east fork of X Creek is not sufficient in quantity to operate the proposed mill. At A's request B gives A permission to divert the water from the west fork of X Creek into the channel of the east fork of the Creek so that there will be sufficient water to operate A's proposed mill. In reliance on the permission given, A builds a dam in the west fork, diverts the water therein to the east fork, builds his mill and begins operating it successfully as a commercial venture. In the building of the dam and the mill A expends $15,000.-00. A has an executed license which is the equivalent of an easement giving him a right to continue indefinitely the diversion of the water from the west fork of X Creek into the east fork, and B has no right to interfere therewith. B is estopped to revoke or terminate the license.

15. Generally, a license is revoked automatically by the licensor's conveyance of the land, or by his doing an act inconsistent with the continuance of the license. In the case of a license coupled with an interest, an executed license, or an oral license acted upon, however, the license is not automatically revoked when the licensor conveys his land.

16. The purpose of the rule that a license relating to the undertaking of activities on another's land is revoked by a conveyance of the land is to protect the marketability of titles. Since the protection is for the benefit of the new landowner, only he can invoke the rule. See infra Case 294.

17. Successors in title take subject to an irrevocable license if they had notice of the license before their purchase.

See Restatement of Property §§ 512–521; Burby, 94–96; Powell, ¶¶ 427, 428.

———

CASE 290: A is the fee simple owner of Blackacre which adjoins B's Whiteacre. B gives A permission to build an irrigation ditch across one edge of Whiteacre for the purpose of carrying water to Blackacre for the purpose of irrigation. The ditch is to be a half mile long, lined with concrete and will cost about $2,000.00, all of which facts are known to B at the time the permission is given. Relying on such permission and with reasonable belief that it will continue indefinitely, A enters on Whiteacre, builds the proposed ditch and by means of water carried through the ditch irrigates Blackacre and raises several crops thereon when B obstructs the flow of water through the ditch and leaves A without water on Blackacre. At the time of B's giving A permission to build the ditch there is no consideration paid to B and there is no deed or writing involved. A brings suit to enjoin B from obstructing the flow of water through the ditch across Whiteacre. Should the injunction issue?

Answer and Analysis

The answer is yes. There are cases which say and hold that every license, executed or unexecuted, is in its very nature revocable, and that when a licensee expends money and labor in pursuance of a license which, contrary to his expectations, is revoked by the licensor, it is just a misfortune the burden of which falls on the licensee and he has no redress in the courts. In short, such a holding is saying in substance, two things, (a) the licensee should not have relied on and had no right to put reliance on a mere license for protection, and (b) the licensee should have procured a grant by deed or a writing under the Statute of Frauds if he expected the law to protect him in his expenditure of labor or capital on the land of the licensor. Legalistically and logically such a holding is on sound ground. However, the result hardly accords with the generally accepted concept of justice, and most of the cases recognize an executed license as the equivalent of an easement and base such holding on the doctrine of estoppel.

In the case given B knew when he gave A permission to construct an irrigation ditch over Whiteacre that such project would involve a large outlay of capital and labor. He knew that a revocation of the permission would result in a complete loss and waste of the capital and labor expended. He knew that the returns expected to be realized on the investment made would fail if the permission were or could be terminated. He knew or should have known that such expenditure would not be made but for the permission given. All of these things B foresaw or should have foreseen under the circumstances. Hence, he is fairly charged with understanding all of these facts and the reasonable inferences to be drawn therefrom. On the other hand, A has relied on B's permission and has made the expected expenditures which both parties foresaw would be made. Under these circumstances it seems quite reasonable and fair to say to B, "By your permission given to A and his acting on such as you expected he would do, you are estopped from revoking the license given because it is now quite inequitable for you to terminate such license". Under such concept A's executed license is the equivalent of an easement for a ditch across Whiteacre appurtenant to Blackacre, and B has no right to interfere with such executed license which has become a right in the land of B. Thus, the injunction should issue prohibiting B from obstructing the flow of water through the ditch over Whiteacre. It should be noticed that estoppel is a doctrine which avoids the harshness of logic and the application of legalistic concepts. It should be used with caution and only when required to do justice. It is justified only by the conduct of the parties. In this case its effect is to give A a right in B's land without the legal requirement of a deed or writing as provided by law or statute. See Restatement of Property § 519; Rerick v. Kern, 14 S. & R. (Pa.) 267, 16 Am.Dec. 497 (1826); Mayor & Council of City of Baltimore v. Brack, 175 Md. 615, 3 A.2d 471, 120 A.L.R. 543 (1939); Stoner v.

Zucker, 148 Cal. 516, 83 P. 808, 113 Am.St.Rep. 301, 7 Ann.Cas. 704 (1906); 6 Col.L.R. 471.

————

CASE 291: A maintains a stadium for the purpose of presenting football and other games to the public for entertainment. B buys a general admission ticket to a football game to be played in A's stadium for which B pays $10.00. When the football game is less than half played A comes to B and advises him that his license to remain in the stadium is revoked and orders him to leave the premises. B objects to such treatment but being assured that if he does not leave voluntarily he will be physically ejected, decides to and does leave the premises on his own power. During B's stay in the stadium his conduct is wholly unobjectionable. A's sole reason for ordering B from the stadium is simply that he, A, does not want B to be there. Upon B's leaving the stadium A offers to return the $10.00 which B has paid for admission and which B refuses to accept. B sues A for damages. The foregoing facts are stipulated as true. May B recover?

Answer and Analysis

The answer is no. This case presents a typical problem in the field of licenses. It is clear that had B paid no consideration for the ticket to the football game there would have been a mere license which is always revocable. It is just as clear that the transaction between A and B does not constitute a lease because the ticket is for general admission and gives B no right to sit in any particular seat in the stadium. A lease transfers to the tenant the right to possession of a particularly described area. Thus, it is always arguable in case of a reserved seat that there may be a lease of a specific seat or space for a definite period of time, the duration of the spectacle. The fact that a consideration is paid in this case does not necessarily take it out of the category of being a mere license.

Whether the $10.00 payment is solely for the purpose of permitting B to come onto A's stadium without being treated as a trespasser by A, in which case there is a mere license, or is solely for an implied promise by A to permit B to remain in the stadium during the entire period of the football game, in which case there is a personal contract between A and B, or whether it is to be for both not being treated as a trespasser and for an implied promise, is usually a fact question to be determined by the trier of fact, and the result will depend upon the finding of such fact. But in this case we are given an agreed set of facts which makes it necessary to determine the question as a matter of law. It is essential first to understand that a license as such deals solely with the privilege of being on the land of another with the possessor's permission, whereas a contract deals solely with the personal relationship between the contracting parties and has nothing to do with land as land. The only connection in such a case as ours is that as an incident the contract may have to be performed on the land. When such is the case the landowner may have a right to eject one from his land as far as the license by itself is concerned, but if such eviction from the land results in a breach of his contract, he may be liable for breach of the contract although not liable for revocation of the license. In such case it is the breach of the personal contract that imposes the liability and not the eviction from the land.

An analysis of this case presents five possible solutions.

(1) It may be inferred that B paid A $10.00 exclusively for an implied promise by A to permit B to remain in the stadium during the entire period of the football game. With such inference there is a revocable license in B as far as remaining in the stadium, that is on the land, is concerned. But there is also a personal promise on the part of A based on a consideration which forms a contract between A and B and for a breach of such promise by A there is liability. Under such theory B can recover from A damages for breach of contract.

(2) It may be inferred that part (say $5.00) of the $10.00 paid by B to A is to induce A not to treat B as a trespasser while in the stadium, and part (say $5.00) of the $10.00 paid by B to A is for an implied promise on A's part to permit B to remain in the stadium throughout the period of the football game. With this inference the solution is exactly the same as under (1) next above. A is not liable for revoking the license but he is liable in damages to B for breach of the personal contract based on the $5.00 consideration.

(3) It may be inferred as in (1) and (2) above that there is a contract between A and B and that because such contract deals with land it is specifically enforceable, in which case B has a right to use self help in remaining on the land and A has neither the right nor the power to break the contract. Under this theory B has a right to specific performance but any attempt to use such remedy is futile because the football game will be over before court action can be commenced. This leaves B to his remedy at law for damages for breach of contract. The objection to this theory is that there is no compliance with the Statute of Frauds and no part performance to take the case outside such Statute.

(4) It may be inferred that there is an intention to create an interest in the land, an interest in rem, which would have to come under the concept of easement. In such case B's right to come into the stadium and remain there would be mere incidents to the right in the land itself. Under this theory A would have no right to terminate B's interest in the land and B would have an action in trespass on the case for damages for A's interfering with the easement. The objection to this theory is that there is neither a deed of conveyance nor a writing to comply with the Statute of Frauds.

(5) It may be inferred that the sole purpose of the $10.00 payment for the ticket is intended as an inducement to A not to treat B

as a trespasser while B is in the stadium on A's land. Under such inference there is no implied promise on the part of A that he will permit B to remain in the stadium for any length of time, definite or indefinite. B is simply not to be liable for trespassing on A's land. B has a mere revocable license with respect to being on A's land, the stadium. Under this theory there is no liability for breach of contract for there is no contract. Neither is there any liability for wrongful interference with an easement or a right in rem for there is no easement or right in the land. Neither is there any liability on the part of B for ejecting A from the stadium because the only interest B has therein is a mere license and such a license is in its very nature always revocable by the licensor. Under B's ticket B was to be permitted to come onto A's land without being a trespasser. That has happened. A is not treating B as a trespasser. He is merely saying to B this, "I gave you a privilege of being on my land, in the stadium, as a licensee without my treating you as a trespasser. You are not a trespasser but your license is revoked so leave my premises forthwith".

After the revocation of his license the most that B can claim under the privilege originally given is a reasonable time to gather up his belongings, if any, brought onto the land and a reasonable time in which to depart. This 5th theory is the commonly accepted orthodox view of the "ticket holder" cases and applies to tickets to theaters, baseball games, horse races, polo and hockey contests and other entertainment spectacles. While there is much to be said on the basis of intention under theory (1) or (2) above, it is believed the best solution is that presented under theory (5) which holds that a ticket holder such as B in this case has neither a contract with the landowner, A, nor a right in rem in the land of the landowner, but has by virtue of such ticket only a revocable license. Under this theory B has no cause of action against A for his being ejected from the stadium. Furthermore, B has no cause of action against A for a return of the $10.00 paid for the ticket because its very purpose has been fulfilled by the protection it has given B in not being a trespasser on A's land, the stadium. It is immaterial that A tendered back to B the admittance fee. The revocable license rationale enables the proprietor to protect more fully members of the public by being able to evict objectionable patrons without having to prove the validity of his reasons, but the proprietor must be careful in his removal of the licensee or he will be liable in damages for unreasonable behavior in the act of revoking the license. See Hurst v. Picture Theatres, Ltd. [1915] 1 K.B. 1; Marrone v. Washington Jockey Club, 227 U.S. 633, 33 S.Ct. 401, 57 L.Ed. 679, 43 L.R.A.,N.S., 961 (1913); 27 Harv.L.R. 495; Clark, p. 38 et seq.; Powell ¶ 428.

————

CASE 292: A is the owner of Blackacre, a section of land used for agricultural purposes. On Blackacre A has a barn with a large expanse of roof area which can be seen by all travelers on a main highway passing in either direction. B is an advertising agent whose business it is to place signs for advertisers of nationally sold products. A signs an acknowledged instrument providing as follows: "I hereby grant to B a license to paint a sign 20 feet by 30 feet on the roof of my barn on Blackacre and to maintain such painted sign for one year from this date, Dec. 1, 1965, for $25.00 with right to renew such license at B's option for 4 more years at $25.00 per year". At the head of the instrument is the word, "Lease". B pays A $25.00 for the first year. Thereafter by letter in which A encloses his check for $25.00, A notifies B that he revokes the license to place the sign on A's barn. B goes to Blackacre to paint the sign on A's barn and A refuses to permit him to do so. B brings suit to enjoin A's interference with placing the sign on A's barn. Should the injunction issue?

Answer and Analysis

The answer is yes. The first thing to determine on this set of facts is the effect of the instrument signed by A. The distinction between a lease and a license is clear although in some cases it is difficult to determine whether a particular instrument creates one or the other. In a lease the lessee is given exclusive possession of the real property. In a license the licensor retains possession of the real property on which the privilege may be exercised. In this case it is clear that A did not intend to give up possession of the roof of his barn. Certainly A intended to retain possession and control for such purposes as maintenance and repair, for example, and would not want to give possession and dominion to B. Hence, even though the word "Lease" appears at the top of the instrument signed by A, it is not a lease. Because an instrument is signed and acknowledged and there is a consideration paid does not necessarily prevent its being a revocable license if such be the intention of the parties. But the fact that the word "license" is used in the instrument is not at all conclusive that it constitutes a license if the instrument taken as a whole evinces a different intention. It is hardly correct to call the instrument a "contract to give a license" for such would seem to be a contradiction in terms. One would hardly be so foolish as to contract for a privilege which is in its nature revocable.

Is the instrument merely a contract between A and B? It might be so construed and if so it would seem to be a specifically enforceable agreement. But taking the instrument as a whole there seems to be an intention to create more than just a personal relationship between A and B. There is a "grant" in the present tense to B to use the roof of A's barn with a "right" to renew such use for 4 years. And there is a consideration paid and accepted to support such "grant". It seems that the words, "lease" and "license" as used in the setting in the instrument are misdescriptions of the concepts sought to be created. To call the instrument a contract seems to fall short of its primary purpose which is to create in B a right in the use of the roof of A's barn. The intention of the parties is to create in B a right in rem, a right in the use of the barn as an accession to the real property on which it is located. It is an intention to grant to B a use in the real property of another, that other being A. And this is the definition of an easement, and in our case an easement in gross. It is believed that the instrument signed and acknowledged by A has created in B an easement in gross in Blackacre for one year, with a specifically enforceable contract obligation on A's part at B's option to grant an easement in gross for 4 more years. Therefore A should be enjoined from interfering with B's painting the sign on the roof of A's barn. See Baseball Pub. Co. v. Bruton, 302 Mass. 54, 18 N.E.2d 362, 119 A.L.R. 1518 (1938); 19 Mich.L.R. 100.

Note

In particular instances where the instrument is informal and does not comply with the conveyancing statute, e. g., it lacks the necessary witnesses or acknowledgment, it may be difficult initially to construe the interest created as an easement since compliance with the conveyancing statute is required for the creation of such an interest. However, if there is a writing signed by the landowner, if consideration is paid, and if the intent to create such an interest is ascertained, then equity, regarding as done that which ought to be done, may grant specific performance of an agreement to create such an interst and grant appropriate relief. In the above case of an acknowledged instrument, it is assumed either that the conveyancing statute is satisfied or that equity will enforce the agreement.

———

CASE 293: A owns Blackacre in fee simple which consists of 10 acres on which pine trees ripe and ready for harvesting stand. A orally agrees to sell the timber on Blackacre to B for a specific price per acre as it is cut together with a license to go onto Blackacre and cut and carry away such timber. B cuts all of the timber on 5 of the 10 acres comprising Blackacre and pays A in full therefor but none of such cut timber is removed from Blackacre. A conveys Blackacre to C without reserving any interest in the timber thereon but at the time of the conveyance A orally notifies C of the oral agreement with B. C takes possession of Blackacre and refuses to permit B to cut any more timber on the property. B sues A in breach of contract for damages. May B recover?

Answer and Analysis

The answer is yes. There are two views concerning the effect of an oral contract to sell standing timber. One view treats the standing timber as part and parcel of the land and requires any contract concerning a sale thereof to be in writing under the Statute of Frauds. This view is quite logical. The second view also recognizes standing timber as part of the land but treats the oral contract to sell such timber as an executory contract to sell the timber when severed, with a license on the part of the landowner to the purchaser to go onto the land and cut the trees. Under such construction of the contract it does not come within the Statute of Frauds and applies only to the trees as personal property when they are severed from the land. The second view seems to be the general rule on the subject and is adopted in the solution of this case. What then is the effect of such contract while A still owns Blackacre? It is this. The contract remains executory as to the trees still standing on Blackacre but as B exercises his license to go onto Blackacre and cut trees the oral contract is executed as to every tree as it is felled by B and becomes personal property. In other words the instant a tree is cut by B the title thereto vests in B under the terms of the oral contract. The result is that when B has cut all of the trees on five acres of Blackacre the title to those trees in their chattel character as logs lying on the ground is in B the purchaser. As to the trees remaining standing on the other five acres of Blackacre, the licensee, B, still has the privilege of cutting same and thereby bringing them as they are severed within the terms of the oral agreement. Such is the situation when A conveys Blackacre to C.

What effect does A's conveyance of Blackacre to C have upon B's license to come onto the land conveyed? It has no effect upon B's license to come onto Blackacre and carry away the logs from the five acres on which B had cut the standing timber. Those trees reduced to logs are personal property and are the property of B under his oral contract with A. B has title to and an interest in that personal property and his license to come onto Blackacre and remove those logs is a "license coupled with an interest" and such a license is irrevocable. Thus, A's conveyance to C does not revoke B's license to take off his logs. But the conveyance does revoke the license of B to come onto Blackacre and cut any more standing timber for the reason that the deed from A to C conveyed Blackacre without reservation as far as the timber standing thereon is concerned. And title to Blackacre includes title to the standing timber. Therefore the standing timber on Blackacre belongs to the grantee, C. A's executory contract to sell standing timber to B includes two distinct items, (a) a license to come onto Blackacre and cut trees, and (b) title to the logs cut is to be in B. A breach of either of these elements constitutes a breach of A's contract with B. When A conveys to C without reserving in A the title to the timber thereon, there is a breach of the contract for which A is liable to B in damages. Hence, B may recover in his action against A. See Emerson v. Shores, 95 Me. 237, 49 A. 1051, 85 Am.St.Rep. 404 (1901); Shipley v. Fink, 102 Md. 219, 62 A. 360, 2 L.R.A.,N.S., 1002 (1906).

CASE 294: In 1957 A Railroad signed an agreement with B City whereby B City was given a license to construct and maintain a sewer upon the railroad's right of way. The agreement provided that B City would indemnify the railroad for liability for any injury resulting from the maintenance of the sewer. In 1972 A Railroad conveyed certain assets including the right of way involved here to C Railroad. Subsequent to this conveyance, an employee of C Railroad was injured by the lid of one of the manholes constructed on the railroad's right of way. C Railroad paid the injured employee in settlement of a claim under the Federal Employee's Liability Act (FELA). C Railroad then sued B City for indemnification pursuant to the 1957 license agreement. B City denied liability on the ground that the 1957 license agreement was revoked by the 1972 conveyance of the right of way involved. Should B City indemnify C Railroad for the loss?

Answer and Analysis

The answer is yes. Generally, a license is revocable upon the conveyance of property. The purpose of this rule is to protect the marketability of titles. However, after the conveyance to it in 1972, and after knowledge of the existence of the license, C Railroad continued to allow B City to use its license to maintain the sewer on the property. Under the circumstances, the conveyance of 1972 did not operate automatically as a revocation of the license or of B City's agreement thereunder to indemnify C Railroad. Since the rule that a conveyance generally revokes a license is only for the benefit of the new landowner, only the new landowner can invoke the rule.

In most instances it is the new landowner who wants the license revoked upon the conveyance rather than the licensee. It is well settled that a license in realty, uncoupled with an interest, is terminated upon the sale or conveyance of that realty. Since a license confers a personal privilege to act and not a possessory estate, it does not run with the land and, therefore, may be revoked by the licensor.

The general rule is subject to the exception that successors-in-title take subject to an irrevocable license if they had notice of the license before purchase, such as in cases where the licensee made expenditures in reliance on the existence of the license and, before the conveyance, the new landowner is made aware of the existence of the license and the expenditures made in reliance thereon. Chicago & Northwestern Transp. Co. v. Winthrop, 257 N.W.2d 302 (Minn.1977).

Note

See Union Travel Associates, Inc. v. International Associates, Inc., 401 A.2d 105 (D.C.App.1979), holding that the arrangement between a hotel and the operator of its gift shop in the lobby constituted a license and not a lease. The instrument labelled a license agreement provided, among other things, that: the licensee would pay $500 each month to the licensor; that the shop was to be operated for the convenience of the hotel guests; that certain type products would be sold and tourist information made available; that the licensor reserved the right to run pipes, wires, and conduits through the premises and that he should have keys to the shop at all times; that the licensor had the right to substitute different space for the location of the shop and that if the operator did not like the new space, then the remainder of the "lease" would be null and void; and that if the hotel were sold the licensor could terminate the agreement.

In deciding that only a license was created the court found that no exclusive possession was given to the operator since the hotel retained the right to run pipes and wires through the shop and had keys at all times; that there was no grant or lease of any specific space in the hotel since the hotel could change the location of the shop; that there was no grant of an estate in real property, but only a privilege to occupy a portion of the hotel; and that the hotel had the right to terminate or revoke the privilege on sale of the hotel, this latter right of revocation said to be a distinct characteristic of a license.

SUMMARY OF CASES IN CHAPTER XXVII

Case 290. When a licensor permits a licensee to come onto the licensor's land, and in pursuance of such license the licensee makes substantial expenditures of labor or capital, and such is foreseen and understood by the licensor, and the licensee proceeds on the reasonable belief that such license will not be terminated, and it becomes inequitable for the licensor to revoke the license, then there is an executed license which is irrevocable. The licensor is estopped to terminate the license, and the licensee has an interest in the licensor's land which is the equivalent of an easement even though no consideration is given for the privilege, and even though the license is oral. The doctrine of estoppel is based on the conduct of the parties and avoids the harshness of applying logic and legalistic concepts which, in such a case, would require a deed or a writing.

Case 291. When a ticket is purchased to a public entertainment such as a theater, football game, baseball game or the like, the question of whether the consideration paid is intended as the basis of a contract to permit the ticket holder to remain on the premises where the spectacle is presented for the entire period of the entertainment, or is intended merely to enable the ticket holder to come onto the premises without being treated as a trespasser in which case there is only a license, is a question of fact to be determined by the trier of fact. If the facts are not in dispute or are agreed upon, then the question of whether there is a contract or only a license or both, is a question of law. If there is a contract and the landowner breaches the contract he is liable in damages for the breach. If there is a license only then the landowner may revoke the license and evict the ticket holder without liability. While it is arguable that such a ticket holder has a contract with the landowner or has a right in rem in the land, and there are cases so holding, it is believed the best view is that such ticket holder has only a license and that such license is revocable without liability on the part of the landowner. Such is the orthodox view in the majority of cases.

Case 292. In construing an instrument the intention of the parties must be gleaned by taking the instrument as a whole. The fact that an instrument is called a "lease" or a "license" or an "easement" is not conclusive that such name is a proper description of the legal effect of the instrument. An instrument which is designated a "lease" and "grants" a "license" may actually constitute a grant of an easement. In a lease the lessee is given exclusive possession of the land. In a license the licensor retains possession of the land on which the privilege is to be exercised. An instrument which grants one person a right to use the land of another in such form that there is a right in rem, creates an easement, and if there is no dominant tenement it is an easement in gross.

Case 293. An oral contract to sell standing timber is considered executory as to the trees until they are severed and become personal property at which time the title to the logs vests in the purchaser. Such a contract is not within the Statute of Frauds. Under such theory the landowner impliedly licenses the purchaser to go onto the land and cut down the trees. If the landowner after making an oral contract to sell standing timber conveys the land without reserving the standing timber thereon, such conveyance revokes the license to come onto the land and cut trees still standing, but such conveyance does not revoke the license of the purchaser of the timber under the oral contract as to any timber which is cut before the conveyance as that is the property of the purchaser of the timber. Such license is one "coupled with an interest", the interest being the title to the logs as personal property lying on the ground conveyed. A "license coupled with an interest" in such personal property on the land of another is irrevocable. The seller of the standing timber under the oral contract is liable in damages for breach of his contract when he conveys the land without reserving the timber and thereby revokes the license of the purchaser of the timber to come onto the land and cut the remaining standing trees.

Case 294. A license is usually revoked on a conveyance of the land subject to the license. The rule, however, is for the benefit of the owner of the land subject to the license; and if the new owner has notice of an "irrevocable" license at time of purchase, or if he consents to the continuation of the license, then such license is not revoked on conveyance.

Chapter XXVIII

LEGISLATIVE CONTROL OVER USE OF LAND—
PLANNING AND ZONING

1. Planning.
   Legal Gems.
   Cases.
2. Zoning.
   Legal Gems.
   Cases.
Summary of Cases in Chapter XXVIII.

---

1. PLANNING

LEGAL GEMS

1. The relationship of traditional land use controls, i. e., zoning to land use planning, has in the past been left primarily to local governments. Recently, however, a renewed concern for the environment and dissatisfaction with the existing system has led to the realization that land use control must have a cohesive policy supporting it, and often this policy must be based upon a much larger geographical area than that covered by a local government. This awareness has led to an upsurge of innovative state legislation in land use control methods, implemented primarily through the use of a "master plan" or "comprehensive plan."

2. The terms "master plan" and "comprehensive plan" have often been used interchangeably, and if the whole political entity was covered by the zoning ordinance, it was likely to be construed as satisfying the required comprehensive plan although there was in fact no separate written instrument depicting a plan as distinct from the ordinance itself.

3. New planning legislation with emphasis on future growth and development, plus compatibility with surrounding areas, requires a separate written plan in addition to the ordinance itself. Further, local municipal plans must be coordinated with those of the county, other municipalities, the appropriate region, and even the state itself.

4. Logically, the distinction between the comprehensive plan and the master plan may be stated thus:

(a) A "comprehensive plan" is one which meets the statutory requirements in a particular state. It is simply a legal concept that must be satisfied in that most enabling legislation requires that zoning be "in accord" with the plan.

(b) A "master plan" is a separate document that historically has not constituted an ordinance and represents a broad state-

623

ment of policies, goals, and objectives for the area it covers. Thus, it is a statement of intent, which is generally implemented through land use regulatory devices, primarily zoning.

It must be emphasized, however, that until recently the courts did not clearly distinguish between the two types of plans, and that the terminology was often used interchangeably without a precise definition.

5. Under recent planning legislation there is definitely required a separate written plan, whether designated as "comprehensive," "master," or otherwise, and such a plan will prevail over an ordinance when there is a conflict. This required plan conforms to the above definition of a "master" plan, but it is unlikely that there will be such conformity in usage in the near future. (See e. g., Fla.Stat. § 163.3177 (1979), using the term comprehensive plan).

See generally: Ravikoff, Land Use Planning, 31 U.Mia.L.Rev. 1119 (1977); Haar, In Accordance with a Comprehensive Plan, 68 Harv.L.Rev. 1154 (1955).

––––––––

CASE 295: Plaintiff, representing a group of homeowners in County X, opposed a requested zoning change by Contractor which would permit mobile homes on the land in question. The Board of County Commissioners approved the change against the recommendation of the Planning Commission. The area had been zoned "single family residential" in accordance with the master plan of the county. A applied for and received a writ of review of the action of the commissioners allowing the change. Should the change be declared invalid?

Answer and Analysis

The answer is yes. The state Supreme Court, sitting en banc, held the zone change invalid. The Court decided that the purpose of the zoning ordinance was to implement the master plan and that both were intended to be parts of a single integrated procedure for land use control. The Court stated that the master plan was a basic document, geared into population, land use, and economic forecasts which should be the basis of zoning ordinances and other land use regulations adopted by the county. The Court held that the state legislature had "conditioned" the county's power to zone upon the prerequisite that the zoning attempt furthers the general welfare of the community. Since the principles and policy determinations regarding the public welfare were embodied in the master plan, the Court concluded that it must be proved that any change was in conformance with the plan.

In proving that the change was aligned with the master plan, the Court required that the proof demonstrate: (1) a public need for a change of the kind in question; and (2) the need will be best served by altering the classification of the property in question as compared with using other available property. The Court concluded that the zone change approved by the County Commission was not in conformance with the master plan and was, therefore, invalid. It is also interesting to note that the Court rejected the general idea that all zoning changes by ordinance are legislative in character and entitled to a full presumption of validity. Rather, it stated that questions concerning changes in a specific piece of property is essentially an exercise of judicial authority and should be subject to a different test than a legislative one. Fasano v. Board of County Com'rs of Washington County, 264 Or. 574, 507 P.2d 23 (1973).

CASE 296: Plaintiff, a landowner in the City of X was protesting the development of property adjacent to his. The property had previously been zoned for residential-business use, allowing 39 units per acre. Subsequent to the enactment of this zoning ordinance, the city adopted a master plan which designated the area as high density residential, allowing 17 units per acre. The present development, authorized by the City Planning Commission, allowed the construction of apartment buildings which would result in 26 units per acre. The density was in conformity with the existing zoning ordinance, but higher than that permitted by the master plan. Plaintiff brought an action to have the city compelled to conform its zoning ordinance to its comprehensive or master plan. The lower court found that there was no requirement that zoning be in accordance with a plan, and that the existing master plan, adopted by resolution, could not be placed in a superior position to a zoning regulation adopted by ordinance. Was the trial court's holding correct?

Answer and Analysis

The State Supreme Court granted review to consider the effect of the adoption by a municipality of a comprehensive or master plan on pre-existing and conflicting zoning ordinances. The Court analogized the function of a master plan and found it similar to a "constitutional" document which provides a broad policy statement that is to be implemented by the local legislature. The plan is the basic instrument for municipal land use planning, and it must be given preference over conflicting prior zoning ordinances in order to be effective.

The Court concluded that the city had a responsibility upon its adoption of a master plan to implement the plan through its zoning ordinances. The Court further held that the zoning decisions of a city must be in accord with that plan, and a zoning ordinance which allows a more intensive use than that prescribed in the plan must fail. Baker v. City of Milwaukie, 271 Or. 500, 533 P.2d 772 (1975).

See also Marracci v. City of Scappoose, 26 Or.App. 131, 552 P.2d 552 (1976), for the proposition that literal conformance with the comprehensive plan is not mandatory in all cases; that the plan sets an outside limit; and a locality can adopt regulations *more* stringent than those called for by the plan and still be in compliance. In Dade County v. Yumbo, S. A., 348 So.2d 392 (Fla. 3d D.C.A.1977), the validity of a master plan was upheld in the absence of a showing that the property could not be put to a reasonable use compatible thereto, or that such plan was so inflexible as to constitute county action precluding all reasonable use of the property.

2. ZONING

LEGAL GEMS

1. All land privately owned is held subject to some controls by

    (a) the common law which prohibits the landowner from committing nuisances, public or private, thereon, or

    (b) the state through legislation exercising either

        (1) the power of eminent domain or

        (2) the police power, including zoning, or

    (c) restrictions voluntarily imposed by individuals including easements, profits, covenants running with the land and equitable servitudes.

2. The state's power over land under eminent domain proceedings in which *just compensation must always be paid* to the landowner includes:

    (a) the power to condemn land for a public purpose; and

    (b) the power to condemn land for a private way of necessity essential to the development of the natural resources of the state.

3. The state's power over land through the police power is exercised only under specific statutes or ordinances under which *no compensation is ever paid to the landowner,* and includes:

    (a) control for the purpose of protecting the health, safety, morals and welfare of the public; and

    (b) zoning ordinances which must be justified as protecting the health, safety, morals or welfare of the public.

4. The police power, especially the general or public welfare aspect, is an expanding concept and today can encompass promoting aesthetics and instituting architectural controls.

5. State statutes or city ordinances attempting to exercise police power must be reasonable and not arbitrary or unreasonable. If a statute or ordinance is arbitrary or unreasonable it either takes property without due process of law or denies equal protection of the laws, or both, under the 14th Amendment of the Constitution of the United States, and is unconstitutional and void.

6. If the validity of a statute or ordinance is fairly debatable, then generally the legislative judgment will control and the enactment is constitutional.

7. Zoning ordinances, being based on the police power, must conform to police power standards. Hence such an ordinance is invalid if it is:

(a) unreasonable or arbitrary (there is no rational basis for the classification as established);

(b) discriminatory (there is no reasonable basis for the classification); or

(c) confiscatory (the property cannot be used for any purpose for which it is reasonably suited).

8. It is normal for a landowner to be able to use his land as he pleases. For such use to be regulated is abnormal. If the regulation is under the police power it must be reasonable. If it is reasonable and still causes damage to the landowner it is damnum absque injuria and the landowner must stand the loss without compensation. If the regulation goes too far it is either (a) unconstitutional and void ab initio, or (b) a "taking" under eminent domain for which just compensation must be paid to the landowner. See special note after Case 299.

9. A regulatory measure or zoning ordinance may be perfectly valid as it is drawn. It may be valid in its application to one set of conditions because it brings about reasonable results. But the same ordinance may be quite invalid in its application to another set of conditions because it brings about arbitrary and unreasonable results. It is in this field where the great bulk of litigation concerning zoning ordinances has centered. And of course it is here where great divergence of opinion occurs.

10. A nonconforming use, not amounting to a nuisance, in effect at the time of the enactment or amendment of a zoning ordinance, probably cannot be constitutionally eliminated at once. Zoning ordinances which permit such nonconforming uses to continue for a reasonable period of time and impose restrictions designed to ensure their eventual elimination are valid.

11. Spot zoning consists of placing a single or limited number of parcels in a classification not in accord with the general scheme or comprehensive plan. It is usually held invalid and appears especially vulnerable to the charge of unreasonable discrimination.

12. A variance from the literal application of a zoning ordinance is granted as a matter of administrative relief on the basis of practical difficulty or unnecessary hardship. An owner would be entitled to a variance under the following conditions:

(a) the land in question cannot yield a reasonable return if used solely as zoned,

(b) the plight of the owner is due to unique circumstances and not to the general conditions in the neighborhood which may reflect the unreasonableness of the ordinance itself, and

(c) the use to be permitted by the variance will not alter the essential character of the locality.

13. An exception is a permitted departure from the restrictions of the ordinance under express provisions of the act, as, for example, when the ordinance authorizes permits for parks, schools or churches in a residential zone under stated conditions.

14. A special use permit performs essentially the same functions as that of an exception, but it probably allows greater discretion.

15. Traditionally, there was no requirement that every community permit every type of use; thus if a municipality was able to anticipate adverse effects of a particular use and its actions were reasonable in excluding such use, the municipality was permitted to do so. A zoning ordinance which was reasonably calculated to advance the community as a social, economic, political and aesthetic unit according to its particular needs was held in furtherance of the general welfare and a proper exercise of the police power even if certain uses were excluded.

Today, however, there is a growing trend which recognizes that each separate community is not an island unto itself. Particularly, if the enacting entity is part of a large metropolitan area, it is then not free to ignore possible adverse effects that an overrestrictive ordinance may have on others. See infra Cases 303 and 304.

16. A city council may not, in enacting a rezoning ordinance, impose conditions and exact concession in connection with the performance of its legislative functions. However, where the property owner voluntarily imposes restrictions and confers on the council the means of enforcing them, an amendment to the ordinance reclassifying land of the owner will not be invalidated on the ground that the action of the council constitutes zoning by contract. Situations of this type, however, are carefully scrutinized and some instances closely analogous have been invalidated as attempted zoning by contract. The legislative body must act in accordance with its conferred powers.

17. Flexible selective zoning or the use of "floating zones" has met with varied success. Under this plan no land at all is originally assigned to the zone in question, but such assignment is made when a landowner requests and is granted such a zone. When a plan of this type is invalidated it is done so on the basis that the zoning is not done pursuant to a comprehensive plan but instead on a case to case basis, and is therefore analogous to spot zoning. See infra Case 306 and the note following for cases reaching divergent results. See Powell, ¶¶ 867–872.

CASE 297: Facts: City X has a neighborhood in which most of the buildings are over 150 years old and are of a unique architectural style. The district is widely known for its quaint and interesting character and attracts thousands of tourists to City X. The appeal of the district is due primarily to the aesthetic, architectural and historical character of the buildings. City X enacted an ordinance to preserve the unique character of the district and set up a commission with authority to approve or disapprove all construction, alteration or demolition within the district. A is the owner of an old residence within the district. A seeks a permit to raze the house and erect a new apartment building in its place. Although apartment buildings are otherwise permitted under the zoning ordinance, a permit is denied because the redevelopment of the property would tend to lessen the aesthetic appeal of the district. A seeks an injunction to prevent the enforcement of the ordinance and to compel the issuance of a permit. Should the injunction issue?

Answer and Analysis

The answer is no. To be a valid exercise of the police power, an ordinance must seek to promote the health, safety, morals or general welfare. But the general welfare is a very broad category and includes the aesthetic appeal of a community, the value of scenic surroundings, and the preservation of environmental quality. So long as the purpose of a zoning or other police regulation appears to be within this broad category, its objective will be sustained. There must then be found a rational nexus between the means adopted in the ordinance and the objectives sought.

In the early days of zoning ordinances, zoning which in fact was enacted to promote aesthetic values had to be justified as somehow promoting health and safety. For example, laws prohibiting billboards were justified on the following grounds: that billboards create a traffic hazard by distracting motorists; that rubbish and garbage tend to accumulate near billboards; and that billboards provide a shield behind which criminals hide and immoral activities take place. Today a court probably would not engage in such patent rationalizations, but would concede that the purpose of such laws is to preserve property values by preventing discordant sights in an attractive, uncluttered community, and the regulations most likely would be sustained.

See: Maher v. City of New Orleans, 516 F.2d 1051 (5th Cir. 1975), rehearing denied 521 F.2d 815, certiorari denied 426 U.S. 905, 96 S.Ct. 2225, 48 L.Ed.2d 830; United Advertising Corp. v. Borough of Metuchen, 42 N.J. 1, 198 A.2d 447 (1964); Reid v. Architectural Bd. of Review of City of Cleveland Heights, 119 Ohio App. 67, 192 N.E.2d 74 (1963).

CASE 298:   City X has a population of about 10,000 people. Within the city limits are about 12½ square miles or 8000 acres of territory, most of which is farm land or unimproved acreage.   A is the owner of 60 acres within the city which are unimproved.   On the north of this property is a railroad, on the south an arterial highway and on the east and west are residential sections.   A comprehensive zoning ordinance passed by the city includes A's property and provides for the regulating of trades, industries, apartment houses, two-family houses, single family houses, the sizes of the lots to be built upon, the size and height of buildings, etc.   The ordinance specifically divides A's property into use zones.   Zone 1 is restricted to use for single family dwellings, public parks, water towers and reservoirs, street railway passenger stations and rights of way, and farming.   Zone 2 includes the uses under Zone 1 and in addition, use for two family dwellings.   Zone 3 includes the uses under Zones 1 and 2 and in addition, use for apartment houses, hotels, schools, churches, public libraries, museums, private clubs, hospitals, sanitariums, public playgrounds, recreation buildings, city hall and courthouse.   Zone 6 includes the uses under the preceding 5 zones and in addition, use for sewage disposal, incinerators, junk yards, aviation fields, cemeteries and other uses not included in the other 5 zones.   These classes of uses covered the various areas within A's 60 acres.

A sues to enjoin the enforcement of any of the provisions of this zoning ordinance contending that to do so would take his property without due process of law and would deny him equal protection of the laws under the 14th Amendment of the U. S. Constitution.   A specifically contends that the zoning ordinance prohibits the use of his property for industrial purposes for which it is peculiarly adapted, that it lies squarely in the path of industrial development from the large city nearby, and that the enforcement of the ordinance will depreciate his property from $10,000.00 per acre to $2,500.00 per acre.   Should the injunction issue?

Answer and Analysis

The answer is no.   Zoning ordinances in this country appeared shortly after the year 1900.   They began with the development of complex urban problems caused by concentrations of population in great metropolitan centers.   For the general welfare freedom in the use of privately owned property is required to be restricted.   Restrictions which are considered arbitrary and oppressive in one generation may be considered quite reasonable in a later period of our development.   Constitutional guaranties must be construed to meet the new conditions in an ever changing world.   The ordinance under discussion must be valid or invalid under the police power of the state.   If it bears some relation to the public health, safety, morals or general welfare and is reasonable in its application, then it cannot offend the constitutional guaranties of the U. S. Constitution. But if it is arbitrary and unreasonable in its operation, then it must fail. Between the uses permitted by the ordinance under the class designated Zone 1 and the uses under Zone 6 there is a broad and readily determined line. It is obviously reasonable to distinguish the use of property for a single family dwelling on one hand from the use of property for a sewage disposal plant on the other. If the power exists to exclude such industrial pursuits as junkyards, aviation fields and factories from residential areas, then it would seem immaterial that the exercise of such power will cause the flow of industrial development in a different direction than it would otherwise take as the plaintiff argues.

But the validity of this ordinance must be determined in the distinction or classification drawn between the use permitted in Zone 1 and that permitted in Zone 2 where the differences become far more minute than those considered above. In other words this ordinance is quite valid if there is a proper justification under the police power for excluding apartment houses, retail stores and shops from the area where single family dwelling houses are permitted. Is the use of an area for an apartment house or for retail stores and shops sufficiently different than the use of the same area for a single family dwelling house as to justify placing it in a different classification under the police power? The validity of the ordinance depends on the answer to this question.

Some differences are both obvious and important. In a residential area most of the houses do not exceed two stories in height and many are only one story high. The houses are usually set well back from the street leaving plenty of open space in front of each house. Seldom does a single family have more than two automobiles to be parked in the street. These conditions constitute a distinct contribution to the safety and health of the neighborhood. There is a minimum of automobile traffic in the streets. The hazards which accompany heavy street traffic are diminished, and the number of accidents resulting therefrom are fewer than where traffic is more congested. The height of the houses permit the sun to shine in and around the living area without being cut off by higher buildings which surely makes a more healthful atmosphere in which to rear children. Around single dwelling units there is room for grass, trees and shrubbery which add to the healthful atmosphere for family life to say nothing of the use of such space for family play and recreation.

When the apartment house moves into an area it is a well known fact that its presence constitutes a blight over the immediate territory for purpose of single dwelling houses. With its coming there appear long rows of automobiles parked solidly along the curbs on both sides of the street. Traffic immediately becomes congested and accidents increase. Such buildings are built at such height as to prevent sunshine from reaching the ground in any direction nearby. Little room is left either in front or on the sides of apartment houses for sunshine, grass, shrubbery or trees and very often there is not even any uncovered space in the rear of such structures. They are built for commercial purposes and to be most economically productive they are constructed to cover the entire area available for building purposes. It may be added that to segregate single dwelling houses from apartment houses makes it possible for fire protection to be provided more economically and effectively because different fire apparatus is necessary to serve an area devoted exclusively to one type of structure from that which serves larger and higher buildings.

What has been said concerning traffic and safety surrounding apartment houses can generally be said also of retail stores and shops in a neighborhood. With the coming of delivery trucks and the cars of customers, the traffic in the community becomes more intensified with accompanying confusion and accidents. From what has been said it is fairly clear that the public health, safety and general welfare may be affected quite differently in an area devoted strictly to single family dwelling houses than in one occupied by apartment houses and retail shops, stores and similar establishments. At least it cannot be said that the distinction and classification is wholly arbitrary and unreasonable. And unless that can be said an ordinance or statute cannot be declared unconstitutional and void. The legislative determination that a certain classification should be made is not conclusive as to its justification under the police power but it is entitled to great weight and when the matter is fairly debatable then the statute should be upheld. Thus, this statute having a reasonable relationship to the public health, safety and general welfare, and not being arbitrary or unreasonable, is a valid legislative exercise of the police power and is not unconstitutional. Hence, the injunction should be denied and the damage to A, if any, is damnum absque injuria. Such is the price of living and owning property in a civilized community. It should be added that the wisdom of such ordinances is not a question for the courts to determine. The question for the judiciary is simply the determination of whether the legislative enactment is within the power of the law making branch. Having determined that question the task of the court is complete. See the leading case of Village of Euclid v. Ambler Realty Co., 272 U.S. 365, 47 S.Ct. 114, 71 L.Ed. 303, 54 A.L.R. 1016 (1926); Powell, ¶¶ 867, 868.

CASE 299: The City of X passed a comprehensive zoning ordinance. Within the city are two intersecting streets, Y and Z. Y Street runs east and west and Z Street north and south. Southeast of the intersection of these two streets and bordering both of them, A owns Blackacre which extends 400 feet along the south side of Y Street and 300 feet along the east side of Z Street. The zoning ordinance classifies the area north of Y Street and west of Z Street and the west 100 feet of A's Blackacre as "residential" and restricts such property to use for residence purposes. Adjacent to Blackacre on the south there is a large Ford Motor Company assembly plant. Immediately to the southeast of Blackacre are the tracks of the J & B Ry. Company and a soap factory. The east 300 feet of A's Blackacre is left unrestricted. Thus A's west 100 feet of Blackacre is left bounded on the north by Y Street with residences beyond, on the east by an unrestricted area 300 feet wide beyond which are railroad tracks and a soap factory, on the south by the Ford Motor Company's assembly plant and on the west by Z Street with residences beyond. This is the tract which the ordinance classifies and restricts to residential use only.

A seeks an injunction against City X to prevent the enforcement of such zoning ordinance as to the west 100 feet of Blackacre claiming such would take his property without due process. The case was submitted to a Master in Chancery who held a hearing and viewed the premises and made findings of fact including this, "No practical use can be made of the west 100 feet of Blackacre for residential purposes because there could be no adequate return on any investment so made. Zoning such property for residential purposes will not promote the health, safety, and general welfare of the inhabitants of that part of X City, taking into account the natural development and the character of the district in which it is located". Should the injunction issue?

Answer and Analysis

The answer is yes. The legislative determination of zone boundaries is not conclusive but should be given great weight by the courts. Further, a zoning ordinance or statute must find its justification in the police power of the state. To be valid it must bear some substantial relation to the protection of the public health, safety, morals and general welfare, and be reasonable in its operation. And the court will not hold such a statute or ordinance invalid unless it is clearly arbitrary and unreasonable in its operation. It should be noticed in our case that A does not attack the validity of the ordinance as such. It is his contention that although the ordinance itself is valid, when it is applied to his particular property, the west 100 feet of his Blackacre, and limits the use of that property to residential purposes only, it is clearly arbitrary, unreasonable and constitutes a taking of his property without due process of law under the 14th Amendment to the United States Constitution. It does not appear why the ordinance did not continue with its line along Y Street to Z Street and then south along Z Street, thus making these two Streets the boundary between residential and non-residential properties. The inclusion of A's property seems quite unnecessary to the zoning scheme.

But it does appear in the Master's findings that A's property which is zoned for residence purposes simply cannot be used for such on an economic basis. Such finding would not necessarily be conclusive if the property could be used for some other proper purpose. But if property can be used for one purpose only and that use will not pay, then the effect of the ordinance is practically to nullify any use at all. That is certainly taking property. Further, here is a piece of land zoned for residence purposes only, when on two sides it is bounded by properties already being used for businesses and a small intervening tract which is unrestricted. On the other two sides are streets. Who would be interested in buying such property on which to build his dwelling house, or be willing to invest in building a dwelling house thereon in such a location? Are the people in the neighborhood any safer or more secure because that corner lot is zoned for residence than for business like the property around it? Is the community made any healthier because that corner lot is to be used for a residence rather than for a business? Are the morals of the community better protected because there is to be a dwelling house on that corner rather than a business house? Is the general welfare improved by such requirement? Of course, the Master's findings determined all of these questions in the negative and unless there is some reason for another hearing such findings should be approved and adopted by the Court.

Hence, it clearly appears that there is no substantial relation between the protection of the public health, safety, morals and general welfare and the application of this ordinance to A's west 100 feet of Blackacre. Furthermore, it clearly appears that to apply such ordinance to such property is arbitrary and unreasonable and results in a taking of A's property contrary to the 14th Amendment of the United States Constitution. Therefore, the injunction should issue and A should be able to use the west 100 feet of Blackacre without regard to the provisions of the zoning ordinance. See Nectow v. City of Cambridge, 277 U.S. 183, 48 S.Ct. 447, 72 L.Ed. 842 (1928).

Special Note

Normally, a property owner challenges a zoning ordinance by seeking either (a) a declaratory judgment that the ordinance is an invalid exercise of the police power, or (b) an injunction to prevent the enforcement of the ordinance to a particular parcel. A third remedy is a suit in "inverse condemnation." This action asks the court to declare that a zoning regulation by restricting the use of property, has to that extent effected a "taking" of property for which just compensation must be paid. This suit does not ask the court to roll back the regulation; it asks the court to recognize the regulation as, in effect, a form of eminent domain.

The courts, however, have generally rejected the inverse condemnation action as a remedy for zoning. Most courts say that inverse condemnation suits will lie only for an actual, physical invasion or physical damage to the property which displaces the property owner. (See, e. g., Cases 153 and 154 supra). The suit will not lie for mere regulation restricting the use of land, even if that restriction causes the land to suffer a severe diminution in its market value. See HFH, Ltd. v. Superior Court of Los Angeles County, 15 Cal.3d 508, 125 Cal.Rptr. 365, 542 P.2d 237 (1975); Agins v. City of Tiburon, 24 Cal.3d 266, 157 Cal.Rptr. 372, 598 P.2d 25 (1979), probable jurisdiction noted 444 U.S. 1011, 100 S.Ct. 658, 62 L.Ed.2d 639 (1980). See also Estuary Properties, Inc. v. Askew, 381 So.2d 1126 (Fla. 1st D.C. A.1979), involving a large development and environmentally sensitive land and water, holding that denial of the requested permit would amount to a taking without compensation, and the case was remanded to the Adjudicatory Commission either to grant the permit or commence condemnation proceedings.

CASE 300: A is the owner and operator of a sanitarium which cares for persons with mild nervous diseases located on A's Blackacre which is outside the city limits of X City. The City of X then extends its boundaries and includes Blackacre in the annexation. The City then passes a zoning ordinance which prohibits the operation of any sanitarium for nervous diseases within the annexed area. A seeks an injunction against the enforcement of the ordinance as to his business contending it would be a taking of his property without due process of law. Should the injunction issue?

Answers and Analyses

The answer is yes. This set of facts makes it imperative that five concepts be distinctly understood.

(1) A nuisance involves the use of property in such a way that it is injurious either to the public or to other property owners. The use may be hazardous or inherently harmful or it may be harmful only because it is a right thing in a wrong place, improperly located. In any event a nuisance may be abated without compensation because it is a nuisance.

(2) The principle underlying zoning is much broader and more comprehensive than nuisance. A perfectly innocuous business involving no harmful effects and no hazard may be prohibited under a proper zoning ordinance even though it has minimal or no effect on the public health, safety or morals. Such prohibition is justified under the broader term "general welfare" and constitutes a sufficiently valid reason for prohibiting an apartment house or a retail store from being operated in a zone restricted to single dwelling houses. The fact that there may be other distinctions based on health and safety does not prevent the operation of this general principle. Such a zoning ordinance may be enforced under the police power without compensation to the landowner simply because it is a case where the individual's interests must give way to the paramount general welfare. And, indeed, this may involve not only inconvenience or slight loss to the landowner; it may even be a real hardship to him. But if the zon-

ing ordinance constitutes a proper exercise of the police power of the state it is, as to the landowner, damnum absque injuria, for which no compensation can be had.

(3) When the use of property is such that it does not constitute a nuisance and a zoning ordinance or statute undertakes to regulate it and such regulation is clearly arbitrary and unreasonable, then such regulation constitutes a "taking" of the property and just compensation must be paid for such. The ordinance or statute is then void and unconstitutional as to the use of that particular property unless condemnation proceedings are had and just compensation is paid.

(4) An ordinance or statute is usually only prospective in its operation. That means it is to be effective only as to the future. It is to affect only acts, operations or use of property which take place after the ordinance or statute is passed. Such a legislative enactment may be quite valid in its prospective operation and quite invalid if it is applied retrospectively.

(5) If a zoning ordinance or statute is intended to be effective retrospectively, that is, effective as to past and present conditions or operations or use of property, it may be invalid as to a use of property which is not a nuisance, and quite valid as to a use of property which is a nuisance. In this latter case the effect of the ordinance or statute may be not only drastic, it may actually destroy an existing business. For example, suppose M is in the business of manufacturing dynamite on a block of land in a rural district. Residences move in all around the block occupied by M's business. If such business has now become a public nuisance it may be completely destroyed by the enforcement of the retroactive terms of an ordinance or statute.

Applying the above propositions to our set of facts it should be noticed that A's sanitarium is an existing and legitimate business. It is neither a nuisance nor is it improperly operated as far as the facts show. By first annexing Blackacre to City X and then passing the zoning ordinance prohibiting sanitariums in the annexed area, City X has said to A this, "Your sanitarium is now in City X. Your sanitarium is hereby destroyed". If this result were permitted to stand, irresponsible city councils or other legislative bodies could legally reduce constitutional guaranties. Therefore the ordinance must fail. A zoning ordinance prospectively may prevent the use of land as a sanitarium but when such business is already in existence a zoning ordinance cannot, unless such business be a nuisance, destroy such business. The ordinance in our case is unconstitutional and void as it applies to A's sanitarium and the injunction should issue in A's favor. See Jones v. City of Los Angeles, 211 Cal. 304, 295 P. 14 (1931); and a case which has nothing to recommend it, State ex rel. Dema Realty Co. v. McDonald, 168 La. 172, 121 So. 613 (1929); 35 Mich.L.R. 644.

Note

Suppose all of the land in a given block is devoted to presently operating businesses. Between two of these business establishments is A's vacant lot. A city ordinance zones A's vacant lot strictly for residential purposes. This would virtually make A's lot totally unusable. As applied to A's lot the ordinance would be a taking of A's property without due process, unconstitutional and void. There is no difference in principle between making vacant land totally unusable and the destruction of an existing business. See Arverne Bay Constr. Co. v. Thatcher, 278 N.Y. 222, 15 N.E.2d 587, 117 A.L.R. 1110 (1938).

Special Note on Nonconforming Uses

As the above case illustrates, the dilemma presented by the nonconforming use in existence at the time of the enactment or amendment of the zoning ordinance presents a difficult problem. To require the immediate cessation of such activity which does not constitute a nuisance appears arbitrary, unreasonable and confiscatory to most individuals, and hence would be unconstitutional. On the other hand, to permit such use to continue indefinitely, to expand and to improve facilities and operations, would be most unfair and detrimental to neighbors and competitors. The continuance of a business as a nonconforming use in an area where no competitors are allowed gives such an owner the advantage of a legally sanctioned monopoly contrary to our instincts and laws for free competition. Such use also is detrimental to the neighbors who wish it discontinued.

The result has been a compromise. Most newly adopted and amended zoning ordinances permit nonconforming uses to continue but with limitations that are designed to ensure their eventual or gradual elimination. Commonly employed devices include:

(a) the setting of a terminal date at which time they must cease and desist;

(b) the prevention of any resumption of such use when and if it has once ceased; and

(c) the curtailment or prevention of new constructions, alterations, enlargements, extensions or even repairs on structures devoted to such uses.

In short, the nonconforming use is regarded something like a necessary evil to be discouraged and eliminated as soon as possible. The validity of the regulations as to such uses is generally tested in the same manner as to the validity of zoning ordinances generally— reasonableness under all the circumstances. The owner or entrepreneur should not have his investment confiscated forthwith but should be given a reasonable opportunity to make a recovery thereof and to make plans for another location; his competitors should not be forced to watch him enjoy indefinitely a monopolistic or semimonopolistic position, and the conforming neighbors should not be compelled to withstand forever such objectionable use.

Amortization

The requirement that a nonconforming use cease within a certain time period is known as "amortization". The amortization of nonconforming uses does not constitute a taking so long as the time period is reasonable. A reasonable time for the elimination of nonconforming uses gives the owner an opportunity to make new plans. The loss he suffers, if any, is offset by the fact that he enjoys a monopoly position with respect to that use for as long as he remains.

Whether the amortization period is reasonable depends upon the facts in each particular case. Where the building itself is nonconforming, as opposed to merely the use of the building, a reasonable period would take into account the expected useful life of the building and may be 20 to 40 years. While an owner does not have the vested right to recoup his investment entirely, the amortization period should not be so short as to result in substantial loss. In determining whether the period is reasonable, a court should look to such factors as: initial capital investment; returns realized to date; life expectancy of the investment; and the existence or nonexistence of a lease obligation.

See: City of Los Angeles v. Gage, 127 Cal.App.2d 442, 274 P.2d 34 (1954); Harbison v. City of Buffalo, 4 N.Y.2d 553, 176 N.Y.S.2d 598, 152 N.E.2d 42 (1958); Modjeska Sign Studios, Inc. v. Berle, 43 N.Y.2d 468, 402 N.Y.S.2d 359, 373 N.E.2d 255 (1977). For an example of the minority view forbidding amortization, see Hoffmann v. Kinealy, 389 S.W.2d 745 (Mo.1965); Powell, ¶ 871.

———

CASE 301: City X passed a comprehensive zoning ordinance under which several blocks were zoned and restricted to single family residences. Many persons, including, A, B and C, built their individual dwelling houses in the restricted area. Through the middle of one block was a ravine into which surface water drained and disappeared as percolating water. The ravine was not more than 200 feet long and about 75 feet wide and the soil in the bottom was sandy and soft. D owned Blackacre which was a lot the exterior boundaries of which were almost coincident with the exterior boundaries of the ravine described. In other words, D owned the ravine in this area restricted by the zoning ordinance to single dwelling houses. D appeared before the zoning commission and sought permission to build an apartment house on his Blackacre, for the reason that the cost of constructing a foundation on the shifting or floating soil in the bottom of the ravine would be wholly prohibitive economically for a single dwelling house, whereas the necessary expenditure or investment could be made for the purpose of erecting an apartment house thereon. The zoning commission was convinced that the ordinance took D's property without due process and recommended to the city council that D's lot be excepted from the operation of the general zoning ordinance. The city council passed the necessary amendment permitting the building of an apartment house on Blackacre. A, B and C bring an action to enjoin D's building of the apartment house contending that they had depended on the continuation of the provisions of the zoning ordinance and had built their single dwelling houses in that area in reliance thereon. It appears that D's building will be carefully built and modern and will in no sense constitute a nuisance. Should the injunction issue?

Answer and Analysis

The answer is no.[1] All privately owned property is held subject to the police power which antedates the constitution. The power to zone emanates from the police power. Therefore, private property is held subject to the power to zone. There is no vested right under the police power or under zoning ordinances because what has been granted by the legislative body can also under proper exercise of the police power, be taken away. There is one possible exception to this principle. It pertains to the property of an owner. For example, A, B and C, in our case, having built their single family dwelling houses or having started to build such under the provisions of the zoning ordinance may have a vested right thereafter that their particular properties will not be hastily rezoned to their detriment. But these same persons, A, B and C, the plaintiffs in this case, have no vested right to have D's Blackacre remain zoned for residence purposes only. Indeed, it appears that the original ordinance might well have been void as it applied to D's Blackacre for the reason that it rendered such property useless and constituted a taking thereof without due process. Neither the courts nor the legislative bodies are in favor of or sympathetic to "spot zoning" which means zoning a small tract here and another one there without an overall plan. Such zoning usually works out very unfairly and inequitably, and therefore is usually invalid. But there are times as in the present case when such cannot be avoided. In the given set of facts the council having heard the evidence and being in a much better position than the court to determine how D's property should be zoned and its decision not appearing to be clearly arbitrary or unreasonable, the ordinance is valid and the injunction should be denied. See Eggebeen v. Sonnenburg, 239 Wis. 213, 1 N.W.2d 84, 138 A.L.R. 495 (1941); 38 Mich.L.R. 431.

Note 1

A number of issues suggested by case 301 are worthy of further attention.

(1) It should be noted that the case dealt with an amendment to the ordinance and not a granting of a variance. Thus, it involved *legislative* action and not an *administrative* procedure.

(2) The court stated that there are generally no vested rights in a particular zoning regulation, especially in the case of restrictions on

---

1. This case raises some interesting questions which are discussed in Note 1 following its report. The result itself, however, of upholding the amendment to the ordinance seems justified and is not questioned.

neighboring property. This may be true generally, but it can be misleading. Residents do have standing to challenge the validity of zoning changes on nearby property. See Frankland v. City of Lake Oswego, 267 Or. 452, 517 P.2d 1042 (1973), citing 3 Anderson, American Law of Zoning 636, § 23.11 (1968).

(3) The court noted that the ordinance before the amendment might have precluded all reasonable use of the property in question and, therefore, would have been void. Thus, it is suggested that an amendment, although limited to a small parcel, especially if it is reasonable, will not be void as spot zoning.

It does appear that the area involved was relatively small, and that the owner did encounter "practical difficulties and unnecessary hardship." Thus, it would seem that the administrative remedy of variance might be more suitable in a situation of this type. Even if the variance procedure should be preferred, it would not necessarily invalidate use of the amendatory powers. As long as the amended classification is reasonable and not arbitrary, discriminatory or confiscatory, and in accordance with the overall plan, it should be upheld.

(4) The court indulged in the presumption of validity because this change was brought about by the legislative process, and thus the presumption of validity applied, and the burden of proof was cast upon those attacking the ordinance to prove its unconstitutionality. This has generally been the approach, but recently some doubt has been raised as to its propriety in the case of amendemnts limited to specific and small areas. In Fasano v. Board of County Comm'rs, Case 295 supra, concerning an amendatory ordinance and the necessity of complying with the master plan, the court referred to such changes as quasi judicial. Thus, the burden of proof would seem to shift from the opponents of the change to prove that it was invalid, to those of the proponents of the change to prove that it was valid.

The issue is discussed, particularly as it relates to Michigan where the "new" approach was short lived, in Cunningham, Rezoning by Amendment As An Administrative or Quasi-Judicial Act: The "New Look in Michigan Zoning," 73 Mich.L.Rev. 1341 (1975); and Cunningham, Reflections on Stare Decisis In Michigan: The Rise And Fall of the "Rezoning As an Administrative Act" Doctrine, 75 Mich.L.Rev. 983 (1977).

Note 2—Spot Zoning Continued

Suppose A owns a parcel of land upon which he grows vegetables and operates a roadside stand. Although the land has been zoned residential, the owner successfully applies to the town council to change part of the land to a business district in order to erect a small shopping center. Since the action of the town council is not in furtherance of the general plan of zoning in the community, it cannot be sustained. The test to be applied in such cases is not the benefit to a particular individual or group of individuals, but rather the good of the community as a whole. See Kuehne v. Town of East Hartford, 136 Conn. 452, 72 A.2d 474 (1950).

See Gruber v. Raritan Twp., 39 N.J. 1, 186 A.2d 489 (Sup.Ct. 1962), for a case in which equitable estoppel was applied against the township on behalf of an owner who spent considerable money in developing his property in accordance with existing regulations before the enactment of zoning. The court indicated that a plan should be evolved by which the owner could recoup his investment.

CASE 302: State X passed a statute which empowered any city within the state to establish a "planning board" to draw up a master plan for zoning areas within the city and within areas adjacent to the city which bear essential relation to the planning for such city. Such master plan is for the purpose of directing the physical development of the city particularly in respect to the general location of streets, bridges, subways, playgrounds, parks, residential areas, zones for apartments, hotels, businesses and industrial establishments, for the purpose of conserving and promoting the public health, safety, morals and general welfare. When the planning board has adopted the master plan it is to present it to the city council, and when the council has adopted it, then it shall have the force of law and its administration is delegated to the planning board which may adopt rules and regulations for the purpose of putting the master plan ordinance into effect.

City Y by ordinance establishes a planning board. The planning board draws up and adopts a master plan and recommends its adoption to the city council which passes an ordinance adopting such master plan. The master plan zones one large area which we shall designate, Whiteacre, for residential purposes only. Within Whiteacre are many single lots containing about 5 acres each and on each of which is a large expensive mansion house. One of these tracts is Blackacre which contains 5 acres and in the center of which is an old mansion house which is totally unsafe for human habitation. A is the owner of Blackacre. He decides to raze the mansion house on his Blackacre and divide the area into 20 smaller lots. Each lot will contain one quarter of an acre, and will be approximately 70 feet wide and 150 feet long. On each lot A plans to build an inexpensive house which houses he will offer for sale to the public. He presents such plan to the planning board.

The board disapproves the plan for the sole reason that nearly all of the other property owners and residents of the residential area, Whiteacre, do not like it ar . are not in favor of it. A appeals to the courts seeking approval of his plan for developing Blackacre and contends that the statute authorizing a planning board and the adoption of a master plan by the board and City Y, is unconstitutional and takes his property without due process because the power to zone does not include the power to plan. He further contends that the disapproval of his plan based on the dislike of it by other residents in Whiteacre is arbitrary and unreasonable and wholly illegal. Should the court approve the action of the planning board?

Answer and Analysis

The answer is no. The first question to determine is the validity of the statute which empowered a city to create a planning board. The validity of the statute and planning board was upheld. The validity of planning is now so well established that the discussion thereon is omitted. See supra part 1 of this chapter for Planning generally.

The next question for consideration is that raised by the fact that the planning board, which is specifically given power to administer the master plan, simply abdicated its position and permitted the disapproval of A's plan for developing Blackacre to be determined or dictated by the residents of Whiteacre. This would seem to be a misunderstanding of its function by the planning board. Statutes and ordinances which leave to the discretion of a percentage of the residents of an area the determination as to whether or not a particular structure or business will be permitted to come into the zoned district, are usually held invalid on the ground that there are no standards set up by which the discretion of the residents is to be controlled or guided, and that without such standards any determination will or may be based entirely on whim and arbitrariness. But in this case it does not appear there is any statute or ordinance which permits the planning board to submit to the residents of any zoned district, including Whiteacre, the power to approve or disapprove any development plan. When the planning board left it to the whim of the residents of Whiteacre to approve or disapprove A's plan for developing Blackacre, and it was disapproved because they "did not like it", these acts were arbitrary, unreasonable and unconstitutional. They constituted a taking of A's property without due process of law.

There appears nothing in A's plan for developing Blackacre which offends the zoning master plan unless the 5 acre area comprising Blackacre is to be forever condemned to a single use for a single mansion house merely because other similar lots in the vicinity are so used, and that on the face of it is absurd. Had the board as a result of its own deliberations reached the conclusion that the general welfare of the community made it desirable or necessary to restrict population density in this whole area to a single family residence on each five acre tract, a different problem would be presented. Under the circumstances, however, the court should disapprove the action of the planning board. See Mansfield & Swett, Inc. v. Town of West Orange, 120 N.J.L. 145, 198 A. 225 (Sup.Ct.1938); Berman v. Parker, 348 U.S. 26, 75 S.Ct. 98, 99 L.Ed. 27 (1954).

CASE 303: Facts: Township X is a rapidly growing suburban area outside an old industrial city. Once entirely rural, the township has experienced sharp population growth as residential subdivisions have been developed. The township has almost no commercial or industrial property; virtually all the developed land is residential. The residential zoning ordinance permits only single family, detached dwellings on large lots. Attached townhouses, apartments and mobile homes are not allowed anywhere in Township X. As a result of these regulations, the average cost of housing in Township X is quite high and only upper and upper-middle income persons can afford to live there.

Meanwhile, the metropolitan region as a whole (city and suburbs) is experiencing a severe shortage of housing suitable for low and moderate income persons, such as apartments, townhouses and mobile homes. Such persons are effectively excluded from Township X. A group of such persons, who live in substandard housing in the city adjacent to Township X, bring an action to declare the ordinance totally invalid. Should the declaratory judgment issue?

Answer and Analysis

The answer is yes. A comprehensive zoning ordinance, to be valid, must promote the general welfare. But the question remains—whose welfare? May a municipality, in designing a zoning plan, consider only the welfare of those currently residing within its boundaries? In the circumstances of this case, the answer is no. Where a developing municipality is part of a larger metropolitan region, its zoning ordinance may have a substantial adverse impact upon persons who live beyond its borders in adjacent communities. Township X is not free to ignore these detrimental effects while pursuing only its narrow, parochial interests. A developing municipality may not, in effect, build a wall around itself to keep out people not adding favorably to the tax base. It cannot preclude the construction of low and moderate income housing merely because residents of such housing are expected to require a greater level of municipal services. A developing municipality must, by its land use regulations, make realistically available an appropriate variety and choice of housing, particularly multi-family housing. As a presumption, a developing municipality must permit the construction of its "fair share" of present and prospective regional needs for low and moderate income housing. The presumption may be rebutted, but the municipality has the burden of showing valid superseding reasons for more restrictive land use policies. Consequently, the zoning ordinance of Township X is invalid to the extent it is inconsistent with these obligations.

See: Southern Burlington County N. A. A. C. P. v. Township of Mount Laurel, 67 N.J. 151, 336 A.2d 713 (1975), appeal dismissed and certiorari denied, 423 U.S. 808, 96 S.Ct. 18, 46 L.Ed.2d 28 (1975); Oakwood at Madison, Inc. v. Township of Madison, 72 N.J. 481, 371 A.2d 1192 (1977); Pascack Ass'n, Ltd. v. Mayor and Council of Township of Washington, 74 N.J. 470, 379 A.2d 6 (1977).

See also: Berenson v. Town of New Castle, 38 N.Y.2d 102, 378 N.Y.S.2d 672, 341 N.E.2d 236 (1975); Gust v. Township of Canton, 342 Mich. 436, 70 N.W.2d 772 (1955), invalidating an ordinance which excluded trailer parks from an agricultural area.

CASE 304: Facts: Town X is a rapidly growing suburb on a fringe of a major metropolitan area. This disorderly development of residential subdivisions in Town X and neighboring suburbs has overwhelmed the ability of Town X to provide the roads, schools, sewers, parks and other municipal services necessary to serve the vastly increased population. To cope with this situation, Town X adopts a comprehensive plan to control development and discourage so-called urban sprawl. The plan does not change any zoning classifications. Rather, it limits the number of development or construction permits which will be granted annually. The number of permits is to be based on the availability of essential public services to serve the new residents. A land developer challenges the ordinance under the state and federal constitutions as being beyond the zoning power of the Town. Should the developer prevail?

Answer and Analysis

The answer is no. It is important to note that the plan does not discriminate on an impermissible basis; nor does it exclude only less expensive housing; nor does it impose any absolute limit on population growth or development. It is merely a plan to insure orderly community growth through sequential development of housing and public services. It is a bona fide effort to maximize population density consistent with orderly growth, and to achieve a balanced community dedicated to the efficient use of land. This type of decision is committed to the discretion of the legislature and will be upheld so long as reasonably related to the public welfare. See: Golden v. Planning Bd. of Town of Ramapo, 30 N.Y.2d 359, 334 N.Y.S.2d 138, 285 N.E.2d 291 (1972), appeal dismissed 409 U.S. 1003, 93 S.Ct. 436, 34 L.Ed.2d 294; and Associated Home Builders v. City of Livermore, 18 Cal.3d 582, 135 Cal.Rptr. 41, 557 P.2d 473 (1976).

A dissenting judge in Ramapo notes that the ordinance provides no incentive for Town X to actually construct the municipal services necessary to serve future residents. The present residents may simply decide not to vote for or pay for such services; the result would be to construct a mythical moat around the perimeter of the Town, excluding all but its fortunate current residents.

CASE 305: Blackacre is an irregular plot of land fronting on a road. Property on both sides of such road is zoned for commercial purposes to a depth of 150 feet. The adjoining area is zoned for residential purposes. Although the front of Blackacre is thereby zoned for commercial use to a depth of 150 feet, its larger rear section, extending from the road in places to a depth of 614 feet, is within a residential zone. A, the owner of Blackacre, seeks to erect a large roller skating rink upon both commercial and residential portions of his land. The zoning board of appeals granted a variance to A on the grounds of unnecessary hardship. Its reasons for doing so were: (1) that the land lies within two zones and the use requested is permitted by right in one of the zones; (2) that the only means of access to the residential portion is by crossing over the portion in the commercial zone; (3) that A could erect the roller skating rink within the commercial zone, but access to the rear portion would be obstructed thereby; and (4) that if the rink is built only upon the commercial portion, parking will have to be in streets in the vicinity causing a traffic problem. A further contends that he could not create a street crossing the commercial portion to the residential portion because of the width and grade required for a village street. A group of neighboring owners of residential property appeal to the courts. Should the board's ruling be overturned?

Answer and Analysis

The answer is yes. The purpose of a variance is to create a safety valve under the control of a board of appeals, which may relieve an individual property owner laboring under restrictions to which no valid general objection may be made. But before such a variance may be granted, it must be shown that: (1) the land in question cannot yield a reasonable return if used only for a purpose allowed in that zone; (2) that the owner's problem is due to unique circumstances and not to general conditions in the neighborhood which may reflect the unreasonableness of the zoning ordinance; and (3) that the use to be authorized by the variance will not alter the essential character of the locality. As to the first requirement, no proof was presented showing that Blackacre may not be reasonably used in conformity with the residential restriction. Another use of the commercial property or a rearrangement of the rink building confined to the commercial portion would appear to leave ample space for a village street. Thus, if the property were usable as zoned, it should yield a fair return. As to the second requirement other owners of property along the road may also have rear portions without direct access to the streets in the residential area. If this is a hardship to them also, then the vice is the legislation itself, not this particular application thereof. As to the third requirement, piecemeal exemption will ultimately change the character of the neighborhood heretofore devoted to residential purposes, since the commercial zone would be extended several hundred feet beyond its present 150 foot limit. Therefore, the determination of the board of appeals is annulled. See Otto v. Steinhilber, 282 N.Y. 71, 24 N.E.2d 851 (1939).

CASE 306: The board of supervisors of City A passed an ordinance which amended its zoning ordinance to provide for a new district called a limited industrial district. The ordinance provides that upon submission of a proper plan with a minimum size of 25 acres, adequate parking space, off-street loading areas, etc., the board of supervisors may permit the use of the land for light industry. The board, however, reserves the right to prescribe particular requirements or other conditions on the owner. Public hearings on the matter as well as a recommendation by the planning commission are also required. The ordinance, however, does not delineate the boundaries of those specific areas within the district. When owner B applied to the board under the above procedure for authorization to build a sewage treatment plant, 300 property owners objected. Nevertheless, the authorization was granted. Residents C and D appeal to the courts on the grounds that the ordinance is unconstitutional and failed to conform to the enabling legislation, seeking to enjoin the board from enforcing the statute. Should the injunction issue?

Answer and Analysis

The answer to the case herein discussed is yes, but the reader is CAUTIONED that the case probably represents the minority view on "floating zones." Flexibility in zoning and land use control is becoming a common practice. See NOTE following this case for contrary holdings and for a brief explanation of a P.U.D.

The reasoning of the *Eves* case, infra, is as follows: the enabling legislation prescribed that the zoning ordinances passed should conform to a comprehensive plan of development. The city supervisors have a duty to implement the comprehensive plan by enacting zoning regulations in accordance therewith. The light industrial district contemplated by the ordinance to be determined on a case by case basis obviously indicates that there was no orderly plan of particular land use. Under this system personal predilections, affluence, or political power could sway zoning permits. Further, it would allow piecemeal placement of light industry in differently zoned areas; and it would give no notice to property owners of the future character of the neighborhood. Under the flexible selective zoning scheme changes would be made not by a specialized body of planners, but by a legislative body without sufficient objective standards for the exercise of its judgment. If such a system were held valid, court review would be limited only to ascertaining whether each legislative act of amending the zoning map by the supervisors was not arbitrary, capricious, or unreasonable. The legislature would have provided for zoning by individual solicitation more clearly if it had meant to do so. See Eves v. Zoning Bd. of Adjustment, 401 Pa. 211, 164 A.2d 7 (1960).

The Pennsylvania Supreme Court is said to have retreated from the *Eaves* case in Donahue v. Zoning Board of Adjustment of Whitemarsh Township, 412 Pa. 332, 194 A.2d 610 (1963). Statutory changes may also have lessened the significance of *Eaves*.

Note

The probable majority view on "floating" zones is illustrated by the following:

The city passed a zoning amendment which permitted multiple dwellings for not more than 15 families on minimum sites of 10 acres anywhere in the village upon approval in the form of a further amendment to the zoning map. When a 10 acre tract was subsequently rezoned pursuant to the amendment, an action was brought by a nearby resident to have the amendments declared invalid. The amendment was upheld since the city's plan contemplated an acute housing shortage, lightening tax loads of small homeowners, and developing otherwise unmarketable and decaying property. If an ordinance is enacted in accordance with a comprehensive zoning plan, it is not spot zoning. The city could have passed an amendment to existing ordinances to allow the erection of garden apartments in all residential areas and the result would have been identical and clearly proper. See Rodgers v. Village of Tarrytown, 302 N.Y. 115, 96 N.E. 2d 731 (1951). See also: Huff v. Board of Zoning Appeals, 214 Md. 48, 133 A.2d 83 (1957).

The PUD, or Planned Unit Development, refers to a large area zoned for a number of different uses with the emphasis on density rather than on specific restrictions on each parcel of land in the area. The objective is a self contained community with the ordinance emphasizing percentages rather than specific regulations. The developer, with the approval and cooperation of the planning commission or other appropriate agency, then promulgates specific plans for the various areas. See Cheney v. Village 2 at New Hope, Inc., 429 Pa. 626, 241 A.2d 81 (1968), upholding a PUD classification; Krasnowiecki, Planned Unit Development: A Challenge to Established Theory and Practice of Land Use Control, 114 U.Pa.L.Rev. 47 (1965); Haar & Hering, The Lower Gwynedd Township Case: Too Flexible Zoning or an Inflexible Judiciary? 74 Harv.L.Rev. 1552 (1961); Reno, Non-Euclidian Zoning: The Uses of the Floating Zone, 23 Md.L.Rev. 105 (1963).

CASE 307: Corporation X obtained an option to purchase a tract of land known as Blackacre and petitioned the town council to rezone the parcel to permit a limited manufacturing use. After receiving a report from the city's planning consultant, the town council voted to approve the petition. In the interim, X in consultation with the planning consultant had agreed to certain restrictions to be recorded in its deed to the property to remain in effect for thirty years. These included a thirty-year option to purchase a thirty-acre strip to be given to the city thereby giving the city a means of enforcing the restrictions; limitation of floor area of the buildings, set back lines, height; providing for a buffer zone between the plant and the neighboring residential district; and regulation of signs and lighting. A memorandum incorporating the tentative deed restrictions was presented to the town council thereafter. An ordinance was then enacted which approved the petition of X as modified. Two weeks later, X took title to the parcel and executed its option agreement with the city. Both were properly recorded. Landowners now seek to have the courts declare the amendment invalid. Should the landowners prevail?

Answer and Analysis

The answer is no. In several jurisdictions votes to rezone on the express condition that the owner impose restrictions—referred to as contract zoning—have been held invalid. The basis for such rule is that it amounts to spot zoning since it is not in accordance with a comprehensive plan. Although legislation by contract is invalid, the form of the matter must control. The induced voluntary action of X imposed the option/restriction, not the vote of the town council. The parcel, as restricted, was zoned for limited manufacturing. That was an appropriate and untainted exercise of the zoning power in both substance and form. The action was in the best interests of the city and inoffensive to public policy. There was no lack of uniformity or failure to conform to the comprehensive zoning plan. Requirements of uniformity and conformity to a plan do not mean that there must be identification of every relevant aspect in areas given the same zoning classification. The actions of the town council together with the planning consultant in encouraging the imposition of restrictions and acceptance of the option was extrastatutory, but nevertheless, proper activity. It should be stressed that this activity was precedent to the exercise of the zoning power, not the exercise thereof. See Sylvania Elec. Products, Inc. v. City of Newton, 344 Mass. 428, 183 N.E.2d 118 (1962).

Note

A city cannot contract away its exercise of the police power. Therefore, a zoning ordinance is invalid which by its terms is contingent upon the subsequent execution of a contract with private parties. If each parcel of property were zoned on the basis of variables that could enter into private contracts, then the whole scheme of community planning would collapse. The residential owner would always be subject to commercial encroachment, since no genuine standards would remain. Uniformity would be destroyed by individual agreements. See Hartnett v. Austin, 93 So.2d 86 (Fla.1956).

CASE 308: Facts: City X has an ordinance requiring land subdividers to dedicate land for park or recreational purposes as a condition to receiving approval of the subdivision map. If the dedication of land is not feasible, the payment of a fee is required instead. The amount of the land or fee, as the case may be, which the ordinance requires, is proportional to the number of persons who would reside in the new subdivision.

A group of land developers argue that the ordinance violates due process by depriving them of their property without compensation. They claim that City X is using the subdivision map as a substitute for eminent domain, since the parkland dedicated would be enjoyed by all citizens of the city and not just by residents of the new subdivision. Should the land developers prevail?

Answer and Analysis

The answer is no. Most states have sustained the power of municipalities to require developers to dedicate land for a park, school or other public purpose. Courts require, however, that certain constitutional safeguards limit and accompany the exaction. Foremost among these is the requirement that the amount of land dedicated bear a reasonable relationship to the expected use of the facilities by future residents of the subdivision. For example, the City X regulation established a ratio of two and one-half acres of park land for each 1,000 new residents. The dedicated park land need not be exclusively reserved to subdivision residents. A municipality could not, however, demand dedication in a way that is arbitrary, discriminatory, or subject to the discretion of city officials. For example, a city could not require dedication of land for a major highway from those properties which happened to lie in its path, while requiring no dedication from other properties. See: Associated Home Builders of the Greater East Bay, Inc. v. City of Walnut Creek, 4 Cal.3d 633, 94 Cal.Rptr. 630, 484 P.2d 606 (1971), appeal dismissed 404 U.S. 878, 92 S.Ct. 202, 30 L.Ed.2d 159; Jenad, Inc. v. Village of Scarsdale, 18 N.Y.2d 78, 271 N.Y.S.2d 955, 218 N.E.2d 673 (1966); Jordan v. Village of Menomonee Falls, 28 Wis.2d 608, 137 N.W.2d 442 (1965), appeal dismissed 385 U.S. 4, 87 S.Ct. 36, 17 L.Ed.2d 3.

Note

The next several cases relate to the relationship between zoning and certain constitutional and personal rights.

CASE 309: Facts: Village X is a small community of 220 homes adjacent to a large state university campus. Its entire area is restricted to single family detached houses. The zoning ordinance prohibits occupancy of any house by more than two persons not related by blood, adoption or marriage. A owns a house in Village X which he leased to two students at the university. Later, four other students moved in; none of the six is related to the other by blood, adoption or marriage. Village X orders A to remedy the violation. A and his tenants bring an action to declare the ordinance invalid on the grounds that it violates constitutionally protected freedoms. Should the landlord and his tenants prevail?

Answer and Analysis

The answer is no. Although the Supreme Court has defined a "freedom of association" and a "right of privacy" as arising from the Bill of Rights, no such fundamental right is involved here. The ordinance involves a piece of economic and social regulation in an area committed to legislative discretion. The Village's action in permitting two unrelated persons to live together, but not three or more, is an example of discretionary line-drawing which will not be disturbed so long as it bears a rational relationship to a permissible state objective. It is permissible to lay out zones of quiet residential neighborhoods where yards are wide and people few, to secure the values of family living, solitude, little traffic and clean air.

See: Village of Belle Terre v. Boraas, 416 U.S. 1, 94 S.Ct. 1536, 39 L.Ed. 797 (1974).

A different situation is presented in City Y, which also restricts housing occupancy to a single family. However, City Y's occupancy ordinance defines "family" narrowly in a way that recognizes only a few categories of blood relationship as constituting a family. The ordinance was held to prohibit a grandmother from occupying the same household with her two grandsons (who were first cousins rather than brothers). Such an ordinance intrudes impermissibly upon the freedom of personal choice in matters of marriage and family life protected by the Fourteenth Amendment. A housing ordinance may not limit the term "family" to the so-called nuclear family, but must respect the venerable tradition of uncles, aunts, cousins and especially grandparents sharing the same household with parents and children.

See: Moore v. City of East Cleveland, 431 U.S. 494, 97 S.Ct. 1932, 52 L.Ed. 531 (1977).

CASE 310: Facts: Village X is a large, rapidly growing suburb outside a major city. Virtually all the residential land is zoned for single family detached houses. A owns a parcel of vacant land in Village X. A agrees to sell a portion of its property to a developer for the purpose of constructing low and moderate income housing under a program subsidized by the federal government.

All federally-assisted housing must be marketed under an affirmative action program designed to assure that the housing is racially integrated. Village X presently has only 27 blacks among its 64,000 residents. By contrast, blacks number over 20% of the metropolitan area as a whole, and constitute 40% of those area residents who would be eligible to become tenants in the project.

The sale is contingent upon obtaining zoning approval. Village X denies the zoning change on the grounds that it would be inconsistent with the single family character of the overall zoning plan, and would cause a measurable drop in the market value of the surrounding property. The developer sues Village X, arguing that the refusal to rezone was unconstitutional because it was motivated by a desire to exclude blacks, and that in any event it had the effect of disproportionately excluding blacks from residing in Village X. Should the developer prevail?

Answer and Analysis

The answer is no under the Equal Protection Clause of the Fourteenth Amendment, but yes under the Fair Housing Act. The court first decided that the developer failed to sustain its burden of proving that Village X was motivated by racial discrimination. The court found as a fact that the Village acted from a desire to protect property values and the integrity of the zoning plan. Consequently, no case can be made out under the Fourteenth Amendment alone. Proof of racially discriminatory intent or purpose is required to show a violation of the Equal Protection Clause.

But the Fair Housing Act of 1968 (Title VIII of the Civil Rights Act of 1968, 42 U.S.C.A. § 3601 et seq.) imposes a national mandate for fair housing practices which goes far beyond minimum constitutional requirements. The Act was passed pursuant to Congress's power under the Thirteenth Amendment to eliminate the badges and incidents of slavery. Under the Fair Housing Act, a plaintiff need not even allege that the decision was racially motivated. He makes out a prima facie case by showing that the government decision has an adverse impact upon a racial minority that is disproportionate to the impact upon the general population. The burden then shifts to the governmental defendant to prove that its action was necessary to promote a compelling governmental interest.

In this case, the plaintiffs showed that the zoning decision had a disproportionate impact upon the blacks who would be potential tenants of the housing project. Consequently, the burden shifts to the government to defend its action. If Village X were to show that other tracts within the village were both properly zoned and suitable for integrated housing, the Village would probably sustain its burden. The Village may not, however, enforce zoning policies that effectively foreclose the construction of any low cost housing within its corporate boundaries.

The governmental interests asserted by the Village for such a prohibition were: (1) to avoid road congestion; (2) to prevent overcrowding of schools; and (3) to prevent devaluation of adjacent single family homes. The Village would have to prove, however, (1) that these interests are in fact futhered by the zoning ordinance; (2) that they are substantial enough to outweigh the private detriment caused; and (3) that no less drastic alternatives are available to achieve the same objectives. Since the Village failed to sustain this burden, the zoning ordinance cannot be enforced against the proposed housing project. See: Village of Arlington Heights v. Metropolitan Housing Dev. Corp., 429 U.S. 252, 97 S.Ct. 555, 50 L.Ed.2d 450 (1977), on remand at 558 F.2d 1283 (7th Cir. 1977), certiorari denied 434 U.S. 1025, 98 S.Ct. 752, 54 L.Ed.2d 772 (1978), on further remand at 469 F.Supp. 836 (N.D.Ill.1979). See also United States v. City of Black Jack, Mo., 508 F.2d 1179 (8th Cir. 1974), certiorari denied 422 U.S. 1042, 95 S.Ct. 2656, 45 L.Ed.2d 694 (1975) rehearing denied 423 U.S. 884, 96 S.Ct. 158, 46 L.Ed.2d 115.

CASE 311: Facts: A is the owner of a mansion in an exclusive neighborhood of City X zoned for single family residential purposes. A is also a member of the Ethiopian Zion Coptic Church, whose members smoke marijuana as an integral part of their religious ritual. At A's invitation, about 30 members of the Church gather at the mansion three times daily to participate in religious worship, which includes praying, loud chanting, and heavy smoking of marijuana. City X seeks an injunction to prohibit the use of the property as a church and to prohibit the smoking of marijuana on the property. In defense, A argues that the activities are protected by the First Amendment right of free exercise of religion, and consequently the zoning ordinance cannot be enforced against her. Should the injunction issue?

Answer and Analysis

The answer is yes. The court first found as a fact that the Ethiopian Coptic Church is a bonafide religion protected by the First Amendment, and that the Church has regularly used marijuana as a sacrament for hundreds of years. The court was even willing to concede that such use of marijuana, if confined strictly to religious worship, would be privileged by the First Amendment for the same reasons that the use of peyote by Navajo Indians was held to be so privileged. However, the facts showed that the use of marijuana was not restricted, either to church services or to church members, but was smoked continually throughout the day and night and was freely shared with casual visitors.

Furthermore, religious worship is not immune from reasonable zoning regulation merely because it enjoys First Amendment protection. Unquestionably, a zoning ordinance can reasonably regulate the location of churches so long as it does not prohibit or burden their existence. In this case, A knew the property was zoned residential before she purchased it for church purposes; further, she did not try to obtain an exception or variance. There is no showing that the ordinance unreasonably burdens the exercise of religion and it will therefore be enforced. See Town v. State ex rel. Reno, 377 So.2d 648 (Fla.1979).

––––––––

Note

The following case is somewhat of a review to illustrate a clear limitation on the zoning power.

CASE 312: The A Company owns a residential complex in City X which includes 10 large apartment buildings and two private parks maintained for the benefit of residents. The A Company threatened to erect, on each park, a building of the maximum size permitted by the existing zoning ordinance. To prevent this development, the zoning board of City X approved an amendment designating the two private parks as a "Special Park District" in which "only passive recreational uses are permitted." In addition, upon the mapping of the Special Park District, the parks would be required to be open to the public daily from 6:00 a. m. to 10:00 p. m. The A Company brings an action to declare the zoning amendment void as going beyond the permissible scope of the police power. Should the injunction issue?

Answer and Analysis

The answer is yes. At the outset, it should be noted that this is not a case like Case 300 where the zoning authority seeks to prohibit an existing use. On the contrary, the zoning is intended to *perpetuate* an existing use against the wishes of the property owner; it is intended to prohibit a prospective use. If the zoning is sustained, the owner will be deprived of the opportunity to redevelop the property to a higher-valued use.

That a zoning ordinance has the effect of reducing the market value of property is not, of itself, grounds for challenging its validity under due process. Many zoning ordinances have been upheld although they reduced the market value of land by over 50 percent. (See Case 298 supra). The market value of land may reflect its current use, or it may reflect the potential use after redevelopment. Case 300 illustrates that a landowner may have a vested right to continue an existing use, at least temporarily. The legality of restrictions on prospective uses is governed by a far looser standard. A landowner has no vested right to redevelop his land to a more profitable use or to the "highest and best use." He has only the legal right to make *some* reasonable productive use of the property. A parcel of vacant land may be bought and sold by speculators on the assumption that it is suitable for a 20-story apartment building. A rezoning of the property to permit only a 4-story apartment building would reduce the market value of the parcel to a small portion of its former value. Yet, assuming the zoning change was properly enacted and that it withstands the unreasonable, arbitrary and discriminatory attacks, the owner's due process rights have not been violated merely because the speculative market value has dropped. A reasonable income producing use of the property is still permitted.

But under the facts of this case, no such reasonable use has been left to the owner of the two private parks. The ordinance requires the two parcels to remain forever vacant. Further, the use of the two parks is no longer restricted to the residents of the adjoining apartments; instead the parks must be open to the public. Not only is the A Company deprived of any income producing use of the property, it is deprived of *any* reasonable private use at all. Consequently, this case presents the rare situation where zoning has gone too far and extends beyond what is permitted under the police power. The zoning is confiscatory and amounts to a taking of A's property. See Fred F. French Investing Co., Inc. v. City of New York, 39 N.Y.2d 587, 385 N.Y.S.2d 5, 350 N.E.2d 381 (1976); also the Arverne Bay Constr. Co. v. Thatcher, 278 N.Y. 222, 15 N.E.2d 587, 117 A.L.R. 1110 (1938).

A different situation is presented by Penn Central Transp. Co. v. City of New York, 438 U.S. 104, 98 S.Ct. 2646, 57 L.Ed.2d 631 (1978). Here the owner was permitted to continue a reasonable, valuable, income producing use of the property, but was forbidden to redevelop the property into an even more profitable use.

SUMMARY OF CASES IN CHAPTER XXVIII

1. PLANNING

Case 295. An official master or comprehensive plan when adopted by the legislative body is the basic and superior document regulating land use. All zoning regulations and ordinances must conform thereto. Subsequent changes in zoning regulations must be in conformity with the master plan.

Case 296. A master plan controls and has priority over then existing conflicting zoning ordinances. The plan is the basic document and the appropriate legislative body has the duty to make its zoning ordinances conform thereto. Ordinances conflicting with the plan are invalid, but more restrictive zoning ordinances may be valid as not being inconsistent therewith.

2. ZONING

Case 297. Zoning for aesthetic purposes is valid under broadened concepts of police power. Preservation of environmental quality and aesthetic appeal are legitimate objectives. Thus, denial of a permit to raze an old residence and substitute therefor a modern apartment house is not per se invalid as not being within the legitimate powers of the zoning authorities.

Case 298. An ordinance having a reasonable relationship to the public health, safety and general welfare is not unconstitutional. If the question is fairly debatable then the doubt is resolved in favor of validity. The classification of uses to which property may be put under a zoning ordinance is not conclusive but is entitled to great weight in the courts. Unless the court can say that an ordinance is clearly arbitrary and unreasonable it will be held constitutional and valid under the police power. An ordinance which limits the use of one zone to single family dwelling houses and excludes therefrom apartment houses, retail shops and stores is a reasonable classification and a valid exercise of the police power.

Case 299. Any zoning ordinance or statute must find its justification in the police power of the state. If such ordinance or statute bears a substantial relation to the protection of the public health, safety, morals and public welfare, and its operation is reasonable, it is valid. If, on the other hand such statute or ordinance bears no substantial relation to the public health, safety, morals or public welfare, or its operation is arbitrary and unreasonable, then it is unconstitutional and void. An ordinance in itself may be valid, but be quite invalid in its application to a specific fact situation.

Case 300. (1) A nuisance involves the use of property which is injurious to the public or other property owners and can be abated without compensation to the landowner. (2) The principle underlying zoning is much broader than nuisance and includes power to control the use of property which is neither hazardous nor affects the public health, safety or morals. Such control comes under the broader term, "general welfare". Such control may be exercised without any compensation to the injured landowner. (3) A zoning ordinance which undertakes to regulate an existing use of land which is not a nuisance, which regulation is arbitrary and unreasonable, constitutes a taking of the property and is unconstitutional and void as applied to that property. (4) A zoning ordinance or statute may be valid in its prospective operation and invalid as to retrospective operation. (5) A zoning ordinance may not in its retroactive operation destroy a presently existing business which is not a nuisance but it may in such operation destroy a nuisance. A zoning ordinance which makes vacant land totally unusable for any purpose is invalid as to that property.

Case 301. All privately owned land is held subject to the police power and is therefore subject to the zoning power properly exercised. No one has a vested right in the exercise of the police power or zoning power thereunder, and amendments are foreseeable. However, if A builds a house in a zone restricted to residences and complies with the ordinance, or he has started to build such, then he has a vested right that his property shall not be hastily rezoned to his detriment. Although generally, he has no right which will prohibit the rezoning of other property, such rezoning may not single out small parcels for rezoning inconsistent with neighboring classifications. Such arbitrary classification would be invalid as spot zoning.

Case 302. Zoning is the districting of the municipality into specifically defined areas and the regulation of the construction and use of buildings and lands in those areas. Planning is a broader term than zoning and consists of the working out of details for the systematic development of municipal growth for the common good of all. Planning is within the police power. When police power is delegated to inferior tribunals there must be general standards set up for their control and guidance, but the details are left to the administrative tribunal. If an administrative tribunal leaves the approval or disapproval of a plan to comply with a zoning ordinance to the whim of the residents of the vicinity, it is arbitrary, unreasonable and unconstitutional as a taking of property without due process of law.

Case 303. A local governmental entity, according to a developing trend of authority, cannot ignore the needs of surrounding areas and consider only its own present inhabitants and their prejudices in enacting zoning ordinances. Thus, a community cannot completely exclude all moderate and low income housing by enacting an ordinance which permits only single family, detached housing on large lots. The needs of surrounding areas must be considered for the ordinance to pass the reasonable test.

Case 304. A zoning regulation designed to permit orderly growth and development and to prohibit disorganized urban sprawl is a valid exercise of the police power. Thus, an ordinance that limits the number of housing permits that may be granted annually, and coordinates the permits with the availability of essential public services and streets, is a valid exercise of the police power so long as it meets the reasonable test.

Case 305. A variance may be granted where property owners are suffering unnecessary hardship because of the application of the zoning ordinance when no general objection to the ordinance may be made. The fault lies in the ordinance's unreasonable application to a particular property, or the result may be caused by conditions in a particular locality.

In the latter situation, the relief is by way of direct attack on the terms of the zoning ordinance. But where a variance is desired upon the ground of unnecessary hardship, the record must show that: (a) the land in question cannot yield a reasonable return if used solely for a purpose allowed in that zone; (2) that the plight of the owner is due to unique circumstances and not to the general conditions in the neighborhood which may reflect the unreasonableness of the zoning ordinance itself; and (3) that the use to be permitted by the variance will not alter the essential character of the locality. If these three requirements are not shown on the record, the variance should not issue.

Case 306. Flexible selective zoning is established when a zoning ordinance provides planning by solicitation and presentment of plans to the designated zoning board. The scheme is invalid if the ordinance was not enacted in accordance with the comprehensive plan of zoning and if it assumes powers in the zoning board quite beyond those duties outlined for them in the enabling legislation. Without a comprehensive plan, the personal predilections of the supervisors or political power of the applicant could determine the zoning application. This is akin to spot zoning. Flexible selective zoning may be upheld if specifically permitted by the enabling legislation or if the court concludes that it is in fact in accordance with a comprehensive plan. Such flexible zoning and the use of PUDs are becoming rather common.

Case 307. All legislation by contract is invalid in the sense that a legislature cannot bargain away or sell its police powers. But when the property owner voluntarily imposes restrictions upon his property, no conditions are imposed by contract by the city council. However, conformity to a comprehensive plan is required. But requirements of uniformity and conformity to a plan do not mean that there must be identity of every relevant aspect in areas given the same zoning classification. The imposition of restrictions by the property owner must occur before the exercise of the zoning power, not afterward as a result of the imposition of a condition subsequent. Zoning regulations are independent of deed restrictions, and only in the case of a direct conflict does the zoning regulation have superiority over the restrictive covenant.

Case 308. An ordinance requiring developers of new subdivisions to dedicate land for park and recreational facilities or to pay a fee in lieu thereof, is valid as long as the amount of land to be dedicated, or the amount of the fee, is reasonable. As long as the costs or fees bear a reasonable relation to the probable increased costs that such development is likely to have on the community, the requirements should be upheld.

Case 309. An ordinance which regulates occupancy of housing units, particularly detached single type units, will be upheld if reasonable. Thus, an ordinance which permitted only two persons not related by blood or marriage to occupy a house was upheld. Although more persons constituting a family were entitled to live in one unit, there would likely be more noise, more traffic, more congestion if a large number of unrelated adults were allowed to live there. Thus, the restriction is reasonable. An ordinance which defines "family", however, so as to prohibit occupancy by related persons is invalid if the definition is too restrictive and arbitrary.

Case 310. A small community near a large metropolitan area may not so zone as to exclude intentionally all low income housing if the effect is racial discrimination. The ordinance would be valid under the 14th Amendment but invalid under the Federal Fair Housing Act. The synopsis of the case supra discusses what must be proved to sustain or invalidate the ordinance.

Case 311. An ordinance restricting land to residential uses may be enforced against one occupying a mansion in the area, but using the mansion daily for religious purposes and the smoking of marijuana throughout the day. First Amendment freedom of religion guarantees does not preclude reasonable zoning regulations. The owner of the home knew of the ordinance at the time of purchase and did not attempt to obtain a variance or exception. The ordinance does not unreasonably restrict the exercise of freedom of religion.

Case 312. A zoning ordinance which prohibits all use of a particular parcel of land, and in effect requires it to be kept undeveloped so that nearby residents can forever use it as a park, is invalid as an unconstitutional taking of private property. The ordinance is confiscatory and therefore void.

Chapter XXIX

COOPERATIVES AND CONDOMINIUMS

1. Introduction.
    Legal Gems.
2. Cooperatives.
    Legal Gems.
    Cases.
3. Condominiums.
    Legal Gems.
    Cases.
Summary of Cases in Chapter XXIX.

---

1. INTRODUCTION

Legal Gems

1. Housing shortages precipitated by two world wars, population explosion and increased urbanization, rising costs of real estate, inflation generally, and the desire for ownership, perhaps stimulated by income tax advantages, have generated the development of cooperative and condominium living.

2. Although cooperatives and condominiums invoke an initial image of vertical subdivisions, neither the high rise nor the housing aspect is critical to this type of development. Both cooperative and condominium concepts can be applied to lateral as well as vertical, and to commercial as well as residential developments.

3. The techniques employed in horizontal subdivisions, such as the covenant running with the land, the property owners' association, easements and licenses, can and necessarily are employed in the creation of cooperatives and condominiums. Also, of course, the project must conform to applicable zoning regulations.

4. The condominium as a separate form of ownership was virtually unknown in the United States prior to the 1960's, although there were isolated instances of this type of development without the aid of statutory authorization. The National Housing Act of 1961 spurred the development of condominiums by authorizing FHA mortgage insurance on a one family unit in a multi-family structure. Legislation aiding in the development of such structures followed rapidly.

5. Principal advantages of cooperative or condominium ownership include:

    a. The acquisition of an ownership interest with the accompanying advantages of pride, security and savings;

    b. The sharing of the high cost of the building site and the cost of maintenance among all the unit owners;

c. The procurement of income tax deductions for interest and taxes which are available to individual home owners;

d. Minimization of the risk of personal liability of the various members; and

e. Greater flexibility in choice of site location since the high cost of real estate prohibits much individual housing on expensive sites which can be feasibly developed only for apartment living.

2. COOPERATIVES

LEGAL GEMS

1. Prior to the advent of the condominium, the term cooperative was used in a generic sense to mean simply several types of organizations whereby the occupants of individual units of a multi-family structure sought to acquire the advantages of joint ownership previously delineated. (Gem 5 supra). As so used, the term would include a form of condominium ownership although such an organization was rarely used in the United States before statutory authorization in the 1960's. The most common types of cooperatives are the corporate or business trust forms depicted in Gem 2 infra.

2. A cooperative can be organized in any of the following manners:

a. Co-ownership in joint tenancy. Title to the premises is vested in all the co-owners as joint tenants with provisions for exclusive occupancy of individual apartments vested in designated co-owners. Because of the characteristic of survivorship and the requirement of the four unities, this plan is feasible only theoretically; it is not practical.

b. Co-ownership as tenants in common. Under this plan the occupants collectively own the entire project as tenants in common, and each occupant acquires the right to occupy a designated apartment exclusively. Covenants running with the land or equitable servitudes are employed to enforce each cotenant's financial obligations in the maintenance and operation of the building. The California tenancy-in-common cooperative appears to be an application of this basic plan and is commonly used in that state.

c. Massachusetts or Business Trust form of organization. Title to the entire premises is vested in the trustees of the Massachusetts type trust; certificates of beneficial interest are issued to the individual tenants or occupants; and each beneficial owner is also assigned an exclusive right of occupancy in a particular unit under a proprietary lease.

d. Corporate form of organization. Title to the entire premises is vested in a corporation, and the corporation leases specific apartments to the tenant-stockholders or members of the corporation. The lease is referred to as a proprietary lease. Its unique feature is that the lessee must own a specified number of shares of the lessor corporation, or otherwise qualify as a member if stock is not issued, in order both to acquire the lease and to continue as lessee.   Ownership of shares or membership as such in the lessor confers no right of occupancy; such occupancy right is conferred by the lease which is obtainable only by members or owners of shares.   This is the most commonly used form of cooperative organization, and is the only one hereinafter discussed.

3.   To create a corporate cooperative organization three documents are essential.   These are:

    a.   a corporate charter or certificate of incorporation;

    b.   a set of by-laws for the corporation; and

    c.   a proprietary lease or occupancy agreement.

These three documents are read together, and together they constitute the contract between the owners and the corporation.

4.   Restriction on the sale of shares or membership are common, and the shares or interest must always be sold in the original block in order to maintain each owner's relative position as a proportionate owner in the cooperative enterprise.

5.   A typical set of by-laws, among other provisions, would include the following:

    a.   name and location of the corporation;

    b.   purpose;

    c.   membership, eligibility, certificates, liens, transfers of membership by death, termination of membership for cause, sales price;

    d.   meetings of members, voting procedures, proxies;

    e.   directors, qualification, removal, compensation, meetings;

    f.   officers, election, removal;

    g.   amendment; and

    h.   fiscal management, fiscal year, books and accounts, audits and inspections.

6.   The lease gives the shareholder-tenant a right to occupy a particular apartment or unit for a stated term.   The rent in a proprietary lease includes the following elements:

    a.   a fixed annual sum which may be nominal if the building and the apartment are free and clear of mortgages and similar encumbrances.

    b.   a further amount fixed annually based on the maintenance and operation costs of the building, mortgage payments and tax assessments.

    c.   an additional sum which may be levied against the individual tenant if that tenant fails to maintain properly the interior of his apartment necessitating the corporation to perform work, and, when applicable, assessment to cover special expenses such as the construction of a new recreational facility.

7. Proprietary leases usually provide for termination on the following grounds:

    a.   failure to pay assessments;

    b.   failure to follow house rules; or

    c.   breach of any covenant required in the by-laws or charter.

8. The relationship of the unit owners to the cooperative corporation is two-fold: they are tenants of the corporation with respect to their individual unit, and they are owner-shareholders of the corporation by virtue of the shares or membership interest they own.

9. Cooperative financing is usually accomplished by a single mortgage executed by the corporation covering the entire project. Separate mortgages on individual units are not common. Thus, each tenant-shareholder is dependent upon the financial ability of his fellow cooperators.

10. Each tenant-stockholder is entitled to deduct on his federal income tax his proportionate share of the interest paid by the cooperative corporation upon its blanket mortgage provided the corporation does not derive more than 20% of its gross income from sources other than its tenant-stockholders.

CASE 313: A is the owner of 500 shares of stock in X corporation, an entity organized for the purpose of providing apartments in a cooperative housing venture. The certificate of incorporation provides that the apartments are to be used for private residential purposes only and by an individual or individuals approved by its board of directors. A is also the tenant under a proprietary lease from the X corporation under provisions that make the ownership of 500 shares of stock a condition precedent to the continuance of the lease. Provisions in the lease and corporate by-laws also provide that neither the stock nor lease is to be assigned without the written consent of the board of directors of the X corporation or of two-thirds of its stockholders. A, being in arrears in her rental and assessment obligations, offered to sell her stock to the X corporation and the offer was declined. Thereafter, she sold her stock and assigned her lease to the P corporation, an entity wholly owned by her husband and which had no other assets. The Board of X corporation refused to consent to the assignment to P corporation; whereupon P and A brought suit to compel X to recognize the assignment as valid and to issue a new stock certificate and new proprietary lease to P. Are P and A entitled to the relief sought?

Answer and Analysis

The answer is no. The legal question involved is the validity of the restraint on alienation. Although there has been a traditional policy of the common law prohibiting or greatly circumscribing restraints on the alienation of property, both realty and personalty, the results in a particular case should not depend upon blind adherence to dogma but upon sound public policy. The validity of a specific restraint should be judged by the purposes to be accomplished, the reasonableness of the restraint imposed, and the evils, if any, likely to result therefrom. The tenant stockholders in a cooperative apartment building are principally interested in the purchase of a home. The success of their individual efforts and of the entire project, however, is closely related to the success of the whole. An individual apartment does not stand or fall as a separate unit; rather the success of each individual unit depends upon the success of the entire complex since there is blanket or unitary financing, operation, and taxation of the entire complex.

Thus, the permanency of the individual occupants as tenant owners is an essential element in the general plan, and their financial responsibility an inducement to the corporation in accepting them as stockholders. Under the plan of organization adopted, each stockholder or his representative is entitled to vote upon the choice of neighbors and their financial responsibility. This latter element is most important when it is remembered that the failure of any tenant to pay his proportionate share of expenses increases the liability of the other tenant stockholders.

The X corporation is in reality a vehicle for the establishment of a community of homes rather than for the pecuniary profit of its stockholders. The primary interest of the shareholders is in the long term proprietary lease, the alienation of which the corporation has the power to restrain. Thus, decisions relating to restrictions on the alienation of stock should not be controlling.

There are, however, also decisions invalidating restrictions on the aliention of real property. Although restraints on the alienation of leasehold estates are generally upheld providing they are not in the form of disabling restraints, restraints on the alienation of fees simple (non-condominiums), have been generally held invalid. The form of the real property ownership in the instant case is that of a leasehold, but it would be inconsistent with the previous discussion to say that the restraint is valid just because the tenant shareholders have only a leasehold interest. In substance they are the owners as well as the tenants; hence the decision should be based on more substantial grounds. As previously indicated, the success of the entire venture depends upon the financial ability of each tenant shareholder, and the proximity of living accommodations and the necessity of cooperating in the management of the building, and in determining the character of the entire project and community, make it very desirable, if not necessary, that the members have a voice in the selection of their neighbors and fellow cooperators.

Further, the social evils frequently asserted to be avoided by invalidating restraints on alienation are not shown to be perpetrated by a cooperative device such as this. The restraints here involved will not tend to keep the property in the same family and concentrate wealth; the member is not prevented from liquidating his interest and consuming the property; creditors are usually not prevented from satisfying their claims; and members are not discouraged from improving their homes. The restrictions on transfer are reasonably necessary to the continued existence of the cooperative association. Of course, the cooperative enterprise should not, and undoubtedly cannot legally be used to achieve racial or other unlawful discrimination in the sale or leasing of housing. See Note following case 268, but there is no evidence of that in this instance. Accordingly, P and A are not entitled to the relief sought. See Penthouse Properties, Inc. v. 1158 Fifth Ave., Inc., 256 App.Div. 685, 11 N.Y.S.2d 417 (1939); LaCaille v. Feldman, 44 Misc.2d 370, 253 N.Y.S.2d 937 (1964), involving priority of liens; Gale v. York Center Community Coop., Inc., 21 Ill.2d 86, 171 N.E.2d 30 (1960), involving a horizontal cooperative organized on a membership rather than a stock basis.

––––––––

CASE 314: A organizes a co-operative apartment house of 45 units under a statute which provides that: "No stockholder at any meeting shall be entitled to more than one vote." A corporate co-operative contracts to purchase the apartments, and 22 of the units are sold to co-operative members. A subscribes to the co-operative and keeps 23 units, and resides in one of them. A is then allowed to sublease his remaining 22 units as ordinary rental apartments to defray the cost burden until they can be sold. A agrees to continue using his best efforts to sell the apartments in order to keep with the co-operative apartment concept. A then assigns to 17 transferees all his interest in the stock and a proprietary lease appurtenant to a particular apartment, but he retains a promissory note on each and, as a condition of each transfer, retains a proxy to vote the shares as he sees fit. Each of the transferees have no intention of becoming residents of the apartments, but purchased the share for "investment purposes" only. A now claims that he has the right to 18 votes: 17 by proxy for his "transferees" and one vote of his own. The 17 transferees now file a writ of mandate ordering the co-op's trustees to count the "proxy" votes. Should the court grant the writ of mandate?

Answer and Analysis

The answer is no. The promoter (A), in this instance, agreed to use his best efforts to sell all the remaining units to tenant-owners. In this context, the promoter should be allowed to subscribe to the remaining units but only as to defray costs while he is exercising his continuing duty to sell the apartments. The interests of the tenants are not thereby unduly prejudiced since the promoter can never obtain more than the one vote he gets by actually living in an apartment, despite his multiple holdings. Control over both conditions and potential buyers or renters therefore remains in the resident-tenant-owners. The statute provides that no "stockholder" shall be entitled to more than one vote. The term "stockholder" is interpreted in light of its underlying purposes; and the only bona fide stockholder in such an association is a resident. When A, as promoter, subdivided his retained apartments among investors rather than residents, he did not increase the number of bona fide stockholders. The non-resident "transferees" held their shares only through A's right as a promoter, and subject to the duty to attempt to sell to third parties who would become residents. The sum total of this subdivided interest equals one stockholder, and therefore, one vote. To hold otherwise would thwart the purpose of cooperative housing and permit control to be vested in one exercising a commercial renting enterprise rather than in the majority of the owner-cooperators. See State ex rel. Leavell v. Nelson, 63 Wash.2d 299, 387 P.2d 82, 99 A.L.R.2d 231 (1963).

CASE 315: Plaintiffs, shareholders in a cooperative corporation, and lessees under a proprietary lease, filed suit against the corporation to recover $400 damages, the cost of repairing rotted underflooring and 2″ x 4″ "sleepers" beneath the floor in their bedroom. The corporation refused to make the repairs or to reimburse the plaintiffs on the basis that it was the plaintiffs' obligation to repair the interior of their apartment. The proprietary lease provided: "Lessor shall keep in good repair the foundations, sidewalks, walls, *supports, beams*." May plaintiffs recover?

Answer and Analysis

The answer is yes. The proper relationship of the parties should be determined. Under the form of cooperation herein employed, the defendant corporation owns the entire building. Plaintiffs own 200 shares of stock in defendant corporation, the amount of stock owned bearing the same relationship to the total amount of stock outstanding as the value of the apartment occupied by the plaintiffs bears to the total value of the building. Ownership of the stock entitles the plaintiffs or other owners to a proprietary lease which in turn entitles them to occupancy privileges. Stock ownership alone is not sufficient.

The legal significance of the proprietary lease is the crucial issue. Is the relationship between the corporation and the shareholder-tenant other than that of any other landlord-tenant relationship for purposes of determining the rights and obligations under the lease? A corporation is normally a legal entity distinct from its shareholders. In an apartment cooperative the corporation is the sole owner of the land and building. The occupancy rights of the shareholders are derived solely through the terms of the proprietary lease, and under the terms of this instrument the relationship is clearly that of landlord and tenant. The shareholders then are in the same position as any other tenants.

For certain limited purposes some courts have referred to cooperative tenant shareholders as owners. See, for example, Case 313 supra, validating the restraints on alienation. Other cases have regarded such a lessee as a title holder so as to permit him to bring dispossess proceedings to recover possession of the cooperative apartment. As to a third party in possession the stockholder-tenant may be a landlord, but as between the parties the relationship between the corporation and shareholders or members is really essentially that of landlord and tenant.

The relationship between the cooperative corporation and the apartment dwellers in an organization of this type is entirely different from that existing between the property owners' association and the apartment dwellers in a condominium organization. In a condominium the individual purchasers acquire title to their respective units and to an undivided interest as tenants in common to all of the common areas and the underlying fee. The whole project is owned directly by the individuals—collectively as to the common areas and individually as to the separate apartments. The association as such owns nothing. In a cooperative, the association owns the entire project—the cooperators own shares of stock and lease a particular apartment. Thus, in the instant case, the parties having chosen the cooperative form of organization, are bound by the usual incidents thereof. Accordingly, their rights in this instance are determined by a construction of the terms of the proprietary lease construed in reference to the usual incidents of a landlord and tenant relationship.

As previously noted, the lessor had agreed to keep in repair "supports" and "beams." Evidence also was introduced to show that on acquiring their interest, the corporation notified the plaintiffs in writing that "the entire interior of the premises is your responsibility." Generally, covenants by a lessee to keep in repair are construed to exclude structural repairs and extraordinary and unforeseen building alterations. Here, the agreement by the tenants should be construed to mean that they covenanted to repair only the visible parts of the interior of their apartment.

Additionally, there are no qualifications, restrictions or limitations to the words supports and beams in the lease under the provision imposing repair obligations on the landlord. The underflooring and "sleepers" can certainly qualify as supports and beams in an ordinary sense since they do hold up the floor. They would seem to be of a structural nature to an ordinary layman, but whether they are or are not, the arrangement between the landlord and tenant would clearly indicate that the obligation to make these repairs fell on the landlord. Such a construction is also consistent with the statutory law in this particular jurisdiction imposing on landlords of multiple family dwellings the obligation to keep in repair. And although failure to make such repairs has resulted in the imposition of tort and not contractual liability on the defaulting landlord, a provision in the lease that repairs required by the lessor shall be made at its expense may be construed as an implied obligation to reimburse a tenant for any repairs made by him on behalf of the lessor. Accordingly, Plaintiffs may recover. See Susskind v. 1136 Tenants Corp., 43 Misc.2d 588, 251 N.Y.S.2d 321 (Civil Ct. of City of N.Y.1964).

3. CONDOMINIUMS

LEGAL GEMS

1.   The term condominium is commonly used in three different ways:

   a.   to denote the system of ownership;

   b.   to denote the entire building devoted to that form of ownership; and

   c.   to denote the individual unit with its accompanying interest in the common elements.

2.   As a system, the term condominium means a form of ownership under which the separate units of a multi-unit improvement of real property are subject to ownership by different owners, and there is appurtenant to each unit an undivided share in the common elements.

3.   As applied to the building, the term condominium simply refers to the entire building which is subject to the condominum form of ownership.

4.   As applied to the individual unit, the term condominium simply means a unit or an apartment which is subject to individual ownership in a multi-unit structure, together with an undivided interest in cotenancy in the common elements or those parts of the realty which are used in common and are owned collectively by all the unit owners in the project.

5.   Since the common law recognizes fee ownership and lesser property interests in usable airspace, it is feasible to create a condominium form of ownership at common law. Precedent for this form of ownership goes back to at least the Middle Ages, but condominium regimes were seldom created in the United States prior to statutory enactments in the 1960's.

6.   All states, Puerto Rico and the District of Columbia have statutes authorizing the creation of condominium regimes. The provisions of these statutes vary considerably, as do the names of the acts themselves. Such phrases as "Apartment Ownership," "Condominium Ownership," and "Horizontal Property" are the most commonly appearing terms in the titles to the various acts.

7.   Unless the statute directly or indirectly provides otherwise, a condominium regime can be constructed on a long term leasehold estate.

8.   The creation of a condominium regime requires four basic documents:

    a.   a declaration of condominium or master deed;

    b.   articles of incorporation or association organizing the association of owners;

    c.   a set of by-laws for governing the association of owners and the operation of the building; and

    d.   a deed for conveying the individual unit.

9.   The declaration or master deed is the instrument by which the property is subjected to or brought under condominium use. It commonly contains provisions covering the following and other items:

    a.   a legal description of all the land, a legal description of each unit, and a description of the common elements;

    b.   restrictions against partition since the continuance of the regime depends upon continued coownership of the common elements and individual ownership of the several units;

    c.   occupancy restrictions and pre-emption rights when a unit owner desires to sell;

    d.   designation of the shares of each unit or fractional interest in the common elements appurtenant to each unit;

    e.   provisions for liens on the units to enforce payment of common expenses;

    f.   casualty loss and rebuilding provisions;

    g.   easements through the units for pipes, wires, and similar essential services;

    h.   voting rights of owners; and

    i.   the method of amending the declaration and by-laws.

10.   The deed to an individual unit must conform to local conveyancing statutes and must sufficiently designate the unit conveyed, the easiest method of which is to incorporate by reference the recorded plan or plat incorporated in the declaration of condominium. The deed frequently includes other matters also, such as covenants and use restrictions which are frequently incorporated by reference, the percentage of interest owned in the common elements, transfer restrictions and similar items.

11. After construction, financing is accomplished by separate mortgages on each unit and its accompanying coownership interest in the common elements. Each unit is also taxed separately.

12. Individual condominium unit owners are entitled to federal income tax deductions for the interest paid on mortgages incumbering their separate units and also for real estate taxes paid thereon.

CASE 316: O, owner in fee simple leased to A for 55 years, the terms of which lease required A to construct an apartment complex within two years. A then recorded the lease and a Declaration of Condominium by which he submitted the leasehold to a horizontal property regime. Thereafter A executed 50 contracts of purchase with various individuals for the purchase of individual apartments, and on the basis of such purchase contracts A borrowed one million dollars for purposes of construction, and executed a mortgage to ME to secure the loan. Thereafter, A defaulted in his payments to the mortgagee; the purchasers made no payments on their purchase contracts, and innumerable mechanics' liens were filed against the project. ME filed an action to foreclose his mortgage and joined all parties. Determine the rights of the parties.

Answer and Analysis

In order to determine the rights and priorities of the parties, it is necessary to determine the legal effect of each of the transactions. The first problem is to determine whether a condominium or horizontal property regime was established. These regimes are now predicated on statutory enabling acts, and the statutes of the various states determine what must be done to comply therewith, as well as the rights of the parties ensuing therefrom. In this particular jurisdiction a condominium regime can be established by recording a master lease or deed and a declaration of submission which is required to contain certain information. The problem states that the lease and declaration were recorded; hence, compliance with the act is established. Once the condominium regime is established, an apartment in the building may be individually conveyed and encumbered and may be the subject of ownership, possession or sale and of all juridic acts inter vivos or mortis causa, as if it were solely and entirely independent of the other apartments in the building.

The statute makes the property susceptible to conveyance of individual units. It, therefore, contemplates the existence of agreements or contracts to convey the developer's interest in individual units within the building. The contracts herein involved were all issued prior to the construction mortgage executed to ME. Although the contracts were not recorded, they were nevertheless known to ME since the problem states that the contracts were the inducement for granting the loan and taking the mortgage.

The vendee under a contract of purchase is usually said to acquire an equitable interest in the land, and usually equity will grant specific performance of such a contract. In this case the principal subject of each contract is an apartment in a building not yet constructed. Equity courts generally refrain from issuing decrees which they cannot enforce, and equity courts generally will not order acts requiring continuous supervision, such as the construction of a building. Does it follow therefore that these purchasers acquired no interest in the land because of the inability to get specific performance before the building is constructed? The answer is no. Recognition of a property interest does not depend upon the availability of any particular remedy to protect that interest.

The public policy behind the condominium statutes which were enacted to further these types of developments suggests that the interests of the purchasers under the contracts should be protected to the fullest extent consistent with established statutory and case law. In the instant case ME had knowledge of the outstanding contracts at the time the mortgage was executed. ME could have refused to proceed with the loan unless the contract purchasers subordinated their interests to the lien of the mortgage. This he failed to do. Normally a subsequent purchaser or mortgagee who takes with notice of an outstanding interest takes subject to such interest. The fact that we are dealing with a condominium regime suggests no adequate reason for varying the normal rules of priority when the subsequent purchaser or mortgagee has notice. Thus, ME's mortgage will be inferior to the rights of those contract purchasers whose contracts were entered into before the mortgage.

At this point, a brief resume of the rights of the parties so far is in order. O is the owner of the fee; he did not join in the mortgage; therefore, his reversion is not subject to the mortgage, and at the end of the leasehold the land will revert free and clear. A has a 55-year term which is encumbered with a condominium regime and 50 outstanding contracts to purchase individual apartments. ME has a mortgage on the leasehold encumbered by the condominium regime and the outstanding contracts. On foreclosure, he will sell the leasehold so encumbered.

The next point is the rights of the mechanics' lien claimants. The rights of such claimants depend entirely upon the statutes affording such rights. The statutes vary considerably among the states as to details of perfecting such liens and as to the effective dates thereof. In order not to prolong the discussion unduly, we will assume that all the statutory requirements were satisfied. Assuming also that the lien statute does not specifically provide that condominium units may be subjected to such liens, the answer nevertheless should be in favor of according liens to those improvers of the realty who would otherwise qualify if the particular land were not subjected to a condominium regime. As previously pointed out, these individual apartments are treated as separate parcels of real property subject to all types of juridic acts. Thus, the lienors acquire a lien superior to the rights of the individual purchasers.

Thus, in brief, ME, the mortgagee can foreclose on the leasehold subject to rights of prior vendees of individual units and subject to the condominium regime, and as to such mortgage the lienors have inferior rights since the mortgage was perfected first. The lienors, however, have valid liens on the equitable interests of the vendees. See State Sav. & Loan Ass'n v. Kauaian Dev. Co., 445 P.2d 109 (Hawaii 1968), containing additional complications.

CASE 317: A was a member of a condominium corporation developed by B corporation. B corporation contracted to sell condominium units in the apartment buildings. Each unit purchaser executed a separate contract with B corporation wherein each purchaser was required to pay to the condominium corporation a monthly maintenance charge. At the closing of each of the condominium purchase transactions, the individual unit owners each executed as guarantor and beneficiary a 99-year lease on the communal recreational facilities which were to be used by unit owners. These leases were between B corporation and the condominium corporation as lessee. The rental under this lease was to be paid by the condominium corporation out of monthly maintenance charges, and each unit owner executed the lease as guarantor and beneficiary. A now brings a class action on behalf of all unit owners for both damages and modification or cancellation of the lease on grounds that B corporation had charged exorbitant rental and made excessive profits.

The pleadings allege several causes of action: (a) breach of fiduciary duties because of the self-dealing lease between the developer and the organization controlled by him; (b) violation of a statute enacted after the lease was in effect providing that such leases shall be fair and reasonable; and (c) that the lease is unconscionable. May A prevail?

Answers and Analyses

The answers are as follows: allegation (a) states a good cause of action but actual recovery may be quite difficult to obtain; allegation (b) will not permit recovery since the statute cannot be applied retroactively; and (c) states a good cause of action but actual recovery will probably be very difficult to achieve.

(a) Until recently the courts of the state in question refused to invalidate the lease or give other relief on the basis of self-dealing. The rationale was that since the officers and directors of the two associations were the same at the time of the lease, and since there was no other members, there was no fiduciary duty, and no liability was incurred because of the lease. Further, purchasers of the condominium apartment units purchased with knowledge of the lease, voluntarily became guarantors thereof, and hence should abide by it. In the case of each condominium purchase, the documents included the Declaration of Condominium, and the articles and by-laws of the condominium corporation. Each purchaser, therefore, was on notice of those documents when he closed. He voluntarily assumed the lease contract and therefore could not later complain.

More recently the state supreme court stated:

> "But there is absolutely nothing to recommend a rule of law which encourages persons in positions of trust secretly to betray their trust for inordinate personal gain, at the expense of those to whom they owe a fiduciary duty." 347 So.2d 601 at 607.

The court stated that self-dealing per se was not actionable, indicated that there was some sort of fiduciary duty to those who would become unit owners and members of the association in the future, and that such self-dealing directors and promoters would be liable for inordinate, excessive profits, or for the amounts by which they unjustly enriched themselves. Avila South Condominium Ass'n, Inc. v. Kappa Corp., 347 So.2d 599 (Fla.1977). Earlier cases upholding self-dealing arrangements: Wechsler v. Goldman, 214 So.2d 741 (Fla. 3d D.C.A. 1968); Fountainview Ass'n, Inc. No. 4 v. Bell, 214 So.2d 609 (Fla. 1968), denying certiorari for 203 So.2d 657 (Fla. 3d D.C.A.1967).

(b) In answering the second question, the court presumed that the statute was not intended to be applied retroactively, (Avila case, supra), and, therefore avoided the constitutional issue. It would appear, however, that if statutes which required the terms of a lease to be fair and reasonable, outlawed escalation provisions, or otherwise affected substantive terms, were to be applied to pre-existing contracts or leases, then the statute would be unconstitutional as an impairment of contractual rights. See, e. g., Fleeman v. Case, 342 So.2d 815 (Fla.1976).

(c) The state supreme court indicated that there might be a cause of action based on unconscionability, but it did not discuss any of the requirements. (Avila case, supra). As of this writing no published decision is known in which a particular condominium "rec" lease has been held unconscionable. One federal trial decision relating to a "rec" lease in connection with single family developments discussed in great detail the concept of unconscionability. It was pointed out that for a contract or lease to be unconscionable it must be so, both procedurally and substantively. For procedural unconscionability there has to be a lack of meaningful choice on the part of one of the parties, and substantive unconscionability is satisfied when the contract is unreasonably favorable to the other party. The particular "rec" lease was not found unconscionable. Bennett v. Behring Corp., 466 F.Supp. 689 (D.C.Fla.1979).

CASE 318: A Corporation, a Condominium Association composed of unit owners, is lessee under a recreation lease with B, the developer and lessor. The lease was assumed by all unit owners as a mandatory condition for purchasing their condominium units. The lease contained an escalation clause calling for periodic adjustments in accordance with the Consumer Price Index. The Declaration of Condominium incorporated all provisions of the Condominiums Act presently existing or as the act may be amended from time to time. Recently, B demanded an increase or escalation of the rental payments as provided for in the lease. A now seeks to invalidate the escalation clause based on a state statute invalidating certain escalation clauses, in particular, condominium leases. The statute was enacted while the lease was in effect. Will A prevail?

Answer and Analysis

The answer is yes. Such a statute will usually be applied prospectively only and, therefore, would have no effect on a lease agreement made prior to the statute's enactment. However, the Declaration of Condominium here provided for the adoption of all subsequent amendments to the Condominium Act. Therefore, although the statute has no retroactive effect, B can not enforce the escalation clause since the statute is adopted into the Declaration of Condominium and becomes binding on all parties. The rent in effect is frozen at the current rate. Previous escalations were valid, but there can be no more escalations. Kaufman v. Shere, 347 So.2d 627 (Fla. 3d D.C.A. 1977). See West's Fla.Stat.Ann. § 718.401(8)(a) (1979), for the statute prohibiting certain escalation clauses.

CASE 319: X Condominium Association decides to bring a suit against the Developer, D, to test the validity of the recreation lease entered into between the association and the Developer when Developer controlled the association. The Association levies an assessment against all the unit owners to finance the law suit. D, Developer, is the owner of one of the condominium units, and he files suit against the association to enjoin the association from making him help finance a suit against himself. Will D succeed?

Answer and Analysis

The answer is no. The association generally has control over the common areas, is responsible for their maintenance and upkeep, and generally represents the unit owners in matters of common interest. The funds of the association are obtained by levying assessments against the unit owners, and if one of the unit owners is a defendant in a suit by the association, he nevertheless is liable for his share of the expenses in maintaining the suit. Thus, the association may assess him. Margate Village Condominium Ass'n, Inc. v. Wilfred, Inc., 350 So.2d 16 (Fla. 4th D.C.A.1977).

CASE 320: At a time when the new Board of Trustees or Directors of X Condominium Association assumed office, the Association was in serious financial difficulties. Huge bills were unpaid; and the condo building was in dire need of repair. Such needs extended to the air conditioning, heating and fire systems, and a "curtain wall" which was in a weakened state. Numerous units suffered water damage from leakage whenever it rained because of the aforesaid "curtain wall" problem. The by-laws of the Association permitted the Board to vote for and collect, without a vote of the unit owners, a special assessment to meet increased operating or maintenance costs, additional capital expenses, or to meet emergencies. The by-laws also required that a majority of unit owners consent to the expenditure of more than $5,000.00 on any item of expense. The Board's assessment amounted to $100,000.00, and was obtained without notice to unit owners and without their vote. Unit owners sought to enjoin the Association from asserting a lien for the assessment. May the unit owners succeed in their action?

Answer and Analysis

The answer is no. The question is whether the Association may validly pass such a large assessment to cover emergency expenses without a vote and approval of the unit owners as required by the by-laws? The Association had fallen heavily into debt and the condominium building was in great disrepair. The Board determined that an emergency existed within the meaning of the by-laws, and that an assessment of $100,000.00 was necessary to resolve the emergency.

The test of a board's actions is that of reasonableness; a court will not second guess the actions of directors or trustees unless it appears that they are the result of fraud, dishonesty or incompetence. The court considered the absence of the unit owners voting for the assessment, and decided that "if an extreme emergency exists, majority approval of the unit owners is not necessary." (401 A.2d at 286). The court concluded that absent a demonstration of the board's lack of good faith, self-dealing, dishonesty or incompetency, its determination that an emergency existed should not be judicially reviewed. Further, it was decided that the board's decision was good-faith motivated, and in the best interests of the unit owners. Papalexiou v. Tower West Condominium, 167 N.J.Super. 516, 401 A.2d 280 (1979).

Note

Community Living and Close Encounters

" . . . [I]nherent in the condominium concept is the principle that to promote the health, happiness and peace of mind of the majority of unit owners since they are living in such close proximity and using facilities in common, each unit owner must give up a certain degree of freedom of choice which he might otherwise enjoy in separate, privately owned property. Condominium unit owners comprise a little democratic sub society of necessity more restrictive as it pertains to use of condominium property than may be existent outside the condominium organization." [1]

The close proximity, the sharing of common facilities, and the divergent interests of the many neighbors often lead to friction and even law suits. Undoubtedly the two subjects that cause the hottest tempers are children and pets, but there are many others. In resolving any controversy concerning condominium living it will be necessary to examine: (1) the applicable statutes; (2) the declaration of condominium or the master deed; (3) the articles of incorporation or association; (4) the by-laws; and (5) the rules promulgated by the Association's Board of Directors. Some changes or restrictions will require an amendment to the declaration or master deed, some can be accomplished by amending the by-laws, and some rules and regulations can be promulgated by the Board of Directors. It is not the purpose of this note to give an in depth study; rather it is just to illustrate some of the cases that have arisen.

Drinking, children and pets. The Board of Directors of a particular association passed a rule prohibiting the use of alcoholic beverages in the club house and adjacent areas. The unit owners approved by a 2:1 majority, but some violently disagreed. The prohibition was upheld since the association has control of the common areas, and the rule was considered reasonable, and not arbitrary or capricious. See Hidden Harbour Estates, Inc. v. Norman, 309 So.2d 180 (Fla. 4th D. C.A.1979).

Restrictions prohibiting occupancy by children under designated ages are rather common and are generally upheld. Problems may arise, and valid defenses asserted, if new restrictions are attempted to be applied retroactively, if the restriction is not uniformly enforced, or if it is not properly enacted, e. g., by a proper amendment to the declaration or by-laws according to the facts and statutes of the particular case. See Riley v. Stoves, 22 Ariz.App. 223, 526 P.2d 747 (1974), not involving a condominium but upholding an age restriction in a recorded declaration of restrictions; White Egret Condominium, Inc. v. Franklin, 379 So.2d 346 (Fla.1979), upholding an age restriction but not enforcing it because of unequal administration and estoppel; Ritchey v. Villa Nueva Condominium Ass'n, 81 Cal.App.3d 688, 146 Cal.Rptr. 695 (1978), upholding age restriction.

Pets appear to be a constant source of friction to apartment dwellers. The following are a sample of some of the litigation: Lin-

---

1. Judge Downey in Hidden Harbour Estates, Inc. v. Norman, 309 So.2d 180 at 181 (Fla. 4th D.C.A.1979).

coln Co-op. Apartments, Inc. v. Zaifert, 23 A.D.2d 796, 258 N.Y.S.2d 903 (1965), holding that the tenant-shareholder was committing a substantial breach of the occupancy agreement by harboring a dog in her apartment, but it was not indicated whether the rule was in effect when the occupant obtained her dog or whether it was subsequently enacted; Johnson v. Keith, 368 Mass. 316, 331 N.E.2d 879 (1975), holding that the association had rule making power only over the common elements, and, therefore, a purported rule prohibiting dogs in the apartment was invalid since such a restriction would have to be enacted by an amendment to the by-laws; Winston Towers 200 Ass'n, Inc. v. Saverio, 360 So.2d 470 (Fla. 3d D.C.A.1978), holding that an amended by-law prohibiting a dog not registered as of a prior date was invalid as an attempt to impose a retroactive regulation; and Wilshire Condominium Ass'n, Inc. v. Kohlbrand, 368 So.2d 629 (Fla. 4th D.C.A.1979), upholding as reasonable a regulation in the declaration of condominium that if a person owned a dog at time of purchase he could keep the dog in his unit, but that no replacement dog would be allowed.

Architectural Control. Declarations of restrictions regulating the size, style and architectural design of homes in subdivision developments are rather common and are generally enforced if reasonable and uniformly administered. See, e. g., Gaskin v. Harris, 82 N.M. 336, 481 P.2d 698 (1971); Huey v. Davis, 556 S.W.2d 860 (Tex.App. 1977), reversed 571 S.W.2d 859, and Dickstein v. Williams, 571 P.2d 1169 (Nev.1977). The importance of architectural symmetry and construction control is even more important in condominium living. Reasonable rules or restrictions will generally be upheld if uniformly enforced. Consider the following cases: Fifty-Six Sixty Collins Ave. Condominium, Inc. v. Dawson, 354 So.2d 432 (Fla. 3d D.C.A.1978), holding the association was estopped to prohibit owner from installing shutters on balcony because the owner believed he had secured approval, the association had passed a general resolution of approval, and the association stood by as the unit owner commenced construction; Fountains of Palm Beach Condominium, Inc. No. 5 v. Farkas, 355 So.2d 163 (Fla. 4th D.C.A.1978), upholding the requirements and enforcing the unit owner to remove a slab from the common elements and finding no basis for an estoppel against the association; and Sterling Village Condominium, Inc. v. Breitenbach, 251 So.2d 685 (Fla. 4th D.C.A.1971), certiorari denied, 254 So.2d 789 (Fla.1971), requiring the unit owner to remove the glass jalousies and restore the screen enclosures.

SUMMARY OF CASES IN CHAPTER XXIX

2. COOPERATIVES

Case 313. Tenant shareholders in a cooperative enterprise are primarily interested in the acquisition of a home, and the success of the entire project, particularly financial but social also, depends upon the exercise of some control in the selection of neighbors. Such control cannot be for the purposes of engaging in unlawful racial discrimination, but otherwise reasonable restraints on the alienation of stock and proprietary leases are valid.

Case 314. A promoter who kept 23 of 45 units pending sale and who was authorized to sublease them in the interim is not entitled to exercise proxy votes from transferees of such units when the transferees signed contracts of purchase for investment purposes only with no intention of occupancy, and there is a statute which provides that each cooperator is entitled to one vote. A cooperative enterprise envisions individual ownership by the cooperators for the purpose of obtaining homes, and to permit the holder or owner of several units to exercise multiple votes could convert the character of the community from one of individual home owners into that of a commercial enterprise.

Case 315. The relationship between a stock cooperative organization and its shareholder tenants under proprietory leases is in fact that of landlord and tenant in relation to the rights and duties of the parties pertaining to the use and occupancy of the premises. The corporation as a distinct entity owns the building and its shareholders under individual leases have a right to occupancy solely as a result of the lease. When the terms of such a lease require the landlord corporation to keep certain parts of the building in repair, including "supports" and "beams," the landlord is obligated to keep in repair the subflooring and 2" x 4" "sleepers" under the flooring of the individual apartments.

3. CONDOMINIUMS

Case 316. A condominium regime may be constructed on a leasehold as well as a fee when the statute so authorizes. Individual condominium units are subject to all types of juridic acts as if they were completely independent, and a vendee under a contract to purchase such a unit acquires an equitable interest therein even if the building is not yet constructed. A subsequent purchaser or mortgagee who acquires his interest with notice of outstanding purchase contracts takes subject to the rights of the vendees under such contracts. Mechanics lien claimants may perfect liens against the owners and contract purchasers of individual units.

Case 317. (a) A recreational lease (or management contract) entered into when the developer controlled both the condominium association and the lessor corporation is not per se invalid because of self-dealing. However, the developer does have some fiduciary obligations, apparently slight, to prospective buyers of the condominium units, and if as a result of self-dealing he obtains "inordinate" profits, he may be liable on the basis of unjust enrichment.

(b) Remedial legislation of a substantive nature such as that which would require leases or contracts to be fair and reasonable, or that which would invalidate escalation clauses, are presumptively intended not to be applied retroactively, and if they are intended to be so applied, then most likely they would be held unconstitutional.

(c) A "rec" lease or contract may be invalidated on the basis of unconscionability even in the absence of a specific statute. To be unconscionable the court must find that there was an absence of meaningful choice on the part of one party, plus contract terms which are unreasonably favorable to the other. These two requirements constitute procedural and substantive unconscionability.

Case 318. Although certain types of statutory regulations affecting substantive contractual rights are prospective only in operation, nevertheless, if a declaration of condominium expressly incorporates the condominium act "as it now exists or as it may be amended," then such amendments will be applicable to that condominium regime. Thus, after a statute was passed prohibiting certain types of escalation clauses in certain leases, previous escalations were valid but no future escalations would be permitted.

Case 319. The Condominium Association has control over the common areas and can sue and be sued on behalf of the unit owners. Thus, the association is authorized to levy assessments for appropriate litigation expenses, and if the defendant in the association's law suit is a unit owner, that unit owner is subject to assessment for his share of the litigation expenses.

Case 320. The association's board of directors or trustees must follow the procedures set forth in the condominium documents and also, of course, adhere to applicable statutes. When the documents require consent of the unit owners for assessments or expenditures in excess of a stated amount, except in the case of an extreme emergency, the board's determination that an emergency exists will not be judicially reviewed in the absence of a showing of the board's lack of good faith, self-dealing, dishonesty or incompetency. Thus, in the instant case a rather large assessment without unit owners' approval was upheld to take care of large deficits and serious building defects.

Part V

PERSONAL PROPERTY

Chapter XXX

POSSESSOR OF PERSONALTY: WILD ANIMALS; FINDERS

Rights of a Possessor of Personal Property.
Legal Gems.
Cases.
Summary of Cases in Chapter XXX.

LEGAL GEMS

1. Possession is a basic property interest entitling the possessor to certain rights such as:

    (a) the right to continue such peaceful possession against everyone except those who have a better right;

    (b) the right to recover the chattel in specie if it is wrongfully taken; and

    (c) the right to recover damages against a wrongdoer.

2. To constitute possession, there must be

    (a) a certain amount of actual control; and

    (b) an intent to possess and exclude others.

3. Possession is a means of acquiring title to wild animals.

    (a) The mere chasing of an animal, although in hot pursuit, does not give one a right to title against another who captures it by intervening.

    (b) If an animal is mortally wounded, or caught in a trap so that capture is certain, the hunter attains a vested right to possession and title which may not be defeated by another's intervention.

4. A *finder* is one who acquires legal possession, that is, one who exercises the prerequisite physical control and appropriate intent, over chattels or goods that have been lost, misplaced, abandoned, or hidden so as to be classified as treasure trove.

5. *Lost property* consists of those chattels whose possession has been parted with casually, involuntarily or unconsciously.

6. *Misplaced or left property* refers to those goods which have been intentionally placed somewhere and then unintentionally left or forgotten.

7. *Abandoned property* consists of those items no longer in the possession of the former owner or bailee, and the beneficial or possessory interest of which has been intentionally relinquished, given up, or released.

8. *Treasure trove* consists of coin or money concealed in the earth or other private place, with the owner unknown.

9. Rights of a Finder:

(a) A finder of *lost property* acquires title as against all but the true owner.

The finder is in a relationship with the true owner similar to that of bailor-bailee. Therefore, he will be guilty of conversion if he appropriates the chattel to his own use with knowledge of the true owner, or if he is reasonably able to discover him.

The weight of authority holds that when one finds a chattel on the property of another, he is entitled to the chattel unless he is a trespasser.

(b) The finder of *misplaced* goods does not obtain title or right to possession, but the owner of the property on which they are found is deemed to be the bailee of the goods for the true owner.

(c) The finder of *abandoned goods* generally is entitled not only to possession but also to ownership as against all others. In the case of abandoned shipwrecks within the territorial waters of a state, there is a conflict of authority—some states holding that such property belongs to the state, and the others holding that it belongs to the finder.

(d) In England *treasure trove* escheated to the crown, but in the United States it is treated as lost property and belongs to the finder.

CASE 321: A was engaged in hunting with his dogs and hounds, and was in hot pursuit of a particular fox. Before A could catch the fox, B killed it and kept it for himself. A sued for its value and received a judgment, B appeals, what result?

Answer and Analysis

The answer is that the appeal should be reversed and judgment entered for B. Wild animals and abandoned goods are things which no one owns. The first person who takes possession or occupancy will become owner of that property. The mere chase of a wild animal, however, will not give possessory rights to the hunter, but, on the other hand, actual manual possession of the wild animal is not necessary to obtain title. It is sufficient that the animal be mortally wounded so that actual possession by the hunter is inevitable, or that the animal be caught in a trap or net of the owner. Once this occurs the owner has a vested property interest which cannot be divested by another. Here A was merely in pursuit of the fox, and had not wounded it; therefore his possession was not certain. Therefore, B rightfully obtained possession and title to the fox. See Pierson v. Post, 3 Caines 175 (Supreme Court of N.Y. 1805).

CASE 322: A being employed as a chimney sweep found a piece of jewelry and took it to a goldsmith to be appraised. An apprentice employed by the goldsmith removed the precious stones from the jewelry while pretending to weigh it. The goldsmith refused to return the stones to A. A now sues the goldsmith in trover for recovery of the value of the stones. May A recover?

Answer and Analysis

The answer is yes. It is a general rule of law that a finder has title against all but the rightful owner. As to the owner, a finder is in the position, similar to that of a bailee, with all the ancillary rights and duties. Therefore, while a finder does not attain absolute ownership, he does have the right of ownership against all but the true owner. Similarly, if the finder now loses the found chattel, he may reclaim it from a subsequent finder. Here A was the finder of the jewelry and was entitled to its possession. A master is responsible for the acts of servants while in his employ; hence, the goldsmith is liable to A for full value of the stones. See Armory v. Delamire, King's Bench, 1722, 1 Strange 505.

CASE 323: A, a young boy, picked up a stocking stuffed with soft material and knotted at both ends, and began playing with it among his friends. The stocking passed from boy to boy until, as one lad was striking another with it, the stocking burst and a large amount of money fell out. A claims the money. Is he entitled to it?

Answer and Analysis

The answer is that A is not entitled to the money exclusively but that all the boys are entitled to a pro rata share as tenants in common. A did not have exclusive possession, and he must share the money with the other boys. A finder, subject to certain exceptions noted in the following cases, is entitled to possession as against all but the true owner, and in the instant case the true owner is unknown and is making no claim. To become a finder, however, one must acquire possession, but possession requires more than physical control. Possession consists of physical control of the chattel plus an intent to assume dominion over it. Here A, at the time of discovery, lacked an intent to take dominion over the stocking and its contents; he merely wanted to use it as a plaything with his friends. The other boys had similar ideas. None desired or attempted to exercise possession or exclusive control over the stocking until the money was discovered. When the stocking burst, all the boys formulated the intent to possess at the same time, and since they were all collectively in physical control, they became co-finders. Other rationales, such as that A did take possession of the stocking but that he acquiesced in the copossession of his friends, is possible. See Keron v. Cashman, 33 A. 1055 (N.J.Ch.1896); Note, 10 Harv.L.Rev. 63 (1896–97). Accord: Edmonds v. Ronella, 73 Misc.2d 598, 342 N.Y.S.2d 408 (1973).

CASE 324: A and B aged eight and ten respectively were employed by C to clean out his henhouse. C's home and henhouse had changed hands frequently throughout their existence. The boys found a tin can full of gold buried in a corner of the henhouse in such a condition to suggest that it had been buried there for quite some time. C took the coins from the boys claiming that they belonged to him. The boys file suit. May they recover the coins?

Answer and Analysis

The answer is yes. At early common law lost articles found concealed in the earth or other private place were called treasure trove. Treasure trove usually consisted of coins or money intentionally hidden for safety and with the owner being either dead or unknown at the time of discovery. This is contrasted with lost property which is defined as chattels found on the surface of the earth the possession of which the owner had casually and involuntarily parted. Treasure trove belonged to the King in England, but in the United States treasure trove merged with the law of lost property. The general rule of lost property gives the finder the right to retain it against all persons except the true owner, and if the true owner never claims it as is most likely in the case of treasure trove, then the property becomes that of the finder. Hence, under the doctrine of treasure trove, A and B are entitled to recover possession of the coins. The claim of A and B is fortified by the fact that they are not trespassers, although in some instances technical trespassers have been allowed to retain treasure trove. Further, the master-servant relationship should not diminish the value of the finders' claim since they were only hired to clean the henhouse. It can hardly be expected that turning in discovered articles, as in the case of the hotel maid, (see infra next case), would be in the normal course of their employment. See Danielson v. Roberts, 44 Or. 108, 74 P. 913 (1904); 15 B.U.L.Rev. 656 (1935).

CASE 325: A was employed as a chamber maid by B hotel to clean rooms on a guest's departure. While cleaning one such room, she discovered eight one hundred dollar bills concealed under the lining of a bureau drawer. She delivered the money to B's manager who attempted without success to find the owner. A now seeks recovery of the bills. May she succeed?

Answer and Analysis

The answer is no. The bills in question are classified as misplaced or left property and not as lost or abandoned property. A person loses property when he parts with its possession casually and involuntarily. The possessor is usually unaware that he is parting with possession in the case of lost property. Misplaced property, on the other hand, is property which has been intentionally placed somewhere and then forgotten. In the instant case the bills were carefully placed under the lining in the bureau drawer. They could not have fallen there; they were obviously intentionally put there and then left. Abandoned property is that the possession of which is voluntarily relinquished with an intent to give up all right, title and interest therein. It is obvious in the instant case that the bills were carefully placed under the lining in the drawer. Hence, they were not abandoned.

As a general proposition the finder of lost property has the right to retain possession as against everybody except the true owner. The finder of abandoned property is entitled to both possession and title of the found goods. Generally, in the case of misplaced or left property, the owner of the locus in quo where the property is found is entitled to retain possession as against the finder. The rationale for this holding is that the owner of the chattel is likely to remember where he placed it and return for it. If a casual finder were entitled to keep it, it would be more difficult for the owner to recover it. The owner of the locus is likely to still be there when the owner of the chattel remembers where he placed it, and thus there is a greater likelihood that the property will be returned to its true owner.

The finder in the instant case is a chamber maid whose general duties encompass the delivery to her employer of all articles left in the hotel rooms by guests thereof. The finding occurred in the course of her employment and she had a duty to surrender the money to the hotel. Thus, for this reason also, the hotel has a better right to possess the found money than the finder, A. See Jackson v. Steinberg, 186 Or. 129, 200 P.2d 376 (1948), rehearing denied 205 P.2d 562 (Or.1949).

CASE 326: A trespassed on the land of a stranger and cut ninety-three pine logs without the consent of the owner. A hauled these logs, marked with his initials to a mill, where B converted them to his own use. A now sues for their market value. What result?

Answer and Analysis

The answer is that A should recover. It is a generally recognized rule that possession is itself a protected property right. Hence a possessor, whether he be a bailee or even a converter who had stolen the goods himself, may recover for their damage, conversion or theft while in his possession. As between a possessor and a wrongdoer, possession is a sufficient title, and only one with a superior title may contest the possessor's right. The rationale behind the rule is the protection of property and the discouragement of breaches of the peace. B's conduct is wrongful and should be discouraged, not encouraged. He should not be allowed to raise the issue of lack of title in the possessor as this would dilute the law's protection whenever goods were not in the immediate possession of their owner. The defendant can only raise the issue of title when he has a superior one to that of the possessor. Here A was clearly the possessor of the logs, and although he acquired possession wrongfully B is not able to raise the issue of A's lack of title. Therefore A should recover. See Anderson v. Gouldberg, 51 Minn. 294, 53 N.W. 636 (1892).

CASE 327: A owned a house which he had never occupied. The house was requisitioned for military use, and B, an enlisted man who was stationed in the house, found a brooch on the top of a window frame behind the blackout curtains and in a crevice. The brooch was unpackaged and covered with cobwebs. The owner of the brooch was not found, and it was turned over to A who sold it and kept the money. B now sues A for the value of the brooch. May he recover?

Answer and Analysis

The answer is yes, but the case is not without difficulty. According to the traditional approach, the found item should be first categorized as lost, misplaced, abandoned or treasure trove. Taking up the various categories in reverse order, the item is not treasure trove. First, it is a single item of jewelry and the circumstances of finding preclude any inference that it was carefully secreted or hidden there. The item was not wrapped or enclosed in a container, but instead it was uncovered and unprotected from dirt and filth. Although it is not necessary under some authorities that treasure trove be buried in the ground, it is necessary that it be intentionally hidden or secreted.

The brooch was not abandoned. The value of the item and its location refute any likelihood of abandonment. If one were to abandon such a piece of jewelry, he would likely throw it in the trash, not in a crevice on top of a window frame.

The two probable categories are those of misplaced and lost property, and the two seem almost equally plausible. A lady wearing the pin could have been adjusting the curtains, cleaning the windows, or performing some other chore at some distant time in the past. The pin could have been loose on her dress and fallen off without her noticing it, in which case it would be lost—the possession being casually and involuntarily parted. On the other hand, she could have voluntarily removed the pin and placed it on the frame until her task was completed, and then gone off and forgotten about it—in which case it would be misplaced property. Under the traditional rules, A would be entitled to the jewelry and the proceeds of the sale if it were misplaced, but if it were lost, then B would be so entitled. Under the particular circumstances of this case where the owner of the pin is very unlikely to reclaim it, where the owner of the house had never lived there and knew nothing about it, where the finder is an honest serviceman whose conduct should be rewarded and encouraged, the better solution is to classify the jewelry as lost property and let B recover.

Once the item is classified as lost property, it is fairly easy to resolve the dispute—recite the general rule that the finder of lost property acquires rights superior to all except the true owner, and then assert that the place of finding makes no difference. Nevertheless, a few other matters and cases should be considered. Frequently when property is found imbedded in the soil, the owner of the locus is preferred over the finder. In this case it cannot be said that the pin became a part of the soil, or even appurtenant to the house. It was found on a ledge in the building, not embedded in the soil. Similarly, the cases dealing with findings by employees should have no bearing. Although B was there as a special type of employee of the government, he had no duties as to finding and surrendering items such as this in the usual course of his employment. Thus, he is not precluded from keeping the item as a result of his status. Finally, although a possessor or owner of land may be regarded as in possession of everything attached to or under his land, he is not necessarily in possession of everything lying unattached on the surface thereof. Further, A was not in possession at the time of finding, and in fact had never been in possession of this land. Thus, B is entitled to recover the value of the brooch. See Hannah v. Peel, 1 K.B. 509 (1945).

CASE 328: In the summer of 1622, a fleet of Spanish galleons, heavily laden with bullion exploited from the mines of the New World, set sail for Spain. As the fleet entered the straits of Florida, it was met by a hurricane which drove it into the reef-laced waters off the Florida Keys. A number of vessels went down, including the richest galleon in the fleet, *Nuestra Senora de Atocha*. Five hundred and fifty persons perished, and cargo with a contemporary value of perhaps $250,000,000 was lost. A later hurricane shattered the *Atocha* and buried her beneath the sands.

For well over three centuries the wreck of the *Atocha* lay undisturbed beneath the wide shoal west of the Marquesas Keys. Then in 1971, after an arduous search aided by survivors' accounts of the 1622 wrecks, and an expenditure of more than $2,000,000, plaintiff located the *Atocha*.

Plaintiff has retrieved gold, silver, artifacts, and armament valued at $6,000,000. Plaintiff's costs have included four lives, among them, the son and daughter-in-law of plaintiff's president and leader of the expedition.

The Plaintiff salvage corporation filed suit to retain possession and confirm title in itself to the wrecked and abandoned vessel. The United States government also claimed title. May the Plaintiff recover?

Answer and Analysis

The answer is yes. The vessel and its cargo belongs to the finder rather than to the United States Government. Insofar as sovereignty claims are concerned, however, there is a conflict of authority, and when the treasure or abandoned ship is found in territorial waters, then depending upon state law, it is sometimes awarded to the state.

The *Atocha* was clearly an abandoned vessel, and the court applied the law of finders thereto. The claim of the United States was based on either or both of the following: (1) the Antiquities Act; [1] or (2) the right of the United States, as heir to the sovereign prerogative asserted by the Crown of England, to goods abandoned at sea and found by its citizens. The court concluded that the Antiquities Act applies by its terms only to lands owned or controlled by the government of the United States, and since the wreck rested on the continental shelf beyond the territorial waters of the United States, that Act did not apply.

The right of sovereignty refers to the right of the sovereign under ancient Roman and early English law to wrecked and derelict property on the seas. Originally, the right was absolute, even to the exclusion of the original owner, but by the time of Edward I, the rule had been softened so that the owner could reclaim such property within a year and a day of its abandonment. [2] Thereafter, it belonged absolutely to the King. Thus, under such a rule of sovereignty, the wrecked vessel and its proceeds would belong to the United States government since it was found beyond the territorial waters. However, since there was no specific act of Congress declaring the right of the United States to such finds, the court decided to follow what it termed the American view and applied the law of finders. Therefore, the company which discovered the wreck and salvaged it, was entitled to its contents and the proceeds thereof. See Treasure Salvors, Inc. v. Unidentified Wrecked and Abandoned Sailing Vessel, 569 F.2d 330 (5th Cir. 1978).

1. 16 U.S.C.A. § 431–433. The act is primarily concerned with designation of historic landmarks and related activity.

   The law of salvage was also discussed at length.

2. This brief reference to the right of the sovereign more closely parallels the explanation in State v. Massachusetts Co., 95 So.2d 902 (Fla.1956), holding contra to the principal case and cited at the end hereof.

Note, however, that there is some authority to the contrary. See, for example, State of Florida v. Massachusetts Co., 95 So.2d 902 (Fla.1956), wherein the "finder" salvage company discovered and removed from time to time various parts of a sunken and abandoned battleship within the territorial waters of the State of Florida. The court held that the State of Florida, which had adopted the English common law, in effect had succeeded to the sovereign rights of the Crown of England, and that the battleship and its contents belonged to the State rather than to the finder.

SUMMARY OF CASES IN CHAPTER XXX

Case 321. Title to wild animals can be acquired by reducing them to possession. Possession requires both an intent and a certain amount of physical control over the object. Pursuit of the animal is not in and of itself sufficient to constitute possession unless the animal is either mortally wounded or so spent that actual manucaption is inevitable. Thus, a hunter in pursuit of a fox has no claim against a third person who interferes, shoots the fox, and actually captures it.

Case 322. The finder of a chattel generally has rights to possession superior to everybody except the true owner. Thus, if a third party converts the chattel in the hands of the finder, the finder may recover the thing in specie if it is still in the possession of the converter, or he may recover the full value from such a wrongdoer.

Case 323. Physical control alone is not sufficient to constitute possession or a finding. Possession and finding both require a certain amount of intent, a conscious desire to control the object, to possess it and to exclude others. Thus, where one boy found a stuffed stocking and joined with his friends in using it as a plaything until it burst open revealing a roll of money, all of the boys formulated the intent to possess the money at one and the same time, and since they had mutual control, they all were entitled to the money as cofinders.

Case 324. Treasurer trove refers to gold and silver coins, bar, plate, valuable objects intentionally hidden or secreted, usually in the earth, but the concept is frequently applied to valuables wherever hidden. The owner is usually unknown and not likely to appear. In England at common law treasure trove belonged to the Crown, but in the United States it belongs to the finder.

Case 325. Misplaced property is that which is intentionally placed somewhere and then forgotten. The owner of the locus where misplaced or mislaid property is found is generally accorded rights to possession superior to that of a finder. Certain employees such as hotel maids are usually obligated as a part of their employment duties to deliver found articles to their employer. Thus, the possession of articles found during and within the scope of one's employment is generally awarded to the employer and not to the finder.

Case 326. A possessor, even a wrongful possessor or thief has the right to possession as against all but the true owner. Such possession is a protected interest, and the party in possession is entitled to recover from a converter either the thing in specie or its value.

Case 327. This case summarizes briefly the classification of found property, i. e., lost, misplaced, abandoned, and treasure trove, and gives the basic rules relating to the rights of the finder. A finder of lost articles on the land of another, especially when the finder is there lawfully and not a trespasser, and the owner of the land has never been in possession, is entitled to possession of the article found as against everybody but the true owner of the chattel.

Case 328. The title to the wreck of a vessel which rests on the continental shelf outside the territorial waters of the United States, where such vessel has been abandoned, vests in the person who reduces that property to his or her possession under the law of finder's. Where such wreck or abandoned property, however, rests within the territorial waters of a state, there is a conflict. Some jurisdictions say that the property belongs to the sovereign state if such property has not been reclaimed within a year and a day of its abandonment. Other jurisdictions follow the law of finders and allow the finder to keep it.

Chapter XXXI

BAILMENT

Legal Gems.
Cases.
Summary of Cases in Chapter XXXI.

LEGAL GEMS

1. A bailment may be broadly defined as a rightful possession of goods by one who is not the true owner.

2. A typical bailment occurs when there is delivery of personalty for a particular purpose, or on deposit upon a contract, express or implied, that after the purpose is accomplished, the property shall be returned.

3. A bailment is frequently said to be based on a contract, expressed or implied, but the obligations may be imposed by law irrespective of the "bailee's" intent; thus any contract in such situations is implied by law and not in fact.

4. The bailee must be in possession of the goods.

5. In order to have possession there must be physical control over the property in question, and an intention to exercise that control.

    (a) Control, for example, is an issue when goods are deposited in a safe deposit box where both the customer and the bank have keys. Courts frequently hold this a bailment although the bailee does not have complete control, and no way of knowing what is in the box. The bailee does intend, however, to control the contents whatever they are.

    (b) There also must be an intent to exercise control. This issue is critical in bailments of parcels or other chattels containing therein items of which the "bailee" is unaware, and in situations where the depositary attempts to prevent himself from becoming a bailee of the particular item.

6. A bailment is distinguished from other legal relationships as follows:

    (a) Custody—When the owner of goods places them in the actual physical control of another, but does not intend to relinquish the right as distinct from the power of dominion over them, there is no bailment or possession but only custody. For example, if a clerk hands goods to a customer to examine, the customer has only custody. Similarly, an employee has only custody of his employer's chattels.

(b) Sale—In a sale, title passes to the purchaser; in a bailment the title remains in the bailor.

(c) Conditional Sale—A purchaser under a conditional sales contract acquires not only possession but also beneficial interest in the goods for which he is under an obligation to pay. The conditional seller retains legal title for security only.

(d) Trust—A trustee acquires legal title for purposes of performing his duties as trustee; a bailee has only possession.

(e) Lease—A landlord-tenant relationship and not a bailment results if there is simply a lease of space for use by the tenant. The automobile parking lot situation results in a landlord-tenant, or licensor-licensee relationship in the case of a park-and-lock operation. In this situation the owner of the car keeps the keys, along with control and constructive possession of the automobile. If the keys are surrendered to the attendant and he assumes control of the car, then a bailment results.

In a lease of personal property where the lessee acquires possession of the goods with an obligation to return them, the lessee is a bailee of the chattels.

7. Although criticized, bailments are frequently classified according to which of the parties derive the most benefit for purposes of imposing liability for negligence on the bailee. According to this scheme, if the bailment:

(a) is for the sole benefit of the bailor, the bailee is liable only for gross negligence;

(b) is for the sole benefit of the bailee, the bailee is liable for even slight negligence;

(c) is for the mutual benefit of both the bailor and bailee, the bailee is liable for ordinary negligence, or failure to observe ordinary care, the care that would be exercised by a reasonably prudent man under the circumstances. The trend is for this standard in all cases.

8. The parties by contract may alter the standard of care owed by the bailee where not contra to public policy. To so contract both parties must accept the terms, and where only a sign is posted by the bailee, there must be proof that the bailor saw and accepted its terms. A limitation of liability on a check or receipt for the bailed goods is only valid if the bailor read the ticket and didn't object, or if a reasonable man would expect a contract under such circumstances.

9. The bailee has a duty to redeliver the goods to the bailor on demand, or if a fixed term has been set for the bailment by contract, at the expiration of that term.

10. The bailee is liable for conversion, regardless of negligence, if he wrongfully refuses to deliver or if he delivers to the wrong party.

11. Liability of the bailee is based on negligence if the goods are lost, destroyed or damaged during the bailment. The burden of proof is normally on the bailor, but once he has proved delivery of the goods and failure to return them, or redelivery in a damaged condition, he has made a prima facie case. At this point, the burden of going forward with the evidence shifts to the bailee. See, however, *infra* case 329, putting the burden of proof on the bailee to show he was not negligent.

CASE 329: A wished to have B repair a ring while B was staying at the C hotel. A took the ring off her finger in the presence of the hotel cashier and asked her to deliver it to B. The cashier placed the ring in an envelope, wrote B's name on it, and placed it on her desk. The ring was either lost or stolen without being delivered to B. A sues the C hotel to recover $2,500, the value of the ring. C defends by saying there was no bailment because A failed to disclose the unusual value of the ring. May A recover?

Answer and Analysis

The answer is yes. A bailment has been broadly defined as the rightful possession of goods by one who is not the owner. This possession of the bailed goods consists of physical control of the chattel with an intent to exercise that control. Where the chattel claimed to be bailed is concealed from the bailee, he will not have intended to assume possession and no bailment will exist. For example, in one case the plaintiff deposited her coat with a fur piece hidden in the sleeve in the defendant's cloakroom, and it was subsequently lost. The court held there was no mutual assent to accept the fur, hence no bailment of the fur. In the instant case, there is no question as to the identity of the thing bailed, namely a ring, but only as to its value. Hence there was an intent on the part of the bailee to accept possession of the ring, resulting in a bailment, and an erroneous estimate of its value will not release the bailee from liability.

The next question is as to the type of bailment and the degree of care owed by the bailee. Formerly, it had been customary to distinguish bailments on the basis of who derived the principal benefit from the relationship. If the bailment was for the chief benefit of the bailor, then the bailee owed the duty of slight care and was liable only for gross negligence. If the bailment was for the mutual benefit of the parties, then the bailee owed the duty of ordinary care and was liable for ordinary negligence. If the bailment was for the sole benefit of the bailee, then he owed the duty of great care and was liable for slight negligence. This classification has been largely discarded, and the standard of ordinary care and the liability for ordinary negligence is imposed in the great majority of cases. Nevertheless, in the instant case, the bailment was one for the benefit of both parties. The ring was accepted by the hotel in the ordinary course of its business, and, therefore, was as a matter of law for its benefit. Thus, the duty of ordinary care and liability for ordinary negligence governs.

In order to recover from the bailee, the bailor generally must prove a lack of ordinary care on the part of the bailee. In the usual case this is impracticable for the bailor is unaware of why the goods were not returned, or why they were returned in a damaged condition. Consequently, the courts have formulated a general rule that when the bailor proves delivery of the chattel to the bailee and a failure to return it, or a return in a damaged condition, then the bailor has presented a prima facie case. The burden of going forward with the evidence now shifts to the bailee and he must explain his failure to return the chattel, or rebut the prima facie case by showing he had exercised the degree of care required by law. While the bailee has the burden at that point of going forward with the evidence or risk a directed verdict for the bailor, the majority of courts hold that the bailor always has the burden of persuasion that the bailee was negligent, and that the presumption of negligence in favor of the bailor disappears once the bailee has introduced evidence to the contrary. However, a large minority of courts hold that the bailee has the burden of persuading the jury the loss of the chattel was not due to his negligence. Here A proved delivery to the hotel, and the hotel was unable to show what happened to the ring, or that it had not been negligent. Therefore, the court should direct a judgment for A at the close of B's case. See Peet v. The Roth Hotel Co., 191 Minn. 151, 253 N.W. 546 (1934), holding that the burden of proof under the above facts was on the hotel to show non-negligence. See generally: Bailment—Allocation of the Burden of Proving the Bailee's Negligence, 43 Mo.L.Rev. 90 (1978).

CASE 330: A's messenger dropped a bond through a letter slot into B's office. An employee of B discovered that the bond had been incorrectly delivered and was not the one ordered by B. The employee then opened the door and called for A's messenger. A boy stepped up to the door, and the employee, not knowing the messengers, handed the bond to the boy. This boy was not the messenger and he absconded with the bond. A brought suit to recover its value and the trial court found in his favor. B appeals, what result?

Answer and Analysis

The appeal should be reversed. In a normal bailment, the bailee intentionally assumes possession of the bailor's chattel, and is aware of his responsibilities in relation to the chattel. Frequently, however, a person comes into possession of a chattel either without his knowledge, or without his consent. While a minority of courts deny the existence of a bailment, the great majority classify such a relationship as a quasi or involuntary bailment. The common law does not thrust the duty of caring for the goods of another on a person against his will. Thus, when possession has been involuntarily cast upon a person he has no affirmative duty to care for the chattel unless he does some act inconsistent with the view he does not voluntarily accept possession. For example, if he uses the chattel for his own purposes, willfully destroys it, or refuses to surrender it to the owner on demand, he then assumes dominion and possession over it. Here the bailee was put in possession without any agreement on his part to accept it. The delivery had been a mistake. The bailee promptly discovered it and immediately attempted to divest himself of possession. Therefore, he was an involuntary bailee and as such had no responsibility to the owner other than that of ordinary care.

In an ordinary bailment, the bailee is held strictly accountable for a misdelivery and is liable for conversion when such misdelivery occurs. However, this is not the rule as to an involuntary bailee. He is held liable only for negligence and the sole issue is whether he used means which were reasonable and proper to return the chattel. Where there is no express obligation to another, a person is held liable for only his negligent or willful acts. In the instant case there was no showing that the means used to return the bond was improper and A should be denied recovery. See Cowen v. Pressprich, 117 Misc. 663, 192 N.Y.S. 242, reversed 202 App.Div. 796, 194 N.Y.S. 926 (1922).

CASE 331: A's scow was chartered to B who then subchartered it to C. D's employees while on a job for C negligently loaded sand and gravel in the scow causing it to capsize. A sued C and D for the damages sustained. The trial court allowed recovery against D but dismissed the claim against C. A appeals the decision dismissing the action against C. What result?

Answer and Analysis

The appeal should be reversed and liability imposed on both C and D. D is primarily liable and C is secondarily liable. A bailment may either be a contractual relation, or created by operation of law. It is the combination of lawful possession and the duty to account for the item as the property of another that creates the bailment. C was the bailee of A even though it received possession from B. As a bailee C has the duty to care properly for the subject matter of the bailment and therefore will be held liable for the acts of negligence of people he entrusts it to. C cannot delegate his duties to others. See Seaboard Sand & Gravel Corp. v. Moran Towing Corp., 154 F.2d 399 (2d Cir. 1946).

CASE 332: A drove her car into B's enclosed parking lot and paid the admission price. She left her keys in the ignition at the request of the attendant and in return was given a receipt. Printed on the ticket was the following:

> Liability. Management assumes no responsibility of any kind. Charges are for rental of space. From 8 AM to 11 PM. Not responsible for articles left in or on the car. Agree to within terms.

She read and understood these words, but did not read a sign which provided:

> Charges are for use of parking space until 11 PM. Not responsible for cars left open after 11 PM. You may lock your car.

When she returned her car had been stolen. A sues B. May she recover?

Answer and Analysis

The answer is yes. Depositing an automobile in a parking lot may constitute either a rental of space or a bailment of the automobile. The difference is whether the owner of the car surrenders possession and the owner of the lot assumes it. Where the attendant collects a fee, designates the area in which to park, and the owner parks and locks the automobile himself, there is no transfer of possession, no bailment, and no liability on the parking lot for theft. But when the attendant takes complete charge of the car, parks it, retains the key and issues a receipt, possession will have passed and a bailment created. This results regardless of what the ticket says. Once the bailment relationship has been created a duty arises to exercise reasonable care to prevent theft. The provisions on the receipt will be of no effect, as a bailee can not by contract relieve himself from *all* liability for losses resulting from his own negligence according to substantial authority.

See Malone v. Santora; Johnson v. Santora, 135 Conn. 286, 64 A. 2d 51 (1949); Ampco Auto Parts, Inc. v. Williams, 517 S.W.2d 401 (Tex.Civ.App.1974), holding that the parking lot was not a bailee of the trunk contents which would not reasonably be expected to be placed therein.

CASE 333: A, a jewelry salesman, while staying at B's hotel, informed the clerk he wished to place a case in the safe. A state statute provides that if the innkeeper provides a safe he shall not be liable for the loss of goods by his guests unless the guest places them in the safe. A second statute fixes $500 as the maximum amount beyond which the guest cannot recover unless the innkeeper consents to a greater liability. A did not inform the clerk that there were jewels in the case. The case was subsequently lost and A seeks to recover its value. What result?

Answer and Analysis

A's recovery will be limited to $500. An innkeeper was liable at common law for any loss of a guest's property unless the loss was occasioned by Act of God, negligence or fraud of the guest, or by the public enemy. However, the modern trend of statutes has modified this insurer's liability. Under the common law the guest did not have to disclose the value of his property in order to impose liability on the Innkeeper, but this has changed. The modern statutes require a guest to use reasonable care and prudence in the protection of his property. One aspect of this care is the disclosing of the value of his property to the innkeeper in order to hold him liable for the excess of that provided for in the statute. Failure to disclose is an act of negligence which will preclude recovery beyond $500. Here A did not disclose the unusual value of the case and therefore his recovery will be limited to the statutory maximum.

See Chase Rand Corp. v. Pick Hotels Corp. of Youngstown, 167 Ohio St. 301, 147 N.E.2d 849 (1958).

––––––

CASE 334: A leased earthmoving equipment from B under a lease-purchase option contract. The contract provided that A would keep and maintain the equipment in good mechanical condition during the term of the agreement and return it to B "in good mechanical condition, save and except the usual wear and depreciation as may be caused by reasonable use and wear thereof." The equipment was destroyed by fire without negligence on the part of A. The trial court held this contract constituted A an insurer of the equipment, and A appealed. What result on appeal?

Answer and Analysis

On appeal the case should be reversed. A bailee is not an insurer of the property in an ordinary bailment; the weight of authority holds that a bailee without fault is not liable for damage to the bailed property. However, a bailee may extend or qualify his liability by contract unless contra to public policy. Therefore, a bailee may become an insurer when he explicitly contracts that he will be absolutely liable irrespective of fault. The general rule however is that a covenant to insure may never be implied and will be imposed only where it is found in the agreement in clear and explicit language. An agreement to return the bailed property in the same condition as when received does not impose such unusual responsibility.

See St. Paul Fire and Marine Ins. Co. v. Chas. H. Lilly Co., 48 Wash.2d 528, 295 P.2d 299 (1956).

CASE 335: A had a trunk transported by the B corp. on its railroad from Providence to Boston. In Boston it was placed in B's warehouse and it could not be found when A came to claim it. The trial judge ruled that if the trunk had been taken from the depot by mistake without negligence on the part of B, he would not be liable. A appeals assigning this ruling as error. What result?

Answer and Analysis

The appeal should be affirmed. A bailee, once the purposes of the bailment have been concluded, owes to the bailor the duty of redelivering the subject matter of the bailment on demand. While the bailee's duty during the bailment is that of using reasonable care, his care in making delivery extends to strict liability. If the bailee misdelivers the goods to an unauthorized third party, he will be liable for conversion of the goods, or for breach of contract regardless of his good faith or lack of negligence. The bailee will also be liable for a conversion if he refuses to deliver the goods to the bailor on his demand. However if the property was stolen from the bailee during the term of the bailment, proof of lack of negligence will relieve him of liability. The case should be affirmed.

See Lichtenhein v. Boston & Providence R.R. Co., 65 Mass. (11 Cush.) 70 (1853).

SUMMARY OF CASES IN CHAPTER XXXI

Case 329. A bailment consists of the rightful possession of another's chattels, but possession requires an intent to control and possess as well as control in fact. The delivery and acceptance of a ring constitutes the receiver a bailee thereof although the receiver may not have been aware of the true value of the ring. Classification of bailments in terms of which party derives the most benefit for purposes of determining the standard of care required by the bailee is becoming less popular, and the general standard of ordinary care under the circumstances is imposed. In jurisdictions where classification is still employed, a bailment for mutual benefit imposes the obligation of ordinary care on the bailee and makes him liable for ordinary negligence. If the bailor shows delivery to the bailee and failure to redeliver, or redelivery in a damaged condition, the bailor makes a prima facie case. At this point most jurisdictions say the burden of going forward with the evidence shifts to the bailee with the ultimate burden of proof resting on the bailor, but some jurisdictions say at this point that the burden of proof shifts to the bailee.

Case 330. The term involuntary bailment is applied to those situations where chattels are placed under the control of a person without his knowledge or consent. In such a situation the only obligation owed by the "bailee" to the owner is that of ordinary care under the circumstances. Absolute liability in conversion for misdelivery, applicable to bailees generally, is not applicable to involuntary bailees. Thus, if an involuntary bailee acts reasonably in attempting to divest himself of possession as soon as he becomes aware of the chattel, such "bailee" is not liable to the owner if the chattel is thereafter lost or damaged.

Case 331. A bailment need not be created by direct contract since it is the combination of lawful possession and the duty to account to the owner of the item that creates the bailment. A person who receives a chattel from a bailee is himself a bailee to the owner. A bailee cannot delegate his duty to others, and he is liable for the negligent acts of persons to whom he entrusts the bailed chattel.

Case 332. A parking lot operation results in a lease of space relationship when the motorist parks and locks his car, but it results in a bailment when the attendant takes possession and control of the car. The conduct of the parties determines the relationship and not the printed words on the ticket. The parties by a voluntary agreement may limit the liability of the bailee, but considerable authority will not permit him to exempt himself from all liability for negligence.

Case 333. At common law an innkeeper was an insurer of the safety of the guest and his property, and was liable for any losses except those occasioned by an act of God, fraud or negligence of the guest, or by the public enemy. Statutes limiting the liability of innkeepers are today very common. Such statutes frequently provide that the innkeeper shall not be liable for the valuables of his guests if the hotel provides a safe for the deposit of articles and the guest does not take advantage of it. The statutes also frequently provide a limit of liability even if the guest deposits his valuables in the safe. Where applicable, the terms of the statute govern the liability of the innkeeper.

Case 334. A bailee is not an insurer but instead is liable only for negligence in the usual case. The parties, however, by a valid contract may agree to expand or limit the liability of the bailee. The liability of an insurer will only be imposed where the contract is explicit in that regard. An agreement to return the bailed property in the same condition as when received does not impose the liability of an insurer.

Case 335. A bailee has an absolute duty to redeliver the bailed goods to the bailor after the purpose of the bailment is accomplished. If the bailee delivers the bailed chattel to the wrong person, the bailee is liable for conversion irrespective of negligence. However, if the chattel is stolen from the bailee without negligence or wrongdoing on his part, the bailee is not liable. His liability is absolute in the case of misdelivery, but he is responsible only for the exercise of due care in his relationship otherwise to the bailed chattel.

Chapter XXXII

GIFTS, INCLUDING JOINT BANK ACCOUNTS

Gifts.
  Legal Gems.
  Cases.
Summary of Cases in Chapter XXXII.

LEGAL GEMS

1. A gift is a voluntary transfer of property by the owner to another without consideration or compensation.

2. A gift is a present transfer of an interest in property. If it is to take effect in futuro it is a mere promise to make a gift and unenforceable for lack of consideration.

3. A present gift of a future interest is valid. There is no necessity that the gift be of the entire interest in the property concerned.

4. A gift by a testamentary disposition does not take effect upon the execution of the instrument, but at death of the testator. Such gifts must comply with the Statute of Wills.

5. Delivery is essential for a gift, but what constitutes delivery depends upon the circumstances.

6. If the subject matter of a gift can not reasonably be delivered manually, or the circumstances do not permit it, a symbolic or constructive delivery will suffice.

7. A delivery is symbolic where something is handed over in place of the actual thing itself; a constructive delivery is the handing over of the means of obtaining possession and control of the property.

8. The delivery must divest the donor of dominion and control over the property given.

9. When the subject matter of the gift is already in the hands of the donee, delivery is not necessary.

10. A delivery to a third person on behalf of the donee is valid if the third person is not the agent, bailee or trustee of the donor.

11. A donative intent is necessary to constitute a valid gift.

12. Donative intent is determined primarily by the words of the donor, but in doubtful cases the court will consider the surrounding circumstances, the relationship of the parties, the size of the gift in relation to the total amount of the donor's property, and the conduct of the donor towards the property after the purported gift.

13. Acceptance by the donee is the final requirement for a valid gift. The donee may refuse to accept since one cannot have property

thrust upon him in an inter vivos transaction against his will. However, acceptance is generally presumed if the gift is beneficial.

14.   A gift may be either inter vivos or causa mortis.

15.   A gift causa mortis is one made in contemplation of imminent death. It becomes absolute on the donor's death from the anticipated peril with the donee surviving and without the donor having revoked the gift. The gift is revocable until the death of the donor, and it is automatically revoked on the donor's recovery.

16.   A bank account made payable on death to one other than the depositor logically is testamentary in character and is ineffective to create presently an interest in the prospective donee. The transaction is also ineffective to transmit the account on the death of the depositor because of noncompliance with the Statute of Wills. There is conflicting authority, however. See paragraph starting "Cf." at end of Case 340.

17.   Joint and survivorship bank accounts when effectively created permit either party to exercise control during their lifetimes, and at the death of one the entire balance belongs to the survivor.

18.   Joint and survivorship bank accounts are frequently used for the purpose of directing the devolution of funds on the death of the depositor. Their effectiveness to accomplish such purpose where one of the parties is the sole depositor depends in part upon the jurisdiction in question and the facts as to the particular joint bank account.

19.   In a jurisdiction following the contract theory of joint bank accounts, the survivor is entitled to the proceeds of the account simply because the contract with the bank so provides.

20.   In a gift theory jurisdiction, the noncontributing survivor will be entitled to the account if he can establish that a gift was effected by which he acquired an interest in the account when it was created. The requirements of donative intent, delivery and acceptance must be proved. The subject matter of the gift is an interest in the account during the joint lives of the depositors and not the entire proceeds of the account. The finding of such a gift is facilitated when both parties make deposits and withdrawals during the joint lives. Any inference of a gift is rebutted by a finding that the account was put in both names merely for the convenience of the principal depositor and that there was no intent to make a gift.

21.   A bank account in the name of the depositor as trustee for another is a valid bank account trust so that on the death of the depositor the proceeds of the account belong to the named beneficiary. Such tentative trusts are revocable and are commonly referred to as Totten trusts.

22.   An oral trust of personal property is valid if the settlor satisfies the requirements of creating a trust. A trust requires a settlor, beneficiary, trustee, res or corpus, and intent to create a trust. A

settlor may also be a trustee, and in a self declaration of trust no delivery of the trust res is required.

CASE 336: O, in accordance with his custom of the past five years, desired to give his son, S, and daughter, D, a Christmas present of one million dollars each. S had physical possession of O's stock and complete access to the vault in which it was stored, O having previously transferred the vault to S, with O not retaining any right of access to the vault. Further, S had a general power of attorney for O as to all the stock in the vault. After O, vacationing in California, had communicated his desire to make the gift, S's bookkeeper in New York wrote to S, by then also in California, suggesting a plan whereby 8,000 shares of stock X would be credited to the accounts of each S and D, and $8,000 in cash, making a total of one million dollars each, would be also credited to the accounts of each S and D. O approved the plan and authorized S to send a telegram "Charge up X stock as indicated in your letter." The bookkeeper changed the books accordingly, the entries indicating that the transfer as to the stock had already taken place. O then dropped dead after the stock entries were made but before the entries as to the cash transfer were recorded. The State Comptroller seeks to tax both the stock and the cash as part of O's estate? May he do so?

Answer and Analysis

The answer is no as to the stock; yes as to the $16,000 in cash. The traditional rule is that for a valid gift there must be both a donative intent to make a gift and a valid delivery of the subject matter of the gift. Delivery of a deed of gift, however, will satisfy the requirements of a delivery of the subject matter itself. The policy behind the rule requiring delivery is to protect alleged donors and their heirs from fraudulent claims of gifts based only on parol evidence. In elementary cases of gifts of tangible personal property, the delivery requirement is most readily satisfied by a transfer of possession to the donee of the subject matter of the gift. Similarly, in the case of certain intangibles such as shares of stock, the delivery requirement is most readily satisfied by a delivery of transfer of possession of the stock certificates themselves.

The requirement of delivery insofar as it entails an actual transfer of the tangible personal property has been considerably diluted over the years. The nature of the requirement depends in a large measure upon the circumstances of the case. Where actual transfer of possession is either impossible or ridiculous, various substitutes have been recognized as sufficient. For example, if the subject matter of the gift is already in the possession of the intended donee, as in the case where he is a bailee of the donor, then the law does not require him to redeliver the items to the donor to have him transfer them back to the donee. Under such circumstances, the requirement of delivery is obviated, and all that is necessary is a donative intent. Under such and similar circumstances, the requirement of delivery is usually satisfied by a clearly expressed intent that the title, or a portion thereof, be presently transferred to the donee.

In the instant case, S was in possession as bailee of all the stock of his father, the donor, O. The stock certificates were physically located in New York, but the donor and S, one of the donees, were in California. As to S physical delivery was not only unnecessary but actually impossible. Hence, as to his gift, any further delivery is unnecessary and all that is required is a complete manifestation of intent to transfer title presently. This was done by the telegram, and further, the book entries were actually made indicating that a transfer had taken place. Therefore, there was a completed gift as to S.

Insofar as the daughter is concerned, delivery need not be made to the donee herself, but it can be made to a third party for the donee. If there is an absolute transfer of possession to a third party for the donee, the fact that the donee is unaware of the transfer is immaterial. In the absence of evidence to the contrary, acceptance by the donee will be presumed. In gifts to third parties for donees, what is required is a transfer of possession of the subject matter of the gift, and a clear manifestation of intent to make a gift, that is, transfer presently some interest in the subject matter. In the instant case, however, S is already in possession of the stock of the donor. Hence, as in the gift to him, any further delivery at this time is not only unnecessary but also impossible. Hence, all that is required is a clear manifestation of intent to release to S the beneficial interest in the stock for the benefit of the donee, D. This was clearly done by the telegram and by the book entries before O's death. Therefore, there was a completed gift of the stock to both S and D.

The cash sums needed to complete the respective gifts of a million dollars each, however, is a different matter. No entries were made upon O's books showing actual payment of this amount until after his death, and the telegram manifesting an intent of a present gift only referred specifically to the stock. Thus, there is insufficient evidence to show an inter vivos gift of the money. See Matter of Mills, 172 App.Div. 530, 158 N.Y.S. 1100, affirmed 219 N.Y. 642, 114 N.E. 1072 (1916). See Jones, Corroborating Evidence as a Substitute for Delivery in Gifts of Chattels, 12 Suff.U.L.Rev. 16 (1978).

––––––––

CASE 337: D, prior to undergoing a serious surgical operation for the removal of a tumor, communicated that fact to X Trust Company and at the same time delivered to it various pieces of jewelry with instructions to give such items to the named donees "in the event of my death from the operation." The surgeon, after making an incision, decided that removal of the tumor was too dangerous and then sewed up the wound. D was released from the hospital and the incision wound healed. Thereafter, D died from the tumor. D was aware that the operation was not performed and the reasons therefor. She expressed a continuing desire that the named donees would receive the items previously designated, but, although advised by her attorney that the gifts were probably no longer valid, she did nothing to change the nature of the deposit, or to make a will bequeathing the items either to the alleged donees or to anybody else. After her death, D's administrator brought an action to recover the items of jewelry from the X Trust Company. May he succeed?

Answer and Analysis

The answer is yes. Gifts are divided into two principal categories—inter vivos and causa mortis. A gift inter vivos is absolute and unconditional, taking effect at the time of delivery. A gift causa mortis is made in contemplation or apprehension of death. It is not absolute but conditional or inchoate and revocable. For a valid gift causa mortis, the peril of death contemplated must be immediate and specific, concern for the normal vicissitudes of life is not sufficient. Further, recovery automatically revokes the gift.

A fully effectuated causa mortis gift is dependent or conditioned on the death of the donor. Whether the condition in such gifts is precedent or subsequent has engendered considerable verbal gymnastics, subtle rationalizations, and frequent disappointed donees. The difficulty with construing the gift as being subject to the condition precedent of the donor's death is that if the gift doesn't take effect until the death of the donor, then it is too late for him to make a gift in this manner since he can only direct the transmission of property after his death by means of a will or last testament, and this requires compliance with the Statute of Wills. Thus, most jurisdictions construe gifts causa mortis as transferring title presently but subject to revocation on recovery by the donor or on his change of mind. Under this rationale, the gift becomes absolute on removal of the conditions subsequent. In effect, the gift operates thus: "This item is yours, take it now and enjoy it, but if I recover from this peril, I want it back." The difficulty of requiring the donor's intent to be expressed in such a manner is that most donors would not be aware of the distinction between conditions precedent and subsequent, and in fact most donors would most likely express the gift in terms of a condition precedent, e. g., "I want you to have this if I die." Thus, some courts may utilize the condition subsequent analysis but liberally construe appropriate statements of satisfying the requirements of a gift causa mortis although they may in fact be in terms of a condition precedent. Some courts simply repudiate the distinction. In the instant case, the facts indicate a gift causa mortis, and for the present we will assume that originally a valid gift causa mortis was effectuated.

The donor wanted the items to be delivered to the donee "in the event of my death from the operation." The facts show that the donor did not die from the operation; in fact the operation was never actually performed, and the donor made a sufficient recovery to return home and have the incision heal. She, in fact, died from the underlying cause. The immediate peril that motivated the gifts was the operation; she did not die therefrom, hence the gift was revoked. The donor did have time after her return home to draft a will or to make an absolute gift of the items, neither of which she did. Therefore, her administrator may recover the items since the gift was revoked. See In re Nols' Estate, 251 Wis. 90, 28 N.W.2d 360 (1947), for a discussion of the condition precedent versus condition subsequent requirement; Brind v. International Trust Co., 66 Colo. 60, 179 P. 148 (1918), for a factual case similar to the above.

Note

Cf. the following case which reached a similar result. On December 23, 1967, A suffered a severe and disabling heart attack from which he remained hospitalized for approximately two months. On March 23, 1968, after returning home from the hospital he gave a check for $10,000.00 to his trusted employee, B. On the check, A penned in the following words, "Only Good In Case of Death." Due to his incapacity, A could only return to his business on a part time basis. A died on October 16, 1972 of "acute pulmonary edema, arteriosclerotic heart disease and chronic congestive heart failure." After his death, A's administrator refused to pay B the $10,000.00 and B sues claiming it was a gift causa mortis. May B succeed?

The answer is no. There is no difficulty in finding that the subject matter of the gift has been delivered by the donor to the donee at a time when the donor was under the apprehension of death from some existing disease; both requirements of a valid gift causa mortis. The difficulty comes with the requirement that the donor must not recover from his infirmity. A finally died of his heart ailment, nearly five years after delivery of the gift to B. The fact that A did leave the hospital and showed some interest in his business is at least convincing evidence that he "recovered" from the depth of the disease that caused him to be concerned about his chances of prolonged life. Therefore, B's claim on the estate must fail. Fendley v. Laster, 260 Ark. 370, 538 S.W.2d 555 (1976).

CASE 338: A, somewhat advanced in years but suffering no particular ill health or peril, endorsed a stock certificate in favor of his daughter, D, placed the stock certificate in an envelope, and delivered the envelope to B, saying that it should be delivered to D in case of the death of A. Sometime later, A died and the certificate was delivered to D. A's administrator brings an action to recover the stock or its value. May he succeed?

Answer and Analysis

The answer is no but a contrary answer is possible. The facts in the instant case indicate somewhat of an ambiguous transaction, and the result depends upon how the court construes the intent of A, the alleged donor. Since A was suffering no ill health and was not facing an immediate peril, it is clear that no gift causa mortis was intended. The general awareness of the inevitability of death is insufficient to support a gift causa mortis. The delivery requirement of a gift is satisfied by delivery to a third person for the benefit of, or for further delivery to, the donee. Thus, the only question, and the crucial one in this case, is the intent of the donor at the time he delivered the certificate of stock to B.

The directions were to deliver the stock to D in case of the death of A. Did he mean by this that D was to get the stock and all interests therein only at the death of A and nothing before? If so, the transaction is testamentary and ineffective because of noncompliance with the Statute of Wills. The direction to deliver "in case of death" does sound as if death is a condition precedent, and hence the transfer should be ineffective. Death, however, is inevitable, and the only contingency is that of time. If the directions were to deliver "on my death" instead of "in case of my death," the transaction would not be testamentary since death is certain to occur. The difference is explained in the next paragraph, but in the meantime, it may be noted that an ordinary layman is just as likely, and perhaps more so, to use the expression "in case of death" as he is to use "on my death," or "when I die."

In the event that a donor transfers chattels to a third person to be delivered to a donee on the death of the donor, meaning whenever and however the donor may die, then the donor has effectively divested himself of sufficient dominion and control over the subject matter of the gift. The inevitability of death makes it certain that the full title will eventually vest in the donee. The situation is analogous to delivery of deeds on similar circumstances, and can be construed as vesting presently a valid future interest in the donee. The relationship can be categorized as that of a life estate and remainder, or absolute ownership and executory interest. Title passes but enjoyment is postponed. Thus, under these circumstances, the fact that the donor collects dividends during his life, or votes the stock, is immaterial. There is a valid gift which takes effect immediately on transfer of the subject matter to the third party, and on the later death of the donor, the future interest previously vested in the donee becomes possessory.

Thus, in the instant case, if the donor's intent can be construed as meaning that the donee is to get the stock on the death of the donor, no matter when or how that event occurs, then the gift is complete on the first delivery and a valid future interest vests at once in the donee. The fact that the donor said "in case I die" instead of "when I die" should not be too significant because of a lack of appreciation of the legal differentiation. Further, natural conceit or reluctance to accept the inevitability of death may lead to the use of a contingent expression when in fact such inevitability is recognized. After delivery to B, A in fact exercised no dominion or control over the stock other than that which was consistent with the reservation of a life estate. We conclude, therefore, that he made a valid gift of a future interest, and that his administrator cannot recover the stock. See Innes v. Potter, 130 Minn. 320, 153 N.W. 604, 3 A.L.R. 896 (1915).

CASE 339: A opened a savings account in the names of "A and B as joint tenants with the right of survivorship" in which the funds were payable to "A or to B or to the Survivor." Both A and B signed the signature cards, but A kept possession of the pass book. All deposits and withdrawals were made by A. After A's death, B withdrew all the funds from the account, and A's administrator then brought an action against B to recover the funds withdrawn. May the Administrator recover?

Answer and Analysis

The answer is no. Joint accounts such as this are in common usage and are the frequent subject of litigation. When one of the parties makes all of the deposits and exercises complete control over the account during his lifetime, the courts follow either one of two theories in determining the rights of claimants after the death of the cotenant who made the deposits. These theories are the contract theory and the gift theory.

The contract theory is predicated on the proposition that a bank deposit constitutes the bank a debtor. Then, when the depositor orders the bank to pay himself or another upon the order of either party, and secures the signature of the second party evidencing an assent to the arrangement and notifies him of the completed transaction, there is created in the second party by contract a joint interest in the account equal to his own. Thus, under this theory, B is entitled to the funds simply because this was the contract with the bank.

Under similar circumstances, however, a majority of jurisdictions follow a gift theory and allow B to get the funds only if it is concluded that a valid gift was made. The requisites of donative intent, delivery, and acceptance must be shown. Acceptance causes little difficulty because of the presumption of accepting beneficial gifts and because of the signing of the signature card. Donative intent and delivery are bigger problems. To sustain a gift it is not necessary that the subject matter of the gift be the entire bank account or that the entire funds be delivered to the donee. In the joint bank account the intended gift and the subject matter thereof is an interest in the account, not the account itself. Delivery is sufficient if there is a vesting of an equal right to control, that is, to deposit and withdraw funds from the account.

Thus, under the gift theory, B will be entitled to the funds if A intended to vest in him presently an interest in the account, and if A did in fact give him an equal right of control. In cases like the present where no dispute arose until after the death of the donor depositor, the form of the account constitutes prima facie evidence of the gift. Thus, if no rebuttal testimony is introduced, B will be allowed to keep the funds. If, however, it is shown that the alleged donee never made any deposits or withdrawals during the lifetime of the donor, that the donor did not intend him to have any such control but that the only purpose of the account was to pass it to the donee on the donor's death, and that until then the funds were to be regarded solely as those of the donor, and that the account was put in both names for the convenience of A, then no present gift was created and the administrator would be entitled to the funds. As may be expected, the degree of liberality with which the courts construe these accounts, varies considerably. In the instant case, however, since there are few, if any, facts to rebut the inference of a gift arising from the joint account, the decision should be in favor of B. That B did not in fact make any deposits or withdrawals is not conclusive that he had no right to do so. See Dyste v. Farmers' & Mechanics' Sav. Bank of Minneapolis, 179 Minn. 430, 229 N.W. 865 (1930); Malone v. Walsh, 315 Mass. 484, 53 N.E.2d 126 (1944); Bachmann v. Reardon, 138 Conn. 665, 88 A.2d 391 (1962), the latter finding against the surviving cotenant.

Note

In case creditors of the non-contributing cotenant seek to reach his interest during the joint lives of both depositors, it would seem clear that in a gift theory jurisdiction which found no gift in the particular case, that such creditors would have no rights. In case a gift were found, then the extent of the gift or the amount of the donee's interest would have to be determined. In the case of a contract theory jurisdiction, it would logically follow that the creditors should be able to reach the codepositor's interest. The amount of such interest might be limited to half on the basis of a presumed equality, or the contract theory might be given full effect so that the creditor could reach the entire account on the basis that the debtor could have withdrawn all the funds. On the other hand, there is also authority for the proposition that in the case of creditors the realities of ownership may be shown, in which case the creditor of the non-contributing depositor would get nothing. See Union Properties, Inc. v. Cleveland Trust Co., 152 Ohio St. 430, 89 N.E.2d 638 (1949); Park Enterprises, Inc. v. Trach, 233 Minn. 467, 47 N.W.2d 194 (1951), both employing the contract theory, but the Ohio case permitting a showing of the realities of ownership.

———

CASE 340: A had an $8,000 deposit in the X bank. He instructed the cashier at the bank that he wanted the funds to go to B on his death. The cashier wrote "pay on death to B" on the account ledger. A made small withdrawals and deposits thereafter. A statute provides that when a deposit is made in the name of two or more persons, payable to survivor, it may be paid to either person. On his death, the estate of A seeks to recover the funds from B. What result?

Answer and Analysis

The answer is that the estate should recover. An instrument which operates only to convey an interest in property after the death of the grantor or donor is testamentary, and passes no present interest in the property. Therefore, such a transaction is void unless it meets the statutory requirements for the execution of a will. The effect of the words on the ledger sheet are clearly testamentary; however, B claims the statute will save the gift. This transaction does not fall into the area covered by the statute, as the deposit was not made in the name of two or more persons, but payable only to A during his lifetime and then to B. The statute contemplates the creation of a present interest with actual enjoyment postponed until death. See Young v. McCoy, 152 Neb. 138, 40 N.W.2d 540 (1950).

Cf. In Re Estate of Wright, 17 Ill.App.3d 894, 308 N.E.2d 319 (1974), which upheld a P.O.D. account on either a theory of "Totten Trust," although no words of trust were used, or on a contract third party beneficiary rationale.

See also Uniform Probate Code §§ 6–101(10) and 6–104(b), which validate qualifying P.O.D. accounts.

———

CASE 341: A opened two savings accounts, the passbooks reading that both accounts were in trust for B. A exercised full control over both accounts, making additional deposits and withdrawals whenever he desired to do so. The money withdrawn was used by A for his own personal uses and he made no effort to set aside for or account for such sums to B. At one time one account had a balance of $10,000, but at the death of A this account was closed. The other account had a balance of $15,000 at the death of A, none of which funds had apparently come from the closed account. At the death of A, both B and A's administrator claimed the right to the proceeds of the remaining account, and B also claimed the $10,000 that had been in the closed account. (1) As between the administrator and B, who is entitled to the proceeds of the active account?　(2) May B recover from A's estate the $10,000 which was in the other account?

Answers and Analyses

The answer to (1) is that B is entitled to the account; and the answer to (2) is that B may not recover.　Bank accounts in the name of the depositor in trust for another person are widely used and are designed for the convenience of the depositor in controlling the account during his lifetime and in determining the disposition of the account in the event of his death.　They are, in effect, tentative trusts, or trusts in which the depositor reserves the right to revoke.　Clearly, no irrevocable trust is intended, but on the other hand, there is an intent that the beneficiary of such an account has an interest in the account from the time that the account is opened.　It is thus a revocable trust, with the grantor depositor reserving complete control and power of revocation in whole or in part.　Thus, when A withdraws money from an account, or closes it entirely, he is in effect revoking the trust either pro tanto or completely.　Until revoked, however, the beneficiary of the trust has a beneficial interest in the account similar to such an interest in a more formally prepared trust in which the settlor reserves the power to revoke.

Thus, in the instant case, the unrevoked account in trust for B became absolute on the death of A.　He no longer had the power to revoke; therefore, the entire beneficial and legal interest vested in B. This is in accordance with the intent of the depositor, and unless some strong public policy should invalidate this type of arrangement, B should get the account.　Substantially, there is no significant difference between this informal type of revocable trust and a more formally created document.　Also, there is no prohibition from the settlor of a trust also being the trustee.　Therefore, B is entitled to the balance of the account.　As to the closed account, however, B is not entitled to recover.　The trust was only tentative or revocable, and A in his lifetime did revoke this trust by closing the account.　Therefore, B is not entitled to recover.　See Matter of Totten, 179 N.Y. 112, 71 N.E. 748 (1904); Dyste v. Farmers' & Mechanics' Sav. Bank of Minneapolis, 179 Minn. 430, 229 N.W. 865 (1930); Uniform Probate Code § 6–104.

CASE 342:　A's minor nephew, B, lived with A as a member of his family for the ten years preceding A's death. During his lifetime A purchased thirteen $1,000.00 bonds and at that time he informed B's father that he was holding the bonds for B.　After A's death the bonds were found in an envelope endorsed: "13 bonds, $1,000 each, held for B, signed A."　In the account books and memoranda of A these bonds and the earned interest on them were entered to the account of B.　A's administrator claims these bonds as a part of A's estate.　Will he be successful?

Answer and Analysis

The answer is no. An owner of personal property wishing to make a voluntary disposition of it, may do so either by gift or by impressing a trust upon the property for the benefit of a donee. Whichever method is decided upon must satisfy the requirements for that particular transaction. In the instant case there was no attempt to make any type of delivery whatsoever of the subject matter of the bonds, and no showing of any reason for not making a delivery; hence the transaction can not be upheld as a gift.

In order to create a trust there must be an intent to create a trust, a trust corpus or subject matter of the trust, a settlor, a beneficiary and a trustee. There is no requirement, however, that the three parties, settlor, trustee and beneficiary be entirely distinct individuals or entities, although, of course, there cannot be a complete identity of the three. Thus, a settlor may also be the trustee, and it is perfectly permissible for an owner to declare himself trustee of designated property for the benefit of a beneficiary. In such cases, the intent to create a trust and the creation of a trust corpus are critical factors. Delivery by the settlor to himself as trustee would be an idle ceremony and is not required.

In the instant case A stated that he was holding the bonds for B, and he communicated this fact to B's father. Further, the bonds were segregated from the personal effects of A and they were clearly marked as being held for B. No precise form of words are needed to create a trust. Although express words of trust may be a clear indication of the settlor's intent, any form of expression indicating such an intent is sufficient. Here there was an expression that the bonds were held for B, and the bonds were earmarked with notations on the envelope to that effect. Further, the interest was credited to the account of B, the intended beneficiary, and the settlor admittedly stood in the position of loco parentis, thus supplying a sufficient motive for the creation of the trust. Hence, there is clear evidence of an intent to create a trust.

Further, there is sufficient evidence that the intent was carried out. Although it may not be sufficient for one in a closed room to declare simply that he is holding property in trust for another, more than that was done in the instant case. Information was communicated to the boy's father, and the writing on the envelope was certainly intended to be seen by someone in the event of the death of the settlor. The subject matter of the trust, the bonds, were set aside, and the trustee's conduct thereto was consistent only with the belief that a valid trust had been created, and that B was entitled beneficially to the proceeds of the bonds. Accordingly, a valid trust was created and B, or his guardian, is entitled to the bonds. See Smith's Estate, 144 Pa. 428, 22 A. 916 (1891).

SUMMARY OF CASES IN CHAPTER XXXII

Case 336. To make a valid gift of personal property there must be a donative intent, delivery and acceptance. Acceptance is generally presumed if the gift is beneficial. Manual tradition of the subject matter of the gift is not required in all circumstances, and delivery can be satisfied by a constructive or symbolic delivery. Further, where actual transfer of possession would serve no useful purpose or is impossible, then it is not required. Thus, if the intended donee is already in possession of the subject matter as bailee, no further delivery is necessary. In such a case, release to the bailee with the proper donative intent is sufficient. Delivery can be made to a third party for the benefit of a donee. Therefore, where a third party is in possession of the subject matter as a bailee, release to the bailee with the requisite intent, that is, with instructions to hold the subject matter for the named donee, is sufficient to constitute a completed gift.

Case 337. Gifts are divided into two principal categories—inter vivos and causa mortis. A gift causa mortis is one made in contemplation of death; it is automatically revoked on the donor's recovery from the contemplated peril, and it is also subject to revocation. The majority construe gifts causa mortis as taking effect immediately but subject to revocation on recovery by the donee. Some cases disregard or minimize formal distinctions in the manner of expression when a donor purports to make a gift causa mortis, since the expression "if I die," expressing a condition precedent, is more likely to be used than the more appropriate words expressing a condition subsequent. A gift causa mortis made on contemplation of death from an operation is revoked automatically if the operation is not performed and death comes later from the underlying cause.

Case 338. A gift, either inter vivos or causa mortis, may be made by delivery to a third party for the donee. If the directions to the third party are to deliver the subject matter to the donee on the death of the donor, meaning whenever and however such death should occur, then, regardless of how the contingency is expressed, the transaction constitutes a valid inter vivos gift. An interest vests presently in the donee with enjoyment postponed. The relationship is similar to that of absolute ownership and executory interest, or life estate and remainder.

Case 339. Joint and survivorship bank accounts, when created by only one of the depositors contributing the funds, are analyzed either on the basis of a contract or gift theory depending upon the jurisdiction. According to the contract theory, the relationship between the depositors and the bank constitutes a contractual one, and either depositor or the survivor, after the death of one of the parties, is entitled to deposit or withdraw funds, including the entire amount. Under this approach, the survivor is entitled to the funds remaining simply on the basis of the contract. Under the gift theory, the non-contributing survivor is entitled to the account only if the court concludes that the contributing depositor did in fact intend to make to the other an inter vivos gift of an interest in the account. The requirements of donative intent, delivery and acceptance must be satisfied. The subject matter of the gift is not of the entire funds in the account but simply of a co-interest therein.

Case 340. A bank account in the name of one person with directions to pay on death to another is a testamentary transaction and void for noncompliance with the Statute of Wills. For a valid joint bank account, each of the codepositors must acquire presently an interest in the account at the time of its creation. Property passes at death only in accordance with testate or intestate laws. There is conflicting authority, however. See paragraph "Cf." at end of principal case.

Case 341. A bank account in the name of the depositor as trustee for another is valid as a tentative or revocable trust with the named beneficiary being entitled to the proceeds of the account on the death of the depositor. During the life of the depositor, however, the account is subject to revocation in whole or in part by the depositor withdrawing funds.

Case 342. A trust creates an equitable or beneficial interest in the beneficiary of the trust. To create such a trust, there must be a trust corpus, manifestation of an intent to create a trust, a settlor, a trustee, and a beneficiary. A trust can be created by a self-declaration of trust in which the settlor is also the trustee, and in such a case, no delivery of the subject matter is required. The trust property must be segregated from the settlor's assets, however.

Chapter XXXIII

BONA FIDE PURCHASER OF PERSONAL PROPERTY

Legal Gems.
Cases.
Summary of Cases in Chapter XXXIII.

LEGAL GEMS

1. The basic common law rule is that one cannot pass a better title than that which he has. Similarly, a purchaser can acquire no better title than that of his vendor.

2. A thief has no title in the stolen goods, and a purchaser from the thief gets no title.

3. An owner who clothes another with indicia of ownership or authority to sell is estopped to deny such authority if the person so clothed sells the property to a bona fide purchaser for value without notice of the owner's rights.

4. Such an estoppel did not apply at common law when an owner delivered his chattel for services or repairs to a dealer in that kind of goods and the dealer in turn wrongfully sold the chattel. Under the UCC, the bona fide purchaser is protected under such circumstances.

5. A person who induces a sale by fraudulent representations acquires a voidable title from the seller. A person with a voidable title has power to transfer a good title to a bona fide purchaser for value without notice of the outstanding equity.

6. The voidable title rule applies when the owner is induced to part with *title* as a result of fraud or deceit; it does not apply when the owner parts with *possession only* as a result of the deception.

7. Holders in due course of negotiable instruments take such paper free of many types of claims which could be asserted between the immediate parties thereto.

CASE 343: A stole B's property and sold it to C, an innocent purchaser for value without notice of the theft. B discovered these facts and demanded that C return the chattels which were still in his possession, and also pay him for the value of that stolen property which C sold to a third person. C refused, and B filed suit. May B recover?

Answer and Analysis

The answer is yes. A thief acquires no title to the goods stolen and he can pass none. The foundation rule at common law is that a

712

purchaser can acquire no better title than that which his vendor has. To this rule there are some exceptions, but the instant case is not within any of the exceptions. In a case such as this one, the law must decide between two innocent parties—the owner whose property was stolen and the innocent purchaser who was misled into buying stolen goods. It is equally harsh on whoever must suffer the loss—the innocent owner or the innocent purchaser. The equities are equal; therefore, the legal title prevails. Note that the innocent purchaser must not only return the goods still in his possession, but that he also must pay the value of the goods which he sold. Such wrongful sale by the purchaser, C, was a conversion of B's goods regardless of the innocence of C. Thus, B can recover. See Morgan v. Hodges, 89 Mich. 404, 50 N.W. 876 (1891); Bolles Wooden-Ware Co. v. United States, 106 U.S. 432, 1 S.Ct. 398, 27 L.Ed. 230 (1882), involving accession and holding that the innocent purchaser from the thief is responsible to the owner for the enhanced (not just the original) value of the goods at the time of his purchase (conversion).

———

CASE 344: A delivers his wrist watch to the B jewelry company for repairs. The company sells new and used watches in addition to repairing watches. C purchases the watch from the B jewelry company without knowledge that the company is not the owner of the watch nor authorized to sell it by the owner. A brings an action in trover against C. May A recover?

Answer and Analysis

The answer is yes at common law, no under the Uniform Commercial Code. The relationship between A and B is that of bailor and bailee. A is the bailor and owner of the watch; B is bailee. C, the innocent purchaser has no way of knowing that B does not own the watch or that he has no authority to sell. Nevertheless, it is A's watch and he did not authorize the sale. The sale then constituted a conversion both by the seller B and by the purchaser C. B had no title to pass, and C could acquire none. Thus, under the rule of the preceding case, C acquires no title to the watch. In some jurisdictions—prior to the UCC, C was protected to the extent that A must make a demand before he had an action against C, but in others the wrongful purchase was itself a conversion without such demand. Of course, in some instances A might be estopped as against an innocent purchaser (see infra case 345), but this common type of bailment situation was not regarded as working an estoppel against A or clothing B with apparent authority to sell.

The Uniform Commercial Code, however, decided that in such circumstances the innocent purchaser should be protected rather than the innocent owner. This no doubt involved a valued judgment that security of transactions under circumstances of the above case was more important than the protection of the innocent owner. The code under both 1962 and 1972 versions provides:

> Any entrusting of possession of goods to a merchant who deals in goods of that kind gives him power to transfer all rights of the entruster to a buyer in the ordinary course of business. UCC § 2-403(2).

Thus, under the Code, which has been adopted (subject to possible modifications in particular instances) in all the states, the innocent purchaser, C, is protected, and A has no action against him. Under the Code, A's action is against B only.

CASE 345: A, the owner of used bicycles, consigned some of his bicycles to B, a licensed dealer in used bicycles. B was to display the bicycles and communicate any offers he received to A for approval. B displayed the bicycles with his stock in trade as he was supposed to, but he sold one of A's bicycles to C. C took possession of the bicycle. Later A, by self help, acquired possession of the bicycle and, knowing of the sale by B to C, nevertheless sold the bicycle to X. C sues A for conversion. May C recover?

Answer and Analysis

The answer is yes. Although the general common law rule is that a purchaser can acquire no better title than that of his vendor, there are exceptions to the rule. In the instant case, A, the owner of the bicycle, delivered possession to B, a dealer in used bicycles. A thus consented to placing the bicycle in the public showroom with similar bicycles of B's own for the purpose of sale. The innocent purchaser, C, would likely believe that all the bicycles either belonged to B or that he had the authority to sell. To third persons B had apparent authority, and A knew that it would thus appear because B was a dealer in bicycles. Thus, A is estopped to deny that B had such authority, and C gets title by estoppel. Therefore, when A took possession of the bicycle, he converted C's property and is liable therefor. The result would be the same under UCC § 2-403(2).

This case differs from Case 344, next preceding, at common law because of the purpose of the bailment and the expected conduct of the bailee. In the previous case A delivered his watch to the jeweler for repairs. Although B also sold watches, it was not anticipated that he would display this particular watch for sale or do anything with it except perform the necessary repairs. In the instant case A delivered the bicycle to a dealer for the express purpose of soliciting offers of purchase, and A knew that the chattel would be displayed with similar chattels for sale. Thus, A intentionally clothed B with apparent authority to sell, the special instructions about taking bids not being known to B's customers and the public at large. Thus, under the circumstances A should be estopped to assert his title as against an innocent purchaser. See Good v. Easy Method Auto Driving Training Sch., 113 A.2d 925 (Mun.Ct.App.D.C.1955)

CASE 346: A, in a face to face conversation with B, represented himself to be someone else. Based upon this fraudulent misrepresentation, B sold jewelry to A on credit. A in turn sold the jewelry to C, a BFP without notice of any defect in title. B now brings an action in replevin against C. May B recover?

Answer and Analysis

The answer is no. Where the vendor of personal property intends to sell his goods to the person with whom he deals, then title passes, even though the vendor would not have sold the property but for the vendee's deception. It is purely a question of the vendor's intention. That the vendor deals with the person personally rather than by letter is immaterial except insofar as it bears upon the question of intent. Where the transaction is by letter, the vendor intends to deal only with the person whose name is signed at the bottom of the letter. Where the transaction is face to face, the vendor intends to deal with the person with whom he is negotiating. In the face to face transaction, title passes; in the other, it does not.

Under the facts of the instant case, B intended to pass title to A and so title passed. Because of the fraud, however, B could have voided the transaction as long as A retained possession of the goods. A acquired a voidable title and B had an equity of rescission. When C enters the picture under the facts of this case, he acquires the legal title from A and also an equity as a result of his good faith purchase without notice of the prior equity. A later equity when combined with the legal title always prevails over a prior equity at common law. Thus, C gets a valid title, and B has no action against him. See Phelps v. McQuade, 220 N.Y. 232, 115 N.E. 441 (1917).

CASE 347: A came to B, a diamond dealer, and fraudulently stated that he (A) had a customer for a diamond ring. A selected a ring which B delivered to him to show to the supposed customer; A to return with either the money or the ring in an hour. A sold the ring to C, an innocent purchaser, though A had no customer in mind when he spoke to B. B now brings suit against C. May B recover?

Answer and Analysis

The answer is yes. If B had sold and delivered the diamond to A upon the fraudulent representations A had made, an innocent purchaser from A would acquire good title and B would not prevail in his action against the innocent purchaser. The question is: Did the owner (B) intend to transfer both the property in and possession of the goods to the person guilty of the fraud? If he did, a voidable title passed and subsequent innocent purchasers for value would be protected.

This rule does not apply, however, unless there is an actual sale of the property by the alleged vendor (B). If one delivers property to another as a mere bailee, a purchaser from the bailee acquires no title, however innocent he may be. He has no more right to assert title to the property than if it had been stolen, and his purchase had been from the thief. The principle upon which this distinction rests is that in the case of the bailment, the vendor (B) does not part with title to the property, nor does he intend to; while in the case of a sale he does.

Nor should B be estopped to assert his ownership. Although B parted with possession and was contemplating a possible sale, A was not a dealer in diamonds operating an established business at which place he publicly displayed such merchandise. There would not be the same degree of apparent authority as if A had such a store. In fact, all that A had here was possession, and possession of goods of another is very commonplace. A casual entrusting of possession for a short period of time is not sufficient to estop the owner from asserting title against an innocent purchaser when the bailee converts the goods. See Baehr v. Clark, 83 Iowa 313, 49 N.W. 840 (1890).

SUMMARY OF CASES IN CHAPTER XXXIII

Case 343. A thief acquires no title to stolen goods and can pass no title. An innocent purchaser from a thief gets no title.

Case 344. An owner who delivers his chattel to a merchant for service does not at common law lose his title to the chattel when the merchant wrongfully sells it to a bona fide purchaser for value without notice. Under the UCC, such a wrongful sale in the ordinary course of business by a merchant to whom the chattel had been entrusted results in the owner being left with an action against the merchant-converter.

Case 345. At common law an owner may be estopped to deny that a person with whom he deposited his chattel had the power or authority to sell it. Such an estoppel occurs when goods are deposited with a merchant selling that kind of merchandise with the owner knowing that the depositary will display the goods as though for sale, but in reality the depositary is only to solicit bids with the owner having the final authority as to whether to sell or not.

Case 346. A face to face sale induced by fraudulent representations results in the purchaser acquiring a voidable title. If the fraudulent purchaser then effects a sale to a bona fide purchaser without notice prior to rescission by the owner, the bona fide purchaser acquires a valid title.

Case 347. The rule protecting the innocent purchaser from the defrauding voidable title holder does not apply if the defrauder doesn't get a voidable title to start with. Thus, if the schemer induces the owner to part with possession only, not title, as a result of the fraudulent representations, then he doesn't acquire a voidable title and an innocent purchaser from him is not protected.

TABLE OF CASES

References are to Pages

Abbott v. Holway, 413
Ackerman v. Hunsicker, 503
Acton v. Blundell, 299
Agins v. City of Tiburon, 635
Akroyd v. Smith, 567
Altman v. Ryan, 321
Ambrosio v. Perl-Mack Constr. Co., 301
Ampco Auto Parts, Inc. v. Williams, 694
Anderson v. Gouldberg, 684
Anderson's Estate, In re, 51
Anthony v. Brea Glenbrook Club, 556
Antley v. Antley, 56
Archer's Case, 129
Arizona Copper Co. v. Gillespie, 292
Arlington Heights, Village of v. Metropolitan Housing Dev. Corp., 652
Armory v. Delamire, King's Bench, 681
Armstrong v. Francis Corp., 300
Arverne Bay Constr. Co. v. Thatcher, 637, 654
Arwe v. White, 418
Asher v. Whitlock, 236
Associated Home Builders v. City of Livermore, 644
Associated Home Builders of the Greater East Bay, Inc. v. City of Walnut Creek, 649
Atchison v. Atchison, 428
Avila South Condominium Ass'n, Inc. v. Kappa Corp., 672
Ayer v. Philadelphia & Boston Face Brick Co., 473, 474

Bachmann v. Reardon, 706
Baehr v. Clark, 716
Baker v. Austin, 471
Baker v. City of Milwaukie, 625
Baker v. Mather, 486
Barber v. Rader, 212
Barrows v. Jackson, 550
Baseball Pub. Co. v. Bruton, 618
Battistone v. Banulski, 14
Belle Terre, Village of v. Boraas, 650
Bennett v. Behring Corp., 672
Beran v. Harris, 15
Berenson v. Town of New Castle, 644
Berman v. Parker, 643
Berman v. Watergate West, Inc., 464
Bernklau v. Stevens, 459, 462

Best Fertilizers of Arizona, Inc. v. Burns, 508
Bethlahmy v. Bechtel, 464
Bick v. Mueller, 375
Black Jack, Mo., City of, United States v., 652
Blackman v. Fysh, 122, 138
Board of Educ. of City of Minneapolis v. Hughes, 488
Boehringer v. Schmid, 86
Bolles Wooden-Ware Co. v. United States, 713
Bond v. O'Gara, 243
Bonomi v. Blackhouse, 273
Boomer v. Atlantic Cement Co., 316
Boone Biblical College v. Forrest, 15
Bove v. Donner-Hanna Coke Corp., 316
Braitman v. Overlook Terrace Corp., 229
Braun v. Hamack, 272
Bray v. Bree, 174
Brind v. International Trust Co., 703
Briz-Ler Corp. v. Weiner, 379
Brown v. Allied Steel Products Corp., 321
Brown v. Fuller, 597
Brown v. Harvey Coal Corp., 471
Brown v. Southall Realty Co., 228
Brumagim v. Bradshaw, 235
Burbank v. Pillsbury, 522
Burnham v. Beverly Airways, Inc., 259
Burns v. McCormick, 375
Butler v. Frontier Tel. Co., 263
Bybee v. Hageman, 442

Cadwalader v. Bailey, 589
Caldwell v. Fulton, 565
Calvert v. Aldrich, 84
Cameron v. Oakland County Gas & Oil Co., 338
Campbell v. Thomas, 426
Canton, City of v. Shock, 290
Capitol Fed. Sav. & Loan Ass'n v. Smith, 551
Carllee v. Ellsberry, 45
Carrig v. Andrews, 267
Carroll, Matter of, 189
Carter v. Adler, 538
Casavant v. Campopiano, 463
Cauble v. Hanson, 216

Causby, United States v., 258, 260, 261

Chalmers v. Smith, 356

Charlotte Park & Recreation Comm'n v. Barringer, 551

Chase Rand Corp. v. Pick Hotels Corp. of Youngstown, 695

Cheney v. Village 2 at New Hope, Inc., 647

Cheshire v. Thurston, 199

Chicago & Northwestern Transp. Co. v. Whinthrop, 620

Chicago Bar Ass'n v. Quinlan & Tyson, Inc., 368

Chicago, Mobile Development Co. v. G. C. Coggin Co., 458, 461

Chillemi v. Chillemi, 416, 424

Chouteau v. City of St. Louis, 49

City of (see name of city)

Claflin v. Claflin, 179

Clay v. Landreth, 378

Cleveland v. Cohrs, 506

Cockson v. Cock, 533

Cohen v. Perrino, 314

Cohodas v. Russell, 371

Collette v. Town of Charlotte, 34, 47, 108

Combs v. Fields, 46

Committee of Protesting Citizens, Etc. v. Val Vue Sewer Dist., 379

Commonwealth Bldg. Corp. v. Hirschfield 77

Condos v. Home Development Co., 550

Conduit v. Ross, 530

Conness v. Pacific Coast Joint Stock Land Bank, 575

Cook v. Stevens, 244

Cooke v. Firemen's Ins. Co., 380

Coquina Club, Inc. v. Mantz, 68

Corporation of Birmingham v. Allen, 273

Cowen v. Pressprich, 693

Cradock v. Cooper, 433

Craig v. Osborn, 484

Dade County v. Yumbo, S. A., 626

Danielson v. Roberts, 682

Dartnell v. Bidwell, 575

David v. B & J Holding Corp., 463

David Properties, Inc. v. Selk, 80

Davis v. Gilliam, 354

Davis v. Lovick, 73

Davis v. Vidal, 218

Davis, Inc., William J. v. Slade, 228

Deery v. Cray, 444

Dema Realty Co., State ex rel. v. McDonald, 636

Dennen v. Searle, 30, 32

D'Ercole v. D'Ercole, 88

Dick v. Sears Roebuck & Co., 538

Dickhut v. Norton, 226

Dickstein v. Williams, 676

DiDonato v. Reliance Standard Life Ins. Co., 378

Doctor v. Hughes, 156

Doe ex dem. Christmas v. Oliver, 468

Dolan v. Cummings, 92

Doll v. Guthrie, 333

Donahue v. Zoning Bd. of Adjustment of Whitemarsh Twp., 647

Dorf v. Tuscarora Pipe Line Co., 31

Dunlap v. Marnell, 428

Duval v. Thomas, 306

Dyste v. Farmers' & Mechanics' Sav. Bank of Minneapolis, 706, 708

Earle v. Arbogast, 355

Easton v. Montgomery, 384

Eastwood v. Shedd, 481

Economy v. S. B. & L. Bldg. Corp., 207

Edmonds v. Ronella, 682

Edwards v. Habib, 226

Edwards v. Lee's Adm'r, 265

Edwards v. Sims, 265

Eggebeen v. Sonnenburg, 639

Ellsworth Dobbs, Inc. v. Johnson, 367

Elwes v. Maw, 338

Emerson v. Shores, 619

Emporia, City of v. Soden, 290

Erbach v. Brauer, 421

Erickson v. Queen Val. Ranch Co., 285

Escher v. Bender, 385

Estate of (see name of party)

Estuary Properties, Inc. v. Askew, 635

Euclid, Village of v. Ambler Realty Co., 632

Evans v. Abney, 551

Evered, In re, 191

Everett v. Paschall, 323

Everts v. Agnes, 429

Eves v. Zoning Bd. of Adjustment, 647

Ewing v. Nesbitt, 60

Exchange Nat'l Bank of Chicago v. Lawndale Nat'l Bank of Chicago, 390

Failoni v. Chicago & N. W. Ry. Co., 249

Fasano v. Board of County Comm'rs of Washington County, 625

Fellmer v. Gruber, 380

Fendley v. Laster, 703

Ferguson v. City of Keene, 260, 261

Fetting Mfg. Jewelry Co., A. H. v. Waltz, 27, 77

Fiduciary Trust Co. v. Mishou, 187

Fifty-Six Sixty Collins Ave. Condominium, Inc. v. Dawson, 676

Finley v. Glen, 494

Finn v. Finn, 90

First Presbyterian Church of Salem v. Tarr, 15

First Universalist Soc'y v. Boland, 14
Fleeman v. Case, 672
Fletcher's Gin, Inc. v. Crihfield, 324
Florida East Coast Properties, Inc. v. Metropolitan Dade County, 323
Florida, State of v. Massachusetts Co., 687
Florio v. State ex rel. Epperson, 306
Foley v. Gamester, 62
Fountains of Palm Beach Condominium, Inc. No. 5 v. Farkas, 676
Fountainview Ass'n, Inc. No. 4 v. Bell, 672
Fox v. Flick, 364
Frankland v. City of Lake Oswego, 640
French Investing Co., Fred F. v. City of New York, 654
Fuentes v. Shevin, 212
Fuglede v. Wenatchee Dist. Co-op. Ass'n, 364

Gable v. Silver, 464
Gaines v. Dillard, 382
Gale v. York Center Community Co-op. Inc., 664
Galjaard v. Day, 9
Galley v. Ward, 485
Gannon v. Peterson, 54
Garrison v. Blakeney, 415
Gaskin v. Harris, 676
Gibson v. Duncan, 317
Gifford v. Yarborough, 441
Glorieux v. Lighthipe, 494
Goldberg v. Housing Auth. of Newark, 228
Golden v. Planning Bd. of Town of Ramapo, 644
Goldfarb v. Virginia State Bar, 369
Good v. Easy Method Auto Driving Training Sch., 715
Goodrich v. McMillan, 296
Gray v. Blanchard, 16
Gray v. City of Cambridge, 582
Gray v. Kaufman Dairy & Ice Cream Co., 399
Greenspan-Greenberger Co. v. Goerke Co., 334
Gruber v. Raritan Twp., 641
Gulf Reston, Inc. v. Rogers, 228
Gust v. Township of Canton, 644

HFH, Ltd. v. Superior Court of Los Angeles County, 635
H & L Land Co. v. Warner, 513
Hacker v. Nitschke, 201
Haferkamp v. City of Rock Hill, 301
Haley v. Morgan, 460
Hall v. Eaton, 446
Hall v. Garson, 212

Hall v. Lawrence, 585
Hammond v. Antwerp Light & Power Co., 296
Hammond v. Thompson, 215
Hannah v. Peel, 685
Hannan v. Dusch, 199
Harbison v. City of Buffalo, 638
Harris v. Harrison, 288
Harris v. Sunset Islands Property Owners, Inc., 552
Harris v. Woodard, 442
Harrison v. Ricks, 75
Hartnett v. Austin, 649
Havana Nat'l Bank v. Wiemer, 505
Hazzard v. Hazzard, 59
Hebert v. Dupaty, 538
Herbert v. Smyth, 319
Heritage Heights Home Owners' Ass'n v. Esser, 556
Herter v. Mullen, 79
Hidden Harbour Estates, Inc. v. Norman, 675
Hillman v. McCutchen, 90
Hinman v. Pacific Air Transport, 258
Hoag v. Hoag, 90
Hoban v. Cable, 446
Hochard v. Deiter, 381
Hoffman v. Semet, 510
Hoffmann v. Kinealy, 638
Hoover & Mooris Dev. Co. v. Mayfield, 68
Horn's Estate, In re, 32
Hornsby v. Smith, 314
Howard v. Kunto, 248
Huey v. Davis, 676
Huff v. Board of Zoning Appeals, 647
Hughes v. Graves, 242
Humber v. Morton, 464
Huntington v. Asher, 567
Hurst v. Picture Theatres, Ltd., 616

Imbeschied v. Lerner, 207
In re (see name of party)
Innes v. Potter, 705

Jackson v. Steinberg, 683
Janofsky v. Garland, 203
Javins v. First Nat'l Realty Corp., 227
Jenad, Inc. v. Village of Scarsdale, 649
Jimerson Housing Co., Earl W. v. Butler, 556
Johnson v. Keith, 676
Johnson v. O'Brien, 201
Johnson v. Santora, 694
Jones v. Alfred H. Mayer Co., 552
Jones v. City of Los Angeles, 636
Jones v. Conn, 289
Jordan v. Village of Menomonee Falls, 649
Judd Realty, Inc. v. Tedesco, 367

Juilliard & Co., A. D. v. American Woolen Co., 217

Kahn v. Wilhelm, 207
Kanawell v. Miller, 420
Kane v. Johnson, 30
Kanter v. Safran, 220, 222
Kaufman v. Shere, 673
Kell v. Belle Vista Vil. Property Owners' Ass'n, 556
Kelly, In re Estate of, 66
Kenney v. Parks, 428
Kentucky Dept. of Highways v. Sherrod, 209
Keron v. Cashman, 682
King v. Wenger, 372
Kirby Lumber Co. v. Temple Lumber Co., 351
Kittrel v. Clark, 389
Klajbor v. Klajbor, 83
Klatzl, Matter of, 86
Klie v. Von Broock, 355
Kline v. 1500 Massachusetts Ave. Apartment Corp., 229
Kohlbrecher v. Guettermann, 371
Kray v. Muggli, 296
Krebs v. Hermann, 319
Kuehne v. Town of East Hartford, 641

LaCaille v. Feldman, 664
Lambert v. Thwaites, Court of Chancery, 188
Larson v. McDonald, 319
LaRue v. Kosich, 573
Leake v. Robinson, 172
Leavell, State ex rel. v. Nelson, 665
Lehigh Val. R. R. Co. v. McFarlan, 575
LeMehaute v. LeMehaute, 418
Lemle v. Breeden, 227
Leonard v. Autocar Sales & Serv. Co., 209
Leonard v. Burr, 107
Lerner Shops of North Carolina, Inc. v. Rosenthal, 424
Lessee of White v. Sayre, 83
Levine v. Blumenthal, 214
Lewis v. Farrah, 237
Licker v. Gluskin, 88
Lichtenhein v. Boston & Providence R. R. Co., 696
Lincoln Co-op. Apartments, Inc. v. Zaifert, 675
Lindenfelser v. Lindenfelser, 31
Lingle Water Users' Ass'n v. Occidental Bldg. & Loan Ass'n, 528
Lloyd v. First Nat'l Trust & Sav. Bank of Fullerton, 365
Los Angeles, City of v. Gage, 638
Low v. Tibbets, 446

Luette v. Bank of Italy Nat'l Trust & Sav. Ass'n, 385
Lunt v. Kitchens, 573

MacQueen v. Lambert, 212
McCray v. Caves, 67
McCullough v. Broad Exchange Co., 603
McCusker v. McEvey, 490
McCutchen v. Crenshaw, 76
McDaniels v. Colvin, 503
McDonald, State ex rel. Dema Realty Co. v. 636
McKee v. Howe, 71
McLain v. Real Estate Bd. of New Orleans, Inc., 369
McManus v. Blackmarr, 386
McRorie v. Creswell, 151
Maas v. Burdetzke, 241
Ma-Beha Co. v. Acme Realty Co., 214
Maher v. City of New Orleans, 629
Malone v. Santora, 694
Malone v. Walsh, 706
Man v. Vockroth, 584
Mandlebaum v. McDonell, 51
Mansfield & Swett, Inc. v. Town of West Orange, 643
Margate Village Condominium Ass'n, Inc. v. Wilfred, Inc., 674
Margosian v. Markarian, 9, 10
Maricopa County Municipal Conservation Dist. No. 1 v. Southwest Cotton Co., 297
Marracci v. City of Scappoose, 626
Marrone v. Washington Jockey Club, 616
Marshall v. Hollywood, Inc., 392
Mar-Son, Inc. v. Terwaho Enterprises, Inc., 219
Martin v. Port of Seattle, 261
Mason v. Wierengo's Estate, 79
Massachusetts Co., State v., 686
Matter of (see name of party)
May v. Emerson, 430
Mayor & Council of City of Baltimore v. Brack, 613
Mays v. Shields, 429
Meade v. Robinson, 432
Meehan's Estate, In re, 460
Meeker v. City of East Orange, 299
Melms v. Pabst Brewing Co., 349
Mettler v. Ames Realty Co., 284
Metzger v. Miller, 411
Meyer v. Law, 254
Meyer v. Meyer, 65
Miami, City of v. St. Joe Paper Co., 392
Midland Realty Co. of Minnesota v. Halverson, 474
Midland Val. R. R. Co. v. Arrow Indus. Mfg. Co., 565
Miller v. Lutheran Conference & Camp Ass'n, 589

Mills, Matter of, 701

Missionary Soc'y of Salesian Congregation v. Evrotas, 582

Mitchell v. Kepler, 459

Mitchell v. W. T. Grant Co., 212

Mitchell's Lessee v. Ryan, 432

Modjeska Sign Studios, Inc. v. Berle, 638

Mooney v. Byrne, 505

Moore v. City of East Cleveland, 650

Morehead v. Hall, 443

Morgan v. Hodges, 713

Morse v. Aldrich, 522

Morse v. Curtis, 493, 494

Morse v. Kelley, 449

Musselman v. Spies, 212

Mustain v. Gardner, 82

National Bellas-Hess, Inc. v. Kalis, 26

Nectow v. City of Cambridge, 634

Nelson, State ex rel. Leavell v., 665

Nols' Estate, In re, 703

Norgard v. Busher, 241

North Georgia Finishing, Inc. v. Di-Chem, Inc., 212

Novak v. Fontaine Furniture Co., 399

Oakwood at Madison, Inc. v. Township of Madison, 644

O'Banion v. Borba, 573

O'Malley v. Central Methodist Church, 555

Otto v. Steinhilber, 646

Papalexiou v. Tower West Condominium, 674

Park v. Stolzheise, 323

Park Enterprises, Inc. v. Trach, 706

Pascack Ass'n, Ltd. v. Mayor & Council of Twp. of Washington, 644

Peck v. Conway, 546

Pedro v. January, 357

Peer v. Wilson, 365

Peet v. The Roth Hotel Co., 692

Pegg v. Pegg, 86

Pendergrast v. Aiken, 288, 300, 301

Penn Central Transp. Co. v. City of New York, 654

Penthouse Properties, Inc. v. 1158 Fifth Ave., Inc. 664

Perkins v. Coleman, 470

Perry v. Farmer, 214

Peters v. Bowman, 462

Phelps v. McQuade, 715

Pierce v. Robinson, Adm'r, 505

Pierson v. Post, 681

Pile v. Pedrick, 265

Pinkerton v. Pritchard, 582

Pitts' Estate, In re, 556

Pollock v. Pittsburgh B. & L. E. R. Co., 272

Post v. Weil, 16

Prete v. Cray, 272

Ralph v. Bayley, 247

Randall v. Hamilton, 483

Rathmell v. Shirey, 427

Reid v. Architectural Bd. of Review of City of Cleveland Heights, 629

Reid v. Wiessner Brewing Co., 217

Rerick v. Kern, 613

Richardson v. Holman, 14, 112

Richardson v. Tumbridge, 601

Ricker v. Rombough, 222

Riley v. Stoves, 675

Ritchey v. Villa Nueva Condominium Ass'n, 68, 675

Robinson v. Blankenship, 104

Robinson v. Diamond Housing Corp., 226, 228

Rodgers v. Village of Tarrytown, 647

Romer v. St. Paul City R. R. Co., 321

Rutherford v. Pearl Assur. Co., 380

St. Paul Fire & Marine Ins. Co. v. Chas. H. Lilly Co., 695

Sakansky v. Wein, 590

Salter v. Jones, 447

Samuels, T. v. Ottinger, 216

Sargent v. Ross, 202

Schall v. Williams Val R. R. Co., 242

Schertz v. Rundles, 241

Schofield v. Iowa Homestead Co., 462

Schuler v. Claughton, 86

Schurtz v. Colvin, 429

Seaboard Sand & Gravel Corp. v. Moran Towing Corp., 693

Seaman v. King Arthur Court, Inc., 366

Seay v. Bennett & Kahnweiler Associates, 366

Seddon v. Harpster, 254

Shaber v. St. Paul Water Co., 528

Shaughnessy v. Eidsmo, 374

Shell Oil Co. v. Henry Ouellette & Sons, Inc., 539

Shelley v. Kraemer, 550

Shelley's Case, 61, 64, 148, 149, 150, 151, 157, 191, 192

Shipley v. Fink, 619

Shreeves v. Pearson, 433

Smiley v. Smiley, 427

Smith v. England Aircraft Co., 259

Smith v. Fay, 427

Smith v. McNew, 75

Smith v. Teel, 63

Smith's Estate, 709

Sniadach v. Family Fin. Corp., 212

Sobel v. Mutual Dev., Inc., 506

Solberg v. Robinson, 461

Southern Burlington County N. A. A. C. P. v. Township of Mount Laurel, 644

Southern New England Ice Co. v. Town of West Hartford, 585

Southern Pacific Co. v. Proebstel, 304

Southwest Weather Research, Inc. v. Duncan, 262

Spur Indus. Inc. v. Del E. Webb Dev. Co., 313

Stamatis v. Johnson, 590

Standard Indus. Inc. v. Smith, 206

Standard Oil Co. v. Buchi, 567, 586

Stanton v. T. L. Herbert & Sons, 589

State v. ——— (see opposing party)

State of (see name of state)

State Bar v. Arizona Land Title & Trust Co., 368

State Sav. & Loan Ass'n v. Kauaian Dev. Co., 671

Steltz v. Shreck, 90

Sterling Village Condominium, Inc. v. Breitenbach, 676

Stiegelmann v. Ackman, 422

Stockport Waterworks Co. v. Potter, 292

Stoddard v. Emery, 536

Stone v. French, 492

Stoner v. Zucker, 613

Stouder v. Dashner, 303

Stratton v. Mount Herman Boys' Sch., 288

Sturges v. Bridgman, 325

Susskind v. 1136 Tenants Corp., 667

Suydam v. Jackson, 205, 206

Sweeney, Adm'x v. Sweeney, 423

Swetland v. Curtiss Airports Corp., 259

Sylvania Elec. Products, Inc. v. City of Newton, 648

Tapscott v. Cobbs, 236

Tavares v. Horstman, 463

Teaff v. Hewitt, 333

Temple v. Benson, 446

Terrell v. Andrew County, 491

Terry v. Heppner, 303

Thellusson v. Woodford, 177

Therrien v. Therrien, 86

Thompson v. Baxter, 28, 62

Thompson v. Leach, House of Lords, 432

Thornburg v. Port of Portland, 260, 261

Thruston v. Minke, 535

Tibbitts v. Openshaw, 463

Tom Reed Gold Mines Co. v. United Eastern Mining Co., 264

Totten, Matter of, 708

Town v. State ex rel. Reno, 653

Townshend v. Moore, 205, 355

Treasure Salvors, Inc. v. Unidentified Wrecked & Abandoned Sailing Vessel, 686

Tristram's Landing, Inc. v. Wait, 367

Tulk v. Moxhay, 546

Tunstall v. Christian, 274

Union Properties, Inc. v. Cleveland Trust Co., 706

Union Travel Associates, Inc. v. International Associates, Inc., 620

United Advertising Corp. v. Borough of Metuchen, 629

United States v. ——— (see name of opposing party)

University Club of Chicago v. Deakin, 211

Van Meter v. Kelsey, 237

Van Sandt v. Royster, 597

Varriale v. Brooklyn Edison Co., 592

Vermes v. American Dist. Tel. Co., 203

Village of (see name of village)

Wack v. Collingswood Extension Realty Co. 474, 489

Wait v. Newman, 592

Walker v. Ireton, 375

Wallach v. Riverside Bank, 386

Wanamaker's Estate, In re, 172

Watergate Corp. v. Reagan, 68

Watson v. Wolff-Goldman Realty Co., 357

Weschsler v. Goldman, 672

Westerlund v. Myrell, 90

Westland Housing Corp. v. Scott, 211

Whaley v. Wotring, 391

Wheeler v. Young, 474

Whitcomb v. Brant, 398

White v. Maynard, 72

White v. Smyth, 351

White Egret Condominium, Inc. v. Franklin, 675

Whitmarsh v. Cutting, 362

Wichelman v. Messner, 388, 391

Willard v. First Church of Christ Scientist Pacifica, 452

Williams v. Bel, 379

Willis v. Kronendonk, 215

Wilshire Condominium Ass'n, Inc. v. Kohlbrand, 676

Wilson v. Kelley, 389

Wilson v. Ruhl, 219

Winston Towers 200 Ass'n, Inc. v. Saverio, 676

Wipfler v. Wipfler, 423

Woods v. Garnett, 494

Wright, In re Estate of, 707

Wright v. Baumann, 219

Young v. McCoy, 707

INDEX

"p." refers to legal gems or text on page cited.

"c., p.," refers to case discussing the point, page citation is to the beginning of the case.

"Note, p." refers to a Note in the text following a case discussion.

ABANDONED PROPERTY
Definition, p. 680; c. 325, p. 682; c. 327, p. 684.
Rights of finder, p. 680; c. 325, p. 682.

ABANDONMENT
Adverse possession, c. 146, p. 247.
By tenant, effect on lease and rental obligations,
 See Rent, subtitle Abandonment; Surrender.
Easement terminated by, p. 598; c. 288, p. 600.
 Non-user not enough, p. 599; c. 288, p. 600.

ABOVE AND BELOW THE SURFACE
See Airspace; Possession; Subsurface.

ACCRETION
 See also Boundaries.
Defined, p. 441.

ACCUMULATIONS
Rule against perpetuities, c. 106, p. 175.

AD COELUM DOCTRINE
Extent of land ownership, c. 153, p. 257.

ADVERSE POSSESSION
Abandonment, c. 146, p. 247.
Actual possession required, p. 236; c. 144, p. 244.
Adverse requirement, p. 236; c. 142, p. 242; c. 143, p. 243; c. 144, p. 244.
 Boundary disputes, c. 140, p. 240.
Boundary disputes, c. 140, p. 240.
Burden of proof, pp. 236–237.
Cause of action necessary, p. 237; c. 147, p. 248.
Claim of title required, p. 237; c. 142, p. 242; c. 143, p. 243.
Color of title, defined, c. 145, p. 246.
 Special note on, p. 253.
Consent of owner to possession, effect, c. 143, p. 243; Note, p. 244.
Constructive adverse possession, p. 237; c. 145, p. 246.
Continuous requirement, p. 236; c. 144, p. 244; c. 146, p. 247.
Conveyance of adversely possessed land, c. 139, p. 239.
Cotenants, between, p. 238.
Disability,
 Accrual of cause of action, at, c. 149, p. 250.
 Caveat as to statutory provisions, note 2, p. 249.
 Effect on, p. 238; cs. 149–152, pp. 250–253.
 Intervening one of no effect, c. 150, p. 251.
 Personal to owner, c. 152, p. 253.
 Simultaneous, effect of, Note, p. 252.
 Subsequent or successive disabilities, c. 150, p. 251; c. 151, p. 252.
 Supervening one of no effect, c. 151, p. 252.
Easements, against, c. 147, p. 248.
Equitable servitudes, effect on, p. 542.
Exclusive possession defined, p. 236; c. 144, p. 244.
Extent of title acquired, p. 237; c. 147, p. 248.
Future interest, effect on, p. 238; c. 148, p. 249.
Hostile requirement, p. 236; c. 142, p. 242; c. 143, p. 243; c. 144, p. 244.

ADVERSE POSSESSION—Continued

Legal gems, p. 236.

Marketable title as, c. 203, p. 385; Note, p. 385.

Mineral rights, against, c. 147, p. 248.

Mistake as to ownership, p. 239; c. 140, p. 240.

Mortgages, against, c. 147, p. 248.

Notorious requirement, p. 236; c. 144, p. 244.

Open possession required, p. 236; c. 144, p. 244.

Peaceable requirement, p. 236; c. 144, p. 244.

Recording acts inapplicable, p. 237; c. 141, p. 241.

Requirements, p. 236.

Tacking periods of possession, p. 238; c. 146, p. 247.

Taxes, payment of, p. 237.

Title acquired by, p. 236; c. 141, p. 241.

Title division after possession begun, p. 239.

Visible possession requirement, p. 236.

ADVERTISING SIGNS

Nature of interest created, c. 292, p. 616.

AGAINST INCUMBRANCES, COVENANT

See Covenants for Title.

AIRCRAFT

Low flights as a taking, p. 257; c. 153, p. 257; c. 154, p. 259.

AIRSPACE

Ad coelum doctrine, c. 153, p. 257.

Aircraft flights as a taking, p. 257; c. 153, p. 257; c. 154, p. 259.

Extent of ownership upward, p. 257; c. 153, p. 257.

Legal gems on, p. 257.

Noise as a taking, p. 257; c. 154, p. 257.

Rainfall, landowner's right to, p. 257; c. 155, p. 262.

Remedies for wrongful invasions, c. 156, p. 263.

Rights of possessor in, p. 257; c. 153, p. 257; c. 154, p. 259; c. 155, p. 262; c. 156, p. 263.

ALIENATION

Restraints on, see Restraint On Alienation.

Statutes prohibiting suspension of the power of, p. 160.

Subinfeudation, by, p. 3.

Substitution, by, p. 3.

ALLODIAL OWNERSHIP

Definition, p. 3.

ALLUVION

See also Boundaries.

Defined, p. 441.

APPOINTEE

See also Powers Of Appointment.

Defined, p. 179.

ARCHITECTURAL CONTROL

Condominiums, p. 676.

ASSIGNMENT

Rent, effect on liability for, p. 213; c. 129, p. 216.

AVULSION

See also Boundaries.

Defined, p. 441.

BAILMENT

Agreement to return in same condition, effect of, c. 334, p. 695.

Bailee's liability for negligence, p. 691; c. 329, p. 691; c. 335, p. 696.

Burden of proof on negligence issue, p. 691; c. 329, p. 691.

Care owed by bailee, p. 690; c. 329, p. 691.

Classification according to benefit, p. 690; c. 329, p. 691.

BAILMENT—Continued

Conditional sale distinguished, p. 690.

Contract altering bailee's liability, p. 690; c. 332, p. 693; c. 334, p. 695.

Contract element, p. 689; c. 329, p. 691.

Control element, p. 689.

Conversion by bailee, what constitutes, p. 690; c. 335, p. 696.

Custody distinguished, p. 689.

Definition, p. 689; c. 329, p. 691; c. 331, p. 693.

Delegation of duties by bailee, c. 331, p. 693.

Innkeeper's liability for guest's property, c. 333, p. 694.

Intent element, p. 689; c. 329, p. 691.

Involuntary bailment, c. 330, p. 692.

    Duty and liability of bailee, c. 330, p. 692.

Lease distinguished, p. 690; c. 332, p. 693.

Legal gems, p. 689.

Misdelivery by bailee, c. 330, p. 692.

Redelivery duty, p. 690; c. 335, p. 696.

Requirements, p. 689; c. 329, p. 691; c. 331, p. 693.

Sale distinguished, p. 690.

Statutory modification of bailee's liability, c. 333, p. 694.

Summary of cases, p. 696.

Title of purchaser from bailee, p. 712; c. 344, p. 713; c. 345, p. 714.

Trust distinguished, p. 690.

Typical example, p. 689.

BANK ACCOUNTS

Joint and survivor, see Joint Bank Accounts.

Payable on death, p. 699; c. 340, p. 707.

Summary of cases, pp. 710–711.

Trustee accounts, p. 699; c. 341, p. 707.

BARGAIN AND SALE

Requirements, p. 406.

BONA FIDE PURCHASER OF PERSONALTY

Apparent authority,

    Bailment, p. 712; c. 344, p. 713; c. 345, p. 714.

    Estoppel against owner, p. 712; c. 345; p. 714.

        Limitations on, c. 347, p. 715.

Bailee, purchaser from, p. 712; c. 344, p. 713; c. 345, p. 714.

    At common law and under UCC, c. 344, pp. 713–714.

Basic rule, p. 712.

Holders in due course of negotiable instruments, p. 712.

Legal gems, p. 712.

Purchaser from thief and accession value, c. 343, p. 712.

Summary of cases, p. 716.

Thief, purchaser from, p. 712; c. 343, p. 712.

Voidable title rule, p. 712; c. 346, p. 715.

    Limitations on, p. 712; c. 347, p. 715.

BOUNDARIES

    See also Land Description.

Accretion, p. 441.

Alluvion, p. 441.

    Ownership of, p. 441.

Avulsion, p. 441.

Ownership of water beds, pp. 440–441.

Parol agreement, p. 441.

Reliction, p. 441.

Summary of cases, p. 453.

Thread of stream a variable, p. 441.

Tidal lands, ownership of, p. 441.

BROKERS' CONTRACTS

Commission, when earned, pp. 366–367.

General principles, p. 366.

Legal documents, authority as to, p. 367; c. 193, p. 368.

Legal gems, p. 366.

BROKERS' CONTRACTS—Continued
Minimum fees, Note, p. 369.
Statute of Frauds, applicability, p. 366.
Types of contracts with seller, pp. 367–368.

CAPTURE
　　See also Powers Of Appointment.
Defined, p. 181.
Illustrated, c. 110, p. 185.

CHAMPERTY
Defined, ftn. 1, p. 111.

CHARITABLE TRUST
Rule Against Perpetuities, exempt, ftn. 1, p. 159.

CHARTS
Base lines and meridians of government survey system, p. 437.
Classification of interests in real property, p. 6.
Concurrent tenancies compared, p. 93.
Delivery of deeds, p. 433.
Future interests compared and distinguished, p. 141.
Possibility of reverter compared with power of termination, p. 114.
Reversion and vested remainder compared, p. 104.
Riparian rights compared with prior appropriation, p. 281.
Rule In Shelley's Cases compared with Doctrine of Worthier Title, p. 157.
Section, map showing fractional portions, p. 439.
Township map showing section numbers, p. 438.
Vested and contingent remainders compared, p. 132.

CHATTEL REAL
Estate for years, as, p. 69; c. 52, p. 70.

CLASS GIFTS
Class closing rules, c. 110, p. 185.
Rule against perpetuities, c. 103, p. 171; Note, p. 172.
　　Class closing rules, c. 110, p. 185.

CLASSIFICATION OF INTERESTS IN REAL PROPERTY
Chart showing, p. 6.

CLASSIFICATION OF POWERS OF APPOINTMENT
See Powers Of Appointment.

CLOGGING EQUITY OF REDEMPTION
　　See also Mortgages.
Defined, p. 501.

CLOUDS
Landowner's rights to, p. 257; c. 155, p. 262.

COMMERCIAL FRUSTRATION
Leases, p. 205; c. 123, p. 207.
Rent extinguished by, p. 213.

COMMON OCCUPANT
Defined, c. 10, p. 22.

COMMON RECOVERY
Device for barring entail, c. 8, p. 19.
Entail and reversion barred by, p. 54; c. 44, p. 56.

CONCURRENT ESTATES
　　See also Joint Tenancy; Tenancy by the Entirety; Tenancy in Common; Tenancy in Coparcenary.
Chart comparing, p. 93.
Classified, p. 6.
Legal gems, p. 80.
Summary of cases, p. 97.

CONDEMNATION
See Eminent Domain; Inverse Condemnation.

CONDITION OF PREMISES
Commercial leases, L's duty, c. 118, p. 202.
    Exculpatory clause, effect, c. 118, p. 202.
Landlords' duty, c. 117, p. 201.
    Common law exceptions to L's immunity, c. 117, p. 201.
    Third parties, to, c. 117, p. 201.
Residential leases, see Landlord and Tenant, Residential leases.

CONDOMINIUMS
Architectural control, p. 676.
Common law recognition, p. 667.
Community living and individual freedom, Note, p. 674.
Condominiums and Close in Living, Note 2, p. 67.
Cooperatives compared, c. 315, p. 665.
Corrective legislation, retroactivity, c. 317, p. 671; c. 318, p. 673.
Covenants running and equitable servitudes, p. 556.
Declaration of condominium, contents and function, p. 668.
    Statutory amendments incorporated into, effect, c. 318, p. 673.
Deeds to units, p. 668.
Definitions, p. 667.
Developer,
    Abuses of, c. 317, p. 671.
    Assessment as unit owner to pay for suit against himself, c. 319, p. 673.
    Remedial legislation, retroactivity, c. 317, p. 671; c. 318, p. 673.
Directors of association,
    Actions tested by reasonableness, c. 320, p. 674.
    Assessments, power of in emergency, c. 320, p. 674.
    Fiducary duties, c. 317, p. 671.
    Self-dealing, c. 317, p. 671.
Documents required for creation, p. 668.
Drinking, children and pets, p. 675.
Exorbitant rental and excessive profits to promoter from recreational lease, c. 317, p. 671.
Federal income tax considerations, p. 669.
Financing, p. 669.
Individual units, juridic acts as to, c. 316, p. 669.
Lease of recreational facilities, c. 317, p. 671.
Leasehold, constructed on, c. 316, p. 669.
Legal gems, p. 667.
Mechanics' lienors, rights of, c. 316, p. 669.
Monthly maintenance charges, c. 317, p. 671.
Mortgagee, rights of, c. 316, p. 669.
Priorities between many claimants in an unsuccessful venture, c. 316, p. 669.
Statutory recognition, p. 668.
Summary of cases, p. 677.
Unconscionability, c. 317 at p. 672.
Unit owner,
    Liable for assessments to finance suit even if the defendant, c. 319, p. 673.
Vendees of individual units, rights of, c. 316, p. 669.

CONSTRUCTION OF DEEDS AND WILLS
    See also Future Interests; Name of Estate or Future Interest.
Alienation, disabling restraint on, p. 43.
All parts considered, p. 41.
Conveyance to self and another, c. 63, p. 85.
Croppers' contracts, c. 56, p. 74.
Death without issue, Note, p. 45.
Defeasible versus absolute fee, c. 38, p. 48.
Determinable life estate or tenancy at will, c. 47, p. 61.
Disabling restraint on alienation ineffective, c. 40, p. 51.
Estate for years subject to termination, c. 55, p. 73.
Executory interests, cs. 85–86, pp. 137–139.
    Limited on an event certain to occur, c. 86, p. 139.
Fee absolute preferred, p. 42.

CONSTRUCTION OF DEEDS AND WILLS—Continued

Fee simple conditional, creation and characteristics, c. 43, p. 55.

Fee simple determinable, c. 37, p. 47.

Fee simple subject to condition subsequent, c. 39, p. 50.

Fee simple subject to executory limitation, c. 41, p. 52.

Fee tail, creation and characteristics, c. 44, p. 56.

Fee tail converted by statute into fee simple, c. 35, p. 46.

"Four corner doctrine," p. 41.

    Intent from entire instrument, c. 34, p. 45.

"Heirs," sense in which used, c. 88, p. 149.

Heirs of body as words of purchase, example of, c. 49, p. 63.

Intent of parties, role of, p. 41.

Joint tenancy, creation of, c. 60, p. 81.

Lease v. License, c. 53, p. 71.

Life estate,

    For joint lives and survivor, c. 50, p. 65.

    Restraint on alienation validity, c. 51, p. 65.

    When Shelley's Rule not applicable, c. 49, p. 63.

Limitation creating both contingent remainder and executory interest, c. 85, p. 137.

Periodic tenancy,

    From invalid lease, c. 54, p. 73.

    Holdover after notice, c. 58, p. 78.

Powers of appointment, cs. 108–113, pp. 182–190.

Remainders, p. 115 et seq.

Repugnant clauses, rule of, p. 42.

Reversion, c. 67, p. 101; c. 68, p. 102.

Reversion subject to defeasance, c. 69, p. 102.

Rule against perpetuities, cs. 93–107, pp. 160–177; c. 110, p. 185.

Rule in Shelley's Case, c. 36, p. 47; cs. 87–89, pp. 148–152.

Rules of construction, p. 41.

    Remainders and executory interests, p. 115; c. 83, p. 129; c. 85, p. 137.

Tenant holding over, effect of, c. 57, p. 77; c. 59, p. 79.

Words of limitation lacking, c. 32, p. 43.

CONSTRUCTIVE ADVERSE POSSESSION

See Adverse Possession.

CONSTRUCTIVE EVICTION

Landlord and tenant, p. 209; c. 125, p. 210.

CONTINGENT REMAINDER

Alienability, p. 116; c. 83, p. 129.

Characteristics, c. 27, p. 37.

Chart comparing future interests, p. 141.

Contingent remainder over executory interest construction preferred, p. 117; c. 83, p. 129; c. 85, p. 137.

Destructibility, c. 27, p. 37.

    See also Destructibility of Contingent Remainders.

Examples of, p. 117; c. 82, p. 127; c. 83, p. 129.

Legal gems, p. 115.

Limitation creating both contingent remainder and executory interest, c. 85, p. 137.

Prohibited after term for years, c. 80, p. 124.

Rule against perpetuities, subject to, p. 117.

Subject to divestment on exercise of power, c. 108, p. 182.

Taxes and interest, rights as to, p. 117.

To heirs of grantor void, p. 153; c. 90, p. 154.

Types of conditions precedent, Note (a), p. 122.

Typical case, c. 27, p. 37.

Vested remainders compared, p. 132.

Waste, rights as to, p. 117.

CONTRACTS

License distinguished, p. 610; c. 291, p. 614; c. 292, p. 616.

Power of appointment, to exercise, p. 182.

CONTRACTS FOR SALE OF LAND
See Equitable Conversion and Risk of Loss; Marketable Record Title Act; Marketable Title; Part Performance; Statute of Frauds; Time of Performance.

CONTRIBUTION
Joint tenants, between, c. 62, p. 84.
Tenants in common, between, c. 66, p. 91.

CONVEYANCES
Common law conveyances outlined, p. 396.
Common law restrictions and modern practices, c. 211, p. 411.
Common law types, p. 396.
    Dedication, p. 397.
    Feoffment, p. 396.
    Grant, p. 396.
    Lease and release, p. 396.
    Surrender, p. 397; c. 208, p. 397.
Effective in the future, c. 211, p. 411.
Informal letters as, c. 210, p. 410.
Land adversely possessed, c. 139, p. 239.
Limitations to grantor's heirs void, p. 153.
Modern, p. 409.
    Legal gems, p. 409.
    Manner of operation, p. 408; c. 209, p. 409.
Modern statutes, under, p. 409.
State power to prescribe form, p. 409; c. 210, p. 410.
Statute of Uses, under, p. 399.
      See also Statute of Uses.
    Outlined, p. 396.
Summary of cases, p. 413.
Surrender, types distinguished, c. 208, p. 397.
Warranties not implied, p. 458.

COOPERATIVES
Community living and individual freedom, Note, p. 674.
Condominiums compared, c. 313, p. 665.
Co-ownership as tenants in common plan, p. 660.
Co-ownership in joint tenancy plan, p. 660.
Corporate form of organization, p. 660.
    Essential documents, p. 661.
    Financing, p. 662; c. 313, p. 662.
    Proprietary lease, function and provisions, pp. 661–662; c. 315, p. 665.
    Repair of individual apartments, c. 315, p. 665.
    Restriction on sale of shares, p. 661; c. 313, p. 662.
    Restriction on voting rights, c. 314, p. 664.
    Typical set of by-laws, provisions of, p. 661.
    Unit owners' relationship to corporation, p. 662; c. 313, p. 662; c. 314, p. 664; c. 315, p. 665.
Definition, p. 660.
Income tax considerations, p. 660.
Legal gems, p. 660.
Massachusetts or business trust form of organization, p. 660.
Methods of organization, p. 660.
Proprietary lease, function and provisions, p. 661; c. 315, p. 665.
Restraint on alienation of corporate shares, policy considerations and validity, c. 313, p. 662.
Summary of cases, p. 676.
Voting rights, restrictions on, c. 314, p. 664.

COOPERATIVES AND CONDOMINIUMS
    See also Condominiums; Cooperatives.
Advantages of, pp. 659–660.
Introduction, p. 659.
Legal gems, p. 659.

COPARCENARY
See Tenancy In Coparcenary.

COURSE
See Land Description.

COVENANTS FOR TITLE
Against incumbrances, p. 455.
    Damages, c. 236, p. 460.
      Scope, pp. 455–456.
      Statute of limitations, c. 236, p. 460.
      Time of breach, p. 455; c. 236, p. 460.
      Zoning restrictions, effect, p. 456.
Enforcement by multiple grantees when covenant runs, p. 456.
Further assurance, p. 456.
    Scope, p. 456.
    Time of breach, p. 456.
General warranty, p. 456.
    Damages, c. 235, p. 459.
    Eviction construed, c. 235, p. 459; c. 237, p. 460.
    Scope, p. 456.
    Time of breach, p. 456; c. 235, p. 459.
Intermediate grantee as plaintiff for breach of running covenant, p. 457.
Legal gems, p. 455.
Listing of, p. 455.
Payment as satisfaction of running covenant, p. 457.
Privity of estate requirement for running, c. 237, p. 460.
Quiet enjoyment, p. 456.
    Damages, c. 235, p. 459.
    Eviction construed, c. 235, p. 459; c. 237, p. 460.
    Time of breach, p. 456; c. 235, p. 459.
    Scope, p. 456.
Right to convey, p. 455.
    Scope, p. 455; c. 234, p. 458.
    Time of breach, p. 456; c. 234, p. 458.
Rights of remote grantees on running covenant, p. 456; c. 237, p. 460.
Running with the land, pp. 456–457; c. 237, p. 460; Note, p. 462.
Seisin, p. 455.
    Scope, p. 455; c. 234, p. 458.
    Time of breach, p. 456; c. 234, p. 458.
Statute of limitations, present covenants, c. 234, p. 458.
Summary of cases, p. 463.
Third party trespasses not protected, p. 456.
"Usual covenants," meaning of, c. 237, p. 460.

COVENANTS IN LEASES
    See also Covenants Running With the Land.
Rent, covenant concerning runs, p. 212; c. 129, p. 216.

COVENANTS RUNNING WITH THE LAND
Benefit and burden tested separately, p. 516.
Condominiums, application to, p. 556.
Cooperatives, application to, p. 556.
Covenants running and equitable servitudes, p. 556.
Drinking, children and pets, p. 675.
Home Owners' Association, application to, p. 555.
In equity, see Equitable Servitudes.
In fee, p. 518.
    Benefit and burden both running, c. 260, p. 524.
    Benefit running, c. 258, p. 518.
    Burden running, c. 259, p. 522.
    Burden running without benefit, c. 262, p. 528.
    Covenant requirement, c. 258, p. 518; c. 261, p. 525.
    Deed poll, created by, c. 258, p. 518.
    Intent requirement, c. 258, p. 518; c. 261, p. 525.
    Legal effect, c. 258, p. 518.
    Party wall agreements, c. 262, p. 528.
    Privity of estate requirement, c. 258, p. 518; c. 261, p. 525.
      Conflicting views, Note, p. 528.
      Cross easements as satisfying, c. 262, p. 528.
      Liberal view, c. 261, p. 525.

COVENANTS RUNNING WITH THE LAND—Continued
In fee—Continued
  Summary of cases, p. 556.
  Touch and concern requirement, c. 258, p. 518; c. 261, p. 525.
   Agreement to pay, c. 262, p. 528.
In landlord-tenant relation, p. 530.
  Assignee's liability, p. 531; c. 263, p. 531.
  Benefit running without burden, c. 266, p. 536.
  Business competition agreement, c. 266, p. 536; Note, p. 538.
  Intent requirement, c. 263, p. 531; c. 265, p. 535; c. 266, p. 536.
  Legal gems, p. 530.
  Original parties' liability, c. 264, p. 533.
  Privity of estate present, p. 530.
  Requirements, p. 530; c. 263, p. 531; c. 266, p. 536.
  Summary of cases, p. 557.
  T's liability, c. 263, p. 531.
  "The land" defined, c. 264, p. 533.
  To repair as continuing covenant, c. 265, p. 535.
  Touch and concern requirement, p. 530; c. 263, p. 531; c. 265, p. 535; c. 266, p. 536; Note, p. 538.
Intention requirement, p. 516.
Introduction, p. 515.
Legal gems generally, p. 515.
Meaning of covenant, p. 515.
Meaning of running, p. 516.
Nature of covenants, pp. 515–516.
Planned Unit Development, application to, p. 555.
Privity of estate requirement, p. 517.
  Meanings of, p. 517.
Requirements, p. 517.
Strict construction policy, p. 517.
Suggested analytical approach, Note, p. 517.
Touch and concern requirement, p. 516.

COVERTURE
Estate during, c. 14, p. 25.

CREDITORS
Appointed property, rights in, p. 181; c. 108, p. 182; c. 109, p. 184.
Deed delivered in escrow, c. 223, p. 430; Note, p. 431.
Executory interests, c. 86, p. 139.
Fee tail, right to reach, c. 45, p. 58; Note, p. 59.
Joint bank accounts, Note, p. 706.
Joint tenancy, rights in, c. 61, p. 82.
Remainders, rights as to, p. 116.
Tenancy by the entirety, rights in, p. 88.
Vested remainder subject to open, c. 77, p. 120.

CROPPERS' CONTRACTS
Estate or interest created, c. 56, p. 74.

CROSS REMAINDERS
Implication of, c. 84, p. 131.

CURATIVE ACTS
  See also Marketable Title.
Marketable title, p. 381.

CURTESY
Extent at common law, c. 13, p. 24.
Initiate and consummate explained, c. 13, p. 24.
Requirements at common law, c. 13, p. 24.
Typical case at common law, c. 13, p. 24.

CY PRES
Rule against perpetuities, p. 160.

DAMAGES
Liquidated in leases, p. 218; c. 132, p. 220.
Support removal, See Lateral And Subjacent Support.

DEATH WITHOUT ISSUE
Definite failure defined, Note, p. 45.
Indefinite failure defined, Note, p. 45.

DEDICATION
Example of, p. 397.
Requirement for subdivision approval, c. 308, p. 649.

DE DONIS
See Statute De Donis.

DEED OF TRUST
Mortgage substitute, as, pp. 510–511.

DEED POLL
Covenants running with the land, c. 258, p. 518; p. 541; c. 267, p. 543.
Defined, c. 258, p. 518.

DEEDS
See also Boundaries; Construction Of Deeds And Wills; Covenants for Title;
  Land Description.
Acceptance, p. 418; c. 224, p. 431.
  Burden to show disclaimer where delivery, p. 418; c. 224, p. 431.
  Presumption of, c. 224, p. 431.
Boundaries, see Boundaries.
Deed absolute as mortgage, p. 510; c. 253, p. 503.
Delivery, p. 415; cs. 212–223, pp. 418–431.
  Burden of proof, c. 215, p. 421; c. 216, p. 421.
  Chart summarizing, p. 433.
  Commercial escrow, p. 416; c. 218, p. 424; c. 219, p. 425.
    See also subheading Escrow.
  Conditional delivery, p. 416; cs. 204–223, pp. 422–430.
  Conditional delivery to grantee, p. 416; c. 217, p. 422; Note, p. 423.
  Defined, p. 415; c. 212, p. 417; c. 213, p. 419.
  Donative escrow, p. 417; c. 220, p. 426; Note, p. 427.
    Grantor relinquishing all control, p. 416; c. 220, p. 426.
    Grantor retaining control, p. 417; Note, p. 427.
    Neither party having control, p. 417; Note, p. 427.
    Title passing, pp. 416–417; c. 220, p. 426; Note, p. 427.
    Types, p. 417; c. 220, p. 426; Note, p. 427.
  Escrow, p. 416; cs. 218–223, pp. 424–430.
    Creditors' rights, c. 223, p. 430; Note, p. 432.
    Death of grantor during, c. 222, p. 429.
    Delivery irrevocable, p. 417.
    Donative type, p. 417; c. 220, p. 426; Note, p. 427.
      See also subheading Donative Escrow.
    Enforceable contract, necessity of, p. 417; c. 219, p. 425.
    First and second deliveries, c. 222, p. 429.
    Grantee as own escrow, p. 416; c. 217, p. 422; Note, p. 423.
    Misappropriation of depositary, Note, p. 432.
    Passing of title in commercial transaction, p. 416; c. 218, p. 424; c. 219,
      p. 425; c. 221, p. 428; c. 222, p. 429.
    Relation back doctrine, c. 222, p. 429.
    Requirements, p. 416; c. 218, p. 424.
    Status of depositary, p. 416; c. 218, p. 424.
    Wrongfully procured deed from, c. 221, p. 428.
  Fact question, as, p. 415; c. 215, p. 421; c. 216, p. 421.
  Intent, p. 415; c. 212, p. 418; c. 213, p. 419; c. 215, p. 421.
  Parol evidence as to, p. 416; cs. 212–219, pp. 418, 425.
  Possession of physical deed not controlling, c. 212, p. 418; c. 213, p. 419.
  Presumption from grantor's recording, c. 216, p. 421.
  Recording undelivered deed immaterial, c. 212, p. 418.
  Return of delivered deed ineffective, c. 214, p. 420.
  Summary of cases, p. 434.

DEEDS—Continued
Form, p. 415.
Incompetents as purchasers, p. 418; c. 224, p. 431.
Land description, see Land Description.
Not contracts, p. 418; c. 224, p. 431.

DEFICIENCY DECREE
See Mortgages.

DELIVERY OF DEEDS
See Deeds.

DELIVERY OF GIFTS
See Gifts.

DESCENT
See also Worthier Title Doctrine.
Title by worthier than title by purchase, c. 90, p. 154.

DESCRIPTION OF LAND CONVEYED
See Land Description.

DESTRUCTIBILITY OF CONTINGENT REMAINDERS
Explanation, c. 27, p. 37.
Methods of destroying, Note (B), p. 129.
Rule against perpetuities, significance in, c. 93, p. 160.
Statement and illustration of rule, p. 118; c. 82, p. 127.
Status today, Note (C), p. 129.

DESTRUCTION OF BUILDING
Rental obligation, effect on, c. 121, p. 205.

DEVISES
Worthier title doctrine inapplicable, pp. 153–154; c. 92, p. 156.

DISABILITY
Adverse possession, effect on, see Adverse Possession.
Legal relation, defined as, p. 4.
Marketable Record Title Acts not tolled by, p. 388.
Prescription, effect on, see Easements and Profits, subheading Prescription, by.

DISPUTED BOUNDARIES
Adverse possession and, c. 140, p. 240.

DISTRESS
Remedy for rent, p. 211.

DOCTRINE OF WORTHIER TITLE
See Worthier Title Doctrine.

DOMINANT TENEMENT
See also Easements And Profits.
Definition, p. 560.

DOWER
Characteristics at common law, c. 12, p. 23.
Joint tenancy, survivorship controls, c. 61, p. 82.
Requirements at common law, c. 12, p. 23.
Typical case at common law, c. 12, p. 23.

DUTY
Legal relation, defined as, p. 4.

EASEMENTS AND PROFITS
Adverse possession against easement, c. 147, p. 248.
Adverseness of user, c. 274, p. 571.
Affirmative easements, p. 562; c. 272, p. 568.
Alienability, p. 563; c. 282, p. 585; c. 283, p. 586.
In gross profits and easements, c. 271, p. 566; c. 282, p. 585; c. 283, p. 586.
Apportionment, p. 563; c. 281, p. 584; c. 283, p. 586.

734 INDEX

EASEMENTS AND PROFITS—Continued

Appurtenant, p. 561.
 Analysis of, p. 561.
  Defined, p. 561; c. 272, p. 568.
  Severance of, Note, p. 589.
Building support, easement for, p. 269; c. 160, p. 273.
Classification, p. 561.
Creation, p. 569.
 Legal gems, p. 569.
 Methods, p. 569.
Deed, by, p. 569.
 Scope determined by terms of instrument, p. 569; c. 279, p. 580; c. 280, p. 582.
Dominant tenement defined, p. 561.
Easement,
 Defined, p. 560.
 Right to take water as, c. 271, p. 566.
Easement and profit distinguished, p. 560.
Easement by implication, pp. 563–564; c. 270, p. 564; pp. 569–570; cs. 286–287, pp. 592–595.
 "Apparent" requirement construed, c. 287, p. 595.
 Evidence as to circumstances, p. 563; c. 270, p. 564; c. 286, p. 592; c. 287, p. 595.
 Extent or scope determined by circumstances, p. 570.
 Intent as basis, p. 563.
 Necessity, role of, c. 286, p. 592; c. 287, p. 595.
 Requirements, c. 286, p. 592; c. 287, p. 595.
Excessive user as suspending, c. 289, p. 601.
Exclusive versus nonexclusive construction, c. 283, p. 586.
Express grant by, p. 569.
Extent or scope, p. 569.
 Changes in use permitted, c. 280, p. 582.
 Express grant, by, c. 279, p. 580; c. 280, p. 582.
 Prescription, c. 278, p. 578.
Extinguishment, p. 598 et seq.
 Abandonment, p. 599.
  Non-user not enough, c. 288, p. 600.
 BFP under recording acts, p. 600.
 Cessation of necessity ends easement by necessity, p. 598.
 Common ownership of dominant and servient estates, pp. 598–599.
 Estoppel, p. 600.
 Excessive user not enough, c. 289, p. 601.
 In gross holder becomes owner of servient estate, p. 599.
 Legal gems, p. 598.
 Prescription, p. 600.
 Release, p. 599.
 Termination by expiration of time specified, p. 598.
Fee versus easement construction, Note, p. 565.
Implied grant, p. 563; c. 286, p. 592.
Implied reservation, p. 563; c. 287, p. 595.
In gross, pp. 561–562.
 Alienability, c. 271, p. 566; c. 282, p. 585; c. 283, p. 586.
 Analysis of, p. 562.
 Defined, pp. 561–562; c. 271, p. 566.
Legal gems, p. 560.
Licenses distinguished, p. 610; c. 292, p. 616.
Location, change of, c. 284, p. 589.
Necessity, easement of, p. 570; Note, p. 597.
Negative easements, p. 562; c. 272, p. 568.
Party wall,
 Extension of and right to contribution, c. 285, p. 590.
 Theories as to ownership and easements, c. 285, p. 590.
Personal property, when, p. 562.
Plat or map, reference to as implication of easement, p. 570.
 Rules as to extent or scope, p. 570.
Preference for nonexclusive construction, c. 283, p. 586.

EASEMENTS AND PROFITS—Continued
Prescription, by, p. 569; c. 273, p. 570; cs. 274–278, pp. 571–578.
    Acquiescence requirement, c. 275, p. 573.
    Adverse possession compared, c. 274, p. 571.
    Change in use after acquisition, c. 278, p. 578.
    Continuity requirement, c. 274, p. 571.
    Continuous and without interruption defined, c. 275, p. 573.
    Disabilities,
        Effect of, p. 570; c. 276, p. 575.
        Intervening and supervening, c. 276, p. 575.
        No tacking of, c. 276, p. 575.
    Duration of easement prescribed by life tenant, c. 276, p. 575.
    Future interests, effect of, p. 570; c. 271, p. 577.
    Letter as interruption, c. 275, p. 573.
    Presumptions as to adverseness, c. 274, p. 571.
    Remainderman, against, c. 277, p. 577.
    Requirements, c. 273, p. 570.
    Scope of easement, p. 569; c. 273, p. 570; c. 278, p. 578.
    Tacking, p. 570; c. 277, p. 577.
    "Without interruption" discussed and applied, c. 275, p. 573.
Profit,
    Defined, p. 560; c. 270, p. 564.
    Divisibility, c. 283, p. 586.
    Ownership of mineral distinguished, c. 270, p. 564; c. 283, p. 586.
    Right to take ice as, c. 271, p. 566.
Real property, when, p. 562.
Repair, right to, c. 279, p. 580.
Reservation or exception, by, p. 569.
Servient tenant, use by, c. 277, p. 577; c. 279, p. 580.
Servient tenement defined, p. 561.
Statute of frauds, applicability to, p. 563.
Summary of cases, p. 603.
Termination, see subheading Extinguishment.

EJECTMENT
Plaintiff's title, strength of, c. 138, p. 235.
Prior possession as sufficient title, c. 138, p. 235.
Wire removal, for, c. 156, p. 263.

EMBLEMENTS
Certainty of term as affecting tenant's rights, p. 361; cs. 190–192, pp. 361–364.
Fructus industriales, p. 359.
    Personalty, when regarded as, p. 360.
    Realty, when regarded as, Note, p. 360.
Fructus naturales, p. 359.
    Realty until severed, p. 359.
Growing crops, oral sale of, p. 360.
Legal gems, p. 359.
Orange crop, status of, c. 192, p. 364.
Perennials as, p. 359; c. 192, p. 364.
Severed crops personalty, p. 360.
Summary of cases, p. 365.
Tenant's right to remove, p. 361; cs. 190–191, pp. 361–364.

EMINENT DOMAIN
Inverse condemnation, p. 257; c. 153, p. 257; c. 154, p. 259.
Landlord and tenant, effect on relationship, p. 208; c. 124, p. 208.
Rent extinguished by, p. 213.
Scope and limitations on power, p. 626.

EMPLOYER AND EMPLOYEE
Landlord and tenant distinguished, Note, p. 75.
Rights of finder, effect on, c. 324, p. 682; c. 325, p. 682; c. 327, p. 684.

EQUITABLE CONVERSION AND RISK OF LOSS
Land contracts, pp. 375 et seq.
    Applicable when, p. 376.
    Basis, p. 375.

EQUITABLE CONVERSION AND RISK OF LOSS—Continued
Land contracts—Continued
　　　Casualty damage during, c. 199, p. 378; Note 1, p. 379.
　　　Effect of, p. 376; c. 199, p. 378.
　　　Illegality of intended use, c. 198, p. 377.
　　　Insurable interest of vendee, p. 377; c. 200, p. 379, Note, p. 380.
　　　Political protest rights, Note 2, p. 379.
　　　Possession, significance of, p. 376.
　　　Risk of casualty during, p. 376; c. 179, p. 378.
　　　Specific performance discretionary, p. 377; c. 198, p. 377.
　　　Taxes accruing, p. 377.
Legal gems, p. 375.
Specific performance of land contracts, p. 377; c. 199, p. 378.
Summary of cases, p. 394.
Uniform Vendor And Purchaser Risk Act, p. 376; c. 199, p. 378.

EQUITABLE SERVITUDES
Adverse possession, effect of, p. 542.
Benefit and burden both running, c. 267, p. 543; c. 268, p. 546.
Burden, requirements for running, p. 543; c. 267, p. 543.
Circumstances justifying non-enforcement, p. 542; c. 269, p. 552.
Common examples, pp. 540, 541.
Condominiums, application to, p. 556.
Cooperatives, application to, p. 556.
Creation, requirements for, pp. 539–540; c. 267, p. 543; c. 268, p. 546; c. 269, p. 552.
Deed poll, created by, p. 541; c. 267, p. 543.
Definition, p. 539.
Duration, c. 269, p. 552.
Enforceable by whom, c. 269, p. 552.
Enforcement basis, p. 539.
Equitable easement equivalent, p. 540.
Extinguishment, p. 542; c. 268, p. 546; c. 269, p. 552.
General scheme, what constitutes, c. 269, p. 552.
Home Owners' Association, application to, p. 555.
Intention requirement, p. 542; c. 267, p. 543; c. 268, p. 546.
Legal gems, p. 539.
Methods of imposing, c. 269, p. 552.
Negative easement, as, c. 267, p. 543.
Notice requirement, pp. 539–543; c. 267, p. 543; c. 268, p. 546.
Planned Unit Developments, application to, p. 555.
Racial restrictions, c. 268, p. 546; Note, p. 550.
Subdivision development scheme, c. 268, p. 546.
Summary of cases, p. 558.

EQUITY
Defined, in reference to mortgages, p. 499.
Uses, relation to, pp. 400–401.

EQUITY OF REDEMPTION
　　　See also Mortgages.
Defined, p. 499.

ESCHEAT
Defined, p. 3.

ESCROW
See Deeds, Delivery, subheading Escrow.

ESTATE BY THE ENTIRETY
See Tenancy by the Entirety.

ESTATE FOR YEARS
　　　See also Landlord and Tenant; Lease; Non-Freehold Estates.
Characteristics, c. 15, p. 25.
Chattel real, as, p. 69; c. 52, p. 70.
Contractual provisions incident to, pp. 69–70.
Croppers' contract, created by, c. 56, p. 74.
Definition, p. 69.

ESTATE FOR YEARS—Continued
Descent of, c. 52, p. 70.
Emblements, c. 190, p. 361.
Holdover, landlord's choices, p. 70; c. 57, p. 77; c. 59, p. 79.
Illustrated, p. 8.
Leasehold elements, p. 70.
Personal property, as, p. 69; c. 52, p. 70.
Restraint on alienation, validity, c. 51, p. 65.
Reversion, incident to, c. 68, p. 102.
Subject to termination, c. 55, p. 73.
Tenancy at will from ineffective attempt to create, p. 69.
Typical case, c. 15, p. 25.
Waste, tenant's liability for, p. 351.

ESTATE FROM YEAR TO YEAR
See Periodic Tenancy.

ESTHETICS
Nuisance, See Nuisance.
Zoning, consideration in, c. 297, p. 629.

ESTOPPEL
Basis of executed license, p. 611; c. 290, p. 612.
Easement terminated by, p. 600.

ESTOPPEL BY DEED
Adverse possessor against grantee claiming benefit, c. 240, p. 468.
Basis, p. 466; c. 240, p. 468.
Bona fide purchaser, rights of, c. 242, p. 471.
Definition, p. 466; c. 240, p. 468.
Election of remedies if covenant in deed, p. 467.
Illustrations, p. 467.
Inapplicable in deed only of grantor's interest, p. 467; c. 241, p. 470.
Leases, application to, c. 239, p. 468.
Misrepresentation not necessary for doctrine, c. 242, p. 471.
Mortgage or conveyance by one entireties tenant, c. 65, p. 89.
Recording act, effect of, c. 242, p. 471; c. 247, p. 489.
Stranger to deed, use by, p. 466; c. 240, p. 468.
Summary of cases, p. 474.
Theories of operation, p. 466; c. 239, p. 468; c. 240, p. 468.

ESTOVERS
Defined, c. 186, p. 352.

EVICTION
Breach of covenant of quiet enjoyment, as, p. 209; c. 125, p. 210.
Rent extinguished by, p. 213.

EXCEPTION
See also Land Description.
Defined, p. 441.
To zoning ordinance, see Zoning.

EXCLUSIVE POWER
See also Power of Appointment.
Defined, p. 180; c. 108, p. 182.

EXECUTORY DEVISE
See Executory Interests.

EXECUTORY INTERESTS
Alienability, c. 83, p. 129; p. 134.
Chart comparing future interests, p. 141.
Contingent interest following term as, c. 80, p. 124.
Contingent remainder construction preferred, p. 134; c. 85, p. 137.
Definition, p. 133.
Examples of, p. 135.
Gaps in successive estates, following, p. 135.
Indestructible, p. 134.

EXECUTORY INTERESTS—Continued

Legal gems, p. 133.

Limitation creating both executory interest and contingent remainder, c. 85, p. 137.

Remainder distinguished, c. 78, p. 122; c. 79, p. 123; Note, p. 122.

Requirements, p. 133.

Rights of creditors, c. 86, p. 139.

Rule against perpetuities, subject to, Note, p. 40.

Shifting type,

    Characteristics, c. 29, p. 39.

    Created by devise, c. 31, p. 40.

    Examples, p. 137.

    Limited on a certain event, c. 86, p. 139.

    Right to prevent waste, c. 42, p. 53.

    Typical case, c. 29, p. 39.

Springing types, pp. 134 et seq.

    By deed, p. 134.

    By devise, p. 134.

    Characteristics, c. 28, p. 38.

    Created by devise, c. 30, p. 39.

    Limited on a certain event, c. 86, p. 139.

    Typical case, c. 28, p. 38.

    Words creating, c. 41, p. 52.

Statute of Uses, effect on, c. 28, p. 38; pp. 133, 134–135.

Term for years, following, p. 136.

Types, p. 134.

Vested estate divested by, p. 134.

Void on remote contingency after fee simple determinable, c. 71, p. 106.

EXTINGUISHMENT OF EASEMENTS

See Easements And Profits.

FAMILY

Zoning restrictions and definitions of single family, c. 309, p. 650.

FEDERAL CIVIL RIGHTS LEGISLATION

Racial restrictions, Note, p. 550.

FEE SIMPLE ABSOLUTE

"And his heirs" explained, c. 1, p. 12.

Characteristics, Special Note, p. 13.

Creation today, Special Note, p. 13.

Duration, Special Note con't., p. 13.

Fee absolute construction preferred, pp. 43–44.

Illustrated, p. 8.

Preferred over defeasible fee construction, c. 38, p. 48.

Repugnant clauses, construction of, c. 33, p. 44.

Restraint on alienation of, c. 40, p. 51; c. 51, p. 65; Note 2, p. 67.

Rule in Shelley's case, result of, c. 36, p. 47.

Statutory conversion of fee tail, c. 35, p. 46.

Typical case, c. 1, p. 12.

Words of limitation,

    Modern law as to, Special Note, p. 13.

    Significance of, c. 32, p. 42.

FEE SIMPLE CONDITIONAL

Characteristics, p. 54; c. 43, p. 55.

Convertible into fee simple absolute, c. 43, p. 55.

Defined and explained, c. 8, p. 19.

Fee tail predecessor, c. 8, p. 19; p. 54.

States where recognized, c. 43, p. 55.

FEE SIMPLE DETERMINABLE

Absolute fee construction preferred, c. 38, p. 48.

Automatic reversion, c. 2, p. 13; c. 37, p. 47.

Characteristics, c. 2, p. 18; c. 37, p. 47.

Covenant distinguished, see Note, pp. 14–15.

Examples of, p. 105; c. 71, p. 106; c. 72, p. 107.

Life estate determinable as alternative, Note 2, p. 62.

FEE SIMPLE DETERMINABLE—Continued
Typical case, c. 2, p. 13; c. 37, p. 47.
Words creating, see Note, pp. 14–15.

FEE SIMPLE SUBJECT TO CONDITION SUBSEQUENT
Characteristics, c. 3, p. 15.
Example of, c. 73, p. 110.
Typical case, c. 3, p. 15.
Words creating, c. 3, p. 15.
    Construction of, c. 39, p. 50.
Words of condition not conclusive, absolute estate preferred, c. 38, p. 48.

FEE SIMPLE SUBJECT TO EXECUTORY DEVISE
Shifting interest, typical case, c. 7, p. 18.
Springing interest, typical case, c. 6, p. 18.

FEE SIMPLE SUBJECT TO EXECUTORY LIMITATION
Shifting type, words creating, c. 42, p. 53.
Springing type, words creating, c. 41, p. 52.
Subject to shifting interest,
    Common law prohibited, c. 5, p. 17.
    Typical case, c. 5, p. 17.
Subject to springing interest,
    Common law prohibited, c. 4, p. 16.
    Typical case, c. 4, p. 16.

FEE TAIL
Common recovery as barring, c. 8, p. 19.
Convertible into fee simple, c. 44, p. 56.
Creation and characteristics, c. 44, p. 56.
Creditor rights where recognized, c. 45, p. 58; Note, p. 59.
Death without issue, meanings of, Note, p. 45.
Fee tail general, examples, Note, p. 57.
Fee tail special, examples, Note, p. 57.
"Heirs of the body" as creating, c. 8, p. 19.
Illustrated, p. 8.
Legal gems on, p. 54.
Possibility of issue extinct, c. 11, p. 22.
Reversion, incident to, p. 54; c. 46, p. 59; c. 67, p. 101.
Rule in Shelley's case, application, c. 49, p. 63.
Status in United States, c. 8, p. 19.
Statute De Donis, created by, p. 54.
Statutory conversion into fee simple, c. 35, p. 46.
Statutory modification, pp. 42, 54.
Types of fee tail, c. 8, p. 19; Note, p. 57.
Typical case, c. 8, p. 19.
Words creating, c. 8, p. 19.

FEOFFMENT
Defined and explained, c. 1, p. 12.
Example of, p. 396.

"FERTILE OCTOGENARIAN"
Rule Against Perpetuities, c. 102, p. 169.

FERTILITY
Rule against perpetuities and presumption of, c. 102, p. 169.

FINDER OF PERSONALTY
Brooch found in requisitioned house, c. 327, p. 684.
Categories of found property, pp. 679–680.
Coins buried in hen house, c. 324, p. 682.
Master-servant relationship, effect of, c. 324, p. 682; c. 325, p. 682; c. 327, p. 684.
Pirate Ship, c. 328, p. 685.
Rights of, p. 680; c. 322, p. 681; c. 325, p. 682; c. 327, p. 684.
Stocking stuffed with money used as plaything, c. 323, p. 681.
Summary of cases, p. 687.

FINE
Device for barring entail, c. 8, p. 19 ; p. 54.

FINE AND RECOVERY
See Fee Tail, Common recovery ; Fine.

FIXTURES
Annexation requirement, p. 327 ; cs. 181, 182, pp. 330, 334.
Appropriated to realty requirement, p. 328 ; cs. 181, 182, pp. 330, 334.
Definition, p. 327.
Efficiency apartment furnishing, c. 181, p. 330.
Fact question, as, p. 329.
Intention requirement, p. 321 ; cs. 181, 182, pp. 330–334.
Intention test, p. 327 ; cs. 181, 182, pp. 330, 334.
Legal gems on, p. 327.
Oral agreement to remain personalty, p. 330.
Priorities between interests in the real estate and interests in the chattel, pp. 338–341 ;
        cs. 183–184, pp. 342–343.
Relationship of parties, significance of, p. 329.
Requirements, p. 327 ; cs. 181–182, pp. 330, 334.
Security interests, p. 338 ; cs. 183–185, pp. 342–344.
    Agreement to remain chattel, p. 340.
    Prior realty interests, c. 183, p. 342.
    Priorities, p. 338 ; cs. 183–185, pp. 342–344.
        UCC, 1962 and 1972 versions, pp. 344–347.
    Right to remove fixture, p. 340 ; c. 185, p. 344.
    Subsequent purchaser or mortgagee of land, p. 339.
    U.C.C. pp. 338–341 ; cs. 183–184 ; pp. 342–343.
Statute of frauds, p. 330.
Stolen chattels annexed, p. 341.
Summary of cases, p. 347.
Trade Fixtures, see Trade Fixtures.

FLOOD WATER
See Water Rights.

FORECLOSURE
See Mortgages.

FOUR CORNER DOCTRINE
Construction of instruments, p. 41.
Controls over rule of repugnant clauses, c. 34, p. 45.

FRAUD ON POWERS
Power of appointment, exercise of, p. 182 ; c. 112, p. 188.

FREE TENURE
Defined, p. 3.

FREEHOLD ESTATES
Classified, p. 6.
Fee simple absolute, see Fee Simple Absolute.
Fee Simple Conditional, see Fee Simple Conditional.
Fee Simple Determinable, see Fee Simple Determinable.
Fee simple illustrated, p. 8.
Fee simple subject to condition subsequent, see Fee Simple Subject to Condition
        Subsequent.
Fee simple subject to executory devise, see Fee Simple Subject to Executory Devise.
Fee simple subject to executory limitation, see Fee Simple Subject to Executory
        Limitation.
Fee Tail, see Fee Tail.
Fee tail illustrated, p. 8.
Life estates, illustrated, p. 8.
Life estates, see Life Estate.
Non freehold, compared and distinguished, p. 8.
Typical cases, list of, p. 11.

FRUCTUS INDUSTRIALES
See Emblements.

FRUCTUS NATURALES
See Emblements.

FRUSTRATION OF PURPOSE
Leases, p. 205; c. 123, p. 207.
Rent extinguished by, p. 213.

FURTHER ASSURANCES, COVENANT
See Covenants for Title.

FUTURE INTERESTS
Adverse possession, effect on, see Adverse Possession.
Characteristics, p. 99.
Classified, p. 7; p. 99.
Compared with and distinguished from each other, chart, p. 141.
Contingent remainder, see Contingent Remainder.
Legal gems, p. 99.
Marketable Record Title Acts, invalidated by, p. 388; Note 2, p. 391.
Possibility of reverter, see Possibility of Reverter.
Power of termination, see Power of Termination.
Remainder, see Contingent Remainder; Vested Remainder.
Reversion, see Reversion.
Right of re-entry for condition broken, see Power Of Termination.
Vested remainder, see Vested Remainder.

GENERAL OCCUPANT
Defined, c. 10, p. 13.

GENERAL POWER
Creditors rights, c. 109, p. 184.
Defined, p. 180.

GENERAL WARRANTY COVENANT
See Covenants For Title.

GESTATION
Period of and the Rule against perpetuities, c. 96, p. 163.
See also Rule Against Perpetuities.

GIFTS
Acceptance, p. 698.
Causa mortis, p. 699; c. 337, p. 701.
Condition precedent versus condition subsequent rationale, c. 337, p. 701.
Peril contemplated, c. 337, p. 701.
Recovery from peril, c. 337, p. 701; Note, p. 703.
Revocation, c. 337, p. 701.
Death as a condition or contingency, c. 338, p. 703.
Definition, p. 699.
Delivery,
Circumstances control, c. 336, p. 700.
Constructive, p. 698.
Donee already in possession, p. 698; c. 336, p. 700.
Symbolic, p. 698.
To third person as bailee, p. 698; c. 336, p. 700; c. 338, p. 703.
Delivery requirement, p. 698; c. 336, p. 700.
Policy behind, c. 336, p. 700.
Donative intent, p. 698; c. 338, p. 703.
Inter vivos defined, c. 337, p. 701.
Legal gems, p. 698.
Oral trusts, requirements, c. 342, p. 708.
Oral trusts compared, p. 699; c. 342, p. 708.
Present gift of a future interest, c. 338, p. 703.
Present versus testamentary gifts, p. 698; c. 338, p. 703.
Summary of cases, p. 710.
Testamentary, p. 698; c. 338, p. 703; c. 340, p. 707.

GRANT
Example of, p. 396.

HEIRS
Limitation to grantor's heirs void, p. 153; c. 90, p. 154.
Limitation to heirs of living person as contingent, c. 80, p. 124; c. 82, p. 127.
Meaning dependent upon context, c. 88, p. 149.
Sense in which used, c. 88, p. 149.

HEIRS OF THE BODY
    See also Fee Tail.
As words of purchase, example of, c. 49, p. 63.

HOLDOVER TENANT
After expiration of notice in periodic tenancy, c. 58, p. 78.
Evictable by new tenant, p. 198; c. 114, p. 198.
Illness, effect of, c. 58, p. 78.
Increased rental demand, c. 59, p. 79.
Landlord's choices, p. 70; c. 57, p. 77; c. 59, p. 79.

HOME OWNERS' ASSOCIATION
Covenants running and equitable servitudes, p. 555.

HUSBAND AND WIFE
    See also Coverture; Curtesy; Dower; Estate by the Entirety.
Conveyance to self and wife, c. 63, p. 85.
Joint tenants, as, p. 81; c. 63, p. 85.

ILLEGALITY
Land contracts, intended use becoming, c. 198, p. 377.
Rental obligation of T, effect on, c. 122, p. 206; p. 223; c. 135, p. 227.

IMMUNITY
Legal relation, defined as, p. 4.

IMPERATIVE POWER
Defined and illustrated, c. 111, p. 187.

IMPLICATION
Easements, see Easements And Profits.
Remainders, c. 84, p. 131.

IMPROVEMENTS
Joint tenancy, contribution, c. 62, p. 84.

INCORPOREAL INTERESTS
Classified, p. 7.

INNKEEPER
Liability for guest's property, c. 333, p. 694.

INSTALLMENT LAND CONTRACT
Mortgage substitute, as, p. 510; c. 257, p. 512.

INTENTION
Construction of deeds and wills, role in, p. 41.

INVERSE CONDEMNATION
Definition, p. 257.

JOINT BANK ACCOUNTS
Contract theory, p. 699; c. 339, p. 705.
Creditors' rights, Note, p. 706.
Gift theory, p. 699; c. 339, p. 705.
    Requirements, c. 339, p. 705.
Legal gems, p. 699.
Nature of, p. 699; c. 339, p. 705.
Summary of cases, p. 710.

JOINT TENANCY
Characteristics, c. 19, p. 28; c. 61, p. 82; c. 62, p. 84.
Chart comparing concurrent tenancies, p. 93.
Common law preference for, p. 80.
Contribution, right between tenants, c. 62, p. 84.

JOINT TENANCY—Continued

Conveyance to self and another as, c. 63, p. 85.

Creditor's rights, c. 61, p. 82.

Devise ineffective, c. 60, p. 81.

Destruction or termination, c. 19, p. 28; p. 81.

Dower superseded by survivorship, c. 61, p. 82.

Husband and wife holding as, p. 81; c. 63, p. 85.

Modification of common law presumption, c. 19, p. 28.

Partition, c. 62, p. 84.

Presumption in creation, p. 80; c. 60, p. 81.

Severance of, p. 81; c. 60, p. 81; c. 61, p. 82; c. 64, p. 87.

    Extent of interest conveyed, c. 64, p. 87.

Statutory changes, c. 19, p. 28.

Survivorship characteristic, c. 19, p. 28; p. 81.

Survivorship substitute when estate prohibited, c. 19, p. 28.

Typical case at common law, c. 19, p. 28.

Unities required, c. 19, p. 28; p. 80.

JUS TERTII

Ejectment, as defense to, c. 138, p. 235.

LAKES

Use of water, see Water Rights.

LAND DESCRIPTION

"All my land" or designated street number, sufficiency of, Note, p. 444.

Boundaries, see Boundaries.

Course defined, p. 440.

Distance defined, p. 440.

Exception applied, c. 231, p. 449.

Exception defined, p. 441; c. 231, p. 449.

Government survey system, p. 436.

    Chart showing base lines and meridians, p. 437.

    Chart showing township section numbers, p. 438.

    Chart showing townships and ranges, p. 437.

    Section map showing fractional portions, p. 439.

    Township and range designation, p. 437.

Inadequate description, instrument void, c. 225, p. 442.

Intent of parties controls, p. 440; c. 229, p. 446.

Legal gems, p. 439.

Map reference incorporated into deed, p. 439; c. 227, p. 443.

Metes and bounds, p. 440.

Monument defined, p. 440.

Parol evidence, p. 440; Note, p. 444.

Reservation construed, c. 232, p. 450; c. 233, p. 451; Note, p. 452.

Reservation defined, p. 442; c. 232, p. 450; c. 233, p. 451; Note, p. 452.

Rules of construction, p. 440; cs. 228–230, pp. 444–448.

    Courses over distances, p. 440; Note, p. 446.

    Intent prevails, p. 440; c. 229, p. 446.

    Monuments over courses and distances, p. 440; c. 228, p. 444.

    Quantity estimate least accurate, p. 440.

    Specific over general, p. 440; c. 230, p. 448.

Summary of cases, p. 453.

"To," "by" or "along" as carrying to center of monument, p. 440; c. 228, p. 444; c. 229, p. 446; Note, p. 446.

Undivided portion of larger tract, p. 439; c. 226, p. 443.

LAND USE CONTROL

See Cooperatives and Condominiums; Covenants Running with the Land; Easements and Profits; Equitable Servitudes; Licenses; Police Power; Zoning.

LANDLORD AND TENANT

    See also Estate for Years; Lease; Non-Freehold Estates; Periodic Tenancy; Tenancy at Sufferance; Tenancy at Will.

Abandonment by T and L's recovery, p. 218; c. 131, p. 219; Note, p. 399.

Abandonment by tenant, see also Rent, subtitle Abandonment.

Advance Rental, p. 218; c. 132, p. 220.

Condemnation, effect on, p. 208; c. 124, p. 208.

LANDLORD AND TENANT—Continued

Condition of premises, see also subheading Residential Leases.
    Commercial leases, L's duty, c. 118, p. 202.
    L's duty to third persons, c. 117, p. 201.
    L's tort liability, c. 117, p. 201.
        Commercial leases, exculpatory clause, c. 118, p. 202.
    Residential leases, see subheading Residential leases.
Covenants running with the land, see Covenants Running with the Land.
    Summary of cases, p. 557.
Damages, mitigation of, c. 208, p. 397.
Delivery of premises,
    Landlord's duty, p. 197; c. 114, p. 198.
    New tenant may evict holdover, p. 198; c. 114, p. 198.
Distress, p. 211.
Employment contract distinguished, Note, pp. 75–76.
Estoppel of T to deny L's title, c. 120, p. 204; p. 209.
Eviction by Landlord, see subheading Quiet Enjoyment.
Exculpatory clause of L, p. 223.
Frustration of purpose, p. 205; c. 123, p. 207.
Illegality, p. 205; c. 122, p. 206.
    See also subheading Residential leases.

Legal gems, p. 197.
Liquidated damages, p. 218; c. 132, p. 220.
Master and servant relationship distinguished, Note, pp. 75–76.
Other relationships distinguished, Note, pp. 75–76.
Penalty void, p. 218; c. 132, p. 220.
Privity of estate and privity of contract explained, c. 208, p. 397.
Purpose frustrated, p. 205; c. 123, p. 207.
Quiet enjoyment,
    Covenant implied, p. 209; c. 125, p. 210.
    Constructive eviction as breach of, p. 209; c. 125, p. 210.
    Eviction by L as breach, p. 209; c. 125, p. 210.
Rent, see Rent.
Repair of premises, p. 203; c. 119, p. 203; c. 120, p. 204.
Rescission, L's breach as justifying, p. 209; c. 125, p. 210.
Residential leases, p. 222.
    Code violations and illegal contract, p. 223; c. 135, p. 227.
    Good faith, p. 224.
    Implied warranty of habitability, p. 223; c. 134, p. 226.
    Landlord and tenant acts, p. 223.
    Legal gems, p. 222.
    Retaliatory eviction, p. 222; c. 133, p. 225.
    Security deposit, p. 224.
    T's right to withhold rent for code violations, p. 223; c. 134, p. 226.
    Torts and crimes of third parties, L's duties as to, p. 225; c. 136, p. 228.
    Unconscionability, p. 224.
Security deposit, residential leases, p. 224.
Security deposits, p. 218; c. 132, p. 220.
Sublease, contingent right of re-entry as, p. 213; c. 130, p. 217.
Summary of cases, p. 229.
Surrender by act of parties and operation of law distinguished, c. 208, p. 397.
Tort liability,
    Exception to L's common law immunity, c. 117, p. 201.
    Landlord to third parties, c. 117, p. 201.
Trade Fixtures, see Trade Fixtures.
Use of premises, p. 199; c. 115, p. 200; c. 116, p. 201.
    Breach by L of covenant for exclusive commercial use, c. 125, p. 216.
    Dangerous condition, p. 199; c. 115, p. 200.
    Furnished dwellings, p. 199; c. 116, p. 201.
    Illegality, effect on rental obligation, c. 122, p. 20.
    Negligent repair by landlord, p. 199; c. 119, p. 203.
    Repair of, p. 200; c. 119, p. 203; c. 120, p. 204.
    Tenant's obligation to repair, p. 203; c. 120, p. 204.
Warranty of Fitness or Suitability,
    Generally, p. 199; c. 115, p. 200; c. 116, p. 201.

LANDLORD AND TENANT—Continued

Warranty of Fitness or Suitability—Continued
> None implied at common law, p. 199; c. 115, p. 200; c. 118, p. 202.
>> Residential leases, p. 223; c. 134, p. 226.

Waste, T's duty in respect thereto, c. 120, p. 204.

LATERAL AND SUBJACENT SUPPORT

Building support,
> Implied easement, p. 269; c. 160, p. 273.
> No prescription for, p. 269; c. 160, p. 273.

Buildings excluded, p. 267; c. 158, p. 269.

Cause of action accrual, p. 268; c. 159, p. 272.

Damages, p. 268; c. 158, p. 269.

Implied easement for building, p. 269; c. 160, p. 273.

Land in natural condition, limited to, p. 267; c. 158, p. 269.

Legal gems, p. 267.

License to shore up, p. 268; c. 158, p. 269.

Negligence,
> Liability for, p. 268.
> Liability not dependent on, p. 268; c. 158, p. 269.

Neighboring land defined, p. 267; c. 159, p. 272.

Semi-solid removal actionable, p. 267; c. 158, p. 269.

Statutes modifying common law, p. 268.

Subjacent support defined, p. 267.

Summary of cases, p. 274.

Water and oil removal not actionable, p. 267.

LEASE
> See also Landlord and Tenant.

Bailment distinguished, p. 690; c. 304, p. 693.

License distinguished, p. 20; c. 53, p. 71; p. 610; c. 291, p. 614; c. 292, p. 616;
> Note, p. 620.

Liquidated damages, p. 218; c. 132, p. 220.

Penalty, p. 218; c. 132, p. 220.

Proprietary lease, see Cooperatives.

LEASE AND RELEASE

Conveyance, as, p. 396.

Example of, p. 396.

LEASEHOLD

Essential elements, pp. 69–70.

Restraint on alienation, validity, c. 51, p. 65.

LEGAL GEMS
> See also principal substantive headings, e. g., Adverse Possession; Deeds;
>> Easements, etc.

Explained, p. 1.

Purpose, p. 2.

LEGAL RELATIONS

Definition, p. 4.

Disability, p. 4.

Duty, p. 4.

Immunity, p. 4.

Liability, p. 4.

"No Right," p. 4.

Power, p. 4.

Privilege, p. 4.

Right, p. 4.

LIABILITY

Legal relation, defined as, p. 4.

LICENSES

Advertising signs, nature of, c. 292, p. 616.

Assignability, p. 611.

Contract distinguished, p. 610; c. 291, p. 614; c. 292, p. 616.

Conveyance of realty as revocation, c. 293, p. 618; c. 294, p. 620.

LICENSES—Continued

Definitions, p. 609.

Easements distinguished, p. 610; c. 292, p. 616.

Estoppel basis of executed license, p. 611; c. 290, p. 612.

Executed license, pp. 609, 611; c. 290, p. 612.

Ineffective attempt to create easement, from, p. 611; Note, p. 618.

Lease distinguished, p. 70; c. 53, p. 71; p. 610; c. 291, p. 614; c. 292, p. 616; Note, p. 620.

Legal gems, p. 609.

License coupled with an interest, pp. 609, 611; c. 293, p. 618.

Mere license, p. 609.

Oral contract to sell timber, effect, c. 293, p. 618.

Oral license acted upon, pp. 609, 611; c. 290, p. 612.

Revocability, pp. 609, 611; c. 290, p. 612; c. 291, p. 614; c. 293, p. 618; c. 294, p. 620.

Sporting events and theatre tickets, c. 291, p. 614.

Summary of cases, p. 621.

Types, p. 609.

LIFE ESTATE

Alienability, c. 10, p. 22.

Characteristics, c. 9, p. 21.

Coverture,
    Characteristics, c. 14, p. 25.
    Typical case during, c. 14, p. 25.

Curtesy, created by, c. 13, p. 24.

Defined, p. 61.

Determinable life estate versus tenancy at will, p. 61; c. 47, p. 61; Note 1, p. 62.

Dower, created by, c. 12, p. 23.

Fee simple determinable as alternative construction, Note 2, p. 62.

Fee tail after possibility of issue extinct, c. 11, p. 22.

For life of tenant, typical case, c. 9, p. 21.

Forfeiture restraint on, valid, p. 61.

Habendum controlling over ambiguous granting clause, c. 34, p. 45.

Illustrated, p. 8.

Joint lives and the survivor, for, p. 61; c. 50, p. 65.

Joint tenancy destroyed by conveying, c. 64, p. 87.

Legal gems on, p. 60.

May last for life, c. 47, p. 61.

Measuring lives too many, effect, p. 61.

Power of sale added, c. 48, p. 63.

Powers may be added, p. 61.

Pur Autre Vie,
    Common occupant defined, c. 10, p. 22.
    Special occupant defined, c. 10, p. 22.
    Typical case, c. 10, p. 22.

Restraint on alienation,
    Forfeiture type, justification on life estate, c. 51, p. 65.
    Validity of, c. 51, p. 65.

Rule in Shelley's case application, c. 36, p. 47; pp. 61, 146.

Shelley's case not applicable, when, c. 49, p. 63; c. 88, p. 149.

Subject to termination, examples of, Note 1, p. 67.

Types, p. 61.

Waste, life tenant's liability for, p. 349; c. 186, p. 352.

Words of limitation lacking, presumption, p. 61.

LIMITATION, WORDS OF

See Words of Limitation.

LIQUIDATED DAMAGES

Landlord and tenant, p. 218; c. 132, p. 220.

LIVERY OF SEISIN

Adversely possessed land, c. 139, p. 239.

LOST PROPERTY

Definition, p. 679; c. 325, p. 682; c. 327, p. 684.

Rights of finder, p. 680; c. 322, p. 681; c. 325, p. 682; c. 327, p. 684.

MAINTENANCE
Defined, ftn. 1, p. 111.

MANDATORY POWER
Defined and illustrated, c. 111, p. 187.

MARIJUANA
Religion and zoning regulations, c. 311, p. 652.

MARKETABLE RECORD TITLE ACT
Claims invalidated by, p. 387, Note 2, p. 391.
Commercially marketable, relation to, p. 388; Note 2, p. 391.
Competing chains of title, effect on, c. 206, p. 389; Note 1, p. 391.
Curative act features, p. 387.
Defeasible fee conversion to absolute fee, Note 2, p. 388.
Disability, no significance, p. 388.
Exceptions provided, p. 387; Note 2, p. 391.
Forged deed as root, c. 207, p. 391.
Future interests invalidated by, p. 388; Note 2, p. 391.
Period specified, p. 387.
Purpose, p. 386.
Quitclaim as root, p. 388; c. 205, p. 388.
Recording act features, p. 387.
Root of title,
    Defined, p. 387.
    Quitclaim as, p. 388; c. 205, p. 388; ftn. 9, p. 389.
Statute of limitations features, p. 387.
Summary of cases, p. 395.
Wild deed as root, c. 206, Note 1, p. 391; end c. 207, p. 392.

MARKETABLE TITLE
Acts of vendor justifying rescission, c. 201, p. 383.
Adverse possession as, c. 203, p. 385.
Contract requirement of abstract showing, p. 382; c. 203, p. 385.
Contract requiring marketable title of record, p. 382; c. 203, p. 385.
Conveyance by quitclaim, effect on requirement, p. 383; c. 204, p. 386.
Curative acts, p. 383.
Defects to be pointed out by vendee, c. 201, p. 383.
Definition, p. 381; ftn. 8, p. 384.
Examples of defects precluding, p. 382.
Executory contract, function limited to, p. 381.
    Exception, c. 203, p. 385; Note, p. 385.
Implication in sales contract, p. 381; c. 201, p. 383.
Insurability, effect on, p. 383.
Legal gems, p. 381.
Matters outside the record, p. 382; c. 203, p. 385.
Slight defect, p. 383.
Specific performance, required for, p. 381.
Summary of cases, p. 394.
Time when required, p. 382; c. 202, p. 384.
Title by acquiescence as, Note, p. 385.
Title search, vendee's obligation, c. 201, p. 383.
Type of estate required, p. 381.

MASTER AND SERVANT
Landlord and tenant distinguished, Note, p. 75.
Rights of finder, effect on, c. 324, p. 682; c. 325, p. 682; c. 327, p. 684.

MERGER
Contract for sale and deed, p. 381; Note, p. 385.
Rent extinguished by, p. 213.

MINERAL RIGHTS
Adverse possession against, c. 147, p. 248.

MISPLACED PROPERTY
Definition, p. 679; c. 325, p. 682; c. 300, p. 684.
Rights of finder, p. 680; c. 325, p. 682; c. 300, p. 684.

MISTAKE
Mutual mistake as basis for rescission, Note, p. 385.

MONUMENT
See Land Description.

MORTGAGES
Adverse possession against, c. 147, p. 248.
Anti-clogging rules, p. 501; c. 253, p. 503.
Assignability, p. 500.
Assignment,
    Note unaccounted for, c. 254, p. 505.
    Recording significance, p. 500.
Break in assumption agreements as affecting personal liability, p. 500; c. 255, p. 506.
Common law, at, p. 499; c. 253, p. 503.
Conveyance "subject to" a mortgage, p. 500; c. 255, p. 506.
Conveyance with assumption agreement, p. 500; c. 255, p. 506.
Debt,
    Evidence of, p. 499.
    Nature of, p. 499.
Deed absolute as mortgage, c. 253, p. 503.
    Parol evidence rule, c. 253, p. 503.
    Recording and third parties, c. 253, p. 503.
    Rights of third parties, c. 253, p. 503.
    Statute of frauds, c. 253, p. 503.
Deficiency decree, p. 501.
    Separate action on note, p. 501.
Definition, p. 499; c. 252, p. 502.
Due on sale clauses, p. 511.
"Equity" defined, pp. 499–500.
Equity of redemption,
    Defined, p. 499.
    Rules against clogging, p. 501; c. 253, p. 503.
Foreclosure, pp. 500–501.
    At common law, p. 501.
    Definition, pp. 500–501.
    Judicial sale, by, p. 501.
    Junior mortgage, rights of parties, c. 256, p. 508.
    Methods, pp. 500–501.
    Multiple mortgages, distribution of proceeds, c. 256, p. 508.
    Parties defendant, c. 256, p. 508.
    Senior mortgage, rights of parties, c. 256, p. 508.
    Strict foreclosure, p. 501.
Future advances for, c. 252, p. 502.
    Nature of, c. 252, p. 502.
    Obligatory or optional nature, c. 252, p. 502.
    Priorities, c. 252, p. 502.
Legal gems, p. 499.
Lien theory, p. 499.
Marshalling, p. 511.
    Inverse order of alienation rule, p. 512.
    "Two funds" doctrine, p. 511.
"Mortgage follows the debt," p. 500; c. 254, p. 505.
Mortgagee in possession, c. 253, p. 503.
Mortgagor defined, p. 499.
Note or bond as evidence of debt, p. 499; c. 254, p. 505.
"Once a mortgage, always a mortgage," p. 501.
Recording significance, p. 500.
Rights and obligations of parties, c. 255, p. 506.
Subrogation, p. 501; c. 255, p. 506.
Substitutes or alternatives, pp. 509 et seq.; c. 257, p. 512.
    Conditional sale, p. 510.
    Deed absolute with oral agreement, p. 510.
    Deed of Trust, pp. 510–511.
    Installment land contract, p. 510; c. 257, p. 512.
Summary of cases, p. 513.

MORTGAGES—Continued
Tenancy by the entirety, one spouse executing, c. 65, p. 89.
Title theory, p. 499.
Wrap-around, defined and explained, p. 511.

NAVIGABLE WATER
Defined, p. 276.

NEGLIGENCE
Bailee liable for, p. 690 ; c. 329, p. 691.
Support of land, see Lateral And Subjacent Support.

NOISE
Nuisance, as, see Nuisance.
Repeated incursions as a taking, p. 257 ; c. 154, p. 259.

NONCONFORMING USE
See Zoning.

NON–FREEHOLD ESTATES
See also Estate for Years ; Estate from Year to Year ; Landlord and Tenant ;
        Lease ; Periodic Tenancy ; Tenancy at Will ; Tenancy at Sufferance.
Classified, p. 6.
Estate for years illustrated, p. 8.
Estate from year to year illustrated, p. 8.
Freehold, compared and distinguished, p. 8.
Legal gems on, p. 69.
Summaries of cases on non-freehold estates, p. 96.
Tenancy at sufferance illustrated, p. 8.
Tenancy at will illustrated, p. 9.
Types, p. 69.

"NO RIGHT"
Legal relation, defined, as, p. 4.

NUISANCE
Accrual of cause of action, c. 180, p. 323.
Average person with ordinary sensibilities test, p. 311 ; c. 177, p. 317 ; c. 179, p. 321.
Business location, may be question of, p. 313 ; c. 179, p. 321.
Definition, p. 310.
Illustrations of, p. 312.
Injunction, scope of relief granted, pp. 312–313 ; c. 177, p. 317.
Liability, basis for, p. 310.
Low wire as, c. 156, p. 263.
Noise as, c. 154, p. 259 ; c. 177, p. 317.
Nonconforming use in zoning, relation to, c. 300, p. 635 ; Special Note, p. 637.
Permanent defined, p. 312.
Pollution of surface water as, c. 176, p. 316.
Prescription as to, p. 313 ; c. 180, p. 323.
Public nuisance defined, p. 310.
Reasonableness as fact question, pp. 312–313 ; c. 175, p. 314 ; c. 178, p. 319.
Recurring trespass as, p. 311.
Remedies for, c. 176, p. 316.
Subsurface encroachment as, c. 157, p. 264.
Summary of cases, p. 325.
Temporary defined, p. 312.
Trespass, same act may be both, p. 311.
Trespass distinguished, p. 310.
Tuberculosis sanitarium as, c. 179, p. 321.
Type of interference or conduct constituting, p. 311.
Unsightliness as, p. 311 ; c. 174, p. 313.

"ONCE A MORTGAGE ALWAYS A MORTGAGE"
Explained, p. 501 ; c. 253, p. 503.

OPTIONS
Cooperatives and condominiums, ftn. 3, p. 67.
Rule against perpetuities, c. 101, p. 168.

ORAL TRUSTS OF PERSONALTY
Gifts compared, pp. 699–700; c. 342, p. 708.

PART PERFORMANCE
Legal gems, p. 372.
Oral land sales contracts, pp. 372–373.
    Acts constituting, p. 373; c. 196, p. 373.
    Collateral acts, Note 2, p. 375.
    Services rendered as constituting, c. 197, p. 374; Notes 1 and 2, p. 375.
    Specific performance, p. 373; c. 196, p. 373.
    Sufficiency of performance depends on jurisdiction, p. 373, c. 196, p. 373.
Services rendered as constituting, c. 197, p. 374.

PARTITION
Joint tenancy, c. 62, p. 84.

PARTY WALL
Covenants concerning as running, c. 262, p. 528.
Extension of and right to contribution, c. 285, p. 590.
Ownership and easements, theories as to, c. 285, p. 590.

PENALTY
Lease provision void, p. 218; c. 132, p. 220.

PERCOLATING WATER
See Water Rights.

PERIODIC TENANCY
Characteristics, c. 16, p. 26.
Continuing tenancy, as, c. 119, p. 203.
Created by ineffective oral lease, c. 16, p. 26.
Emblements, c. 191, p. 362.
Estate from year to year,
    Illustrated, p. 6.
    Typical case, c. 16, p. 26.
Holding over after notice to quit, c. 58, p. 78.
Notice to terminate, c. 16, p. 26.
Tenancy at will transformed into, p. 70; c. 54, p. 73.

PERPETUITIES, RULE AGAINST
See Rule Against Perpetuities.

PLANNED UNIT DEVELOPMENT
Covenants running and equitable servitudes, p. 555.
Explained, p. 555.
Floating zones, relation to, Note, p. 647.

PLANNING
Comprehensive plan,
    Defined, p. 623.
        See also master plan, infra.
Legal gems, p. 623.
Master plan, p. 623.
    Defined, p. 623.
More stringent zoning, effect, c. 296, p. 626.
Zoning, relation to, p. 623; cs. 295–296, pp. 624–625; c. 302, p. 641.
Zoning must conform thereto, c. 295, p. 624; c. 296, p. 625.

POLICE POWER
Arbitrary and unreasonable ordinance invalid, c. 299, p. 632; c. 302, p. 641.
Definition and scope, p. 626; c. 298, p. 630; c. 299, p. 632.
Delegation of, necessity of standards, c. 302, p. 641; c. 307, p. 648; Note, p. 648.
Excessive regulation, effect of, p. 627; c. 300, p. 635.
Fairly debatable rule, p. 627; c. 298, p. 630.
Flexibility and changing circumstances, c. 302, p. 641.
General welfare concept, c. 298, p. 630.
Limitations on, p. 626; c. 299, p. 632.
Promotion of health, safety, welfare and morals as objective, cs. 298–299, pp. 630–634.

POLICE POWER—Continued

Reasonable ordinance valid, c. 311, p. 652.

Summary of cases, p. 655.

Zoning, basis of, pp. 626, 627; cs. 298, 299, pp. 630–634.

POSSESSION

Ejectment, prior possession as title, c. 138, p. 235.

Land, p. 233.

    Acts constituting, p. 233; c. 137, p. 233.

    Airspace, see Airspace.

    Court role in determining, c. 137, p. 233.

    Jury role in determining, c. 137, p. 233.

    Jus tertii as defense to ejectment, c. 138, p. 235.

    Legal gems, p. 233.

    Prior possessor, rights of, c. 138, p. 235.

    Protected interest, as, p. 233.

    Real property, as, p. 233.

    Rights incident to, p. 257.

    Subsurface rights, c. 157, p. 264.

Lease versus employment contract, significance in,
    Comment, p. 76.

Lease versus license, significance in, p. 70, c. 53, p. 71.

Personalty,

    Legal gems, p. 679.

    Physical control and intent required, c. 323, p. 681.

    Rights incident to, p. 679; c. 326, p. 683.

    Summary of cases, p. 687.

    What constitutes, p. 679; c. 323, p. 681.

    Wrongful possessor may recover from converter, c. 326, p. 683.

Wild animals,

    Acquisition of title by, p. 679; c. 321, p. 680.

    Pursuit not sufficient, c. 321, p. 680.

    What constitutes, p. 679.

POSSIBILITY OF REVERTER

Alienability, Note, p. 14, c. 24, p. 33; p. 105; c. 72, p. 107.

Automatic reversion chief characteristic, p. 105.

Characteristics, c. 24, p. 33.

Chart comparing future interests, p. 141.

Created by implication of law, p. 105.

Definition, p. 105.

Descendability, c. 24, p. 33; p. 105; c. 71, p. 106.

Devisable, p. 105; c. 71, p. 106.

Example of, pp. 105, 106.

Explained, Note, p. 14.

Express reverter and absence of "so long as," c. 72, p. 107.

Express words of reverter not necessary, p. 105.

Incident to void executory interest after fee simple determinable, c. 71, p. 106.

Legal gems, p. 105.

Nature of, Note, p. 107.

Power of termination distinguished, Note, p. 35; pp. 114–115.

Reversion, may be incident to, p. 105.

Rule against perpetuities not applicable, Note, p. 49; p. 105.

Typical case, c. 24, p. 33.

POWER

Legal relation, defined as, p. 4.

POWER IN TRUST

Defined, p. 180, c. 111, p. 187.

Failure to exercise, p. 182; c. 111, p. 187.

POWER OF SALE

Appended to life estate, c. 48, p. 63.

POWER OF TERMINATION

Alienability, Note, p. 16; c. 25, p. 34; p. 110; c. 74, p. 112.

    Maintenance and champerty, basis of nonassignability rule, ftn. 1, p. 111.

POWER OF TERMINATION—Continued

Characteristics, c. 25, p. 34.
Chart comparing future interests, p. 141.
Definition, p. 109.
Descendability, c. 25, p. 34; p. 110; c. 73, p. 110.
Devisable, p. 110; c. 73, p. 110.
Equitable relief from forfeiture, p. 110.
Examples, pp. 109–110; c. 73, p. 110; c. 74, p. 112.
Forfeiture of estate results from exercise, p. 109.
Legal gems, p. 109.
Possibility of reverter distinguished, Note, p. 35; chart, p. 114.
Requirements for exercise, p. 109; c. 73, p. 110.
Reversion, may be incident to, p. 109, c. 74, p. 112.
Rule against perpetuities not applicable, Note, p. 49; p. 110.
Rules of construction, p. 110.
Typical case, c. 25, p. 34.
Typical words creating, p. 109.
Waiver, c. 55, p. 73; p. 110; c. 74, p. 112.
Waiver and multiple conditions, c. 74, p. 112.

POWERS OF APPOINTMENT

Appointee defined, p. 179.
Appointment, validity under perpetuities, p. 182; c. 110, p. 185.
    General power presently exercisable, p. 182; c. 110, p. 185.
    General testamentary power, p. 182; c. 110, p. 185.
    Measurement of period, c. 110, p. 185.
    Special power, p. 182; c. 110, p. 185.
Capture doctrine, p. 181, c. 110, p. 185.
Classification, p. 179.
Contract not to appoint, c. 113, p. 190.
Contract to exercise, p. 182; c. 113, p. 190.
Creditors, rights in appointive property, p. 181; c. 108, p. 180; c. 109, p. 184.
Definition, p. 179.
Exclusive power, presumption favors, p. 181; c. 108, p. 182.
Exclusive power defined, p. 180; c. 108, p. 182.
Exercise,
    Contract to, p. 182; c. 113; p. 190.
    Failure when power in trust, p. 182; c. 111, p. 187.
    Fraudulent, p. 181; c. 112, p. 188.
    In favor of non-objects, p. 182; c. 112, p. 188; c. 113, p. 190.
    Ineffective or void,
        Capture, p. 181; c. 110, p. 185.
        Result, p. 182; c. 110, p. 185.
    Limitations on control, p. 180.
    Restrictions in creating instrument, p. 180.
Fraudulent exercise, p. 182; c. 112, p. 188.
General power defined, p. 180.
General power presently exercisable,
    As equivalent to ownership, c. 104, p. 173.
    Validity under perpetuities, c. 104, p. 173.
General testamentary power, validity under perpetuities, c. 105, p. 174.
Legal gems, p. 179.
Non-exclusive power defined, p. 180; c. 108, p. 182.
Power appendant defined, p. 180.
Power in gross defined, p. 180.
Power in trust defined, p. 180; c. 111, p. 187.
Power purely collateral defined, p. 180.
Release, p. 182; c. 113, p. 190.
Remainder or interest following, effect on, c. 76, p. 119.
Rule against perpetuities, validity of appointment, p. 182.
Special power,
    Defined, p. 180; c. 108, p. 182.
    Validity under perpetuities, c. 105, p. 174.
Summary of cases, p. 194.
Takers in default defined, p. 179.
Title from donor to appointee, c. 108, p. 182.
Typical case, c. 108, p. 182.

PRESCRIPTION
Building support, p. 269.
Easement created by, see Easements And Profits, subheading Prescription, by.
Easement terminated by, p. 600.
Nuisance, may acquire right to maintain, p. 313.

PRIMOGENITURE
Defined, p. 4.

PRIOR APPROPRIATION DOCTRINE
See Water Rights.

PRIORITIES AND RECORDING
Actual notice, effect of, c. 244, p. 484.
Adverse possession and recording, p. 237; c. 141, p. 241; p. 482.
BFP requirements, p. 481; c. 244, p. 484.
Chain of title, p. 480; c. 246, p. 486.
    Estoppel by deed, c. 247, p. 489.
    Missing link or break in chain, p. 480; c. 245, p. 485; c. 246, p. 486.
    Prior deeds to other land from common grantor, c. 251, p. 494.
    Recording out of turn, c. 250, p. 493.
Charts comparing recording acts, pp. 495, 496.
Common law, priority of title under, p. 476.
Constructive notice,
    Deeds to other land by common grantor, c. 251, p. 494.
    Defined, p. 478; c. 244, p. 484.
    Effect of, p. 478; c. 244, p. 484.
    Imputed by recording, p. 478; c. 244, p. 484.
    Significance of tract index, Note 2, p. 488.
Defects or interests not covered by recording, p. 482; c. 249, p. 491.
Estoppel by deed, effect of recording act, c. 242, p. 471; c. 247, p. 489.
Fraudulent conveyances void, p. 482.
Improperly executed deeds not constructive notice, p. 479.
Indexing mistakes, p. 482.
Indices, type of, p. 482.
Inquiry notice, gap in chain of title, c. 245, p. 485.
Legal gems, p. 476.
Mortgagee as purchaser, p. 481.
Persons not protected by recording, p. 482; c. 245, p. 485.
Persons protected by recording, p. 481.
Possession as notice, p. 481; c. 244, p. 484.
Pre-existing debt and qualification as purchaser, p. 481.
Properly recorded defined, p. 479.
Purchaser defined, p. 481; c. 230, p. 484.
Quitclaim grantee as purchaser, p. 481.
Recorder's mistakes, p. 479; c. 248, p. 490.
Recording construed, Note 1, p. 488.
Reliance on records by subsequent BFP, p. 480.
Subsequent purchaser subject to prior interests properly recorded, p. 480.
Summary of cases, p. 497.
Tract index, significance, Note 2, p. 488.
Types of recording statutes, p. 477.
    Notice, p. 477; c. 243, p. 482; c. 244, p. 484; c. 250, p. 493.
        Operation and effect, c. 243, p. 482; c. 244, p. 484.
    Period of grace, p. 478; ftn. 1, p. 487.
    Race, p. 477; ftn. 1, p. 487.
    Race-Notice, p. 477; ftn. 1, p. 487; c. 250, p. 493.
    Results compared in one case, ftn. 1, p. 487; Charts, pp. 495–496.
Undelivered but recorded deeds, p. 482; c. 249, p. 491.
Void instruments, pp. 479, 482; c. 249, p. 491.
Wrongfully procured and recorded deed from escrow, c. 221, p. 428.

PRIVILEGE
Legal relation, defined as, p. 4.

PRIVITY OF CONTRACT
Rent, liability based on, p. 213; c. 129, p. 216.

PRIVITY OF ESTATE
Covenants running with the land, see Covenants Running with the Land.
Rent, liability based on, p. 213; c. 129, p. 216.

PROFIT A PRENDRE
See Easements And Profits.

PROMISES RESPECTING LAND USE
See Covenants Running with the Land.

PROPERTY
Legal relation, defined as, p. 4.

PROPRIETARY LEASE
See Cooperatives.

PUR AUTRE VIE
See Life Estate.

PURCHASE, WORDS OF
See Words of Purchase.

QUIET ENJOYMENT
Deeds, in, See Covenants for Title.
Leases in,
        Constructive eviction, p. 209; c. 125, p. 210.
        Covenant implied, p. 209; c. 125, p. 210.
        Eviction as breach, p. 209; c. 125, p. 210.

QUITCLAIM DEED
Root of title, as, p. 388; c. 205, p. 388.

RACIAL RESTRICTIONS
Validity of, c. 268, p. 546; Note, p. 550.

RAINFALL
Landowner's right to, p. 257; c. 155, p. 262.

RANGES
Chart showing how designated, p. 437.

REAL PROPERTY
Interests classified, p. 6.
        Concurrent estates, p. 6.
        Freehold estates, p. 6.
        Future interests, p. 7.
        Incorporeal interests, p. 7.
        Non-freehold estates, p. 6.

RECORDING ACTS
        See also Priorities and Recording.
Adverse possession and, p. 237; c. 141, p. 241.
Easement terminated by BFP under, p. 600.
Estoppel by deed, relation to, c. 242, p. 471.

RELEASE
Easement extinguished by, p. 599.
Powers of appointment, p. 182; c. 113, p. 190.
Rent extinguished by, p. 213.

RELICTION
        See also Boundaries.
Defined, p. 441.

REMAINDER
        See also Contingent Remainder; Vested Remainder.
Cannot cut short prior estate, c. 78, p. 122.
Classification or types, p. 116.
Contingent and vested remainders compared, p. 132.
Creditors' rights, p. 116.
Death Without Issue, following, Note, p. 45.

REMAINDER—Continued

Doesn't cut short prior estate, p. 116.

Executory interest distinguished, c. 78, p. 122; c. 79, p. 123; Note, p. 122.

Following fee simple prohibited, c. 42, p. 53.

Heirs of grantor, limitation to void, p. 153; c. 90, p. 154.

Implication, created by, p. 118; c. 84, p. 131.

Legal gems, p. 115.

Personal property and chattels real, Note, p. 126.

Requirements for creating, p. 115; c. 75, p. 118.

Requirements of particular estate supporting, p. 115.

Reversion ancillary thereto, when possible, p. 117.

Rules of construction, p. 116; c. 83, p. 129; c. 85, p. 137.

Term for years, following, c. 80, p. 124.

Types differentiated and explained, c. 81, p. 126.

Waste, action of holder for, p. 351.

REMOTENESS OF VESTING

See Rule against Perpetuities.

RENT

Abandonment of tenant, p. 218; c. 131, p. 219; c. 132, p. 220.

    Anticipatory breach resulting therefrom, p. 218; c. 131, p. 219.

    Landlord's remedies on, p. 218; c. 131, p. 219; c. 132, p. 220.

    Mitigation of damages by landlord, p. 218; c. 131, p. 219; c. 132, p. 220.

    Surrender resulting therefrom, p. 218; c. 131, p. 219.

Advance rentals not recoverable, p. 218; c. 132, p. 220.

Apportionable as to amount, p. 212.

Assignment, effect on liability for, p. 213, c. 129, p. 216.

Classification at common law, p. 211.

Contractual nature of, p. 211; c. 126, p. 213.

Covenant concerning runs, p. 212; c. 129, p. 216.

Definition, p. 211.

Destruction of building, effect on, p. 205; c. 121, p. 205.

Extinguished or suspended,

    Acts constituting, p. 213.

    Eminent domain, p. 213.

    Eviction, p. 213.

    Expiration of lease, p. 213.

    Frustration of purpose, p. 213.

    Merger, p. 213.

    Release, p. 213.

    Surrender, p. 213; p. 218; c. 131, p. 219.

Frustration of purpose, effect on, p. 205; c. 123, p. 207.

Legal gems, p. 211.

Liquidated damages, p. 218; c. 132, p. 220.

Modification of, necessity of consideration, c. 126, p. 213.

Not apportionable as to time, p. 212; c. 127, p. 214.

Penalty void, p. 218; c. 132, p. 220.

Privity of contract, liability based on, p. 213; c. 129, p. 216.

Privity of estate, liability based on, p. 213; c. 129, p. 216.

Rent charge defined, p. 211.

Rent seck defined, p. 211.

Rent service defined, p. 211.

Reversion, as incident thereto, p. 212.

Security deposit, landlord's duty to return, p. 218; c. 132, p. 220.

Sublease, effect on, p. 213; c. 130, p. 217.

Third person, wrongful acts of not affecting, c. 128, p. 215.

REPAIR OF LEASED PREMISES

See Landlord and Tenant, Use of premises, Repair.

REPAIRS

Joint tenancy, contribution, c. 62, p. 84.

RESERVATION

    See also Land Description.

Defined, p. 442.

RESTRAINT ON ALIENATION
Condominium and Close in Living, effect on, Note 2, p. 67.
Corporate cooperative shares, p. 661; c. 313, p. 662.
Disabling type,
Limited validity in Mississippi, c. 51, p. 65.
Void, p. 43; c. 40, p. 51.
Forfeiture restraint on life estate, p. 61.
Forfeiture type,
Justification on life estate, c. 51, p. 65.
Valid on leaseholds, c. 51, p. 65.
Reasonable valid, Note 2, p. 67.
Types, see caveat, p. 51; Note 2, p. 67.
Types and validity, c. 51, p. 65; Note 2, p. 67.

RETALIATORY EVICTION
T's defense to L's ouster, p. 222, c. 133.

REVERSION
Alienability, c. 23, p. 33.
Assignment of, c. 69, p. 102.
Characteristics, c. 23, p. 33.
Chart comparing future interests, p. 141.
Created by operation of law, p. 100.
Definition, p. 100.
Fee simple conditional, incident to, c. 43, p. 55.
Fee tail, incident to, p. 54; c. 46, p. 59; c. 67, p. 101.
Legal gems, p. 100.
Rent as incident thereto, p. 211.
Term for years, incident to, c. 68, p. 102.
Typical case, c. 23, p. 33.
Vested indefeasibly, examples, p. 100.
Vested interest, as, c. 23, p. 33; p. 100.
Vested remainder compared, p. 104.
Vested subject to divestment, examples, p. 100; c. 69, p. 102.
Waste, action of holder for, p. 351.
Worthier title, effect, p. 101; c. 70, p. 103.

REVIEW
Review suggestions for use of text, p. 2.

RIGHT
Legal relation, defined as, p. 4.

RIGHT OF FIRST REFUSAL
Cooperatives and condominiums, in, p. 67, ftn. 3.

RIGHT OF RE-ENTRY FOR CONDITION BROKEN
See Power of Termination.

RIGHT TO CONVEY, COVENANT OF
See Covenants for Title.

RIPARIAN RIGHTS
See Water Rights.

RISK OF LOSS
See Equitable Conversion And Risk Of Loss.

ROOT OF TITLE
See also Marketable Record Title Act.
Defined, p. 387.

RULE AGAINST PERPETUITIES
Accumulations and, c. 106, p. 175.
Administrative contingency cases, c. 100, p. 167.
Alienation, policy to further, p. 158.
Analysis, p. 158.
Appointment, validity under power, p. 182; c. 110, p. 185.
Charitable trusts, application to, ftn. 1, p. 159.

RULE AGAINST PERPETUITIES—Continued

Class gifts, c. 103, p. 171.
    Unit rule, c. 103, p. 171.
    Unit rule exceptions, c. 103, p. 171; Note, p. 172.
Contingent remainder subject to, p. 117.
Criticism of common law rule, p. 160.
Cy pres and, p. 160.
Destructibility of contingent remainders, significance, c. 93, p. 160.
Effect of violation, c. 93, p. 160.
Executory interests subject to, Note, p. 40; c. 99, p. 166.
"Fertile octogenarian," c. 102, p. 169.
Fertility, presumption of, c. 102, p. 169.
Gestation,
    May precede as well as follow lives, c. 106, p. 175.
    Period of included, c. 96, p. 163.
"If at all," meaning of, p. 158; c. 94, p. 161; c. 95, p. 162.
Indestructible trusts and c. 107, p. 177.
Interests excepted, p. 159.
Interests subject to, p. 159.
Legal gems on, p. 158.
Lives in being, requirements as to, p. 159.
Measuring lives, c. 96, p. 163; c. 97, p. 164.
Modern reforms, p. 160.
"Must vest" meaning of, p. 158; c. 94, p. 161.
Options in leases, Note, p. 169.
Options unconnected with leases, c. 101, p. 168.
Period from which measured, c. 98, p. 165; c. 110, p. 185.
    Deeds, c. 98, p. 165.
    Wills, c. 98, p. 165.
Period in gross, c. 100, p. 167.
Period of rule, p. 158.
Possibilities not probabilities, c. 93, p. 160.
Possibility of reverter excepted, Note, p. 49; p. 105.
Power of appointment,
    Validity of general power presently exercisable, c. 104, p. 173.
    Validity of general testamentary power, c. 105, p. 174.
    Validity of special power, c. 105, p. 174.
Power of termination exempt from, Note, p. 49; p. 110; c. 99, p. 166.
Remoteness of vesting, policy against, p. 158.
Statement of rule, p. 158.
Status of rule today, p. 160.
Statutes prohibiting suspension of power of, p. 160.
Statutory modifications, p. 160.
Summary of cases, p. 192.
Terms analyzed, p. 158.
Trust duration, p. 159; c. 106, p. 175; c. 107, p. 177.
Unborn widow case, Note, p. 166.
Unlikely possibilities, Note, p. 166.
Vested remainder excepted, p. 117.
Vesting, time for, c. 96, p. 163.
Vesting requirement explained, c. 94, p. 161.
Wait and see doctrine, p. 160.

RULE IN SHELLEY'S CASE

Abolition, c. 89, p. 152.
Estates to which applicable, c. 49, p. 63; p. 147.
Legal gems, p. 146.
Life estate, effect on, pp. 61, 147.
Not applicable when, case illustrating, c. 49, p. 63; c. 88, p. 149.
Operation of rule, examples, p. 147.
Personalty, applicability to, p. 148.
Requirements, p. 147; c. 87, p. 148.
Rule of law, not of construction, p. 147; c. 87, p. 148.
Statement of rule, p. 146.
Technical use of "heirs" required, c. 88, p. 149.
Typical case, c. 36, p. 47.
Worthier title compared, chart, p. 157.

RULE OF REPUGNANT CLAUSES
Caution use indicated, c. 33, p. 44.
Construction of instruments, p. 42 ; c. 33, p. 44.
Specific intent controls, c. 34, p. 45.

RULES OF CONSTRUCTION
See also Boundaries ; Construction Of Deeds And Wills ; Land Description.
Land conveyed, see Land Description.

SALES CONTRACTS
See Equitable Conversion and Risk of Loss ; Marketable Record Title Act ; Marketable Title ; Part Performance ; Statute of Frauds ; Time of Performance.

SECTION
See also Land Description.
Map showing fractional portions, p. 439.

SECURITY DEPOSIT
Landlord's duty to return, p. 218 ; c. 132, p. 220.

SECURITY INTERESTS IN FIXTURES
See Fixtures.

SEISIN
Abeyance prohibited, c. 4, p. 16 ; c. 27, p. 37.
Defined or explained, p. 5.
Livery, c. 4, p. 16 ; c. 139, p. 239.

SEISIN, COVENANT FOR
See Covenants for Title.

SERVIENT TENEMENT
See also Easements And Profits.
Definition, p. 561.

SHELLEY'S CASE, RULE IN
See Rule in Shelley's Case.

SHIFTING USE OR INTEREST
See Executory Interests ; Future Interests.

SPECIAL OCCUPANT
Defined, c. 10, p. 22.

SPECIAL POWER
See also Powers of Appointment.
Creditors rights, c. 108, p. 182.
Defined, p. 180.

SPECIFIC PERFORMANCE
Oral land sales contracts, see Part Performance.

SPENDTHRIFT TRUSTS
Disabling restraint on alienation valid, c. 40, p. 51.

SPOT ZONING
See Zoning.

SPRINGING USE OR INTEREST
See Executory Interests ; Future Interests.

STATUTE DE DONIS
Fee tail created by, p. 54 ; c. 43, p. 55 ; c. 44, p. 56.

STATUTE OF FRAUDS
Brokers' Contracts, p. 366.
Delivery of deeds in escrow, applicability, c. 219, p. 425.
Fixtures, p. 330.
Growing crops, oral sale of, p. 361.
Land contracts, p. 369.
    Agent's authority, p. 370.
    Agreements included, p. 369.

STATUTE OF FRAUDS—Continued

Land contracts—Continued

    English origin, p. 369.

    Executed contracts excepted, p. 369.

    Executory contracts, p. 369.

    Legal gems, p. 369.

    Memorandum,

        Customary matters, c. 194, p. 370.

        Incidental items implied, c. 194, p. 370.

        Intent, role of, c. 195, p. 372.

        Parties' identity, c. 194, p. 370.

        Promises of parties, c. 194, p. 370.

        Purchase price and terms of sale, c. 194, p. 370.

        Requirements, pp. 369–370; c. 194, p. 370.

        Several writings connected, p. 370.

        Sufficiency of, p. 369; c. 194, p. 370.

        Sufficiency of land description, c. 194, p. 370.

    Signature required, p. 370.

Part performance, see Part Performance.

Periodic tenancy,

    Effect in creating, c. 16, p. 26.

    Resulting from non-compliance and conduct of parties, p. 70; c. 54, p. 73.

Summary of cases, land contracts, p. 393.

STATUTE OF TENURES

Operation and effect, p. 5.

STATUTE OF USES

Active uses unexecuted, pp. 407, 409.

Conveyances, pp. 399 et seq.

    Outlined, p. 396.

    Resulting use, p. 402.

    Use raised by bargain and sale, p. 404.

    Use raised by consideration recited, p. 403.

    Use raised by declaration of use, p. 404.

    Use raised on consideration paid, p. 402.

    Use raised without transmutation of possession, p. 404.

    Uses executed on feoffment, p. 401.

    Uses executed on transmutation of possession, p. 401.

Effect of statute, p. 399.

Enforcement of uses, p. 400.

Executory interests made possible by, c. 28, p. 38.

Historical note, conveyances under, p. 399.

Modern law, effect on, p. 408.

Periods of development, p. 401.

Shifting interests made possible, c. 5, p. 17.

Springing interests made possible, c. 4, p. 16.

Unexecuted uses, p. 407.

Unexecuted uses as trusts, pp. 407, 409.

Use on chattel interests unexecuted, p. 407.

Use on use unexecuted, p. 408.

What's a Use, p. 399; p. 401.

Why a use, p. 400.

STATUTE OF WILLS

Executory devises made possible by, c. 30, p. 39; c. 31, p. 40.

Shifting interests permitted, c. 7, p. 18.

Springing interests permitted, c. 6, p. 18.

STATUTE QUIA EMPTORES

Effect of, p. 5.

Subinfeudation prohibited, p. 5.

STUDY METHODS

Study tips for use of book, p. 2.

SUBJACENT SUPPORT

See Lateral and Subjacent Support.

SUBLEASE
See Landlord and Tenant; Rent.

SUBMERGED LAND
Title to, see Water Rights, Land under water.

SUBROGATION
Mortgages, p. 501; c. 255, p. 506.

SUBSURFACE
Caves and minerals, note, p. 265.
Rights of possessor generally, p. 257; c. 157, p. 264.

SUMMARIES OF CASES
Above and below the surface, p. 265.
Adverse possession, p. 255.
Bailment, p. 696.
Bona fide purchaser of personalty, p. 716.
Brokers' contracts, p. 393.
Concurrent estates, p. 97.
Conveyances, p. 413.
Cooperatives and condominiums, p. 676.
Covenants for title, p. 464.
Covenants running with the land, p. 556.
Delivery of deeds, p. 434.
Easements and profits, p. 603.
Emblements, p. 365.
Equitable conversion and risk of loss, p. 394.
Equitable servitudes, p. 558.
Estoppel by deed, p. 474.
Executory interest, p. 145.
Fee simple, p. 94.
Fee simple conditional and fee tail, p. 94.
Fixtures, p. 347.
Future interests, p. 142.
Gifts, p. 710.
Joint bank accounts, p. 710.
Land contracts, p. 393.
Land description and boundaries, p. 453.
Landlord and tenant, p. 229.
Lateral and subjacent support, p. 274.
Licenses, p. 621.
Life estates, p. 95.
Marketable record title acts, p. 395.
Marketable title, p. 394.
Mortgages, p. 513.
Non-freehold estates, p. 96.
Nuisance, p. 325.
Part performance, p. 393.
Planning, p. 655.
Police power, p. 655.
Possession and prior possession, p. 255.
Possession of personalty, rights incident to, p. 687.
Possibility of reverter, p. 142.
Power of termination, p. 143.
Powers of appointment, p. 194.
Priorities and recording, p. 497.
Remainders, p. 143.
Rent, p. 231.
Residential leases, p. 232.
Reversion, p. 142.
Rule against perpetuities, p. 192.
Rule in Shelley's Case, p. 191.
Vendor and purchaser, p. 393.
Warranty of fitness or habitability in deeds, p. 465.
Waste, p. 358.
Water rights, p. 306.

SUMMARIES OF CASES—Continued
Worthier title, p. 192.
Zoning, p. 655.

SUPPORT
See Lateral and Subjacent Support.

SURFACE WATER
See Water Rights.

SURRENDER
Act of parties and operation of law distinguished, c. 208, p. 397.
Example of, p. 397.
Rent extinguished by, p. 213; c. 127, p. 214; c. 131, p. 219.

SURVIVORSHIP
Joint tenancy,
   See also Joint Tenancy.
  Incident of, c. 19, p. 28.
Life estate for joint lives and the survivor, c. 50, p. 65.
Severance in joint tenancy, what constitutes, c. 64, p. 87.
Tenancy by the entirety, characteristic of, p. 88.

TACKING
Periods of adverse possession, see Adverse Possession.

TAKERS IN DEFAULT
Definition, p. 179.

TENANCIES LESS THAN FREEHOLD
See Estate For Years; Landlord and Tenant; Lease; Non-Freehold Estates; Periodic Tenancy; Tenancy at Sufferance; Tenancy at Will.

TENANCY AT SUFFERANCE
 See also Holdover Tenant; Non-Freehold Estates.
Illustrated, p. 9.
Typical case, c. 18, p. 28.

TENANCY AT WILL
Characteristics, c. 17, p. 27.
Determinable life estate as alternative construction, c. 47, p. 61; Note 1, p. 62.
From invalid attempt to create a term, p. 70.
Illustrated, p. 8.
Typical case, c. 17, p. 27.

TENANCY BY THE ENTIRETY
Characteristics, c. 20, p. 31; p. 88.
Chart comparing concurrent tenancies, p. 93.
Conveyance to self and wife as, c. 63, p. 85.
Creditors rights, p. 88.
Divorce, terminated by, c. 20, p. 31; p. 88; c. 65, p. 89.
Legal gems on, p. 88.
Mortgage by one spouse, effect, c. 65, p. 89.
Partition disallowed, p. 88.
Typical case, c. 20, p. 31.
Unities required, c. 20, p. 31; p. 88.

TENANCY FOR YEARS
See Estate for Years.

TENANCY FROM YEAR TO YEAR
See Periodic Tenancy.

TENANCY IN COMMON
Characteristics, c. 21, p. 31; p. 90.
Chart comparing concurrent tenancies, p. 93.
Contribution, cotenant's right to, c. 66, p. 91.
Cotenants, relations between, c. 66, p. 91.
Creation, c. 21, p. 31; p. 90; c. 66, p. 91.
Destruction or termination of, p. 90.

TENANCY IN COMMON—Continued
Interest alienable and descendable, p. 90; c. 66, p. 94.
Legal gems, p. 90.
Possession, cotenants' right to, c. 46, p. 59; c. 66, p. 91.
Preferred over joint tenancy, p. 90.
Typical case, c. 21, p. 31.

TENANCY IN COPARCENARY
Characteristics, c. 22, p. 32.
Chart comparing cotenancies, p. 93.
Typical case at common law, c. 22, p. 32.

TENURE
Defined, p. 5.
Free tenure, p. 5.
Types of, p. 5.
Unfree tenure, p. 5.

TENURES, STATUTE OF
Defined and explained, p. 5.

TENURIAL SYSTEM
Explained, p. 5.

THIRD PERSON
Wrongful acts of, no effect on L–T relationship, c. 128, p. 215.

TIDAL LANDS
Abutting owner's extent of title, p. 276.
Ownership of, p. 441.

TIME OF PERFORMANCE
Land contracts, p. 381.
    Reasonable time, p. 381.
    Time not of essence but later made so, p. 381.
    Time of essence, p. 381.
    Waiver of time of essence, p. 381.
Legal gems, p. 381.

TITLE
Submerged land, see Water Rights, Land under water.

TITLE COVENANTS
Construction of, p. 458.

TOTTEN TRUSTS
Nature of, c. 341, p. 707.

TOWNSHIPS
Chart showing how designated, p. 437.
Chart showing section numbers, p. 438.

TRADE FIXTURES
Date for removal, p. 333.
Definition, p. 333; c. 182, p. 334.
Farm buildings and implements, c. 182, p. 334.
Forfeiture for non-removal, p. 333.
Legal gems, p. 333.

TREASURE TROVE
Definition, p. 680; c. 324, p. 682; c. 327, p. 684.
Rights of finder, p. 680; c. 324, p. 682.

TRESPASS
Low flights as, c. 153, p. 257; c. 154, p. 259.
Low wire as, c. 156, p. 263.
Nuisance, same act may be both, p. 311.
Nuisance distinguished, p. 310.
Recurring may be nuisance, p. 311.
Subsurface intrusion as, c. 157, p. 264.

TRUST
Bailment distinguished, p. 690.
Indestructibility and the rule against perpetuities, c. 107, p. 177.
Power in, defined, p. 180.
Rule against perpetuities, applicability, p. 159; c. 106, p. 175; c. 107, p. 177.
    Charitable trust not applicable, ftn. 1, p. 159.
Unexecuted uses as, pp. 407, 409.

UNFREE TENURE
Defined, p. 5.

UNIFORM COMMERCIAL CODE
Fixtures, see Fixtures, subtitle Security interests.

UNIFORM VENDOR AND PURCHASER RISK ACT
Land contracts, p. 376; c. 199, p. 378.

USE OF PREMISES
Landlord and tenant, see Landlord and Tenant, Use of premises.
Nuisance, see Nuisance.

USE ON USE
Unexecuted by Statute of Uses, p. 407.
    For uses generally, see Statute of Uses.

VARIANCE
See Zoning.

VENDOR AND PURCHASER
See Brokers' Contracts; Equitable Conversion and Risk of Loss; Marketable
    Record Title Acts; Marketable Title; Part Performance; Statute of Frauds;
    Time of Performance.

VESTED REMAINDER
Alienable, devisable and descendible, p. 116.
Characteristics, c. 26, p. 35.
Chart comparing future interests, p. 141.
Contingent remainders compared, p. 132.
Examples of, p. 117; c. 75, p. 118; c. 76, p. 119; c. 77, p. 120; c. 81, p. 126; c. 84,
    p. 131.
For life, characteristics, c. 67, p. 101.
Illustrations, see Note, p. 36.
Legal gems, p. 115.
Reversion compared, p. 104.
Rules against perpetuities, excepted from, p. 117.
Surplus words of contingency ignored, c. 81, p. 126.
Taxes and interest, rights as to, p. 117.
Typical case, c. 26, p. 35.
Vested absolutely, Note, p. 36; p. 116; c. 75, p. 118; c. 80, p. 124; c. 81, p. 126.
Vested rather than contingent construction preferred, p. 117; c. 83, p. 129; c. 85,
    p. 137.
Vested subject to open or partial defeasance, Note, p. 36; p. 117; c. 77, p. 120.
    Rights of creditors, c. 77, p. 120.
Vested subject to total defeasance, Note, p. 36; p. 117; c. 76, p. 119; c. 83, p. 129.
    Power of appointment, effect, c. 76, p. 119.
Waste, rights as to, p. 117.

WAIT AND SEE DOCTRINE
Rule against perpetuities, p. 160.

WAIVER
Power of termination, p. 110; c. 74, p. 112.

WARRANTY OF FITNESS OR HABITABILITY
Residential leases, in, p. 223, c. 134, p. 226.
Sale of housing, p. 462; c. 238, p. 463.
    Parameters of the doctrine, Note, p. 463.

WARRANTY OF HABITABILITY
See supra, Warranty of Fitness or Habitability.

WASTE

Accident excluded, c. 187, p. 354.

Act of God excluded, c. 187, p. 354.

Ameliorating, p. 350; c. 186, p. 352.

Contingent future interest holder, rights as to, p. 351; c. 189, p. 356.

Contingent remainderman, rights as to, p. 351; c. 189, p. 356.

Cotenants, p. 351.

Definition, p. 349; cs. 186–188, pp. 352–356.

Equitable, p. 350.

Examples, p. 349; cs. 186–188, pp. 352–356.

Executory interest holder, rights of, c. 42, p. 53.

Failure to extinguish fire, c. 187, p. 354.

Legal gems, p. 349.

Permissive, p. 350; c. 187, p. 354.

Persons liable, p. 351; cs. 186–188, pp. 352–356.

Proceeds of sale from, p. 351.

Purpose, p. 351.

Remainderman, rights as to, p. 351.

Remedies for, p. 351; cs. 186–188, pp. 352–356.

Summary of cases, p. 358.

Tenant's duty not to commit, c. 120, p. 204.

Timber cutting, c. 186, p. 352.

Types generally, p. 350.

Unreasonable use of premises, c. 188, p. 355.

Voluntary, p. 350; cs. 186–188, pp. 352–356.

WATER RIGHTS

Accrual of cause of action, c. 163, p. 286; c. 167, p. 292.

Classification of waters, p. 276.

    Criticized, Note, p. 288.

Flood water,

    Defined, p. 277; c. 172, p. 303.

    Rights as to, c. 172, p. 303.

Hydrological cycle, Note, p. 288.

Lakes,

    Rights of abutters, p. 277.

    Use of waters in privately owned lakes, c. 173, p. 304.

Lakes and streams defined, pp. 276–277; c. 168, p. 296.

Land under water, title to, p. 276.

Legal gems, p. 276.

Natural flow theory, see subtitle Riparian Rights.

Navigable water,

    Defined, p. 276.

    Federal control, p. 276.

New conditions as natural, c. 167, p. 292.

Percolating water,

    Defined, p. 277.

    English rule, c. 169, p. 297.

    Reasonable use rule, c. 169, p. 297.

    Rules concerning, p. 280; c. 169, p. 297.

    Sale of water for use elsewhere, c. 169, p. 297.

Prior appropriation doctrine,

    Generally, p. 277.

    Applied, c. 161, p. 283; c. 162, p. 284.

    Chart comparing prior appropriation and riparian rights, p. 281.

    Explanation, p. 280.

Reasonable use theory, see subtitles Riparian rights; Percolating water.

Riparian land, extent of, c. 164, p. 288.

Riparian rights,

    Generally, p. 277.

    Chart comparing riparian rights and prior appropriation, p. 281.

    Diversion of water from riparian land, c. 161, p. 283; c. 164, p. 288; c. 165, p. 290.

    Municipality's Use for inhabitants, c. 165, p. 290.

    Natural flow theory, p. 277; c. 161, p. 283; cs. 163–167, pp. 286–292.

        Distinguished from reasonable use, p. 278.

WATER RIGHTS—Continued

Riparian rights—Continued

Pollution, c. 166, p. 291.
Prescription as to, c. 163, p. 286 ; c. 167, p. 292.
Reasonable use theory, p. 278 ; c. 161, p. 283 ; cs. 163–167, pp. 286–292.
Distinguished from natural flow, p. 278.
Stream, what constitutes, c. 168, p. 296.
Transfer of, c. 166, p. 291.
Summary of cases, p. 306.
Surface water,
Defined, p. 277 ; c. 170, p. 299.
Drainage of land, c. 171, p. 302.
Impounding of, c. 170, p. 299.
Pollution as nuisance, c. 176, p. 316.
Rules concerning, p. 280 ; c. 170, p. 299.
Tidal lands, extent of abutting owner's title, p. 276.
Underground waters, defined, p. 277.
Water skiing as nuisance, c. 173, p. 304.

WILD ANIMALS

Acquisition of title by possession, p. 679 ; c. 321, p. 680.
Pursuit not sufficient for possession, c. 321, p. 680.

WILLS

Worthier title doctrine inapplicable, p. 153.

WORDS OF LIMITATION

Defined, p. 5.
Estate created when absent, c. 32, p. 43.
Explained, c. 1, p. 12.
Modern law as to, Special Note, p. 13 ; p. 42 ; c. 32, p. 43.
Words of purchase distinguished, c. 1, p. 12.

WORDS OF PURCHASE

Defined and explained, p. 5 ; c. 1, p. 12.
"Heirs of the body" as, c. 49, p. 63.
Words of limitation distinguished, c. 1, p. 12.

WORTHIER TITLE DOCTRINE

Conveyances, limited to, p. 153 ; c. 92, p. 156.
Definition, p. 153.
Estate given to heirs immaterial, p. 153.
Estate preceding immaterial, p. 153.
Feudal origins of rule, p. 153.
Heirs used in a technical sense, p. 153.
Legal gems on, p. 153.
Limitations to heir of named person not covered, p. 153.
Limitations to heirs of grantor void, p. 153 ; c. 90, p. 154.
Requirements of rule, p. 153 ; cs. 90–92, pp. 154–156.
Rule in Shelley's Case compared, chart, p. 157.
Rule of construction, as, p. 154 ; c. 91, p. 155.
Rule of law, as, c. 70, p. 103 ; p. 154 ; c. 91, p. 155.
Statement of rule, p. 153 ; c. 70, p. 103 ; c. 90, p. 154.
Status of rule today, p. 154 ; c. 91, p. 155.
Wills, not applicable to, p. 153 ; c. 92, p. 156.

WRAP–AROUND MORTGAGE

Defined and explained, p. 511.

ZONING

See also Police Power.
Aesthetic purposes, for, c. 297, p. 629.
Amendment affecting single parcel, c. 301, p. 638.
Amendment versus variance, Note 1, p. 640.
Amendments and burden of proof, Note 1, p. 640.
Arbitrary ordinance invalid, p. 627 ; c. 299, p. 632 ; c. 302, p. 641.
Circumstances affect validity, p. 627 ; c. 299, p. 632.
Comprehensive zoning valid, c. 298, p. 630.

ZONING—Continued

Confiscatory ordinance invalid, p. 627; c. 299, p. 632; c. 300, p. 635; c. 312, p. 653.

Dedication required for subdivision approval, c. 308, p. 649.

Determination based on popular vote as arbitrary, c. 302, p. 284.

Discriminatory ordinance invalid, p. 627.

Equitable estoppel precluding change, Note 2, pp. 640–641.

Exception, p. 628.

Exclusion of some uses permissible, p. 628.

Existing regulation and vested rights, Note 1, p. 639.

Flexible selective zoning, p. 628; c. 306, p. 646; Note, p. 647.

"Floating" zones, p. 628; c. 306, p. 646; Note, p. 647.

Floating zones and the PUD, Note, p. 647.

Invalidity tests, p. 627; c. 298, p. 630; c. 299, p. 632.

Inverse condemnation, challenge by, Special Note, p. 634.

Living together, zoning restrictions as to unrelated persons, c. 309, p. 650.

Low and moderate income housing, discrimination against c. 303, p. 643.

Marijuana smoking and religion, c. 311, p. 652.

Neighboring areas, necessity of considering, c. 303, p. 643.

No vested right to a classification, c. 301, p. 638; Note 1, p. 639.

Nonconforming use,
    Amortization, Note, p. 637.
    Elimination of, p. 627; c. 300, p. 635; Special Note, p. 637.
    Relation to nuisance, c. 300, p. 635; Special Note, p. 637.
    Techniques for eliminating, Special Note, p. 637.

Orderly growth, permissible objective, c. 304, p. 644.

Plan, necessity of, c. 306; p. 646; Note, p. 647.

Planning, relation to zoning, p. 623; c. 302, p. 641.

Police power basis, p. 626; c. 298, p. 630; c. 299, p. 632.

Racial discrimination invalid, c. 310, p. 651.

Religious activities, restrictions on, c. 311, p. 652.

Residential classification invalid when land unsuitable for such use, c. 299, p. 682.

Retrospective operation, c. 300, p. 635.

Review case showing clear limitation on zoning power, c. 312, p. 653.

Single family restrictions, validity, c. 390, p. 650.

Spot zoning, p. 627; c. 301, p. 638; Note 2, p. 640; Note, p. 647; c. 307, p. 648.

Summary of cases, p. 655.

Trailer camps, exclusion of, see paragraph preceding, c. 304, p. 644.

Unreasonable ordinance invalid, p. 627; c. 299, p. 632; c. 302, p. 641.

Use separations valid, c. 298, p. 630.

Variance, p. 627; c. 305, p. 645.
    Amendment compared, Note 1, p. 640.
    Basis for granting, p. 627; c. 305, p. 645.
    Requirements for granting, p. 627; c. 305, p. 645.
    Unique versus general hardship, c. 305, p. 645.

Zoning by contract, p. 628; c. 307, p. 648; Note, p. 648.

†